Agency, Partnership, and the LLC: The Law of Unincorporated Business Enterprises

Agency, Partnership, and the LLC: The Law of Unincorporated Business Enterprises

Cases, Materials, Problems

TENTH EDITION

J. Dennis Hynes
NICHOLAS A. ROSENBAUM PROFESSOR OF
LAW EMERITUS UNIVERSITY OF COLORADO

Mark J. Loewenstein
MONFORT PROFESSOR OF COMMERCIAL LAW
UNIVERSITY OF COLORADO

CAROLINA ACADEMIC PRESS
Durham, North Carolina

ISBN: 978-1-5310-0813-0
e-ISBN: 978-1-5310-0814-7
LCCN: 2019930391

Carolina Academic Press
700 Kent Street
Durham, North Carolina 27701
Telephone (919) 489-7486
Fax (919) 493-5668
www.cap-press.com

Printed in the United States of America

First through Fifth Editions (from Professor Hynes)
To my children

Professor Loewenstein dedicates this Tenth Edition
to his family.

Contents

Table of Cases   xxi
Preface   xxxv
Glossary   xxxvii

Introduction • The Law of Unincorporated Business Enterprises   3
  A. The Corporation   3
  B. The Different Forms of Unincorporated Businesses   6
    1. The Sole Proprietorship   6
    2. The Business Trust   7
    3. The Partnership   8
    4. The Limited Liability Partnership (LLP)   9
    5. The Limited Partnership   9
    6. The Limited Liability Limited Partnership (LLLP) 10
    7. The Limited Liability Company (LLC)   10

Chapter 1 • The Agency Relationship; The Ambiguous Principal
           Problem; Subagency   13
           Carrier v. McLlarky   14
           United States v. Bonds   15
           Notes   24
  A. Agency or Sale   29
           Hunter Mining Laboratories, Inc. v. Management
             Assistance, Inc.   29
           Notes   31
           United States v. General Electric Co.   33
           Notes   35
  B. Agency or Debtor-Creditor Relationship   36
           A. Gay Jenson Farms Co. v. Cargill, Inc.   36
           Notes   42
  C. Agency and the Law of Trusts   44
           Notes   46
  D. Agent or Escrow Holder   46
           Notes   47
  E. Dual Agency; The Ambiguous Principal Problem   49
    1. The Dual Agency Rule   49
           Notes   49

2. The Ambiguous Principal Problem   50
    Norby v. Bankers Life Co.   51
    Notes   54
F. Subagency   55
    Notes   56
G. Agency Distinguished from Other Relationships   57
  1. The Franchise Relationship   57
  2. The Marriage Relationship   58
  3. Property Relationships   59
    a. Co-ownership   59
    b. Landlord-Tenant   59
  4. Corporate Relationships   59
    a. The Agency Status of Corporate Directors   59
    b. The "Mere Instrumentality" or "Alter Ego" Doctrine
    Contrasted with Traditional Agency Liability   60
H. The History of Agency and Other Matters   62
    Problems   63

Chapter 2 · Rights and Duties between Principal and Agent   67
A. Duties of Principal to Agent   68
  1. Duty of Exoneration and Indemnification   68
    Admiral Oriental Line v. United States   68
    Notes   70
  2. Duty to Pay Compensation   72
    Notes   72
  3. Duty of Care   73
    Notes   74
  4. Social Legislation   75
    a. Worker's Compensation Legislation   75
    b. Other Social Legislation   76
  5. Duty to Deal Fairly and in Good Faith   77
    Taylor v. Cordis Corp.   77
    Deonier & Associates v. Paul Revere Life Insurance Company   79
    Notes   85
B. Duties of Agent to Principal   87
  1. Duty of Good Conduct and to Obey   87
  2. Duty to Indemnify Principal for Loss Caused by Misconduct   88
  3. Duty to Account   90
  4. The Fiduciary Duties of Agents   90
    a. Commencement of Fiduciary Relationship   90
    b. Duty of Care   92
    Carrier v. McLlarky   93
    Notes   95
    c. Duty of Disclosure   95

Estate of Eller v. Bartron	95
Note	100
d. Duty of Loyalty	101
i. Loyalty During the Relationship	101
Gelfand v. Horizon Corp.	101
Notes	105
ii. Post-Termination Competition	111
Notes	112
Notes	113
iii. Dealing at Arm's Length	115
Pappas v. Tzolis	115
Note	118
Problems	118
Chapter 3 • Vicarious Tort Liability	**121**
A. The Master-Servant Relationship	121
1. The Concept	121
Jones v. Hart	121
Notes	122
a. The History of Respondeat Superior Liability	126
i. The Holmes Thesis	126
ii. The Wigmore Rebuttal	127
b. Is an Employment Relationship Necessary to Respondeat Superior Liability?	128
Heims v. Hanke	129
Sandrock v. Taylor	130
Notes	131
c. Rationale for Respondeat Superior	133
i. Arguments Questioning the Theory	133
ii. Arguments in Favor of or Explanations for the Theory	136
d. Imputed Contributory Negligence	137
e. Limitation to Losses Caused by Tortious Behavior	137
f. Direct Tort Liability of an Employer	138
2. The Independent Contractor Exception	138
a. The Concept	138
Kane Furniture Corp. v. Miranda	139
Note	143
Lazo v. Mak's Trading Co.	143
Notes	146
Soderback v. Townsend	147
Hunter v. R.G. Watkins & Son, Inc.	149
Notes	151
Sandrock v. Taylor	155
Note	156

      b. The Independent Contractor Exception in the Modern Economy   157
      c. Limitations to the Independent Contractor Exception   159
        Hixon v. Sherwin-Williams Co.   159
        Notes   161
        Kleeman v. Rheingold   162
        Notes   166
        Problems   168
   3. Borrowed Servants   170
      Charles v. Barrett   170
      Notes   171
      ATS, Inc. v. Beddingfield   173
      Sparger v. Worley Hospital, Inc.   177
      Note   180
      Problems   181
   4. The Scope of Employment Limitation   181
      a. Negligent Acts   182
        Joel v. Morison   182
        Notes   183
        Fiocco v. Carver   187
        Notes   190
        Clover v. Snowbird Ski Resort   192
        Note   197
        Spencer v. V.I.P., Inc.   199
      b. Intentional Torts   203
        Bremen State Bank v. Hartford Accident & Indemnity Co.   204
        Note   205
        i. The Assault on § 228(1)(c)   206
        Ira S. Bushey & Sons v. United States   206
        Notes   209
        Lisa M. v. Henry Mayo Newhall Memorial Hospital   211
        Notes   220
        ii. Restatement (Second) § 219(2)(d)   222
        Costos v. Coconut Island Corp.   222
        Notes   226
        iii. The Implied Contract Theory   228
        Nazareth v. Herndon Ambulance Service   228
        Adams v. New York City Transit Authority   230
        iv. Punitive Damages   233
        v. Non-Physical Torts   236
B. The Partnership Relationship   236
C. The Unincorporated Nonprofit Association Relationship   238
   1. Liability of the Members   238
   2. Liability of the Association   239
      a. In General   239

  b. For the Actions of Its Affiliates and Chapters   239
  c. To Its Members   239
 D. Three Unusual Examples of Vicarious Tort Liability   241
  1. Vicarious Liability by Estoppel   241
  2. The "Family Car" Doctrine   241
  3. Owner Consent and Other Legislation   242
   Problems   242

Chapter 4 • Contractual Powers of Agents   **245**
 A. Authority   245
  1. Express Authority   245
   King v. Bankerd   246
   Lamb v. Scott   250
   Notes   251
  2. Implied Authority   253
   a. Delegation of Authority   254
    Notes   254
   b. Incidental Authority   255
 B. Apparent Authority   255
   H. H. Taylor v. Ramsay-Gerding Construction Company   255
   Smith v. Hansen, Hansen & Johnson, Inc.   260
   Notes   263
   Sauber v. Northland Insurance Co.   266
   Notes and Questions   268
 C. Estoppel   272
   Estate of Cordero v. Christ Hospital   272
   Notes   277
 D. The Inherent Agency Power Concept   279
   Autoxchange.Com, Inc. v. Dreyer and Reinbold, Inc.   281
   Note   284
   Problems   284

Chapter 5 • Fraudulent Acts of Agents   **287**
 A. The Unscrupulous Agent   288
   Grease Monkey International, Inc. v. Montoya   288
   Notes   293
   Entente Mineral Co. v. Parker   293
   Hydrolevel Corp. v. American Society of Mechanical
    Engineers, Inc.   298
   Notes   300
   Rothman v. Fillette   303
   Note   306
 B. Limits to Liability for Fraud   307
   Light v. Chandler Improvement Co.   307

Notes   310
Leafgreen v. American Family Mutual Insurance Co.   311
Notes   317
Problems   318

Chapter 6 · The Undisclosed Principal   **321**
A. Rights of the Undisclosed Principal   322
1. Assertion of Rights by the Undisclosed Principal   322
2. Parol Evidence Rule   324
3. Sealed Contracts   324
4. Exceptions   326
Kelly Asphalt Block Co. v. Barber Asphalt Paving Co.   326
Finley v. Dalton   328
Notes   331
B. Liabilities of the Undisclosed Principal   332
1. Authorized Transactions   332
a. Remedies of the Third Party   333
b. The Election Rule   333
2. Unauthorized Transactions   335
Watteau v. Fenwick   336
Note   337
Senor v. Bangor Mills   339
Notes   342
C. Payment and Setoff   343
1. Payment by the Third Party   343
2. Payment to the Third Party   344
3. Setoff   346
Oil Supply Company, Inc. v. Hires Parts Service, Inc.   346
Note   349
Question   350
Problems   350

Chapter 7 · Liability of the Agent to Third Persons   **353**
A. Liability on the Contract   353
1. Liability When the Principal Is Unintentionally Undisclosed   353
Jensen v. Alaska Valuation Service   353
Notes   356
2. Liability When the Principal Is Disclosed: Special Circumstances   359
Copp v. Breskin   359
Notes   361
3. Liability When the Principal Is Partially Disclosed or Unidentified   364
Van D. Costas, Inc. v. Rosenberg   364
Notes   366
B. The Agent's Warranty of Authority   369

Husky Industries v. Craig Industries 369
Notes 371
C. Harm to the Economic Interests of Others 373
Coker v. Dollar 373
Note 375
D. Liability in Tort 375
Problems 376

Chapter 8 • The Doctrine of Ratification 377
A. The Concept 377
Evans v. Ruth 377
Dempsey v. Chambers 379
1. Justification for the Concept 381
Notes 383
2. Implied Ratification 385
Manning v. Twin Falls Clinic & Hospital, Inc. 385
Notes 389
B. The Knowledge Requirement 390
Lewis v. Cable 391
Computel, Inc. v. Emery Air Freight Corp. 393
Inn Foods, Inc. v. Equitable Cooperative Bank 396
C. Can Silence Constitute Affirmance? 399
Bruton v. Automatic Welding & Supply Corp. 399
Notes 403
D. The No Partial Ratification Rule 406
Rakestraw v. Rodrigues 406
Notes 409
E. Changed Circumstances 411
Notes 411
Problems 413

Chapter 9 • Notice and Notification; Imputed Knowledge 417
A. Introduction 417
B. Notification 417
Montana Reservoir & Irrigation Co. v. Utah Junk Co. 423
Note 424
C. Imputed Knowledge 425
Constant v. University of Rochester 426
Notes 428
Bird v. Penn Central Co. 432
Notes and Questions 435
D. The Adverse Interest Qualification 436
Kirschner v. KPMG LLP 438
Notes 442

E. The Sole Actor Doctrine 443
    Munroe v. Harriman 445
    Notes 448
    Problems 449

Chapter 10 · Termination of the Agency Relationship 451
A. Termination Between the Parties to an Agency Relationship 451
  1. Termination by Will 451
    a. Some Consequences of Termination of an Agency Relationship 452
      Want v. Century Supply Co. 454
    b. Irrevocable Powers Phrased in Agency Terms 455
  2. Termination by Operation of Law 456
    a. Death 456
      Hunt v. Rousmanier's Administrators 456
      Notes 459
    b. Loss of Capacity 460
      In re Berry's Estate 460
      Campbell v. United States 462
      Notes 465
    c. Bankruptcy 467
    d. War 467
B. Notice of Termination to Third Parties 467
  1. Termination by Will 467
  2. Termination by Operation of Law 469
    Problems 471

Chapter 11 · The Creation of a Partnership 473
A. Introduction 473
B. The Limited Liability Partnership (LLP) 474
C. The Partnership Relationship Defined and Distinguished from
    Other Relationships 476
  1. Historical Background 476
  2. An Early Test of Partnership 476
    Questions 477
  3. The Uniform Partnership Act (1914), the Revised Uniform
    Partnership Act (1997) and the 2013 Amendments to RUPA 477
    Notes and Questions 481
    Martin v. Peyton 482
    Notes 486
    Byker v. Mannes 487
    Notes 491
    Note on Non-Equity Partners 493
D. The Underlying Theory of Partnership — Aggregate or Entity? 494
    Fairway Development Co. v. Title Insurance Co. of Minnesota 496

Notes 500
E. Income Tax Considerations — A Brief Summary 501
F. Contributions of Property to the Partnership 502
  1. Ambiguities Concerning Ownership of Particular Property 502
    Notes 504
  2. The Special Matter of Title to Real Property 506
  3. The Property Rights of a Partner 506
    Groff v. Citizens Bank of Clovis 507
    Notes 509
    Problems 511

Chapter 12 · The Operation of a Partnership 515
A. Contractual Powers of Partners 515
  1. Actual Authority 516
    Elle v. Babbitt 516
    Summers v. Dooley 518
    National Biscuit Co. v. Stroud 520
    Notes 522
  2. Apparent Authority 523
    Burns v. Gonzalez 523
    Notes 527
    RNR Investments Limited Partnership v. Peoples
      First Community Bank 529
    Note 534
  3. Liability of Purported Partner 534
    a. Is There a Duty to Speak? 536
    b. The Reliance Conundrum 536
    c. The Release Conundrum 537
    Note 537
B. Tort Liability for the Wrongs of Partners 538
  1. In General 538
  2. The Fraudulent Partner 538
    a. The Traditional View 539
    Rouse v. Pollard 539
    b. A Conflicting View 541
    Cook v. Brundidge, Fountain, Elliott & Churchill 541
C. The Nature of a Partner's Liability — Joint as Opposed to Joint
  and Several Liability 547
D. Suits against the Partnership 550
E. Suits by the Partnership 551
    Adams v. Land Services, Inc. 551
    Note 556
F. Notice and Notification to the Partnership 556
    Federal Deposit Insurance Corp. v. Braemoor Assocs. 556

      Notes   558
G. Keeping Track of Things — A Brief Look at Partnership Accounting   559
H. Rights and Duties Among Partners   560
  1. Fiduciary Duties   560
    a. The Duty of Loyalty   561
      i. Duty During Formation of Partnership   561
       Corley v. Ott   561
       Note   562
      ii. Pre-Empting Business Opportunities   563
       Meinhard v. Salmon   563
       Notes   568
      iii. Leaving the Business   570
       Note   571
       Gibbs v. Breed, Abbott & Morgan   572
      iv. Dealing with Conflicts of Interest   578
       J & J Celcom v. AT&T Wireless Services, Inc.   582
       Note   588
      v. Fiduciary Duties and Freedom of Contract   589
       Labovitz v. Dolan   589
       Question   593
       Singer v. Singer   593
       Notes   595
    b. The Duty of Care   597
      Duffy v. Piazza Construction, Inc.   597
      Notes   598
      Moren v. Jax Restaurant   600
      Note   602
    c. The Duty of Full Disclosure   602
      Walter v. Holiday Inns, Inc.   602
    d. The Duty of Good Faith and Fair Dealing   605
      Holman v. Coie   606
      Note   610
      Bohatch v. Butler & Binion   611
      Cadwalader, Wickersham & Taft v. Beasley   617
      Note   623
  2. The Right to an Accounting and Suits Among Partners   623
    Question   627
I. Claims by Creditors of the Partnership   627
  1. Rights Against Partnership Assets   627
  2. Rights Against the Personal Assets of Individual Partners   627
J. Claims by Personal Creditors of a Partner against the Partnership
  Interest of the Partner   629
    Tupper v. Kroc   630
    Notes   634
    Bauer v. Blomfield Co./Holden Joint Venture   634

K. The LLP Shield 637
  Ederer v. Gursky 637
  Notes 642
  Problems 643

Chapter 13 • Dissociation of a Partner and Dissolution of a Partnership 647
  Dreifuerst v. Dreifuerst 648
  Notes 651
A. Causes of Dissolution Under UPA and RUPA 653
  1. Dissolution at Will 654
    Girard Bank v. Haley 654
    Page v. Page 656
    Notes 659
  2. Judicial Dissolution 661
    *Horizon/CMS Healthcare Corp. v. Southern Oaks
      Health Care, Inc.* 661
    Note 666
  3. Wrongful Dissociation 666
    Saint Alphonsus Diversified Care, Inc. v. MRI Associates, LLP 666
    Notes 669
  4. Judicial Expulsion 670
    Brennan v. Brennan Associates 670
    Notes 675
B. Notice of Dissolution and Termination of Authority among Partners 676
  1. Termination of Authority 676
  2. Notice of Dissolution — Lingering Apparent Authority 677
    Note 678
C. Continuing the Business 679
  1. The Buy-Sell Agreement 679
    Estate of Cohen, Ex rel. Perelman v. Booth Computers 679
    Note 683
  2. Continuation Clauses 683
  3. Liability of an Incoming Partner 684
  4. Liability of a Withdrawing Partner 685
    Redman v. Walters 685
    Note 688
  5. Creditors' Claims 688
    Case v. Paul Troester Maschinenfabrik 689
  6. The Treatment of Goodwill 693
    Dawson v. White & Case 693
    Notes 696
  7. Calculation of Buy-out Price Under RUPA § 701 697
    Notes 700
D. Winding Up; Liquidation; Terminating the Business 701
  1. Winding Up and Liquidation 701

Resnick v. Kaplan	701
Notes	703
Marr v. Langhoff	705
Ohlendorf v. Feinstein	707
2. Termination	709
a. Settlement of Accounts	710
b. The Losing Venture: Claims Among Partners	711
Kovacik v. Reed	711
Notes	713
Problems	714
Chapter 14 • The Limited Partnership	**717**
A. Historical Background	720
B. Organizational Defects	721
Briargate Condominium Ass'n v. Carpenter	722
C. The Agreement of Limited Partnership	727
Note	728
D. The Limited Partner	728
1. The Control Question	728
a. In General	728
Holzman v. DeEscamilla	728
Note	730
Gateway Potato Sales v. G.B. Investment Co.	730
Notes	734
b. Control of the Corporate General Partner	736
Zeiger v. Wilf	736
c. Piercing the Veil of a Limited Partnership	742
Canter v. Lakewood of Voorhees	742
Question	748
2. Removal of the General Partner by the Limited Partners for Cause	748
DV Realty Advisors v. Policemen's Annuity	748
3. Suits by Limited Partners	752
Anglo American Security Fund v. S.R. Global International Fund	755
Notes	762
4. Limitations on Distributions and Transfer of Interests	763
Temple v. White Lakes Plaza Assocs., Ltd.	764
5. Duties of Limited Partners	767
KE Property Management, Inc. v. 275 Madison Management Corp.	767
Note	770
6. Rights of Personal Creditors of Partners	770
7. Withdrawal Rights of a Limited Partner	771
8. Merger of a Limited Partnership into Another Entity	771

9. Inspection Rights of Limited Partners 772
10. Dissolution of a Limited Partnership 772
E. The General Partner 772
   1. Powers of a General Partner 772
   2. Fiduciary Duty of the General Partner 773
      Appletree Square I Limited Partnership v. Investmark, Inc. 773
      Notes 776
      Gotham Partners, L.P. v. Hallwood Realty Partners, L.P. 777
      Notes 784
      Brickell Partners v. Wise 787
      Notes 790
   3. The General Partner's Obligations Under the Implied Covenant
      of Good Faith and Fair Dealing 791
   4. Withdrawal of General Partner 794
      Problems 794

Chapter 15 • The Limited Liability Company **797**
A. Introduction 797
B. Tax Matters 800
   1. The Kintner Regulations 800
   2. The Check-the-Box Regulations 800
C. Securities Laws Issues 801
D. The Creation of an LLC 801
      Notes 802
      Elf Atochem North America, Inc. v. Jaffari 803
      Notes 810
E. The Entity Theory and the LLC 811
      Litchfield Asset Management Corporation v. Howell 811
      Notes 817
      Abrahim & Sons Enterprises v. Equilon Enterprises, LLC 819
      Notes 823
      Turner v. Andrew 824
      Questions 825
      Note 826
      Weber v. U.S. Sterling Securities, Inc. 827
      Notes 829
F. The Operation of an LLC 831
   1. The Management of an LLC 831
      Pinnacle Data Services, Inc. v. Gillen 831
      Note 834
     a. Authority and Apparent Authority of Members 834
      Note 835
     b. Fiduciary Duties of Members 837
      McConnell v. Hunt Sports Enterprises 838
      Notes 841

VGS, Inc. v. Castiel   842

Notes   847

Katris v. Carroll   850

Note   854

c. Use of Corporate Structure   854

2. Claims Among Members   855

a. Derivative Claims   855

Wood v. Baum   855

Notes   860

CML V, LLC v. BAX   862

Note   868

b. Direct Claim for Oppression   869

Pointer v. Castellani   869

Notes   877

c. Direct Claim for Breach of Fiduciary Duty   879

Feresi v. The Livery, LLC   879

Notes   883

3. Limitations on Distributions   884

4. Transferability of Interests   885

Condo v. Conners   885

In re Carlisle Etcetera LLC   890

5. Exit Privileges   893

6. Expulsion of a Member   894

Walker v. Resource Development Company Limited, L.L.C.   894

Note   900

7. Claims of Creditors of Members   900

8. Inspection of Books and Records   901

9. Bankruptcy of a Member   902

G. Series LLCS   902

H. LLCs as Social Enterprise Vehicles: The L3C and the Benefit LLC   903

I. LLCs as Estate Planning Devices   904

J. Dissolution of an LLC   904

1. Judicial Dissolution   905

Haley v. Talcott   905

R & R Capital, LLC v. Buck & Doe Run Valley Farms, LLC   912

Notes   918

In re Carlisle Etcetera LLC   920

Holdeman v. Epperson   925

2. Winding Up   931

Hurwitz v. Padden   931

Notes   933

Problems   934

Index   937

Table of Cases

1515 North Wells, L.P. v. 1513 North Wells, L.L.C., 777

8182 Maryland Assoc. v. Sheehan, 685

A.G. Ship Maintenance Corp. v. Lezak, 623

A.J. Richey Corp. v. Garvey, 664

Abraham v. E.H. Porter Constr. Co., 190

Abrahim & Sons Enterprises v. Equilon Enterprises, LLC, 819

Achaian, Inc. v. Leemon Family LLC, 893

Act II Jewelry, LLC v. Mu Ying Zhu, 538

Adams' Express Co. v. Trego, 249

Adelphia Communications Corp., In re, 734

Adler v. Helman, 302

Admiral Oriental Line v. United States, 68

Aegis Corp. v. United Builders of Washington, Inc., 666

Ahn v. Rooney, Pace, Inc., 26

Aiello v. Ed Saxe Real Estate, Inc., 302

Ak's Daks Communications, Inc. v. Maryland Securities Division, 801

Albright, In re, 901

Aldridge v. Franco-Wyoming Sec. Corp., 467

Alexander Myers & Co. v. Hopke, 310

Alma W. v. Oakland Unified School District, 216, 220

American Nat'l Bank v. Miller, 446, 447

Anderson v. Abbott, 44

Anderson v. United States, 633

Angelo Tomasso, Inc. v. Armor Construction & Paving, Inc., 813

Apcar Investment Partners VI, Ltd. v. Gaus, 475

Apex Smelting Co. v. Burns, 205

Application of the County Collector, In re, 853

Arbor Place, L.P. v. Encore Opportunity Fund, L.L.C., 901

Armoneit v. Elliott Crane Serv., Inc., 175

Arnold's of Mississippi v. Clancy, 331

Aronson v. Lewis, 857, 858, 859

Arsand v. City of Franklin, 123

Arthur v. St. Peters Hosp., 273

Arvizu v. Estate of Puckett, 133

ASB Allegiance Real Estate Fund v. Scion Breckenridge Managing Member, LLC, 792

Ash v. Georgia- Pacific Corp., 444

Asociation de Prejudcicos v. Citibank, F.S.B., 480

Atlantic & Gulf Stevedores v. Revelle, 48

Atlas Tack Corp. v. DiMasi, 535

Atwood v. Chicago, Rock Island & Pac. Ry., 49

Aupied v. Joudeh, 66

Auriga Capital Corp. v. Gatz Properties, LLC, 878

Awuah v. Coverall North America, Inc., 58

Azioni v. City of Los Angeles, 132

Azzolina v. Sons of Italy, 238

B.B. Walker Co. v. Burns Int'l Sec. Servs., Inc., 205

Babbitt Bros. Trading Co. v. New Home Sewing Mach. Co., 415

Bailly v. Betti, 621

Bakalis v.Bressler (1953), 592

Balaban v. Bank of Nevada, 631, 633

Balinovic v. Evening Star Newspaper Co., 243

Baltrusch v. Baltrusch, 529

BancInsure, Inc. v. U.K. Bancorporation, Inc., 436

Bancroft-Whitney Co. v. Glen, 576

Band v. Livonia Assocs., 774

Bandringa v. Bandringa, 591

Barnes v. Costle, 225

Barnes v. Lopez, 310

Basil v. Wolf, 273, 274

Basile v. H & R Block, Inc., 29

Bassan v. Investment Exchange Corp., 583, 584

Batzel v. Smith, 21

Baxter Int'l, Inc. S'holders Litig., In re, 858

Baxter v. Morningside, Inc., 132

Baybank v. Catamount Construction, Inc., 771

Bayless v. Christie, Manson & Woods Int'l, Inc., 265

Beals v. Superior Welding Co., 701

Beatty v. H.B. Owsley & Sons, 171

Beckenstein v. Potter & Carrier, Inc., 54

Beckett v. H & R Block, Inc., 29

Beebe v. Columbia Axle Co., 455

Bell v. N. Ohio Tel. Co. (1948), 928

Bell v. Riggs, 54

Belmont v. MB Inv. Partners, Inc., 443

Belt Railway Co. v. Banicki, 205

Benjamin Plumbing, Inc. v. Barnes, 366

Bernier v. Bernier, 876

Berry v. Ostrom, 627

Bescor, Inc. v. Chicago Title & Trust Co., 375

Biever, Drees & Nordell v. Coutts, 111

Billups Petroleum Co. v. Hardin's Bakeries Corp., 296

Bilonoha v. Zubritzky, 180

Bird v. Penn Central Co., 432

Birkner v. Salt Lake County, 193, 194, 196

Birmingham Matinee Club v. McCarty, 332

Birnbaum v. Birnbaum, 568

Bischoff Realty, Inc. v. Ledford, 348

Blackmon v. Hale, 544

Blackmore Partners, L.P. v. Link Energy LLC, 848, 849

Blanchette v. Cataldo, 56

Blum v. Kauffman, 783

Bobrow v. United States Casualty Co., 434

Boehmer v. Norton, 205

Bohatch v. Butler & Binion, 611, 614

Boise Dodge v. Clark, 387

Bolinger, Estate of, In re, 683

Bonds, United States v., 15

Bourjaily v. United States, 18

Boykin v. District of Columbia, 215

Brcka v. Falcon Electric Corp., 803

Brehm v. Eisner, 858

Briargate Condominium Ass'n v. Carpenter, 722

Brickell Partners v. Wise, 787

Brinkley v. Farmers Elevator Mut. Ins. Co., 153

BRJM, LLC v. Output Systems, Inc., 372

Brodie v. Jordan, 873, 876

Brooks v. Shaw, 341

Brown & Bigelow v. Roy, 536

Brown v. Owen Litho Service, Inc., 355

Browne v. Maxfield, 280

Bryant v. Better Bus. Bureau of Greater Md., 138

BT-I v. Equitable Life Assurance Society, 579, 776

Bucher & Willis v. Smith, 263

Burg v. Miniature Precision Components, 106

Burke v. Farrell, 604

Burlington Industries, Inc. v. Ellerth, 227

Bushard v. Reisman, 704

Bushey & Sons, Inc. v. United States, 197, 206

Bushi v. Sage Health Care, PLLC, 884

Byker v. Mannes, 491

Byker v. Mannes, 492

Cahn v. Fisher, 362

Campbell v. United States, 462

Campen v. Stone, 234

Cange v. Stotler & Co., 266, 280

Cannon v. Goodyear Tire & Rubber Co., 194, 196

Canon v. Chapman, 103

Cantor Fitzgerald, L.P. v. Cantor, 770

Cantor v. Cochran, 139

Capital Wireless Corp. v. Deloitte & Touche, 440

Carden v. Arkoma Associates, 823

Caremark Int'l Inc. Deriv. Litig., In re, 857

Carlisle Etcetera LLC, In re, 890, 920

Carr v. Wm. C. Crowell Co., 212

Carter v. Bessey, 193

Carter v. Reynolds, 202

Carter v. Walton, 366

Case v. Paul Troester Maschinenfabrik, 689

Casey Ranch LP v. Casey, 529

Cassano v. Aschoff, 161

Cassiday v. McKenzie, 470

Cates v. International Telephone & Telegraph Corp., 553, 554, 555

Cede & Co. v. Technicolor, Inc., 599

Cefaratti v. Aranow, 278

Cenco Inc. v. Seidman & Seidman, 441, 442

Cencom Cable Income Partners, L.P. Litig., In re, 757, 782

Centro Empresarial Cempresa S.A. v. América Móvil, S.A.B. de C.V., 117

Chalupiak v. Stahlman, 109

Chapel v. Mitchell, 84 N.Y.2d 345, 622

Chase v. Consolidated Foods Corp., 265

Chemical Bank v. Security Pacific Nat'l Bank, 95

Christensen Group v. Puget Sound Power & Light, 59

Citigroup Inc. S'holders Litig., In re, 860

Clapp v. JMK/Skewer, Inc., 25

Clark v. Gunn, 621

Clawson v. Pierce-Arrow Motor Car Co., 185, 186

CML V, LLC v. Bax, 752, 753, 818, 862

Coastal Barge Corp. v. Coastal Zone Indus. Control Bd., 863

Cohen v. Blank, 311

Cohen, In re, 480

Coker v. Dollar, 373

Colby v. Riggs Nat'l Bank, 431

Coleman v. Lofgren, 604

Collins v. Cooper, 525

Colony Assocs. v. Fred L. Clapp & Co., 56

Colorado Accounting Machines, Inc. v. Mergenthaler, 114

Combes v. Montgomery Ward & Co., 194

Combined Ins. Co. v. Sinclair, 75

Computel, Inc. v. Emery Air Freight Corp., 393

Condo v. Conners, 885

Cooke v. E.F. Drew & Co., 152

Cordero v. Christ Hospital, Estate of, 272

Corrales v. Corrales, 479

Cory Bros. & Co. v. United States, 68, 71

Cosgrove v. Bartolotta, 823

Costa v. Borges, 509, 667

Costos v. Coconut Island Corp., 222

Cotten v. Perishable Air Conditioners, 687

Countryman, Estate of, 125, 830

Craig v. Parsons, 103

Creel v. Lilly, 652

Crinkley v. Holiday Inns, Inc., 241

Crozier, Rhea & Co. v. Kirker, 526

Cruz v. S. Dayton Urological Assocs., Inc., 840

CSX Transp., Inc. v. Recovery Express, Inc., 266

Cunard Line Ltd. v. Abney, 549

Cunningham v. BHP Petroleum Great Britain PLC, 486

Cupples, Matter of, 575, 576

Currie v. Land Title Bank & Trust Co., 391

Currier v. Abbott, 150

Curtis v. A. Garica y Cia., Ltda., 167

Curtis, Collins & Holbrook Co. v. United States, 447

Cyrus v. Cyrus, 505

D & G Equip. Co. v. First Nat'l Bank, 469

D. Costas, Inc. v. Rosenberg, 364

Darling Apartment Co. v. Springer, 866

Darling-Singer Lumber Co. v. Commonwealth, 323

Dass v. Yale, 830

Davenport v. Quinn, 813, 814, 816

Davidson v. Harris, 190

Davis v. Dunnet, 252

Davis v. Lane, 462

Dawson v. White & Case, 619, 693, 694

Day v. Parachute Invest. Holdings, LLC, 763

De Pratt v. Sergio, 172

Delaney v. Rochereau & Co., 125

Della Ratta v. Larkin, 481, 771, 776, 794

Deloitte LLP v. Flanagan, 569

Dembrowski v. Central Construction Co., 317

Denburg v. Parker Chapin Flattau & Klimpl, 576

Deonier & Associates v. Paul Revere Life Insurance Company, 79

DeRuyter v. Wis. Elec. Power Co., 203

Desert Equities v. Morgan Stanley Leveraged Fund II, 776

Desimone v. Barrows, 858

DeVaux v. American Home Ins. Co., 264

Diamond v. Oreamuno, 577

Diamond v. Pappathanasi, 762

Dierksen v. Albert, 46

Direct Mail Specialist Inc. v. Brown, 721

Ditzel v. Kent, 528

Dixon v. Crawford, McGilliard, Peterson & Yelish, 697

Dobson, Inc. v. Richard, 383

Doe v. Forrest, 227

Doettl v. Colonial Life & Accident Insurance Company, 80, 81, 83

Douglas Reservoirs Water Users Ass'n v. Maurer & Garst, 543

Dow v. Connell, 152

Dreier, In re, 301

Dreifuerst v. Dreifuerst, 648

Drennis v. Haligiannis, 763

Driscoll v. Towle, 171

Duray Development, LLC v. Perrin, 803

Dynamex Operations West, Inc. v. Superior Court, 158

Eastman v. Clark, 237

Eden v. Spaulding, 147

Edlebeck v. Hooten, 131

Edwards v. National Speleological Soc'y, 239

Effort Enters., Inc. v. Crosta, 205

Eisenberg v. Redd, 688

Elf Atochem North America, Inc. v. Jaffari, 896, 915, 917

Eliason v. Englehart, 865

Eller v. Bartron, Estate of, 95

Elsbury, State v., 631, 633

Emerald Partners v. Berlin, 858

Enea v. Superior Court, 578, 582, 882

Engalla v. Permanente Med. Group, 53

Entente Mineral Co. v. Parker, 293

Eppler, Guerin & Turner, Inc. v. Kasmir, 362

Essex Trust v. Enwright, 120

F & G Investments, L.L.C. v. 1313 Hickory, Ltd., 364

F.C. Adams, Inc. v. Elmer F. Thayer Estate, 66

Faegre & Benson, LLP v. R & R Investors, 510

Fairway Development Co. v. Title Insurance Co. of Minnesota, 496

Faragher v. City of Boca Raton, 227

Farm Bureau Co-op Mill & Supply, Inc. v. Blue Star Foods, 317

Farmers Insurance Group v. County of Santa Clara, 218

Farnsworth v. Deaver, 710

Farwell v. Boston & W.R. Corp., 74

Federal Deposit Insurance Corp. v. Braemoor Assocs., 556

Feldman v. Upton, Cohen & Slamowitz, 165

Feresi v. The Livery, LLC, 79

Ferrer v. Okbamicael, 198

Fiocco v. Carver, 184

First American Title v. Lawson, 435

First Bank v. S & R Grandview, L.L.C., 900

First Nat'l Bank of Cicero v. Lewco Securities Corp., 448

First Nat'l Bank of Cicero v. United States, 444

Fisher v. Fisher, 666

Fisk Ventures, LLC v. Segal, 912, 919

Fitz-Gerald v. Hull, 613

Flippo v. CSC Associates III, L.L.C., 847

Flynn v. Gold Kist, Inc., 205

Flynn v. Reaves, 601

Foley v. Allard, 268

Foley v. Interactive Data Corp., 453

Ford v. Williams, 324

Ford v. Wisconsin Real Estate Examining Bd., 88

Forsythe v. CIBC Employee Private Equity Fund (U.S.) I, 772

Fox v. Abrams, 932

Frank Rizzo, Inc. v. Alatsas, 740

Frank v. United States, 59

Frankel v. Moody, 243

Franklin v. Gupta, 180

Frates v. Nichols, 702

Fravega v. Security Savings & Loan Ass'n, 602

Frederick Inv. Co. v. American Sur. Co., 64

Freeman v. Superior Court, 418

Frontier Traylor Shea, LLC v. Metropolitan Airports Commission, 823

Funds for Business Growth, Inc. v. Woodland Marble & Tile Co., 410

Fuqua v. Taylor, 568

Gandy v. Cole, 406

Garbish v. Malvern Fed. Sav. & Loan Ass'n, 95

Gardner v. Hermann, 269

Gaston v. Sharpe, 176, 177

Gates v. Life of Montana Ins. Co., 453

Gaughan v. Nickoloff, 249

Gavette v. Warner & Swasey Co., 693

Gebhardt Family Investment, L.L.C. v. Nations Title Insurance of New York, Inc., 826

Gelber v. Kugel's Tavern, 825

Gelder Med. Group v. Webber, 613, 694

Gelfand v. Horizon Corp., 101

Gelfand v. Tanner Motor Tours, 231, 232

General Electric Co., United States v., 33

General Overseas Films, Ltd. v. Robin Int'l, Inc., 265

Gerber v. Enterprise Products Holdings, LLC, 792

Gibbs v. Bardahl Oil Co., 455

Gibbs v. Breed, Abbott & Morgan, 572

Gigandet v. Lighting Galleries, Inc., 359

Gildon v. Simon Property Group, Inc., 550

Gilman Paint & Varnish Co. v. Legum, 725

Gilman, United States v., 89

Glanding v. Indus. Trust Co., 921

Glendale Realty, Inc. v. Johnson, 311

Goldstick v. ICM Realty, 382

Golf Digest/Tennis, Inc. v. Diode, Inc., 359

Gorco Construction Co. v. Stein, 58

Gordon v. Pettingill, 394

Gordon v. S.M. Byers Motor Car Co., 172

Gotham Partners, L.P. v. Hallwood Realty Partners, L.P., 784

Gotthelf v. Property Mgt. Sys., 205

Gottsacker v. Monnier, 848

Grace v. Smith, 477

Grainger v. Antoyan, 795

Grant-Howard Assocs. v. General Housewares Corp., 691

Graphic Directions, Inc. v. Bush, 107

Graybar Electric Co. v. Lowe, 723

Grease Monkey International, Inc. v. Montoya, 288

Grede v. McGladrey & Pullen LLP, 440

Green v. Bellerive Condos. Ltd. Pshp., 771

Green v. H & R Block, Inc., 29

Grieb v. Hammerle, 186

Groff v. Citizens Bank of Clovis, 507

Grosboll, Estate of, In re, 505

Grossberg v. Haffenberg, 591

Grotelueschen v. Am. Family Ins. Co., 601

Grove v. Brown, 850

Grubb & Ellis Co. v. First Texas Sav. Ass'n, 363

Guinand v. Walton, 715

Guttman v. Huang, 858

H & R Block, Inc. v. Lovelace, 208 Kan. 538, 57

Hagan v. Adams Property Associates, Inc., 826

Hale Propeller, LLC v. Ryan Marine Products Pty., Ltd., 815

Hamilton v. Natrona County Educ. Ass'n, 221

Hammon v. Paine, 350

Harle v. Krchnak, 180

Harper ex rel. Al-Hamim v. Denver Health and Hosp. Authority, Estate of, 154

Harrelson v. Lee, 818

Harris v. Mardan Business Sys., Inc., 932

Hartell v. Simonson & Son Co., 171

Hartford Elevator v. Lauer, 106

Hausman, In re, 803

Heart of Am. Lumber Co. v. Belovee, 351

Heller Ehrman LLP v. Davis Wright Tremaine LLP, 704

Heller v. Pillsbury Madison & Sutro, 613

Hendrix v. First Bank of Savannah, 404

Henshaw v. Kroenecke, 113

Herbert Constr. Co. v. Continental Ins. Co., 270, 468

Hewitt v. First Nat'l Bank, 421

Heydon v. Heydon, 506

Higgins v. Shenango Pottery, 558

Hinman v. Westinghouse Elec. Co., 197

Hinson v. United States, 150

Hirsch v. Jones Intercable, Inc., 762, 763

Hirzel Funeral Homes, Inc. v. Equitable Trust Co., 413

Historic Hermann, Inc. v. Thuli, 28

Hixon v. Sherwin-Williams Co., 159

Holdeman v. Epperson, 925

Holly Hill Lumber v. McCoy, 329

Holm v. C.M.P. Sheet Metal, Inc., 383

Horecker v. Pere Marquette R. Co., 205

Horne v. Aune, 652

Horning v. Horning Construction, LLC, 918

Howe v. Buffalo, 68

Howell v. First of Boston Int'l Corp., 350

Howell v. Smith, 356, 376

Huatuco v. Satellite Healthcare and Satellite Dialysis of Tracy, LLC, 923

Hubbard v. Tenbrook, 341

Hull, United States v., 125

Hunt v. Rousmanier's Adm'rs, 459

Hunter v. Straube, 683

Huong Que, Inc. v. Luu, 114

Hurney v. Locke, 107

Huston v. Greene, Estate of, 385

Hutchins v. Insurance Co., 150

Hyde v. Cooper, 380

Hydrolevel Corp. v. American Society of Mechanical Engineers, 298, 301

Illinois Central R. Co. v. King, 205

Independent Harvester Co. v. Malzohn, 411

Industrial Mfrs., Inc. v. Bangor Mills, Inc., 342

Industries, Inc. v. DeVilbiss Health Care, 727

Ingram v. Deere, 492

Ingram v. Lupo, 362

Inn Foods, Inc. v. Equitable Cooperative Bank, 396

Instituto Cubano v. The S.S. Theotokos, 368

Inter-Tel Technologies, Inc. v. Linn Station Properties, LLC, 825

Investcorp, L.P. v. Simpson Investment Co., L.C., 933

Investment Management, Inc. v. Jordan Realty, Inc., 653

IOS Capital, LLC v. Allied Home Mtg. Capital Corp., 265

Iron v. Sauve, 237

J & J Builders Supply v. Caffin, 536

J & J Celcom v. AT&T Wireless Servs., Inc., 582, 583, 584, 586

Jahncke Service, Inc. v. Heaslip, 355

Jamison v. Morris, 57

Jennings v. Pittsburgh Mercantile Co., 264

Jensen Sound Lab. v. Long, 678

Jerger v. Rubin, 310

Jessen v. National Excess Ins. Co., 391

Jewel v. Boxer, 703

John Chezik Buick v. Friendly Chevrolet Co., 272

John R. v. Oakland Unified School Dist., 219

Johnson Realty v. Bender, 71

Johnson v. Bernheim, 521

Johnson v. Hunnicutt, 59

Jones v. Healthsouth Treasure Valley Hospital, 278

Jones v. Mutual Creamery Co., 413

Jones v. Wells Fargo Bank, 579

Kahn v. Seely, 703

Kaminski v. Wladerek, 247

Kaplan v. Coldwell Banker Residential Affiliates, Inc., 279

Karle v. Seder, 583, 584

Karrick v. Hannaman, 621

Katris v. Carroll, 850

Kaufman v. IBM, 575

Kaycee Land and Livestock v. Flahive, 817

KE Property Management, Inc. v. Madison Management Corp., 275, 767

Keller v. Gunn Supply Co., 194

Kelley v. Rossi, 153

Kelly v. Blum, 878

Kenai Peninsula Borough v. State, 132

Kilbourne v. Henderson, 50

King v. Bankerd, 247

King v. Barnes, 563

King v. First Nat'l Bank, 47

King v. Horizon Corp., 318

Kingston v. Booth, 122

Kirsch v. Leventhal, 621

Kirschner v. KPMG LLP, 438

Klebanow v. New York Produce Exch., 752

Klein v. Weiss, 248

Kline Bros. v. Royal Ins. Co., 412

Kline Hotel Partners v. Aircoa Equity
    Interests, Inc., 553

Kline v. Gutzler, 331

KMK Factoring, L.L.C. v. McKnew
    (In re William McKnew), 841

Konick v. Berke Moore Co., 150, 151

Kozasa v. Guardian Elec. Mfg. Co.,
    106

Kuehn v. White, 222

Kuznik v. Bees Ferry Associates, 598

L.C.S. Colliery, Inc. v. Mack, 48

Labovitz v. Dolan, 589

Lachmann v. Houston Chronicle Pub'g
    Co., 376

LaFleur v. LaFleur, 147

LaFountain v. Webb Industries Corpo-
    ration, 692

Lampe v. Williamson, 492

Lane v. Cotton, 125

Lauer Const., Inc. v. Schrift, 770

Lavazzi v. McDonald's Corp., 46

Lawlis v. Kightlinger & Gray, 610

Lawrence Co. v. Twohig, 78

Lazo v. Mak's Trading Co., 143

Leafgreen v. American Family Mutual
    Insurance Co., 311

Leff v. Gunter, 579

Leight v. Osteosymbionics, L.L.C., 802

Lenart v. Ragsdale, 323

Leon v. Kelly, 482

Levy & Surrick v. Surrick, 568

Levy v. Nassau Queens Med. Group,
    613

Lewis v. Cable, 391

LiButti v. United States, 814

Licocci v. Cardinal Assocs., 113

Light v. Chandler Improvement Co.,
    307

Liike, Matter of, 504

Lindsay, Marcel, Harris & Pugh v. Har-
    ris, 933

Link v. Kroenke, 266

Lio v. Zhong, 861

Litchfield Asset Management Corp. v.
    Howell, 811

LLC v. RR Donnelley & Sons Co., 819

LNYC Loft, LLC v. Hudson Opportu-
    nity Fund I, LLC, 861

Lola Cars Intern. Ltd. v. Krohn Racing,
    LLC, 919

Lou-Con, Inc. v. Gulf Building Ser-
    vices, Inc., 314

Loughry v. Lincoln First Bank, N.A.,
    234

Lowery, SEC v., 801

Lowman v. Sheets, 644

Lucas v. Liggett & Myers Tobacco Co.,
    314

Luddington v. Bodenvest Ltd., 773

Lumer v. Marone, 368

Luster, State v., 27

Luth v. Rogers & Babler Constr. Co.,
    197

Lyons v. American Legion Post No. 650
    Realty Co., 239

Lyons v. Brown, 201

MacDonald v. Gough, 472

Madden v. Kaiser Found. Hosps., 53

Maddex v. Ricca, 210

Mahan v. Mahan, 710

Mahar v. Stonewood Transport, 226

Main Bank of Chicago v. Baker, 60

Maloney v. Rath, 166

Malpiede v. Townson, 858

Mann v. Adventure Quest, Inc., 436

Marks' Dependents v. Gray, 185

Marley, Estate of, 236

Marqusee v. Hartford Fire Ins. Co., 412

Marsh v. Delta Air Lines, Inc., 88

Marshall v. International Longshore-
    man's Union, 239

Martin v. Heinold Commodities, Inc.,
    90

Mary M. v. City of Los Angeles, 214,
    218, 219

Massachusetts Casualty Insurance
    Company v. Forman, 80

Matanuska Valley Bank v. Arnold, 443

Matulis v. Gans, 383

Matz v. Ibach, 431

Mayer v. Buchanan, 368

Mays v. Brighton Bank, 28, 58

McBriety v. Phillips, 536

McCarthy v. Souther, 150

McCollum v. Clothier, 72

McCombs Constr., Inc. v. Barnes, 59

McConnell v. Williams, 179

McCormick v. Brevig, 502, 652

McCracken v. Hamburger, 341

McCrillis v. A & W Enterprises, Inc., 383

McGee v. Best, 837

McKinney v. Tromly, 180

McKnight v. Peoples-Pittsburgh Trust Co., 73

McLain v. Training & Dev. Corp., 224

MDM Group Associates, Inc. v. CX Reinsurance Co. Ltd, U.K., 85

Mduba v. Benedictine Hosp., 274

Mediacomp, Inc. v. Capital Cities Communication, Inc., 359

Meehan v. Shaughnessy, 570, 574, 578, 706

Meinhard v. Salmon, 105, 883

Merritt v. Merritt, 462

Mervyn Investment Co. v. Biber, 657

Messenger, In re, 644

Metzler v. Layton, 205

Mieuli v. DeBartolo, 719

Mifflin Chem. Corp., In re, 437

Milbank, Tweed, Hadley & McCloy v. Boon, 577

Milford Power Company, LLC v. PDC Milford Power, LLC, 902

Miller v. American Real Estate Partners, L.P., 784

Miller v. Paducah Airport Corp., 824

Miller v. Quarles, 375

Miller v. Westcor Ltd. Pt'ship, 161

Minute Maid Corp. v. United Foods, Inc., 512

Mitchell v. Reed, 565

Mock v. Bigale, 652

Mogensen v. Mogensen, 502

Monin v. Monin, 645

Monroe Park v. Metro. Life Ins. Co., 924

Montoya v. Grease Monkey Holding Corp., 289, 293

Monty v. Orlandi, 214

Moore & Co. v. T-A-L-L, Inc., 105

Moore v. Seabaugh, 356

Morgan v. Harper, 468

Morris v. Brown, 714

Morriss v. Coleman Co., 452

Mortgage Grader, Inc. v. Ward & Olivio, L.L.P., 643

Moses v. Diocese of Colorado, 289

Mosser v. Darrow, 103, 104

Mount Vernon Sav. & Loan v. Partridge Assocs., 730

Moye White LLP v. Beren, 101

Mrachek v. Sunshine Biscuit, Inc., 170

Mundorff v. Wickersham, 434

Munroe v. Harriman, 445

Murphy v. American Home Prods. Corp., 453

Murray v. Standard Pecan Co., 411

Mussey v. Beecher, 285

Mutual Service Cas. Ins. Co. v. Midway Massage, Inc., 154

Mutzenbecher v. Ballard, 467

Myers v. Cook, 405

Napp v. Liberty National Life Insurance Co., 296

National Biscuit Co. v. Stroud, 520

Nationwide Mutual Insurance Co. v. Darden, 157

Naviera Despina, Inc. v. Cooper Shipping Co., 49

Navrides v. Zurich Ins. Co., 415

NCP Litigation Trust v. KPMG LLP, 443

Neal v. Cincinnati Union Stock Yards Co., 431

Nelson v. American-West African Line, 207

Nemec v. Shrader, 85

Nepstad v. Lambert, 172

Nicholes v. Hunt, 651

Nightingale & Associates, LLC v. Hopkins, 878

Nixon v. Blackwell, 878

NLRB v. Friendly Cab Co., Inc., 18

Noonan v. Texaco, Inc., 146

Norby v. Bankers Life Co., 51

North American Catholic Educational Programming Foundation, Inc. v. Gheewalla, 818, 863

Northeast Gen. Corp. v. Wellington Advertising, Inc., 107

Northern Tankers (Cyprus) Ltd. v. Backstrom, 815

Norton v. K-Sea Transp. Partners L.P., 791

Nowell v. Union Mut. Fire Ins. Co., 14

O'Connor v. Uber Techs., Inc., 157, 158

O'Malley v. Putnam Safe Deposit Vaults, 310

O'Neal v. Employment Sec. Agency, 88

O'Toole v. Carr, 244

Ochoa v. Vered, 180

Ohlendorf v. Feinstein, 707

Olmstead v. F.T.C., 900, 901

Olsen v. Vail Associates Real Estate, Inc., 100

Olson v. Halvorsen, 810

Olson v. Staggs-Bilt Homes, Inc., 190

Oneta v. Paul Tocci Co., 145

Opinions of the Justices, In re, 866

Oregon RSA No. 6, Inc. v. Castle Rock Cellular of Oregon Limited Partnership, 606

Owen v. Cohen, 657, 676

Owens v. Palos Verdes Monaco, 527

Owensboro v. Dark Tobacco Growers' Ass'n, 64

Oxford Lake Line v. First Nat'l Bank of Pensacola, 394, 395

P.D. 2000, L.L.C. v. First Financial Planners, Inc., 803

Pacific Landmark Hotel v. Marriott Hotels, 460

Page v. Suraci, 390

Palo Alto Ass'n v. First Nat'l Bank, 687

Pankratz Farms, Inc. v. Pankratz, 652

Pannell v. Shannon, 933

Papp v. Rocky Mountain Oil & Minerals, 479

Pappas v. Tzolis, 837

Parker v. Vanderbilt Univ., 176

Paro v. Trust Co., 150

Parrish Chiropractic Centers, P.C. v. Progressive Casualty Insurance Co., 889, 890

Partners, LLC v. America First Real Estate Investment Partners, L.P., 772

Patmon v. Hobbs, 884

Paul v. Kennedy, 48

PB Real Estate, Inc. v. DEM II Properties, 813, 900

Pee Dee State Bank v. Prosser, 430

Pena v. Greffert, 227

Petersen v. Schneider, 131

Peterson v. Brinn & Jensen Co., 152

Peterson v. Peterson, 468

Petrikis v. Hanges, 527

Phansalkar v. Andersen Weinroth & Co., L.P., 106

Phil Watson, P.C. v. Peterson, 571

Phoenix Airline Svcs. v. Metro Airlines, 861

Phoenix Canada Oil Co. v. Texaco, Inc., 61

Phung v. Waste Mgt., 453

Pierson v. Houston Indep. Sch. Dist., 239

Ping v. Beverly Enterprises, Inc., 252

Plastering Institute Pension Trust v. Elite Plastering Co., Inc., 430

PNC Bank, N.A. v. Farinacci, 549

Pohl v. National Benefits Consultants, Inc., 569

Polikoff v. Levy, 624
Popricki, State v., 137
Port Ship Serv. v. Norton, Lilly & Co., 368
Posner v. Bayless, 248
Potter v. Brown, 675
Potter v. Chaney, 355
Potts v. BE & K Constr. Co., 390
Premier Van Schaack Realty, Inc. v. Sieg, 826
Primary Investments, LLC v. Wee Tender III, Inc., 831
Printing Mart-Morristown v. Sharp Electronics Corp., 739
Prod. Res. Gp., L.L.C. v. NCT Gp., Inc., 863
Puckett v. Codisco, Inc., 363
Pullen v. Dale, 401
Putnam v. Shoaf, 510
Quinn v. Leidinger, 502
R & R Capital, LLC v. Buck & Doe Run Valley Farms, LLC, 912, 922
R.C.M. Executive Gallery Corp. v. Rols Capital Co., 691
R.N.R. Oils, Inc. v. BP West Coast Products, LLC, 823
R.R. Passenger Corp. v. Notter, 429, 431
R.S.M. Inc. v. Capital Management Holdings L.P., 786
Radzvilowicz, State v., 813
Rakestraw v. Rodrigues, 406
Ramlall v. MobilePro Corp., 818
Randall v. Meredith, 526, 544, 546
Rappaport v. Gelfand, 642, 700
Rathke v. Griffith, 720
Rattner v. Bidzos, 859
Rayvid v. Burgh, 360
Red-E-Gas Co. v. Meadows, 454
Redman v. Walters, 685
Reed v. Hinderland, 137
Reisen Lumber & Millwork Co. v. Simonelli, 537
Remora Investments, L.L.C. v. Orr, 884

Resnick v. Kaplan, 932
Rev O, Inc. v. Woo, 885
Richardson-Merrell, Inc., 233
Richert v. Handly, 713
Richmond v. White Mount Rec. Ass'n, 162
Ricketts v. Pennsylvania R. Co., 300
Ridgely v. First National Bank, C.C., 528
Riggs Inv. Mgmt. Corp. v. Columbia Partners, L.L.C., 106
Riley v. Standard Oil Co., 184, 188
Rinke v. Rinke, 650, 651
Riveredge Assocs. v. Metropolitan Life Ins. Co., 643
Robarge v. Bechtel Power Co., 197
Robbins v. Finlay, 112, 113
Roberts Assocs. v. Blazer Int'l Corp., 72
Robertson v. Jacobs Cattle Co., 675, 697
Robinson Bank v. Miller, 502
Robinson v. Glynn, 801
Rocky Mountain Exploration, Inc. v. Davis Graham & Stubbs LLP, 369
Rodgers v. Kemper Constr. Co., 213
Rodliff v. Dallinger, 327
Roepke v. Western Nat'l Mutual Ins. Co., 825
Roginsky v. Richardson-Merrell, Inc., 234
Rohe Scientific Corp. v. National Bank of Detroit, 270
Roll v. Tracor, Inc., 692
Rosenbaum v. Texas Energies, Inc., 431
Rosenblum v. Jacks or Better of Am. West, Inc., 264
Roth v. First Nat'l State Bank, 319
Rothman v. Fillette, 303
Rouse v. Pollard, 546
Royal Carbo Corp. v. Flameguard, Inc., 106
Rumbin v. Utica Mutual Insurance Co., 889
Russell Realty Associates v. Russell, 676
Rykaczewski v. Kerry Home, Inc., 304

S.B. McMaster, Inc. v. Chevrolet Motor Co., 33

Salazar v. McDonald's, 159

Salmon v. Commissioner, 568

Sandrock v. Taylor, 130, 155

Sanford v. Goodridge, 156

Santiago v. Phoenix Newspapers, Inc., 147

Saphir v. Neustadt, 813

Sauter v. New York Tribune, 210

SBC Pledgor 1 2012-1 Trust v. Clark/School, LLC, 934

Schanc v. Conrad, 624

Schoeller v. Schoeller, 708

Schoonover v. Carpet World, Inc., 263

Schroer v. Schroer, 666

Schueler v. Blomstrand, 591

Schuette v. Winternitz, 301

Schuler v. Birnbaum, 625

Scott v. Randle, 282

Security Servs., Inc. v. K Mart Corp., 451

Segars v. McCormick, 550

Seifert v. Union Brass & Metal Mfg. Co., 411

Senor v. Bangor Mills, 339

Serio v. Baystate Properties, LLC, 819

Sexton v. United States, 431

Shank, Irwin, et al., v. Durant, et al., 71

Shannon v. Hudson, 657

Shapiro v. American Home Assurance Co., 435

Sheets v. Teddy's Frosted Foods, Inc., 453

Sheffield Services Company v. Trowbridge, 818

Shephard, In re, 509

Shifrin v. Forest City Ents., Inc., 927

Shimko v. Guenther, 736

Shiner, SEC v., 801

Shoemaker v. Shoemaker, 701

SI Management L.P. v. Wininger, 727

Siddall v. Keating, 695

Simmons v. United States, 216

Simpson v. Thorslund, 626

Simpson v. Union Oil, 35

Sims v. Bergamo, 145

Sladen v. Lance, 522

Slates v. International House of Pancakes, 57

Smith v. Manchester Mgt. Corp., 625

Smith v. Thompson, 121

Soberg v. Sanders, 548

Solar Cells, Inc. v. True North Partners, LLC, 847

Solomon v. Gibson, 445

Sonet v. Plum Creek Timber Co., 776, 789

Soo Line R.R. Co. v. B.J. Carney & Co., 691

Sorenson v. H & R Block, Inc., 29

Southern Bell Tel. & Tel. Co. v. WRNO, Inc., 407

Spaulding v. Benenati, 696

Spayd v. Turner, Granzow & Hollenkamp, 841

St. James Recreation, LLC v. Rieger Opportunity Partners, LLC, 829

St. Louis & St. Charles Bridge Co. v. Union Elec. Light & Power Co., 420

St. Paul Ins. Co. v. Industrial Underwriters Ins. Co., 66

Stanford v. Dairy Queen Products, 57

Stansifer v. Chrysler Motors Corp., 32

Starr v. Fordham, 598

State ex rel. Clarke v. Ripley Sav. Bank & Trust Co., 431

State Farm Mutual v. Johnson, 253

Steckroth v. Ferguson, 675

Stefanski v. Gonnella, 696

Stein Bros. & Boyce, Inc., 66

Sterud v. Chugach Elec. Ass'n, 147

Stewart v. Brooklyn & Crosstown R.R. Co., 231, 233

Stockwell v. Morris, 151

Stoker v. Bellemeade, LLC, 861

Stone ex rel. AmSouth Bancorporation v. Ritter, 857, 858, 860

Stone v. Hurst Lumber Co., 194

Stortroen v. Beneficial Finance Co., 55

Stott v. Greengos, 66

Strain v. Ferroni, 132

Stroll v. Epstein, 359, 363

Sullivan, Bodney & Hammond v. Bodney, 932

Summers v. Dooley, 518

Sunflower Bank, N.A. v. Airport Red Coach Inn of Wichita, L.L.C., 835

Sunset-Sternau Food Co. v. Bonzi, 409

Superior Vending, LLC, In re, 933

Sweeney v. Otter, 669

T & T Communications v. State, Department of Labor and Employment Security, 140

T.G. Slater & Son, Inc. v. The Donald P. and Patricia A. Brennan LLC, 384

Tarnowski v. Resop, 105

Tarron v. Bowen Machine & Fabricating, Inc., 172

Taslich v. Industrial Comm'n, 414

Tauscher v. Puget Sound Power & Light Co., 161

Tedder v. Riggin, 373

Teed v. Parsons, 480

Thayer v. Pacific Elec. Ry., 49

Theis v. duPont, Glore Forgan, Inc., 405

Thelen LLP, In re, 704

Thomas v. Hutchinson, 179

Thompson v. Sun Oil Co., 418

Thomson-Houston Electric Co. v. Capitol Electric Co., 447

Thorn v. City of Glendale, 214

Throop v. F.E. Young & Co., 152

Tiller v. Atlantic Coast Line R. Co., 179

TM2008 Investments, Inc. v. Procon Capital Corp., 884

Tonsic v. Wagner, 180

Tooley v. Donaldson, Lufkin & Jenrette, Inc., 860

Toothman v. Freeborn & Peters, 801

Torrence v. Chicago Tribune Co., 156

Town & Country House & Home Serv. v. Newbery, 111

Travel Centre, Ltd. v. Starr-Mathews Agency, Inc., 251

TravelCenters of Am., LLC v. Brog, 912

Travers, People v., 236

Triple Five of Minnesota, Inc. v. Simon, 569

Trover v. 419 OCR, Inc., 810

Tucker v. Jerris, 380

Tupper v. Kroc, 630

Turner v. Andrew, 824

Tyson Fresh Meats, Inc. v. Lauer Ltd. LLC, 819

Tzolis v. Wolff, 861

United Carolina Bank v. Caroprop, Ltd., 430

United States Cellular Investment Co. of Allentown v. Bell Atlantic Mobile Systems, Inc., 786

USACafes, L.P. Litigation, In re, 790

Utah State Univ. v. Sutro & Co., 50

Valone v. Valone, 772

Vangel v. Vangel, 657

Venture Sales, LLC v. Perkins, 919

Vette v. Giles, 723, 725

VGS, Inc. v. Castiel, 842

Viado v. Domino's Pizza, LLC, 133, 279

Vidricksen v. Grover, 725

Violette v. Shoup, 24

Von Wedel v. McGrath, 251

W.J. Howey Co., SEC v., 801

W.M. Webb, Inc., United States v., 77

Waggaman v. General Fin. Co., 255

Wagner v. City of Globe, 412

Wah Chang Smelting & Ref. Co. of America, Inc. v. Cleveland Tungsten Inc., 909

Walker v. Pacific Mobile Homes, Inc., 263

Walker v. Resource Dev. Co., 783

Walter v. Holiday Inns, Inc., 602

Want v. Century Supply Co., 454

Warren v. McLouth Steel Corp., 167

Water, Waste & Land, Inc. v. Lanham, 357
Watson v. Schmidt, 413
Waugh v. Carver, 476
Webb v. Jorns, 180
Weber v. Stokely-Van Camp, 137
Weil v. Diversified Props., 730
Weinstein v. Colborne Foodbotics, LLC, 818, 885
Weir v. JMACK, Inc., 920
Wellman v. Dow Chemical Co., 829
Wendt v. Fischer, 105, 564
West v. Hartford Fire Ins. Co., 35
Western Alliance Corp. v. Western Reliance Corp., 110
Western Blue Print Co., LLC v. Roberts, 107
White v. Consumers Fin. Serv., Inc., 254
Wiersma v. City of Long Beach, 216
Wilkins v. Waldo Lumber Co., 384
Willey v. Mayer, 292

William Penn Partnership v. Saliba, 848
Williams v. Feather Sound, Inc., 138, 317
Williams v. Good Health Plus, Inc., 154
Wilson v. Joma, Inc., 190
Wilzig v. Sisselman, 684
Winchester v. Howard, 328
Winslow v. Wellington, 150
Wirum & Case Architects v. Cash, 569
Wolfe v. Harms, 601
Wright v. United States, 146, 147
Wylie v. Bushnell, 624
Young v. Nevada Title Co, 50
Zaist v. Olson, 813
Zeiger v. Wilf, 745
Zimmerman v. Hogg & Allen, P.A., 544
Zito v. Fischbein Badillo Wagner Harding, 493
Zito v. United States, 437
Zsigo v. Hurley Medical Center, 227

Preface

This Tenth Edition seeks to incorporate developments in the law of agency and unincorporated business entities since the publication of the Ninth Edition of this casebook in 2015. The courts have considered many issues arising under the revised general and limited partnership acts as well as the limited liability company acts, and I have sought to capture the most important of those cases. Significant developments have occurred in relation to limited liability companies, where the courts have decided numerous cases in the past several years.

As in previous editions, most textual omissions, whether of a few words, a paragraph, or several pages, are indicated by an ellipsis. Occasionally the ellipsis is not used where the nature of the text is such that its use would be excessive or distracting, and sometimes text is slightly rearranged for ease of reading. In addition, omissions consisting of footnotes or of citations to cases or articles are not indicated. Under no circumstances has editing altered the substance of the text being presented. Footnotes that have been retained from cases retain their original numbers in brackets at the start of the text of the footnote. All citations in court opinions to legislation based on one of the uniform acts are treated as if made directly to the uniform act. This avoids the problem of forcing the reader to cope with the different numbering systems of the various states.

I am deeply indebted to my colleague, Professor J. Dennis Hynes, whose meticulous scholarship is reflected in the first five editions of this book and, of course, greatly influences the most recent five editions for which I have been responsible.

Mark J. Loewenstein
Boulder, Colorado
August 2018

Glossary

Agency   The agency relationship is a consensual relationship created when one person (the agent) acts on behalf of and subject to the control of another (the principal).

Agent   An agent is a person (which can include an entity, like a corporation, partnership, or LLC) who acts on behalf of and subject to the control of another.

Agent's agent   This sometimes confusing phrase describes the situation where a person acts on behalf of and subject to the control of an agent for another (the agent's principal) but is not responsible to and does not have the power to create liability for the agent's principal. The phrase is confusing because a subagent (see below) also is an agent of an agent. (The difference is that the subagent is also the agent of, and thus possesses the power to create liability for, the remote principal.) The confusion can be dispelled only by seeing the language in context. Although sometimes ambiguous, the phrase can serve the useful purpose, once a situation is analyzed, of sharply delineating the relationship of the parties in just a few words.

Apparent authority   Apparent authority is the power of an agent to bind the principal to unauthorized contracts. The power is created by manifestations, which can be subtle and indirect, of the principal to the third party that are reasonably relied upon by the third party.

Borrowed servant   A servant (employee) is borrowed when exposure to vicarious liability for the torts of the employee is shifted from the lending employer to the borrowing employer. The standards for determining when an employee is borrowed are in conflict and confusion in the law of many states today. The majority rule appears to require both a transfer of the allegiance of the employee and control by the borrowing employer before vicarious liability is shifted from the lending employer to the borrowing employer.

Business trust   This is a form of doing business through use of a trust. The business trust recently has received significant statutory treatment in some states. At the present time it is infrequently used except in specialized security transactions. It is covered in the Introduction immediately following this glossary.

Co-agent   A co-agent is one of two or more agents of a principal. Co-agents can be in a hierarchical relationship, like that of a president of a corporation and her secretary. Under such circumstances, co-agency appears confusingly like agency because the secretary functions throughout the working day under the direction and control of the president and may even have been hired by the president. Yet the secretary is a co-agent, not the president's agent, because both the president and the secretary work on behalf of their common employer.

Control   To exercise authority over; dominate; direct; regulate. This word has different meanings in the law of agency depending upon context. If, for example, the issue being pursued is liability for the physical torts of another, a special kind of control, over physical conduct and over the details of the activity, is required.

Disclosed principal   A principal is disclosed when a third party has notice of the principal's existence and identity. Under such circumstances, the agent acting in the transaction is not a party to the resulting contract in the absence of special facts, like guaranteeing the contract.

Employee   The term *employee* is a defined term in the Restatement (Third) of Agency § 7.07 and is used to describe an agent for whose torts the principal is vicariously liable. Thus, an employee is "an agent whose principal controls or has the right to control the manner and means of the agent's performance or work." It replaces the term "servant," used in earlier Restatements of Agency and in many common law cases. The new definition makes clear that the term is not limited to traditional, compensated employees, as the definition goes on to provide that "the fact that work is performed gratuitously does not relieve a principal of liability." The term might also exclude an agent who is an employee for purposes of federal and state laws, but whose principal lacks the right to control the manner and means of the agent's performance of work.

Employer   This term is used in the Restatement (Third) of Agency to describe a principal who is vicariously liable for the torts of its "employee" agent. See the definition of "employee." The term "employer" replaces the term "master," used in earlier Restatements of Agency and in many common law cases. As used in the Restatement (Third) of Agency, the term "employer" includes principals who, for other purposes (such as coverage under various federal and state laws regulating the employment relationship), are not "employers."

General agent   A general agent is an agent authorized by the principal to conduct a series of transactions involving a continuity of service, like a manager of a business.

Independent contractor   This is an ambiguous phrase in the law of agency. It can mean a nonagent, such as a building contractor who contracts to build something for an owner but who is not subject to control over the physical conduct of the work and who does not act on the owner's behalf, but rather merely benefits the owner by the work being done as performance under an ordinary contract. The phrase "independent contractor" also refers to a nonservant agent, such as a real estate broker or a lawyer, who acts as agent for another but who is not subject to control over the physical conduct of the work. A principal is not liable for the physical torts of a nonservant agent (independent contractor).

The Restatement (Third) of Agency abandons this term. To determine whether a principal is vicariously liable for the tortious conduct of its agent, the Restatement (Third) has a special definition of the term "employee." If the agent falls within this definition (which focuses on the degree of control that the principal has over the agent), the agent is an employee and the principal has respondeat superior liability for the employee's tortious conduct. The Restatement (Third) also uses the term "nonagent service provider" in some comments to capture one of the meanings of "independent contractor" set forth here.

Inherent agency power   This is a controversial doctrine in the literature of agency. It states that a general agent has the power to bind a principal to unauthorized acts beyond the customary doctrines of apparent authority and estoppel if the acts done "usually accompany or are incidental to" authorized transactions. The Restatement (Third) of Agency abandons this term.

LLC   The acronym "LLC" stands for "limited liability company." This relatively new form of doing business in an unincorporated form is described in the Introduction immediately following this glossary and is covered in detail in Chapter 15. All states allow the creation of LLCs.

LLLP   The acronym "LLLP" stands for "limited liability limited partnership." It refers to a limited partnership in which not only the limited partners but also the general partners have limited liability. This form of doing business is described in the Introduction immediately following this glossary and is covered in Chapter 14.

LLP   The acronym "LLP" stands for "limited liability partnership." It is a recent innovation in the law of partnership, following the widespread adoption of statutes authorizing the LLC. It refers to a general partnership in which the partners have limited liability. This form of doing business is described in the Introduction immediately following this glossary and is covered in Chapter 11. All states have legislation providing for the LLP.

Master   The word "master" is a term of art in the law of agency. It identifies a principal who employs an agent to perform services and who controls or has the right to control the physical conduct of the agent in the performance of the service. A master is vicariously liable for the physical torts of its servant under the doctrine of respondeat superior. The Restatement (Third) of Agency has abandoned this term in favor of the term "employer." See the definition of "employer" above.

On behalf of   This is an essential element of the agency relationship. It means acting *primarily* for the benefit of another, not merely benefiting another by one's actions. A person who acts on behalf of another ordinarily is a fiduciary of the other, due to the trust being placed in the actor under such circumstance.

Partially disclosed principal   A principal is partially disclosed when the third party has notice that the agent is acting on behalf of someone but does not know the identity of the principal. Under this circumstance it is inferred, subject to agreement, that the agent is a party to the contract. The Restatement (Third) of Agency abandons this term in favor of the term "unidentified principal."

Partnership   A partnership is an association of two or more persons to carry on as co-owners a business for profit. It can be formed without any papers being filed and without the owners even realizing that they are creating a partnership. The partnership is described more fully in the Introduction immediately following this glossary and is covered in detail in Chapters 11–13.

Principal   A principal is the one for whom action is taken. The action is taken on behalf of and subject to the principal's control.

Respondeat superior   This Latin phrase means "let the master answer." It is a shorthand and classic expression for the doctrine that a master (or employer) is vicariously liable for the torts of its servant (or employee) committed within the scope of employment.

Servant   The word "servant" is a term of art in the law of agency. A servant is an agent who is employed to perform service and whose physical conduct in the performance of the service is controlled or is subject to the right of control by the master. Janitors and construction workers are examples of servants, although they are unlikely to appreciate being called servants. In part because the word "servant" is passé in today's language, the word "employee" is usually used in its place. "Employee" is less exact, however, because there are servants who are not employees and employees who are not servants. Despite this possible confusion, the Restatement (Third) of Agency abandons the term "servant" in favor of the term "employee," albeit one specially defined. See the definition of "employee" above.

Sole proprietorship   A sole proprietorship occurs when a person carries on a business as its sole owner. No forms need be filed with the state in order to create a sole proprietorship. The proprietor is personally liable for the debts of the business and pays income taxes on the net income of the business. The sole proprietorship is covered in the Introduction immediately following this glossary.

Special agent   A special agent is an agent who is authorized to conduct a single transaction or a series of transactions not involving continuity of service, such as a real estate broker.

Subagent   Subagency exists when an agent (A) is authorized expressly or (more commonly) implicitly by the principal (P) to appoint another person (B) to perform all or part of the actions A has agreed to take on behalf of P. If A remains responsible to P for the actions taken, B is a subagent and A is both an agent (to P) and a principal (to B). B is an agent of P as well as A, which underscores the importance of P's express or implied consent to this relationship.

Undisclosed principal   A principal is undisclosed when the third party is unaware that the agent is acting for a principal and thus assumes that the agent is contracting on its own behalf. Under these circumstances the agent is a party to the contract (as is the undisclosed principal).

Unidentified principal   This term is employed in the Restatement (Third) of Agency to describe what many courts and the earlier Restatements referred to as a "partially disclosed principal." See the definition of that term above.

Agency, Partnership, and the LLC: The Law of Unincorporated Business Enterprises

Introduction

The Law of Unincorporated Business Enterprises

Contained below is an overview of the various ways of doing business in unincorporated form. It is placed here, prior to studying the law of agency, in part because the study of agency may acquire added meaning if one is aware in a preliminary way of the distinct risks run by co-owners in their relations to each other, their employees, and third parties, when operating under different forms of doing business. Most of the forms of doing business discussed in this overview are covered in detail in Chapters 11–15.

There are several matters of common concern for persons who contemplate becoming co-owners of a business with others. These include (1) the right to manage or at least share in the management of the business, (2) the option to avoid personal liability for the debts[1] of the business, (3) enjoyment of favorable tax treatment, and (4) the right to exit the business and cash out one's holdings in a reasonably prompt way. These are not the only issues of importance to co-owners. For example, owners may be concerned about what statutory limitations, if any, exist on distributions to them and what fiduciary obligations they might be subject to, among other things. But the four matters listed above are of such common concern and vary sufficiently among the different business forms that it is useful to look at the different ways of doing business from this perspective.

This overview will commence with a brief look at the main features of the corporation. An understanding in broad terms of the corporate form should provide useful contrast and focus to a discussion of the unincorporated forms of doing business.

A. The Corporation

The topic of the corporation appears to fit poorly into material covering the law of unincorporated business organizations. Nevertheless, a brief introduction to the

---

1. Throughout this essay the word "debts" is used in its broadest sense to include both contract obligations and tort liabilities. The standard statutory phrase for expressing this meaning is "debts, obligations and liabilities," but it seems unnecessary to burden the reader with repetition of that phrase under these circumstances.

law of corporations may prove helpful to those readers who have not yet studied that subject; also, as noted above, it provides a useful contrast to the different forms of unincorporated business associations. A full development of the concepts mentioned below, as well as the application in detail of the law of agency specifically to corporations, will have to await the course on corporations. It is important to note that some (but not all) states have adopted legislation that allows the closely held business (one with a relatively limited number of owners) to be operated in corporate form with less formality than that described below.

———————

A corporation is a legal entity formed under a state statute by filing articles of incorporation with the proper state office.[2] The articles designate, among other things, the number and kinds of shares of stock, which may differ, by classes, in such rights as voting, share of profits, and property rights on liquidation. A corporation is owned by persons who hold shares of its stock. As a legal entity a corporation can sue and be sued, own property, and be required to pay taxes on its income. General policy is set by a board of directors, which is elected by the shareholders. The board of directors in turn appoints officers, who are employees and run the day-to-day business of the corporation.

A corporation can act only through its employees-agents. The board of directors may act only as a group. Individual directors have no authority to establish policy or run the business unless they also are officers.

Debts of a corporation ordinarily are satisfied only out of the assets of the corporation. Thus, the shareholders, members of the board, and officers all enjoy limited liability in the sense that they are not personally liable for the debts of the business.[3] Corporations are required in most states to file reports with the state and to operate with a certain degree of formality. A corporation may be established with a perpetual life.

With regard to the four main concerns of co-ownership expressed above: (1) Management is not in the hands of the owners. Instead, the board of directors manages the corporation, assisted by officers appointed by the board. Thus, ownership and control are separated in a corporation, although individual owners can become officers and members of the board. (2) Liability of owners is limited, as explained above. (3) Taxation is a problem, due to the double taxation created by the corporate form. Income generated by a corporation is taxed first to the corporation. Then, when income is distributed to the shareholders, usually in the form of dividends, it is taxed again as income to the shareholders.[4] (4) Exiting from the

———————

2. Some corporations are organized under federal law, but their numbers are small.

3. This limitation on liability does not apply to personal tortious acts or to personal guarantees of corporate obligations.

4. Double taxation can be avoided by forming an S corporation, but that form is subject to a number of technical restrictions. Also, double taxation is avoided and limited liability available for members of a limited liability company and for the limited partners in a limited partnership, but

business and cashing out are extremely easy when the shares of a corporation are publicly traded. Exit is more of a problem for the closely held corporation where there is no established market in the shares, and usually depends on contractual buyout arrangements.

The corporate form is most widely used for large businesses where there is a need to accumulate substantial amounts of capital and where there is a public market (like the New York Stock Exchange) for trading in the shares of a corporation. Historically the corporate form also has been used for closely held businesses where limited liability for owners of the business was so important that it outweighed the income tax and operational irritations and drawbacks posed by operating in corporate form.

The Historical Price Paid for Limited Liability

Although, as noted above, some states have legislated ways in which the closely held corporation can be operated informally, it is nevertheless true that in most instances the corporate form entails some inconvenience structurally and managerially, in addition to the problems created by double taxation. This was the price paid for limited liability for all owners of a business. That price existed for many years. It no longer need be paid by closely held businesses because of the recent availability of limited liability, and a change in the income tax laws, which make operating in unincorporated form much more attractive, as explained below.

Recent Changes in Limited Liability and Pass-Through Taxation for Unincorporated Businesses

It seems a safe assumption that today many lawyers think first about recommending that clients do business in LLC (limited liability company) or LLP (limited liability partnership) form when dealing with a closely held business. In large part this is because operating as an LLC or LLP can be informal and flexible, carries no disadvantage in terms of limited liability, and provides the benefits of partnership taxation, where the income of the partnership flows directly through to the partners and is not first taxed separately to the partnership.

Limited liability is available to unincorporated businesses (partnerships and limited liability companies) if the entity complies with the appropriate state statute. The change in taxation came about as a result of the adoption of "check-the-box" regulations by the Internal Revenue Service in 1997, abandoning the rigid four-part test used for years by the IRS for distinguishing between corporations and partnerships for tax purposes.[5] It is now possible for an unincorporated business involving

---

limited liability is not available to the general partners of a limited partnership unless the limited partnership qualifies as a limited liability limited partnership.

5. The check-the-box regulations, Treas. Reg. §301.7701 (effective January 1, 1997), provide that an unincorporated business is taxed as a partnership unless it elects to be taxed as a corporation. These regulations replace the Kintner regulations, which stated that any entity having

more than one owner to be taxed as a partnership even if its owners have limited liability and the business has other corporate characteristics, like centralized management, free transferability of interests, and continuity of life.

B. The Different Forms of Unincorporated Businesses

The sole proprietorship and the business trust will receive most of their coverage at this point. A more detailed treatment of the partnership, the LLP, the limited partnership, the LLLP (limited liability limited partnership), and the LLC will take place in Chapters 11–15.

1. The Sole Proprietorship

In one sense, this is not a "form" of doing business at all. A sole proprietorship is simply one person going into business without making any plans for an entity to carry on the business. No papers are filed in order to create the business. The sole proprietorship is one of the two "default" ways of doing business, in the sense that it applies if no other form is chosen. (The other default form, covering the situation where there is more than one owner, is the general partnership.)

The business may be carried on in the owner's (proprietor's) name or it may be given a trade name.[6] The net income from the business is taxable income to the proprietor. All losses are indistinguishable from losses related to the proprietor's personal life and thus can be paid from personal assets. Although it is wise to separate business and personal assets and have a separate accounting for the business, there is no significance in doing so with regard to taxation or liability.

The sole proprietorship is widely used in this country. Over 22,000,000 nonfarm sole proprietorships were active in 2008, the most recent year for which statistics are available, with the number constantly rising (there were 5 million in 1970 and 15 million in 1990). This is more than two and one-half times the combined number of partnerships (3,146,000) and corporations (5,847,000) in 2008.[7] Nearly half of sole proprietorships are in services, and the next largest number are in wholesale and retail trade.

---

a majority of the four corporate characteristics of limited liability, continuity of life, free transferability of interests, and centralized management, was taxed as a corporation. A considerable amount of business planning prior to adoption of check-the-box was devoted to ensuring that unincorporated entities did not have more than two corporate characteristics.

6. If the business is given a trade name, many states require that a filing be made that identifies the owners of the business. These statutes exist largely to protect creditors of the business.

7. http://www.census.gov/compendia/statab/2012/tables/12s0744.pdf.

This surprisingly large number may reflect the informality and small size of most sole proprietorships.[8] Also, the incentive to spend time and money adopting a limited liability form is minimal for a business owned and operated by one person because of the reality that individuals always are liable for their personal wrongdoing and for the contracts they guarantee, and thus nothing significant is gained by doing so.[9] In addition, many people tend not to revisit arrangements when a business starts to grow and hire employees, and thus are perhaps a bit slow about consulting an attorney and obtaining protection from vicarious liability for the torts of their employees by, for example, becoming a single member LLC or a sole shareholder corporation. It is important to emphasize that liability protection does not exist for the personal wrongdoing of an owner in *any* form of doing business; thus the issue of limited liability becomes important only when the owner starts to engage the services of others in an agency capacity.[10]

2. The Business Trust

The business trust originated at common law, utilizing the trust concept first recognized by equity to create an unincorporated business association, commonly known as the Massachusetts trust. It was used earlier in this century primarily as a device designed to provide limited liability for owners of a business while avoiding certain restrictions in some states (in particular, Massachusetts) on operating in corporate form. The business trust is used today primarily for asset securitization ventures in which income-generating assets, such as mortgages, are pooled in a trust, with participation (ownership) interests in the trust sold to investors.[11] The common law business trust has certain drawbacks, as explained below. In 1990

---

8. The accounting, hiring, tax, and operational complexities of operating in sole proprietorship form are well explained in Robert W. Hamilton, BUSINESS ORGANIZATIONS— ESSENTIAL TERMS AND CONCEPTS 29–49 (1996).

9. It may be useful to note that protection from liability is not the only reason some sole proprietorships decide to incorporate or become a single member LLC (most states now allow this). Some accounting efficiencies are achieved by doing so because the LLC and the corporation are entities and the owner is an employee of the entity. In addition, although liability for personal wrongdoing is unaffected, the owner may avoid some small contractual liabilities because the contract is entered into by the entity, with the owner signing as agent. (The reality is, however, that the personal guarantee of the owner will be required by the other party for most contracts involving substantial commitments.) Also, in corporate form, income to the owner can be reported as W-2 income, bypassing the need to use Schedule C on federal income tax form 1040. And, although a minor point, it is possible to borrow from the retirement plan of a corporation, but not from a personal retirement plan.

10. All employees are agents by definition, even though many employees do not contract on behalf of their employer, because they agree to act on behalf of and subject to the control of their employer.

11. *See* Dale A. Oesterle, *Subcurrents in LLC Statutes: Limiting the Discretion of State Courts to Restructure the Internal Affairs of Small Business*, 66 U. Colo. L. Rev. 881, 917 (1995); *see also* Dale A. Oesterle & Wayne M. Gazur, *What's in a Name? An Argument for a Small Business "Limited in Liability Entity" Statute*, 32 Wake Forest L. Rev. 101, 123, n. 117 (1997) (containing a detailed discussion of the use and taxation of business trusts, with citation to other literature).

Delaware passed a statute that avoids the common law defects and provides considerable freedom of contract among the owners and managers.[12] The Uniform Law Commission proposed a uniform act in 2009, The Uniform Statutory Trust Act. It has been adopted by only a few jurisdictions.

A business trust is created by placing the assets of a business in trust under trustees who hold title to the property for the benefit of holders of shares in the trust. The holders contribute capital, receiving shares reflecting the extent of each individual's contribution, and thus are the beneficial owners of the trust. The shares can be made freely transferable without disrupting the continuity of the organization. The trustees manage the business. In the absence of statute to the contrary, the trustees sue and are sued in their individual names, and as legal owners of the business are personally liable for obligations incurred in the business. However, they have a right to reimbursement from the trust assets if the obligation paid does not stem from their own wrongdoing.

One concern at common law is the risk of liability of the beneficial owners if they exercise control over the trustees. Liability is based on the reasoning that the trustees become the agents of the beneficial owners under such circumstance, or the trust may be classified as a partnership. The Delaware statute resolves this by expressly stating that beneficiaries of a Delaware business trust cannot be held responsible for the debts of the trust beyond their original investment. Also, the Delaware statute specifies that the trustees are not personally responsible for the obligations of the business, and that a business trust has a perpetual existence unless the governing instrument provides otherwise.

With regard to the four common concerns: (1) Management is in the hands of the trustees. With respect to common law trusts, the owners cannot control the trustees in any substantial way without running the risk of personal liability; this risk does not exist by statute in some jurisdictions. (2) Liability for owners is limited at common law because they are not the legal owners of the business, and it is limited by statute in Delaware and some other states. (3) Taxation may be on a flow-through basis if business trusts take advantage of the check-the-box change in the tax laws; like public limited partnerships, business trusts that are traded on national exchanges are subject to taxation as corporations pursuant to a special provision of the Internal Revenue Code. IRC §7704. (4) Exit is accomplished by a routine sale of shares and does not cause a dissolution of the trust.

3. The Partnership

As explained in the Glossary, a general partnership is created when two or more persons carry on as co-owners a business for profit. No documents need be filed to create a partnership. It exists as soon as two or more people start doing business

---

12. Del. Code Ann. tit. 12 §§ 3801–3862 (2006).

together without choosing another form of business. In that respect the partnership is a "default" form of doing business. People can become partners without realizing they have done so and with no understanding of the consequences of being in this relationship. Chapters 11–13 are devoted to the partnership.

The law has for centuries provided the two default forms of business operation, the sole proprietorship and the partnership, as a "back-up" for people who enter into business without planning. It is important to note that people sometimes choose these forms deliberately. It is only the default status that is being emphasized at this stage, due to its importance to an overall understanding of the legal consequences of certain decisions relating to business. The other alternatives of doing business in unincorporated form require filing a document with a designated office in the state of origin before the particular entity can come into existence.

With regard to the four matters of common concern: (1) Partners have equal rights to manage the business, unless they agree otherwise. (2) Partners are personally liable for the debts of the firm. (3) Partnership taxation is on a flow-through basis, which means that income is taxed only once, a desirable feature in small business where most income is paid out to the owners. (4) Partners can exit a business whenever they desire, although contractual liability to fellow partners may result from this under some circumstances. Cashing out one's partnership interest can be difficult due to the absence of a ready market for the interest in nearly all cases. Contractual buyout arrangements with fellow partners are common. In the absence of such arrangements, a departing partner has a liquidation right against the partnership, as explained in Chapter 13. Unless otherwise agreed, partners share income and losses equally and must unanimously agree on new partners, thus reducing exit options as a practical matter. Each partner is a general agent of the partnership.

4. The Limited Liability Partnership (LLP)

The limited liability partnership ("LLP") makes available limited liability for all partners of a general partnership if a proper filing is made with the state. An LLP is a general partnership in all other respects. All states have amended their partnership acts to make filing for LLP status possible.

The limited liability made available by the LLP shields partners from vicarious liability for the acts of others. Some states ("full shield" states) provide more protection than others ("partial shield" states), as developed in Chapter 11. All partners in full shield states may avoid vicarious liability for the debts of the business, just as if they were shareholders of a corporation, simply by filing a certificate in a designated office in the state.

5. The Limited Partnership

The limited partnership is a creature of statute. It is quite distinct from the LLP, although the names are confusingly similar. It is formed by filing a document with a designated office in the state. All states recognize the limited partnership, which is covered in detail in Chapter 14.

The limited partnership has general and limited partners. General partners in a limited partnership are like general partners in a conventional partnership, which includes having personal liability for the debts of the business.[13] Limited and general partners are owners and enjoy the tax benefits of being partners in a partnership. By statute the limited partners are not liable for the debts of the business, although care must be exercised in some states about their participation in control. They do not have management rights in their status as limited partners, although they can contract otherwise.

With regard to the four common concerns of co-ownership: (1) As noted above, limited partners do not have management rights as a matter of status. Management of a limited partnership is in the hands of its general partners. Because of this clear-cut separation of managerial rights and responsibilities, limited partnerships are regarded as "hard-wired." (2) Limited partners are exempt from liability for the debts of the firm, unlike the general partners of the firm. (3) The taxation benefits of operating in partnership form are fully available to general and limited partners in a limited partnership. (4) Exit privileges are more confined for limited partners. Under some statutes, limited partners are entitled to a return of their capital after some period after giving notice of withdrawal, unless the partnership agreement specifies otherwise, as almost all agreements do. In some cases the limited partnership interests are, by agreement, freely transferable, and may even be evidenced by certificates and traded on national securities exchanges.[14]

6. The Limited Liability Limited Partnership (LLLP)

The limited liability limited partnership ("LLLP") is an entity authorized by statute and has only recently arrived on the scene. A filing with the state is required to create an LLLP. If a filing is properly made, limited liability is extended to the general partners of a limited partnership in the same manner as it is to partners in an LLP. In all other respects the LLLP is like a regular limited partnership. Legislation enabling the creation of LLLPs is rapidly being adopted by the states.

7. The Limited Liability Company (LLC)

The limited liability company ("LLC") offers owners the benefits of limited liability, taxation as a partnership, and management flexibility. Liability is limited in the sense that owners (called "members") are not liable as such for the debts of the

---

13. Often a limited partnership will have solely a corporate general partner, as an "end run" around the liability issue.

14. As noted previously when discussing the business trust, public limited partnerships are taxed as corporations by special provision of the Internal Revenue Code.

business, and in that sense are in a similar position to shareholders of a corporation. The LLC is covered in detail in Chapter 15.

It is necessary to file a document with the state in order to create an LLC. All states have adopted enabling legislation for LLCs, with considerable variation from state to state. The Uniform Law Commission promulgated a Uniform Limited Liability Company Act (1995) ("ULLCA"), which is set forth in the statutory supplement to this book together with the 2006 (with further amendments in 2013) revision of that Act, referred to herein as RULLCA. As of this writing, 18 jurisdictions had adopted RULLCA.

With regard to the four major concerns: (1) Management is shared among the owners, just as it is among partners in a partnership, in a "member-managed" LLC. Owners are free to form a "manager-managed" LLC, placing management in the hands of managers (who may or may not be members). (2) Liability of owners is limited, as explained above. (3) Taxation, as in a partnership, is on a pass-through basis, unless an election is made under the check-the-box regulations to be taxed as a corporation. (4) Exit from the entity need not cause dissolution of the LLC under statutes that have been amended following adoption of the check-the-box regulations.

The organizing document of an LLC is referred to nearly everywhere as an "operating agreement." The LLC is desirable for small businesses due to the enactment of LLC legislation in all 50 states and the flexible management and operational structure of the LLC, as contrasted with the corporation.

Chapter 1

The Agency Relationship; The Ambiguous Principal Problem; Subagency

Most chapters will begin with questions about the law to be covered in the chapter before introduction of the legal principles that have been adopted for the resolution of such matters. This is done in order to encourage the reader to formulate answers to the questions based on common sense and fairness prior to exposure to the thinking of others, which may encourage a sense of measured skepticism when approaching the law.

Several hypotheticals are set forth below. In working through them, assume that a "yes" answer should be given to the questions posed if you resolve that an agency relationship exists. A widely recognized definition of the agency relationship will be set forth shortly.

1. *B* entered into a one-year lease of a single-family residence with *O*, owner of the house, and took occupancy. Six months later a saleswoman for Ace Home Improvement stopped at the house and, seeing *B*, offered a contract to paint the house for $1,500. *B* said, "OK, but not on my liability. I'm renting the place from *O*. I'll enter into this contract for him." The contract was entered into. Subsequently *O* refused to let Ace's crew do any painting. Ace sues *O* for breach of contract. Is *O* liable to Ace?

2. *P*, an Italian who understands no English, employs *A*, an interpreter, to make an offer to *T* that *P* will buy certain described goods from *T*. *A* misunderstands *P* and makes an offer for different goods also sold by *T*, which *T* in good faith accepts. Is *P* bound to *T*?

3. *H* and *W* are husband and wife. *W* runs an interior decorating business. *H* is a school administrator. Recently *W* bid on a redecorating job for *R*, an acquaintance of *H* and *W*. *R* has decided to accept the bid. She sees *H* at a local cross-country race and says to him, "Tell *W* I've decided to accept her bid on the redecorating job for me." *H* agrees to do so, but later forgets to pass on the information. Is the attempted acceptance effective?

4. Able is a neighbor of Parr. One day Able mentions to Parr that she is going to the local hardware store to buy some materials. Parr responds, "While you're there would you get me four pounds of eight-penny nails? Just charge it to my account."

Able assents, charges the goods to Parr's account, and thereafter decides to make personal use of them. Would Parr nevertheless be liable to the store?

The Agency Relationship

The definition of an agency relationship is set forth in § 1.01 of the Restatement (Third) of Agency:

> Agency is the fiduciary relationship that arises when one person (a "principal") manifests assent to another person (an "agent") that the agent shall act on the principal's behalf and subject to the principal's control, and the agent manifests assent or otherwise consents so to act.

The next two cases demonstrate the breadth of this definition. In the first, *Carrier v. McLlarky*, the court finds an agency relationship, and in the second, *U.S. v. Bonds*, the court does not, over a vigorous dissent. Consider the extent to which the Restatement definition, which is widely accepted, influenced the outcome in these cases and whether you agree with those outcomes.

Carrier v. McLlarky
Supreme Court of New Hampshire
693 A.2d 76 (1997)

Johnson, Justice.

The defendant, Bruce M. McLlarky d/b/a Assured Plumbing & Heating, appeals an adverse judgment by the Derry District Court (Warhall, J.) in a small claims matter. We reverse.

The defendant installed a replacement hot water heater in the home of the plaintiff, Janet Carrier, in September 1994. The existing water heater had been installed by a different plumber approximately four years prior to its failure. When the defendant installed the new water heater, he told the plaintiff that he believed the old unit was under warranty, and that he would try to obtain a credit against the cost of the new water heater from the manufacturer. The defendant subsequently returned the defective unit to a supplier. The defendant has not given the plaintiff the desired credit and claims that he has failed to do so because he has not received payment from the manufacturer. The plaintiff sued the defendant in small claims court for the replacement value of the water heater and assorted costs. The district court rendered judgment in favor of the plaintiff, and this appeal followed.

The district court held: "The defendant in accepting the duty of returning the unit for the benefit of his [principal], the plaintiff[,] either obtained a credit or failed to pursue a credit to the detriment of the plaintiff." We interpret the court's holding as imposing liability under a theory of breach of duty on the part of an agent. *See Nowell v. Union Mut. Fire Ins. Co.*, 119 N.H. 855, 857, 409 A.2d 784, 786 (1979) (breach of agent's duty to principal can subject him to liability for damages).

We find no error in the district court's determination that the parties had entered into an agency agreement whereby "the defendant would on behalf of the plaintiff return the old water heater for credit, which the plaintiff would [recoup]," and that "[t]he defendant accepted the authority to act for the plaintiff and took the old water heater to return it to the manufacturer for credit." Whether an agency agreement has been created is a question of fact. An agency relationship is created when a principal gives authority to another to act on his or her behalf and the agent consents to do so. The granting of authority and consent to act need not be written, but "may be implied from the parties' conduct or other evidence of intent." *93 Clearing House, Inc. v. Khoury*, 415 A.2d [671] at 673 (N.H. 1980). This court will not overturn a factual finding of the trial court unless it is unsupported by the evidence. Here, both the testimony and documentary evidence submitted by the parties support a finding that an agency agreement had been formed.

The question thus becomes whether there is evidence in the record to support a finding of breach. Agents have a duty to conduct the affairs of the principal with a certain level of diligence, skill, and competence. "A determination that an agent was not sufficiently diligent is a question of fact that will not be disturbed unless it can be said that no rational trier of fact could come to the conclusion that the trial court has reached." 409 A.2d at 786. We find that in this case the trial court's findings were unreasonable and unsupported by the record.

"Under ordinary circumstances, the promise to act as an agent is interpreted as being a promise only to make reasonable efforts to accomplish the directed result." *Restatement (Second) of Agency* § 377, Comment b at 174 (1957). The court's own findings show that the defendant did make a reasonable attempt to obtain a refund for the plaintiff. Specifically, the court found that after agreeing to act on behalf of the plaintiff, "[t]he defendant then gave the old water [heater] to [a supplier] to return it to the manufacturer." . . . The record shows only that the defendant was charged with returning the defective water heater for a possible credit; he did not guarantee that a credit would be obtained. . . .

Consequently, because the district court's ruling was unsupported by the evidence, we reverse.

Reversed.

All concurred.

United States v. Bonds

United States Court of Appeals, Ninth Circuit
608 F.3d 495 (2010)

Before: MARY M. SCHROEDER, STEPHEN REINHARDT and CARLOS T. BEA, CIRCUIT JUDGES.

SCHROEDER, CIRCUIT JUDGE:

In 2001, Barry Bonds hit 73 home runs for the San Francisco Giants. Also in 2001, as well as in prior and succeeding years, BALCO Laboratories, Inc. in San Francisco recorded, under the name "Barry Bonds," positive results of urine and blood tests for performance enhancing drugs. In 2003, Bonds swore under oath he had not taken performance enhancing drugs, so the government is now prosecuting him for perjury. But to succeed it must prove the tested samples BALCO recorded actually came from Barry Bonds. Hence, this appeal.

. . . .

I. Background

BALCO Laboratories, Inc. was a California corporation that engaged in blood and urine analysis, and was located in San Francisco. In 2003, the IRS began to investigate BALCO, suspecting the company of first, distributing illegal performance enhancing drugs to athletes, and then, laundering the proceeds. In September 2003, the government raided BALCO and discovered evidence which it contends linked both trainer Greg Anderson ("Anderson") and BALCO to numerous professional athletes. One of these athletes was professional baseball player and Defendant Barry Bonds ("Bonds"). The government also found blood and urine test records which, it asserts, established that Bonds tested positive for steroids.

On multiple occasions Anderson took blood and urine samples to BALCO Director of Operations James Valente ("Valente") and identified them as having come from Bonds. According to Valente, when he received a urine sample from Bonds, he would assign the sample a code number in a log book, and then send the sample to Quest Diagnostics ("Quest") for analysis. Quest would send the result back to BALCO. BALCO would then record the result next to the code number in the log book. Also, according to Valente, BALCO would send Bonds' blood samples to Lab-One & Specialty Lab ("LabOne") for analysis. The government seized the log sheets from BALCO, along with the lab test results.

Before the grand jury in the probe of BALCO, the questioning by the government focused extensively on the nature of Bonds' relationship with Anderson. Bonds testified that he had known Anderson since grade school, although the two had lost touch between high school and 1998. In 1998, Anderson started working out with Bonds and aiding him with his weight training. Anderson also provided Bonds with substances including "vitamins and protein shakes," "flax seed oil," and a "cream." According to the government, some or all of these items contained steroids. Anderson provided all of these items at no cost to Bonds. Bonds testified he took whatever supplements and creams Anderson gave him without question because he trusted Anderson as his friend. ("I would trust that he wouldn't do anything to hurt me."). Bonds stated that he did not believe anything Anderson provided him contained steroids. He specifically denied Anderson ever told him the cream was actually a steroid cream.

With respect to blood sample testing, Bonds testified before the grand jury that Anderson asked Bonds to provide blood samples on five or six occasions, telling Bonds he would take the blood to BALCO to determine any nutritional deficiencies in his body. Bonds said that he would only allow his own "personal doctor" to take the blood for the samples.

Bonds also testified he provided around four urine samples to Anderson and he believed the urine samples were also going to be used to analyze his nutrition. Anderson also delivered these samples to Valente at BALCO for analysis. ("Greg went [to BALCO] and dealt with it."). Bonds did not question Anderson about this process because they "were friends."

The government showed Bonds numerous results of blood and urine tests but Bonds denied ever having seen them before. Rather Bonds contended that Anderson verbally and informally relayed the results of any tests to him. Bonds stated that Anderson told him that he tested negative for steroids. ("Greg just said: "You're— you're negative."). Bonds trusted what Anderson told him. ("He told me everything's okay. I didn't think anything about it.").

With respect to the relationship between Bonds and Anderson, Bonds admitted to paying Anderson $15,000 a year for training. Bonds stated that this payment was not formally agreed to. Rather, Bonds contended that he "felt guilty" and "at least [wanted to give Anderson] something." ("Greg has never asked me for a penny."). Bonds had several trainers and considered some of the trainers employees, but considered Anderson a friend whom he paid for his help. ("Greg is my friend. . . . Friend, but I'm paying you."). Bonds made his payments to Anderson in lump sums. In 2001, the year he set the Major League Baseball single season home run record, Bonds also provided Anderson, along with other friends and associates, a "gift" of $20,000. Bonds spent considerable time with Anderson in San Francisco but Bonds noted that Anderson only visited during weekends during spring training.

On February 12, 2004, a grand jury indicted Anderson and other BALCO figures for their illegal steroid distribution. Anderson pled guilty to these charges and admitted to distributing performance enhancing drugs to professional athletes. The government also commenced an investigation into whether Bonds committed perjury by denying steroid use during his grand jury testimony. Anderson, since that time, has continuously refused to testify against Bonds or in any way aid the government in this investigation and has spent time imprisoned for contempt.

II. Procedural History of this Appeal

On December 4, 2008, the government indicted Bonds on ten counts of making false statements during his grand jury testimony and one count of obstruction of justice. They included charges that Bonds lied when he 1) denied taking steroids and other performance enhancing drugs, 2) denied receiving steroids from Anderson, 3) misstated the time frame of when he received supplements from Anderson.

The next month, in January 2009, Bonds filed a motion in limine to exclude numerous pieces of evidence the government contends link Bonds to steroids. As relevant to this appeal Bonds moved to exclude two principal categories of evidence: the laboratory blood and urine test results, and the BALCO log sheets of test results.

When the government sought to introduce as business records the lab test results from Quest (urine) and LabOne (blood) seized from BALCO, Anderson's refusal to testify created an obstacle. The essence of the government's identification proof was Anderson's identification of the samples to Valente as Bonds'. The government wanted to introduce Valente's testimony that Anderson told him for each sample that "This blood/urine comes from Barry Bonds," in order to provide the link to Bonds. Because the government was attempting to use Anderson's out of court statements to prove the truth of what they contained, Bonds argued that Anderson's statements were inadmissible hearsay and that the lab results could not be authenticated as Bonds' in that manner. *See* Fed. R. Evid. ("FRE") 802 ("Hearsay is not admissible except as provided by these rules or by other rules prescribed by the Supreme Court pursuant to statutory authority or by Act of Congress.").

The government sought to fit the statements within a hearsay exception. In its response to the defense motion in limine the government countered that Anderson's statements were admissible ... as statements of an agent (Anderson as Bonds' agent) under FRE 801(d)(2)(D). The court held that the government, as the proponent of hearsay, had failed to prove by a preponderance of the evidence that any of the exceptions or exemptions applied. *See Bourjaily v. U.S.*, 483 U.S. 171, 175, 107 S. Ct. 2775, 97 L. Ed. 2d 144 (1987) (holding that proponent of hearsay must prove exception or exemption by preponderance of the evidence).

III. Discussion

. . . .

B. Admissibility of Anderson's Statements Under 801(d)(2)(C) and (D).

... FRE 801(d)(2)(D) provides that a statement is not hearsay if it "is offered against a party and is ... a statement by the party's agent or servant concerning a matter within the scope of the agency or employment, made during the existence of the relationship." ... Subsection (D) authorizes admission of any statement against a party, but only provided it is made within the scope of an employment or agency relationship.

. . . .

To determine whether Anderson's statements are admissible under Rule 801(d)(2)(D), we must "undertake a fact-based inquiry applying common law principles of agency." *NLRB v. Friendly Cab Co., Inc.*, 512 F.3d 1090, 1096 (9th Cir. 2008). For Anderson's statements to fall under this exception, he would have to have been Bonds' ... agent.

. . . .

Accordingly, we must now address the government's argument that ... Anderson ... acted as an agent in delivering Bonds' blood and urine to BALCO. An agent is one who "act[s] on the principal's behalf and subject to the principal's control." *Restatement (Third) Agency § 1.01.* To form an agency relationship, both the principal and the agent must manifest assent to the principal's right to control the agent. *Id.*

As is clear from the above description of Anderson's and Bonds' relationship, Anderson did not generally act subject to Bonds' control in his capacity as a some-time trainer, nor did he or Bonds manifest assent that Bonds had the right to control Anderson's actions as a trainer. There is no basis in the record to differentiate between Anderson's actions in his capacity as a trainer and his conduct in delivering the samples to BALCO. There is little or no indication that Bonds actually exercised any control over Anderson in determining when the samples were obtained, to whom they were delivered, or what tests were performed on them. Nor, contrary to the dissent's assertion, is there any indication that either Bonds or Anderson manifested assent that Bonds would have the right to instruct Anderson in these respects. It was Anderson who proposed to Bonds that he have his blood and urine tested. Bonds provided samples to Anderson when requested by the latter, and according to Bonds' testimony, "didn't think anything about it" after doing so. It was, further, Anderson who selected BALCO as the location for testing. In short, it was Anderson who defined the scope of the testing. Bonds provided Anderson no guidance or direction in terms of what specific tests BALCO would run on the samples. Bonds did not even inquire into the results of the tests. Rather, Anderson would, apparently on his own initiative, inform Bonds of results. The dissent says that Bonds instructed Anderson to deliver the samples to BALCO within 30 minutes of extraction, but this is not correct. The record shows that it was Anderson who told Bonds about the 30-minute time constraint. Moreover, the samples were taken at Bonds' house not because Bonds so ordered, but because his house was close to BALCO and taking the samples there made it possible for them to be delivered in time. Bonds quite understandably would allow only his own doctor to take the samples, but this does not show that he also had reserved the right to instruct Anderson as to what to do with the samples. *See Restatement (Third) of Agency § 1.01 cmt. f* (stating that the fact that a service recipient imposes some constraints on the provision of services does not itself mean that the recipient has a general right to instruct and control the provider).

While the dissent focuses on whether, as a practical matter, Bonds had the "capacity" to assess Anderson's performance and give Anderson instructions as to how to have the testing performed, it ignores the key question: whether Bonds and Anderson ever agreed that Bonds could do so. These are very different inquiries. Any time one person does something for another, the latter is in all likelihood capable of evaluating and instructing the first. The Restatement provision on which the dissent relies makes it clear, however, that not all service providers and recipients stand in agency relationships. *Restatement (Third) of Agency § 1.01 cmt f.* Rather, as we have seen, an agency relationship exists only if both the provider and the recipient have manifested assent that the provider will act subject to the recipient's control and instruction. *Id.* The question whether Bonds had the ability, in a practical sense, to prevent Anderson from having the testing carried out similarly fails to resolve the question whether Anderson was Bonds' agent. Obviously Bonds could have put an end to the testing by refusing to provide Anderson with samples of his blood and urine, but that does not establish an agency relationship. There is nothing in the record that requires a finding that Bonds actually controlled Anderson with respect to the testing or that Bonds and Anderson had agreed that Anderson would be obligated to follow Bonds' instructions if Bonds chose to provide them. Contrary to the dissent's contention, we do not maintain there needs to be an explicit agreement, but there must be at least some manifestation of assent to the principal's right to control. Here, the testing was performed on Anderson's own initiative and not at the request of Bonds. The dissent incorrectly assumes otherwise. Thus, the district court did not abuse its discretion in finding that Anderson was not an agent for the limited purpose of the drug testing.

IV. Conclusion

The district court's evidentiary rulings are AFFIRMED and the case is remanded for further proceedings consistent with this opinion.

Bea, Circuit Judge, dissenting:

I dissent.

. . . .

The district court, and then the majority, err in holding Anderson's statements were hearsay. Statements made by a party's agent that are related to a matter within the scope of his agency or by a person's authorized speaker are not hearsay under Federal Rules of Evidence 801(d)(2)(D). . . . Instead, such statements are considered admissions of a party litigant. . . . This is not a situation where overwhelming evidence supports the district court's holding, such that we should affirm despite the presence of one or two isolated errors in the district court's opinion. To the contrary, the evidence here strongly supports a finding that Anderson's statements were admissible in evidence because they (1) were statements about a matter related to a matter within the scope of Anderson's agency for Bonds, for the purposes of Rule 801(d)(2)(D). . . .

B. Anderson's Task

The district court and the majority's error, in holding that Anderson's statements are inadmissible under Rules 801(d)(2)(D) . . . seems a consequence of their focus on Anderson's role as Bonds's trainer—a red herring—and their overly narrow characterization of the task the evidence proves Bonds entrusted Anderson to perform. It is not necessary for the government to rely on some professional label, such as trainer or coach, for Anderson's statements to be admissible. As I will discuss below, it is enough that Bonds authorized Anderson to be his agent for the purpose of the specific task of setting up tests and procuring accurate test results from BALCO, or, that Bonds authorized Anderson to make statements that would be usual and ordinary in accomplishing that task. For the sake of clarity, I set forth at the outset of this analysis a complete description of what I see as Anderson's task (the "Task").

Bonds assented that Anderson perform the following actions on Bonds's behalf: (1) procure the vials which were to contain the blood and urine samples, and furnish such vials to Bonds and Bonds's doctor; (2) once the vials were filled with Bonds's samples, collect such samples from Bonds at Bonds's home; (3) deliver the samples to BALCO within 30 minutes of collection of the bodily fluids; (4) deal with BALCO to procure testing of the samples; (5) learn the test results from BALCO; and (6) report the test results to Bonds. For Anderson to accomplish this Task successfully, it was necessary for him to identify the samples in a manner that would later allow BALCO accurately to report test results to Anderson and for Anderson to know the results were truly of Bonds's samples, so he could accurately report to Bonds his BALCO results. Anderson's Task included each and all of the above-enumerated actions.

C. Anderson's Statements Are Admissible Under Rule 801(d)(2)(D) (statements of an agent concerning a matter within the scope of the agency or employment).

. . . .

(1) *Anderson was Bonds's agent for the Task.* Agency is the fiduciary relationship that arises when one person, the principal, manifests assent to the agent for the agent to act on the principal's behalf and subject to the principal's control, and the agent agrees or otherwise consents. *Batzel v. Smith*, 333 F.3d 1018, 1035 (9th Cir. 2003); *accord* Restatement (Third) of Agency § 1.01 (2006). In short, agency requires (a) the principal's assent; (b) the principal's right to control; (c) the agent acting on the principal's behalf or benefit; and (d) the agent's consent.

(a) *Bonds assented to Anderson's performance of the Task.* Bonds testified that he agreed to have Anderson take his blood and urine samples to BALCO. Moreover, Bonds manifested such assent not only to Anderson, but to BALCO, for Bonds testified he met with Conte, CEO of BALCO, and Anderson at BALCO's facilities. There, Conte, Bonds, and Anderson discussed testing Bonds's bodily fluids and the consequent results as to his nutrient levels. Bonds did not object to Anderson's dealing with BALCO to procure the testing and results discussed. Bonds also asked Anderson to have him tested to check Major League Baseball's tests for errors.

(b) *Bonds had the right to control Anderson's performance of the Task.* "The principal's right of control presupposes that the principal retains the capacity throughout the relationship to assess the agent's performance, provide instructions to the agent, and terminate the agency relationship by revoking the agent's authority." Restatement (Third) of Agency § 1.01 cmt. f (2006). This is a key point of dispute between my analysis and that of the majority; I think the evidence shows Bonds had the capacity to control Anderson's performance of the Task and the panel does not. Admittedly, Bonds testified he did not exercise much supervisory authority over Anderson. But our inquiry is not whether Bonds *exercised* his authority, but only whether Bonds *had* the authority to exercise in the first place. *Id.* cmt. c ("A principal's failure to exercise the right of control does not eliminate it."). For example, just because a movie actor does not exercise his right to reject a screen role through his agent does not mean that he no longer has an agent, or that he can no longer reject roles through the agent.

Here, Bonds had the capacity to assess Anderson's performance. For example, Bonds could have called BALCO to verify Anderson was procuring testing and successfully delivering the samples within 30 minutes of collection. Or, Bonds could have reviewed the test results documents. Bonds's own testimony creates an inference that Bonds could have done so: "So, I never saw the documents. I should have. Now that I think of it with the situation that is now, I should have." The fact that Bonds did not assess and modify or terminate Anderson's performance of the Task does not mean, as a matter of law, that Bonds lacked the *right* to do so.

Bonds also had the right to instruct Anderson. Not only did Bonds have that right, but he exercised it by instructing Anderson when and where Anderson was to collect Bonds's samples and when and where Anderson was to deliver the samples. The majority is correct that Bonds did not instruct Anderson regarding the 30-minute limit, but that limit did provide one measure by which Bonds could evaluate Anderson's actions. The point, however, is that Bonds did instruct Anderson when and where to collect his samples—at his home in San Francisco. The majority seems to argue that the fact that Bonds's house was also a suitable location under the 30-minute requirement is incompatible with Bonds's instructing Anderson, but that is illogical. There were many places they could meet that were within 30 minutes of BALCO; Bonds instructed Anderson to come to Bonds's house and not to another location, most likely because it was a private place where Bonds's personal doctor would be comfortable drawing his blood and collecting his urine. Further, Bonds controlled when he could be tested because Anderson could not complete his task without Bonds's samples.

Moreover, the majority completely omits the fact that Bonds met with BALCO's CEO Conte to discuss, in Anderson's presence, the procedure for testing his blood and urine. This fact strongly supports the conclusion that Bonds was intimately familiar with BALCO's testing procedures, and therefore able to assess and instruct Anderson, even if he "didn't think anything about it" after doing so.

Most importantly, Bonds had the right and ability to terminate the agency relationship—a factor essentially ignored by the majority. Were Bonds to decide to terminate the relationship, he could simply have stopped giving samples of his blood and urine to Anderson. Without Bonds's samples, Anderson could not perform the Task. It would be implausible to find Anderson had access to some reserve of Bonds's blood or urine that he could have tested despite Bonds's terminating his agency relationship with Anderson. Besides, any such reserves could not meet the 30-minutes-from-draining "shelf life" requirement. The majority simply asserts, without explanation, that Bonds's right to terminate Anderson's role in dealing with BALCO was not enough to prove Bonds had control over Anderson's actions.

The majority also asserts Bonds and Anderson never manifested an agreement as to control. I can only interpret this point to be based on the majority's confusion between the requirement that the principal and agent respectively manifest assent and consent to the agency relationship and the requirement that the principal has the right to control the agent's actions. The majority suggests there must be an explicit agreement between a principal and agent that the principal may control the agent's actions. There is no support for that claim in the Restatement or the law generally. The majority points to the Restatement (Third) of Agency's distinction between agents and service providers. § 1.01 cmt. f. Nothing in the comment to the Restatement section cited states how the principal and agent must manifest assent and consent to the right of control; to the contrary "[a] principal's power to give instructions" is "created by the agency relationship." *Id.* Further, none of the illustrations provided in Restatement (Third) of Agency § 1.01, comment f, mention anything about an agreement as to control. Instead, the illustrations contemplate that an agent has a right to resign as the principal's agent if the agent does not wish to follow an instruction. *Id.* The reference to "service providers," relied on by the majority, is explained by turning to § 1.01, comment c, which distinguishes service providers on the basis that agents deal with third parties while service providers do not. *Id.* cmt. c. Here, Anderson dealt with a third party, BALCO; that is an attribute of an *agent*, not of a service provider.

By demanding affirmative evidence of a manifestation of assent and consent to the right to control, the majority puts the cart before the horse. As the Restatement explains:

> If the principal requests another to act on the principal's behalf, indicating that the action should be taken without further communication and the other consents so to act, an agency relationship exists. If the putative agent does the requested act, it is appropriate to infer that the action was taken as agent for the person who requested the action unless the putative agent manifests an intention to the contrary or the circumstances so indicate.

Id. cmt. c. Bonds requested Anderson act on his behalf by taking his samples to BALCO and having them tested. Anderson did so. There is no evidence Anderson manifested an intention to refuse the Task, nor are there circumstances that indicate he did not consent. Therefore, the evidence gives rise to a compelling inference that Anderson acted as Bonds's agent, subject to Bonds's control.

The majority's application of the law of agency to the facts in this case imposes unwarranted obstacles to the government's showing that Anderson was Bonds's agent. The holding in this case is flatly inconsistent with how this court has handled similar cases in the past.

. . . .

(c) *Anderson acted on Bonds's behalf, or for his benefit.* Anderson performed his Task so that Bonds would better be able to manage his nutrition and diet. The parties do not dispute that Anderson acted on Bonds's behalf.

(d) *Anderson consented to perform the Task.* Bonds testified that Anderson took Bonds's samples and reported back with the results, and Valente testified that Anderson arrived at BALCO with blood and urine samples that Anderson identified as Bonds's. Anderson's performance is sufficient to show his consent. Restatement (Third) of Agency § 1.01 cmt. c. Therefore, Anderson was Bonds's agent for the purpose of the Task. This conclusion is obvious if one considers similar facts in a slightly different legal context. Imagine that Anderson were not quite so loyal. Had

Anderson sold documents showing Bonds tested positive for steroids to a celebrity gossip publication, would Bonds have a cause of action against Anderson for breach of Anderson's duty of confidentiality? Yes: "An agent's relationship with a principal may result in the agent learning information about the principal's health, life history, and personal preferences that the agent should reasonably understand the principal expects the agent to keep confidential. An agent's duty of confidentiality extends to all such information concerning a principal even when it is not otherwise connected with the subject matter of the agency relationship." Restatement (Third) of Agency §8.05 cmt. c. Bonds could assert a cause of action only if Anderson were his *agent*, but I have no doubt a court evaluating Bonds's relationship with Anderson in that context would hold Anderson was Bonds's agent for the purpose of the Task. It would not even be necessary for Bonds to adduce facts supporting the claim that Anderson was his friend or trainer.

. . . .

Because the district court erred as to a matter of law, the majority is wrong to apply a deferential standard of review. Moreover, the majority fails in its attempt to distinguish *Jones* or *Itzhaki*, two cases where the agency relationship at issue was far more attenuated than is the case here. Reviewing the record below to determine only if the district court's misstatements of law caused the government prejudice, the ineluctable conclusion is that the district court's error did prejudice the government and its decision should be reversed.

Notes

1. In *Violette v. Shoup*, 16 Cal. App. 4th 611, 619 (1993), Rod Violette asked Richard Shoup, his neighbor, if he knew anyone who sold aggressive tax shelters. Shoup, an independent insurance agent, introduced Violette to Margaret Sciaroni, a financial planner he had met at a seminar. Sciaroni commenced discussions with Violette, which resulted in a substantial investment on Sciaroni's recommendation. Subsequently Sciaroni gave Shoup $2400 for referring this business to her. Shoup said that he did not know how the amount was calculated and that he had not expected to receive any compensation for introducing Violette to Sciaroni. Shoup had no further contact with either party on this matter and did not know what investment Violette ultimately made.

Sciaroni had recommended that Violette invest $60,000 in an aggressive tax shelter involving a private wind energy investment offering. The shelter subsequently became insolvent and the Internal Revenue Service determined that it was a potentially abusive tax shelter. Violette sued Shoup, claiming an agency relationship, for breach of a duty of care to refer him to a competent financial planner. What result?

The court held that Shoup was not subject to a duty of care to Violette. It rejected the agency argument (which would create a duty of care, as noted in *Carrier*) in the following terms:

> A person does not become the agent of another simply by offering help or making a suggestion. As the court stated in *Edwards* [212 P.2d 883 (Cal.

1949)]: "To permit a finding of agency upon this evidence would be, in effect, to hold that one who performs a mere favor for another, without being subject to any legal duty or service and without assenting to any right of control, can be an agent. This is not the law."

Is this holding consistent with the holding in *Carrier*? Was the defendant in *Carrier* doing a favor for the plaintiff?

Can a persuasive argument be made that Shoup, while not the agent of Violette, was the agent of Sciaroni? Admittedly, even if that were the case, one has trouble finding a cause of action against Shoup. Sciaroni, not Shoup, was the one with the contractual relationship with Violette. Agents do not engage in personal contractual relationships with their principal's clients except in unusual circumstances, covered in Chapter 7. The court nevertheless addressed the question, holding that no agency relationship between Shoup and Sciaroni existed despite the payment of the $2400.

2. In *U.S. v. Bonds,* under the majority's view, did any aspect of the relationship between Bonds and Anderson meet the Restatement definition of an agency relationship? What additional facts might have convinced the majority that Anderson was an agent for Bonds? The opinion in *Carrier* focuses on one of the three elements in the agency relationship: acting "on behalf of." The other two elements, consent and control, are not at issue in *Carrier*, are they? Should they be? Which elements are at issue in *Bonds*?

3. *The elements of the agency relationship.* The Restatement definition of agency quoted above enjoys nearly universal usage by the courts. Contained below is a brief commentary on its main elements.

(i) *On behalf of.* This element means literally what it says. The acting party must be acting "on behalf of" the principal in order to create the special powers and liabilities that accompany the agency relationship. If the acting party is acting on its own behalf, it is not a fiduciary, nor is it fair, in the eyes of many courts, to subject the other party to the special burdens (to be developed throughout this book) of being a principal. It is true that a paid agent is motivated to act by the prospect of compensation and thus has a personal stake in the situation. But compensation is earned by acting in a manner that advances the interest of the principal, and thus the paid agent is considered to be *primarily* acting for the benefit of another.

"On the principal's behalf" and acting "primarily" for the principal's benefit are different ways of expressing the same requirement. Merely benefiting another by one's conduct does not qualify. It is too far removed in degree. While this proposition is well accepted, the task of distinguishing between actions that merely benefit persons and actions taken on behalf of persons is not always easy. It sometimes involves drawing a fine line, subject to debate.

As an example of a case where the court expressly distinguishes between acting on behalf of (which the court describes as "carrying out the principal's affairs") and merely benefiting another, consider *Clapp v. JMK/Skewer, Inc.,* 484 N.E.2d 918, 921 (Ill. App. Ct. 1985), involving a suit against the owners of a shopping mall

("Northwoods") by persons who suffered food poisoning at a restaurant ("Skewer") in the mall. Northwoods exercised considerable control over all the tenants in the mall, including Skewer, by regulating the hours of operation, restricting the kinds of advertising its tenants may publish and the scope of the wares offered for sale, reserving the right to inspect the premises, and requiring all tenants to belong to a tenant's association, which was formed to promote the mall. Also, and most important for these purposes, Northwoods required as rent a fixed minimum amount plus a percentage of the gross sales of Skewer. The plaintiffs contended that these facts created an agency relationship, rendering Northwoods strictly liable for the tortious conduct of Skewer. The court responded as follows:

> The parties do not take issue with the general proposition that when a landlord turns over possession and control of the premises, he is not liable for injuries to invitees which arose from the operation of the tenant's business. The argument pressed by plaintiffs is that the relationship created by the lease between Northwoods and Skewer Inn was different in kind from that of merely landlord and tenant. . . .
>
> Plaintiffs have focused on one aspect of the law of principal and agent (right of control) and seek to fashion an agency relationship therefrom. Even conceding that Northwoods retained broad rights of control over Skewer, it does not follow that Skewer was the agent of Northwoods. A true agency requires that the agent's function be the carrying out of the principal's affairs. There is nothing to suggest that the instant relationship involved Skewer's tending to the affairs of Northwoods. It just so happens that in the course of furthering its own business (in fact, as the principal thereof), Skewer benefits Northwoods as one element of the retail gestalt. That hardly renders Skewer the agent of Northwoods for purposes of imputing liability in tort.

(ii) *Control.* Again, there is a sense in which this element is self-explanatory. The word "control" is in constant use in oral and written communication. People assume that its meaning is obvious, which may not always be the case with this ambiguous word. Also, this presumed clarity of meaning masks complexity in the law of agency. The word "control" takes on different meaning, for example, when the focus shifts from contractual liability to liability for physical torts. There a narrower meaning of control is used, as will be seen in Chapter 3.

One useful judicial explication of control is that it involves an "element of subservience." *Ahn v. Rooney, Pace, Inc.*, 624 F. Supp. 368, 370 (S.D.N.Y. 1985). The meaning of control and the attitude of courts toward proof of control in a particular case—whether to be demanding and strict in the requirement of proof, or casual to the point of virtually ignoring that element (as in *Carrier*)—seems sometimes to depend on the court's view of the equities of the case before it.

As noted above, the "on behalf of" and "control" elements are both necessary to prove an agency relationship. Neither element is alone sufficient, perhaps because agency liability is strict liability and it seems unfair to subject a person (the principal) to common law strict liability except under circumstances where action is being taken both on behalf of and under the control of the principal. Yet as you read these materials you will see that sometimes the "on behalf of" element is overshadowed by the control element in a particular case. Occasionally it is forgotten altogether when a court focuses with singular intensity on control, allowing that element to dominate a case, doubtless with a particular result in mind and perhaps without full consideration of the costs of uncertainty and confusion incurred by the law as a consequence of paying inconsistent attention to the basic elements of the agency relationship.

(iii) *Consent.* The consent of both parties is a required element of the agency relationship. Entering into an agency relationship involves risk as well as reward for both parties. No useful policy is fulfilled by forcing people to assume such risks without their consent. The matter of the principal's consent is involved in one form or another throughout these materials. The requirement of the agent's consent is infrequently addressed by courts, which makes the following judicial language a matter of some interest:

> We find the phrase "unwitting agent" to be a contradiction in terms . . . . An agency relationship must be created by mutual agreement. It cannot be created by one party *in invitum.* If the existence of an alleged agency relationship is unknown to the "agent," the "agent's" authority is without scope or definition — a situation which invites abuse and far-reaching legal ramifications.

State v. Luster, 295 S.E.2d 421, 425 (N.C. 1982).

Consent can exist even where the parties involved fail to recognize that they have created an agency relation. See Restatement (Second) § 1, Comment b, which bears some resemblance to *Carrier*:

> Thus, when one who asks a friend to do a slight service for him, such as return for credit goods recently purchased from a store, neither one may have any realization that they are creating an agency relation or be aware of the legal obligation which would result from performance of the service.

With regard to proof of consent, it is important to remember that consent can be implied as well as express. Also, if the underlying transaction is contractual in nature, the principal must have the capacity to contract. This is not ordinarily required for the agent, as will be developed below.

The electronic agent. The revision of Article Two of the Uniform Commercial Code contains an intriguing new phrase: the "electronic agent." This term is defined in § 2-103(1)(g) as follows:

> "Electronic agent" means a computer program or an electronic or other automated means used independently to initiate an action or respond to electronic records or performances in whole or in part, without review or action by an individual.

One has a difficult time identifying consent between agent and principal in this context. The Uniform Commercial Code is a statute, however, and can give the word "agent" whatever meaning it wishes. *See, generally,* Samir Chopra and Laurence F. White, A Legal Theory for Autonomous Artificial Agents, (Univ. Mich. Press 2011).

4. *Proof of agency.* The resolution of the question whether an agency relationship exists is ordinarily one of fact. If the facts are not in dispute, however, and the inference that there is, or is not, an agency relationship is clear, the court will decide the question as one of law. The burden of proof is on the one asserting the existence of an agency relationship. "The law does not indulge in a presumption of agency, if an agency is to be inferred it must be inferred from a natural and reasonable construction of the facts, and not from a forced, strained or distorted construction." *Historic Hermann, Inc. v. Thuli,* 790 S.W.2d 931, 935 (Mo. App. 1990).[1]

It will sometimes be the case that the relationship in question cannot easily be characterized. Elements of several different legal relationships may be combined in a confusing way. When this is so, it may be that the consequences of characterizing a relationship as one of agency will as a practical matter carry substantial weight in the determination of the court.

5. *When agency can be used; ambiguity of the word "agency."* With regard to the circumstances under which one can act through an agent, consider the following language from *Mays v. Brighton Bank,* 832 S.W.2d 347, 351 (Tenn. App. 1992):

> Unless prevented by public policy, a statute, or a contract requiring personal performance, what a person can lawfully do himself, he can do through an agent. This delegation may be manifested by an express authorization or it may be implied from the circumstances and the conduct of the parties . . .

6. *The Restatement of Agency.* The opinion in *Carrier* quoted several times from the Restatement (Second) of Agency, while the *Bonds* opinion draws on the Restatement (Third) of Agency. The Restatement (Second) of Agency (1958) was published by the American Law Institute ("ALI"), a voluntary, nonofficial association of lawyers, judges and law teachers. In May 2005, the ALI completed work on the Restatement

---

1. *See also* Seibert v. Noble, 499 N.W.2d 3, 8 (Iowa 1993) ("While the issue of agency is ordinarily a fact question, there must be more than a scintilla of evidence."); Hector v. Metro Centers, Inc., 498 N.W.2d 113, 118 (N.D. 1993) ("A person is presumed to act for himself and not as the agent of another."); Volunteer Fire Co. v. Hilltop Oil Co., 602 A.2d 1348, 1351 (Pa. Super. 1992) ("Agency cannot be assumed from the mere fact that one does an act for another."); CKP, Inc. v. GRS Constr. Co., 821 P.2d 63, 67 (Wash. App. 1991) ("The agency concept is flexible. The relation may be established for a limited purpose, or it may be broad. . . . Under lien statutes which [apply when work is being done to real property] at the request of an owner or his agent, very clear proof of strong circumstances showing an intimate relationship between the owner and the making of the improvement are required to give rise to an implied agency.").

(Third) of Agency, which was published in July 2006. This edition contains references to the new Restatement, together with references to the Restatement (Second), which has been widely cited by the courts.

The two Restatements differ markedly in style. The Restatement (Third) consists of eight chapters and 73 sections, while the Restatement (Second) consists of 14 chapters and over 500 sections. Thus, while the drafters of the Restatement (Second) opted for narrow statements of the law, capturing the holdings of numerous cases as precisely as possible, the drafters of the Restatement (Third) opted for broad statements of the law. Given this difference in approach, it is possible that courts will continue to rely on the Restatement (Second) when its provisions apply directly to the facts of a case before the court. The extent to which the Restatement (Third) will displace the Restatement (Second) remains, of course, to be seen. To avoid confusion, this book will indicate which edition of the Restatement of Agency is being referenced.

7. *Tax refund loan programs.* The courts have decided a number of cases involving H & R Block and its tax refund anticipation loan program, under which Block arranges bank loans for its customers who are entitled to a tax refund and who want the money quickly. The loans are secured by the anticipated refund. Block facilitates loans between its customers and a third-party bank by transmitting the loan application to the bank.

The suits, most of them class actions, are based on Block's failure to disclose its financial stake in such loans. Block received from the banks a percentage of the finance charge paid to the bank by the taxpayer. The plaintiffs claimed that this violated a fiduciary duty of full disclosure that Block owed to plaintiffs based on an alleged agency relationship between Block and plaintiffs. Among the recent cases are: *Sorenson v. H & R Block, Inc.*, 2004 U.S. App. LEXIS 17723 (1st Cir. Aug. 20, 2004) (no agency relationship under Massachusetts law); *Beckett v. H & R Block, Inc.*, 714 N.E.2d 1033 (Ill. App. 1999) (no agency as a matter of law); *Basile v. H & R Block, Inc.*, 761 A.2d 1115 (Pa. 2000) (no agency as a matter of law); and *Green v. H & R Block, Inc.*, 735 A.2d 1039 (Md. App. 1999) (question of fact as to existence of agency relationship precluded summary judgment).

A. Agency or Sale

Hunter Mining Laboratories, Inc. v. Management Assistance, Inc.

Supreme Court of Nevada
763 P.2d 350 (1988)

Per Curiam:

In January and February of 1981, appellant Hunter Mining Laboratories, Inc. ("Hunter") and Hubco Data Products Corporation ("Hubco") signed contracts in which Hubco agreed to sell and Hunter to buy Basic Four computer equipment.

Hubco also agreed to install the equipment and customize some of the stock Basic Four software to accommodate the specific needs of Hunter's business.

Hubco delivered most of the equipment, but closed its business in Nevada without completing the installation or the specialized software programming.

Hunter hired The Data Doctors Corporation ("Data Doctors") to complete the software programming which Hubco had begun. Unfortunately, Data Doctors, like Hubco, did not fulfill its part of the agreement.

Respondents Management Assistance, Inc. ("MAI") and M.A.I. Application Software Corporation ("MAI Software"), an MAI subsidiary, manufactured the computer products which Hubco sold to Hunter. Both Hubco and Data Doctors were licensed distributors of MAI computer products in the Reno, Nevada area.

Hunter brought this action against MAI and MAI Software for breach of the contracts that Hunter signed with Hubco and Data Doctors.[2] Because neither MAI nor MAI Software was a party to either of the two contracts upon which Hunter bases its action, liability on the part of the MAI companies was dependent upon an agency relationship between Hubco and Data Doctors, the contracting parties in the Hunter agreements, and the MAI companies.

Although the jury did find the MAI companies liable for breach of contract, the trial court determined that no evidence supported the jury's implicit finding of an agency relationship. Consequently, the court granted MAI's motion for judgment notwithstanding the verdict.

In light of the review standards for judgments n.o.v., the issue before this court is whether any evidence, viewed in the light most favorable to Hunter, tends to support the jury's finding of agency and its verdict against the MAI companies.

Given the necessary elements of an agency relationship, we conclude that the district court was correct in determining that no evidence supports the jury's verdicts against MAI and MAI Software.

In an agency relationship, the principal possesses the right to control the agent's conduct. Restatement (Second) of Agency § 14 (1958). This principle of agency, however, does not mean that an agency relationship exists every time one party has a contractual right to control some aspect of another party's business.

The MAI/Hubco dealership agreement gave MAI some degree of control over the manner in which Hubco handled MAI products. For example, the agreement required Hubco to maintain an "appropriate" premises, to inform MAI of changes in Hubco management, and to submit monthly reports to MAI indicating the number of prepackaged Basic Four software units it installed. The agreement also granted MAI the right to monitor Hubco's advertisement of Basic Four products,

---

2. [1] Hubco and Data Doctors were also defendants in this lawsuit but are not parties to this appeal.

the right to refuse to sell to Hubco if Hubco did not meet certain credit standards, and the right to rescind the dealership contract under specified conditions.

These types of controls, typical in manufacturer/distributor agreements, protect MAI's goodwill and the integrity of the Basic Four products line. They are not, however, the types of control that create a question of fact regarding agency. . . . MAI had no power to control Hubco business expenditures, fix Hubco customer rates, or demand a share in Hubco's profits. Neither did MAI Software possess a power to control these aspects of Data Doctors' business. . . .

Another essential element of agency missing in this case is a fiduciary obligation on the part of the alleged agents to "act primarily for the benefit of [MAI] in matters connected with [their] undertaking." Restatement (Second) of Agency § 13 Comment a. MAI sold computer equipment to Hubco and Data Doctors who resold that equipment to the public. Title to the goods and an obligation to pay a set price for them passed to the dealers as soon as MAI delivered. The dealers set the price at which they then sold the MAI products to their customers, and neither Hubco nor Data Doctors had any duty to account to MAI for prices charged or profits received. All companies at all times acted independently and in their own names.

In short, the only relationship which the evidence supports between the MAI companies and the two distributors is that of seller and buyer. See Restatement (Second) of Agency § 14 J. . . .

Neither Hubco nor Data Doctors had . . . authority to create a contractual relationship between MAI or MAI Software and Hunter or any other purchaser of Basic Four computer goods. The MAI dealership agreements with both parties specifically negated such authority; nothing else in the parties' agreements or conduct contradicted those disclaimers.

The district court was justified in concluding that, as a matter of law, the relationship between MAI and Hubco and MAI Software and Data Doctors was not that of principal and agent, but rather that of seller and buyer.

The judgment notwithstanding the verdict is affirmed.

Notes

1. The opinion in *Hunter* focuses on two key elements of the agency relationship: control and "on behalf of" (which the court describes as acting "primarily for the benefit of" the principal). The element of control plays a significant role in the analysis of the court, in large part because MAI exerted considerable control over Hubco. Yet, despite this, the court did not find Hubco to be the agent of MAI. In understanding this, the reader might want to think back to the definition of co-agent in the Glossary, where the hypothetical president exercises considerable control over her secretary, yet the secretary is not her agent. Co-agency is not involved in *Hunter*, but both situations illustrate the independent significance of the "on behalf of" element.

2. See also *Stansifer v. Chrysler Motors Corp.*, 487 F.2d 59 (9th Cir. 1973), where the issue was whether Fisher Motors, a distributor and wholesaler of Chrysler cars, was a "straw man" or agent of Chrysler when entering into a written dealership agreement with Stansifer covering the city of Tacoma. The issue was important to Stansifer because he was attempting to sue Chrysler for violation of the Automobile Dealer's Day in Court Act following termination of his dealership. If Fisher was an agent of Chrysler, then the written dealership agreement between Fisher and Stansifer was in reality an agreement between Chrysler and Stansifer, making the Day in Court Act applicable. The court stated the following with regard to the control Chrysler had over Fisher:

> In contending that Chrysler reserved substantial control over the dealer's method of operation, [Stansifer] relies upon provisions in the distributorship agreements that (1) the form of dealership agreements would be furnished to Fisher by Chrysler; (2) Fisher was obliged to use these forms in appointing dealers; (3) Chrysler could terminate the distributorship if sales volume was insufficient; (4) Chrysler could veto prospective appointments of dealers; (5) Fisher's method of distribution and location of dealers was subject to the approval of Chrysler; (6) Chrysler could give directives to Fisher's dealers, and Fisher agreed to enforce compliance; and (7) Chrysler required Fisher to maintain minimum inventories of parts and automobiles.

The court also looked at other facts defining the relationship of Chrysler and Fisher, as follows:

> It is clear from the testimony of J. O. Fisher, Jr., which is uncontradicted, that in conformity with the distributorship agreements Fisher purchased the automobiles and parts from Chrysler, obtained title thereto, could resell at wholesale to any automobile dealer or to any person at retail, could resell at any price, and dealt with its purchasers in its own name. Fisher could decide which dealers to appoint if the prospective dealer had the necessary capital requirements, facilities and services. Fisher assumed the credit risks for any automobiles it sold, at wholesale and retail, and carried liability insurance for various risks of loss.

The court quoted § 14 J of the Restatement (Second), a provision cited and relied upon by the court in *Hunter*. Section 14 J reads as follows:

> One who receives goods from another for resale to a third person is not thereby the other's agent in the transaction: whether he is an agent for this purpose or is himself a buyer depends upon whether the parties agree that his duty is to act primarily for the benefit of the one delivering the goods to him or is to act primarily for his own benefit.

The court affirmed a trial court holding that no agency existed as a matter of law on the reasoning that the "on behalf of" element was not satisfied, doubtless because Fisher was bargaining for its own account when negotiating the price of cars with Stansifer, having paid a set price to Chrysler.[3]

3. *A quote from Mechem.* The courts in *Hunter* and *Stansifer* dealt with the question whether the relationship between the parties was one of agency or of seller and buyer. The following brief passage from the classic treatise on the law of agency, 1 F. Mechem, Law of Agency 30–31 (2nd ed. 1914), addresses the question of agency or sale:

> These doubtful cases are to be determined, not by the name which the parties have seen fit to apply to their contract but by its true nature and effect. The essence of sale is the transfer of the title to the goods for a price paid or to be paid. Such a transfer puts the transferee, who has obtained the goods to sell again, in the attitude of one who is selling his own goods, and makes him liable to the person from whom he received them as a debtor for the *price* to be paid and not liable as an agent for the *proceeds* of the resale. The essence of agency to sell is the delivery of the goods to a person who is to sell them, not as his own property but as the property of the principal, who remains the owner of the goods and who therefore has the right to control the sale, to fix the price and terms, to recall the goods, and to demand and receive their *proceeds* when sold, less the agent's commission, but who has no right to a *price* for them before sale or unless sold by the agent.

United States v. General Electric Co.

Supreme Court of the United States

272 U.S. 476 (1926)

Mr. Chief Justice Taft delivered the opinion of the Court.

This is a bill in equity brought by the United States in the District Court for the Northern District of Ohio to enjoin the General Electric Company . . . from violation of the Anti-Trust Act of July 2, 1890.

[The Government argued that the General Electric Company was requiring the 21,000 distributors of its product to sell at prices fixed by the Company, which constituted an unlawful restraint of trade because price competition among the

---

3. The court quoted the following language from *S.B. McMaster, Inc. v. Chevrolet Motor Co.*, 3 F.2d 469 (E.D. S.C. 1925), in support of its opinion:

> As I view this contract, the case is simply this: The manufacturer desires to sell his products in such manner only that his interests may be promoted. He therefore demands as a part of the price in the making of the contract that the person to whom he sells his goods shall submit to certain restrictions. The person desiring to buy the manufacturer's goods is anxious to purchase them, and in order to purchase them is willing to submit to the conditions and restrictions named. A consideration of the whole contract and all its terms shows that the parties were studiously careful to make a contract of sale and not a contract of agency. They certainly had a right to do this, and if that was their real intention it is the duty of this court to give effect to that intention.

distributors was eliminated. General Electric argued there was no "resale" price maintenance by it because the 21,000 distributors were its agents under consignment contracts, rather than buyers. Title passed directly from the Company to the ultimate purchaser with no intermediate sale to the distributor, contended the Company. The details of the contractual arrangement with the distributors are set forth below.]

. . . Each . . . agent is appointed by the Electric Company by the execution and delivery of a contract for the appointment, which lasts a year from a stated date, unless sooner terminated. It provides that the company is to maintain on consignment in the custody of the agent a stock of lamps, the sizes, types, classes and quantity of which, and the length of time which they are to remain in stock, to be determined by the company. . . . All of the lamps in such consigned stock are to be and remain the property of the company until the lamps are sold, and the proceeds of all lamps are to be held in trust for the benefit and for the account of the company until fully accounted for. . . . The agent . . . is not to control or attempt to control prices at which any purchaser shall sell any of such lamps. The agent is to pay all expenses in the storage, cartage, transportation, handling, sale and distribution of lamps, and all expenses incident thereto and to the accounting therefor and to the collection of accounts created. . . . The agent guarantees the return to the company of all unsold lamps in the custody of the agent within a certain time after the termination of his agency. The agent is to pay over to the company, not later than the 15th of each month, an amount equal to the total sales value, less the agent's compensation, of all of the company's lamps sold by him — that is, first, of the collections that have been made, second of those customers' accounts which are past due. This is to comply with the guaranty of the agent of due and prompt payment for all lamps sold by him from his stock. Third, the agent is to pay to the company the value of all of the company's lamps lost or missing from or damaged in the stock in his custody. . . . If the agent becomes insolvent, or fails to make reports and remittances, or fails in any of his obligations, the appointment may be terminated; and, when terminated, either at the end of the year or otherwise, the consigned lamps remaining unsold are to be delivered to the manufacturer. . . . The plan was of course devised for the purpose of enabling the company to deal directly with consumers and purchasers, and doubtless was intended to avoid selling the lamps owned by the company to jobbers or dealers, and prevent sale by these middle men to consumers at different and competing prices. The question is whether, in view of the arrangements, made by the company with those who ordinarily and usually would be merchants buying from the manufacturer and selling to the public such persons are to be treated as agents, or as owners of the lamps consigned to them under such contracts. If they are to be regarded really as purchasers, then the restriction as to the prices at which the sales are to be made is a restraint of trade and a violation of the Anti-Trust law.

We find nothing in the form of the contracts and the practice under them which makes the . . . agents anything more than genuine agents of the company, or the delivery of the stock to each agent anything more than a consignment to the agent for his custody and sale as such. He is not obliged to pay over money for the stock held by him until it is sold. As he guarantees the account when made, he must turn over what should have been paid whether he gets it or not. This term occurs in a frequent form of pure agency known as sale by *del credere* commission. There is no conflict in the agent's obligation to account for all lamps lost, missing or damaged in the stock. It is only a reasonable provision to secure his careful handling of the goods entrusted to him. We find nothing in his agreement to pay the expense of storage, cartage, transportation (except the freight on the original consignment), handling and the sale and distribution of the lamps, inconsistent with his relation as agent. The expense of this is of course covered in the amount of his fixed commission. The agent has no power to deal with the lamps in any way inconsistent with the ownership of the lamps retained by the company. When they are delivered by him to the purchasers, the title passes directly from the company to those purchasers. . . . The circumstance that the agents were in their regular business wholesale or retail merchants, and under a prior arrangement had bought the lamps, and sold them as their owners, did not prevent a change in their relation to the company. We find no reason in this record to hold that the change in this case was not in good faith and actually maintained. . . .

The decree of the trial court dismissing the bill is affirmed.

Notes

1. The question of who had title to the goods played an important role in the *Hunter, Stansifer* and *General Electric* cases and in the test posed by Mechem, doubtless for the reason that one who has title to property is more likely to deal with it on his own behalf than in a representative capacity. Title is not always determinative, however. The subsequent history of the *General Electric* case casts doubt on the use of the consignment arrangement as a device to avoid the antitrust laws, at least with regard to unpatented products. *See Simpson v. Union Oil*, 377 U.S. 13 (1964), where a consignment arrangement between Union Oil and its lessee dealers concerning gasoline was invalidated in a controversial 6–3 decision. *See also West v. Hartford Fire Ins. Co.*, 248 Iowa 993, 997, 83 N.W.2d 465, 468 (1957) ("It has also been held that there is no magic in the words 'consignment' or 'agency' which can change the real character of a transaction from a sale to a consignment or agency contract"). The ultimate test, as noted in Restatement (Second) § 14 J quoted above, is whether the actor is acting primarily for his own benefit or for the benefit of the other party when acting pursuant to the arrangement between the parties.

2. *Terminology.* Historically an agent employed to sell goods entrusted to his possession and control by consignment was called a *factor*; he sold the goods in his own name and was paid by commission.[4] A *broker* is an agent paid by commission who

---

4. Today this type of agent is sometimes called "commission merchant" or "commercial agent," and the word "factor" is commonly used to refer to financial intermediaries who supply funds to businesses, taking back accounts receivable.

ordinarily acts as an intermediary between buyer and seller, does not have control or possession of the property, and does not sell in his or her own name. These definitions are not always followed consistently. The meaning of "broker" can be greatly varied by trade usage or by statute.

B. Agency or Debtor-Creditor Relationship

A. Gay Jenson Farms Co. v. Cargill, Inc.

Supreme Court of Minnesota
309 N.W.2d 285 (1981)

PETERSON, JUSTICE.

Plaintiffs, 86 individual, partnership or corporate farmers, brought this action against defendant Cargill, Inc. (Cargill) and defendant Warren Grain & Seed Co. (Warren) to recover losses sustained when Warren defaulted on the contracts made with plaintiffs for the sale of grain. After a trial by jury, judgment was entered in favor of plaintiffs, and Cargill brought this appeal. We affirm.

This case arose out of the financial collapse of defendant Warren and its failure to satisfy its indebtedness to plaintiffs. Warren, which was located in Warren, Minnesota, was operated by Lloyd Hill and his son, Gary Hill. Warren operated a grain elevator and as a result was involved in the purchase of cash or market grain from local farmers. The cash grain would be resold through the Minneapolis Grain Exchange or to the terminal grain companies directly. Warren also stored grain for farmers and sold chemicals, fertilizer and steel storage bins. In addition, it operated a seed business which involved buying seed grain from farmers, processing it and reselling it for seed to farmers and local elevators.

Lloyd Hill decided in 1964 to apply for financing from Cargill.[5] Cargill's officials from the Moorhead regional office investigated Warren's operations and recommended that Cargill finance Warren.

Warren and Cargill thereafter entered into a security agreement which provided that Cargill would loan money for working capital to Warren on "open account" financing up to a stated limit, which was originally set as $175,000.[6] Under this contract, Warren would receive funds and pay its expenses by issuing drafts drawn on Cargill through Minneapolis banks. The drafts were imprinted with both Warren's and Cargill's names. Proceeds from Warren's sales would be deposited with Cargill

---

5. [1] Prior to this time, Atwood Larson had provided working capital for Warren, and Warren had used Atwood Larson as its commission agent for the sale of market grain on the grain exchange.

6. [2] Loans were secured by a second mortgage on Warren's real estate and a first chattel mortgage on its inventories of grain and merchandise in the sum of $175,000 with 7% interest. Warren was to use the $175,000 to pay off the debt that it owed to Atwood Larson.

and credited to its account. In return for this financing, Warren appointed Cargill as its grain agent for transactions with the Commodity Credit Corporation. Cargill was also given a right of first refusal to purchase market grain sold by Warren to the terminal market.

A new contract was negotiated in 1967, extending Warren's credit line to $300,000 and incorporating the provisions of the original contract. It was also stated in the contract that Warren would provide Cargill with annual financial statements and that either Cargill would keep the books for Warren or an audit would be conducted by an independent firm. Cargill was given the right of access to Warren's books for inspection.

In addition, the agreement provided that Warren was not to make capital improvements or repairs in excess of $5,000 without Cargill's prior consent. Further, it was not to become liable as guarantor on another's indebtedness, or encumber its assets except with Cargill's permission. Consent by Cargill was required before Warren would be allowed to declare a dividend or sell and purchase stock.

Officials from Cargill's regional office made a brief visit to Warren shortly after the agreement was executed. They examined the annual statement and the accounts receivable, expenses, inventory, seed, machinery and other financial matters. Warren was informed that it would be reminded periodically to make the improvements recommended by Cargill.[7] At approximately this time, a memo was given to the Cargill official in charge of the Warren account, Erhart Becker, which stated in part: "This organization [Warren] needs *very strong* paternal guidance."

In 1970, Cargill contracted with Warren and other elevators to act as its agent to seek growers for a new type of wheat called Bounty 208. Warren, as Cargill's agent for this project, entered into contracts for the growing of the wheat seed, with Cargill named as the contracting party. Farmers were paid directly by Cargill for the seed and all contracts were performed in full. In 1971, pursuant to an agency contract, Warren contracted on Cargill's behalf with various farmers for the growing of sunflower seeds for Cargill. The arrangements were similar to those made in the Bounty 208 contracts, and all those contracts were also completed. Both these agreements were unrelated to the open account financing contract. In addition, Warren, as Cargill's agent in the sunflower seed business, cleaned and packaged the seed in Cargill bags.

During this period, Cargill continued to review Warren's operations and expenses and recommended that certain actions should be taken.[8] Warren purchased from

---

7. [3] Cargill headquarters suggested that the regional office check Warren monthly. Also, it was requested that Warren be given an explanation for the relatively large withdrawals from undistributed earnings made by the Hills, since Cargill hoped that Warren's profits would be used to decrease its debt balance. Cargill asked for written requests for withdrawals from undistributed earnings in the future.

8. [4] Between 1967 and 1973, Cargill suggested that Warren take a number of steps, including: (1) a reduction of seed grain and cash grain inventories; (2) improved collection of accounts

Cargill various business forms printed by Cargill and received sample forms from Cargill which Warren used to develop its own business forms.

Cargill wrote to its regional office in 1970 expressing its concern that the pattern of increased use of funds allowed to develop at Warren was similar to that involved in two other cases in which Cargill experienced severe losses. Cargill did not refuse to honor drafts or call the loan, however. A new security agreement which increased the credit line to $750,000 was executed in 1972, and a subsequent agreement which raised the limit to $1,250,000 was entered into in 1976.

Warren was at that time shipping Cargill 90% of its cash grain. When Cargill's facilities were full, Warren shipped its grain to other companies. Approximately 25% of Warren's total sales was seed grain which was sold directly by Warren to its customers.

As Warren's indebtedness continued to be in excess of its credit line, Cargill began to contact Warren daily regarding its financial affairs. Cargill headquarters informed its regional office in 1973 that, since Cargill money was being used, Warren should realize that Cargill had the right to make some critical decisions regarding the use of the funds. Cargill headquarters also told Warren that a regional manager would be working with Warren on a day-to-day basis as well as in monthly planning meetings. In 1975, Cargill's regional office began to keep a daily debit position on Warren. A bank account was opened in Warren's name on which Warren could draw checks in 1976. The account was to be funded by drafts drawn on Cargill by the local bank.

In early 1977, it became evident that Warren had serious financial problems. Several farmers, who had heard that Warren's checks were not being paid, inquired or had their agents inquire at Cargill regarding Warren's status and were initially told that there would be no problem with payment. In April 1977, an audit of Warren revealed that Warren was $4 million in debt. After Cargill was informed that Warren's financial statements had been deliberately falsified, Warren's request for additional financing was refused. In the final days of Warren's operation, Cargill sent an official to supervise the elevator, including disbursement of funds and income generated by the elevator.

After Warren ceased operations, it was found to be indebted to Cargill in the amount of $3.6 million. Warren was also determined to be indebted to plaintiffs in the amount of $2 million, and plaintiffs brought this action in 1977 to seek recovery of that sum. Plaintiffs alleged that Cargill was jointly liable for Warren's indebtedness as it had acted as principal for the grain elevator.

---

receivable; (3) reduction or elimination of its wholesale seed business and its specialty grain operation; (4) marketing fertilizer and steel bins on consignment; (5) a reduction in withdrawals made by officers; (6) a suggestion that Warren's bookkeeper not issue her own salary checks; and (7) cooperation with Cargill in implementing the recommendations. These ideas were apparently never implemented, however.

The jury found that Cargill's conduct between 1973 and 1977 had made it Warren's principal.[9] Warren was found to be the agent of Cargill with regard to contracts for:

1. The purchase and sale of grain for market.
2. The purchase and sale of seed grain.
3. The storage of grain.

The court determined that Cargill was the . . . principal of Warren. It was concluded that Cargill was jointly liable with Warren for plaintiffs' losses, and judgment was entered for plaintiffs. . . .

The major issue in this case is whether Cargill, by its course of dealing with Warren, became liable as a principal on contracts made by Warren with plaintiffs. Cargill contends that no agency relationship was established with Warren, notwithstanding its financing of Warren's operation and its purchase of the majority of Warren's grain. However, we conclude that Cargill, by its control and influence over Warren, became a principal with liability for the transactions entered into by its agent Warren.

. . . An agreement may result in the creation of an agency relationship although the parties did not call it an agency and did not intend the legal consequences of the relation to follow. The existence of the agency may be proved by circumstantial evidence which shows a course of dealing between the two parties. . . .

Cargill contends that the prerequisites of an agency relationship did not exist because Cargill never consented to the agency, Warren did not act on behalf of Cargill, and Cargill did not exercise control over Warren. We hold that all three elements of agency could be found in the particular circumstances of this case. By directing Warren to implement its recommendations, Cargill manifested its consent that Warren would be its agent. Warren acted on Cargill's behalf in procuring grain for Cargill as the part of its normal operations which were totally financed by Cargill.[10] Further, an agency relationship was established by Cargill's interference with the internal affairs of Warren, which constituted de facto control of the elevator.

---

9. [6] At trial, plaintiffs sought to establish actual agency by Cargill's course of dealing between 1973 and 1977 rather than "apparent" agency or agency by estoppel, so that the only issue in this case is one of actual agency.

10. [7] Although the contracts with the farmers were executed by Warren, Warren paid for the grain with drafts drawn on Cargill. While this is not in itself significant—see *Lee v. Peoples Cooperative Sales Agency*, 201 Minn. 266, 276 N.W. 214 (1937)—it is one factor to be taken into account in analyzing the relationship between Warren and Cargill.

A creditor who assumes control of his debtor's business may become liable as principal for the acts of the debtor in connection with the business. Restatement (Second) of Agency § 14 O (1958).[11] It is noted in Comment a to section 14 O that:

> A security holder who merely exercises a veto power over the business acts of his debtor by preventing purchases or sales above specified amounts does not thereby become a principal. However, if he takes over the management of the debtor's business either in person or through an agent, and directs what contracts may or may not be made, he becomes a principal, liable as a principal for the obligations incurred thereafter in the normal course of business by the debtor who has now become his general agent. The point at which the creditor becomes a principal is that at which he assumes de facto control over the conduct of his debtor, whatever the terms of the formal contract with his debtor may be.

A number of factors indicate Cargill's control over Warren, including the following:

(1) Cargill's constant recommendations to Warren by telephone;

(2) Cargill's right of first refusal on grain;

(3) Warren's inability to enter into mortgages, to purchase stock or to pay dividends without Cargill's approval;

(4) Cargill's right of entry onto Warren's premises to carry on periodic checks and audits;

(5) Cargill's correspondence and criticism regarding Warren's finances, officers' salaries and inventory;

(6) Cargill's determination that Warren needed "strong paternal guidance";

(7) Provision of drafts and forms to Warren upon which Cargill's name was imprinted;

(8) Financing of all Warren's purchases of grain and operating expenses; and

(9) Cargill's power to discontinue the financing of Warren's operations.

We recognize that some of these elements, as Cargill contends, are found in an ordinary debtor-creditor relationship. However, these factors cannot be considered in isolation, but, rather, they must be viewed in light of all the circumstances surrounding Cargill's aggressive financing of Warren.

---

11. [The full text of § 14 O reads as follows:
   A creditor who assumes control of his debtor's business for the mutual benefit of himself and his debtor, may become a principal, with liability for the acts and transactions of the debtor in connection with the business.
— Eds.]

It is also Cargill's position that the relationship between Cargill and Warren was that of buyer-supplier rather than principal-agent. Restatement (Second) of Agency § 14 K (1958) compares an agent with a supplier as follows:

> One who contracts to acquire property from a third person and convey it to another is the agent of the other only if it is agreed that he is to act primarily for the benefit of the other and not for himself.

Factors indicating that one is a supplier, rather than an agent, are:

> (1) That he is to receive a fixed price for the property irrespective of price paid by him. This is the most important. (2) That he acts in his own name and receives the title to the property which he thereafter is to transfer. (3) That he has an independent business in buying and selling similar property.

Restatement (Second) of Agency § 14 K, comment a (1958).

Under the Restatement approach, it must be shown that the supplier has an independent business before it can be concluded that he is not an agent. The record establishes that all portions of Warren's operation were financed by Cargill and that Warren sold almost all of its market grain to Cargill. Thus, the relationship which existed between the parties was not merely that of buyer and supplier.

In this case . . . Cargill furnished substantially all funds received by the elevator. Cargill did have a right of entry on Warren's premises, and it . . . required maintenance of insurance against hazards of operation. Warren's activities . . . formed a substantial part of Cargill's business that was developed in that area. In addition, Cargill did not think of Warren as an operator who was free to become Cargill's competitor, but rather conceded that it believed that Warren owed a duty of loyalty to Cargill. The decisions made by Warren were not independent of Cargill's interest or its control.

Further, we are not persuaded by the fact that Warren was not one of the "line" elevators that Cargill operated in its own name. The Warren operation, like the line elevator, was financially dependent on Cargill's continual infusion of capital. The arrangement with Warren presented a convenient alternative to the establishment of a line elevator. Cargill became, in essence, the owner of the operation without the accompanying legal indicia.

The amici curiae assert that, if the jury verdict is upheld, firms and banks which have provided business loans to county elevators will decline to make further loans. The decision in this case should give no cause for such concern. We deal here with a business enterprise markedly different from an ordinary bank financing, since Cargill was an active participant in Warren's operations rather than simply a financier. Cargill's course of dealing with Warren was, by its own admission, a paternalistic relationship in which Cargill made the key economic decisions and kept Warren in existence.

Although considerable interest was paid by Warren on the loan, the reason for Cargill's financing of Warren was not to make money as a lender but, rather, to establish a source of market grain for its business. As one Cargill manager noted, "We were staying in there because we wanted the grain." For this reason, Cargill was willing to extend the credit line far beyond the amount originally allocated to Warren. It is noteworthy that Cargill was receiving significant amounts of grain and that, notwithstanding the risk that was recognized by Cargill, the operation was considered profitable.

On the whole, there was a unique fabric in the relationship between Cargill and Warren which varies from that found in normal debtor-creditor situations. We conclude that, on the facts of this case, there was sufficient evidence from which the jury could find that Cargill was the principal of Warren within the definitions of agency set forth in Restatement (Second) of Agency §§ 1 and 14 O. . . .

It is also Cargill's position that the trial court erred in failing to submit certain requested jury instructions. . . .

Cargill asserts, second, that the trial court erred in refusing to instruct on the issue that agency to perform a particular act cannot be inferred by the existence of agency relationship at another time and in a different capacity. Cargill is concerned that the testimony regarding the agency relationship in the sunflower and Bounty 208 program between Cargill and Warren created an inference that this relationship extended to other aspects of Warren's operations. The court, however, is not required to instruct against every improper inference that a jury could draw. . . .

Cargill's third contention is that the trial court erred in not submitting to the jury an instruction, in the form of Restatement (Second) of Agency § 14 K and comment a to that section, which would serve to focus on some, but not all, of the applicable factors. . . . The court's instruction on general agency law was adequate to inform the jury of the applicable principle of law. . . .

Finally, Cargill claims that the trial court's denial of its motion for a change of venue was improper. Cargill moved for a change of venue because it was not satisfied with the impartiality of the jury.[12] . . . The mere fact that the jury had knowledge of the financial collapse of Warren and its connection with Cargill does not indicate that it could not render a fair decision. . . .

Affirmed.

Notes

1. The following quotation is taken from pages 13–15 of the appellant's (Cargill's) brief in *Jenson v. Cargill*:

> [T]he evidence overwhelmingly establishes that Warren acted solely on its own account and for its own benefit. . . .

---

12. [As the court noted in a subsequent passage, "Warren was a small community and jurors from that area could be presumed to have some association with the elevator or with one of the 86 plaintiffs." — Eds.]

Each of the farmers, including plaintiffs herein, sold and delivered their grain to Warren. With the exception of those persons delivering grain for storage, title to the grain passed to Warren. Warren received for its benefit any profit from its purchase and resale of grain by way of margin or the difference between the price at which Warren purchased and the price at which it could sell. Mr. Hill testified that margin would normally range from 7 to 10 cents per bushel. On purchases of seed grain from farmers, Warren profited by even greater margins, sometimes of $1.50 to $2.00 per bushel. Warren consistently maintained large grain inventories which it held and/or sold depending upon prices. Warren at times lost money on its purchases, especially in purchases of barley on which it misjudged the grade when buying from farmers.

Warren neither accounted to Cargill for profits derived nor losses sustained. This was consistent with the fact that it was acting for its own account. Warren considered itself to be "an independent operator," rather than a mere agent of Cargill.

Ironically, the exhibits introduced by plaintiffs to sustain the relationship of agency are replete with references regarding the independence of Warren and the fact that both Warren and Cargill intended and expected Warren to profit.[13] . . .

Further evidence that Warren was dealing on its own account and not on behalf of Cargill was that while Warren sold approximately 90 percent of its market grain to or through Cargill, when higher prices could be obtained elsewhere for greater profit to Warren, it sold to others at the higher prices. . . .

It is clear that Cargill never requested nor manifested any consent that Warren act on its behalf in regard to any of the subject transactions and equally clear that Warren never assumed to act as Cargill's agent, but rather that Warren was at all times acting on its own behalf and for its own benefit.

2. The appellee's brief did not challenge the factual assertions described above in note 1. Instead, on pages 30–31, it responded to the above argument as follows:

Cargill's argument is without basis. The transactions "in question" were all directly or indirectly potentially beneficial to Cargill. Every cent of net income obtained by Warren from *any* transaction was beneficial to Cargill in that it reduced Warren's debt to Cargill by so much. Every transaction which generated grain for sale to Cargill afforded Cargill an opportunity to make a profit out of the transaction [presumably by resale in the national

---

13. As example: Exhibit 211 states that Lloyd Hill "feels by making a change to Cargill that they could increase their grain volume and also improve their profit picture." Exhibit 229, wherein Cargill states to Warren that it would like to see "a reduction in your interest cost as every dollar saved in that fashion is one more dollar of profit for you." . . .

or international markets]. The greater Warren's purchases, the greater Cargill's potential profit.

Do you find this rebuttal convincing?

3. The court opinion quotes from and relies heavily upon §140 of the Restatement (Second). Do you think that the proposition set forth by the Restatement is undebatable? Certainly, a party in control of an activity should be subject to standards of liability, such as requiring the exercise of due care. Negligence and dishonesty would be penalized by all courts under such circumstances. But should a party's liability be extended to full responsibility for all debts of a business, as if it were a co-owner of the business, solely as a result of its exercise of control as a creditor? What are the arguments on both sides of this? *See* J. Dennis Hynes, *Lender Liability: The Dilemma of the Controlling Creditor*, 58 Tenn. L. Rev. 635 (1991).

C. Agency and the Law of Trusts

A *trust* is defined in the Restatement (Second) of Trusts §2 as follows:

A trust is a fiduciary relationship with respect to property, subjecting the person by whom the title to the property is held to equitable duties to deal with the property for the benefit of another person, which arises as a result of a manifestation of an intention to create it.

As noted earlier, a *fiduciary* is defined in the Restatement (Second) of Agency §13, Comment a, as "a person having a duty, created by his undertaking, to act primarily for the benefit of another in matters connected with his undertaking."

Is an agent who receives title to property of his principal always a trustee? The answer to this question is yes, isn't it? Do you see why?

The case of *Anderson v. Abbott*, 61 F. Supp. 888, 891–93 (W.D. Ky. 1945), contains a lengthy discussion distinguishing agency from trust. The following is an excerpt from the opinion:

A trust involves control over property. The trustee holds legal title. The agent may hold legal title but usually does not hold any title at all. The trustee may act in his own name; the agent usually acts in the name of the principal. In the restatement of the law of trusts by the American Law Institute, the following enumerated distinctions are given:

a. Title: A trustee has title to the trust property; an agent as such does not have title to the property of his principal, although he may have powers with respect to it.

b. Control: An agent undertakes to act on behalf of his principal and subject to his control (see Restatement of Agency, §1); a trustee as such is not subject to the control of his beneficiary, except that he is under a duty to deal with the trust property for his benefit in accordance with the terms of the trust and can be compelled by the beneficiary to perform this duty.

c. Liability: An agent may subject his principal to personal liabilities to third persons; a trustee cannot subject the beneficiary to such liabilities (see § 274).

d. Consent: An agency is created by the consent of the principal and the agent (see Restatement of Agency, § 1); a trust may be created without the knowledge or consent of the beneficiary or of the trustee (see §§ 35, 36).

e. Termination: An agency can be terminated at the will of either the principal or the agent and is terminated by the death of either (see Restatement of Agency, §§ 118–121). A trust is not ordinarily terminable at the will of either the beneficiary or the trustee or by the death of either (see §§ 330, 337).

f. Agent May Also Be Trustee: A person may be at the same time both an agent and a trustee for the same person. If an agent is entrusted with the title to property for his principal, he is a trustee of that property.

An illustration is given:

1. A, the owner of shares of stock, delivers the certificates to the B Trust Company to hold and deal with as custodian, to receive the income and pay it to A, and with power to sell the shares and to reinvest the proceeds as A may direct. In order to carry out these purposes the shares are registered in the name of the trust company. The trust company is agent of A, and, since it holds the title to the shares because of the registration of the shares in its name, it is also trustee of the shares for A.

... In the case of an express trust the beneficial owner has little or no control of the trustee. ... An agent, on the other hand, is ever-mindful of the presence and desires of the principal, even though the principal has no active part in the management of the estate.

In the Restatement of the Law of Agency [§ 14, Comment b], we find this language:

Where it is otherwise clear that there is an agency relationship, as in the case of recognized agents such as attorneys at law, factors, or auctioneers, the principal, although he has contracted with the agent not to exercise control and to permit the agent the free exercise of his discretion, nevertheless has power to give lawful directions which the agent is under a duty to obey if he continues to act as such (see § 385). Where the existence of an agency relationship is not otherwise clearly shown, as where the issue is whether a trust or an agency has been created, the fact that it is understood that the person acting is not to be subject to the control of the other as to the manner of performance determines that the relationship is not that of agency.

Section 385 referred to in this quotation . . . provides:

> Except where he is privileged to protect his own or another's interests, an agent is subject to a duty not to act in matters entrusted to him on account of the principal contrary to the directions of the principal, even though the terms of the employment prescribe that such directions shall not be given.

Notes

1. Agency principles predominate when a relationship is agent-trustee. See *Dierksen v. Albert*, 254 A.2d 809 (N.J. App. Div. 1969), where plaintiffs had transferred stocks into the name of their daughter pursuant to an arrangement under which they retained control. The daughter later disappeared, and plaintiffs sought to have title to the stock revested in them. Their request was denied by the trial court on the reasoning that the plaintiffs had created a trust and could not revoke it absent an express reservation of the power to do so. On appeal, the court held that the control reserved by the plaintiffs made the relationship one of agency and trust, which they could revoke at will because under such circumstances agency principles predominate. What reasoning do you think underlies this rule?

2. As noted above, the element of control plays a major role in distinguishing agency from trust. Can one legitimately infer that control exists solely from an unrestricted right to terminate a relationship? See Restatement (Second) § 14 B, Comment f, noting that one must look to the amount of control agreed to be exercised "or, in doubtful situations, upon the amount of control in fact exercised." The implication is that a power of termination is not alone sufficient to infer control. *See also Lavazzi v. McDonald's Corp.*, 606 N.E.2d 845, 852 (Ill. App. 1992) ("A right to rescind a contract or call off the work is generally insufficient to establish control and impose liability. . . .").

3. As discussed in the above materials, although a trustee acts on behalf of its beneficiary, usually a trustee is not subject to the beneficiary's control. Thus, an agency relationship does not ordinarily exist between trustee and beneficiary. This also is true of guardians, executors, and receivers, who act on behalf of persons but are not subject to their control and thus are not agents.

Note that the above situations are the reverse of the *Hunter* situation, where the actor does *not* act on behalf of the purported principal but *is* subject to the control of the principal. In neither circumstance does a true agency relationship exist.

D. Agent or Escrow Holder

The following quotation is taken from the comments to § 8.09 of the Restatement (Third).

> *d. Duty of escrow holder to comply with terms of escrow agreement.* A holder of an escrow contracts to hold money, a deed, or some other asset until the

occurrence or nonoccurrence of a specified event before a specified date; the escrow contract states the holder's duties to deliver or return the escrow upon the occurrence or nonoccurrence of the specified event. An escrow arrangement places the escrowed deed or other property beyond the control of parties to a transaction for a specified time and determines when the holder may properly make delivery. Prior to the occurrence or nonoccurrence of the specified event, an escrow holder is not an agent as defined in § 1.01 because the holder does not assent to acting subject to the control of the parties to the escrow contract. An escrow holder, although often termed an "escrow agent," is more precisely comparable to a holder of a power given as security for the benefit of a third party other than the power holder. *See* § 3.12, Comment b.

To achieve the purposes for which an escrow is created, the escrow holder has a duty to adhere to the terms of the escrow agreement. If an escrow holder breaches its duty to adhere to the terms of the agreement, the holder is subject to liability to parties for whose benefit the escrow was created for loss caused by the holder's failure to adhere to the terms of the agreement. The stringency of an escrow holder's duty of compliance provides security to parties who structure transactions that involve a risk of nonconsummation. For example, in an "all or nothing" offering of stock, subscribers to the offering make payment into an escrow account, to be held for the corporation that will issue its stock to them if subscriptions are received for the number of shares set in the escrow agreement. If subscriptions are not received for that number of shares by a date set in the escrow agreement, the escrow holder has a duty to return the funds to the subscribers. The escrow structure provides investors with an assurance that the issuer will receive capital in a sufficient amount and that their money will be returned by a certain date if the conditions stated in the escrow agreement are not met.

Notes

1. *X* delivers property to *A* to be delivered by *A* to *Y* upon performance of an act by *Y* within a certain time. Is this an escrow?

2. *X, Y,* and *A* agree that *X* shall deliver property to *A* to be delivered by *A* to *Y* upon performance of an act by *Y* within a certain time. *X* delivers the property to *A*. Is this an escrow?

3. In *King v. First Nat'l Bank*, 647 P.2d 596 (Alaska 1982), the Kings contracted to buy land from Olson, who was making payments to the state of Alaska under an installment land contract. It was arranged that the Kings would make payments to Olson's bank, which would remit a portion of each payment to the state toward satisfying Olson's purchase contract and would remit the balance of the payment to a savings account Olson had with the bank. The bank was acting pursuant to a document titled "Collection Instructions," signed only by Olson. Soon after the Kings began making payments, Olson altered the instructions to the bank, telling it to remit all the proceeds to his savings account. This was unknown to the Kings, who kept making payments. The state ultimately terminated its contract with Olson for failure to make the necessary payments. The Kings sued the bank for violation of escrow instructions. The court rejected this claim, holding that the Kings were not parties to the Collection Instructions document and thus an escrow did not exist. Instead, the bank was merely an agent for Olson, who as principal was free to make any change he wished in his instructions. The case was remanded, however, for trial under a third-party beneficiary theory, the court noting that "[a]n agent acting on behalf of one person may be held liable to a third person for failure to perform a contract intended to benefit the third person. . . . The original [Collection] instructions were drafted by the Kings' attorney with particular sections intended to protect the Kings' interest. . . ."

4. The third-party beneficiary theory invoked by the court in *King* can prove hazardous to an agent under some circumstances. First, there can be an element of surprise in the application of this soft-edged, fact-specific theory. A court may hold that enforceable rights exist outside of the principal-agent relationship under circumstances where the agent had not even considered that possibility. Second, there is a risk that an agent may be presented with conflicting demands from the principal and the third party. The agent is accustomed to obeying the principal, yet is exposed to contractual liability to the third party. See § 14 L(2), Comment e, of the Restatement (Second), addressing this dilemma by declaring that the agency relationship terminates for these purposes. Perhaps with the above problems in mind, some courts take a narrow approach to the recognition of third-party beneficiary rights. See *Atlantic & Gulf Stevedores v. Revelle*, 750 F.2d 457, 459 (5th Cir. 1985), where agent ("A") used funds planned for payment to T to pay P's "most pressing debts" instead. The court, in rejecting T's claim against A, required that a promise of A to P to pay T must be "for the primary benefit" of T before T can claim third-party beneficiary rights. See also *L.C.S. Colliery, Inc. v. Mack*, 290 A.2d 260 (Pa. 1972), rejecting a claim by T against A, observing that there was no agreement between A and T that A would pay T.

5. Sometimes an arrangement that closely resembles escrow instead will be characterized by a court as an agency relationship, resulting in a major shift in the risks and liabilities of the parties. *Paul v. Kennedy*, 102 A.2d 158 (Pa. 1954), is an example of this. In that case the owner of a trucking business (Kennedy) engaged a business broker (Brenner) to sell his business. Brenner found a buyer (Paul) and drafted a contract of sale that was signed by both Kennedy and Paul. It called for Paul to deposit the purchase price in escrow with Brenner until the state approved the transfer of the public utility license. Paul deposited the money, which Brenner embezzled. Paul sued Kennedy for specific enforcement of the sale, alleging that full payment had been made to Kennedy. Kennedy attempted to invoke the rule that the loss should be on the party who deposited the funds in escrow. *Held:* Paul prevails. The usual rule of escrow does not apply because Brenner remained Kennedy's agent and thus was not a true escrow holder.

E. Dual Agency; The Ambiguous Principal Problem

This section differs from the preceding material in that it does not distinguish the agency relationship from other relationships. Instead, it has as its subject the problem of identifying the principal when the facts seem to be confusingly neutral on the issue of for whom the agent is acting.

1. The Dual Agency Rule

The dual agency rule states that an agent cannot act on behalf of the adverse party to a transaction connected with the agency without the permission of the principal. *See Naviera Despina, Inc. v. Cooper Shipping Co.*, 676 F. Supp. 1134, 1141 (S.D. Ala. 1987) ("It is wrong, except where there is full disclosure and consent, for an agent to attempt to serve two masters with differing interests."). The reasoning behind the rule is expressed in *Atwood v. Chicago, Rock Island & Pac. Ry.*, 72 F. 447, 455 (W.D. Mo. 1896) ("It is a doctrine as old as the Bible itself, and the common law of the land follows it, that a man cannot serve two masters at the same time; he will obey the one and betray the other. He cannot be subject to two controlling forces which may at the time be divergent."). If the two principals are unaware of the double employment, the transaction between them is voidable. *See* Restatement (Second) § 391, Comment g. If one principal secretly employs the agent to act on its account knowing that the other principal is unaware of the double employment, the defrauded principal can rescind or choose to affirm the transaction and recover damages from the other principal or the knowing agent.

Notes

1. In *Thayer v. Pacific Elec. Ry.*, 360 P.2d 56, 62 (Cal. 1961), Hileman, a station agent for the defendant railroad, went to the office of plaintiff, whose precision grinding machine had been damaged in shipment, and sought to collect the freight charges. Plaintiff objected to paying, noting that the damage exceeded the amount of the freight charge. Hileman stated that these were two separate matters, but plaintiff continued to object, stating that he did not want to waive his right to collect for damages. Hileman then wrote on the freight bill, "Damages on this shipment, 4/20/55, C.D. Hileman." Ten months later, after lengthy exploration of the alternatives of repair or replacement of the machine, plaintiff made a written claim for the damages. His claim was rejected on the ground that the nine-month limitation period for claims had expired. He sued, arguing that the writing of Hileman satisfied the requirement that written claims must be submitted within nine months.

The court saw the issue as turning on whether Hileman had acted as plaintiff's agent in making the notation on the freight bill. It approved a trial court finding of agency, stating that "even though Hileman was employed by the defendant railway, he became plaintiff's agent for the purpose of noting on the freight bill that plaintiff intended to claim damages. . . . The existence of an agency is a question of fact, which may be implied from the conduct of the parties."

2. Is *Thayer* consistent with the dual agency rule? Can you make an argument that it is, based on a commonsense limitation to the rule? 1 Restatement (Second) § 391, Comments b and d, observing that the agent can deal with the other party "if such dealing is not inconsistent with his duties to his principal." *Accord Young v. Nevada Title* Co, 744 P.2d 902 (Nev. 1987).

3. *Utah State Univ. v. Sutro & Co.*, 646 P.2d 715, 722 (Utah 1982), contains language relevant to this matter:

> It is not necessarily always true that a party acting as an agent in a transaction must be exclusively the agent of one party or the other. When he is requested and performs duties for each of the parties, with the knowledge and consent of both, he may very well be considered as an agent for each for the particular services he renders that principal.

This language makes clear what is suggested in the above introductory text, that the dual agency rule does not apply when both principals consent to the situation. It is addressing a matter distinct from that raised in note 2, however.

2. The Ambiguous Principal Problem

This topic focuses on the problem of identifying the principal when the facts are confusingly neutral on the issue of for whom the agent is acting. One context in which this problem frequently arises is that of group insurance, where an employer contracts for and administers a group policy for its employees. The employer makes a mistake in administering a policy or gives bad advice to an employee, resulting in loss to the employee. The issue of who bears the loss turns on the agency status of the employer, who appears to be acting on behalf of both the employee and the insurance company. Courts have split on this matter. Contained below are excerpts from opinions that take conflicting positions on this question. With which opinion do you agree?

The case of *Kilbourne v. Henderson*, 577 N.E.2d 1132, 1136 (Ohio App. 1989), involved group health insurance coverage where the employer's health plan administrator (Fitzgerald) unwittingly overstated the coverage available to an employee (Kilbourne), who incurred substantial medical bills in reliance on coverage. The insurance company (CNA) refused to pay the bills, invoking the terms of the policy. Kilbourne sued CNA, arguing that it was bound by Fitzgerald's statements because she was its agent for those purposes. The appellate court upheld a summary judgment rejecting Kilbourne's argument, in an opinion stating in part as follows: "An employer's administration of a group insurance plan does not create an agency relationship between the employer and the insurance carrier since the employer is acting only for the benefit of its employees and the employer's own benefit in promoting better relations between itself and its employees."

A contrasting view is represented by the following case.

Norby v. Bankers Life Co.

Minnesota Supreme Court
231 N.W.2d 665 (1975)

Heard before PETERSON, MACLAUGHLIN, and YETKA, JJ., and considered and decided by the court en banc.

PETERSON, JUSTICE.

Important issues in the administration of group insurance programs for the benefit of employees are raised in this appeal.

The issues arise out of an uncomplicated factual situation. Hoffman Brothers, Inc. (hereafter Hoffman) . . . is a member of the Upper Midwest Employers Association. The association is named as policyholder in a group accident and sickness policy issued by The Bankers Life Company of Des Moines, Iowa (hereafter Bankers Life), defendant. The policy provides for reimbursement of a portion of the medical bills incurred by covered employees of the association's employer members, including dependents of employees. Plaintiff, Fred G. Norby, is an employee of Hoffman, and claims benefits for the expense of medical care for his injured child in the undisputed amount of $3,460.49.

Plaintiff commenced his employment with Hoffman in August 1970. He completed an application for coverage under the policy in September 1970, which was thereupon delivered to his employer, Hoffman. If Hoffman had transmitted the application to Bankers Life, plaintiff's insurance coverage would have begun immediately and his subsequent claim would have been paid. But, through oversight or neglect, Hoffman failed to forward the application.

Plaintiff, on discovering Hoffman's error, completed a second application on December 31, 1970, which was promptly transmitted to Bankers Life. Because of an intervening period of temporary layoff, plaintiff's coverage, under the terms of the policy, was not effective until January 20, 1971 that is, unless the initial, untransmitted application was binding upon Bankers Life. Plaintiff's child, for whom the claim is made, was injured on January 19, 1971.

Bankers Life denied the claim, asserting that plaintiff was not effectively covered until it had received his application form from Hoffman. Plaintiff then brought this action on the policy against Bankers Life. . . . The trial court ordered judgment for plaintiff, finding and concluding that Hoffman stood in the relationship of agent to Bankers Life with authority to accept the application, thus binding Bankers Life at the time of plaintiff's initial application. . . . This appeal followed, raising the primary issue of whether such an agency relationship existed. . . .[14]

---

14. [1] Defendant, Bankers Life, contends additionally that, because the group insurance policy was written in the name of Upper Midwest Employers Association, the association alone has standing. It is elementary, however, that an employee who otherwise satisfies the conditions of a group plan may maintain an action against the insurer as a third-party beneficiary.

The principal issue for determination is whether an employer may be held to be acting as an agent of a group insurer for the purpose of accepting insurance applications from eligible employees. If, as the trial court here found, Hoffman acted as the agent of Bankers Life with respect to plaintiff's timely initial application, Bankers Life is bound by Hoffman's action, since a principal is bound by the acts of its agent. We hold that it was.

Conventional wisdom has been that the employer functions in the administration of a group insurance policy solely for its own interests or for the benefit of its employees, rather than serving the purposes of the insurer, and that the employer and the employees are allied in their interests adverse to the insurer. Judicial precedent, including the older precedents, are numerically weighted against finding the existence of an employer-insurer agency relationship.

Pragmatic, as well as theoretical, considerations induce us to undertake, as others have, a reappraisal of these concepts.[15] Group insurance is today a widespread and most significant form of insurance protection, particularly for employee groups . . . .

Administration of group insurance policies entails some rather routine functions, such as enrolling employees through their completing applications for themselves and dependents; collecting employee contributions, if any, and remitting premiums to the insurer; terminating and reinstating insurance; and assisting in the processing of claims. Employers may have a role in determining eligibility for coverage, at least to the extent that the classification and employment status of employees relates to whether or not an employee is within the insured group. There may be situations where the insurer performs all these functions itself, in which case the plan is wholly "insurer-administered," and in which case no issue of agency between the employer and insurer arises. There are the other situations, as in this case, in which the employer performs such a number of these functions that, at least as a shorthand expression, it may be considered, in whole or in part, to be "employer-administered." To the extent the employer, with the consent of the insurer, performs the functions of the insurer, it may properly be considered the insurer's agent.

An agency relationship is based upon consent by one person that another shall act in his behalf and be subject to his control. Restatement, Agency 2d, § 1. These aspects of the relationship in employer-sponsored insurance plans should be realistically viewed from the various perspectives of the insurer, the employer, and the employee. The insurer has an obvious choice as to whether or not to authorize the performance of administrative functions by the employer and, if it does so, is in a position to exercise effective control over the performance of those functions; the employer, likewise, has a choice of whether or not to purchase an insurance policy

---

15. [4] Discussion of the issue may be found in Note, 1968 Duke L.J. 824; Eugster, Group Insurance: *Agency Characterization of the Master Policyholder*, 46 Wash. L. Rev. 377; 1 Appleman, Insurance Law and Practice, § 43.

under those conditions, recognizing that the choice may have an effect upon the premium it pays. The employee-beneficiary, however, ordinarily has no choice with respect to the policy purchased or the manner of its implementation. He usually knows only that he is entitled to stated insurance benefits. He does not ask whether the insurance plan is "insurer-administered" or "employer-administered." He may reasonably assume that his employer and the insurer will, in their dealings with each other, do that which is necessary to provide him with the promised benefits. It is, therefore, unreasonable and inequitable to frustrate the employee's expectations because of an employer's negligence in administering the insurance agreement.

This is substantially the rationale of that minority of the courts which hold that the employer, in circumstances similar to these, acts as the agent of the insurer. . . . We now hold that the employer policyholder may, in appropriate circumstances, be found to be the agent of the group insurer of employees and affirm the trial court's finding that third-party defendant, Hoffman, was in this case the agent of defendant, Bankers Life.

We do not undertake to anticipate what may constitute appropriate circumstances to support a finding of agency in any future case, except to make two clarifying points. . . . First, the use of the terms, "employer-administered" and "insurer-administered" is not necessarily of determinative significance, for it would seem that few insurance plans for employee groups are likely to be wholly one or the other. The focus, instead, should be on which specific and relevant administrative functions are performed by the employer on behalf of the insurer, with respect to the particular ground asserted for noncoverage or nonpayment under the policy. An employer may be considered an agent of an insurer for some purposes but not for others.[16] Here, the employee was plainly eligible for coverage but was denied coverage only because the function of enrollment, clearly delegated to the employer by the insurer, was mishandled. The delegated act was specifically relevant to the particular ground upon which the insurer denied coverage. Whether the insurance plan was or was not "employer-administered" in other respects, is, in this situation, of little relevance. That is, in essence, the basis upon which the trial court made its finding and is the basis upon which it is affirmed.

Second, we take anticipatory note of the danger of collusion between an employer and employee to defeat the insurer for each other's benefit. . . . Those courts which

---

16. [The case of *Madden v. Kaiser Found. Hosps.*, 131 Cal. Rptr. 882, 552 P.2d 1178 (1976), is an illustration of this point. The court held that in negotiating a group medical plan for state employees the board of administration acted as the agent of the employees. The court cited to an earlier California case which had held an employer to be the agent of the insurance company while administering a group insurance policy, and expressly approved this distinction in legal status based on different activities. With regard to the characterization of an employer as agent while negotiating a plan, see *Engalla v. Permanente Med. Group*, 938 P.2d 903, 919, n. 11 (Cal. 1997) ("We recognize, of course, that this inverse agency relationship between the employer and its employees is a narrow one, and does not preclude an employer from acting in its own interests to obtain cost savings for the enterprise as a whole when choosing a group health plan.").—Eds.]

have rejected a finding of agency have done so on the assumption that the interests of both the employer and employee are adverse to the insurer. Although we depart from those precedents, we agree that whenever it is established that the employer and employee have colluded adversely to the insurer, no agency may be found to exist. Any authority of an agent clearly terminates if, without knowledge of the principal, he acquires adverse interests or if he is otherwise guilty of a breach of loyalty to the principal. A principal is not bound by an agent's actions where the agent acts adversely to the principal and the party with whom the agent deals is aware of such adverse dealing. . . .

Affirmed.

Notes

1. Suppose that the application for coverage in the *Norby* case, signed by Norby, had included the following language: "I hereby constitute and appoint Hoffman Brothers, Inc., as my agent to procure insurance for me from the Bankers Life Company." How would such language affect the arguments of the parties? For the response of one court to language in a contract describing a relationship between the parties as an agency relationship, see *Bell v. Riggs*, 34 Okla. 834, 841–43, 127 P. 427, 430 (1912):

> The mere use of the word "agent," as thus applied by parties in their contract, cannot be held to have the effect to make one an agent who, in view of the law under the evidence, is not such. A legal relation of one to another is not the fruit of a name, but is to be determined from all of the evidence in the case. . . . As is well said in *Insurance Co. v. Ives*, 56 Ill. 402: "There is no magic power residing in the words of the stipulation to transmit the real into the unreal."

While the above language makes an indisputable point, this does not mean that contractual language characterizing a relationship has no effect under any circumstance. Consider the following quotation from *Beckenstein v. Potter & Carrier, Inc.,* 464 A.2d 6, 16 (Conn. 1983):

> We have noted that the labels which the parties attach to their descriptions of their relationship is not a conclusive factor. In this case, however, where the provision in the agreement disclaiming an agency relationship is consistent with the provisions of the rest of the agreement, that statement can and should be given credence as indicative of the intent of the parties.

2. In an omitted passage, the court in *Norby* rejected an argument that, while Hoffman may have been an agent of Bankers Life for some purposes, such as assisting in the processing of claims, nevertheless it was an agent for the employee while engaged in the act of transmitting the application form. The argument apparently involved an effort by defendant's counsel to apply the principles of the *Thayer* case, *supra*, by arguing that in processing and transmitting the application Hoffman was primarily benefiting the employee and thus was, for that act, the employee's agent. Consider the following language from *Bell*, note 1, *supra*, with regard to this question.

> It is true the courts have held . . . that the same person can be the agent of both borrower and lender for different purposes in connection with the loan. Certainly the proof should be clear that would permit the same man to be agent of both parties. It is hardly in human nature for him to serve both sides with the same zeal and fidelity.

F. Subagency

This section deals with agents acting for other agents. An understanding of the relationships can get tricky in this setting, in part because one person is functioning in a dual capacity, acting both as agent and as principal. Also, subagency must be distinguished from co-agency, where two agents both act for one principal. Sometimes in co-agency one agent is in a superior position to the other and gives orders to the other, so that the relationship looks confusingly like subagency. It is not always apparent at a glance what type of relationship one is dealing with.

The case of *Stortroen v. Beneficial Finance Co.*, 736 P.2d 391 (Colo. 1987), involved subagency in the real estate brokerage context. The decision turned on the characterization of the relationship between a listing broker (who contracts with the property owner to list the property for sale) and a selling broker (the broker who obtains a contract for sale of the property) in a multiple listing setting, where property is listed by the listing broker on a multiple listing service, inviting any broker to show and sell it in return for a percentage of the commission promised to the listing broker. The court held that the selling broker was an agent of the listing broker and a subagent of the seller, even though the selling broker and the seller had never met, with the result that notice to the selling broker of acceptance of an offer bound the unwilling seller. In reaching its decision the court stated as follows:

> . . . We hold that in a multiple listing real estate transaction involving residential property the selling broker or salesperson, in the absence of a written agreement creating a different agency relationship, is an agent of the listing broker and, as such, is within a chain of agency to the seller. . . .

> . . . A subagent is "a person appointed by an agent empowered to do so, to perform functions undertaken by the agent for the principal, but for whose conduct the agent agrees with the principal to be primarily responsible." [Restatement] § 5(1). A subagent is the agent of both the appointing agent and the principal. *Id.* § 5 comment d. Notice to an agent given in the course of a transaction which is within the scope of the agency is notice to the principal. So too, notice to a subagent who is under a duty to communicate the notice to the agent is effective to the same extent as if notice had been given to the agent.

In the context of residential real estate transactions, it is a widely accepted rule of agency law that a real estate broker operating under an exclusive listing contract with the seller of the property stands in an agency relationship to the seller. . . . Because it is customary for a real estate broker to employ salespersons to deal with prospective purchasers of the listed property, the authority given to the broker by the listing agreement will generally include the implied authority to appoint these salespersons as subagents to perform the tasks assigned to the broker by the listing agreement.

The listing agreement may authorize the broker to list the property with a multiple listing service. A multiple listing service is basically an arrangement for brokers in a given locality to pool their listings and split their commissions. . . . Under traditional agency principles, a listing contract which authorizes the listing broker to list the property with a multiple listing service permits the listing broker to create a subagency with other members of the multiple listing service. . . .

Notes

1. *Terminology.* The words "principal" and "agent" are ambiguous in the subagency context because one agent is both an agent and a principal. Thus it may sometimes prove helpful to refer to the original principal as the remote principal and the agent as the immediate principal, depending on context.

2. The relationship of subagency has consequences beyond those involved in the *Stortroen* case. Some complex questions arise when defining rights and duties among principal, agent, and subagent. Those matters will be covered in Chapter 2. In addition, questions arise concerning the liability of the remote principal for the mistakes or misconduct of the subagent. *Blanchette v. Cataldo*, 734 F.2d 869, 874–75 (1st Cir. 1984), involved liability for the filing of nearly 2,000 groundless lawsuits by an employee of one Cataldo, a claims agent hired by the defendant freight receivers to file claims on their behalf. The trial court declined to impose liability on the freight receivers because Cataldo's employee "while indirectly an agent of the receivers was not their employee." This decision was reversed on appeal on the reasoning that, "A principal's liability for the acts of its agents' employees — its subagents — is normally the same as its liability for the acts of the agents themselves." *Id.* at 874–75.

3. Another consequence of subagency is the liability of the agent for the mistakes and misconduct of the subagent. *Colony Assocs. v. Fred L. Clapp & Co.*, 60 N.C. App. 634, 300 S.E.2d 37, 38 (1983), involved the following fact situation. Plaintiff (Colony) hired defendant (Clapp) to obtain refinancing for an apartment complex that Colony owned. Clapp contacted Global, which represented a lender. Clapp and Global agreed to work on a "fifty-fifty net split fee basis." An $11,000 deposit was required as part of the loan application. Global requested that the deposit be made payable to it so that if anything went wrong the deposit could be refunded quickly. Colony sent $11,000 to Global. The loan did not go through. Global refused to return the deposit. Suit was brought by Colony against Clapp. Colony prevailed

on the reasoning that its agent Clapp, as principal of Global, was liable for the misconduct of Global.

G. Agency Distinguished from Other Relationships

1. The Franchise Relationship

Franchisors are often sued for the tortious conduct of their franchisees, on the theory that the franchisee is an agent of the franchisor. Generally, the franchisor prevails, but sometimes only after an appeal. *See, e.g., Jamison v. Morris*, 684 S.E.2d 168 (S.C. 2009) (jury award of $30 million against franchisor reversed on appeal).

A franchise is defined in *H & R Block, Inc. v. Lovelace*, 208 Kan. 538, 545, 493 P.2d 205, 211–12 (1972), as "a license from the owner of a trademark or trade name [the franchisor] permitting another [the franchisee] to sell a product or service under that name or mark." It usually includes "an exclusive right to sell the product in a specified territory."

The franchise arrangement often provides for the exercise of a considerable amount of control by the franchisor. *See Slates v. International House of Pancakes*, 90 Ill. App. 3d 716, 724, 413 N.E.2d 457, 465 (1980), where the franchise agreement included the following terms concerning control:

> The agreement further provides that the restaurant may serve and sell only such items and products as shall be expressly from time to time designated and approved in writing by the defendant [franchisor]. The franchisee may purchase all flour and pancake mixes only from the franchisor or from suppliers approved in writing by the franchisor. The franchisor is specifically given the power to promulgate a standard operational procedures manual which will be binding upon the franchisee covering the following subjects: training and supervision of franchisees and restaurant managers, quality control, record keeping and account controls, administrative assistance, periodic inspections, appearance of the premises, hours of operation, merchandise sold, employees' appearance and demeanor, the personal standards in training, promotions, advertising and signs, preparation and service of food and beverages, and relations with suppliers.

Despite the above reservation of substantial control, the court in *Slates* found that the relationship was not an agency relationship, holding that service of process on the franchisee of a claim against the franchisor was ineffective in the absence of an agency relationship. Which element of an agency relationship is missing? *See Stanford v. Dairy Queen Products*, 623 S.W.2d 797, 803 (Tex. App. 1981):

> With respect to appellee [franchisor], the manifest purpose and object of the contract was to exploit for profit its ownership of the exclusive right to license others to use the trade name "Dairy Queen," while simultaneously

preserving the value of the name in the market place. With respect to a licensee under such a contract, the manifest purpose and object of the contract was to obtain the right to use the trade name because of its market value, which the licensee had in a business decision determined to be worth the consideration demanded, namely: the franchise fee, the two-percent "royalty," and a promise to abide by those contract provisions which appellee considered necessary and exacted to maintain the value of the trade name. We believe that the numerous contract provisions dealing with an alleged retention of excessive control by appellee must be read in this light. The parties simply had *different* purposes and objects.

We hold that the evidence does not conclusively establish the relation of "agency" or "representative." . . . Specifically, the record includes substantial and probative evidence from which the trial court could conclude that the typical restaurant operator did not *act for* appellee and *in its behalf.*

The above materials have as their subject the existence of an actual agency relationship. Questions of apparent agency and of estoppel will be covered in later chapters.

Aside from whether a franchisor-franchisee relationship qualifies as an agency relationship, merely calling an arrangement a "franchise" does not automatically assure that the courts will recognize it as such. For instance, in *Awuah v. Coverall North America, Inc.*, 707 F. Supp. 2d 80 (D. Mass. 2010), the court considered a case in which a "franchisor" of janitorial services entered into "franchise agreements" with individuals who, in turn, would provide janitorial services to customers obtained by the franchisor. The franchisor billed the customers and only paid the "franchisees" when the customer paid. To become a franchisee, the individual paid a fee to the franchisor and, thereafter, "royalty and management fees" of various amounts. In effect, the individual franchisees paid for their jobs and assumed the risk of nonpayment by the customers. The federal district court concluded that the franchisees were actually employees (that is, agents) of the franchisor.

2. The Marriage Relationship

As you know, the agency relationship is a consensual relationship involving one party acting on behalf of another on a matter entrusted to the acting party. It thus involves elements of trust and confidence. The marriage relationship also is a consensual relationship involving trust and confidence. Yet it does not in itself create an agency between husband and wife. This is because in particular transactions it is not necessarily—or even usually—the case that one spouse is acting on behalf of and subject to the control of the other spouse. *See Gorco Construction Co. v. Stein*, 256 Minn. 476, 99 N.W.2d 69 (1959). With regard to the weight to be given to such relationship, however, see the following language from *Mays v. Brighton Bank*, 832 S.W.2d 347, 351 (Tenn. App. 1992):

While the existence of marital or family ties between the alleged agent and principal, unaccompanied by any other facts or circumstances, will not justify an inference of agency, such relationship is entitled to great weight, when considered with other circumstances, as tending to establish the fact of agency.

3. Property Relationships

This brief note will address in a preliminary way two property relationships where the law of agency can surface on occasion.

a. Co-ownership

This relationship does not in itself establish agency because one cannot fairly infer that one co-owner consents to another acting on his behalf merely from the fact that they are joint owners of property. *See Johnson v. Hunnicutt*, 358 S.E.2d 74, 77 (N.C. App. 1987) (two of five tenants in common had no power to sell the subject property without the consent of the other three; there was "no evidence from any source that the other three defendants had authorized" such conduct).

b. Landlord-Tenant

In general, the landlord-tenant relationship in itself does not involve agency. *See Frank v. United States*, 797 F.2d 724, 726 (9th Cir. 1986) ("The lessee's status does not make him an agent authorized to enter contracts on behalf of the lessor."); *see also McCombs Constr., Inc. v. Barnes*, 645 P.2d 1131, 1134 (Wash. App. 1982) ("A lessor's knowledge of, and acquiescence in, the making of improvements by the tenant, are insufficient to establish agency."). The nature of a lease can change things, however. In *Christensen Group v. Puget Sound Power & Light*, 723 P.2d 504, 507 (Wash. App. 1986), the court stated, "Washington case law supports the proposition that if a lessee makes improvements because it is required to do so under the terms of the lease, it [becomes] the lessor's agent."

4. Corporate Relationships

A brief explanation of the key features of the corporation is set forth in the Introduction preceding this chapter. Contained below are two features of the law of corporations that involve the law of agency. A full development of the concepts mentioned below, and a detailed application of the law of agency specifically to corporations, will have to await the course on corporations.

a. The Agency Status of Corporate Directors

The agency status of a board of directors of a corporation is covered in Comment (f)(2) to Restatement (Third) § 1.01, stating in part as follows:

> Although a corporation's shareholders elect its directors and may have the right to remove directors once elected, the directors are neither the

shareholders' nor the corporation's agents as defined in this section, given the treatment of directors within contemporary corporation law in the United States. Directors' powers originate as the legal consequence of their election and are not conferred or delegated by shareholders. Although corporation statutes require shareholder approval for specific fundamental transactions, corporation law generally invests managerial authority over corporate affairs in a board of directors, not in shareholders, providing that management shall occur by or under the board of directors. Thus, shareholders ordinarily do not have a right to control directors by giving binding instructions to them. If the statute under which a corporation has been incorporated so permits, shareholders may be allocated power to give binding instructions to directors through a provision in the corporation's articles or through a validly adopted shareholder agreement. The fact that a corporation statute may refer to directors as the corporation's "agents" for a particular purpose does not place directors in an agency relationship with shareholders for purposes of the common law of agency. In any event, directors' ability to bind the corporation is invested in the directors as a board, not in individual directors acting unilaterally. . . .

The Restatement (Second) also notes that an individual director "has still less resemblance to an agent" because he has no power to act on his own.[17] He may, however, be appointed by the board to an agency position, such as executive officer.

b. The "Mere Instrumentality" or "Alter Ego" Doctrine Contrasted with Traditional Agency Liability

A subsidiary corporation is one in which at least a majority of its voting shares is held by another corporation, called the parent corporation or a holding company. Does this status mean that a parent corporation runs the risk of liability for the acts of its subsidiary as a result of its stock control? *Main Bank of Chicago v. Baker*, 427 N.E.2d 94, 101–02 (Ill. 1981), addresses this matter in the following terms:

> It is a well-established principle that a corporation is separate and distinct as a legal entity from its shareholders, directors and officers and, generally, from other corporations with which it may be affiliated. Stock ownership alone in one corporation by another does not create an identity of interest between the two or create the relation of principal and agent,

---

17. Suppose a director is elected by a group of shareholders who cast their votes solely for him by design and with an intent to get a member on the board who will act in their interest. Is the director the agent of the group that elected him to the board by prearrangement and with a specific agenda in mind? See *Sassower v. Field*, 752 F. Supp. 1182, 1186 (S.D.N.Y. 1990), stating, "Once elected, a member of a board of directors acts for the corporation and his actions will be attributed to the corporation. Although the member of the board may consider the interests of those who elected him and may act in furtherance of their goals, he is not, by virtue of his election, their designated agent."

representative, or alter ego between the two. Nor does the use of common officers and directors of itself render one corporation liable for the obligations of another. These practices are common and exist in most parent-subsidiary relationships. Generally, before the separate corporate identity of one corporation will be disregarded and treated as the alter ego of another, it must be shown that it is so controlled and its affairs so conducted that it is a mere instrumentality of another, and it must further appear that observance of the fiction of separate existence would, under the circumstances, sanction a fraud or promote injustice.

While, ordinarily, when multiple corporations are involved, a party seeks to pierce the corporate veil to hold a parent liable for its subsidiary's acts or the subsidiary responsible for the acts of its parent, . . . the doctrine of piercing the corporate veil is not limited to the parent and subsidiary relationship; the separate corporate identities of corporations owned by the same parent will likewise be disregarded in an appropriate case.

Phoenix Canada Oil Co. v. Texaco, Inc., 842 F.2d 1466, 1476–77 (3d Cir. 1988), distinguishes the above doctrine from traditional agency liability in the corporate context:

The relationship between parent and subsidiary corporations has been a fruitful source of litigation and although the case law on the subject is extensive, it is neither uniform nor clear. Some decisions apply an agency theory to assess parental liability, others focus on an alter ego basis, and some speak in terms of "piercing the corporate veil." Much of the confusion stems from a failure to distinguish between subsidiaries treated as independent entities and those in fact not independent, but considered part of the parent corporations.

[I]ndependent corporate status may be disregarded when such factors as gross undercapitalization, fraud, failure to observe corporate formalities, non-functioning of officers and directors, or similar circumstances indicate that the subsidiary is merely the shadow of the parent. If, as in this case, the shareholder happens to be another corporation, piercing the corporate veil results in disregard for the separate existence of parent and subsidiary. . . . The activities bearing on the issue of corporate independence need not have any particular relationship to the cause of action being asserted.

There is a second theory under which a parent may be held liable for the activities of its subsidiary: an application of general agency principles. One corporation whose shares are owned by a second corporation does not, by that fact alone, become the agent of the second company. However, one corporation—completely independent of a second corporation—may assume the role of the second corporation's agent in the course of one or more specific transactions. This restricted agency relationship may develop whether the two separate corporations are parent and subsidiary or are completely unrelated outside the limited agency setting. See Restatement (Second) of Agency § 14 M, comment (a) (1958). Under this second theory, total domination or general alter ego criteria need not be proven. . . . Unlike the alter ego/piercing the corporate veil theory, when customary agency is alleged the proponent must demonstrate a relationship between the corporations and the cause of action. Not only must an arrangement exist between the two corporations so that one acts on behalf of the other and within usual agency principles, but the arrangement must be relevant to the plaintiff's claim of wrongdoing.

As the court in *Phoenix* recognized, there are situations where a genuine agency relationship can exist between corporations. See the Reporter's Notes to § 14 M of the Restatement (Second), stating: "It is an accepted principle of agency that the term 'agent' includes both natural persons and corporations . . . [likewise the terms principal, master and servant], notwithstanding the anthropomorphic sound of the titles. It follows that a corporation can be an agent for another corporation."

H. The History of Agency and Other Matters

1. *Etymology.* The word "agent" is derived from the Latin word *agens*, the present participle of *agere*, to drive, act, do. The Indo-European root *ag* is also contained in the Greek word *agein*, to drive, lead.

2. *Capacity to be an agent.* Ordinarily an agent acts only in a representative capacity, binding his principal to a contract but not himself. Thus, it frequently is said that anyone can be an agent, even one who has no capacity to enter into a contract.[18] While this is true concerning contracts between the principal and third persons, one without capacity may not be held to full fiduciary duties to his principal, and any contractual rights and duties between principal and agent would have to meet capacity requirements. *See* WARREN A. SEAVEY, HANDBOOK OF THE LAW OF AGENCY 27 (1964).

3. *History of agency.* The history of agency will be treated only briefly at this stage. A further look at history will be taken when we cover specific subjects that will give the matter more definition and focus, such as respondeat superior liability in Chapter 3.

---

18. The classic illustration of this is the medieval monk, who became "civilly dead" upon becoming professed in religion, taking a vow of obedience and poverty and "quitting this world." *See* 1 F. Pollock & F. Maitland, THE HISTORY OF ENGLISH LAW 433 (2nd ed. 1898). "When a man becomes 'professed in religion,' his heir at once inherits from him any land that he has, and, if he has made a will, it takes effect at once as though he were naturally dead." *Id.* at 434. A monk could not make a contract "but he was fully capable of acting as the agent of his sovereign." *Id.* (It should be noted that the fiction of civil death had its limits. A monk was not fair game for any tortfeasor who came along, and a monk remained subject to personal criminal and tort liability.)

The law of agency involves some fairly sophisticated legal concepts, including the principle of direct representation. This principle recognizes that a legal transaction by *A* acting manifestly on behalf of *P* and with *P*'s authority binds or benefits *P* without creating liability for *A*.

Agency does not exist in primitive legal systems, where all legal transactions must be done in person. *See* 2 WILLIAM S. HOLDSWORTH, A HISTORY OF ENGLISH LAW 311–12 (4th ed. 1936) ("The idea that one man can stand in the place of another does not come naturally to primitive systems of law."). Surprisingly, even Roman law, an advanced legal system, did not recognize the principle of direct representation. With only a few exceptions, the Roman citizen could not act through a representative in contractual matters, due to the personal nature of contracts. An agent could not contract with a third person without becoming a party to the contract, nor could his principal acquire any rights or liabilities under the contract. *See* WILLIAM BUCKLAND, A TEXT-BOOK OF ROMAN LAW FROM AUGUSTUS TO JUSTINIAN 533 (3rd ed. 1963).

The principle of direct representation was recognized early in English law, which was not bound to Roman law. There is written evidence of the use of agency in the twelfth century by the king, who would issue letters of credit empowering agents to borrow money and to promise repayment in the name of the king. Monasteries necessarily had to act through agents because, as footnoted earlier, monks, through whom most matters were accomplished, were regarded as civilly dead. Also, trading companies, which came to be recognized in the fourteenth and fifteenth centuries, had to act through agents because the trading company was an artificial entity and hence incapable of acting on its own.

The common law in medieval times and for many centuries afterward held the principal to contractual and tort liability only for acts that the agent was ordered to do. "In both cases there must be a particular authority to do the act complained of." 4 WILLIAM S. HOLDSWORTH, A HISTORY OF ENGLISH LAW 411 (1924). We shall deal later with the gradual expansion of liability beyond these limitations.

Problems

As you go through the problems in this casebook, you are encouraged to analyze the facts of each problem first from the perspective of the lawyer for the aggrieved party, asking what arguments you would make through use of the preceding materials, and then do the same from the perspective of the defending lawyer. Then put on yet another hat, that of a judge trying the matter without a jury, and decide the case.

Many of the problems are drawn from actual cases. As you will observe below, sometimes the case upon which a problem is based is cited in the problem. We strongly encourage the student reader to take the time, which sometimes may be of considerable length, to think through the problems on his or her own *before* consulting the reports, however. The learning experience of formulating one's own analysis of a fact situation otherwise is considerably weakened.

1. Some growers of dark tobacco entered into an agreement to form a nonprofit corporation, The Dark Tobacco Growers' Association. The agreement provided that the Association "shall have absolute title to the tobacco upon delivery to it by the grower" and shall resell the tobacco at the best prices obtainable and "pay over the net amounts received therefrom . . . as payment in full to the grower." The municipality of Owensboro assessed for tax purposes $350,000 worth of tobacco that the Association had on hand in the city. A state statute exempts from local taxation unmanufactured agricultural products in the hands of the producer or his agent. The Association sought to enjoin collection of the tax on the ground that it was holding the tobacco as the agent of the growers. Advance and evaluate the arguments that can be made on behalf of the Association and of Owensboro. *See Owensboro v. Dark Tobacco Growers' Ass'n*, 222 Ky. 164, 300 S.W. 350 (1927).

2. Grosvenor, who was in business under the name of Grosvenor Music House, entered into an agreement called a Consignment Contract with a piano company (the "Company"). Grosvenor agreed to take on consignment merchandise shipped to him by the Company, which he agreed to sell "for the Company" for cash or on an installment payment basis. The installment contracts were to be evidenced by notes payable to the Company and guaranteed by Grosvenor. During the period of payment, the merchandise would remain the property of the Company. Grosvenor agreed to keep the merchandise fully insured at his expense. It was also stipulated in the contract "the Consignee [Grosvenor], when requested by the Company or its assigns, will assist in making collections on sales made by the Consignee; and also will foreclose mortgages and/or repossess musical instruments; all without expense to the Company." Grosvenor was to receive as his remuneration any amount for which the instruments consigned were sold in excess of the consignment price.

Six months after the Contract was executed Grosvenor decamped, owing the Company over $5,000. The Company sought to obtain the sums lost from a surety company that had agreed to pay the Company "such pecuniary loss . . . sustained . . . by an act of dishonesty on the part of any of the agents and employees named in the schedule attached to this bond." Grosvenor was among the persons named in the schedule, listed as a "collector." The surety company refused to pay, claiming that, at the time his defalcations occurred, Grosvenor was not an agent within the meaning of the bond. Instead, the surety company claimed that Grosvenor was conducting a business of his own. The piano company sued on the bond. What result? *See Frederick Inv. Co. v. American Sur. Co.*, 314 Pa. 1, 169 A. 155 (1933).

3. Voss was engaged in the business of banking, abstracting titles, and making real estate loans, under his name and also under the name Bank of Denison. Some years ago he was appointed the "loan correspondent" of the Prudential Insurance Company with authority to submit applications for and close real estate mortgage loans located in the state of Iowa. The contract between them read in part as follows:

> [The] party of the first part [Voss] desires to submit to the insurance company applications for loans upon the security of mortgages on lands located in the state of Iowa, and the insurance company is willing to receive such

applications, and make loans where said applications are approved, ... [providing, after an application is accepted, for credits to Voss's account of any amounts that may have been advanced by Voss to close the loans.]

Voss agreed to purchase from Prudential all loans that contained errors and to pay to Prudential all amounts in excess of one-half of the value of the security. The following language was also part of the contract:

> It is further mutually understood and agreed that in all transactions arising out of the performance of this agreement, the party of the first part is acting and will act as agent of the borrower in negotiating said loans, and in no instance is acting or shall be authorized to act as agent for the said insurance company.

This relationship continued for several years, with occasional letters from Prudential in its files calling Voss's attention to such matters as commission charges for securing loans, and exhorting him to exercise unusual care "in connection with all applications where the loan per acre is in excess of $500."

Recently, Betsy and Tom Argot, who had an $18,000 mortgage outstanding on their property to the Burlington Savings Bank, contacted Voss about obtaining a new mortgage to secure an increased loan. Voss prepared on their behalf an application to Prudential for a loan of $24,000, it being intended that the proceeds of this loan would be used in part for the payment of the $18,000 mortgage held by Burlington Bank. The Argots executed to Prudential a note for $24,000 and a mortgage on the land. Voss forged and recorded a release of Burlington's $18,000 mortgage and furnished Prudential an abstract of title showing the release. This was unknown to the Argots. Prudential then loaned the $24,000, of which Voss appropriated $18,000, remitting the balance to the Argots. Burlington's mortgage was not paid, of course, and it foreclosed. In the foreclosure proceedings the court canceled the Prudential mortgage except for $6,000, for which amount personal judgment was rendered against the Argots. Prudential appeals, contending that the Argots should be responsible for the full amount of the mortgage to them. What result?

4. Larry and his wife Mildred entered into a divorce property settlement which provided that Larry would quitclaim his share of the jointly owned family residence to Mildred and that, in return, she would execute a second mortgage on the property in favor of Larry's brother. The mortgage was to secure the payment of a $4,000 loan the brother had made to them for the purchase of the home. They were jointly liable on the debt. Mildred agreed to pay off the second mortgage and, if she sold the property prior to full repayment, she would pay the brother from the proceeds. Hardesty, Mildred's attorney, prepared all the documents. Larry executed and delivered the quitclaim deed to Hardesty, but Mildred and the brother were unable to agree on the terms for repayment of the mortgage. Hardesty nevertheless recorded the deed, Mildred sold the house free and clear of the contemplated second mortgage and left for Florida, having paid nothing to the brother. Larry sues Hardesty for $4,000 damages. What result?

5. Thayer called Adams, a stockbroker, and gave him an order for the purchase of 30 shares of a particular company at a stated price of $1,000. Adams bought the stock on two separate occasions at a price several points below the stated price, taking title in his name. He then sent a bill to Thayer for the stated price with no commission charged. Thayer refused to take or pay for the stock. Adams sued for the price and was met at trial with the defense of Statute of Frauds. (The Uniform Commercial Code § 8-319 made, with some qualifications, a contract for the sale of securities unenforceable in the absence of a writing meeting certain requirements. Section 8-319 was repealed with the 1994 revisions to the UCC.) The statute was not applicable if the transaction was one of agency.

a. Advance and evaluate the arguments that can be made on behalf of Thayer and Adams.

b. Would Adams' case be stronger or weaker if the more traditional brokerage transaction had been entered into, where the broker is instructed to "get me the best deal you can," and the compensation for the broker is a commission? Assume that Adams got the stock as cheaply as he could, took title in his name and sent Thayer a bill for the price paid for the stock plus the customary commission.

See F.C. Adams, Inc. v. Elmer F. Thayer Estate, 85 N.H. 177, 155 A. 687 (1931), *aff'd on rehearing*, 85 N.H. 184, 156 A. 697 (1931), *exception to denial of petition for new trial overruled*, 86 N.H. 555, 171 A. 771 (1934), noted in 45 HARV. L. REV. 739 (1932); *see also Stott v. Greengos*, 95 N.J. Super. 96, 230 A.2d 154 (1967); *Lindsey v. Stein Bros. & Boyce, Inc.*, 222 Tenn. 149, 433 S.W.2d 669 (1968).

6. *S* advertised her car for sale. *B*, a prospective purchaser, expressed interest in the car and wanted to test drive it. *S* consented to this, but only after imposing certain conditions of use, such as specifying that only *B* can drive the car. While test driving the car, *B* negligently caused an accident with *C*, who also drove negligently and contributed to the accident. *S* sues *C* for the damage to her car. What defense can *C* make? What difference, if any, would it make if *S* had requested *B* to stop at a nearby gas station and "get some gas" on her account (she gave *B* a business card to show the attendant at the station) because the car was low on gas, and *B* had done that, and then got into the accident while test driving the car? *See St. Paul Ins. Co. v. Industrial Underwriters Ins. Co.*, 262 Cal. Rptr. 490 (Cal. App. 1989); *see also Aupied v. Joudeh*, 694 So. 2d 1012 (La. App. 1997).

Chapter 2

Rights and Duties between Principal and Agent

The subject matter of this chapter develops the concepts involved in Chapter 1, where the agency relationship was defined and applied to a variety of situations. Once a relationship is defined, it is important to know what the rights and duties are between the parties to the relationship.

The topic of this chapter breaks down into the duties the principal owes the agent and the agent owes the principal. It will probably come as no surprise to the reader that the larger part of the chapter is devoted to the duties the agent owes the principal. It is the agent who is the active party in the relationship, the party in whom trust is placed. The great majority of the internal disputes between principal and agent are generated by the misuse or perceived misuse of that trust.

With regard to the duties of the principal, when and under what circumstances is an agent entitled to compensation, if the parties have not expressly agreed on that issue? If an agent suffers losses as a result of the agency (stemming from lawsuits by third parties, for example), is the principal required to reimburse the agent, even if there is no agreement to do so? Is a principal required to reimburse a subagent for similar expenses, even if the principal has never met the subagent?

An agent is a fiduciary. Fiduciary concepts are so basic to the agency relationship that the definition of the relationship in § 1.01 of the Restatement (Third) contains the word "fiduciary," even though one ordinarily would consider the fiduciary characterization to be a consequence of the relationship, not part of its definition. What does it mean to be a fiduciary? Does it mean that an agent can never deal with the principal as an adverse party? Can an agent profit from a transaction beyond the compensation agreed to be paid by the principal if the principal receives everything the bargain calls for? Is an agent able to make use of knowledge and skills obtained during employment with the principal in competition against the principal after quitting the employment? Is an agent liable to the principal for errors innocently made while performing the duties of the agency? Is an agent required to disclose a conflict of interest to the principal even if the agent in good faith believes that the conflict will have no effect on the underlying transaction?

A. Duties of Principal to Agent

1. Duty of Exoneration and Indemnification

Admiral Oriental Line v. United States

United States Court of Appeals, Second Circuit

86 F.2d 201 (1936)

Before L. Hand, Swan, and Augustus N. Hand, Circuit Judges.

L. Hand, Circuit Judge.

These appeals are from decrees dismissing two libels in personam in the admiralty. In the first the libellant, the Admiral Oriental Line, alleged that it had been employed by the respondent, the Atlantic Gulf & Oriental Company, as ship's agent in the Philippines, and had had charge of fitting out the steamship, "Elkton," on a voyage out of Pulupandan, on which she was lost with all hands in a typhoon. The "Elkton" was owned by the United States, and had been entrusted to the Atlantic Gulf & Oriental S. S. Co. as ship's agent under an operating contract. The "Elkton's" cargo owners sued the Admiral Oriental Line for its loss, and the Line was put to certain expenses in defending the suit, in which it was, however, successful. It claimed these expenses on the theory that as agent it had paid them upon its principal's account. The Atlantic Gulf & Oriental S. S. Co. answered and attempted to bring in the United States under the Fifty-Sixth Rule (28 U.S.C.A. following section 723). It alleged that the United States was the principal in the whole venture and as such responsible to its immediate agent, the Atlantic Gulf & Oriental S. S. Co. not only for any expenses to which it was put in its own defense, but for any which it might be compelled to pay to the sub-agent, the Admiral Oriental Line, under decree in the main suit. The second suit was filed directly under the Suits in Admiralty Act (46 U.S.C.A. § 741 et seq.) against the United States by the Atlantic Gulf & Oriental S. S. Co. for its own expenses in defending itself in the suit by the "Elkton's" cargo to which it too had been made a party. Each libellant appealed, and the Atlantic Gulf & Oriental S. S. Co. filed assignments of error in the suit of the Admiral Oriental Line.

An agent, compelled to defend a baseless suit, grounded upon acts performed in his principal's business, may recover from the principal the expenses of his defense. We considered the question in *Cory Bros. & Co. v. United States*, 51 F.(2d) 1010, where we did not have to rule upon it; but the cases are unanimous, so far as we have found. In *Howe v. Buffalo, etc., R. R. Co.*, 37 N.Y. 297, and *Clark v. Jones*, 16 Lea (Tenn.) 351, notwithstanding that the agent had lost the suit brought by the third party against him, he recovered of the principal because his conduct was within the scope of his authority, though it was wrongful. The right of recovery in all these instances is only an example of the general doctrine that an agent may recover any expenditures necessarily incurred in the transaction of his principal's affairs.

The doctrine stands upon the fact that the venture is the principal's, and that, as the profits will be his, so should be the expenses. Since by hypothesis the agent's outlay is not due to his mismanagement, it should be regarded only as a loss, unexpected it is true, but inextricably interwoven with the enterprise. The Atlantic Gulf & Oriental S. S. Co. insists, on its part, that the Admiral Oriental Line should have given it notice to defend the suit on its behalf. We can see no reason for this and none is suggested; the Atlantic Gulf & Oriental S. S. Co. was itself a party to the suit, and the Admiral Oriental Line had a separate interest of its own to defend; certainly until the Atlantic Gulf & Oriental S. S. Co. volunteered to defend that interest, it was justified in protecting it itself. No doubt the amount of its expenditures is always open to contest, but their necessity is undoubted and it is that which imposes the liability.

The contract between the Admiral Oriental Line and the Atlantic Gulf & Oriental S. S. Co. appointed the Line "General Freight Agents" for all ships which the principal was operating on behalf of the United States in the "Far East." The Line agreed to have sub-agents at all ports where it had no offices of its own, and to perform all the principal's duties under its contract with the United States; it was to receive for its services a commission on the gross freights with brokerage. Thus, if Atlantic Gulf & Oriental S. S. Co. was an agent of the United States, the Line was an agent of the Atlantic Gulf & Oriental S. S. Co. We therefore turn to the relations between that company and the United States. These were set forth in a contract whose substance was as follows. The Shipping Board appointed the company "its Agent to manage, operate and conduct the business of such vessel as it . . . may assign to the Agent," and the company agreed to act as such "in accordance with the directions" of the Board. The company was to "man, equip, victual and supply" the vessels as the Board required, and to pay all expenses and maintain them in seaworthy condition, all on the Board's account. It was to issue all documents on the Board's form, appoint sub-agents, collect freights which it must deposit in a bank approved by the Board and in the Board's name, and for which it was to account on forms prescribed by the Board. For this the company was to be paid in percentages on the gross receipts including salvage; out of these it was to bear its "administrative and general expenses of every nature," not including brokerage however, or commissions "for agency services rendered at foreign ports." The company was to furnish a bond for faithful performance of its duties and was forbidden to profit in any way from the services rendered. We find it difficult to see how this contract can be construed as creating anything but a straight agency for operating the Board's ships. As we have already said, the question at bar turns chiefly upon whose the venture is; upon who stands to win or lose. The United States not only described itself throughout as owner, but was in that position, letter for letter. It chose, not to charter its ships to the company, but to put them in trade on its own account; why it should not bear the hazard of defending unwarranted suits we cannot see. We have so construed almost identical contracts. . . . The argument of the United States that the conduct of the parties put another interpretation on their relations is wholly unsupported by the evidence, and would in any event have been irrelevant. Had the Atlantic Gulf & Oriental S. S. Co. paid the Admiral Oriental Line, it would therefore have been in position to recover of the United States, for there is no difference between payment by an agent of his sub-agent's recovery against him, and payment of his own expenses. Obviously the same considerations apply to the suit of the Atlantic Gulf & Oriental S. S. Co. against the United States.

. . . This does not, however, dispose of the petition of the Atlantic Gulf & Oriental S. S. Co. . . . [T]he only question would be whether it stated a cause of action, which in turn depends upon whether an agent may sue before he has suffered loss, even when a third party is suing him. As a complaint in an action at law, such a petition would be premature; the plaintiff having paid nothing, may not yet call for indemnity. . . . In equity, however, the rule is otherwise; before paying the debt a surety may call upon the principal to exonerate him by discharging it; he is not obliged to make inroads into his own resources when the loss must in the end fall upon the principal. . . . [I]t is enough that if the Atlantic Gulf & Oriental S. S. Co. had paid the Admiral Line, the disbursement would have been recoverable like any other; the eventual loss was to fall on the United States, which was for this reason in the position of a principal, and could be compelled to exonerate the surety. The United States was fully protected; it was able to contest both the liability of its agent—the surety—to the sub-agent, the creditor, and its liability to the agent, and it was required to pay only the sub-agent. . . .

The Atlantic Gulf & Oriental S. S. Company should therefore have recovered upon its libel against the United States, treated as a petition at law under the Tucker Act. The Admiral Oriental Line should have recovered upon its libel against the Atlantic Gulf & Oriental S. S. Co., treated as a complaint at law. The Atlantic Gulf & Oriental S. S. Co. should have had a decree upon its intervening petition . . . directing the United States to pay the claim of the Admiral Oriental Line.

Decrees reversed; causes remanded with instructions to proceed according to the foregoing.

Notes

1. The opinion in *Admiral Oriental* cites to *Howe v. Buffalo Railroad* in support of the proposition that an agent is entitled to indemnity even if the agent loses the suit brought against him, if his conduct was within the scope of his authority. The plaintiff in *Howe* was a conductor for defendant Buffalo Railroad. He was instructed not to accept any ticket presented more than six days beyond the date of its issuance. He followed the instruction and ejected a passenger who presented such a ticket. Plaintiff was sued by the passenger and lost because his employer did not possess the authority it presumed to have. He suffered body execution, was arrested and imprisoned. He eventually paid the judgment and sued for indemnity. The court held he was entitled to it, since he acted in obedience to defendant's instructions and in good faith without realizing he was committing a wrong.

Although not applicable in the *Howe* case, the Restatement (Third) in §8.14, Comment b recognizes a limitation on the indemnity principle as follows:

> A principal's duty to indemnify does not extend to losses that result from the agent's own negligence, illegal acts, or other wrongful conduct.

2. The agent's right to indemnity, unless expressly agreed to, depends on reasonable inferences drawn from the circumstances. Thus, a real estate broker, who is paid by commission, ordinarily is expected to bear certain expenses, like the cost of gasoline used in transporting potential purchasers to the property her principal is trying to sell. The general standard is expressed by Seavey: "[T]he principal bears the burdens to the extent that courts believe to be just, considering the customs of the business and the nature of the particular relation." WARREN A. SEAVEY, LAW OF AGENCY 266 (1964).

3. Does a principal whose agent is being sued have standing to enter the suit and raise defenses, on the reasoning that the agent's right to indemnity creates an interest of the principal in the litigation? See *Shank, Irwin, et al., v. Durant, et al.*, 748 S.W.2d 494, 501 (Tex. App. 1988), denying the right of a principal (Hill) to raise defenses by way of a cross action in a suit by a third party against his agent, saying, "As a principal, Hill has the right to *demand of his agent* the opportunity to defend the agent. Hill has no standing to enter the lawsuit and assert defenses to [third party's] claim against [agent] in an action independent of that right."

4. *Admiral Oriental* discusses subagency, a concept introduced in Chapter 1. A subagent is entitled to indemnity against either the immediate or the remote principal for appropriate expenses or losses. Restatement (Third) §8.14, cmt. b. This can have serious consequences for the remote principal. In order to establish subagency, a principal must know or have reason to know that the agent will hire someone else to act on behalf of the principal and consent, expressly or impliedly, to such arrangement. If there is no knowledge, or knowledge and no consent and no estoppel to deny consent, the actor is an agent's agent, not a subagent, and has no indemnity rights against the remote principal. Consistent with this notion, an agent has a duty to notify the principal of a claim against the agent and give the principal the opportunity to defend the claim. Failure to do so may affect the agent's ability to obtain reimbursement. Moreover, if the principal and agent are co-defendants represented by separate counsel, "the agent may not obtain reimbursement for his or her separate defense costs unless it is shown that joint representation would have left the agent's interests unprotected." *Johnson Realty v. Bender*, 39 P.3d 1215, 1220 (Colo. App. 2002). The court in *Johnson Realty* did not give an example of a situation in which an agent's interests might be unprotected. What might it have had in mind?

5. In *Cory Bros. & Co. v. United States*, 51 F.2d 1010, 1013 (2d Cir. 1931), Cory Brothers & Co. had contracted with the United States "to attend to the discharge of the cargo [of the steamship Milwaukee Bridge, in Brazil] and to book cargo for points beyond." It did so, and subsequently was sued by a shipper for cargo damage. It prevailed in the suit and then sued the United States for reimbursement of the litigation expenses incurred in defending the suit. The court rejected the claim, stating as follows:

> Whether [the contract] be interpreted as employing [Cory Bros.] to engage others to do the stevedoring in discharging the flour or to perform the stevedoring business itself makes no difference; in either case [Cory Bros.] is an independent contractor. The principle that an agent is entitled

to reimbursement in successfully defending a suit . . . should have no application to an independent contractor. The risks of the independent contractor's business are his own.

2. Duty to Pay Compensation

The duty to pay compensation ordinarily is defined contractually by the principal and the agent, although that can involve problems of interpretation. See, for example, *Roberts Assocs. v. Blazer Int'l Corp.*, 741 F. Supp. 650, 657 (E.D. Mich. 1990), containing an extensive discussion of the rights between agent and principal in sales contracts, including the meaning of the ambiguous phrase "exclusive representation." Sometimes, however, services are rendered by one party on behalf of another and nothing is said about compensation. Under what circumstances can the party rendering services successfully bill the other party? This issue was raised in *McCollum v. Clothier*, 241 P.2d 468, 470 (Utah 1952), where plaintiff secured bidders on machinery and equipment of a beet harvester company that had gone into bankruptcy. Defendant held a mortgage on the property of the company and thus stood to gain from active bidding at the bankruptcy sale. Plaintiff admitted there was not an express contract to pay him but argued that the facts established an implied contract. He had previously worked for the bankruptcy trustee on this matter, had been paid for that work, and was asked by defendant's attorney to continue his work. After noting that defendant was aware of plaintiff's efforts and had conversed with plaintiff about his activities (the substance of the conversations was in dispute), the court in finding for plaintiff first quoted Restatement (Second) § 441: "Except where the relationship of the parties, the triviality of the services, or other circumstances indicate that the parties have agreed otherwise, it is inferred that one who requests or permits another to perform services for him as his agent promises to pay for them." The court then stated as follows:

> It is appreciated that this rule should not be applied to bind one under implied contract who merely permits services to be rendered him, or accepts benefits from another, under such circumstances that he may reasonably assume they are given gratuitously. The law should not require everyone to keep on guard against such possibilities by warning persons offering services that no pay is to be expected. It is, therefore, essential that the court should exercise caution in imposing the obligations of implied contract. . . . With such caution in mind, the test for the court to apply was: Under all the evidence, were the circumstances such that the plaintiff could reasonably assume he was to be paid and that the defendant should have reasonably expected to pay for such services. . . .

Notes

1. *The agent's lien.* Subject to agreement otherwise, an unpaid agent rightfully in possession of property of the principal has a lien upon it for the amount the agent is due from the principal. In general, the lien consists of a right to retain possession

of the property, including documents, until the amount due the agent is paid. Certain agents, such as factors, also have a right after notice to the principal to sell the goods. *See generally* WARREN A. SEAVEY, LAW OF AGENCY 281–82 (1964). Seavey also distinguishes between general and special liens: the general lien is "a right to hold goods until payments are completed on the general balance of accounts due from the principal for agency transactions." *Id.* at 281. The special lien is for agents employed only for single transactions and confines the agent's right to satisfaction of the claim arising out of the transaction in which possession was obtained.

2. *Subagents.* We have seen that a subagent has a right of indemnity against the remote principal. Does the subagent also have a right to receive compensation from the remote principal? Assume that *P*, who lives in New York, seeks to collect on a large claim she has in Florida. She hires a New York lawyer *(A)* to collect the claim, promising to pay *A* $2,000. *A* in turn hires *B*, a Florida lawyer, to search title, obtain documents, and so forth, promising *B* $500 as payment. *B* does the work, *A* collects the claim and, deducting $2,000, remits the proceeds to *P*. *A* becomes insolvent and never pays *B*. Can *B* make a valid claim against *P* for the $500? What are the arguments on both sides of this question?

A claim by a subagent against the remote principal for compensation was litigated in *McKnight v. Peoples-Pittsburgh Trust Co.*, 61 A.2d 820, 822 (Pa. 1948). Plaintiff McKnight was employed by George Brothers, a Pittsburgh real estate firm. The defendant bank held a mortgage on a theatre in Pittsburgh that was in financial trouble. Pursuant to an arrangement with George Brothers, the bank in lieu of foreclosure had the owners of the theatre convey title to it to McKnight, as straw man for the bank. McKnight thereafter managed the theatre under the direction of W.D. George, a partner in George Brothers. Ultimately the theatre was sold. McKnight received no part of the commission on the sale. Claiming he was entitled to extra compensation for his services in developing the property for sale, and being denied this by George Brothers, he sued the bank, arguing that he had managed the theatre for the bank under the direction of its agent, W.D. George. The court denied the claim, quoting Restatement (Second) § 458, Comment a: "If an agent employs a subagent, the agent is the employing person and the principal is not a party to the contract of employment, except where, by express promise or otherwise, he becomes a surety. He is not, therefore, subject to pay the agreed compensation. . . ." An additional feature of the case was the introduction into evidence of an affidavit of defendant in unrelated litigation, admitting that plaintiff was its agent. The court found this insignificant, reasoning that it is understood that a subagent is an agent. "The distinction between agency and subagency is important only in its effect upon the relations between the principal, agent, and subagent." (quoting Restatement (Second) § 142, Comment b).

3. Duty of Care

A master (employer) is subject to a common law duty of care toward its servants (employees), arising from its control over the work environment. The employer can discharge this duty by providing reasonably safe working conditions. This includes using due care in the construction, inspection, and maintenance of the premises where employees work, in the selection of fellow employees and in the management of work. The duty of care can be discharged by warning employees of the risks of unsafe conditions that the employer should realize may not be discovered by the employees in the exercise of due care. *See* Restatement (Second) § 492.

The employer's duty of care is nondelegable. This means that, although an employer is free to arrange for performance of the duty by someone else, it cannot avoid liability for the fault worthy acts of the person to whom performance was delegated. Thus, if an employer directs one of its employees to repair a stairway on the plant premises and the employee does the work in a negligent manner, the employer will incur liability for injuries caused to other employees who use the stairway even if due care was exercised in selecting and instructing the employee who did the work. The same result would follow if the employer instead had made arrangements with an independent business to undertake the repair.

Suppose, however, that one employee is negligent while engaging in an act involved in the operation of the business that is not connected with creating safe conditions for workers and injures another employee. Assume that no case of negligence can be established against the employer. If the victim had been a stranger to the business, he would have a respondeat superior claim against the employer. Should an injured employee also have a respondeat superior claim against the employer? *Farwell v. Boston & W.R. Corp.*, 45 Mass. (4 Met.) 49 (1842), denied such a cause of action, arguing that there is a distinction between the claim of a stranger and that of an employee, who has a contractual relationship with the employer. "The general rule is that he who engages in the employment of another for the performance of specified duties for compensation, takes upon himself the natural and ordinary risks and perils incident to the performance of such services, and in legal presumption the compensation is adjusted accordingly. . . . Each [employee] is an observer of the conduct of the others, can give notice of any misconduct, and leave the service, if the common employer will not take precautions. By these means, the safety of each will be more effectually secured than could be done by a resort to the common employer for indemnity." This is the fellow servant rule.

Notes

1. The fellow servant rule articulated in *Farwell*, denying strict liability of employer to employee, did not receive a warm reception in some academic and political circles. Also, even when an employer was found negligent in a particular situation, the common law defenses of contributory negligence and assumption of risk held down recovery by injured workers. Consider the reaction of Warren Seavey, a widely respected legal scholar, in his article *The Rationale of Agency*, 29 YALE L.J. 859, 861, n.5 (1920) ("The aberration of the courts in creating the fellow servant rule has been one of their most unfortunate errors and the one requiring most legislation to correct"). An argument on the other side by Richard Posner, also a widely respected

legal scholar, is presented in *A Theory of Negligence*, 1 J. Legal Stud. 29, 44–46 (1972). Professor Posner observes that, unlike a stranger to a business, a fellow employee is in a good position to identify and report careless workers in proximity to him.

> The fellow-servant rule, as the exception to respondeat superior is known, provides, in principle at least, a powerful instrument for industrial safety when combined with the rule making the employer liable for injuries inflicted on an employee through the negligence of a fellow employee if the employer was on notice of the fellow employee's habitual neglect or incompetence. The effect of the two rules is to give employees a strong incentive to report careless fellow workers to their supervisors.

Professor Posner notes that a major limitation on the fellow servant rule expressed in *Farwell*, is that the employer is not immunized from liability for the negligence of those employees responsible for the conditions in which the injured employees work, is consistent with his thesis. "Such work is not done in proximity to the operating employees and the latter will neither know who the responsible workers are nor have any basis for evaluating the care with which they have worked until an accident occurs."

2. The fellow servant doctrine has other limitations, including the "vice-principal" doctrine, which covers any servant "who represented the employer in his responsibility to plaintiff." Prosser and Keeton on Torts at 529. Typically, it covers servants performing maintenance and repair work on the premises, but it has also been expansively interpreted to include supervisory employees as a group. *See, e.g., Combined Ins. Co. v. Sinclair*, 584 P.2d 1034 (Wyo. 1978) (company sales manager was driving in his car with a saleswoman of the company. He injured her as a result of his negligent driving. She recovered on respondeat superior grounds against their employer, invoking the vice-principal doctrine.).

3. With the exception of agricultural and household employment in some states, the fellow servant rule is infrequently used today. Worker's compensation legislation, covered immediately below, has for most employees replaced the common law with a legislative and administrative system for compensating injuries on the job.

4. Social Legislation

a. Worker's Compensation Legislation

The defenses of contributory negligence and assumption of risk, and the fellow servant rule, are still part of the common law today in many jurisdictions (although contributory negligence has been changed to comparative negligence by statute in a number of states). Their impact on the law has been substantially affected, however, by the enactment of worker's compensation acts in all states, as noted above. This is the corrective legislation Professor Seavey referred to in discussing the fellow servant rule.

Worker's compensation is the best-known example of social legislation concerning the employment relationship. It swept the state legislatures of this country in the early 1900s, apparently in response to the low rate of compensation received by workers for on-the-job injuries under the common law. According to some sources, anywhere from 70 percent to 94 percent of industrial accidents went uncompensated under the common law system. *See* PROSSER AND KEETON ON TORTS 572, n.43.

Although there is diversity among the states with respect to detail, worker's compensation requires employers to pay premiums for insurance (or set aside reserves) for compensating employees according to a detailed schedule of recoveries for injuries incurred in the course of employment. An administrative agency acting under statutory authority promulgates regulations for the system and adjudicates contested cases. Medical care is paid for. Also, cash payments to the employee or dependents reflecting income loss for disability or death are calculated as a percentage (usually 66 percent) of the employee's weekly earnings at the time of injury, subject to a maximum amount. There is no recovery for pain and suffering.

An employee is entitled to compensation even if the injury was not the fault of the employer and, more controversially, even though it was caused solely by the employee's own negligence. Employees who are covered by worker's compensation do not retain their common law actions against their employer, with the result that a trade-off takes place, involving a more certain recovery for less damages (usually) as against the opposite condition under the common law.

Problems of interpretation and thus of litigation remain, of course, through the need to apply terms which have so long troubled the common law, like who is an "employee," whether the employee was working within the "course of employment," and so forth, to a vast array of accident situations. See IC, ARTHUR LARSON, THE LAW OF WORKMEN'S COMPENSATION §§ 43–46 (1986), noting that precedents can be found in borderline cases on both sides of almost every situation.

b. Other Social Legislation

Other examples of legislation affecting the employer-employee relationship are: (1) unemployment compensation laws, which partially cover the loss of wages for up to 26 weeks when a worker is involuntarily unemployed for such nonfault reasons as reduction in the work available; (2) laws requiring employers to rehire returning veterans; (3) the 1964 Civil Rights Act fair employment provisions, forbidding employers of 15 or more employees to discriminate on the basis of race, color, religion, sex or national origin; (4) the Age Discrimination in Employment Act, placing restrictions on employers of 20 or more employees; (5) minimum wage laws; (6) laws regulating the relationship between management and labor; (7) employee safety legislation, such as the federal Occupational Safety and Health Act of 1970, the Federal Mine Safety and Health Act of 1977, and similar legislation on the state level; (8) the Employee Polygraph Protection Act (1988); (9) the Worker Adjustment and Retraining Notification Act (1988) (requires 60 days' notice of plant closings or mass layoffs for employers of 100 or more); (10) the Americans with Disabilities Act of 1990; and (11) the Family and Medical Leave Act of 1993, applicable to employers of 50 or more employees.

As one would expect, litigation concerning such legislation has been active, a large share of it initiated by employers wishing to avoid government regulation, paying taxes or being unionized. The opinion in *United States v. W.M. Webb, Inc.*, 397 U.S. 179 (1970), summarizes the judicial and legislative experience in this area since the 1930s. *See also* JOSEPH W. LITTLE, THOMAS A. EATON & GARY R. SMITH, WORKERS' COMPENSATION (1993).

5. Duty to Deal Fairly and in Good Faith

Taylor v. Cordis Corp.

United States District Court, Southern District of Mississippi
634 F. Supp. 1242 (1986)

TOM S. LEE, DISTRICT JUDGE.

This cause came before the court on the complaint of plaintiff Daniel J. Taylor for a declaratory judgment that a non-competition agreement in Taylor's contract of employment with defendant Cordis Corporation (Cordis) is void and unenforceable. Cordis counterclaimed for a preliminary injunction to enforce the agreement. . . .

Taylor began his employment with Cordis on February 13, 1981. The Cordis products line which Taylor was authorized to sell included heart pacemakers, pacemaker lead introducers and vascular catheters. . . . Although Taylor had extensive experience in sales of medical supplies in the Mississippi area and was familiar with the local physicians who regularly implanted pacemakers, he received technical training on pacemakers during his employment with and at the expense of Cordis. It appears that it took him over a year to develop sufficient technical expertise, combined with cultivating the trust and confidence of the implanting physicians, to attract any significant portion of the market. . . .

On February 13, 1981, the first day of Taylor's employment with Cordis, he signed [an agreement not to compete for one year after termination of employment].

Plaintiff testified that in 1984, 1985 and early 1986, he became increasingly concerned about the quality and marketability of Cordis pacemakers. His concern stemmed from the frequency of recalls of Cordis pacemakers issued by the United States Food and Drug Administration (FDA) and the frequency with which notices were distributed by Cordis to its sales force and physicians with respect to defects in design and performance of its pacemakers. On December 5, 1983, Cordis issued an "Urgent Medical Device Notification" for certain Gamma series pacemakers which were experiencing "early battery depletion" due to "self-discharge." This notice was followed by an "Important Update on Notification Concerning Gamma Series Pacers" issued on April 18, 1984. These notices recommended close supervision of patients with Gamma series implants, especially pacer-dependent patients. . . .

Taylor contends that as a result of the recalls and reliability problems of Cordis pacemakers, he suffered repeated humiliation and embarrassment when he had to inform the physicians of the recalls or notifications. He avers that these constant problems diminished the confidence that the physicians had in him and the products he sold, thus damaging his business reputation and credibility. . . .

On February 18, 1986, Taylor voluntarily resigned from Cordis. He filed this declaratory judgment action the same day. On the next day, Taylor began promoting the sale of medical products on behalf of Cardio-Life Systems, Inc. of Baton Rouge, Louisiana. . . .

Taylor contends that the contract of employment he signed with Cordis is void and unenforceable [because] Cordis has breached the implied duty of good faith and fair dealing it owed to its agent Taylor in failing to timely provide him with material information relating to problems it had discovered in its pacemakers. . . . Taylor concludes that such action by Cordis entitles him to the equitable remedy of rescission.

The court recognizes that a principal has a duty to deal fairly and in good faith with an agent and to provide the agent with any information which might subject the agent to physical or pecuniary loss in dealing with the product. *See Restatement, Agency* (2d ed.) § 35; 3 Am. Jur. 2d *Agency* § 238; *Lawrence Co. v. Twohig*, 224 F.2d 493, 497 (8th Cir. 1955). The principal's good faith duty to the agent also demands that the principal must maintain a standard of conduct which will not harm the agent's business reputation or reasonable self-respect. *Restatement, Agency* § 437 (comment).

Taylor alleges that Cordis breached its duty of good faith by failing to provide its sales force with timely, accurate information concerning the serious problems it had found in its Gamma series pacemakers. Taylor makes no allegation that Cordis failed to provide him with the various notifications it issued beginning in December 1983. Harold Hershenson, executive vice president of Cordis in charge of corporate product assurance, testified by deposition that sales agents "always" receive copies of the notifications sent to doctors, and that usually the agents are notified first and asked to consult with the doctors before their notifications arrive. Specifically, however, Taylor contends that Cordis became aware of the battery-depletion problem with its Gamma series pacemakers as early as 1980 but failed to inform the sales force of such problems until the December 1983 notification. Taylor further alleges that Cordis was aware of problems in all its pacemakers for a considerable period before notifying its sales force.

This court does not agree with Taylor's construction of the principal's good faith duty to inform the agent of product problems. The duty cannot be interpreted to require the principal to distribute to the agent copies of consumer complaints relating to product performance or to report the progress of all ongoing research into product efficiency. It appears to the court that Cordis' actions, beginning in 1980, to identify and remedy the battery-depletion and other related problems in its pacemakers were reasonable under the circumstances. The duty to inform its sales agents of product problems attached only when the company, in the exercise of reasonable diligence, knew that specific product defects posed a threat of harm to consumers and a concomitant threat to the professional reputation of the sales agent. Therefore, the court concludes that Cordis' failure to inform Taylor of all product problems before the issuance of the notifications does not entitle him to the equitable remedy of rescission.

[Injunction issued].

Deonier & Associates v. Paul Revere Life Insurance Company

Supreme Court of Montana
301 Mont. 347, 9 P.3d 622 (2000)

JUSTICE TERRY N. TRIEWEILER delivered the Opinion of the Court.

Factual Background

The Plaintiff, Marie Deonier, was a licensed disability and life insurance agent. In 1986, Paul Revere appointed Deonier as one of its independent agents and expressly authorized Deonier to solicit applications, deliver policies, collect premiums, and service Paul Revere's clients. Deonier did not have an exclusive relationship with any disability insurance carrier, nor was Paul Revere the primary company for which Deonier sold insurance policies.

The original Plaintiff, Kathryn Vestal, enrolled in the University of Montana School of Law in 1988. On May 24, 1989, Vestal sought medical help from the University of Montana Student Health Services for insomnia that she was experiencing. Vestal was prescribed low dose antidepressants over the next several months.

In 1990, Vestal accepted employment as a staff attorney in the Billings Office of Hearings and Appeals of the Social Security Administration. Vestal met with Deonier in June 1991 to discuss Vestal's desire to purchase a disability insurance policy. Because of Vestal's special needs as a federal employee, Deonier recommended a Paul Revere policy. Deonier completed the insurance application based on information provided by Vestal. The insurance application expressly disclosed the fact that Vestal had suffered insomnia for a period of time during law school.

On June 27, 1991, Paul Revere issued Vestal a disability insurance policy which did not exclude any preexisting conditions. Vestal's policy contained the following provisions pertinent to this case:

9.2 INCONTESTABLE

a. After your policy has been in force for two years, excluding any time You are Disabled, We cannot contest the statements in the application.

b. No claim for Disability beginning after two years from the Date of Issue will be reduced or denied because a disease or physical condition that existed before the Date of Issue unless it is excluded by name or specific description.

3.2 PRE-EXISTING CONDITION LIMITATIONS

We will not pay benefits for a Pre-Existing Condition if it was not disclosed on Your application. You are responsible for verifying the accuracy of each and every statement on Your application. Also, We will not pay benefits for any loss We have excluded by name or specific description.

DEFINITIONS

"Sickness" means sickness or disease which first manifests itself after the Date of Issue and while Your Policy is in force.

"Pre-existing Condition" means a Sickness or physical condition for which, prior to the Date of Issue:

a. Symptoms existed that would cause an ordinarily prudent person to seek diagnosis, care, or treatment; or

b. Medical advice or treatment was recommended by or received from a Physician.

In 1975, the Fifth Circuit Court of Appeals decided *Massachusetts Casualty Insurance Company v. Forman* (5th Cir. 1975), 516 F.2d 425. In *Massachusetts Casualty Insurance Company*, the insurance company asserted a legal defense to the incontestable clause in its policy based on its definition of "sickness" which excluded disabilities that manifested themselves prior to the issue date of the policy. This legal position is presently known as the "*Forman* defense."

In 1981, a Montana Federal District Court decided the case of *Doettl v. Colonial Life & Accident Insurance Company* (D. Mont. 1981), 505 F. Supp. 127. The *Doettl* case discussed an insured's reliance on an incontestable clause, citing *Massachusetts Casualty Insurance Company*, 516 F.2d 425, and stating that "[t]he almost universal rule is that incontestable clauses do not abrogate defenses going to coverage." *Doettl*, 505 F. Supp. at 128.

In 1987, counsel for Paul Revere presented a paper to the Association of Life Insurance Counsel entitled: "The *Forman* Defense in Disability Insurance." The paper outlined Paul Revere's position as follows:

> The *Forman* defense permits a company to deny beyond the two-year contestable period, a disability claim for a disease which had clearly manifested itself prior to the policy date, on the ground that it is not a covered sickness under the policy. It is available in approximately 40 states and can be asserted in the remaining states with the right set of facts or by filing for declaratory relief and continuing to pay the claim. However, in many of these states, there is no clear authority pro or con and the company will be making new and hopefully favorable law. Accordingly, it is imperative that corporate counsel review carefully each claim where the *Forman* defense would be involved and select only those which have "clean" facts for the company and amply demonstrate the insured's duplicity.

Id. at 779.

Based on the Montana Federal District Court's decision in *Doettl*, 505 F. Supp. 127, Montana was listed as a state with favorable authority in support of the *Forman* defense. Paul Revere Life Insurance Co., *The Forman Defense in Disability Insurance* at 777. However, Paul Revere did not inform any of its insurance agents of its intention to assert the *Forman* defense in Montana. Following the *Doettl* decision in 1981, no Montana state or federal court has discussed the application of the *Forman* defense in Montana.

On February 18, 1992, Vestal was admitted to the emergency room at Billings Deaconess Hospital for treatment of depression and suicidal tendencies. In September 1993, Vestal was diagnosed with major depression and was unable to work. On November 9, 1993, Vestal submitted an application for social security disability benefits. Vestal was awarded social security benefits following her appeal to an administrative law judge.

On November 29, 1993, Vestal filed a disability claim with Paul Revere. Paul Revere initially paid disability benefits, but after obtaining Vestal's University of Montana health services medical records, Paul Revere denied Vestal's claim. In a letter to Vestal dated June 16, 1994, Paul Revere stated:

> A review of your records indicated that you received treatment from February 4, 1989 to May 16, 1989 at the University of Montana Student Health Center. These records also indicate that you received treatment for depression and that you were treated with low doses of anti-depressants. . . .

> In reviewing your application for insurance which was signed on June 27, 1991, we find no indication of any treatment for depression. Paul Revere had no prior knowledge of your depression.

> Your policy defines sickness as a sickness or disease which first manifests itself after the date of issue and while your policy is in force. Since your condition manifested itself prior to the issuance of this coverage, it would not be a covered sickness under your contract. Therefore, we are unable to consider any further benefits with regard to this claim.

On August 28, 1995, Vestal filed a complaint against Paul Revere and Deonier. Vestal alleged that Paul Revere breached the disability insurance contract and acted in bad faith, and that both Paul Revere and Deonier negligently misrepresented the policy provisions to Vestal. On October 30, 1995, Deonier filed an answer and cross-claim against Paul Revere which alleged that Paul Revere breached its duty to indemnify Deonier.

On February 6, 1998, Deonier filed an amended answer and cross-claim against Paul Revere. The amended cross-claim further alleged that Paul Revere breached its fiduciary duties to Deonier, and in doing so, Paul Revere acted with actual malice and committed actual fraud, entitling Deonier to punitive damages.

On April 23, 1998, Vestal's claims were dismissed pursuant to a settlement agreement reached between the parties. The District Court realigned the remaining parties-Deonier as the Plaintiff and Paul Revere as the Defendant. On May 8, 1998, Paul Revere filed a motion for summary judgment. Paul Revere's motion requested that the District Court dismiss Deonier's claim for breach of fiduciary duty, and grant partial summary judgment on Deonier's claim for indemnity. On June 17, 1998, the District Court entered its order and memorandum granting Paul Revere's motion for summary judgment on Deonier's claim for breach of fiduciary duty. On July 1, 1998, the District Court entered its order denying Paul Revere's motion for partial summary judgment on Deonier's claim for indemnity.

A nonjury trial on Deonier's claim for indemnity was held on July 6 and 7, 1998. On November 24, 1998, the District Court entered its findings of fact and conclusions of law. The District Court concluded that Paul Revere owed Deonier indemnity for attorney fees expended by Deonier in defense of Vestal's claims against her.

Issue 1

Did the District Court err when it dismissed Deonier's claim for breach of fiduciary duty by summary judgment?

Deonier asserts that the District Court erred when it granted Paul Revere's motion for summary judgment. Deonier contends that, although the District Court correctly determined that Paul Revere owed Deonier a fiduciary duty pursuant to the Restatement (Second) of Agency §435, the District Court erred when it concluded that Paul Revere did not breach this duty. Deonier asserts that there was a significant amount of evidence presented that Paul Revere planned to assert the *Forman* defense in Montana and, therefore, Paul Revere's failure to inform Deonier of its intention to invoke the *Forman* defense was a clear breach of Paul Revere's duty to inform Deonier, its agent, of a risk of pecuniary loss from potential lawsuits.

In response, Paul Revere asserts that the District Court was correct in its determination that Paul Revere did not breach its duty by failing to inform Deonier of its intention to assert a legal defense. Moreover, Paul Revere contends that, pursuant to *Doettl*, in which a Montana Federal District Court endorsed the *Forman* defense, Paul Revere had no reason to believe that its policy interpretation might be in violation of Montana law and, therefore, it did not violate its duty to inform its agents of risk of pecuniary loss.

In its Order and Memorandum granting Paul Revere's motion for summary judgment, the District Court concluded:

> The duty claimed by Deonier to have been breached by Revere is the duty provided by Restatement (Second) of Agency §435 which provides, in applicable part "A principal contracts to use care to inform the agent of risks of . . . pecuniary loss which, as the principal has reason to know, exist in the performance of authorized acts and which he has reason to know are unknown to the agent."

Clearly such a duty would be owed to Deonier as the agent of Revere.

There is no genuine issue of material fact concerning a breach of duty in this case. Revere was entitled to assert an arguable legal position concerning the policy written here. It would be an impossible duty to contend that insurance companies are required to inform agents in advance, prior to the time that arguments are even known, that certain legal positions may be asserted concerning various clauses in a policy that is written. That certainly is not a fact unknown to the agent which should be disclosed by the principal within the concept of Restatement (Second) of Agency § 435.

. . . Revere had an arguable position that it was entitled to assert in defending the claim of Vestal. Without deciding how the Montana Supreme Court would rule on the interpretation of the policy today, it is apparent that under a number of cases which are cited by Revere in its brief it was entitled to assert that a manifestation of disease or sickness prior to the time the policy was purchased by Vestal precluded her recovery as not being within the definition of the policy as to disease or sickness despite the fact that the two year contestability time had lapsed. Case law from Montana and other jurisdictions supported such argument. The language in *Doettl v. Colonial Life & Accident Insurance Company*, 505 F.Supp. 127, 128 (D.Mont.1981) stating "[t]he almost universal rule is that incontestable clauses do not abrogate defenses going to coverage" . . . at least allowed Revere to make the argument in this case.

The District Court's analysis appears to apply the terms of § 33-18-242(5), MCA, which provides a defense to an Unfair Trade Practices Act or bad faith action against an insurance company. That statute provides that "[a]n insurer may not be held liable under this section if the insurer had a reasonable basis in law or in fact for contesting the claim or the amount of the claim, whichever is in issue." The District Court concluded that Paul Revere was entitled to assert the *Forman* defense because several jurisdictions, including a Montana federal district court, had issued opinions which accept that defense. Accordingly, the District Court concluded that there was no requirement that Paul Revere inform Deonier in advance that a *Forman* defense may be asserted and, therefore, there was no genuine issue of material fact concerning a breach of Paul Revere's duty to Deonier.

The District Court's apparent application of § 33-18-242(5), MCA, is misplaced. The proper analysis is simply whether or not Paul Revere breached the following duty, as set forth in the Restatement (Second) of Agency § 435 (1958):

Unless otherwise agreed, it is inferred that a principal contracts to use care to inform the agent of risks of physical harm or pecuniary loss which, as the principal has reason to know, exist in the performance of authorized acts and which he has reason to know are unknown to the agent. His duty to give other information depends upon the agreement between them.

Comment (a) to Restatement (Second) of Agency § 435 (1958) states:

> The duty may require not only warning the agent against physical dangers, as when the principal directs an agent to go to a place which is dangerous, but also disclosing facts which, if unknown, would be likely to subject the agent to pecuniary loss. Thus, a principal employing a factor to sell goods which appear to be but are not sound is subject to liability to the agent if the agent is led to incur personal liability to a buyer through mistaken statements concerning the condition of the goods.

Black's Law Dictionary defines "risk" as a "chance of injury, damage or loss." Black's Law Dictionary 1328 (7th Ed.1999). Accordingly, the analysis the District Court should have applied is whether Paul Revere had knowledge that it might assert the *Forman* defense in order to deny coverage on a policy sold by Deonier; and, if so, that there was a risk Deonier would incur pecuniary loss, such as attorney fees, as a result of her unknowingly false or misleading statements concerning coverage provided by the policy.

The District Court stated that "[i]t would be an impossible duty to contend that insurance companies are required to inform agents in advance, prior to the time that arguments are even known, that certain legal positions may be asserted. . . ." While we agree with the District Court that a principal has no duty to inform its agent of unknown future legal positions we disagree with the District Court's conclusion that potential consequences of the *Forman* defense were unknown.

Paul Revere's corporate counsel's paper, presented and published in 1987, illustrates the company's level of awareness of the *Forman* defense and its consequences.

The disability policy at issue in this case was issued to Vestal in 1991. The paper written by Paul Revere's corporate counsel was published in 1987 and clearly contemplates a future application of the *Forman* defense in Montana. Accordingly, we disagree with Paul Revere's assertion and the District Court's conclusion that there was no genuine issue of material fact concerning a breach of duty in this case.

Moreover, Paul Revere's assertion that, based on the decision in *Doettl*, it had no reason to inform its agents of its intention to assert the *Forman* defense because it had no reason to believe that its policy interpretation might involve its agents in litigation, is without merit. The federal district court's decision in *Doettl*, while it applies some Montana law, is not binding on this Court. Moreover, the portion of the decision that discusses the *Forman* defense contains no citations to Montana authority and, instead, relies on a New York Court of Appeals' decision for the principle that the "almost universal rule is that incontestable clauses do not abrogate defenses going to coverage."

Because the issue was still an issue of first impression in Montana, never having been decided by this Court, Paul Revere cannot rely on the decision in *Doettl* to support its position that as a matter of uncontroverted fact and law, it had no knowledge of risk to its agents.

For these reasons, we conclude that whether Paul Revere breached its duty to inform Deonier of the risk of litigation from the policy she sold on its behalf, involves issues of material fact. Therefore, we further conclude that the District Court erred when it granted Paul Revere's motion for summary judgment and dismissed Deonier's claim for breach of fiduciary duty. Accordingly, we reverse the District Court's award of summary judgment in favor of Paul Revere.

Issue 2

Did the District Court err when it refused to decide the issue of the legality of Paul Revere's disability policy?

[Based on a review of Montana statutory provisions on insurance and a 2000 California appellate court decision, the court concluded "that the incontestability clause bars insurers from denying coverage for a disability, whether or not the causative sickness first manifested itself before the policy's date of issue. We further conclude that Paul Revere's assertion of the *Forman* defense to deny Vestal's disability claim was in violation of Montana law." The court also ruled that Paul Revere was required to indemnify Deonier for her legal expenses incurred in defending Vestal's suit against her.]

Notes

1. The lower court decision in *Deonier & Associates* proceeded on the basis that the insurer as principal owed a fiduciary duty to its agent. Not all courts would agree with that characterization and it is worth noting that the Montana Supreme Court, although agreeing that the insurer owed a duty to the agent, did not characterize that duty as a fiduciary duty. *See, e.g., MDM Group Associates, Inc. v. CX Reinsurance Co. Ltd, U.K.*, 165 P.3d 882 (Colo. Ct. App. 2007) (citing Restatement (Third) of Agency § 1.01, cmt. e: "[The] obligations that a principal owes an agent . . . are not fiduciary"). What practical difference does it make if the duty is characterized as a fiduciary duty?

2. Contract law recognizes that the implied covenant of good faith and fair dealing is a part of every contract. This fundamental principle of contract law plays an important role in shaping the contractual relationship of agents and principals; partners; and members and managers of limited liability companies. (In the materials that follow in this casebook, we will see this concept applied in each of these relationships.) It allows a court to imply a term that, presumably, the parties would have agreed to had the matter been brought to their attention. It serves to preserve the expectations of the parties and is based on the express provisions to which the parties have consented. Thus, if the parties addressed a concern, there is no room for a court to imply a term. Not surprisingly, parties disappointed with the behavior of their counterparties frequently argue that such behavior violates the implied covenant. In *Nemec v. Shrader*, 991 A.2d 1120 (Del. 2010), for instance, retired corporate officers complained when their former employer redeemed their corporate stock prior to a corporate reorganization with the effect that they received far less

than they would have had the redemption taken place after the reorganization. The court refused to find a violation of the implied covenant:

> The implied covenant of good faith and fair dealing involves a "cautious enterprise," inferring contractual terms to handle developments or contractual gaps that the asserting party pleads neither party anticipated. "[O]ne generally cannot base a claim for breach of the implied covenant on conduct authorized by the agreement." We will only imply contract terms when the party asserting the implied covenant proves that the other party has acted arbitrarily or unreasonably, thereby frustrating the fruits of the bargain that the asserting party reasonably expected. When conducting this analysis, we must assess the parties' reasonable expectations at the time of contracting and not rewrite the contract to appease a party who later wishes to rewrite a contract he now believes to have been a bad deal. Parties have a right to enter into good and bad contracts, the law enforces both.

> The plaintiffs lacked "a reasonable expectation of participating in the benefits" of the [reorganization]. . . .

> The implied covenant only applies to developments that could not be anticipated, not developments that the parties simply failed to consider-particularly where the contract authorizes the Company to act exactly as it did here.

> The Chancellor found no cognizable claim for a breach of the implied covenant because the Stock Plan explicitly authorized the redemption's price and timing, and [the parties] received exactly what they bargained for under the Stock Plan. The Chancellor wrote "[c]ontractually negotiated put and call rights are intended by both parties to be exercised at the time that is most advantageous to the party invoking the option."

> . . . .

> The Company's redemption of the retired stockholders' shares now produces the retirees' accusation that the Company breached the covenant of fair dealing and good faith implied in the stock plan. The directors did nothing unfair and breached no fiduciary duty by causing the Company to exercise its absolute contractual right to redeem the retired stockholders' shares at a time that was most advantageous to the Company's working stockholders.

> . . . Delaware's implied duty of good faith and fair dealing is not an equitable remedy for rebalancing economic interests after events that could have been anticipated, but were not, that later adversely affected one party to a contract. Rather the covenant is a limited and extraordinary legal remedy. As the Chancellor noted in his opinion, the doctrine "'requires a party in a contractual relationship to refrain from arbitrary or unreasonable conduct which has the effect of preventing the other party to the contract from receiving the fruits of the bargain.'" These plaintiff-appellants got

the benefit of their actual bargain, and now urge us to expand the doctrine of the implied duty of good faith and fair dealing. A party does not act in bad faith by relying on contract provisions for which that party bargained where doing so simply limits advantages to another party. We cannot reform a contract because enforcement of the contract as written would raise "moral questions." The policy underpinning the implied duty of good faith and fair dealing does not extend to post contractual rebalancing of the economic benefits flowing to the contracting parties. Accordingly, we affirm the Chancellor's dismissal of Count I.

B. Duties of Agent to Principal

The relationship of principal and agent ordinarily is based on a contract between the two parties. The contract is of a special nature, however, because an agent is a fiduciary and is subject to the directions of the principal. As noted in Chapter 1, a "fiduciary" is defined in §13 of the Restatement (Second) as "a person who has a duty, created by his undertaking, to act primarily for the benefit of another in matters connected with his undertaking." Some of the responsibilities attached to the agent's status as fiduciary are described as follows in WARREN A. SEAVEY, THE LAW OF AGENCY 236 (1964):

> He has a duty to account for money or property received on account of the principal [and to keep his principal's assets separate from his own]. In his dealings with the principal, he has the duty of full disclosure; in acting for the principal he must not prefer his own [or others'] interests, he cannot compete with the principal nor, without disclosure of his interest, sell his own property to the principal. In carrying out the directions of the principal, he has the duty to use normal care.

See Deborah A. DeMott, *Beyond Metaphor: An Analysis of Fiduciary Obligation*, 1988 DUKE L.J. 879; Tamar Frankel, *Fiduciary Law*, 71 CAL. L. REV. 795 (1983); Austin W. Scott, *The Fiduciary Principle*, 37 CAL. L. REV. 539 (1949).

Most authorities break fiduciary duties down into three categories: care, disclosure, and loyalty. These materials will adopt that format, after briefly describing several other duties that agents owe their principals. These duties are not customarily described as fiduciary duties but nevertheless are regarded as part of the agency relationship.

1. Duty of Good Conduct and to Obey

An agent is subject to a duty not to act in a manner that makes continued friendly relations with the principal impossible. Also, the agent must not bring disrepute to the principal. Many of the cases involving these limitations arise in the context of an employee's claim for unemployment compensation benefits. Cases where an employee has been held in breach include a clerk of a merchant making disparaging remarks at a social function about the quality of merchandise sold by his employer and a bank teller engaging in repeated acts of gambling while off-duty. *See also Marsh v. Delta Air Lines, Inc.*, 952 F. Supp. 1458 (D. Colo. 1997) (upholding discharge of employee for writing sharply critical letter about employer airline to newspaper); *O'Neal v. Employment Sec. Agency*, 89 Idaho 313, 404 P.2d 600 (1965) (upholding firing of postal employee after conviction of a morals charge involving a minor); W. Sell, Agency 116 (1975).

The agent must obey all reasonable directions of the principal. The duty to obey is unique to agency in the commercial world and distinguishes the agent from all other fiduciaries. An agent "has no duty to perform acts which are illegal, unethical or unreasonable," however. *Id. See Ford v. Wisconsin Real Estate Examining Bd.*, 48 Wis. 2d 91, 179 N.W.2d 786 (1970) (real estate broker has no duty to obey principal's instruction to engage in racial discrimination in showing principal's property).

2. Duty to Indemnify Principal for Loss Caused by Misconduct

A principal has an action in tort or in contract against an agent who wrongfully causes it loss, as where the agent negligently damages the property of the principal, or exceeds his authority, or by negligence or fraud causes the principal to be liable to a third person, or violates a duty of loyalty owed the principal. Thus, a servant is subject to a duty to indemnify the master for damages the master had to pay resulting from the servant's negligence while acting within the scope of employment. *Fireman's Fund Am. Ins. Co. v. Turner*, 488 P.2d 429 (Ore. 1971), contains a lengthy discussion of the policy behind the right of indemnification in such situations. The court upheld a claim of indemnification made by the employer's insurer against an employee who was driving his own car on company business when he negligently caused an accident. The injured person sued both the employer and employee and obtained a judgment against them. The liability insurer of the employer paid the judgment and, acting under a subrogation clause in the policy, brought suit against the employee for indemnification. The employee had his own automobile insurance; doubtless his insurance company handled the defense in the indemnification suit.

The theory of the defense was that the rule granting an employer indemnification against an employee was out of date; that it was inevitable that an employee driving many miles each year on the job would have an accident; that the employer had insurance coverage, which is sufficient protection for it; that the accident involved "mere inadvertent negligence," not drinking or gross negligence, and thus "the employer should not, as a matter of public policy, be entitled to pass the economic loss off on to the employee when it is foreseeable at the outset."

The trial court agreed with the above argument and entered judgment in favor of the defendant. It was reversed unanimously on appeal on the ground that "the 'fault concept'—that all persons should be held responsible for the consequences of their wrongful acts, including 'inadvertent negligence' — while subject to criticism, is still firmly established as the foundation of tort liability." The Oregon Supreme Court stated, with this as a premise and citing the Restatement of Restitution § 96, that it is not contrary to public policy to permit the employer, who is held liable without fault on its part, to obtain indemnity from the person at fault. The court noted that some of the cases upholding indemnification did so on the alternative ground of breach by the employee of an implied term of the employment contract to perform his duties with reasonable care. It observed that no cases have abolished the rule of indemnity, although the United States Supreme Court declined to create such a rule when faced with the question in a case under the Federal Tort Claims Act. *United States v. Gilman*, 347 U.S. 507 (1954). *See* Seavey, *"Liberal Construction," and the Tort Liability of the Federal Government*, 67 Harv. L. Rev. 994 (1954) (commenting on the lower court decision); Note, 63 Yale L.J. 570 (1954).

A leading English case, after lengthy consideration, reached the same result as the *Turner* court. *See Lister v. Romford Ice & Cold Storage Co.*, [1957] A.C. 555 (H.L.) (upholding, with several dissents, indemnification on the basis of breach of an implied term in the employment contract to use due care); *see also* Prosser & Keeton, Law of Torts 311 (5th ed. 1984); Restatement § 401, cmt. d.

The master's right of indemnification has been sharply criticized. *See* Steffen, *The Employer's "Indemnity" Action*, 25 U. Chi. L. Rev. 465 (1958); Williams, *Vicarious Liability and the Master's Indemnity*, 20 Mod. L. Rev. 220, 437 (1957). Both of these articles were inspired by the *Lister* case. For literature in support of the case, see Jolowicz, *The Right to Indemnity Between Master and Servant*, [1956] Camb. L.J. 101; Sandford & McMullin, *Master and Servant: Employer's Claim Against Negligent Employee*, 33 N.Z.L.J. 252 (1957).

Professor Steffen argued that it is unfair and unjust to hold an employee liable for mere inadvertence so long as he was rendering faithful service to his employer. Professor Williams argued that it would misallocate costs to put the loss on the employee; losses occasioned by unintended accidents instead should be left on the business and passed on to the persons who choose to benefit from the business, the customers. Arguments along these lines were rejected by the Oregon court in *Turner*.

Both the *Turner* and *Lister* cases involved income-generating enterprises. In evaluating the soundness of continuing to recognize the right to indemnity in master-servant situations, consider the fact that respondeat superior liability extends beyond such enterprises, as noted in Chapter 3 when discussing nonemployment vicarious liability.

See Restatement (Third) of the Law of Torts: Apportionment of Liability, stating, in the Reporter's Notes:

This section [§ 22] and Illustration 2 follow the normal legal rule that an innocent employer who is vicariously liable is entitled to indemnity from the employee. Not surprisingly, actual collection is rare. *See* Schwartz, *The*

Hidden and Fundamental Issue of Employer Vicarious Liability, 69 S. Cal. L. Rev. 115, 126–29 (1996).

3. Duty to Account

Section 382 of the Restatement (Second) asserts that an agent has a duty to keep and render accounts, stating: "Unless otherwise agreed, an agent is subject to a duty to keep, and render to his principal, an account of money or other things which he has received or paid out on behalf of the principal." Comment a to § 382 notes that this duty includes keeping an accurate record of the persons involved, of payments made, and taking such receipts as are customarily taken in business transactions.

4. The Fiduciary Duties of Agents

a. Commencement of Fiduciary Relationship

When does a fiduciary relationship begin? This question was addressed by the court in *Martin v. Heinold Commodities, Inc.*, 510 N.E.2d 840, 844–45 (Ill. 1987), involving a class action claim by customers of a commodities broker that the broker failed to disclose the material fact that it charged substantial additional commissions on each London Commodities Option, which it concealed in a fee labeled "foreign service fee." Defendant responded that it was not bound by a fiduciary duty during pre-agency bargaining and thus was under no duty to communicate additional information concerning the fee. Instead, it was up to the customers to ask about the fee if it was a matter of concern to them. Defendant argued that its fiduciary duty of full disclosure attached only after it was agreed that defendant would act as plaintiff's broker.

The lower court granted summary judgment in favor of the plaintiff. The appellate court split 4–3 on its decision to reverse. The majority of the court responded as follows:

> We agree [with defendant] that, as a general rule, an agent's fiduciary duty is limited to actions occurring within the scope of his agency and that the creation of the agency relationship is not itself within that scope. However, we are unwilling to conclude, as a matter of law, that a fiduciary duty can never be imposed upon a prospective agent prior to the formal creation of an agency relationship. Thus, while the general rule governing preagency contacts does not require disclosure of the terms of a prospective agent's compensation, we believe that facts could be established which would support imposition of a fiduciary duty upon a prospective agent applicable to preagency contacts. . . .

> We intimate no view as to the specific facts which would support imposition of a fiduciary duty prior to the formal creation of an agency relationship between members of the plaintiff class and the defendant. Our holding

is limited to recognizing the possibility of a factual exception to the general rule that no fiduciary duty attaches prior to the creation of an agency relationship.

We also note that, where the very creation of the agency relationship involves a special trust and confidence on the part of a principal in the subsequent fair dealing of an agent, the prospective agent may be under a fiduciary duty to disclose the terms of his employment as an agent. (Restatement (Second) of Agency sec. 390, comment e (1958)). Determination of whether or not this exception applies to the case at bar is also a matter of fact.

It is clear therefore that summary judgment was not appropriate in this case.

The dissent, at 847–49, stated in part as follows:

Justice Simon, dissenting:

> ... Heinold's disclosure statement misrepresented the nature of its $1,200 foreign-service fee. Rather than informing its prospective customers that 75% of the foreign-service fee was an additional commission—a kickback to the broker and regional office manager from the London office—Heinold described the fee as necessary to cover expenses such as overseas telephone calls and telexes. Heinold contends, and the majority agrees, that this deception, as a matter of law, fails to breach the fiduciary duty Heinold owed to the plaintiff. ... My colleagues have become so concerned with the exact point at which the fiduciary duty attaches that they have totally overlooked the fundamental principles governing fiduciary relationships. ... This court has concluded that a fact is material within the meaning of the Restatement:

>> if it is one which the agent should realize would be likely to affect the judgment of the principal in giving his *consent to the agent to enter into the particular transaction on the specified terms.* Hence, the disclosure must include ... facts which he [the broker] should realize have or are likely to have a *bearing upon the desirability of the transaction from the viewpoint of the principal.*

> (Emphasis added.) (Quoting Restatement (Second) of Agency § 390, Comment a (1958).)

> An additional cost of approximately $1,200 (or even $900, as was the charge to the named plaintiff) per transaction would be a material factor in a customer's decision to enter into a contract which, in the case of the named plaintiff, involved approximately $3,547. Knowing that a major portion of the charge is a brokerage fee rather than an expense of doing business abroad would clearly influence a customer in deciding whether to enter into a transaction in which the broker is so handsomely compensated.

> The majority's formalistic conception of a fiduciary duty drains the obligation of its substance. It permits an agent to deceive a prospective customer

by partially disclosing information and omitting certain details so that further customer inquiry becomes a slim possibility. . . .

Can one fairly argue that the dissent's citation to Restatement (Second) § 390 begs the question before the court?

The Restatement (Third) § 8.11, Comment c endorses the notion that certain prospective agents have enhanced duties of disclosure:

> Moreover, if the creation of the relationship between an agent and a principal involves peculiar trust and confidence, and the prospective principal relies on the prospective agent to deal fairly with the prospective principal, the prospective agent is subject to a duty to deal fairly in arranging the terms of the agency relationship, as if the prospective agent were an agent dealing as an adverse party with a principal, with the principal's knowledge. See § 8.06. The duty to deal fairly may require a prospective agent to furnish the prospective principal with information that is not otherwise reasonably available to the prospective principal and that is material to the principal's decision whether to engage the agent.

Interestingly, the Restatement (Third) illustrates this concept with the facts of the *Martin v. Heinhold Commodities, Inc.* case, thus suggesting that the broker in that case had a duty of disclosure, notwithstanding the appellate court's more cautious approach.

It is worth noting that just as a prospective agent may have some duties to a prospective principal at the time the agency relationship is formed, an agent dealing at arm's length with the principal during the course of the agency relationship may have duties. Section 8.06 of the Restatement (Third) states that an agent acting as an adverse party with the principal's consent has a duty to deal fairly and to disclose all facts that the agent should know would reasonably affect the principal's judgment. Why doesn't the fact that the agent is openly acting as an adverse party transform the relationship to that of ordinary contracting parties, where no such burdens exist? That is, why continue to treat the relationship as if it were one of agency when the agent is not acting on the principal's behalf and the principal knows it? The Comments to Restatement (Second) § 390 appear to address this issue in Comment c: "If the agent is one upon whom the principal naturally would rely for advice, the fact that the agent discloses that he is acting as an adverse party does not relieve him from the duty of giving the principal impartial advice based upon a carefully informed judgment as to the principal's interests. If he cannot or does not wish to do so, he has a duty to see that the principal secures the advice of a competent and disinterested third person."

b. Duty of Care

The following case is also set forth in Chapter 1, as part of introducing the agency relationship. The facts are again described here for the convenience of the reader. The portion of the opinion dealing with the care issue, which was severely edited in Chapter 1, is set forth in full below.

Carrier v. McLlarky

Supreme Court of New Hampshire
693 A.2d 76 (1997)

JOHNSON, JUSTICE.

The defendant, Bruce M. McLlarky d/b/a Assured Plumbing & Heating, appeals an adverse judgment by the Derry District Court (Warhall, J.) in a small claims matter. We reverse.

The defendant installed a replacement hot water heater in the home of the plaintiff, Janet Carrier, in September 1994. The existing water heater had been installed by a different plumber approximately four years prior to its failure. When the defendant installed the new water heater, he told the plaintiff that he believed the old unit was under warranty, and that he would try to obtain a credit against the cost of the new water heater from the manufacturer. The defendant subsequently returned the defective unit to a supplier. The defendant has not given the plaintiff the desired credit and claims that he has failed to do so because he has not received payment from the manufacturer. The plaintiff sued the defendant in small claims court for the replacement value of the water heater and assorted costs. The district court rendered judgment in favor of the plaintiff, and this appeal followed.

[The appellate court approved the district court's determination that the parties had entered into an agency relationship and turned its attention to the duty of care defendant owed his principal, Carrier.]

The question thus becomes whether there is evidence in the record to support a finding of breach. Agents have a duty to conduct the affairs of the principal with a certain level of diligence, skill, and competence. "A determination that an agent was not sufficiently diligent is a question of fact that will not be disturbed unless it can be said that no rational trier of fact could come to the conclusion that the trial court has reached." [*Nowell v. Union Mut. Fire Ins. Co.*,] 409 A.2d [784] at 786 [(N.H. 1979)]. We find that in this case the trial court's findings were unreasonable and unsupported by the record.

"Under ordinary circumstances, the promise to act as an agent is interpreted as being a promise only to make reasonable efforts to accomplish the directed result." *Restatement (Second) of Agency* § 377, comment b at 174 (1957). The court's own findings show that the defendant did make a reasonable attempt to obtain a refund for the plaintiff. Specifically, the court found that after agreeing to act on behalf of the plaintiff, "[t]he defendant then gave the old water [heater] to [a supplier] to return it to the manufacturer." The court's subsequent statement that "[t]he plaintiffs contacted the defendant numerous times regarding the credit and were told they would receive their money as soon as he received the credit," is insufficient to support a finding that the defendant breached his duty of diligence. This is especially true given that "[t]he duties of an agent toward his principal are always to be determined by the scope of the authority conferred." 3 Am. Jur. 2d *Agency* § 209; *see*

Restatement (Second) of Agency § 376. The record shows only that the defendant was charged with returning the defective water heater for a possible credit; he did not guarantee that a credit would be obtained.

In addition, the degree of skill required by an agent in pursuit of the principal's objective is limited to the level of competence which is common among those engaged in like businesses or pursuits. *See Restatement (Second) of Agency* § 379, comment c at 179. There is no indication from the evidence on the record that more was required of the defendant in his agent capacity beyond executing the actual return and seeking the credit. The invoices and work orders provided to the court by the plaintiff do not indicate that the defendant guaranteed a refund. Rather, he merely promised to attempt to obtain a credit from the manufacturer. The invoice drawn up by the defendant and submitted as evidence by the plaintiff stated only that a refund under a warranty may be possible. Further, the record contains a letter from a supplier stating that the defendant "acted in a normal manner as any dealer would under these circumstances," and "was right to withhold credit . . . until the factory actually covered the unit."

Furthermore, an agent cannot be held liable to the principal simply "because he failed to procure for him something to which the latter is not entitled." 3 Am. Jur. 2d *Agency* § 215. The defendant correctly argues that any finding by the court that there was a valid warranty in place is unsupported by the record. The evidence submitted regarding the existence of a warranty included only two undated sales brochures claiming that a similar unit would be covered by a five to ten-year warranty and a letter dated approximately six months after the unit was replaced noting that a warranty currently offered to customers was valid for five to twelve years. Notably, the plaintiff did not produce a warranty for her actual unit. No evidence in the record established that the actual heater returned by the plaintiff was in fact covered by a warranty with terms identical to those described in the sales brochures or letter. Moreover, the defendant's supplier stated in a letter that the unit in question was not covered under a valid warranty.

There is also no support in the record for the holding that the defendant failed to turn over a refund actually received from the manufacturer. As noted above, the record contains a letter from a supplier stating that "[t]echnically, the unit was out of warranty." While the court did find the defendant to be less credible than the plaintiff, there is simply no evidence on the record that the defendant ever received the credit at all. Hence, there is no evidence to support a finding that the defendant breached his duty to remit funds actually received on behalf of the plaintiff. Cf. *Restatement (Second) of Agency* § 427 (agent who has received money on behalf of principal has duty to deliver it to principal on demand).

Consequently, because the district court's ruling was unsupported by the evidence, we reverse.

Reversed.

All concurred.

Notes

1. As noted in *Carrier*, subject to agreement, a paid agent is under a duty to act with the ordinary skill of persons performing similar work. Restatement (Second) § 379. With respect to a higher standard of skill, see the following language from *Garbish v. Malvern Fed. Sav. & Loan Ass'n*, 517 A.2d 547, 554 (Pa. Super. 1986):

> The standard of care imposed on the fiduciary depends on whether or not the fiduciary is or claims to be an expert in the area to which his fiduciary duty relates. When the fiduciary either has or procures his appointment by asserting that he has skill beyond that of the ordinary prudent person, he will be judged by the level of skill that he has or that he claims to have, whichever is higher.

The standard of care for the gratuitous agent is described in Restatement (Third) § 8.01, Comment e:

> In general, the standard of care applicable to a gratuitous agent should reflect what it is reasonable to expect under the circumstances. Relevant circumstances include the skill, experience, and professional status that the agent has or purports to have. Thus, providing a service gratuitously may subject an agent to duties of competence and diligence to the principal that do not differ from the duties owed a principal who agrees to compensate the agent. See Restatement Third, The Law Governing Lawyers § 16 (lawyer's duties to client); § 38, Comment c (lawyer may agree to represent client without payment); and § 50 (lawyer's duty of care to client). It is also relevant whether the principal is aware of any limitations or shortcomings in the agent's skills.

2. The principal and agent can agree on the appropriate level of care owed to the principal. *See Chemical Bank v. Security Pacific Nat'l Bank*, 20 F.3d 375, 377 (9th Cir. 1994) ("Beyond question [agent] acted negligently [by failing to file for $10 a financing statement, resulting in losses exceeding $1 million]. But there is no law against parties to a contract relieving themselves of liability by contract, particularly when they are sophisticated institutions represented by knowledgeable counsel.... According to the credit agreement, [agent] was liable only for its own gross negligence or willful misconduct; [the neglect of the agent] was insufficient to prove either willful misconduct or gross negligence.").

c. Duty of Disclosure

Estate of Eller v. Bartron

Supreme Court of Delaware
31 A.3d 895 (2011)

Before Steele, Chief Justice, Berger and Ridgely, Justices.

Steele, Chief Justice:

A real estate agent served as the seller's agent for two sales of the same house. The initial purchaser submitted a bid for the house and, the same day, hired the initial seller's agent to serve as seller's agent for the second sale. A few days later, the agent convinced the initial seller to accept the initial purchaser's bid without disclosing his conflict of interest or the purchaser's interest in flipping the house. After one day of trial concerning the initial seller's complaint against the agent alleging, *inter alia,* a breach of fiduciary duties, the trial judge granted the defendant's motion for a directed verdict. Because the plaintiff raised issues of material fact concerning whether the defendant breached his fiduciary duties to the seller, we remand the case for a new trial.

Factual and Procedural Background

Loretta Eller decided to sell her mother's house after her mother entered a nursing home. Acting on her mother's behalf, Eller entered into a listing agreement with Wayne Bartron, a real estate agent, on July 22, 1998. The contract awarded Bartron the exclusive right to list the house for one year, specified a sale price of $152,000, and set the commission at seven percent. The contract also included a waiver of Eller's right to object to dual agency, meaning that Eller relinquished her common law right to object to Bartron representing both her and a buyer in the sale of the house. As a result, Bartron could earn the full seven percent, rather than splitting it with a buyer's agent, if he solely found a buyer.

Several months passed uneventfully, then a flurry of activity occurred during January, 1999. On January 20, 1999, Bartron showed the house to Brian Pierce, a person Bartron knew to be a real estate investor. Pierce was part owner of Pierce/O'Neill Ltd., a firm that purchases real estate at distressed prices in the hope of quickly reselling it for a profit. Two days later, Pierce/O'Neill made a $96,000 offer, in writing. Bartron read his notes from that day into evidence:

> O'Neill/Pierce made an offer with stipulation they can access prior to settlement for repairs and showings. Loretta agreed with the condition that she/I be there for all entry. . . . O'Neill/Pierce signed contract with a promise to list with me for a reduced commission to solve problems with entry prior to.

After a brief delay, Eller signed the contract on January 28. She testified that she only decided to accept the offer after a conversation Bartron initiated, at her house, after work hours.

As Bartron's notes indicate, the same day Pierce/O'Neill made an offer to Eller, Pierce/O'Neill engaged Bartron to serve as Pierce/O'Neill's agent for reselling the property. Bartron arranged for Wayne Knierim, a potential buyer who knew Pierce socially, to tour the property. Knierim entered into a contract on January 27 to purchase the house from Pierce/O'Neill, for $130,000. Section 11 of that contract stated that Pierce/O'Neill sold the property "as is." But Knierim testified that he entered into a handshake agreement with Pierce, obligating Pierce/O'Neill to both foot the bill for some repairs to the house and also provide raw materials for Knierim to use to accomplish other improvements. Knierim testified that he would not have paid the $130,000 if Pierce/O'Neill had not agreed to this other help.

On March 30, 1999, the settlements for both sales occurred in the same law firm. The first sale consummated that day transferred the house from Eller's mother to Pierce/O'Neill; the next sale transferred it from Pierce/O'Neill to Wayne Knierim.

Months later, a realtor who happened to notice that Eller's mother's house was sold twice on the same day mentioned that oddity to Eller. After learning of the second sale, Eller filed a suit against Bartron that alleged a number of claims, including a breach of fiduciary duty.

At trial, Eller testified that Bartron never told her that he had agreed to sell the house on behalf of Pierce/O'Neill. Nor, she testified, did Bartron inform her about the second sale. Eller testified that she only learned the house was sold a second time on the same day because a realtor thought it was odd, and so mentioned the second sale to Eller when the two happened to speak some months later.

Other factual disputes arose at trial. First, Eller contended that Bartron knew about the January 27 contract on January 28, when he convinced Eller to sign the offer. Eller could offer no specific evidence supporting this contention, instead she relied on the nature of the relationship between Bartron and Pierce/O'Neill to support a finding that Bartron knew of the contract. Despite the circumstances underlying the Bartron and Pierce/O'Neill relationship, the trial judge found that Eller put forward no particular evidence sufficient to create a dispute about a genuine issue of material fact in the face of Bartron's direct testimony that he did not know about the January 27 contract on January 28.

Second, Eller contended that the two transactions cheated her out of the difference between the two sales prices. Bartron introduced evidence suggesting, to the contrary, that the price difference reflected Pierce/O'Neill's willingness to finance some renovations to the house.

After a one day trial, the trial judge issued an oral order granting the defendant's motion for a directed verdict. Although Eller's complaint asserted that Bartron breached his fiduciary duty, the trial judge's oral order included no specific findings about that claim. The trial judge concluded that the existence of Bartron's notes "does necessarily indicate that he told her that he was working with [Pierce/O'Neill]."

Standard of Review

We review a trial judge's decision on a motion for a directed verdict to determine "whether the evidence and all reasonable inferences that can be drawn therefrom, taken in a light most favorable to the nonmoving party, raise an issue of material fact for consideration by the jury."

Discussion

To establish liability for the breach of a fiduciary duty, a plaintiff must demonstrate that the defendant owed her a fiduciary duty and that the defendant breached it. Because Bartron acted as Eller's agent, and therefore owed her traditional fiduciary duties, the trial judge should have permitted the jury to determine whether

Bartron breached his fiduciary duties, and if so, what damages proximately resulted from the breach.

. . . Delaware courts consider real estate agents to be agents as recognized at common law.

The existence of an agency relationship empowers an agent to act on behalf of his principal. When accompanied by trust that the agent will use the principal's confidential information to pursue the principal's ends, that relationship also imposes fiduciary duties on the principal [sic-agent?].

To protect the social gains resulting from fiduciary relationships, the courts, in appropriate circumstances, afford a remedy to those parties whose trust has been unlawfully abused, often referred to as the "exclusive benefit" rule, which unless modified by contract "flatly forbid[s]" fiduciaries from gaining personally from the agency relationship.

Agents owe their principals a duty to disclose certain information, and a duty to avoid gaining an interest adverse to their principal.

It is true, of course, that under elemental principles of agency law, an agent owes his principal a duty of good faith, loyalty and fair dealing. Encompassed within such general duties of an agent is a duty to disclose information that is relevant to the affairs of the agency entrusted to him. There is also a corollary duty of an agent not to put himself in a position antagonistic to his principal concerning the subject matter of his agency.

An agent who acquires a position adverse to the principal, but fails to disclose it, simultaneously breaches the duties of loyalty and care.

The evidence developed after one day at trial created genuine, disputed issues of material fact about whether Bartron breached his fiduciary duties. First, the evidence at trial created an issue about whether Bartron informed Eller that Pierce/O'Neill's bid for her property was accompanied with a promise that Pierce/O'Neill would use Bartron as its listing agent to sell the property. An agent cannot accept another agency that creates tension with an earlier agency unless he first informs the principal and receives the principal's consent. If an agent "acts for more than one principal in a transaction," he must "disclose to each principal . . . all other facts that the agent knows, has reason to know, or should know would reasonably affect the principal's judgment unless the principal has manifested that such facts are already known by the principal or that the principal does not wish to know them." This requirement ensures that the principal will have "a focused opportunity to assess risks" once the agent identifies potentially problematic circumstances.

Bartron's failure to explain his dual agency role to Eller prevented her from having an opportunity to assess her risks. Bartron's agreement to act as the seller for Pierce/O'Neill's second transaction affected the weight Eller should assign to his views, so Bartron had a duty to refuse to act for Pierce/O'Neill until he informed Eller of his opportunity to benefit and secured Eller's consent. When Eller consented to dual agency, she consented only to Bartron representing her and the buyer in a single transaction. She would have reasonably expected Bartron to sell the house at a price approximating fair market value. She reasonably could have objected to Bartron, as her agent, representing the buyer's resale so quickly as detrimental to her receiving the highest available price in the initial sale. The agent's loyalty to both parties, coupled with the fact that the second sale enhances the returns from the agent's commissions, suggests that Eller would be worried about her price reflecting real market value. But if the real estate agent agrees to sell that same property a second time on behalf of the prospective buyer, the agent faces a set of incentives that can destroy the agent's incentives to get the best deal for the initial seller. An agent who stands to earn a second commission on the same property, immediately, has reason to make sure that the prospective buyer secures the property. The commission that he would stand to earn from a second sale could typically more than compensate him for a lower commission in the first transaction. Eller should have had a focused opportunity to assess whether she would permit an agent with those arguably competing interests to act on her behalf.

Eller's contractual consent to Bartron representing her and a buyer's interest in a single sale does not remove Bartron's duty to fully disclose his January 22 agreement to serve as Pierce/O'Neill's agent to resell the house. A real estate agent who accepts a dual agency represents both the seller and the agent [sic-buyer] in a single transaction. On January 28, when Bartron convinced Eller to accept Pierce/O'Neill's offer even though it was significantly beneath the price she expected, Eller did not know she was dealing with a conflicted advisor. Eller thought Bartron expected to receive a commission as the seller's agent and one as the buyer's agent. She did not know he also expected to receive another commission — as the seller's agent for an immediate resale of the same property. Therefore, Eller did not consent to a situation where she might reasonably expect Bartron to recommend she sell the property for less than his estimate of its market value.

Second, Bartron should have told Eller that Pierce/O'Neill planned to immediately resell the house. The seller of a house, a person interested in receiving the best possible price for the property, would want to know if the purchaser planned to flip the house. That information would at least suggest that the house could be sold for a higher price. Eller testified that Bartron did not tell her that Pierce/O'Neill planned to attempt to resell Eller's mother's house before her sale to Pierce/O'Neill even closed. Bartron's notebook offers evidence that he told Eller about this plan. But the conflict between Bartron's notebook and Eller's testimony creates a genuinely disputed issue about a material fact. The jury should have resolved the issue of whether Bartron told Eller Pierce/O'Neill planned to flip the property.

Factual arguments advanced by Bartron's counsel misconceive the problem with Bartron's behavior. For instance, it does not matter that Eller put forward no particular facts suggesting that Bartron knew O'Neill/Pierce had signed a contract with Knierim when it happened. Had facts suggested that Bartron knew of the January 27 contract while he was persuading Eller to sign the offer on January 28, his violation of the duty of loyalty would have been patently obvious. But even assuming that Bartron did not know of the contract between Knierim and Pierce/O'Neill, Bartron still should have told Eller of his conflict of interest and of Pierce/O'Neill's intent to resell the house.

Similarly, the argument that the higher price in the second sale was justified because a handshake deal between Pierce/O'Neill and Knierim explained the price increase misses the point. Financial support given from Pierce/O'Neill to Knierim only demonstrates that Pierce/O'Neill's profits from the two sales might be less than is suggested by the difference between the first and second sale prices. That Pierce/O'Neill might have made a smaller profit than the facts at first suggest does not affect whether Bartron should have told Eller about those two points. In any event, a jury need not credit Knierim's testimony that a handshake deal existed. Since Pierce/O'Neill, an experienced real estate investment firm, bargained for the contractual right to receive payment without improving the property in any way, a reasonable jury could very well consider the contractual language to be a better guide to the content of the deal than the contradictory testimony.

. . . .

Conclusion

We reverse the judgment of the Superior Court and remand for a new trial.

Note

The duty of disclosure relates to material information:

> A breach of fiduciary duty occurs if the broker, as agent, conceals from the seller, as principal, "material" information, i.e., "information that bears upon the transaction in question." *Moore & Co. v. T.A.L.L.*, 792 P.2d [794] at 799 (Colo. 1990). An agent is thus required to disclose to the principal any facts "which might reasonably affect the principal's decision." *Wheeler v. Carl Rabe*, 599 P.2d [902] at 904 (Colo. 1979). However, the burden is on the principal to demonstrate that the agent was aware of the nondisclosed fact, that the nondisclosed fact is material, and that the agent breached his or her fiduciary duty.
>
> In terms of what constitutes "material" information in the present case, we find instructive . . . Restatement (Second) of Torts § 538(2)(a) (1977) ("The matter is material if a reasonable [person] would attach importance to its existence or nonexistence in determining his choice of action in the transaction in question."). Thus, the question presented here is whether the information known to and withheld by [the agent] would, if disclosed, have assumed actual significance in the deliberations of the [principal] in regard to the sale of the estate property or significantly altered the total mix of information available to them.

Olsen v. Vail Associates Real Estate, Inc., 935 P.2d 975, 978–79 (Colo. 1997).

In *Moye White LLP v. Beren*, 320 P.3d 373 (Colo. Ct. App. 2013) a client of a law firm, counterclaiming to the firm's suit for an unpaid legal fee, asserted that the firm breached its fiduciary duty for failing to disclose that an attorney it had assigned to the client's case had a history of disciplinary proceedings, mental illness, alcoholism, and related arrests. (The attorney's disciplinary record was public, although the firm did not call this to the attention of the client.) There was no evidence that these circumstances affected the attorney's performance in the client's case. The appellate court, affirming the trial court, concluded that the firm's failure to disclose this information was not material, "because the evidence presented at trial demonstrated that [the attorney's] medical and arrest history did not adversely affect the quality of [the firm's] representation. . . . Even a reasonably prudent person, concerned about the quality of his or her legal representation, would not find such a speculative risk significant in his or her decision to retain a particular law firm." Is the fact that the attorney's performance was unaffected relevant? Should it be? Drawing on the definition of materiality in *Vail Associates*, would the client have "attach[ed] importance" to such information in deciding whether to retain the firm?

d. Duty of Loyalty

Suppose Ann, an agent, negotiates a transaction her principal wants and takes a little "gratuity" that the third party has offered her in order to hurry the deal through. The principal, satisfied with the transaction, pays Ann her commission and then learns about the gratuity. Has Ann violated her fiduciary duty to her principal? What incentive is there for the law to act, since the principal got what it wanted at no extra cost to it?

i. Loyalty During the Relationship

Gelfand v. Horizon Corp.

United States Court of Appeals, Tenth Circuit
675 F.2d 1108 (1982)

Before Seth, Chief Judge, Doyle, Circuit Judge, and Anderson, District Judge.

William E. Doyle, Circuit Judge.

Gelfand sued Horizon Corporation, a real estate concern, which was engaged in the owning and marketing of real estate around the country. Gelfand began working for Horizon in 1966. He served first as a real estate salesman and later as a sales manager. In recent times he was transferred to New Mexico and became the district manager in charge of Paradise Hills and Rio Communities which were located near Albuquerque. He had been paid a salary, but in 1977 it was decided by Horizon to pay him a lower salary, plus commissions and overrides based on real estate sales in his district. The percentages paid to the district manager were called overrides and were established by an inter-office memorandum in 1976.

Gelfand was terminated in January, 1979. Horizon's management apparently felt that Gelfand's success was benefiting him more than the company. Soon after that Gelfand claimed Horizon owed him commissions and overrides on some completed transactions. These Horizon refused to pay. Eventually, however, Gelfand filed suit in the Federal District Court in New Mexico, alleging that he was owed parts of some twelve different sales. Trial was to the court and it was concluded that Gelfand was entitled to commissions of eleven of the twelve sales, and judgment was entered in favor of Gelfand in the sum of $140,322.88.

On this appeal Horizon raises two points. First, that Gelfand was guilty of a breach of fiduciary duties with respect to one of the sales. There does not seem to be much controversy on this; it is the amount of the offset against Gelfand's claim which is in dispute. Horizon maintains that as a result of the breach of the fiduciary relationship, Horizon was entitled to an offset not only for profits accruing directly to the agent, but also for profits which accrued to third parties allied with the agent. The trial court gave damages based upon only those profits which had accrued directly to the agent. . . .

The Barranca Estates

This is the property which Gelfand sold to a corporation in which his wife had a one-third interest. Horizon was not apprised of the details of this transaction. The purchaser corporation was apparently formed for this particular conveyance; it was organized almost contemporaneously with the sale.

Horizon maintains that due to the breach of the fiduciary relationship, Gelfand was not entitled to a commission, but that Horizon was entitled to set off against Gelfand's other claims all of the profits that were made by the dummy corporation on the Barranca Estates transaction. The trial court, after hearing all the evidence, concluded that Horizon was entitled to an off-set, but only as to the one-third share of the profits from the sale. On this appeal, Horizon contends that three-thirds should have been the award.

The Barranca Estates tract had been for sale for some time (one or two years) prior to Gelfand's arrival in New Mexico. The home office of Horizon in Tucson had set the sales price at $165,000. On November 10, 1977, Gelfand, working as an agent of Horizon, sold an option to buy the tract to B & C Enterprises, a New Mexico corporation, which is mentioned above, and in which Gelfand's wife and son were principals. B & C Enterprises had been incorporated October 27, 1977. Gelfand's wife had advanced the $2,500 price of the option herself. Within the ensuing month, B & C sold the option to Professional Homes, and received a $57,500 profit. Professional Homes paid B & C $60,000 for the option, and then exercised it, and paid Horizon $165,000 for the property. The profit was split three ways; $20,000 went to Mrs. Gelfand, and the balance was divided between Stewart Braums and David Simms, who were the other partners in B & C. B & C apparently went out of business immediately after this transaction.

The law regarding fiduciary relationships in New Mexico is generally similar to the laws throughout the United States. An agent occupies a relationship in which trust and confidence is the standard. When the agent places his own interests above those of the principal there is a breach of fiduciary duty to the principal. The fiduciary is duty bound to make a full, fair and prompt disclosure to his employer of all facts that threaten to affect the employer's interests or to influence the employee's actions in relation to the subject matter of the employment.

In the present case, the facts giving rise to the breach of the fiduciary relationship are undisputed. That Gelfand failed to disclose the relevant facts to Horizon at the time of the transaction cannot be questioned. Also, it is certain that the company would have objected to the sale to B & C Enterprises which had been formed the previous month. The violation of the fiduciary relationship was, indeed, blatant and the court was entirely correct in concluding that there was a breach of fiduciary duty owed by Gelfand to Horizon.

What should be the remedy for breach of fiduciary duty? The trial court refused to give Gelfand a commission on the sale. This was plainly correct. See *Canon v. Chapman*, 161 F. Supp. 104, 111 (D. Okla. 1958), holding that a broker is not entitled to compensation where he acts adversely to his principal's interest; *Craig v. Parsons*, 22 N.M. 293, 161 P. 1117, 1119 (1916). In this latter case, an agent's fraudulent conduct prevented him from receiving or retaining any benefit whatever from the transaction. Cf. *Iriart v. Johnson, supra*, 411 P.2d [226] at 230 [(N.M. 1965)], holding that a commission is a profit which the principal is entitled to recover. *See also* Douthwaite, *Profits and Their Recovery*, 15 VILLANOVA L. REV. 346, 373–74 (1970). Where an agent seeks to recover compensation growing out of the same transaction in which he was guilty of being disloyal to his principal, the court is justified in denying the compensation, and the equitable principle applicable to the fiduciary that he is not to profit from his own wrong comes into play.

We now turn to the issue whether the wife can be forced to return the $20,000 profit made in the transaction. We conclude that this is all part of the breach of fiduciary relationship, and that Gelfand was using his wife for the indirect purpose of gaining a profit which could not be given to him directly. Surely the principal is entitled to recover that sum of money. . . . Bogert, Trusts and Trustees, Sec. 543, 543(A), 543(T), at 218, 225–26, 231–32 (rev. 2d ed. 1978) (profit made by fiduciary's wife is attributable to fiduciary and may be taken from him).

But the court's refusal to hold Gelfand liable for the profits made by the third parties is a more difficult problem.

It would appear from the cases that a fiduciary who has, by violating his obligation of loyalty, made it possible for others to make profits, can himself be held accountable for that profit regardless of whether he has realized it. *See* Douthwaite, *Profits and Their Recovery, supra*, at 370; Bogert, Trusts and Trustees, Sec. 543(V) at 393 (rev. 2d ed. 1978). *See also Mosser v. Darrow*, 341 U.S. 267, 271–73 (1951). There a trustee was surcharged for profits made by employees who traded in securities of trust subsidiaries. The theory is that the trustee is not to be free to authorize others to do what he is forbidden. There are a good many other cases which give support to this proposition. The liability of the fiduciary and of the profiting third party in such cases is said to be joint and several. Douthwaite, *Profits and Their Recovery, supra*, at 371. The cases hold that the purpose for restoring profits is to discourage potential conflicts of interest and duty; the complaining principal or employer need not prove that any loss was caused by fiduciary's misconduct. Douthwaite, *Profits and Their Recovery, supra*, at 335; Dobbs, Handbook on the Law of Remedies 683–84 (1973). This differs from the damages remedy, the purpose of which is to compensate the plaintiff for proven loss. The restitution of profits remedy serves primarily as a deterrent. Bogert, Trusts and Trustees, *supra*, Sec. 543 at 218. Requiring the fiduciary to disgorge his own unjustly acquired gains serves a punitive as well as a compensatory function if no loss to the beneficiary is proven. To require him to account for the gains of others still more plainly operates to deter him and other fiduciaries from disloyalty. *Id.*; D. Dobbs, Handbook on the Law of Remedies, *supra*, at 224.

So the trial court could have held Gelfand accountable for the $37,500 profit made by Braums and Simms. We do not hold that the trial court was incorrect in refusing to exercise its broad equity powers to this extent. Several reasons for the court's staying its own hand are suggested. First, the court is not obligated to compel a fiduciary to reimburse the beneficiary for third party profits. Thus, the authorization for such a remedy is not a mandatory one. Rather, it partakes of a discretionary equitable character. Second, the flexibility and concern for doing justice that are central to equity are another factor. It requires a case by case evaluation of all relevant circumstances whenever restitution of third party profits is sought.

From consideration of the evidence and the court's findings, it is our conclusion that the facts support the trial court's decision.

One factor which deserves prominent mention is that Horizon did not have a policy which forbade land purchases by employees or required disclosure in such situations. Other Horizon executives had bought property from Horizon for their own business interests. As a matter of fact, the evidence shows that Horizon employees could obtain a 20% discount on purchases of unimproved property. With respect to the sale of Barranca Estates to B & C Enterprises, Horizon's management executives were not wholly ignorant of the circumstances surrounding the transaction. The Tucson central office set the $165,000 sales price for the tract, and Horizon's Vice-President in Charge of Sales, S.P. Abrams, signed the B & C option purchase agreement himself.

Further elements supporting the trial court's decision are the non-existence of a strict trusteeship applicable to the two-thirds interest, see *Mosser v. Darrow*, 341 U.S. 267, 271 (1951) (trustee was held liable for profits made by employees, in part because the case involved "a strict trusteeship, not one of those quasi-trusteeships in which self-interest and representative interests are combined"), and the susceptibility of the other two B & C partners, Braums and Simms, to an action to recover profits (though Braums now lives in Florida). There are special rationales for holding fiduciaries liable for third-party profits, such as the possibility of reciprocal tipping arrangements. There is no evidence that Braums and Simms were in any position to return Gelfand's favor through questionable real estate transactions or other means. In addition, the Barranca Estates transaction appears to be an isolated incident in a long term of useful service by Gelfand to Horizon. *See* Douthwaite, *Profits and Their Recovery, supra*, at 374 (total forfeiture may be inappropriate where transaction complained of was isolable from fiduciary's conduct in general). . . .

It is our conclusion that substantial evidence supports the trial court's decision across the board. Accordingly, even if this court can find some support for the appellant's position, the ruling of the trial court should stand. "If, from established facts, reasonable men might draw different inferences, appellate courts may not substitute their judgment for that of the trial court."

Judgment . . . affirmed.

Notes

1. The following quotation on the fiduciary duty of loyalty is taken from the opinion of Judge Cardozo in the case of *Meinhard v. Salmon*, 164 N.E. 545 (N.Y. 1928). It is one of the most frequently quoted passages in the law. It was written in the context of a dispute involving the application of partnership law (the *Meinhard* case is contained in Chapter 12), but the passage has been quoted and applied in contexts extending well beyond the law of partnership.

> Many forms of conduct permissible in a workaday world for those acting at arm's length, are forbidden to those bound by fiduciary ties. A trustee is held to something stricter than the morals of the market place. Not honesty alone, but the punctilio of an honor the most sensitive, is then the standard of behavior. As to this there has developed a tradition that is unbending and inveterate. Uncompromising rigidity has been the attitude of courts of equity when petitioned to undermine the rule of undivided loyalty by the "disintegrating erosion" of particular exceptions (*Wendt v. Fischer*, 243 N.Y. 439, 444). Only thus has the level of conduct for fiduciaries been kept at a level higher than that trodden by the crowd. It will not consciously be lowered by any judgment of this court.

2. *Remedies.* In addition to the extensive discussion in *Gelfand* of the principal's remedies for breach of fiduciary duty, see *Tarnowski v. Resop*, 51 N.W.2d 801 (Minn. 1952), in which a principal in a suit against his agent recovered the agent's secret commission even though the principal had rescinded the underlying contract and recovered his down payment; he also recovered attorney's fees, all expenses, and loss of time devoted to the matter. *See also Moore & Co. v. T-A-L-L, Inc.*, 792 P.2d 794 (Colo. 1990) (agent forfeits commission retained by it even though principal

unable to prove damages). With regard to the liability of the person who has aided the agent in breach of the fiduciary relation, see *Donemar, Inc. v. Molloy*, 169 N.E. 610 (N.Y. 1930), where the third party was ordered to pay a $4,555 "gratuity" to the principal, even though he had already paid it to the agent.

Does the remedy of forfeiture of profits include a right of the principal to recover whatever compensation was paid to the agent during the period of disloyalty? Courts split on this. *See Phansalkar v. Andersen Weinroth & Co., L.P.*, 344 F.3d 184 (2d Cir. 2003) (all compensation forfeited during period of disloyalty, including investment opportunities); *Riggs Inv. Mgmt. Corp. v. Columbia Partners, L.L.C.*, 966 F. Supp. 1250 (D.D.C. 1997) (all compensation forfeited from time disloyalty took place until termination of agent's employment, a period of six months); *Royal Carbo Corp. v. Flameguard, Inc.*, 645 N.Y.S.2d 18 (N.Y. App. Div. 1996) (all compensation forfeited during period of disloyalty, and agent held accountable to principal for profits lost on accounts agent diverted to others). But see *Hartford Elevator v. Lauer*, 289 N.W.2d 280 (Wis. 1980), rejecting a rule of per se forfeiture in favor of a consideration of all the circumstances, including the damage done to the employer and the value of the services of the employee. See also *Burg v. Miniature Precision Components*, 330 N.W.2d 192 (Wis. 1983), apparently narrowing the *Hartford Elevator* rule by placing the burden of proof on the employee under some circumstances to show that his service during the period of disloyalty was of some value to his employer after deducting the damage done to the employer.

3. *The middleman.* With regard to forfeiture of compensation and the duty of full disclosure, some jurisdictions distinguish the "middleman" from an agent, allowing the middleman to work for both parties to a transaction and receive compensation from each without disclosure. The following language from the opinion in *Kozasa v. Guardian Elec. Mfg. Co.*, 425 N.E.2d 1137, 1143–44 (Ill. App. 1981), addresses this topic:

> Defendant claims that plaintiff was its agent and therefore had a duty to inform defendant of the 2% royalty plaintiff was receiving from Koike [the other party]. Plaintiff's failure to disclose this, defendant says, amounted to fraud which should foreclose plaintiff from collecting commissions. Plaintiff asserts that he was not defendant's agent but rather a middleman. Defendant agrees that a middleman need not disclose to all parties his acceptance of dual commissions.... When properly authorized, [the agent] makes contracts or other negotiations of a business nature on behalf of his principal, by which his principal is bound. On the other hand, the "middleman" or "go-between" has nothing to do with negotiations and thus it is of no importance that both parties pay him.... Plaintiff did not have the authority to negotiate on defendant's or Koike's behalf or bind [either] contractually. He played no part in the negotiating or drafting of the contract between defendant and Koike. Defendant's president testified that plaintiff's role was that of a "finder." ... [Plaintiff] was not agent of either and therefore was not guilty of fraud.

See also *Northeast Gen. Corp. v. Wellington Advertising, Inc.*, 624 N.E.2d 129, 131 (N.Y. 1993), where a finder, an independent business consultant, located a buyer for plaintiff-seller's business. Before the introduction of the parties, the finder learned that the purchaser had a reputation for buying companies, removing assets, and leaving minority investors unprotected. Finder did not disclose this information to seller. Seller's minority investors suffered loss as a result of purchaser's actions. Finder sued to recover its fee and won, despite an argument that it had failed a duty of disclosure. The New York Court of Appeals reasoned that there was no fiduciary relationship and therefore no duty of disclosure because a finder merely introduces and brings the parties together "without any obligation or power to negotiate the transaction, in order to earn the finder's fee." The court distinguished a finder from a broker by saying, "While a broker performs the same introduction task, the broker must ordinarily also bring the parties to an agreement." The court concluded that, "If the seller wanted fiduciary-like responsibilities, it could have bargained for them."

See *Hurney v. Locke*, 308 N.W.2d 764, 768 (S.D. 1981), recognizing the above category for middlemen but describing it as "an extremely limited exception to the rule that an agent cannot be compensated by the third party without the informed consent of his principal."

4. Is an hourly employee with no management or administrative authority a fiduciary? This question was raised in *Graphic Directions, Inc. v. Bush*, 844 P.2d 1190 (Colo. App. 1992), remanded 862 P.2d 1020 (Colo. App. 1993), by a defendant in a breach of loyalty case involving pre-termination solicitation of customers of the employer. The defendant employee argued that fiduciary duties extend only to corporate officers and high-echelon employees. He had no duty of loyalty because he handled only the technical art aspects of his employer's accounts, he contended. This argument was rejected by the court, in an opinion indirectly acknowledging that the scope of a duty of loyalty can vary with the position of the employee and with the nature of the alleged violation.

The Missouri Supreme Court seemed to reach a different result in *Western Blue Print Co., LLC v. Roberts*, 367 S.W.3d 7 (Mo. 2012). In this case, an at-will employee (Myrna), who managed a branch office for her employer (Western Blue), planned to compete with Western Blue during the course of her employment. After leaving Western Blue, Myrna induced others in her branch office to join her and, shortly after launching her business, submitted a successful competing bid for a key piece of business. Western Blue's loss of this business ultimately resulted the closure of the branch office. In addition to other claims, Western Blue sued Myrna for breach of fiduciary duty and obtained a jury award on this claim. On appeal, the Supreme Court of Missouri reversed, writing:

> Every employee owes his or her employer a duty of loyalty. *Scanwell*, 162 S.W.3d at 479. *Scanwell* left open the question of whether or to what extent an employee owes the employer a fiduciary duty separate from the duty of loyalty. *Scanwell, supra*. Western Blue abandoned its separate claim of breach of loyalty against Myrna at trial in favor of pursing its breach of

fiduciary duty claim only. Hence, the discussion will focus on this specific issue.

Missouri law is clear that officers and directors of public and closely held corporations are fiduciaries because they occupy positions of the highest trust and confidence and are required to exercise the utmost good faith when using the powers conferred upon them to both the corporation and their shareholders. Myrna was not an officer or director of Western Blue, but held the title of division vice president. Western Blue argues that although Myrna was an at-will employee, she operated as a "de facto officer" causing a fiduciary duty to arise because she was vested with broad control and responsibility over the Columbia branch office.

. . . .

Myrna exercised a substantial degree of control over the day-to-day operations of the Columbia branch in her capacity as division vice president. However, the Columbia branch office comprised merely 5 percent of Western Blue's total business operations. As such, Myrna was not within the "top echelon of corporate officials" when carrying out her job duties, nor was her authority so substantial that she was free to disregard Western Blue's directives as to how she performed those duties.

. . . .

Generally, "an employer-employee relationship, without more, is insufficient to cause a confidential relationship to exist as to knowledge naturally acquired during employment." To establish a confidential relationship between an employer and an employee, "[t]here must be either an express understanding as to the confidential nature of the information or it must be acquired under such circumstances that the employee must necessarily be aware of the confidence reposed in him."

. . . .

Myrna gained her knowledge and expertise through the general course of her employment. She was not restricted by a non-compete agreement, and she was not asked to maintain the alleged confidential nature of the information she obtained through her work at Western Blue. Much of the information entrusted to her was also entrusted to other individuals. . . .

Finally, Western Blue failed to provide this Court with any case law from any other jurisdiction that has held that an at-will employee who is not subject to a non-compete agreement and is neither an officer, director, partner or member of a limited liability corporation owes a fiduciary duty to his or her employer. This Court declines to extend the law of fiduciary duty as Western Blue suggests to include at-will employees who are not constrained by a non-compete agreement under the particular facts of this case and this state's precedent.

It is curious that the Missouri Court distinguished breach of fiduciary duty from a breach of the duty of loyalty. Typically, the duty of loyalty is described as one of the fiduciary duties that an agent owes to a principal. Is it fair to read the opinion as implying that Myrna did not have a duty of loyalty to Western Blue? Assuming that she did have a duty of loyalty, did her conduct amount to a breach of that duty?

5. The duty of loyalty includes a duty not to use confidential information in competition with or to the injury of the principal. See, for example, *Chalupiak v. Stahlman*, 81 A.2d 577, 580–81 (Pa. 1951), where the defendant was engaged to draft several deeds for a subdivision of some land that plaintiff mistakenly thought he owned. Defendant looked at some maps and questioned plaintiff's ownership, but plaintiff said his attorney and engineer assured him he had good title. Defendant prepared the deeds. Thereafter he purchased the property for himself at a tax sale. In a suit by plaintiff to compel conveyance of the land to him, the court, in finding for plaintiff, stated as follows:

> Here defendant acted, at plaintiff's request and on plaintiff's behalf, in drawing the deeds in question, subject to plaintiff's control. Because of his knowledge as tax collector and as an agent or conveyancer, he was aware . . . that . . . plaintiff's title was doubtful. Defendant secured, *during the course of his service to plaintiff,* the knowledge that plaintiff was attempting to convey land which plaintiff did not own. *It was this knowledge that defendant utilized against the interests of plaintiff.* Defendant, on the basis of this knowledge, went to a commissioners' sale and purchased the land which he knew or suspected that plaintiff mistakenly thought he had already validly conveyed to others. . . .

Defendant violated the duty of loyalty and fidelity he owed to plaintiff. In Restatement, Agency, sec. 395, it is stated:

> Unless otherwise agreed, an agent is subject to a duty to the principal not to use or to communicate information confidentially given him by the principal or acquired by him during the course of or on account of his agency or in violation of his duties as agent, in competition with or to the injury of the principal, on his own account or on behalf of another, although such information does not relate to the transaction in which he is then employed, unless the information is a matter of general knowledge.

Comment (a) reads:

> . . . The agent also has a duty not to use information acquired by him as agent or by means of opportunities which he has as agent to acquire it, or acquired by him through a breach of duty to the principal, for any purpose likely to cause his principal harm or to interfere with his business,

although it is information not connected with the subject matter of his agency.[1]

It is not of controlling importance that defendant utilized information which related to defect in *title*. True, defendant was not employed to search *title* but to prepare or draw a deed. However, . . . "The relation between him and his client is confidential, and whether he acts upon information derived from him or from any other source, he is affected with a trust." . . .

There was a vigorous dissent from the decision. The dissenting judge argued that: "Whatever information defendant acquired as to the ownership of the land was never secured by him from plaintiff and plaintiff never relied upon defendant, but instead on the advice of plaintiff's counsel and engineer."

The citations in *Chalupiak* are to § 395 of the Restatement (Second). The language in § 395 is broad, including within its sweep information "not connected with the subject matter of the agency" and "information [that] does not relate to the transaction in which [the agent] is then employed." Section 395 focuses upon actions of an agent that injure the principal. Would the prohibition be so far-reaching if instead the conduct of the agent involved a failure to enrich the principal? Suppose a ranch hand finds oil on open land adjacent to his employer's land while riding herd and repairing fences. Would he have to forego taking personal profit on that information? The comparable provision in Restatement (Third) is § 8.05:

An agent has a duty

(1) not to use property of the principal for the agent's own purposes or those of a third party; and

(2) not to use or communicate confidential information of the principal for the agent's own purposes or those of a third party.

Does it help resolve this problem?

The duty not to compete is not violated if the principal knows or has reason to know that the agent believes he is privileged to compete or self-deal. An illustration of this is provided by *Western Alliance Corp. v. Western Reliance Corp.*, 643 P.2d 1382 (Or. 1982), a case involving the VSI (vendor's single interest) insurance business in Oregon. The business provides physical damage coverage to financing agents in automobile sales transactions. The insurance is not sold to the general public. The custom in the business tolerated agents switching their customers from one insurance carrier or agency to another. It was understood that the customers belonged to the agent and not the agency for which he worked. Thus an unfair competition case

---

1. Comment b of § 395 includes the following language: "The rule stated in this Section applies not only to those communications which are stated to be confidential, but also to information which the agent should know his principal would not care to have revealed to others or used in competition with him. . . . It does not apply to matters of common knowledge in the community."

by one agency against another complaining about customer switching failed. This situation involving a custom allowing competition between agent and principal is rare, however.

ii. Post-Termination Competition

One of the most difficult and frequently litigated questions involves what rights and duties continue between parties after termination of their relationship. Although this topic is related to Chapter 10, which deals with termination, it also fits naturally into the present topic, dealing with the agent's duty to be loyal and respect confidences, and thus is treated here.

Can an agent, after learning a particular skill, quit her principal's business and set up a competing business, assuming there is no agreement in her contract relating to this? In general, the common law will not stand in the way of competition, so long as it is fair. One factor that may prove important in assessing the fairness of the competition relates to the circumstances under which the employee left the business. See *Biever, Drees & Nordell v. Coutts*, 305 N.W.2d 33, 36 (N.D. 1981), a case where a former employee of an accounting partnership was enjoined from performing accounting services for certain clients of the partnership. There was no written employment agreement between the parties, nor was there an oral agreement with regard to competition after employment. Defendant had solicited certain clients of plaintiff for his business while still employed by plaintiff, however. The court quoted with approval the following language dealing with a similar situation: "While it is true that an employee may take steps to insure continuity in his livelihood in anticipation of resigning his position, he cannot feather his own nest at the expense of his employer while he is still on the payroll."

Trade Secrets

A common situation involves the use by a former employee of information obtained during employment in competition with the former employer. *Town & Country House & Home Serv. v. Newbery*, 147 N.E.2d 724, 726 (N.Y. 1958), is a classic case on this issue. In *Newbery* three employees who had not signed noncompete covenants, quit their jobs as members of a cleaning crew of the plaintiff home cleaning service and started their own company. After terminating their employment, they solicited the customers of their former employer. The employer sued, proving that its list of customers had been obtained at considerable effort and expense by telephoning neighborhoods at random, obtaining 8 to 12 customers out of every 200–300 telephone calls. The court classified the customer list as a trade secret and enjoined defendants from further solicitation of plaintiff's customers. The court also required payment to plaintiff of profits obtained by reason of those customers whom defendants enticed away, stating as follows:

> [A former employee] may not solicit the [employer's] customers who are not openly engaged in business in advertised locations or whose availability as patrons cannot readily be ascertained but "whose trade and patronage have

been secured by years of business effort and advertising, and the expenditure of time and money, constituting a part of the good-will of a business which enterprise and foresight have built up" [citations omitted]. In [an omitted case] it was pointed out by the Appellate Division that although there was no evidence that the former employee had a written customers list, "[t]here was in his head what was equivalent. They were on routes, in streets and at numbers revealed to him through his service with plaintiff. Their faces were familiar to him, and their identity known because of such employment."

Notes

1. The litigation on the issue involved in *Newbery* is substantial. See the extensive annotation in 28 A.L.R.3d 7 (originally published in 1969), dealing solely with the use of customer lists by former employees, and the annotation in 30 A.L.R.3d 631 (originally published in 1970), dealing with the use or disclosure by former employees of special skills or techniques acquired in the earlier employment. *See* Epstein & Levi, *Protecting Trade Secret Information: A Plan for Proactive Strategy*, 43 Bus. Law. 887 (1988).

2. The *Newbery* opinion mentioned the term "trade secret" several times. As you can imagine, defining what is or is not a trade secret, and the scope of protection to be granted to one, can be a complex task. In addition, the problems of enforcing this aspect of the fiduciary relationship are compounded by the presence of conflicting interests: protecting the property interests of the employer and discouraging unethical conduct by employees versus encouraging competition and allowing a person to derive maximum benefit from his or her knowledge and skills.

A trade secret is defined in the Uniform Trade Secrets Act, which is adopted in the majority of states, as:

> information, including a formula, pattern, compilation, program, device, method, technique, or process that: (i) derives independent economic value, actual or potential, from not being generally known to, and not being readily ascertainable by proper means by, other persons who can obtain economic value from its disclosure or use, and (ii) is the subject of efforts that are reasonable under the circumstances to maintain its secrecy.

Covenants Not to Compete

A significant aspect of the *Newbery* case is the absence of a covenant not to compete. Such covenants are quite common and can provide powerful support to an employer's case. Their enforceability depends in part on the breadth of their terms and on the validity of the underlying interests the employer is seeking to protect. The case of *Robbins v. Finlay*, 645 P.2d 623 (Utah 1982), is representative. Defendant (Finlay) was employed by plaintiff (Robbins) to sell hearing aids. Finlay had signed a contract expressly declaring a list of prospects and users given to him by Robbins a trade secret and containing a promise by Finlay to pay $5,000 in liquidated damages if the list was used to the detriment of Robbins. The contract contained a separate clause specifying that Finlay would not compete for one year in Utah upon resignation, with damages for breach set at $3,000. Finlay quit some time later and immediately began competing with Robbins in Utah. Robbins sued and prevailed on the trade secrets clause. Robbins lost on enforcement of the noncompete clause, however, on the ground that it did not protect a legitimate interest because Finlay had not received any particular training nor were his services unique or extraordinary. The court stated as follows:

> Covenants not to compete are enforceable if carefully drawn to protect only the legitimate interests of the employer. The reasonableness of a covenant depends upon several factors, including its geographical extent; the duration of the limitation; the nature of the employee's duties; and the nature of the interest which the employer seeks to protect such as trade secrets, the goodwill of his business, or an extraordinary investment in the training or education of the employee. . . . Covenants not to compete which are primarily designed to limit competition or restrain the right to engage in a common calling are not enforceable. . . .

> We recognize that to some extent the customer leads which Finlay had were in the nature of trade secrets due to the time, expense, and effort which went into discovering the leads. However, the customer leads were specifically protected by the [other] provision and the covenant not to compete was not justified as an additional protection.

Id. at 627–28.

Notes

1. Sometimes a court will "blue pencil" an overly broad covenant if enforceable language can be severed from the unenforceable portion. *See Licocci v. Cardinal Assocs.*, 445 N.E.2d 556 (Ind. 1983) (contract that restricted competition in three ways held enforceable as to two of the ways). Other courts will issue an injunction that cuts down the area or time covered by the contractual provision even though the precise language cannot be penciled out, thus taking a more flexible approach. *See* Blake, *Employee Agreements Not to Compete*, 73 HARV. L. REV. 625, 681–82 (1960). Neither of these approaches would have saved the clause in *Robbins*, however. In some jurisdictions there exist statutory restrictions on covenants not to compete.

2. The court in *Robbins* includes goodwill as an interest that will support a covenant not to compete. The following language, taken from *Henshaw v. Kroenecke*, 656 S.W.2d 416, 418 (Tex. 1983), provides an elaboration of what the court in *Robbins* may have meant by good will:

> Henshaw [owner] had a right to protect himself from the possibility that Kroenecke [newcomer] would establish a rapport with the clients of the business and upon termination take a segment of that clientele with him.

Henshaw had a legitimate interest to protect, and therefore the covenant was reasonable.

3. *In Huong Que, Inc. v. Luu*, 150 Cal. App. 4th 400, 411 (2007), the defendants sold a calendar distribution business to the plaintiffs and agreed to stay on five years as "managing agents" for the business. The sale contract included a non-compete agreement, which provided that the defendants would not compete "as owners" with the business that they had sold to plaintiffs. While employed with plaintiff, the defendants furnished the business's customer list to a competitor, presumably for some compensation, although they were not "owners" of the competitor. When plaintiff sought to enjoin the use of the customer list and defendants' conduct that interfered with plaintiffs' business, the defendants argued that the contract controlled and their conduct did not amount to a breach of that contract. In affirming the lower court's preliminary injunction, the appellate court held that the contract did not supplant the common law fiduciary duties, including the duty of loyalty, that arose from the principal-agent relationship of the parties: "We are directed to nothing on the face of the contract, and certainly to no extrinsic evidence, that would support the supposition that the parties intended to excuse appellants from the duty of loyalty otherwise flowing from their agency relationship. . . . The non-competition clause could readily be understood as intended not to affect appellants' duties as agents or employees, but only to obligate them as sellers." In any case, contracting around the duty of loyalty is subject to certain limitations.

4. In some jurisdictions there are statutory restrictions on covenants not to compete. See, for example, Colo. Rev. Stat. §8-2-113(2):

> (2) Any covenant not to compete which restricts the right of any person to receive compensation for performance of skilled or unskilled labor for any employer shall be void, but this subsection (2) shall not apply to:
>
>   (a) Any contract for the purchase and sale of a business or the assets of a business;
>
>   (b) Any contract for the protection of trade secrets;
>
>   (c) Any contractual provision providing for recovery of the expense of educating and training an employee who has served an employer for a period of less than two years;
>
>   (d) Executive and management personnel and officers and employees who constitute professional staff to executive and management personnel.
>
> (3) [prohibiting injunctive relief for covenants that bind physicians post-termination]

This statute was interpreted in *Colorado Accounting Machines, Inc. v. Mergenthaler*, 609 P.2d 1125, 1126 (Colo. App. 1980), a case in which the employment contract between plaintiff and defendant contained a nondisclosure of trade secrets clause and a separate noncompetition clause that was limited as to time and proximity. Defendant went to work for a competitor of plaintiff. In a suit for breach of the noncompetition covenant, plaintiff apparently argued that the covenant was valid despite the above statute because, realistically, it was the only means by which plaintiff could get protection from disclosure of its trade secrets; if defendant could work for a competitor, the trade secret protection would exist in name only. This argument was rejected by the court on the reasoning that the separate clause relating to trade secrets "adequately protects plaintiff's interests, and the restrictive covenant is not limited to enhancing this protection." Could the contract involved in the *Mergenthaler* case have been drafted more skillfully?

iii. Dealing at Arm's Length

Restatement (Third) sec. 8.06 allows a principal to waive a fiduciary obligation of its agent, subject to certain conditions. It provides, in relevant part:

> Conduct by an agent that would otherwise constitute a breach of duty . . . does not constitute a breach of duty if the principal consents to the conduct, provided that
>
> > (a) in obtaining the principal's consent, the agent
> >
> > > (i) acts in good faith,
> > >
> > > (ii) discloses all material facts that the agent knows, has reason to know, or should know would reasonably affect the principal's judgment unless the principal has manifested that such facts are already known by the principal or that the principal does not wish to know them, and
> > >
> > > (iii) otherwise deals fairly with the principal; and
> >
> > (b) the principal's consent concerns either a specific act or transaction, or acts or transactions of a specified type that could reasonably be expected to occur in the ordinary course of the agency relationship.

In the following case, the New York Court of Appeals treated a member of a limited liability company, who was buying out his co-members, as an agent and the sellers as his principal. Assuming that to be the case, would the sellers' waiver of the buyer's fiduciary duties pass muster under Sec. 8.06?

Pappas v. Tzolis
Court of Appeals of New York
982 N.E.2d 576 (2012)

PIGOTT, J.

Plaintiffs Steve Pappas and Constantine Ifantopoulos along with defendant Steve Tzolis formed and managed a limited liability company (LLC), for the purpose of entering into a long-term lease on a building in Lower Manhattan. Pappas and

Tzolis each contributed $50,000 and Ifantopoulos $25,000, in exchange for proportionate shares in the company. Pursuant to a January 2006 Operating Agreement, Tzolis agreed to post and maintain in effect a security deposit of $1,192,500, and was permitted to sublet the property. The Agreement further provided that any of the three members of the LLC could "engage in business ventures and investments of any nature whatsoever, whether or not in competition with the LLC, without obligation of any kind to the LLC or to the other Members."

Numerous business disputes among the parties ensued. In June 2006, Tzolis took sole possession of the property, which was subleased by the LLC to a company he owned, for approximately $20,000 per month in addition to rent payable by the LLC under the lease. According to plaintiffs, they "reluctantly agreed to do this, because they were looking to lease the building and Tzolis was obstructing this from happening." Pappas, who wanted to sublease the building to others, alleges that Tzolis "not only blocked [his] efforts, he also did not cooperate in listing the Property for sale or lease with any New York real estate brokers." Moreover, Pappas claims that Tzolis "had not made, and was not diligently preparing to make, the improvements . . . required to be made under the Lease. Tzolis was also refusing to cooperate in [Pappas's] efforts to develop the Property." Further, Tzolis's company did not pay the rent due.

On January 18, 2007, Tzolis bought plaintiffs' membership interests in the LLC for $1,000,000 and $500,000, respectively. At closing, in addition to an Agreement of Assignment and Assumption, the parties executed a Certificate in which plaintiffs represented that, as sellers, they had "performed their own due diligence in connection with [the] assignments . . . engaged [their] own legal counsel, and [were] not relying on any representation by Steve Tzolis [,] or any of his agents or representatives, except as set forth in the assignments & other documents delivered to the undersigned Sellers today," and that "Steve Tzolis has no fiduciary duty to the undersigned Sellers in connection with [the] assignments." Tzolis made reciprocal representations as the buyer.

In August 2007, the LLC, now owned entirely by Tzolis, assigned the lease to a subsidiary of Extell Development Company for $17,500,000. In 2009, plaintiffs came to believe that Tzolis had surreptitiously negotiated the sale with the development company before he bought their interests in the LLC.

Plaintiffs commenced this action against Tzolis in April 2009, claiming that, by failing to disclose the negotiations with Extell, Tzolis breached his fiduciary duty to them. They alleged, in all, 11 causes of action.

Tzolis moved to dismiss plaintiffs' complaint. Supreme Court dismissed the complaint in its entirety, citing the Operating Agreement and Certificate. A divided Appellate Division modified Supreme Court's order, allowing four of plaintiffs' claims to proceed—breach of fiduciary duty, conversion, unjust enrichment, and fraud and misrepresentation—while upholding the dismissal of the rest of the complaint (87 AD3d 889 [1st Dept 2011]). The dissenting Justices would have dismissed all the causes of action, relying on our recent decision in *Centro Empresarial Cempresa S.A. v. América Móvil, S.A.B. de C.V.* (17 NY3d 269 [2011]).

The Appellate Division granted Tzolis leave to appeal, certifying the question whether its order was properly made (2012 NY Slip Op 61541[U] [2012]). We now answer the certified question in the negative, and reverse.

In their first cause of action, plaintiffs claim that Tzolis was a fiduciary with respect to them and breached his duty of disclosure. Tzolis counters that plaintiffs' claim fails to state a cause of action because, by executing the Certificate, they expressly released him from all claims based on fiduciary duty.

In *Centro Empresarial Cempresa S.A. v. América Móvil, S.A.B. de C.V.*, we held that "[a] sophisticated principal is able to release its fiduciary from claims—at least where . . . the fiduciary relationship is no longer one of unquestioning trust—so long as the principal understands that the fiduciary is acting in its own interest and the release is knowingly entered into" (*Centro Empresarial Cempresa S.A.*, 17 NY3d at 278). Where a principal and fiduciary are sophisticated entities and their relationship is not one of trust, the principal cannot reasonably rely on the fiduciary without making additional inquiry. For instance, in *Centro Empresarial Cempresa S.A.*, plaintiffs—seasoned and counseled parties negotiating the termination of their relationship—knew that defendants had not supplied them with the financial information to which they were entitled, triggering "a heightened degree of diligence" (*id.* at 279). In this context, "the principal cannot blindly trust the fiduciary's assertions" (*id.*). The test, in essence, is whether, given the nature of the parties' relationship at the time of the release, the principal is aware of information about the fiduciary that would make reliance on the fiduciary unreasonable.

Here, plaintiffs were sophisticated businessmen represented by counsel. Moreover, plaintiffs' own allegations make it clear that at the time of the buyout, the relationship between the parties was not one of trust, and reliance on Tzolis's representations as a fiduciary would not have been reasonable. According to plaintiffs, there had been numerous business disputes, between Tzolis and them, concerning the sublease. Both the complaint and Pappas's affidavit opposing the motion to dismiss portray Tzolis as uncooperative and intransigent in the face of plaintiffs' preferences concerning the sublease. The relationship between plaintiffs and Tzolis had become antagonistic, to the extent that plaintiffs could no longer reasonably regard Tzolis as trustworthy. Therefore, crediting plaintiffs' allegations, the release contained in the Certificate is valid, and plaintiffs cannot prevail on their cause of action alleging breach of fiduciary duty.

Practically speaking, it is clear that plaintiffs were in a position to make a reasoned judgment about whether to agree to the sale of their interests to Tzolis. The need to use care to reach an independent assessment of the value of the lease should have been obvious to plaintiffs, given that Tzolis offered to buy their interests for 20 times what they had paid for them just a year earlier.

. . . .

Accordingly, the order of the Appellate Division, insofar as appealed from, should be reversed, with costs, plaintiffs' complaint dismissed in its entirety, and the certified question answered in the negative.

CHIEF JUDGE LIPPMAN and JUDGES CIPARICK, GRAFFEO, READ and SMITH concur.

Note

The duties of members of a limited liability company to the LLC (in which the members are responsible for managing the company, as was the case in *Pappas*) and the duties of partners to their partnership are based on principal-agent law. As will be discussed more fully below, each partner is an agent of the partnership and each member of a member-managed LLC is an agent the LLC. The fiduciary duties that partners and LLC members owe include the duties of loyalty and care, although the duty of care is somewhat relaxed. In any case, whether the relationship is that of partners, LLC members or a garden variety principal-agent relationship, there may come a time in which the fiduciary seeks to deal at arm's length with its principal. The law has struggled with this situation, and the Restatement (Third) sought to clarify the relevant doctrine, at least in the principal-agent relationship. *Pappas* suggests that in an LLC context, the rigid requirements of the Restatement are not applicable.

Problems

1. The real estate branch of Harrods Limited, a large company that deals with real estate, building construction, and so forth, was employed by Mrs. Lemon as real estate agent to find a purchaser for her property known as "Blythswood," located at Ascot. On July 3, Harrods arranged for the sale of the property to one Mrs. Campbell "subject to contract and a surveyor's report" (the latter meaning a building inspection). On July 8, Mrs. Campbell, who had had previous business dealings with the building department of Harrods (which was situated in a separate building from that of the real estate department) called upon the manager of the building department, told him she had contracted for a house at Ascot, and asked him to inspect it. He did so and suggested that the drains be repaired, which was a fairly expensive proposition. On July 16, the solicitor for Mrs. Campbell wrote the solicitor for Mrs. Lemon calling this defect to their attention and specifying either that it be repaired before the sale or that the cost of repair be deducted from the purchase price. Soon thereafter the relationship between the two branches was discovered, and the solicitors for Mrs. Lemon complained of this. Harrods replied, offering to advise Mrs. Campbell to have an independent firm test the drains. Nothing further was done by Mrs. Lemon and the contract was signed on July 31, with a discount for the cost of repairing the drains. Mrs. Lemon thereafter refused to pay the real estate department their commission. Harrods sued for the commission. What result? *See Harrods Ltd. v. Lemon*, [1931] 2 K.B. 157, noted in 4 CAMBRIDGE L.J. 373 (1932), 44 HARV. L. REV. 1294 (1931).

Would it change your analysis if the sale had been completed, with a discount from the purchase price, and then for the first time Mrs. Lemon and Harrods discovered the involvement of both departments?

Suppose the discovery of the involvement of both departments had resulted in the transaction being called off. How would you assess the rights between the parties?

2. After foreclosure proceedings against the mortgagor of the Half Moon Hotel on Coney Island, a trustee was appointed for the benefit of the holders of the first mortgage certificates. The attorneys for the trustee bought some of the certificates for themselves. They bought in their own names from brokers and dealers only, not directly from certificate holders; they alleged that they did not act on any inside or secret information, and that they consistently advised the certificate holders to keep their certificates rather than sell them. The average cost per certificate to the attorneys was less than 16 cents on the dollar. Distributions on the certificates amounted to nearly 56 cents on the dollar up to the time that the attorneys, who made a $22,000 profit on the certificates, requested in the final accounting a legal fee of $25,000, having previously received a legal fee of $10,000. The fee was objected to by the present certificate holders. On what grounds, do you think? What remedy (assuming they were successful) do you think the holders would get?

3. A medium-size law firm employed Jane Smith as an associate attorney seven years ago. During that time she came to work almost exclusively with the Acme Corporation, a major client of the firm. The work nominally was done under the supervision of one of the senior partners of the firm, who signed the opinion letters, attended the closings, and so forth, but actually was done by Smith, and the officers of Acme knew this.

About three months ago Smith inquired about partnership status for herself and was curtly informed, "We don't respond to associates' requests about such matters." Offended, Smith decided to quit. Before quitting, she telephoned several of the key officers of Acme with whom she had worked extensively, told them she was leaving to enter her own practice, and said, "I would be delighted, of course, to continue handling your work." The officers decided to keep their business with her and accordingly withdrew their account from the firm. One of the partners of the firm has come to you for advice as to what, if anything, they can do about this. What is your advice?

a. What difference would it make if Smith had first left the firm and then made her telephone calls to the Acme officers?

b. Would it affect your analysis of the above facts if Smith had brought the client into the firm in the first place?

c. What difference would it make if, instead of only one person, five associates quit together to establish their own practice, the other facts and variations remaining the same?

4. F.W. Enwright was a part-time reporter for the Lynn Publishing Company, which published a daily newspaper. The Company leased the basement and first floor of a building in the town of Lynn. It had substantial amounts of heavy equipment in the basement, including a press embedded in concrete that would take two weeks to move at considerable expense.

Enwright was given an assignment to write a story on the rental market in Lynn. In the process of researching the story, he talked to an officer of the International Trust Company, the lessor of the building, and learned that the newspaper's lease was about to expire. The newspaper was in economic trouble and was behind on its rent. Enwright persuaded the lessor to grant a new lease to him. Upon obtaining the lease, he gave the publishers notice to quit.

The publishers do not intend to leave. They have come to you for advice. What arguments would you make in their behalf? Would you advise your clients that you have a good chance of succeeding? *See Essex Trust v. Enwright*, 214 Mass. 507, 102 N.E. 441 (1913).

a. Would it change your analysis if Enwright had learned of the imminent expiration of the lease by seeing a "For Lease" sign on the main entrance to the building while going to work one day? What if he had seen a sign saying "Premises for Lease" (and specifying the building in question) in a window of the International Trust Company while taking a Sunday stroll?

b. Would it affect your analysis if Enwright had been a trustee for the newspaper rather than a part-time reporter? If he had been the janitor for the paper and had discovered the facts (i) by overhearing a conversation between an officer of the lessor and the office manager of the newspaper, or (ii) by seeing documents disclosing the lease situation while emptying the trash from the office of the office manager?

Chapter 3

Vicarious Tort Liability

A. The Master-Servant Relationship

1. The Concept

It is accepted doctrine that one is liable for the damages caused when directing or participating in the commission of a tort by someone else. Thus, if an employer directs an employee to restrain physically an obviously innocent customer or to arrange a display containing dangerous objects in a negligent manner, or participates in this, and someone is injured as a result, the liability of the employer to the injured person is clear. *See* Restatement (Second) § 212; *Smith v. Thompson*, 655 P.2d 116, 118 (Idaho App. 1982) ("All persons who command, . . . aid or abet the commission of a trespass by another are co trespassers with the person committing the trespass.")

But the above is not *vicarious* liability, is it? Webster's International Dictionary, Second Edition, defines "vicarious" as "of or pertaining to a vicar, substitute or deputy" and notes that it is derived from the Latin word "vicarius," meaning the place or office of one person as assumed by another. These definitions would lead one to infer that vicarious liability is some form of substitute liability for the employer. It is technically more accurate, however, to describe vicarious liability as liability *in addition* to the liability of the employee, who remains personally liable for tortious conduct, as will be developed below.

Suppose, for example, that the employee described above restrained the customer or negligently arranged the display and someone was injured, but the employer was absent, knew nothing of this, and had instructed the employee to always be careful. Could you reasonably argue that nevertheless the employer should be held liable for the harm caused? What sort of argument would you make?

Jones v. Hart

Court of King's Bench
Holt K.B. 642, 90 Eng. Rep. 1255 (1698)

A servant to a pawn-broker took in goods, and the party came and tendered the money to the servant, who said he had lost the goods. Upon this, action of trover was brought against the master; and the question was, whether it would lie or not?

HOLT C.J. The action well lies in this case: If the servants of A. with his cart run against another cart, wherein is a pipe of wine, and overturn the cart and spoil the wine, an action lieth against A. So where a carter's servant runs his cart over a boy, action lies against the master for the damage done by this negligence: and so it is if a smith's man pricks a horse in shoeing, the master is liable. For whoever employs another, is answerable for him, and undertakes for his care to all that make use of him.

The act of a servant is the act of his master, where he acts by authority of the master.

Notes

1. Chief Justice Holt's statement that "whoever employs another, is answerable for him," is commonly cited as the beginning of the modern law of vicarious liability. Prior to that time a master could not be made liable for his servant's torts unless the servant had "special authority" to do the act that caused damage to the plaintiff. The following language from *Kingston v. Booth*, Skinner 228, 90 Eng. Rep. 105 (1685), expressed the policy underlying the special authority rule: "If I command my servant to do what is lawful, and he misbehave himself or do more, I shall not answer for my servant, but my servant for himself, for that it was his own act; otherwise it was in the power of every servant to subject his master to what actions or penalties he pleased." Although this language has some rhetorical force, the law moved in a different direction with *Jones v. Hart*.

Note that *Jones v. Hart* was decided almost 300 years ago and that the court talked of imposing strict liability on masters, in that they would be subject to liability for the negligence of their servants without any inquiry into the nature of their conduct toward their servants or the injured third party. This form of vicarious liability is usually referred to as respondeat superior (let the master answer) liability. The maxim, *qui facit per alium facit per se* (he who acts through another acts himself) reflects this concept.

2. The words "master" and "servant" used by Chief Justice Holt are passé today in ordinary speech but retain significance in the law as terms of art used to describe the two parties involved in this common form of vicarious liability. This usage is reflected in the following Restatement (Second) of Agency definition of these words. The independent contractor concept mentioned below will be developed in Section 2 of this subchapter.

§ 2 Master; Servant; Independent Contractor

(1) A master is a principal who employs an agent to perform service in his affairs and who controls or has the right to control the physical conduct of the other in the performance of the service.

(2) A servant is an agent employed by a master to perform service in his affairs whose physical conduct in the performance of the service is controlled or is subject to the right to control by the master.

(3) An independent contractor is a person who contracts with another to do something for him but who is not controlled by the other nor subject to

the other's right to control with respect to his physical conduct in the performance of the undertaking. He may or may not be an agent.

Comment:

b. Servant contrasted with independent contractor. The word "servant" is used in contrast with "independent contractor." The latter term includes all persons who contract to do something for another but who are not servants in doing the work undertaken. An agent who is not a servant is, therefore, an independent contractor when he contracts to act on account of the principal. Thus, a broker who contracts to sell goods for his principal is an independent contractor as distinguished from a servant. Although, under some circumstances, the principal is bound by the broker's unauthorized contracts and representations, the principal is not liable to third persons for tangible harm resulting from his unauthorized physical conduct within the scope of the employment, as the principal would be for similar conduct by a servant; nor does the principal have the duties or immunities of a master towards the broker. Although an agent who contracts to act and who is not a servant is therefore an independent contractor, not all independent contractors are agents. Thus, one who contracts for a stipulated price to build a house for another and who reserves [is subject to? — Ed.] no direction over the conduct of the work is an independent contractor; but he is not an agent, since he is not a fiduciary, has no power to make the one employing him a party to a transaction, and is subject to no control over his conduct.

3. As noted in § 2 of the Restatement (Second) quoted above, the word "master" is included within the broader word "principal." The same is true for the words "servant" and "agent." The use of these terms of art, while widespread, is not universal nor is court usage always consistent. Sometimes, for example, a court will use the broad word "agent" to refer to the type of agent known as a servant. (See *Arsand v. City of Franklin*, 83 Wis. 2d 40, 264 N.W.2d 579 (1978), for a careful opinion distinguishing between the words "agent" and "servant," and reversing a trial court judgment for improper use of the word "agent" in its instructions to the jury.) It will be necessary for the reader to glean the narrower meaning from the context of the language. Also, the words "employer" and "employee" are frequently used today in place of master and servant and will sometimes be so used in these materials.

4. As noted in the Glossary, the Restatement (Third) of Agency abandons the terms "master" and "servant." In their place, the new Restatement uses the terms employer and employee. It is important to note, however, that the terms employer and employee are specially defined terms for purposes of vicarious liability. Restatement (Third) § 7.07 defines such an employee as "an agent whose principal controls or has the right to control the manner and means of the agent's performance of work." The section goes on to provide that "the fact that work is performed gratuitously does not relieve a principal of liability." Thus, it is clear that a principal may be vicariously liable for the torts of its agent even if the agent is not, *for other purposes*, an "employee" of the principal.

The definition of "servant" in the Restatement (Second) was substantially the same as the Restatement (Third) definition of "employee." The shift from servant to employee has the advantage of removing from the legal discourse a term (servant) that carries some unwanted implications. However, its replacement (employee) is less than ideal because employee is a well-accepted term that suggests a compensated relationship with certain responsibilities accruing the employer (such as paying employment taxes, providing worker's compensation insurance, etc.). In addition to the problem of uncompensated agents, there are some cases in which employers are not liable for the torts of their employees because the employer lacks the necessary control over the employee. This concept is developed more fully below.

Nevertheless, as a matter of fact, in most cases in which a principal has the necessary degree of control over its agent to result in vicarious liability, the agent will be an employee for all purposes. And the instances in which a true employer lacks the necessary control over its employees to result in vicarious liability are rare. Indeed, many courts today classify an employee as a servant even when the employer does not actually exercise control over physical conduct due to the specialized nature of the work of the employee, like lawyers or doctors working full-time for one employer. Those courts seem to be creating a conclusive presumption that full-time employment creates a *right* of control over physical conduct, which satisfies the test for respondeat superior liability. Whether the courts will embrace this new terminology, however, remains to be seen.

5. The decision whether a master-servant or employer-employee relationship exists in a particular case normally is made by the trier of fact. "If the inference is clear that there is, or is not, a master and servant relation, it is made by the court; otherwise the jury determines the question after instruction by the court as to the matters of fact to be considered." Restatement (Second) § 220, cmt. c.

6. Is the president of General Motors a servant for some purposes? See Restatement (Third) § 7.07, cmt. f: "[S]enior corporate officers, like captains of ships, may exercise great discretion in operating the enterprises entrusted to them, just as skilled professionals exercise discretion in performing their work. Nonetheless, all employers retain a right of control, however infrequently exercised."

7. *Another view of* Jones v. Hart. T. BATY, VICARIOUS LIABILITY 24–25 (1916), states the following with regard to *Jones v. Hart*:

> The importance of *Jones v. Hart* lies in its dicta, and not in its decision. The reporter nonchalantly introduces into his memorandum . . . an account of certain dicta of Holt, to the effect that *A*'s servant runs with his cart against another cart, or against a boy, and spoils a barrel of sack in the one case, or injures the passerby in the other. Here, at nisi prius,[1] with

1. *Nisi prius* refers to a trial court proceeding. *See* BLACK'S LAW DICTIONARY (6th ed. 1990).

his fancies unchecked by other lawyers, Holt clearly lays down the modern principle, which thus rests on the precarious foundation of an obiter dictum in a nisi prius case.

The actual case itself is, so far as its own facts are concerned, a case of contract. A pawnbroker's servant took an article in pledge, and a contract thereupon arose between the broker and the pledger. When the latter, through the servant's default, was unable to restore the goods he was of course liable. The gist of the action was, however, not assumpsit but trover; and this contributed to reinforce the notion of the master's liability for all torts of his servant committed in the course of employment.[2]

8. *Liability of the employee.* As noted above, an employee is personally liable for affirmative acts of wrongdoing committed while acting on behalf of the employer. Acting as an employee does not somehow confer personal immunity on the acting party. *See* Restatement (Third) §7.01; Seavey, *Liability of an Agent in Tort*, 1 So. L.Q. 16 (1916), *reprinted in* W. SEAVEY, STUDIES IN AGENCY 1–27 (1949); *United States v. Hull*, 195 F.2d 64 (1st Cir. 1952); *Lane v. Cotton*, 12 Mod. 472, 88 Eng. Rep. 1458 (1701). To find otherwise would be to take the fiction of identification of principal and agent (that the agent is simply the alter ego of the principal) to an extreme that no court or commentator has recognized. See the excerpt immediately below from Holmes, discussing his view of the role of the fiction of identification in the history of agency.

A more troubling question involves the personal liability of an agent for nonfeasance where the agent fails to perform a duty owed to the principal, such as a failure to repair certain property of the principal contrary to instructions, and a person is injured as a result. A well-known and frequently quoted case held an agent not liable under such circumstances, based on both common law and civil law principles. *Delaney v. Rochereau & Co.*, 34 La. Ann. 1123, 1128, 44 Am. Rep. 456, 457–58 (1882), saying: "At common law, an agent is personally responsible to third parties for doing something which he ought not to have done, but not for not doing something which he ought to have done, the agent, in the latter case, being liable to his principal only. . . . No man increases or diminishes his obligations to strangers by becoming an agent." The "increases" aspect of this view is criticized by Seavey in the article cited above, principally by stressing the control that an agent may have under some circumstances because of the agency status (such as being in control of property), which should create a duty of care toward strangers under such circumstances. Not all courts recognize the misfeasance/nonfeasance distinction, at least in the case of personal injury. See, e.g., *Estate of Countryman*, 679 N.W.2d 598 (Iowa 2004), which is discussed, *infra*, Chapter 15, Section F.

---

2. Trover is an action in damages to recover the value of goods wrongfully appropriated by another. Assumpsit is a suit for breach of contract.

a. The History of Respondeat Superior Liability

i. The Holmes Thesis

Oliver Wendell Holmes, Jr., *Agency*, 4 HARV. L. REV. 345, 347–51 (1891), advances the following thesis on the history of respondeat superior liability:

> [I]t is plain good sense to hold people answerable for wrongs which they have intentionally brought to pass, and to recognize that it is just as possible to bring wrongs to pass through free human agents as through slaves, animals, or natural forces. This is the true scope and meaning of *"Qui facit per alium facit per se,"* and the English law has recognized that maxim as far back as it is worth while to follow it. . . . In such cases there is nothing peculiar to master and servant; similar principles have been applied where independent contractors were employed. . . .
>
> If agency is a proper title of our *corpus juris*, its peculiarities must be sought in doctrines that go farther than any yet mentioned. Such doctrines are to be found in each of the great departments of the law. In tort, masters are held answerable for conduct on the part of their servants, which they not only have not authorized, but have forbidden. . . .
>
> There is an antecedent probability that the *patria potestas*[3] has exerted an influence at least upon existing rules. I have endeavored to prove elsewhere that the unlimited liability of an owner for the torts of his slave grew out of what had been merely a privilege of buying him off from a surrender to the vengeance of the offended party, in both the early Roman and the early German law. I have shown, also, how the unlimited liability thus established was extended by the praetor in certain cases to the misconduct of free servants. Of course it is unlikely that the doctrines of our two parent systems should have been without effect upon their offspring, the common law.
>
> It will be easy to see how this tended toward a fictitious identification of agent with principal, although within the limits to which it confined agency the Roman law had little need and made little use of the fiction. . . . The fiction is merely a convenient way of expressing rules which were arrived at on other grounds. The Roman praetor did not make innkeepers answerable for their servants because "the act of the servant was the act of the master," any more than because they had been negligent in choosing them. He

---

3. [For an explanation of the concept of *patria potestas*, see W. Buckland, A Text-book of Roman Law 599–601 (3d ed. 1963) ("We have now to consider the circumstances in which one might be responsible for another's delict. . . . [T]here was what was called noxal liability for delicts committed by members of the familia, i.e., liability either to pay the damages or to hand over the offender. . . . The master's liability depended on his having potestas, which here meant power to produce the slave. If, when sued, he would not defend, his proper course was to produce the man . . . which released the master."). — Eds.]

did so on substantive grounds of policy — because of the special confidence necessarily reposed in innkeepers. . . .

But when such a formula is adopted, it soon acquires an independent standing of its own. Instead of remaining only a short way of saying that when from policy the law makes a master responsible for his servant, . . . the formula becomes a reason in itself for making the master answerable and for giving him rights. If "the act of the servant is the act of the master," or master and servant are "considered as one person," then the master must pay for the act if it is wrongful, and has the advantage of it if it is right. And the mere habit of using these phrases, where the master is bound or benefited by his servant's act, makes it likely that other cases will be brought within the penumbra of the same thought on no more substantial ground than the way of thinking which the words have brought about.

ii. The Wigmore Rebuttal

John Wigmore, *Responsibility for Tortious Acts: Its History*, 7 Harv. L. Rev. 315, 330–36, 391–99 (1894), offers a different view of the history of respondeat superior liability, as reflected in the following passages from his article.

There was certainly a time when the master bore full responsibility for the harmful acts of his serf or his domestic. It is worth while to emphasize this by quoting [the following] passage. . . .

". . . According to Germanic law . . . the house-master was responsible to third persons for those attached to his house. This responsibility extended not merely to bondsmen, but also to half-free and free persons. If a free but landless man remained for some time in the house of another, he acquired a relation of dependency which established the responsibility of the house-master. . . . The responsibility for free persons shows itself in the form of a duty upon the master to answer for the freeman's misdeeds."

This responsibility disappeared in the case of freemen, as time went on, so that the master could relieve himself by handing them over to the regular courts. . . .

In Norman England we find this notion, "se hoc non conscium esse,"[4] . . . distinctly reappearing in the idea that it made a difference whether the master consented to or commanded the harm done by the servant or other member of his household. . . .

We see here going on the process of a general leavening by the principle of "se hoc non conscium esse"; and apparently we are safe in concluding that by the end of the 1200s . . . so far as any penal results were concerned, the master could pretty generally exonerate himself by pleading that he had not commanded or consented to the act. . . . As we shall see later, the test

---

4. [Freely translated, "This was not done with his knowledge." — Eds.]

of command or consent was soon after extended generally to civil liability also; and even in the 1200s we seem to see it coming. . . .

. . . Now, whether or not such a limited rule would have been desirable, it is certain that the circumstances of the time [of Lord Holt] forced upon the judges a serious consideration of the expediencies of such a rule. The nation was reaping in commercial fields the harvest of prosperity sown in the Elizabethan age and destined to show fullest fruition in the age of Anne. The conditions of industry and commerce were growing so complicated, and the original undertaker and employer might now be so far separated from the immediate doer, that the decision of questions of masters' liability must radically affect the conduct of business affairs in a way now for the first time particularly appreciated. . . . "Whoever employs another is answerable"; "acting in the execution of authority"; "acting for the master's benefit"; "being about the master's business,"—these appear as tentative expressions in the general effort to re-state on a rational basis. . . .

. . . So that what we have to remember about the employment of the . . . fiction of Identification, in the history of the present doctrine, is, (1) that it was merely a reason, an easy, lazy reason, which was put forth to sanction and support a rule of whose practical expediency the Courts were perfectly satisfied; (2) that it was merely one of several reasons, and by no means the most common, and that, in short, the rule would have stood substantially as it does now, if all reference to the Identification fiction were wanting. In what may be taken as the next stage, the balance is seen to change gradually; the Command test disappears as a regular one, and "scope of employment" and its congeners come into full control.

b. Is an Employment Relationship Necessary to Respondeat Superior Liability?

It is clear from *Jones v. Hart* that an employment relationship immediately raises the possibility of vicarious liability for the employer. Is, however, an employer-employee relationship *the* threshold to respondeat superior liability? In other words, does a person run the risk of vicarious liability only by the act of hiring someone else to work for her? Should this be the law, if it is not?

Assume, for example, that *B* drove some friends to her summer cabin in order to show off the freshly stocked private pond that she recently had constructed. She left the car with the keys in it 500 feet down the road and walked in with one of the friends in order to check that the road was safe. After she ascertained that it was in good condition, her accompanying friend said, "I'll drive in the others." *B* nodded approval. Her friend, unfortunately, drove badly and turned the car over, seriously injuring one of the other occupants.

It is obvious that the friend is liable for her own negligence. The interesting question, though, is whether *B* is also liable.

Heims v. Hanke

Supreme Court of Wisconsin
93 N.W.2d 455 (1958)

Action for personal injuries sustained when plaintiff slipped and fell on a patch of ice on a sidewalk. The case was tried by the court without a jury, and . . . judgment was entered for the plaintiff. Defendant appeals.

The accident occurred about 11 A.M. on April 3, 1954, when the temperature was below freezing. A few minutes before the accident, defendant had finished washing his car at the street curb across the sidewalk from a house which he owned. His sixteen-year-old nephew, William Hanke, helped him as an unpaid volunteer. Defendant washed the street side of the car and William the side next to the curb. Water was obtained by the pailful from a faucet on the outside of the house across the sidewalk. The court found on sufficient evidence that defendant several times requested or directed William to get more water, and William did so, and that in carrying the water from the faucet to the automobile some of it was spilled on the sidewalk, where it froze. After the car washing was finished and defendant and William had left and the water had frozen, plaintiff walked along the sidewalk in an easterly direction, failed to see the ice, and slipped and fell on it.

WINGERT, J.

Appellant contends that there was no evidence of actionable negligence on his part, that William's negligence, if any, could not properly be imputed to defendant, that no nuisance was established, that plaintiff's negligence was the sole cause of the accident, and that the trial court erred in excluding certain evidence.

1. *Defendant's negligence.* The finding that the icy condition of the sidewalk was caused by the negligence of the defendant is supported by sufficient evidence.

The court could properly find that William, the nephew, was negligent in spilling water on the sidewalk in freezing weather and doing nothing to prevent the formation of ice or to remove or sand it, or to warn pedestrians of it. While the day was not too cold for washing a car barehanded, the car was in the bright sunlight while the sidewalk where the water was spilled was then or soon would be in the shade of the house. The court could well infer that one in the exercise of ordinary care would have foreseen the formation of a slippery condition and would have done something to protect users of the sidewalk.

It was also permissible to conclude from the evidence that defendant was liable for injuries resulting from William's negligence, on the principle *respondeat superior.* Probably William was defendant's servant in carrying the water. A servant is one employed to perform service for another in his affairs and who, with respect to his physical conduct in the performance of the service, is subject to the other's control or right to control. Restatement, 1 Agency (2d), p. 485, sec. 220. The evidence permits the inference that William was in that category, although he was an unpaid volunteer. One volunteering service without any agreement for or expectation of reward may be a servant of the one accepting such services. Restatement, 1 Agency (2d), p. 497, sec. 225. The illustration given in comment *a* under that section is pertinent:

> A, a social guest at P's house, not skilled in repairing, volunteers to assist P in the repair of P's house. During the execution of such repair, A negligently drops a board upon a person passing upon the street. A may be found to be a servant of P.

Since the finding of negligence attributable to defendant is sustainable, there is no need to consider whether the condition constituted a nuisance. . . .[5]

Judgment affirmed.

Sandrock v. Taylor

Supreme Court of Nebraska
174 N.W.2d 186 (1970)

McCown, J.

This is an action for damages for the death of the plaintiff's decedent in a motor vehicle accident at a country road intersection. . . .

The decedent, George B. Sandrock, was a guest passenger in an automobile driven by the defendant Casper B. Meirose. The Meirose car was proceeding north. The defendant Robert L. Taylor was driving a partially loaded milk tank truck in a westerly direction. . . . The two vehicles collided approximately in the center of the intersection and George B. Sandrock was killed. . . .

The jury brought in a verdict of $46,712 against all defendants, and all defendants have appealed. . . .

The next group of assignments of error rest on the premise that the negligence of the defendant Meirose should have been imputed to the plaintiff's decedent, and that the negligence of Meirose barred any recovery by the plaintiff.

The defendant Meirose resided in the buildings on his farm but leased the farm land to his son, who lived on a nearby farm. The decedent Sandrock also lived on a nearby farm and exchanged work with Meirose's son. On the date of the accident, the decedent Sandrock was helping the younger Meirose mow hay when a part on Sandrock's mower broke. After the noon meal, Sandrock asked the defendant Meirose to take him to town. Meirose agreed to take Sandrock to town so that Sandrock could get the broken part repaired. There was no other purpose for the trip.

---

5. [The omitted material contains, among other matters, language dealing with the scope of liability of a doctor who subsequently aggravated the plaintiff's injuries due to malpractice. Such language was overturned by the Wisconsin Supreme Court in *Butzow v. Wausau Memorial Hosp.*, 51 Wis. 2d 281, 187 N.W.2d 349 (1971). The agency aspect of the *Heims* case was not relevant to or discussed in *Butzow.* — Eds.]

On the basis of these facts, Taylor and Co-op contend that the defendant Meirose was acting as an agent on behalf of Sandrock and subject to Sandrock's direction and control and solely for Sandrock's purposes and benefit. Therefore, they assert that Meirose's negligence is imputed to Sandrock and bars any recovery as against them.

This case was tried and the instructions were given on the basis of a host-guest relationship rather than that of agent and principal. [The court quotes §1 of the Restatement (Second).]

There is no evidence here that the transportation was anything but gratuitous, resulting from a friendly and neighborly favor. There is no evidence of any mutual understanding that Sandrock had any right or power to control Meirose's operation of the car, nor that Meirose consented to act subject to Sandrock's control. There is no evidence whatever that Sandrock exercised or attempted to exercise any direction or control over the operation of the car. The fact that Sandrock requested the ride is not controlling.

This state, for many years, has followed the rule that the negligence of a driver is not imputable to a passenger except where the driver is the servant or agent of the passenger, or where the driver and passenger are engaged in a joint enterprise or where the passenger assumes to direct operation of the automobile and to exercise control over it. See *Petersen v. Schneider*, 154 Neb. 303, 47 N.W.2d 863. Such cases probably reflect the view that ordinarily an agency does not arise out of purely social relationships. The rule of nonimputation of negligence has been extended to cases where an owner is a passenger in his own automobile. See *Petersen v. Schneider, supra.* Unless some relationship existed between the passenger and the driver which gave a passenger authority to direct or assist in the operation of the automobile, a passenger has ordinarily been classified as a guest, and the negligence of a driver has not been imputed to the passenger. Where there is no evidence of a relationship between the driver of an automobile and a passenger other than that of a gratuitous social host and guest, the mere fact that the trip is for the passenger's benefit and that he happens to have a business purpose, does not make the driver a controlled agent and the passenger a controlling principal; and the negligence of the driver is not ordinarily imputable to the passenger.

The district court was correct in concluding that the defendant Meirose was a host driver and the decedent Sandrock a guest passenger. . . .

Notes

1. The court in dictum stated that the rule of nonimputation of negligence applies even in cases where the owner is a passenger in his own automobile. This is true, but the reader should be aware that some jurisdictions hold that ownership of the car by a passenger raises a rebuttable presumption of the agency of the driver. *Edlebeck v. Hooten*, 20 Wis. 2d 83, 121 N.W.2d 240 (1963).

2. *Biedenbach v. Teague*, 194 Pa. Super. 245, 166 A.2d 320 (1960), is a case involving a fact situation very similar to that presented immediately before the *Heims* case,

supra, dealing with the friend who volunteered to drive the car up to the cabin. The defendant-owner was held liable for the negligence of the friend who drove the car. See also *Baxter v. Morningside, Inc.*, 10 Wash. App. 893, 521 P.2d 946 (1974) (charitable organization vicariously liable for negligence of volunteer driver), citing cases in accord with the principle applied in *Heims. Accord General Acc. Group v. Frintzilas*, 111 Misc. 2d 306, 443 N.Y.S.2d 989 (1981) (defining "employed" as the act of performing services, even without wages).

3. Does it make any difference if the person who is gratuitously aiding the defendant acts for her own motives and not with an intention to help the defendant? Suppose, for example, that a car is stalled in traffic and another driver, Jones, gets out of her own car and assists in pushing the stalled car to the curb under the directions— limited as they are—of the owner of the stalled car. Is Jones the servant of the owner of the stalled car if her purpose is to remove an obstruction to her own progress down the street? Should this make any difference? See Restatement (Second) §225, Comment b, stating (without explanation) that it does. Why?

Suppose, on the other hand, that Jones intends to aid the owner of the stalled car, but the owner has not asked her to help. Would the owner be liable if Jones was negligent and somehow caused a loss?

4. Assume that a pilotage statute requires shipowners whose ships are entering or leaving port to accept the navigation services of licensed pilots who are not in the shipowner's employ. Is a shipowner liable for the negligence of a pilot during navigation of the ship under such circumstances? *See* Restatement (Second) §223, cmt. c (saying no). *Accord Societa per Azioni v. City of Los Angeles*, 31 Cal. 3d 446, 183 Cal. Rptr. 51, 645 P.2d 102 (1982). Do you see why there is no vicarious liability? (This situation should be distinguished from the converse situation where the actor is compelled to serve someone, like a convict serving a consenting person. There the person being served is subject to liability as if there were a master-servant relation. *See Kenai Peninsula Borough v. State*, 532 P.2d 1019 (Alaska 1975); Restatement (Second) §224.)

5. Control over physical conduct is important to a master-servant relationship. It is difficult to imagine a more genuine instance of such control than that of a construction foreman in charge of a crew of workers. Would the foreman be vicariously liable for the negligence of one of the workers while on duty that causes injury to a passerby? The answer is clearly no, isn't it? Do you see why? *See Strain v. Ferroni*, 592 A.2d 698, 704 (Pa. Super. 1991) ("[T]he right to supervise, even as to the work and the manner of performance, is not sufficient; otherwise a supervisory employee would be liable for the negligent act of another employee though he would not be the superior or master of that employee in the sense the law means it."). Would the foreman be subject to any standard of liability? If so, what standard, and why?

6. Vicarious liability can be imposed even when actual control over the tortfeasor at the time of the accident is absent. As noted in Warren A. Seavey, Studies in Agency 133 (1949), "The *de facto* control is frequently absent; the relationship having been created, it is convenient for the law to generalize and to extend the liability on the assumption that there is control."

7. An "employment" relationship can exist between two entities, and the argument is often made that, for purposes of respondeat superior, a franchisor is the employer or master of its franchisee. If successful, the franchisor would then be vicariously liable for the tortious conduct of the franchisee's employees. This argument is rarely successful, however, with courts often concluding that the franchisor cannot control the physical details of the franchisee's employees performance, even if the franchisor can set the standards applicable to that performance: "Setting those standards for a franchisee's employees and having the right to actually control how the franchisee's employees perform the physical details of driving are two different things." *Viado v. Domino's Pizza, LLC*, 217 P.3d 199 (Or. Ct. App. 2009).

8. The Texas courts have developed a theory of respondeat superior liability called "nonemployee mission liability." *See, Arvizu v. Estate of Puckett*, 364 S.W.3d 273 (Tex. 2012). Under this doctrine, respondeat superior liability can result when a person performs a service for another and is subject to that other's control. In the *Arvizu* case, a driver employed by an auto auctioneer negligently injured the plaintiff, who sued the auctioneer and the auctioneer's client, an auto dealer. The auto dealer, who owned the vehicle driven by the negligent driver, had instructed the auctioneer to deliver the vehicle to another auction house. On these facts, the jury found both the auctioneer and the auto dealer liable and the Texas Supreme Court upheld the judgment. The Court held that the relationship between the driver and the auto dealer was one of subagency; that is, the auto dealer was the principal, the auctioneer was the agent of the auto dealer, and the driver was a subagent. The negligence of the subagent was imputed to the remote principal. In this context, the term employed by the court—nonemployee mission liability—does not really add to a subagency analysis.

c. Rationale for Respondeat Superior

In considering the fairness of the imposition of respondeat superior liability, recall that in most jurisdictions the master (principal) has a right of indemnification against the wrongdoing servant (agent) for the losses sustained through vicarious liability. As noted in Chapter 2, this right usually is based on the principle of restitution that the party actually at fault in causing a loss should be the one ultimately to bear the loss.

i. Arguments Questioning the Theory

Oliver Wendell Holmes, Jr., *Agency*, 5 HARV. L. REV. 1, 14 (1891), states the following opinion on respondeat superior liability:

> I assume that common-sense is opposed to making one man pay for another man's wrong, unless he actually has brought the wrong to pass according to the ordinary canons of legal responsibility,—unless, that is to say, he has induced the immediate wrong-doer to do acts of which the wrong, or, at

least, wrong, was the natural consequence under the circumstances known to the defendant. . . . I therefore assume that common sense is opposed to the fundamental theory of agency, although I have no doubt that the possible explanations of its various rules which I suggested at the beginning of this chapter,[6] together with the fact that the most flagrant of them now-a-days often presents itself as a seemingly wholesome check on the indifference and negligence of great corporations, have done much to reconcile men's minds to that theory.

T. BATY, VICARIOUS LIABILITY (1916), cited in the notes following *Jones v. Hart, supra,* is a small and provocative book that criticizes the adoption of respondeat superior liability. Although the concept of respondeat superior liability is no longer questioned, serious issues exist as to how far the doctrine should be carried, as you will see in the sections to come. In that sense, the distinctions and criticisms of Baty are relevant today even beyond their importance as a part of the history of this doctrine. The following excerpts from pages 7–13 of his book will serve to introduce his thesis.

> The earliest real trace of any broad principle that the employer is liable for the unauthorized acts of his employee perpetrated "within the scope," as the ironical phrase goes, "of his employment," appears to be found in the . . . case of *Hern v. Nichols* (1709) 1 Salk. 289, decided by Lord Holt. This case is quoted . . . as the earliest authority for the proposition in question. But it seems to fall very far short of it.
>
> For what were the facts in *Hern v. Nichols?* Simply these: that a merchant had entrusted goods (silk) to an agent abroad; the agent sold them with an incidental fraud, representing them to be of different and superior quality. The purchaser brought an action of "deceit," i.e. fraud. It was doubted whether it lay properly against the merchant. Holt C. J. decided — at nisi prius — that it did, and that the merchant was liable *civiliter* (though not *criminaliter*): "For, seeing somebody must be a loser by this deceit, it is more reason that he that employs and puts a trust and confidence in the deceiver, should be a loser, than a stranger." . . .
>
> It was decided expressly on the ground of confidence. Two persons had reposed confidence in the factor — the seller and the buyer. . . . Holt's language in *Hern v. Nichols* might lead a superficial reader to conclude that only the principal had reposed "trust and confidence" in the agent — of course the buyer must have done so, otherwise the gist of the action of deceit would be gone. . . . In what Holt says, stress must be laid on the word "employs." The principal employs the agent, trusts him, and induces other people to trust him.

---

6. [See the section on the history of respondeat superior liability, *supra.* — Eds.]

. . . If a merchant invites other people to repose confidence in, and to make contracts with, his agent, he cannot be surprised if he is called upon to justify that confidence and to fulfil those contracts. . . .

The principle thus emerges that, alike in questions of contract and confidence, it is the individual relation between the principal and the third party, created by this invitation of confidence, which is the foundation of liability should it prove misplaced. . . .

This explains the liability of innkeepers for the torts of their servants. Innkeepers invite the public to rely on the safety and honesty of their houses. . . .

Unfortunately, when the time came to put limits on the doctrine flowing from *Hern v. Nichols*, the limitation was not founded on the fact of a subsisting relation, invited by the principal, and carrying with it an invitation to trust the agent; but on that of the acts having been committed "in the course of employment."

Unfortunately: because the whole sense of the rule is thus departed from. When an agent's employment is to make contracts, the principal knows that he will make contracts. He knows that he may make unprofitable contracts, stupid contracts — and he takes that risk. But he takes no incalculable risks. The risk of the contracts involving loss are measurable: They are limited by the common usage of business people. The invitation to confide is solely an invitation to confide within business limits.

. . . You clothe a factor with credit, and he may involve you up to the hilt of that credit. But if you clothe a coachman with livery he may involve you in damages without any limit whatever.

The moral foundation of the rule also disappears. Instead of sustaining a credit which you have deliberately invited, you are asked to compensate a casual stranger between whom and yourself there is no privity — no moral responsibility — whatever. In the one case, you have invited me to trust your agent: he has deceived me: you are responsible. In the other, you have invited no confidence, and have entered into no moral bond for his good behaviour. [Baty noted in a prior passage that, "The owner of a carriage does not invite the public to use the roads in reliance on the care and skill of his coachman."]

Baty suggested that the real basis for respondeat superior is that servants ordinarily are impecunious and masters usually solvent. Thus, satisfaction of the judgment is the goal. "[T]he damages are taken from a deep pocket." *Id.* at 154. Similarly, see Glanville Williams, *Vicarious Liability and the Master's Indemnity*, 20 Mod. L. Rev. 220, 232 (1957):

What other theory is there? Well, there is the purely cynical theory that the master is liable because he has a purse worth opening. The master is frequently rich, and he is usually insured—two arguments that might be used by any burglar, if he ever troubled to justify his thefts. The strange thing is to find them put forward by judges of eminence.

ii. Arguments in Favor of or Explanations for the Theory

Professor Warren Seavey, one of the principal architects of modern agency law,[7] stated his position on the legitimacy of vicarious tort liability in *Speculations as to "Respondeat Superior,"* Harv. Legal Essays 433, 447 (1934), *reprinted in* W. SEAVEY, STUDIES IN AGENCY 129, 147 (1949), from which the following excerpt is taken:

> Perhaps the strongest reason which can be given for the imposition of "absolute" liability applies even more strongly in the case of vicarious liability, that is, the fact that one who is responsible for all consequences is more apt to take precautions to prevent injurious consequences from arising. If the law requires a perfect score in result, the actor is more likely to strive for that than if the law requires only the ordinary precautions to be taken. . . .
>
> Another reason for liability without fault in many cases is the difficulty of proving negligence. This reason is particularly cogent in imposing liability upon a master. Whether an employee was unfit at the time of the accident or whether there was improper supervision would ordinarily have to be proved by the testimony of fellow workers. Truthful testimony in such cases is difficult to obtain from the members of a well-disciplined organization. Aside from self-interest, which is obvious, only disgruntled fellow-workers are likely to subject themselves to the name commonly applied to a "tattle tale" within the organization.

See also Posner, *A Theory of Negligence*, 1 J. LEGAL STUD. 29, 43 (1972), noting that under a negligence system the courts would have "to regulate in great detail the company's method of selecting, supervising, and disciplining employees" and suggesting that this is why strict liability was chosen.

Professor Young B. Smith of Columbia Law School justified the existence of respondeat superior liability on the ground that "it is socially more expedient to spread or distribute among a large group of the community the losses which experience has taught are inevitable in the carrying on of industry, than to cast the loss upon a few; . . . the master should be made responsible not merely because he is better able to pay, but because he is best able to effectuate the spreading (by means of insurance) and the distribution (by enhanced price) of such losses." *Frolic and Detour*, 23 COLUM. L. REV. 444, 716 (1923). This rationale is sometimes referred to as the entrepreneur theory.

---

7. Professor Seavey was the Reporter for the first two editions of the Restatement of Agency (as noted earlier, the first edition was published in 1933; the second in 1958). He authored a short hornbook on the law of agency in 1964, and wrote a number of articles on the subject, most of which are reprinted in his book STUDIES IN AGENCY (1949). (The Reporter for Restatement (Third) of Agency (2006) was Professor Deborah DeMott.)

See also Gary T. Schwartz, *The Hidden and Fundamental Issue of Employer Vicarious Liability*, 69 So. Cal. L. Rev. 1739 (1996); Alan O. Sykes, *The Economics of Vicarious Liability*, 93 Yale L.J. 1231 (1984); Guido Calabresi, *Some Thoughts on Risk Distribution and the Law of Torts*, 70 Yale L.J. 499 (1961); 1939 N.Y. L. Rev. Comm'n 616–31; Douglas, *Vicarious Liability and Administration of Risk I and II*, 38 Yale L.J. 584, 720 (1929); Laski, *The Basis of Vicarious Liability*, 26 Yale L.J. 105 (1916).

d. Imputed Contributory Negligence

In discussing vicarious liability, the preceding materials dealt with imputed negligence. Under what circumstances does the master-servant relationship have a bearing on imputed *contributory* negligence?

The widely adopted rule is that a master is barred from recovery against a third person who negligently caused a loss to the master if the servant also was negligent in the accident giving rise to the loss. Restatement (Second) of Agency § 317. (You may recall that the concept of imputed contributory negligence was involved in *Jones v. Taylor*, the agency versus bailment case in Chapter 1, and in *Sandrock v. Taylor*.) Does this rule make sense? The immediately preceding materials have summarized some of the painstaking efforts that have been made to explain the imputed negligence involved in vicarious liability. In reviewing these arguments, are they equally persuasive (or unpersuasive) with the matter of contributory negligence in mind?

In *Weber v. Stokely-Van Camp*, 274 Minn. 482, 144 N.W.2d 540 (1966), the "both ways" test (if negligence is imputed, so is contributory negligence) set forth above in the Restatement (Second) and in earlier Minnesota cases was rejected. The court held that an employer who was injured while riding with his employee could recover against the negligent driver of the other vehicle even though his employee was contributorily negligent. The "both ways" test was criticized as illogical and unfair. The court identified the deep pocket theory as the underlying policy of vicarious liability; it then noted that it makes no sense to use this theory to block a suit *by* the employer. Thus the court concluded that the "both ways" test should be rejected. Accord *Reed v. Hinderland*, 135 Ariz. 213, 660 P.2d 464, 37 A.L.R.4th 555 (1983) (citing cases from several states joining *Weber* in rejecting imputed contributory negligence) and *State v. Popricki*, 89 A.D.2d 391, 456 N.Y.S.2d 850, 851 (1982), where the court stated:

> These cases repudiated the doctrine of imputed contributory negligence, particularly where the passenger-owner sued for damages, because the doctrine relies on the implausible fiction that the owner has control over the operator's conduct. In our view, no tenable justification exists to retain imputed contributory negligence. . . . We agree that theoretical control fails to justify the [doctrine].

e. Limitation to Losses Caused by Tortious Behavior

Liability under respondeat superior is limited to the tortious acts of servants. Some commentators have argued that an employer's liability should also include nontortious harms committed by employees in the course of their employment so long, at least, as such harms are predictably recurring losses caused by the enterprise. *See* Guido Calabresi, *Some Thoughts on Risk Distribution and the Law of Torts*, 70 YALE L.J. 499, 544–45 (1961).

For an interesting discussion supporting the existing status of the law, see CLARENCE MORRIS, TORTS 254–55 (1953). Morris takes the position that a substantial justification for respondeat superior liability is that it provides an incentive for masters to exercise their "considerable measure of control over [the] lives of their workmen" and to discipline them for misconduct. This incentive is not present when the behavior of the servant is nonfaulty. Morris argues that this fact, combined with the fact that the master's risk-bearing capacity is sometimes not superior to that of the injured third person, supplies a reason for hesitating to extend liability to losses caused by nonfaultworthy behavior.

f. Direct Tort Liability of an Employer

Although direct tort liability is more properly a topic for the torts course, the tort of negligently hiring an employee is often involved as an additional claim in vicarious liability cases, especially those involving intentional torts. It comes up with sufficient frequency that it is worth a brief reference. In general, see *Bryant v. Better Bus. Bureau of Greater Md.*, 923 F. Supp. 720, 751 (D. Md. 1996), stating, "[T]here is a rebuttable presumption that an employer uses due care in hiring an employee." Nevertheless, with regard to specific situations, see *Williams v. Feather Sound, Inc.*, 386 So. 2d 1238 (Fla. App. 1986), involving a suit against a condominium developer arising out of an assault against a homeowner in her home by an employee of the developer. The court discussed the scope of an employer's duty to check into the character of applicants for employment. The court differentiated between an employee hired to do only outside work (no duty to inquire beyond information supplied by the applicant for the job) and one who will have access to the inside of homes (a duty to make an independent inquiry exists). The court held that an employer is chargeable with such information concerning the more trusted employee's background as it could have obtained upon reasonable inquiry.

2. The Independent Contractor Exception

a. The Concept

A local bank does all its considerable legal business through Jones, a partner in a partnership of seven lawyers. One day Jones, while driving directly from her office to the courthouse solely in order to represent the bank in a lawsuit, negligently drives into and injures Smith. Is the bank vicariously liable to Smith for the negligence of Jones? What argument would you make that the bank should not be held liable?

As the material already covered makes clear, you run a risk of liability if you hire a neighborhood boy to mow your yard using your mower and he negligently injures someone while throwing an impeding object off of your yard during the mowing job. Suppose, however, that the same negligent act takes place but the person doing it was an employee of Ace Lawn Service, a large company that specializes in lawn care, supplying its own tools and equipment, but also installs fences, removes trees, and so forth. Can you think of any reason why you would not be held liable for the harm caused by Ace Lawn Service?

Kane Furniture Corp. v. Miranda

Court of Appeals of Florida
506 So. 2d 1061 (1987), *review denied*, 515 So. 2d 230 (1988)

RYDER, ACTING CHIEF JUDGE.

Kane is a furniture store which also sells carpeting. Kane sold its carpet installation business to Perrone in 1975, and since that time, Kane has provided carpet installation services through Perrone's installation business (known as Service) as well as through other independent carpet installers.

For the past ten years, however, Perrone has been the principal carpet installer at Kane's St. Petersburg store. Initially, Kane put Perrone on a two-week probationary period during which Kane inspected Perrone's work to determine that Perrone was qualified. Thereafter, Perrone was given a small work area from which to assign installation jobs. Perrone hired other independent carpet installers, such as Kraus, to complete jobs which he could not perform.

On the morning of Saturday, August 6, 1983, Perrone assigned Kraus two installation jobs from Kane. Kraus completed the installation called for by the jobs around noon. Thereafter, Kraus, in his own truck, drove to a bar with his helper, Kevin Carleton, as a passenger. After drinking for approximately four hours, Kraus attempted to drive Carleton to Kane's warehouse parking lot in order that Carleton could retrieve his car. On the way to the parking lot, Kraus, traveling at a speed in excess of 50 m.p.h., ran a stop sign and collided broadside with the Miranda vehicle. Dr. Miranda's wife, Zenaida Quintos-Miranda, a passenger in the Miranda vehicle, died in a hospital soon after the accident.

This consolidated appeal arose from a wrongful death action which Dr. Romulo Miranda brought against Kane Furniture Corporation and Joseph P. Perrone for the death of Zenaida Quintos-Miranda. Kane appeals from the trial court's final summary judgment finding that Perrone was Kane's employee and that Kraus was Kane's subemployee. Kane also appeals the jury verdict award of 2.3 million dollars to Dr. Miranda.

We hold that the trial court erred in ruling that Perrone and Kraus were Kane's employees as a matter of law. We order the trial court to enter summary judgment for Kane finding that Perrone and Kraus are independent contractors.

Analysis of Restatement Factors

In *Cantor v. Cochran*, 184 So. 2d 173 (Fla. 1966), the Supreme Court of Florida approved the test set out in Restatement (Second) of Agency §220 (1958) for determining whether one is an employee or independent contractor:

(2) In determining whether one acting for another is a servant or an independent contractor, the following matters of fact, among others, are considered:

(a) the extent of control which, by the agreement, the master may exercise over the details of the work;

(b) whether or not the one employed is engaged in a distinct occupation or business;

(c) the kind of occupation, with reference to whether, in the locality, the work is usually done under the direction of the employer or by a specialist without supervision;

(d) the skill required in the particular occupation;

(e) whether the employer or the workman supplies the instrumentalities, tools, and the place of work for the person doing the work;

(f) the length of time for which the person is employed;

(g) the method of payment, whether by the time or by the job;

(h) whether or not the work is a part of the regular business of the employer;

(i) whether or not the parties believe they are creating the relationship of master and servant; and

(j) whether the principal is or is not in business.

Upon applying the Restatement test to the facts before us, we come to the conclusion that Perrone and Kraus were independent contractors, not employees.

(a) The extent of control which, by the agreement, the master may exercise over the details of the work

It has been said that the extent of control is the most important factor in determining whether a person is an independent contractor or an employee. *T & T Communications v. State, Department of Labor and Employment Security*, 460 So. 2d 996 (Fla. 2d DCA 1984). The right of control as to the mode of doing the work is the principal consideration. If a person is subject to the control or direction of another as to his results only, he is an independent contractor; if he is subject to control as to the means used to achieve the results, he is an employee. . . .

In *T & T Communications*, the court found cable installers to be independent contractors primarily because the company's only concern was with the final product or result. Although the cable installers agreed with the cable company to complete the cable installations pursuant to the cable company's plans and specifications, the installers themselves determined the method by which to accomplish the installation. The court stated that further indicia that they were independent contractors were:

The fact that cable installers are normally unsupervised . . . are skilled tradesmen . . . provide their own tools and transportation . . . are not employed for any length of time, are paid per installation, and receive no vacation and fringe benefits.

In the instant case, although Kane's salesmen diagrammed the installation lay-out plan, the carpet installers, Perrone and Kraus, had unbridled discretion in the physical performance of their tasks. Perrone did not report to anyone at Kane and had absolute discretion in contracting out installation jobs. The only instructions Kane gave Perrone were that he and the other carpet installers should be neatly attired and not intoxicated while on the job. Kane also instructed Perrone on customer satisfaction.

Once the carpet installer got the job, he was on his own. He performed his work completely without Kane's supervision or any other involvement. Upon completion of his task, the installer was free to go where he pleased: to another job or, unfortunately, to the local bar.

(b) Whether or not the one employed is engaged in a distinct occupation or business

Carpet installing can be viewed as a distinct occupation. Perrone and Kraus each had their own independent installation businesses. Perrone performed his services through a company which he purchased from Kane in 1975. Kraus performed his services through his own company, Mike's Carpet Service.

(c) The kind of occupation with reference to whether, in the locality, the work is usually done under the direction of the employer or by a specialist without supervision

Carpet installers are skilled workers who routinely perform without supervision. Perrone and Kraus performed work which emanated through Kane sales on an "as needed" basis. Both performed without Kane's supervision. Each was responsible for his own work. Kraus guaranteed his work for one year. Each, personally, was responsible for replacing carpeting he lost or damaged.

(d) The skill required in the particular occupation

Testimony at trial indicated that carpet installers are required to complete an apprenticeship in order to acquire the necessary skill to perform installation. As was aforementioned, Perrone also underwent a two-week probationary period at Kane.

(e) Whether the employer or the workman supplies the instrumentalities, tools, and the place of work for the person doing the work

Perrone and Kraus supplied their own installation equipment: knives, kickers, seaming irons, etc. They owned and insured their own trucks for work. Kane did not reimburse them for mileage and other expenses, such as gasoline.

While Kane supplied Perrone with a small space and a telephone from which to assign installation jobs, such accommodations did not make Perrone Kane's employee.

(f) The length of time for which the person is employed

Again, Perrone and Kraus worked for Kane on an "as needed" basis. The time spent on each job varied in length. The installation jobs were assigned on an "A.M. job or P.M. job." Neither was obligated to work exclusively for Kane. Kane was not obligated to use only Perrone and Kraus.

(g) The method of payment, whether by time or by job

While Kane determined the amount Perrone was paid, Perrone was paid strictly on a per yard basis. Kane made its checks out to Perrone's company. Perrone, in turn, paid Kraus and the other installers to whom he had assigned jobs.

Independent contractors are normally paid "per installation" rather than "by time." For instance, in *VIP Tours* [449 So. 2d 1307] a tour company was not deemed employer of tour guides using company vehicles who worked on a per job basis. In *T & T Communications*, cable splicers were found to be independent contractors where they were not employed for any length of time, were paid per installation and received no vacation or fringe benefits.

(h) Whether or not the work is part of the regular business of the employer

Kane is engaged in the retail furniture business. As a part of that business, Kane also sells carpeting and advertises installation as included in the purchase price. This is the only factor favoring the conclusion that Perrone and Kraus are employees. With all the other factors pointing to the conclusion that they are independent contractors, this factor alone is insufficient to sustain a holding that they are employees.

(i) Whether or not the parties believe they are creating the relation of master and servant

The parties' intent and course of dealing are important factors in determining their legal status. Clearly, the parties believed they were entering into an independent contractor relationship. Perrone and Kraus paid taxes as the owners of independent carpet installation businesses. Kane did not withhold social security or income taxes. Kane filed a Form "1099" for Perrone which is the IRS tax form a company files for nonemployees. A person who is responsible for paying all taxes due has been found to be an independent contractor.

Both Perrone and Kraus were free to accept or reject Kane's work. Perrone and Kraus were also able to work for companies in addition to Kane. Kane was not obligated to use Perrone or Kraus exclusively and, in fact, did not. Both Perrone and Kraus could hire their own employees.

Neither Perrone nor Kraus had employment agreements with Kane. Neither enjoyed the usual amenities associated with an employment relationship: fringe benefits, health care insurance, unemployment compensation, worker's compensation and paid vacations or holidays.

(j) Whether the principal is or is not in business

We concur that "the relevance of this factor is obscure, but for what it is worth, appellant is in business." [458 So. 2d 894, 898].

Measured against the Restatement criteria, we hold that Perrone and Kraus are independent contractors. Perrone and Kraus were independent contractors . . . just as the cable splicers were in *T & T Communications*.

Appellee argues that we should not hold that Perrone and Kraus were independent contractors as a matter of law. Rather, appellee contends that it is a question of fact for the jury. . . .

Even if the Restatement factors favored a finding of Perrone as Kane's employee, an application of the Restatement factors to Kraus and Kane's business relationship would indicate that Kraus was an independent contractor, not a subemployee. This alone would be sufficient to reverse the trial court's summary judgment finding of an employer/employee relationship. . . .

Reversed and remanded with instructions.

LEHAN and FRANK, JJ., concur.

Note

The Restatement (Third) § 7.07, Comment f sets forth a list of similar factors:

> Numerous factual indicia are relevant to whether an agent is an employee. These include: the extent of control that the agent and the principal have agreed the principal may exercise over details of the work; whether the agent is engaged in a distinct occupation or business; whether the type of work done by the agent is customarily done under a principal's direction or without supervision; the skill required in the agent's occupation; whether the agent or the principal supplies the tools and other instrumentalities required for the work and the place in which to perform it; the length of time during which the agent is engaged by a principal; whether the agent is paid by the job or by the time worked; whether the agent's work is part of the principal's regular business; whether the principal and the agent believe that they are creating an employment relationship; and whether the principal is or is not in business. Also relevant is the extent of control that the principal has exercised in practice over the details of the agent's work.

Lazo v. Mak's Trading Co.

Court of Appeals of New York
644 N.E.2d 1350 (1994)

OPINION OF THE COURT.

Memorandum

The order of the Appellate Division, 199 A.D.2d 165, 605 N.Y.S.2d 272, should be affirmed, with costs.

Plaintiff, the operator of a tractor trailer, delivered a shipment of rice to defendant, a wholesale and retail grocer in New York City. Defendant grocer engaged three neighborhood men to help unload the trailer. During the unloading, one of the three individuals got into an altercation with plaintiff, resulting in personal injuries.

The alleged tortfeasor came and went as he and his companion pleased, worked at their own convenience, were free to hold other employment, were never placed on defendant's payroll, received no fringe benefits, and had no taxes withheld from the flat rate, single payment for all three. Defendant paid $80 in cash to one of the three workers and left it up to them to divide the payment. While they had performed other unloading tasks for defendant previously, they did so on a random, on-inquiry-for-work basis. In the circumstances of this case, defendant did not exercise actual or constructive control over the performance and manner in which the work of these unloaders was performed. We agree with the Appellate Division that this record does not support the existence of any question of fact that could lead to the conclusion that defendant supervised these day laborers' activities for vicarious liability purposes. Also, in the circumstances of this case, there is no duty to conduct background inquiries in the selection of individuals for this as-needed task.

TITONE, ASSOCIATE JUDGE, concurring.

I agree with the Court's holding that defendant cannot be held liable, vicariously or otherwise, for the injuries plaintiff sustained when he was assaulted by a worker whom defendant had engaged. I part company with the majority, however, in its analysis of both the facts and the applicable legal principles. Accordingly, I write separately to explain the basis of my vote to affirm.

Initially, I note my disagreement with the conclusion, critical to the majority's rationale, that defendant did not exercise any actual or constructive control over "the performance and manner in which the work of these unloaders was performed." The "unloaders" were individuals who frequented the neighborhood looking for odd jobs. They had no special expertise and no special relationship to defendant's business such as would empower them to make the necessary decisions as to how the unloading work was to be performed. The sole function of these itinerant workers was to remove the sacks of rice they were told to remove from plaintiff's truck and to place those sacks where defendant's owner-manager wanted them placed. Indeed, defendant's owner-manager testified during his deposition that he told the apparent leader of the three workers where the men were to place the sacks of rice each time they unloaded the truck. Moreover, it is apparent from the agreed-upon facts that the men did not have the authority to choose when or where to perform the unloading.

It is at best implausible to suggest under these circumstances that *as a matter of law* it was the workers, rather than defendant, who were in control of the conduct of the work. As the comments to the Restatement (Second) of Agency indicate, "[u]nskilled labor is usually performed by those customarily regarded as servants, and *a laborer is almost always a servant* in spite of the fact that he may nominally contract to do a specified job for a specified price" (§ 220 [2][d], comment i [emphasis supplied]). Further, where, as here, the workers have neither control over the results produced nor the means used to achieve the results, they could readily be found not to be in control of the work. Accordingly, in my view, it is unreasonable to hold, as the majority has, that there was not even a fair question of fact as to the status of the itinerant workers.

More importantly, it is not necessary in this case to grapple with the question of who had control over the work, since the answer to that question has no legal significance in the context of the present dispute. The control question is relevant to resolving whether the three itinerant workers were "independent contractors" or were instead "employees" of defendant. However, in this case involving an assault, it is not important whether the workers were "employees" or "independent contractors," since, regardless of the status of the three men, there is no legal basis for holding defendant vicariously liable for the assault.[8]

Although an employer is often held liable for the torts of employees, an employer cannot be held liable for an employee's assaultive acts where the tortious conduct was not undertaken within the scope of employment, the employer did not authorize the violence and the use of force is not within the discretionary authority afforded the employee.... Almost directly on point is *Oneta v. Paul Tocci Co.*, 75 N.E.2d 743, which has twice been cited by this Court with approval. In *Oneta*, an employee of a waste-paper collection service assaulted a building's porter during an altercation over the location of a hand truck. This Court affirmed a ruling denying the injured porter recovery from the waste-paper collection concern. The Court subsequently explained the *Oneta* holding by stressing that although the precipitating dispute concerned a tool related to the tortfeasor-employee's job duties, "there was no basis for an inference that the assault was in furtherance of the employer's interests" (*Sims v. Bergamo*, 147 N.E.2d 1).

Here, as in *Oneta*, the assault occurred while the tortfeasor-worker was engaged in the employer's business, but there was no connection between the assault and the tortfeasor's duties as a day laborer. The assault was not undertaken in furtherance of defendant's business, nor was the use of force implicit in the tortfeasor's duties. Finally, there was no claim that the assault was authorized, instigated or condoned by defendant's manager. Thus, even if we were to assume that the assaultive worker was an employee of defendant, defendant could not be held vicariously liable for the worker's wrongful act.

Based on the foregoing, I would hold that the Court below properly granted defendant's motion for summary judgment dismissing the complaint. Inasmuch as plaintiff could not benefit from a finding that the tortfeasor was an "employee" of defendant, I find no need to explore the status or degree of control over the work that these itinerants had, nor do I perceive a reason to enmesh the Court in the essentially factual question of a particular hiree's status. Accordingly, my vote is to

---

8. [*] I have no quarrel with the majority's conclusion that there was no basis for holding defendant liable for its own alleged negligence in failing adequately to screen its laborers or in failing to intervene at an earlier point, when plaintiff complained about the assaultive worker's verbal abuse.

affirm for the simple reason that regardless of defendant's control over the unloading work, it was not liable for the worker's entirely separate assaultive conduct.

Order affirmed, with costs, in a memorandum.

KAYE, C.J., and SIMONS, BELLACOSA, SMITH and CIPARICK, JJ., concur.

TITONE, J., concurs in result in an opinion in which LEVINE, J., concurs.

Notes

1. With regard to the list of factors in Restatement (Second) § 220 used to determine servant versus independent contractor status set forth in *Kane*, consider whether it might be appropriate to add factors relating to modern employment legislation, like whether the employer files a W-2 form for the actor, whether the actor is eligible for unemployment compensation, worker's compensation, and so forth.[9] Note that Restatement (Third) does not include these additional factors.

2. Suppose a contract between a hospital and an independent ambulance service provides that the hospital can "investigate, inspect and supervise" the work to be performed by the ambulance service. Would such provision compromise the hospital's claim that it is not liable for the negligence of the ambulance service because the service is an independent contractor? *See Wright v. United States*, 537 F. Supp. 568, 570 (N.D. Ill. 1982) ("IM-C" is the ambulance service; "VA" is the hospital):

> The contract between IM-C and the VA establishes the independent contractor status of IM-C employees. Under the terms of that contract, the VA simply reserved the right to furnish "technical guidance and advice or generally supervise the work to be performed," and the right to "inspect and investigate" the operations of IM-C. Although reservation of the right to supervise the work is not irrelevant to this Court's determination, it does not describe the kind of control necessary to establish an agency relationship. The VA did not reserve the right to control the day-to-day "details and means" by which the contractor's work was to be accomplished.
>
> Even a cursory review of the relationship between the parties supports this conclusion. IM-C is a separate business entity providing ambulance service to a variety of patients and hospitals not covered by the contract at issue here. Unlike most agency relationships, this contract provides that IM-C is alone responsible for all injuries resulting from its own negligence, and requires IM-C to procure and maintain its own workman's compensation, employer's liability, general liability and automobile liability insurance coverage. In light of these circumstances, there can be no genuine dispute that IM-C was an independent contractor of the United States.

See also Noonan v. Texaco, Inc., 713 P.2d 160, 167 (Wyo. 1986) ("We think an owner who undertakes to see that an independent contractor operate [*sic*] in a safe

---

9. See ROBERT W. HAMILTON, BUSINESS ORGANIZATIONS, ESSENTIAL TERMS AND CONCEPTS 16 (1996), making this suggestion.

manner ought not be penalized. The reservation of a right to require safe equipment, material, and supplies to be used by the contractor is not without justification or reason."); *Eden v. Spaulding*, 218 Neb. 799, 359 N.W.2d 758, 762 (1984) ("[T]he employer of an independent contractor may, without changing the status, exercise such control as is necessary to assure performance of the contract in accordance with its terms"); *Sterud v. Chugach Elec. Ass'n*, 640 P.2d 823 (1982) (holding that the employer's right to order any worker of the independent contractor fired was not, "standing alone, sufficient to raise a reasonable inference that a master-servant relationship existed . . .").

3. Does the reservation in the contract of a right to inspect and supervise create a duty to exercise that right? *See Wright v. United States, supra* note 2, at 571:

> Plaintiff's complaint also alleges rather vaguely that the decedent's injury and subsequent death was proximately caused by the VA's own failure "to properly supervise the loading of the decedent and his wheelchair into the van." . . .

> As a matter of law, however, the VA cannot be found negligent for its failure to supervise the loading of the decedent into the van in the absence of a legal duty to conduct such supervision. Plaintiff has not alleged nor will this Court infer the existence of such a duty.[10]

4. The independent contractor concept can be difficult to apply. *Compare LaFleur v. LaFleur*, 452 N.W.2d 406 (Iowa 1990) (newspaper carrier an independent contractor as a matter of law), *with Santiago v. Phoenix Newspapers, Inc.*, 794 P.2d 138 (Ariz. 1990) (reversing judgment that newspaper carrier was an independent contractor as a matter of law).

Soderback v. Townsend

Court of Appeals of Oregon
644 P.2d 640, *petition for review denied*, 650 P.2d 927 (1982)

Before RICHARDSON, P. J., JOSEPH, C. J., and VAN HOOMISSEN, J.

VAN HOOMISSEN, JUDGE.

Plaintiff appeals from a summary judgment in favor of defendant American Quasar Petroleum Company (Quasar) in this action for damages arising out of an automobile accident. The issue is whether the trial court was correct in concluding that there was no genuine issue of material fact and that Quasar was entitled to a judgment as a matter of law. . . .

Defendant Townsend was retained by Quasar to negotiate gas leases. The accident occurred while Townsend was driving a rental car from St. Helens to Mist to check

---

10. [4] The contract between the VA and IM-C simply reserves VA's right to inspect and supervise IM-C's operation; it does not create a legally enforceable duty to do so on a patient-by-patient basis. . . .

on some leases. Plaintiff contends that Townsend was the agent of Quasar. Quasar contends that Townsend was an independent contractor. In *Kowaleski v. Kowaleski*, 235 Or. 454, 457–58, 385 P.2d 611 (1963), quoting the comment to section 250 of the Restatement (Second) of Agency, the Supreme Court explained:

> A principal employing another to achieve a result but not controlling or having the right to control the details of his physical movements is not responsible for incidental negligence while such person is conducting the authorized transaction. Thus, the principal is not liable for the negligent physical conduct of an attorney, a broker, a factor, or a rental agent, as such. In their movements and their control of physical forces, they are in the relation of independent contractors to the principal. It is only when to the relation of principal and agent there is added that right to control physical details as to the manner of performance which is characteristic of the relation of master and servant that the person in whose service the act is done becomes subject to liability for the physical conduct of the actor. . . .

In support of its motion for summary judgment, Quasar submitted affidavits describing in detail its employment arrangement with Townsend. Townsend had been in business for more than 26 years as an independent oil and gas broker. He was retained by various clients to negotiate and purchase leases. In April, 1979, he was retained by Quasar to negotiate gas leases in Oregon. He was told generally the areas in which Quasar was interested. Quasar placed maximum limits on Townsend's negotiating authority as to price and the duration of leases, but otherwise he was given a free hand. The manner and means by which he obtained leases were up to him. He set his own work schedule and had no quotas. He did not contract for any specific piece of work. He was paid a *per diem* of $175 plus expenses and accounted to Quasar at two-week intervals. . . .

Quasar's employee Kerr, who had responsibility for overseeing Quasar's lease acquisitions, stated in his deposition that he knew that Townsend had rented a car, but that:

> American Quasar had no control over the broker's operation of the vehicle. Of course, he was told the specific land in which the company was interested and, as part of this work, he would have to go to that particular area. However, American Quasar had no right to tell Townsend when he would drive the car, how to drive it or what route he was to travel.

These facts are distinguishable from those found in *Knapp v. Standard Oil Co.*, 156 Or. 564, 572, 68 P.2d 1052 (1937), in which the court noted that:

> . . . the defendant company had the right to control the operation of the automobile by Hampton. It had the right to say: "You will return to John Day by way of Baker and not by way of Long Creek," and how and when the automobile should be operated by him when transacting its business.

Plaintiff's affidavits did not dispute the description of the employment relationship between Townsend and Quasar contained in Quasar's affidavits, nor do they contain any evidence that might support an inference that Quasar had the right to control the manner or means by which Townsend went about his work. Plaintiff relied primarily on the affidavits of persons who Townsend had contacted and to whom Townsend had represented that he "worked for" Quasar. That Townsend may have represented himself as "working for" Quasar did not present any evidence to dispute Quasar's evidence on its lack of any right to control the means whereby Townsend accomplished his mission for Quasar. . . .

Here, we cannot discern any disputed issue of fact concerning the right of Quasar to control the activities of Townsend.

Affirmed.

Hunter v. R.G. Watkins & Son, Inc.

Supreme Court of New Hampshire
265 A.2d 15 (1970)

Griffith, J.

These are actions for wrongful death, personal injuries and property damage brought as a result of an accident on Route 4A in Enfield, New Hampshire, on August 6, 1965, involving motor vehicles operated by Edgar H. Hunter, Ralph F. Davis, Jr., and Chester D. Abbott.

Ralph F. Davis, Jr. was an employee of R. G. Watkins & Son, Inc. driving his own automobile at the time of the accident. All parties have agreed that it is desirable to have certain legal issues relating to the chargeability of R. G. Watkins & Son, Inc. for the acts of Ralph F. Davis, Jr. determined in advance of trial. These issues were reserved and transferred by Keller, J. without ruling, on an agreed statement of facts.

On August 6, 1965 Ralph F. Davis, Jr. was an employee of R. G. Watkins & Son, Inc. operating an L. V. truck on a road construction project in Lyme, New Hampshire. The truck operated by Davis broke down and a replacement part needed to repair it was located in Lawrence, Massachusetts. Davis was instructed to pick up the part and bring it back to the job site the next morning. He left about noon in his own car, stopping in Lebanon, New Hampshire at his apartment on the way down and in Salem, New Hampshire on the way back for personal errands.

The accident happened about 5:00 p.m. in Enfield, New Hampshire when Davis was on his way back to his apartment in Lebanon. His normal work day was from 7:30 a.m. until 5:00 p.m. and he was kept on the payroll until 5:00 p.m. on August 6, 1965 to compensate him for his time and gasoline in getting the part. It is agreed for the purpose of this transfer only that he was acting within the scope of his employment at the time of the accident. The defendant reserves the right to contest this issue at trial.

The questions presented on these agreed facts are:

1. Is R. G. Watkins & Son, Inc. liable for the negligence of its employee, Davis, in the operation of a motor vehicle owned by Davis and operated while on company business within the scope of his employment?

2. If it is necessary to show control or right to control by R. G. Watkins & Son, Inc. what constitutes "control" or "right to control" within the meaning of New Hampshire decisions on this general subject?

Counsel for both the plaintiffs and the defendant expect us to reexamine the rule of *McCarthy v. Souther*, 83 N.H. 29, 137 A. 445 in answering the transferred questions. *McCarthy v. Souther, id.*, and its descendant *Hutchins v. Insurance Co.*, 89 N.H. 79, 192 A. 498 both involved salesmen operating their own cars on business of their employers. Recovery against the employers was denied on the ground that there was no evidence from which it could be found the employers had any control over the employees in the "management and operation of the latter's automobile." *McCarthy v. Souther, supra* at 37. In following this rule it is apparent that we belong to a dwindling minority. *Konick v. Berke Moore Co.*, 245 N.E. 2d 750 (Mass. 1969), overrules Massachusetts' previous acceptance of the rule and its citations indicate our lonely situation. See also cases cited in Annot., 53 A.L.R.2d 631. . . .

The vicarious liability of a master for the wrongs of a servant acting on the master's business has been firmly established in our law from earliest times. See Prosser, Torts 471 (3d ed. 1964).

The simple statement of the rule of respondeat superior, unchanged over the years, has not resulted in simple application. . . .

Restatement, Second, Agency retained without change the definition of a servant contained in section 220 of the first Restatement. In order to put into proper perspective the control test of *McCarthy v. Souther, supra*, this definition must be considered.

The facts listed by the Restatement as relevant in determining whether an employer-employee relationship exists require consideration of many factors unless control is decisive. . . . Where other facts indicate the nonexistence of an employer-employee relationship, control may be a decisive factor as in *Paro v. Trust Co.*, 77 N.H. 394, 92 A. 331 and *Winslow v. Wellington*, 79 N.H. 500, 111 A. 631, dealing with employees of an otherwise independent contractor, and *Currier v. Abbott*, 104 N.H. 299, 185 A.2d 263, dealing with a borrowed employee.

Generally the control factor has been overemphasized in judicial reasoning (2 Harper & James, Torts 1400 (1956)) and we are usually concerned with whether on all the facts the community would consider the person an employee. Prosser, Torts 472 (3d ed. 1964). The fact that the employer in this case lacked control of the method by which the employee operated his car does not make the employee an independent contractor. The same may be said of the fact that the employee owned the automobile. In some cases this could be very material but in the present case it is not a controlling factor. *Hinson v. United States*, 257 F.2d 178.

"We are of opinion that we should no longer follow our cases to the extent that they indicate that a master-servant relationship does not exist unless the employer has a right to control the manner and means (the details, in other words) of operating the car." *Konick v. Berke Moore Co.*, 245 N.E.2d 750, 753 (Mass. 1969). Thus in this case where it is agreed that a regular employee is sent upon a specific errand, using his own car with the knowledge and permission of the employer, and it is agreed he was acting within the scope of his employment at the time of the accident, the employer is liable for his acts whether it had control of his detailed operation of the motor vehicle or not. We answer the first question transferred in the affirmative and the second question then requires no answer. . . .

Remanded.

All concurred.

Notes

1. *A look at history.* A brief treatment of the history of the independent contractor exception to respondeat superior liability is contained in the comprehensive and thoughtful opinion of Justice Blume in *Stockwell v. Morris*, 22 P.2d 189 (Wyo. 1933), noted in 32 MICH. L. REV. 276 (1933). The case involved the liability of Maytag Company for the negligent driving (to the home of a customer to look at a malfunctioning washing machine) of a full-time salesman for the company who worked solely on commission, drove his own car, paid his own expenses, and worked according to his own schedule. In the course of affirming a trial court verdict for the company, Justice Blume had the following to say on the history of the independent contractor concept:

> Prior to the latter part of the seventeenth century, a master was not responsible for the torts of his servants, unless committed by his express command or subsequent assent. But in the case of *Jones v. Hart*, it was held that if a servant driving a cart negligently runs into another cart, the master is liable. And from about that time commenced to be developed the modern doctrine that a master is responsible for the torts of his servant committed within the scope of his employment. . . . The doctrine was carried to its logical conclusion. Independent agents or contractors were treated the same as servants. It was not until the second quarter of the nineteenth century that it was doubted that the doctrine of respondeat superior should be applied in all cases in which one man was employed to perform an act for another. . . . Two decisions rendered in 1840, namely, *Milligan v. Wedge*, 12 A. & E. 737, and *Quarman v. Burnett*, 6 M. & W. 497, took a definite departure from the then generally accepted rule, and by the middle of that century it came to be recognized that there are many cases in which a man should not be held responsible for the acts of a representative, if the latter is not under his immediate control, direction or supervision. Such representative has generally been called an independent contractor, a phrase that has acquired almost a technical meaning, originally, of course, applied to one who actually performed services under an independent contract. It is not altogether appropriate to apply the term in all cases, or in the case at

bar, and various other terms have been sought to be substituted, such as entrepreneur or enterpriser.

2. *Inferring the right of control.* In making his decision to affirm a verdict for defendant, Justice Blume noted that, "The fact that [Maytag] did not exercise control does not show that it did not have the right of control, though it may be some evidence thereof. The right must be determined by reasonable inferences shown by the evidence. In view of the fact that actual control of an automobile driven hundreds of miles away from the place of the employer can at best be theoretical only, . . . the right of such control should, in a case of this character, be able to be implied only from reasonably clear evidence showing it. We think, accordingly, that the employer in this case ought not to be held liable."

Justice Blume refused to infer a right of control because of the nature of the relationship in the *Stockwell* case, where Morris, the salesman, drove his own car and worked on commission. See *Cooke v. E.F. Drew & Co.*, 319 F.2d 498, 500 (2d Cir. 1963), drawing an inference of right of control when an employee was paid by salary since "his time belonged to his employer and he was entitled to be paid irrespective of results." See also Warren A. Seavey, Studies in Agency 74 (1949), stating that, "the more complete control over the servant" results "from the sale of his time to the employer."

3. The facts that Morris owned his own car and chose his own route (within bounds) obviously were important to the *Stockwell* decision described in Note 1, above. These factors have not proved impressive to some courts subsequently deciding the question, even when the tortfeasor was not otherwise clearly a servant. *See Peterson v. Brinn & Jensen Co.*, 134 Neb. 909, 911–12, 280 N.W. 171, 172 (1938). With regard to other factors considered by courts in resolving the servant or independent contractor issue, see *Dow v. Connell*, 448 F.2d 763 (10th Cir. 1971). In classifying a traveling salesman as an independent contractor (on much easier facts, however; he worked for several firms), the court placed emphasis on the absence of liability insurance, worker's compensation insurance, and unemployment insurance coverage on the salesman by the defendants. The court also observed that none of the defendants deducted social security or federal or state income tax from his compensation. These factors can be important in establishing an employment relationship, from which the courts presumably will more readily draw an inference of right of control. They are not conclusive in all jurisdictions, however. See *Throop v. F.E. Young & Co.*, 94 Ariz. 146, 382 P.2d 560 (1963), where a traveling salesman was classified as an independent contractor as a matter of law despite being carried on personnel records of the defendant as an employee, with withholding and unemployment compensation taxes deducted from his income. See also *Cooke v. E.F. Drew & Co.*, 319 F.2d 498 (2d Cir. 1963), rejecting an argument that an actor is a servant as a matter of law "merely because he devoted his full time to the business of Drew [his employer] or because there was a written contract of employment with Drew and the company deducted social security and withholding taxes." Perhaps a useful approach to this problem would be for courts to recognize a rebuttable presumption of servant status whenever there is full-time employment.

4. It is well known that some prominent chefs are touchy about control over their preparation of food and running of the kitchen. Apparently there frequently is an understanding with the employer-restaurant owner that no control shall be exercised in these areas. Suppose a chef at a famous restaurant, having retained such control, even to the extent of excluding the owner from the kitchen when the chef is preparing meals, negligently prepares and serves some bad food. The ill patrons sue the owner. Would the owner be liable vicariously for the chef's negligence? Restatement (Second) § 220, Comment d, indicates there is liability. How can this be so?

5. Suppose a negligent employee is exercising a skill that requires a license from the state. A license is issued only after testing following considerable training. The expertise of the licensed person is considerable, thus rendering impractical any effective control over many details of the work. Does this mean that the employee would be classified as an independent contractor rather than as a servant? See Restatement (Second) § 223, Comment a, noting that:

> The fact that the law requires an examination and a certain standard of skill does not prevent the relation of master and servant from arising; it may, however, indicate . . . that such a relation is not contemplated, as in the case of attorneys and surgeons, whereas in other cases, as in the case of chauffeurs, the fact . . . has little bearing on the inference to be drawn. Even in the case of attorneys and physicians there may be the master and servant relation. . . . [I]t may be found that the house physician or [hospital] interns, if subject to directions as to the manner in which their work is performed, are servants . . . while in the performance of their ordinary duties.

Kelley v. Rossi, 481 N.E.2d 1340, 1343 (Mass. 1985), addresses this issue in the context of negligence by a doctor in the second year of her residency at a hospital; the court stated that the "position of a physician normally is not that of a servant to anyone," but also noted that, "The general rule is that a resident is a servant of the hospital." With regard to the lawyer hypothetical at the beginning of this section, see *Brinkley v. Farmers Elevator Mut. Ins. Co.*, 485 F.2d 1283 (10th Cir. 1973) (insurance company not liable for negligent driving of lawyer who worked 90 percent of his time for defendant, on ground of no control or right of control over the lawyer's physical movements. The lawyer was driving home from a case, making it possible to raise a scope of employment issue, but the opinion was worded broadly enough to classify the lawyer as a nonservant agent, or independent contractor, even with regard to his courtroom activities.).

6. *The independent calling test.* This alternative approach to identifying servant status is suggested in Leidy, *Salesmen as Independent Contractors*, 28 MICH. L. REV. 365, 370 (1930). Professor Leidy would define an independent contractor as follows:

> [The term independent contractor] has come to be used with special reference to one who, in *pursuit of an independent business*, undertakes to do

a specific piece of work for other persons, using his own means and methods, without submitting to their control in respect of all its details. . . . [T]he true test of a "contractor" would seem to be that he renders the services in the course of an independent occupation, representing the will of his employer only as to the result of the work and not as to the means by which it is accomplished.

Professor Leidy bases much of his analysis on *Milligan v. Wedge*, 12 A. & E. 737, 113 Eng. Rep. 993 (1840), one of the first English cases to recognize the independent contractor doctrine. In *Milligan*, defendant butcher purchased a bullock (a steer) in the city of London. He employed a licensed drover to drive the steer to defendant's slaughterhouse, which was outside the city. On the way, the steer got away from the drover and ran into plaintiff's showroom, destroying some marble chimney pieces. Plaintiff sued defendant on respondeat superior grounds. The court held for the defendant, with one of the opinions stating that: "The party sued has not done the act complained of, but has employed another who is recognized by the law as exercising a distinct calling. . . . The mischief was done in the course not of the butcher's business, but of the drover's."

Professor Leidy argues that the above test makes more sense than the right to control over details test. He criticizes the "almost universal attention to the right to control," including that of the Restatement (Second). His criticism of the right to control test is that it is too indeterminate. "[O]n the same facts, . . . with two courts applying the same test, one will say 'there is' and the other will say 'there is not,' such control, or right of control, as to produce the master-servant relation." 28 MICH. L. REV. at 372.

Justice Blume, in the *Stockwell* case described in note 1, made the following comment about the above remarks: "Some criticism has been leveled at courts for . . . not finding a more decisive and clear-cut test. But it must be remembered that the rule [of respondeat superior] is founded not upon a rule of logic, but upon a rule of public policy . . . and it is not to be wondered at that one court answers the question one way, another way."

7. Many states recognize the "corporate practice of medicine" doctrine, meaning that only licensed physicians can render medical services. *See, e.g., Estate of Harper ex rel. Al-Hamim v. Denver Health and Hosp. Authority*, 140 P.3d 273 (Colo. App. 2006) ("under this doctrine, a corporation may not employ physicians, perform medical services, or interfere with a physician's independent medical judgment"); *Mutual Service Cas. Ins. Co. v. Midway Massage, Inc.*, 695 N.W.2d 138 (Minn. App. 2005); *Williams v. Good Health Plus, Inc.*, 743 S.W.2d 373 (Tex. App. 1988). In Colorado, however, the courts have interpreted the doctrine to preclude vicarious liability for corporations that are affiliated in some ways with physicians who commit medical malpractice. The courts reason that inasmuch as the corporation cannot "control" the conduct of the physician, the physician could not be an employee (or servant, to use the vernacular of the Second Restatement) of the corporation and therefore the corporation cannot be vicariously liable. Does it necessarily follow

from the corporate practice of medicine that a corporation can never be liable for a physician's malpractice?

Sandrock v. Taylor

Supreme Court of Nebraska
174 N.W.2d 186 (1970)

[A portion of this case was reproduced in Part A, *supra*. It involved a motor vehicle accident. The defendant Taylor was driving a milk tank truck. The defendant Co-op was joined on the allegation that Taylor was its servant driving in the course of its business.]

The next issues involve Co-op's assertions that Taylor was an independent contractor, and was not acting as a servant or agent of Co-op. Co-op contends that it is therefore absolved from liability because there was no master-servant relationship.

Prior to September 19, 1961, Co-op owned all of the milk trucks used in the business and the drivers, including the defendant Taylor, were employees. At about that time, at the instigation of the drivers during a strike, arrangements were changed and a form of "carrier's contract" was executed with the individual drivers, including the defendant Taylor. Taylor was designated the "carrier" and the contract provided that he was to render daily fresh sweet milk delivery, including Sundays and holidays, between Co-op's creamery and the respective farms on its bulk routes. The transportation service was to be furnished by suitable insulated equipment supplied, maintained, and operated by Taylor at his own expense and required him to deliver whatever milk was tendered to him from each and every place situated on Co-op's milk route. It also required him to deliver butter, calf feeds, and products used in sanitation for the production of milk as directed by Co-op. Co-op reserved the right to revise bulk routes at 3-month intervals. . . .

Transportation service was to be satisfactory to Co-op and all shippers on the route and Co-op agreed to collect from each shipper and pay to Taylor the amounts each shipper authorized Co-op to deduct for that purpose from any payments due the shipper on milk delivered to Co-op. . . .

Taylor was required to perform his obligations under the contract personally except for use of a relief man paid by Taylor. Taylor could not employ any person objectionable to Co-op and was forbidden to continue employment of any employee beyond 2-weeks notice who was objectionable to Co-op. The contract was not assignable by Taylor.

The contract provided that Taylor should have complete liberty to use his own discretion and judgment as to the method and manner of performance without any right on the part of Co-op to direct or control his performance. It also required him to furnish and maintain in effect workmen's compensation insurance on his own employees if required by law, and public liability, property damage, and cargo insurance on the equipment. Taylor was to pay all taxes and license fees. The parties expressly disclaimed possession by either of any rights with respect to the other except those conferred by law applicable to an independent contractor. . . .

The contract also provided for purchase of the tank truck from Co-op by Taylor and for the method of payment. "As a deterrent toward violation of this contract," Co-op reserved the right to consider all payments made by Taylor forfeited if he "solicits business for a competitor or . . . breaks contract by working for a competitor."

The contract was for a period of 1 year. It was automatically renewable from year to year in the absence of written notice by either party not later than 30 days prior to the end of the year. Co-op, however, reserved the right to terminate the contract by 30-days written notice to Taylor at any time. . . .

. . . The case of *Sanford v. Goodridge*, 234 Iowa 1036, 13 N.W.2d 40, is similar to the one at bar in many respects, including the general nature of the contract as well as the type of business and vehicle involved. The language of the court in that case is appropriate here. "An employer cannot insulate himself against the burdens of the employer-employee relationship by a contract that leaves him with the control benefits of that relationship. Nor can he escape his liability under the doctrine respondeat superior by a contract that expressly provides that the workman is an independent contractor, if in fact, under the entire contract, the workman only possesses the same independence that employees in general enjoy."

Here the evidence could have justified a finding by the jury that the written contract did not constitute the entire agreement between the parties and that Co-op maintained control over the methods of carrying out the contract. The facts justified a finding that Taylor had no more independence than employees in general enjoy. The effect upon control involved in Co-op's right to terminate the contract on short notice without liability to Taylor was clearly material. The issue of whether the defendant Taylor was an independent contractor, or a servant, or employee of Co-op was properly submitted to the jury.

The judgment is affirmed as against Robert L. Taylor and against Osceola County Cooperative Creamery Association, a corporation.

Note

As was noted in Chapter 2, the classification of a person as a servant (employee) or an independent contractor carries legal significance well beyond the risk of exposure to vicarious tort liability. Worker's compensation coverage depends on the existence of an employment relationship. Matters of taxation (such as the employer's share of social security tax), susceptibility to service of process, and the burdens of social legislation often turn on whether a relationship is one of employee or independent contractor. These matters may have played an important role in the decision of the Creamery Association in the *Sandrock* case to attempt to place its drivers on independent contractor status. See *Torrence v. Chicago Tribune Co.*, 535 F. Supp. 743 (N.D. Ill. 1981), for an opinion discussing the tests used to determine employment status in most social legislation and quoting from the United States Supreme Court that "the total factual context is assessed in the light of pertinent common law agency principles." In general, see Annot., 55 A.L.R.3d 1216 (1974).

b. The Independent Contractor Exception in the Modern Economy

With the growth of the "sharing economy," where workers are hired as independent contractors for part-time or temporary work, and the "on-demand economy," where employers use staffing companies to provide labor (often temporarily), the number of classification cases, and the stakes in those cases, has increased dramatically. Workers in both categories and government regulators have argued that such workers are employees. For the most part, the common law definition of employee and independent contractor, as set forth in this chapter, has guided the courts, even when a statute was involved. In *Nationwide Mutual Insurance Co. v. Darden*, 301 U.S. 318 (1992), the United States Supreme Court decided that unless Congress indicated otherwise, when it used the term "employee" in a statute the courts should assume Congress meant the common law definition. Thus, a person who sold insurance as an independent contractor for Nationwide could not claim the protections of the federal Employee Retirement Income Security Act (ERISA). Avoiding ERISA and other state and federal laws designed to protect employees has been an important incentive for many businesses to structure their workforce, or at least part of it, as independent contractors or use staffing companies to supply their labor needs. On the other hand, the impact of these laws, such as ERISA or the federal Fair Labor Standards Act, which sets a minimum wage for workers (among other things), is diminished if large numbers of workers are not covered. As a result, the courts (both federal and state) have become somewhat more willing in recent years to find an employment relationship where, in the past, they might have determined that the worker was an independent contractor.

The Sharing Economy

Uber is a prominent example of a company in the sharing economy that has faced this issue. It styles itself as a technology company that makes its electronic app available to individual drivers and people looking for transportation so that they can connect with one another. Its business plan is that Uber drivers are independent contractors simply licensed to use the Uber app. The company has argued that Uber drivers drive their own vehicles, are free to pick their own hours, are not supervised, have an independent business (as drivers), are paid on the basis of the fares they generate, enter into contracts that identify them as independent contractors and, in short, meet the traditional criteria as set forth in the case law and Restatements of Agency. Uber has had mixed success when challenged by their drivers and government regulators. In the most prominent case to date, *O'Connor v. Uber Techs., Inc.*, 82 F. Supp. 3d 1133 (N.D. Cal. 2015), the court denied Uber's motion for summary judgment. Although citing the traditional criteria the courts use to decide a classification case, the *O'Connor* court determined that there were questions of fact precluding summary judgment. In accordance with California precedent, the court focused on control and noted the various ways that Uber exercised control over its drivers (e.g., Uber sets fares and prohibits drivers from answering passenger inquiries about booking directly with a driver). The court concluded that there remained questions of material fact regarding the determination of whether the control exercised by Uber over its drivers was sufficient to establish that the drivers were employees. The determination was a mixed question of fact and law, the court said, requiring further proceedings. *Id.* at 1152.

The California Supreme Court, in a 2018 decision involving the California wage and hours law, *Dynamex Operations West, Inc. v. Superior Court*, 416 P.3d 1 (Cal. 2018), announced a rather radical departure from the common law. In *Dynamex*, the California Court essentially rejected the multifactor common law test used by the federal court in O'*Connor* and opted for a simpler test that starts with the presumption that anyone with whom a business engages, suffers, or permits to work for it is its employee. To rebut this presumption, an employer must show a worker is free from its control and direction, performs work that is outside the usual course of a hiring entity's business, and is engaged in an independently established trade, occupation, or business. Only if the employer satisfies all three tests will the worker be considered an independent contractor.

The *Dynamex* decision is, of course, a case interpreting a California statute that is designed to protect workers in the California economy. The Court recognized that the common law definition was developed to determine whether *respondeat superior* should apply and a different test may be better suited to its regulatory statutes. It remains to be seen whether this case will have an impact on the common law and future Restatements of Agency.

The On-Demand Economy

The use of staffing companies is becoming increasingly common in the U.S. economy. Essentially, many businesses outsource the regulatory burdens of the employment relationship, which includes, among other things, compliance with Social Security contributions, income tax withholding, workers' compensation, family leave, etc. to a staffing company that, for a fee, takes on these obligations. (The *ATS, Inc. v. Beddingfield* case, in Section 3 *infra*, provides an example of a staffing company.) The staffing company's client—the business where the workers actually provide their services—inevitably exercises at least some control over the workers. As that control edges up, the risk that the client firm will be considered the workers' employer or a joint employer with the staffing company increases. In a case decided by the National Labor Relations Board, *In re Browning-Ferris Industries of California, Inc.,*[11] the NLRB decided that a client firm (Browning-Ferris) was a joint employer, together with the staffing company, of the employees supplied by the

11. 362 N.L.R.B. No. 186 (2015).

staffing company. As a result, Browning-Ferris could be required to bargain with the union representing workers at its facility even though, technically, those workers were employed by the staffing company.

Some commentators have expressed the view that the reasoning of the *Browning-Ferris* case could be extended to other business structures, such as franchises. If so, a franchisor might be considered a joint employer, together with the franchisee, of the franchisee's employees, with the result (for instance) that a franchisor could be found vicariously liable for the wrongful actions of the franchisee's employee. In *Salazar v. McDonald's*, 2016 WL 4394165 (N.D. Cal. Aug. 16, 2016), for instance, the plaintiffs, employees at a franchised McDonald's restaurant, sued McDonald's under the California Labor Code and claimed that McDonald's was their employer together with the franchisee. The trial court granted summary judgment in favor of McDonald's because, among other things, the plaintiff did not prove that McDonald's exercised the necessary control. But, interestingly, the court would not grant summary judgment on plaintiffs' claim that the franchisee was McDonald's "ostensible" agent. Under California law an ostensible agent is an apparent agent. *See generally* Mark J. Loewenstein, *Agency Law and the New Economy*, 27 Bus. Law. 1009 (2017).

c. Limitations to the Independent Contractor Exception

Hixon v. Sherwin-Williams Co.

United States Court of Appeals, Seventh Circuit
671 F.2d 1005 (1982)

Before Cummings, Chief Judge, Swygert, Senior Circuit Judge, and Posner, Circuit Judge.

Posner, Circuit Judge.

In this diversity case we decide a question of federal jurisdiction plus several questions under the common law of Indiana.

Mr. and Mrs. Chess, who are not parties to this litigation, sustained several hundred dollars in water damage to the kitchen floor of their home in Indiana. Their homeowner's insurer, American States Insurance Company, a nonresident corporation, hired a local contractor, Marv Hixon, to install a new linoleum floor in the kitchen. Too busy to attend to the contract himself, Hixon subcontracted the job to the Sherwin-Williams Company, another nonresident corporation. Sherwin-Williams is a manufacturer of linoleum and other products rather than a building contractor, but it undertook to install its linoleum in the Chesses' kitchen rather than just sell the linoleum to Hixon for installation. The local office of Sherwin-Williams hired Louis Benkovich to do the installation. Benkovich had been in the linoleum installation business for many years and had done previous jobs for Sherwin-Williams. His reputation was good; people said, "Louie puts in a nice floor." He had never been known to have an accident or otherwise fail to render adequate service. He was self-employed, and was retained by Sherwin-Williams as an independent contractor rather than an employee. Sherwin-Williams did not supervise his work and knew nothing about the particulars of the Chess job beyond the fact that Hixon wanted a new linoleum floor installed.

The new linoleum could not be attached directly to the cement floor beneath it because of dampness; a plywood layer was required between the cement and the linoleum. Benkovich used a glue that happened to be extremely flammable to fasten the plywood to the cement. The label on the can contained explicit and emphatic warnings concerning the flammability of the glue and the importance of good ventilation. Benkovich had never used this brand of glue before; in fact, he had never in his many years as a linoleum contractor fastened a plywood layer to a cement floor. He proceeded to ignore the warnings on the can; he may not even have read them. Instead of opening the windows and turning off the pilot light in the hot water heater in the Chesses' kitchen, he closed the windows and left the pilot light on. The glue exploded; and pursuant to its homeowner's policy American States found itself having to indemnify the Chesses for some $27,000 in additional damage to their house.

American States ... brought this lawsuit in a federal district court in Indiana against Sherwin-Williams. ... At the close of the plaintiffs' evidence the defendant moved for a directed verdict. The district court granted the motion and dismissed the complaint on the merits. This appeal followed. ...

We come at last to the merits of American States' claim against Sherwin-Williams. Benkovich was an independent contractor rather than an employee of Sherwin-Williams, and at common law a principal is not liable for the torts of his independent contractors; respondeat superior (employer liability for the torts committed by its employees in furtherance of their employment) is inapplicable. In an age when tort law is dominated by the search for the deep pocket, which Benkovich does not have, the common law rule may seem an anachronism; on the other hand, since by definition an independent contractor, unlike an employee, is an agent the details of whose work are not supervised by his principal, making the principal liable for the torts of his independent contractors would have little positive effect on the amount of care taken by them. But we need not take sides in the policy debate. The Indiana courts, explicitly adopting an accident-prevention rather than deep-pocket approach to the question, have decided—whether rightly or wrongly is not our business—to retain the independent-contractor rule in full force.

This case is not within the exception to the rule for inherently hazardous activities. The more hazardous an activity is, the higher is the cost-justified level of care; and if it is hazardous enough, the principal should take his own precautions even though he does not supervise the details of the independent contractor's work. But there is nothing hazardous about laying a linoleum floor. It becomes so only if the installer misuses one of the inputs, the glue. This kind of hazard is present in almost all construction work and does not make construction a hazardous activity. If the presence of a hazardous input made the principal liable for the torts of his independent contractors, then if the employee of a building contractor sawed off his finger while repairing a house the owner of the house would be liable, at least if it turned out that the accident had been due to negligence by the contractor. The exception would swallow the rule.

A principal is liable, however, for the consequences of negligently failing to select a competent contractor, and American States argues that Sherwin-Williams was negligent in failing to ask Benkovich whether he had ever laid plywood on cement. But Benkovich had a good reputation as an installer of linoleum, and Sherwin-Williams had no duty to quiz him concerning the details of his experience.

Even if Sherwin-Williams was negligent in selecting Benkovich because he had no experience with this particular type of job, its negligence was not the proximate cause of the accident. The accident resulted from Benkovich's unaccountable failure to read or pay attention to the warnings on the can of glue rather than from his lack of experience in laying this type of floor. Such an accident was no more probable because Benkovich was inexperienced; it was if anything less probable—a novice might be expected to pay more attention to warnings and directions than an experienced man. Therefore, making Sherwin-Williams liable in this case would not result in fewer accidents of this type. . . .

[Judgment affirmed on the independent contractor issue.]

Notes

1. A person who engages an independent contractor to do inherently dangerous work is vicariously liable for the negligence of the contractor, as noted in the *Hixon* opinion. "Inherently dangerous" work has been defined as work "which, in its nature, will create some peculiar risk of injury to others unless special precautions are taken—as, for example, excavations in or near a public highway." PROSSER & KEETON ON TORTS 472. *See Miller v. Westcor Ltd. Pt'ship*, 831 P.2d 386 (Ariz. App. 1991) (public fireworks exhibition in shopping mall is inherently dangerous). See also *Tauscher v. Puget Sound Power & Light Co.*, 96 Wash. 2d 274, 635 P.2d 426 (1981), a case involving the inherently dangerous activity doctrine in the interesting context of a suit by an injured employee of an independent contractor against the company that engaged the services of the independent contractor. The court denied liability in a 5-4 decision, noting that the majority of courts deny liability under such circumstances and citing to decisions on both sides of the question. Liability is denied despite the inherently dangerous nature of the activity (working with high voltage electric lines), in part because the injured employee had available the remedy of worker's compensation, which the owner had in effect paid for in the fees it paid the independent contractor, who is the employer of the injured party.

2. The *Hixon* opinion also states that a person can be liable for negligently failing to select a competent contractor. Does this include inquiring into financial stability and insurance before hiring an independent contractor? See *Cassano v. Aschoff*, 543 A.2d 973, 976 (N.J. Super. 1988), involving an accident that occurred during removal of a tree by an independent contractor hired by landowners, who did not

know the contractor was uninsured. The court rejected an argument that "concepts of distributive justice might support the imposition of liability against those who hire financially irresponsible contractors if the contractor injures an innocent third person." The *Cassano* court stated that, "no court in this state has chosen to apply that concept," and "it is by no means clear that property owners will always, or even usually, be able to better bear the burden of a loss."

See also *Richmond v. White Mount Rec. Ass'n*, 674 A.2d 153 (N.H. 1996), stating that hiring an independent contractor without researching the adequacy of his equipment and personnel is not negligence. The court quotes with approval Restatement (Second) of Torts § 411 as follows:

> [O]ne who employs a carpenter to repair the ceilings of his shop or [a plumber] to install plumbing in his hotel is entitled to assume that a carpenter or plumber of good reputation is competent to do such work safely . . . . Indeed, there is no duty to take any great pains to ascertain whether his reputation is or is not good. The fact that he is a carpenter or plumber is sufficient, unless the employer knows that the contractor's reputation is bad or knows of facts which should lead him to realize that the contractor is not competent.

3. *Hixon* sets forth two of the widely accepted limitations on the independent contractor defense: Contracting for work on inherently dangerous activities (vicarious liability) and negligently hiring an independent contractor (direct liability). The third limitation is the nondelegable duty doctrine, covered below.

Kleeman v. Rheingold

Court of Appeals of New York
614 N.E.2d 712 (1993)

TITONE, JUDGE.

In a prior action brought to recover damages for alleged medical malpractice, plaintiff was nonsuited for failure properly to serve the defendant doctor before the Statute of Limitations on her claim expired. The threshold issue in this second malpractice action, which was brought by plaintiff against the lawyers she retained to prosecute the first, is whether an attorney may be held vicariously liable to his or her client for the negligence of a process server whom the attorney has hired on behalf of that client.

According to the allegations in the present complaint, plaintiff, a victim of alleged medical malpractice, had originally retained defendant and his law firm to pursue her claim against Dr. Neils Lauersen. With only five days remaining before the Statute of Limitations on the claim would expire, defendant promptly prepared a summons and complaint. On November 5, 1978, two days before the Statute of Limitations was to run, defendant delivered the prepared documents to Fischer's Service Bureau, a process service agency regularly used by defendant's law firm, with the instruction that process was to be served "immediately." It is undisputed that Fischer's, not defendant, selected the licensed process server who would actually deliver the papers and that Fischer's and the process server, rather than defendant, determined the precise manner of effecting service.

Although the process server used by Fischer's apparently delivered the papers on time, plaintiff's medical malpractice claim was ultimately dismissed when a traverse hearing revealed that the process server had given the papers to Dr. Lauersen's secretary rather than Dr. Lauersen himself. . . .

Plaintiff subsequently commenced the present legal malpractice action against defendant and his law firm, claiming that they should be held liable for the negligence of the process server who had been retained to serve Dr. Lauersen on plaintiff's behalf. Defendants moved for summary judgment and plaintiff cross-moved. . . .

The trial court . . . concluded that a process server is an "independent contractor" rather than an agent of the employing attorney, since "[t]he attorney does not have control over the manner in which the task is performed." Accordingly, the court held, the relationship between the process server and the attorney here did not provide a cognizable basis for holding the latter vicariously liable for the acts of the former. . . .

On plaintiff's appeal, a divided Appellate Division affirmed for essentially the same reasons. We now modify by denying defendants' motion for summary judgment. . . .

The general rule is that a party who retains an independent contractor, as distinguished from a mere employee or servant, is not liable for the independent contractor's negligent acts. Although several justifications have been offered in support of this rule, the most commonly accepted rationale is based on the premise that one who employs an independent contractor has no right to control the manner in which the work is to be done and, thus, the risk of loss is more sensibly placed on the contractor.

Despite the courts' frequent recitation of the general rule against vicarious liability, the common law has produced a wide variety of so-called "exceptions." . . . These exceptions, most of which are derived from various public policy concerns, fall roughly into three basic categories: negligence of the employer in selecting, instructing or supervising the contractor;[12] employment for work that is especially or "inherently" dangerous; and, finally, instances in which the employer is under a specific nondelegable duty.

The exception that concerns us here—the exception for nondelegable duties—has been defined as one that "requires the person upon whom it is imposed to answer for it that care is exercised by anyone, even though he be an independent contractor,

---

12. [1] Notably, although often classified as an "exception," this category may not be a true exception to the general rule, since it concerns the employer's liability for its own acts or omissions rather than its vicarious liability for the acts and omissions of the contractor.

to whom the performance of the duty is entrusted" (Restatement of Torts at 394). The exception is often invoked where the particular duty in question is one that is imposed by regulation or statute. However, the class of duties considered "nondelegable" is not limited to statutorily imposed duties. To the contrary, examples of nondelegable common-law duties abound.

There are no clearly defined criteria for identifying duties that are nondelegable. Indeed, whether a particular duty is properly categorized as "nondelegable" necessarily entails a sui generis inquiry, since the conclusion ultimately rests on policy considerations.

The most often cited formulation is that a duty will be deemed nondelegable when "'the responsibility is so important to the community that the employer should not be permitted to transfer it to another'" (quoting Prosser and Keeton at 512). This flexible formula recognizes that the "privilege to farm out [work] has its limits" and that those limits are best defined by reference to the gravity of the public policies that are implicated.

Viewed in the light of these principles, the duty at issue here — that owed by an attorney to his or her client to exercise care in the service of process — fits squarely and neatly within the category of obligations that the law regards as "nondelegable." Manifestly, when an individual retains an attorney to commence an action, timely and accurate service of process is an integral part of the task that the attorney undertakes. Furthermore, proper service of process is a particularly critical component of a lawyer's over-all responsibility for commencing a client's lawsuit, since a mistake or oversight in this area can deprive the client of his or her day in court regardless of how meritorious the client's claim may be. Given the central importance of this duty, our State's attorneys cannot be allowed to evade responsibility for its careful performance by the simple expedient of "farming out" the task to independent contractors. . . .

Our conclusion is also supported by the perceptions of the lay public and the average client, who may reasonably assume that all of the tasks associated with the commencement of an action, including its formal initiation through service of process, will be performed either by the attorney or someone acting under the attorney's direction. While it may be a common practice among attorneys to retain outside agencies like Fischer's to assist them in effecting service, that custom is not necessarily one of which the general public is aware. Even where a client is expressly made aware that a process serving agency will be retained, it is unlikely that the client will understand or appreciate that the process serving agency's legal status as an "independent contractor" could render the retained attorney immune from liability for the agency's negligence. Under established principles, the client's reasonable expectations and beliefs about who will render a particular service are a significant factor in identifying duties that should be deemed to be "nondelegable." . . .

Before closing, we note that, contrary to the concurrer's suggestion that our ruling has a far broader application, the nondelegable duty of care that we have recognized in this case is limited to the discrete and unique function of commencing an action through service of process. Furthermore, the duty extends only to clients who have retained an attorney for the purpose of commencing a lawsuit. We do not decide here the entirely separate question of an attorney's liability for the wrongs that a retained process server may commit against a potential defendant or another third party.[13] Nor do we consider the right of an attorney who has been held liable for the negligence of a retained process server to pursue whatever contractual or tort remedies that the attorney may have against that process server. We hold only that an attorney has a nondelegable duty to his or her clients to exercise due care in the service of process and that, accordingly, an attorney may be held liable to the client for negligent service of process, even though the task may have been "farmed out" to an independent contractor.[14]

In view of this conclusion, it is evident that the courts below erred in granting defendants' motion for summary judgment dismissing the complaint. . . . We note, however, that plaintiff is not herself entitled to summary judgment on the liability question at this point in the litigation, since she still must demonstrate both that the retained process server acted negligently and that she would have prevailed in the underlying action against Lauersen if the negligence had not occurred. Thus, the denial of plaintiff's cross motion for partial summary judgment was proper. . . .

Accordingly, the order of the Appellate Division should be modified, with costs to plaintiff, by denying defendants' motion for summary judgment dismissing the complaint and, as modified, affirmed.

BELLACOSA, JUDGE (concurring).

While I agree with the Court's result, I am unable to join in the broad rationale upon which it is premised. This case should be more prudently resolved on the narrower ground that questions of fact exist as to whether the defendant law firm was negligent in choosing its process server. . . . [P]laintiff alleges that the entity chosen by defendants, Fischer's Service Bureau, Inc., had a reputation for poor and sloppy service. [T]here are fact issues here which suffice to defeat defendants' summary judgment motion for dismissal.

The Court's result is reached instead by classifying service of process, for the first time, as a nondelegable duty of the attorney. This rationale opens up an unrealistic and undue liability channel. . . . For practical purposes, it will compel attorneys to

---

13. [A lower New York did resolve this issue in *Feldman v. Upton, Cohen & Slamowitz*, 740 N.Y.S.2d 790 (N.Y. Dist. Ct. 2002), deciding that the attorney is not vicariously liable to third parties for the tortious conduct of a process server.—Eds.]

14. [3] Contrary to the concurrer's concern about the practical implications of our holding, we find nothing untoward or "unrealistic" about a rule that holds practicing attorneys responsible to their clients for the negligence of the process servers they choose to retain. Further, we see no sound reason for permitting attorneys who happen to use outside process servers to escape liability while attorneys who use in-house staff to perform the same functions can be held liable under ordinary principles of respondeat superior.

assume the role of process servers themselves. While many large firms already have such in-house operatives, attorneys practicing in small firms and solo practitioners may now also have no choice but to hire in-house process servers so that the lawyers can always maintain direct supervision and control over them. No other way is left to avoid potential liability to disgruntled or harmed clients. . . .

[A]ttorneys in these situations have no effective control over the particular manner in which selected process servers do their jobs. The long-standing classification of process servers as independent contractors should be retained, with the result that attorneys would not be liable to plaintiff on a respondeat superior basis for the negligent acts of process servers.

KAYE, C.J., and SIMONS, HANCOCK and SMITH, JJ., concur with TITONE, J.

BELLACOSA, J., concurs in result in a separate opinion.

Notes

1. Is the inherently dangerous activity exception just another example of a nondelegable duty?

2. Many nondelegable duty cases involve either a special status of the defendant (such as a common carrier), a contractual relationship between plaintiff and defendant (such as landlord and tenant) or circumstances where defendant has extended an invitation to plaintiff, such as opening premises to the public. These categories can overlap in a particular case.

Maloney v. Rath, 445 P.2d 88 (Cal. 1968), extended nondelegable duty liability to a car owner who had recently had her car brakes overhauled at a service station. With no warning, her brakes failed and she hit plaintiff's car. The decision cited to a California statute requiring that vehicles must be equipped with adequate brakes, and held the innocent owner liable for the negligence of the service station on nondelegable duty grounds. The *Maloney* case is unusual and controversial because of its expansion of the concept of nondelegable duty to include routine automobile maintenance. For a forceful criticism of the expansion of vicarious liability to include such circumstances, see Williams, *Liability of Independent Contractors*, [1956] CAMBRIDGE L.J. 180, 194–96:

> The question to be asked about every form of vicarious liability, or liability without fault, is: What is to be gained from it? Let us grant, for the sake of argument, that vicarious responsibility for servants is regarded as socially justifiable, as it commonly is, and that several of the reasons traditionally given for this form of liability apply equally to suggest vicarious liability for contractors. Even so, there is one great difference, in general, between a contractor and a servant. This is that the contractor is likely to be a person of substance, with machinery and plant that can if necessary be sold to satisfy the judgment debt. It is unlikely that vicarious liability for servants would ever have been developed if servants as a class had been capable of paying damages and costs. The argument from poverty hardly

applies to contractors, who are often far wealthier than their employers. Where both employer and contractor are large firms or covered by insurance the incidence of tort liability may not greatly matter, but where the employer is an individual, who is not likely to be insured, the imposition of liability upon him may bring about the gravest hardship. He can, of course, obtain an indemnity from the contractor, if, perhaps after being sold up to pay the judgment debt, he is still able to carry on a legal battle. But it is not an argument for putting liability on the wrong person that he is able to obtain an indemnity from the real culprit.

From the point of view of the plaintiff, the only case in which the liability of the employer is advantageous is where the contractor is unable to pay the damages. Quite apart from the question of justice, it may be doubted whether this situation is sufficiently frequent to warrant provision being made for it, particularly when it adds so greatly to the difficulty of the law. . . . A rule of law that requires the victim to proceed in the first instance against the employer, on the basis of strict or vicarious liability, and then allows the employer to recover an indemnity from the contractor, is defective, because by creating the circuity of action it wastes the time and money of a person who need never have been brought in. It is platitudinous to remark that litigation in itself entails an economic loss to the parties and to society, so that a rule that needlessly extends the number of persons involved, and therefore the complexity of the litigation, is open to objection. So also is a rule that in effect requires double insurance, and moreover imposes the necessity of insurance upon a person who would not normally expect to bear the risk.

3. It should be noted that the above exceptions to the independent contractor doctrine often involve a nonagent independent contractor, which means that the question is one of general tort law. The concepts are closely related to the agency questions we have covered, however, and thus are treated here as a matter of convenience. Sometimes, for example, a case will involve a plaintiff arguing in the alternative that a negligent actor was the defendant's servant or, if not, nevertheless defendant is liable under an exception to the independent contractor doctrine.

4. With regard to the right of a person held vicariously liable for the tort of an independent contractor to indemnity from the contractor, see *Curtis v. A. Garica y Cia., Ltda.*, 272 F.2d 235, 237 (3d Cir. 1959) ("[A] general undertaking of an independent contractor to perform a job carries with it a promise, implied in fact, that the operation will be conducted in a safe, skillful and generally workmanlike manner. Though such a contract may contain no express agreement to indemnify, a breach of this warranty of workmanlike performance which results in a loss to the owner by way of liability to a third person in damages, is redressed by imposing an obligation to indemnify upon the responsible contractor."). See also *Warren v. McLouth Steel Corp.*, 111 Mich. App. 496, 314 N.W.2d 666 (1981), stating that indemnification can be based on the theory that the party entitled to indemnification was a passive tortfeasor as opposed to the active tort of the independent contractor or its servant.

5. Some commentary.

a. The following excerpt is taken from Guido Calabresi, *Some Thoughts on Risk Distribution and the Law of Torts*, 70 YALE L.J. 499, 545–46 (1961):

> *Independent Contractor.* An employer is not liable for the torts committed by independent contractors in his hire. This doctrine is justified in terms of our analysis if an independent contractor is defined as a party who would, *a priori*, be more likely to consider the risk in his market decisions than would his employer. Thus, a taxi driver is better suited to bear the risk of taxi accidents than the man who hires a cab. For the rider will almost certainly not carry insurance; and even if he does, he will not be influenced in his use of taxis by the fact that part of the cost of his general liability insurance stems from taking taxis. The taxi driver, on the other hand, will make his insurance cost part of the cost of riding cabs. [Calabresi argues that it is desirable to make taxi driving and other activities bear their full costs, since the consumer is then able to make an effective economic choice among competing activities. All other things being equal, the safest activity will be the least expensive; thus the level of accidents in general may be reduced through consumer choice of least costly activities. — Eds.]

b. Richard A. Posner, *A Theory of Negligence*, 1 J. LEGAL STUD. 29, 43 (1972), argues that the independent contractor exception to vicarious liability is economically justifiable. He observes that, since the person hiring the independent contractor does not control the details of the work, "there is no basis for anticipating that the work will be done more safely if the principal is liable. Nor is there a presumption that an independent contractor is insolvent and therefore undeterrable by the threat of tort liability from behaving, or permitting his employees to behave, carelessly." Professor Posner became a federal judge in 1981 and authored the opinion in the *Hixon* case, reproduced earlier in this section.

c. For a forceful dissent from the policy of broad exceptions to the independent contractor doctrine, see G. Williams, *Liability for Independent Contractors*, [1956] CAMBRIDGE L.J. 180, and *Some Reforms in the Law of Tort*, 24 MOD. L. REV. 101, 112–15 (1961). The first article was cited earlier in these materials.

d. For literature on the other side, urging severe limitation of or even abolition for the independent contractor doctrine, see McHugh, *Risk Administration in the Marketplace: A Reappraisal of the Independent Contractor Rule*, 40 U. CHI. L. REV. 661 (1973); Steffen, *Independent Contractor and the Good Life*, 2 U. CHI. L. REV. 501 (1935); Morris, *The Torts of an Independent Contractor*, 29 ILL. L. REV. 339 (1934).

Problems

1. Augustus Juilliard was the owner of a six-story office building in Manhattan, the various floors of which he rented to separate tenants. He furnished these tenants with passenger and freight elevator service. He did not, however, operate and

maintain the elevators using his own employees, but had a yearly contract with the Edward Engineering Company to do this work. Edward Engineering furnished an elevator attendant in uniform to operate the passenger elevator, one freight elevator attendant to operate that elevator, plus maintenance and cleaning service. The contract had been renewed from year to year for some four years at the time of the accident explained below.

The Department of Labor of New York City directed Juilliard to provide properly constructed sliding doors at all openings in the freight elevator shaft. Juilliard contracted with the Smith Company to do this work. Smith Company in turn sublet the contract to the National Sash & Door Company. Soon thereafter two employees of National Door began to install the sliding doors. In doing this it was necessary at times for the workmen to enter a portion of the freight elevator shaft. The work proceeded for about two weeks, during which time the freight elevator was used by the various tenants. An arrangement was made with the operator of the elevator to stop his car before reaching the place where the men were at work, or to give notice of its descent.

On the day of the accident Besner, one of the workmen, was leaning over into the shaft at the same time the operator was descending in the elevator with a shipment of 500 paper boxes from one of the tenants. The operator lowered the elevator without warning and knocked Besner into the shaft, killing him. His widow sued Juilliard for wrongful death. What result? As attorney for Mrs. Besner, what authority contained in the preceding materials would you rely upon in arguing on her behalf? What authority would you anticipate the defendant using?

2. Sunshine Biscuit is in the business of manufacturing food products. Ms. Mrachek, a woman 42 years of age, applied for a position at the New York City factory of the company. She was required to submit to a physical examination and to a blood test for the purpose of determining whether she was suffering from a communicable disease. Such testing was required by the regulations of the Board of Health of New York City. Sunshine Biscuit maintained for this purpose a pre-employment room for examinations, where it kept medical equipment for the use of its employees and where it also had available nurses and a physician. The nurses and the physician were employees of the company. They were carried on its payroll and were covered under the worker's compensation law.

The physician proceeded to take a blood test, with gruesome results for Ms. Mrachek. He attempted again and again to draw blood from her left arm, unsuccessfully. Apparently her veins were not discernible in the left arm but were in her right arm, where he ultimately took the sample. Ms. Mrachek is able to prove that as a result of negligent insertion of the needle she suffered severe and painful damage to the median and ulna nerves of the left arm, resulting in a permanent "claw-hand."

a. Make a case on Ms. Mrachek's behalf against Sunshine Biscuit, using the authority contained in the preceding materials. Then defend against it as the lawyer for the Company. What result would you predict?

b. Would it change your analysis if the physician had his own practice and dropped over to Sunshine's plant three afternoons a week to give physicals? If so, why? Would it change anything from the perspective of Ms. Mrachek?

c. Would it make any difference if the physician maintained his own office (which, together with many other offices, was near the plant) and Sunshine Biscuit always sent its applicants over to his office for testing? Again, if so, why, and from whose perspective? See, with respect to the original set of facts, *Mrachek v. Sunshine Biscuit, Inc.*, 283 App. Div. 105, 126 N.Y.S.2d 383 (1953), *aff'd*, 308 N.Y. 116, 123 N.E.2d 801 (1954), noted in 3 Buffalo L. Rev. 311 (1954).

3. *A* plans to sell her house without the services of a real estate broker. She plans to be away one weekend, so she asks her friend *B*, a musician, to show the house for her while she is gone, giving *B* authority to sign a contract of sale for her if that proves necessary. *B* locates an interested person and, while driving the prospective purchaser to the house, negligently causes an accident. Is *A* vicariously liable for *B*'s negligence?

3. Borrowed Servants

As we have seen, the relationship between an independent contractor and the person engaging its services is not one upon which the law imposes vicarious liability, although liability can be incurred under several exceptions to this doctrine. Suppose, however, the tortfeasor (Baker), the operator of a bulldozer, is employed and paid on a full-time basis by a separate business (sometimes called the "general employer") that specializes in renting operators and equipment. For several weeks Baker has been working as operator of a bulldozer for a party (sometimes called the "special employer") who is paying the general employer for Baker's time and for the use of the bulldozer. Baker reports to work to the special employer every day and takes all his orders from the foreman of the special employer.

One day Baker negligently injures someone with the bulldozer. The special employer is sued on vicarious liability grounds. Does the resolution of the question "servant or independent contractor" end the inquiry?

Perhaps it should. As you will see, however, the law in this area has specialized to some extent, with its own terminology, and poses a hard question concerning the shifting between employers of exposure to vicarious liability on vaguely defined grounds.

Charles v. Barrett

Court of Appeals of New York
135 N.E. 127 (1922)

Cardozo, J.

One Steinhauser was in the trucking business. He supplied the Adams Express Company, the defendant, with a motor van and a chauffeur at the rate of $2 an hour.

The defendant did the work of loading at its station and unloading at the railroad terminal. It sealed the van at the point of departure and unsealed at the point of destination. Between departure and destination, the truck remained without interference or supervision in charge of the chauffeur. While so engaged, it struck and killed the plaintiff's son. Negligence is not disputed. The question is whether the defendant shall answer for the wrong. The trial judge ruled as a matter of law that it must; the Appellate Division, holding the contrary, dismissed the complaint.

We think that truck and driver were in the service of the general employer. There was no such change of masters as would relieve Steinhauser of liability if the driver of the van had broken the seals, and stolen the contents. By the same token, there was no such change as to relieve of liability for other torts committed in the conduct of the enterprise. Where to go and when might be determined for the driver by the commands of the defendant. The duty of going carefully, for the safety of the van as well as for that of wayfarers, remained a duty to the master at whose hands he had received possession. Neither the contract nor its performance shows a change of control so radical as to disturb that duty or its incidence. The plaintiff refers to precedents which may not unreasonably be interpreted as pointing in a different direction. Minute analysis will show that distinguishing features are not lacking. Thus, in *Hartell v. Simonson & Son Co.* (218 N.Y. 345) the special employer used his own truck. The submission to a new "sovereign" was more intimate and general (*Driscoll v. Towle*, 181 Mass. 416, 418). We do not say that in every case the line of division has been accurately drawn. The principle declared by the decisions remains unquestioned. At most the application is corrected. The rule now is that as long as the employee is furthering the business of his general employer by the service rendered to another, there will be no inference of a new relation unless command has been surrendered, and no inference of its surrender from the mere fact of its division.

The judgment should be affirmed with costs.

Hiscock, Ch. J., Pound, McLaughlin, Crane and Andrews, JJ., concur; Hogan, J., not voting.

Judgment affirmed.

Notes

1. In accord with *Charles*, see *Beatty v. H.B. Owsley & Sons*, 53 N.C. App. 178, 182, 280 S.E.2d 484, 487, *petition for review denied*, 304 N.C. 192, 285 S.E.2d 95 (1981). This case involved responsibility for an injury caused by a crane operator (Thompson) employed by Owsley, the general employer. Thompson had worked in the special employer's (Kaiser) plant for several months prior to the accident. Owsley contended that Thompson had become a borrowed servant of Kaiser in view of Kaiser's control over Thompson's work. The court addressed the issue in the following terms:

> The North Carolina Supreme Court has ... held a general employer liable even when the special employer controlled the details of the work

and the manner of doing the work. . . . Consequently, the fact that Kaiser instructed Thompson when to lift panels, how to lift panels, and where and how to place them is not enough, standing alone, to make Thompson an employee of Kaiser.

It is significant that Owsley had the power to hire and fire Thompson, that Thompson was a specialist — a skilled crane operator — and that Owsley was in the business of renting heavy equipment and people to operate the equipment. We quote relevant portions of Restatement (Second) of Agency § 227, Comment c (1958):

> [A] continuation of the general employment is indicated by the fact that the general employer can properly substitute another servant at any time, that the time of the new employment is short, and that the lent servant has the skill of a specialist.

> A continuance of the general employment is also indicated in the operation of a machine where the general employer rents the machine and a servant to operate it, particularly if the instrumentality is of considerable value. . . . [T]he fact that the general employer is in the business of renting machines and men is relevant, since in such case there is more likely to be an intent to retain control over the instrumentality.

> . . . In the case at bar, we find Thompson to be the agent of Owsley as a matter of law.

2. Many borrowed servant cases, like *Charles v. Barrett*, involve the loaning of an employee and equipment from a company that has trained the employee and owns the specialized equipment that the employee uses in the service of the special employer. In determining which employer is liable to third parties injured by the employee, the focus of many courts has been on which employer had the right to control the employee's conduct at the time of the negligent act, on the rationale that such employer was in the best position to prevent the injury. *E.g., Tarron v. Bowen Machine & Fabricating, Inc.*, 213 P.3d 309 (Ariz. Ct. App. 2009) (summary judgment against general employer reversed because general employer offered evidence to controvert that it had right to control employee); *Nepstad v. Lambert*, 50 N.W.2d 614 (Minn. 1951) (holding the special employer liable on the basis of its "on-the-spot" control of the employee at the time that the accident occurred); Restatement (Third) of Agency § 7.03, cmt. (d)(2) ("Liability should be allocated to the employer in the better position to take measures to prevent the injury suffered by the third party. An employer is in that position if the employer has the right to control an employee's conduct. When both a general and special employer have the right to control an employee's conduct, the practical history of direction may establish that one employer in fact ceded its right of control to the other, whether through its failure to exercise the right or otherwise."). In some instances, the courts have imposed liability on both the general and special employer. *E.g., Gordon v. S.M. Byers Motor Car Co.*, 164 A. 334 (Pa. 1932); *contra, De Pratt v. Sergio*, 306 N.W.2d 62 (Wis. 1981) ("the dual liability approach, though having some merit, does not offer a simple and easily applicable alternative to the borrowed servant rule, and we decline to [adopt it]").

In recent years, many companies have gone into the business of "loaning employees." They typically provide no training or equipment and, indeed, generally exercise no role in the hiring decision. All of that is left to the special employer, with the general employer just providing payroll services, including the provision of medical insurance, etc., for the special employer. The next case considers whether the general employer retains any vicarious liability for the acts of the loaned employee, an important question in this growing industry.

ATS, Inc. v. Beddingfield

Supreme Court of Alabama
878 So. 2d 1131 (2003)

SEE, JUSTICE

ATS, Inc., and ATS, Inc. of Georgia (hereinafter collectively referred to as "ATS") appeal from a judgment entered on a jury verdict in favor of the plaintiffs, Glenn Beddingfield and Stephanie Beddingfield, Roger Nash and Tami Nash, and Leo Byrtice Crawford (hereinafter collectively referred to as "the plaintiffs"). ATS argues that it was entitled to a judgment as a matter of law on the plaintiffs' vicarious-liability claims based on the loaned-servant doctrine. We reverse and remand.

I.

ATS is an employee-leasing company; it contracts with small businesses to consolidate their employees into a single entity for purposes of providing payroll services and benefits such as medical insurance, retirement plans, and workers' compensation. Under those contracts, the employees of the small businesses become employees of ATS. Thereafter, ATS leases the employees back to its customer-the small business. This arrangement is essentially one of form instead of substance. That is, ATS's leasing contract does not otherwise alter an employee's job responsibilities or supervisory setting at the customer's business.

Mercer Trucking, Inc., a Georgia corporation ("Mercer Trucking"), became an ATS customer in 1997. Erwin Mercer, president of Mercer Trucking, became interested in the employee-leasing concept as a way to provide his drivers with workers' compensation benefits and to reduce some of the payroll duties associated with running a business. ATS and Mercer Trucking entered into a "Personnel Payroll Service Agreement" on April 16, 1997. This agreement provided, in relevant part:

"2. ATS, Inc. of Georgia will pay the employee's wages, provide any applicable benefits, and will pay all applicable federal and state taxes with respect to the employment of such personnel including social security, [and] federal and state unemployment compensation taxes. ATS, Inc. of Georgia further will maintain payroll records and reports for all employees.

"3. ATS, Inc. of Georgia will procure and maintain Worker's Compensation Insurance on all personnel supplied [to Mercer Trucking] hereunder as required by applicable law. . . .

"5. *Work related instructions of personnel will be handled by [Mercer Trucking] personnel.*" (Emphasis added.)

Mercer retained primary responsibility for hiring and firing drivers in the same manner as he had before Mercer Trucking entered into the payroll-service agreement with ATS. That is, Mercer chose the drivers ATS employed and leased back to Mercer Trucking. Because ATS was technically the employer of Mercer Trucking's drivers, it did have the authority to fire any of the drivers at will. However, the president of ATS testified that he never exercised this authority with any of ATS's customers. Instead, ATS removed employees from its payroll only at the direction of the business that was its customer.

As an additional service, ATS sponsored safety meetings for its payroll-service customers at no additional cost. The safety meetings were tailored to a customer's business and were provided only at a customer's request. ATS conducted one such safety meeting on Mercer Trucking's behalf on December 1, 1997.

In May 1999, Roger Walker responded to a newspaper advertisement, which stated that Mercer Trucking was looking for truck drivers. On May 22, 1999, Walker had an interview with Mercer at Mercer Trucking. After Walker filled out some paperwork and took a road test to assess his driving abilities, Mercer hired Walker. At this time, Mercer explained to Walker that he would be an employee of ATS but that Walker would still receive orders from Mercer.

Mercer also gave Walker ATS's employment policies manual, which ATS had prepared exclusively for Mercer Trucking. This manual contained rules and regulations that all ATS employees working for Mercer Trucking were expected to follow. Those rules set forth the duties required of ATS employees in their "general conduct" of Mercer Trucking's business. Mercer Trucking, as a payroll-service customer, was primarily responsible for enforcing those employment policies.

One of the documents Walker signed on his date of hire was an "Acceptance of Employment" form that contained the following provision:

"I, Roger D. Walker, do hereby accept employment with ATS, Inc. of Georgia, with the following express understanding [sic] agreements [sic]:

"I do expressly acknowledge, agree, and understand that I am to be employed solely by ATS, Inc. of Georgia, and that, *although I may be under some day-to-day supervision from someone other than ATS, Inc. of Georgia,* I hereby expressly do not consent to any employer-employee relationship with any other party. I further expressly object to, and reject being a special or other classification of employee, either expressly or by implication, of anyone other than ATS, Inc. of Georgia." (Emphasis added.)

May 26, 1999, was Walker's first day driving for Mercer Trucking. Walker received instructions directly from Mercer as to where he should pick up and drop off loads. Walker telephoned Mercer for instructions each time he finished unloading his truck.

On May 27, 1999, Walker dropped off a truckload of cargo at Tom's Potato Chips in Knoxville, Tennessee. After unloading, Walker telephoned Mercer for further instructions. Mercer told Walker to drive to Chattanooga for a possible pickup. Walker drove south on Interstate 75 toward Chattanooga. Seeing a sign warning of road work ahead, Walker slowed his truck to 50 miles per hour. Walker then realized that the traffic ahead of him had stopped, and he started to brake. Walker attempted to maneuver his truck into the emergency lane, but it continued to slide forward and collided with a minivan stopped in the traffic. All four occupants in the minivan were killed.

Walker telephoned Mercer to report the accident. Walker had no contact with anyone at ATS regarding the accident. . . .

In January 2000, the plaintiffs, as personal representatives of the estates of the deceased victims, initiated wrongful-death actions against Walker, Mercer Trucking, ATS, and other defendants in the Jefferson Circuit Court. The plaintiffs asserted claims against both ATS and Mercer Trucking of (1) negligence and recklessness under the doctrine of respondeat superior and (2) negligent and reckless hiring. On April 3, 2001, ATS moved for a summary judgment. On August 2, 2001, the trial court denied ATS's motion. . . .

ATS moved for a judgment as a matter of law ("JML") both at the close of the plaintiffs' evidence and at the close of all the evidence. The trial court denied each motion and submitted interrogatories to the jury. The jury answered the special interrogatories, finding that Walker's conduct was negligent and reckless and that both ATS and Mercer Trucking were vicariously liable for Walker's conduct.

. . . [T]he jury [also] found that ATS and Mercer Trucking were not liable on the negligent- and reckless-hiring claims [and imposed compensatory and punitive damages against ATS amounting to $24.5 million]. . . .

ATS argues that under the loaned-servant doctrine it is not vicariously liable for Walker's negligent and reckless actions. We agree.

Because the accident giving rise to this action occurred in Tennessee, the parties agree that the substantive issues in this case are governed by Tennessee law. Under Tennessee law, an employer is liable for an employee's negligence based solely upon the doctrine of respondeat superior. To determine whether a master-servant or employer-employee relationship exists, "control is a key element." *Armoneit v. Elliott Crane Serv., Inc.*, 65 S.W.3d 623, 629 (Tenn. Ct. App. 2001). Unlike Alabama, "[i]n Tennessee, the right to control the result is not determinative of the existence of the relation of master and servant, but the actual control of means and methods is." *Id.* (citing *McDonald v. Dunn Constr. Co.*, 182 Tenn. 213, 220, 185 S.W.2d 517, 520 (1945)).

Under the loaned-servant doctrine, "[a]n employee of one employer may become the servant of another and shift the liability for his negligent acts to the second employer." *Parker v. Vanderbilt Univ.*, 767 S.W.2d 412, 416 (Tenn. Ct. App. 1988). In *Gaston v. Sharpe*, 179 Tenn. 609, 614, 168 S.W.2d 784, 786 (1943), the Supreme Court of Tennessee adopted the *Restatement of Agency* view in fashioning a test to determine whether an employee of one employer is the loaned servant of another employer:

> "'Since the question of liability is always raised because of some specific act done, the important question is not whether or not [the employee] remains the servant of the general employer as to matters generally, but whether or not, as to the act in question, he is acting in the business of and under the direction of one or the other. It is not conclusive that in practice he would be likely to obey the directions of the general employer in the case of conflict of orders. The question is as to whether it is understood between him and his employers that he is to remain in the allegiance of the first as to a specific act, or is to be employed in the business of and subject to the direction of the temporary employer as to the details of such act. This is a question of fact in each case.'"

As the above rule acknowledges, whether an employee of one becomes the loaned servant of another is a question of fact. *Id.* However, in this case, there is no conflicting evidence as to where authority to direct the specific act that caused the deadly accident lay.

First, the authority vested in Mercer Trucking as to its leased employees is set forth in the payroll-service agreement between Mercer Trucking and ATS. "The interpretation of an unambiguous written agreement is a question of law for the court." *Parker*, 767 S.W.2d at 417. In *Parker*, the Tennessee Court of Appeals, applying the test set forth in *Gaston* and relying on the terms of an unambiguous agreement between Vanderbilt University and a local hospital, held that a doctor was the loaned servant of the hospital. *Id.* Pursuant to the agreement, Vanderbilt University provided the local hospital with surgical residents. The agreement specifically provided that the residents, as members of the hospital's surgical staff, were accountable solely to the hospital.

Similarly, in this case, the payroll-service agreement between Mercer Trucking and ATS states that Mercer Trucking was responsible for providing any "work related instructions" to its leased personnel. On May 27, 1999, Mercer, exercising the authority vested in him by the payroll-service agreement, instructed Walker to proceed to Chattanooga for a possible pickup on Mercer Trucking's behalf. While Walker was en route to Chattanooga, he was "acting in the business of and under the direction of [Mercer]." *Gaston*, 179 Tenn. at 614, 168 S.W.2d at 786. Thus, under the *Gaston* test, Walker was acting as the loaned servant of Mercer Trucking at the time of the fatal accident.

The plaintiffs argue that because Mercer Trucking did not provide Walker with specific instructions as to how to drive the truck, Walker cannot be deemed to be a loaned servant of Mercer Trucking. They claim that ATS retained responsibility for training and supervising the drivers it leased, and that, therefore, ATS retained authority over the specific act that caused the accident, namely, Walker's driving. In support of this argument, the plaintiffs point to the employment policies manual Walker received when he was hired.

Contrary to the plaintiffs' suggestion, the manual does not contain any instructions on how to drive a truck. The manual actually directs employees to communicate with Mercer Trucking, not with ATS, "for matters pertaining to [their] dispatch." Walker's driving caused the accident, not his failure to perform the general tasks described in the manual, and it is Walker's driving, not ATS's retention of control regarding Walker's general conduct in performing Mercer Trucking's business, that is relevant to this analysis. *Gaston*, 179 Tenn. at 614–15, 168 S.W.2d at 786. . . .

We conclude that, as a matter of law, Walker was the loaned servant of Mercer Trucking at the time of the accident, and, therefore, that ATS is not liable for Walker's negligent and reckless actions. The trial court's order denying ATS's motion for a JML is reversed, and this cause is remanded to the trial court to enter a judgment in favor of ATS consistent with this opinion.

HOUSTON, LYONS, BROWN, JOHNSTONE, HARWOOD, WOODALL, and STUART, JJ., concur. MOORE, C.J., concurs in the result.

The Captain of the Ship Doctrine
Sparger v. Worley Hospital, Inc.

Supreme Court of Texas
547 S.W.2d 582 (1977)

POPE, JUSTICE.

This is a medical malpractice case. The plaintiff Sylvia Caldwell sued Worley Hospital, Inc. and Dr. C. F. Sparger for injuries resulting from the failure to remove a sponge from Mrs. Caldwell's abdominal cavity after an operation. The trial court rendered judgment on a jury verdict for plaintiff against Worley Hospital only. The court of civil appeals reversed that judgment and held that Dr. Sparger under the captain of the ship doctrine was liable as a matter of law and that the defendants were jointly and severally liable. 529 S.W.2d 639. We reverse the judgment of the court of civil appeals and affirm the judgment of the trial court.

The jury by its verdict found that someone in the group comprising Dr. Sparger, Dr. Bellamy, and the surgical nurses was negligent with respect to the sponge that was found in Mrs. Caldwell's abdomen. The jury found that this negligence was the proximate cause of Mrs. Caldwell's injury. The jury refused to find that Dr. Sparger failed to exercise ordinary care by looking for the sponge in question before closing the incision in plaintiff's abdomen. The jury did find that Wanda Ensey, Marjie Holland, Geneva Finney, (nurses) or any of them, failed to make a correct sponge count and this negligence was the proximate cause of Mrs. Caldwell's injury. The jury refused to find that in watching after the sponges the three nurses were the borrowed servants of Dr. Sparger.

The plaintiff did not sue the nurses, and Dr. Bellamy has gone out of the case by reason of an instructed verdict in his favor. The jury answers exonerated Dr. Sparger from every act of negligence for which he was charged and found instead that the nurses were negligent. Dr. Sparger is therefore before us with an application for writ of error in which he insists that the court of civil appeals should not have held him vicariously liable as a matter of law for the negligence of the nurses under the so-called captain of the ship doctrine. Worley Hospital's application contends that Dr. Sparger must bear the sole liability since the captain of the ship doctrine made the nurses his exclusive employees. The issue presented is whether Dr. Sparger is liable as captain of the ship notwithstanding the finding that the nurses were not his borrowed servants.

If this was anything but a malpractice case, the question before us would be resolved by the jury's refusal to find that Dr. Sparger had borrowed the Worley Hospital's nurses so as to make them his employees. Mrs. Caldwell sought to hold Dr. Sparger vicariously liable for the improper sponge count by submitting the following special issue concerning the employment relationship between the surgeon and the assisting nurses:

Special Issue Number Four:

Do you find from a preponderance of the evidence that in watching after the lap packs Wanda Ensey, Marjie Holland and Geneva Finney were borrowed employees of Dr. Sparger?

A "Borrowed Employee," as used in this charge, means one, who, while in the general employment of the hospital, is subject to the right of the physician to direct or control the details of the particular work inquired about, and is not merely cooperating with suggestions of said physician.

An employee in the general employment of one employer may be temporarily loaned to another so as to become a borrowed employed [sic] of the second employer. Under these circumstances, a person may serve two masters simultaneously and at times only momentarily.

Answer "Yes" or "No"

ANSWER: No

. . . Under the borrowed servant doctrine the essential inquiry would be whether or not the surgeon had the *right to control* the assisting nurses in the details "of the specific act raising the issue of liability." The right of control is ordinarily a question of fact.

The principle of borrowed servant cuts across the entire law of principal and agent and employer and employee, and is therefore also applicable to the legal relationships between a physician or surgeon and a nurse. Physicians and surgeons are and should be subject to the usual rules applicable to borrowed servants. In some jurisdictions, however, there has been imposed upon the medical profession, a special and more onerous form of vicarious liability. Our question is whether they should have an extra liability imposed upon them.

The phrase "captain of the ship," was first employed in the medical malpractice context in the case of *McConnell v. Williams*, 361 Pa. 355, 65 A.2d 243 (1959). It was used in that case as an apt analogy but in some jurisdictions the phrase has grown into a separate and independent concept of agency which specially applies to medical malpractice cases.

In naval parlance, the captain of a ship is in total command and is charged with full responsibility for the care and efficiency of the ship and the welfare of all hands. His authority over his own ship and crew is supreme. The captain does not, however, assume personal responsibility for the acts of misconduct or for the criminal deeds committed by the individual men aboard his ship. The court in *McConnell* did not in fact, impose liability upon the surgeon under its handy phrase which characterized him as the captain of the ship. The court instead ruled that "[i]t is for the jury to determine whether the relationship between defendant and the interns, at the time the child's eyes were injured, was that of master and servant. . . ." The court remanded the cause for the factual determination. Other medical malpractice cases have treated the disputed borrowed servant issue in the same manner, as one of fact.

Similes sometimes help to explain a factual situation, but in legal writing, phrases have a way of being canonized and of growing until they can stand and walk independently of the usual general rules. Mr. Justice Frankfurter once wrote concerning such phrase-making in judicial opinions: "The phrase . . . is an excellent illustration of the extent to which uncritical use of words bedevils the law. A phrase begins life as a literary expression; its felicity leads to its lazy repetition; and repetition soon establishes it as a legal formula, undiscriminatingly used to express different and sometimes contradictory ideas." *Tiller v. Atlantic Coast Line R. Co.*, 318 U.S. 54, 68, 63 S. Ct. 444, 452, 87 L. Ed. 610 (1942). The result in the use of captain of the ship is that a surgeon or physician may be held liable, not as others upon the basis of the general rule of borrowed servant, but as captain of the ship.

The jurisdiction which first employed the metaphor has now retreated from the concept so that occurrences in the operating room might be brought back to the confines of the more general borrowed servant concept. The court in *Thomas v. Hutchinson*, 442 Pa. 118, 275 A.2d 23 (1971), said that the captain of the ship example was intended as an adaptation of the familiar borrowed servant principle that applies generally in the law of agency. See Note, *Malpractice-Vicarious Liability of an Operating Surgeon*, 10 DUQUESNE L. REV. 117 (1971). Hence, where there are inconsistent factual inferences concerning the servant's employer which can be reasonably drawn from evidence, the issue should be resolved factually as any other borrowed servant issue.

This court has not previously addressed the question of the adoption of the captain of the ship doctrine as a basis for a surgeon's liability in addition to his responsibility under the borrowed servant doctrine. In *Webb v. Jorns*, 488 S.W.2d 407 (Tex. 1973), the application of the captain of the ship doctrine was not an issue since the physicians conceded that they were subject to liability for actions of any of the persons under their supervision in the operating room. 488 S.W.2d at 411. In *McKinney v. Tromly*, 386 S.W.2d 564 (Tex. Civ. App. 1965, writ ref'd n.r.e.), the court approved the doctrine. The judgment in that case, however, was not grounded upon the mere presence of the surgeon in the operating room but, as the opinion stated, upon the admitted fact that the doctor had absolute right of control of all personnel in the operating room during the operation. Later, *Harle v Krchnak*, 422 S.W.2d 810 (Tex. Civ. App. 1968, writ ref'd n.r.e.), followed *McKinney* without discussion.

We now disapprove *McKinney* and *Harle* insofar as they suggest that a surgeon's mere presence in the operating room makes him liable as a matter of law for the negligence of other persons. We disapprove the captain of the ship doctrine and hold that it is a false special rule of agency. Operating surgeons and hospitals are subject to the principles of agency law which apply to others. *Tonsic v. Wagner*, [329 A.2d 497 (Pa. 1974)], *supra*; *Bilonoha v. Zubritzky*, 233 Pa. Super. 136, 336 A.2d 351 (1975). The state of the facts may in some cases be such as to make one a surgeon's employee or borrowed servant as a matter of law, but that is not the factual situation before us in this case.

The question remains whether the facts show that, as a matter of law, the nurses were the borrowed servants of Dr. Sparger. . . .

Wanda Ensey, the scrub nurse, testified that Dr. Sparger did not direct her and Mrs. Holland to make the sponge count. Mrs. Ensey stated that the two nurses knew how to perform the sponge count, because it was part of the manual regulations which they followed. Reasonable minds might differ as to the facts which presented the borrowed servant issue.

We conclude, therefore, as did the trial court, that plaintiff should have judgment against Worley Hospital since the jury made a finding that it was hospital's employees who were negligent. Since the captain of the ship idea is a false issue and the jury found as a fact that the nurses were not the borrowed servants of Dr. Sparger, plaintiff was not entitled to a judgment against Dr. Sparger. . . .

SAM D. JOHNSON, J., dissents. . . .

Note

Although rejected in *Sparger*, the doctrine is recognized in other jurisdictions. *See, e.g., Ochoa v. Vered*, 212 P.3d 963 (Colo. App. 2009). For a scholarly discussion of the history and various formulations of the "captain of the ship" theory, see *Franklin v. Gupta*, 567 A.2d 524 (Md. App. 1990).

Problems

1. Suppose a crane operator is injured by the negligence of one of the laborers on the job site. What legal position would the operator want to take?

2. The following hypothetical is from § 227, illustration 3, of the Restatement (Second) of Agency:

> *P*, a master carpenter, by agreement with *B*, sends *A*, a skilled cabinetmaker, to work with *B*'s servants for a week, under the direction of *B*'s foreman, in the reconstruction of a stairway. For this *B* is to pay *P* an agreed amount. *A* acts as the servant of *B* in building the stairway.

Can you explain this result?

3. A doctor left at a hospital a post-operative order that his patient was to be given an injection of tetracycline every 12 hours. The nurse on duty, acting under this order, negligently injected the prescribed dosage into the patient's sciatic nerve, causing permanent foot paralysis. Both the doctor and the hospital are sued.

a. Which party will be held responsible for the acts of the nurse? Approach your analysis of this problem from two perspectives: (i) using the preceding materials, argue the case for the hospital, the doctor and the plaintiff (who will be proceeding against both, presumably); (ii) acting as judge, to which party would you allocate the loss?

b. Would your analysis change if the nurse had committed the same act pursuant to the same instructions during the course of the operation? Immediately after it?

4. The Scope of Employment Limitation

As was stated in *Jones v. Hart*, a master is vicariously liable for the negligence of his servant when the servant "runs his cart over a boy." As we have seen, this concept won overwhelming approval in the common law, with the only serious questions that remain centering on the scope of the concept and its underlying rationale, and with the answers to those questions seemingly interdependent.

Suppose, however, that the servant had "run his cart over a boy" while returning from a 10-block side trip (off an 18 block route) to the office of a competitor of his master to look for another job at a higher wage. Or suppose he had injured someone while taking a load of personal goods home in the cart after work. Or suppose he had intentionally run his cart into a personal enemy while directly on his route making a delivery.

Should the above variations be treated differently than when the servant negligently runs over a boy while delivering his master's goods pursuant to orders and while on the shortest route between the master's and the customer's places of business? If so, why?

Pause at this point and try to work out your own answers to the above questions. Then, as you read through this chapter, test your answers against those that various judges and writers have advanced. Have you or have they come up with a rationale that would satisfy you as a judge in making decisions on the myriad fact situations that can arise in this area?

a. Negligent Acts

Joel v. Morison

England, Nisi Prius (Exchequer)
6 Car. & P. 501, 172 Eng. Rep. 1338 (1834)

The declaration stated, that, on the 18th of April, 1833, the plaintiff was proceeding on foot across a certain public and common highway, and that the defendant was possessed of a cart and horse, which were under the care, government, and direction of a servant of his, who was driving the same along the said highway, and that the defendant by his said servant so carelessly, negligently, and improperly drove, governed, and directed the said horse and cart, that, by the carelessness, negligence, and improper conduct of the defendant by his servant, the cart and horse were driven against the plaintiff, and struck him, whereby he was thrown down and the bone of one of his legs was fractured, and he was ill in consequence, and prevented from transacting his business, and obliged to incur a great expense in and about the setting the said bone, &c., and a further great expense in retaining and employing divers persons to superintend and look after his business for six calendar months. Plea — Not guilty.

From the evidence on the part of the plaintiff it appeared that he was in Bishops-gate-street, when he was knocked down by a cart and horse coming in the direction from Shoreditch, which were sworn to have been driven at the time by a person who was the servant of the defendant, another of his servants being in the cart with him. The injury was a fracture of the fibula.

On the part of the defendant witnesses were called, who swore that his cart was for weeks before and after the time sworn to by the plaintiff's witnesses only in the habit of being driven between Burton Crescent Mews and Finchley, and did not go into the City at all.

Thesiger, for the plaintiff, in reply, suggested that either the defendant's servants might in coming from Finchley have gone out of their way for their own purposes, or might have taken the cart at a time when it was not wanted for the purpose of business, and have gone to pay a visit to some friend. He was observing that, under these circumstances, the defendant was liable for the acts of his servants.

PARKE, B. — He is not liable if, as you suggest, these young men took the cart without leave; he is liable if they were going *extra viam* in going from Burton Crescent Mews to Finchley; but if they chose to go of their own accord to see a friend, when they were not on their master's business, he is not liable.

His Lordship afterwards, in summing up, said—This is an action to recover damages for an injury sustained by the plaintiff, in consequence of the negligence of the defendant's servant. There is no doubt that the plaintiff has suffered the injury, and there is no doubt that the driver of the cart was guilty of negligence, and there is no doubt also that the master, if that person was driving the cart on his master's business, is responsible. If the servants, being on their master's business, took a detour to call upon a friend, the master will be responsible. If you think the servants lent the cart to a person who was driving without the defendant's knowledge, he will not be responsible. Or, if you think that the young man who was driving took the cart surreptitiously, and was not at the time employed on his master's business, the defendant will not be liable. The master is only liable where the servant is acting in the course of his employment. If he was going out of his way, against his master's implied commands, when driving on his master's business, he will make his master liable; but if he was going on a frolic of his own, without being at all on his master's business, the master will not be liable. As to the damages, the master is not guilty of any offence, he is only responsible in law, therefore the amount should be reasonable.

Verdict for the plaintiff—damages, £ 30.

Notes

1. We are unable to ascertain from the opinion the distance that defendant's servants deviated from their authorized route. A look at the literal language of the opinion leaves the impression that the extent of the deviation was immaterial, so long as the servant was "at all" on his master's business. As you read through the remaining materials, recall the breadth of the court's language, written before liability insurance was available. (Liability insurance apparently was not generally available until the latter part of the nineteenth century. *See* Douglas, *Vicarious Liability and Administration of Risk I*, 38 YALE L.J. 584, 591 (1929).)

2. The *Joel* case introduced the language of "frolic or detour" into this area of the law. As the opinion notes, when a servant is on a frolic, he is outside of the scope of his employment and his master is no longer vicariously liable for his actions. A detour is a deviation within the scope of employment. For an economic analysis of the concept of scope of employment, see Alan O. Sykes, *The Boundaries of Vicarious Liability: An Economic Analysis of the Scope of Employment Rule and Related Legal Doctrines*, 101 HARV. L. REV. 563 (1988).

3. Defendant sent a truckload of its merchandise from Manhattan to Staten Island, instructing its driver to bring the truck back to its garage at 23rd Street and 11th Avenue on the west side of Manhattan. After making the delivery, the driver instead drove to Hamilton Street on the east side of Manhattan to visit his mother, where a neighborhood carnival was in progress. He took a group of boys in fantastic costumes on a tour of the district, stopping at a pool room on Catherine Street to say a word to a friend. As he drove off, with some of the boys still on the truck, an 11-year-old boy trying to join them was injured. The driver stated at the trial that

his purpose was to return to the garage. The boy sued defendant on respondeat superior grounds.

Upon the above facts a jury found that the driver was in the course of his employment and the defendant was held liable at the trial level. *See Fiocco v. Carver*, 234 N.Y. 219, 137 N.E. 309 (1922). What would be your argument on appeal on behalf of the defendant? What would be your decision as a judge?

Do the following quotes from the Restatement (Second) and three other New York cases affect the decision you reached?

Title B — Torts of Servant, Scope of Employment

§ 228. *General Statement*

(1) Conduct of a servant is within the scope of employment if, but only if:

(a) it is of the kind he is employed to perform;

(b) it occurs substantially within the authorized time and space limits;

(c) it is actuated, at least in part, by a purpose to serve the master, and

(d) if force is intentionally used by the servant against another, the use of force is not unexpectable by the master.

(2) Conduct of a servant is not within the scope of employment if it is different in kind from that authorized, far beyond the authorized time or space limits, or too little actuated by a purpose to serve the master.

§ 229. *Kind of Conduct within Scope of Employment*

(1) To be within the scope of the employment, conduct must be of the same general nature as that authorized, or incidental to the conduct authorized. . . .

The succeeding 20 sections of the Restatement (Second) treat in more detail the general standards set forth above. Section 237 deals with the subject of "re-entry" after a frolic, stating that a servant does not re-enter the scope of employment "until he is again reasonably near the authorized space and time limits and is acting with the intention of serving his master's business."

In *Riley v. Standard Oil Co.*, 231 N.Y. 301, 308, 132 N.E. 97, 99 (1921), noted in 31 YALE L.J. 99 (1921), and 20 MICH. L. REV. 98 (1921), a driver for the defendant was instructed to obtain some paint from the Long Island Railroad freight yards 2½ miles away from defendant's mill and to return at once. After the truck was loaded at the freight yards, the driver picked up some waste pieces of wood and left the yards in the opposite direction from the mill to take the wood to his sister's house four blocks away. This accomplished, he started back to the mill. His course would have led him directly past the freight yards, but he negligently caused an accident after he had driven only a short distance from his sister's house.

The court, in a 4–3 decision, held that the servant was within the scope of employment, apparently as a matter of law (the exact holding of the court is unclear, since a new trial was directed with no explanation of what issue was left to be tried). The majority opinion did note that a question of fact would have been raised for the jury had the accident occurred between leaving the yards and arriving at the sister's house. The dissent, per McLaughlin, J., stated that the driver's act was not a "mere deviation," he was doing an independent act of his own, and he could not as a matter of law re-enter the employment "until he had again reached the yard. . . . I cannot believe that the liability of the defendant here is to be determined by the way in which the truck was headed. Rights of property do not rest upon such a slender thread."

In *Clawson v. Pierce-Arrow Motor Car Co.*, 231 N.Y. 273, 275, 277, 131 N.E. 914, 915 (1921), a servant of defendant drove the manager of defendant's sales department home in one of defendant's demonstrator cars. The manager then directed him to drive a seamstress personally employed by the manager to her home (five miles away) and then return the car to the defendant's repair shop (four miles away and on the same route). It was clear that the manager had no authority to direct that the defendant's car be used to take the seamstress home.[15] The accident occurred after the driver had proceeded but a short distance away from the manager's home and at a place the car would have passed on its way to the repair shop even if the seamstress had not been in it.

The plaintiff, who was injured by the servant's negligent driving, sued and won a verdict in the trial court. The trial court judgment was reversed by the appellate division, on the ground that "the car on its path to the garage was withdrawn from the defendant's service by the dual purpose of the errand." In a 5-2 decision, the court of appeals reversed the appellate division. The opinion was written by Judge Cardozo and read in part as follows: "How the case would stand if the collision had occurred in the course of deviation from the route, we need not now inquire. Deviation there never was. The unfulfilled intention of passing the repair shop and returning did not transform the trip in its entirety, and vitiate that part of the service which was legitimate and useful." The dissent, per McLaughlin, J., stated, "The fact that the defendant had the repair shop on the route is of no importance, since it played no part in the object of the journey. . . ."

And finally, consider *Marks' Dependents v. Gray*, 251 N.Y. 90, 93, 94, 167 N.E. 181, 182–83 (1929), noted in 9 B.U. L. Rev. 310 (1929), a worker's compensation case. Marks was a plumber's helper who worked at Clifton Springs, New York, and one day was going to Shortsville, New York, after work to pick up his wife. Marks' employer heard of this proposed journey and asked him to take his tools and fix

---

15. Indeed, one could argue that the entire trip was unauthorized, from the company's perspective. The manager was an invalid, however, and for several years had been driven home by one of the salesmen in a demonstrator car, apparently with the knowledge of higher officials in the company. Does this resolve the broader question for you?

some faucets at a house in Shortsville. The job was a small one, calling for 15 or 20 minutes of work. Although nothing was said about paying Marks for the job, the expectation was that he would be paid at the usual rate for overtime work. Marks used his own car rather than the employer's truck, and was killed in an automobile accident about a mile out of Clifton Springs, while on the way to Shortsville.[16]

Marks' dependents received an award by the State Industrial Board under the worker's compensation law, on the theory that the accident was one "arising out of and in the course of the employment." The award was unanimously affirmed by the appellate division, but was thereafter reversed by the court of appeals.

The 5–2 decision of the court of appeals was written by Judge Cardozo. The basis of the decision in this interesting case was explained as follows:

> Unquestionably injury through collision is a risk of travel on a highway. What concerns us here is whether the risks of travel are also risks of the employment. In that view the decisive test must be whether it is the employment or something else that has sent the traveler forth upon the journey or brought exposure to its perils. A servant in New York informs his master that he is going to spend a holiday in Philadelphia, or perhaps at a distant place, at San Francisco or at Paris. The master asks him while he is there to visit a delinquent debtor and demand payment of a debt. The trip to Philadelphia, the journey to San Francisco or to Paris, is not a part of the employment. A different question would arise if performance of the service were to occasion a detour, and in the course of such detour the injuries were suffered. So here, a different question would arise if Marks after making the trip to Shortsville had met with some accident while repairing the defective faucets. (*Grieb v. Hammerle*, 222 N. Y. 382). The collision occurred while he was still upon the highway, a mile or less from home.
>
> In such circumstances we think the perils of the highway were unrelated to the service. We do not say that service to the employer must be the sole cause of the journey, but at least it must be a concurrent cause. To establish liability, the inference must be permissible that the trip would have been made though the private errand had been canceled. We cannot draw that inference from the record now before us. On the contrary, the evidence is that a special trip would have been refused since the pay would be inadequate. The test in brief is this: If the work of the employee creates the necessity for travel, he is in the course of his employment, though he is serving at the same time some purpose of his own (*Clawson v. Pierce-Arrow Co.*, 231 N.Y. 273). If, however, the work has had no part in creating the necessity for travel, if the journey would have gone forward though the business errand had been dropped, and would have been canceled upon failure of

---

16. The distance between the two small communities is approximately seven miles by the shortest route. They are located in upstate New York, north of the Finger Lakes.

the private purpose though the business errand was undone, the travel is then personal, and personal the risk.

Although *Marks* involved a decision under the New York worker's compensation law, Cardozo cited a vicarious liability case (*Clawson v. Pierce-Arrow*) as authority for his major premise; also, *Marks* subsequently has been cited and relied upon by vicarious liability cases in New York. Is there any reason why the scope of employment tests in the two fields should be interpreted differently?

Has the material in this note affected your earlier conclusion with respect to vicarious liability for the acts of the carnival-loving employee? In addition to reaching your own conclusion, speculate as to the conclusion you think the court of appeals reached in view of the case authority it had before it (which did not include the *Marks* case). The opinion on these facts is contained immediately below.

Fiocco v. Carver
Court of Appeals of New York
137 N.E. 309 (1922)

CARDOZO, J.

The defendants, engaged in business in the city of New York, sent a truckload of merchandise from Manhattan to Staten Island. The duty of the driver when he had made delivery of the load was to bring the truck back to the garage at Twenty-third street and Eleventh avenue on the west side of the city. Instead of doing that, he went, as he tells us, to Hamilton street on the east side, to visit his mother. A neighborhood carnival was in progress in the street. A crowd of boys, dressed in fantastic costumes, as Indians, Uncle Sam, cowboys, and the like, were parties to the frolic. They asked the driver for a ride, and in response to the request, he made a tour of the district, going from Hamilton street to Catherine, then through other streets, and back again to Catherine. At this point he stopped in front of a pool room, and left his truck for a moment to say a word to a friend. It is here that the plaintiff, a child of eleven years, arrived upon the scene. The merrymakers were still crowding about the truck. The plaintiff with a playmate tried to join them. While he was climbing up the side, the driver came back and three times ordered him to get off. As the third order was given, the plaintiff started to come down, but before he could reach the ground, the truck, as he tells us, was started without warning, and his foot was drawn into a wheel. The driver gives a different story, insisting that the boy ran after the moving truck and climbed on the side when it was impossible to see him. All the witnesses agree that the truck as it left Catherine street was still carrying the boys. The driver adds that his purpose then was to go back to the garage. Upon these facts a jury has been permitted to find that [he] was in the course of his employment. The ruling was upheld at the Appellate Division by a divided court.

We think the judgment may not stand.

The plaintiff argues that the jury, if it discredited the driver's narrative of the accident, was free to discredit his testimony that there had been a departure from the course of duty. With this out of the case, there is left the conceded fact that a truck belonging to the defendant was in the custody of the defendant's servant. We are reminded that this without more sustains a presumption that the custodian was using it in the course of his employment. But the difficulty with the argument is that in this case there *is* more, though credit be accorded to the plaintiff's witnesses exclusively. The presumption disappears when the surrounding circumstances are such that its recognition is unreasonable. We draw the inference of regularity, in default of evidence rebutting it, presuming, until otherwise advised, that the servant will discharge his duty. We refuse to rest upon presumption, and put the plaintiff to his proof, when the departure from regularity is so obvious that charity can no longer infer an adherence to the course of duty.

Such a departure is here shown, apart altogether from the narrative put before us by the driver. The plaintiff's testimony, confirmed by the testimony of his witnesses, breaks the force of the presumption that might otherwise be indulged, and leaves his case unproved unless something is in the record, in addition to the presumption, to show that the defendant's servant was in the course of the employment. The wagon was an electric truck intended for the transportation of merchandise in connection with the defendants' business. At the time of the accident it was crowded with boys, "packed as thick as sardines," whom the driver was taking on a frolic. They filled, not only its body, but also the roof and sides and box. Plainly on proof of these facts the presumption vanishes that the driver was discharging his duty to the master. The character of the transaction is so extraordinary, the occupation of the truck by the revellers so dominant and exclusive, as to rebut the inference that the driver was serving his employer at the same time that he was promoting the pleasure of his friends. The dual function, if it existed, can no longer rest upon presumption. Regularity will no longer be taken for granted when irregularity is written over the whole surface of the picture. We will no longer presume anything. What the plaintiff wishes us to find for him, that he must prove.

We turn, then, to the driver's testimony to see whether anything there, whether read by itself or in conjunction with the plaintiff's narrative, gives support for the conclusion that the truck was engaged at the moment of the accident in the business of the master. All that we can find there, when we view it most favorably to the plaintiff, is a suggestion that after a temporary excursion in streets remote from the homeward journey, the servant had at last made up his mind to put an end to his wanderings and return to the garage. He was still far away from the point at which he had first strayed from the path of duty, but his thoughts were homeward bound. Is this enough, in view of all the circumstances, to terminate the temporary abandonment and put him back into the sphere of service? We have refused to limit ourselves by tests that are merely mechanical or formal (*Riley v. Standard Oil Co. of N.Y.*, 231 N.Y. 301). Location in time and space are circumstances that may guide the judgment, but will not be suffered to control it, divorced from other circumstances that may characterize the intent of the transaction. The dominant purpose must be proved to be the performance of the master's business. Till then there can be no resumption of a relation which has been broken and suspended.

We think the servant's purpose to return to the garage was insufficient to bring him back within the ambit of his duty. He was indisputably beyond the ambit while making the tour of the neighborhood which ended when he stopped at Catherine street upon a visit to a pool room. Neither the tour nor the stop was incidental to his service. Duty was resumed, if at all, when, ending the tour, he had embarked upon his homeward journey. It was in the very act of starting that the injury was done. The plaintiff had climbed upon the truck while it was at rest in front of the pool room, still engaged upon an errand unrelated to the business. The negligence complained of is the setting of the truck in motion without giving the intruder an opportunity to reach the ground. The self-same act that was the cause of the disaster is supposed to have ended the abandonment and re-established a relation which till then had been suspended. Act and disaster would alike have been avoided if the relation had not been broken. Even then, however, the delinquent servant did not purge himself of wrong. The field of duty once forsaken, is not to be re-entered by acts evincing a divided loyalty and thus continuing the offense. Many of the illicit incidents of the tour about the neighborhood persisted. The company of merry-makers was still swarming about the truck. The servant was still using the property of the master to entertain his friends and help the merriment of the carnival. The presence of these merrymakers was the very circumstance that had prompted the little boy to jump upon the truck, and make himself a party to all the fun and frolic. Add to this that the truck was still far away from the route which it would have traveled if the servant had followed the line of duty from the beginning. We do not need to separate these circumstances and to insist that any one of them alone would be strong enough to shape the judgment. Our concern is with the aggregate. We are not dealing with a case where in the course of a continuing relation, business and private ends have been co-incidently served. We are dealing with a departure so manifest as to constitute an abandonment of duty, exempting the master from liability till duty is resumed. Viewing the circumstances collectively, we are constrained to the conclusion that at the moment of the wrong complained of, the forces set in motion by the abandonment of duty were still alive and operative. Whether we have regard to circumstances of space or of time or of causal or logical relation, the homeward trip was bound up with the effects of the excursion, the parts interpenetrated and commingled beyond hope of separation. Division more substantial must be shown before a relation, once ignored and abandoned, will be renewed and re-established.

The judgment of the Appellate Division and that of the Trial Term should be reversed, and the complaint dismissed, with costs in all courts.

HISCOCK, CH. J., HOGAN, POUND, McLAUGHLIN, CRANE and ANDREWS, JJ., concur.

Judgments reversed, etc.

Notes

1. *Fiocco* is a re-entry case. In addition to the sophisticated analysis contained in the opinion, another way to define the test for re-entry into the scope of employment is to say that an employee re-enters after a frolic when the employee "breathes a sigh of relief." On a separate matter, although it may not seem like it so far, the scope of employment issue does involve more than automobile accidents.

2. What effect does an employee's disobedience of express instructions have on the matter of scope of employment? Can an employer successfully argue that such disobedience always takes the employee outside of the scope of employment? What if the instruction violated is to "drive carefully"? Or suppose the owner of a sporting goods store directs her employees never to insert a bullet while exhibiting a gun for sale. An employee does so anyway, and someone is injured as a result. Is the employee's act within the scope of employment? *See* Restatement (Second) § 230, illustration 1 (yes).

3. As noted above, a servant is within the scope of employment while acting on the master's business, or in a manner incidental to performance of the business. Does this mean that conduct of a personal nature is outside of the scope of employment? One answer may be, "It depends." If the personal business consists of going one block off of a 10-mile delivery trip in order to buy a soda, that almost certainly would be within the scope of employment. Suppose, however, that an employee injures someone while on her lunch hour, away from her employer's premises. Would the employer face respondeat superior liability for the tortious conduct? *See Abraham v. E.H. Porter Constr. Co.*, 354 Mass. 757, 235 N.E.2d 782 (1968) (negligence of builder's employees while on their lunch hour and away from the construction site not chargeable to their employer, as a matter of law). *Accord Davidson v. Harris*, 79 Ga. App. 788, 54 S.E.2d 290 (1949) (Waitress on her lunch hour was on her way to a rest room on a different floor from the restaurant. She was running, laughing and jostling with another employee. She fell down a stairway, struck and injured plaintiff. *Held:* The waitress was outside of the scope of employment, as a matter of law.). Does this mean, however, that tortious conduct while on one's lunch break is never within the scope of employment? *See Wilson v. Joma, Inc.*, 537 A.2d 187 (Del. 1988) (evidence raised issue of fact whether trip on motorcycle during employee's lunch break to sandwich shop to pick up sandwiches for himself and fellow employees was within the scope of employment).

The exception for personal conduct can include horseplay. *See Olson v. Staggs-Bilt Homes, Inc.*, 23 Ariz. App. 574, 576, 534 P.2d 1073, 1075 (1975). In this case, defendant builder's employee (Urban), who was hired to patrol several construction projects, stopped for gas while on duty. Urban pulled his gun out of its holster and apparently started to brandish it at or hand it to Olson, the service station attendant, either as part of horseplay or for Olson's inspection. The gun discharged and Olson was injured. The court held that Urban's conduct was outside the scope of employment as a matter of law, as the gun "was not drawn for any conceivable purpose pertinent to Urban's employment."

4. The Restatement (Third) differs from the Restatement (Second) in its formulation of respondeat superior liability. First, as is typical with the Restatement (Third), the formulation is state in broad terms. Section 7.07(2) provides:

> (2) An employee acts within the scope of employment when performing work assigned by the employer or engaging in a course of conduct subject to the employer's control. An employee's act is not within the scope of employment when it occurs within an independent course of conduct not intended by the employee to serve any purpose of the employer.

The drafters of Restatement (Third) expanded on this section and distinguished it from Restatement (Second) in Comment b:

> Under subsection (2), an employee's tortious conduct is outside the scope of employment when the employee is engaged in an independent course of conduct not intended to further any purpose of the employer. An independent course of conduct represents a departure from, not an escalation of, conduct involved in performing assigned work or other conduct that an employer permits or controls. When an employee commits a tort with the sole intention of furthering the employee's own purposes, and not any purpose of the employer, it is neither fair nor true-to-life to characterize the employee's action as that of a representative of the employer. The employee's intention severs the basis for treating the employee's act as that of the employer in the employee's interaction with the third party.
>
> The formulation of the scope-of-employment doctrine in subsection (2) differs from its counterparts in Restatement Second, Agency §§ 228 and 229 because it is phrased in more general terms. Under Restatement Second, Agency § 228(1)(b), conduct falls within the scope of employment when it "occurs substantially within the authorized time and space limits." This formulation does not naturally encompass the working circumstances of many managerial and professional employees and others whose work is not so readily cabined by temporal or spatial limitations. Many employees in contemporary workforces interact on an employer's behalf with third parties although the employee is neither situated on the employer's premises nor continuously or exclusively engaged in performing assigned work. Moreover, under § 228(1)(c), conduct is not within the scope of employment unless "it is actuated, at least in part, by a purpose to serve" the employer. Under § 228(2), conduct is not within the scope of employment if it is "too little actuated by a purpose to serve" the employer. Under § 235, conduct is not within the scope of employment "if it is done with no intention" to perform an authorized service or an incidental act. These formulations are not entirely consistent; an act motivated by *some* purpose to serve

the employer could still be "*too little actuated*" to be within the scope of employment.

In contrast, under subsection (2) of this section, an employee's conduct is outside the scope of employment when it occurs within an independent course of conduct intended to serve no purpose of the employer. Most cases apply the standard stated by this section.

Clover v. Snowbird Ski Resort

Supreme Court of Utah
808 P.2d 1037 (1991)

HALL, CHIEF JUSTICE:

Plaintiff Margaret Clover sought to recover damages for injuries sustained as the result of a ski accident in which Chris Zulliger, an employee of defendant Snowbird Corporation ("Snowbird"), collided with her. From the entry of summary judgment in favor of defendants, Clover appeals.

At the time of the accident, Chris Zulliger was employed by Snowbird as a chef at the Plaza Restaurant. Zulliger was supervised by his father, Hans Zulliger, who was the head chef at both the Plaza, which was located at the base of the resort, and the Mid-Gad Restaurant, which was located halfway to the top of the mountain. Zulliger was instructed by his father to make periodic trips to the Mid-Gad to monitor its operations. Prior to the accident, the Zulligers had made several inspection trips to the restaurant. On at least one occasion, Zulliger was paid for such a trip. He also had several conversations with Peter Mandler, the manager of the Plaza and Mid-Gad Restaurants, during which Mandler directed him to make periodic stops at the Mid-Gad to monitor operations.

On December 5, 1985, the date of the accident, Zulliger was scheduled to begin work at the Plaza Restaurant at 3 p.m. Prior to beginning work, he had planned to go skiing with Barney Norman, who was also employed as a chef at the Plaza. Snowbird preferred that their employees know how to ski because it made it easier for them to get to and from work. As part of the compensation for their employment, both Zulliger and Norman received season ski passes. On the morning of the accident, Mandler asked Zulliger to inspect the operation of the Mid-Gad prior to beginning work at the Plaza.

Zulliger and Norman stopped at the Mid-Gad in the middle of their first run. At the restaurant, they had a snack, inspected the kitchen, and talked to the personnel for approximately fifteen to twenty minutes. Zulliger and Norman then skied four runs before heading down the mountain to begin work. On their final run, Zulliger and Norman took a route that was often taken by Snowbird employees to travel from the top of the mountain to the Plaza. About mid-way down the mountain, at a point above the Mid-Gad, Zulliger decided to take a jump off a crest on the side of an intermediate run. He had taken this jump many times before. A skier moving relatively quickly is able to become airborne at that point because of the steep drop off on the downhill side of the crest. Due to this drop off, it is impossible for skiers above the crest to see skiers below the crest. The jump was well known to Snowbird. In fact, the Snowbird ski patrol often instructed people not to jump off the crest. There was also a sign instructing skiers to ski slowly at this point in the run. Zulliger, however, ignored the sign and skied over the crest at a significant speed. Clover, who had just entered the same ski run from a point below the crest, either had stopped or was traveling slowly below the crest. When Zulliger went over the jump, he collided with Clover, who was hit in the head and severely injured.

Clover brought claims against Zulliger and Snowbird, alleging that (1) Zulliger's reckless skiing was a proximate cause of her injuries, (2) Snowbird is liable for Zulliger's negligence because at the time of the collision, he was acting within the scope of his employment, (3) Snowbird negligently designed and maintained its ski runs, and (4) Snowbird breached its duty to adequately supervise its employees. Zulliger settled separately with Clover. Under two separate motions for summary judgment, the trial judge dismissed Clover's claims against Snowbird for the following reasons: (1) as a matter of law, Zulliger was not acting within the scope of his employment at the time of the collision, (2) Utah's Inherent Risk of Skiing Statute, Utah Code Ann. §§ 78-27-51 to -54 (Supp.1986), bars plaintiff's claim of negligent design and maintenance, and (3) an employer does not have a duty to supervise an employee who is acting outside the scope of employment.

Under the doctrine of respondeat superior, employers are held vicariously liable for the torts their employees commit when the employees are acting within the scope of their employment. Clover's respondeat superior claim was dismissed on the ground that as a matter of law, Zulliger's actions at the time of the accident were not within the scope of his employment. In a recent case, *Birkner v. Salt Lake County*,[17] this court addressed the issue of what types of acts fall within the scope of employment. In *Birkner*, we stated that acts within the scope of employment are "'those acts which are so closely connected with what the servant is employed to do, and so fairly and reasonably incidental to it, that they may be regarded as methods, even though quite improper ones, of carrying out the objectives of the employment.'"[18] The question of whether an employee is acting within the scope of employment is a question of fact. The scope of employment issue must be submitted to a jury "whenever reasonable minds may differ as to whether the [employee] was at a certain time involved wholly or partly in the performance of his [employer's] business or within the scope of employment."[19] In situations where the activity is so clearly within or without the scope of employment that reasonable minds cannot differ, it lies within the prerogative of the trial judge to decide the issue as a matter of law.

---

17. [6] 771 P.2d 1053 (Utah 1989).
18. [7] *Birkner v. Salt Lake County*, 771 P.2d at 1056 [quoting W. Keeton, *Prosser and Keeton on the Law of Torts* § 70, at 502 (5th ed. 1984)].
19. [8] *Carter v. Bessey*, 97 Utah 427, 93 P.2d 490, 493 (1939).

In *Birkner*, we observed that the Utah cases that have addressed the issue of whether an employee's actions, as a matter of law, are within or without the scope of employment have focused on three criteria.[20] "First, an employee's conduct must be of the general kind the employee is employed to perform. . . . In other words, the employee must be about the employer's business and the duties assigned by the employer, as opposed to being wholly involved in a personal endeavor."[21] Second, the employee's conduct must occur substantially within the hours and ordinary spatial boundaries of the employment.[22] "Third, the employee's conduct must be motivated at least in part, by the purpose of serving the employer's interest."[23] Under specific factual situations, such as when the employee's conduct serves a dual purpose or when the employee takes a personal detour in the course of carrying out his employer's directions, this court has occasionally used variations of this approach. These variations, however, are not departures from the criteria advanced in *Birkner*. Rather, they are methods of applying the criteria in specific factual situations.

In applying the *Birkner* criteria to the facts in the instant case, it is important to note that if Zulliger had returned to the Plaza Restaurant immediately after he inspected the operations at the Mid-Gad Restaurant, there would be ample evidence to support the conclusion that on his return trip Zulliger's actions were within the scope of his employment. There is evidence that it was part of Zulliger's job to monitor the operations at the Mid-Gad and that he was directed to monitor the operations on the day of the accident. There is also evidence that Snowbird intended Zulliger to use the ski lifts and the ski runs on his trips to the Mid-Gad. It is clear, therefore, that Zulliger's actions could be considered to "be of the general kind that the employee is employed to perform."[24] It is also clear that there would be evidence that Zulliger's actions occurred within the hours and normal spatial boundaries of his employment. Zulliger was expected to monitor the operations at the Mid-Gad during the time the lifts were operating and when he was not working as a chef at the Plaza. Furthermore, throughout the trip he would have been on his employer's premises. Finally, it is clear that Zulliger's actions in monitoring the operations at the Mid-Gad, per his employer's instructions, could be considered "motivated, at least in part, by the purpose of serving the employer's interest."[25]

---

20. [10] *See* Restatement (Second) of Agency § 228 (1958); W. Keeton, *Prosser and Keeton on the Law of Torts* § 70, at 502 (5th ed. 1984).

21. [11] *Birkner v. Salt Lake County*, 771 P.2d 1053, 1056–57 (Utah 1989); *see also Keller v. Gunn Supply Co.*, 62 Utah 501, 220 P.1063, 1064 (1923).

22. [12] *Birkner v. Salt Lake County*, 771 P.2d at 1057; *see also Cannon v. Goodyear Tire & Rubber Co.*, 60 Utah 346, 208 P. 519, 520–21 (1922).

23. [13] *Birkner v. Salt Lake County*, 771 P.2d at 1057; *see also, e.g., Whitehead v. Variable Annuity Life Ins.*, 801 P.2d at 936; *Stone v. Hurst Lumber Co.*, 15 Utah 2d 49, 386 P.2d 910, 911 (1963); *Combes v. Montgomery Ward & Co.*, 119 Utah 407, 228 P.2d 272, 274 (1951).

24. [16] *Birkner v. Salt Lake County*, 771 P.2d at 1057.

25. [17] *Id.*

The difficulty, of course, arises from the fact that Zulliger did not return to the Plaza after he finished inspecting the facilities at the Mid-Gad. Rather, he skied four more runs and rode the lift to the top of the mountain before he began his return to the base. Snowbird claims that this fact shows that Zulliger's primary purpose for skiing on the day of the accident was for his own pleasure and that therefore, as a matter of law, he was not acting within the scope of his employment. In support of this proposition, Snowbird cites *Whitehead v. Variable Annuity Life Insurance*.[26] *Whitehead* concerned the dual purpose doctrine. Under this doctrine, if an employee's actions are motivated by the dual purpose of benefiting the employer and serving some personal interest, the actions will usually be considered within the scope of employment. However, if the primary motivation for the activity is personal, "even though there may be some transaction of business or performance of duty merely incidental or adjunctive thereto, the [person] should not be deemed to be in the scope of his employment."[27] In situations where the scope of employment issue concerns an employee's trip, a useful test in determining if the transaction of business is purely incidental to a personal motive is "whether the trip is one which would have required the employer to send another employee over the same route or to perform the same function if the trip had not been made."[28]

In *Whitehead*, we held that an employee's commute home was not within the scope of employment, notwithstanding the plaintiff's contention that because the employee planned to make business calls from his house, there was a dual purpose for the commute. In so holding, we noted that the business calls could have been made as easily from any other place as from the employee's home. The instant case is distinguishable from *Whitehead* in that the activity of inspecting the Mid-Gad necessitates travel to the restaurant. Furthermore, there is evidence that the manager of both the Mid-Gad and the Plaza wanted an employee to inspect the restaurant and report back by 3 p.m. If Zulliger had not inspected the restaurant, it would have been necessary to send a second employee to accomplish the same purpose. Furthermore, the second employee would have most likely used the ski lifts and ski runs in traveling to and from the restaurant.

There is ample evidence that there was a predominant business purpose for Zulliger's trip to the Mid-Gad. Therefore, this case is better analyzed under our decisions dealing with situations where an employee has taken a personal detour in the process of carrying out his duties. This court has decided several cases in which employees deviated from their duties for wholly personal reasons and then, after resuming their duties, were involved in accidents. In situations where the detour was such a substantial diversion from the employee's duties that it constituted an abandonment of employment, we held that the employee, as a matter of law, was acting outside the scope of employment. However, in situations where reasonable

---

26. [18] 801 P.2d 934 (Utah 1989).
27. [20] *Id.* (citing *Martinson v. W-M Ins. Agency*, 606 P.2d 256, 285 (Utah 1980)).
28. [21] *Id.*

minds could differ on whether the detour constituted a slight deviation from the employee's duties or an abandonment of employment, we have left the question for the jury.

Under the circumstances of the instant case, it is entirely possible for a jury to reasonably believe that at the time of the accident, Zulliger had resumed his employment and that Zulliger's deviation was not substantial enough to constitute a total abandonment of employment. First, a jury could reasonably believe that by beginning his return to the base of the mountain to begin his duties as a chef and to report to Mandler concerning his observations at the Mid-Gad, Zulliger had resumed his employment. In past cases, in holding that the actions of an employee were within the scope of employment, we have relied on the fact that the employee had resumed the duties of employment prior to the time of the accident.[29] This is an important factor because if the employee has resumed the duties of employment, the employee is then "about the employer's business" and the employee's actions will be "motivated, at least in part, by the purpose of serving the employer's interest."[30] The fact that due to Zulliger's deviation, the accident occurred at a spot above the Mid-Gad does not disturb this analysis. In situations where accidents have occurred substantially within the normal spatial boundaries of employment, we have held that employees may be within the scope of employment if, after a personal detour, they return to their duties and an accident occurs.

Second, a jury could reasonably believe that Zulliger's actions in taking four ski runs and returning to the top of the mountain do not constitute a complete abandonment of employment. It is important to note that by taking these ski runs, Zulliger was not disregarding his employer's directions. In *Cannon v. Goodyear Tire & Rubber Co.*,[31] wherein we held that the employee's actions were a substantial departure from the course of employment, we focused on the fact that the employee's actions were in direct conflict with the employer's directions and policy. In the instant case, far from directing its employees not to ski at the resort, Snowbird issued its employees season ski passes as part of their compensation.

These two factors, along with other circumstances — such as, throughout the day Zulliger was on Snowbird's property, there was no specific time set for inspecting the restaurant, and the act of skiing was the method used by Snowbird employees to travel among the different locations of the resort — constitute sufficient evidence for a jury to conclude that Zulliger, at the time of the accident, was acting within the scope of his employment.

Although we have held that Zulliger's actions were not, as a matter of law, outside the scope of his employment under the *Birkner* analysis, it is important to note that Clover also argues that Zulliger's conduct is within the scope of employment

---

29. [27] *See Burton v. La Duke*, 210 P. [978] at 979–81 [(Utah 1922)].
30. [28] *See id.* 210 P. at 981; *see also Birkner v. Salt Lake County*, 771 P.2d at 1057.
31. [30] 60 Utah 346, 208 P. 519 (1922).

under two alternative theories. First, she urges this court to adopt a position taken by some jurisdictions that focuses, not on whether the employee's conduct is motivated by serving the employer's interest, but on whether the employee's conduct is foreseeable.[32] Such an approach constitutes a significant departure from the *Birkner* analysis.

Second, Clover urges this court to apply the premises rule, a rule developed in workers' compensation cases, to third-party tort-feasor claims. Under this rule, employees who have fixed hours and places of work will usually be considered to be acting outside of the scope of employment when they are traveling to and from work. However, they will be considered to be in the course of employment while traveling to and from work when they are on their employer's premises. In this instance, we decline to adopt such an approach. It is to be noted that the policies behind workers' compensation law differ from the policies behind respondeat superior claims. Furthermore, the premises rule departs from the analysis in *Birkner* in that it focuses entirely upon the second criterion discussed in *Birkner*, the hours and ordinary spatial boundaries of the employment, to the exclusion of the first and third criteria. Situations like the instant case, where the employee has other reasons aside from traveling to work to be on the employer's premises, demonstrate the need for a more flexible and intricate analysis in respondeat superior cases. In fact, it is not entirely clear that the premises rule would apply in a workers' compensation case if the only connection an employee had with work was that the employee, after some recreational skiing, was returning to work on the employer's ski runs. We therefore, in this instance, decline to adopt these approaches.

Reversed and remanded for further proceedings.

Note

1. In *Robarge v. Bechtel Power Co.*, 131 Ariz. App. 280, 640 P.2d 211 (1982), the court held that an employee is not considered to be within the scope of employment when traveling to and from work. This is consistent with the prevailing view on the question. For a case contra to *Robarge*, see *Luth v. Rogers & Babler Constr. Co.*, 507 P.2d 761 (Alaska 1973), where a going and coming case was sent to the jury. The tortfeasor (Jack) was a flagman on a construction job, returning home from the jobsite at the end of the working day. The majority opinion found that the $8.50 per day additional remuneration paid to Jack (and all other employees) may have enabled laborers to commute to the job site, "thus benefiting Rogers," the defendant construction company. Under such circumstances, the court held, "It would not be unfair to require Rogers to pay for the [plaintiff's] resulting injuries."

---

32. [32] *See Bushey & Sons, Inc. v. United States*, 398 F.2d 167, 171 (2d Cir. 1968); *Hinman v. Westinghouse Elec. Co.*, 2 Cal. 3d 956, 88 Cal. Rptr. 188, 190, 471 P.2d 988, 990 (1970).

The language in *Luth* of "benefit" to the employer is borrowed from the law of worker's compensation. Under worker's compensation a far broader range of acts is included within the scope of employment (called "course of employment" in the language of worker's compensation) than under the law of respondeat superior. This difference between the two systems may be explained in part by the fact that in worker's compensation the exposure to liability for the employer is more confined. Liability extends only to the employer's workers. Also, payments to an injured worker are made according to a schedule and do not include pain and suffering, as noted earlier.

The exposure to liability under respondeat superior is much greater. The range of potential plaintiffs is undefined but potentially large, and the damages can be exceptionally high because pain and suffering and other open-ended features of tort damages are available to persons injured by an employee. Liability is strict under both systems, but the potential for severe loss for an innocent employer is far greater under vicarious tort liability. In addition, under worker's compensation the injured party has only one defendant; under respondeat superior the injured person has two defendants: the tortfeasor and the tortfeasor's employer.

Perhaps for these reasons, most courts tend to draw tighter limits on what actions are within the scope of employment when dealing with vicarious tort liability. In most jurisdictions courts look for some evidence of intent, at least in part, by the employee to serve the employer at the time of the loss, plus evidence meeting the other factors of time, place, and kind of work, with the objective of confining liability to acts that might fairly be said to have been performed as part of discharging the employee's obligation to the business. Admittedly, this distinction sometimes is lost sight of by courts when dealing with particularly troubling cases.

2. As noted above, plaintiffs often combine claims for vicarious liability with direct claims against the employer for negligent hiring and/or negligent supervision. It is worth noting that there is a line of authority, not followed in all states, that holds that when an employer is sued on direct and vicarious liability claims, the direct negligence claims against the employer will be dismissed if the employer concedes that the employee was acting within the scope of employment. *See, e.g., Ferrer v. Okbamicael*, 390 P.3d 836 (Colo. 2017). The case involved a taxi driver who negligently injured two pedestrians. At first, the employer claimed the driver was an independent contractor, but then conceded he was an employee. The employer then sought dismissal of the direct claims and the *Ferrer* court agreed that those claims should be dismissed, reasoning that because "both vicarious liability and direct negligence claims are tethered to the employee's tortious acts," allowing the direct claims would be duplicative and unnecessary, while not increasing the possible recovery for the plaintiff. The Court also noted that evidence relevant to the employer's negligence—such as the employee's prior driving record—could be unfairly prejudicial to the employee.

Spencer v. V.I.P., Inc.

Supreme Judicial Court of Maine
910 A.2d 366 (2006)

DANA, J.

James Spencer, individually and as the personal representative of Nancy Spencer's estate, and Brittany Spencer appeal from a summary judgment entered in the Superior Court (Oxford County, *Gorman, J.*) in favor of V.I.P., Inc. They contend that the court erred in concluding that, when V.I.P. employee Justin Laliberte's vehicle collided with the Spencers' vehicle, Laliberte was not acting within the scope of his employment, and V.I.P., consequently, could not be held vicariously liable. Finding genuine issues of material fact as to whether Laliberte was acting within the scope of his employment, we vacate the summary judgment.

I. Background

The following facts are undisputed. Laliberte, an hourly employee at V.I.P.'s Lewiston warehouse, volunteered to help set up for the 2002 Show, Shine & Drag, an annual promotional event sponsored by V.I.P. and held at the Oxford Plains Speedway, during which the public is invited to view cars, vendor products, and drag racing. Hourly employees who volunteered to help set up received $25 cash and a T-shirt.

Pursuant to his commitment, Laliberte awoke at 4:30 A.M. on July 20, 2002, and drove to the Oxford Plains Speedway where he began setting up at 6:00 A.M. He completed his work in approximately one hour and then departed. While driving home, Laliberte's vehicle crossed into the on-coming lane and collided with the vehicle containing James, Nancy, and Brittany Spencer. As a result of the collision, Nancy was killed and James and Brittany were injured.

James, individually and as the personal representative of Nancy's estate, and Brittany commenced this action against Laliberte and V.I.P., seeking damages for James's and Brittany's personal injuries and Nancy's suffering and wrongful death. V.I.P. moved for a summary judgment arguing that, inasmuch as Laliberte was not acting within the scope of his employment at the time of the accident, V.I.P. could not be held vicariously liable. The court granted V.I.P.'s motion, and James and Brittany brought this appeal.

II. Discussion

In determining whether an employer is vicariously liable for the actions of an employee, Maine follows the Restatement (Second) of Agency (1958) and holds an employer liable only if its employee's action occurred within the scope of employment. Under Restatement (Second) of Agency § 228(1) as it applies in the present case, an employee's action occurs within the scope of employment if "(a) it is of the kind he is employed to perform; (b) it occurs substantially within the authorized time and space limits; [and] (c) it is actuated, at least in part, by a purpose to serve the master."[33]

To determine whether there is a genuine issue of material fact as to whether the travel to and from the Oxford Plains Speedway was within the scope of Laliberte's employment, we begin by considering whether the statements of material facts and referenced record evidence support a finding that the travel was part of a task Laliberte was employed to perform. James referenced testimony that the $25 received by hourly employees who helped set up was intended to cover any expenses, including gas.[34] James further referenced testimony that hourly employees who traveled more than two hours to help set up could, upon approval, receive mileage in addition to the $25 and that salaried employees could receive only mileage. Inasmuch as these references suggest that the $25 was intended, at least in part, as compensation, they support a finding that the travel was part of a task Laliberte was employed to perform.

We next consider whether the statements of material facts and referenced record evidence support a finding that the travel occurred substantially within the authorized time and space limits. Certain references indicating that the travel at issue occurred at the time reasonably expected—i.e., immediately before and after Laliberte completed his set-up work-support such a finding.

We finally consider whether the statements of material facts and referenced record evidence support a finding that the travel was actuated, at least in part, by a purpose to serve V.I.P. Inasmuch as it was necessary in order to perform the set-up work, the travel might be found to have been actuated by a purpose to serve V.I.P. Because the statements of material facts and referenced record evidence reveal a genuine issue of material fact as to whether the travel was within the scope of Laliberte's employment, the summary judgment cannot stand.

Summary judgment vacated. Remanded to the Superior Court for further proceedings consistent with this opinion.

SAUFLEY, C.J., dissenting, with whom, LEVY, J., joins.

I must respectfully dissent. The decision of the court today may ultimately cause employers to become the insurer for all harm caused on the highways by their employees while driving to or from work. It also changes Maine law, and moves Maine out of step with tort law across the country. This extraordinary expansion of liability without limitations or guidance is unprecedented. I would affirm the judgment because the Superior Court correctly concluded, as a matter of law, that Justin Laliberte was not acting within the scope of his employment with V.I.P., Inc., at the time his car collided with the car of James, Nancy, and Brittany Spencer.

---

33. [1] The Restatement (Third) of Agency (2006) is now extant. At the time of the events at issue, the Restatement (Second) of Agency (1958) was operative and relied on by this Court.

34. [2] A supervisor stated: "The $25 was to cover any expenses they would have, whether it was gas on the way up, or they could use the money any way they wanted."

If Justin Laliberte was negligent, it is he who must be held responsible. However, to reach for other methods to compensate the family for their loss by making Laliberte's employer responsible for his nonwork-related driving will have profound consequences on the economics of employment. Such a shift in fiscal responsibility for the act of a single person who was not at work should be brought about by legislative action where the costs and risk assessment can be debated and discussed. To shift responsibility to the employers of the people driving on Maine roads through the sweep of the judicial pen moves the Court outside of its constitutional role. We should apply the law that exists today: a person who is going to or coming from work is responsible for his or her own actions.

This result is dictated first of all by our precedent, which requires us to follow the principles of vicarious liability set forth in the Restatement (Second) of Agency (1958). The Court acknowledges the existence of the Restatement by quoting section 228(1)(a)–(c), which provides the relevant test for determining whether a servant's conduct is within the scope of employment. The Court's opinion, however, applies section 228 in a vacuum, without acknowledging that its rule "is given more content by . . . subordinate rules, commentary and illustrations" within the Restatement, as well as "by case law and rules of thumb." *Lyons v. Brown*, 158 F.3d 605, 609 (1st Cir. 1998) (applying Maine law).

The Restatement commentary provides useful guidance. It notes that section 228 is governed by an important rule found in a previous section:

> As stated in Section 220, one is a servant only if, as to his physical conduct in the performance of the service, he is subject to the control or to the right to control of the master. Hence, there is no liability for the conduct of one who, although a servant in performing other service, is doing work as to which *there is no control or right to control by the master.*

Restatement (Second) of Agency § 228 cmt. c (1958) (emphasis added). This rule is central to the issue in this case. Equally important is the rule of section 228(1) (c) & (2), expanded upon by section 235, that conduct is not within the scope of employment if it is not actuated by a purpose to serve the master. The Restatement commentary explicitly applies these rules to the issue of employer liability for the torts of a commuting employee. *See id.* §§ 229 cmt. d, 233 cmt. c, illus. 3.

These rules leave no doubt about the correct result in this case. When the collision with the Spencers occurred, Laliberte was driving home from Oxford Plains Speedway after performing work there for V.I.P. At the time Laliberte was driving home, V.I.P. had no control over, and no right to control, his conduct; it did not dictate what vehicle he drove, the route he took, his speed, or even whether he drove home at all. What Laliberte did that day after leaving the Show, Shine & Drag was of no concern to V.I.P. at all. He thus was not V.I.P.'s servant at the time of the accident. In addition, Laliberte's purpose after he left the speedway was entirely personal. It is undisputed that he intended to drive home, pick up his daughter, and take her to York's Wild Kingdom. He no longer had any purpose to serve V.I.P., and thus, even if he were a servant, he was not acting within the scope of his employment at the time of the accident. Under the principles of the Restatement, therefore, V.I.P. may not be held vicariously liable for any negligence by Laliberte.

Although the Restatement alone is clear enough, the same result is also suggested by the case law. We have not addressed this specific issue before, but we are not the first appellate court to consider whether an employee driving to or from work is within the scope of employment for purposes of imposing vicarious liability on the employer. There are dozens, perhaps hundreds, of cases from across the country on point.

Most courts also recognize some exceptions to the going and coming rule, but there is substantial disagreement about the nature of the exceptions. In an insightful recent opinion, the New Jersey Supreme Court explained that

> *respondeat superior* has been held to apply to a situation involving commuting when: (1) the employee is engaged in a special errand or mission on the employer's behalf; (2) the employer requires the employee to drive his or her personal vehicle to work so that the vehicle may be used for work-related tasks; and (3) the employee is "on-call."
>
> Those so-called "dual-purpose" exceptions cover cases in which, at the time of the employee's negligence, he or she can be said to be serving an interest of the employer along with a personal interest. It makes sense that those exceptions to the going and coming rule exist. Unlike ordinary commut[ing] in which an employer really has no interest, *each of the noted exceptions involves some control over the employee's actions and a palpable benefit to be reaped by the employer*, thus squarely placing such conduct back into the vicarious liability construct of the Restatement.

Carter v. Reynolds, 175 N.J. 402, 815 A.2d 460, 467 (2003) (citations omitted) (emphasis added). . . .

Laliberte was not on call on the day of the accident, and V.I.P. did not require him to drive his car to Oxford so he could use it for work-related tasks. The Spencers contend, however, that Laliberte was on a special errand or mission for V.I.P. It appears that a few courts have formulated the special errand exception so broadly that it might possibly encompass the facts of this case. *See, e.g., Chevron, U.S.A., Inc. v. Lee*, 847 S.W.2d 354, 356 (Tex. App. 1993) (holding that the employer could be liable when the employee was driving to a mandatory seminar on what was normally his day off, because his attendance at the seminar "was for the ultimate benefit of his employer").

Most courts, however, have applied the special mission exception more narrowly. In many cases where courts have found the exception applicable, the employee's driving was a necessary part of the errand in a way that Laliberte's driving was not necessary to his work at the Show, Shine & Drag.

On the other hand, courts have found the special mission exception inapplicable in cases where, as in this case, the employee was merely driving to or from work at an unusual location or on a day the employee would not normally have worked. In cases similar to the one at bar, many courts have found no employer liability. The Nevada Supreme Court concluded in 2003 that an employee who was required to report to different job sites was not on a special errand while driving to work at the job site assigned for that particular day. *See Kornton*, 67 P.3d [316] at 317 [(Nev. 2003)]. Other courts have ruled similarly. At least one court has gone further and declined to recognize any exception for special missions because under the Restatement a commuting employee is acting within the scope of employment only if the employer has control over the method or route of the employee's travel. *DeRuyter v. Wis. Elec. Power Co.*, 200 Wis.2d 349, 546 N.W.2d 534, 537, 540–42 (Ct. App. 1996), *aff'd by an equally divided court*, 211 Wis.2d 169, 565 N.W.2d 118 (1997).

Although we need not reach as far as the Wisconsin Court, in my view, the Restatement's principles of vicarious liability do not comport with the more expansive approach to the special mission exception. Exceptions to the going and coming rule should be recognized only in cases where some unique aspect of the employee's travel is within the control of, or for the benefit of, the employer. In the absence of facts asserting those fundamental aspects of vicarious liability, liability may be imposed on any driver's employer without adhering to the foundational principles of tort liability and in a random, unpredictable, and arbitrary fashion.

The concepts in the Restatement accepted previously by this Court compel the conclusion that Laliberte was not acting in the scope of his employment at the time of the accident because he was not subject to V.I.P.'s control and was not acting with a purpose to serve V.I.P. He thus was not within the special mission exception as correctly understood, and the trial court correctly ruled that V.I.P. should not be liable for his allegedly tortious acts.

I would affirm the summary judgment of the Superior Court.

b. Intentional Torts

As we have seen, there has been surprisingly little controversy about holding a master liable for a servant's unintentional torts, although there is dispute about the limits to be drawn. What happens, however, when the servant commits an intentional tort? Does this so completely shift the ground that the doctrine of vicarious liability should not apply? Or should it make no difference at all, so long as the conduct was "expectable"? Would you anticipate that courts dealing with responsibility for intentional torts would give extra weight to the requirement in Restatement (Second) § 228(1)(c), that such conduct be "actuated, at least in part, by a purpose to serve the master"? And the relevance of § 228(1)(d) is clear, isn't it?

Suppose, for example, that a seaman who worked on a vessel that was being overhauled in a floating dry dock got drunk one night while on shore leave. Upon returning to the vessel late at night, he turned some wheels on the dry dock wall. In doing this he opened some valves, which resulted in flooding the tanks on one side of the dry dock, causing a listing of the ship and damage to the dry dock. The dry dock owner sued the ship owner. The defense was that the seaman was acting out-side his scope of employment. How would you argue against that as the plaintiff's lawyer? How would you decide the issue as a judge? Would your answer change if the seaman had been cold sober and acted out of hostility, planning to quit the next day?

A deliveryman for the New York Tribune negligently ran into Smith while on route. Both drivers stopped. The deliveryman refused to identify himself to Smith and gave Smith a shove. After regaining his balance, Smith kneeled down to look at the license plate of the delivery truck. The driver kicked him in the face. Smith sues the New York Tribune on respondeat superior grounds. The defense is obvious. What result would you reach if you were the judge in the case?

Finally, suppose a bartender while on duty has a patron call to his attention the fact that a car engine is boiling over in the parking lot of the bar. The bartender goes out to the lot and turns off the engine. The owner of the car, a drunk bar patron who was sitting in the car, resents this. Words are exchanged and the bartender savagely beats the patron up while still out in the parking lot. The bar owner is sued by the injured patron. What result?

Bremen State Bank v. Hartford Accident & Indemnity Co.

United States Court of Appeals, Seventh Circuit
427 F.2d 425 (1970)

SWYGERT, CHIEF JUDGE.

Plaintiff, Bremen State Bank, brought this diversity action in the district court to recover $10,342.03, which sum was lost during a move by the bank from one location to another within the village of Tinley Park, Illinois. On the day before the move the bank instructed its tellers to put their money at the end of the day in canvas bags on the floor of the vault rather than in metal lockers inside the vault, the usual prac-tice. One teller, Mrs. Laucke, did not receive these instructions and thus put her cash drawer money, $10,342.03, in her metal locker instead of on the vault floor.

Arrangements had been made for the Tinley Park police to move the bank's money and for defendant, Bekins Van & Storage Company, to move the office equip-ment, including the metal lockers, inside the vault. After the police, under guard, had moved the money from the vault floor to the new location, Bekins' employees entered the bank and began their job. While removing some of the metal lockers from the vault, one of Bekins' employees, Danny Francis, noticed that something was inside one of the lockers. After placing them in a van, he opened the locker used by Mrs. Laucke and discovered the money. Francis finished working that day and later absconded with the $10,342.03, none of which was ever recovered.

Plaintiff's complaint . . . sought recovery . . . against Bekins on the theory of *respondeat superior.* The district court granted summary judgment against the bank. . . .

The bank's claim against Bekins rests on the theory that since Francis stole the money during the performance of his employment by Bekins the latter is civilly liable for the loss occasioned by the criminal act of its employee. We think the bank has misinterpreted the applicable Illinois law. Our reading of the cases leads us to conclude that the rule in Illinois is that the employer is liable for the negligent, wilful, malicious, or criminal acts of its employees when such acts are committed during the course of employment and in furtherance of the business of the employer; but when the act is committed solely for the benefit of the employee, the employer is not liable to the injured third party.

Thus, an employer was not liable for the criminal act of its employee-watchman in setting fire to the building which he had been employed to guard, *Apex Smelting Co. v. Burns*, 175 F.2d 978 (7th Cir. 1949), or for the shooting of a trespasser who was leaving the employer's premises by a guard who was armed without the knowledge or permission of the employer, *Belt Railway Co. v. Banicki*, [102 Ill. App. 642 (1902)], *supra*, or where the employee engaged in a fistfight for purposes unrelated to his job, *Horecker v. Pere Marquette R. Co.*, 238 Ill. App. 278 (1925), or where the employee-driver deviated from the route leading to the destination assigned by the employer, *Boehmer v. Norton*, 328 Ill. App. 17, 65 N.E.2d 212 (1946). On the other hand, the employer was held liable where an employee-brakeman who had been instructed to remove unauthorized riders on railroad cars willfully and maliciously pulled a boy off a moving train, crushing the latter's foot in the process, *Illinois Central R. Co. v. King*, 179 Ill. 91, 53 N.E. 552 (1899), and where the employee mistakenly injured the plaintiff in defending the employer's property against robbers, *Metzler v. Layton*, 298 Ill. App. 529, 19 N.E.2d 130, *aff'd*, 373 Ill. 88, 25 N.E.2d 60 (1939).

In the instant case, there is no contention that Francis stole the money in furtherance of the business of his employer. In fact, the money came into his hands by inadvertence and without the knowledge or permission of either his employer or the bank. Under Illinois law, therefore, the employer was not liable for Francis' act and the granting of summary judgment in favor of Bekins was correct.

Note

For cases in accord with *Bremen State Bank*, see *B.B. Walker Co. v. Burns Int'l Sec. Servs., Inc.*, 424 S.E.2d 172 (N.C. App. 1993) (theft by security guards); *Effort Enters., Inc. v. Crosta*, 391 S.E.2d 477 (Ga. App. 1990) (theft by movers); *Flynn v. Gold Kist, Inc.*, 181 Ga. App. 637, 353 S.E.2d 537 (1987) *Gibbs v. Air Canada*, 810 F.2d 1529 (11th Cir. 1987), *rehearing denied en banc*, 816 F.2d 688 (11th Cir. 1987) (theft of cargo by employee of airline ramp services provider); *Gotthelf v. Property Mgt. Sys.*, 189 N.J. Super. 237, 459 A.2d 1198, *petition for certification denied*, 95 N.J. 219, 470 A.2d 435 (1983) (theft in apartment complex by employee of defendant, apparently the manager of the property).

i. The Assault on § 228(1)(c)

Ira S. Bushey & Sons v. United States[35]

United States Court of Appeals, Second Circuit

398 F.2d 167 (1968)

Before WATERMAN, FRIENDLY and KAUFMAN, CIRCUIT JUDGES.

FRIENDLY, CIRCUIT JUDGE. While the United States Coast Guard vessel Tamaroa was being overhauled in a floating dry dock located in Brooklyn's Gowanus Canal, a seaman returning from shore leave late at night, in the condition for which seaman are famed, turned some wheels on the drydock wall. He thus opened valves that controlled the flooding of the tanks on one side of the drydock. Soon the ship listed, slid off the blocks and fell against the wall. Parts of the drydock sank, and the ship partially did—fortunately without loss of life or personal injury. The drydock owner sought and was granted compensation by the District Court for the Eastern District of New York in an amount to be determined, 276 F. Supp. 518; the United States appeals. . . .

The Tamaroa had gone into drydock on February 28, 1963; her keel rested on blocks permitting her drive shaft to be removed and repairs to be made to her hull. The contract between the Government and Bushey provided in part:

> (o) The work shall, whenever practical, be performed in such manner as not to interfere with the berthing and messing of personnel attached to the vessel undergoing repair, and provision shall be made so that personnel assigned shall have access to the vessel at all times, it being understood that such personnel will not interfere with the work or the contractor's workmen.

Access from shore to ship was provided by a route past the security guard at the gate, through the yard, up a ladder to the top of one drydock wall and along the wall to a gangway leading to the fantail deck, where men returning from leave reported at a quartermaster's shack.

Seaman Lane, whose prior record was unblemished, returned from shore leave a little after midnight on March 14. He had been drinking heavily; the quartermaster made mental note that he was "loose." For reasons not apparent to us or very likely to Lane,[36] he took it into his head, while progressing along the gangway wall, to turn each of three large wheels some twenty times; unhappily, as previously stated, these wheels controlled the water intake valves. After boarding ship at 12:11 A.M., Lane mumbled to an off-duty seaman that he had "turned some valves" and also muttered something about "valves" to another who was standing the engineering watch. Neither did anything; apparently Lane's condition was not such as to encourage proximity. At 12:20 A.M. a crew member discovered water coming into the drydock.

---

35. Noted in 82 HARV. L. REV. 1568 (1969).

36. [4] Lane disappeared after completing the sentence imposed by a court-martial and being discharged from the Coast Guard.

By 12:30 A.M. the ship began to list, the alarm was sounded and the crew were ordered ashore. Ten minutes later the vessel and dock were listing over 20 degrees; in another ten minutes the ship slid off the blocks and fell against the drydock wall.

The Government attacks imposition of liability on the ground that Lane's acts were not within the scope of his employment. It relies heavily on § 228(1) of the Restatement of Agency 2d which says that "conduct of a servant is within the scope of employment if, but only if: . . . (c) it is actuated, at least in part by a purpose to serve the master." Courts have gone to considerable lengths to find such a purpose, as witness a well-known opinion in which Judge Learned Hand concluded that a drunken boatswain who routed the plaintiff out of his bunk with a blow, saying "Get up, you big son of a bitch, and turn to," and then continued to fight, might have thought he was acting in the interest of the ship. *Nelson v. American-West African Line*, 86 F.2d 730 (2 Cir. 1936), *cert. denied*, 300 U.S. 665, 57 S. Ct. 509, 81 L. Ed. 873 (1937). It would be going too far to find such a purpose here; while Lane's return to the Tamaroa was to serve his employer, no one has suggested how he could have thought turning the wheels to be, even if—which is by no means clear—he was unaware of the consequences.

In light of the highly artificial way in which the motive test has been applied, the district judge believed himself obliged to test the doctrine's continuing vitality by referring to the larger purposes *respondeat superior* is supposed to serve. He concluded that the old formulation failed this test. We do not find his analysis so compelling, however, as to constitute a sufficient basis in itself for discarding the old doctrine. It is not at all clear, as the court below suggested, that expansion of liability in the manner here suggested will lead to a more efficient allocation of resources. As the most astute exponent of this theory has emphasized, a more efficient allocation can only be expected if there is some reason to believe that imposing a particular cost on the enterprise will lead it to consider whether steps should be taken to prevent a recurrence of the accident. Calabresi, *The Decision for Accidents: An Approach to Non-fault Allocation of Costs*, 78 HARV. L. REV. 713, 725–34 (1965). And the suggestion that imposition of liability here will lead to more intensive screening of employees rests on highly questionable premises, see Comment, *Assessment of Punitive Damages Against an Entrepreneur for the Malicious Torts of His Employees*, 70 YALE L.J. 1296, 1301–04 (1961).[37] The unsatisfactory quality of the allocation of resource rationale is especially striking on the facts of this case. It could well be that application of the traditional rule might induce drydock owners, prodded by their insurance companies, to install locks on their valves to avoid similar incidents in the future,[38] while placing the burden on shipowners is much less likely to lead

---

37. [5] We are not here speaking of cases in which the enterprise has negligently hired an employee whose undesirable propensities are known or should have been.

38. [6] The record reveals that most modern dry docks have automatic locks to guard against unauthorized use of valves.

to accident prevention.[39] It is true, of course, that in many cases the plaintiff will not be in a position to insure, and so expansion of liability will, at the very least, serve *respondeat superior's* loss spreading function. See Smith, *Frolic and Detour*, 23 Colum. L. Rev. 444, 456 (1923). But the fact that the defendant is better able to afford damages is not alone sufficient to justify legal responsibility, see Blum & Kalven, Public Law Perspectives on a Private Law Problem (1965), and this overarching principle must be taken into account in deciding whether to expand the reach of *respondeat superior.*

A policy analysis thus is not sufficient to justify this proposed expansion of vicarious liability. This is not surprising since *respondeat superior, even* within its traditional limits, rests not so much on policy grounds consistent with the governing principles of tort law as in a deeply rooted sentiment that a business enterprise cannot justly disclaim responsibility for accidents which may fairly be said to be characteristic of its activities. It is in this light that the inadequacy of the motive test becomes apparent. Whatever may have been the case in the past, a doctrine that would create such drastically different consequences for the actions of the drunken boatswain in *Nelson* and those of the drunken seaman here reflects a wholly unrealistic attitude toward the risks characteristically attendant upon the operation of a ship. We concur in the statement of Mr. Justice Rutledge in a case involving violence injuring a fellow-worker, in this instance in the context of workmen's compensation:

> Men do not discard their personal qualities when they go to work. Into the job they carry their intelligence, skill, habits of care and rectitude. Just as inevitably they take along also their tendencies to carelessness and camaraderie, as well as emotional make-up. In bringing men together, work brings these qualities together, causes frictions between them, creates occasions for lapses into carelessness, and for fun-making and emotional flare-up. . . . These expressions of human nature are incidents inseparable from working together. They involve risks of injury and these risks are inherent in the working environment.

Put another way, Lane's conduct was not so "unforeseeable" as to make it unfair to charge the Government with responsibility. We agree with a leading treatise that "what is reasonably foreseeable in this context [of *respondeat superior*] . . . is quite a different thing from the foreseeably unreasonable risk of harm that spells negligence. . . . The foresight that should impel the prudent man to take precautions is not the same measure as that by which he should perceive the harm likely to flow from his long-run activity in spite of all reasonable precautions on his own part. The proper test here bears far more resemblance to that which limits liability for workmen's compensation than to the test for negligence. The employer should be held to expect risks, to the public also, which arise 'out of and in the course' of his

39. [7] Although it is theoretically possible that shipowners would demand that drydock owners take appropriate action, see Coase, *The Problem of Social Cost*, 3 J.L. & Econ. 1 (1960), this would seem unlikely to occur in real life.

employment of labor." 2 Harper & James, The Law of Torts 1377–78 (1956). See also Calabresi, *Some Thoughts on Risk Distribution and the Law of Torts*, 70 Yale L.J. 499, 544 (1961). Here it was foreseeable that crew members crossing the drydock might do damage, negligently or even intentionally, such as pushing a Bushey employee or kicking property into the water. Moreover, the proclivity of seamen to find solace for solitude by copious resort to the bottle while ashore has been noted in opinions too numerous to warrant citation. Once all this is granted, it is immaterial that Lane's precise action was not to be foreseen. . . .

Consequently, we can no longer accept our past decisions that have refused to move beyond the *Nelson* rule, since they do not accord with modern understanding as to when it is fair for an enterprise to disclaim the actions of its employees.

One can readily think of cases that fall on the other side of the line. If Lane has set fire to the bar where he had been imbibing or had caused an accident on the street while returning to the drydock, the Government would not be liable; the activities of the "enterprise" do not reach into areas where the servant does not create risks different from those attendant on the activities of the community in general.

We agree with the district judge that if the seaman "upon returning to the drydock, recognized the Bushey security guard as his wife's lover and shot him," 276 F. Supp. at 530, vicarious liability would not follow; the incident would have related to the seaman's domestic life, not to his seafaring activity, and it would have been the most unlikely happenstance that the confrontation with the paramour occurred on a drydock rather than at the traditional spot. Here Lane had come within the closed-off area where his ship lay, to occupy a berth to which the Government insisted he have access, cf. Restatement, Agency 2d, §267, and while his act is not readily explicable, at least it was not shown to be due entirely to facets of his personal life. The risk that seamen going and coming from the Tamaroa might cause damage to the drydock is enough to make it fair that the enterprise bear the loss. It is not a fatal objection that the rule we lay down lacks sharp contours; in the end, as Judge Andrews said in a related context, "it is all a question [of expediency,] . . . of fair judgment, always keeping in mind the fact that we endeavor to make a rule in each case that will be practical and in keeping with the general understanding of mankind."

Affirmed.

Notes

1. Did the court reject Calabresi's allocation of resources analysis? It is argued in *Respondeat Superior — Vicarious Liability Imposed for the Willful Tort of a Drunken Employee Not Motivated by a Purpose to Serve His Employer*, 82 Harv. L. Rev. 1568, 1570 (1969), that the rationale behind the resource allocation thesis would not apply in Bushey because the tortfeasor's victim was also a business organization, able to take safety measures and to spread costs.

> The broad purposes purportedly served by respondeat superior might then be best served by refusing to impose vicarious liability and leaving

losses where they lie. . . . If respondeat superior is simply a means of social engineering—not founded in notions of the employer's causation of or responsibility for the injury—the doctrine might be applied only when it best serves the purposes of cost-spreading and long-run injury prevention.

Do you agree?

2. The deliveryman and bartender hypotheticals raised at the beginning of this section are drawn from actual cases. *See Sauter v. New York Tribune*, 305 N.Y. 442, 113 N.E.2d 790 (1953) (noted in 39 CORNELL L.Q. 505 (1954)); *Maddex v. Ricca*, 258 F. Supp. 352 (D. Ariz. 1966) (noted in 9 ARIZ. L. REV. 110 (1967)). In both cases the plaintiff lost on the ground that the employee did not intend to serve, even in part, the interests of his employer. How would the court in *Bushey* have resolved these cases?

3. The Restatement (Third) rejects the use of the foreseeability test, preferring instead a test that focuses exclusively on the employee's motive or intent. In Comment b to § 7.07 the drafters explain:

> Alternative formulations avoid the use of motive or intention to determine whether an employee's tortious conduct falls within the scope of employment. These tests vary somewhat in how they articulate the requisite tie between the tortfeasor's employment and the tort. In general, such a tie is present only when the tort is a generally foreseeable consequence of the enterprise undertaken by the employer or is incident to it. In this context, "foreseeability" means that, in the context of the employer's particular enterprise, the employee's conduct is not so unusual or startling that it seems unfair to include the loss resulting from it in the employer's business costs. This is a separate inquiry from whether an employer acted negligently. One test directs the trier of fact to determine whether an employee's tort was "engendered by the employment," or an "outgrowth" of it, or whether the tort arose out of a personal dispute or other causative factor unrelated to employment. An alternative looks to whether the employment furnished the specific impetus for a tort or increased the general risk that the tort would occur. These tests leave to the finder of fact the challenge of determining whether a tortfeasor's employment did more than create a happenstance opportunity to commit the tort.

> Although formulations that focus on an employee's intention may be difficult to apply in some cases, formulations based on assessments of "foreseeability" are potentially confusing and may generate outcomes that are less predictable than intent-based formulations. "Foreseeability" has a well-developed meaning in connection with negligence and to use it, additionally, to define a different boundary for respondeat superior risks confusion. Moreover, references to "foreseeability" in the respondeat superior context tend to conflate the foreseeable likelihood, from an employer's standpoint, that mishaps and slippage will occur in connection with the

performance of assigned work, with the possibility that the work may lead to or somehow provide the occasion for intentional misconduct that is distinct from an employee's actions in performing assigned work. To be sure, the latter possibility is indeed always "foreseeable," given human frailty, but its occurrence is not a risk that an employer can effectively control and its occurrence may be related causally to employment no more than to other relationships and circumstances in an errant employee's life more generally.

Lisa M. v. Henry Mayo Newhall Memorial Hospital
Supreme Court of California
907 P.2d 358 (1995)

WERDEGAR, ASSOCIATE JUSTICE. . . .

On July 9, 1989, plaintiff, 19 years old and pregnant, was injured in a fall at a movie theater and sought treatment at Hospital's emergency room. At the direction of the examining physicians, ultrasound technician Bruce Wayne Tripoli performed obstetrical and upper-right-quadrant ultrasonic imaging examinations.

Tripoli took plaintiff to the ultrasound room on a gurney. She remained in her street clothes, shorts and a maternity top. No one else was present during the examination; plaintiff had asked that her boyfriend accompany her, but Tripoli refused the request, as was his practice in conducting emergency obstetrical examinations. Tripoli turned out the room lights but left the adjacent bathroom door ajar to admit dim light.

Tripoli first conducted the prescribed examinations. Plaintiff pulled up her shirt and pushed her shorts down to expose the area to be examined. The obstetrical or "general pelvic" examination requires passing an ultrasound-generating wand across the patient's lower abdomen. The sound waves must be mediated by a gel, which Tripoli testified must be worked into the skin somewhat to displace all the air. The exact placement and movement of the wand varies with the patient's body type, and on some patients the best images are obtained by passing the wand as much as an inch below the pubic hairline. Tripoli found it necessary to do so in plaintiff's case. In performing the upper-right-quadrant examination (to see the liver), Tripoli had to lift plaintiff's right breast, which he did through a towel with the back of his hand.

After conducting the ordered examinations, Tripoli left the room for about 10 minutes to develop the photographic results. On his return, Tripoli asked plaintiff if she wanted to know the sex of the baby, and she said she did. He told her, falsely, that to determine the sex he would need to scan "much further down," and it would be uncomfortable. [Tripoli inappropriately touched plaintiff.] Tripoli eventually stopped molesting plaintiff and returned her to the emergency room.

At the time of the misconduct, plaintiff thought it was part of a "regular procedure," albeit "kind of weird." Later that day, however, she began to suspect Tripoli's actions were improper, a suspicion confirmed the next morning when she talked to her regular obstetrician. Tripoli was criminally prosecuted and pleaded no contest to a felony charge arising out of his molestation of plaintiff.

Plaintiff's suit named Tripoli, Hospital and others as defendants, and contained causes of action for professional negligence, battery and intentional and negligent infliction of emotional harm. In opposition to Hospital's motion for summary judgment, plaintiff maintained triable issues of fact existed as to whether Hospital was vicariously liable for the battery as a tort committed within the scope of Tripoli's employment, or was directly liable for its own negligence in failing to have a third person present during the examination. The superior court granted the summary judgment motion, rejecting both arguments.

The Court of Appeal reversed. The court relied only on the theory of respondeat superior and expressly declined to reach the question of Hospital's negligence. We granted Hospital's petition for review in order to decide the vicarious liability question.

The rule of respondeat superior is familiar and simply stated: an employer is vicariously liable for the torts of its employees committed within the scope of the employment.[40] Equally well established, if somewhat surprising on first encounter, is the principle that an employee's willful, malicious and even criminal torts may fall within the scope of his or her employment for purposes of respondeat superior, even though the employer has not authorized the employee to commit crimes or intentional torts. What, then, is the connection required between an employee's intentional tort and his or her work so that the employer may be held vicariously liable?

It is clear, first of all, that California no longer follows the traditional rule that an employee's actions are within the scope of employment only if motivated, in whole or part, by a desire to serve the employer's interests. Our departure from that limiting rule dates at least from the leading case of *Carr v. Wm. C. Crowell Co.*, 171 P.2d 5.

In *Carr*, this court held a building contractor liable for injuries caused when an employee, angry at a subcontractor's employee for interfering in his work, threw a hammer at the other worker's head. We rejected the defendant's claim its employee was not acting within the scope of employment because he "could not have intended by his conduct to further" the employer's interests. . . .

While the employee thus need not have intended to further the employer's interests, the employer will not be held liable for an assault or other intentional tort that

---

40. [2] . . . Tripoli was not formally employed by Hospital, but by Mediq Imaging Services, Inc., with which Hospital contracted for his services. Hospital, however, concedes it did not seek summary judgment on the ground Tripoli was not its employee, did not argue that issue in the Court of Appeal, and does not rely on it in this court. For purposes of reviewing the ruling on summary judgment, therefore, we will treat Tripoli as Hospital's employee, without considering or deciding whether Tripoli was Hospital's nonemployee agent or ostensible agent or a special employee for whose torts Hospital is liable under the "borrowed servant" rule.

did not have a causal nexus to the employee's work. This rule, too, can be traced to *Carr.* There the court acknowledged that "[i]f an employee inflicts an injury out of personal malice, *not engendered by the employment*, the employer is not liable." (italics added.) . . .

Because an intentional tort gives rise to respondeat superior liability only if it was engendered by the employment, our disavowal of motive as a singular test of respondeat superior liability does not mean the employee's motive is irrelevant. An act serving only the employee's personal interest is less likely to arise from or be engendered by the employment than an act that, even if misguided, was intended to serve the employer in some way.

The nexus required for respondeat superior liability—that the tort be engendered by or arise from the work—is to be distinguished from "but for" causation. That the employment brought tortfeasor and victim together in time and place is not enough. We have used varied language to describe the nature of the required additional link (which, in theory, is the same for intentional and negligent torts): the incident leading to injury must be an "outgrowth" of the employment; the risk of tortious injury must be "'inherent in the working environment'" or "'typical of or broadly incidental to the enterprise [the employer] has undertaken.'"

Looking at the matter with a slightly different focus, California courts have also asked whether the tort was, in a general way, foreseeable from the employee's duties. Respondeat superior liability should apply only to the types of injuries that "as a practical matter are sure to occur in the conduct of the employer's enterprise." The employment, in other words, must be such as predictably to create the risk employees will commit intentional torts of the type for which liability is sought.

In what has proved an influential formulation, the court in *Rodgers v. Kemper Constr. Co.*, 124 Cal. Rptr. 143, held the tortious occurrence must be "a generally foreseeable consequence of the activity." In this usage, the court further explained, foreseeability "merely means that in the context of the particular enterprise an employee's conduct is not so unusual or startling that it would seem unfair to include the loss resulting from it among other costs of the employer's business." . . .

"Ordinarily, the determination whether an employee has acted within the scope of employment presents a question of fact; it becomes a question of law, however, when 'the facts are undisputed and no conflicting inferences are possible.'" Neither plaintiff nor Hospital has pointed to factual disputes that would prevent us in this case from deciding the applicability of respondeat superior as a matter of law.

Was Tripoli's sexual battery of Lisa M. within the scope of his employment? The injurious events were causally related to Tripoli's employment as an ultrasound technician in the sense they would not have occurred had he not been so employed. Tripoli's employment as an ultrasound technician provided the opportunity for him to meet plaintiff and to be alone with her in circumstances making the assault possible. The employment was thus one necessary cause of the ensuing tort. But, as previously discussed, in addition to such "but for" causation, respondeat superior liability requires that the risk of the tort have been engendered by, "typical of or broadly incidental to," or, viewed from a somewhat different perspective, "a generally foreseeable consequence of," Hospital's enterprise.

At the broadest level, Hospital argues sex crimes are never foreseeable outgrowths of employment because they, unlike instances of nonsexual violence, are not the product of "normal human traits." Hospital urges us not to "legitimize" sexual misconduct by treating it on a par with mere fights. These generalized distinctions are not, however, compelling. Neither physical violence nor sexual exploitation are legitimate, excusable or routinely expected in the workplace. In *Carr* this court did not "legitimize" the act of the construction worker who, on trivial provocation, threw a carpenter's hammer at the plaintiff, "striking him on the head and seriously injuring him," any more than we excused, condoned or otherwise "legitimized" a police officer's forcible rape of a detainee in *Mary M. v. City of Los Angeles*, [814 P.2d 1341]. The references in certain cases to "the faults and derelictions of human beings" (*Carr*) thus must be taken in context to include not only minor character flaws, but also the human tendency toward malice and viciousness. We are not persuaded that the roots of sexual violence and exploitation are in all cases so fundamentally different from those other abhorrent human traits as to allow a conclusion sexual misconduct is per se unforeseeable in the workplace.

Focusing more specifically on the type of sexual assault occurring here, we ask first whether the technician's acts were "engendered by" or an "outgrowth" of his employment. They were not.

Nonsexual assaults that were not committed to further the employer's interests have been considered outgrowths of employment if they originated in a work-related dispute. "Conversely, vicarious liability [has been] deemed inappropriate where the misconduct does not arise from the conduct of the employer's enterprise but instead arises out of a personal dispute (e.g., *Monty v. Orlandi* (1959) 337 P.2d 861 [bar owner not vicariously liable where on-duty bartender assaulted plaintiff in the course of a personal dispute with his common law wife]), or is the result of a personal compulsion (e.g., *Thorn v. City of Glendale* (1994) 28 Cal. App. 4th 1379, 1383, 35 Cal. Rptr. 2d 1 [city not vicariously liable where fire marshal set business premises on fire during an inspection])."

As with these nonsexual assaults, a sexual tort will not be considered engendered by the employment unless its motivating emotions were fairly attributable to work-related events or conditions. Here the opposite was true: a technician simply took advantage of solitude with a naive patient to commit an assault for reasons unrelated to his work. Tripoli's job was to perform a diagnostic examination and record the results. The task provided no occasion for a work-related dispute or any other work-related emotional involvement with the patient. The technician's decision to engage in conscious exploitation of the patient did not arise out of the performance of the examination, although the circumstances of the examination made it possible. "If . . . the assault was not motivated or triggered off by anything in the employment activity but was the result of only propinquity and lust, there should be no liability." (*Lyon v. Carey*, 533 F.2d [649] at 655 [(D.C. Cir. 1976)].)

Our conclusion does not rest on mechanical application of a motivation-to-serve test for intentional torts, which would bar vicarious liability for virtually all sexual misconduct. Tripoli's criminal actions, of course, were unauthorized by Hospital and were not motivated by any desire to serve Hospital's interests. Beyond that, however, his motivating emotions were not causally attributable to his employment. The flaw in plaintiff's case for Hospital's respondeat superior liability is not so much that Tripoli's actions were personally motivated, but that those personal motivations were not generated by or an outgrowth of workplace responsibilities, conditions or events.

Analysis in terms of foreseeability leads to the same conclusion. An intentional tort is foreseeable, for purposes of respondeat superior, only if "*in the context of the particular enterprise* an employee's conduct is not so unusual or startling that it would seem unfair to include the loss resulting from it among other costs of the employer's business." (*Rodgers, supra*, italics added.) The question is not one of statistical frequency, but of a relationship between the nature of the work involved and the type of tort committed. The employment must be such as predictably to create the risk employees will commit intentional torts of the type for which liability is sought.

In arguing Tripoli's misconduct was generally foreseeable, plaintiff emphasizes the physically intimate nature of the work Tripoli was employed to perform. In our view, that a job involves physical contact is, by itself, an insufficient basis on which to impose vicarious liability for a sexual assault. (Accord, *Boykin v. District of Columbia* (D.C. 1984) 484 A.2d 560, 562 "[[T]hat physical touching was necessarily a part of the teacher-student relationship" held insufficient to impose liability on employer for teacher's molestation of deaf and blind student, who could be taught only through touch.]). To hold medical care providers strictly liable for deliberate sexual assaults by every employee whose duties include examining or touching patients' otherwise private areas would be virtually to remove scope of employment as a limitation on providers' vicarious liability.[41] . . .

---

41. [6] We part company at this point with the dissenting justices, who would hold summary judgment improper because either the patient's vulnerability or the intimate physical contact inherent in the examination might have encouraged or incited Tripoli to assault her. On the present record, such inferences would be wholly speculative. Lacking evidence the assault was a product of the therapeutic relationship, to impose vicarious liability on a hospital for a technician's deliberate sexual assault on a patient would stretch the rationale of respondeat superior too far. To do so would make the hospital potentially liable, irrespective of its actual fault, whenever an employee used force, coercion or trickery to exploit criminally a patient's physical or psychological vulnerability, vulnerability that is characteristic of hospitalized patients generally. An analysis that, in the field of health care, deems a conscious sexual assault to have arisen from the employment simply because the patient involved was vulnerable, surrendered his or her privacy or submitted to physical contact unusual for strangers in a nonmedical context, would, in effect, expose

Here, there is no evidence of emotional involvement, either mutual or unilateral, arising from the medical relationship. Although the procedure ordered involved physical contact, it was not of a type that would be expected to, or actually did, give rise to intense emotions on either side. We deal here not with a physician or therapist who becomes sexually involved with a patient as a result of mishandling the feelings predictably created by the therapeutic relationship (see, e.g., *Simmons v. United States* (9th Cir. 1986) 805 F.2d 1363, 1369–1370; *Doe v. Samaritan Counseling Center* (Alaska 1990) 791 P.2d 344, 348–349), but with an ultrasound technician who simply took advantage of solitude, access and superior knowledge to commit a sexual assault.

Although the routine examination Tripoli was authorized to conduct involved physical contact with Lisa M., Tripoli's assault on plaintiff did not originate with, and was not a generally foreseeable consequence of, that contact. Nothing happened during the course of the prescribed examinations to provoke or encourage Tripoli's improper touching of plaintiff. (See *Alma W. v. Oakland Unified School District, supra,* 123 Cal. App. 3d at p. 141, 176 Cal. Rptr. 287 [contrasting assault cases, in which a work-related quarrel preceded the assault, with school custodian's rape of student, which was held unrelated to custodian's duties]; *Wiersma v. City of Long Beach* (1940) 41 Cal. App. 2d 8, 11, 15, 106 P.2d 45 [producer of wrestling exhibition not vicariously liable for injuries caused by wrestler who "suddenly and, apparently without provocation" attacked spectator].) The assault, rather, was the independent product of Tripoli's aberrant decision to engage in conduct unrelated to his duties. In the pertinent sense, therefore, Tripoli's actions were not foreseeable from the nature of the work he was employed to perform.

Plaintiff contends the battery in this case, like the police officer's rape of a detainee in *Mary M. v. City of Los Angeles, supra,* "arose from an abuse of job-created authority." More accurately, Tripoli abused his position of trust, since he had no legal or coercive authority over plaintiff. Assuming an analogy can be fully maintained between authority and trust, *Mary M.* still provides less than compelling precedent for liability here. In *Mary M.,* we held a police officer's assault was a generally foreseeable consequence of his position. "In view of the considerable power and authority that police officers possess, it is neither startling nor unexpected that on occasion an officer will misuse that authority by engaging in assaultive conduct." We expressly limited our holding: "We stress that our conclusion in this case flows from the unique authority vested in police officers. Employees who do not have this authority and who commit sexual assaults may be acting outside the scope of their employment as a matter of law."

While a police officer's assault may be foreseeable from the scope of his unique authority over detainees, we are unable to say the same of an ultrasound technician's assault on a patient. Hospital did not give Tripoli any power to exercise general

---

health care providers to potential liability without fault for sexual assault by virtually any employee on any patient.

control over plaintiff's liberty. He was not vested with any coercive authority, and the trust plaintiff was asked to place in him was limited to conduct of an ultrasound examination. His subsequent battery of the patient was independent of the narrow purpose for which plaintiff was asked to trust him. Whatever costs may be fairly attributable to a police officer's public employer in light of the extraordinary scope of authority the community, for its own benefit, confers on the officer, we believe it would not be fair to attribute to Hospital, which employed Tripoli simply to conduct ultrasound examinations, the costs of a deliberate, independently motivated sexual battery unconnected to the prescribed examination.

In reaching our conclusion we have consulted the three identified policy goals of the respondeat superior doctrine—preventing future injuries, assuring compensation to victims, and spreading the losses caused by an enterprise equitably—for additional guidance as to whether the doctrine should be applied in these circumstances. In this case, however, we have drawn no firm direction from consideration of the first two policy goals. Although imposition of vicarious liability would likely lead to adoption of some further precautionary measures, we are unable to say whether the overall impact would be beneficial to or destructive of the quality of medical care. Hospital and its amici curiae predict imposition of respondeat superior liability would lead health care providers to overreact by monitoring, for possible sexual misconduct, every interaction between patient and health care worker. Published research, on the other hand, indicates providers have available several other approaches to preventing sexual misconduct by employees.

As for ensuring compensation, the briefing does not enable us to say with confidence whether or not insurance is actually available to medical providers for sexual torts of employees and, if so, whether coverage for such liability would drastically increase the insurance costs—or, if not, the uninsured liability costs—of nonprofit providers such as Hospital. The second policy consideration is therefore also of uncertain import here; imposing vicarious liability is likely to provide additional compensation to some victims, but the consequential costs of ensuring compensation in this manner are unclear.

Third and finally, we attempt to assess the propriety of spreading the risk of losses among the beneficiaries of the enterprise upon which liability would be imposed. As Hospital points out, this assessment is another way of asking whether the employee's conduct was "so unusual or startling that it would seem unfair to include the loss resulting from it among other costs of the employer's business." For reasons already discussed, we conclude the connection between Tripoli's employment duties—to conduct a diagnostic examination—and his independent commission of a deliberate sexual assault was too attenuated, without proof of Hospital's negligence, to support allocation of plaintiff's losses to Hospital as a cost of doing business. Consideration of the respondeat superior doctrine's basis in public policy, therefore, does not alter our conviction that an ultrasound technician's sexual assault on a patient is not a risk predictably created by or fairly attributed to the nature of the technician's employment.

Although, as we have concluded, Tripoli's criminal acts were not engendered by or broadly incidental to his work so as to render Hospital vicariously liable, Hospital's duty of due care to its patient obliged it to take all measures dictated by ordinary prudence to protect against even such unusual sources of injury. The Court of Appeal declined to decide whether plaintiff's cause of action for negligence could survive summary judgment. The court therefore did not decide whether Hospital fulfilled its duty of care under the circumstances. . . . Consequently, we consider it appropriate to remand the matter to the Court of Appeal for decision in the first instance on plaintiff's negligence cause of action.

The judgment of the Court of Appeal is reversed and the matter is remanded to that court for further proceedings consistent with this opinion.

LUCAS, C.J., and ARABIAN, BAXTER, GEORGE, JJ., concur.

GEORGE, ASSOCIATE JUSTICE, concurring.

I concur in the result and reasoning of the majority, and I have signed the majority opinion. I write separately because, for the reasons expressed in my concurring opinion in *Farmers Insurance Group v. County of Santa Clara* (1995), 906 P.2d 440, I would go further and overrule the decision in *Mary M. v. City of Los Angeles* (1991) 814 P.2d 1341.

LUCAS, C.J., concurs.

MOSK, ASSOCIATE JUSTICE, dissenting.

I dissent. Justice Kennard demonstrates that the Court of Appeal's decision is without error and hence that its judgment should be affirmed. I join in her opinion. . . .

KENNARD, ASSOCIATE JUSTICE, dissenting.

I dissent.

The majority holds that, as a matter of law, a hospital employee was not acting within the scope of his employment when he sexually molested a pregnant woman while purportedly conducting an ultrasound examination necessitating that he have physical contact with intimate areas of the woman's body. I disagree. Scope of employment in this case, as in most cases, is a question of fact to be resolved by the trier of fact.

The scope-of-employment question presented here is very similar to one this court addressed just a few weeks ago in *Farmers Insurance Group v. County of Santa Clara* (1995) 906 P.2d 440. In that case, an employee had sexually harassed coemployees, whereas here an employee sexually assaulted a nonemployee, but both cases pose the question whether an employee's on-the-job sexual misconduct arises in the scope of employment. In *Farmers*, as here, the majority concluded, as a matter of law, that the sexual misconduct was outside the scope of employment. In *Farmers*, as here, I have concluded that because reasonable minds may differ as to the proper resolution of the issue, it should not be resolved as a matter of law. . . .

More recent cases . . . have said that scope of employment is a question of fact unless "the facts are undisputed and *no conflicting inferences are possible.*" (*Mary M. v. City of Los Angeles, supra*, 814 P.2d 1341, italics added.) In other words, if the parties agree as to the underlying facts, but dispute the inferences as to scope of employment that may reasonably be drawn from those facts, scope of employment is a question of fact. . . . [T]he majority concludes, Tripoli's sexual assault on plaintiff "is fairly attributed not to any peculiar aspect of the health care enterprise, but only to 'propinquity and lust' [citation]."

Perhaps. But a trier of fact might also reasonably conclude that Tripoli's employment as an ultrasound technician did have certain "peculiar aspects" that played a not insignificant role in the sexual assault. To perform an ultrasound examination on a pregnant woman, a technician rubs a gel on the woman's exposed lower abdomen. This intimate contact, inherent in the job, put plaintiff in a vulnerable position and permitted Tripoli to dupe plaintiff into believing that his sexual assault was actually part of a standard medical procedure, thereby giving Tripoli a basis to hope that his misconduct would remain undetected. Moreover, it is not unreasonable to infer that the intimate contact inherent in the job contributed to Tripoli's sexual arousal and incited him to engage in the misconduct. In short, a reasonable trier of fact could conclude that this sexual assault would never have occurred had Tripoli been employed by defendant in a capacity other than ultrasound technician, and that therefore the misconduct may fairly be attributed to risks arising from, and inherent in, the "peculiar aspects" of Tripoli's employment. . . .

When an employee's personal motivations are so enmeshed with the employee's performance of occupational duties that reasonable minds can differ as to whether the employee's tortious act is incidental to those duties, the issue of whether the act arose in the scope of employment should be resolved by the trier of fact, rather than a trial court acting on a motion to dismiss. . . .

I do not suggest, by the foregoing comments, that the question whether an employee's tortious conduct is within the scope of employment may never be resolved on summary judgment. Although scope of employment is ordinarily a question of fact, it becomes a question of law "where the undisputed facts would not support an inference that the employee was acting within the scope of his employment." (*John R. v. Oakland Unified School Dist., supra*, 769 P.2d 948 [(Cal. 1989)].) Thus, this court held in *John R.* that, as a matter of law, a junior high school teacher acted outside the scope of his employment when he molested one of his students, and that therefore no liability could be imposed on the school district that employed him. But the converse is also true: when an employee's tortious acts, although personally motivated, are so integrally entwined with his or her employment that reasonable minds can differ as to whether the acts arose in the scope of employment, then scope of employment is a question of fact, rather than one of law, and may not be decided on a motion for summary judgment. This is the case here.

Notes

1. *Alma W. v. Oakland Unified School Dist.*, 176 Cal. Rptr. 287, 290–91 (Cal. App. 1981), cited in *Lisa M.*, is a case dealing with a sexual assault by a school janitor in his office during working hours in an elementary school. The court's opinion contains several useful observations on the troubling issue of scope of employment in such a context. Selected quotations from the opinion are contained below:

> Similarly, [A. B.]'s use of the janitor's office, which arguably furnished a unique opportunity for his action, does not impute liability to the school district. The mere fact that an employee has the opportunity to abuse facilities necessary to the performance of his duties does not render an employer vicariously liable for the abuse. Nor does the fact that the offense occurred during working hours make A. B.'s action incidental to his employment. Although appellant strenuously argues that the janitor's presence at his workplace and his attendance to his duties immediately before and immediately after the offense is a determinative factor in resolving the issue of scope of employment, he is unable to cite any authority for that proposition.

> [In this passage the court is addressing the foreseeability test suggested by Judge Friendly in the *Bushey* case. That test was adopted in California in the *Rodgers* case referred to in *Lisa M.*] ". . . However, 'foreseeability' in this context must be distinguished from 'foreseeability' as a test for negligence. In the latter sense 'foreseeable' means a level of probability which would lead a prudent person to take effective precautions whereas 'foreseeability' as a test for *respondeat superior* merely means that in the context of the particular enterprise an employee's conduct is not so unusual or startling that it would seem unfair to include the loss resulting from it among other costs of the employer's business. [Citations.] . . ." [T]he [*Rodgers*] decision also limits liability to those torts which "may fairly be said to be characteristic" of the enterprise's activities. . . . [I]t defies every notion of fairness to say that rape is characteristic of a school district's activities.

> The fact that the Legislature has taken the action it has [to weed out sex offenders] in no way alters the fact that sexual molestation is an *aberrational* act. Although appellant argues that the Legislature's anticipation of such an eventuality proves that sexual molestation was foreseeable, the legislative action does not in itself meet the foreseeability test that is the law of this state. The test is not whether it is foreseeable that one or more employees might at some time act in such a way as to give rise to civil liability, but rather, whether the employee's act is foreseeable *in light of the duties* the employee is hired to perform. (Rest. 2d Agency (1957) § 245.) Thus, while it might be foreseeable for a school custodian to become involved in a dispute over the manner in which he swept the floors or cleaned a classroom and for the dispute to end in someone being hit with a mop, the same statement cannot be made with reference to rape. There is no aspect of a

janitor's duties that would make sexual assault anything other than highly unusual and very startling.

2. An alternative theory of liability was advanced in *Doe v. Samaritan Counseling Center*, 791 P.2d 344 (Alaska 1990), cited in *Lisa M.*, a case involving sexual misconduct in the counseling profession. Plaintiff sued Samaritan Counseling for emotional harm suffered as a result of the sexual misconduct of one of its pastoral counselors. The majority of the court reversed summary judgment for the defendant below and remanded the case for jury determination. The court explained its decision as follows:

> We are not unmindful of the force of those authorities which hold that an employee's tortious sexual behavior is impelled by motivations other than a desire to further the interests of the employer. However, we are of the view that the "motivation to serve" test, so construed, would too significantly undercut the enterprise liability basis of the respondeat superior doctrine we have previously articulated. In *Fruit*, [502 P.2d 133 (Alas. 1972)] we discussed this basis for the doctrine, saying,
>
> > "Scope of employment" as a test for application of respondeat superior would be insufficient if it failed to encompass the duty of every enterprise to the social community which gives it life and contributes to its prosperity. . . . The basis of respondeat superior has been correctly stated as "the desire to include in the costs of operation inevitable losses to third persons incident to carrying on an enterprise, and thus distribute the burden among those benefited by the enterprise."
>
> . . . .
>
> Although not usually enunciated as a basis for liability, in essence the enterprise may be regarded as a unit for tort as opposed to contract liability purposes. Employees' acts sufficiently connected with the enterprise are in effect considered as deeds of the enterprise itself. Where through negligence such acts cause injury to others it is appropriate that the enterprise bear the loss incurred.

The majority opinion in *Doe* rejects the "motivation to serve" test by pointing to the "enterprise liability" doctrine, under which employees' acts "sufficiently connected" with the enterprise are considered "as deeds of the enterprise itself." The enterprise liability doctrine reflects the desire to include in the costs of operation "inevitable losses incident to carrying on the enterprise."[42] One response to this thesis may be

---

42. For a different perspective on the use by courts of an enterprise liability doctrine to displace traditional respondeat superior doctrine, see *Hamilton v. Natrona County Educ. Ass'n*, 901 P.2d 381, 387 (Wyo. 1995), stating:

> Courts generally "decline to impose a rule, the ramifications of which would be far-reaching and which would rearrange, across the state, the responsibility of employers for the conduct of their employees. Such a redirection of social policy is, more appropriately,

that the enterprise liability theory clearly states a worthy goal, and analysis need go no further. An argument on the other side might be that the enterprise liability theory begs the question before the court. That is, the issue before the court is whether a loss is "sufficiently connected" with the defendant's activity to justify imposing the loss on defendant. The enterprise liability theory simply restates the question as if that supplied the answer, the argument goes. Instead what is needed are some tools of analysis to assist in deciding the issue of "sufficient connection."

3. *Lisa M.* in part of the opinion applies the three policy goals used in prior California authority for determining the limits of respondeat superior liability, posing broad questions about accident prevention, assuring compensation to victims and equitable distribution of losses. That approach does not seem much different from the enterprise liability approach of *Doe*. Also, it can be argued that asking whether a loss is "incident" to the enterprise, a test that played a central role in *Doe*, poses a standard so vague and open-ended that it is hard to frame arguments about whether an act is or is not within the scope of employment. An argument under that test might be: "This *is* incident to the enterprise." A rebuttal might be: "This is *not* incident to the enterprise." In some cases it might be difficult to take the arguments much beyond such an exchange of conclusory assertions.

4. With regard to tools of analysis, one virtue of the standards set forth in § 228 is that they provide something more specific to consider when deciding these complex and emotional cases that deal with conduct everywhere viewed as offensive and repellent. With regard to the intent to serve test, one can argue that it should not be discarded too readily, for it serves as a moral foundation for agency law. Conduct of an agent must be subject to the control of and on behalf of the principal before it is fair to hold the principal to the strict liability of respondeat superior. If there is no "intent, even in part, to serve," there is no action "on behalf of" and therefore no moral justification for strict liability, it can be argued. Perhaps in part for this reason, the intent to serve test is still followed by the overwhelming majority of courts. *See* 1980 Duke L.J. 742; 39 S.D. L. Rev. 570 (1994).

The following cases discuss alternative modes of analysis for these difficult scope of employment cases.

ii. Restatement (Second) § 219(2)(d)

Costos v. Coconut Island Corp.

United States Court of Appeals, First Circuit
137 F.3d 46 (1998)

Before Torruella, Chief Judge, Boudin and Lynch, Circuit Judges.

---

the function of the legislature." *Kuehn v. White*, 600 P.2d 679, 683 (Wash. App. 1979). We agree with this rationale and reject the theory of enterprise liability.

LYNCH, CIRCUIT JUDGE.

A jury found the defendants vicariously liable for the act—rape—committed by their employee Charles Bonney. Bonney, the manager of the Maine inn owned by defendants, let himself into the room of the plaintiff, a guest at the inn, in the early morning hours and raped her. The jury awarded plaintiff $50,000 on that count, and $5,000 on a negligence count.

Defendants say the issue of vicarious liability never should have gone to the jury. They argue that under the Restatement (Second) of Agency § 219(2)(d), adopted by Maine law, vicarious liability may not be imposed for acts committed by the employee outside the scope of employment unless the employee has acted with apparent authority or deceit, and that the evidence does not support such a finding. Under present Maine law, and on the evidence of record, the issue was, we believe, properly submitted to the jury. The Maine courts may decide, as have other courts, that some limiting principles should evolve to prevent § 219(2)(d) from being used to erode the distinction between acts committed within the scope of employment and those outside the scope. But this case does not present the occasion to do so. We affirm. . . .

In the early morning of August 14, 1993, Charles Bonney raped Patricia O'Boyle Costos in her room at the Bernard House in Old Orchard Beach, Maine. The Bernard House was a small seasonal inn owned by defendant Neal Weinstein and managed through the Coconut Island Corporation. The Coconut Island Corporation was wholly owned by Weinstein in 1993.

The day before, Costos and her friend Lynn Tierney travelled to Maine for the weekend. Tierney knew Charles Bonney, knew that he worked at the inn, and suggested that she and Costos spend the weekend at the Bernard House. When they arrived at the inn, Costos and Tierney paid Bonney for two nights' accommodation. Bonney told Costos that he was the manager and future owner of the Bernard House.

Bonney escorted the women to Room 23 on the third floor. He carried a plastic bag full of keys with him, and rummaged through it looking for the room key. Bonney eventually gave Tierney and Costos a key from his pocket, telling them that it was a master key and that they should not lose it.

That evening Costos, Tierney, Bonney, and two of Bonney's male friends socialized together at the Bernard House and later at a local club. Costos and Tierney eventually returned to their room at the inn, Costos to go to bed, and Tierney to keep her company back to the room.

Costos went to bed, but Tierney decided to go out again. Tierney left, taking the room key with her. Costos remembered that Tierney locked the door to their room.

Costos fell asleep. She awoke to find Bonney in the bed, having intercourse with her. She threw Bonney out of the bed, punching and kicking him. Bonney stood over her, laughing, and then left the room.

Bonney has fled the jurisdiction and remains at large. He is wanted on a federal fugitive warrant.

Costos sued the defendants in federal court, alleging the defendants were negligent and were vicariously liable for Bonney's torts. . . . At the close of the plaintiff's case, the defendants moved for a directed verdict, inter alia, on the vicarious liability count. That motion was denied. This appeal is from the denial of that motion and the denial of the renewal of that motion. . . .

The district court, sitting in diversity, applied the substantive law of Maine. The plaintiff's vicarious liability claim was based upon § 219(2)(d) of the Restatement (Second) of Agency, which has been adopted as the law of Maine. *See McLain v. Training & Dev. Corp.*, 572 A.2d 494 (Me. 1990) (holding a jury could find employer vicariously liable under § 219(2)(d) for the intentional torts of its employee). That section states:

Section 219. When Master is liable for Torts of His Servants

. . .

(2) A master is not subject to liability for the torts of his servants acting outside the scope of their employment, unless:

. . .

(d) the servant purported to act or speak on behalf of the principal and there was reliance upon apparent authority, or he was aided in accomplishing the tort by the existence of the agency relation.

Maine has also adopted the Restatement's definition of agency. . . . It is plain that there was an agency relationship between Bonney and defendants, and that Bonney, as manager of the inn, was the defendants' "servant". . . .

Defendants argue that they cannot be liable under § 219(2)(d) because it requires the use of "apparent authority" or deceit by the servant to facilitate the tort. Defendants argue that there is no evidence that Costos believed that Bonney was acting on his employer's behalf when he assaulted her, or that the use of apparent authority in any way aided Bonney in accomplishing the tort.

Defendants attempt to construe the final clause of § 219(2)(d), "or he was aided in accomplishing the tort by the existence of the agency relation," as merely a reiteration of the prior language in subpart (d) on apparent authority. If the phrase was meant to be independent of an apparent authority analysis, defendants argue, it would have been put into a separate subsection. We conclude that under Maine law, as articulated in *McLain*, a master may be liable for the torts of his or her servants who are acting outside the scope of their employment when they are aided in accomplishing the tort by the existence of the agency relation.

In *McLain*, a client of a Jobs Corps program sued the agency operating the program after a counselor directed him to perform painful and humiliating "tests." The counselor said those "tests" would help the client gain admission to the U.S.

Marine Corps. The client was rejected by the Marines, and sued the agency for the injuries he suffered as a result of the counselor's intentional torts. The Supreme Judicial Court of Maine held that a jury could find the agency vicariously liable for the client's injuries under §219(2)(d), because "the jury could rationally find from the evidence that [the counselor's] employment made possible the tortious assault and battery he imposed upon McLain, rendering [the agency] liable for all of McLain's injuries at [the counselor's] hand, on the alternative theory of vicarious liability." 572 A.2d at 498. The court said the jury could find either that the tort was within the scope of employment or that it was outside the scope but within the §219(2)(d) exception.

McLain does not say that the use of apparent authority is required for vicarious liability under §219(2)(d). Instead, the Maine courts have thus far followed the plain meaning of §219(2)(d). Indeed, defendants' reading would violate another rule of statutory construction because the broad reading proffered by defendants would render the second clause of subpart (d) superfluous.

Defendants argue that this reading of §219(2)(d) will result in a vast expansion of employer liability in Maine and will render every intentional tort committed outside the scope of employment as equivalent to those committed within the scope of employment. Defendants ask us to interpret §219(2)(d) in light of the evolving rules for vicarious liability for sexual harassment in Title VII cases. We need not speculate whether Maine courts would follow such an analogy or otherwise narrowly gloss the Restatement because, even if narrowing limitations were to be assumed *arguendo*, the appeal would still fail.

In general terms, defendant's argument as to the scope of §219(2) finds some support in case law elsewhere. As noted by Judge MacKinnon, concurring in a Title VII case, *Barnes v. Costle*, 561 F.2d 983, 996 (D.C. Cir. 1977), "Concerning the second part of the [§219(2)(d)] exception, at first reading it seems to argue too much. In every case where vicarious liability is at issue, the agent will have been aided in some way in committing the tort by the position that he holds." The Court of Appeals for the D.C. Circuit, citing the *Barnes* concurrence, recently sounded the same cautionary note. "In a sense, a supervisor is always 'aided in accomplishing the tort by the existence of the agency relation' because his responsibilities provide proximity to and contact with the victim." *Gary v. Long*, 59 F.3d 1391, 1397 (D.C.Cir.1995). In attempting to find a narrowing principle, that court referred to the commentary of the Restatement: that an employer is liable only if the tort "was accomplished by an instrumentality, or through conduct associated with the agency status." *Id.* (citing Restatement (Second) of Agency §219 cmt. e (1958)).[43]

---

43. [1] Other Comment to subsection (2)(d) in the Restatement says:
   Clause (d) includes primarily situations in which the principal's liability is based upon conduct which is within the apparent authority of a servant, as where one purports to speak for his employer in defaming another or interfering with another's business. . . . *In other situations, the servant may be able to cause harm because of his position as agent,*

Even viewing this case through the narrower focus of the commentary on Restatement § 219, which the *Gary* court found helpful, defendants are well within the scope of § 219(2)(d) liability. By virtue of his agency relationship with the defendants, as manager of the inn, Bonney was entrusted with the keys to the rooms, including Costos' room, at the Bernard House. Because he was the manager of the inn, Bonney knew exactly where to find Costos. The jury could find that Bonney had responsibilities to be at the inn or to have others there late at night. In short, because he was the defendants' agent, Bonney knew that Costos was staying at the Bernard House, he was able to find Costos' room late at night, he had the key to the room and used the key to unlock the door, slip into bed beside her as she slept, and rape her.

We hold that the district court correctly denied the defendants' motion for judgment as a matter of law. The record shows sufficient evidence to hold the defendants vicariously liable under § 219(2)(d) for Bonney's acts.

The judgment of the district court is *affirmed*.

Notes

1. Five years after the First Circuit decided the *Costos*, the Maine Supreme Judicial Court decided *Mahar v. Stonewood Transport*, 823 A.2d 540, 546 (Me. 2003), a case in which the plaintiffs sought to rely on Restatement (Second) § 219(2)(d) in the context of a case of road rage. The Maine court seemed to reject the application of § 219(2)(d) in cases involving physical torts that would typically be viewed as outside the scope of employment. The court noted the origins of § 219(2)(d):

> Comment e to section 219(2)(d) acknowledges that the section is limited in its application to cases within the apparent authority of the employee, or when the employee's conduct involves misrepresentation or deceit ... ("Clause (d) includes primarily situations in which the principal's liability is based upon conduct which is within the apparent authority of a servant ... [which] may also be the basis of an action of deceit, and even physical harm."); *see also* Daniel M. Combs, Casenote, Costos v. Coconut Island Corp.: *Creating a Vicarious Liability Catchall Under the Aided-by-Agency-Relation Theory*, 73 U. Colo. L. Rev. 1099, 1105 (2002) ("The limitations contained in Comment e ... prevent the aided-by-agency-relation basis for liability from potentially swallowing agency law's general scope of employment rule"). Additionally, the deliberations preceding section 219(2)(d)'s adoption demonstrate an intent to limit the section's application to cases involving apparent authority, reliance, or deceit. Combs, *supra*, at 1107–11

---

as where a telegraph operator sends false messages purporting to come from third persons. .... The enumeration of such situations is not exhaustive, and is intended only to indicate the area within which a master may be subjected to liability for acts of his servants not in the scope of employment. Restatement (Second) of Agency § 219 cmt. e (1958) (emphasis added).

(providing a detailed synopsis of the drafters' discussions while formulating section 219(2)(d)).

The court went on to distinguish its case from *Costos*, noting that the tortfeasor in *Mahar* "did not purport to act on behalf of [the employer], and he engaged in no misrepresentation or deceit; rather, he committed an assault and thereafter drove in a threatening manner." *Id*. Is this a convincing distinction?

2. Until relatively recently, § 219(d)(2) received little judicial attention other than its use in fraud cases. See Chapter 5, Fraudulent Acts of Agents, where § 219(2)(d) is used in its customary manner, as persuasive authority in a fraud case. The court in *Costos*, a physical tort case, thus is confronted with a new and distinctive use of § 219. In casting about for analogous authority, the court refers to Title VII sexual harassment cases. Although those cases involve interpretation of a federal statute, with independent underlying policy grounds, it is of interest that the United States Supreme Court recently has decided two landmark cases under Title VII, with both opinions making use of § 219(2)(d). *See Faragher v. City of Boca Raton*, 524 U.S. 775 (1998); *Burlington Industries, Inc. v. Ellerth*, 524 U.S. 742 (1998).

3. Relying on *Faragher, Burlington Industries* and *Costos*, among other authorities, and expressly rejecting *Mahar*, the Vermont Supreme Court embraced a robust reading of Restatement § 219(2)(d) in a lengthy opinion. In *Doe v. Forrest*, 853 A.2d 48, 67 (Vt. 2004) the Vermont court held that a sheriff's department may be vicariously liable for the sexual assault committed by a deputy while on patrol, even if the deputy did not use employer-supplied handcuffs or weapons to commit the assault. Rather, the court reasoned, "if plaintiff can show that an on-duty law enforcement officer was aided in accomplishing an intentional tort involving a sexual assault on the plaintiff by the existence of the employment relationship with the law enforcement agency, vicarious liability will apply." *See also Pena v. Greffert*, 110 F. Supp. 3d 1103 (D.N.M. 2015) (applying New Mexico law). For a case rejecting both *Doe v. Forrest* and a broad reading of § 219(2)(d), see *Zsigo v. Hurley Medical Center*, 716 N.W.2d 220 (Mich. 2006).

4. The Restatement (Third) does not embrace the use of § 219(d)(2) reflected in the *Costos* case. Regarding that section, see Restatement (Third) § 7.08, Comment b:

> This Restatement does not include "aided in accomplishing" as a distinct basis for an employer's (or principal's) vicarious liability. The purposes likely intended to be met by the "aided in accomplishing" basis are satisfied by a more fully elaborated treatment of apparent authority and by the duty of reasonable care that a principal owes to third parties with whom it interacts through employees and other agents. See § 7.05.

For a defense of § 219(2)(d) and criticism of the Restatement (Third), see Alan J. Oxford, II, *When Agents Attack: Judicial Misinterpretation of Vicarious Liability Under "Aided in Accomplishing the Tort by the Existence of the Agency Relation" and Restatement 3rd's Failure to Properly "Restate" the Ill-Fated Section 219(2)(d) Provision*, 37 Okla. City U. L. Rev. 157 (2012).

iii. The Implied Contract Theory

Nazareth v. Herndon Ambulance Service

Court of Appeals of Florida
467 So. 2d 1076, *review denied*, 478 So. 2d 53 (1985)

SHARP, JUDGE.

Ruth Ann Nazareth appeals from a summary judgment determining that Herndon Ambulance Service, Inc. is not liable for a sexual assault and battery which allegedly occurred while appellant was being transported by ambulance from her home to Florida Hospital North and which was allegedly perpetrated by Herndon's employee [Barrett] who was attending her in the passenger portion of the ambulance. . . .

The record conclusively establishes no basis to charge Herndon with negligence in hiring Barrett, and nothing to put Herndon on notice of any tendencies on Barrett's part to commit such an assault. Barrett's record as an employee for Herndon was excellent; and there was nothing in Barrett's past to indicate he would commit such an act. The fact that Herndon did not make a detailed check of Barrett's background before hiring him, therefore, was irrelevant since if such a check had been made nothing would have been discovered. Nor do we think Nazareth's contention that Herndon should have had a policy that only female attendants attend female passengers has any merit in view of the evidence in the record that no such policy exists anywhere in the ambulance business, and that it would not be feasible. . . .

In addition, the punitive damage claim by Nazareth against Herndon could also have been properly disposed of by the trial judge, since the record shows the sexual assault was clearly not within the scope of Barrett's employment, and it was not directed or authorized by Herndon.

Generally, sexual assaults and batteries by employees are held to be outside the scope of an employee's employment and, therefore, insufficient to impose vicarious liability on the employer. The general rule is that an employer cannot be held liable for the tortious or criminal acts of an employee, unless they were committed during the course of the employment and to further a purpose or interest, however excessive or misguided, of the employer. . . .

[An] exception to the general rule is where the employer is a common carrier for hire to the public, and the tort or attack is by an employee upon a passenger while the contract for transport is being accomplished. Such circumstances were clearly established by the record in this case. Herndon was licensed and generally operating an ambulance business in Orange County, Florida; Nazareth was a paying passenger; and the tort allegedly took place en route to the hospital.

Florida has long recognized vicarious liability on the part of a carrier-employer for torts of employees under such circumstances without regard to whether they were committed within the scope of employment. . . .

The rationale for imposing vicarious liability on the employer in such cases is the existence of an implied contract between the victim-passenger and the carrier for safe passage, free from attack by the carrier's employees. Once the undertaking to transport a passenger has begun, this extraordinary duty to the passenger arises, and does not terminate until the journey is complete. This is characterized in terms of tort liability as a non-delegable duty owed by the employer. These two causes of action, one in tort and one in contract, may coexist in an action against a carrier.

The source of this high standard of care imposed on carriers is in part the nature of the carrier's undertaking whereby the passenger must entrust his or her bodily safety to the care and control of the carrier's vehicle and employees, and he or she cannot freely or independently walk away, once the undertaking has commenced. This situation creates a special duty to protect. This is the basis for such tort liability having been applied in other similar situations not involving carriers, such as innkeepers, hospitals, and pullman car companies. . . .

We conclude that ambulances in Florida are common carriers for purposes of imposing on them a high degree of care owed their passengers during the fulfillment of their contract of carriage. This duty includes vicarious liability for the torts of employees visited upon a passenger while the contract for transport is being accomplished. We therefore do not reach the question of whether such vicarious liability would be imposed on Herndon if it were not a "common carrier," although the technical classification appears to us less significant than the nature and scope of its undertaking on behalf of its users.

Because Nazareth's complaint sufficiently alleged facts supported by the record, creating viable causes of action against Herndon for vicarious liability and breach of implied contract of safe carriage, we reverse the final summary judgment and remand this cause for trial on the merits.

Reversed and remanded.

COBB, CHIEF JUDGE, concurring in part and dissenting in part: . . .

It is patently clear from the record that Herndon's liability as a common carrier is not a legitimate issue in this case. Even if it were, the determination that Herndon is a common carrier is wrong. . . . Nazareth does not allege, and offered no proof, that Herndon was legally obligated to accept her business. . . .

The doctrine assessing strict liability against a common carrier for the independent torts (*i.e.*, those unrelated to the employer's business) of its employees is outmoded and unfair; this court should not expand its applicability, especially in a case where no party has asked, by pleadings or argument, that we do so. The plaintiff's cause of action, based on the factual allegations of her complaint, is an action in tort, not in contract. That action properly is against Barrett, not Herndon.

I would affirm the summary judgment discharging Herndon from the case.

Adams v. New York City Transit Authority

Court of Appeals of New York
666 N.E.2d 216 (1996)

TITONE, JUDGE.

In 1882, this Court held that a common carrier is liable to passengers for the torts of its employees regardless of whether those torts were committed within or outside the scope of their employment. This appeal requires us to determine whether the New York City Transit Authority may be held liable under this holding for injuries sustained by a subway rider as a result of an unprovoked attack by a Transit Authority token booth clerk. Concluding that the liability rule enunciated in 1882 is no longer viable as a matter of law or policy, we hold that the token booth clerk's assaultive conduct, which was indisputably outside the scope of her employment, does not give rise to vicarious liability on the part of her employer.

According to the complaint allegations and deposition testimony, plaintiff Margaret Adams was waiting in line to purchase a subway token when she heard the clerk inside the token booth yelling at the man immediately in front of her. After the man walked away, plaintiff stepped up to the booth, slid her fare through the opening in the window and asked for directions to her destination. Inexplicably, the clerk responded with a barrage of verbal abuse.

Shocked by the clerk's reaction, plaintiff walked away from the booth, placed her token in the slot and attempted to proceed through the turnstile. Her movement was interrupted, however, when she was assaulted from behind by the token clerk, pushed to the ground and choked. The incident ended when plaintiff's companion, who had been waiting in line with her, called for help and obtained the assistance of a man who pulled the assailant away from plaintiff. According to plaintiff, she suffered physical and emotional injury as a result of the assault.

Plaintiff commenced the present action for damages against the Transit Authority, alleging several causes of action.[44] On cross motions for summary judgment, plaintiff's claims based on negligent hiring, training and supervision and the Authority's alleged acquiescence in its employee's misconduct were dismissed for lack of factual or legal support. The Supreme Court concluded, however, that plaintiff had established entitlement to summary judgment on her cause of action that was based on defendant Authority's breach of its carrier's duty to provide its passengers with transportation "'free from insults or assaults by [its employees].'"

On defendant Authority's appeal, the Appellate Division reversed this aspect of the Supreme Court's ruling and modified its order accordingly by dismissing plaintiff's remaining cause of action. After reviewing the legal history of the special

---

44. [*] Plaintiff also sued the token booth clerk, Christine Bowman, but Bowman has apparently never appeared in the action.

common-carrier rule of vicarious liability on which the Supreme Court relied, the Appellate Division concluded that the rule was no longer viable. . . .

As a general rule, employers are held vicariously liable for their employees' torts only to the extent that the underlying acts were within the scope of the employment. The scope-of-employment limitation on employers' vicarious liability is a logical consequence of the policies underlying the vicarious liability doctrine itself. The modern justification for the doctrine lies in the view that "[t]he losses caused by the torts of employees, which as a practical matter are sure to occur in the conduct of the employer's enterprise," are most fairly allocated to the employer "as a required cost of doing business" (Prosser and Keeton, Torts § 69, at 500 [5th ed.]). It follows from this rationale that torts which are outside the scope of employment and are therefore not part of the "conduct of the employer's enterprise" should not be made the responsibility of the employer.

One particularly significant exception to the general rule is the expansive liability that has been imposed on common carriers for the torts of their employees. In *Stewart v. Brooklyn & Crosstown R.R. Co.*, 90 N.Y. 588, this Court held that carriers are liable for their employees' torts regardless of whether those torts were committed within the scope of employment. The *Stewart* decision was premised principally on the carrier's implicit contract with its passengers, which was held, as a matter of law, to require the carrier to transport its passengers "'safely and properly, and to treat [them] respectfully.'" An assault on a passenger by a carrier's employee constituted a breach of this contractual duty and, in the *Stewart* Court's view, should therefore be actionable without regard to the relationship between the employee's conduct and the master's business.

In subsequent cases applying the rule, the Court retained the breach of contract theory but also acknowledged the rule's equally important underpinnings in tort law. Modern authorities have recognized that the special duty of a common carrier to its passengers is a tort-based duty rather than an obligation derived from an implied contract between the carrier and the passenger. Prosser & Keeton § 12 at 57–58. As one court has noted in a somewhat different context, "'the tickets [issued by a carrier to a passenger] do no more than evidence a relation of common carrier and passenger for hire; it is the law of torts that imposes the standard of care and responsibility appropriate to the carrier-passenger relationship, but that standard, and any consequent liability, are not creatures of contract'" (*Gelfand v. Tanner Motor Tours*, 339 F.2d 317, 322) (2d Cir.). Accordingly, if the special rule adopted in *Stewart* is to retain its force in our contemporary body of law, it must find some justification in modern tort principles.

Consideration of the broad policies underlying the vicarious liability doctrine does not reveal such a justification. Where an unprovoked assault or other intentional tort committed by a carrier's employees is determined to be outside the scope of the actor's employment, it is, by definition, not of the kind of activity that is "as a practical matter . . . sure to occur in the conduct of the [carrier's] enterprise" (Prosser and Keeton, *op. cit.*, at 500). Thus, it makes no more sense to treat the cost of such misconduct as "a required cost" of the carrier's business (see *id.*) than it would to treat the same class of misconduct as a required cost of the business of a restaurateur, storekeeper or any other class of proprietor.

Since the general vicarious-liability principles that are applicable to all employers do not suggest a sound basis for the *Stewart* rule, its justification, if any, must be found in the special characteristics of common carriers. The lengthy history of the law's attempt to address common-carrier liability suggests several possibilities. However, as the Appellate Division correctly found, none of these furnishes a wholly satisfactory ground for applying the 100-year-old *Stewart* rule to contemporary controversies.

In the past, carriers were held subject to a higher duty of care, and terms like "absolute liability" and "duty of an *absolute nature*" were often used to explain why "the usual distinctions which attend the doctrine of respondeat superior cut little or no figure" in cases involving common-carrier liability. Thompson, Negligence § 3186. However, the higher duty of care imposed on carriers has been subject to considerable criticism and is no longer applied in many quarters. Moreover, there is no real logical connection between a carrier's higher duty of care and the imposition of "absolute" liability for the unforeseeable acts of employees that are both beyond the employer's control and outside the reasonable scope of the employer's enterprise.

Further, the apparent historic underpinnings of the carrier's absolute liability for employee misconduct are of dubious validity under current social and legal conditions. Any analogy between the carrier's absolute responsibility as a bailee of inanimate goods and its responsibility to human passengers has long been discredited. Similarly, although the special hazards once posed by rail travel have sometimes been cited as an important source of the absolute liability imposed on carriers, that rationale has long since become outdated as public conveyances like trains, planes and boats have become at least as safe as private modes of travel. Moreover, even if travel by common carrier could still fairly be regarded as an especially hazardous activity, that circumstance would not provide a persuasive explanation for the *Stewart* rule's retention, since the risks arising from the independent non-work-related tortious actions of an employee are unrelated to the hazards of travel and, in fact, are essentially the same regardless of whether the individual is hurtling through a subway tunnel or is instead leisurely sipping a cup of coffee in a quiet restaurant.

The status of passengers as helpless prisoners confined within the carriers' travel compartments is another factor that has been mentioned in support of the absolute liability rule. Like the ultrahazardous activity rationale, this theory proves too much. As one court has noted, the same factors that appear to enhance the risk of assault in public conveyances, i.e., the difficulty of escape and the involuntary exposure to many strangers, may actually operate as deterrents to would-be wrongdoers and thereby reduce the risk of harm from third-party attacks. Furthermore, modern life includes a host of other situations in which a consumer of services, such as a hospital patient or movie theater patron, might be confined to a limited area or find his or her movements similarly curtailed. It is doubtful that a court today would hold the proprietor of these classes of enterprises absolutely liable for an employee's intentional torts solely because of the existence of those conditions.

Finally, the former absolute duty of carriers to protect their passengers from criminal attacks by third parties is an unconvincing reason for imposing absolute liability for assaults by employees. Since this Court decided *Basso v. Miller*, [352 N.E.2d 868], in 1976, landowners have been absolved of the heightened duties of care that they previously owed their business invitees and guests. *Basso*'s holding undermines the basic notion that owners of particular businesses should be held to special or different duties of care that are determined solely by their relationship to or the status of the injured party. Moreover, where governmentally operated carriers like the Transit Authority are concerned, the premise that carriers should be liable at all for third-party criminal assaults has been drastically curtailed. Thus, the theoretical predicate for the third-party liability rule has itself been substantially eroded.

Even more importantly, the *Stewart* Court's reasoning on the point is fundamentally flawed. The Court concluded in *Stewart* that carriers should be held liable for the irrational and gratuitous *intentional* misconduct of their employees, since it would be anomalous to deny liability in those circumstances while imposing liability when an employee *negligently* permits a passenger to be attacked by a stranger. First, this syllogism, if valid, is as pertinent to all other service enterprises as it is to common carriers and is therefore not a sound basis for a special rule for the common carriers. Second, the syllogism is logically defective because it overlooks that liability in situations involving employee negligence requires the existence of an analytically critical fact not present in cases involving gratuitous intentional employee misdeeds, i.e., employee misconduct occurring *within the scope* of employment. As previously noted, it is only that condition that justifies the imposition of vicarious liability on an otherwise faultless employer.

In this case, plaintiff's only cause of action against the Transit Authority that was not dismissed for want of proof is her claim based on the Authority's vicarious liability for the tortious acts of its employee. Plaintiff does not contend that those acts were within the scope of her assailant's employment and, accordingly, her claim depends wholly on the special rule of "absolute liability" that was previously applied to carriers under *Stewart v. Brooklyn & Crosstown R.R. Co., supra.* Since that rule is no longer viable, we conclude that plaintiff's remaining cause of action was properly dismissed.

Accordingly, the order of the Appellate Division should be affirmed, with costs.

KAYE, C.J., and SIMONS, BELLACOSA, SMITH, LEVINE and CIPARICK, JJ., concur.

iv. Punitive Damages

Can an employer be held liable in punitive damages for the fraud, malice or gross negligence of its employees acting within their scope of employment? Should the answer depend on whether the employer authorized or ratified the act? *See Toole v. Richardson-Merrell, Inc.*, 251 Cal. App. 2d 689, 60 Cal. Rptr. 398, 29 A.L.R.3d

988 (1967) (upholding a $250,000 punitive damages award against defendant drug company for injuries caused by "MER/29," noting that there was ample evidence to show that high-level management knew of the wrong-doing—primarily falsification of data—of its employees). *Cf. Roginsky v. Richardson-Merrell, Inc.*, 378 F.2d 832 (2d Cir. 1967). See also Note, *The Assessment of Punitive Damages Against an Entrepreneur for the Malicious Torts of His Employees*, 70 Yale L.J. 1296 (1961), noting two divergent lines of authority. One group of opinions permits assessment of punitive damages in any case where the employer would be liable for compensatory damages under respondeat superior. The other rule, applied in the majority of states that have considered the question, allows the imposition of punitive damages on the employer only on the basis of culpability, such as authorizing or ratifying the tortious behavior. The note writer urges the adoption of a third rule, allowing the imposition of punitive damages only against individuals, on any level of employment, who expressly or impliedly authorized or participated in the tortious behavior, and not against the employer. For a case fully discussing both sides of the matter in majority and dissenting opinions, see *Campen v. Stone*, 635 P.2d 1121, 1124 (Wyo. 1981). The majority opinion, which rejected assessing an innocent employer for punitive damages, cited the following in support of its opinion:

> The punitive and deterrent underpinnings of a punitive damages award explain this divergence in vicarious liability doctrine. For whereas the purpose of compensatory damages—compensation of the victim—is accomplished whether payment comes from the master or his misbehaving servant, that of punitive damages—to punish the wrongdoer and deter him and others from duplicating his misconduct—is not. Unless the employer is himself guilty of some tortious act (or omission) because his employee has misbehaved, an award punishing the employer and deterring him and others situated to act likewise (i.e., other employers) makes no sense at all. *Williams v. City of New York*, 508 F.2d 356, 360 (2nd Cir. 1974).[45]

See also the discussion in *Loughry v. Lincoln First Bank, N.A.*, 494 N.E.2d 70, 74–76 (N.Y. 1986), where the court stated as follows:

> ... But punitive damages are a different matter entirely. Unlike damages that compensate an individual for injury or loss, punitive damages—damages over and above full compensation, and in that sense a windfall for the plaintiff—serve the societal purposes of punishing and deterring the wrongdoer, as well as others, from similar conduct in the future. Because of a dual recognition that blameless shareholders or owners likely suffer the ultimate burden of punitive damages vicariously imposed on an employer, and yet vicarious punitive damages can advance the goal of deterrence by

---

45. [See *Jones v. Compagnie Generale Maritime*, 882 F. Supp. 1079, 1086 (S.D. Ga. 1995), stating, "The retribution and deterrence objectives of punitive awards are not achieved 'when courts drop the punitive damage hammer on the [innocent] principal for the wrongful acts of [an employee].'" (*Quoting* P & E Boat Rentals, 872 F.2d [642] at 652 [(5th Cir. 1989)]—Eds.).]

motivating the employer to take corrective action, the issue of vicarious liability for punitive damages has for decades fueled heated controversy among courts and commentators. Indeed, it has been described as "chief" among the debates surrounding punitive damages.

In this State, the question has long been settled: an employer is not punished for malicious acts in which it was not implicated. While the decision to award punitive damages in any particular case, as well as the amount, are generally matters within the sound discretion of the trier of fact, there is a threshold issue: punitive damages can be imposed on an employer for the intentional wrongdoing of its employees only where management has authorized, participated in, consented to or ratified the conduct giving rise to such damages, or deliberately retained the unfit servant, or the wrong was in pursuance of a recognized business system of the entity. Put another way, this "complicity rule"—in essence the position adopted by the Restatement (Second) of Torts §909 and the Restatement (Second) of Agency §217C—results in employer liability for punitive damages only when a superior officer in the course of employment orders, participates in, or ratifies outrageous conduct.[46]

No serious contention is made before us that [employer] authorized or ratified the statements, or deliberately retained unfit employees, or promulgated such statements as part of its regular business policy. The issue thus is whether [the employee] was a "superior officer" so as to provide a basis for imposing punitive damages on the bank. . . .

The term "superior officer" obviously connotes more than an agent, or "ordinary" officer, or employee vested with some supervisory or decision-making responsibility. Indeed, since the purpose of the test is to determine whether an agent's acts can be equated with participation by the employer, the term must contemplate a high level of general managerial authority in relation to the nature and operation of the employer's business. This is not to suggest, however, that a "superior officer" can only be found in the executive suite or topmost reaches of corporate government. The agent's level of responsibility within the entity should be sufficiently high that his participation in the wrongdoing renders the employer blameworthy, and arouses the "institutional conscience" for corrective action, thus serving both the punishment and the deterrence goals for punitive damages. . . .

Could an employer be held criminally liable for the crimes of her employees? It is not reasonable to argue that an innocent employer would be criminally liable for an aggravated assault of her employee, is it? But suppose the crime consisted of price-fixing? Or selling liquor in a tavern to a minor? Or selling short weight? With

---

46. [2] Apparently 24 states have adopted the complicity rule, and 18 states have the vicarious liability rule.

respect to the last example, see *Ex parte Marley*, 29 Cal. 2d 525, 175 P.2d 832 (1946) (owner, absent from the store at the time, was convicted under the short weight statute for the unauthorized actions of his employee and sentenced to 90 days in jail). The rationale for this criminal liability in the absence of proof of criminal intent is set forth in *People v. Travers*, 52 Cal. App. 3d 111, 124 Cal. Rptr. 728, 729–31 (1975), a case dealing with the criminal liability of an employer for his employee's sale of mislabeled motor oil. The owner was absent from the station, did not condone such activity and was not aware of such sales, apparently. The court addressed the rationale in the following terms:

> It is a settled rule of law that a principal is not criminally liable for the criminal act of his agent unless he authorized, consented to, advised, aided or encouraged the specific act. An exception to this rule is the doctrine of criminal liability without fault which has been applied to criminal statutes enacted for the public morals, health, peace and safety. In general, such statutes deal with offenses of a regulatory nature and are enforceable irrespective of criminal intent or criminal negligence.
>
> In California the doctrine of criminal liability without fault has been applied to the misbranding of drugs; misbranding of onions as to weight; compounding and sale of prescriptions by nonregistered pharmacist; mislabeling of eggs; shortweighting of meat; adulterated food; and unsanitary conditions in a nursing home.
>
> The rationale of the doctrine of strict criminal liability is that, although criminal sanctions are relied upon, the primary purpose of the statutes is regulation rather than punishment or correction, and that the interest of enforcement for the public health and safety requires the risk that an occasional non-offender may be punished in order to prevent the escape of a greater number of culpable offenders. . . . To permit the owner, operator or employer to plead ignorance of the quality or the contents of that which he undertakes to sell as meeting the standards imposed by law could result in the escape of culpable offenders.

v. Non-Physical Torts

The vicarious liability of a principal for the intentional torts of agents extends beyond personal injury and property damage to include liability for fraud and deceit. The law concerning fraud is intimately bound up with the authority or appearance of authority of the agent and the reasonable reliance of the injured party, however, and thus will be covered in Chapter 5.

B. The Partnership Relationship

The doctrine of vicarious liability as it relates to the partnership will be noted briefly at this point because it fits naturally into treatment of the topics addressed in Sections B and D. More extensive coverage of this issue will take place in Chapter 12.

A partnership is defined as "an association of two or more persons to carry on as co-owners a business for profit." Uniform Partnership Act ("UPA"), §6(1). The definition in the revised Uniform Partnership Act (1994) ("RUPA") makes no substantive change.

With respect to tort liability, UPA §§ 13–15 establish joint and several liability of all partners for "any wrongful act or omission of any partner acting in the ordinary course of the business of the partnership." RUPA establishes the same standard of liability in its § 306. (This assumes that the partnership in question has not filed a statement to become an LLP. *See* Glossary, Chapters 11 and 12. All states make that option available to partnerships today.)

Wrongful acts in the "ordinary course of the business" of a partnership. The "ordinary course of the business" language comes from UPA § 13 and is directed toward a partner's vicarious liability for the torts of co-partners. Vicarious liability of the partnership and of individual partners as principals for the torts of their employees is like that of any other employer, of course.

You would not be surprised, would you, to discover that the above language dealing with torts by partners is interpreted by the courts in a manner similar to the interpretation of "scope of employment"? Can you think of any reason why it might be interpreted more narrowly? More broadly? Does the rationale behind vicarious liability for masters also underlie this aspect of the doctrine?

With respect to the questions raised above, the following passage from *Iron v. Sauve*, 27 Wash. 2d 562, 568, 179 P.2d 327, 330 (1947), is typical:

> "In truth, 'the law as to partnership is undoubtedly a branch of the law of principal and agent; and it would tend to simplify and make more easy of solution the questions which arise on this subject, if this true principle were more constantly kept in view.' Lord Wensleydale, in *Cox v. Hickman*, 8 House of Lords' Cases 268, . . . 'All questions between partners are no more than illustrations of the same questions as between principal and agent.' Parke, B., in *Beckham v. Drake*, 9 M. & W. 79, p. 98. . . . The real and ultimate question in all cases like the present is one of agency." *Eastman v. Clark*, 53 N. H. 276, 289 [16 Am. Rep. 192].

> It is not enough for appellants to establish an agency relationship; it must be established that [the tortfeasor] was doing something in furtherance of the purpose for which the relationship was created. In other words, it must be within the scope of the partnership.

See generally 1 R. ROWLEY, ROWLEY ON PARTNERSHIP § 13.1 (2nd ed. 1960) (describing specific torts and concluding in general that "the law of agency" applies); A. BROMBERG & L. RIBSTEIN, BROMBERG & RIBSTEIN ON PARTNERSHIP § 4.07 (2006) (hereafter BROMBERG & RIBSTEIN ON PARTNERSHIP); *see also Wheeler v. Green*, 286 Or. 99, 126, 593 P.2d 777, 792 (1979). Both Green and Wassenberg were sued as partners in the business of racing horses for damages for defamatory statements made by Green about plaintiff, who had been a trainer for Green and Wassenberg. Green made the statements during a social dinner conversation. The court held that Wassenberg was entitled to a directed verdict of no liability. It found that there was "no basis for finding that this kind of dinner conversation was within the ordinary course" of the partnership business.

C. The Unincorporated Nonprofit Association Relationship

Unincorporated nonbusiness associations, such as clubs, fraternal societies, parent soccer organizations, and so forth, are usually formed for some sort of nonprofit continuous operation. The forming of such associations raises a variety of contractual and tort liability problems, developed below.

It should be noted at the outset that two uniform acts have been promulgated on unincorporated nonprofit associations, the Uniform Unincorporated Nonprofit Association Act (1992) and the Revised Uniform Unincorporated Nonprofit Association Act (2008). The former has been adopted in 12 states (Alabama, Arkansas, Colorado, Delaware, District of Columbia, Hawaii, Idaho, North Carolina, Texas, West Virginia, Wisconsin and Wyoming) and the revised act in one state to date (Nevada). The acts declare a nonprofit association a legal entity separate from its members and expressly states that members are not liable in contract or tort for liabilities of the association absent special circumstances, like a personal guaranty or personal misconduct. The distinctive feature of these uniform acts is that the association is declared an entity without the necessity of any filing with the state. This is not true of any other association whose members enjoy limited liability.

The materials contained below describe the situation at common law for voluntary nonbusiness associations. These concepts apply to the jurisdictions that have not adopted the uniform act, although some states have adopted specific statutes addressing some of the problems that are posed by the voluntary association.

1. Liability of the Members

The usual rule is that members of voluntary nonprofit associations are regarded as co-principals of each other. Although membership alone in an unincorporated association does not render one vicariously liable for the torts committed by its officers, other members, or employees, a member can become liable by authorizing or ratifying the tortious acts. *See generally,* 1 R. ROWLEY, ROWLEY ON PARTNERSHIP §6.8, B.2 (2nd ed. 1960). The same rule applies with respect to liability for contracts made by the association, as will be developed further in Chapter 7. *Azzolina v. Sons of Italy,* 119 Conn. 681, 179 A. 201 (1935); *Cousin v. Taylor,* 115 Or. 472, 239 P. 96, 41 A.L.R. 750 (1925). Unlike the partnership, there is no *delectus personae* (choice of person) (*See* UPA § 18(g)), no dissolution by death of a member (*See* UPA § 31(4)), and no mutual agency. Rowley, at § 6.8, B.1. Note, however, that if a particular association starts generating and dividing income among its members it may be held to be a partnership, with the contract and tort liability consequences for the members then being considerably broader.

2. Liability of the Association

a. In General

Unincorporated associations are not recognized as entities by the common law and thus are not suable. This has been changed by statute in some jurisdictions, with the question of personal liability of members of such organizations sometimes remaining unresolved. See *Lyons v. American Legion Post No. 650 Realty Co.*, 175 N.E.2d 733, 735 (Ohio 1961), construing such a statute to the effect that individual members actively participating in the event giving rise to the injury (a fish fry), and who knew or should have known of the defective condition of the instrumentality causing harm (an unsafe heating system) remained personally liable, despite language in the Ohio statute that: "A money judgment against such unincorporated association shall be enforced only against the association as an entity and shall not be enforceable against the property of an individual member of such association." The plaintiffs in the *Lyons* case had not joined the association itself as a party, and the court held that the statute did not take away rights previously existing at common law.

b. For the Actions of Its Affiliates and Chapters

This application of vicarious liability ordinarily rests on control or ratification. *See Pierson v. Houston Indep. Sch. Dist.*, 698 S.W.2d 377 (Tex. App. 1985) (explosion on homecoming float; summary judgment granted defendant Future Farmers of America on ground that it had no control over its local chapter which built the float); *Edwards v. National Speleological Soc'y*, 502 So. 2d 337 (Ala. 1987) (summary judgment granted in favor of national organization on ground of no right of control over local chapter).

c. To Its Members

Suppose a member of an association (a labor union) is injured on the union premises due to negligent maintenance of the premises, which she did not participate in or authorize. Can she successfully sue her association and recover? See *Marshall v. International Longshoreman's Union*, 57 Cal. 2d 781, 22 Cal. Rptr. 211, 213, 371 P.2d 987, 989 (1962), holding yes, and that "reality is apt to be sacrificed to theoretical formalism" if the concepts of partnership (explained immediately below) are applied to voluntary organizations like labor unions, "which act normally through elected officers and in which the individual members have little or no authority in the day-to-day operations of the association's affairs." *Accord White v. Cox*, 17 Cal. App. 3d 824, 95 Cal. Rptr. 259, 45 A.L.R.2d 1161 (1971). The court in *Cox* held that a condominium owner and member has a cause of action against the nonprofit unincorporated association of owners of the condominium for a personal injury sustained due to negligently maintained premises. The question concerning what assets the member could execute against if liability insurance was inadequate or nonexistent was not addressed by the majority opinion of the court.

The opinion in *Marshall* noted substantial authority against its position. The contrary authority holds the association immune from liability to one of its members for the tortious actions of another of its members, or of an employee of the group, on the reasoning that each member acting with consent is an agent of every other member and employees are agents of all members. Thus the wrongdoer, whether a member or an employee, is an agent of the plaintiff as well as the other members for the purpose of determining group liability. Since one cannot base a cause of action on a wrong attributable to him, the association is immune from liability. *See* 14 A.L.R.2d 470. This concept is also applied to members of a partnership for similar reasons, and is reflected in § 13 of UPA (this limitation does not exist in RUPA, however, because a partnership is characterized as an entity in that act; see Chapter 11). This explains the "concepts of partnership" language used in *Marshall*. *See* Bromberg & Ribstein on Partnership 6.98 n.14; *see also* Crane, *Liability of Unincorporated Association for Tortious Injury to a Member*, 16 Vand. L. Rev. 319 (1963). This doctrine is known as the "co-principal doctrine." It should be emphasized that the actual wrongdoer remains personally liable to the injured party under either line of authority.

The co-principal doctrine obviously may result in apparently unjust results, which places the doctrine under pressure. The *Marshall* court thus avoids that result, as did the Indiana Supreme Court in *Hanson v. St. Luke's United Methodist Church*, 704 N.E.2d 1020 (1998), holding that a member of an unincorporated association — a church — can maintain an action against the association for injuries suffered as a result of the association's negligence. Overruling prior precedent, the Indiana Supreme Court joins a growing number of jurisdictions that, by judicial decision and legislative action, have reversed the common law rule that prohibited such actions.

The Indiana court decided that the unfairness of the common law, together with the change in Indiana to comparative fault, justified abandonment of the common law rule. Of some interest is the fact that the court of appeals had reached the same conclusion, despite contrary Indiana Supreme Court precedent. The appellate court, however, seemed to write more narrowly, deciding that because of the size of the church's congregation, the existence of by-laws, etc., the common law should not be applied. The combination of the appellate court and supreme court decisions raise the question of whether, in future cases, the particular circumstances of the unincorporated association will be irrelevant.

D. Three Unusual Examples of Vicarious Tort Liability

1. Vicarious Liability by Estoppel

This section raises the question whether one can be vicariously liable for the torts of another in the absence of an agency relationship between the two. The response would seem to be obviously no. There are, however, a number of cases in which courts have estopped a party from denying that another was its agent and then held the estopped party liable for the tort of the alleged agent. In *Crinkley v. Holiday Inns, Inc.*, 844 F.2d 156 (4th Cir. 1988), for instance, Holiday Inns, Inc., was held liable for the negligence of its franchisee because the plaintiffs believed that the motel in which they were staying was owned by Holiday Inns. We will return in Chapter 4 to agency by estoppel, sometimes called apparent agency.

2. The "Family Car" Doctrine

Although vicarious liability almost always arises out of a relationship or apparent relationship between persons and while the family involves relationships among its members, the common law, as a general matter, has not chosen to base vicarious liability on family relationships.[47] Thus, parents are not liable for their children's negligent or intentional torts in the absence of their own negligence — for example, handing a loaded gun to a young child or negligently supervising their child after receiving notice that a situation exists where control should be asserted over the child's behavior. Some states have legislated exceptions to this exclusion from vicarious liability, most frequently by imposing liability on parents for the delinquent acts of their children, covering vandalism and similar misconduct, whether or not the parent was aware of the child's misbehavior and had an opportunity to correct it.

The common law in some states has also carved out an exception, usually called the family car doctrine, to the above principle. The owner of a car "who permits members of his household to drive it for their own pleasure or convenience is regarded as making such a family purpose his 'business,' so that the driver is treated as his servant" (PROSSER & KEETON ON TORTS 524), with the result that the owner is vicariously liable for the damage caused by the driver. Based on what you have read and studied to date, can such liability legitimately be explained on the basis of agency law, or is the family car doctrine, which Prosser and Keeton indicate has

---

47. One major exception to this statement was the common law rule that a husband was liable for the torts of his wife. This was usually explained on the grounds of the husband's control of his wife's property, his authority over her, and the fact that a wife was incapable of being sued alone. PROSSER & KEETON ON TORTS 912 (5th Ed. 1984). This rule is now "almost entirely abrogated by statute" and is a matter of "purely historical interest." *Id.* at 912–13.

lately been rejected in most jurisdictions, based upon a legal fiction? If it is based on fiction, why was this done?

3. Owner Consent and Other Legislation

A similar result for car owners has been reached by "owner consent" statutes, which make the owner liable for the negligence of any person, whether a member of his family or not, who is driving the car with his express or implied consent. Apparently about a dozen states have enacted such legislation. *See* Prosser & Keeton on Torts 527.

The evident intent of this legislation and the family car doctrine is to increase the chance that victims in automobile accidents will obtain recourse against solvent persons. This is accomplished by expanding vicarious liability.[48] The omnibus clause in a liability insurance policy, which, as noted earlier, provides insurance coverage for the named insured and "any other person using such automobile with the permission of the named insured," achieves the same result, although not through vicarious liability. Apparently almost all automobile liability policies today contain such a clause. *See* C. Gregory, H. Kalven & R. Epstein, Cases and Materials on Torts 770 (3d ed. 1977).

Problems

1. Smith, who makes deliveries for the Jones Drug Company, while on route negligently flips her cigarette out the window onto dry land, causing a brush fire. Is Jones Drug liable? Would your answer change if instead Smith, while driving on route, had taken both hands off the wheel in order to light the cigarette and had caused an accident? For a discussion of these questions, see P. Mechem, Outlines of the Law of Agency §§ 375–377 (4th ed. 1952) and 20 A.L.R.3d 893 (1968).

2. White, a truck driver for Ace Trucking Company, while on a direct route to a delivery, negligently parked his truck on the side of the road while coming to the aid of a stranded motorist. An accident results. Is Ace Trucking liable? Would your answer change if the motorist had offered to pay White for the assistance, and White had accepted?

3. While driving on her route, a delivery truck operator for the Evening Star Newspaper is commandeered by a municipal policeman to chase an escaping convict and, driving negligently (measured even by the emergency conditions), causes an accident. Is the newspaper liable? Is the municipality, assuming no sovereign immunity

---

48. Another example of legislation mandating vicarious liability beyond the limits of the common law is the legislation in several states mandating liability for car rental companies for the negligent driving of persons renting their cars. See *Car Rental Firms Decry Vicarious Liability*, Wall St. J., Jan. 14, 1992 at B1, describing a $7.8 million judgment obtained against Alamo Rent A Car when a car it rented to four British sailors in Florida, a state with such legislation, went out of control, causing fatal injuries.

problems? See *Balinovic v. Evening Star Newspaper Co.*, 113 F.2d 505 (D.C. Cir. 1940), noted in 29 Cal. L. Rev. 223, 41 Colum. L. Rev. 136, 25 Minn. L. Rev. 244, and 26 Wash. U. L.Q. 123 (among others). In what manner, if at all, would your response vary if the operator had been commandeered at gun point by an escaping criminal and had caused the same accident?

4. At 8 p.m. one evening, Moody, a Philadelphia police officer on duty at the time, entered the store of Fred Ashley. Ashley was seated in a swivel chair behind a small desk in the office portion of his store, to the right of the front door. His arms were folded across his chest and he was talking to his stepson. Moody entered the office, made a complete turn and faced Ashley while at the same time drawing his revolver. The gun discharged. A bullet struck Ashley in the head, killing him instantly.

Assess the impact, if any, the following facts might have on the case: Moody and Ashley had been friends for several years and on various occasions in the spirit of horse-play had engaged in mock "quick draw" contests in which each would pretend to draw his revolver and shoot the other. Ashley had never actually drawn his revolver; Moody had drawn his at least once in the dozen or so contests. Also, Moody visited Ashley occasionally in order to cultivate informants for his police work.

Could you, as counsel for Ashley's survivors, put together a successful case against the city of Philadelphia on respondeat superior grounds (assume that sovereign immunity does not apply)? How would you do so and what problems would you face? Assume the counsel for the city has cited to you a Pennsylvania case holding that a railroad was not liable as a matter of law to an injured child when one of its engineers, "solely in a spirit of mischief," discharged steam on the child, on the ground that the act was "solely a personal one of the engineer, outside the scope of his duty." What argument would you make in attempting to persuade the court not to apply this precedent? Are there any other factual inquiries you would want to make? See *Frankel v. Moody*, 393 F.2d 279 (3d Cir. 1968).

5. Charles A. Tribbey was the bookkeeper and cashier of the White Oak Coal Company. His duties were to keep the books, take off balances, render bills and take care of the office. One day, while the general manager was gone, Tribbey noticed that the deliveries of coal to customers were falling far behind the daily schedule. He resolved to aid his employer and, leaving the office, drove a loaded truck from the yard to deliver coal to several long-term customers of the company. He had not driven a coal truck before and negligently caused an accident while in route to a customer's place of business. The person he injured has come to you for advice. Assume that Tribbey has insufficient assets to pay the judgment. Can a good case be made against White Oak Coal Company? What problems would you face?

6. Paul Carr was a lawyer in the firm of Murray & Carr. He had a part-time job as a municipal judge and did not share his income from this position with his firm. While driving from the firm's office to his judgeship, he negligently injured Adrienne O'Toole. The vehicle that Carr was driving was leased to him and paid for by

him from distributions that he received from the law firm. O'Toole sued the law firm, claiming it was vicariously liable for Carr's negligence. Is it? Suppose O'Toole argued that the firm should be liable because it benefited indirectly from the prestige that attached to Carr's position. Would it make a difference if, immediately before the accident, Carr used his cell phone in the automobile and conducted firm business? (Assume alternatively that he completed the call before the accident and that he was on the phone at the time of the accident.) *See O'Toole v. Carr*, 815 A.2d 471 (N.J. 2003).

7. While delivering a load of lumber for her employer, Mary Smith stuck the vehicle in front of her while texting on her cell phone to her friend. Mary was responding to her friend's inquiry on where they should meet for lunch. Assuming that Mary is at fault in the collision, is Mary's employer vicariously liable for the damages? Should it be?

8. Wallace, the son of the coach of University of Hawaii basketball team, served as the student manager for the team. During a game, he became agitated by the taunting of a fan directed against UH players and its coach. In response, Wallace yelled racial slurs at the fan. Subsequently, the fan brought a claim against Wallace and the University under a Hawaii statute that allows a person who has suffered discrimination to recover monetary damages. Assuming Wallace's behavior justifies recovery against him under the statute, is the University vicariously liable?

9. Audrey, a pharmacist at Acme Drugstore, viewed the prescription records of one of Acme's customers, Gail. Audrey printed out the list of prescriptions that Gail had filled at Acme and gave that printout to Gail's former boyfriend, Devon. (Devon wanted to know whether Gail had filled her birth control prescription in recent months. Devon became suspicious that Gail had not when she told him that she was pregnant with Devon's child and that she could not understand how that had happened, as she was taking birth control pills.) Gail found out about Audrey's actions when Devon confronted her with the printout. Gail sued Audrey on theories of negligence/professional malpractice, invasion of privacy/public disclosure of private facts, and invasion of privacy/intrusion. She also sued Acme on a theory of respondeat superior. Is Acme liable?

A Concluding Question

This material essentially concludes our inquiry into questions of vicarious liability in tort under agency principles. Can you describe to your own satisfaction the paramount criteria for determining when one person may be liable vicariously for the physical torts of another? Are they satisfactory? If you think they are not, what principles for deciding the cases would you suggest?

Chapter 4

Contractual Powers of Agents

"That portion of the field of law that is classified and described as the law of contracts attempts the realization of reasonable expectations that have been induced by the making of a promise." 1 A. Corbin, Contracts 2 (1963).

A. Authority

1. Express Authority

Von Wedel, a German national, left the United States for Europe in 1939. Apprehensive that war might break out and prevent his return, prior to leaving he signed a general power of attorney to his friend Kooiman, authorizing Kooiman:

> to do any and all acts which I could do if personally present, hereby intending to give him the fullest power and not intending by anything hereinafter contained to limit or cut down such full power, giving and granting unto him . . . full power and authority to sell, transfer or do any other acts concerning any stocks and bonds which I may have . . . [other language in the power granted authority to demand rent and payment of debts, to give receipts therefore, to write checks, and to commence, defend against, and settle lawsuits]; hereby giving to my said attorney power and authority to do, execute and perform for me and in my name all those things which he shall judge expedient or necessary in and about the premises as fully as I could do if personally present. . . .

Von Wedel was prevented from returning to the United States. In 1940 Kooiman transferred Von Wedel's property to Mrs. Von Wedel, an American citizen. The property was seized by the Alien Property Custodian after declaration of war against Germany on December 11, 1941. Von Wedel's wife filed a claim for its return, arguing that it had been transferred to her prior to the declaration of war and thus was not property of an enemy alien at the time the Custodian seized it. The court saw the issue as turning on the authority of Kooiman to transfer the property to Mrs. Von Wedel. What are the arguments in favor of holding Kooiman authorized to make the transfer? What are the arguments against such a result?

King v. Bankerd

Court of Appeals of Maryland
492 A.2d 608 (1985)

COLE, JUDGE.

The single issue presented in this case is whether a power of attorney authorizing the agent to "convey, grant, bargain and/or sell" the principal's property authorizes the agent to make a gratuitous transfer of that property.

The facts are uncomplicated. Howard R. Bankerd (Bankerd) and his wife, Virginia, owned, as tenants by the entirety, a home in Montgomery County, Maryland. They resided there until 1966 when Mrs. Bankerd moved out as a result of marital problems. Bankerd continued to live at the property until July 1968, when he "left for the west." Mrs. Bankerd thereupon resumed residency of the property. For the ensuing twelve years, Bankerd lived at various locations in Nevada, Colorado, and Washington, and he made no payments on the mortgage, for taxes, or for the maintenance and upkeep of the home.

Before Bankerd's departure, he executed a power of attorney to Arthur V. King, an attorney with whom he was acquainted. From 1971 to 1974, Bankerd did not communicate or correspond with King in any manner. In 1975, however, King sent Bankerd a letter enclosing an updated power of attorney because the Washington Suburban Sanitary Commission was about to put a sewer adjacent to the subject property, and King believed the new power would be beneficial. This power of attorney, which is the center of the instant litigation, was executed by Bankerd and returned to King. Dated October 30, 1975, this power of attorney provides:

> KNOW ALL MEN BY THESE PRESENTS, that I, Howard R. Bankerd, hereby make, constitute and appoint ARTHUR V. KING, my attorney for me, and in my name to convey, grant, bargain and/or sell the property designated in the Montgomery County land record as Lot 9 of an unrecorded subdivision as recorded in Liber 3027 at folio 293, situated at 14026 Travilah Road, Rockville, Maryland on such terms as to him may seem best, and in my name, to make, execute, acknowledge and deliver, good and sufficient deeds and conveyances for the same with or without covenants and warranties and generally to do and perform all things necessary pertaining to the future transfer of said property, and generally to do everything whatsoever necessary pertaining to the said property.

After granting this power of attorney, Bankerd had no further communication with King until 1978.

Mrs. Bankerd, who as noted above had been residing at and maintaining the subject property since 1968, requested King in September 1977 to exercise the power of attorney and to transfer Bankerd's interest in the property to her. King was aware that Mrs. Bankerd was nearing retirement and that she was "saddled" with a property she could neither sell nor mortgage. Consequently, King attempted to locate

Bankerd. . . . King also made several other efforts, albeit unsuccessful, to obtain Bankerd's address.

Mrs. Bankerd informed King that her husband had once attempted to give the property away to a neighbor on the condition that the neighbor assume the mortgage payments. Consequently, King asserted that he believed Bankerd "didn't give a damn" about the property, that Bankerd had abandoned his interest in the property, and that given Bankerd's age (approximately sixty-nine years), King believed that Bankerd might even be deceased. King therefore conveyed Bankerd's interest in the property to Mrs. Bankerd by deed dated June 21, 1978. Mrs. Bankerd paid no consideration for the transfer and King received no compensation for the conveyance on behalf of Bankerd. Mrs. Bankerd thereafter sold the property to a third party for $62,500.

In 1981 Bankerd filed suit against King in the Circuit Court for Montgomery County alleging breach of trust and breach of fiduciary duty in King's conveyance of Bankerd's interest in the subject property in violation of the power of attorney. After the completion of the discovery proceedings each party moved for summary judgment. On August 12, 1982, the trial court granted summary judgment to Bankerd against King and awarded $13,555.05 in damages on the basis that King had negligently violated the fiduciary relationship that existed between those two parties. The Court of Special Appeals affirmed, holding that the broad language of the power of attorney did not authorize the conveyance without consideration in favor of Bankerd. *King v. Bankerd*, 55 Md. App. 619, 465 A.2d 1181 (1983).[1] We granted King's petition for certiorari to consider the issue of first impression presented in this case.

King basically contends that the language contained in a document granting a broad power of attorney be viewed in light of the surrounding circumstances to determine whether the attorney in fact had authority to transfer the property without consideration. Based on this contention, King concludes that the second power of attorney did not as a matter of law preclude him from gratuitously transferring Bankerd's property. We disagree.

Similar to other jurisdictions, Maryland appellate courts have had relatively few occasions to analyze powers of attorney. Because we last addressed the substantive law relating to powers of attorney over a half century ago, see *Kaminski v. Wladerek*, 149 Md. 548, 131 A. 810 (1926), we shall review the relevant rules relating to powers of attorney again.[2]

---

1. [1] The Court of Special Appeals also rejected King's argument that Bankerd had abandoned his interest in the subject property and that summary judgment should have been denied on the basis of equitable estoppel.

2. [2] In this regard we note that Md. Code (1981 Repl. Vol.), § 4-107 of the Real Property Article, which requires that an agent's authority to grant property be executed in the same manner as a deed, is not at issue here.

Broadly defined, a power of attorney is a written document by which one party, as principal, appoints another as agent (attorney in fact) and confers upon the latter the authority to perform certain specified acts or kinds of acts on behalf of the principal.

Various rules govern the interpretation of powers of attorney. As Chief Judge Murphy observed for this Court in *Klein v. Weiss*, 284 Md. 36, 61, 395 A.2d 126, 140 (1978), one "well settled" rule is that powers of attorney are "strictly construed as a general rule and [are] held to grant only those powers which are clearly delineated[.]" Although our predecessors recognized this rule over a century ago in *Posner v. Bayless*, 59 Md. 56 (1882), they were careful to note that the rule of strict construction "cannot override the general and cardinal rule" that the court determine the intention of the parties. To ascertain this intent, the *Posner* Court emphasized that the language used in the instrument and the object to be accomplished be viewed in light of the surrounding circumstances. Other courts of last resort have likewise embraced the rule of strict construction of powers of attorney. See generally Comment, *Construction of Written Powers of Attorney*, 18 Ohio St. L.J. 129, 130 (1957) (indicating that American courts follow the strict construction principle).

Another accepted rule of construction is to discount or disregard, as meaningless verbiage, all-embracing expressions found in powers of attorney. Restatement, *supra*, §34 comment h. Because powers of attorney are ordinarily very carefully drafted and scrutinized, courts give the terms used a technical rather than a popular meaning. Restatement, *supra*, §34 comment h. In addition, ambiguities in an instrument are resolved against the party who made it or caused it to be made, because that party had the better opportunity to understand and explain his meaning. Finally, general words used in an instrument are restricted by the context in which they are used, and are construed accordingly.

In accordance with these principles, nearly every jurisdiction that has considered the issue in the case *sub judice* has concluded that a general power of attorney authorizing an agent to sell and convey property, although it authorizes him to sell for such price and on such terms as to him shall seem proper, implies a sale for the principal's benefit. Such a power of attorney, however, does not authorize the agent to make a gift of the property, or to convey or transfer it without a present consideration inuring to the principal.

For the reasons below, we conclude that an agent holding a broad power of attorney lacks the power to make a gift of the principal's property, unless that power (1) is expressly conferred, (2) arises as a necessary implication from the conferred powers, or (3) is clearly intended by the parties, as evidenced by the surrounding facts and circumstances.

First, the power to make a gift of the principal's property is a power that is potentially hazardous to the principal's interests. Consequently, this power will not be lightly inferred from broad, all-encompassing grants of power to the agent.

Accordingly, "the agent must be circumspect with regard to the powers created—or the lack of them." [Citation omitted.]

Second, the main duty of an agent is loyalty to the interest of his principal. See Restatement, *supra*, §39 ("Unless otherwise agreed, authority to act as agent includes only authority to act for the benefit of the principal."); *id.* §387 ("Unless otherwise agreed, an agent is subject to a duty to his principal to act solely for the benefit of the principal in all matters connected with his agency."). Thus, in exercising granted powers under a power of attorney, the attorney in fact is bound to act for the benefit of his principal and must avoid where possible that which is detrimental unless expressly authorized. We recognized these principles well over a century ago in *Adams' Express Co. v. Trego*, 35 Md. 47 (1872), where our predecessors quoted Judge Story's treatise on agency:

> Even if a general discretion is vested in the agent, it is not deemed to be unlimited. But it must be exercised in a reasonable manner, and cannot be resorted to in order to justify acts, which the principal could not be presumed to intend, or which would defeat, and not promote, the apparent end or purpose, for which the power was given.

Id. at 66–67 (quotation marks omitted). . . . In light of the duties of loyalty that arise from the fiduciary relation, it is difficult to imagine how a gift of the principal's real property would be to the benefit of the principal when the power of attorney does not authorize such a gift or the principal does not intend to authorize such a gift. In short, the agent is under a duty to serve his principal with only his principal's purposes in mind.

Third, "[i]t would be most unusual for an owner of property to grant a power of attorney authorizing the attorney in fact to give his property away. If a person has decided to make a gift of property, he or she usually decides as to who is going to be the donee." Gaughan v. Nickoloff, *supra*, 214 N.Y.S.2d [487] at 490 [(1961)]. . . .

The facts and surrounding circumstances presented in this case do not give rise to any fact or inference that King was authorized to make a gift of Bankerd's real property. In arguing that his conduct was reasonable under the circumstances, King points to his "beliefs" that Bankerd had abandoned the property, that Bankerd did not care about the property, and that Bankerd might be deceased. These arguments completely miss the mark. King's conduct could only be "reasonable" if Bankerd intended for King to give the property away. Although the facts and surrounding circumstances to which King points suggest reasons why he made the gift, they do not support an inference that Bankerd intended to authorize the gift.

Furthermore, the only evidence before the trial court that was relevant to this issue indicated that Bankerd did not intend to authorize King to give the subject property to Bankerd's wife or anyone else. In a letter Bankerd sent to King along with the executed power of attorney, Bankerd wrote that "[y]ou know if I outlive Va., [Bankerd's estranged wife] (and I'm ornery enough) you would certainly have a job on that Travilah Road (sic) [the subject property] bit *if* you would accept it, that is." [Emphasis in original.] Nothing could more clearly belie an assertion that Bankerd authorized any gift of the property. Bankerd, by virtue of this correspondence, notified King that he clearly anticipated maintaining his interest in the property. Furthermore, King wrote Bankerd assuring him that if the latter executed the new power of attorney he would do nothing detrimental to Bankerd's interests. Certainly, had King believed that he was acquiring the authority to give away Bankerd's property, King would not have made this representation.

In sum, there is no genuine dispute as to any material fact. Moreover, the facts are not susceptible of more than one permissible inference. We therefore hold that the trial court did not err in granting Bankerd's motion for summary judgment.

Judgment affirmed.

Lamb v. Scott

Supreme Court of Alabama

643 So. 2d 972 (1994)

SHORES, JUSTICE.

The issue in this case is the validity of a deed executed by Rita D. Lamb, the donee of a durable power of attorney, to herself and her sister, Judy C. Heliste.

Timothy D. Scott sued Lamb and Heliste, asking that the deed executed by Rita Lamb to Rita Lamb and Judy Heliste be set aside and held for naught. The complaint also asked that the property described in that deed be sold for a division of the proceeds among joint owners. (Scott claimed to be a joint owner.) Scott moved for a summary judgment. The trial court granted Scott's motion and declared the deed void. Lamb and Heliste appeal.

Dollie Scott executed a durable power of attorney to her daughter, Rita Lamb. Almost a year later, Dollie executed a will leaving all her property, including a farm located in Etowah County, to her two daughters, Rita Lamb and Judy Heliste, and her stepson, Timothy Scott, the three to share equally. About a month after Dollie executed the will, she suffered a stroke and became incapacitated; a month after Dollie suffered the stroke, Rita, as attorney in fact for Dollie, deeded Dollie's farm to herself and her sister, Judy Heliste, with right of survivorship. Dollie subsequently died.

The first issue is whether the deed executed by Rita Lamb, as attorney in fact for Dollie Scott, is valid as to Rita. Our case law is clear that powers of attorney will be construed strictly, restricting the powers to those *expressly* granted. Because Lamb's power of attorney did not specifically state that Lamb could convey land to herself, she was without the power to do so.

Lamb and Heliste argue that Ala. Code 1975, §26-1-2, supersedes the case law regarding durable powers of attorney. We disagree. Lamb and Heliste specifically refer to §26-1-2(b) as the subsection that supersedes our case law. That section provides:

(b) All acts done by an attorney in fact pursuant to a durable power of attorney during any period of disability, incompetency or incapacity of the principal have the same effect and inure to the benefit of and bind the principal and his successors in interest as if the principal were competent, not disabled and not incapacitated.

That subsection merely provides that the incapacity of the donor of a durable power of attorney does not change the effect of actions of the donee taken in conformity with the authority conferred by the power of attorney. It does not supersede the common law rules for determining the authority conferred by a power of attorney. Because the common law rule that a power of attorney grants only those powers expressly conferred remains unchanged, the trial court correctly held that the deed was void as to Lamb.

The second issue is the effect of the deed as to Heliste. It is obvious from Dollie's will, executed after she had executed the power of attorney, that Dollie's intention was to leave all her property to her two daughters and her stepson equally. . . . Therefore, Lamb was also without the power to deed Dollie's farm to Heliste.

> . . . One who accepts a power of attorney covenants to use the power for the sole benefit of the one conferring the power and to use it in a manner consistent with the purposes of the agency relationship created by the power of attorney. For the foregoing reasons, we affirm the judgment of the trial court.

Affirmed.

HORNSBY, C.J., and MADDOX, STEAGALL and INGRAM, JJ., concur.

Notes

1. In its footnote 2, the court in *King* refers to a statute that requires that an agent's authority to grant property be executed in the same manner as a deed. This is known as the "equal dignity" rule. It is adopted in one form or another in many states. It was applied in *Travel Centre, Ltd. v. Starr-Mathews Agency, Inc.,* 175 Ga. App. 175, 333 S.E.2d 26 (1985), to nullify a transaction (a lease) entered into by an otherwise clearly authorized agent on the ground that the agent was not appointed with the requisite written formality.

2. The fact situation in the introductory problem was taken from *Von Wedel v. McGrath,* 180 F.2d 716 (3d Cir. 1950). An excerpt from the majority opinion (denying Mrs. Von Wedel's claim) follows, as does the concurring opinion. In reading the opinions, ask yourself whose interest the court is protecting in this case.

> In the absence of ambiguity or incompleteness, we must deal with the intent as actually expressed in the document itself. The power of attorney before us is neither ambiguous nor incomplete. Under the settled law, the specific language governs. That language refers solely to von Wedel's ordinary business affairs. It contains nothing that can be reasonably construed

as authority for the attorney in fact to make gifts of von Wedel's property. The principle of ejusdem generis squarely applies and the command of the specific language must be pursued with legal strictness. . . .

GOODRICH, CIRCUIT JUDGE (concurring). I go along with the result because I think it is supported by authority and the subject is not one on which to try to start a revolution. But it seems to me that the whole thing is incongruous. A man has said, in effect, that he gives another the power to do everything for him. Then he enumerates certain specific things which the other may do, carefully saying, however, that he does not mean to alter the general power by stating specific powers. Then he ends up by saying that he means his language to be as broad as he stated it. Yet the rule seems to be that he is held to mean something much less than indicated by the language he used. Perhaps the law cannot quite say that white is black. But in this instance it certainly can make white look a pretty dark grey.

3. Would a power of attorney saying only that *A* can "do and perform all and every act and thing" that *P* herself could do if she were present, and containing no specific recitals, be effective? Compare *Davis v. Dunnet*, 239 N.Y. 338, 146 N.E. 620 (1925), indicating a negative response. Why wouldn't it be effective?

4. Based on the above, does the inclusion of general language serve any apparent purpose? Would you in drafting a power of attorney feel free to leave it out of the document?

5. One interesting approach to the law of powers of attorney is the statutory route taken in New York and a few other states. See New York General Obligations Law § 5-1501 *et seq.*, containing a statutory short form of power of attorney. The statutory form contains a general declaration of appointment, followed by 12 specific subdivisions setting forth particular kinds of transactions (e.g., "real estate transactions" or "banking transactions"), followed by a general "all other matters" subdivision. Each specific subdivision is defined in the statute in some detail, describing routine circumstances where the power would be effective. The policy seems to be to standardize powers of attorney, making their use more convenient and reliable.

6. The *Lamb* case involves interpretation of a durable power of attorney that apparently was a general power relating to financial and property matters. Durable powers are made possible by statute, bypassing the common law rule that all agency powers, including powers of attorney, are revoked upon the incapacity of the principal. Durable powers can cover health care issues, if so drafted, as well as financial matters. This problem is covered in Chapter 10, dealing with termination of agency, but it seems appropriate to raise it at this stage when introducing powers of attorney, in view of the importance of the durable power of attorney today.

7. A durable power of attorney, like any power of attorney, is narrowly construed. In *Ping v. Beverly Enterprises, Inc.*, 376 S.W.3d 581, 593 (Ky. 2012), the executrix of the

estate of a former nursing home resident brought a wrongful death action against the nursing home. The defendant sought to enforce an arbitration agreement that the holder of a durable power of attorney had signed as agent for the decedent when she was admitted to the nursing home. The executrix resisted enforcement of the arbitration agreement, arguing that the durable power of attorney did not authorize its holder to agree to arbitrate claims against the nursing home. Rather, she argued, the durable power of attorney only authorized the agent to manage the decedent's property and finances and to make health-care decisions. The Kentucky Supreme Court agreed: "Absent authorization in the power of attorney to settle claims and disputes or some such express authorization addressing dispute resolution, authority to make such a waiver is not to be inferred lightly."

2. Implied Authority

Courts and commentators often refer to an agent's "implied authority." The Restatement (Third) has this to say about the term:

> The term "implied authority" has more than one meaning. "Implied authority" is often used to mean actual authority either (1) to do what is necessary, usual, and proper to accomplish or perform an agent's express responsibilities or (2) to act in a manner in which an agent believes the principal wishes the agent to act based on the agent's reasonable interpretation of the principal's manifestation in light of the principal's objectives and other facts known to the agent. These meanings are not mutually exclusive. Both fall within the definition of actual authority. Section 2.02, which delineates the scope of actual authority, subsumes the practical consequences of implied authority.

Restatement (Third) § 2.01, cmt. b. Later, in Comment c to § 2.02, the drafters add: "Thus, it is often said that implied authority is actual authority proved circumstantially, which means it is proved on the basis of a principal's conduct other than written or spoken statements that explicitly authorize an action."

A good example of implied authority can be seen in *State Farm Mutual v. Johnson*, 396 P.3d 651, 656 (Colo. 2017), in which an owner of an automobile (the principal) authorized his co-owner (the agent) to buy insurance for the vehicle. The agent rejected Uninsured/Underinsured Motorist (UM/UIM) coverage. A short time later, the principal was seriously injured when his vehicle was hit by another vehicle driven by an underinsured motorist. He sued the insurance company, claiming that his agent lacked to authority to reject the UM/UIM coverage. The Colorado Supreme Court, citing the Restatement (Third), held that while the agent lacked the express authority to reject such coverage, because the "no facts indicate that Johnson [the principal] gave his friend [the agent] express authority to waive UM/UIM coverage on his behalf," the agent had implied authority to do so.

a. Delegation of Authority

The problem of delegation of authority by an agent has generated a fair amount of case law. Consider the following situation: an agent (Smith) sent out to repossess a car picks up a friend (Huddy) to help him. Huddy is driving the repossessed car to the car lot to be sold when he negligently causes an accident. Is the employer of Smith liable for the loss? See *White v. Consumers Fin. Serv., Inc.*, 339 Pa. 417, 15 A.2d 142 (1940), where the court held there was no liability, explaining its decision in the following terms:

> . . . The general rule applicable to situations of this type is stated in many of our decisions. We said in *Corbin v. George*, 162 A. 459, at page 460, speaking by the present Chief Justice: "The relation of master and servant cannot be imposed upon a person without his consent, express or implied. The exception to this rule is that a servant may engage an assistant in case of an emergency, where he is unable to perform the work alone." . . . [*See*] *Kirk v. Showell, Fryer & Co., Inc.*, where it appeared (120 A. at page 672): ". . . that the article, carried by direction of the master, was of such size and weight as to require the aid of an assistant in handling, thus creating a necessity which justified the driver in securing aid."
>
> We fail to see that there was any emergency confronting Smith which made it essential that he entrust the operation of the repossessed car to Huddy. The fact that the automobile failed to start, and that Smith, alone, was unable to push it, created a difficulty in the performance of his task, but did not constitute an emergency. Smith was in possession of the keys to the car, and the situation was not one of such urgency that he could not have requested further instructions from his employer. It is only where "an unforeseen contingency arises making it impracticable to communicate with the principal and making such an appointment reasonably necessary for the protection of the interests of the principal entrusted to the agent," that an agent may be said to have implied authority to employ an assistant. See Restatement, 1 Agency, § 79, subd. (d).

Notes

1. The *White* case involves the well-established common law rule that normally an agent owes the principal a duty to personally discharge his employment and thus is unable to delegate his authority unless the principal so consents, or the particular circumstances of the case indicate that the principal's consent could reasonably be implied. The Latin phrase *delegatus non potest delegare* (a delegate cannot delegate) reflects the general rule that an agent's powers cannot be delegated in the absence of authority to do so; it carries particular weight when the agent's undertaking calls for judgment or discretion. *See* F. MECHEM, THE LAW OF AGENCY §§ 302–342 (2nd ed. 1914).

Two situations should be distinguished in dealing with delegation of authority by an agent. One situation is that described above, where the agent is either delegating authority or procuring assistance in the exercise of the powers conferred upon him. The other, and distinct, situation is where an agent is employed to hire (or "appoint") other agents for the principal. In this latter situation the agent is not delegating authority, but instead is simply exercising it.

2. *Waggaman v. General Fin. Co.*, 116 F.2d 254, 258–59 (3d Cir. 1940), was decided a few months after *White* and also involved the tort liability of a finance company for the negligence of a driver (Houston) who was assisting a repossessor (McWilliams). The court let a jury verdict against defendant stand, noting that the arrangement between defendant and McWilliams "contemplated McWilliams' hiring drivers" to deliver the repossessed cars. The court stated in part:

> It was not intended that McWilliams should personally drive the repos-
> sessed cars to the appellant in Philadelphia. Indeed, it was not possible for
> him to make all of the deliveries, a fact known to the appellant. . . . McWil-
> liams' authority to hire another to assist him in performing his work for the
> appellant may be reasonably inferred from the evidence. . . .

b. Incidental Authority

Although the Restatement (Third) abandons the term "incidental authority," many cases employ the term, and the Second Restatement explanation is useful. Restatement (Second) § 35, entitled, "When Incidental Authority Is Inferred," states that, "Unless otherwise agreed, authority to conduct a transaction includes author-ity to do acts which are incidental to it, usually accompany it, or are reasonably necessary to accomplish it." For example, an agent who has authority to borrow has incidental authority to give a promissory note in the principal's name. Restatement (Second) § 75(b). As stated in Comment c to § 35, "[I]t is inferred that the principal is not doing a vain thing, but intends to give a workable and effective consent. It is not essential to the authorization of an act that the principal should have contem-plated that the agent would perform it as incidental to the authorized performance."

B. Apparent Authority

H. H. Taylor v. Ramsay-Gerding Construction Company

Supreme Court of Oregon
196 P.3d 532 (2008)

Balmer, J.

This breach of warranty action requires us to determine when an agent has apparent authority to bind a principal under Oregon law. Apparent authority arises when actions of a principal cause a third party reasonably to believe that an agent has authority to act for the principal on some particular matter. While constructing a hotel, plaintiffs became concerned about the possibility that their new stucco sys-tem might rust, and their contractor organized a meeting with the stucco installer and an agent of the stucco manufacturer, among others. At that meeting, the agent made a number of representations to plaintiffs, including that they had a five-year warranty, which he later confirmed in writing. A jury found that the agent had apparent authority to provide the warranty and that the principal had breached that warranty, and the trial court entered judgment for plaintiffs. The Court of Appeals reversed, holding that the agent did not have apparent authority to bind the principal. . . . For the reasons set out below, we reverse and remand to the Court of Appeals.

We state the facts in the light most favorable to plaintiffs, because they prevailed before the jury. . . . In 1998, plaintiffs, H. H. (Todd) Taylor and his wife, C. A. Taylor, began construction of a hotel in Lincoln City. They hired Ramsay-Gerding Construction Company as their general contractor. In turn, Ramsay-Gerding hired a subcontractor to install stucco plaster exterior siding and accompanying accessories. Pursuant to the stucco installer's recommendation, Ramsay-Gerding proposed using a stucco system called "SonoWall," manufactured by ChemRex, Inc., and plaintiffs approved that proposal.

During construction, plaintiff Todd Taylor grew concerned about possible rusting of the galvanized fittings that were included in the stucco system. In September 1998, Ramsay-Gerding halted construction until the problem could be solved and organized a meeting to discuss the situation. Among those present at the meeting were Taylor, a representative of Ramsay-Gerding, and a representative of the stucco installer. Additionally, Ramsay-Gerding's representative, pursuant to communications with the stucco installer, brought Mike McDonald, ChemRex's territory manager for Oregon, to the meeting as a ChemRex "representative." In response to Taylor's concerns, McDonald asserted that the SonoWall system was "bullet-proof" against rust but noted that a corrosion inhibitor would provide further protection. When Taylor was still unconvinced, McDonald stated, "Mr. Taylor, did you know you're getting a five-year warranty?" By the end of that meeting, Taylor agreed to go forward, with the addition of the corrosion inhibitor.

In July 1999, after construction had been completed, but before all construction funds had been disbursed, McDonald sent a letter to the stucco installer on ChemRex letterhead. The letter stated, in part, "This letter is to confirm that [ChemRex] will warrantee the Sonowall stucco system for five years covering the material and labor on this project starting in March of 1999," and was signed "Mike McDonald, Territory Manager OR." The stucco installer eventually sent that letter to Ramsay-Gerding, who sent it to plaintiffs, and McDonald stated at trial that he had intended the warranty to extend to plaintiffs.

At some point in late 1999, an employee of plaintiffs' company noticed discoloration on the exterior walls of the hotel. By the spring of 2000, the employee had realized that the discoloration was rust and contacted Taylor. In the summer of 2000, Taylor informed Ramsay-Gerding of the problem, and representatives from ChemRex and the stucco installer came to the hotel to examine the stucco system. However, no one ever fixed the problem.

In 2001, plaintiffs initiated this action against Ramsay-Gerding for breach of the construction contract. In April 2002, Ramsay-Gerding filed a third-party complaint against ChemRex, alleging, among other things, that ChemRex had breached its warranty of the stucco system. Ramsay-Gerding also sought indemnity and contribution from ChemRex for any damages that plaintiffs might recover from them. In August 2003, plaintiffs amended their complaint to add a claim against ChemRex for breach of express warranty.

In 2004, plaintiffs and Ramsay-Gerding moved to bifurcate their breach of express warranty claims against ChemRex from the other claims and defenses in the case. The trial court granted that motion, and, in July 2004, the express warranty claims were tried to a jury. At the close of the evidence, ChemRex moved for a directed verdict, arguing that there was insufficient evidence for the jury to find that McDonald had authority to act for ChemRex in giving the warranty. The trial court determined that the evidence did not support a finding of actual authority but allowed the jury to determine whether McDonald had apparent authority. The jury found for plaintiffs on the breach of warranty claim, which necessarily included a determination that McDonald had apparent authority to provide the warranty.

. . . .

ChemRex . . . appealed, arguing, *inter alia*, that the trial court had erred in denying its motion for a directed verdict on the issue of apparent authority. The Court of Appeals agreed with ChemRex that its motion for a directed verdict should have been granted and remanded for entry of judgment in favor of ChemRex . . . As to the apparent authority issue, the Court of Appeals applied this court's decision in *Badger v. Paulson Investment Co., Inc.*, 311 Or. 14, 803 P.2d 1178 (1991), reasoning that McDonald's role as selling agent and his title of territory manager were insufficient to establish apparent authority to provide a warranty on ChemRex's behalf. . . .

We begin with a review of some basic principles of agency law. Generally speaking, an agent can bind a principal only when that agent acts with actual or apparent authority. Actual authority may be express or implied. When a principal explicitly authorizes the agent to perform certain acts, the agent has express authority. However, most actual authority is implied: a principal implicitly permits the agent to do those things that are "reasonably necessary" for carrying out the agent's express authority. In contrast, a principal also may be bound by actions taken that are "completely outside" of the agent's actual authority, if the principal allows the agent to appear to have the authority to bind the principal. Such a circumstance is called "apparent authority."

For a principal to be bound by an agent's action, the principal must take some affirmative step, either to grant the agent authority or to create the appearance of authority. An agent's actions, standing alone and without some action by the principal, cannot create authority to bind the principal. . . .

Here, the key issue is whether the principal—ChemRex—took sufficient action to create the appearance of authority on the part of McDonald. Apparent authority requires that the principal engage in some conduct that the principal "'should real-ize'" is likely to cause a third person to believe that the agent has authority to act on the principal's behalf. Although the focus of that inquiry is on the principal's conduct, the third party need not receive information respecting either the nature or the extent of that conduct directly from the principal:

> "'The information received by the third person may come directly from the principal by letter or word of mouth, from authorized statements of the agent, from documents or other indicia of authority given by the principal to the agent, or from third persons who have heard of the agent's authority through authorized or permitted channels of communication.'"

Thus, information that has been channeled through other sources can be used to support apparent authority, as long as that information can be traced back to the principal.

A principal can create the appearance of authority "by written or spoken words or any other conduct * * *." For example, when a principal clothes an agent with actual authority to perform certain tasks, the principal might create apparent authority to perform other, related tasks. Additionally, by appointing an agent to a position that carries "'generally recognized duties[,]'" a principal can create apparent authority to perform those duties. Similarly, when a distant principal places an agent "in charge of a geographically distinct unit or branch[,]" that may lend weight to a finding of apparent authority, depending on the circumstances. For example, if the principal structures its organization so that the "branch manager"—or terri-tory manager—"makes decisions and directs activity without checking elsewhere in the organization[,]" that may create apparent authority to commit the principal to similar transactions. *Id.*

We turn to the application of those principles to the actions of ChemRex at issue here. Using the standards discussed above, we conclude that there is suffi-cient evidence in the record to support the jury's finding that McDonald acted with apparent authority when he warranted the stucco system to plaintiffs. The first issue is whether ChemRex took sufficient steps to create the apparent author-ity to provide a warranty. Significantly, ChemRex gave McDonald actual author-ity to help in processing warranties and to communicate with customers—about warranties—using ChemRex letterhead. Indeed, McDonald used that authority to confirm, in his July 1999 letter, that plaintiffs had a five-year warranty. Fur-thermore, ChemRex clothed McDonald with the title of "territory manager" and gave him the actual authority to visit job sites and to solve problems, such as plain-tiffs' rust problem, that he found there. McDonald also had the authority to sell an additional product intended to address the very performance at issue here and to answer plaintiffs' questions about the system, which he did in response to plain-tiffs' stated concerns.

The next issue is whether there was evidence from which the jury could have concluded that those actions by ChemRex reasonably led plaintiffs to believe that

McDonald was authorized to provide the warranty. ChemRex argues that McDonald's title could not have led plaintiffs to believe that McDonald was so authorized, because plaintiffs were unaware of that title until after construction was completed. However, Taylor testified that he believed that McDonald "was the person that was in charge of or supervising this area, the coastal area. He was the guy that you had to get your answers from." He also stated that he knew that McDonald "represented" ChemRex. It is not necessary that plaintiffs knew McDonald's exact title; they knew generally that McDonald was in charge of the geographical area in which their project was located and that he represented ChemRex. In any event, McDonald used his title of territory manager for Oregon when signing the July 1999 letter confirming the five-year warranty. Because, as discussed below, the jury was permitted to find that plaintiffs relied on that letter, it is further evidence that plaintiffs knew of McDonald's position.

ChemRex also implies that McDonald's position is irrelevant because ChemRex did not directly inform plaintiffs of that position. But it was not necessary that plaintiffs learn of McDonald's position directly from ChemRex; receiving that information through an intermediary, such as a contractor, would be sufficient. The general contractor knew that McDonald was the territory manager for Oregon, or "[ChemRex] for Oregon, so to speak," and the stucco installer knew that he was in charge of the "Oregon area." It was permissible for the jury to infer that plaintiffs learned the information from the general contractor and the stucco installer.

Because of McDonald's position and his actual authority to help allay plaintiffs' concerns about rust, it was reasonable for plaintiffs to infer that one of the ways in which McDonald had authority to allay their concerns was by warranting the system for five years. That is particularly true here, because there was evidence in the record that five years was a reasonable length of time for such a warranty.

The third issue is whether plaintiffs reasonably relied on McDonald's apparent authority to provide the warranty. ChemRex does not dispute that plaintiffs relied on McDonald's statements and conduct at the September 1998 meeting in moving forward with the construction project. However, ChemRex argues that the evidence was insufficient to show that plaintiffs had relied on the 1999 letter, because construction already had been completed when plaintiffs received the letter. We disagree. Plaintiffs' general contractor testified that it was customary to obtain all warranties in writing before completing the "close-out" process and paying the retainage. Although he could not recall specifically whether that had happened here, he was confident that that procedure had been followed. Further, plaintiffs' stucco installer testified that he had asked for the warranty in writing because of plaintiffs' concerns, and Taylor testified that obtaining the warranty in writing was "important" to him. Although the evidence does not conclusively demonstrate that plaintiffs relied on the letter from McDonald, the jury was entitled to find, from the evidence discussed above, that plaintiffs did so rely.

In sum, plaintiffs presented sufficient evidence for the jury to find that McDonald had apparent authority to provide the warranty on ChemRex's behalf. . . .

The decision of the Court of Appeals is reversed, and the case is remanded to the Court of Appeals for further proceedings.

Smith v. Hansen, Hansen & Johnson, Inc.

Court of Appeals of Washington
818 P.2d 1127 (1991)

MORGAN, JUDGE.

The owner of a building hired Hansen, Hansen & Johnson, Inc. (HH & J) to renovate it. The renovation included design and construction of an exterior glass wall. A year or so after the new wall was finished, it began to leak. The owner of the building sought redress from HH & J, which settled with the owner for $81,000. HH & J then sued Fentron, a corporation in the business of designing and installing glass walls. HH & J sought reimbursement plus other damages. [After a bench trial,] the trial court awarded damages, but we reverse. . . .

Fentron employed Everett Foster as a "manager of manufacturing services." Fentron furnished Foster with business cards, an office and a telephone. Foster's duties included purchasing material needed for manufacturing, but did not include selling products to customers. He was employed in the manufacturing department, and sales to customers were handled through the sales department.

In 1982, Foster visited Hansen [an architect and partner in HH & J, who was acquainted with Foster socially] at HH & J's offices. At this time, HH & J was the general contractor for construction of the Tacoma Dome Hotel, and Foster's purpose was to solicit sales for Fentron products and services in the construction of the hotel. In the course of the conversation Foster told Hansen that Fentron had salvage glass available and was trying to find a use for it. During this visit or at a later time, Foster "presented his business card showing that he was a manager of Fentron's manufacturing services division." Foster led Hansen to believe that Foster had authority to sell materials on behalf of Fentron, but in fact Foster's efforts were unknown to Fentron and contrary to its policies and direction.

Later, apparently in late 1982, Hansen called Foster at Fentron and inquired about salvage glass. Foster called back later and indicated that certain salvage glass, hereinafter called the ARCO glass, was available. In effect, Foster offered to sell the ARCO glass to HH & J at a reduced price, so that HH & J could use it on the 1111 Fawcett Building, the Tacoma office building that HH & J had been asked to renovate. Foster ostensibly made the offer on behalf of Fentron. The offer was oral, and HH & J did not request a written quotation from either Foster or Fentron. Foster told Hansen that the glass had been rejected from Fentron's ARCO project in Anchorage only because of its color, when in fact Fentron had rejected the glass for other manufacturing deficiencies. HH & J accepted the offer . . . [believing] it was dealing with Fentron. It would not have accepted had it known it was dealing with Foster individually. . . .

Starting on January 7, 1983, HH & J wrote a series of 29 checks, totaling about $20,000, in order to pay for the materials being delivered by Foster. According to the findings, the checks were made payable "to Foster," or "on his behalf," or "at his request." The first check, for $6,300, was dated January 7, 1983; the second, for $8,300, was dated February 16, 1983. At Foster's request, Roger Hansen, another principal in HH & J, made both checks payable to Foster personally. Foster said he needed the first check because the glass was at a salvage yard and was about to be destroyed. He said he needed the second check in order to obtain metal extrusions for the project. In mid-May, 1983, Foster absconded to California. . . . [The court turned to the issue whether Foster had apparent authority to bind Fentron to a contract for the sale of merchantable glass, among other things.]

Whether apparent authority exists in a particular case is a question of fact. The trial court resolved that question in favor of HH & J and against Fentron. On appeal, then, the issue is whether the court's finding of apparent authority is supported by substantial evidence. In deciding that issue, we view the evidence and the reasonable inferences therefrom in the light most favorable to HH & J, who was the prevailing party below.

Both actual and apparent authority depend upon objective manifestations.[3] The objective manifestations must be those of the principal. . . . With actual authority, the principal's objective manifestations are made to the agent; with apparent authority, they are made to a third person. . . .[4]

Manifestations to a third person can be made by the principal in person or through anyone else, including the agent, who has the principal's actual authority to make them—e.g., an advertisement in the newspaper, provided it is placed by the principal or an agent with actual authority. However, such manifestations will support a finding of apparent authority only if they have two effects. First, they must

---

3. [12] Although agency relationships do not always stem from contract, Restatement (Second) of Agency, § 1, comment b, at 8, this objective manifestation requirement is similar to that which governs contract formation.

4. [13] These rules are well summarized in the Restatement (Second) of Agency. With respect to actual authority, Restatement § 26 says in pertinent part:

> [A]uthority to do an act can be created by written or spoken words or other conduct of the principal which, reasonably interpreted, causes the agent to believe that the principal desires him so to act on the principal's account.

With respect to apparent authority, Restatement § 27 says in pertinent part:

> [A]pparent authority to do an act is created as to a third person by written or spoken words or any other conduct of the principal which, reasonably interpreted, causes the third person to believe that the principal consents to have the act done on his behalf by the person purporting to act for him.

And with respect to how the creation of actual and apparent authority differs, comment a to Restatement § 27 says in pertinent part:

> Apparent authority is created by the same method as that which creates [actual] authority, except that the manifestation of the principal is to the third person rather than to the agent.

cause the one claiming apparent authority to actually, i.e., subjectively, believe that the agent has authority to act for the principal. Second, they must be such that the claimant's actual, subjective belief is objectively reasonable.[5] Obviously, manifestations must be communicated to the claimant before they can have either effect.

The Restatement of Agency summarizes some of the specific manifestations that can, in appropriate circumstances, support a finding of apparent authority. Restatement § 27, Comment a, says:

> The information received by the third person may come directly from the principal by letter or word of mouth, from authorized statements of the agent, from documents or other indicia of authority given by the principal to the agent, or from third persons who have heard of the agent's authority through authorized or permitted channels of communication. Likewise, as in the case of [actual] authority, apparent authority can be created by appointing a person to a position, such as that of manager or treasurer, which carries with it generally recognized duties; to those who know of the appointment there is apparent authority to do the things ordinarily entrusted to one occupying such a position, regardless of unknown limitations which are imposed upon the particular agent.

. . . The evidence is insufficient to support a reasonable inference that Foster had apparent authority to sell materials and designs on Fentron's behalf. Fentron did not represent to HH & J or anyone else that Foster had authority to contract, nor did it authorize Foster or anyone else to do so on its behalf. It did not furnish Foster with documents or other indicia of authority that could be shown to others, other than business cards and a telephone number. If it objectively manifested that Foster had authority, it did so because (1) it employed him as a "manager of manufacturing services," or (2) because it furnished him with an office, telephone number, and business cards that said he was a "manager of manufacturing services."

By employing Foster as a manager of manufacturing services, Fentron did not manifest that Foster had authority to sell materials and designs on its behalf. Although a general manager may have apparent authority to sell products, Fentron did not title Foster as its general manager, but instead titled him a "manager of manufacturing services." There is no evidence in the record that one titled "manager of manufacturing services" is customarily or generally understood in the business community to have the authority to sell, and we are unwilling to assume that the title is so understood. Therefore, the fact that Fentron employed and titled Foster as it did is not, by itself, sufficient to support the finding of apparent authority.

---

5. [14] Again, these rules are well summarized in the Restatement. In § 8, comment c, it states: Apparent authority exists only to the extent that it is reasonable for the third person dealing with the agent to believe that the agent is authorized. Further, the third person must believe the agent to be authorized. In this respect apparent authority differs from [actual] authority since an agent who is authorized can bind the principal to a transaction with a third person who does not believe the agent to be authorized.

Even when the fact that Fentron furnished Foster with an office, telephone, and business cards is combined with his employment and qualified title, there is still insufficient evidence to support a reasonable inference that Fentron manifested that Foster had authority to sell products on its behalf. Taken in the light most favorable to HH & J, this combination of facts shows only that Foster was a Fentron employee whose authority was not apparent. Absent additional relevant evidence, it says nothing about whether he did or did not have Fentron's authority to sell products.[6] . . .

Finally, the evidence amply showed that HH & J subjectively believed that Foster [was] authorized by Fentron, but it is insufficient to support a reasonable inference that that belief was objectively reasonable. Before HH & J gave the first $6,300 check to Foster, it knew that Foster had requested that the check be made payable to him personally, that the glass was at a salvage yard instead of being in the control of Fentron, and that the glass was to be broken up and reprocessed almost immediately. Even if Fentron had engaged in more objective manifestations than it did, this knowledge by HH & J put it on notice as a matter of law that further inquiry of Fentron was needed.

Reversed with directions to dismiss the complaint.

WORSWICK, C.J., and ALEXANDER, J., concur.

Notes

1. The court quoted from the Restatement (Second) about the creation of apparent authority by appointing a person to a position that carries generally recognized powers. As one example of apparent authority by position, see *Bucher & Willis v. Smith*, 643 P.2d 1156, 1159 (Kan. App. 1982), involving the apparent authority of an estate's attorney (Johnson) to order a survey of the property owned by the estate. The court stated that in some situations:

> the mere relationship between the agent and principal or the title conferred upon the agent by the principal is sufficient to constitute a representation of some authority. Illustrative cases include the so-called "powers of position," examples of which are: general manager [citations omitted]; president; and partner. Into this category, the relationship of attorney-client falls. In our view, the mere appointment of Johnson as attorney for the estate clothed

---

6. [18] *Schoonover v. Carpet World, Inc.*, 91 Wash. 2d 173, 588 P.2d 729 (1978), and *Walker v. Pacific Mobile Homes, Inc.*, 68 Wash. 2d 347, 413 P.2d 2 (1966), contrast interestingly with the present case. In *Schoonover*, the principal, a carpet retailer, placed Rodriguez in sole control of one of its stores. The result was an appearance that Rodriguez had the authority to hire and fire persons to work at the store, and the plaintiff reasonably relied on that appearance. In *Walker*, the principal placed Stewart and Henderson in sole control of its mobile homes sales lot. The result was an appearance that they had the authority to receive the plaintiff's mobile home on consignment, and the plaintiff reasonably relied on that appearance. In the present case Fentron employed a number of employees at its office, and other than what is discussed in the text, it did nothing to create an appearance that Foster was in control of its office or its operations.

him with sufficient apparent authority to obligate the estate for services, such as the survey, which were routinely and directly connected with the administration of the estate. This apparent authority, conferred by the employment of the attorney to represent the estate, is precisely the type of authority recognized in *Reimer v. Davis*, 224 Kan. 225, 580 P.2d 81 (1978) (an attorney has apparent authority to control procedural matters incident to litigation) and *Smith v. Ward*, 161 Kan. 453, 169 P.2d 93 (1946) (an attorney who has recovered judgment for a client has authority, by virtue of his employment, to receive payment and enter satisfaction of that judgment). In our view, these cases are in accord with the better reasoned of the general authorities recognizing the apparent authority of an attorney to obligate the client to pay for expenses incurred incidental to litigation, such as witness, detective, appraiser, stenographer, expert, and printing fees.

The case of *Rosenblum v. Jacks or Better of Am. West, Inc.*, 745 S.W.2d 754, 760 (Mo. App. 1988), states the following with regard to the authority and apparent authority of an attorney:

> [W]e adhere to the general principle that the fact of an attorney's employment alone implies no authority to settle or compromise the client's case. *A fortiori*, the fact of employment implies no authority in an attorney to rescind a settlement, for rescission of a settlement is the surrender of a substantial right of the client. . . . In conformity to the principles discussed above, attorneys have been held not to have had implied or apparent authority to renounce a devise, to confess liability on a debt, to create a client's obligation to pay a fee to another attorney, or to endorse a client's name on a settlement check. [Citing cases.]

As a matter of collateral interest, issues of apparent authority also arise in the context of an attorney as employer. See *DeVaux v. American Home Ins. Co.*, 387 Mass. 814, 444 N.E.2d 355 (1983), in which a legal malpractice action was brought against an attorney for the error of his secretary. Plaintiff had called defendant attorney's office after an accident involving a fall in a store. A secretary in the office advised plaintiff to inform the store of her fall and arranged a medical examination for plaintiff with the store's insurance company. She also advised plaintiff to write a letter to defendant attorney requesting legal assistance. Plaintiff wrote the letter, which the secretary accidentally misfiled. The letter was not discovered until the statute of limitations had passed. Defendant apparently never had the matter called to his attention. He argued that the attorney-client relationship had never arisen. The court held that it was a question of fact to be determined on remand whether the secretary was apparently authorized to establish an attorney-client relationship on behalf of defendant.

2. A power of position argument was made with regard to corporate officers in *Jennings v. Pittsburgh Mercantile Co.*, 202 A.2d 51, 54–55 (Pa. 1964), involving the apparent authority of the vice-president and treasurer-comptroller of a corporation to accept an offer of a sale and leaseback of all of the real property of the corporation for a period of 30 years. The court saw the issue as being "the apparent authority

possessed *virtute officii* to consummate an extraordinary transaction." The court denied apparent authority, stating that "any other conclusion would improperly extend the usual scope of authority which attaches to the holding of various corporate offices, and would greatly undercut the proper role of the board of directors in corporate decision-making. . . ."

Would it make any difference if the officer had falsely stated to plaintiff (who was suing for a brokerage commission) that the board of directors had met and accepted the offer, and had authorized him to inform plaintiff of this? The fact situation in the case came close to this. The court denied apparent authority under this circumstance, stating: "An agent cannot, simply by his own words, invest himself with apparent authority." *See also Chase v. Consolidated Foods Corp.*, 744 F.2d 566, 569 (7th Cir. 1984) ("Even . . . the title of 'president' [does not invest the holder] with apparent authority to 'make a contract which is unusual and extraordinary,' that is, beyond the usual authority of a president, as a contract to sell a major corporate division would be."); *General Overseas Films, Ltd. v. Robin Int'l, Inc.*, 542 F. Supp. 684, 689 (S.D.N.Y. 1982), *aff'd without opinion*, 718 F.2d 1085 (2d Cir. 1983) (vice president-treasurer of a corporation, although "in a high and visible corporate position, with broad powers over financial affairs," does not have the apparent authority to issue a guarantee by the corporation of the debt of an unrelated corporation).

With regard to inferences that can be drawn from the agent's position, consider the language of Comment b of Restatement (Third) § 1.03:

> [A]n agent is sometimes placed in a position in an industry or setting in which holders of the position customarily have authority of a specific scope. Absent notice to third parties to the contrary, placing the agent in such a position constitutes a manifestation that the principal assents to be bound by actions by the agent that fall within that scope. A third party who interacts with the person, believing the manifestation to be true, need not establish a communication made directly to the third party by the principal to establish the presence of apparent authority as defined in § 2.03.

Consider, in light of Restatement (Third) § 1.03, *IOS Capital, LLC v. Allied Home Mtg. Capital Corp.*, 150 S.W.3d 148 (Mo. App. 2004), where the appellate court upheld a trial court judgment that a branch manager of a business that originated and processed home mortgage loans lacked the apparent authority to enter into a lease for a photocopy machine. The plaintiff failed to prove that it actually relied on the branch manager's apparent authority to enter into the lease. What evidence, beyond entering into the lease, would demonstrate plaintiff's reliance?

3. What effect does knowledge that an agent has a power of attorney have on apparent authority? See *Bayless v. Christie, Manson & Woods Int'l, Inc.*, 2 F.3d 347, 353 (10th Cir. 1993), quoting the following language from § 167 of the Restatement (Second): "[I]f a person has means of knowledge reasonably open to him as to the limits of the agent's authority, he cannot hold the principal unless he uses ordinary diligence to ascertain them, even in those situations in which a principal is otherwise held although the agent goes beyond his authority. He has means of knowledge if he knows or has reason to know that the authority is evidenced by a document open to and intended for his inspection."

4. Courts sometimes cite to a duty to inquire into an agent's apparent authority. *See, e.g., Link v. Kroenke*, 909 S.W.2d 740, 745 (Mo. App. 1995) ("A person dealing with a supposed agent has a duty to ascertain for themselves the fact and scope of agency and must display that degree of common sense which distinguishes good faith from blind faith."). Is the following language inconsistent with a duty of inquiry? "[A] principal is bound by all that his general agent has done within the scope of the business in which he was employed, and this, though the agent may have violated special or secret instructions given him, but not disclosed to the party with whom the agent deals." *Cange v. Stotler & Co.*, 826 F.2d 581, 590 (7th Cir. 1987) (quoting from *Butler v. Maples*, 76 U.S. 766, 776 (1869)).

5. What sort of authority, if any, does the authorized use of a company's email account confer on the user? If the seller of goods is contacted via email by someone who purports to be an agent of the XYZ Company and the purported agent has an email address that includes XYZ Company (e.g., smith@xyzcompany.com), can Smith bind XYZ Company to a contract? The answer is probably not, if Smith lacks the actual authority to bind XYZ Company and XYZ did not make any other representations regarding Smith to the seller. Access to an email account might be seen as no different than supplying the person with a business card which, in and of itself, is a limited representation of the person's authority. See, *CSX Transp., Inc. v. Recovery Express, Inc.*, 415 F. Supp. 2d 6 (D. Mass. 2006) (email account, standing alone, is insufficient to confer apparent authority on person with account).

Sauber v. Northland Insurance Co.

Supreme Court of Minnesota
87 N.W.2d 591 (1958)

Knutson, Justice.

On June 18, 1953, R. J. McDonald was the owner of a 1952 Hudson automobile. On that date he procured a policy of insurance on the car from defendant. Among other things, the policy covered damages caused by collision or upset. The policy ran for two years, and the premium was paid for that length of time.

On November 20, 1953, McDonald sold the car to his brother-in-law, John E. Sauber. The transfer was completed in a bank at Farmington. After transferring the title card to Sauber, McDonald handed him an envelope containing the insurance policy. Sauber then called Northland Insurance Company, defendant herein, on the telephone about the insurance. His testimony is that a woman answered the telephone. She inquired whether she could help him, and his testimony in that regard was as follows:

> "I was informed, naturally, it was the Northland Insurance Company; I didn't know her name or whether she said this was the Northland Insurance

Company, but she knew I was talking to the right place; the purpose was, I told her I had purchased the car and it was transferred to me and I was the new owner of the car and I had the insurance policy and I wanted to know if it was all right I would drive the car with this insurance and she said it is perfectly all right, go ahead and that is about the summary of the whole deal; I was the new owner of the car and it was insured by them people."

One of defendant's employees, Helen Serres, was called as a witness by defendant. She testified that on November 20, 1953, she answered a telephone call at the company office. She said that the call came from a man, but she did not remember whether he identified himself or not; he did tell her, however, that he was calling in regard to insurance issued to McDonald on the 1952 Hudson; and she checked the files in the office and found the policy. She denied that she told the person calling that it would be all right to drive or that the policy would be transferred. She said: "He only asked if it could be done." It was her testimony that she informed the person calling that the policy could not be transferred until the Industrial Credit Company, which carried a finance contract on the car, had been paid. . . . On cross-examination, Mrs. Serres admitted that it was part of her duties to answer inquiries coming over the telephone about insurance policies. . . .

When McDonald sold the car to Sauber he reserved the right to use it when he wished and to buy it back if he chose to do so. He did borrow the car on two occasions, and on the last occasion, March 24, 1954, he was forced off the highway by another automobile, and the Hudson was badly wrecked. A joint action originally was commenced by McDonald and Sauber to collect on the collision insurance coverage of the policy involved. The action brought by McDonald was dismissed by the trial court, and the jury returned a verdict in favor of Sauber in his action. . . .

On its appeal, defendant contends that it is entitled to judgment notwithstanding the verdict for the reason: . . . (2) that plaintiff has failed to establish that the person with whom he claims to have talked was an agent of defendant or had authority to bind defendant by waiving any of the provisions of the policy. . . .

[W]e long ago indicated that we favored the so-called liberal view, followed by a majority of the courts, that, where a place of business installs a telephone and invites the public to use it in the transaction of business by listing its name in the telephone directory, one who answers a call at such place of business and undertakes to respond as the agent of the business establishment is presumed to have authority to speak in respect to matters of the general business carried on at such establishment. Here, identification of a particular person who answers the telephone is not essential. In a truer sense, we are concerned with the identity of the place of business rather than with a certain individual. In order for the conversation to be admissible, all that is necessary is to show that the place of business was called and that someone at that place answered and purported to act for the business establishment. . . .

When the conversation becomes admissible, the authority of the person who answers to speak for the business establishment becomes important. Here, again, we have indicated that we favor the rule that, when an employee of the business place answers the telephone at such established place of business and purports to act for such concern, a presumption arises that such person has authority to act. . . .

This presumption rests on the apparent authority of an agent and is based on the law that a principal is bound by the acts of his agent within the apparent authority which he knowingly or negligently permits the agent to assume or which he holds the agent out as possessing. . . . Restatement, Agency, § 8, defines apparent authority as follows:

> Apparent authority is the power of an apparent agent to affect the legal relations of an apparent principal with respect to a third person by acts done in accordance with such principal's manifestations of consent to such third person that such agent shall act as his agent.[7]

Apparent authority in cases of this kind arises by virtue of the fact that: (1) The business has invited the public to use the telephone to transact business with it; (2) the business has permitted an employee to answer the telephone; (3) such person has purported to act for the business with authority; and (4) the person calling the place of business had a right to assume that the person permitted to answer the telephone had authority to act. The presumption is not conclusive, but, once the basic facts giving rise to the presumption are proven, it is incumbent upon the defendant to produce evidence to rebut it. It might be rebutted, for instance, by showing plaintiff was not acting in good faith or had no reason to believe that defendant's employee had authority to act. But, in the absence of evidence rebutting the presumption, it controls as a matter of law. Once evidence competent to rebut the presumption is introduced, it becomes a question of fact whether plaintiff had good reason to rely on the apparent authority. . . .

Mrs. Serres' authority to act is established by the unrebutted presumption discussed above. The case then rested upon the determination of whose testimony was to be accepted. The jury accepted plaintiff's version of the telephone conversation. The credibility of the witnesses and weight to be given to their testimony was for them to determine. . . . It follows that the verdict for plaintiff should stand.

Notes and Questions

1. The Minnesota court faced a similar issue 30 years later in *Foley v. Allard*, 427 N.W.2d 647 (Minn. 1988), where Allard, a customer at a brokerage firm (Steichen & Company), told plaintiff (Foley) at a social gathering that he was a "securities dealer" with "a major desk" at the firm and could make her money with "no

---

7. [The wording of § 8 was changed slightly in the second edition of the Restatement. It reads in the second edition as follows:

> Apparent authority is the power to affect the legal relations of another person by transactions with third persons, professedly as agent for the other, arising from and in accordance with the other's manifestations to such third persons.

—Eds.]

risk" to her. Foley called Allard at the firm several times. The calls were transferred to Allard in the company lunchroom by a receptionist who had been told by Allard that he was expecting calls from his girlfriend. Foley wrote Allard a personal check for $10,000, payable to Allard, because he told her that Steichen would not take a personal check made out to them. Allard lost all of Foley's money. She sued the brokerage firm, invoking the *Sauber* case. The court declined to grant her relief, stating as follows:

> . . . [I]n *Sauber*, we held that a presumption of apparent authority was raised by the fact that an employee answered the business phone and purported to act for the business. . . . Under the facts of that case, however, the insurer's agent had the authority to answer inquiries regarding insurance policies and had assured Sauber that he could drive the car with a transferred insurance policy. . . . The *Sauber* holding is made clearer by reference to another insurance case, *Gardner v. Hermann*, 133 N.W. 558 (Minn. 1911). On very similar facts, the *Gardner* court found apparent authority, but indicated that the result would be different if the telephone conversation had been carried on with a "mere switchboard operator or janitor, with no authority. . . ." In any case, the *Sauber* court did not extend the principal's liability to non-employees.
>
> In the instant case, . . . Allard was neither an employee or agent of Steichen's, and Foley had no assurances that Allard could act on behalf of Steichen. . . . [W]e find no evidence of affirmative conduct on Steichen's part holding out Allard as its authorized agent. Steichen's customers, including Allard, were merely permitted to receive calls. Nor is there any evidence that Foley relied on or even knew of Steichen's general policy of transmitting telephone messages to customers through their brokers. Finally, Foley did not discharge her duty to inquire into Allard's authority. The fact that Allard gave her no records or documents, that she made her check payable directly to Allard, that she received assurances of "no risk," and that she was charged no commission were all highly irregular activities that would have acted as signals to a person of ordinary prudence. [Summary judgment for brokerage firm reinstated.]

Id. at 652–53.

2. a. P wrote to A directing A to act as her agent to contract for the sale of a valuable oil painting P owned. P sent a copy of the letter to T, a prospective purchaser. The next day P told A in a private conversation not to sell until she (P) had approved the price. One week later A sold the painting to T without communication to P about the price. P is dissatisfied with the price and wants to avoid the sale. T wants to enforce the bargain he struck with A. Can T do so?

b. Suppose P had not sent a copy of the letter to T, but A displayed the letter sent to him to T and the facts were otherwise the same. Would T have a strong claim against P?

c. What effect would it have on your answer under (b) if *P* had instructed *A* not to show her letter to anyone?

d. Suppose that *P* had included in the letter a paragraph stating that *A* was not authorized to sell until *P* had approved the price. *A* artfully covers over that paragraph, displays the letter to *T*, and sells the painting without communicating with *P*. Is *P* bound to the sale?

e. Would your answer to part (a) change if *A*, with no relationship to *P*, had himself typed a letter identical to that in (a) above, convincingly forged *P*'s signature, and sent it to *T*, who contracted in reliance on it? The expectations of *T* would be identical to the expectations created in (a) above, would they not? *See Rohe Scientific Corp. v. National Bank of Detroit*, 350 N.W.2d 280, 283 (Mich. App. 1984) ("The trial court found that each of the nine documents given to defendant's loan officer was fraudulent. . . . None of these documents was sufficient to show apparent authority, even assuming that defendant relied upon them in good faith.").

3. *Lingering apparent authority.* The topic of termination of agency is taken up in Chapter 10, but the lingering apparent authority issue is so closely tied to the subject matter of this chapter that it seemed appropriate to cover it here. Section 3.11 of the Restatement (Third), in terse language, covers this concept:

> (1) The termination of actual authority does not by itself end any apparent authority held by an agent.
>
> (2) Apparent authority ends when it is no longer reasonable for the third party with whom an agent deals to believe that the agent continues to act with actual authority.

Restatement (Second) § 130 incorporates an example of the concept:

> If the principal entrusts to the agent a power of attorney or other writing which manifests that the agent has authority and which is intended to be shown to third persons, and this is retained by the agent and exhibited to third persons, the termination of the agent's authority by causes other than incapacity or impossibility does not prevent him from having apparent authority as to persons to whom he exhibits the document and who have no notice of the termination of the authority.

Herbert Constr. Co. v. Continental Ins. Co., 931 F.2d 989 (2d Cir. 1990) is an example of the complexities of lingering apparent authority. In this case, the authority of an agent (Dixon) to issue payment and performance bonds was revoked by Continental because of poor performance. Continental retrieved the power of attorney forms and corporate seals in Dixon's possession. Dixon was allowed to keep blank bond forms because his authority to solicit applications for insurance bonds for execution by Continental was continued. He thereafter committed Continental to a $680,000 bond by altering a valid power of attorney issued before the revocation, which was returned to him by a customer whose bid had been rejected. Dixon deleted the date on the power of attorney form and then affixed it to the unauthorized bond, stamping the bond with another insurance company's seal. He later admitted that he did this to "get even" with Continental. He also appropriated the premiums. The contractor whose work was bonded failed, and Continental was sued for $680,000. The court noted that § 130 of the Restatement did not apply because Continental indeed had retrieved all the power of attorney forms and the corporate seals. The court also stated that, although allowing Dixon to retain the blank bond forms facilitated the ensuing fraud, "absent a power of attorney or a corporate seal, Dixon's possession of a blank bond form could not have amounted to a manifestation by Continental to third parties that it consented to have Dixon act on its behalf [in executing the bonds]." The court nevertheless sent the case to a jury, stating as follows:

> It may be, as Herbert contends, that Continental bears some responsibility for Dixon's reacquisition of a Continental power of attorney. Continental, for instance, could have used original, not facsimile powers of attorney. It also could have numbered and dated each form. Each of these precautions would have helped Continental account for the powers that had been given to Dixon. Failure to adopt these or other precautionary measures in this instance, however, does not make Continental responsible as a matter of law for Dixon's possession of the principal indicia of authority, the power of attorney. In our view, whether Continental bears any responsibility for not tracking down the re-acquired power of attorney form and preventing the subsequent doctoring of that form presents a substantial question of material fact, one best left to the collective judgment of a jury.

Id. at 994. How would the court's suggestion that Continental number and date each form prove effective in a case where the agent reacquired an already used document and altered it? For a stricter approach to the issue of termination of authority (not involving alteration of documents), see *Continental Ins. Co. v. Gazaway*, 453 S.E.2d 91 (1994).

4. *Agency costs.* As *Herbert* and many other cases in this book demonstrate, principals run risks and incur costs when they use the services of agents. *See* Richard A. Posner, Economic Analysis of the Law 392 (4th ed. 1992), noting "the control problem, or as it is called in modern economics, the problem of agency costs (the costs to the principal of obtaining faithful and effective performance by his agents)." These costs include the costs of monitoring the behavior of agents. *See* Evelyn Brody, *Agents without Principals: The Economic Convergence of the Nonprofit and For-Profit Organizational Forms*, 40 N.Y.L. Sch. L. Rev. 457, 462 (1996) ("Agency costs are the heart of the maxim: 'If you want something done right, you have to do it yourself.' To an economist, agency costs arise because the agent simply does not have the same incentives as the principal. Agency costs include, among other things, the principal's costs of monitoring the agent (against misunderstanding, shirking, and even theft). . . .") See also Frank H. Easterbrook & Daniel R. Fischel, *The Corporate Contract*, 89 Colum. L. Rev. 1416, 1424 (1989), observing that monitoring can be costly and imperfect, and noting that "another way around the difficulty of monitoring the work of the firm's employees is to give each the right to claim the profits from the firm's success. Then he will work hard.... But [this allocation] is just another cost. It reduces the return of those who contribute the venture's capital.... The trick is to hold the total costs of these things as low as possible."

5. Apparent authority can be established by prior dealings between the parties, but the dealings must be similar to the one at issue and there must be a "degree of repetitiveness." *John Chezik Buick v. Friendly Chevrolet Co.*, 749 S.W.2d 591, 594 (Tex. App. 1983), involved this matter. In this case, Chevrolet (a Dallas dealership) sold a Corvette to Buick (an out-of-state dealership) through one Tschirner, who had walked into Chevrolet's offices that day. Chevrolet had first called Buick and ascertained that it would honor a draft for the car. It had never dealt with Tschirner or Buick before. Buick said yes, and the sale went through. Nine days later Tschirner again approached Chevrolet, and Chevrolet sold another Corvette to Buick through him, this time without checking with Buick. Unfortunately, this time Tschirner and car disappeared. Buick disclaimed liability, proving that it had no agency relationship with Tschirner. Chevrolet sued Buick on apparent authority grounds and recovered $37,000 at trial. On appeal, the decision was reversed, the appellate court stating, "Buick and Chevrolet only communicated once concerning any transaction involving Tschirner. One prior transaction, as a matter of law, is insufficient evidence to establish an agency relationship [based on apparent authority]. The one prior transaction rule has long been recognized in Texas."

6. Does the use of stationery containing the letterhead of a company by one who has consensual possession of the stationery itself confer apparent authority to contract on the company's behalf? *See Drake v. Maid-Rite Co.*, 681 N.E.2d 734 (Ind. App. 1997) (no).

C. Estoppel

Estate of Cordero v. Christ Hospital

Superior Court of New Jersey, Appellate Division
958 A.2d 101 (2008)

Before SKILLMAN, GRAVES and GRALL.

GRALL, J.A.D.

Plaintiffs, the estate and husband of Ramona Cordero, appeal from an order granting summary judgment in favor of defendant Christ Hospital on claims of [...] vicarious liability for the negligence of defendant Dr. Selvia G. Zaklama. Dr. Zaklama, an anesthesiologist and a member of defendant Hudson Anesthesia Group, practices in Christ Hospital pursuant to the hospital's contract with Hudson. Dr. Zaklama attended to Ramona Cordero (Cordero) during surgery performed at Christ Hospital....

Plaintiffs contend the evidence was adequate to permit a jury to find Christ Hospital liable for Dr. Zaklama's negligence under a theory of "apparent authority," which applies when a "hospital, by its actions, has held out a particular physician as its agent and/or employee and . . . a patient has accepted treatment from that physician in the reasonable belief that it is being rendered in behalf of the hospital." *Basil v. Wolf*, 193 N.J. 38, 67, 935 A.2d 1154 (2007) (quoting and approving *Arthur v. St. Peters Hosp.*, 169 N.J. Super. 575, 581, 405 A.2d 443 (Law Div. 1979)). Based on the absence of evidence that Christ Hospital "actively held out" Dr. Zaklama as its agent or "misled Cordero into believing" Dr. Zaklama was its agent, or that Cordero was misled, the trial court dismissed plaintiffs' claim. . . .

I

The facts viewed in the light most favorable to plaintiffs are as follows. On the morning of September 14, 2003, Cordero, a fifty-one-year-old insulin-dependent diabetic, woke up vomiting. When her condition did not improve, she sought care in Christ Hospital's emergency room. She was diagnosed with renal failure, admitted to Christ Hospital and underwent dialysis while there. Surgery to implant a catheter that would facilitate ongoing dialysis was done on September 22.

Dr. Zaklama, who is on the staff of Christ Hospital's anesthesiology department through Hudson's contract with Christ Hospital, was on call on September 22. Dr. Zaklama was assigned, randomly, to provide services during Cordero's procedure. Dr. Zaklama did not meet Cordero or any member of her family before September 22.

Dr. Zaklama had one brief conversation with Cordero before the procedure. The doctor gave this account: "I just introduced myself, 'I am Dr. so and so who is the anesthesia [sic] and I'm going to take care of you.'" Dr. Zaklama wore no identification to disclose her affiliation with Hudson and did not tell Cordero that Christ Hospital assumed no responsibility for the care she would provide. Christ Hospital's website identifies Dr. Zaklama as a member of its anesthesia department without reference to Hudson.

During Cordero's operation, the surgeon implanted the catheter without incident, but while the surgeon was dictating his report in the operating room he noticed that Cordero's blood pressure and heart rate had dropped. He alerted Dr. Zaklama, who was still with Cordero. Dr. Zaklama was unable to stabilize the patient, and Christ Hospital's "Code" team was summoned. Although Cordero was resuscitated, she suffered brain damage and never regained consciousness. She remained in a vegetative state until she died approximately three-and-one-half years later.

II

Generally, a principal is immune from liability for the negligence of "an independent contractor, or that of its employees, in the performance of the contracted services." *Basil, supra*, 193 N.J. at 62, 935 A.2d 1154; *Restatement (Second) of Torts* §409 (1965). There are exceptions to that general rule. *See id.* at comment b (noting that the exceptions are generally "stated . . . as particular detailed rules for particular situations").

The exception at issue here is based on what our courts have termed "apparent authority."[8] "[A]pparent authority imposes liability on the principal 'not as the result of the reality of a contractual relationship but rather because of the actions of a principal or an employer in somehow misleading the public into believing that the relationship or the authority exists.'" *Basil, supra*, 193 N.J. at 67, 935 A.2d 1154 (quoting *Arthur, supra*, 169 N.J. Super. at 580, 405 A.2d 443 and noting that the passage quoted "best explain[s]" apparent authority).

Imputation of liability based on apparent authority prevents a principal from "choos[ing] to act through agents whom it has clothed with the trappings of authority and then determin[ing] at a later time whether the consequences of their acts offer an advantage." *Restatement (Third) of Agency*, § 2.03 comment c (2006). On that ground, a principal is vicariously liable for its agent's tortious conduct "when actions taken by [an] agent with apparent authority constitute the tort. . . ." Id. at § 7.08; *see id.* at comment b (discussing the rationale for tort liability based on apparent authority). When a hospital's conduct permits a patient to "properly assume" a doctor is rendering treatment in behalf of the hospital, principles of apparent authority prohibit the hospital from avoiding liability by relying on "secret limitations . . . in a private contract between the hospital and the doctor." *Mduba v. Benedictine Hosp.*, 52 A.D.2d 450, 384 N.Y.S.2d 527, 529 (1976).

With few exceptions, courts considering the issue have concluded that liability for a doctor's negligence should be imputed to a hospital when apparent authority, as defined in that jurisdiction, is established.

Under decisions of our courts, apparent authority is demonstrated when the "'hospital, by its actions, has held out a particular physician as its agent and/ or employee and . . . a patient has accepted treatment from that physician in the reasonable belief that it is being rendered in behalf of the hospital.'" *Basil, supra*, 193 N.J. at 67, 935 A.2d 1154 (quoting and approving *Arthur, supra*, 169 N.J. Super. at 581, 405 A.2d 443). In this case, the trial court erred in concluding that Christ Hospital was entitled to summary judgment because there was no evidence that the hospital actively held out Dr. Zaklama or misled Cordero and no proof that Cordero was misled.

The trial court read the conditions for liability stated in *Arthur* too strictly. The facts of *Arthur* demonstrate that a hospital can act to "hold out" a doctor as its agent without actively misrepresenting the doctor's agency or affirmatively misleading the patient. In that case, a patient sought treatment in the hospital's emergency room for an injured wrist, was sent to the radiology department for an x-ray and was erroneously advised that there was no fracture. The only evidence of action by the

---

8. [1] Other courts have employed different labels and theories in addressing the vicarious liability of hospitals. *See* Sword v. NKC Hosps., Inc., 714 N.E.2d 142, 148–51 (Ind. 1999) (discussing cases using the terms "apparent agency," "ostensible agency," and "agency by estoppel").

hospital "holding out" the doctors to the patient was that the hospital provided doctors to treat an emergency.

The *Arthur* court assessed whether the hospital's conduct amounted to holding out the doctors by considering the totality of the circumstances created by the hospital's action-establishing and staffing an emergency room-and its inaction-failing to give the patient notice of the doctor's independence or an opportunity to select a different doctor. Viewing the resulting "factual setting" from the perspective of a reasonable patient in the same situation, who would not be aware of the doctors' status, the court concluded that the evidence was sufficient to support an inference that the hospital held out the doctors in a manner that would lead a reasonable patient to assume that the doctors were rendering care in its behalf.

The *Arthur* court's consideration of the hospital's entire course of conduct and the impression it would convey to a reasonable patient in the same situation is consistent with section 2.03 of the *Restatement (Third) of Agency* and with section 429 of the *Restatement (Second) of Torts*, upon which the court relied in *Arthur, supra*.... Under section 2.03, apparent authority exists "when a third party reasonably believes the actor has authority to act on behalf of the principal and that belief is traceable to the principal's manifestations." *Restatement (Third) of Agency, supra*, § 2.03. Under section 429, liability for negligent care is imputed to a principal who "employs an independent contractor to perform services for another which are accepted in the reasonable belief that the services are being rendered by the employer or by his servants." *Restatement (Second) of Torts, supra*, § 429. Although section 429 does not expressly require manifestations by the principal, section 429 applies only if the principal has acted to manifest assent "by employing an independent contractor to perform services" for another and allowing the independent contractor to perform under circumstances that lead the person who accepts the service to reasonably believe it is rendered in behalf of the principal.

The standards for apparent authority employed in *Arthur* and stated in sections 2.03 and 429 have two essential elements: 1) conduct by the principal that would lead a person to reasonably believe that another person acts on the principal's behalf—*i.e.*, conduct by the principal "holding out" that person as its agent; and 2) acceptance of the agent's service by one who reasonably believes it is rendered on behalf of the principal.[9]

---

9. [3] There is a notable difference between sections 2.03 and 429 and the standard for apparent authority provided in section 267 of the Restatement (Second) of Agency (1958), which includes an element of reliance. Reliance is an element of apparent authority under sections 2.03 and 429 only to the extent that it is subsumed in the requirement that the person accepting an agent's services do so in the "reasonable belief" that the service is rendered in behalf of the principal.

The elements of agency by estoppel also differ from the elements of apparent authority stated in sections 2.03 and 429. Agency by estoppel requires proof of detrimental reliance. Restatement (Third) of Agency, *supra*, § 2.05 introductory note.

Active or explicit misrepresentations of agency by the principal are not required. A principal can manifest assent to a person's action on its behalf by employing an independent contractor and sending that contractor to render performance requested by another without disclosing the relationship. And, a principal also may manifest such assent by placing a person in a position from which third parties will infer that the principal assents to acts necessary to fulfill the responsibilities of that position.

In *Arthur*, the court found conduct manifesting agency primarily because of the position in which the hospital placed the doctors who misdiagnosed the patient's condition. Courts of other jurisdictions take that approach when a hospital has established and staffed facilities or departments through which patients receive specialized care from medical professionals with whom they do not have a prior or ongoing relationship-emergency rooms, operating rooms and anesthesiology and radiology departments.

When a hospital provides such a medical specialist for a patient without taking action to dispel the appearance of authority implied by the specialist's position and action, courts generally treat the hospital's inaction as additional conduct manifesting the hospital's assent to having the specialist care for the patient in its behalf. The rationale is that "silence" is a "manifestation when, in light of all the circumstances, a reasonable person [in the principal's position] would express dissent to the inference that other persons will draw from silence." *Restatement (Third) of Agency, supra,* § 1.03 comment b. Courts have relied on inactions such as a hospital's failure to give the patient notice of the specialist's independent status, a disclaimer of responsibility for the specialist's care, or a role in selecting the specialist.

On the foregoing authorities, we hold that when a hospital provides a doctor for its patient and the totality of the circumstances created by the hospital's action and inaction would lead a patient to reasonably believe that the doctor's care is rendered on behalf of the hospital, the hospital has held out that doctor as its agent.[10]

When a hospital provides a doctor for a patient under circumstances in which a reasonable patient would believe the service is rendered in behalf of the hospital, a strong inference arises that a patient who accepts the doctor's care does so in that reasonable belief. For that reason, we hold that when a hospital patient accepts a doctor's care under such circumstances, the patient's acceptance in the reasonable belief that the doctor is rendering treatment in behalf of the hospital may be presumed unless rebutted.

Based on the cases discussed above, we conclude that the following are among the relevant circumstances that should be considered in their totality when determining whether the hospital's conduct would lead a patient in the same situation to

10. [4] The reasonableness of a patient's belief should be measured from the perspective of a patient of ordinary prudence and understanding of the hospital's procedures. . . .

reasonably believe that the doctor acts on the hospital's behalf: whether the hospital supplied the doctor; the nature of the medical care and whether the specialty, like anesthesiology, radiology or emergency care, is typically provided in and an integral part of medical treatment received in a hospital; any notice of the doctor's independence from the hospital or disclaimers of responsibility; the patient's opportunity to reject the care or select a different doctor; the patient's contacts with the doctor prior to the incident at issue; and any special knowledge about the doctor's contractual arrangement with the hospital.

Assessing the adequacy of Christ Hospital's manifestations of authority under the foregoing standards and viewing the facts in the light most favorable to plaintiffs, the evidence was adequate to withstand Christ Hospital's motion for summary judgment on apparent authority. By its action in contracting with Hudson to staff its anesthesiology department with doctors for its patients, Christ Hospital put in place a system under which Dr. Zaklama arrived, without explanation, on the day of Cordero's surgery to provide specialized care in the hospital's operating room. The doctor had no prior contact with the patient. The totality of these circumstances would lead a reasonable patient in the same situation to assume that Christ Hospital furnished the services of the anesthesiologist along with those of other members of the operating room staff.

Having created a misimpression of agency, Christ Hospital failed to take any action to correct it. There is no evidence that Christ Hospital issued, or required Dr. Zaklama to issue, any disclaimer of its responsibility and no evidence that Cordero was given an opportunity to reject Dr. Zaklama's services or select a different doctor. Nothing suggests that Cordero had special knowledge about the administration of Christ Hospital or its relationship with Dr. Zaklama.

Under these circumstances, created by Christ Hospital's action and its inaction, a reasonable patient in Cordero's position would have every reason to believe and little reason to doubt that Dr. Zaklama was rendering care in Christ Hospital's behalf. That evidence is sufficient to permit a jury to find that Christ Hospital, by its conduct, held out Dr. Zaklama as its agent.

Because Cordero accepted Dr. Zaklama's care under circumstances that would lead a reasonable patient to believe the care was rendered in behalf of Christ Hospital, plaintiffs are entitled to a rebuttable presumption that Cordero accepted Dr. Zaklama's care in that reasonable belief.

[The lower court's grant of summary judgment on this issue was reversed.]

Notes

1. The *Cordero* court uses the term "apparent authority" to describe "apparent agency." This is not uncommon in judicial opinions, but is confusing as the issue is not what authority an agent might have had (apparent authority), but whether the person should be considered an agent for purposes of vicariously liability (apparent agency). (The *Codero* court does note this in the first footnote in its opinion.) See

Jones v. Healthsouth Treasure Valley Hospital, 206 P.3d 473 (Idaho 2009), where, in a fact situation similar to *Cordero*, this distinction is discussed in some detail.

2. The Idaho Supreme Court noted that the doctrine of agency by estoppel requires justifiable reliance and a detrimental change in position, while apparent authority only requires plaintiff to "show a reasonable belief the actor had the authority to act on behalf of the principle that is traceable to the principal's manifestations to the plaintiff." *Jones v. HealthSouth Treasure Valley Hosp.*, 206 P.3d 473, 480–81 (2009). *Cordero* opted for this lesser standard, as did the court in *Jones*, relying on *Cordero*. Does this formulation mean that agency by estoppel is no longer needed in those jurisdictions? Does this suggest that the doctrine describing the apparent authority of an actual agent may not be appropriate to determine whether a person should be estopped to deny that another is that person's agent? In *Cefaratti v. Aranow*, 141 A.3d 752, 771–72 (Conn. 2016), the Connecticut Supreme Court, in a case with facts similar to *Cordero*, adopted a new, alternative test for tort plaintiffs when the claim was based on apparent agency:

> Accordingly, we adopt the following alternative standards for establishing apparent agency in tort cases. First, the plaintiff may establish apparent agency by proving that: (1) the principal held itself out as providing certain services; (2) the plaintiff selected the principal on the basis of its representations; and (3) the plaintiff relied on the principal to select the specific person who performed the services that resulted in the harm complained of by the plaintiff. Second, the plaintiff may establish apparent agency in a tort action by proving the traditional elements of the doctrine of apparent agency, as set forth in our cases involving contract claims, plus detrimental reliance. Specifically, the plaintiff may prevail by establishing that: (1) the principal held the apparent agent or employee out to the public as possessing the authority to engage in the conduct at issue, or knowingly permitted the apparent agent or employee to act as having such authority; (2) the plaintiff knew of these acts by the principal, and actually and reasonably believed that the agent or employee or apparent agent or employee possessed the necessary authority; and (3) the plaintiff detrimentally relied on the principal's acts, i.e., the plaintiff would not have dealt with the tortfeasor if the plaintiff had known that the tortfeasor was not the principal's agent or employee. We emphasize that this standard is narrow, and we anticipate that it will be only in the rare tort action that the plaintiff will be able to establish the elements of apparent agency by proving detrimental reliance.

How would the plaintiff in *Cordero* have fared under the Connecticut tests?

3. Note how the *Cordero* opinion avoids all mention of whether the hospital could control the actions of Dr. Zaklama, even assuming she was an actual agent of the hospital. In other words, the opinion seems to assume that if Zaklama was an actual agent or an apparent agent, the hospital would be vicariously liable for her negligent conduct. This is particularly noteworthy because the hospital's contract was with Zaklama's employer, Hudson Anesthesia Group. Nevertheless, the law appears

settled that if a principal contracts with another entity that is an "employee" or "servant" agent of the principal (by virtue of the control exercised by the principal), the principal may be vicariously liable for the tortious conduct of the employees of that entity. *Viado v. Domino's Pizza, LLC*, 217 P.3d 199 (Or. Ct. App. 2009).

4. Based on *Cordero*, how would you advise a hospital that employs a contractor, such as Hudson Anesthesia Group, to proceed in order to minimize its risk of vicariously liability?

5. In California, the courts have employed the term "ostensible agent" to describe when the concept of estoppel is appropriate:

> It is elementary that there are three requirements necessary before recovery may be had against a principal for the act of an ostensible agent. The person dealing with the agent must do so with belief in the agent's authority and this belief must be a reasonable one; such belief must be generated by some act or neglect of the principal sought to be charged; and the third person in relying on the agent's apparent authority must not be guilty of negligence. . . .

> Liability of the principal for the acts of an ostensible agent rests on the doctrine of 'estoppel,' the essential elements of which are representations made by the principal, justifiable reliance by a third party, and a change of position from such reliance resulting in injury.

Kaplan v. Coldwell Banker Residential Affiliates, Inc., 69 Cal. Rptr. 4th 741, 747 (Cal. App. 1997) (internal citations omitted).

6. The Restatement (Third) provision on estoppel reads in part as follows:

> **§ 2.05 Estoppel To Deny Existence Of Agency Relationship**

> A person who has not made a manifestation that an actor has authority as an agent and who is not otherwise liable as a party to a transaction purportedly done by the actor on that person's account is subject to liability to a third party who justifiably is induced to make a detrimental change in position because the transaction is believed to be on the person's account, if

>> (1) the person intentionally or carelessly caused such belief, or

>> (2) having notice of such belief and that it might induce others to change their positions, the person did not take reasonable steps to notify them of the facts.

D. The Inherent Agency Power Concept

The Restatement (Second) includes a concept called "inherent agency authority" which is defined in § 8A: "Inherent agency power is a term used . . . to indicate the power of an agent which is derived not from authority, apparent authority or estoppel, but solely from the agency relation and exists for the protection of persons harmed by or dealing with a servant or other agent." In § 161, the drafters apply this concept:

> A general agent for a disclosed or partially disclosed principal subjects his principal to liability for acts done on his account which usually accompany or are incidental to transactions which the agent is authorized to conduct if, although they are forbidden by the principal, the other party reasonably believes that the agent is authorized to do them and has no notice that he is not so authorized.

Section 161 seems like an application of the concept of apparent authority, because a general agent is one who, by definition, has broad authority, typically a manager of the principal's business. *See* Restatement (Third) § 2.01, cmt. d. A third party would rely on the authority that a general manager typically has in contracting with the manager, and thus could cite apparent authority to hold the principal to the contract. So what does the concept of inherent authority add to the concept of apparent authority? The drafters of Restatement (Second) gave an illustration that responds to this question:

> P employs A as the general manager of his foundry, instructing A to purchase his alloys from a certain firm. A, finding the alloys to be unsatisfactory, and without consultation with P, purchases alloys from another firm, T, writing to T upon personal stationery and signing the letter only "A, agent of P". P is bound upon this transaction.

If T knew that A was a general manager, and a general manager of a foundry customarily has the authority to purchase alloys, T could rely on A's apparent authority to bind P. Therefore, the illustration seems to contemplate a situation in which A was the general manager, but T did not know that. If so, the illustration, particularly with A using his personal stationery, is peculiar, to say the least. Courts and scholars have been critical of the doctrine of inherent agency authority. See, e.g., the following statement of Easterbrook, J., concurring in *Cange v. Stotler & Co.*, 826 F.2d 581, 598 (7th Cir. 1987):

> [The majority makes] repeated references to an agent's "inherent authority" to do certain things. I do not understand my colleagues to add to the categories of actual and apparent authority, the new brand of "inherent" authority. If a limit *known to third parties* confines the agent's actual authority, then there is also no authority at all. The third party cannot get around this actual, known limitation by appealing to "inherent" authority. Neither agents nor third parties may engage in such bootstrapping.

See also Browne v. Maxfield, 663 F. Supp. 1193, 1200 (E.D. Pa. 1987) ("As this theory [inherent agency power] would, if broadly applied, substitute the general principle of *respondeat superior* for the more carefully drawn rules of agency law, we hesitate to rule on its applicability on the record before us."). Law review authors are similarly critical. *See, e.g.,* John Dwight Ingram, *Inherent Agency Powers: A Mistaken Concept Which Should be Discarded*, 29 OKLA. CITY U.L. REV. 583 (2004); Stephen A.

Fishman, *Inherent Agency Powers—Should Enterprise Liability Apply to Agents' Unauthorized Contracts?*, 19 Rutgers L.J. 1 (1987). *But see* Edward Means, Jr., Comment, *Vicarious Liability for Agency Contracts*, 48 Va. L. Rev. 50 (1962) (supporting the concept).

The Restatement (Third) has abandoned the concept entirely, because "[o]ther doctrines stated in this Restatement encompass the justifications underpinning §8 A, including the importance of interpretation by the agent in the agent's relationship with the principal, as well as the doctrines of apparent authority, estoppel, and restitution." Restatement (Third) §2.01, Comment b. Despite the view of the drafters of Restatement (Third), and because the concept of inherent agency authority has been reflected in the cases for many years, it is important to see how at least one court has employed the concept.

Autoxchange.Com, Inc. v. Dreyer and Reinbold, Inc.

Court of Appeals of Indiana
816 N.E.2d 40 (2004)

Riley, Judge.

Appellants-Third Party Plaintiffs, AutoXchange.com, Inc. (AutoXchange) and Donald Tabor (Tabor) (collectively, Appellants), appeal the trial court's denial of their motion to strike [the] award of partial summary judgment in favor of Appellee-Third Party Defendant, Dreyer & Reinbold, Inc. (Dreyer & Reinbold).

In March of 2001, Dreyer & Reinbold, an automobile retailer operating several locations in and out of Marion County, Indiana, purchased three automobiles from AutoXchange for a total amount of $148,208. During the negotiations leading up to this transaction, Dreyer & Reinbold dealt solely with Scott Ellingwood (Ellingwood), AutoXchange's corporate officer and minority shareholder. Tabor was AutoXchange's corporate president and majority shareholder.

At Ellingwood's request, Dreyer & Reinbold paid the purchase price directly to [Automative Finance Corporation (AFC)], AutoXchange's floorplan lender and secured creditor, which would ensure Dreyer & Reinbold's receipt of free and clear title to the vehicles. Dreyer & Reinbold's payment to AFC was credited to AutoXchange's account by AFC following receipt of the purchase price. Under the terms of the financing agreement between AutoXchange and AFC, AutoXchange was required to hold the proceeds of the sale of any floorplanned vehicles in trust for AFC, and to transfer those proceeds to AFC within forty-eight hours of the sale.

Appellants contend that the trial court erred by granting Dreyer & Reinbold's motion for partial summary judgment. Initially, we note that at the trial court, Appellants alleged a myriad of claims in tort against Dreyer & Reinbold as part of their third party complaint, which included: (1) a request for mandatory injunctive relief; (2) wrongful diversion and misappropriation of corporate funds; (3) fraud; (4) intentional and malicious interference with a business relationship; (5) intentional infliction of emotional distress; and (6) unfair business practices.

Appellants' litany of causes of action against Dreyer & Reinbold all stem from one event: Dreyer & Reinbold's payment to AFC at Ellingwood's request. In this vein, Appellants first maintain that the trial court erred in its award of partial summary judgment in favor of Dreyer & Reinbold on the basis of apparent and inherent agency authority. Specifically, Appellants insist that under the circumstances, Dreyer & Reinbold did not act in good faith when it complied with Ellingwood's instructions to transfer the purchase price for the vehicles directly to AFC.

Our established case law recognizes a difference between apparent agency authority and inherent agency authority. An agent possesses apparent authority when a third person reasonably believes the agent possesses authority due to some act by the principal. *Scott v. Randle*, 697 N.E.2d 60, 67 (Ind.Ct.App. 1998). Whereas the focus of apparent authority is the reasonable belief of the third party, inherent authority refers to acts done on the principal's account which accompany or are incidental to transactions which the agent is authorized to conduct if, although they are forbidden by the principal, the third party reasonable believes that the agent is authorized to do them and has no notice that he is not so authorized.

In *Scott*, we stated that placing an agent in a position to act and make representations which appear reasonable is sufficient to endow him with apparent authority. *Scott*, 697 N.E.2d at 67. However, we also added that a communication of authority made solely by the agent is inadequate, instead it is essential that there be some form of communication, direct or indirect, by the principal, which instills a reasonable belief in the mind of the third party. *Id.* In the present case, Ellingwood was a corporate officer and minority shareholder of AutoXchange, and was authorized to sell vehicles. The designated evidence shows Ellingwood to be Dreyer & Reinbold's sole contact at AutoXchange and sole negotiator for sale terms. Despite Dreyer & Reinbold's claim that Ellingwood's request to submit payment directly to AFC was reasonable, this communication was made by Ellingwood personally, and not by his principal, AutoXchange. *See id.*

Nevertheless, when a party places an agent in the position of sole negotiator on his behalf, it may be reasonable for the third person to believe that the agent possesses authority to act for the principal. *See id.* In such instance, the conduct of the principal, although indirect, constitutes the requisite manifestation or communication. *Id.* This is exactly the case here. Ellingwood's sole negotiating position in the commercial transactions with Dreyer & Reinbold resulted in an indirect manifestation by AutoXchange which could reasonably be relied upon by Dreyer & Reinbold. As a result, we conclude that Ellingwood had apparent authority to instruct Dreyer & Reinbold to make payment directly to AFC.

Furthermore, Ellingwood also possessed inherent agency authority during his discussions with Dreyer & Reinbold. Distilling inherent authority to its basics, we have to analyze whether: (1) Ellingwood acted within the usual and ordinary scope of his authority as corporate officer and sole negotiator; (2) Dreyer & Reinbold reasonably believed Ellingwood was authorized to dictate the payment terms in this commercial transaction; and (3) Dreyer & Reinbold had no notice that Ellingwood was not so authorized.

In examining whether Ellingwood acted within the usual and ordinary scope of his authority, we find that the record supports that Ellingwood, as corporate officer and minority shareholder, was authorized to sell vehicles. Additionally, since Ellingwood was the sole negotiator of the transactions between AutoXchange and Dreyer & Reinbold, we conclude that the formulation of payment terms was a necessary accompaniment to the ordinary scope of Ellingwood's authority.

Next, we determine the reasonableness of Dreyer & Reinbold's belief that Ellingwood had the authority to instruct the payment to be made directly to AFC. Because the inherent agency theory "originates from the customary authority of a person in the particular type of agency relationship," we examine the agent's indirect or direct manifestations to find whether Dreyer & Reinbold's reliance on Ellingwood's authority was reasonable. The record shows that from AutoXchange's inception, Ellingwood served as a corporate officer and minority shareholder. During all commercial transactions with Dreyer & Reinbold, Ellingwood held himself out as the sole negotiator and only contact with AutoXchange. Considering that AutoXchange placed Ellingwood in the position of corporate officer and sole negotiator, we conclude that Dreyer & Reinbold should not be required to scrutinize too carefully the mandates of this agent, who did nothing more than what is usually done by a corporate officer. Therefore, we find it reasonable that Dreyer & Reinbold did not question Ellingwood's instruction to transfer the purchase price of the vehicles directly to AFC.

Finally, we analyze whether Dreyer & Reinbold had notice that Ellingwood was not authorized to change the payment terms in this particular purchase. The trial court did not mention any evidence, nor does our review of the record reveal any indication that Dreyer & Reinbold was aware of the alleged limitations to Ellingwood's authority as a corporate officer. Appellants mere statement that Dreyer & Reinbold knew or should have known that Ellingwood lacked the requisite authority does not make it so. Thus, based on the foregoing, we conclude that Ellingwood had inherent authority to request Dreyer & Reinbold to transfer the purchase price for the vehicles directly to AFC.

However, Appellants contend that Ellingwood's reason to change the payment terms, *i.e.*, so Dreyer & Reinbold could receive clear and free title to the vehicles, should logically have put them on notice that Ellingwood did not have inherent agency authority to direct AutoXchange's funds. Thus, Appellants argue, Dreyer & Reinbold failed to act in good faith by not investigating whether Ellingwood had AutoXchange's authorization for changing the payment terms. We are not persuaded. According to Appellants' assertion, anyone dealing with a corporate agent would be required to determine the identity of the corporate officers and their hierarchy in the corporation and then seek confirmation of the corporate officer's authority from the highest ranking officer each time this corporate officer makes a reasonable request during a regular commercial relationship. Affirming Appellants would then effectively impede commerce and result in a paralysis of speedy business transactions with repeated inquiries and attempts to contact corporate executives who would become flooded with requests for numerous confirmations of authority. This would completely defeat the purpose of agency law.

The language of the agreement explicitly requires that once a vehicle financed by AFC is sold, AutoXchange must repay AFC within forty-eight hours of the transaction. Accordingly, pursuant to the terms of the financing agreement, we fail to see what use, if any, AutoXchange could have made of the funds during this very limited time period even if Dreyer & Reinbold had remitted the funds to Appellants, rather than AFC.

. . . .

Based on the foregoing, we conclude that Ellingwood possessed apparent and inherent agency power on which Dreyer & Reinbold could reasonably rely when complying with his request to transfer the purchase price directly to AutoXchange's floorplan lender. These funds were immediately credited towards AutoXchange's balance and resulted in diminishing AutoXchange's debt to AFC. . . . Accordingly, we find that the trial court did not err in its award of partial summary judgment in favor of Dreyer & Reinbold on the basis of apparent and inherent agency authority.

Note

It is not an easy task to distinguish inherent agency power from apparent authority in the *AutoXchange.com* case. For a case that can be described as applying the concept of inherent agency power in its purest form, although not by name, see *Watteau v. Fenwick*, Chapter 6, *infra*. In *Watteau* there is no room for an argument based on apparent authority because the principal in that case was undisclosed. The general manager of a tavern ran the tavern in his own name, with the permission of the owner. The case involved the purchase on credit by the manager of goods he was not authorized to buy. The unpaid creditor later discovered the existence of the undisclosed owner of the business and sued him. The owner was held liable in a decision that might best be explained on estoppel grounds, but which has been embraced by proponents of the inherent agency power doctrine because of the breadth of the language in the court's opinion.

Problems

1. Parker had a claim against Thomas and wanted to settle it. She hired Adams to contact Thomas and negotiate an offer of settlement from him. In order to increase the chance that Thomas would take negotiating with Adams seriously, Parker authorized Adams to represent that he was authorized to settle the claim. At the same time, however, Parker said to Adams, "Now don't *actually* settle. Just bring an offer back to me."

Adams contacted Thomas and represented that he was authorized to negotiate and settle the claim. Thereafter, without checking back with Parker, Adams settled with Thomas. Parker doesn't like the deal. Is she bound by it?

2. A leather dealer named Beecher appointed Pierce by written instrument to carry on a business for him (apparently a branch shop) in Andover, including "to do and perform such matters and things as are necessary and proper for the carrying on and conducting said business. Provided, however, that said Pierce shall not make purchases or incur debts exceeding in amount at any one time the sum of $2,000." Pierce showed this document to one Mussey, who asked Pierce if a sale on credit to him for $1,000 would mean that his indebtedness would exceed $2,000. No, said Pierce, misrepresenting the fact that he was already considerably over the $2,000 limit. Mussey made the sale. Upon being unable to collect his money, he sued Beecher for the full amount. What arguments could be advanced by Mussey and Beecher?

The following language is drawn from the opinion of one of the judges in the case.

> But an agent cannot enlarge his authority any more by his declarations, than by his other acts; and the rule is clear, that the acts of an agent, not within the scope of his authority, do not bind the principal. . . . But it is urged, that, upon this construction, no one could safely deal with the agent. This objection . . . is answered by the consideration, that no one is bound to deal with the agent. . . . It is he himself [the seller of goods to the agent on credit], and not the principal, who trusts the agent beyond the expressed limits of the power; and, therefore, the maxim, that where one of two innocent persons must suffer, he who reposed confidence in the wrongdoer must bear the loss, operates in favor of the constituent, and not in favor of the seller of the goods.

Another judge hearing the case viewed the matter as follows:

> [I]f [Mussey] might not rely on the representations of the agent, the consequence would be, that no sale could safely be made on credit under the power. But the power was given to be used for the benefit of the defendant, and if given in such a form as to enable the agent to perpetrate a fraud, by obtaining credit by false representations, and credit was so obtained, and a loss occurred, it should be sustained by the defendant, and not by the plaintiff, who dealt with the agent in good faith, without knowing, or having any means of knowing, that he was exceeding his authority.

Which judge do you agree with and why? Are there any other arguments that could be made? *See Mussey v. Beecher,* 57 Mass. (3 Cush.) 511 (1849); *see also* Restatement (Second) § 171. Would it change your analysis if Mussey had not seen the power of attorney?

3. Parsons, who lives in New York, bought a ranch in Montana. She hired Able to manage it, instructing Able not to sell any cattle for six months. Unknown to Parsons, ranch managers in the area where the ranch is located have the customary power to sell cattle. One month later Able sold some cattle that were not in his possession to Treece, who knew that Able was the manager of the ranch but did not know of the local custom. Can Parsons disaffirm the sale? Would it change your analysis if Treece knew that Able was Parsons' agent but did not know that Able was the manager?

4. Katy Jacobs owned a retail store in Miami, Florida that specialized in selling kites. She hired her brother, Paul Jacobs, to run the shop and executed a power of attorney that read, in part, as follows:

> I hereby constitute and appoint Paul Jacobs as my attorney in fact in and throughout the State of Florida for me and in my name to purchase and to make and enter into, sign and execute any contract or agreement with any persons, firm, company or companies for the purchase of any goods or merchandise in connection with the business carried on by me as aforesaid . . . and to make such purchase either for cash or for credit, as my attorney shall in his discretion think advisable. . . . And for me and on my behalf, and where necessary in connection with any purchases made on my behalf as aforesaid or in connection with my said business, to make, draw, sign, accept or indorse any bill or bills of exchange, promissory note or promissory notes, . . . and to sign my name or my trading name to any checks or orders for payment of money on my banking account in Miami, Florida.

Soon thereafter Paul Jacobs, purporting to act on behalf of his principal, applied to Kites International, Inc., a firm that imported "stunt kites," for a loan of $50,000. Jacobs represented that he was authorized to borrow by the power of attorney, which he had with him, and that his principal contemplated manufacturing traditional kites. Jacobs stated he wanted cash for machinery for this purpose. Without looking at the power of attorney, Kites International granted the loan, upon condition that Jacobs would push the sale of Kites International's stunt kites. Paul Jacobs applied the money "to his own purposes."

The loan by Kites International was not repaid and they are asserting a claim against Katy Jacobs. Describe what arguments you would make against Katy Jacobs if you were retained on behalf of Kites International after the true facts were discovered and the money lost. Would it have made any difference if Kites International had looked at the power of attorney, and then loaned the money?

5. A group of neighbors have come to you with the following problem. It appears that a pleasant, well-dressed individual appeared at their homes during the last three weeks selling subscriptions to popular magazines at a good rate. With each solicitation he displayed a card indicating that he was an authorized representative of Ace Wholesale Magazines, Inc. He also had with him a large pad of order forms and some colorful advertising flyers. Each person who bought some subscriptions from him gave him a check for the first six months of the subscriptions (which usually ran around $25 to $50 and covered a number of magazines) made out to "John Smith, Agent for Ace Wholesaler, Inc." No magazines ever arrived. It turns out that the person selling the subscriptions had stolen the card, order forms and flyers from a magazine salesman in Portland, Oregon, and was working his way around the country with considerable success. Can you bring a successful suit against Ace?

Chapter 5

Fraudulent Acts of Agents

Fraud is a tort, exposing a principal to vicarious liability for misconduct of its agents. The subject of fraud was not included in Chapter 3, which focuses on vicarious liability for physical torts, because reliance of the victim on impressions created by the principal is an important element of fraud. Chapter 4, which covers protection of the expectations of third persons for which the principal is responsible under the doctrine of apparent authority, thus precedes naturally a treatment of fraud.

It is difficult to draw a bright line between the agent misconduct covered in Chapter 4 and that covered here. Nevertheless, the topic of fraud is sufficiently specialized, containing hard questions about how far to extend liability of an innocent principal, what remedies are appropriate, what burdens are placed on the third party, and the effect of disclaimer or merger clauses, among others, that it seems appropriate to treat fraud as a separate matter.

As noted above, fraud (deceit) is a tort. The elements of fraud are set forth in W. Page Keeton, Prosser and Keeton on Torts 728 (5th ed. 1984). The following is a close paraphrase of that text:

1. A representation made by the defendant;
2. knowledge of the defendant that the representation is false, or that he has not a sufficient basis of information to make it;
3. intention of defendant to induce the plaintiff to act (or refrain from action) in reliance upon the misrepresentation;
4. justifiable reliance by the plaintiff upon the representation; and
5. damage to the plaintiff resulting from such reliance.

As we saw in Chapter 3 when considering the liability of employers for the torts of their employees, the great majority of courts take into account the motive of the employee. The employee's intention must be to serve a purpose of the employer (Restatement (Third) §7.07(2)) before tortious conduct will be characterized as within the scope of employment. Can you identify one aspect of the tortious behavior that is the subject of this chapter that distinguishes it from that involved in Chapter 3, creating the potential for a broader standard of liability for the principal?

A. The Unscrupulous Agent

Grease Monkey International, Inc. v. Montoya

Supreme Court of Colorado (en banc)
904 P.2d 468 (1995)

JUSTICE ERICKSON delivered the Opinion of the Court. . . .

Grease Monkey Holding Corporation is a Utah corporation, and Grease Monkey International is a wholly-owned subsidiary of Grease Monkey Holding Company. [The two corporations are referred to collectively as "Grease Monkey."] From 1983 through 1991, Arthur Sensenig was Grease Monkey's President, Chief Operating Officer, and Chairman of the Board. During that time, Sensenig ran Grease Monkey and had broad authority to act as general officer and agent for Grease Monkey. Sensenig had authority to raise capital from banks and other lenders. The trial court found that Sensenig "had implied or had apparent authority to raise capital by borrowing or obtaining loans on behalf of Grease Monkey from private citizens like the . . . [respondents] in this case." Sensenig did not need Board approval for these loans unless they exceeded $500,000.

Respondents Nick and Aver Montoya were married for over fifty years. Nick Montoya worked for the railroad approximately ten years, and he was sole proprietor of a barber shop for about thirty years. He kept the financial records for his church and household. In 1985, he sold a parcel of land he owned with his two sons for $1.2 million. The trial court found Nick Montoya to be a person of "average investor sophistication." Aver Montoya was a factory worker for approximately seventeen years, and she left financial matters primarily to her husband.

Nick Montoya met Arthur Sensenig in the mid-1960's. Sensenig was a teller at a bank where Mr. Montoya was a customer. During the 1960's and 1970's, Sensenig gave Mr. Montoya investment advice. Mr. Montoya was impressed by Sensenig and his progress at the bank. Sensenig ultimately achieved the position of vice-president before leaving the bank. Mr. Montoya also knew Sensenig through a church connection.

From 1983 through 1991, Sensenig secured payments from respondents under the guise that the payments were investments in Grease Monkey. Sensenig secured the payments by representing that, because Grease Monkey was a new company, it did not have its own account, and that as President and Chairman of the Board, Sensenig used his personal account as the corporate account. In furtherance of his scheme, Sensenig took Mr. Montoya to the Grease Monkey offices and showed him a promotional slide show presentation used by Grease Monkey to solicit franchise business. However, none of the payments were invested in Grease Monkey, and Grease Monkey did not receive any of the funds. Rather, Sensenig used respondents' money for his own personal benefit.

Generally, about a week after writing out an investment check, respondents received a promissory note as evidence of their investment. When Sensenig delivered interest payments to respondents, he brought charts showing the growth and success of Grease Monkey. Mailings to respondents concerning their investments were on Grease Monkey letterhead and calls regarding the investments were made to Sensenig at Grease Monkey. Sensenig gave respondents many Grease Monkey promotional items, such as pens, hats, and sweatshirts.

Respondents filed a complaint against Grease Monkey, as Sensenig's employer, for breach of contract, fraud, misrepresentation, breach of duty of good faith and fair dealing, promissory estoppel, extreme and outrageous conduct, and negligent hiring and supervision. After a trial to the court, respondents prevailed on their fraud and misrepresentation claims, and their other claims for relief were dismissed. The trial court entered judgment against Grease Monkey for the outstanding balance due on the promissory notes. The trial court made the following findings: (1) the respondents reasonably believed they were investing in Grease Monkey; (2) Sensenig's representations to respondents were material, false representations, upon which respondents relied to their detriment; (3) Sensenig was acting within his apparent authority when he made the representations regarding the nature of the investments; and (4) Grease Monkey is liable with regard to the investments.

The trial court concluded that the Restatement (Second) of Agency § 261 established Grease Monkey's liability. According to the trial court, "[s]ection 261 is nothing more than a refinement of the principle of apparent authority, which is well established in Colorado law by other cases." The trial court denied respondents' other claims, including the claim of negligent hiring and supervision. In *Montoya v. Grease Monkey Holding Corp.*, 883 P.2d 486 (Colo. App. 1994), the court of appeals affirmed the trial court's judgment. . . .

Section 261 of the Restatement (Second) of Agency provides that "[a] principal who puts a servant or other agent in a position which enables the agent, while apparently acting within his authority, to commit a fraud upon third persons is subject to liability to such third persons for the fraud." The application of section 261 is not limited to principals and agents but extends also to masters and servants. Grease Monkey primarily relies upon footnote twenty-seven of *Moses v. Diocese of Colorado*, 863 P.2d 310 (1993), for its claim that section 261 is precluded from being applied as Colorado law. Footnote twenty-seven states:

> . . . Although the commission of an intentional tort may sometimes be within the scope of employment, the agent's intent in committing the tortious act must be to further the employer's business. [I]f an employee commits an intentional tort solely for reasons that do not further his employer's business or cannot be considered a natural incident of employment, the employer cannot be vicariously liable.

. . . Apparent authority liability is not based upon the rules of respondeat superior, and it is not "essential to find that the agent was motivated by an intent to act for his master's purposes." See Seavey, Handbook of the Law of Agency § 91(C) (1964). Actions for misrepresentations and fraud generally fit into the category of torts which do not lie within the scope and principles of respondeat superior. In many of these situations, the agent's position enables him to perpetrate the fraud, and the agent acted for his own purposes. However, "[t]he fact that the agent is acting from purely personal motives is immaterial unless this is known to the other party." *Id.* § 92(F).

The application of section 261 to the present case squares with the misrepresentation or fraud analysis of the principal-agent doctrine. Footnote twenty-seven of *Moses* refers to respondeat superior as applied to the master-servant doctrine. Respondeat superior and master-servant principles constitute an aspect of agency law distinct from fraud based on the apparent authority analysis of section 261.

In *Moses*, a church parishioner with a history of mental illness sought counseling from an assistant priest. While counseling the parishioner, the priest entered into a sexual relationship with her. . . . The parishioner commenced a civil action against the priest and the Episcopal Diocese of Colorado. [W]e determined "[t]he evidence . . . was not sufficient to prove that . . . [the priest] was acting within the scope of his employment when he . . . [entered into a sexual relationship with the parishioner]; therefore, the Diocese is not vicariously liable for . . . [the priest's] sexual acts with . . . [the parishioner]." In *Moses*, we addressed the scope of employment aspect of the master-servant doctrine. We did not discuss an agent's apparent authority to perpetrate fraud.

The priest in *Moses* was not a non-servant agent who had the power to bind the principal (the Diocese) contractually. Rather, he was a servant, and the Diocese was his master. The Diocese had the right to control the priest's physical activities. Because the Diocese controlled the priest's physical activities, *Moses* existed in the realm of the master-servant doctrine, and respondeat superior analysis was appropriate. Applying respondeat superior principles, we concluded that a priest acts outside the scope of employment when he engages in sexual acts with a mentally ill parishioner.

In the present case, Grease Monkey did not possess the right to control the physical movements or activities of Sensenig, who was the Chief Operating Officer of Grease Monkey. Sensenig was expected to perform certain tasks for Grease Monkey. Grease Monkey did not monitor Sensenig's physical activities, but was only concerned with the results achieved. See Seavey, *supra*, § 84(A) ("[A] servant sells or gives his time, while a non-servant agent is paid primarily for results rather than for the time which it takes to accomplish them."). Sensenig acted as a non-servant agent for Grease Monkey. Unlike the priest in *Moses*, Sensenig committed fraud while acting within his apparent authority. Factually, the present case requires a different analytical framework than *Moses*, and the trial court properly applied section 261 and did not address respondeat superior considerations. . . .

Under section 261, a plaintiff must establish that the servant or other agent was put in a position which enabled the agent to commit fraud, the agent acted within his apparent authority, and the agent committed fraud. See Restatement (Second) of Agency § 261 (1958). First, the trial court found that Sensenig was the highest authority at Grease Monkey. He had authority to raise up to $500,000 without Board approval, and as general officer and agent for Grease Monkey, he had broad authority to act without corporate restrictions. The findings of the trial court support a conclusion that Grease Monkey put Sensenig in a position where he could commit fraud if he had a mind to.

Second, the trial court found that Sensenig acted within his apparent authority when he raised capital from individuals such as respondents. A finding of fact as to the existence of apparent authority should not be disturbed on appeal.

Third, the trial court found that Sensenig made false representations to respondents. Sensenig made these representations with the awareness they were false and with intent to induce respondents to rely on the representations. The representations were material, and respondents reasonably relied on the representations to their detriment. The trial court found for respondents on their claim of fraud and misrepresentation, and we are unwilling to disturb that finding on review.

Grease Monkey contends that the use of section 261 amounts to strict liability for the principal. However, "'few doctrines of the law are more firmly established or more in harmony with accepted notions of social policy than that of the liability of the principal without fault of his own.'" *ASME*, 456 U.S. [556] at 568 [(1982)]. Our decision recognizes the legal principle that "when one of two innocent persons must suffer from the acts of a third, he must suffer who put it in the power of the wrongdoer to inflict the injury." *Richards*, 866 F.2d [1570] at 1572–73 [(10th Cir. 1989)]. This policy motivates organizations to see that their agents abide by the law.

Accordingly, we affirm the judgment of the court of appeals.

Justice Mullarkey concurring in the result and specially concurring:

I concur in the result reached in the majority opinion but write separately because my analysis differs from that of the majority. I agree with the majority that section 261 provides the appropriate framework for the present case and that the findings of the trial court support imposing liability on Grease Monkey for Sensenig's misrepresentations and fraud pursuant to section 261. However, I disagree with the majority that footnote 27 of *Moses* is inapplicable in this case because the priest whose sexual activities were at issue in *Moses* was a servant to whom the master-servant doctrine applies, while Sensenig was a "non-servant agent" to whom the doctrine of apparent authority applies. It appears to me that the application of apparent authority analysis, as opposed to *respondeat superior* analysis, is triggered by the nature of the tort, not by the relationship of the agent to the principal.[1]

---

1. [6] While I do not find the distinction between servant and non-servant agents to be relevant in this case, typically corporate executives are considered "servants" rather than "non-servant agents" for purposes of *respondeat superior* analysis. See, e.g., Restatement (Second) of Agency

The distinction between a servant and a non-servant agent is important for purposes of determining the liability of a principal for a physical tort committed by an agent incident to the performance of the agent's duties. . . .

The concept of apparent authority, however, applies to determine the liability of a principal when either a servant or non-servant agent has committed a tortious representation. See Restatement §219 ("A master is not subject to liability for the torts of his servants acting outside the scope of employment, unless . . . the servant purported to act or speak on behalf of the principal. . . ."); §257 ("A principal is subject to liability for loss caused to another by the other's reliance upon a tortious representation of a servant or other agent, if the representation is: (a) authorized; (b) apparently authorized; or (c) within the power of the agent to make for the principal.") . . . Where apparent authority has been employed to commit a tort, a principal may be held liable whether or not the servant or non-servant agent intended to further the principal's interests.

The rationale behind this rule is that it "place[s] the risk that an agent may abuse his authority for his own benefit on the principal, rather than on the [innocent third party]." *Willey v. Mayer*, 876 P.2d 1260, 1266 (Colo. 1994). Thus, the rule provides an incentive for a principal to select reliable agents. It also recognizes that benefits accrue to a principal by employing an agent and that the principal is in a better position to supervise an agent's conduct than a third party relying on the agent's representations. Accordingly, where an agent acts with actual or apparent authority in transacting business with a third party, we have held the principal liable even where the third party [agent?] acts for his own purposes.

Therefore, I agree with the majority that footnote 27 of *Moses* states master-servant principles that do not apply when determining the liability of a principal for a tortious representation where, as in this case, an agent acts with apparent authority. However, the apparent authority doctrine of section 261 applies to this case because the Montoyas were injured when they relied on Sensenig's purported authority and apparent authority to raise money and to enter into secured transactions on behalf of Grease Monkey, not because Sensenig was a "non-servant agent." The female parishioner who became involved in sexual relations with a male Episcopal priest in *Moses* did not rely on the priest's apparent or purported authority to engage in such acts. Instead, she was injured by the sexual misconduct itself. Therefore, the diocese could not be liable except to the extent that the priest acted with intent to promote the purposes of the diocese.

For these reasons, I would base the analysis of this case on apparent authority, not on the distinction between agents who are servants and those who are not. Accordingly, I specially concur.

---

§220 cmt. a (1958) ("managers of great corporations are normally superior servants, differing only in the dignity and importance of their positions from those working under them").

I am authorized to say that JUSTICE LOHR and JUSTICE KOURLIS join in this special concurrence.

Notes

1. The majority opinion in *Grease Monkey* seems to proceed on the assumption that Restatement (Second) § 261 does not apply to servants. In assessing the accuracy of that assumption, consider the fact that the language of § 261 itself expressly includes servants when describing agents who have the power under some circumstances to subject their principals to liability for fraud. This appears to underscore the validity of the analytical approach of the concurring opinion.

2. On a collateral matter, in assessing the merits of the assumption made by both the majority and concurring opinions that Sensenig was acting within his apparent authority, consider the facts that the promissory notes mentioned in the majority opinion were executed by Sensenig personally and all amounts loaned by the Montoyas were reflected by checks written out to Sensenig personally, as noted in the court of appeals opinion in this case. *Montoya v. Grease Monkey*, 883 P.2d 486, 487 (Colo. App. 1994). Also, all of the checks sent to the Montoyas representing interest payments were executed by Sensenig personally, drawn against his own bank account. Opening Brief for Petitioners 1. This went on for eight years. Sensenig's explanation to the Montoyas was that Grease Monkey was a new company and did not have its own account. The doctrine of apparent authority includes a requirement of reasonable reliance by the third party. Can a plausible argument be made that this aspect of apparent authority is in serious doubt in this case?

3. Unlike the Restatement (Second) § 261, which specifically addresses fraud committed by an agent on a third party, Restatement (Third) § 7.08 more broadly provides: "A principal is subject to vicarious liability for a tort committed by an agent in dealing or communicating with a third party on or purportedly on behalf of the principal when actions taken by the agent with apparent authority constitute the tort or enable the agent to conceal its commission." Illustration 9 to that section is based on the *Grease Monkey* case, suggesting that the same result would be reached under Restatement (Third). The illustration, however, does not include the additional facts, discussed in note 2 above, that raise the issue of the reasonableness of the Montoyas' reliance.

Entente Mineral Co. v. Parker

United States Court of Appeals, Fifth Circuit
956 F.2d 524 (1992)

Before THORNBERRY, GARWOOD, and DAVIS, CIRCUIT JUDGES.

THORNBERRY, CIRCUIT JUDGE:

This is an appeal from a directed verdict. The defendant-appellee law firm was sued for vicarious liability. The district court directed a verdict in favor of the firm, concluding as a matter of law that the jury could not find vicarious liability. . . .

In February 1987, H.B. Sneed ("Sneed"), a petroleum landman employed by Entente Mineral Company ("Entente"), negotiated with McKinley Young ("Young") to purchase one-half of Young's royalty interest in certain property. On February 23, Young and Sneed orally agreed that Entente would purchase one-half of Young's interest for $25,000. Sneed then presented a $25,000 draft and a royalty deed to Young. Young, who does not read well if at all, stated that he wanted his banker, Bruce Edwards, ("Edwards") to review the deed to ensure that it accurately reflected the terms of the oral agreement. Young and Sneed took the deed to Edwards, who suggested that Young's attorneys at the firm of Barrett, Barrett, Barrett, and Patton ("the firm") review the deed. Edwards telephoned Derek Parker, a partner in the firm, and arranged for Sneed and Young to meet with Parker.

That afternoon, Sneed and Young drove to the firm and met with Parker. Parker reviewed the deed and told Young that the deed reflected the terms and conditions of the oral agreement. He also advised Young that before signing the deed, he should have a title search performed to guarantee that he owned a one-sixteenth royalty, the one-half of one-sixteenth that he intended to sell to Entente and the one-half of one-sixteenth that he intended to retain. Young then asked Parker to perform the title search. Parker instructed Sneed and Young to return the next day at one o'clock p.m. to close the deal. Sneed left the royalty deed and the $25,000 draft with Parker.

After Sneed and Young left the firm, Parker telephoned his brother, who was an oil and gas lease and royalty speculator. Parker asked his brother whether he knew about a well being drilled on Young's property. After doing some research, Parker's brother informed him that the well looked promising and that he would provide financing to Parker if he attempted to purchase the royalty from Young. Parker's brother suggested offering Young $30,000 for the one-half royalty. Parker replied that he did not want to pay $30,000 and that he could probably buy it for $27,000. Later that day, Parker asked his partner Pat Barrett, Jr. whether he thought there was anything wrong with a lawyer's purchasing mineral interests from a client, and Barrett replied that he did not see anything wrong with it.

The following morning, Parker called Edwards and told him that he knew of someone who could make Young a better offer. He asked Edwards to have Young contact him. Young returned Parker's call and the two agreed to meet that afternoon at Edwards's bank. Once at the bank, Parker informed Young that he wanted to purchase the one-half royalty for $27,000. Young agreed, and they executed the same deed that Sneed had prepared except that Parker's name appeared in the Grantee blank.

When Sneed arrived at the firm, prepared to close the sale, he was informed that Young had received a better offer for the one-half royalty. Sneed asked who purchased the one-half royalty but was not given an answer. Eventually, Sneed discovered from the officially recorded deed that Parker had purchased the one-half royalty.

In June, 1987, Entente sued Parker and the firm in federal district court based on diversity jurisdiction. Entente asserted that Parker's actions constituted tortious interference with business relations and contract in violation of Mississippi law, and that the firm was vicariously liable for Parker's tortious conduct. The court held a jury trial. At the close of Entente's evidence, the firm moved for a directed verdict on the ground that Parker's purchase of the royalty was not within the scope of his employment, and hence, the firm could not be vicariously liable for any tort he may have committed in purchasing the royalty. The district court concluded that Parker had not been acting within the scope of his employment when he purchased the royalty and granted the firm's motion for directed verdict. . . .

Mississippi law applies in this diversity case. Accordingly, the law firm's vicarious liability for Parker's conduct is assessed under agency principles. See Miss. Code Ann. [UPA § 9(1)] ("Every partner is an agent of the partnership for the purpose of its business. . . ."); Id. [UPA § 13] ("Where, by any wrongful act . . . of any partner acting in the ordinary course of business of the partnership . . . loss or injury is caused to any person . . . the partnership is liable therefor to the same extent as the partner so acting. . . ."). We are also guided by the Restatement (Second) of Agency, as the Mississippi Supreme Court has cited with approval various sections of the treatise.

Section 219 of the Restatement (Second) of Agency discusses the circumstances in which a master or principal is liable for the torts of his servant or agent. Subsection (1) of § 219 provides that a principal or master is vicariously liable for the torts of his agent or servant that are committed within the scope of employment. [The court quotes § 228.] Section 228 of the Restatement clearly requires that, in order to be within the scope of employment, the agent's conduct must be actuated, at least in part, by a purpose to serve the master.

Subsection (2) of § 219 lists four situations in which conduct that fails to satisfy the "within the scope of employment" test found in § 228, may still provide a basis for imposing vicarious liability. Subsection (2) provides in part that

> (2) A master is not subject to liability for the torts of his servants acting outside the scope of employment, unless:
>
> . . . .
>
> (d) the servant purported to act or to speak on behalf of the principal and there was reliance upon apparent authority, or he was aided in accomplishing the tort by the existence of the agency relation.

Thus, under the Restatement, a principal is liable for the torts of his agent if the agent commits the tort while acting within the scope of his employment as defined by § 228, or if § 219(2) applies. The situations listed in § 219(2)[2] are not necessarily exceptions to the scope of employment doctrine, but rather situations in which courts have decided to impose liability on the principal or employer even if the

2. [The other three situations are (1) the master intended the conduct; (2) the master was negligent; and (3) the conduct violated a nondelegable duty of the master. —Eds.]

agent's conduct does not meet all of the traditional "within the scope of employment" criteria.

Section 261 is an extension of § 219(2)(d), and states that

> A principal who puts a servant or other agent in a position which enables the agent, while apparently acting within his authority, to commit a fraud upon third persons is subject to liability to such third persons for the fraud.

Unlike § 228, § 261 assesses vicarious liability even though the agent's conduct was not actuated by a purpose to serve the principal. Although Mississippi case law has not expressly differentiated between the two types of vicarious liability found in § 219(1) and § 219(2) of the Restatement, the distinction is implicit. . . .

1. Was Parker's Conduct Within the Scope of His Employment?

The district court concluded that Parker's purchase of the royalty from Young was an "abandonment of employment" and therefore, not within the scope of his employment with the firm. Entente does not dispute that the firm is not in the business of buying minerals or that the firm received no gain from Parker's purchase of the royalty. Instead, Entente asserts that the district court improperly focused on the last event, the purchase itself, and that if the transaction is viewed in the proper context, Parker's conduct satisfies each element of § 228.

In essence, Entente contends that Parker purchased the royalty while acting as Young's attorney, and was motivated by the firm's purposes both when he agreed to meet with Young, a longstanding client, and when he agreed to perform the title search. Entente maintains that Parker's conduct, from the time he agreed to meet with Young to the time he purchased the royalty, is only one series of conduct that cannot be separated into distinct acts; in Entente's words, Parker's "legal engagement could not be turned on and off." . . .

There is no dispute that Parker purchased the royalty for himself and was acting in his own interest, not in the interest of the firm. There is also no dispute that the firm did not receive any benefit from Parker's purchase of the royalty. In fact, Young was never billed by Parker or the firm. In order to satisfy the § 228 definition of "within the scope of employment," Parker's conduct must have been motivated, at least in part, by a desire to serve the firm. It is undisputed that Parker was motivated only by a desire to serve himself when he purchased the royalty. Viewing the conduct from the proper perspective, as a matter of law, Parker could not have been acting within the scope of his employment when he purchased the royalty interest.

2. Did the Agency Relationship Aid Parker in Committing Allegedly Tortious Acts, Within the Meaning of §§ 219(2)(d) and 261?

Entente claims that two cases, *Billups Petroleum Co. v. Hardin's Bakeries Corp.*, 217 Miss. 24, 63 So. 2d 543 (1953), and *Napp v. Liberty National Life Insurance Co.*, 248 Miss. 320, 159 So. 2d 164 (1963), support its argument that conduct need not be motivated by any desire to serve a master in order to be within the scope of a servant's employment. . . . Entente's argument conflates two theories of liability.[3] We examine the *Billups* and *Napp* cases, however, to determine whether the type of liability anticipated by § 261 exists in this case. After a careful examination of the cases and the underlying theories of liability, we find that as a matter of law, the liability described in §§ 219(2)(d) and 261 does not exist in this case.

In *Billups*, a salesman for Hardin's Bakeries overcharged Billups for bread over a period of several months, and kept the excess for himself. The Mississippi Supreme Court held Hardin's Bakeries vicariously liable for its agent's fraud. . . . Contrary to some of the language in the *Billups* case, the principal's liability is based on the theory embodied in §§ 219(2)(d) and 261 of the Restatement, rather than traditional "scope of employment" liability contained in § 219(1). The four cases the *Billups* court discusses in support of its holding evidence that the court imposed § 219(2)(d) liability. Each of the four cases involves fraud by an agent upon the principal's customer. Each case involved a situation in which the principal delegated to the agent the power to perform a certain task, such as collect monies for the principal. In each case, the agent acted for his own purposes, but the fraud transpired as part of the very duty that the principal authorized the agent to perform. Because the customers had a relationship with the principal that induced the customers to rely on the principal's agent, and the agent defrauded the customers in the performance of the duty entrusted to him by the principal, the agent was "aided in accomplishing the tort by the existence of the agency relation." Restatement (Second) of Agency, § 219(2)(d) (1958).

In *Napp*, the insurance company's agent defrauded a beneficiary by painstakingly convincing her that her husband's policy had lapsed before his death, but that the insurance company would pay half of the benefit she otherwise would have been due. In fact, the policy had not lapsed, and when the agent delivered a check for the full amount of the benefit to the beneficiary, he told her that the check had been made out for the incorrect amount, and that she would have to give half of it back to him to return to the company. He induced her to sign a receipt for the full amount and he kept one half of the money for himself. The court found that even though this conduct was not within the scope of the agent's employment contract, the company elected to have the agent deliver the check, and "could not delegate to one certain duties and then deny agency because the written contract between them limited his activities to other matters." *Napp*, 159 So. 2d at 166. Thus, as in *Billups*, the fraud in *Napp* transpired as part of the very duty that the agent was authorized to perform for the principal and customer.

Entente contends that, just as in *Billups* and *Napp*, Parker was aided in purchasing the royalty by the existence of his agency relationship with the firm. Entente advances that but for his employment at the firm, Parker never would have met

---

3. [4] Although the holding of the *Billups* case is framed in "scope of employment" language, upon close examination, the underlying theory of liability is that expressed in § 219(2)(d) of the Restatement. See Restatement (Second) of Agency § 219 cmt. e (1958).

Young and never would have had the opportunity to purchase the royalty; yet, but-for causation is irrelevant in this case. The proper inquiry for determining vicarious liability of a principal whose agent defrauds the principal's customer is the relationship between the principal and the customer. In *Billups*, the four cases it discusses, and *Napp*, the principal had a relationship with the customer and the customer was defrauded by the principal's agent. The courts reasoned that a principal who provides his agent with the tools or position necessary to perpetrate a fraud on the principal's customers, should be held responsible to the innocent customers who relied on the agent. In this case, there was no relationship between the firm and Entente that could be imputed to the firm's agent. It is undisputed that neither Parker nor the firm represented Entente. The premise underlying § 219(2)(d) and § 261 liability, a relationship between the principal and an innocent third party, is absent in this case. Therefore, as a matter of law, the firm could not have been held vicariously liable for Parker's acts.

We AFFIRM the verdict directed by the district court.

Hydrolevel Corp. v. American Society of Mechanical Engineers, Inc.

United States Court of Appeals, Second Circuit
635 F.2d 118 (1980), *aff'd*, 456 U.S. 556 (1982)

Before LUMBARD, FRIENDLY and MESKILL, CIRCUIT JUDGES.

LUMBARD, CIRCUIT JUDGE:

The American Society of Mechanical Engineers (ASME) appeals from a judgment of $7.5 million [resulting from trebled damages under the antitrust laws].... We affirm the judgment of liability on a theory different from that of the district court, and remand for a new trial on damages, with instructions regarding the treatment of the settlement payments and the assessment of legal fees.

ASME is a tax-exempt technical and scientific society founded in 1880 and based in New York. It has more than 90,000 members, drawn from all fields where mechanical engineers are active—including industry, academia, insurance and government—and has an annual operating budget of over $12 million. It conducts educational and research programs, publishes a national magazine devoted to mechanical engineering, and, principally important to this case, promulgates over 400 codes and standards. Those codes have great influence in the profession and the marketplace. Although ASME employs a full-time staff, much of its work is done by volunteers from its membership who participate in ASME as individuals, not as representatives of their employers. The question in this appeal is whether ASME is liable for the restraint of trade that resulted when two of its highly placed volunteers caused it to issue a misinterpretation of one such code so as to frustrate competition at the expense of Hydrolevel Corporation.

At all relevant times, the Boiler and Pressure Vessel Code set standards for the performance of various components of steam and water boilers and pressure vessels.

Section IV of the Code set standards specifically for components of heating boilers, including a device whose name wholly describes its function: the low-water fuel cut-off. If the water inside a boiler drops below a level that is sufficient to moderate the boiler's temperature, the boiler will "dry fire" and can explode. A low-water fuel cut-off cuts off fuel to the boiler, and thus stops it, when the water reaches a certain low point. To ensure that the cut-off operates before the water reaches a dangerously low level, Paragraph HG-605 of Section IV of the Code required that each boiler "have an automatic low-water fuel cut-off so located as to automatically cut off the fuel supply when the surface of the water falls to the lowest visible part of the water-gauge glass" attached to the outside of the boiler.

The leading manufacturer of cut-offs for the last fifty years has been McDonnel & Miller, Inc. (M&M), of Chicago, which annually makes 70%–85% of the sales of "float" cut-offs. The literal nomenclature of this area of mechanical engineering almost wholly explains function: when water in the boiler falls to the critical level, a floating bulb falling with the water trips a switch mechanically linked to the bulb and thus cuts off the fuel. Hydrolevel began in 1965 to manufacture and market a "probe" cut-off which, as its name suggests, penetrates into the water in the boiler. So long as water covers an electrode in the probe, a completed electrical circuit will cause fuel to flow to the boiler; when the water drops below the probe, the circuit is broken and the fuel stops. [The probe included a time delay feature that neutralized the effects of fluctuating levels of water due to boiling.]

In early 1971, a major purchaser of cut-offs, Brooklyn Union Gas Co., had decided to change to Hydrolevel's time-delay probe after years of purchasing M&M's float. At the same time, M&M arranged to use ASME code interpretation procedures to stifle Hydrolevel's competition. [One Hardin, who was closely associated with M&M and also was Chairman of the committee that interpreted Section IV, arranged for the issuance of a letter on ASME letterhead that discouraged the use of time delay features on safety grounds. The court characterized the reasoning in the letter as misleading].

[T]he ASME [letter] proved to be valuable M&M propaganda. M&M included a copy of [it] in its booklet entitled "The Opposition—Who They Are, How to Beat Them," which M&M distributed to its salesmen. Not surprisingly, copies of ASME's [letter] soon reached the hands of customers in the cut-off market. [Hydrolevel eventually went out of business.]

The district court charged the jury that ASME could be held liable [for fraud] only if the jury found that ASME had ratified the acts of its agents or if the agents had acted to advance ASME's interests. That is the appropriate theory for conventional torts. See Restatement (2d) of Agency §§ 235, 236. The conduct at issue here, however, is far closer to the torts discussed in § 247 (defamation); § 248 (interference with business relations); § 257 (misrepresentation); and §§ 261 and 262 (fraud). None of these sections ties the principal's liability to a requirement that the agent act at least in part for the principal's benefit, and several expressly reject such a requirement. See § 257, comment d; § 261, comment a; § 262. Under these sections it is likewise immaterial that the agent knows the transaction to be a sham. See § 261, comment a and illustration 3.

The reasons for this stringent treatment of [such] intentional torts are not difficult to find. Such torts arise from and are enhanced by the agent's appearance of authority. Third persons—here the customers to whom M&M circulated the misleading ASME letter—are entitled to rely on that appearance. Moreover, as stated in § 247, dealing with defamation, the act of the agent "is effective, in part at least, because of the personality" of the principal. Or, as said in § 261, comment a, dealing with fraud:

> (L)iability is based upon the fact that the agent's position facilitates the consummation of the fraud, in that from the point of view of the third person the transaction seems regular on its face and the agent appears to be acting in the ordinary course of the business confided to him.

Imposing liability on the principal will induce greater care to prevent misconduct by agents occupying especially sensitive or responsible positions that invite reliance—a consideration of great importance in cases such as this where misuse of quasi-official standards and codes can so easily injure competitors.

Hardin's conduct here was essentially a fraud, a willful and knowing misrepresentation of the Code. The victims, however, were those customers to whom he knew M&M would circulate the letter as well as, ultimately and most seriously, the plaintiff. This difference from the more usual situation in which the injured party relies directly on the culpable misrepresentations can hardly be material. In *Ricketts v. Pennsylvania R. Co.*, 153 F.2d 757, 759 (2d Cir. 1946), we held that there is "no distinction in principle" between the situation in which the agent deceives the third person "and one in which the agent deceives, not the third person, but his principal." Alternatively, the tort could be regarded as "injurious falsehood." See Prosser, Torts § 128 at 915–26 (4th ed. 1971). As to this, the Restatement (2d) of Agency tells us, § 248 comment b, that where "harm to business relations is accomplished by defamation or other methods of untruthful publicity, a servant with apparent authority to make statements binds his employer, irrespective of his motive. . . ."

A conspiracy to restrain trade is so similar to fraud, injurious falsehood, and tortious interference with business relations that application of the Restatement rules governing those torts is appropriate. For ASME to be liable, then, Hydrolevel had to demonstrate only that ASME's agents acted within their apparent authority when participating in the conspiracy; it did not have to demonstrate that they also acted in part to benefit ASME or that ASME later ratified their actions. The district court's charge required either one of those two additional aspects and consequently was more favorable to ASME than it should have been. As the jury found for Hydrolevel on a charge that was more favorable to the defendant than the law requires, we affirm the judgment on liability.

Notes

1. This case was affirmed by the United States Supreme Court by a vote of 5 to 3, with one justice concurring in the result. *American Soc. of Mechanical Eng'rs v. Hydrolevel*

Corp., 456 U.S. 556, 579 (1982). Justice Powell in dissent stated, "In this case, the Court specifically holds that standard-setting organizations may be held liable for the acts of their agents even though the organization never ratified, authorized, or derived any benefit whatsoever from the fraudulent activity of the agent and even though the agent acted solely for his private employer's gain." Justice Powell argued against this, questioning in particular the use of the apparent authority doctrine to impose strict liability when the damages are in part punitive in nature. He stated, "It would be enlightening if the Court would explain how [ASME] can protect itself even from 'mere tort' liability, much less the treble-damages liability imposed in this case, in light of the Court's adoption of the apparent authority theory of liability. . . . No set of rules and regulations, and no procedures however elaborate, can protect adequately against fraud and disloyalty. . . . A member bent on fraud could forge evidence or otherwise circumvent most safeguards." *Id.* at 591, n.17.

A case from the bankruptcy court, *In re Dreier*, 450 B.R. 452, 457–58 (Bankr. S.D.N.Y. 2011), posed a similar problem. An attorney represented his client on a dispute with a third party on an investment that the client made with the third party. The client rejected a settlement that the attorney had negotiated and insisted that the settlement include a mutual non-disparagement clause. The client then signed a new settlement agreement the attorney prepared with the non-disparagement clause. The attorney then forged his client's signature to the original agreement and sent it to the adverse party, who signed it and wired to the attorney's trust account the amount agreed upon in the original settlement amount. The attorney converted those funds to his own use and never informed his client that the funds had been received. When these facts came to light, the client sought to set aside the settlement on the basis that his attorney lacked the apparent authority to settle the dispute. Rejecting this argument, the court ruled that apparent authority was irrelevant; the attorney did not purport to act on behalf of his client but rather forged his client's signature. The court wrote that the client "appeared to agree to the settlement in his own name based on his forged signature without regard to [the attorney's] apparent authority to settle. [The attorney] duped both parties and the well-settled rule of agency law dictates that as between two innocent parties, 'the risk of loss from the unauthorized acts of a dishonest agent falls on the principal that selected the agent.'"

2. For an approach to the problem of an innocent principal's liability for an agent's fraud that bears some similarity to the philosophy expressed by Justice Powell, see *Schuette v. Winternitz*, 498 P.2d 1183, 1185 (Colo. App. 1972) ("A principal is not bound by the false representations of his agent made without his knowledge, consent or authority and without ratification by him after receipt of a benefit. . . . The only remedy against the principal is rescission and restitution."). Apparently the rationale behind this approach is that fraudulent acts of agents are regarded as beyond the scope of employment in view of their intentionally tortious nature. The one aspect of this tortious behavior that distinguishes it from that involved in Chapter 3, namely that here the victim has acted in reliance on expectations for

which the principal is at least partly responsible, is taken into account by allowing rescission and restitution to the victim. The victim also has a full set of remedies, including money damages, against the agent. This is as far as protection should go when the principal is innocent, the *Schuette* court seems to be saying. *Schuette* was not cited in the opinions in *Grease Monkey*, the first case in this chapter, although they both are Colorado cases.

As noted, a similar approach appears to be expressed in the language of Justice Powell in the *Hydrolevel* case (the remedy of rescission and restitution can play no role in the fact situation of that case, however, and perhaps one could argue that the rule of the *Schuette* case should be limited to cases where the parties can be restored to the status quo). Although directly attacked by Restatement (Second) § 261 and the great weight of authority, there is a certain tenacity to this line of reasoning. See, for example, *Adler v. Helman*, 564 N.Y. Supp. 2d 828, 830 (App. Div. 1991), stating, "When an agent abandons the object of his agency and acts for himself, by committing a fraud for his own exclusive benefit, he ceases to act within the scope of his employment and, to that extent, ceases to act as agent." The court notes in *Adler* that liability of the principal under that circumstance must be based on ratification, usually by retention of the benefits of the fraudulent acts, assuming that the facts of a particular case include retention of benefits.

3. Section 261 of the Restatement (Second) would appear to endorse the award of money damages to a defrauded third party who wants to keep the property purchased through an agent and sue the principal for damages occasioned by the fraud. One court, *Aiello v. Ed Saxe Real Estate, Inc.*, 508 Pa. 553, 499 A.2d 282, 287–88 (1985), articulated the rationale for this in the following terms (the case involved a suit for money damages by the purchaser of a home against a real estate broker (Saxe) for the fraud (misrepresenting availability of a sewage disposal system) of Jones, his salesman):

> Today we reaffirm the longstanding and widely held rule of law that a principal is liable to innocent third parties for the frauds, deceits, concealments, misrepresentations, torts, negligences and other malfeasances or misfeasances of his agent committed in the course of his employment, although the principal did not authorize, justify or participate in, or indeed know of, such misconduct, or even if he forbade the acts or disapproved of them.

> To hold otherwise is to violate public policy and permit the person who held out his agent as worthy of trust and confidence, to escape liability for his agent's deceits and frauds, while at the same time reaping the fruits of his agent's fraud, all at the expense of an innocent third party. Such a holding would be contrary to natural justice and common honesty. . . .

> . . . It is clear that Saxe cannot retain the commission earned by the sale and at the same time repudiate Jones's agency or the statements made by him by means of which it obtained that commission. Saxe accepted the

commission subject to Jones's fraudulent statement and the maxim *qui sentit commodum sentire debet et onus* (he who receives the advantage ought also to suffer the burden) applies.

Is this explanation of the rationale underlying liability of an innocent principal for the fraud of its agent the same as that articulated in the *Hydrolevel* case and Restatement (Second) § 261?

4. Is *Hydrolevel* consistent with the *Entente* case? Was there "a relationship between the principal and an innocent third party" in *Hydrolevel*?

5. The Restatement (Third) § 7.08 is consistent with these cases, with this broad statement of the law:

> A principal is subject to vicarious liability for a tort committed by an agent in dealing or communicating with a third party on or purportedly on behalf of the principal when actions taken by the agent with apparent authority constitute the tort or enable the agent to conceal its commission.

Rothman v. Fillette

Supreme Court of Pennsylvania
469 A.2d 543 (1983)

Before Roberts, C.J., and Nix, Larsen, Flaherty, McDermott, Hutchinson and Zappala, JJ.

Nix, Justice.

We are here called upon to resolve the difficult problem of who must bear the burden of loss between innocent parties where the attorney for one of the parties has acted beyond the scope of his authority and has misappropriated funds. . . .

Appellee, Philip Rothman, was involved in an automobile accident which occurred on November 15, 1971 and, as a result thereof, sustained personal injuries. He retained Irving Madnick, Esq., to institute suit to recover for the loss sustained. A complaint . . . was filed on November 2, 1972 . . . against Gloria and Ronald Fillette. The Fillettes were insured by the Liberty Mutual Insurance Company. After negotiations, Liberty Mutual, in 1974, agreed to settle the case for the sum of Seven Thousand ($7,000) Dollars. Pursuant to the settlement agreement, Liberty Mutual delivered to Madnick a release containing the terms of the proposed settlement and requiring the signature of appellee. The release was returned to Liberty Mutual purportedly signed by Philip Rothman and attested to by two witnesses. In return, Liberty Mutual presented to Madnick a check in the amount of Seven Thousand ($7,000) Dollars, payable to Philip Rothman and Irving L. Madnick. This check was thereafter purportedly endorsed by Philip Rothman and cashed. On order of Madnick, the case was marked settled, discontinued and ended on September 9, 1974.

Approximately five years later on November 20, 1979, Rothman filed a petition seeking a rule to remove the Order marking the case settled, discontinued and ended. In that petition it was alleged that Rothman had no knowledge of the purported settlement and that he did not sign the release nor did he endorse the check. It was his contention that since he was neither aware of, nor had he authorized the settlement and that his agent acted without authority, he should not be prevented from pursuing his claim against the Fillettes and their insurer. The court below granted the prayer of the petition and reinstated the action against the Fillettes. That ruling was affirmed by the Superior Court, 305 Pa. Super. 28, 451 A.2d 225.

At the outset, it must be understood that under the facts of this case there is no question of an implied or an apparent agency. The law in this jurisdiction is quite clear that an attorney must have express authority to settle a cause of action of the client.

The issue that is presented here relates to where the allocation of loss should fall as a result of the agent's unfaithful performance. It must be emphasized that in our judgment both of the parties of this action were innocent and free of any fault. Mr. Rothman in selecting his counsel, a person at that time certified to practice law by this Court, had no reason to suspect misconduct. Likewise, the Fillettes and their insurer bargained in good faith with appellee and Mr. Madnick under circumstances that would not reasonably give rise to any inference that counsel was breaching a trust to the client. The Fillettes and their insurer had every reason to believe under the facts presented that the purported settlement had been expressly approved by Mr. Rothman.

Under these circumstances, we believe applicable here the long recognized principle that where one of two innocent persons must suffer because of the fraud of a third, the one who has accredited him must bear the loss. As was stated in *Rykaczewski v. Kerry Home, Inc.*, 192 Pa. Super. 461, 465, 161 A.2d 924, 926 (1960):

> Where one of two innocent persons must suffer, the loss should be borne by him who put the wrongdoer in a position of trust and confidence and thus enabled him to perpetrate the wrong.

. . . In such instances the lack of authority of the agent has been rejected as a basis for shifting the principal's losses onto the innocent third party. The fact that the agent has wronged his principal through the agent's unlawful act does not provide a predicate for insulating the principal against the harm caused by the agent at the expense of the innocent third party who had no responsibility for the conduct of the agent. We believe that this view is consistent with fundamentally sound principles of agency and equity and that there were no other additional factors here present to justify ignoring its applicability.

It is argued that the fact that appellant was insured should compel a different result. Such an argument must be summarily rejected. Liberty Mutual undertook to indemnify the Fillettes against the damages arising from the motor vehicle accident; it did not assume the responsibility of insulating a plaintiff bringing action against its insured from the losses incurred by the defalcation of plaintiff's counsel. The fact that an insurance carrier may be in an apparently better financial position to absorb the loss does not justify creating a liability where none exists. Thus it is clear, at the very least, that the Fillettes must be credited with the payment to Rothman of the $7,000 towards the payment of the damages sustained as a result of the accident which occurred on November 15, 1971.

The next step in the analysis must address the question as to whether the unauthorized actions of the agent bars Rothman's further pursuit of the claim.[4] Logical consistency would not be offended by a finding that although the Fillettes were entitled to a credit for the payment made, the unauthorized settlement should be set aside and Rothman provided an opportunity to establish that the damages exceeded the amount received. However, such a view must be rejected as being inescapably disruptive of established settlement policies. There is a strong judicial policy in favor of parties voluntarily settling lawsuits. . . .

The lower court suggested the following methods for an insurer to ascertain the attorney's authority prior to consummating settlement: (1) compare the signature on the release with signature in the files; (2) require the release to be notarized; (3) request the claimant to personally execute the release in their presence; and/or, (4) obtain permission to contact the claimant in order to verify settlement.

In our judgment these suggestions are impractical and of little utility for the objectives sought to be achieved. The requirement that the release must be notarized will not deter an individual bent on committing a forgery. Nor does the requirement that the release be signed in the presence of an agent of the insurer offer any meaningful protection against such criminal conduct. In most cases, the insurance company would not be aware of the appearance of the claimant so that an impostor could sign the release without detection. Moreover, such a requirement would unduly burden the settlement process. The requirement that the insurer compare the signature with samples of the signature of the claimant, first assumes that the company has such signatures in its files. Such an assumption is unwarranted in the normal course of our settlement practice. The final suggestion that the defendant or his insurer obtain permission to contact the claimant personally is directly in conflict with the strong policy against interference by an opposing party with a relationship between attorney and client.

In summary, we are satisfied that the procedures followed by appellants and their insurer in this case were well established and that the suggested changes would be more harmful and obstructive to the settlement process than any possible benefit that may be derived therefrom. We cannot design our rules on the assumption that the members of our Bar will participate in criminal behavior. We must rely upon the fidelity of our Bar and in the main, experience has demonstrated the justification for that reliance. Where the unusual and unfortunate case of breach of trust occurs, such as here, we must rely upon the other procedures

---

4. [4] The harshness of this result is to some extent ameliorated by this Court's establishment of a client security fund which was designed to assist clients of defalcating attorneys.

established in our law to provide punishment and to serve as a deterrent against repetition of such conduct.

Accordingly, the Order of the Superior Court affirming the Court of Common Pleas is reversed. The petition to strike the order to settle, discontinue and end is dismissed.

Hutchinson, J., concurs in the result.

Larsen, Justice, dissenting.

I agree with the majority's determination that as between appellants and appellee Rothman, appellee must bear the loss of the $7,000 settlement which his attorney misappropriated. I disagree, however, with the majority's conclusion that appellee is barred from pursuing his claim against appellants for amounts in excess of the $7,000 settlement with which appellants have been credited. Accordingly, I dissent.

Since appellee never authorized the $7,000 settlement, there is no reason to believe that that amount was reasonable to compensate him for his injuries. In addition, I fail to see how prohibiting appellee from establishing the true value of his loss at trial will promote our policy favoring settlement. The only thing that would be accomplished by disallowing a suit such as appellee's is the further punishment of a plaintiff and the provision of a bonanza to a defendant for conduct which was beyond their control. In this case, I do not think that appellee should be further penalized; rather, appellee should have an opportunity to establish at trial his actual damages.

Further, the fact that a client security fund exists is no reason to deny appellee his right of action against appellants. The client security fund is funded by attorneys and its purpose is to assist clients who have suffered losses due to the misconduct of their attorneys. The fund's purpose is not, however, to reimburse appellee for any injuries resulting from the negligence of appellants. While it is true that appellants should not bear the loss occasioned by appellee's dishonest counsel, neither should appellants be permitted to profit from counsel's misconduct. If appellants actually caused injury to appellee in an amount in excess of $7,000, then they should be responsible for that excess.

I would hold that appellee may proceed to trial against appellants for any damages in excess of the $7,000 unauthorized settlement.[5]

Note

The *Rothman* case resolves a dispute created by an agent's fraud without citing § 219(2)(d) or § 261 of the Restatement (Second). Is the court proposing a different standard of liability?

---

5. [*] In those cases in which settlement negotiations and the subsequent striking of a settlement have created a long lapse of time between the filing of suit and trial, any allegation of actual prejudice to the defendant, such as the unavailability of witnesses, such that requiring defense of the suit would be patently unfair, must be disposed of by the trial court.

B. Limits to Liability for Fraud

Light v. Chandler Improvement Co.

Supreme Court of Arizona
261 P. 969 (1928)

LOCKWOOD, J.—

Chandler Improvement Company, a corporation, hereinafter called plaintiff, brought suit against G. P. Light, H. A. Berry, and May W. Berry, his wife, hereinafter called defendants, to foreclose a mortgage on twenty acres of land situated near Chandler, Arizona, to secure part of the purchase price. The defense to the suit was fraud and deceit in inducing the purchase, with a prayer that the notes and mortgage involved be adjudged to be fully paid and satisfied, that the notes be surrendered and canceled, that the mortgage be released of record, and that defendants recover from plaintiff judgment in the sum of $945, being the excess actually paid in cash for the land over the real value thereof. The issues were presented to a jury, and at the close of defendants' case plaintiff moved for an instructed verdict, which motion was by the court granted, and, after the usual motion for new trial was overruled, defendants appealed. . . .

In the fall of 1919, defendants saw an advertisement that the land in question, then owned by plaintiff, was offered for sale, and that one Crenshaw had it listed with him for that purpose. Defendants called upon him and were taken out to examine the land. They spent some half hour's time going over it, and were informed by Crenshaw that all of said land was fertile and would produce good crops, and in particular that it would produce a reasonable crop of cotton; that about eight acres thereof was quite heavy, but that there was no so-called "slick" or "tight" land thereon. Defendants thereupon closed the deal, paying $1,500 in cash, receiving a deed to the land from plaintiff, and giving notes and a mortgage back for $4,500, being the balance of the purchase price. Defendants did not attempt to farm the land themselves, but rented it from 1920 to 1924, inclusive. The tenants first planted it to Sudan grass, and later to oats and alfalfa, and in 1924 it was planted to cotton. During none of these years was a reasonable crop grown upon the land, although all of the tenants had given it at least ordinary care and culture. In 1923, for the first time, the defendants suggested to plaintiff that the transaction was unsatisfactory. At this time in a conversation with one of its officers, defendant Light said:

"I told him we weren't producing anything off of it, and asked him if he would take it back. We were unable to make our payments. . . ."

On cross-examination, the witness was questioned:

"Q. Did you ever go to the Chandler Improvement Company and say to them that you wanted to rescind this land because false representations had been made to you? A. I didn't give that reason. I said we weren't getting anything off of it, and we couldn't make our payments. . . ."

"Q. You never hinted to them, did you, that you had been led to buy this land by false representations of anybody, did you? A. No."

This is the only evidence in the record in regard to any offer on the part of the defendants to rescind the contract, or in regard to any alleged false representations of Crenshaw being communicated to plaintiff at any time before filing the answer herein. The evidence also shows that of the twenty acres in question, considerably over half is what is known as "tight land"; that is, it is land covered with a fine sediment from flood water. These soils are very rich, but take water very slowly when irrigated, due to their high content of deflocculated clay. They are better adapted to grain and fine-rooted crops than deep-rooted plants, and require the introduction of some other substance such as straw, manure or Bermuda sod to make them available for general crop production.

... It is contended by defendants that a real estate broker in the selling of land is impliedly authorized by his principal to make representations in regard to the quality and value of the land, and that the principal is bound by such representations as though he had himself made them. It is insisted, on the other hand, by plaintiff that a real estate broker who is not authorized to convey land, but who merely may find a purchaser upon the terms fixed by his principal, cannot bind the principal by representations in regard to the quality and value of the land, unless he was expressly authorized to make such representations, or unless they are known to his principal before the sale is consummated. There are authorities upon both sides of the question.

The matter is one of first impression in this jurisdiction, and we are therefore at liberty to adopt the rule which seems to us best in consonance with our general practice, conditions, and public policy. We are of the opinion that plaintiff's position on this issue is the soundest. The other rule originated in England, where land is transferred with comparative rarity, and where an agent dealing with land is impliedly given far more authority over it than is the case with the ordinary real estate broker in western America. There lands were and generally are handled by exclusive agents in whom the owner reposes a special confidence, and to whom a prospective purchaser might well look as being, if not the *alter ego*, at least the *fides Achates*[6] of such owner. With us, on the contrary, it is the general custom, when an owner desires to sell his land, to list the same with as many real estate brokers as possible, with specific instructions given to them as to price and conditions of sale, and with an authority which is ordinarily assumed to extend only to showing prospective purchasers over the premises, stating the terms, and, if the property and terms are satisfactory, taking them to the owner for completion of the transaction. If we are to hold the owner of property bound by any and all representations made by any one of a dozen brokers under such circumstances, and liable in an action for

---

6. [Trusted bargainer.—Eds.]

fraud and deceit because of such representations, when they are entirely unknown to him and would have been indignantly repudiated, had they been called to his attention, the door to fraud upon the owner will be thrown wide open. We think the authorities supporting plaintiff's position lay down the better rule, and we adopt that as the one to be followed in Arizona.

But, it will be said, has the purchaser no rights, and must he go remediless, or at most have an action against a possibly irresponsible and insolvent agent, when, relying on the latter's conduct, he has entered into a contract with the owner from which the latter has received a pecuniary profit? If such were the result necessarily flowing from the rule laid down, it would, indeed, work with harshness and injustice. The authorities which follow that rule, however, also indicate the proper remedy for the defrauded purchaser. When he discovers the fraud, he has two courses open to him. He may either ratify the transaction so far as the owner is concerned and make the payments, notwithstanding the false representations, reserving the right to sue the agent in damages for such fraud and deception, or he may go to the owner and, stating the fraud, offer to rescind. If the owner, after due notice of the fraud and offer of rescission, insists upon holding the purchaser to his bargain, he will then be deemed to have ratified the alleged representations of the agent and the purchaser may pursue as against such owner any remedy which he would have had, had the false representations been made by the owner in person. If, on the other hand, the owner accepts the rescission and returns the purchase price, the parties are in *status quo* and justice, as between them, is satisfied.

In the case at bar there is no evidence that any false representations, even if they were made by the agent, were ever communicated or known to plaintiff or any of its officers until the filing of the answer herein. There is no evidence of any offer of rescission on the ground of fraud. One of defendants, it is true, said that he asked plaintiff to take the land back, but expressly stated that the only reason he gave was that the land was unproductive, and that defendants could not make the payments thereon, and that he never at any time suggested that defendants had been deceived or defrauded by any false representations made at the time of their purchase of the property in question. Further, not even in the answer do defendants offer to rescind, but on the contrary, insist on retaining the land in question. To allow a recoupment under such circumstances would, in effect, be compelling an innocent owner of land to sell it against his will on terms to which he had never agreed.

We are of the opinion that before a purchaser who has been deceived by unauthorized false and fraudulent representations as to quality and value made by a real estate broker with whom land has been placed for sale may set up the defense of recoupment for such false and fraudulent representations in an action by the vendor for the purchase price, it must be alleged and proved, in addition to the false representations by the broker, that the vendor, after knowledge of such representations and an offer of rescission on that ground by the purchaser, refused to accept the rescission. No such knowledge and offer having either been pleaded or proved by defendants, the trial court properly directed the jury to return a verdict in favor of plaintiff. The judgment of the superior court of Maricopa county is affirmed.

Ross, C. J., and McAlister, J., concur.

Notes

1. See *O'Malley v. Putnam Safe Deposit Vaults*, 458 N.E.2d 752 (Mass. App. 1983), *rev. denied*, 461 N.E.2d 1219 (Mass. 1984), involving a suit by a depositor (O'Malley) of gold coins against a safe deposit company for losses sustained by the conversion of O'Malley's gold coins by Caten, the vice-president of defendant company. O'Malley had given Caten permission to borrow coins from O'Malley's box in order to provide "quick delivery" to other customers. *Held*: O'Malley could not establish a case for apparent authority under Restatement (Second) § 261. "Not only was there no evidence suggesting that Caten's borrowing was known to, or acquiesced in by, his superiors, but there was no showing that borrowing gold from one customer to deliver to another was within the usual responsibility of a person in Caten's position or that such practice could be viewed as reasonably necessary to his authorized duties." Is the reasoning of *O'Malley* similar to that contained in *Light*? (The court in *O'Malley* held alternatively that a jury question existed whether defendant was negligent in failing to establish more safeguards or provide more supervision.)

2. The *Light* case was cited with approval in *Jerger v. Rubin*, 471 P.2d 726 (Ariz. 1970), a unanimous en banc decision. The court added one point to the ratification analysis in *Light*, noting that a principal who insists on a contract after being informed of his agent's fraud is not deemed to have ratified it if he had changed his position in good faith prior to being informed of the fraud, citing Restatement (Second) § 99.

3. In *Barnes v. Lopez*, 544 P.2d 694, 698 (Ariz. App. 1976), the purchasers of property brought suit against the seller (Barnes) and his broker for damages for fraud based on the broker's misrepresentation that the property was zoned entirely for business, whereas it was partially zoned residential. The court held that the purchasers were not required to make an offer to rescind to Barnes before suing him for damages because the listing agreement signed by Barnes with his broker stated that the property was zoned for business. "He therefore cannot be heard to say that the representation was unknown to him."

4. In *Alexander Myers & Co. v. Hopke*, 565 P.2d 80, 83 (Wash. 1977), Hopke engaged a realty agent (Estvold) to sell an unimproved and irregularly shaped tract of land. The broker prepared an earnest money agreement that plaintiff, an interested buyer, signed. The agreement falsely stated that the parcel contained 70 acres; it was actually 50 acres. The court held that plaintiff was entitled to specific performance with abatement of the purchase price since Hopke was bound to the representation, on the following reasoning:

> The scope of the authority of a real estate broker who is engaged only to find a purchaser includes at least authority to state the area of the parcel when the area and boundary lines, as in the instant case, are not apparent

from inspection. Since it is clear defendant entrusted Estvold not only with obtaining a purchaser but with all negotiations up to the sale itself, he certainly had authority to state the acreage of the tract.

5. The agent is liable for his own fraud, of course. See *Glendale Realty, Inc. v. Johnson*, 495 P.2d 1375 (Wash. App. 1972), and authorities cited therein.

6. In *Cohen v. Blank*, 518 A.2d 582 (Pa. Super. 1986), the buyer of a townhouse sued the seller for the value ($10,000) of a parking space that seller's agent had said was included in the sale of the townhouse and that buyer did not receive. Seller was unaware of the agent's representation. The opinion of the court stated that many things were discussed between buyer and seller at the five-hour settlement and closing, but parking was not among them. Nothing was said about parking in the written documents. The suit was for money damages rather than rescission. The agent making the misrepresentation apparently was an agent for the listing broker. *Held*: Seller is liable in damages for the statement of the agent that a parking space would be included in the sale. Is this case inconsistent with the *Light* case?

Leafgreen v. American Family Mutual Insurance Co.

Supreme Court of South Dakota
393 N.W.2d 275 (1986)

Wuest, Justice.

Floyd and Joyce Leafgreen (Leafgreens) appeal from a grant of summary judgment in an action charging American Family Insurance Company (American Family) with vicarious liability for conversion committed upon the Leafgreens by American Family Insurance Agent Edmund K. Arndt (Arndt). We affirm.

In February 1968, American Family and Arndt entered into an agreement whereby Arndt became an independent agent for the sale of insurance policies issued by American Family. Prior to the agreement, American Family investigated Arndt's background. Several individuals were interviewed in connection with the investigation, all of whom recommended Arndt for the position. A security check performed by Retail Credit of Minneapolis, Minnesota, indicated Arndt had no criminal record and his driving record showed no offense other than a 1963 speeding violation. After the South Dakota Insurance Department conducted its own investigation, Arndt was issued a license by the State to sell insurance.

From 1968 through 1981, Arndt had an extremely good record for insurance sales and service. During this period, his conduct was exemplary. Affidavits and exhibits reflect that Arndt was one of American Family's top agents. Not only was he an outstanding sales leader in the Rapid City District and the whole State of South Dakota, but in some months and years Arndt was considered one of the company's outstanding salesmen throughout the nation.

On May 22, 1981, Arndt went to the Leafgreens' residence for the apparent purpose of correcting certain lot descriptions and writing liability insurance for them.

In providing the lot descriptions, Leafgreens produced their hidden lockbox to examine a deed and thereby disclosed to Arndt the existence of their jewelry and other valuables. Leafgreens claim Arndt was really getting this information to assist two professional burglars, who later burglarized the residence.

It is undisputed that Arndt and the Leafgreens were personal friends. On Friday, June 26, 1981, Leafgreens went to Arndt's office and invited Arndt and his wife on a trip to Rapid City on Saturday. Floyd Leafgreen phoned Arndt on Saturday morning, June 27, 1981, and asked if Arndt and his wife had decided to join them. Arndt told Leafgreen he had made other plans. The Leafgreens' home was burglarized that day while they were in Rapid City.

On March 3, 1983, Jack DeFea, American Family's Rapid City District Manager, was advised by Arndt's secretary, Donna Kemery, that a search warrant had been issued for Arndt's home and that property belonging to Leafgreens had been found in the home. DeFea consulted with American Family executives and counsel and, on May 16, 1983, Arndt was advised that his contract with American Family would terminate on May 31, 1983. On April 1, 1983, a Hughes County Grand Jury filed a three-count indictment against Arndt. On April 4, 1984, Arndt pleaded guilty to Count III of the indictment, aiding and abetting second-degree burglary. He is presently incarcerated in the South Dakota Penitentiary.

On April 18, 1984, Leafgreens filed a complaint against American Family, which alleged: Arndt used his status as an American Family insurance agent to gain entry into the Leafgreens' home on May 22, 1981; he gathered information concerning Leafgreens' valuables with the intent to promote and facilitate the crime of burglary; and used the information to advise two co-conspirators — convicted felons — who committed the burglary on Saturday, June 27, 1981. The Leafgreens argued that Arndt's tortious conduct should be imputed to American Family because it placed Arndt in a position which enabled him, while apparently acting within his authority as an agent of American Family, to commit a fraud[7] upon Leafgreens; namely, the June 27, 1981, burglary of their home.[8]

On June 28, 1985, American Family filed a motion for summary judgment, contending Leafgreens' complaint contained no genuine issue of material fact and that American Family was entitled to judgment as a matter of law because Arndt was not acting within the scope of his employment when he conspired to burglarize

---

7. [1] In their complaint, Leafgreens use the term fraud; however, the facts they state really allege a conversion.

8. [2] Leafgreens' complaint contained a second cause of action alleging that American Family owed them a duty to exercise reasonable care in the selection, retention and review of Arndt, its resident agent, and that American Family breached the duty by negligently retaining Arndt when it knew or should have known he was untrustworthy and dishonest. However, the trial court also granted summary judgment on this cause of action for negligence and appellants did not appeal that portion of the judgment. At oral argument, they made it very plain they had abandoned that theory and were relying upon vicarious liability.

Leafgreens' home. The trial court granted summary judgment in favor of American Family on the issue of vicarious liability, stating in its memorandum decision that Arndt's tortious acts were not reasonably foreseeable by American Family and, consequently, it would be inequitable to impute Arndt's conduct to the company. Leafgreens appeal.

The issue for our determination is whether the doctrine of *respondeat superior* warrants that American Family be held vicariously liable in tort for the burglary of Leafgreens' home, because Arndt used his status as an American Family insurance agent to gain information regarding the property stolen in the burglary. The issue is one of first impression in South Dakota and we are guided, in part, by various rules set out in the Restatement (Second) of Agency.

Under general rules of agency law, a principal may be held liable for fraud and deceit committed by an agent within his apparent authority, even though the agent acts solely to benefit himself. [The court quotes § 261 of the Restatement (Second).]

Comment a to section 261 states:

> The principal is subject to liability under the rule stated in this Section although he is entirely innocent, has received no benefit from the transaction, and, as stated in Section 262, although the agent acted solely for his own purposes. Liability is based upon the fact that the agent's position facilitates the consummation of the fraud, in that from the point of view of the third person the transaction seems regular on its face and the agent appears to be acting in the ordinary course of the business confided to him.

While the boundaries of a principal's liability under this rule are not easily drawn, as the Reporter's Notes to section 261 suggest, they do exist:

> It is difficult to state more definitely than is done in this section the limits of liability. It would seem to be clear that if the agent is purporting to act as an agent and doing the things which such agents normally do, and the third person has no reason to know that the agent is acting on his own account, the principal should be liable because he has invited third persons to deal with the agent within the limits of what, to such third persons, would seem to be the agent's authority. To go beyond this, however, and to permit the third persons to recover in every case where the agent takes advantage of the standing and position of his principal to perpetuate a fraud would seem to go too far. . . . In some cases the situation is ambiguous: the agent performs his primary function as an agent . . . acting within the scope of his powers as such agent without loss to the other from the transaction itself, but the transaction is used as a means by which the agent may defraud such other. If in such cases the principal benefits from the agent's act, his liability to the extent of the benefits received is clear. If, however, the principal is not benefited, and the transaction which actually causes the loss is not one in which the agent purports to represent the principal, liability should not follow.

The situation in the present case is indeed ambiguous. Arndt entered Leafgreens' home and gained information concerning the location of their valuables by purporting to act within the scope of his powers as an American Family insurance agent, without loss to Leafgreens. The transaction, however, was used to facilitate the burglary which occurred approximately five weeks later.

A review of several foreign cases demonstrates the manner in which courts of other jurisdictions have applied the foregoing principles.... In *Lucas v. Liggett & Myers Tobacco Co.*, 50 Haw. 477, 442 P.2d 460 (1968), the owner of a supermarket sued a cigarette manufacturer for the value of cigarettes stolen by a cigarette sales representative. The evidence showed that while servicing a cigarette rack in the store, the representative had stolen a quantity of the product over an extended period of time. The stolen cigarettes were billed to the supermarket by the wholesale supplier, to which the supermarket owners had made payments. Rejecting the argument that the tobacco company was not liable because the sales agent was acting outside the scope of his employment when he committed the thefts, the Supreme Court of Hawaii held the company liable for the acts of its agent. The court relied on the foregoing Restatement rules and pointed out that the company put the agent in a position to commit the thefts and that from the plaintiff's point of view all of the agent's activities connected with servicing the cigarette rack were apparently authorized by the principal. The court emphasized that company's division manager often accompanied the agent and gave no indication that he disapproved of the agent's activities....

In *Lou-Con, Inc. v. Gulf Building Services, Inc.*, 287 So. 2d 192 (La. App. 1973), the client of a janitorial service brought an action against the service and its insurer for damages to the customer's building which was burned down by the janitorial company's employee. The employee was given the keys to the building in connection with his janitorial duties without any restrictions except that he was to use the keys to perform the services agreed to on certain evenings. The plaintiff cited Restatement (Second) of Agency §261, *supra*, and several cases applying the section — including *Lucas v. Liggett & Myers Tobacco Co., supra,* — to support its contention that the janitorial service should be held liable for the arson committed by the employee under the theory of apparent authority. The Louisiana Court of Appeal held that under the facts of the case, section 261 must be read in connection with section 231 of the Restatement.

> The fact that the servant intends a crime, especially if the crime is of some magnitude, is considered in determining whether or not the act is within the employment, since the master is not responsible for acts which are clearly inappropriate to or unforeseeable in the accomplishment of the authorized result. The master can reasonably anticipate that servants may commit minor crimes in the prosecution of the business, but serious crimes are not only unexpectable but in general are in nature different from what servants in a lawful occupation are expected to do.... A servant selling goods for his master may cause the master to be liable in an action of deceit,

although the servant was guilty of obtaining property by false pretenses in making the sale. . . . As in other cases, it is a matter of degree, the question being whether or not the conduct is so unlike that authorized that it is a substantially different thing.

Restatement (Second) of Agency § 231 Comment a (1958).

The Louisiana Court took the facts of the case and applied section 231 and comment a to section 231. The court held that the janitor's freedom of access to the building did not form a basis for tort liability on the part of the janitorial service because it was not foreseeable that he would commit the crime of arson simply because he had the keys in his possession and could gain access to the building.

Restatement (Second) of Agency § 231 focuses on startling or outrageous actions of an agent used as a means of achieving an authorized result. The section deals with the foreseeability of an agent's criminal or tortious conduct from the principal's point of view. Under section 261 and the theory of apparent authority, however, the agent's conduct is seen through the eyes of the third party. The principal is estopped from asserting the agent's lack of authority because he clothed the agent with the authority to act, and the third party reasonably relied on that authority to his detriment. Nevertheless, in ambiguous situations like the case before us, section 231 imparts an element of foreseeability which helps to delineate the limits of liability under the doctrine of *respondeat superior* for acts done within the scope of an agent's apparent authority. . . .

We think it fairly stated that a principal is liable for tortious harm caused by an agent where a nexus sufficient to make the harm foreseeable exists between the agent's employment and the activity which actually caused the injury; foreseeable is used in the sense that the employee's conduct must not be so unusual or startling that it would be unfair to include the loss caused by the injury among the costs of the employer's business.

Applying this test to the facts before us, with a view toward the propriety of summary judgment, we believe there was not such a connection between Arndt's employment as an American Family insurance agent and the burglary which actually caused the harm to Leafgreens, as to make the harm foreseeable. Arndt's conduct was outrageous and, as the trial court stated, unforeseeable by American Family or anyone else for that matter. It would be unfair to impute liability to American Family for Arndt's felonious acts for various reasons. First, we note that American Family was defrauded by Arndt as well, inasmuch as the stolen property was covered under American Family policies. Indeed, American Family received no benefit from the transaction; but, rather, it incurred a liability. Second, the burglary occurred some five weeks after Arndt used his employment with American Family as a subterfuge to enter the Leafgreen home and gather information used in the burglary. While it may be said Arndt's entrance into the home was incidental to his employment with American Family, the burglary clearly was not. Thirdly, Arndt learned that Leafgreens would be in Rapid City the day of the burglary through his friendship with Leafgreens, and not because of his status as an American Family insurance agent. To hold employers liable in such situations as a cost of doing business would be unfair.

Accordingly, the judgment is affirmed.

FOSHEIM, C.J., and MORGAN, J., concur.

HENDERSON and SABERS, JJ., dissent.

HENDERSON, JUSTICE (dissenting).

. . . When zeroing in on the bottom rationale of the majority opinion, it becomes apparent that the majority opinion relies upon "foreseeability" and then pegs a definition of foreseeability to an "unfair" concept, i.e., that a loss to an insurance company caused by the injury of its agent should not be borne as costs of the employer's business. Who put the fox in the hen house? . . . Would it be such a leap of unreasonable logic to assume that an insurance company would monitor the conduct and honesty of its agent? And from a standpoint of fairness, would it not be more fair for the insurance company to bear the loss than the innocent victim?

That the Leafgreens were friends of the agent is totally immaterial. Is the majority suggesting that this is some type of contributory negligence? Likewise, that Arndt was a capital fellow with only a speeding offense, as the majority opinion suggests, has no probative force. Leafgreens were deceived, burglarized, taken advantage of, but this hint of friendship in the majority opinion is not a contributory negligence defense.

> Contributory negligence on the part of the deceived person is not generally recognized as a defense. However, if a third person should know or otherwise has notice that an agent is acting for his own purposes or is otherwise violating his authority, the principal is not liable.

Restatement (Second) of Agency § 262 comment c, at 573 (1958). Contributory negligence is a defense to an action for negligence, not a willful tort.

Contracts of insurance result from personal calls by agents upon prospects at their home. Insurance companies know this is a part of the salesmanship game. Unquestionably, insurance companies would not fare well if agents did not enter the privacy of homes. Were this salesmanship closed down, sales would drop. When an insurance agent goes to the home of a prospective customer, he has an insignia of approval by his insurance company; if he goes sour and cheats, deceives, or even burglarizes that home based upon knowledge he gained by getting into the front door, the insurance company wants to say: "He's not our boy. We claim him not." I say: "It's too late for that Pontius Pilate attitude." The insurance company cannot wash its hands. It clothed him with an aura of honesty and respectability. Arndt was its agent when he was hired, its agent when he tried to sell insurance, its agent when he went into the home to obtain a sale, its agent when he obtained money for them, its agent when he surveilled the home for his burglar-friends, its agent when he learned of the steel lockbox and its contents, and was still acting as its agent when he conspired to have the insurance company's customer burglarized. American Family Insurance does not advocate that Arndt was not its agent when he called on the Leafgreens on May 22, 1981. The Leafgreens trusted this insurance agent. . . .

. . . Accordingly, under the facts of this case, and authorities cited herein, this family is entitled to a jury trial. I would therefore reverse.

SABERS, JUSTICE (dissenting). [Justice Sabers argued that defendant's responsibility to obtain information about Arndt's character and conduct was increased because Arndt had authority to enter the dwellings of others, citing to *Williams v. Feather Sound*, 386 So. 2d 1238 (Fla. App. 1980), the case mentioned briefly in Chapter 3 when discussing the duty of care of an employer.]

Notes

1. The opinions in the above case recognize that in some circumstances a defrauded person can lose his claim if he has not acted reasonably. Although the defense of contributory negligence ordinarily is rejected when dealing with an intentional tort (query, however, whether this applies when the liability being asserted for the intentional tort is vicarious, as it is with an innocent principal, rather than direct), nevertheless the defrauded person is not able to hold the principal liable if he "should know or otherwise has notice that an agent is acting for his own purposes or is otherwise violating his authority. . . ." Restatement (Second) § 262, cmt. c.

An example of a defense based on the plaintiff's conduct is provided by the case of *Farm Bureau Co-op Mill & Supply, Inc. v. Blue Star Foods*, 238 F.2d 326, 335–36 (8th Cir. 1956). In that case, plaintiff, a seller of goods to the defendant principal, endorsed in blank five sight drafts drawn on the principal and made payable to plaintiff. Defendant's agent, through whom plaintiff dealt, cashed the drafts and appropriated the money to his own use. The court stated:

> If we assume that plaintiff and defendant were equally innocent of the fraud, then the rule that, where one of two innocent parties must suffer, he who made the fraud possible must bear the loss, is applicable. Plaintiff endorsed these five sight drafts without ever looking to see what they were. . . . [T]he plaintiff, and not the defendant, should bear the loss resulting from his negligence.

Another way of expressing this, using the language of economic analysis, is that the plaintiff in *Blue Star Foods* was the cheapest cost avoider.

2. *Exculpatory clauses.* The risk that an agent will make misrepresentations to a third party that it is not authorized to make is a real one. Principals often try to avoid the consequences of unauthorized, or even tortious, misrepresentations by including a provision in the contract with the third party disclaiming the agent's authority and limiting the principal's liability to the representations and warranties contained in the written agreement. The extent to which such disclaimers are effective is a question of both contract law and agency law. *See* Restatement (Third) § 7.08, cmt. (c)(4). In *Dembrowski v. Central Construction Co.*, 186 Neb. 624, 185 N.W.2d 461 (1971),

for instance, a home improvements contract providing for the purchase and installation of aluminum siding contained a clause that disclaimed the agent's authority to represent to purchasers that purchasers' home would be designated as a "model home" entitling the purchasers to a rebate on their contract. Nevertheless, the agent told purchasers that they would not have to pay for the improvements because their home would be designated as a model home. The purchasers were aware of the disclaimer, but there was no evidence that the principal was aware of its agents' misconduct. When the purchasers subsequently sued for reformation, the Supreme Court of Nebraska reversed a lower court ruling in their favor, citing Restatement (Second) § 166: "A person with notice of a limitation of an agent's authority cannot subject the principal to liability upon a transaction with the agent if he should know that the agent is acting improperly."

In contrast to *Dembrowski*, the court in *King v. Horizon Corp.*, 701 F.2d 1313, 1318 (10th Cir. 1983) affirmed a lower court judgment that awarded plaintiff damages for the deceit of defendant's agent. Plaintiffs purchased property from the defendant pursuant to a land sale contract that included an acknowledgment by the purchasers "that [they have] relied solely upon the representations contained herein . . . that no guarantee of appreciation, resale or repurchase has been given." Seller's agent, however, orally represented to purchasers that the land had a then present value far in excess of its actual value. The court noted the limitations on the effectiveness of a disclaimer:

> The fraud of an agent may be attributed to the principal in a number of ways. First, it is clear that where the principal knows of and encourages the fraudulent behavior of his agent he is going to be liable for that fraudulent behavior himself and cannot avoid that liability through the use of a disclaimer clause. Second, if the principal accepts the fruits of the fraud, with knowledge of the misrepresentations by which the fraud was accomplished, he has ratified the fraudulent act and will be liable for it. Third . . . a principal may be liable for the fraud of his agent where he exercises an inadequate amount of supervision over that agent.

As the facts indicated that the defendant was aware of its agent's fraudulent conduct, the court held that the disclaimer was ineffective to protect the principal:

> In spite of this knowledge [defendant] failed to put a stop to the misrepresentations and continued to accept the sales procured by the defrauding agents. By virtue of [defendant's] lack of action the trial court could have reasonably determined . . . that [defendant] either ratified a sale that it knew was procured by fraud or had engaged in such inadequate supervision that it ought to have reasonably anticipated the further fraud of its agent and taken supervisory steps to avoid it. *Id.* at 1319.

Problems

1. Every morning, Roth, a customer of First National State Bank, would withdraw substantial amounts of cash to use in his check cashing business. A teller employed by the bank who was aware of Roth's routine tipped off several unsavory friends of hers, describing Roth, his car and his habits. Roth was robbed of his cash and, upon discovering the facts, sued the bank. Would it be relevant whether the teller handled Roth's withdrawal transaction on the day of the robbery? Would it make a difference if she did not generally handle his transactions and instead obtained the information she passed on to the robbers through observation of others while at work? *See Roth v. First Nat'l State Bank*, 404 A.2d 1182 (N.J. Super. 1979).

2. Art Tucker was a truck driver for the Sanitary Milk Company for four years. The Milk Company sold milk to Brook Store, a large retail grocery store. After delivery, Tucker routinely presented a bill for the milk delivered to Brook's receiving clerk, who would check off the items and sign the bill. Tucker would then take the signed bill to the cashier, Brook's paying clerk, in a different part of the store, for payment in cash. Unfortunately, Tucker devised a scheme by which he inserted carbon paper and an additional sheet, showing a much larger delivery, directly underneath the true bill prior to presenting the true bill to the receiving clerk for signature. He would then present the false bill, complete with the signature of the receiving clerk, to the paying clerk and pocket the difference. This went on for nearly three years. Tucker pocketed over $20,000 from this fraudulent activity. Brook has discovered the scheme and sues the Milk Company for the losses. Should Brook prevail?

Chapter 6

The Undisclosed Principal

Assume that Ms. Jones, a wealthy woman, arranges with a resident of a resort community to have the resident purchase in his own name but actually on behalf of Jones substantial tracts of land in his community, such as a wealthy industrialist from Chicago is reported to have had done for him in Aspen, Colorado after World War II. Jones is an "undisclosed principal" under this arrangement. After a number of contracts have been made, Jones wants to step in and enforce them against the owners in her own name. Should she be able to do so? What, if anything, would give you pause before answering yes, assuming that no misrepresentations had taken place?

Would your answer change or be easier to reach if the agent had disclosed to the contracting parties that he was acting on "someone's" behalf, but refused to disclose his principal's identity? The principal under this circumstance is referred to as a "partially disclosed principal" [a term apparently coined by the Restatement (First) of Agency][1] or as an "unidentified principal," which is the term adopted by the Restatement (Third) in § 1.04(2)(c).

Would you have any difficulty answering the initial question if the agent expressly disclosed that he was acting on behalf of Jones, the out-of-town principal?

Under which of the above situations would the agent personally be liable on the contract?

---

1. The terminology of the Restatement (Second) is defined in § 4 as follows:
   (1) If, at the time of a transaction conducted by an agent, the other party thereto has notice that the agent is acting for a principal and of the principal's identity, the principal is a disclosed principal.
   (2) If the other party has notice that the agent is or may be acting for a principal but has no notice of the principal's identity, the principal for whom the agent is acting is a partially disclosed principal.
   (3) If the other party has no notice that the agent is acting for a principal, the one for whom he acts is an undisclosed principal.

A. Rights of the Undisclosed Principal

Restatement (Third) of Agency

§ 6.03 Agent For Undisclosed Principal

When an agent acting with actual authority makes a contract on behalf of an undisclosed principal,

(1) unless excluded by the contract, the principal is a party to the contract;

(2) the agent and the third party are parties to the contract; and

(3) the principal, if a party to the contract, and the third party have the same rights, liabilities, and defenses against each other as if the principal made the contract personally, subject to §§ 6.05–6.09.

What accounts for this unusual doctrine, where a person can become a party to a contract in the absence of a manifestation of mutual assent? Also, the doctrine appears to endorse prearranged misleading behavior. The agent is pretending to be contracting on his own behalf, like the agent for Ms. Jones, when actually he is acting on behalf of and pursuant to the instructions of a principal who is camouflaging her role in the transaction. Why do courts tolerate this?

The above questions will be answered in part as these materials address the protections extended to the third party. Also, the law of assignment of rights and duties under contracts makes a substantial inroad into the notion that a contractual relationship is inherently personal. In addition, it can be argued that the undisclosed principal doctrine fills a practical need. Consider, for example, the problem of the holdout in a land acquisition setting. Suppose a person who does not enjoy the power of eminent domain attempts to assemble a tract of land for a large-scale project. The land currently is owned by many different people. The early purchases will be at current market value. But as the word gets out, the remaining owners, aware of the vulnerable position of the buyer, will hold out for a price vastly inflated over current market value. *See* RICHARD A. POSNER, ECONOMIC ANALYSIS OF LAW 56 (4th ed. 1992). In this situation the undisclosed principal doctrine becomes of practical importance to the buyer. *See* Peter Hellman, *How They Assembled the Most Expensive Block in New York's History*, 7 NEW YORK, Feb. 25, 1974, at 30 (describing the land assemblage for the Citicorp building); Charlotte Allen, *The Mouse That Roared into Orlando's Economy*, INSIGHT, Oct. 30, 1989, pp. 8, 13 ("So, using middlemen, stealth, and more than 100 dummy corporations, he [Walt Disney] went on a secret land-buying spree near Orlando, paying about $400 an acre." Disney bought "28,000 acres—an area twice the size of Manhattan.").

1. Assertion of Rights by the Undisclosed Principal

As is made clear by Restatement (Third) § 6.03, when a contract is made by an agent for an undisclosed principal, the principal can enforce the contract. One important application of this concept is that if the principal notifies the third party who entered into the contract with the agent to make payment under the contract directly to the principal, the third party is bound to do so, and payment to the agent after such notice will not relieve the third party of liability to the principal. To some extent, this rule of law is counterintuitive, as many people would believe that making payment in accordance with the contract should relieve the payor of further liability. For instance, in *Darling-Singer Lumber Co. v. Commonwealth*, 290 Mass. 488, 195 N.E. 723 (1935), the defendant, a contractor, ordered a large amount of lumber from A. C. Place, to be shipped from the west coast to defendant's job site. Place ran his own business and defendant thought he was dealing directly with him. Place was in fact acting for the plaintiff Darling-Singer Lumber Company. The lumber arrived with an invoice on the letterhead of Darling-Singer Lumber Company accompanying the bill of lading. Also accompanying the invoice and bill of lading was a notice from F. P. Gram Co., reading, "We enclose herewith duly assigned to us invoice and bill of lading covering cars containing lumber sold and shipped to you by Darling-Singer Lumber Company. . . . We are entitled to the proceeds under this assignment and look to you for payment of the same. Please remit directly to us." On the invoice was typed what purported to be an assignment of the account by Darling-Singer Co. to F. P. Gram Co. Both companies were located in Portland, Oregon.

Defendant had never heard of either company. He paid Place in full and in good faith, having been told at the time he ordered the lumber that the lumber was being shipped from Place's western office in Portland or from his mill. He did not understand the legal significance of the documents mailed to him, and regarded Place as the only one with whom he had contracted and the only one to whom he owed any obligation of payment.

Place failed to remit to plaintiff. Thereafter F. P. Gram Co. reassigned the account to plaintiff. Plaintiff successfully sued defendant for the full contract price.

For a more recent case recognizing the right of an undisclosed principal to be treated as a party to the contract, see *Lenart v. Ragsdale*, 385 N.W.2d 282, 284 (Mich. App. 1986). In that case a land contract was executed by plaintiffs as vendors and one Gorecki as vendee. The following day the contract was assigned by Gorecki to defendant, with plaintiffs' consent. Payments were not made under the contract and plaintiffs sued to foreclose. Defendant raised a usury defense, contending that she was an undisclosed principal and Gorecki her agent. The trial court rejected this defense and granted a summary judgment for plaintiff. This decision was reversed on appeal. The opinion of the appellate court stated in relevant part as follows:

> Assuming that a usury defense is available, there exists a material issue of fact concerning whether defendant was an assignee or an undisclosed principal. If defendant is an assignee, she may not avail herself of a usury defense since such a defense is personal and not available to assignees. However, under Michigan law, an undisclosed principal may sue on his own behalf for the breach of a contract entered into on his behalf by his agent or for the breach of a legal duty related to that contract and may claim the benefits

of such contract. Since an undisclosed principal is treated as a party to the contract with respect to the obligations and benefits under the contract, it follows that the principal would be entitled to raise the defense of usury absent a statute to the contrary.

Are the outcomes in *Darling-Singer* and *Lenart* equitable?

2. Parol Evidence Rule

What effect does the parol evidence rule, which ordinarily does not allow variations from or additions to an integrated contract, have on application of the undisclosed principal doctrine? The following language from the classic case of *Ford v. Williams*, 62 U.S. (21 How.) 287, 289 (1858), expresses the nearly universal response of courts to this issue:

> Notwithstanding the rule of law that an agreement reduced to writing may not be contradicted or varied by parol, it is well settled that the principal may show that the agent who made the contract in his own name was acting for him. This proof does not contradict the writing; it only explains the transaction. But the agent, who binds himself, will not be allowed to contradict the writing by proving that he was contracting only as agent, while the same evidence will be admitted to charge the principal. "Such evidence (says Baron Parke) does not deny that the contract binds those whom on its face it purports to bind, but shows that it also binds another, by reason that the act of the agent is the act of the principal." See *Higgins v. Senior* (8 Messon & Wilsby 834).

Accord Restatement (Third) § 6.03, cmt. c. Parol evidence is forbidden, however, if the contract by its terms excludes the principal as a party.

3. Sealed Contracts

Suppose that a contract bears a seal. At common law this had specific legal consequences. The authority of an agent signing a sealed instrument had to be under seal. Also, the agent's principal could not sue or be sued unless his name appeared on the instrument. The latter rule affected the undisclosed principal doctrine, of course. A number of states have passed legislation abolishing the legal effect of the seal. *See* P. MECHEM, OUTLINES OF THE LAW OF AGENCY §§ 25, 318 (4th ed. 1952); Uniform Commercial Code § 2-203 (1978 Official Text) (abolishing the legal effect of seals insofar as contracts for sale of or offers to buy or sell goods are concerned). The Restatement (Third) § 6.03, Comment f, emphatically rejects the common law and Restatement (Second) view on the effect of sealed instruments:

> *f. Sealed and negotiable instruments.* Unless a statute provides otherwise, a principal has rights under and is subject to liability on a contract whether or not the contract is under seal. This is so whether the principal

is disclosed, unidentified, or undisclosed. See § 6.01, Comment *f*, for discussion of this point as it concerns disclosed principals. In contrast, under Restatement Second, Agency § 191, an undisclosed principal is not liable as a party to a sealed instrument in the absence of a statute providing otherwise. Under Restatement Second, Agency § 296, in the absence of statute, an obligor named in a sealed instrument given to an agent on behalf of a principal is not subject to liability to the principal in an action at law unless the principal appears in the instrument as a covenantee.

Any general distinction between sealed and unsealed contracts has been abolished by statute in many states. Additionally, U.C.C. § 2-203 makes law respecting sealed instruments inapplicable to contracts for the sale of goods or offers for such contracts. At the time of completion of Restatement Second, Contracts, the seal's "decay" had reached the point that it had come to seem "archaic" and its principal legal consequence was often only the application of a longer statute of limitations, as opposed to more substantive consequences. *See* Restatement Second, Contracts, Chapter 4, Topic 3, Introductory Note. Many cases from the 20th century that consider the question do not permit an undisclosed principal to avoid liability on a contract when the contract recites that it is made under seal. Some cases reach this conclusion in the absence of legislation abolishing distinctions between sealed and unsealed contracts.

In the absence of a controlling statute, ascribing significance to the presence or absence of a seal is inconsistent with the expectations of most contemporary parties. Many parties, if they are aware of the question, may well believe that sealing no longer carries operative significance because so many significant transactions may be undertaken without seals. This likelihood is enhanced by the fact that legislative and common-law changes in many states have eliminated many operative consequences that sealing carried in the past. Moreover, legislation concerning the effect of seals is far from uniform and, as noted above, some courts have concluded that the presence or absence of a seal on a contract should not affect the rights or liabilities of an undisclosed principal even in the absence of legislation abolishing the effect of sealing as a general matter.

Moreover, the functional argument in support of the rule stated in Restatement Second, Agency §§ 191 and 296 is not strong, at least in the contemporary environment described above. The common-law rule excluding the liability of an undisclosed principal when an instrument is sealed is not necessary to enable parties, if they wish, to exclude an undisclosed principal from a contract. This is because the parties may accomplish this objective by so providing in the contract. See Comment *d* for discussion. A provision that explicitly excludes an undisclosed principal as a party from a contract, such as the provision in Illustration 5, is likely to be a more accurate manifestation of the parties' intention than the fact that the writing states that it is made "under seal," because most parties are unaware of the consequences of so stating.

4. Exceptions

The rule stated above in §6.03 of the Restatement (Third) is not without its exceptions. Suppose, for example, that a person knows that the party she wants to contract with will not deal with her due to personal enmity. She therefore hires an agent to enter into the transaction on her behalf but with instructions not to disclose the fact that he is doing so. Can she step in after the contract is made and enforce it? Would your answer vary if the undisclosed principal merely suspected that the third party would not deal with her personally? An example of this would be where the undisclosed principal and the other party are competitors, and the principal is afraid that the other party will not deal with her. The following case addresses these questions.

Kelly Asphalt Block Co. v. Barber Asphalt Paving Co.

Court of Appeals of New York
105 N.E. 88 (1914)

Appeal from a judgment of the Appellate Division of the Supreme Court in the second judicial department, entered November 6, 1912, affirming a judgment in favor of plaintiff entered upon a verdict.

The nature of the action and the facts, so far as material, are stated in the opinion.

CARDOZO, J.

The plaintiff sues to recover damages for breach of an implied warranty. The contract was made between the defendant and one Booth. The plaintiff says that Booth was in truth its agent, and it sues as undisclosed principal. The question is whether it has the right to do so.

The general rule is not disputed. A contract not under seal, made in the name of an agent as ostensible principal, may be sued on by the real principal at the latter's election. The defendant says that we should establish an exception to that rule, where the identity of the principal has been concealed because of the belief that, if it were disclosed, the contract would not be made. We are asked to say that the reality of the defendant's consent is thereby destroyed, and the contract vitiated for mistake.

The plaintiff and the defendant were competitors in business. The plaintiff's president suspected that the defendant might refuse to name him a price. The suspicion was not based upon any previous refusal, for there had been none; it had no other origin than their relation as competitors. Because of this doubt the plaintiff availed itself of the services of Booth, who, though interested to the defendant's knowledge in the plaintiff's business, was also engaged in a like business for another corporation. Booth asked the defendant for a price and received a quotation, and the asphalt blocks required for the plaintiff's pavement were ordered in his name. The order was accepted by the defendant, the blocks were delivered, and payment was made by Booth with money furnished by the plaintiff. The paving blocks were unmerchantable, and the defendant, retaining the price, contests its liability for damages on the ground that if it had known that the plaintiff was the principal it would have refused to make the sale.

We are satisfied that upon the facts before us the defense cannot prevail. A contract involves a meeting of the minds of the contracting parties. If "one of the supposed parties is wanting," there is an absence of "one of the formal constituents of a legal transaction." (*Rodliff v. Dallinger*, 141 Mass. 1, 6). In such a situation there is no contract. A number of cases are reported where A has ordered merchandise of B, and C has surreptitiously filled the order. The question has been much discussed whether C, having thrust himself without consent into the position of a creditor, is entitled to recover the value of his wares. That question is not before us, and we express no opinion concerning it. We state it merely to accentuate the distinction between the cases which involve it and the case at hand. Neither of the supposed parties was wanting in this case. The apparent meeting of the minds between determinate contracting parties was not unreal or illusory. The defendant was contracting with the precise person with whom it intended to contract. It was contracting with Booth. It gained whatever benefit it may have contemplated from his character and substance. An agent who contracts in his own name for an undisclosed principal does not cease to be a party because of his agency. Indeed, such an agent, having made himself personally liable, may enforce the contract though the principal has renounced it. As between himself and the other party, he is liable as principal to the same extent as if he had not been acting for another. It is impossible in such circumstances to hold that the contract collapses for want of parties to sustain it. The contractual tie cannot exist where there are not persons to be bound, but here persons were bound, and those the very persons intended. If Booth had given the order in his own right and for his own benefit, but with the expectation of later assigning it to the plaintiff, that undisclosed expectation would not have nullified the contract. His undisclosed intention to act for a principal who was unknown to the defendant, was equally ineffective to destroy the contract in its inception.

If, therefore, the contract did not fail for want of parties to sustain it, the unsuspected existence of an undisclosed principal can supply no ground for the avoidance of a contract unless fraud is proved. We must distinguish between mistake, such as we have been discussing, which renders the contract void *ab initio*, because the contractual tie has never been completely formed, and fraud, which renders it voidable at the election of the defrauded party. *Rodliff v. Dallinger*, 141 Mass. 1, 6. In the language of Holmes, J., in the case cited: "Fraud only becomes important, as such, when a sale or contract is complete in its formal elements, and therefore valid unless repudiated, but the right is claimed to rescind it." If one who is in reality an agent denies his agency when questioned, and falsely asserts that his principal has no interest in the transaction, the contract, it may be, becomes voidable, not because there is a want of parties, but because it has been fraudulently procured. That was substantially the situation in *Winchester v. Howard*, 97 Mass. 303. When such a case arises, we shall have to consider whether a misrepresentation of that kind is always so material as to justify rescission after the contract has been executed. But no such situation is disclosed in the case at hand. Booth made no misrepresentation to the defendant. He was not asked anything, nor did he say anything, about the plaintiff's interest in the transaction. Indeed, neither he nor the plaintiff's officers knew whether the defendant would refuse to deal with the plaintiff directly. They suspected hostility, but none had been expressed. The validity of the contract turns thus, according to the defendant, not on any overt act of either the plaintiff or its agent, but on the presence or absence of a mental state. We are asked to hold that a contract complete in form becomes a nullity in fact because of a secret belief in the mind of the undisclosed principal that the disclosure of his name would be prejudicial to the completion of the bargain. We cannot go so far. It is unnecessary, therefore, to consider whether, even if fraud were shown, the defendant, after the contract was executed, could be permitted to rescind without restoring the difference between the price received for the defective blocks and their reasonable value. It is also unnecessary to analyze the evidence for the purpose of showing that the defendant, after notice of the plaintiff's interest in the transaction, continued to make delivery, and thereby waived the objection that the contract was invalid.

Other rulings complained of by the defendant have been considered, but no error has been found in them.

The judgment should be affirmed, with costs.

WILLARD BARTLETT, CH. J., WERNER, CHASE, COLLIN, CUDDEBACK and HOGAN, JJ., concur.

Judgment affirmed.

Finley v. Dalton

Supreme Court of South Carolina
164 S.E.2d 763 (1968)

LEWIS, JUSTICE.

Plaintiff brought this action in equity to rescind a deed to real estate because of alleged fraudulent misrepresentations or concealment on the part of the buyer relative to his intended use of the property. The matter is here on appeal by plaintiff from an order of the lower court sustaining a demurrer to the complaint for failure to state a cause of action.

The factual allegations of the complaint, which are deemed true for the purposes of demurrer, are to the effect that prior to February 10, 1964, unknown to plaintiff, the defendant Duke Power Company formulated a plan to acquire a large area of land in Pickens and Oconee Counties, South Carolina, for the purpose of constructing a large hydroelectric power project; that on or about February 8, 1964 the defendant, Roy S. Dalton, who was then an undisclosed real estate acquisition agent for the defendant Duke Power Company, went to plaintiff's office and represented that he, Dalton, was interested in acquiring a 138 acre tract of land in Pickens County, to which plaintiff held equitable title, and wished to complete the purchase promptly. Plaintiff thereupon inquired of Dalton "why he wished to purchase this property and why he wished to conclude the transaction so rapidly." In response to this inquiry, instead of truthfully disclosing his purchase of the property for defendant Duke Power Company at a large profit for himself, Dalton falsely "represented to plaintiff that he had just come into a large sum of money which he wished to reinvest promptly in a long range timber investment for his children and that he wished to purchase plaintiff's land for that purpose since he already owned an adjoining tract." It is then alleged "that such tract of land had a value for hydroelectric purposes, and other purposes for which the corporate defendants were acquiring property, of approximately Two Hundred and No/100 ($200.00) Dollars an acre and that, if it had not been for the false and fraudulent representations of the defendant, Dalton, the plaintiff could have disposed of such property to the corporate defendants for a price of not less than Twenty-seven Thousand and No/100 ($27,000.00) Dollars."

Following the foregoing negotiations, plaintiff sold the 138 acre tract of land to defendant Dalton on February 10, 1964 for the sum of $4100.00 and transferred to him a fee simple title to the property. On March 31, 1965, about thirteen months later, plaintiff attempted to rescind the deed and tendered to Dalton the purchase price paid, with interest to the date of tender. Dalton refused to agree to a rescission of the deed and, on July 15, 1967, approximately three and one-half years after the sale, this action was brought by plaintiff seeking to have the deed rescinded upon the ground that Dalton had misrepresented to plaintiff at the time of sale the purpose for which he was buying the land.

We agree with the trial judge that the complaint fails to allege facts sufficient to show that the alleged misrepresentation or concealment was a material one and that plaintiff was induced to sell because thereof. Such showing is necessary to maintain an action for rescission. . . .

The general rule governing the necessity of disclosure by a vendee of facts relative to the intended use of property being purchased by him was thus stated in *Holly Hill Lumber v. McCoy*, 23 S.E.2d 372 as follows:

> The conclusion is clearly established by the decisions that under ordinary circumstances, there being no previously existing fiduciary relation between the parties, and no confidence being expressly reposed by the vendor in the vendee with reference to the particular transaction, no duty rests upon the vendee to disclose facts which he may happen to know advantageous to the vendor, facts concerning the thing to be sold which would enhance its value or tend to cause the vendor to demand a higher price, and the like; so that failure to disclose would not be a fraudulent concealment. The reason is evident. If it were otherwise, such a principle must extend

to every case in which the buyer of an estate happened to have a clearer discernment of its real value than the seller. It is, therefore not only necessary that great advantage should be taken in such a contract, and that such advantage should arise from superiority of skill or information; but it is also necessary to show some obligation binding the party to make such a disclosure. Of course, each case must depend upon its own circumstances.

A misstatement or misrepresentation made in the negotiations for the purchase of land as to the use which the purchaser intends to make of the land or the purpose for which he wants it does not necessarily constitute fraud, especially where the use for a different purpose from that stated does not injuriously affect the vendor by reason of his ownership of other land in the vicinity. A false statement or representation relating to the purpose for which the purchaser is buying the land or to the use which he intends to make of it is of no consequence unless it appears that the statement or representation made was material, and that the vendor relied upon it and was induced to enter into the contract thereby. 55 Am. Jur., Vendor and Purchaser, Section 95.

The representation allegedly made in response to plaintiff's inquiry as to why Dalton wished to buy the property, while it was, under the pleadings, false, was not a representation as to the value of the land and in no way operated as an inducement to plaintiff to sell. It is conceded that no fiduciary relationship existed between the parties. Nothing appears which would indicate that plaintiff in any way relied upon the statement of Dalton, nor is there any indication that plaintiff intended the inquiry as a solicitation of information upon which to base the sale. Presumably plaintiff was familiar with the land and there is no allegation that it did not bring its fair market value at the time of the sale. The alleged misrepresentation simply amounted to a failure to disclose the fact that the land was being acquired for Duke Power Company for its planned hydroelectric project. While plaintiff alleges that the value of the land for hydroelectric purposes was in excess of that received by him, this allegation, when construed with other parts of the complaint, is nothing more than a statement that he would have demanded more money if Dalton had revealed the purpose for which the property was being purchased.

Plaintiff contends however that he made inquiry of defendant Dalton as to the purpose of his buying the property and that, when the inquiry was made, a duty arose on the part of Dalton to either remain silent or else give a full and truthful answer, relying upon the following statement from *Holly Hill Lumber Co. v. McCoy, supra*:

> While the rules of equity which we have hereinabove stated, as they relate to fraud and concealment on the part of a vendee, are generally recognized and accepted by the Courts, it is agreed that an informed vendee must limit himself to silence in order to escape the imputation of fraud. If in addition to the party's silence there is any statement, even in word or act on his part, which tends affirmatively to a suppression of the truth, or to a withdrawal

or distraction of the other party's attention or observation from the real facts, the line is overstepped, and the concealment becomes fraudulent.

While the foregoing is a sound principle, it applies only to material representations and is inapplicable to the present factual situation. Here, as previously pointed out, the complaint fails to allege facts sufficient to show that the alleged misrepresentation or concealment was material and that plaintiff was thereby induced to sell.

Affirmed.

Moss, C.J., Bussey and Littlejohn, JJ., and Clarence E. Singletary, Acting Associate Justice, concur.

Notes

1. As indicated above, the law is clear that a third party is not bound if an agent falsely states that he is not acting for a principal and if the third party would not have dealt with the principal as a party to the contract (thereby making the misrepresentation material to the contract, an important point as *Finley* demonstrates). Restatement (Third) §6.11(4). The comments to §6.11 also apply this limitation to the situation where no express misrepresentation is made, but the undisclosed principal and the agent know that the third party would not deal with the principal, and the agent fails to disclose the existence of the principal. In addition, the third party is not bound where the agent is innocent.

What is the effect of the law allowing assignment of contracts on this? Could the principal avoid these limitations on the undisclosed principal doctrine by having her agent contract directly with the third party and then assign the contract to her? The answer is no, isn't it, if the facts subsequently are fully revealed? Do you see why? *See Kline v. Gutzler*, 464 N.E.2d 399 (Mass. App. 1984). In this case co-plaintiff (Shada), who had been told by defendant (Gutzler) that she did not want to sell the property in dispute to him under any circumstances, obtained specific performance as assignee of a contract of sale of the property that Gutzler made with Kline, who represented to her that he was buying it for himself. Shada brought the suit jointly with Kline. He succeeded because Gutzler was unable to prove that Kline was acting on Shada's behalf at the time the contract to buy her property was made. The court strongly implied that Shada would not have been able to enforce the contract if a pre-existing relationship between Shada and Kline had been proven.

2. There also is authority stating that if a contract expressly refers to the agent as principal, or if the language of the contract indicates an intent to treat the agent as a sole contracting party, the undisclosed principal cannot enforce it as a party, or be held liable in such capacity. *See Arnold's of Mississippi v. Clancy*, 171 So. 2d 152, 154 (Miss. 1965) (clause in lease prohibiting subletting without landlord's consent held to exclude undisclosed principal. "The [provision against subletting] is an express exclusion of liability to any other lessee than Arnold's, Inc.. . . . Lessor has a right to elect the person with whom he will deal. There are elements of confidence other than credit involved in leasing property."); *Cooper v. Epstein*, 308 A.2d 781,

783 (D.C. App. 1973) (an undisclosed principal "simply cannot sue where to do so would violate a term of the written contract"). Does a clause prohibiting assignment of the contract without consent operate to trigger this limitation? Comment c to Restatement (Second) § 303 states that such clause may operate "as evidence" of intent to exclude an undisclosed principal, but does not in itself prevent suit by the principal on the contract. Similarly, Comment d to Restatement (Third) § 6.03 states: "An undisclosed principal is not excluded from a contract by language stating that the contract is not assignable."

3. Another limitation on the rights of an undisclosed principal to enforce in its own name the contract made by its agent is that it cannot tender its own performance if the third party has a substantial interest in receiving the performance of the agent. Restatement (Third) § 6.03, cmt. d; *Birmingham Matinee Club v. McCarty*, 152 Ala. 571, 44 So. 642 (1907) (undisclosed principal cannot, over the objection of the third party, tender its warranty deed in substitute for warranty deed of its agent).

4. Assume that the agent of Ms. Jones, the undisclosed principal mentioned at the beginning of this chapter, transfers the land he has purchased for Jones to someone else. Can Jones assert any rights against that party? See § 307A of the Restatement (Second), noting that the transferee will prevail against the undisclosed principal if he pays value and takes without notice of the principal's interest, on the reasoning that the agent is transferring legal title to the property. The principal "has only an equitable interest, as indicated by the fact that his rights in the contract are limited by the agent's rights." *Id.*, cmt. a.

B. Liabilities of the Undisclosed Principal

1. Authorized Transactions

It is clear from the above authority that ordinarily an undisclosed principal can sue as a party to the contract. Should the converse be true, and the third party be able to hold a reluctant undisclosed principal as a party to the contract, if it discovers the principal's existence? One might ask why the third party should be able to since it was satisfied with the name and credit of the agent at the time it entered into the contract. An inability to sue the principal would not result in any loss of reasonable expectations, would it?

Restatement (Third) § 6.03 states the general rule, which is that the principal is bound by the contract and can be sued by the party contracting with the agent. The theory behind this rule is that, since the principal initiated the activities of the agent and has a right to control them, he is liable in accordance with the ordinary principles of agency. *See also* W. Muller-Freienfels, *The Undisclosed Principal*, 16 Mod. L. Rev. 299, 300 (1953) ("It is the undisclosed principal who gets the advantages and disadvantages of the contract in the end. He is the one who authorized the agent and thereby induced the whole transaction...."); Mechem, *The Liability of an Undisclosed Principal*, 23 HARV. L. REV. 513 (1910); Lewis, *The Liability of the Undisclosed Principal in Contract*, 9 COLUM. L. REV. 116 (1909); Ames, *Undisclosed Principal—His Rights and Liabilities*, 18 YALE L.J. 443 (1909).

a. Remedies of the Third Party

The third party has the customary contractual remedies against the agent, of course. The agent signed the agreement as a contracting party. The fact that, unknown to the third party, he was acting on behalf of an undisclosed principal does not reduce or destroy his contractual liability. And, as noted above, the undisclosed principal is liable to the third party in accordance with principles of agency law.

b. The Election Rule

Can the third party sue both the principal and the agent in one suit and get judgments against both, followed by execution against the assets of either or both until the amount owing is paid? Comment a to § 186 of the Restatement (Second) states the following with respect to the rights of the third party against both the agent and the undisclosed principal:

> The American decisions are illogical, but more equitable[2] in holding that if the third person with knowledge of the facts obtains judgment against either one, he cannot have judgment against the other, although if he obtains judgment against the agent with no knowledge of the identity of the principal, he can later get judgment against the principal. Neither the American nor English courts give reasons, aside from authority, why the third person should not have a right to two judgments, one based on the agreement itself, the other based on the contract created by law upon the agreement.

The traditional American rule thus did not allow the third party to sue both the agent and the principal, obtain judgments against them, and execute on the judgments until it receives satisfaction. Although it is procedurally possible to join both the agent and the principal in the suit, the third party was forced to choose from whom it wishes to obtain judgment. This is known as the election rule. It has been the target of considerable criticism. *See* Michael L. Richmond, *Scraping Some Moss from the Old Oaken Doctrine: Election Between Undisclosed Principals and Agents and Discovery of Their Net Worth*, 66 MARQ. L. REV. 745 (1983); Mark A. Sargent & Arnold Rochvarg, *A Reexamination of the Agency Doctrine of Election*, 36 U. MIAMI L. REV. 411 (1982); Merrill, *Election (Undisclosed Agency) Revisited*, 34 NEB. L. REV. 613 (1955); Merrill, *Election Between Agent and Undisclosed Principal: Shall We Follow the Restatement?*, 12 NEB. L. BULL. 100 (1933).

---

2. [More equitable, in the Restatement view, than the English decisions, which hold that the third person has only one right that can be exercised in the alternative against the principal or the agent, but not against both, regardless of his knowledge. —Eds.]

The Restatement (Third) § 6.09 abandoned the election rule. Comment c explains the rationale that underlay the reversal from the Restatement (Second):

Although the election rule is supported by many cases, the better rule, stated in several recent and well-reasoned opinions and by statute in New York, is that only the satisfaction of a judgment discharges the liability of an undisclosed principal or an agent who made a contract on behalf of an undisclosed principal. The "satisfaction" rule is consistent with the contemporary view that a judgment against one person who is liable for a loss does not terminate the claim that the injured party may have against another party who may also be liable for the loss. See Restatement Second, Judgments § 49.

Whatever may have been the theoretical justification for the election rule, its practical consequences are not justifiable. The election rule operates adversely to third parties who, at the point of obtaining judgment, err in predicting whether principal or agent will have sufficient assets to satisfy the judgment at the later point when execution is attempted on the judgment. The rule also operates adversely when neither principal nor agent alone has sufficient assets to satisfy a judgment. Sections 210 and 337 in Restatement Second, Agency, attempted to ameliorate the third party's predicament by noting that it may be procedurally possible to join both principal and agent in the same action and to elect between them only once evidence has been taken. Some states permit judgment to be entered against both principal and agent when they do not force the third party to make an election. See Restatement Second, Agency § 210, Comment b. Moreover, if an agent has a right to indemnity or exoneration from the principal, the third party may be able to reach that right as an asset of the agent. Id.

Notwithstanding these ameliorative possibilities, Comment a to Restatement Second, Agency § 210 characterized as "inconsistent with the basic reason underlying the liability of the undisclosed principal" the doctrine that a third party's claim under a contract is discharged when the third party obtains judgment against the agent with knowledge of the principal's identity. This basic reason is that an undisclosed principal is a party to the contract made on the principal's behalf by an agent as stated in § 6.03(1). As a party to the contract, the principal may require the third party to tender performance to the principal, unless the burdens imposed on the third party would be materially enhanced. See § 6.03, Comment d. However, the election rule operates asymmetrically. Once a third party has notice of the principal's existence, the third party's payment to or other settlement of accounts with the agent does not discharge the third party's liability to the principal unless the agent acts with actual or apparent authority. See § 6.08(2)(b). Thus, a third party may not elect between agent and principal in performing duties under the contract, and a third party may not elect whether to be sued by principal or agent.

Additionally, the election rule may be triggered by action by a third party that does not reflect a fully considered choice, as when the third party joins both principal and agent in an action on a contract and obtains a default judgment against one of them. Even when the third party joins principal and agent and, at the point of obtaining judgment, makes a considered choice between them, the third party's information about their respective abilities to satisfy a judgment may be limited.

Discharging the liability of principal and agent only upon satisfaction of a judgment is consistent with the parties' expectations. A contract creates a right to receive the agreed-to performance. Both principal and agent know that either may be called upon to satisfy the duty of performance owed to the third party. Both are in this position because they consented to a relationship of agency in which the principal's existence and identity were not revealed to third parties. As agent for an undisclosed principal, the agent is subject to the duty because the agent is the person whom the third party expected to owe a duty of performance. The principal is subject to the duty because the agent made the contract on the principal's behalf. Although the third party has a right to one full performance under the contract, principal and agent separately owe obligations to the third party. Moreover, no windfall is conferred on the third party because the contract gave the third party the right to receive the agreed-to performance.

Additionally, the election rule is not a basis on which parties plan transactions or evaluate their prospective liabilities. Its operation is not predictable because a creditor's election determines whether the judgment will run against principal or agent.

If a third party obtains a judgment against a principal or against the agent and the judgment is not fully satisfied, the third party's recovery against both parties may not exceed the amount of the judgment. See Restatement Second, Judgments § 49, Comment c.

2. Unauthorized Transactions

On first impression one would think that the undisclosed principal would not be exposed to liability for unauthorized transactions. The third party is not even aware that an agency relationship exists. It has no expectation of holding anyone liable other than the person with whom it is dealing. Thus, if a transaction is unauthorized, one could argue that the undisclosed principal should have a complete defense and the third party should have only a claim against the agent as a full contracting party, which is all it bargained for. Can you think of any argument against this position?

Watteau v. Fenwick

Queen's Bench Division
[1893] 1 Q.B. 346

Appeal from the decision of the county court judge of Middlesborough.

From the evidence it appeared that one Humble had carried on business at a beer-house called the Victoria Hotel, at Stockton-on-Tees, which business he had transferred to the defendants, a firm of brewers, some years before the present action. After the transfer of the business, Humble remained as defendants' manager; but the license was always taken out in Humble's name, and his name was painted over the door. Under the terms of the agreement made between Humble and the defendants, the former had no authority to buy any goods for the business except bottled ales and mineral waters; all other goods required were to be supplied by the defendants themselves. The action was brought to recover the price of goods delivered at the Victoria Hotel over some years, for which it was admitted that the plaintiff gave credit to Humble only: they consisted of cigars, bovril, and other articles. The learned judge allowed the claim for the cigars and bovril only, and gave judgment for the plaintiff for £22 12 s. 6 d. The defendants appealed.

Dec. 12. LORD COLERIDGE, C.J.

The judgment which I am about to read has been written by my brother Wills, and I entirely concur in it.

WILLS, J.

The plaintiff sues the defendants for the price of cigars supplied to the Victoria Hotel, Stockton-upon-Tees. The house was kept, not by the defendants, but by a person named Humble, whose name was over the door. The plaintiff gave credit to Humble, and to him alone, and had never heard of the defendants. The business, however, was really the defendants', and they had put Humble into it to manage it for them, and had forbidden him to buy cigars on credit. The cigars, however, were such as would usually be supplied to and dealt in at such an establishment. The learned county court judge held that the defendants were liable. I am of opinion that he was right.

There seems to be less of direct authority on the subject than one would expect. But I think that the Lord Chief Justice during the argument laid down the correct principle, viz., once it is established that the defendant was the real principal, the ordinary doctrine as to principal and agent applies—that the principal is liable for all the acts of the agent which are within the authority usually confided to an agent of that character, notwithstanding limitations, as between the principal and the agent, put upon that authority. It is said that it is only so where there has been a holding out of authority—which cannot be said of a case where the person supplying the goods knew nothing of the existence of a principal. But I do not think so. Otherwise, in every case of undisclosed principal, or at least in every case where the fact of there being a principal was undisclosed, the secret limitation of authority would prevail and defeat the action of the person dealing with the agent and then discovering that he was an agent and had a principal.

But in the case of a dormant partner it is clear law that no limitation of authority as between the dormant and active partner will avail the dormant partner as to things within the ordinary authority of a partner. The law of partnership is, on such a question, nothing but a branch of the general law of principal and agent, and it appears to me to be undisputed and conclusive on the point now under discussion. . . .

In my opinion this appeal ought to be dismissed with costs.

Appeal dismissed.

Note

Some doubts were raised about *Watteau* soon after it was decided. In a brief essay in 9 LAW Q. REV. 111 (1893), Sir Frederick Pollock stated as follows: "The objection that in such a case there is no holding out at all, and therefore no question of apparent authority, was met by the analogy of a dormant partner. But is a dormant partner liable merely because he is an undisclosed principal? Is it not rather because he is, by the partnership contract, liable to the same extent as the known partners?" In addition, in 39 Solicitor's J. 280, Feb. 25, 1893, an essay on the case, after observing that no room exists for liability based on any expectation of plaintiff that Humble represented another, made the following argument: "Humble being unauthorized by Messrs. Fenwick to purchase the goods in question, Humble was not in fact, on the occasion of that purchase, the agent of Messrs. Fenwick at all, and the fact that he was, unknown to the creditors, their agent on other occasions does not seem to strengthen the case against the defendants. It is clear that if Humble had paid for the goods, he could not have obtained repayment from Messrs. Fenwick on the ground of agreement. The agreement, therefore, seems to have been an immaterial circumstance in the consideration of the case."[3]

There is judicial authority in Canada that rejects the reasoning of *Watteau*. See *Sign-O-Lite Plastics v. Metropolitan Life Ins. Co.*, (1990), 73 D.L.R. (4th) 541, 547–48 (B.C.C.A.), in which the court, in strongly rejecting *Watteau*, quoted the following language from an earlier Canadian opinion:

> It seems to be straining the doctrine of ostensible agency or of holding out, to apply it in a case where the fact of agency and the holding out were unknown to the person dealing with the so-called agent at the time, and to permit that person, when he discovered that his purchaser was only an agent, to recover against the principal, on the theory that he is estopped from denying that he authorised the purchase. *It appears to me that the fact*

---

3. One would want to consider restitution liability under this analysis. That is, if the cigars had been sold in the ordinary course of business and income generated for Fenwick, principles of unjust enrichment would call for the restoration to plaintiff of benefits conferred on Fenwick.

that there was a limitation of authority is at least as important as the fact that the purchaser was an agent. The vendor did not know either of these facts, and so did not draw any conclusion involving the principal when he sold and delivered the goods. Should he be permitted, when he elects to look to the principal, to do so upon any other terms than in accordance with the actual authority given at that time? It is entirely different where there is a holding out as agent and the fact of agency is known, but where neither is an element in the bargain nor the reason why credit was given, and so not an additional security known to the vendor at the time, no equity should be raised in favour of the vendor as against the principal so as to make the latter liable. (Emphasis added by court.)

See also G.H.L. Fridman, *Agency-Agent Acting Beyond Actual Authority-Liability of Undisclosed Principals—The Demise of* Watteau v. Fenwick, 70 Can. Bar Rev. 329, 330 (1991), expressing approval of the Sign-O-Lite decision in the following terms:

One who is not apparently an agent cannot logically be said to have been held out as having any authority at all, whether based on custom, what is usual, or otherwise. The only logical way in which such a conclusion [of liability for unauthorized acts] can be reached is by starting from the premise that anyone who employs an agent and does not disclose that he is an agent, inferentially accepts liability for any and every transaction into which the undisclosed agent enters as long as such transaction has a connection with the business or other activity which has been entrusted to the undisclosed agent. The difficulty about this, however, from a practical, if not a logical point of view, is that it would expose the undisclosed principal to a potentially very wide, almost limitless liability for what the agent does. This might protect third parties transacting with the agent. It would mean that the principal has accepted a very great risk by employing an agent and allowing him to appear to be the principal.

The arguments made above are forceful. Nevertheless, a troubling fact in *Watteau* is that the arrangement adopted by Fenwick created a misleading impression that Humble was the apparent proprietor of an established business. Should Fenwick bear some responsibility for this? One could answer yes, but liability should be based on estoppel, not inherent agency power. (The concept of inherent agency power, seen earlier in Chapter 4, is expressed in the undisclosed principal context in §§ 194 and 195 of the Restatement (Second), which adopts the approach of *Watteau*. Inherent agency power liability is not based on estoppel.) Under this approach Fenwick would be estopped from denying that Humble was the owner. This would subject the apparent assets of the business to execution on a judgment against Humble. See J.S. Ewart, Estoppel by Misrepresentation 247 (1900), expressing this idea. The exposure to liability thus would be consistent with the expectations of the party (Watteau) dealing with Humble believing that Humble was the owner of the business. Watteau would have the personal liability of Humble plus a claim against the apparent assets of the business, which is all he expected to have.

As noted above, the Restatement (Third) abandons the term "inherent agency." In §2.06, however, the Restatement (Third) adopts *Watteau v. Fenwick* in these terms:

> An undisclosed principal may not rely on instructions given an agent that qualify or reduce the agent's authority to less than the authority a third party would reasonably believe the agent to have under the same circumstances if the principal had been disclosed.

Comment c following this black-letter rule explains that the focus of the rule is on the reasonable expectations of the third party. Not knowing that it is dealing with an agent, the third party has no reason to inquire into the extent of the agent's authority. To allow the principal to escape liability under these circumstances "might otherwise permit the principal opportunistically to speculate at the expense of third parties."

Senor v. Bangor Mills[4]
United States Court of Appeals, Third Circuit
211 F.2d 685 (1954)

HASTIE, CIRCUIT JUDGE.

This is a diversity case presenting a Pennsylvania controversy between a seller of certain goods and a purchaser of the same goods who did not deal with each other, but rather with a third person as a result of whose improper conduct and financial irresponsibility one of the present parties must bear a loss. The district court found that the defendant buyer was not liable to the plaintiff seller either for goods bought and sold or on a check given to the seller by the wrongdoer. The plaintiff has appealed.

These are the facts. At the time in question the demand for nylon yarn exceeded the supply which the sole producer of such yarn allocated among the members of the trade. This shortage had led to the development of a so-called "secondary" market in which some of those who purchased from the manufacturer resold yarn at a profit rather than using it themselves. Plaintiff Senor was such a seller. Defendant Bangor Mills, a very large user of nylon yarn in the manufacture of tricot, was able to maintain its production level only by frequent substantial purchases in the "secondary" market. But its known needs and economic position were such that it was asked to pay prices that were very high even for that market. Accordingly, it sought to get yarn cheaper through an intermediary.

Beginning in January 1951, Bangor utilized William Shetzline as such an intermediary. The district court found that Shetzline "was, among other things, a hosiery jobber . . . in practical control . . . of two manufacturing concerns, River Lane and H & S. . . . He also had or was supposed to have contacts with various

---

4. Noted in Warren Seavey, *Undisclosed Principal; Unsettled Problems*, 1 How. L.J. 79 (1955).

other manufacturers, which put him in a position to obtain their surplus yarn." However, Shetzline had no substantial credit of his own and thus had to make most of his purchases in the "secondary" market for cash. To enable him to proceed in this way in its interest Bangor established an account in the Peoples Bank of Langhorne, Pennsylvania in both its name and Shetzline's, upon which Shetzline could draw without using Bangor's name. As to the actual purchase of yarn, the district court found that the agreement between Bangor and Shetzline was as follows:

> Shetzline had no authority to buy any yarn at all for Bangor, except as specified and agreed to from time to time by Bangor. Originally, each time that he was able to purchase yarn he had to get in touch with Bangor and advise it of the quantity and the price and get its consent; otherwise there would be no sale. Later on, Bangor, in effect, gave its consent in advance by telling Shetzline how much yarn it would buy and at what price, but Shetzline had no more authority to buy more than the amount specified or to pay more than the price fixed than he had before.

The record further shows, and it is not disputed, that under this arrangement at the time of the transactions here in dispute Bangor had stipulated that Shetzline was not to buy yarn for Bangor at a price exceeding $10 per pound and that his purchases for its account should not exceed the unobligated balance in the bank account which Bangor had placed at his disposal. At the same time, again in the language of the district court, "Shetzline was under no obligation to buy any yarn at all for Bangor. He was entirely free to purchase as much as he wanted on his own account and sell it to manufacturers other than Bangor, or if he wished he could use it in his own manufacturing business." The record also shows that when Shetzline did supply yarn to Bangor he was not required to reveal the source.

With the foregoing arrangement in effect, Shetzline purchased yarn from many persons, paying for it out of the above described account and forwarding the yarn, after he received it, to Bangor. As to the particular transaction in suit the district court found:

> On June 19 Shetzline bought about 1250 pounds of nylon yarn from the plaintiff at $11.35 a pound and directed him to ship the yarn to River Lane, one of Shetzline's corporations, to whom Senor had shipped and billed goods on a number of prior occasions. The plaintiff sent the yarn as directed and [on June 29] received a check signed by Shetzline drawn, . . . upon the . . . account in the Peoples Bank. The yarn was delivered at Shetzline's place of business and was invoiced by Shetzline to Henry Mills [a dummy corporation for Bangor] at $10.00 a pound, but was delivered by him directly to Bangor. The check was returned unpaid because of insufficient funds.

> The plaintiff knew nothing whatever of any relationship between Shetzline and Bangor. He intended to sell the yarn to River Lane, understood

that River Lane was the buyer and made the sale entirely upon the credit of River Lane.

On all the facts one of the district court's conclusions was that "The result [of the arrangement between Shetzline and Bangor] was that a separate agency was created each time Shetzline bought yarn with Bangor's money." As we see it, this conclusion is both correct and in the present circumstances decisive against plaintiff on its claim against Bangor for goods sold and delivered.

It is axiomatic that the existence of an agency relationship and, in large measure, the area it covers are determined by whatever agreement the parties have made as to the circumstances under which the agent may and will act for the principal. In this case the district court quite properly found that Shetzline had not undertaken to buy any yarn at all for Bangor. He was free to buy for others or for himself and to disregard Bangor's needs entirely. He did not go into the market subject to an agent's fundamental undertaking and fiduciary obligation to act primarily in the interest of his principal. It was not until Shetzline actually made a particular purchase such as Bangor had agreed to accept and, by using Bangor's money to pay for it or in some other proper way, indicated the appropriation of that acquisition to Bangor's account, that Shetzline came under any obligation to Bangor. The purchase in this case made on Shetzline's credit at a price prohibited by Bangor was not within the terms of the agency. There is nothing in the record to suggest any duty of Shetzline, after the goods were delivered to him, to appropriate and redirect them to Bangor. The goods as received by Shetzline belonged to him and he was free to keep them or dispose of them to whomever he would and could.

Therefore Bangor cannot be liable as a principal on Shetzline's purchase unless some special doctrine of apparent authority, estoppel or something akin to fraud extends Bangor's responsibility beyond the agreed limits of Shetzline's agency. The only such rule which suggests itself as possibly applicable appears in Section 195 of the Agency Restatement:

> An undisclosed principal who entrusts an agent with the management of his business is subject to liability to third persons with whom the agent enters into transactions usual in such businesses and on the principal's account, although contrary to the directions of the principal.

The typical application of this rule is to a going concern with an established place of business and obvious assets operated by one who ostensibly is the proprietor but secretly is agent for an undisclosed principal. *McCracken v. Hamburger*, 1890, 139 Pa. 326, 20 A. 1051; *Hubbard v. Tenbrook*, 1889, 124 Pa. 291, 16 A. 817, 2 L.R.A. 823; *Brooks v. Shaw*, 1908, 197 Mass. 376, 84 N.E. 110; *Watteau v. Fenwick*, 1892, 1 Q.B. 346. In such cases liability is imposed upon the undisclosed principal because he has placed the agent in such apparent relationship to an observable enterprise as is likely to induce reliance upon him as a responsible proprietor. But there is no rational or equitable basis for such a doctrine unless the person dealing with the agent finds him in charge of a "business" in this sense of a functioning enterprise with observable assets. Obviously Bangor has not put Shetzline in any such deceptive situation of apparent proprietorship of a "business." Section 195 of the Restatement is not applicable to the facts of this case.

Beyond this, plaintiff has urged that we consider other doctrines enlarging the power of an agent to bind a partially disclosed principal beyond his actual authority, although such rules admittedly have no application to an undisclosed principal. But the contention that Bangor was partially disclosed misconceives the character of a partially disclosed principal. Senor thought Shetzline was the real and sole party in interest as purchaser, acquiring goods for his own personally controlled business carried on in corporate form under the River Lane name. There was no suggestion that behind Shetzline there stood any unidentified independent personality whose credit and responsibility backed the Shetzline purchase. Without such an understanding there can be no case of a partially disclosed principal.

Neither is the plaintiff's case improved by the fact that Bangor accepted the yarn from Shetzline and presumably used it in its own business. For Bangor already had supplied Shetzline with more than sufficient funds to pay for this quantity of yarn with the understanding that Shetzline would pay cash for any goods purchased on Bangor's account. Whatever Shetzline actually did with the money, Bangor having thus fully settled with him in advance, the delivery of the goods in controversy and the attendant transfer of title from Shetzline to Bangor imposed no duty of further payment to Shetzline upon Bangor. In these circumstances any claim the seller asserts against Bangor as alleged undisclosed principal of Shetzline is not strengthened by Bangor's receipt and use of the merchandise. Indeed, the majority of the American decisions hold that such good faith settlement by an undisclosed principal with his agent gives the principal a complete defense even against the third person who, on tardily discovering the principal's existence, establishes that the agent acted within the scope of his authority and asserts that the principal should bear the burden of the agent's authorized contract from which the principal has benefited. We need not decide which view represents the law of Pennsylvania, which governs this case. For even where the minority view prevails, we think the additional fact here that Bangor did not authorize the Senor-Shetzline sale would leave no room for doubt that Bangor's only duty with respect to the goods was that which it owed Shetzline as a result of the transactions between them and had satisfied before Senor made any claim.

The judgment will be affirmed.

Notes

1. See *Industrial Mfrs., Inc. v. Bangor Mills, Inc.*, 126 N.Y.S.2d 508 (App. Div. 1953), which deals with the same relationship as that involved in *Senor*. The court holds that an agent who is supplied with cash does not have the power to bind his principal to a credit transaction, under the circumstances involved in the case. (The opinion contains facts from which one can infer that Shetzline had embezzled over $50,000 from the account established by Bangor Mills.)

2. In addition to § 195 of the Restatement (Second), which is quoted in *Senor*, see Restatement (Third) § 2.06(2), quoted below, on the topic of unauthorized acts in the undisclosed principal setting:

> (2) An undisclosed principal may not rely on instructions given an agent that qualify or reduce the agent's authority to less than the authority a third party would reasonably believe the agent to have under the same circumstances if the principal had been disclosed.

What is the rationale behind this rule? Note that it is not limited to apparent ownership situations. Instead, it adopts the same broad standard of liability for the acts of general agents in disclosed agency situations (see Chapter 4).

3. *Intent of agent to act for his own purposes.* The disclosed or partially disclosed principal is liable to a third party even if its agent acts for the agent's own or other improper purposes, unless the other party has notice that the agent is not acting for the principal's benefit. Restatement (Second) § 165. Is this also true with respect to the undisclosed principal? See Restatement (Second) § 199, saying no, because there is no reliance by the other party upon the fact of an agency relationship. "The fact that the existence of the agency suggested or created the opportunity for the act is not sufficient. The only basis for the principal's liability [when it is undisclosed] is the intent of the agent to act in the principal's business." The motive of the agent can be improper and still bind the undisclosed principal, however, "if the act is performed as part of [but not necessarily in furtherance of] the principal's business." The example given is an agent deliberately ordering and selling substandard goods because she disliked her principal and wanted to give the principal's store a bad reputation.

4. Suppose an agent combines the orders of several undisclosed principals in one contract. Assume, for example, that an agent orders 500 tons of coal from T: 300 for principal A, 100 for principal B, and 100 for herself. Is each principal bound to the contract? See § 187 of the Restatement (Second), stating no (absent authorization), because neither principal has agreed to be responsible for the single, entire contract created by the agent. The principals may, however, be subject to restitutional liability for benefits received. Also, the third party could attach the agent's rights to reimbursement or exoneration. *Id.*, cmt. a.

C. Payment and Setoff

1. Payment by the Third Party

Suppose the third party pays the agent the amount owed under a contract and the agent fails to remit to his undisclosed principal, who at this stage remains unknown to the third party. Can the principal successfully sue the third party for the amount it should have received? There is no doubt about the answer to this question, at least if the agent was authorized to conceal the existence of the principal, is there? *See*

Restatement (Third) §6.07(3)(a) ("When an agent has made a contract on behalf of an undisclosed principal, until the third party has notice of the principal's existence, the third party's payment to or settlement of accounts with the agent discharges the third party's liability to the principal.").

2. Payment to the Third Party

This topic was discussed in the opinion in *Senor*, endorsing the majority rule. The minority rule was adopted by the Restatement (Second) §208 and by the Restatement (Third) §6.07, which provides:

(1) A principal's payment to or settlement of accounts with an agent discharges the principal's liability to a third party with whom the agent has made a contract on the principal's behalf only when the principal acts in reasonable reliance on a manifestation by the third party, not induced by misrepresentation by the agent, that the agent has settled the account with the third party.

(2) A third party's payment to or settlement of accounts with an agent discharges the third party's liability to the principal if the agent acts with actual or apparent authority in accepting the payment or settlement.

(3) When an agent has made a contract on behalf of an undisclosed principal,

(a) until the third party has notice of the principal's existence, the third party's payment to or settlement of accounts with the agent discharges the third party's liability to the principal;

(b) after the third party has notice of the principal's existence, the third party's payment to or settlement of accounts with the agent discharges the third party's liability to the principal if the agent acts with actual or apparent authority in accepting the payment or settlement; and

(c) after receiving notice of the principal's existence, the third party may demand reasonable proof of the principal's identity and relationship to the agent. Until such proof is received, the third party's payment to or settlement of accounts in good faith with the agent discharges the third party's liability to the principal.

In Comment d, Restatement (Third) §6.07 explains why the minority rule was preferred:

d. Undisclosed principal who pays or otherwise settles with agent. This section does not deal symmetrically with settlements made with agents by third parties and by principals who remain undisclosed at the time of the settlement. When an agent has made a contract on behalf of an undisclosed principal and while the principal's existence remains undisclosed, the rule stated in subsection (1) does not treat a payment that a principal makes in good faith to the agent as effective to discharge the principal's duty of performance to the third party unless the principal makes the payment on the basis of a manifestation from the third party that the agent has settled the account. In contrast, under subsection (3), a third party who lacks notice of the principal's existence may discharge the third party's duty to the principal by paying or otherwise settling with the agent.

This asymmetry is justified on theoretical as well as pragmatic grounds. When an agent makes a contract on behalf of an undisclosed principal, the principal becomes a party to the contract unless excluded from it, see § 6.03(1), and has the right to receive the third party's performance unless rendering performance to the principal would materially change the nature of the third party's performance. See § 6.03, Comment *d*. In exchange, an undisclosed principal has a duty of performance to the third party. That duty is not discharged by rendering performance to someone else, including the agent. Unless a duty created by a contract may be discharged on some other basis, only full performance is effective to discharge it. See Restatement Second, Contracts § 235, Comment *a*.

A principal may protect its position by making its existence credibly known to the third party and by demanding that the third party pay only the principal. The principal chose to deal on an undisclosed basis through an agent whom the principal also chose and whom the principal had the right to control. See § 1.01, Comment *f(1)*. It is the principal's choice whether to remain undisclosed after the agent has made a contract on the principal's behalf. By revealing its identity after the agent has made the contract, the principal does not risk losing the contract that binds the third party. Thus, the rule as stated in subsection (1) does not require a principal to sacrifice the benefits the principal may anticipate receiving by dealing through an agent who may make contracts on the principal's behalf without disclosing the principal's existence.

The rule stated in subsection (1) is articulated in Restatement (Second) Agency § 208. The contrary rule discharges an undisclosed principal's duty of performance to the third party when the principal pays the agent in good faith. This rule is followed by statutory codifications in five states and by a majority of U.S. cases as of the time of the drafting of Restatement Second. Subsequent cases are sparse; one controlled by a statutory codification applies the contrary rule, but those not so controlled apply the rule as stated in § 208 and subsection (1) of this Restatement.

Pragmatic grounds also justify the rule stated in subsection (1) and explain why it is preferable to the contrary rule. Under the contrary rule, the dispositive question is whether the principal paid or settled with the agent in good faith. The contrary rule places on the third party, who did not observe the interactions between agent and principal, the burden of establishing that the principal had knowledge or reason to know that the agent was insolvent or otherwise unreliable when the principal paid or otherwise settled with the agent. It may be impossible for the third party to establish, even when it is true, that the principal doubted the agent's solvency or other indicia of reliability when the principal settled with the agent. The contrary rule may also require a court to draw distinctions among fine shadings of culpability that depend on whether and why the principal may have doubted the agent's reliability. The rule stated in subsection (1) is simpler to apply than the fact-intensive and generally formulated contrary rule. Additionally, by placing the risk of an agent's dishonesty on the principal, the rule stated in subsection (1) encourages principals to exercise diligence in selecting and monitoring their agents.

3. Setoff

Section 6.06(2) of the Restatement (Third) states the rights of a third party to setoff amounts owed to it by the agent when dealing with an undisclosed principal:

(2) When an agent makes a contract on behalf of an undisclosed principal,

    (a) the third party may set off

        (i) any amount that the agent independently owed the third party at the time the agent made the contract and

        (ii) any amount that the agent thereafter independently comes to owe the third party until the third party has notice that the agent acts on behalf of a principal against an amount the third party owes the principal under the contract;

    (b) after the third party has notice that the agent acts on behalf of a principal, the third party may not set off any amount that the agent thereafter independently comes to owe the third party against an amount the third party owes the principal under the contract unless the principal consents. . . .

Oil Supply Company, Inc. v. Hires Parts Service, Inc.

Supreme Court of Indiana
726 N.E. 2d 246 (2000)

SHEPARD, CHIEF JUSTICE.

. . . In the summer of 1988, William Dolin [a commodities broker] was indebted to Oil Supply Company, Inc. in an undetermined, but substantial, amount of money. In an effort to get paid by Dolin on this outstanding debt, Oil Supply entered into an agreement with Dolin under which Dolin would arrange sales through Oil Supply. The profits of these sales would be split between Oil Supply and Dolin. A percentage of Dolin's share of the profits would be credited toward Dolin's debt with Oil Supply.

During the fall of 1988, Dolin was also indebted to Hires Parts Service, Inc., d/b/a Hires Auto Parts, in the amount of $28,080. To remedy this debt, Dolin represented to Hires in October 1988 that he had a load of 720 cases of antifreeze that he would ship to Hires in exchange for release of his debt to Hires. Hires agreed to this arrangement.

Dolin telephoned Craig Dyas, general manager of Oil Supply, and said, "Craig, I got an order here, Hires Automotive, Fort Wayne, Indiana. Ship them 720 cases of antifreeze, no matter what it is." Oil Supply ran a financial check on Hires but did not contact Hires to confirm the sales order.

Oil Supply sent 720 cases of antifreeze to be delivered to Hires. Hires received the antifreeze on November 7, 1988; an agent of Hires signed and dated a document indicating that Oil Supply was the shipper of the antifreeze. Prior to this transaction, Oil Supply and Hires were unaware of each other's existence.

Hires has neither paid for nor returned the 720 cases of antifreeze, despite demands by Oil Supply. Oil Supply sued Hires for the cost of the antifreeze, $28,900.80, plus prejudgment interest. The trial court awarded Oil Supply the value of the antifreeze and set off the debt Dolin owed Hires, leaving a judgment of $820.80. It declined to award prejudgment interest. Oil Supply appealed. The Court of Appeals largely affirmed, although it ordered prejudgment interest. . . .

An agent is one who acts on behalf of some person, with that person's consent and subject to that person's control. If a party to a transaction has no notice that the agent is acting for a principal, the party for whom he acts is called an undisclosed principal, and the relationship between the agent and the principal is called an undisclosed agency. Both the trial court and the Court of Appeals concluded that an undisclosed agency existed between Dolin, the agent, and Oil Supply, the principal. We agree.

Those courts also concluded that Hires was entitled to set off Dolin's debt against the value of the goods shipped by Oil Supply, relying heavily on the well-recognized rule of agency law outlined in 3 American Jurisprudence 2d § 341:

> [O]ne who contracts with the agent of an undisclosed principal, supposing that the agent is the real party in interest, and not being chargeable with notice of the existence of the principal, is entitled, if sued by the principal on the contract, to set up any defenses and equities which he could have set up against the agent had the latter been in reality the principal suing on his own behalf.

While we agree that this established rule informs the case, we think our colleagues have drawn the wrong conclusion from it. Both courts focused on Hires' assumption "that the agent [wa]s the real party in interest." We think the case turns instead on the fact that Hires cannot set up its defense against Oil Supply unless it is "not . . . chargeable with notice of the existence of the principal."

When Hires received the cases of antifreeze as payment of Dolin's antecedent debt, it signed shipping documents that made no mention of Dolin at all, but declared instead that the goods were from Oil Supply. This declaration should have alerted Hires to question the provenance of the cases and the nature of the transaction. Of course, the goods belonged to Oil Supply, who intended to sell them to Hires rather than pay on Dolin's pre-existing debt.

Not only did Hires have *an* opportunity to question the transaction, it had *the last* opportunity to do so before the matter was complete and Dolin absconded, leaving the parties to sort out who must bear the loss. Hires, therefore, was chargeable with notice of the existence of Oil Supply as the principal. As a result, Hires is not entitled to assert the defense it would have had against the agent, Dolin, in this lawsuit brought by the principal, Oil Supply.

This conclusion is bolstered by section 306 of the Restatement (Second) of Agency, which reads, in pertinent part:

> (2) If the agent is authorized only to contract in the principal's name, the other party does not have set-off for a claim due him from the agent unless the agent had been entrusted with the possession of chattels which he disposes of as directed or unless the principal had otherwise misled the third person into extending credit to the agent.

The illustration provided after that section is also helpful:

> 1. A is authorized by P to contract to sell to T in P's name goods of which A does not have possession. A sells the goods in his own name and causes them to be delivered to T. At this time A owes T $500. In an action by P against T, T may not set off the claim which he has against A.

We find nothing in the record to support the notion that Dolin was authorized to conceal the existence of Oil Supply as his principal. In fact, that Oil Supply's name was printed on the shipping receipt suggests the contrary—that Oil Supply had no desire to hide its existence. Section 306(2) prevents Hires from claiming a right of set off in this action by Oil Supply. [As the dissenting opinion in the Court of Appeals decision stated, "A purchaser from an agent having neither the possession or indicia of property in himself may not set off a debt due him from the agent when sued by the undisclosed principal. The reason for the rule is that the absence of apparent title should put the purchaser on inquiry as to the true status of the agent in the matter."]

. . . In resolving the present case, [our Court of Appeals] relied on *Bischoff Realty, Inc. v. Ledford*, 562 N.E.2d 1321 (Ind. Ct. App.1990), which observed that the burden of an agent's fraud ought rightly be placed "on the principal who hired him rather than on a third party stranger to the agency relationship." The object of agency law in cases such as the one before us should be the deterrence of absconding agents. Commerce will be facilitated where the law allocates burdens to those best able to thwart the absconders.

To be sure, principals are generally in a better position to prevent potential fraud by their agents than are buyers. Oil Supply could have prevented this situation by making a confirmation, or by closer supervision of its agent Dolin. The Court of Appeals was correct to characterize these failings as neglectful.

On the other hand, Hires might just as easily prevented the defalcation by taking the time to ponder why some company it had never heard of had just deposited a truckload of antifreeze on its doorstep. [As the dissenting opinion in the Court of Appeals decision stated, "This principle [between two innocent parties, the loss should be placed upon the party who put the agent out to deal] does not apply, however, if the party seeking refuge in the principle has wittingly or otherwise aided an unscrupulous agent to defraud the principal."]

Because Hires was chargeable with notice of the existence of Oil Supply as Dolin's principal before it accepted the goods, and because Hires had the last opportunity to prevent the loss before the transaction was complete, Hires should bear the loss. . . .

We conclude that Hires was not entitled to set off its Dolin debt in the lawsuit brought by Oil Supply. Accordingly, we affirm the trial court's finding for Oil Supply on the value of its antifreeze and reverse with respect to the set-off of Dolin's debt.

DICKSON, SULLIVAN, and RUCKER, JJ., concur.

BOEHM, J., concurred and filed separate opinion [omitted] in which DICKSON, J., joined.

Opinion, 670 N.E.2d 86, vacated.

Note

Note that while *Oil Supply* relied on Restatement (Second), it is consistent with Restatement (Third) § 6.06, which uses the case in illustration 4. The two Restatements do differ, however, in the treatment of the third party's right to setoff if the third party had no notice that it was dealing with an agent. Under Restatement (Second) § 306, if the agent is not authorized to conceal the principal's identity, the third party's setoff right exists only if the agent has been entrusted with possession of goods or if the principal has otherwise misled the third party into extending credit to the agent. Under Restatement (Third) § 6.06, however, the third party's setoff rights are not affected if the agent acted without actual authority in not revealing the principal's existence or identity. The drafters of the Restatement (Third) note that "[w]hether an agent acted with actual authority depends on interactions between the principal and agent that the third party is not in a position to observe. Regardless of instructions the principal has given the agent, a principal may be tempted to claim that the agent acted without actual authority in not revealing the principal's identity if by so doing the principal may defeat the third party's right to set off amounts that the agent owes the third party." [Restatement (Third) § 6.06, cmt. c.] For this reason, the drafters reject the rule of the Second Restatement.

Question

Doesn't Hires have the protection of § 6.06(2)(a)(i), if read literally?

Problems

1. As we have seen, § 6.03 of the Restatement (Third) states that when an agent contracts on behalf of an undisclosed principal, the principal and the third party "have the same rights, liabilities, and defenses against each other as if the principal made the contract personally. . . ." Suppose that the Jones Corporation in Massachusetts sold some of its shares to a trust company. The shares were not registered under the "blue-sky" laws of Massachusetts and therefore were not available for sale and distribution to the public. The sale appeared proper on its face because sales to trust companies are not within the provisions of the blue-sky law, the theory being that they are able to look out for themselves. It turns out, however, that the trust company was buying the shares for an elderly lady, Mrs. Means. Upon receiving the shares, Mrs. Means discovered they were unregistered and, tendering back the shares, sued the Jones Corporation to recover the purchase price plus interest.

Analyze the rights of the parties. *See Howell v. First of Boston Int'l Corp.*, 309 Mass. 194, 34 N.E.2d 633 (1941).

2. Mary Hammon, desiring to engage in stock transactions but not in her own name, turned her 5000 shares of Ventura Corporation over to one John Cuniff on the understanding that he was to use the shares as margin on a trading account for her. Cuniff proceeded to do this, employing the partnership of Paine, Webber & Co. as his brokers. The identity of Mrs. Hammon was not disclosed to them, with her knowledge and consent. Cuniff already had five different accounts of his own with Paine, Webber, numbered consecutively from 1 to 5. This was unknown to Mrs. Hammon. The account carried for Mrs. Hammon was entered on the books of Paine, Webber as account number 6.

Several years later, Mrs. Hammon directed Cuniff to deliver the stock and cash in her account to a certain bank in Boston. Cuniff was unable to comply fully because his account number 5 showed a debit balance and Paine, Webber claimed the right to apply the credit balance in number 6 to the debit balance in number 5. Cuniff did, however, obtain the $19,461 cash balance and 2500 shares of stock, which he transferred to the Boston bank. Paine, Webber retained the remaining shares of stock.

Mrs. Hammon sent notice of her interest in account number 6 by telegram to Paine, Webber. Upon receipt of the telegram, Paine, Webber transferred the remaining shares of stock and accumulated dividends from account 6 to account 5, sold the stock and applied the proceeds to reduce the debit balance in number 5.

Mrs. Hammon has come to you in a state of rage. Can you advise her that there is something you can do to help her? *See Hammon v. Paine*, 56 F.2d 19 (1st Cir. 1932).

3. A lease was entered into by J. E. Turner as lessee with Sarah Belove, the lessor. Turner was acting on behalf of an undisclosed principal. The lease contained

a clause that it would be binding on "the heirs, assigns and legal representatives" of the parties, and that it could not be assigned or transferred by the lessee without the written consent of the lessor. The lease did not purport to be binding on "successors."

A fire destroyed the building during the term of the lease. At this stage The Heart of America Lumber Company appeared and, as undisclosed principal, sued the lessor for breach of a covenant to repair. Could the lessor successfully assert a defense against the Lumber Company, other than a defense based on interpretation of the repair clause? If so, how would you evaluate the defense?

Would it affect your analysis if the lease contained an endorsement by the Lumber Company guaranteeing "the performance by J. E. Turner of each and all of the terms, conditions and provisions in said lease contained, including the prompt payment of the monthly rental therein provided," and the endorsement was signed on behalf of the Company by J. E. Turner, Treasurer? *Heart of Am. Lumber Co. v. Belove*, 111 F.2d 535, 130 A.L.R. 658 (8th Cir. 1940).

4. McCorkle ordered chemicals and laboratory supplies from Fisher Chemical Company for a friend named Mills. The order was placed in the name of McCorkle's employer, Jones Steel Company, because Fisher does not sell chemical supplies to individuals. When the materials were delivered to Jones Steel, McCorkle informed Mills, who picked them up. It is disputed whether Jones Steel knew of this activity. It denies it. McCorkle claims that it gave him permission to order in its name. Fisher has not been paid. What are the rights and liabilities of the parties?

Chapter 7

Liability of the Agent to Third Persons

A. Liability on the Contract

1. Liability When the Principal Is Unintentionally Undisclosed

As noted in Chapter 6, an agent is liable as a party to a contract with a third person when the agent's principal is undisclosed by design. Suppose, however, that no such prearrangement exists between principal and agent and instead the agent unwittingly fails to disclose and identify the principal. Does this affect the agent's liability and, if so, under what circumstances is the third party charged with notice of the principal? The following case deals with this issue in a modern and frequently recurring context.

Jensen v. Alaska Valuation Service

Supreme Court of Alaska
688 P.2d 161 (1984)

Before Burke, C.J., and Rabinowitz, Compton and Moore, JJ.

Compton, Justice.

Arthur Jensen, Inc. was an Alaska corporation, incorporated in 1972, engaged in the housing construction business. Arthur Jensen owned over half of the corporation's stock and served as its president. The corporation became insolvent in 1980.

Alaska Valuation Service (AVS) conducted appraisals for Arthur Jensen from the early 1970s until 1979. On July 19, 1979, Jensen ordered by telephone appraisals on five single family homes. AVS was to appraise these residences from plans and blueprints rather than from an actual inspection of the sites. AVS's president, Alfred Ferrera, who took the order, recorded it as being for "Art Jensen." Invoices for the appraisals were later sent to "Art Jensen, Jensen Builders" at the corporation's Anchorage post office box address. Arthur Jensen, Inc. was not mentioned in AVS's records until late 1979, when Jensen specifically informed AVS of his company's corporate status. Thereafter, a statement of lien filing fee was addressed to Arthur Jensen, Inc. The appraisals were completed but never paid for.

In 1982, AVS filed a complaint for $823.00 against Jensen in small claims court. Jensen admitted the amount of the debt, but denied any personal liability. At trial,

Ferrera testified that he had not been aware that Jensen was doing business as a corporation until late 1979. He stated that AVS's records had always shown Jensen as "Arthur Jensen, Jensen Builders," and that he had assumed that the company was a sole proprietorship. He claimed that "[i]t's just not typical . . . for most of the builders we do business with to be corporations," and that it had not occurred to him that Jensen might be incorporated.

Jensen testified that he had always paid for appraisal services with the corporation's checks, and introduced four checks dated prior to July 1979 into evidence. He also testified that he placed signs with the corporation's name on each of the houses he built. He conceded, however, that appraisals were completed before construction on the houses began. He testified that he could not think of anything besides the checks which might have put AVS on notice that it was dealing with a corporation.

The small claims court concluded that "just writing checks after the fact to a bookkeeper" did not provide AVS with adequate notice of Arthur Jensen's position as an agent of a corporation. It awarded AVS $831.00.

Jensen appealed the decision to superior court and requested leave to submit the contractor's plans from which the appraisals were made. He alleged that these plans contained information identifying Arthur Jensen, Inc., and would have given AVS notice that it was dealing with a corporation before the actual appraisals could be done. The superior court affirmed the district court ruling without mentioning the request to supplement the record.

In his petition for hearing, Jensen asks that we hold that payments to a creditor by corporate checks over the course of several years adequately notifies that creditor of a company's corporate status.

Although officers of a corporation will not ordinarily be held personally liable for contracts they make as agents of the corporation, they must disclose their agency and the existence of the corporation before they will be absolved from liability. An agent who makes a contract for an undisclosed or partially disclosed principal will be liable as a party to the contract. Restatement (Second) of Agency, §§ 321, 322 (1958). Thus, Jensen can avoid liability only if his use of corporate checks disclosed the existence of Arthur Jensen, Inc. and Jensen's intention to contract on its behalf.

An agent who attempts to avoid liability on a contract has the burden of proving that the agency relationship and the identity of the principal were in fact disclosed. A third party with whom the agent deals is not required to inquire whether the agent is acting for another. The third party will be held to have notice of the agency relationship, however, "if he knows [about it], has reason to know [about] it, should know [about] it, or has been given notification of it." Restatement (Second) of Agency § 9 (1958).

The question before us, then, is whether Jensen's continuing use of corporate checks gave AVS "reason to know" about the existence of Arthur Jensen, Inc. Courts in a number of jurisdictions have considered similar questions and reached varying conclusions. The holdings of these courts have fallen into three categories: 1) that use of corporate checks is sufficient, as a matter of law, to provide notice; 2) that it is insufficient as a matter of law; and 3) that the question is one of fact which must be decided by the court.

The first category of holdings is best exemplified by *Potter v. Chaney*, 290 S.W.2d 44 (Ky. App. 1956). In that case, the defendant was president of a coal company which bought coal from the plaintiff over the course of four years and paid him with corporate checks. The court held that the corporation's existence before the plaintiff began delivering coal and its consistent use of corporate checks were sufficient, as a matter of law, to have put the seller on notice that the buyer transacted business with it on behalf of a corporation.

The Louisiana Court of Appeals reached the opposite conclusion in *Jahncke Service, Inc. v. Heaslip*, 76 So. 2d 463 (La. App. 1954). In that case, the defendant conducted business with the plaintiff over the course of several years, and incorporated during that time. He argued that his use of corporate checks should have put the defendant on notice that it dealt with a corporation rather than with an individual. The court held that the use of five or six corporate checks did not provide the plaintiff with legally sufficient notice to relieve the corporation's agent of liability. . . .

We conclude that the third category of holdings — that the question of whether an agent's use of corporate checks provides sufficient notice of the corporation's existence is a factual one — is best supported by case law and by reason. . . .

Ordinarily, the question of whether a corporate agent acts for a disclosed or an undisclosed principal is one of fact. An agent's use of corporate checks is one factor for the trier of fact's consideration, but it is not necessarily determinative. The reasonableness of a third party's failure to deduce the existence of a corporate principal from its agent's use of corporate checks varies from case to case. In *Brown v. Owen Litho Service, Inc.* [384 N.E.2d 1132 (Ind. 1979)], for example, where all meetings took place in the agent's house, and the transaction at issue involved the printing of four issues of a new magazine, a court could reasonably conclude that the third party had insufficient notice of the corporation's existence. In *Potter v. Chaney*, on the other hand, where the transactions took place entirely in the corporation's offices, the corporation involved was a coal distributor, and $170,000 changed hands, the existence of the corporation was much more evident from the circumstances surrounding the use of corporate checks. We see no reason to attempt to fashion a rule of law which assumes that corporate checks provide equivalent notice in such widely differing factual settings. Since we have determined that the small claims court's finding that Jensen did not sufficiently disclose his agency is one of fact, we will not disturb it unless it is clearly erroneous. . . .

In his appeal to superior court, Jensen moved to supplement the record with the plans from which AVS performed the appraisals. These plans, which identified Arthur Jensen, Inc. as the builder, were not introduced at trial. Jensen urges us to remand for consideration of the plans if we find that the corporate checks provided insufficient notice of the corporation's existence.

Jensen placed his order for the appraisals by telephone, and submitted the plans to AVS sometime thereafter. AVS thus did not see the plans until after it had agreed to perform the appraisals. An agent is liable for a contract he or she enters into unless the principal is disclosed at the time the contract is formed. As comment *c* to the Restatement (Second) of Agency § 4 notes:

> Whether a principal is a disclosed principal, a partially disclosed principal or an undisclosed principal depends upon the manifestations of the principal or agent and the knowledge of the other party *at the time of the transaction.* The disclosure of the existence or identity of the principal subsequently has no bearing upon the relations created at the time of the transaction. [Emphasis added].

Jensen argues that the plans were incorporated by reference into the contract, since AVS' order form notes that the appraisals were to be made "from plans." This argument is without merit. We are not concerned here with the integral parts of the contract, but with AVS' knowledge when it entered that contract. The plans had no bearing on AVS' actual or constructive notice of the existence of Arthur Jensen, Inc. at the time of the contract, since AVS did not see them until *after* the contract was formed. Hence, there is no need for remand to allow consideration of the plans.

Affirmed.

Notes

1. *The Divisible Contract.* As *Jensen* indicates, an agent for an undisclosed principal is liable as a party to the contract in recognition of the expectations of the person contracting with the agent. This is true even when the agent did not intend such liability and had unintentionally failed to disclose the principal. The extent of the liability can depend on the nature of the contract, however. Suppose, for example, that the third party discovers the existence of the agency and the identity of the principal while a continuing, divisible contract is not yet fully performed, and thereafter continues to perform. Would the agent be liable for obligations incurred thereafter under that circumstance? *See Howell v. Smith,* 134 S.E.2d 381 (N.C. 1964) (no).

2. *The Parol Evidence Rule.* The *Jensen* court's language concerning the burden of proof on disclosure is supported by other authority. See *Moore v. Seabaugh,* 684 S.W.2d 492, 495 (Mo. App. 1984), where the court stated:

> Indeed, it seems the better rule is that upon proof that an agent signed his signature without limitations, to an instrument and with no limitations stated in the body of the instrument, the other party to the agreement has made a prima facie case for the agent's personal liability, and the agent bears the burden of proving both disclosure of the principal and the intention of the parties not to impose personal liability on the agent.

The above quotation does not mention the parol evidence rule, which limits the introduction of evidence extrinsic to an integrated writing. That rule would seem to pose serious problems for the agent in the situation described by the court in

Moore. See § 323(1) of the Restatement (Second), stating as follows: "If it appears unambiguously in an integrated contract that the agent is a party or is not a party, extrinsic evidence is not admissible to show a contrary intent, except for the purpose of reforming the contract."[1]

3. *The Notice Provision of Entity Statutes.* The case of *Water, Waste & Land, Inc. v. Lanham,* 955 P.2d 997 (Colo. 1998) resolved an important question of statutory interpretation. The Colorado limited liability company act, like many statutes, included this provision:

> The fact that the articles of organization are on file in the office of the secretary of state is notice that the limited liability company is a limited liability company and is notice of all other facts set forth therein which are required to be set forth in the articles of organization. C.R.S. § 7-80-208.

An agent of a limited liability company argued that this provision relieved him of liability to a third party who did not know he was acting on behalf of an LLC. The agent, Lanham (and second agent, named Clark), entered into an oral contract with Westec, the third party, for engineering services. Lanham and Clark were acting on behalf of Preferred Income Investors, L.L.C., a Colorado limited liability company, but Lanham's business card did not include the name of the company; instead, it included the initials PII and the address of the company. There was no indication on Lanham's card, or on any materials that Westec received, that indicated that Lanham represented an LLC. The court held that the above-quoted provision did not change the common law of agency:

> In order to relieve Lanham of liability, this provision would have to be read to establish a conclusive presumption that a third party who deals with the agent of a limited liability company always has constructive notice of the existence of the agent's principal. We are not persuaded that the statute can bear such an interpretation.
>
> Such a construction exaggerates the plain meaning of the language in the statute. Section 7-80-208 could be read to state that third parties who deal with a limited liability company are always on constructive notice of the company's limited liability status, without regard to whether any part of the company's name or even the fact of its existence has been disclosed. However, an equally plausible interpretation of the words used in the statute is that once the limited liability company's name is known to the third party, constructive notice of the company's limited liability status has been

---

1. Reformation is an equitable remedy that corrects mutual mistakes made in the transcription of an agreement to writing. It requires proof by clear and convincing evidence. *See* JOHN D. CALAMARI & JOSEPH M. PERILLO, THE LAW OF CONTRACTS 392 (3d ed. 1987). Reformation is not available against one who has changed position in good faith reliance on a document, nor is it available against a bona fide purchaser for value or a holder in due course of a negotiable instrument. *See* Restatement § 8D.

given, as well as the fact that managers and members will not be liable simply due to their status as managers or members.

Moreover, the broad interpretation urged by Lanham would be an invitation to fraud, because it would leave the agent of a limited liability company free to mislead third parties into the belief that the agent would bear personal financial responsibility under any contract, when in fact, recovery would be limited to the assets of a limited liability company not known to the third party at the time the contract was made. While Westec has not alleged that Clark or Lanham deliberately tried to conceal the Company's identity or status as a limited liability company, Lanham's construction would open the door to sharp practices and outright fraud. We may presume that in adopting section 7-80-208, the General Assembly did not intend to create a safe harbor for deceit. For this reason alone, a broad reading of the notice provision would be suspect.

In addition, statutes in derogation of the common law are to be strictly construed. For the reasons outlined above, the interpretation urged by Lanham would be a radical departure from the settled rules of agency under the common law. If the legislature had intended a departure of such magnitude, its desires would have been expressed more clearly. . . .

For these reasons, we conclude that where an agent fails to disclose either the fact that he is acting on behalf of a principal or the identity of the principal, the notice provision of our LLC Act, section 7-80-208, cannot relieve the agent of liability to a third party. When a third party deals with an agent acting on behalf of a limited liability company, the existence and identity of which has been disclosed, the third party is conclusively presumed to know that the entity is a limited liability company and not a partnership or some other type of business organization. Where the third party does not know the identity of the principal entity, however, the situation is fundamentally different because the third party is without notice and the law does not contemplate that he has any way of finding the relevant records.

If Clark or Lanham had told Westec's representatives that they were acting on behalf of an entity known as "Preferred Income Investors, LLC" the failure to disclose the fact that the entity was a limited liability company would be irrelevant by virtue of the statute, which provides that the articles of organization operate as constructive notice of the company's limited liability form. The [lower] court, however, found that Lanham and Clark did not identify Preferred Income Investors, LLC, as the principal in the transaction. The "missing link" between the limited disclosure made by Clark and the protection of the notice statute was the failure to state that "P.I.I.," the Company, stood for "Preferred Income Investors, LLC."

2. Liability When the Principal Is Disclosed: Special Circumstances

In general, an agent for a disclosed principal is not liable on the contract arranged by the agent. See *Stroll v. Epstein*, 818 F. Supp. 640, 644 (S.D. N.Y. 1993), stating that under New York common law an agent for a disclosed principal will not be held personally liable "unless there is clear and explicit evidence of the agent's intention to substitute or superadd his own personal liability for, or to, that of his principal." Another court stated that, in a disclosed principal situation, "There is a presumption that it was the agent's intention to bind his principal and not to incur personal liability. . . ." See *Golf Digest/Tennis, Inc. v. Diode, Inc.*, 849 S.W.2d 617, 618 (Mo. App. 1993). An example of a clear expression of intent of an agent to be bound is provided by *Gigandet v. Lighting Galleries, Inc.*, 382 S.E.2d 600, 601 (Ga. App. 1989), where an open account agreement contained the following language: "If the above account debtor is a corporation, the undersigned agree to personally guarantee, jointly and severally, payment of any charges which the corporation fails to pay when due." An example of implied intent is provided by *Mediacomp, Inc. v. Capital Cities Communication, Inc.*, 698 S.W.2d 207 (Tex. App. 1985), where an advertising agency was held liable for its clients' accounts in a decision based in part on industry custom.

Is the following case inconsistent with the above authority?

Copp v. Breskin

Court of Appeals of Washington
782 P.2d 1104 (1989)

Webster, Judge.

Breskin & Robbins, a law firm, appeals a summary judgment in favor of Harley Copp, an expert witness hired by the firm on behalf of a client. Copp successfully claimed $14,789 for expert services.

Breskin & Robbins advised Copp before hiring him that fees "were being paid, and were to be paid" by the client. . . . Copp sent Breskin & Robbins an initial bill which the firm paid with a "trust check" for $1,424. An accompanying letter assured Copp that any future charges would be paid within 30 days of his testimony. Breskin & Robbins claims it gave the assurance on behalf of the client and did not intend a guaranty. The client paid some of Copp's bills directly while he was in town for the trial. After trial, Copp sent Breskin & Robbins a final bill. He said he expected payment within 30 days, as previously agreed.

Breskin & Robbins replied that the client was willing to pay only 30 per cent of the bill. The firm offered to commence litigation on Copp's behalf, and eventually sued the client on its own behalf. It claimed $37,000 in litigation expenses allegedly incurred at the client's request, including amounts owing to Copp.

Subsequently, Copp filed this action against Breskin & Robbins. Breskin & Robbins admitted the amount owed, but averred as an affirmative defense that it hired Copp as agent of a disclosed principal, the client. Breskin & Robbins relies on dictum to the effect that an attorney, as agent of a client, is not responsible for litigation costs, such as expert witness fees, unless the attorney personally agrees with the litigation service provider to pay them. [Citations omitted.]

Washington State Bar Association, Ethics Opinion 140 (1969), states:

> [W]hen the attorney has directly and personally ordered or arranged for services in circumstances under which . . . the attorney . . . did not make it clear (if such were [the] intent) to the person rendering the services that such person must look to the client alone for payment, the attorney has been derelict in . . . preserving a good public image of the legal profession. *The primary responsibility of making it clear that the attorney acts in an agency capacity with no personal liability rests upon the attorney.* If [the attorney] has been derelict herein, others may reasonably be misled into believing that the attorney is agreeing to pay or to guarantee the payment of the obligation so created.

(Emphasis added). The Rules of Professional Conduct prohibit attorneys from using the ignorance of litigation service providers to their financial advantage. . . .

Other jurisdictions are split as to whether an attorney is responsible to an expert or other service provider in the absence of a disclaimer. Since 1955, three jurisdictions deciding the issue as a matter of first impression have reasoned that the attorney is an agent of a disclosed principal and, as such, is not liable unless the attorney expressly or impliedly agrees to be bound. During the same period, nine jurisdictions considering the issue anew or for the first time have held that formal agency reasoning does not accurately reflect the attorney's role as a strategist in litigation or the common understanding of litigation service providers. The clear trend is to hold the attorney liable. One court, bound by prior cases siding with the attorney, nevertheless expressed the view that the attorney should be liable in the absence of a disclaimer, because the service provider deals with the attorney, not the client, and generally accepts employment based on the attorney's credit, not the client's. See *Rayvid v. Burgh*, 37 Misc. 2d 963, 234 N.Y.S.2d 868 (1962).

Justification for the disclosed agency rule is the probable intention of the parties, objectively manifested. Restatement (Second) of Agency § 320, Comments *a–c*; § 321, Comment *a*; § 328, Comment *a* (1958). When the circumstances indicate a probable intention that is contrary to the general rule, the reason for the rule is gone, and the rule should be modified to reflect this fact. Otherwise, the purpose of the rule—giving effect to the intentions of the parties—is lost. When a litigation service provider contracts with an attorney based on the attorney's credit, and the attorney is aware, or should be aware of this, it should not matter that the client's identity is known. The service provider reasonably expects that the attorney will be responsible, as surety or guarantor of the client's performance,[2] and any contrary expectation of the attorney is unreasonable, if not fraudulent.

An agent may guarantee performance by the principal, and the existence of a guarantee "may be shown by proof of a custom to that effect." Restatement (Second) of Agency § 328, Comment *b*. Custom is determinative of the parties' intent where both parties are aware of it, and neither knows or should know that the other party has an intention contrary to it.

Here, Copp's testimony establishes that he relied upon a custom whereby experts look to attorneys for payment of their fees. Breskin & Robbins was aware of an identical custom locally. The statement that litigation costs were being paid and were to be paid by the client does not address the situation when the client is unwilling or unable to pay. Therefore, under the circumstances of this case, it was insufficient as a matter of law to apprise Copp of a change from customary practice. . . .

Breskin & Robbins offered to commence litigation against the client on Copp's behalf without any indication that there would be a charge for this service. The firm's offer reveals an understanding on its part that it was indebted to Copp. The lawsuit commenced by Breskin & Robbins on its own behalf against the client admits amounts owing to Copp as its damages. The firm would not have acted in this way if it believed it had adequately apprised Copp of an intention not to be liable for his services.

We hold that in these circumstances an attorney owes an expert or other litigation service provider an express disclaimer of responsibility if the attorney intends not to be bound by a contract for litigation services. This reflects the modern trend, which is to hold the attorney liable in the absence of an express disclaimer or other clear indication not to be bound. Putting the burden on the attorney promotes public trust and confidence in the legal profession, the supervision of which is the exclusive province and responsibility of the courts. Public trust in the profession and the courts would be "greatly endangered and jeopardized" by a technical defense of disclosed agency. Ethics Opinion 140.

The judgment is affirmed.

COLEMAN, C.J., and PEKELIS, J., concur.

Notes

1. The Restatement (Third) § 6.01, Comment c, is consistent with the *Copp* case ("[a] lawyer who contracts with a third party for goods or services used by lawyers is subject to liability to the third party when the lawyer knows or reasonably should know that the third party relies on the lawyer's credit although the third party knows the identity of the lawyer's client, unless at the time of contracting the lawyer

---

2. [Would this promise of guaranty have to be in writing and signed by the attorney in order to satisfy the Statute of Frauds? *See generally*, E. ALLAN FARNSWORTH, CONTRACTS 400–412 (2nd ed. 1990). Perhaps the "main purpose" exception would make this unnecessary. *Id.* at 408.—Eds.]

has disclaimed such liability.") See also *Ingram v. Lupo*, 726 S.W.2d 791, 798 (Mo. App. 1987), where an attorney was sued by a court reporter for the costs incurred in preparing a transcript. The court held the attorney liable, stating:

> Many modern decisions now take the position that an attorney ordering a transcript in connection with litigation is ordinarily to be treated as a principal, so that even when he is known to be an attorney acting for a particular client, he is personally liable in the absence of an express disclaimer of such responsibility.

Is the following case inconsistent with *Copp* and *Ingram*? In *Eppler, Guerin & Turner, Inc. v. Kasmir*, 685 S.W.2d 737, 739 (Tex. Civ. App. 1985), an investment banking firm that had performed appraisal services sued the law firm that had retained it for payment of its fees. The law firm defended on the ground that it was acting only as agent for a disclosed principal, its client. The court stated as follows in the course of upholding the defense:

> Except in the case of negotiable instruments, the general rule is that when an agent contracts for the benefit of a disclosed principal, the agent is not liable on the contract he makes. Of course, the parties to a contract can alter this general rule by agreement so that the agent will be liable on the contract. The agent may bind himself to such a contract by expressly or impliedly agreeing either to substitute his own responsibility for that of his principal or to add his personal responsibility. Thus, it is clear that if an agent is liable on a contract he has made for the benefit of a disclosed principal, his liability is predicated upon his specific contractual obligation and not upon his agency relationship.

Plaintiff argued that its letter agreement with the law firm, which stated that billings "shall be rendered to [the] firm," constituted an implied assumption of liability by the law firm. This argument was rejected by the court. "Attorneys routinely receive such billings for their clients. In this context such a provision means only that the attorney is designated as the agent of the corporate client to whom bills should be sent." *Id.* at 739. *See also Cahn v. Fisher*, 805 P.2d 1040, 1042–43 (Ariz. Ct. App. 1990) ("We disagree that there is one rule of law for principals and agents generally, and another for principals and agents who happen to be lawyers and their clients. There is no sound reason for such a distinction. The idea that lawyers are 'in charge' of the client's business is no less true of many other agents, who may exercise a great degree of control over their principal's affairs.").

2. *Form of signature.* Suppose a written contract contains the following sentence: "In your capacity as both an officer of Intercontinental Asset Group and as agent for the joint venture, you [Jeffrey Epstein] verbally agreed to . . . return all amounts contributed by me to the venture. . . ." Epstein signed the contract as follows: "/s/ Jeffrey Epstein I.A.G." Epstein later is sued for nonperformance of the contract. Is he liable? Was he skillful in the way he signed the contract? If you had been representing Epstein, what would you have recommended that he do? The court resolving this dispute first said that a signature in a clearly representative capacity would have been "Jeffrey Epstein for I.A.G." or "I.A.G., by Jeffrey Epstein." *See Stroll v. Epstein*, 818 F. Supp. 640, 644 (S.D. N.Y. 1993). The court concluded, however, that the contract, "when read as a whole, is unambiguous on its face and indicates the parties' intention that Epstein was acting in a representative capacity when he agreed to return Stroll's capital contribution." *Id.* at 645.

As noted above, the safest form of signature is "P by A, agent." Other acceptable forms are "A as agent for P" or "A on behalf of P." Corporate titles are commonly used in place of the word "agent" as in "P by A, President." *See* Restatement (Second) § 156.

One form of signature to avoid, as *Stroll* suggests, is that of the name of the agent simply followed by the name of the principal, as in "Mary Smith, President, Seattle Laundry Co." This runs the risk of triggering the doctrine of *descriptio personae*, which characterizes the words "President, Seattle Laundry Co." as merely descriptive of the person and not as indicating Mary Smith's intention not to be bound. *See* PHILIP MECHEM, OUTLINES OF THE LAW OF AGENCY 208 (4th ed. 1952). Most of the authority embracing this approach is older, but it seems prudent to avoid any risk of litigation over the meaning of the instrument by drafting the signature line more carefully.

Finally, consider *Puckett v. Codisco, Inc.*, 440 So. 2d 596, 599 (Fla. Ct. App. 1983), where Puckett, the president of Fan World, Inc., signed an application for credit for Fan World in the following form:

Fan World, Inc.

Charles Puckett

The print in the contract immediately above the signature line included the language "the undersigned personally guarantees payment of its accounts. . . ." Puckett was sued for the obligations of Fan World. The trial court refused to permit him to introduce parol evidence that he had signed only as president of Fan World, holding that as a matter of law Puckett's signature constituted a personal guaranty on his part. The appellate court reversed, holding that the application was ambiguous and thus parol evidence should be admitted, stating in part as follows: "If Fan World was to sign the application, merely writing the name of the corporation would not suffice. Someone would have to sign on the corporation's behalf and it would be logical for its president to do so." Doubtless Puckett ultimately prevailed on remand, but at considerable expense and inconvenience, which reinforces the wisdom of signing in a skillful manner.

On a related matter, "[a]n agent is not required, in the text of the contract, to constantly refer to itself as the agent for the principal." *Grubb & Ellis Co. v. First Texas Sav. Ass'n*, 726 F. Supp. 1226, 1228 (D. Colo. 1989). The written contract in *Grubb & Ellis* commenced with the sentence, "This letter shall serve as a commission agreement between Paragon Group as agent for First Texas Savings and Grubb & Ellis. . . ." Paragon was sued on promises made in its name in the contract. The court stated, "Although the commission agreement contains expressions of Paragon's intention to perform certain acts, this language is not sufficient to . . . impose liability on Paragon [since it does not indicate that the reference to Paragon] is other than a reference to Paragon as agent for First Texas." It may be of interest that the contract was signed by Paragon clearly in a representative capacity.

3. Yet another twist is furnished by *F & G Investments, L.L.C. v. 1313 Hickory, Ltd.*, 807 So. 2d 1004 (La. App. 2002), where the signature page in a commercial lease appeared as follows:

> F & G Investments, L.L.C.
>
> /s/ Glenn Gaeth
>
> Lessor: Glenn Gaeth, Managing Member
>
> 1313 Hickory, Ltd.
>
> /s/ Sean T. Reynolds
>
> Lessee: Sean T. Reynolds

The court ruled that Reynolds, an agent for the lessee, was not personally liable, reasoning that where the capacity of the agent signing the lease is ambiguous (as it was in this case), and the lease was prepared by the lessor, the ambiguity would be construed against the lessor.

3. Liability When the Principal Is Partially Disclosed or Unidentified

At times, it will be clear to a third party that it is dealing with an agent but unclear who that principal is. The Restatement (Second) and many cases refer to such a principal as "partially disclosed," while the Restatement (Third) uses the term "unidentified principal." The Restatement (Third) § 6.02 succinctly states the well-accepted rule regarding the liability of the principal, third party and the agent:

> When an agent acting with actual or apparent authority makes a contract on behalf of an unidentified principal,
>
> (1) the principal and the third party are parties to the contract; and
>
> (2) the agent is a party to the contract unless the agent and the third party agree otherwise.

Van D. Costas, Inc. v. Rosenberg

District Court of Appeal of Florida
432 So. 2d 656 (1983)

GRIMES, JUDGE.

This is an appeal from a final judgment denying appellant's claims for mechanic's lien foreclosure and breach of contract.

Gilbert Rosenberg owned a parcel of real property on Siesta Key upon which the Magic Moment Restaurant was located. Seascape Restaurants, Inc., operated the restaurant and paid a monthly rental to Rosenberg for use of the property. Gilbert Rosenberg, his son Jeff Rosenberg, and Chris Moore each owned one third of Seascape. Jeff was president of Seascape and Moore was vice president, and the two of them operated the restaurant. . . .

In November of 1980, appellant's president, Van D. Costas, met with Gilbert and Jeff to discuss the creation of a "magical entrance" for the restaurant. The following month, appellant entered into a contract to remodel the entrance. Jeff Rosenberg signed the contract on a line under which appeared "Jeff Rosenberg, The Magic Moment." After the work commenced, the parties became involved in a dispute over performance and payment, and appellant filed a claim of lien on the real estate. Appellant thereafter . . . sued Jeff Rosenberg for breach of contract. Following a trial, the court entered a final judgment against the appellant which stated in pertinent part:

> Jeff Rosenberg signed his name on the line provided. Obviously he signed for "The Magic Moment," and there is no dispute that the plaintiff knew he was contracting with "The Magic Moment Restaurant." Plaintiff did testify that he thought the Rosenbergs owned the restaurant. However, there is also no dispute that the business was owned by Seascape Restaurants, Inc. who were doing business under the trade name of "The Magic Moment Restaurant." Under all these circumstances, there is no individual responsibility and the proper party to this suit, as to both claims and counterclaims, is Seascape Restaurants, Inc.

. . . The extent to which an agent must make disclosure of his principal in order to avoid personal liability is explained in 3 Am. Jur. 2d *Agency* § 320 (1962):

> In order for an agent to avoid personal liability on a contract negotiated in his principal's behalf, he must disclose not only that he is an agent but also the identity of his principal, regardless of whether the third person might have known that the agent was acting in a representative capacity. It is not the third person's duty to seek out the identity of the principal; rather, the duty to disclose the identity of the principal is on the agent. . . .

Section 321 of the Restatement (Second) of the Law of Agency (1957) discusses the liability of the agent under circumstances in which it appears that he is acting for someone else but the identity of his principal is unknown to the other party.

Comment:

> a. . . . The fact that, to the knowledge of the agent, the other party does not know the identity of the principal is of great weight in ascribing to the other party the intention to hold the agent liable either solely, or as a surety or co-promisor with the principal. The inference of an understanding that the agent is a party to the contract exists unless the agent gives such

complete information concerning his principal's identity that he can be readily distinguished. If the other party has no reasonable means of ascertaining the principal, the inference is almost irresistible and prevails in the absence of an agreement to the contrary.

In view of the contractual reference to the Magic Moment trade name, the annotation at 150 A.L.R. 1303 (1944) entitled "Use of tradename in connection with contract executed by agent as sufficient disclosure of agency or principal to protect agent against personal liability" is directly on point. The annotator points out that with the possible exception of a single decision, all of the prior cases on the subject have held that the use of a trade name is not a sufficient disclosure of the identity of the principal so as to eliminate the liability of the agent.

. . . Illustrative of the cases cited in the supplement to the annotation is *Carter v. Walton*, 469 S.W.2d 462 (Tex. Civ. App. 1971), holding that the fact that the defendant signed contracts as agent for the Tally-Ho Motor Hotel, actually a trade name of its corporate owner, did not constitute a sufficient disclosure of his principal to avoid personal liability.

Of course, if the contracting party knows the identity of the principal for whom the agent purports to act, the principal is deemed to be disclosed. A dispute concerning such knowledge presents an issue of fact. Here, however, nothing indicates that appellant had ever heard of Seascape at the time the contract was signed. Subsequent knowledge of the true principal is irrelevant where performance of an indivisible contract has commenced. The trial court emphasized that Costas drafted the contract. However, it was not incumbent upon him to ferret out the record ownership of the Magic Moment. . . . Jeff knew that the owner was Seascape, and he had it within his power to avoid personal liability by properly disclosing his principal. Since there is no evidence that the appellant knew or should have known the true principal, the law holds Jeff legally responsible.

That portion of the judgment exonerating Jeff Rosenberg from liability is reversed, and the case is remanded for further proceedings. . . .

Notes

1. In *Benjamin Plumbing, Inc. v. Barnes*, 470 N.W.2d 888, 894–96 (Wis. 1991), William Whitcomb, a director of Response to Hunger Network, Inc., a nonprofit corporation, ordered $10,000 worth of plumbing work from Benjamin Plumbing on a canning project for RHN. The signature on the contract read, "William K. Whitcomb, Canning Committee — RHN." The letterhead was captioned RESPONSE TO HUNGER NETWORK. Only $5,000 of the bill was paid. Whitcomb was sued for personal liability and held liable as a matter of law. The court reasoned that:

> The general rule that agents are contractually liable where the principal is partially disclosed has produced the rule that an agent is liable where the contracting party is not aware of the corporate status of the principal. . . . The failure to use the "Inc." notation in correspondence between the agent

and third party or in the contract itself is often critical in the determination of whether there was adequate disclosure of corporate status.

[T]he fact that Benjamin Plumbing was aware that Whitcomb was acting on behalf of an entity called RHN reveals nothing of Benjamin's awareness of the type of business organization it was dealing with. All business entities are not corporations. . . . RHN was essentially using a tradename.

[T]he fact that RHN was manifestly a charitable, nonprofit organization does not lead to the inference that it was a corporation. [It] might just as well have been an unincorporated association. . . . Whitcomb did not expressly disavow personal liability on the contract as he so easily could have. . . . Had Benjamin Plumbing known RHN was a corporation with limited liability, it might well have taken precautionary measures to protect its interests.

Whitcomb points out, however, that the statutes only expressly require nonprofit corporations to use their corporate name when suing and being sued. He states that it is well accepted that corporations need not contract in their legal corporate name. . . . The legal principles presented by Whitcomb are inapposite. These general rules only relate to the corporate principal's liability on a contract, not the agent's.

2. Why is an agent who acts on behalf of a partially disclosed principal liable as a party to the contract? Usually agents, who function as the representatives of others, do not intend to commit themselves personally to perform the underlying transaction. The agent in a partially disclosed principal setting can always so specify, but in the absence of wording making that clear, courts infer that the third party's expectation is that the agent is a party to the contract on the assumption that ordinarily one would not rely solely upon the credit of an unknown person.

Is the partially disclosed principal a party to the contract? Section 6.02 of the Restatement (Third) says yes. Why? If the third party is willing to contract without knowing the identity of the principal, isn't it reasonable to assume that it is satisfied with the liability of the agent as a party to the contract? One could so assume, but the inference is drawn that normally a party dealing with an agent desires the liability of the one on whose account the contract is made. *See* SEAVEY ON AGENCY §70E (1964).

If the third party obtains a judgment against either the agent or the partially disclosed principal, knowing of the existence of both, is it thereafter barred from suing the other party, as in the undisclosed principal situation in states that apply the election doctrine? Section 336 of the Restatement (Second) denies this, stating that the third party "has the same opportunity to select his debtors as where the principal is wholly disclosed. Unless otherwise agreed, the third party has cumulative and not alternative rights against agent and principal." *Id.*, cmt. c. The Restatement (Third) §6.09 rejects the election rule both for disclosed and unidentified principals.

3. Suppose an agent signs a contract in a manner clearly indicating its agency status ("Transworld Marine Transport Corp., As Agents for Owners of the good ship Theotokos"), but the contract does not specifically identify the principal. Assume that the identity of the principal can be discovered through public records, as apparently was true with the Magic Moment restaurant in the principal case. Is the agent nevertheless personally liable on the contract? Courts have split on this. One line of authority, in addition to the principal case, is reflected in *Mayer v. Buchanan*, 50 A.2d 595 (D.C. Mun. App. 1946), where a rental agent signed a lease "A, as agent for the owner only." The agent tried to avoid personal liability for collecting rent in excess of rent control ceilings by arguing that the identity of the owner was a matter of public record under the address of the building. The court held the agent liable. See also *Lumer v. Marone*, 569 N.Y.S.2d 321 (N.Y. App. Term 1990), where a corporation known as "Mar-1 Power Systems, Inc." operated under the name "Corvette Station." It had filed a certificate of assumed name, as required by New York law, disclosing the ownership of Corvette Station. Plaintiffs sued to recover a deposit they had given to the individual defendants for work to be done on a 1972 Corvette. Defendants argued that they had acted only as agents for the corporation, that the work authorization was on the stationery of Corvette Station, and that a certificate explaining the ownership behind the assumed name was on file in the public records. The court rejected this defense, explaining the underlying policy as follows:

> While it may be true that plaintiffs could have ascertained the identity of defendants' principal by checking the records on file with the Secretary of State, they were not required to do so. It would be unreasonable to place upon the consumer the burden of checking the records on file with the Secretary of State and with the County Clerk every time he enters into a contract with a party using an assumed name.

The other line of authority is reflected in *Instituto Cubano v. The S.S. Theotokos*, 155 F. Supp. 945 (S.D.N.Y. 1957), involving the "Transworld Marine" signature noted above. The court relied on the fact that the name of the owner of the ship could be learned by checking the Shipping Index. See also *Port Ship Serv. v. Norton, Lilly & Co.*, 883 F.2d 23, 24 (5th Cir. 1989), where Port Ship, a water taxi service that ferries crew members, customs agents, and supplies between ships and the shore at the Port of New Orleans, sued Norton, a maritime agent that provides husbanding services for ships, for services performed for Norton's unidentified principals. The court affirmed a judgment of nonliability for Norton, noting that, "Norton had twenty-four hour per day telephone service through which Port Ship could ascertain principals' identities." Although not invoked by the court, custom and usage would seem to play a major role in defining expectations among commercial enterprises like those involved in the *Port Ship* case.

With which line of authority do you agree?

4. Can an agent who signs a contract "A, Agent" introduce parol evidence to show that the parties did not intend her to be bound personally? See § 323 of the Restatement (Second), Comment d, stating yes, on the ground that the contract is ambiguous.

5. Questions involving the form of signatures also are of major importance in the laws involving negotiable instruments. Uniform Commercial Code § 3-402 and comments prescribe the standards for negotiable instruments.

6. The rule reflected in note 1 following the *Finley v. Dalton* case in Chapter 6, that a contract is not binding on a third party if the undisclosed principal or the agent *knew* the third party would not contract with principal, does not apply to contracts entered into on behalf of unidentified principals. *Rocky Mountain Exploration, Inc. v. Davis Graham & Stubbs LLP*, 420 P.3d 223 (Colo. 2018).

B. The Agent's Warranty of Authority

Husky Industries v. Craig Industries

Court of Appeals of Missouri
618 S.W.2d 458 (1981)

TITUS, JUDGE.

Plaintiff Husky Industries, Inc., sued defendants Craig Industries, Inc., and D. C. Craig in the Circuit Court of Howell County via a four-count Second Amended Petition. Counts I, II and III of the pleading sought of Craig Industries, Inc., specific performance of an alleged contract for the sale of its Mountain View charcoal plant, or, in the alternative, damages for breach of the agreement. By Count IV, plaintiff asked money damages from D. C. Craig averredly resulting from Craig's misrepresentation anent his authority to contractually bind Craig Industries, Inc., to sell the charcoal plant and real estate. Following a court trial, judgment in favor of defendant Craig Industries, Inc., was entered on Counts I, II, and III; judgment on Count IV was rendered in favor of plaintiff and against D. C. Craig in the sum of $14,400. Only D. C. Craig has appealed.

Defendant D. C. Craig was in the business of manufacturing charcoal in two plants—one at Mountain View, the other at Summersville. The two businesses were incorporated into a single corporation in 1972 under the name of Craig Industries, Inc. Craig (as president), his wife, daughter, son-in-law and Kay Clarkson constituted the corporation's board of directors and sole shareholders. Via Leon Gideon, its vice president of production, plaintiff had long expressed interest in purchasing the plants of Craig to augment its business of producing and selling charcoal briquets. On September 12, 1977, "Craig Charcoal Industries," via a written agreement signed on its behalf only by "D. C. Craig (Seller)," contracted to sell for two years 1,500 tons of charcoal per month to "The Kingsford Company," plaintiff's competitor. According to trial-testimony estimates of Mr. Craig, the amount of charcoal contracted to be sold, exceeded the output capabilities of both Craig's Mountain View and Summersville plants. Nevertheless, seven days later or on September 19, 1977, Mr. Craig telephoned Mr. Gideon, plaintiff's vice president, to inquire if the plaintiff corporation was interested in buying the Mountain View plant. Upon receiving an affirmative reply, Messrs. Craig and Gideon arranged a meeting for the morrow.

Craig, Gideon and plaintiff's attorney met on September 20, 1977, inspected and inventoried the Mountain View plant. In anticipation of a deal being made, the lawyer had prepared a partially completed typewritten "Letter Offer to Purchase" wherein "Dwane [sic] Craig and ___ Craig, his wife, d/b/a Craig Charcoal Company" were designated as sellers. After the price and terms of the sale and purchase of the plant (including both real and personal property) had been reached, the attorney completed the purchase offer form in his handwriting. When Craig disclosed he did not personally own the property to be sold, the typed names of the sellers, *supra*, were marked out and "Craig Industries, Inc." was inserted as the seller. "D. C. Craig, Pres." signed the completed form on behalf of the corporation. Inter alia, the form stated that plaintiff's attorney would prepare a "formal contract for execution within ten (10) days from this date." Mr. Gideon gave Mr. Craig his $25,000 check as the down payment on the transaction. The check was made payable to "Craig Industries, Inc." For inclusion in the formal contract to be prepared, the attorney obtained the names of the selling corporation's board of directors and stockholders. He also received from Mr. Craig possession of the abstract of title to the real estate being sold.

Under date of September 27, 1977, the attorneys for Craig Industries, Inc., wrote the plaintiff's lawyer to the effect that the corporation's board of directors had met that date and "voted to reject the offer." Mr. Gideon's uncashed $25,000 check was returned with the letter. Plaintiff thereafter commenced suit.

Craig's sole point relied on in this appeal reads: "The trial court erred in entering judgment against D. C. Craig on the theory that he, as agent, exceeded his authority and should be held liable as being the party in the best position to know of his lack of authority, because in so holding the court erroneously announced and applied the law to the facts, in that all facts touching D. C. Craig's lack of authority were equally within the knowledge of both parties, and [plaintiff] had actual or presumptive knowledge that D. C. Craig lacked authority to bind his principal."

. . . [The trial court] was not asked to and did not give any findings of fact on the issue here presented. Consequently, all fact issues affecting this appeal are presumed to have been found in accordance with the court's judgment.

Having represented himself as an agent of a disclosed principal, an individual who purports to contract in the name of his principal without or in excess of his authority to do so, becomes personally subject to liability to the other contracting party. Unless the agreement also expressly binds him personally, the liability of the agent is not predicated upon the contract itself, but rather upon the agent's breach of the express or implied covenant or warranty of authority. The individual liability of the agent is fixed unless he manifests that he does not make such a warranty or the other contracting party knows the agent is not so authorized. The agent is personally liable even if he acts in the utmost good faith and honestly believes he was authorized and regardless of whether he has falsely represented his authority with intent to deceive. . . . As stated in the Restatement [§ 329], Comment *a*, p. 726: "Where an agent purports to make a contract . . . for a principal, the other party thereto may reasonably assume from such conduct that the agent represents that he has power so to bind the principal. Hence, the rule stated in this Section [i.e., 329] results from the mere fact that the agent purports to act as such, although he makes no express representation as to his authority." Though the agent acts bona fide, yet if he has no authority he still does a wrong to the other party. If that wrong produces damage to the other party, owing to his confidence in the truth of an express or implied assertion of authority by the agent, it is deemed just and proper that the agent who makes such an assertion should be personally liable for the consequences, rather than that the damage should be borne by the other party who has been misled.

The sum and substance of the trial testimony from both sides was that Mr. Craig at no time, either before or after revealing his principal was a corporation, said or indicated anything to the effect that he possessed or did not possess authority to make an agreement binding on the corporation. Likewise, the evidence was void of even a suggestion that plaintiff's vice-president and attorney were aware or should have known of any limitation on the authority ostensibly possessed by Mr. Craig to make a binding contract on behalf of the corporation he purported to represent. In short, nothing was mentioned or discussed regarding the apparent authority Mr. Craig was using to contract on behalf of the corporation.

[T]he question here is not whether defendant Craig did, in fact, have authority to bind his principal via the agreement he made with plaintiff's agent. That question was answered by the trial court in favor of Craig's purported principal and has not been appealed. Rather, the questions for us are whether defendant Craig, representing himself as an agent, undertook to contract in the name of his disclosed principal without or in excess of his authority to do so; whether plaintiff's agents were unaware of such lack of authority; and whether plaintiff was damaged by defendant Craig's breach of his express or implied covenant or warranty of authority. The ruling of the trial court makes it patent that it answered each question in the affirmative. Under the facts and circumstances presented, we cannot say of the trial court's judgment on Count IV of the petition that there was no substantial evidence to support it, that it is against the weight of the evidence, that it erroneously declares the law or that it erroneously applies the law. We harbor no firm belief that the judgment nisi was wrong. Therefore . . . the judgment is affirmed.

GREENE, P. J., and FLANIGAN, J., concur.

Notes

1. The liability of an agent to a person who contracts in reliance on the agent's authority to bind his principal, and who is unable to hold the principal liable because the agent had no power to make the contract, has never been in doubt. The theoretical basis for such liability has varied at different times and in different jurisdictions,

however. P. Mechem, Outlines of Agency §§ 322–331 (4th ed. 1952), states that early cases held the agent liable as a party to the contract. Another basis of liability, made by some courts in recognition that it was illogical to hold the agent on a promise he never made, is in tort for misrepresentation. This works until the situation arises where the agent makes an innocent misstatement as to his authority, raising problems as to the vaguely defined limits of the tort of misrepresentation. As a result, most jurisdictions have adopted the implied warranty of authority theory, apparently first set forth in *Collen v. Wright*, 8 E. & B. 647, 120 Eng. Rep. 241 (Ex. 1857), where an agent made an agreement in good faith with plaintiff to execute a 12–year lease on behalf of his principal. His authority did not extend to executing that long a lease, and he was held liable to the plaintiff. Justice Willes of the court stated in part, "[The agent's] moral innocence, so far as the person whom he has induced to contract is concerned, in no way aids such person or alleviates the inconvenience and damage which he sustains." This view is adopted by Restatement (Third) § 6.10. An agent does not, in the absence of an express agreement, warrant his principal's honesty or solvency, however.

Such liability does not come into effect where the third party knows that the agent lacks authority, although having reason to know of the agent's lack of authority apparently will not prevent a claim based on warranty of authority. *Id.* (Why not, if the interest being protected is *T*'s expectation that *A* is authorized to do what he is purporting to do? *T*'s expectation is not reasonable if he has reason to know that *A* is not authorized, is it? Perhaps the answer is that of the two parties, the agent is more at fault.) Does an agent who is unauthorized but who has apparent authority breach his warranty of authority? Consider in answering this question exactly what is warranted by a warranty of authority and what powers are held by an agent who is apparently authorized.

An agent can avoid personal liability by expressly disclaiming it or by fully laying all the facts concerning his authority before the other party and letting the other party decide for itself whether the transaction should go forward. See *Cousin v. Taylor*, 239 P. 96 (Ore. 1925), a classic case on warranty of authority.

2. In the absence of special agreement, an agent is held liable if his principal is completely lacking in capacity. Lack of capacity arises frequently in the context of contracts entered into by promoters of entities not yet formed. For instance, *BRJM, LLC v. Output Systems, Inc.*, 917 A.2d 605 (Conn. App. 2007) involved a real estate purchase agreement between M & K Realty, LLC, as purchaser, and Englesen, as seller. Kepple executed the contract on behalf of the LLC, but it was never formed. Prior to bringing suit, Kepple, again acting on behalf of the nonexistent M & K Realty, LLC, assigned the contract to BRMJ, LLC, which did exist. Englesen sought to resist BRMJ's suit for specific enforcement on various grounds, including that the contract was void *ab initio* because M & K did not exist when the contract was entered into on its behalf. The court rejected this argument, reasoning that Kepple had capacity to contract as an individual and, therefore, he was a party to the contract. Englesen, as seller, could have held Kepple personally liable and this persuaded the court that

a contract entered into by an individual acting on behalf of an unformed entity is enforceable by that individual or his assignee. The court cited Restatement (Third) of Agency § 6.04 and Comment b for support.

3. There are two theories on how damages should be measured for breach of the warranty of authority. Under the Restatement (Third) § 6.10, damages against the agent may include "the loss of the benefit expected from performance." In a number of states, however, damages are limited to the actual loss: "the measure of recovery is not the difference between the plaintiff's pecuniary condition if the representation had been true and his condition under the actual facts, but rather the difference between what the plaintiff had before he acted on the representation and what he had afterward. This represents his actual loss." *Tedder v. Riggin*, 61 So. 244, 245 (Fla. 1913) (quoted in *Hettinger v. Kleinman*, 733 F. Supp. 2d 421, 435 (S.D.N.Y. 2010)). Most courts opt for the Restatement benefit-of-the-bargain rule. See Reporter Note 1 to § 6.10. The "actual loss" rule is similar to tort damages, while the benefit-of-the-bargain rule is similar to contract damages. What rationales might support each alternative?

4. For another aspect of an agent's liability, see MECHEM, OUTLINES OF AGENCY §§ 332–342, and Restatement (Second) §§ 339–342, discussing the liability of an agent for money had and received. Generally, an agent is required to return funds received (or their equivalent) that were paid by the third party by mistake or as a result of the fraud of the principal, if the agent has not already transferred the funds to the principal. The defense of a good faith transfer to the principal would not be available to the agent if the principal was undisclosed.

C. Harm to the Economic Interests of Others

Coker v. Dollar

United States Court of Appeals, Eleventh Circuit
846 F.2d 1302 (1988)

TJOFLAT, CIRCUIT JUDGE:

[In May 1978, Jackson purchased an apartment complex in Florida, planning to convert the apartments into condominiums and then sell them. On October 31, 1979, he contracted with the Dollars, promising them that 30% of all net proceeds derived from the sale of the condominium units would be placed in an escrow account for them. In turn, the Dollars assigned their 30% interest in the project to Jackson.]

Meanwhile, Jackson had entered into a contract with Barry W. Coker, one of the appellants here, pursuant to which Coker agreed to act as project manager for the condominium conversion. After Jackson executed the October 31, 1979 contract with the Dollars, he had a copy of the contract sent to Coker, with instructions to set up the escrow account provided for therein. Coker received the instructions, but misunderstood them and failed to set up the account. The Dollars were unaware of this failure. . . .

As of February 1980, no condominium sales had yet occurred. On February 28, 1980, Coker and Harold J. Vucovich entered into a joint venture with Jackson. Under the joint venture agreement, Jackson was to receive the first net $1,000,000 from the condominium sales, and Coker and Vucovich were to receive all proceeds in excess of that amount. In June 1980, sixty of the units were sold, and Jackson was paid out. On June 21, 1980, Jackson deeded to Coker and Vucovich the remaining units.

Throughout all this time, the Dollars remained unaware that Jackson had failed to set up an escrow account as required under the October 31, 1979 contract. When the sixty units were sold in June 1980, none of the proceeds were set aside for them. . . .

[In October 1982, the Dollars filed a claim against Coker, alleging in Count III] that Coker had injured them by negligently failing to set up the escrow account.

After a bench trial, the district court, applying Florida law, found for [the Dollars] on count III.

We begin with Coker's appeal of the district court's finding of liability on count III. As we have already noted, that count sounds in negligence: the Dollars claim that Coker, by failing to set up the escrow account, caused them to suffer an injury that is actionable under Florida law.

It is of course a basic principle of tort law that one cannot be held liable for negligence unless one is deemed to have breached some legal duty owed to the injured party. Here, the Dollars entered into a contract with Jackson; as part of the agreement, Jackson was to set up an escrow account. Jackson did not himself set up the account, but instructed his agent to do it for him. That agent, Coker, did not follow these instructions, and the Dollars claim that they suffered an injury as a result. Now, there can be no question that Jackson had a contractual obligation to the Dollars to set up the escrow account. And Coker probably had an obligation to Jackson to carry out his instructions. But did Coker owe a legal duty to the Dollars such that they are now entitled to recover damages from him for his failure to set up the account?

We can assume that Coker, as Jackson's agent, had an obligation to carry out Jackson's instructions, and that the Dollars were injured by his failure to perform that obligation. The general rule, however, is that an agent is not liable for pecuniary harm to a person other than his principal that results from his failure adequately to perform his duties to his principal. Restatement (Second) of Agency §§ 352, 357. The Dollars have not directed us to any Florida case holding otherwise, and our own research has uncovered no such case.

The Dollars argue that Coker is nevertheless liable to them because he voluntarily undertook to set up the escrow account. As support for this theory, the Dollars refer us to cases holding that one who voluntarily attempts to rescue another or otherwise perform a service for another assumes a duty to exercise due care in performing the rescue or service. One problem with applying this principle to the facts of this case is that the district court found that Coker never actually took any action to set up the escrow account. Coker's failure to read carefully the copy of the October 31, 1979 contract sent him by Jackson is irrelevant; the fact remains that he never actually did *anything* in connection with any escrow account. Thus, the Dollars' reliance on the "rescue" cases, which is questionable in any event,[3] is clearly misplaced under the facts of this case.[4]

We therefore conclude that the district court erred in holding Coker liable under count III. . . .

[Judgment] reversed in part.

Note

See also *Bescor, Inc. v. Chicago Title & Trust Co.* 113 Ill. App. 3d 65, 446 N.E.2d 1209, 1212, 68 Ill. Dec. 812 (1983), where the court said: "Traditionally, an agent is not liable for injuries to third persons resulting solely from a mere breach of duty which he owes to his principal, unless at the same time the agent owes a separate duty to the third party." (Sometimes the third-party beneficiary doctrine can create a duty for an agent under certain circumstances; see Chapter 1, Section E (*King v. First National Bank* and the Notes following).) For a rare case on the other side, see *Miller v. Quarles*, 410 S.E.2d 639 (Va. 1991), holding an agent liable in tort to the third party. The agent had negligently performed his principal's contract by failing to check into the reliability of an escrow holder in Europe who was given $50,000 to hold under a contract between plaintiff and the agent's principal, and who disappeared with the money.

D. Liability in Tort

This topic was covered briefly in Chapter 3, where the point was made that an agent is fully liable for personal tortious behavior. Acting as the agent of another does not confer immunity upon the actor for personal torts. The more subtle question of liability for nonfeasance also was addressed, noting that control by an agent over an activity or physical area can create liability for inactivity in the eyes of some courts, if it poses foreseeable risks of physical harm to others.

---

3. [6] One rationale for the "rescue" rule is that the defendant, by his actions, may have discouraged or prevented a more able rescuer from aiding the injured party. That rationale has no relevance to the facts of this case. Additionally, to the extent that the rule is based on some theory of reliance, that rationale is also irrelevant here. The district court specifically found that the Dollars were unaware that Coker had been delegated the job of setting up the escrow account.

4. [7] The Dollars argue as an alternative theory that Coker, a licensed real estate agent, is liable to them because real estate agents have a duty under Florida law to be honest, open, and fair with their clients. The short answer to this argument is that the Dollars were never Coker's clients.

Problems

1. For years Howell Oil Company had sold petroleum products to one A. J. Marlow, who was doing business under the name Atlantic Building Block Company. Two years ago Marlow introduced Combs, Howell's salesman at the time, to H. Smith and informed Combs that he was selling out to Smith. Combs and Smith agreed that Howell would sell petroleum products to Smith just as it had to Marlow.

A few days later, Combs delivered 160 gallons of gasoline to Smith, who signed a ticket made out to him in his own name. At that time Smith told Combs he was changing the name of the business to Atlantic Block Company. He did not tell Combs that the business was incorporated and that he had purchased Marlow's business by buying the stock of the corporation. Apparently Smith assumed that Combs knew Marlow's business was a corporation. Combs was unaware of that.

Howell's credit manager checked the credit rating of H. Smith, and then set up the account on her ledger in the name of Atlantic Block Company. Deliveries were made to Smith over the next 18 months. Occasionally payments on account were made by Smith by checks with the name Atlantic Block Company printed above the signature line and signed by Smith without any official designation.

One year after the deliveries commenced Howell purchased some blocks from the Atlantic Block Company. A bill was rendered to Howell. At the top of the statement was imprinted the name "Atlantic Building Block Company, Inc." The amount of the bill was credited by Howell against the account of Atlantic Block Company.

Ten thousand dollars remains outstanding on the account. Despite repeated requests, Howell has not received payment. Howell intends to bring suit. Is Smith vulnerable to suit on a personal basis? What would be his defense to such a claim? *See Howell v. Smith*, 261 N.C. 256, 134 S.E.2d 381 (1964).

2. Household Manufacturing Company, Inc. does business under several trade names, including "Artcraft Mattress Company." Recently the Houston Chronicle Publishing Company, as publisher, entered into a contract with Artcraft Mattress Company for the sale of 5,000 lines of advertising over the next year. The acceptance by Artcraft was in the following form: "Artcraft Mattress Company by Albert Bench." The Houston Chronicle ran the advertising as promised. Its bill remains unpaid. Household Manufacturing Company is insolvent. Does Houston Chronicle have anyone else it can look to for payment of the bill? *Should* it have anyone else it could look to for payment? *Lachmann v. Houston Chronicle Pub'g Co.*, 375 S.W.2d 783 (Tex. Civ. App. 1964).

Chapter 8

The Doctrine of Ratification

A. The Concept

Acting wholly without authority, on Monday morning Able contracted as agent to sell Parr's car to Todd. On Tuesday Parr hears about the deal, likes the price, and says to Able, "I'll go along with that." Is the sale now binding on Parr? If so, is the effective date of the contract the time when the deal was made by Able or when agreed to by Parr? Is it necessary for Parr to notify Todd of her affirmance? If Todd changed his mind and told Able on Monday afternoon he was not going through with the deal, could Parr on Tuesday affirm the deal anyway?

Suppose instead that Able, acting wholly on her own initiative, drove her car to pick up some law books for Parr. On the way Able negligently caused an accident. Later, upon hearing of this, Parr said, "Able was only trying to help me out. I'll take care of the damage." Is Parr now bound to pay for the damage, even though no consideration was given for this voluntary assumption of liability?

Evans v. Ruth

Superior Court of Pennsylvania
195 A. 163 (1937)

Baldrige, J.

James S. Evans brought an action in assumpsit against Homer Ruth, trading as the Ruth Lumber and Supply Company, to recover $131.11 alleged to be due for hauling stone under an oral contract. . . .

It appears from the evidence that in the fall of 1933, Ruth was awarded by the State Department of Property and Supplies two purchase orders under which he was to furnish crushed stone to certain state highways being constructed. Evans, having learned that there was work to be obtained at Bradford Woods stone quarry, applied there to an unidentified foreman, and was employed to haul stone. In answer to his inquiries, Evans was told that the Ruth Lumber & Supply Company of Scottdale had charge of the work and that he would be paid 40 cents per ton. Each load of stone was weighed and slips bearing the name of the Ruth Lumber Company, admittedly furnished by Ruth, were made out, in triplicate, containing the weight and other necessary data. Ruth acknowledged that one of these slips was then given to him, one was delivered to the State Highway Department, and the third was retained by Evans.

377

From October 30th to November 23, 1933, the plaintiff hauled stone, and it is conceded that there was due him the sum for which he sued.

On December 5th, after the work was completed, the plaintiff, together with four or five other truckers, went to Ruth's place of business in Scottdale and presented him with their bills. After examining these accounts, Ruth said: "Well, I see you finished the work for me. . . . If you will have a sworn affidavit to that statement, I will pay you. I have the money right in the safe there." Ruth was furnished this affidavit, but Evans was not paid. Later, at a squire's office in Warrendale, Ruth offered to pay, and did pay, 53 per cent of the claims to some of the claimants, but Evans refused to accept that proposition.

Ruth denied any liability to Evans, alleging that he had never entered into a contract of employment with him. He offered in evidence a written contract between himself and George Darr, subletting all the work allotted to him under the purchase orders to Darr as an independent contractor. He stated that he, personally, was never on the job, or had anything to do with it, other than to furnish two trucks on one occasion to hasten delivery of the stone. Darr testified to the existence of the contract, that he had two foremen on the job who kept the records, and that he was in complete control of the work. There was no evidence that Evans knew or had any way of knowing that Darr had this subcontract. Darr got into financial difficulty and whatever money may have been due him from Ruth was attached by one of Darr's creditors.

The plaintiff obtained a judgment. This appeal followed.

The plaintiff relied primarily upon an oral contract with an agent, subsequently ratified by the principal. Affirming agency, the burden rested upon him to prove it. The agency could not be established by the declaration of the agent alone. If plaintiff's case depended solely on the statements of the unidentified foreman, admitted in evidence without objection, the position of the appellant that the agent's authority was not shown would be well taken. But the proof that Ruth furnished the weigh slips and received a copy after each load of stone hauled by the plaintiff had been weighed, which was the basis upon which Ruth was paid by the state, and Ruth's failure to disavow the contract, instead . . . affirming it by stating that the work was done for him and that he would pay for it provided an affidavit was furnished, were sufficient for the jury's consideration.

It is a well-recognized rule of law that, if A assumes to act for B without precedent authority, and B subsequently affirms A's act, it is a ratification which relates back and supplies original authority for the act. B is bound then to the same extent as if previous authority had been granted A.

Ruth could have previously authorized the plaintiff's employment, and it follows that he could subsequently ratify it. "Ratification is the affirmance by a person of a prior act which did not bind him but which was done or professedly done on his account, whereby the act, as to some or all persons, is given effect as if originally authorized by him": Restatement, Agency § 82, p. 197. "Affirmance is a manifestation of an election by the one on whose account an unauthorized act has been performed to treat the act as authorized, or conduct by him justifiable only if there is such an election": Restatement, Agency § 83, p. 198. Our own cases are in accord with this pronouncement of the law.

The verbal agreement of Ruth to pay Evans did not fail for consideration, as appellant argues, as ratification does not require a new consideration. . . .

We find no error in this record.

Judgment . . . is affirmed.

Dempsey v. Chambers
Supreme Judicial Court of Massachusetts
28 N.E. 279 (1891)

Tort. Trial in the Superior Court, before Thompson, J., who allowed the following bill of exceptions:

"This was an action to recover for an injury to the plaintiff's building, the injury consisting in the breaking of a light of plate glass in the front of said building. . . . It appeared at the trial, that the glass was broken by one McCullock, while he was engaged in delivering a load of coal to the plaintiff, which had been ordered by the plaintiff of the defendant, who was a dealer in coal. The defendant claimed, and offered evidence tending to show, that at the time of the delivery of the coal McCullock was not his servant or in his employ, and undertook to deliver the coal without his direction or knowledge. It appeared that McCullock was a member of the defendant's household, accustomed to be in and about the defendant's coalyard, and that he took the coal from the defendant's yard and on one of the defendant's wagons. It also appeared at the trial that, subsequent to the delivery of the coal and with a full knowledge of the accident and of the delivery of the coal by McCullock, the defendant presented a bill for the coal to the plaintiff, and claimed that the plaintiff owed him for the same. The court found as a fact that the glass was broken by the carelessness of McCullock in delivering the coal, and that at the time of the delivery of the coal McCullock was not in fact the agent or servant of the defendant, or in his employ, but found that the delivery of the coal by McCullock was ratified by the defendant, and that such ratification made McCullock in law the agent and servant of the defendant in the delivery of the coal. And the court ruled that the defendant, by his ratification of the delivery of the coal by McCullock, became responsible for his negligence in the delivery of the coal. To this ruling the defendant excepted, and now excepts, and prays that his exceptions may be allowed.

"The case was tried by the court without a jury, and the finding of the court was for the plaintiff."

Holmes, J. [after restating the facts].

If we were contriving a new code to-day, we might hesitate to say that a man could make himself a party to a bare tort in any case merely by assenting to it after it had been committed. But we are not at liberty to refuse to carry out to its consequences any principle which we believe to have been part of the common law simply because the grounds of policy on which it must be justified seem to us to be hard to find, and probably to have belonged to a different state of society.

It is hard to explain why a master is liable to the extent that he is for the negligent acts of one who at the time really is his servant, acting within the general scope of his employment. Probably master and servant are "feigned to be all one person" by a fiction which is an echo of the *patria potestas* and of the English frankpledge. Possibly the doctrine of ratification is another aspect of the same tradition. The requirement that the act should be done in the name of the ratifying party looks that way.

The earliest instances of liability by way of ratification in the English law, so far as we have noticed, were where a man retained property acquired through the wrongful act of another. But in these cases the defendant's assent was treated as relating back to the original act, and at an early date the doctrine of relation was carried so far as to hold that, where a trespass would have been justified if it had been done by the authority by which it purported to have been done, a subsequent ratification might also justify it. . . .

If we assume that an alleged principal by adopting an act which was unlawful when done can make it lawful, it follows that he adopts it at his peril, and is liable if it should turn out that his previous command would not have justified the act. It never has been doubted that a man's subsequent agreement to a trespass done in his name and for his benefit amounts to a command so far as to make him answerable. . . .

Doubts have been expressed, which we need not consider, whether this doctrine applied to the case of a bare personal tort. If a man assaulted another in the street out of his own head, it would seem rather strong to say that if he merely called himself my servant, and I afterwards assented, without more, our mere words would make me a party to the assault, although in such cases the canon law excommunicated the principal if the assault was upon a clerk. Perhaps the application of the doctrine would be avoided on the ground that the facts did not show an act done for the defendant's benefit. As in other cases it has been on the ground that they did not amount to such a ratification as was necessary. *Tucker v. Jerris*, 75 Maine 184; *Hyde v. Cooper*, 26 Vt. 552.

But the language generally used by judges and text writers, and such decisions as we have been able to find, is broad enough to cover a case like the present when the ratification is established.

The question remains whether the ratification is established. As we understand the bill of exceptions, McCullock took on himself to deliver the defendant's coal for his benefit and as his servant, and the defendant afterwards assented to McCullock's assumption. The ratification was not directed specifically to McCullock's trespass, and that act was not for the defendant's benefit if taken by itself, but it was so connected with McCullock's employment that the defendant would have been liable as master if McCullock really had been his servant when delivering the coal. We have found hardly anything in the books dealing with the precise case, but we are of the opinion that consistency with the whole course of authority requires us to hold that the defendant's ratification of the employment established the relation of master and servant from the beginning, with all its incidents, including the anomalous liability for his negligent acts. The ratification goes to the relation, and establishes it *ab initio*. The relation existing, the master is answerable for torts which he has not ratified specifically, just as he is for those which he has not commanded, and as he may be for those which he has expressly forbidden. . . . For these reasons, in the opinion of a majority of the court, the exceptions must be overruled.

Exceptions overruled.

1. Justification for the Concept

Evans involved ratification in a contractual context, and *Dempsey* was a tort case. In both cases the fiction of relation back applied. In neither case was any consideration given for the voluntary assumption of liability. Also, in neither case does the law of restitution seem to play a role. (In *Evans*, Ruth may have already paid for the work done by paying Darr, his subcontractor. In *Dempsey*, defendant was merely seeking payment for goods sold and delivered.) Estoppel clearly does not apply in *Dempsey* and is doubtful in *Evans* because there is no indication until after plaintiff had already changed his position that Ruth knew or should have known that Darr was not assuming responsibility for the work he had contracted to do. What accounts, therefore, for this extraordinary doctrine? Comments c and d to §82 of the Restatement (Second), quoted below, address this matter:

> *c. A unique concept.* The concept of ratification . . . is unique. It does not conform to the rules of contracts, since it can be accomplished without consideration to or manifestation by the purported principal and without fresh consent by the other party. Further, it operates as if the transaction were complete at the time and place of the first event, rather than the last, as in the normal case of offer and acceptance. It does not conform to the rules of torts, since the ratifier may become responsible for a harm which was not caused by him, his property or his agent. It can not be justified on a theory of restitution, since the ratifier may not have received a benefit, nor the third person a deprivation. Nor is ratification dependent upon a doctrine of estoppel, since there may be ratification although neither the agent nor the other party suffers a loss resulting from a statement of affirmance or a failure to disavow. However, in some cases in which ratification is claimed, the principal's liability can be based upon unjust enrichment or estoppel, either in addition to or as alternative to his liability based on ratification. See §§ 103, 104.
>
> *d. Justification.* That the doctrine of ratification may at times operate unfairly must be admitted, since it gives to the purported principal

an election to blow hot or cold upon a transaction to which, in contract cases, the other party normally believes himself to be bound. But this hardship is minimized by denying a power to ratify when it would obviously be unfair. See §§ 88–90. Further, if the transaction is not ratified normally the pseudo-agent is responsible; if not, it is because the third party knew, or agreed to take the risk, of lack of authority by the agent. In many cases, the third person is a distinct gainer as where the purported principal ratifies a tort or a loan for which he was not liable and for which he receives nothing. This result is not, however, unjust, since although the creation of liability against the ratifier may run counter to established tort or contract principles, the liability is self-imposed. Even one who ratifies to protect his business reputation or who retains unwanted goods rather than defend a law suit, chooses ratification as preferable to the alternative. Further, the sometimes-derided doctrine of relation back not only is one used in other parts of the law, but it tends to give the parties what they wanted or said they wanted. If it sometimes happens that a mistaken or over-zealous agent is relieved from liability to the third person, the net result causes no harm to anyone. However, perhaps the best defense of ratification is pragmatic; that it is needed in the prosecution of business. It operates normally to cure minor defects in an agent's authority, minimizing technical defenses and preventing unnecessary law suits. In this aspect, it is a beneficial doctrine, which has been adopted in most systems of law.

Restatement (Third) § 4.01, Comment b adds another justification:

Ratification often serves the function of clarifying situations of ambiguous or uncertain authority. A principal's ratification confirms or validates an agent's right to have acted as the agent did. That is, an agent's action may have been effective to bind the principal to the third party, and the third party to the principal, because the agent acted with apparent authority. See § 2.03. If the principal ratifies the agent's act, it is thereafter not necessary to establish that the agent acted with apparent authority. Moreover, by replicating the effects of actual authority, the principal's ratification eliminates claims the principal would otherwise have against the agent for acting without actual authority. See § 8.09, Comment b. The principal's ratification may also eliminate claims that third parties could assert against the agent when the agent has purported to be authorized to bind the principal but the principal is not bound. See § 6.10. Ratification is effective even when the third party knew that the agent lacked authority to bind the principal but nonetheless dealt with the agent.

Finally, in *Goldstick v. ICM Realty*, 788 F.2d 456, 460 (7th Cir. 1986), Judge Posner offered the following rationale for the concept of ratification:

As an original matter one might wonder *why* ratification should make the principal liable. The effect seems to be to confer a windfall on the other party to the contract, who did not bargain for this additional promisor.

The explanations that have been offered have been conclusional. See, e.g., Seavey, Handbook of the Law of Agency 57–59 (1964). The best explanation may be that the principal would not have ratified the contract unless he had seen a commercial advantage in doing so, and that advantage would be less if the ratification had no binding effect. Ordinarily a principal ratifies an agent's unauthorized transaction in order to protect the principal's relationship with the other party to the transaction, usually a customer or supplier; and for ratification to have this protective effect it has to be more than an idle gesture, signifying nothing because unenforceable.

Notes

1. The court in *Dempsey* noted that McCullock undertook to act on behalf of defendant. Is such intent a required element for ratification of a tort? *See Matulis v. Gans*, 107 Conn. 562, 566–67, 141 A. 870, 872 (1928). In this case, Gans, the defendant, said he would assume responsibility for an injury to plaintiff caused by the negligent driving of Gans' car by one Inturisi, a prospective purchaser of the car. Inturisi was driving around with two women friends at the time of the accident. *Held:* Judgment for Gans. "If Inturisi was assuming to act on behalf of Gans, but beyond the scope of his authority, such an act would be ratified, but Gans could not ratify an act which was not done in his behalf." *See also Dobson, Inc. v. Richard*, 17 Ark. App. 155, 705 S.W.2d 893 (1986) (son drove car registered in name of parents' business and negligently injured plaintiff; father told plaintiff that his insurance would take care of the loss; within a few days the parents learned that their insurance would not cover the loss and they informed plaintiff they would not pay. *Held*: no ratification because son was not acting as agent); *Holm v. C.M.P. Sheet Metal, Inc.*, 89 A.D.2d 229, 455 N.Y.S.2d 429 (1982) (subsequent owner of building may not ratify actions taken on behalf of previous owner). These cases seem consistent with the doctrine of ratification set forth in the opinion in *Evans*. Although physical torts rarely are "professedly done" on defendant's behalf, that is not a necessary element of ratification so long as the act "was done" on defendant's behalf.

2. Should ratification be effective if an agent admits to the third party at the time of the agreement that she is not authorized to act? See Restatement (Third) §4.01, stating in Comment b that this does not affect the power of the principal to ratify. Why not, if it is assumed that the doctrine of ratification exists at least in part to realize the expectations of the third party? Perhaps the answer to this depends on how the word "expectations" is defined. If it means the expectation that one has a binding contract at the time the deal is struck with the agent, then the rule is hard to explain, since by hypothesis it was understood that the agent was not authorized to make the contract. But if "expectations" is defined to include the expectation that one has a contract "subject to ratification" by the party on whose behalf the agent is purporting to act, then there is nothing unusual about recognizing ratification. Admittedly, this is drawing a fine line, but see *McCrillis v. A & W Enterprises, Inc.*, 155 S.E.2d 281 (N.C. 1967) (ratification even though third party knew agent

unauthorized); and *Wilkins v. Waldo Lumber Co.*, 153 A. 191 (Me. 1931) (involving a home office approval clause in the contract signed by agent and plaintiff).

Wilkins raises the possibility that some of these cases can be explained on offer-acceptance grounds rather than ratification. One can argue that the "contract" proposed for ratification is in reality nothing more than an offer from the third party that becomes a contract upon the principal's acceptance, with an express or implied understanding that the effective date of the contract shall be as of the time the offer was signed by the third party. What difference does it make whether one characterizes this situation as ratification or offer-acceptance?

3. Can an undisclosed principal ratify a contract? What conceptual problems are involved? See § 85 of the Restatement (Second), stating, "Ratification does not result from the affirmance of a transaction with a third person unless the one acting purported to be acting for the ratifier." For a dissent from this position, see Arnold Rochvarg, *Ratification and Undisclosed Principals*, 34 McGill L.J. 287 (1989). *See also* Warren Seavey, *Ratification — Purporting to Act as Agent*, 21 U. Chi. L. Rev. 248 (1954); Goddard, *Ratification by an Undisclosed Principal*, 2 Mich. L. Rev. 25 (1903). Section 4.03 of the Restatement (Third) of Agency departs from the earlier Restatement: "A person may ratify an act if the actor acted or purported to act as agent on the person's behalf." The drafters of Restatement (Third) explain this difference in Comment b to § 4.03:

> The formulation in this section does not distinguish among disclosed principals, unidentified principals, and undisclosed principals. It is contrary to the rule in Restatement Second, Agency § 85(1), which states that an act may be ratified only if the actor purported to act as an agent. That rule limited ratification to situations in which the principal was disclosed or unidentified. For definitions of these terms, see § 1.04(2). In contrast, under the formulation in this section, an undisclosed principal may ratify an agent's unauthorized act. This is consistent with the result reached in a number of relatively recent cases but inconsistent with the often-stated (but rarely directly dispositive) proposition that it is a requisite for ratification that the actor have purported to act as an agent.

4. Suppose a promoter for a corporation not yet formed enters into several contracts on its behalf. The corporation thereafter is formed and the Board of Directors at its first meeting seeks to ratify the promoter's contracts. Can it do so? What conceptual problems are involved? See Restatement (Third) § 4.04, which permits ratification only if the person ratifying the act "existed at the time of the act." This conceptual problem was resolved by courts holding that the corporation can "adopt" the promoter's contracts, with the problems surrounding adoption sounding very similar to those surrounding ratification. The Virginia courts have gone a step further, allowing "an agent or promoter of a business entity to bind the entity to contracts even before that entity is formed." *T.G. Slater & Son, Inc. v. The Donald P. and Patricia A. Brennan LLC*, 385 F.3d 836, 842 (4th Cir. 2004).

5. Restatement (Second) §93 states in part that "[w]here formalities are requisite for the authorization of an act, its affirmance must be by the same formalities in order to constitute a ratification." An illustration of this concept is provided by *Estate of Huston v. Greene*, 60 Cal. Rptr. 2d 217 (Cal. App. 1997). In this case an annuity was purchased by the holder of a power of attorney acting on behalf of Ms. Huston; the annuity was made payable to a person who had devotedly cared for the elderly Ms. Huston long after others had abandoned her. The holder of the power was not authorized by the power to make gifts. Ms. Huston orally approved the gift in a conversation with the manager at her bank, among others. She was mentally alert up to the time of her death, and clearly wanted this gift to go to her friend. After her death her relatives challenged the gift on the ground that it was not properly authorized. The court agreed with this, noting that "a power of attorney is a written authorization to an agent to perform specified acts on behalf of the principal.... Because a power of attorney must be in writing, any act performed by the agent acting under the power of attorney must therefore be ratified in writing to be valid. Even though, from the evidence at trial, it is apparent decedent in fact wished to make [the] gift, nonetheless, she failed to comply with the formalities necessary to do so.... We therefore conclude the gift was void."

2. Implied Ratification

Manning v. Twin Falls Clinic & Hospital, Inc.

Supreme Court of Idaho
830 P.2d 1185 (1992)

PER CURIAM.

This is a medical malpractice case wherein the decedent's family brought an action seeking an award of damages for the wrongful death of Daryl Manning, negligent and intentional infliction of emotional distress, and punitive damages. We affirm the jury verdict awarding compensatory damages and emotional distress damages. We also affirm the punitive damage award against nurse Anderson. However, we reverse the award of punitive damages against the hospital.

Daryl Manning, a sixty-seven-year-old man with a lengthy history of respiratory ailments, was admitted to the Twin Falls Clinic & Hospital on April 17, 1987, with chronic obstructive pulmonary disease (COPD).... Manning had previously been hospitalized several times, including hospitalization for episodes of COPD that were life threatening, and for two years prior to his last admission to the hospital, he had been on prescribed twenty-four-hour-a-day supplemental oxygen which was administered through a nasal canula.

At the time of his hospitalization on April 17, 1987, Manning's disease was in its final stage and the treating physician, Dr. Kassis, told Manning's family that his death was imminent. Upon his admission, and at the request of the family, the record indicates that Manning was classified as a "no code" patient meaning the hospital and its employees were directed by the family not to place Manning on a respirator or resuscitate him if he were to suddenly expire. The family and Dr. Kassis agreed this was to be Manning's last hospital admission. Subsequent to Manning's admission to the hospital, arterial blood gas tests indicated a continual deterioration of his condition. Virtually all of Manning's strength and energy were needed for breathing and he was unable to sleep or eat.

On April 20, 1987, the day of the event in question, a decision was made by the hospital staff to move Manning to a private room. At that time the treating physician estimated Manning had 24 hours to live. Just prior to the attempted move, an arterial blood gas test was taken. Although the results were not available at the time nurses Anderson and Austin attempted to move Manning, the results of the blood gas test indicated Manning's condition had deteriorated to a point precariously close to cessation of the body's ability to sustain life. Preparatory to the move, Manning's supplemental oxygen was temporarily disconnected. Despite the request of family members present who strenuously urged that Manning be given a portable oxygen unit during the move, the nurses declined to do so because of the relatively short distance of the transfer. Manning's bed was pushed no more than fifteen feet when his condition suddenly and dramatically worsened. In the few seconds that the supplemental oxygen was disconnected, Manning suffered extreme respiratory distress and, according to the record, he may have stopped breathing altogether. Resuscitation efforts were attempted and a doctor was summoned. However, when Manning was identified as a "no code" patient, the doctor provided no treatment. Manning died shortly thereafter.

At the time of Manning's death the hospital had a standing committee in place which was responsible for reviewing all deaths occurring in the facility. After reviewing the circumstances, the committee determined that removal of the supplemental oxygen did not cause Manning's death because an arterial blood gas test taken minutes before the incident indicated his condition had deteriorated to a point nearly incompatible with the sustaining of life. Because the committee concluded the brief removal of the supplemental oxygen probably did not cause Manning's death, the hospital did not reprimand or fire the nurses involved. Even at the time of trial, the hospital and nursing staff maintained the nurses had done nothing wrong because the removal of oxygen did not cause Manning's death. Notwithstanding the committee's determination that the removal of oxygen did not cause Manning's death, a policy was implemented shortly after the incident requiring patients who were on prescribed oxygen to be moved with portable supplemental oxygen.

At trial, evidence was presented indicating nurses at the hospital regularly moved patients from room to room without supplemental oxygen. . . . The nurses defended the practice contending the small size of the hospital allowed patient moves to be made quickly, and that there had never been a problem in the past. The hospital administration and doctors testified this practice was conducted without their knowledge or authorization. At trial, one of the hospital's doctors testified that it was a breach of the standard of nursing care for Manning to be moved without his prescribed oxygen. Dr. Kassis also testified that Manning's death was "caused by a sudden plummet of his already terribly low oxygen level" and that the plummet was the result of Manning's prescribed oxygen being removed.

After a jury trial, plaintiffs were awarded $3,500 compensatory damages and plaintiff Helen Jane Heiskell was awarded $1,000 for emotional distress. In addition, the jury awarded $300 punitive damages against nurse Anderson and $180,000 punitive damages against the hospital. Nurse Austin was relieved of all liability.

The issues we find dispositive on appeal [include] whether the issue of punitive damages should have been submitted to the jury. . . . At trial, the plaintiffs asserted that the hospital ratified the conduct of its nurses. . . . The hospital, on the other hand, contends as a matter of law, that its conduct cannot constitute ratification and that because ratification was alleged as the sole basis for an award of punitive damages, the issue of punitive damages against it should never have been submitted to the jury. We agree. [The court quotes as follows from two Idaho opinions:]

> We recognize that Idaho is one of those states which applies the rule that a principal is liable for punitive damages based upon the acts of his agents only in which the principal participated or which he authorized or ratified.

Boise Dodge v. Clark, 92 Idaho 902, 905, 453 P.2d 551, 554 (1969). Furthermore, as we stated in *Openshaw v. Oregon Automobile Insurance Co.*:

> To be entitled to an award of punitive damages against a corporation the complaining party must show that the principal (or when the principal is a corporation, its directors and managing officers) participated in or authorized or ratified the agent's acts. . . .

. . . As we have previously noted, "ratification is the affirmance by a person of a prior act which did not bind him but which was done or professedly done on his account, whereby the act as to some or all persons, is given effect as if originally authorized by him." [citing Restatement §82] The "essence of ratification by principal of act of agent is manifestation of mental determination by the principal to affirm the act, and this may be manifested by written word or by spoken word or by conduct, or may be inferred from known circumstances and principal's acts in relation thereto." Black's Law Dictionary 1262 (6th ed. 1990). . . . Consequently, our analysis must focus on whether substantial evidence exists in the record upon which a jury could find that subsequent to Manning's death, the hospital with knowledge of all material facts, expressed an intent to approve or sanction the nurses' conduct.

In support of its position that the hospital ratified the conduct of the nurses, the plaintiffs argue that the nurses were not reprimanded or criticized for their conduct, that the hospital maintained that nurses Anderson and Austin had done nothing wrong, and that the hospital never apologized to the Mannings for the conduct of the nurses. The Mannings contend this constitutes substantial evidence of implied ratification. We disagree.

In *Carpenter* [578 P.2d 1074 (Idaho 1978)], we considered the doctrine of implied ratification in a contract setting. We noted that ratification

> may also be implied if the principal, with full knowledge of the material facts, receives, accepts and retains benefits from the contract; remains silent, acquiesces in or fails to repudiate or disaffirm the contract; or otherwise exhibits conduct demonstrating an adoption and recognition of the agent's act as binding.

Id., 578 P.2d at 1078. We also observed in *Carpenter* that implied ratification is a means by "which the principal is estopped from denying the unauthorized act of his agent because to do so would result in the unjust enrichment of the principal." *Id.*, 578 P.2d at 1078 n.5. In addition to principles of unjust enrichment, an additional rationale for implied ratification is based on principles of estoppel.[1]

The requirement of a clear showing of ratification is particularly important when the doctrine of implied ratification is asserted. The plaintiffs' contention that the hospital's failure to punish or reprimand the nurses constitutes sufficient evidence of ratification is not persuasive. In addition to falling short of a clear showing of ratification as required by *Hatfield* [606 P.2d 944 (Idaho 1980)], such conduct is not indicative of an intent to ratify. A review of the jurisdictions that have considered the issue indicates that as a general rule, the failure to punish or reprimand, at least standing alone, is insufficient evidence to support a finding of ratification.

An employer's reasons for continuing an employment relationship or declining to reprimand an employee may be varied, and in the absence of clear evidence of an intent to ratify cannot be the basis to uphold an award of punitive damages. Furthermore, from a public policy standpoint, it would be an unwise rule of law that mandates disciplinary action whenever misconduct is alleged. As the Supreme Court of Hawaii reasoned in *Abraham v. S.E. Onorato Garages*, 446 P.2d 821, 827 (1968):

> The continuance of [the defendant's] employment alone is insufficient to show such approval. Such continuance is "too readily open to explanation on other grounds." If we held otherwise, we would in effect be requiring the discharge of an employee whenever an employer learns of an employee's wrongful act. Surely we should wish to promote a policy of clear and objective reflection when a man's job is at stake. Since we are all subject to human frailties, we think that the law should permit an employer to retain and give an opportunity to an employee to redeem himself where he has acted tortiously, without the employer being found to have ratified the tort. Of course, the employer would thereafter be on notice that such

---

1. [9] For example, where a principal undertakes an "act which is inconsistent with the nonexistence of affirmance, such as bringing an action upon a prior contract purported to be made for him, the principal is estopped from denying ratification of the prior contract." Warren A. Seavey, *Ratification by Silence*, 103 U. Pa. L. Rev. 30–31 (1955). Similarly, where a principal's act or omission does something which misleads a third party into believing a prior transaction was authorized or ratified, the principal is estopped to deny the validity of the transaction. *Id.*

conduct on the part of the employee is a future possibility, and he would be required to take reasonable steps to assure it would not occur again. (Citations omitted).

. . . .

Similarly, we are satisfied that the hospital's failure to apologize, and the hospital's defense at trial that the nurses did nothing wrong does not constitute sufficient evidence to support a finding of ratification. In addition to the lack of evidence indicating an intent to ratify, the plaintiffs' position, if adopted, would effectively require a principal to admit its agent's negligence or wrongdoing in every case to avoid a finding of ratification. Such a double-edged position is not sound policy.

In Mannings' case-in-chief, uncontroverted evidence was presented showing that shortly after his death, the hospital adopted a policy requiring all patients on prescribed supplemental oxygen to be moved in the future with supplemental oxygen in place. This act of the hospital clearly rejects any contention that the hospital acquiesced, or failed to repudiate or disaffirm the conduct of the nurses. . . .

After reviewing all of the evidence presented in the Mannings' case-in-chief, and drawing all inferences available, we are unable to conclude that substantial evidence was presented upon which a jury could have found a clear showing of ratification. . . . The judgment of the district court is affirmed, except as to the award of punitive damages against the defendant Twin Falls Clinic & Hospital, Inc., which is reversed. The cause is remanded to the district court to enter an amended judgment excluding the award of punitive damages against the hospital. Costs to appellants. No attorney fees allowed. [Bistline, Justice, concurred in part and dissented in part.]

Notes

1. In a case decided the same year as *Manning*, the following was said about proving ratification of an employee's tort: "Among other factors which may be considered evidence of ratification on the part of a superior are a failure to investigate and discipline an employee . . . and failure to disavow an employee's unauthorized action and to mitigate the harm caused once the facts are ascertained." *Pinshaw v. Metropolitan Dist. Comm'n*, 604 N.E.2d 1321 (Mass. App. 1992). Is that language inconsistent with *Manning*? Compare this statement from Restatement (Third) § 4.01, Comment d: "[A] principal's failure to terminate or reprimand an employee by itself is not likely to ratify the employee's unauthorized action because the employer may have varied reasons for failing to take action adverse to an employee. On the other hand, if the employer is aware of ongoing conduct encompassing numerous acts by the employee, failure to terminate may constitute ratification, as in some circumstances may the promotion or celebration of such an employee."

2. The above cases deal with the difficult problem of indirect ratification through conduct or lack of conduct. Sometimes the equities of a case will lead a court to draw an inference of ratification under ambiguous circumstances. An active area of

litigation today involves sexual harassment cases, where ratification frequently is an alternative ground of recovery against an employer. *See Potts v. BE & K Constr. Co.,* 604 So. 2d 398, 400 (Ala. 1992) ("An employer's failure to stop the tortious conduct after it learns of the conduct will support an inference that the employer tolerated the conduct.").

3. As the above cases indicate, it is possible for an employer to subject itself to compensatory and punitive damages through approval of an employee's wrongdoing. Yet in *Dempsey v. Chambers* and the notes following it, the point was made that a tort cannot be ratified unless the actor intends to act on behalf of the party being sued on the basis of ratification. In what sense, then, can a tortious act that is outside the scope of employment because it was engaged in for purely personal reasons, with no interest even in part to serve the employer, be found to be ratifiable? This may be one of several "rough edges" in the doctrine of ratification, where the doctrine does not appear fully to match the decisions being made by courts.

B. The Knowledge Requirement

One of the conventional rules of ratification is that the purported principal must have knowledge of all the material facts before being held to an apparent affirmance. *See* Restatement (Third) §4.06; *see also Page v. Suraci,* 483 A.2d 601 (Vt. 1984) (retention by plaintiff buyers of second deed for eight months before objection was not ratification of attorney's unauthorized act of recording the deed because plaintiffs were unaware of the material fact that the second deed differed substantially from the first).

One way of characterizing the effect of this rule is that it allows avoidance of a contract on the ground of unilateral mistake. Ordinarily the law is reluctant to allow this in the absence of an unconscionable injury to the mistaken party. *See* E. ALLAN FARNSWORTH, CONTRACTS 631 (3rd ed. 1999). This strict standard does not apply to ratification. Why not? The drafters of Restatement (Third) suggest, in Comment b to §4.06, that "[t]he grounds for avoiding a ratification are broader, perhaps because the principal's ignorance is often attributable to the agent's failure to make disclosure." Perhaps another explanation for this is that if a ratification is rescinded, presumably the third party's breach of warranty claim against the person who acted as agent would be revived, and thus unilateral rescission would not result in the same frustration of expectations that an ordinary contract case would involve. Rescission by the ratifying party for mistake is limited only by its assumption of the risk of mistake or by change of position by the third party in reliance on the affirmance.

Would the following illustration fall within the above rule? *P*'s agent in this country advanced *P*'s money to a mutual friend to enable the friend to save stock that she was carrying on a margin account. This was done without authority. *P*, in Europe, on being informed of *A*'s action, expressly approved. Later, however, he attempted to disavow the ratification on the ground that he had no idea what a critical condition the mutual friend's account was in. Can he escape under the general principle that one must have knowledge of all material facts before he is held to a ratification? *See Currie v. Land Title Bank & Trust Co.*, 5 A.2d 168 (Pa. 1939) (no). Why not? Is it because he was aware of his ignorance? *See* W. Seavey, Law of Agency 66–67 (1964); *Jessen v. National Excess Ins. Co.*, 776 P.2d 1244, 1249 (N.M. 1989) ("Ratification requires either knowledge of the material facts or circumstances sufficient to put a reasonable person on notice to inquire into the facts."). Can estoppel be an alternative ground of decision under some circumstances?

Lewis v. Cable

United States District Court, Western District of Pennsylvania
107 F. Supp. 196 (1952)

Marsh, District Judge.

This action was instituted by plaintiffs to recover from defendant 20¢ for each ton of coal produced by defendant for use or sale during the life of the National Bituminous Coal Wage Agreement of 1948 and to recover 30¢ for each ton of coal produced by defendant for use or sale during the life of the National Bituminous Coal Wage Agreement of 1950. Plaintiffs allege that said Agreements were signed on behalf of defendant by the Somerset County Coal Operators Association of Pennsylvania (Association) of which defendant is a member.

Plaintiffs filed a motion for summary judgment. In support of their motion, they contend that the Association had apparent authority to execute the contracts on behalf of the defendant; or, if the Association did not have apparent authority then defendant ratified the contracts by making payments thereunder.

Defendant made payments on the production of coal up to April 30, 1949. These payments were 20¢ for each ton of coal produced for use or sale. On October 10, 1949, counsel for plaintiffs sent defendant a letter demanding payment for coal produced "due and owing in accordance with and pursuant to the terms and provisions of the National Bituminous Coal Wage Agreement of 1948. . . . If the aforesaid debt is not paid within a reasonable time, it will be necessary for the Trustees of the United Mine Workers of America Welfare and Retirement Fund to take the legal steps necessary to compel compliance of your contractual obligations." Defendant, on October 12, 1949, replied: "In reference to your letter of Oct. 10, 1949, regarding the Welfare fund I owe the U.M.W.A. Right now I'm in no position to pay anything on this debt. But just as soon as we go back to work my broker will advance the money on the output for the first two days, this will be sent to you at once to apply on the welfare fund."

In opposition to plaintiffs' motion, defendant filed an affidavit in which he states that "The payments made as aforesaid were made by me under the influence of fear of strike and repercussions which I was convinced would inevitably result if such payments had not been made and which would entail irreparable loss to me in my business, and were in nowise made pursuant to any legal obligation known by me to exist at that time and, on the contrary, I was not cognizant of any legal obligation incurred by me at any time for making such payments."

Defendant's defense, therefore, appears to be that subjectively he did not intend to ratify the 1948 Agreement. But the court is of the opinion that it is the manifestation and not the undisclosed intention of the alleged principal which controls. . . . Defendant cannot by his acts and declarations pretend to be bound by the Agreement so as to prevent strikes and repercussions and then, when full liability under said Agreement is asserted, seek to disaffirm it. . . .

Defendant further urges, however, that he did not ratify the 1948 Agreement because it is not shown that he had full knowledge of all the material facts concerning the Agreement. We do not agree with this contention. If he did not have full knowledge of all the material facts, the payments and the above letter of defendant indicate to the court a willingness on the part of defendant to ratify the contracts without complete knowledge. See Restatement of the Law of Agency, § 91. . . . From defendant's acts and declarations, we find, as a matter of law, that he did ratify the 1948 agreement.

Although defendant did not make payments under the 1950 Agreement, we find that the ratification of the 1948 Agreement created apparent authority in the Association to enter into the later Agreement on defendant's behalf. The ratification of the prior Agreement appears to the court to be such "conduct of the principal which, reasonably interpreted, causes a third person to believe that the principal consents to have the act done on his behalf by the person purporting to act for him." Restatement of the Law of Agency, § 27.

It further appears to the court that the motion for summary judgment should be granted because the defendant is estopped from denying the authority of the Association to act on his behalf. Defendant's affidavit indicates that he made payments under the 1948 Agreement in order to circumvent strikes and other repercussions. Obviously this course of action was taken to insure continued production at defendant's mines by inducing the employees and their union to believe that defendant had a contract with the union. The success of this deception is demonstrated by the fact that the 1950 Agreement was entered into in the same manner as the 1948 Agreement. As a result, the employees and their union did not undertake to enter into a separate contract with defendant although they have the right to insist that defendant bargain collectively. Defendant's action and declarations caused the employees and their union to forego this valued right of labor. If we were to sustain defendant's contention, the employees and their union would be prejudiced after they had relied on the only reasonable inference to be drawn from defendant's course of conduct. Thus, the elements of estoppel are present. See Restatement of the Law of Agency, § 103.

The motion, therefore, will be granted and summary judgment will be entered for the amount shown to be due by the number of tons admittedly produced by defendant.

Computel, Inc. v. Emery Air Freight Corp.

United States Court of Appeals, Eleventh Circuit
919 F.2d 678 (1990)

Fay, Circuit Judge:

Computel, Inc. ("Computel") [was] granted summary final judgment on a breach of contract claim against Emery Air Freight Corp. ("Emery") in the amount of $38,625.21. . . . Computel contracted with Emery in Miami, Florida, for delivery of various computer goods to American Shop at Home, Inc. ("Consignee") in New York. "C.O.D. Cashier Check" was written in the "Special Instructions" box of the waybill. . . . Emery delivered the shipment to the Consignee, and collected a corporate check payable to Computel, bearing the Consignee's name and address. Emery then delivered the check to Computel, who received, accepted, stamped and deposited the check unconditionally in its bank account. Computel's president, Claudio Osorio, did not discover that the check in question was not a cashier's check until the check was returned to Computel stamped "Account Closed." After receiving the dishonored check, Computel brought a multi-count action against Emery, essentially maintaining that the carrier failed to fulfill a contract to deliver computer products to a third party and obtain, in return, a valid cashier's check. . . .

. . . Did Computel, the principal, by accepting and unconditionally depositing the Consignee's corporate check, ratify its agent Emery's unauthorized acceptance and delivery of a form of payment other than that specified in the carriage contract? . . . "In actions such as this where a shipping customer sues his carrier for allegedly collecting an unauthorized form of payment, the vast majority of jurisdictions agree that ratification will be found where the shipping customer unconditionally deposits this unauthorized form of payment into its account, knowing that it deviates from the form of payment specified." [citations omitted] One of the primary elements of the doctrine of ratification is knowledge of the material facts. . . . In deposition testimony, the president of Computel, Claudio Osorio, stated that the checks that come into the company are simply stamped and processed by administrative employees who "don't have to qualify or evaluate the type of payments they receive."[2] Because the check in question was processed by a ministerial employee "who was without knowledge that the check did not conform to the requirements of the contract," Computel argues that depositing Consignee's check was not a "fully

---

2. [6] The key exchange was as follows:

Q:

So, your testimony is that prior to the deposit of this in the bank, this check, that nobody checked it to determine whether it conformed to the method of payment that you had requested from [the Consignee]?

A:

That's correct. They just received the check and stamped it. There is no signature on the bank [*sic*] as you can see. And they deposit it. *Deposition of Claudio Osorio* (SR1).

informed knowing act of ratification." We disagree, at least for purposes of summary judgment.

In this case, the undisputed evidence established that Computel was the party who imposed the requirement of payment by cashier's check. Further, the waybill in the record is clearly marked "shipper's copy." Knowledge of the "C.O.D. cashier check" requirement thus was apparently available to Computel's officers and employees in the shipper's files. In addition, cashier's checks are clearly marked, and generally, a recipient is charged with knowledge when a check is not a cashier's or certified check.

Section 91(1) of the Restatement (Second) of Agency dealing with the knowledge of a principal at the time of affirmance or ratification is instructive. . . . Specifically, Comment e speaks to when a principal assumes the risk of lack of knowledge:

> If the purported principal is shown to have knowledge of facts which would lead a person of ordinary prudence to investigate further, and he fails to make such investigation, his affirmance without qualification is evidence that he is willing to ratify upon the knowledge which he has. Likewise, if, learning that one who had no authority acted for him, he affirms without qualification and without investigation, when he has reason to believe that he does not know all the facts, it may be inferred that he is willing to assume the risks of facts of which he has no knowledge.

Id. Indeed, in *Oxford Lake Line v. First Nat'l Bank of Pensacola*, 40 Fla. 349, 359–60, 24 So. 480, 483 (1898), the Supreme Court of Florida observed:

> Generally speaking, it does not devolve upon the principal to make inquiries as to the facts. He has a right to presume that his agent has followed instructions, and has not exceeded his authority. Whenever he is sought to be held liable on the ground of ratification, either express or implied, it must be shown that he ratified upon full knowledge of all material facts, *or that he was willfully ignorant, or purposely refrained from seeking information, or that he intended to adopt the unauthorized act at all events, under whatever circumstances.*

(Emphasis added); *see also Gordon v. Pettingill*, 105 Colo. 214, 218, 96 P.2d 416, 418 (1939) (principal's lack of knowledge cannot be established by showing that he was "ignorant of facts it was in his interest to know, and which, if awake, he would have known").

Claudio Osorio, the president of Computel, in effect testified that no one at the company analyzes the quality of incoming payments or the payments' conformity with prior instructions before they are deposited by administrative clerks. Osorio's awareness of such a structure for accepting incoming payments, considered in the light most favorable to Emery, could be found to reasonably imply that Computel intentionally refrains from checking incoming payments against the form of payment specified to its carriers. Computel appears to deposit checks unconditionally "whatever the circumstances." We believe that the above-mentioned authority suggests that Computel cannot specify one form of payment, set up a procedure whereby it is *willfully ignorant* of whether the incoming payment conforms with the company's original payment instructions (copies of which are presumably readily available in its files), unconditionally accept and deposit a varying form of payment, and then argue lack of knowledge when an unfortunate dishonoring or "bouncing" of payment occurs.

Further, Florida case law acknowledges the general principle of agency law that knowledge of, or notice to an agent or employee is imputed to the principal when it is received by the employee within the scope of her employment, and when it is in reference to matters over which the employee's authority extends. Thus, if 1) Computel's ministerial employees were on notice that cashier's checks differ from corporate checks; 2) if Computel kept Emery's waybill on file, i.e. possessed the means to easily verify whether the payments were conforming but, as Osorio's testimony suggests, chose not to do so; and 3) Computel nonetheless deposited the payments unconditionally, it seems that "full knowledge" could be imputed to Computel for ratification purposes.

At the very least, we think that when the facts and testimony are considered in the light most favorable to Emery . . . Computel's intent to ratify is a jury question not appropriately decided on summary judgment. Accordingly, the order of the district court is . . . VACATED and REMANDED for trial on the issue of ratification.

Johnson, Circuit Judge, dissenting:

I agree with the panel's holding that Emery breached its contract with Computel. I cannot agree, however, with the panel's holding that Computel may have ratified Emery's action by simply depositing the non-conforming check. I therefore dissent.

As the majority observes, under Florida law, one asserting ratification must show that the principal accepted the agent's conduct "upon full knowledge of all material facts, or that [the principal] was willfully ignorant, or purposely refrained from seeking information, or that he intended to adopt the unauthorized act at all events, under whatever circumstances." *Oxford Lake Line v. First Nat'l Bank of Pensacola*, 40 Fla. 349, 24 So. 480, 483 (1898). The majority takes the position that, based on the deposition of Claudio Osorio, Computel may have ratified Emery's acceptance of the non-conforming payment by remaining "willfully ignorant." Osorio's deposition shows that he was aware that the office clerks at Computel did not analyze the quality of incoming payments or attempt to confirm the payments' compliance with prior instructions before depositing them. From this fact, the majority infers that Computel may have intentionally refrained from investigating whether its carriers complied with instructions regarding the form of payment the carrier was to accept. In my view, such an inference requires a long leap. Though it is possible to infer from Osorio's statement that the system has the effect of keeping the company in the dark as to whether the carrier has performed as promised, I do not believe that we can also infer that Osorio "willfully" or intentionally established this office procedure in order to insulate the company from an affirmative defense of ratification.

This long leap is especially troublesome because it goes directly against the language of *Oxford Lake Line*. That case states that "it does not devolve upon the principal to make inquiries as to the facts. He has a right to presume that his agent has followed instructions. . . ." *Id.* This language clearly places the burden of showing that the principal remained "willfully ignorant" upon the defendant who asserts ratification as an affirmative defense. If we allow the fact that Computel's office procedure presumes that Emery has followed instructions to stand as the basis for a showing that Computel was "willfully ignorant," then we inappropriately shift this burden. I find no precedent in Florida law for such a shifting of the burden in an affirmative defense, even when viewing the facts in a light most favorable to the nonmovant on a summary judgment motion.

I would therefore affirm the district court's grant of summary judgment in favor of Computel.

Inn Foods, Inc. v. Equitable Cooperative Bank

United States Court of Appeals, First Circuit
45 F.3d 594 (1995)

Before TORRUELLA, CHIEF JUDGE, CYR and STAHL, CIRCUIT JUDGES.

STAHL, CIRCUIT JUDGE.

Plaintiff-appellant Inn Foods, Inc. ("Inn Foods"), secured a default judgment in the amount of $1,084,524.13 against Atlantic Brands, Inc. ("Atlantic"). During discovery to determine the availability of assets to satisfy the judgment, Inn Foods learned that Atlantic's president, Paget T. Hodge ("Hodge"), had indorsed a $523,744.18 United States Treasury check ("Treasury check"), payable to Atlantic, for deposit into his personal account at defendant-appellee Equitable Co-operative Bank ("Equitable"). In the present case, Inn Foods seeks to reach and apply a never-asserted cause of action for conversion of the Treasury check that it contends Atlantic has against Equitable. . . .

In the early 1980's, Hodge formed Atlantic, a closely held corporation based in Boston, Massachusetts, with Hodge serving as Atlantic's president. The primary business of Atlantic was food distribution. In 1988, Atlantic obtained from the Department of Defense Personnel Support Center ("DOD") a contract to supply frozen vegetables to DOD. Atlantic subcontracted some of its supply obligations to Inn Foods, a California-based wholesale food supplier, which agreed to provide a portion of the contracted-for frozen vegetables to DOD, thus partially fulfilling Atlantic's contract obligations with DOD. In November of 1988, Atlantic breached its contract with Inn Foods by failing to pay Inn Foods for the vegetables it had delivered to DOD. Inn Foods then sued Atlantic for the amount due and, in March of 1989, obtained a default judgment.

In their discovery efforts seeking assets to satisfy the judgment, Inn Foods learned the following. Hodge maintained a personal checking account at Equitable, where he had been a regular customer for more than ten years. Equitable officials knew that Hodge was president of Atlantic. On December 8, 1988, Hodge appeared at Equitable's office in Lynn, Massachusetts, where he indorsed to himself the Treasury check which was in partial payment to Atlantic for the vegetables actually supplied to DOD by Inn Foods. Equitable accepted the check for deposit into Hodge's personal account. Equitable then issued to Hodge a bank check payable to the Bank of New England in the amount of $450,000. Equitable debited Hodge's account accordingly. The next day, Equitable took the Treasury check directly to the Federal Reserve Bank of Boston, which credited Equitable's account. Eventually, Hodge withdrew from his personal account the balance of the funds obtained from the Treasury check.

By deposition, Equitable's senior vice president and treasurer, Arthur E. Horgan, testified that he was "uncomfortable" about the Hodge transaction in light of both the sum involved and the fact that Hodge had deposited the Treasury check into his personal account. As a result, Horgan "contacted counsel and they suggested we get something, a certificate of vote from the company indicating that ... Hodge has authority to transact business." Equitable's president, James G. Perkins, then called Hodge and requested that Atlantic provide a written corporate resolution stating that Hodge had authority to indorse the Treasury check and that he was authorized to deposit the check into his personal account. Thereafter, Perkins received a resolution ("resolution"), dated December 17, 1988, and signed by Wallace Johnson, the corporation's secretary, which stated that the Board of Directors of Atlantic had unanimously:

> VOTED: That, Paget Hodge, President of Atlantic Brands, Inc. is hereby authorized to endorse on behalf of the Corporation any checks to his order, said checks being drawn or endorsed payable to said Corporation, and deposit said checks to his personal account.

After Atlantic defaulted, Inn Foods brought the present action against Equitable and others to satisfy its judgment. As alluded to above, Inn Foods' theory of recovery against Equitable has two principal elements. First, Inn Foods argues that Atlantic has a cause of action for conversion against Equitable. Second, as a judgment creditor, it seeks to reach and apply Atlantic's unfiled conversion claim.[3] As noted, Atlantic has never filed such a claim, nor has it ever indicated an intent to do so.[4] The parties entered cross-motions for summary judgment. After a hearing, the district court denied Inn Foods' motion and granted Equitable's. . . .

Inn Foods' conversion theory rests on the premise that Hodge was not authorized to indorse the Treasury check to himself for deposit into his personal account.

---

3. [3] Mass. Gen. L. ch. 214, §3(6) authorizes an action by creditors to reach and apply an unsatisfied debt.

4. [4] From the record, it appears that Atlantic ceased to function as an ongoing enterprise before the default judgment occurred. As for Hodge, he was a named defendant below, but failed to answer. Service of process on Hodge was made at the Wormwood Scrubs prison in London, England.

Under the Code, conversion takes place when an instrument "is paid on a forged indorsement." § 3-419(1)(c). This section has generally been interpreted to permit actions for conversion where a negotiable instrument has been paid on either an "unauthorized" or a "forged" indorsement. Under the Code, "[a]ny unauthorized signature may be ratified" by the principal. § 3-404(2). We assume but do not decide that Inn Foods met its initial burden of establishing that Hodge's signature on the Treasury check was unauthorized when presented. Thus, we proceed directly to the question of whether Atlantic ratified Hodge's signature.

Unless they are displaced by a particular provision, general common law principles, including those of agency, supplement the Code. Under Massachusetts law, ratification of an agent's acts may be express or implied and, as a general proposition, the principal must have full knowledge of all material facts. Massachusetts courts, however, do not always require that the principal have actual knowledge. There may be ratification when the principal "purposely shut[s] his eyes to means of information within his own possession and control." See also *Puritan Medical Ctr. v. Cashman*, 596 N.E.2d [1004] at 1008 (Mass. 1992) (ratification may be implied where corporation directors have "knowledge of such facts or circumstances as would put a reasonable person on inquiry and which would lead to full discovery").

Inn Foods argues that because the record is devoid of any indication that Atlantic had full knowledge of the facts, no ratification occurred. We do not agree. We think the only reasonable conclusion to be drawn from the record is that Atlantic ratified the transaction with knowledge at least sufficient to satisfy the "deliberate ignorance" standard recited above. The language of the resolution itself speaks directly to the two critical elements of the Treasury check transaction. The resolution authorizes Hodge to both indorse checks on behalf of the corporation, and to deposit those checks into his personal account. Moreover, the resolution was dated nine days after Hodge presented the Treasury check to Equitable. At a minimum, the terms of the resolution as well as the surrounding circumstances should have alerted Atlantic's directors that "something was afoot," *Perkins v. Rich*, 415 N.E.2d [895] at 898 (Mass. App. 1981).

Inn Foods makes the additional argument that the resolution does not ratify the Treasury check transaction because its language is cast in prospective terms only. Even if we were to agree, Massachusetts law makes clear that ratification can be implied when a principal with knowledge makes no effort to repudiate a transaction.[5] See also Restatement of Agency 2d § 94 ("An affirmance of an unauthorized transaction can be inferred from a failure to repudiate it."). The rationale for this

5. [7] On this point, we disagree with Inn Foods' contention that *Puritan*, 596 N.E.2d at 1008, should be read as requiring that a benefit accrue to the principal from the disputed transaction before an implied -ratification can be found. While benefits received are certainly strong evidence that the principal acquiesced in the agent's transaction, other Massachusetts cases make clear that ratification can take place in the absence of such a benefit. See, e.g., *Boice-Perrine Co. v. Kelley*, 243 Mass. 327, 137 N.E. 731 (1923).

rule is plain. When a principal fails to disavow promptly an act of his agent, such a failure both thwarts a damaged third party's ability to mitigate the effects of an unauthorized act and perpetuates an inference of authority reposed in the would-be agent. Again, we do not think there can be reasonable dispute that Atlantic had sufficient knowledge for ratification, and there is no indication in the record that Atlantic ever sought to repudiate this transaction.

In short, Atlantic had sufficient knowledge to ratify by either acting (as it purported to do in the resolution) or not acting (thereby acquiescing in the Treasury check transaction). Either route leads to the same conclusion: Atlantic ratified Hodge's indorsement and deposit. Because Hodge's signature was authorized, Atlantic has no conversion cause of action against Equitable and, thus, Inn Foods' claim must fail.

For the reasons discussed above, the decision of the district court is Affirmed. Costs to appellee.

C. Can Silence Constitute Affirmance?

Bruton v. Automatic Welding & Supply Corp.

Supreme Court of Alaska
513 P.2d 1122 (1973)

Before Rabinowitz, C.J., and Connor, Erwin, Boochever, and Fitzgerald, JJ.

Boochever, Justice.

We are here confronted with the question of whether the owner of a tractor or the person using it with his permission is liable to a repair shop for major repairs undertaken at the request of the borrower without prior authorization of the owner.

In the fall of 1969, appellant Jerry Bruton loaned a D8 Caterpillar rent-free to appellee Dr. David Ekvall, who wanted to clear some of his land as a field for horse riding activities. By their informal oral agreement, Ekvall was to provide an operator, pay for the fuel consumed and perform routine maintenance. Nothing was said about major repairs or overhauls.

Bruton delivered the Cat to Ekvall's property where it was driven by one or more operators under the direction of Mike Fontana, Ekvall's foreman. Problems developed which required repairs. The Cat kept slipping out of gear, cables broke, and there was damage to the radiator. Ekvall called Appellee Automatic Welding & Supply [hereinafter AWS], which did maintenance and repair work. At first AWS sent men out to the Ekvall site to make field repairs; but those proved only temporarily effective. During the period in which field repairs were attempted, several conversations ensued between Emmett Roetman, owner and manager of AWS, and Ekvall, and between Roetman and Fontana, in which the possibility of a major repair was discussed.

Thereafter on authorization by Ekvall AWS removed the machine to its shop where extensive repairs were undertaken, valued at $2340.89. While the Cat was there, Bruton entered the shop on other business, recognized his Cat and authorized some additional work to be done on it, at a cost of $387.80. At the time of Bruton's visit to the shop, the major repairs authorized by Ekvall were either completed or nearly completed; Bruton learned from Ed Dow, an AWS mechanic, of the scope of the major repairs but their cost was not discussed.

When the repairs were completed, the Cat was returned to Ekvall's property and used for some time thereafter. AWS billed Bruton for all the repairs, including those authorized specifically by Bruton while in the AWS shop, those made in the field on Bruton's Cat and authorized by Ekvall, some other repairs wholly unrelated to Bruton's Cat which Ekvall had authorized on a different Cat, and the major repairs which had been performed in the AWS shop. Ekvall was sent copies of the bill.

Unable to get any portion of the bill paid, AWS brought suit against both Bruton and Ekvall in District Court. Bruton contended that Ekvall was liable and cross-claimed against him for the cost of the repairs during the period that he had used the Cat, and for damage to the Cat that Bruton claimed was the result of Ekvall's negligence. The District Court held that Ekvall was severally liable to AWS for $757.90 plus interest, which represented the field repairs specifically authorized by Ekvall prior to the major repair, and the cost of the repairs which were unrelated to Bruton's Cat. Bruton was found severally liable for the $387.80 plus interest. Each was held jointly and severally liable for the major repairs, with Ekvall to have judgment against Bruton for any part of the joint and several liability which Ekvall would be compelled to pay. Attorney's fees were awarded to AWS on the principal suit and to Ekvall on the crossclaim. Bruton was to pay Ekvall for any part of the attorney's fees assessed against them jointly which Ekvall might be compelled to pay. On appeal to the Superior Court, the judgment was affirmed, and Bruton has appealed from that affirmance.

Because at oral argument Bruton's counsel conceded liability to AWS for the $387.80 which he specifically authorized, we need focus only on the District Court's findings that Bruton is jointly and severally liable with Ekvall to AWS for the major repairs, and that he is liable to Ekvall for any part of the major repair bill that Ekvall might be required to pay.

The District Court based its judgment against Bruton on three theories, each of which is argued by Ekvall as sufficient to justify Bruton's liability: (1) Ekvall had apparent authority to order major repairs for Bruton to the Cat; (2) Bruton ratified Ekvall's actions when he went to the AWS shop; and (3) Bruton rather than Ekvall should be ultimately liable for the repairs, as otherwise he would be unjustly enriched.

Apparent Authority

The District Court listed as a finding of fact: "The court specifically finds that Ekvall had apparent authority to order major repairs to the D-8." We must thus ascertain whether such ultimate finding was clearly erroneous. . . .

[H]ere there were no words or conduct of Bruton which could have caused AWS to believe that Bruton consented to have the repairs made on his behalf. There was no testimony to the effect that Bruton made any representation to AWS that Ekvall was authorized to order repairs on his behalf. The mere fact that Bruton permitted Ekvall to use the Cat did not constitute any representation to AWS that Ekvall was authorized to make repairs to it on Bruton's behalf.

[T]he gratuitous loan constituted a bailment.... While the relations of bailment and agency are not mutually exclusive, the ordinary bailment does not involve authorization from the bailor for the bailee to act for him in such a way that an agency may be inferred. The crucial distinction between the two relations for our purposes is that "a bailee has, *as such*, no power to subject the bailor to liability in contract or tort." (Emphasis supplied.)[6] We find no element of an agency relationship in the bailment entered into by the parties.... To conclude from the record that Ekvall had apparent authority was clearly erroneous.

Ratification

The District Court found that at the time Bruton went into the AWS shop and specifically authorized further minor repairs to the Cat, his "assent and/or lack of protest ... constituted ratification of Ekvall's actions."

As with apparent authority, ratification is an agency doctrine. It was created by common law courts to deal with a situation where, *after* a transaction is entered into by a second party purporting to act for a principal, the principal manifests an intent to be bound by the acts of the second party. Thus ratification is unnecessary where a person acts with a principal's authority or apparent authority; in those situations the third party has reason to believe, by communication *prior* to the transaction either from the principal directly or through another, that the principal is liable.

But ratification was wrongly applied in the instant case. As stated in *Pullen v. Dale*, 109 F.2d 538, 539, 9 Alaska 643, 646 (9th Cir. 1940), "It is sufficient to say that for the doctrine of ratification to apply, it is a requisite that the act sought to be ratified be done by someone who held himself out to the third party as an agent."[7]

No evidence was presented below that Ekvall purported to be acting for Bruton when he authorized the Cat to be brought into the AWS shop. In fact the testimony of Roetman indicated that Ekvall, who up until that time had explicitly authorized all repair bills for the D8 Cat, had the major repairs done on his own account. Roetman testified:

> I explained to him what we were trying to do, and that in the event this didn't work, it would then become a major repair job, and have to go to the

---

6. [5] Restatement (Second) of Agency § 12, comment *c* (1958); [additional citations omitted].
7. [9] To the same effect is the Restatement (Second) of Agency § 85(1) (1958):
Purporting to Act as Agent as a Requisite for Ratification.
(1) Ratification does not result from the affirmance of a transaction with a third person unless the one acting purported to be acting for the ratifier.

shop, and he said well, we don't want to put any more money into it, in so many words anyway, that any more money in it than we have to, but we've got to repair it, so do whatever you see fit. . . .

Ekvall testified that he did not remember authorizing major repairs to the best of his knowledge; but he did not testify at all about representing himself to Roetman as Bruton's agent. In short, our search of the transcript reveals no evidence that Ekvall was purporting to act for Bruton in authorizing the repairs. Absent Ekvall giving Roetman a reasonable basis for assuming that Bruton would be paying the bill, no subsequent ratification is possible.

But even if Ekvall had purported to act for Bruton in authorizing the major repairs, there was no ratification for yet another reason. Neither through conduct nor speech did Bruton affirm any responsibility to pay for repairs authorized by Ekvall. Affirmance is defined in the Restatement (Second) of Agency § 83 as:

(a) a manifestation of an election by one on whose account an unauthorized act has been done to treat the act as authorized, or

(b) conduct by him justifiable only if there were such an election.

Though there is no evidence of an express election by Bruton to pay for the major repairs, appellee argues that a finding of implied affirmance may be justified because Bruton, upon finding that major repairs were being done to his Cat, did not question Dow or Roetman about the cost or his liability. Appellee also argues that by receiving or by retaining the benefit of the work done on the Cat without protest, Bruton impliedly affirmed his liability for the repairs.

But none of these theories will justify a finding of affirmance. A failure to act may of course constitute an affirmance if, "according to the ordinary experience and habits of men, one would naturally be expected to speak if he did not consent. . . ." Restatement (Second) of Agency § 94, Comment a; see Seavey, *Ratification by Silence*, 103 U. Pa. L. Rev. 30 (1954). Bruton could be deemed to have elected to pay for the major repairs only if, based on what he knew, he should have denied liability.

But up until the time that Bruton went into the AWS shop, Ekvall had completely authorized all the repairs on the Cat. The evidence shows that Bruton received no notification from Ekvall that the major repairs were to be made. Bruton testified that he never discussed with Roetman the cost of the repairs authorized by Ekvall:

I wasn't even concerned with it and didn't see any need to even discuss the terms that had been made or the cost of the repair at all. I assumed as I thought that Mr. Roetman did, that Dr. Ekvall would be taking care of the repairs on it.

We think it was reasonable for Bruton to assume that Ekvall would pay for the repairs which were nearly complete when Bruton came into the AWS shop. Only if Roetman could reasonably assume from Bruton's silence that Bruton agreed to pay for the repairs would his silence serve as affirmance. Here no facts giving rise to a duty on Bruton's part to discuss liability or cost were ever communicated to him.

Receipt of benefits and retention of benefits were also inappropriately applied. Both rest on the notion that the acquiescence of the principal through acceptance of the benefits of an unauthorized transaction may reasonably be assumed to be authorization. But Bruton never realized that he was considered responsible for the cost of repairs until after he received the bill from AWS. After the major repair, the Cat was returned to Ekvall, who continued to use it for some length of time. When it was finally returned to Bruton there was no way for him to have the repairs undone.

Unjust Enrichment

The trial court found unjust enrichment to be a third legal theory on which Bruton could be held liable to Ekvall for whatever portion of the joint and several damages that Ekvall might be required to pay AWS. But Ekvall never filed a cross-claim against Bruton, and the record does not indicate that the issue was tried with the consent of the parties. Accordingly, we need not entertain an opinion on the merits of a recovery by Ekvall against Bruton based on unjust enrichment.[8] It was error for the trial court to consider it.

. . . We hold that Bruton is neither jointly nor severally liable to AWS for the cost of the major repairs. We affirm Bruton's several liability for the cost of the repairs that he authorized specifically in the AWS shop.

Reversed in part.

Notes

1. The *Bruton* court discussed ratification by receipt and retention of benefits. Section 99 of the Restatement (Second) describes this concept as follows:

> The retention by a purported principal, with knowledge of the facts and before he has changed his position, of something which he is not entitled to retain unless an act purported to be done on his account is affirmed, and to which he makes no claim except through such act, constitutes an affirmance unless at the time of such retention he repudiates the act. Even if he repudiates the act, his retention constitutes an affirmance at the election of the other party to the transaction.

The rationale underlying this concept is explained in Comment c to § 83:

> This rule is based upon the belief that one should not be permitted to obtain or retain the benefits of an act purported to be done on his account unless he is made responsible for the means by which they have been obtained. This equitable result is to be contrasted with the rule which enables a contracting party to keep the profits from a transaction induced by the fraud of

---

8. [10] Even if unjust enrichment had been pleaded however, any recovery thereon would have been questionable. Although Ekvall had ample opportunity, Bruton was never notified that major repairs to the Cat were necessary. See generally Restatement of Restitution §§ 2, 112 (1937). . . .

a third person not purporting to act as his agent, if he did not know of the fraud until after the transaction was completed.

If you were counsel for Bruton and wanted to distinguish §99 from your case, what argument would you make?

The Restatement (Third) §4.01 is consistent with Restatement (Second) §99. Restatement (Third) provides, in relevant part:

(2) A person ratifies an act by

(b) conduct that justifies a reasonable assumption that the person so consents.

Specifically regarding retention of benefits, Comment g to Restatement (Third) §4.01 states:

A person may ratify an act under subsection (2)(b) by receiving or retaining benefits it generates if the person has knowledge of material facts, see §4.06, and no independent claim to the benefit. If a principal retains a benefit, and additionally, manifests dissent to the agent's act, the third party has a choice. The third party may elect to treat the principal's retention of the benefit as a ratification or may rescind the transaction.

2. According to *Hendrix v. First Bank of Savannah*, 394 S.E.2d 134, 136 (Ga. App. 1990):

The acts of a principal are to be liberally construed in favor of an adoption of the acts of the agent, and when the unauthorized act of the agent is done in the execution of power conferred, but in excess or misuse thereof, a presumption of ratification readily arises from slight acts of confirmation, or from mere silence or acquiescence, or where the principal receives and holds the fruits of the agent's act.

Note that the quoted language is written in the context of a pre-existing agency relationship where the act being ratified was pursuant to at least a partial grant of power by the principal. It may be that the standard would be less liberal if the act sought to be ratified was that of a stranger to the principal.

3. The subject of ratification by silence was visited again in Alaska in *Sea Lion Corp. v. Air Logistics of Alaska, Inc.*, 787 P.2d 109 (1990). A summary judgment of ratification by silence was approved on appeal. The court quoted Comment b of Restatement (Second) §94 as follows:

A principal's silence is usually more significant if an agent has exceeded his powers in the particular transaction, especially if the agent acted from an excess of zeal. If such an agent reports the matter to the principal at a time or in a manner calculated to call for dissent if the principal were unwilling to affirm, the latter's failure to dissent, if unexplained, furnishes sufficient evidence of affirmance.

The court then stated:

> This fact pattern is indistinguishable from the Restatement §94, Comment b. An admitted agent exceeded his authority in a moment of zeal to avoid a loss of an investment opportunity for his principal [by signing a contract committing the principal to deliver services in excess of what the principal wanted]. He reported the matter to his principal. . . . [T]he secretary/treasurer of the principal chastised the agent, realizing the risk created. The principal then said nothing to the third party to disavow the agent's signature until it was sued about a year later. This is "sufficient evidence of affirmance" absent an adequate explanation. There is no adequate explanation on the record.

4. *Y* sold *X* a piece of property on credit. *X* signed his wife's name as well as his to the note. The signing of the wife's name was done without her consent. The wife later found out about this and said nothing to *Y*. Should *Y* bear the risk of loss? He did act without knowledge that the additional signature was authorized, and there is no apparent authority in the case or it would be unnecessary to worry about ratification. (Of course, both grounds may be pursued in the alternative in a close case.) See *Myers v. Cook*, 87 W. Va. 265, 104 S.E. 593 (1920), holding no ratification, on the ground that the wife's silence after being informed by her husband of his use of her name was not sufficient evidence of ratification in the absence of a pre-existing agency relationship or of receipt and retention of benefits. See Restatement (Second) §94, requiring circumstances "which reasonably justify an inference of consent" before there is ratification by silence.

5. In *Theis v. duPont, Glore Forgan, Inc.*, 212 Kan. 301, 304–05, 510 P.2d 1212, 1215–16 (1973), a customer of the defendant brokerage firm suffered loss through unauthorized transactions in his commodities market trading account by an employee of the firm. The unauthorized transactions took place over a two-month period, with plaintiff repeatedly raising objections with the employee involved. Finally, plaintiff closed the account and sued for the losses occasioned over the two-month period. The court affirmed a trial court judgment limiting plaintiff's recovery to the last transaction, on the ground that he had ratified the 35 prior transactions. The court stated as follows:

> On acquiring knowledge of the unauthorized act of an agent, the principal should promptly repudiate the act, otherwise it will be presumed that he has ratified and affirmed the act. . . . [T]he requirement of prompt repudiation is to prevent an investor from withholding his disapproval until the market has taken a turn for the worse, and then deciding to assert the alleged wrongdoing. In such case if prompt repudiation were not required he might sit back and quietly accept profits resulting from an unauthorized trade when it turned out to be to his advantage.

See also Ellwood v. Mid States Commodities, Inc., 404 N.W.2d 174 (Iowa 1987) (court found ratification by silence of unauthorized trades over a two-month period in customer's commodities trading account; customer had received confirmations of all trades; contract with defendant firm stated that reports of trades shall be deemed conclusive if not objected to within five days after receipt). *But see Karlen v. Ray E. Friedman & Co. Commodities*, 688 F.2d 1193 (8th Cir. 1982) (no ratification where customer testified that he did not know how to interpret confirmation slips and monthly statements).

6. The opinion of the court in *Bruton* carefully distinguishes ratification from restitution. You should be forewarned that sometimes these two concepts are blurred together in a confusing way, with facts calling for the application of restitution principles instead being labeled ratification. *See Candy v. Cole*, 193 N.W.2d 58, 63 (Mich. 1971) ("There is another class of cases to which the term ratification has unfortunately been applied. Although there may be no ratification under agency law, the element of unjust enrichment may be present and thus recovery may be had under the law of restitution.").

D. The No Partial Ratification Rule

Rakestraw v. Rodrigues

Supreme Court of California
500 P.2d 1401 (1972)

Wright, C. J.—

Cross-defendant Sherwood T. Rodrigues (Rodrigues) appeals from a judgment upon a jury verdict for $30,000 in favor of cross-complainant Joyce Rakestraw (Joyce). His claimed liability arises out of involvement in a transaction whereby Joyce's name was forged on a promissory note and a deed of trust in order to obtain funds for a business venture of her then husband, William Rakestraw (William), who was also a cross-defendant. We have concluded that as a matter of law the alleged fraudulent acts of Rodrigues in connection with the forgeries were ratified by Joyce and that he was thereby absolved of liability to her.

The action was initiated by Acme Financial Corporation (Acme) and Security Title Insurance Company (Security) to enforce payment of a $75,000 promissory note bearing Joyce's purported signature which in fact had been forged and which was secured by a deed of trust (also forged) covering property owned by her. . . . Joyce asserted the forgeries as a defense to the action and cross-complained against . . . Rodrigues and William. . . .

Joyce entered into a stipulated judgment with Acme and Security by which she agreed to be bound by the note and deed of trust and to dismiss her cross-complaint as against them. . . .

Joyce's cross-complaint against . . . Rodrigues and William proceeded to trial and resulted in a jury verdict in her favor. Rodrigues' motion for judgment notwithstanding the verdict was denied. . . .

... William ... signed Joyce's name to both a promissory note for $75,000 in favor of Acme and a deed of trust on her Woodside property securing the loan. The signature on the deed of trust was notarized by Ellinghouse on February 18, 1965. Although Rodrigues, an auditor and a close friend and business associate of William, denied any participation in the execution and notarization of the deed of trust, the evidence supports implied findings that he told Ellinghouse he had seen Joyce sign the document and requested Ellinghouse to attest that she had acknowledged the execution of the instrument.

William took the forged documents to Acme and arranged for the loan. A check was drawn by Acme payable to William and Joyce which she endorsed without realizing that she was purportedly liable on the note or that her property had purportedly been encumbered. The major portion of the proceeds of the loan was used to satisfy obligations incurred in connection with a supermarket which was owned and operated by the William Rakestraw Co., Inc. (the corporation).

Joyce concedes that within a few days after she endorsed the check she learned of the forgeries. Later in conversations with her husband and others she claimed that she was the owner of the supermarket since her property had been used as security to finance it. She also demanded that stock in the corporation be issued to her. William, however, refused to issue or transfer any stock to her and initially refused to permit her to take any active role in the operation of the business.

Shortly after the discovery of the forgeries Joyce consulted an attorney who advised her to report the matter to the trustee designated in the deed of trust. Joyce, however, did not follow this advice and sought no remedy until three years later when both the business and her marriage had failed and the complaint had been filed by Acme and Security....

... Rodrigues asserts that because Joyce ratified the forgeries he is relieved from any liability in damages to her.[9] We agree.

The issues we deal with involve the application of traditional principles of agency law. Two basic rules are involved: (1) ratification by a person of an act purportedly done on his behalf not only creates the relationship of principal and agent but also constitutes approval by the ratifier of the purported agent's act, relieving such agent

---

9. [4] The theory of Rodrigues' defense is that by adopting the loan transaction as her own, Joyce not only ratified the unauthorized signings, but also ratified any misrepresentations claimed to have been made by Rodrigues to the extent that they implemented the forgeries. (Cf. *Southern Bell Tel. & Tel. Co. v. WRNO, Inc.* (1950) 216 S.C. 533, 536 [59 S.E.2d 146]: "'... a principal who ratifies the unauthorized act of his agent also ratifies his representations and warranties, as well as all other instrumentalities employed by the agent as an inducement to the action of the third person involved in the unauthorized transaction.' 2 C.J.S. Agency, §66, page 1145.") It is established agency doctrine that ratification of part of a transaction is deemed to be ratification of the whole transaction.

of liability to the ratifier for the act; and (2) forgeries can be ratified thereby relieving the wrongdoer agent of liability to the principal.[10]

. . . Ratification is the voluntary election by a person to adopt in some manner as his own an act which was purportedly done on his behalf by another person, the effect of which, as to some or all persons, is to treat the act as if originally authorized by him. A purported agent's act may be adopted expressly or it may be adopted by implication based on conduct of the purported principal from which an intention to consent to or adopt the act may be fairly inferred, including conduct which is "inconsistent with any reasonable intention on his part, other than that he intended approving and adopting it." It is essential, however, that the act of adoption be truly voluntary in character. Moreover, there can be no adoption if the act, although voluntary, is done only because the purported principal is obligated to minimize his losses caused by the agent's wrongful act or because of duress or misrepresentation by the agent (Rest. 2d Agency, § 416).[11]

As to the second rule here involved, it is well settled in California that a principal may ratify the forgery of his signature by his agent.[12] We conclude that the ratification of an act of forgery by one held out to be a principal creates an agency relationship between such person and the purported agent and relieves the agent of civil liability to the principal which otherwise would result from the fact that he acted independently and without authority.

We now turn to the facts of this case. Joyce concedes that she became aware of the forgeries within a few days after she had endorsed the check from Acme and thereafter consulted an attorney in connection therewith. Accordingly, the requirement of knowledge of the material facts essential to voluntary ratification is satisfied. . . . Here it is clear that Joyce elected not to rescind at a time when she was fully informed and had power to do so and had been advised of her rights. . . .

---

10. [5] We note, although the issue is not before us, a technical difference in the effect of Joyce's ratification as between William and Rodrigues. Although we do not now so determine it is probable that a principal-agent relationship between Joyce and William pre-dated the unauthorized forgeries, in which event her ratification of such acts would merely relieve the agent of personal responsibility to the principal. In Rodrigues' case, however, Joyce's ratification served first to create an agency where none existed before and then to relieve the agent of personal responsibility to the principal.

11. [The reader may wish to exercise caution about generalizing too broadly from this language. The court's discussion is in the context of determining rights between principal and agent. Section 416 of the Restatement (Second), cited by the court, is in the same context. It may be that the requirement of voluntariness would not be so strictly applied if instead third-party interests were involved. Note the language of Restatement (Second) § 82 comment d, recognizing the validity of a ratification even when it is motivated by a desire to protect the ratifier's business reputation or involves the decision to ratify rather than defend a lawsuit. The context of Restatement (Second) § 82 involves third-party interests. — Eds.]

12. [6] Restatement Second, Agency, section 85, comment b, provides in part: ". . . if one impersonates another . . . , or executes or delivers an instrument purportedly signed by another, the rationale of ratification is applicable and the act or transaction can be ratified by affirmance if it does not involve an illegal agreement."

Joyce also contends that there can be no ratification of Rodrigues' acts since such ratification had to be in writing. Civil Code section 2310, a codification of the "equal dignities" doctrine, provides: "A ratification can be made only in the manner that would have been necessary to confer an original authority for the act ratified, or where an oral authorization would suffice, by accepting or retaining the benefit of the act, with notice thereof." Since authorization to bind a principal to a deed of trust must be in writing (Civ. Code, § 2309) and because her consent to or adoption of the fraudulent acts was not in writing, Joyce argues that there has been no valid ratification.

Joyce's liability, however, arises from the promissory note; the deed of trust only secured the note. An agent's authority to execute a promissory note need not be in writing. . . .

Finally, Civil Code section 2310 was not intended to apply to a ratification as between a principal and agent. (See *Sunset-Sternau Food Co. v. Bonzi* (1964) 60 Cal. 2d 834 [36 Cal. Rptr. 741, 389 P.2d 133].) In *Sunset-Sternau* we held that Civil Code section 2309,[13] requiring that authorization for a contract required in law to be in writing must also be in writing, was not intended to apply as between an agent and principal. The decision's rationale applies with equal force to Civil Code section 2310. That section, therefore, is inapplicable as between the principal and the agent, and thus inapplicable in the present case.

As Joyce's ratification of the fraudulent transaction relieved Rodrigues of liability to her as a matter of law, the trial court improperly denied his motion for judgment notwithstanding the verdict. Since that motion should have been granted, we may order that judgment be so entered. (Code Civ. Proc., § 629.) The judgment insofar as it relates to Rodrigues is therefore reversed and the cause remanded with directions to enter judgment in his favor.

McComb, J., Peters, J., Tobriner, J., Mosk, J., and Burke, J., concurred.

Notes

1. As the court observed in an omitted footnote, because a promissory note was involved in the case, Article 3 of the Uniform Commercial Code (UCC) should be consulted. UCC § 3-403 (1990 revision) declares that an unauthorized signature (which includes both a forgery and a signature made by an agent in a transaction that exceeds his actual or apparent authority) may be ratified, a point also made in *Inn Foods*. Part (c) of § 3-403 notes that "the civil or criminal liability of a person who makes an unauthorized signature is not affected by" ratification. The counterpart provision in the original article three is § 3-404.

---

13. [8] Civil Code section 2309 provides: "An oral authorization is sufficient for any purpose, except that an authority to enter a contract required by law to be in writing can only be given by an instrument in writing."

2. As noted above, the UCC provides that a forgery may be ratified. The common law split on this question. The Negotiable Instruments Law § 23 declared that ratification of a forgery was not possible. The UCC has displaced the NIL. What conceptual problem underlies this difference in views on the question of forgery? See *Funds for Business Growth, Inc. v. Woodland Marble & Tile Co.*, 278 A.2d 922, 925 (Pa. 1971), stating that a forgery of a non-negotiable instrument may not be ratified in Pennsylvania "since it is a crime the adjustment of which is forbidden by public policy." Also, forgery is neither acting on behalf of the victim, nor purporting to act on the victim's behalf, and thus has difficulty meeting the technical limits of ratification. Nevertheless, the overwhelming majority of courts today recognize ratification in forgery situations, perhaps in part because, from the third party's perspective, acting *as* the victim is not so different from purporting to act *on behalf of* the victim.

3. Purporting to act on behalf of *P* but without authority, *A* sells some of *P*'s property. *P* decides to ratify. Is *P* liable to *A* for the customary commission for such services? See Restatement (Second) § 462, stating that *A* ordinarily is entitled to the customary compensation unless the ratification is made only to avoid losses or was induced by *A*'s fraud or duress. *A* also would not be entitled to compensation if the transaction is fraudulent as to a third person because such conduct could not lawfully be authorized initially. The word "customary" could be read to condition *A*'s right to compensation on whether *P* ratified knowing or having reason to know that *A* intended to claim compensation. Thus it might make a difference whether *A* is a real estate broker or a well-meaning next-door neighbor, if there is no express claim for compensation prior to ratification.

The principal and agent can by agreement modify the normal effect of ratification by, for example, reducing the amount of compensation the agent would normally receive. The agent may be agreeable to doing this because ratification releases him from liability to the third person under his warranty of authority.

4. The court in *Rakestraw* noted in footnote 4 that one cannot ratify only part of a transaction. See § 4.07 of the Restatement (Third), stating, "A ratification is not effective unless it encompasses the entirety of an act, contract, or other single transaction." This is the no partial ratification rule, which is also reflected in Restatement (Second) § 96. The Comments to § 96 state that the purported principal "cannot affirm a sale and disavow unauthorized representations or warranties which the purported agent made to induce it. He cannot affirm a contract and disavow unauthorized terms which the purported agent included." It may be, however, that the Restatement language should be qualified if the third party was put on clear notice of an agent's lack of authority to make representations and dealt anyway, later claiming he relied on the representations.

Consider the following fact situation: Nicholson was a special agent of Standard Pecan Company, with authority to sell its stock for cash at the rate of $10 per share. He was equipped with blank certificates, signed by the president and the secretary, with authority to fill in the name of the purchaser and deliver them for sale. He had no authority to enter into any agreements for repurchase or to vary the transaction in any way.

Nicholson sold 100 shares to Mrs. Murray and wrote on the back of the certificate: "It is hereby agreed that the Standard Pecan Co. shall at the end of three years from this date repurchase this stock at $11 per share upon 30 days' notice." The certificate was delivered to Mrs. Murray. She gave Nicholson $1,000, which he paid to the Company. The Company did not know of the endorsement until three years later, when the heirs of Mrs. Murray demanded a repurchase of the stock. The Company refused to repurchase and repudiated the agreement of Nicholson. Counsel for Mrs. Murray's heirs argued the "no partial ratification." Should this argument prevail? What arguments would you make on behalf of the Company in rebuttal?

The court rejected the argument based on § 96, stating that it devolved upon Mrs. Murray to acquaint herself with the extent of the agent's authority, and limiting the rule of § 96 to executory contracts. *See Murray v. Standard Pecan Co.*, 309 Ill. 226, 140 N.E. 834, 31 A.L.R. 604 (1923).

Would it make any difference if Mrs. Murray had paid for the stock with a promissory note and the procedural context of the suit was switched, with the corporation as plaintiff suing for the purchase price? *See Independent Harvester Co. v. Malzohn*, 147 Minn. 145, 179 N.W. 727 (1920). In this case the court invoked the rule of no partial ratification where a corporation was suing for the purchase price on a stock subscription agreement. The defense was that the agent as part of the sale promised the stock buyer a job, a promise the corporation repudiated. Judgment was rendered in favor of the defendant. Also, would it make any difference if the plaintiffs in *Murray* had pleaded in the alternative for rescission and restitution? See *Seifert v. Union Brass & Metal Mfg. Co.*, 191 Minn. 362, 254 N.W. 273 (1934), holding that it does.

E. Changed Circumstances

Suppose that *A*, purporting to act for *P* but without power to bind *P*, contracts to sell Blackacre with a house on it to *T*. The next day the house burns to the ground. The following day *P* discovers the facts and hastily ratifies. Is the ratification effective, with the consequence that the contract of sale was effective from the moment of its making? Restatement (Second) § 89, from which this hypothetical was taken, states that "when the situation has so materially changed that it would be inequitable to subject the other party to liability thereon, the other party has the election to avoid liability." Restatement (Third) § 4.05(2) is to the same effect.

Notes

1. Does the changed circumstances limitation on ratification apply to the situation where the unauthorized act is one of contracting for insurance, and the party on whose behalf the insurance contract was made seeks to ratify after a loss that would be covered by the insurance? One would assume that of course one cannot ratify under such circumstances, since the aleatory nature of the insurance contract no longer exists. Judge Learned Hand agreed with this and refused to allow ratification in *Kline Bros. v. Royal Ins. Co.*, 192 F. 378 (S.D.N.Y. 1911) (Note, 25 Harv. L. Rev. 729 (1912)). But see P. MECHEM, OUTLINES OF AGENCY (4th ed. 1952), stating in § 252 that the prevailing American view is that the principal can ratify in the insurance situation if he does so before the insurance company withdraws. Although the result of this is that the principal is able to insure lost property, Mechem argues that this is not so anomalous because the premium will have been paid or must be accounted for and "the transaction from the standpoint of the insurance company will be completely routine." *See also Marqusee v. Hartford Fire Ins. Co.*, 198 F. 475, *aff'd on rehearing*, 198 F. 1023 (1912) (holding, in litigation arising from the same facts as *Kline*, that the principal can ratify even after the insured property is destroyed); Robinson, *Ratification After Loss in Fire Insurance*, 18 Cornell L.Q. 161 (1933).

2. The factor of changed circumstances has relevance beyond disputes between the immediate parties. *See* SEAVEY, LAW OF AGENCY 77 (1964) ("The fiction of relation back can not be used to deprive others of accrued rights."). An example of this is provided by Illustration 2 of § 101 of the Restatement (Second):

> Purporting to act for P but without power to bind him, A makes a contract for the sale of P's land to T and records the contract. P's creditor, B, makes an attachment on the land. P affirms T's contract. B's right is prior to that of T. P is subject to liability to T on the contract.

3. On a related matter, see § 90 of the Restatement (Second): "If an act to be effective in creating a right against another or to deprive him of a right must be performed before a specific time, an affirmance is not effective against the other unless made before such time." An illustration of this is where an option is by its terms to expire on July 1. *A*, acting without authority, accepts on *P*'s behalf on June 30. *P* seeks to ratify on July 2. The ratification will be ineffective. In *Wagner v. City of Globe*, 150 Ariz. 82, 722 P.2d 250 (1986), the plaintiff police officer was fired on August 2, 1974, by the chief of police. Plaintiff contended that only the city council had the power to fire him. The city council voted to affirm the police chief's action on July 7, 1975. This was nearly two months after plaintiff had filed suit against the city. The court denied ratification, stating, "Allowing the city to retroactively affirm [the chief's] actions after the commencement of the lawsuit would divest the [plaintiff] of a 'right or defense' in derogation of his right to bring a cause of action" (citing § 90, cmt. a). Restatement (Third) § 4.05(3) states the same principal.

4. The other party is free to withdraw prior to ratification. In the ordinary case, does the other party need to notify either the agent or the principal of its withdrawal? *See* Restatement § 88; SEAVEY ON AGENCY § 35A (implying yes); *see also Rescission by Third Party Prior to Principal's Ratification of Agent's Unauthorized Action*, 2 VAND. L. REV. 100 (1948); Wambaugh, *A Problem as to Ratification*, 9 HARV. L. REV. 60 (1895).

Problems

1. In *Jones v. Mutual Creamery Co.*, 81 Utah 223, 17 P.2d 256, 85 A.L.R. 908 (1932), Sager, an employee of the defendant Creamery Company who as part of his duties gathered eggs from farmers for the Company using his own truck, was informed one day while at work that a customer had some eggs to sell to the Company. Sager's friend Mecham was with him at the time. Sager told Mecham that he would be unable to pick up the eggs, complete the other work he had to do, and still go "to a show" with Mecham, as previously planned. Mecham then volunteered to get the eggs. Sager agreed and let Mecham use his truck. Mecham negligently injured the plaintiff while en route to the farm. Thereafter he picked up the eggs and brought them back to the Company. The eggs were used and paid for by the Company.

Frame an argument for the plaintiff in her suit against the Company. Then change hats and defend the Company against the claim. What material distinctions are there, if any, between this case and the *Dempsey* case, *supra.*? Finally, decide the case.

2. John Kreggenwinkel died, leaving no estate other than certain insurance policies, of which his father was the beneficiary. The father was in a convalescent home. Deceased's mother, who was divorced from the father, went to the funeral home of Hirzel, arranged for the burial and charged the account to the father. At the time she had in her possession the policies of insurance naming the father as beneficiary. She left the funeral home, "stating in substance that she would talk to the father at the convalescent home; that she was on friendly terms with him." Hirzel then sent a bill to the father, who signed a document saying he authorized payment of the bill out of the proceeds of the insurance policies. (Whether he signed the document before or after the funeral is not clear from the opinion. Does it make any difference?) The document, which was introduced into evidence in court, never came into Hirzel's possession and the bill was not paid. The father died, and his estate is being sued for the bill. What result? See *Hirzel Funeral Homes, Inc. v. Equitable Trust Co.*, 46 Del. 334, 83 A.2d 700 (1951), commented on in 56 DICK. L. REV. 263 (1952) and 21 CHI. L. REV. 248 (1954). The latter comment was authored by Warren Seavey.

3. Blanche Watson was in severe financial straits. The Farmers' Supply Company was about to attach some of her property for a $1,700 feed bill, so she wired Holman, her agent, to sell a filly, Easter by name, for $300. On October 15, Holman wired Watson the following: "We are lucky. Sold Kadiak for two thousand dollars. Took up draft Farmers' Supply Company." Watson received this telegram and the rest of the money and said nothing. On December 26 of the same year she sued the purchaser of Kadiak for return of the horse, tendering $2,000. What result? *See Watson v. Schmidt*, 173 La. 92, 136 So. 99 (1931).

a. Would it affect your answer to know that Kadiak ran in six races between October 15 and December 26 and won four times?

b. Suppose Watson had been away on a trip from October 15 to December 15 and could not be contacted. This fact was unknown to her agent. Would that affect the result? In answering this, look at it from the purchaser's perspective too.

4. Leibsohn, Sr., was authorized in writing by his son-in-law, Schurman, "to list it [a hotel Schurman owned in Leibsohn's town] for sale, if you want to." Leibsohn then contracted with one Estes, a real estate agent, on the following terms:

> I hereby grant you the sole and exclusive right to sell the property described on the reverse side hereof and I hereby relinquish my right to sell the said property. Should said property be sold or exchanged . . . by you, or by myself, or by any other person, . . . I agree to pay you the commission. This contract shall terminate on 25 September of this year.

On September 18, Leibsohn's son, Sidney, acting without knowledge of his father's agreement and without authority from Schurman, negotiated a sale of the hotel to an out-of-state investor. Sidney called Schurman's attention to the purported sale and on September 28, Schurman ratified the sale by Sidney. The deed was executed on October 28.

Upon discovering this, Estes sued Leibsohn, Sr., who knew nothing about the sale by Sidney, for his commission. What argument can be made on behalf of Estes? What defense, if any, is available to Leibsohn, Sr.?

Would your analysis change if Leibsohn, Sr., had been the owner of the property and had himself ratified the sale on September 28, not having heard of the sale by Sidney before that day? Assume all the other facts remained the same.

5. While employed by the Lion Coal Company at Wattis, Utah, Janko Taslich sustained injuries from which he died on April 13, 1923. The Utah compensation statute requires that, "Any claim for compensation must be filed with the commission within one year from the death of the deceased." On February 15, 1924, an application for compensation was filed on behalf of Taslich's widow, who was living in Europe, by one Milka Skrinarich, her friend and countrywoman. The application was filed without authority from Mrs. Taslich.

The Lion Coal Company discovered the lack of authority and objected to the power of the commission to grant an award. Thereafter a formally executed power of attorney was presented to the commission, signed by Mrs. Taslich, ratifying the act of Milka Skrinarich. The document was executed on May 29, 1924, and filed with the commission on August 16, 1924. Assume that the communication of the need for authorization, and the response thereto, was done as rapidly as the passage of mail would permit in those days before airmail delivery was possible.

You are the attorney for Mrs. Taslich. What arguments would you make on her behalf, and what do you anticipate would be the defense of the coal company? How would you assess the chances of her succeeding on her claim? *See Taslich v. Industrial Comm'n*, 71 Utah 33, 262 P. 281 (1927).

6. Audrey Navrides was injured on the premises of one Crancer who was insured by Zurich Insurance Company. She employed an attorney, Robert S. Forsyth, who filed an action for damages on her behalf. Forsyth negotiated a settlement of the claim with Zurich for $9,000. Navrides rejected the settlement but Forsyth represented to Zurich that she had approved it. Zurich then delivered to Forsyth for signature a release of all claims and a request for the dismissal of the pending action. It also delivered to Forsyth a check in the sum of $9,000 payable to "Audrey R. Navrides and Robert S. Forsyth, her attorney." Forsyth cashed the check and returned to Zurich the other documents with the forged signature of Navrides. The request for dismissal was filed and the action dismissed. One year later, Navrides discovers the facts and comes to you as an attorney. What course of action would you recommend for her?

What her second attorney did was to sue Zurich, alleging that Zurich had for a valuable consideration drawn, executed and delivered a check to Navrides, that the check was wrongfully paid on a forged endorsement, that Zurich "has not paid said check, or any part thereof, to plaintiff, and that by reason of said fact there has been a failure of consideration" and that defendant owed plaintiff the sum of $9,000. What arguments could be made in Zurich's defense? What arguments would plaintiff's attorney make? How should the case be decided? *See Navrides v. Zurich Ins. Co.*, 97 Cal. Rptr. 309, 488 P.2d 637 (1971).

7. The charter of the City of San Francisco states that the city can sell city property only at public auction after appropriate notice in the public journals. Some city property is sold informally by an employee acting on the city's behalf to a private person at a price which is very advantageous to the city. The matter comes up before the city council for approval. The members of the council want to ratify the deal. You are the city attorney. What would you advise?

8. Dockery is a salesman for the New Home Sewing Machine Company. His authority extends merely to soliciting orders for the Company, subject to acceptance and approval by the head office. He uses order blanks containing the following sentence immediately above the signature line:

> It is understood that no conditions agreed to by any salesman or agent and not embodied herein will be binding on The New Home Sewing Machine Company, and it is understood and agreed that The New Home Sewing Machine Company shall not be in any way liable under any separate agreement made between the undersigned and its salesman.

Babbitt, on being solicited by Dockery, said he would buy a carload of machines only if the seller would furnish experienced salesmen to sell them and would guarantee their resale within a reasonable time. Dockery, to induce the purchase, agreed to these terms in a separate piece of writing. He sent in the signed order but not the separate agreement. The machines were sent to Babbitt and he was billed for the contract price of $9,096.60. Later Babbitt called the Company's attention to the separate agreement, but they disclaimed the unauthorized terms. Babbitt refused to pay and is now being sued by the Company. What arguments would you make as the lawyer for the Company? As the lawyer for Babbitt? And what decision of this case would you make as judge? *See Babbitt Bros. Trading Co. v. New Home Sewing Mach. Co.*, 62 F.2d 530 (9th Cir. 1932).

Chapter 9

Notice and Notification; Imputed Knowledge

A. Introduction

This chapter will draw the customary distinctions made concerning this subject. The following summary from W. Seavey, Law of Agency 17–18 (1964), may prove helpful in understanding the use by the Restatement and many courts of the words "notice, notification and knowledge":

> [N]otice will be herein used only to indicate the legal consequence which follows when a person has received a notification or has acquired relevant knowledge. . . .
>
> A notification is an act intended to give information to another, which for most purposes has the same legal effect as if the other had received the information. . . . There may be a notification of an action brought against an individual, effected by leaving the required document at his last legal abode. . . .
>
> Knowledge, on the other hand, is subjective, although the evidence to prove it is objective. It is entirely factual. . . .

Not all courts and commentators use the words "notice, notification, and knowledge" consistently. Sometimes it will be necessary to glean the meaning from the context of the language. The major articles in this area include Seavey, *Notice Through an Agent*, 65 U. Pa. L. Rev. 1 (1916), *reprinted in* W. Seavey, Studies in Agency 29–64 (1949); Merrill, *The Anatomy of Notice*, 3 U. Chi. L. Rev. 417 (1936), and Merrill, *Unforgettable Knowledge*, 34 Mich. L. Rev. 474 (1936). Also, there exists a three-volume treatise on the subject of notice. *See* M. Merrill, Merrill on Notice (1952).

B. Notification

Notification involves a deliberate effort to bring some fact to the attention of a person or group of persons, or all present or future persons who may have or claim an interest in the subject matter (made through a valid recording, for example). The major question to be explored in this section is under what circumstances will notification to an agent be effective in binding the principal? As with most legal problems, common sense can take us a long way toward answering this. Consider and answer the following questions (some, as you will see, are drawn from actual cases or Restatement (Second) illustrations), and then try to define the principles upon which you based your answers.

1. *P* tells *A*, a cashier, to do no business between the hours of 12:00 and 1:00, and to direct all customers to cashier *B*. In *P*'s absence, *T* enters the bank between 12:00 and 1:00 and, for the purpose of notifying it of a default by the maker of a negotiable instrument upon which the bank is an endorser, hands to *A* a letter indicating the facts. *A* puts the letter into a large and disorganized stack of materials on her desk and later loses it. Has *P* been "notified"? This hypothetical is drawn from Restatement (Second) §268, illustration 1. What analysis would you go through in answering this question? Would you look to the law of apparent authority? (Suppose notification of the assignment of the lease of a gasoline station is given to an attendant at the station. Would the notification be effective? *See Thompson v. Sun Oil Co.*, 185 So. 837 (Fla. 1939) (no).)

2. In a pending action, *T* "serves notice" of a motion upon *P*'s attorney, *A*. Intending to injure *P, A* does not inform him of the motion and does not appear against it. The motion is granted to *T*. Is *P* bound by the notification?

This hypothetical, taken from Restatement (Second) §271, illustration 3, includes an element not present in the off-duty cashier hypothetical. What element? And how would you resolve the question?

For a case somewhat related to the above, see *Freeman v. Superior Court*, 44 Cal. 2d 533, 537–38, 282 P.2d 857, 860 (1955), where the court unanimously upheld a criminal contempt conviction of the petitioner, who had failed to pay counsel fees and court costs in a divorce action after being ordered to do so. Petitioner testified that he had not known of the order. He had been represented in court, however, by counsel at the time the order was made. The court held that the presence of petitioner's attorney created a rebuttable presumption that he had received knowledge, and this could support the finding of fact of knowledge "even though the accused may give uncontradicted evidence to the contrary." The court stated that the presumption would be conclusive in civil actions.

The reasoning of the court is as follows:

> The general rule of agency, that notice to or knowledge possessed by an agent is imputable to the principal, applies for certain purposes in the relation of attorney and client. The rule rests on the premise that the agent has acquired knowledge which it was his duty to communicate to his principal, and the presumption is that he has performed that duty.

Are you satisfied that the analysis should stop at this point? What policy considerations are involved in holding a client to the consequences of his attorney's failure to transmit information received by her in her capacity as attorney? Do these considerations extend to criminal liability?

3. Plaintiff owns a toll bridge across the Missouri River at St. Charles, Missouri. Defendant is an electric utility, located in St. Louis. By agreement with plaintiff, defendant transmits electricity to St. Charles through uninsulated high-tension wires strung on spans above the superstructure of the bridge. It was agreed that defendant would indemnify plaintiff from liability resulting from the presence of the wires. It was further agreed:

> Eighth. It is necessary and may from time to time become necessary during the term of this contract for said Bridge Company to paint said bridge and add to, alter and repair the same, in which event, and when it becomes necessary for it to do so in the opinion of said Bridge Company, the said Electric Company in order to secure the safety of the persons making said repairs, additions, alterations or painting of said bridge shall, upon notice by the Bridge Company, arrange to have a representative in attendance during such repairing or construction for the purpose of instructing the workmen to maintain a safe distance between the wires and themselves, and the Electric Company, in the event the same becomes necessary, will at its own expense so adjust the wires on said bridge as to render the condition of the workmen of the Bridge Company reasonably safe from danger.

Subsequently a workman, who was painting the bridge, was severely injured by contact with the wires. There was no representative of the electric company there at the time. The bridge company settled with the injured employee and brought suit against the defendant for reimbursement. The defense was that no notice of the repair and maintenance work was ever received by the defendant. This was denied by the plaintiff. The following facts were before the court:

> It was shown that Jones was a new manager [for defendant] at St. Charles, having been appointed to that position shortly before the commencement of the painting of the bridge.

> The evidence for the plaintiff shows that shortly after the painting of the bridge was commenced and while the work was in progress the plaintiff's president, Charles D. Bolin, casually met the new local manager at a restaurant in St. Charles, being introduced to him by some citizen of that city; that the two gentlemen had lunch together, engaged in social conversation, and incidentally discussed a business matter. Concerning this Mr. Bolin testified:

> I told Mr. Jones that we were going to double the bridge toll houses, that the tolls had all been collected at the St. Charles side, that we were going to build a toll house on the east side, and we had no way to get light on the east side, and that I would like to have arrangements made for wires to run down to light the toll house on the east side. Mr. Jones said that those were high-power wires on the bridge and that the wire for the light would have to be run back across the bridge from St. Charles. He said it would be an expensive proposition to bring the light wire off from the high-power wires

on the east side, and that he would get the necessary information . . . and take the matter up with me later. I told him we were painting the bridge and expected to paint the bridge from one end to the other. We walked out in front of the restaurant and I pointed to the painters painting the bridge and said that we were going to commence at this end and paint from one end to the other, and that I would like to get the wires put in on the east side in the toll house. He said to come back in a few days and he would let me know what could be done and what would be the cost. I went back afterwards and he told me it would be necessary to bring the wires from St. Charles back across the bridge. I said, "Here are the workmen painting the bridge and we won't do anything about wiring until we are through painting the bridge, that we didn't want them stringing wires while the painters were working." At the time I had these conversations with Mr. Jones I was not familiar with the contract in question and was not intending to give any notice under the contract. These conversations occurred some time before Corder was injured. . . . It is this testimony of the plaintiff's president that counsel rely on in support of their insistence that defendant had sufficient notice and knowledge of the painting of the bridge to meet the requirements of the contract.

What result, and why? Explain the distinction between this question and the questions asked previously. And try slight variations of the facts to see if you come out with different results and, if you do, can you explain them? For example, would the result be different if the same conversation had taken place in the office of the new manager? Would it make any difference if Bolin *was* "intending to give . . . notice" under the contract?

The above quotation is taken from *St. Louis & St. Charles Bridge Co. v. Union Elec. Light & Power Co.*, 216 Mo. App. 385, 268 S.W. 404 (1925). The decision unanimously adopted by the court is contained in the following passage:

The law is well settled in this State and elsewhere that knowledge which comes to an officer or agent of a corporation through his private transactions, and beyond the range of his duties as such officer or agent is not notice to the corporation. The rule that notice to an officer or agent is notice to the corporation applies only where the matter with reference to which notice is given or acquired is within the scope of his authority and has some direct connection with his agency, and the notice or knowledge comes to, or is possessed by, him in his official or representative capacity, and where the officer or agent in the line of his duty ought, and could reasonably be expected, to act upon or communicate the knowledge to the corporation.

Under these well-established principles it is clear that the evidence relied on is insufficient to show any such notice to the defendant corporation of the painting of the plaintiff's bridge as was required to meet the condition of the contract. The notice or knowledge which the defendant's local manager obtained concerning the painting of the bridge was not obtained in his official or representative capacity, nor within the scope of his authority, and was therefore not imputable to the corporation. The knowledge was obtained by him through mere casual remarks of the plaintiff's president while the parties were engaged in a discussion of a business proposition relating to a matter having not the remotest connection with the respective rights and obligations of the plaintiff and the defendant under the provisions of the contract in question. In the casual notice thus given to the defendant's local manager there was no suggestion or intimation that it was given under the contract or that any action was desired or expected to be taken thereunder. In fact the president conceded that the notice or information given by him was not intended as a notice under the contract. It does not appear that this local manager in the line of his duty as such ought to have communicated to his principal the knowledge he thus obtained, or that he could reasonably have been expected to do so.

4. The drawer of a check on defendant bank, issued Saturday night, called the cashier of the bank at his home on Sunday and told him to stop payment. The cashier said he would do so, but arrived to work late on Monday, and the check had already been paid. Is the bank liable to the drawer? The court deciding this question held that notice to the cashier was notice to the bank and thus the bank was held liable. *Hewitt v. First Nat'l Bank*, 113 Tex. 100, 252 S.W. 161 (1923). The court stated that the drawer had the right to expect the cashier to "diligently execute the promise he had given." Would you expect the case to come out the same today? See UCC § 4-403(1), stating that the customer's order "must be received at such time and in such manner as to afford the bank a reasonable opportunity to act."

Suppose the same facts except the cashier had said, "If I remember, I'll let the right people know." Would you advise the drawer of the check that she could safely rely on that? Or suppose the cashier had said, "Don't bother me at home. Call me Monday." Would you predict different results for the above variations, and if so, why?

5. You represent a client who owns an unrecordable equitable interest in some land in midtown Manhattan. She has heard that General Motors Corporation is about to buy the land and place an office building on it. You want to effectively notify GM of the equitable interest, and your time is very limited. How would you go about doing so?

6. Suppose an effective notification of an assignment of a contract is made to an agent authorized to receive the notification, and the agent thereafter in good faith and honestly asserts that he forgot about it. Is this lapse of memory a defense to the principal? *See* SEAVEY, LAW OF AGENCY 173 (1966) ("Since a notification, as such, operates to determine the rights of the parties to it, the effect continues indefinitely.").

7. The terms "notice" and "notification" are defined in Restatement (Third) §§ 1.04(4) and 5.01(1), respectively. Set forth below are those sections and excerpts from the comments to § 5.01:

§ 1.04(4) *Notice.* A person has notice of a fact if the person knows the fact, has reason to know the fact, has received an effective notification of the fact, or should know the fact to fulfill a duty owed to another person. Notice of a fact that an agent knows or has reason to know is imputed to the principal as stated in §§ 5.03 and 5.04. A notification given to or by an agent is effective as notice to or by the principal as stated in § 5.02.

§ 5.01(1) A notification is a manifestation that is made in the form required by agreement among parties or by applicable law, or in a reasonable manner in the absence of an agreement or an applicable law, with the intention of affecting the legal rights and duties of the notifier in relation to rights and duties of persons to whom the notification is given.

b. "Notice" defined. Within this Restatement, "notice" is used as an inclusive term. . . . A person may acquire notice of a fact through several routes. A person has notice of a fact if: (1) the person has actual knowledge of the fact; (2) the person has reason to know a fact on the basis of an inference reasonably to be drawn from facts of which the person has actual knowledge; (3) an effective notification of the fact has been made to the person; (4) the person should know the fact to fulfill a duty owed to others; or (5) the law charges the person with the legal consequences of another person's knowledge of a fact or reason to know the fact or with the legal consequences of a notification made to another person. In ordinary usage, the meanings of these terms may overlap. For example, a person often "should know" what the person has "reason to know," such as the consequences that typically follow an action.

For purposes of this Restatement, it is important to distinguish between facts that a person has "reason to know" and facts that a person "should know." If an agent has no knowledge of a fact and no reason to know the fact on the basis of inferences reasonably to be drawn from facts known to the agent, the principal is not charged with notice of the fact. The fact, however, may be one that the agent should know in order to discharge a duty that the agent owes to the principal or to a third party, and the agent's failure to know that fact may cause the principal to breach a duty that the principal owes to the third party. The principal's breach of duty does not turn on imputing to the principal notice of a fact not known to the agent. For further discussion, see § 5.03, Comment b.

A person may have notice of a fact because the person has received an effective notification of it. Section 5.02 states when a notification received by an agent is effective as to the principal. If a manifestation is ineffective as a notification, a person may receive notice of a fact if, through the manifestation, the person acquires knowledge of the fact or reason to know it. See § 5.02, Comment b.

. . .

c. "Notification" defined. "Notification" is a narrower term than "notice." Agency law itself does not determine whether a notification is effective. Some manifestations that constitute notifications are made through public filings. For example, a person who files a lien does so to affect that person's rights against a property in relation to its owner and other persons. . . . In all cases, however, a person who gives a notification intends by so doing to affect that person's legal relations with persons to whom the notification is given, whether indirectly and generally, as in the case of the publicly filed lien, or directly, as when a tenant receives an eviction notice.

Montana Reservoir & Irrigation Co. v. Utah Junk Co.[1]

Supreme Court of Utah
228 P. 201 (1924)

Action by the Montana Reservoir & Irrigation Company against the Utah Junk Company and others. From a judgment for plaintiff, defendants appeal.

GIDEON, J.

[Utah Junk Company had an agent named Rosenblatt who, on behalf of Utah Junk, had purchased surplus metal from Montana Power Company from time to time. Utah Junk terminated its agency relationship with Rosenblatt on May 31, 1917, and, the court found, failed to so notify Montana Power. Subsequently, the plaintiff, Montana Reservoir & Irrigation Co., had some metal to sell. The plaintiff was a subsidiary of Montana Power and plaintiff's officers were also officers of Montana Power. Plaintiff sold its surplus metals to Rosenblatt, believing that he was acting on behalf of Utah Junk. The junk company failed to pay plaintiff for the materials that had been shipped to it, claiming that Rosenblatt had no authority to bind Utah Junk. The trial court gave judgment for plaintiff and Utah Junk appealed.]

There is no controversy, nor can there be, as to the general rule of law that one who has dealt with an agent in a matter within the agent's authority has the right to assume, if not otherwise informed, that such authority continues, and unless notice of revocation of such agency is brought to his knowledge, the principal is bound, if the dealings continue after the authority is actually revoked. No citation is necessary in support of that general proposition. Clearly, under that, if the purchase in this instance had been from the Montana Power Company, in the absence of any notice of the revocation of Rosenblatt's agency, the junk company would be liable, assuming as the proof in this case shows, that Rosenblatt represented himself to be such agent, and the power company acted in good faith in dealing with him as such.

---

1. Noted in 23 MICH. L. REV. 285 (1925).

As above stated, the officers of the Montana Power Company were likewise officers of the plaintiff. The agent, in transacting business with the plaintiff, was dealing with the same individuals that he had dealt with in making the purchase from the Montana Power Company. The Montana Power Company and the plaintiff company are two distinct legal entities. It does not appear that the plaintiff had ever dealt with the junk company through the agency of Rosenblatt. On the contrary, it appears that no such relationship existed.

The concrete question presented may be stated: Did the officers of the Montana Reservoir & Irrigation Company have the legal right to rely upon their knowledge gained while acting as officers of the Montana Power Company that Rosenblatt had been the agent of the junk company, and then representing himself to be such agent, and thereby bind the junk company?

I have found no case dealing with a like situation. The authorities cited by counsel do not aid in the solution of the problem here presented. Corporations act, and can act, only through and by their officers or agents designated by such officers. Knowledge imparted to the officers is generally held to be knowledge of the corporation. If the Utah Junk Company, by its acts and conduct, is estopped to deny the agency of Rosenblatt while dealing with the officers of the Montana Power Company, it would be illogical to hold that it would not be estopped while dealing with the same individuals as the officers of another or different corporation, especially so when, as shown here, the two corporations have the same ownership. The author, in 1 Mechem on Agency (2d ed.) § 628, says:

> Where a general authority is once shown to have existed, it may be presumed to continue until it is shown to have been revoked, and persons who have dealt with the agent as such, or who have had knowledge of his authority, and are therefore likely to deal with him, may very properly expect that if the authority be withdrawn, reasonable and timely notice of the fact will be given and they may therefore lawfully presume, in the absence of such notice, that the authority still continued.

We are of the opinion, and so hold, that the findings of the court are supported by substantial competent testimony.

Errors are assigned respecting the admission of certain testimony. That testimony was offered to show the good faith of the plaintiff in dealing with Rosenblatt as the agent of the junk company, and was properly admitted for that purpose, and in no way was prejudicial to any substantial right of the junk company.

The judgment of the district court is affirmed, with costs.

WEBER, C. J., did not participate herein.

Note

While the general principles of law articulated by the court are correct, it may be that the application by the court of those principles in the unusual context of this case, involving interlocking officers of related corporations, could be given further thought. As a first step in further analysis, ask yourself if the quotation from Mechem, while sound as it stands, is correctly applied by the court. Think carefully about the word "persons" in the context of this case.

C. Imputed Knowledge

Suppose that Baker, an attorney, represented Peters in obtaining a mortgage on the Johnson farm to secure a loan from Peters to Johnson. Through mistake, Baker failed to record the mortgage. Six months later Baker represents Smith, who is in the process of buying the Johnson farm. Baker says nothing to Smith about the outstanding mortgage in favor of Peters, and Smith buys in good faith thinking there are no liens against the farm. Is the knowledge of Baker imputed to Smith? Does it make any difference whether Baker remembered the Peters mortgage and deliberately said nothing, or simply had forgotten about it? If the time period between transactions was six years rather than six months? What legal principle would you resort to in order to decide these questions?

Assume that a cashier at the Reliable Bank is involved in a conspiracy with one partner to defraud the other partner of a two-person partnership by accepting checks drawn on the partnership account by the defrauding partner that the cashier knows are drawn without the actual authority of the innocent partner. Reliable Bank, the payee of the checks, seeks to collect against the innocent partner. The cashier has left town with the defrauding partner, having embezzled other bank funds as well. Is the knowledge of the cashier imputed to the bank? Would your answer vary if he was still an employee of the bank? For that matter, can the bank successfully argue that the knowledge of the defrauding partner is imputed to her innocent partner? How would you resolve this? Would you be able to make use of the principles you used in resolving the first hypothetical?

The treasurer of Merrill Corporation, acting pursuant to a resolution of the Board of Directors, negotiates and signs an employee fidelity bond with a bonding company. The application states that Merrill Corporation has no knowledge that any of its officers or employees are dishonest. It is a condition of coverage that all statements made in the application are true. Unfortunately, the treasurer herself has been embezzling funds from the corporation. She leaves town suddenly. The corporation demands payment under the bond. The bonding company refuses and is sued by the corporation. The defense of the bonding company is that the knowledge of the treasurer that the application contained a false statement is imputed to the corporation with the result that the bond is void. What result?

The following quotation from the Restatement (Third) § 5.03, Comment b, explains the concept of imputation of knowledge.

> b. Justifications for imputation; limitations on relevance of imputation. A principal's agents link the principal to the external world for purposes of

taking action, including the acquisition of facts material to their work for the principal. An agent undertakes to act on behalf of a principal; at the time the agent determines how to act, facts known to the agent at the time should guide the agent's determination of what action to take, if any . . . An agent also has a duty, unless otherwise agreed, to use reasonable effort to transmit material facts to the principal or to coagents designated by the principal. . . . A principal's right to control an agent enables the principal to consider whether and how best to monitor agents to ensure compliance with these duties. A principal may not rebut the imputation of an agent's notice of a fact by establishing that the agent kept silent.

Imputation creates incentives for a principal to choose agents carefully and to use care in delegating functions to them. Additionally, imputation encourages a principal to develop effective procedures for the transmission of material facts, while discouraging practices that isolate the principal or coagents from facts known to an agent. Notice is not imputed for purposes of determining rights and liabilities as between principal and agent. Thus, imputation does not furnish a basis on which an agent may defend against a claim by the principal.

. . .

Imputation charges a principal with the legal consequences of having notice of a material fact, whether or not such fact would be useful and welcome. If an agent has actual knowledge of a fact, the principal is charged with the legal consequences of having actual knowledge of the fact. If the agent has reason to know a fact, the principal is charged with the legal consequences of having reason to know the fact. A principal may not rebut the imputation of a material fact that an agent knows or has reason to know by establishing that the principal instructed the agent not to communicate such a fact to the principal. Imputation thus reduces the risk that a principal may deploy agents as a shield against the legal consequences of facts the principal would prefer not to know.

Constant v. University of Rochester

Court of Appeals of New York
19 N.E. 631 (1889)

[Plaintiff Constant sued to foreclose a mortgage executed by Mrs. Meehan to plaintiff's testator on February 17, 1883. The defendant university had acquired title to the land in question through purchase at a foreclosure sale on a mortgage executed to it by Mrs. Meehan dated January 10, 1884, and recorded the next day. Plaintiff's mortgage had not been recorded at the time that defendant took its mortgage nor at the time of sale. Defendant denied any notice or knowledge of the existence of plaintiff's mortgage until the commencement of this action, and thus asserts that its title, having been purchased in good faith and without notice, is not subject to plaintiff's lien. Plaintiff won below, and defendant appealed.]

Peckham, J.

In taking the mortgage of January, 1884, we think the university occupied the position of mortgagee for a valuable consideration.... If the university be not chargeable with notice of the prior mortgage to Constant, which was unrecorded, then its own mortgage is the prior lien as between the two. The first important question arising is, did Deane, who acted in the transaction as the attorney and agent for the university at the time of the existence of the mortgage to the university, have knowledge of the existence of the prior mortgage to Constant, executed in February, 1883, and which he then took as agent for Constant? In other words, is there any proof that he in January, 1884, had that fact present in his mind and recollection, so that it can be said from the evidence that he then had knowledge of its existence as an unpaid, outstanding obligation? The transaction out of which the mortgage to the university arose occurred eleven months subsequent to the transaction out of which the mortgage in suit arose; and the former mortgage was neither a part of the same transaction as the latter, nor had it the least connection therewith. Under the law, as decided by the older cases in England, such fact would have been an absolute defense to the claim that there was any constructive notice to the defendant arising out of notice to its agent, because such notice was in another and entirely separate transaction. In *Warrick v. Warrick*, decided by Lord Chancellor Hardwicke in 1745 (3 Atk. 291, 294), that able judge assumed it as unquestioned law that notice to the agent, in order to bind his principal by constructive notice, should be in the same transaction. He said: "This rule ought to be adhered to, otherwise it would make purchasers' and mortgagees' title depend altogether on the memory of their counselors and agents, and oblige them to apply to persons of less eminence as counsel, as not being so likely to have notice of former transactions."...

But in *Mountford v. Scott*, 1 Turn. & R. Ch. 274, upon an appeal from a decision of the vice-chancellor, Lord Chancellor Eldon said that the vice-chancellor proceeded upon the notion that notice to a man in one transaction is not to be taken as notice to him in another transaction. The lord chancellor continued: "In that view of the case it might fall to be considered whether one transaction might not follow so close upon the other as to render it impossible to give a man credit for having forgotten it." He further said that he would be unwilling to go so far as to say that if an attorney has notice of a transaction in the morning he shall be held in a court of equity to have forgotten it in the evening; that it must, in all cases, depend upon the circumstances....

From all these various cases it will be seen that the farthest that has been gone in the way of holding a principal chargeable with knowledge of facts communicated to his agent, where the notice was not received, or the knowledge obtained, in the very transaction in question, has been to hold the principal chargeable upon clear proof that the knowledge which the agent once had, and which he had obtained in another transaction, at another time and for another principal, was present to his mind at the very time of the transaction in question. Upon a careful review of the testimony in this case, we have been unable to find any such proof....

The other facts in the case uncontradicted are that, for some years prior to January, 1884, Deane and the plaintiffs' decedent were acting together, and that the plaintiffs' decedent was, weekly and even almost daily, in the habit of investing large amounts of money upon mortgages of this nature, and that the dealings of plaintiffs' decedent in these various building mortgages, through Deane's office, had amounted, at the time of the mortgage to the university, in the aggregate, to three millions of dollars, if not more; that the mortgages were of all sizes, from six up to forty thousand dollars. It also appears that this very mortgage in suit was found after the execution of the university mortgage in a pigeon-hole in which satisfied mortgages were kept, and was found by the assignee of Deane after the assignment was made.

There is no proof in the case showing that Deane made any pretense of remembering, at the time of the execution of the mortgage to the university, that, eleven months before, he had taken a mortgage on the same property for the plaintiffs' decedent, which was not recorded. Taking into consideration the enormous amount of business done by Deane for Constant of this same general nature, and the length of time that elapsed since the taking of the Constant mortgage by him, and the fact that it was never taken from the office by the mortgagee, and that it remained there and was found in a pigeon-hole appropriated to satisfied mortgages . . . ; all these facts would tend to show very strongly that Deane had no recollection whatever of the existence of the Constant mortgage as an existing lien at the time he took the mortgage to the university. . . .

For the reasons already given the judgment should be reversed and a new trial ordered, with costs to abide the event.

GRAY, J. (dissenting). . . .

The trial judge found that Deane had knowledge of the Constant mortgage at the time of the transaction of the university loan, and I think the evidence supports such a finding in the proof of the circumstances attending it.

. . . If the agent has knowledge of a fact, while he is acting for the principal, in the course of the very transaction which becomes the subject of the suit, this operates as constructive notice to the principal himself. For, upon general principles of policy, it must be taken for granted that the principal knows what the agent knows. . . .

All concur with PECKHAM, J., for reversal, except ANDREWS and GRAY, JJ., dissenting.

Judgment reversed.

Notes

1. The terminology in the *Constant* opinion is not always consistent with the distinctions we have drawn. For example, the statement in the first paragraph of the opinion that "such fact would have been an absolute defense to the claim that there was any constructive notice to the defendant arising out of notice to its agent, . . ."

talks of "notice" to the agent, when the Restatements would talk of the agent's knowledge. The court also mentions "constructive notice" to the principal rather than "imputed knowledge," which is the term more frequently used today. As noted above, the Restatement (Third) rejects the term "constructive notice."

2. What is the policy underlying the doctrine of imputed knowledge? See *National R.R. Passenger Corp. v. Notter*, 677 F. Supp. 1, 6 (D.D.C. 1987), quoting language stating that the imputed knowledge rule seeks to prevent "the injustice of allowing the principal to avoid, by acting vicariously, burdens to which he would become subject if he were acting for himself." The underlying theory of imputed knowledge also is explored at length in *First Ala. Bank v. First State Ins. Co.*, 899 F.2d 1045, 1061 (11th Cir. 1990), in the following language:

> Two basic theories ... attempt to explain the rule's existence. The first and oldest finds the reason for the rule in the legal identity of the agent with the principal during the continuance of the agency. In other words, the agent, while acting within the scope of his agency is, as to matter embraced within the agency, the principal himself or the *alter ego* of the principal. See Holmes, The Common Law 232 (1880). The other theory ... is based on the conclusive presumption that the agent has discharged his duty to impart the principal with all his knowledge which is necessary for the principal's protection or guidance.... Both the alter ego theory and the presumed communication theory are mere legal fictions which common law judges employed as shorthand to impose liability upon ostensibly "ignorant" principals. It is important to recognize that the reason courts impose constructive knowledge upon a principal is to avoid the injustice which would result if the principal could have an agent conduct business for him and at the same time shield himself from the consequences which would ensue from knowledge of conditions or notice of the rights and interests of others had the principal transacted his own business in person. [As a corollary to this policy, the court notes that "[t]he rule imputing an agent's knowledge to the principal is designed to protect only those who exercise good faith, and is not intended to serve as a shield for unfair dealing by the third person."]

For an insightful discussion of the imputation doctrine in agency law, see Deborah A. DeMott, *When is a Principal Charged with an Agent's Knowledge?*," 13 DUKE J. COMP. & INT'L L. 291 (2003) (suggesting that the doctrine is representative of agency doctrines more generally and recognizes that in a principal-agent relationship, the agent may be reticent to transmit information that the agent believes that principal may prefer not to know).

3. Note that "clear proof" that the knowledge was "present to his mind" at the time of the transaction in question is required by the court in *Constant*. The fact to be proved (the state of mind of the agent) will in many cases be impossible to present direct evidence on, with the opposing party instead often forced to rely upon proof

by inference from collateral facts, underscoring the importance of the burden of proof.

4. The principle of law established in the *Constant* case is widely accepted in this country. *See* Restatement (Third) § 5.03, cmt. b. See also *Pee Dee State Bank v. Prosser*, 367 S.E.2d 708, 714 (S.C. App. 1988),[2] a case involving facts remarkably similar to those of the *Constant* case. The court stated in relevant part as follows:

> As a general rule, a principal is charged with the knowledge an agent acquired before the relationship only when the knowledge can reasonably be said to have been in the mind of the agent while acting for the principal or where he acquired it so recently as to raise the presumption he still retained it in his mind. No testimony was offered to establish the state of mind of the attorney. The title searches performed by the attorney [for plaintiff] took place over a year before the attorney [handled the closing for the interest claiming title superior to the plaintiff]. Under this record, we decline to find actual notice.

The Restatement (Third) § 5.03, Comment b suggests that the principal should bear the burden of proving that the agent forgot the information (from a previous transaction) that the third party seeks to impute to the principal and that the third party should not "because principal and agent are more likely to know facts relevant to proving that the agent has forgotten what the agent once knew." What evidence would be relevant?

5. Of course, as noted in the introductory materials to this chapter, to be imputed, the knowledge of the agent must be acquired in the course of the agency relationship. A good example of how this principle operates is evident in *Trustees of Chicago Plastering Institute Pension Trust v. Elite Plastering Co., Inc.*, 603 F. Supp. 2d 1143, 1150 (N.D. Ill. 2009). A lawyer represented a company (G & J) in the sale of its assets. At the time, he was also representing G & J in connection with a lawsuit brought against it by a pension trust alleging that G & J failed to make required contributions to the trust. The buyer of G & J's assets asked the lawyer to form a corporation to acquire the assets and, with the consent of G & J, the lawyer did so. The lawyer at no time revealed the pending lawsuit against G & J to the buyer. The trust, in a lawsuit against the buyer claiming the buyer should be liable for G & J's contributions under a theory of successor liability, argued that the lawyer's knowledge of the trust's suit against G & J should be imputed to the buyer because he served, albeit briefly, as the buyer's lawyer. The court rejected the argument, noting that the lawyer's work for the buyer was very limited — simply doing the paperwork

---

2. *Pee Dee Bank* was overruled on other grounds by *United Carolina Bank v. Caroprop, Ltd.*, 446 S.E.2d 415 (S.C. 1994).

for incorporation. The performance of these "ministerial acts," the court said, did not create "a duty to warn [the buyer] about all potential pitfalls of the sale."

6. Suppose no single employee of a bank has knowledge of a breach of trust affecting a customer of the bank with respect to whom the bank is handling documents, but if all the facts known to the different employees were pieced together, the breach of trust would become apparent. Should the bank be held to the composite knowledge of its agents? *Compare Colby v. Riggs Nat'l Bank*, 92 F.2d 183 (1937), *with Neal v. Cincinnati Union Stock Yards Co.*, 15 Ohio Cir. Ct. Dec. 299, 1 Ohio C.C.R. (n.s.) 13 (1903). In general, courts will invoke composite knowledge only when each employee is under a duty to transmit the information he has to someone who is charged with responsibility for the information. With regard to duty, see *Sexton v. United States*, 797 F. Supp. 1292, 1304 (E.D.N.C. 1991), where the knowledge of a welder's assistant (Rosser) that a scuttle door had fallen into a pit on a construction site, posing a safety hazard, was not imputed to his employer, a subcontractor on the job. The court stated, "[T]he general rule is that a principal is chargeable with, and bound by, the knowledge of or notice of defects to his agent which are received while the agent is acting as such within the scope of his authority and in reference to a matter over which the agent's authority extends, even though the agent does not in fact inform his principal of such defects.... Rosser was not a supervisory employee or one engaged in safety concerns" for his employer. Thus, the matter was not one "over which his authority extended." The point made by the *Sexton* court is well accepted. The following statement from *National R.R. Passenger Corp. v. Notter*, 677 F. Supp. 1, 7 (D.D.C. 1987), adds a useful collateral point: "A corporation may limit the authority of its agents but it cannot disable itself entirely to receive information or notice of facts affecting its interests."

7. Is knowledge imputed when an agent of two principals embezzles from one of the principals by misusing a position she has with the other principal? For example, suppose a bank cashier who is also a guardian deposits the guardian's money in the bank and then, through manipulation of fictitious accounts, embezzles funds from the guardianship. Is the cashier's knowledge of the misdeeds imputed to the bank? *See Matz v. Ibach*, 235 Wis. 45, 291 N.W. 377 (1940) (no, in the absence of estoppel or unjust enrichment). *But cf. State ex rel. Clarke v. Ripley Sav. Bank & Trust Co.*, 25 Tenn. App. 490, 160 S.W.2d 189 (1941) (bank liable; cashier was its sole representative). *See Seavey, Embezzlement by Agent of Two Principals: Contribution?*, 64 HARV. L. REV. 431 (1951).

8. We have seen that an agent's knowledge can be imputed to the principal. Conversely, is a principal's knowledge imputable to the agent? Suppose, for example, that a third person wants to sue an agent for fraud, based on a representation the agent made innocently. The principal knows the true facts. Is the knowledge of the principal imputed to the agent? What is your common-sense response to this? *See Rosenbaum v. Texas Energies, Inc.*, 736 P.2d 888, 892 (Kan. 1987) ("We have found no rule of law which imputes the knowledge of the principal to its agent.").

Bird v. Penn Central Co.

United States District Court, Eastern District of Pennsylvania
341 F. Supp. 291 (1972)

Joseph S. Lord, III, Chief Judge.

This is a diversity case governed by Pennsylvania law. Plaintiffs in this action are certain named underwriters trading under the name of Lloyds of London. On July 2, 1968 they issued what we construe as two separate policies providing coverage for the defendants. The Directors and Officers Liability policy (hereinafter referred to as D & O policy) provides coverage for the individual defendants, all present or past officers and/or directors of the Penn Central Company. The Company Reimbursement policy provides coverage for the defendant Penn Central Company.

There was one application completed to obtain both policies. This application, which was specifically incorporated as part of the policies, was executed by defendant David C. Bevan, Chairman of the Finance Committee of the defendant corporation. It is alleged by the plaintiffs that defendant Bevan's response to Item 10 of the application was falsely made in bad faith, was material to the risk, and was justifiably relied on so as to entitle them to rescind the policy because of fraud.

Three of the defendants, Kattau, Kirk and Annenberg, moved for summary judgment under F.R. Civ. P. 56, advancing many arguments. We rejected those arguments in an opinion filed on November 15, 1971 (334 F. Supp. 255) and denied summary judgment. In that opinion, among other things, we said that if the contract of insurance was a unitary one, with Lloyds of London and Penn Central Company the only contracting parties, the officers and directors would all be in the position of third-party beneficiaries, their rights rising no higher than those of their contracting party, Penn Central. Under this construction of the contract of insurance, if defendant Bevan's response on the application was proven fraudulent, this fraud would be imputed to his principal, Penn Central Company, regardless of the innocence of movants or other officers and directors.

We said that another construction of the "policy" would consider each officer and director assured as a contracting party rather than a third-party beneficiary.[3]

---

3. [The opinion contains the following language with regard to that construction:
   If we were to accept this construction of the policy, each insured would have to be considered a separate principal for the purposes of agency law. Movants' affidavits are uncontroverted that defendant Bevan had no actual authority to answer questions on an insurance application on their behalf as individuals. There would, nevertheless, still remain the question regarding each principal, of whether he was apparently authorized to act when he completed the application. Restatement, Law of Agency 2d sec. 257 (1958). This unresolved factual question alone would be enough to deny summary judgment. However, more fundamental is the fact that movants are by this argument attempting to affirm this contract, not avoid it. Movants cannot have it both ways. They may not in the same breath deny that defendant Bevan had any authority to act, and thus attempt to dissociate themselves from any statements he made in obtaining the policy, while at

We did not resolve this question of the construction of the "policy" because we said that the result would be the same in any event — if there was a material fraud in the application, and the other elements of rescission were present, the entire "policy" could be rescinded.

Having some doubts about whether our conclusion was correct if we considered the proper construction of the "policy" to be that the individual officers and directors are contracting parties, we granted reargument limited to the following questions:

> (a) Was the contract of insurance a unitary contract with Penn Central as the other contracting party, or a series of individual contracts with each officer and director; (b) if the latter, is the knowledge of Bevan imputed to each individual officer and director? . . .

We conclude that the Company Reimbursement insurance was a separate policy intended to protect the company's interest in the event it indemnified its officers and directors for personal liability. The D & O insurance has for its purpose the protection of the individual officer or director from personal liability, and each officer and director is a separate promisee under this policy. . . .

Item 10 of the application which was the basis for both the Company Reimbursement policy and the D & O policy provides as follows:

> No person proposed for this insurance is cognizant of any act, error, or omission which he has reason to suppose might afford valid grounds for any future claim such as would fall within the scope of the proposed insurance except as follows:

Defendant Bevan's response to this, which is alleged to have been knowingly false, and which is the basis for this rescission action, was "None known." Defendant Bevan, himself, was one of the assureds under the D & O policy. Movants argue that since the answer called for a subjective response, defendant Bevan's answer, if a misrepresentation was made, was a misrepresentation only of his own state of knowledge, but was a true response in his capacity as agent for each individual officer and director (such as movants) who would have truthfully responded "None known" to Item 10.

It is contended that defendant Bevan was acting in three capacities in signing the application: (a) as agent for Penn Central,[4] (b) as principal for his own account as

---

the same time claim to have a binding policy and seek coverage under it. It is a matter of hornbook law that a contract must be affirmed in its entirety in order to effect its ratification. A principal may not claim the benefits of a contract without accepting the consequences of statements made by his agent, or apparent agent, which induced the contract in the first place.

334 F. Supp. at 262. — Eds.]

4. [3] In consideration of this motion, we are unconcerned with his actions as agent for Penn Central since movants are individual assureds seeking summary judgment only as to their rights as individuals under the D & O policy.

one of the assureds, and (c) as agent for each of the other individual assureds. Recognizing these various capacities, movants in effect then ask us to consider defendant Bevan's single response to Item 10 as being over sixty separate responses, his own plus one representing the knowledge of each officer and director. See *Bobrow v. United States Casualty Co.*, 231 App. Div. 91, 246 N.Y.S. 363 (Sup. Ct. 1930). Thus, it is urged that plaintiffs should be able to rescind the D & O policy only as to defendant Bevan, for if he answered Item 10 fraudulently it was only in his capacity as principal for his own account. If it was held that the entire D & O policy could be subject to rescission because defendant Bevan happened to be the officer who signed the insurance application, it would be manifestly unfair to the directors and officers who are completely blameless, such as movants.

While we sympathize with movants' position, and recognize that innocent officers and directors are likely to suffer if the entire policy is voidable because of one man's fraudulent response, it must be recognized that plaintiff insurers are likewise innocent parties. Defendant Bevan was not plaintiffs' agent. Movants do not deny that he was their agent in completing the application by which the policy was obtained.

The general rule in this type of situation was stated by the Pennsylvania Supreme Court over 100 years ago.

> Where the agent of the insured, in effecting an insurance, makes a false and unauthorized representation, the policy is void. Where one of two innocent persons must suffer by the fraud or negligence of a third, whichever of the two has accredited him, ought to bear the loss. . . . *Mundorff v. Wickersham*, 63 Pa. 87, 89 (1870) (dictum).

That the fraud of the agent in inducing a contract is binding on an innocent principal is a well established doctrine of agency law in other jurisdictions as well.

The leading case in Pennsylvania is *Gordon v. Continental Casualty Co.*, 319 Pa. 555, 181 A. 574 (1935). There a trust company obtained a banker's blanket bond to insure it against any loss due to the dishonesty of its officers and employees. The application which was signed by its secretary and treasurer, Ralph E. Mathews, represented that no losses had been sustained by it during the preceding five years because of employee dishonesty, and that the company had no notice or knowledge of any facts indicating that any of the officers were dishonest or unworthy of confidence. Mathews at that very time, without the trust company's knowledge, was an embezzler of the company's funds to the tune of $26,000, and was of course aware of his own misconduct. The court held that the innocent trust company could not recover on the bond because it was bound by Mathews' misrepresentations. Stated another way, recovery was barred because the knowledge of Mathews' own misdeeds was imputed to the company.

Movants wish to limit the Gordon decision strictly to its facts, arguing that the fact that a corporation is an artificial entity and can "know" only through its agents is a reason that the trust company there was bound by the fraudulent knowledge of its agent who completed the insurance application. We do not, however, read the crucial fact in Gordon to be that the principal was a corporation, rather than an individual or a group of individuals. It is rather an application of the usual rule that a principal is bound by the fraud of his agent in procuring a contract.

> Where a principal sends forth his agent to conduct his affairs and contract for his benefit and the agent procures a contract by fraudulent or corrupt practices, although the principal may not have been privy in any way to such conduct of his agent, yet by claiming the benefits of the contract he must take it tainted as it may be by such practice. *Gordon, supra,* 319 Pa. at 566, 181 A. at 578, quoting Thompson on Corporations, volume 3, section 1769.

We do not think that the fact that defendant Bevan signed the application on behalf of numerous principals including himself alters the force of this rule. It would be extremely artificial to read defendant Bevan's response to Item 10 as being multiple separate responses on behalf of himself, the company, and each of the individual assureds under the D & O policy. No matter how the policies for Company Reimbursement insurance and D & O insurance are characterized, the simple inescapable fact is that both policies were issued on the basis of a single application, and only one response was made to Item 10 of that application. Defendant Bevan, movants' agent, made that response. As we said in our previous opinion, we construe Item 10 as being directed at gaining information regarding the nature and scope of the insured risk. If the answer to Item 10 is fraudulent, we cannot say with assurance that plaintiffs would not have acted differently before issuing the policies if they had been given a truthful response, either issuing the policies only if a higher premium were paid, or refusing to issue any policy at all.

Therefore, the motions for summary judgment will be denied.

Notes and Questions

1. Different courts have approached the issue raised in *Bird v. Penn Central Co.* in different ways. In *Shapiro v. American Home Assurance Co.,* 584 F. Supp. 1245 (D. Mass. 1984), for instance, the court rejected the agency analysis in *Bird* and, instead, based its decision on the principle of contract interpretation: the contract simply precluded coverage "if any Director or Officer [had] knowledge or information of any act, error or omission which might give rise to a claim under the proposed policy" and that information was not disclosed to the insurer. On the other hand, the court in *First American Title v. Lawson,* 827 A.2d 230, 240 (N.J. Sup.Ct. 2003) held that the insurer did have to provide coverage to an innocent partner in a law firm under its malpractice insurance policy notwithstanding the fraudulent misrepresentations in the application. The court said that the insurer could rescind the coverage as to the firm, the managing partner, and another partner. The latter two were aware of the facts and the managing partner had completed the application. But the third partner was unaware of the wrongdoing and, as a matter of equity, should be afforded coverage under the policy. The Court wrote:

> [V]oiding the policy in respect of Snyder [the innocent partner] would mean that he no longer would possess coverage for any of his actions in unrelated matters, including simple malpractice, that might have occurred during the period of anticipated coverage. Thus, applying the rule of law advocated by Underwriters could leave members of the public, whom Snyder had represented throughout that period, unprotected even though the insured himself committed no fraud. In our view, that harsh and sweeping result would be contrary to the public interest. More specifically, it would be inconsistent with the policies underlying our Rules of Court that seek to protect consumers of legal services by requiring attorneys to maintain adequate insurance in this setting.

Would this reasoning support a different conclusion in *Bird* or *Shapiro*?

2. The insurance policy in *Mann v. Adventure Quest, Inc.*, 974 A.2d 607 (Vt. 2009), excluded coverage if the insured, Adventure Quest (a private school), had "personal knowledge of any sexual abuse, sexual molestation, sexual exploitation, or sexual injury." The founder of Adventure Quest, Drutchal, served as coach and chaperone at the school and, while so serving, sexually abused students. The insurer sought to avoid coverage when the victims of Drutchal's abuse sued, arguing that Drutchal's knowledge should be imputed to Adventure Quest. The court ruled against the insurer, reasoning, in part, that "personal knowledge" means something more than imputed knowledge so that insurance coverage would not be excluded if Adventure Quest's "knowledge" was only based on imputation of Drutchal's knowledge. The court provided no guidance as to how an entity would have personal knowledge of a fact if not through imputation. What sort of evidence might be persuasive?

3. The court in *BancInsure, Inc. v. U.K. Bancorporation, Inc.*, 830 F. Supp. 2d 294 (E.D. Ky. 2011) took a different approach to preserving coverage under a fidelity bond. The president of a bank executed an application for a fidelity bond that included a representation that she had no knowledge of any act that might give rise to a claim under the bond. In fact, she did have such knowledge, as she had been embezzling money from the bank. The court applied the adverse interest exception, reasoning that her knowledge of her own wrongful acts should not be imputed to the bank because in making the misrepresentation she was acting adversely to the bank, her principal, and in her own interest. The adverse interest exception is taken up in the next section.

D. The Adverse Interest Qualification

During prohibition the defendant's salesmen collaborated with bootleggers in diverting the denatured alcohol that defendant manufactured to alcoholic beverage purposes, thus increasing sales for the company and commissions for the salesmen.

Defendant was sued by the federal government to recover the high taxes due upon alcohol withdrawn and distributed in violation of regulations. Defendant argued that the knowledge of its salesmen should not be attributed to it because they were acting contrary to the company's interests, and for their own gain. What result? Consider, in formulating your answer, Restatement (Second) § 282, stating in part that, "A principal is not affected by the knowledge of an agent in a transaction in which the agent secretly is acting adversely to the principal and entirely for his own or another's purposes."

The above facts, modified slightly, were drawn from *In re Mifflin Chem. Corp.*, 123 F.2d 311, 315–16 (3d Cir. 1941). The decision of Judge Goodrich reads in part as follows:

> The scheme for the illegal diversion of this alcohol was carried out by salesmen for Mifflin in New York and Philadelphia. There is no dispute that these men had full knowledge of the transactions. Mifflin argues, however, that such knowledge is not to be attributed to it because in carrying out the unlawful plans its agents were acting contrary to the company's interests; therefore, their knowledge is not attributable to the employer. The evidence on this point is somewhat equivocal. But for the purpose of the discussion it may be assumed that the salesmen did not tell their superiors for fear of disapproval of the scheme. Added to that is another piece of evidence to the effect that one of them received a commission or gift from one of the bootleggers for help given.

> Even then, we believe unquestionably that Mifflin is charged with responsibility for the knowledge of its employees. As Judge Holly puts the legal proposition: "It is elementary law that the knowledge of an agent or employee obtained within the sphere of his agency or employment will be imputed to the corporation." The very job these salesmen were employed to do was to sell alcohol and selling alcohol they were, although in an improper way. Of course they were doing it to make money; the difference between doing it in a proper and an improper way was that doubtless they made more by the latter course. But: "The mere fact that the agent's primary interests are not coincident with those of the principal does not prevent the latter from being affected by the knowledge of the agent if the agent is acting for the principal's interests." Restatement, Agency § 282, Comment b.

> Counsel for Mifflin have cited authorities where courts have held that when an agent departs from his employment and acts adversely to his principal the latter is no longer responsible for facts known to the wrongdoing employee. But in these cases the agent was found either to be actively cheating or defrauding his principal or acting adversely as the other party to the same transaction in which he was serving as his principal's agent.

> *Zito v. United States*, 7 Cir., 1933, 64 F.2d 772 is a case presenting facts not dissimilar in this respect to the case at bar. The knowledge of the agent in

that case was sufficient to charge the company with criminal responsibility. In the instant case the question is not that of punishment or penalty, but simply that of the payment of a tax because the conditions on which non-liability was conditioned have not been complied with. One need not talk about actual knowledge by Mifflin or a presumption that the employer knows everything that the employee knows. It has been conceded that these employees were violating instructions and that they concealed from their superiors in the Mifflin organization the knowledge of their activities in promoting illegal diversion of the alcohol. That does not, on principles of agency, ipso facto relieve the employer of liability. Responsibility of an employer for things his agent does is not imposed on the basis of knowledge in fact, but under the general rule of respondeat superior. No reliance need be made on any fictional attributing of knowledge to Mifflin. The employers are responsible for the knowledge of the facts had by their agents in doing the very business for which they were employed. The learned trial judge correctly concluded that the tax was due and payable.

Kirschner v. KPMG LLP

Court of Appeals of New York

938 N.E.2d 941 (2010)

Before GRAFFEO, SMITH, JONES, CIPARICK, LIPPMAN and PIGOTT

READ, J.

In these two appeals, plaintiffs ask us, in effect, to reinterpret New York law so as to broaden the remedies available to creditors or shareholders of a corporation whose management engaged in financial fraud that was allegedly either assisted or not detected at all or soon enough by the corporation's outside professional advisers, such as auditors, investment bankers, financial advisers and lawyers. For the reasons that follow, we decline to alter our precedent relating to in pari delicto, and imputation and the adverse interest exception, as we would have to do to bring about the expansion of third-party liability sought by plaintiffs here.

[The case was before the New York court as a result of requests from two different courts—the United States Court of Appeals for the Second Circuit and the Delaware Supreme Court—in two unrelated cases in which corporations sued their independent outside auditors. Both courts sought clarification from the New York court on the questions noted above based on similar fact patterns: accounting fraud committed by management of the companies involved and a failure of the independent outside auditors to detect and report the fraud. The federal case related to Refco, a provider of brokerage and clearing services, while the Delaware case involved AIG, a large insurance and financial company. Refco declared bankruptcy and the suit against its auditors, KPMG LLP, was brought by the Liquidation Trustee. The AIG suit was a derivative action on behalf of AIG against its auditors, PricewaterhouseCoopers LLP.] . . . .

In pari delicto

The doctrine of in pari delicto mandates that the courts will not intercede to resolve a dispute between two wrongdoers. This principle has been wrought in the inmost texture of our common law for at least two centuries. The doctrine survives because it serves important public policy purposes. First, denying judicial relief to an admitted wrongdoer deters illegality. Second, in pari delicto avoids entangling courts in disputes between wrongdoers. . . .

The justice of the in pari delicto rule is most obvious where a willful wrongdoer is suing someone who is alleged to be merely negligent. A criminal who is injured committing a crime cannot sue the police officer or security guard who failed to stop him; the arsonist who is singed cannot sue the fire department. But, as the cases we have cited show, the principle also applies where both parties acted willfully. Indeed, the principle that a wrongdoer should not profit from his own misconduct is so strong in New York that we have said the defense applies even in difficult cases and should not be "weakened by exceptions."

Imputation

Traditional agency principles play an important role in an in pari delicto analysis. Of particular importance is a fundamental principle that has informed the law of agency and corporations for centuries; namely, the acts of agents, and the knowledge they acquire while acting within the scope of their authority are presumptively imputed to their principals. A corporation must, therefore, be responsible for the acts of its authorized agents even if particular acts were unauthorized. After all, the principal is generally better suited than a third party to control the agent's conduct, which at least in part explains why the common law has traditionally placed the risk on the principal.

Agency law presumes imputation even where the agent acts less than admirably, exhibits poor business judgment, or commits fraud. As we explained long ago, a corporation "is represented by its officers and agents, and their fraud in the course of the corporate dealings [ ] is in law the fraud of the corporation." Like a natural person, a corporation must bear the consequences when it commits fraud.

When corporate officers carry out the everyday activities central to any company's operation and well-being-such as issuing financial statements, accessing capital markets, handling customer accounts, moving assets between corporate entities, and entering into contracts-their conduct falls within the scope of their corporate authority. And where conduct falls within the scope of the agents' authority, everything they know or do is imputed to their principals.

Next, the presumption that agents communicate information to their principals does not depend on a case-by-case assessment of whether this is likely to happen. Instead, it is a legal presumption that governs in every case, except where the corporation is actually the agent's intended victim. Where the agent is defrauding someone else on the corporation's behalf, the presumption of full communication remains in full force and effect.

In sum, we have held for over a century that all corporate acts-including fraudulent ones-are subject to the presumption of imputation. And, as with in pari delicto, there are strong considerations of public policy underlying this precedent: imputation fosters an incentive for a principal to select honest agents and delegate duties with care.

Adverse Interest Exception to Imputation

We articulated the adverse interest exception in *Center* [*v. Hampton Affiliates*] as follows:

> "To come within the exception, the agent must have *totally abandoned* his principal's interests and be acting *entirely* for his own or another's purposes. It cannot be invoked merely because he has a conflict of interest or because he is not acting primarily for his principal" (*Center*, 66 N.Y.2d [782] at 784– 785 [emphasis added]).

This rule avoids ambiguity where there is a benefit to both the insider and the corporation, and reserves this most narrow of exceptions for those cases-outright theft or looting or embezzlement-where the insider's misconduct benefits only himself or a third party; i.e., where the fraud is committed *against* a corporation rather than on its behalf.

The rationale for the adverse interest exception illustrates its narrow scope. As already discussed, the presumption that an agent will communicate all material information to the principal operates except in the narrow circumstance where the corporation is actually the victim of a scheme undertaken by the agent to benefit himself or a third party personally, which is therefore entirely opposed (i.e., "adverse") to the corporation's own interests. Where the agent is perpetrating a fraud that will benefit his principal, this rationale does not make sense.

A fraud that by its nature will benefit the corporation is not "adverse" to the corporation's interests, even if it was actually motivated by the agent's desire for personal gain. Thus, "[s]hould the 'agent act[ ] both for himself and for the principal,' . . . application of the exception would be precluded" (*Capital Wireless Corp. v. Deloitte & Touche*, 216 A.D.2d 663, 666, 627 N.Y.S.2d 794 [3d Dept 1995] [quoting *Matter of Crazy Eddie Sec. Litig.*, 802 F. Supp. 804, 817 (E.D.N.Y. 1992)]; *see also Center*, 66 N.Y.2d at 785, 497 N.Y.S.2d 898, 488 N.E.2d 828 [the adverse interest exception "cannot be invoked merely because. . . . (the agent) is not acting primarily for his principal"]).

New York law thus articulates the adverse interest exception in a way that is consistent with fundamental principles of agency. To allow a corporation to avoid the consequences of corporate acts simply because an employee performed them with his personal profit in mind would enable the corporation to disclaim, at its convenience, virtually every act its officers undertake. "[C]orporate officers, even in the most upright enterprises, can always be said, in some meaningful sense, to act for their own interests" (*Grede v. McGladrey & Pullen LLP*, 421 B.R. 879, 886 [ND Ill 2008]). A corporate insider's personal interests—as an officer, employee, or shareholder of the company—are often deliberately aligned with the corporation's interests by way of, for example, stock options or bonuses, the value of which depends upon the corporation's financial performance.

Again, because the exception requires adversity, it cannot apply unless the scheme that benefitted the insider operated at the corporation's expense. The crucial distinction is between conduct that defrauds the corporation and conduct that defrauds others for the corporation's benefit. "Fraud on behalf of a corporation is not the same thing as fraud against it" (*Cenco Inc. v. Seidman & Seidman*, 686 F.2d 449, 456 [7th Cir. 1982]), and when insiders defraud third parties *for* the corporation, the adverse interest exception is not pertinent. Thus, as we emphasized in *Center*, for the adverse interest exception to apply, the agent "must have *totally abandoned* his principal's interests and be acting *entirely* for his own or another's purposes," not the corporation's (*Center*, 66 N.Y.2d 784–785 [emphasis added]). So long as the corporate wrongdoer's fraudulent conduct enables the business to survive-to attract investors and customers and raise funds for corporate purposes-this test is not met.

The Litigation Trustee suggests that, to the extent that the adverse interest exception requires harm, "bankruptcy is harm enough" and that, whenever the corporation is bankrupt, "it is fair to assume at the pleading stage" that the adverse interest exception applies. But the mere fact that a corporation is forced to file for bankruptcy does not determine whether its agents' conduct was, at the time it was committed, adverse to the company. Even where the insiders' fraud can be said to have caused the company's ultimate bankruptcy, it does not follow that the insiders "totally abandoned" the company. . . .

Critically, the presumption of imputation reflects the recognition that principals, rather than third parties, are best-suited to police their chosen agents and to make sure they do not take actions that ultimately do more harm than good (*see Cenco*, 686 F.2d at 455 ["if the owners of the corrupt enterprise are allowed to shift the costs of its wrongdoing entirely to the auditor, their incentives to hire honest managers and monitor their behavior will be reduced"; *see also* Restatement [Third] of Agency § 5.03, Comment b ["Imputation creates incentives for a principal to choose agents carefully and to use care in delegating functions to them"]).

Consistent with these principles, any harm from the discovery of the fraud-rather than from the fraud itself-does not bear on whether the adverse interest exception applies. The disclosure of corporate fraud nearly always injures the corporation. If that harm could be taken into account, a corporation would be able to invoke the adverse interest exception and disclaim virtually every corporate fraud-even a fraud undertaken for the corporation's benefit-as soon as it was discovered and no longer helping the company.

Finally, to focus on harm from the exposure of the fraud would be a step away from the requirement of adversity. Generally, a fraud will suit the interests of both a company and its insiders for as long as it remains a secret (sometimes a considerable number of years, as was the case with Refco), and leads to negative consequences for both when disclosed.

[The court declined to adopt exceptions to the adverse interest exception based on public policy and concluded that imputation and in pari delicto applied to the claims against the auditors]

JUDGES GRAFFEO, SMITH and JONES concur.

JUDGE CIPARICK dissents in an opinion in which CHIEF JUDGE LIPPMAN and JUDGE PIGOTT concur.

[Dissenting opinion of CIPARICK, J. omitted.]

Notes

1. *Kirschner* is one of many cases in which companies that have committed fraud have turned around and sued their outside auditors for failing to detect the fraud. These cases invariably involve fraudulent accounting entries and altered or fabricated documentation by management of the company, bankruptcy or near bankruptcy of the company and restatement of the company's financial statements. In nearly all cases, the auditor prevails on the theory that the knowledge of the wrongdoers in management is imputed to the corporation and, therefore, *in pari delicto* precludes suit by one wrongdoer, the company, against a second wrongdoer, the auditor. *See* Restatement (Third) of Agency § 5.03. But is imputation the correct doctrine to apply? After all, the employees actively misled the auditors, providing them with inaccurate information, false documentation and concealing the truth. Would not respondeat superior be a better doctrine? In response to this question, the court in *Cenco Inc. v. Seidman & Seidman*, 686 F.2d 449, 454 (7th Cir. 1982), suggested that applying respondeat superior in such cases "would exonerate auditors from all liability for failing to detect and prevent frauds by employees of the audited company." But is this accurate?

2. The Restatement (Third) of Agency § 5.04 states the adverse interest exception in narrow terms:

> For purposes of determining a principal's legal relations with a third party, notice of a fact that an agent knows or has reason to know is not imputed to the principal if the agent acts adversely to the principal in a transaction or matter, *intending to act solely* for the agent's own purposes or those of another person. Nevertheless, notice is imputed
>
> (a) when necessary to protect the rights of a third party who dealt with the principal in good faith; or
>
> (b) when the principal has ratified or knowingly retained a benefit from the agent's action.
>
> A third party who deals with a principal through an agent, knowing or having reason to know that the agent acts adversely to the principal, does not deal in good faith for this purpose.

How does this section affect the outcome in cases such as *Kirschner*? A plain reading of the section suggests that notice of the employees' fraud is imputed to the employer because the employees were not acting solely in their own interests. Under this reading, the words beginning with the word "[n]evertheless" are irrelevant to an analysis of the problem; they only come into play if the employees intended to act solely for their own purposes. An early draft of the Restatement (Third) of Agency included an illustration similar to the facts of *Kirschner* with the conclusion that the adverse interest exception did not apply. The final draft of the Restatement, however, replaced that illustration with a new one reaching the opposite conclusion:

> A, the chief financial officer of P Corporation, withholds material financial information from T, P Corporation's auditor. T does not independently discover the information and certifies materially inaccurate financial statements for P Corporation . . . T knows or has reason to know that A has withheld material information from T. P Corporation sues T, claiming that T is subject to liability to P for loss suffered by P Corporation due to its inaccurate financial statements. T may not assert, as a defense to P Corporation's claim, that A's knowledge of P Corporation's true financial condition is imputed to P Corporation. T has not dealt with P Corporation in good faith. (combining illustrations 3 and 5)

Why is T's lack of good faith a bar to the imputation defense?

3. There is some authority contrary to *Kirschner*. See, e.g., *NCP Litigation Trust v. KPMG LLP*, 901 A.2d 871 (N.J. 2006). The *Kirschner* court considered, but rejected, following the New Jersey decision. *See, generally*, Mark J. Loewenstein, *Imputation, The Adverse Interest Exception, and the Curious Case of the Restatement (Third) of Agency*, 84 U. COLO. L. REV. 305 (2013).

4. The analysis of whether *knowledge* of an agent should be imputed to the principal is similar to whether the *actions* of an agent should give rise to liability to the principal under the doctrine of respondeat superior. The excerpt from *In re Mifflin Chem. Corp.*, in the introduction to this section, suggests as much. In the case of imputation of knowledge, the relevant inquiry is whether the agent was acting adverse to the principal, while for respondeat superior liability, the inquiry is whether the agent was acting within the scope of employment. In the former, the courts focus on whether the principal benefited from the conduct of the agent, although opinions do differ on how much benefit suffices to impute knowledge. *See, Belmont v. MB Inv. Partners, Inc.*, 708 F.3d 470, 495–96 (3d Cir. 2013). For respondeat superior, the focus is generally on whether the employee's actions were intended to serve any purpose of the employer. *See* Chapter 3, Section A, *supra*.

E. The Sole Actor Doctrine

The Reliable Bank (defrauding cashier) hypothetical, *supra* Section C, was based on the case of *Matanuska Valley Bank v. Arnold*, 116 F. Supp. 32, 35–36 (D. Alaska 1953). The court decided that the knowledge of the cashier was imputed to the bank, destroying its cause of action against the innocent partner. The following language reflects the basis of decision:

> The well-established principle that the knowledge of the agent is the knowledge of the principal as to acts done by the agent within the scope of his authority and in furtherance of the principal's business is of course applicable to banking corporations and their agents. The knowledge of a bank officer which will be imputed to the bank is knowledge concerning matters within the scope of his authority that he is under a duty to communicate to the bank.
>
> The exception to this rule, known as the "adverse agent doctrine," does not seem applicable to this case. The gist of this exception is that the knowledge of the agent will not be imputed to the principal if the agent is engaged in fraudulent activities which it is necessary to conceal in the perpetration of the fraud. But even if the adverse agent exception would seem to be applicable to a situation of this kind, the sole actor qualification prohibits the application of the exception where, as here, only one agent of the bank deals with the third party. The apparent basis of the qualification is estoppel. The Courts refuse to permit a bank to recognize the agency of its officer for the purpose of accepting the benefit of a note obtained through him and at the same time deny the knowledge the officer had when the note was made. The same result may be reached on the theory of ratification. The bank cannot sue on the notes and then attempt to escape the imputed knowledge rule by setting up the fraudulent scheme of its officer.

The sole actor rule is an interesting and somewhat vague qualification of the adverse interest exception. Although the above quotation from the *Matanuska* case explains it on estoppel grounds, restitution of benefits received, based on unjust enrichment, seems a more fitting explanation for that case. *See First Nat'l Bank of Cicero v. United States*, 653 F. Supp. 1312, 1317 (N.D. Ill. 1987), *rev'd*, 860 F.2d 1407 (7th Cir. 1988) ("The law will charge the principal with whatever the agent knew, as the fair price of claiming the benefit through the agent."); SEAVEY, LAW OF AGENCY §§ 38F, 98D (1964).

An additional feature of the sole actor doctrine, explained in *Ash v. Georgia-Pacific Corp.*, 957 F.2d 432, 436 (7th Cir. 1992), is that, "None of the 'sole actor' cases we could find allows the imputation of knowledge to the principal where the adverse party knew that the agent was acting adversely to his employer. . . ." Although the facts of *Matanuska* involved participation in the fraud by a partner of the plaintiff, the court viewed the plaintiff as innocent. It did not discuss the possibility of imputing knowledge the other way, that is, imputing the knowledge of plaintiff's partner to plaintiff, thus triggering this limitation on the sole actor doctrine.

The sole actor rule applies to circumstances beyond those involved in *Matanuska*, where an asset is acquired for the principal by the agent while acting or purporting to act in an agency capacity and where ratification can serve as an alternative ground for liability. It also applies to situations where the agent acquires property by fraud from a third party, then transfers it to his principal in the capacity of an adverse party. Under this circumstance, ratification is not available as a ground for liability. If the principal pays for the asset, which surely would almost always be the case in a transaction involving the acquisition of property or of a security interest in property, the restitution rationale also would not seem applicable. And estoppel presumably would almost never apply in these situations because the principal usually does not act until after the transaction between the agent and the third party has been completed, thus making unlikely any change of position by the third party in reliance on the principal's conduct.

Under these circumstances, one would assume in the ordinary case that the defense of bona fide purchaser for value would be available to the principal. See *Solomon v. Gibson*, 615 A.2d 367 (Pa. Super. 1992), quoting § 282, Comment j, of the Restatement (Second) to the effect that, "if he [the principal] deals with the agent as an adverse party and receives as a purchaser property which the agent had obtained by fraud, he may keep it. So, if an agent having embezzled from his principal has replaced the embezzled funds with others which he has stolen, the principal is protected if, with or without knowledge of the embezzlement, he settles accounts with the agent."

When, if at all, considering the above doctrine, would the guilty knowledge of an agent be imputed in a transaction where the agent acts as an adverse party to the principal? The following case addresses this question.

Munroe v. Harriman

United States Court of Appeals, Second Circuit
85 F.2d 493 (1936)

Bill in equity by Charles A. Munroe against Joseph W. Harriman, the Harriman National Bank & Trust Company of the City of New York, Frederick V. Goess, as receiver of the Harriman National Bank & Trust Company, and others, to rescind a loan of securities made by the complainant to Joseph W. Harriman and to recover such securities from the Harriman National Bank & Trust Company, to whom Harriman had pledged them. Decree for complainant (16 F. Supp. 341), and the bank and its receiver appeal.

Affirmed.

Before MANTON, L. HAND, and SWAN, CIRCUIT JUDGES.

SWAN, CIRCUIT JUDGE.

By this suit Charles A. Munroe seeks to recover possession of securities (shares of stock) which he lent to Joseph W. Harriman on June 14, 1932, to be used by the latter as he saw fit to secure personal loans. The lending of the securities was procured by fraud, which concededly gave ground for rescission of the transaction as against Harriman. The controversy is whether rescission is available against the bank, to which Harriman pledged the securities as collateral for a loan. While the suit was pending, the bank was put into liquidation and a receiver was appointed. By supplemental complaint, the receiver was made a party defendant.

Harriman was president of the bank and dominated its other officers and employees. Upon obtaining Munroe's securities he caused the bank to make a time loan of $380,000 to M. H. O. Company, Inc., one of his dummy corporations, and pledged as collateral therefor the Munroe securities plus some shares of Standard Oil stock. Later, $14,000 more was advanced on the same collateral. The proceeds of the original loan of $380,000 were used as follows: $150,000, taken from the bank at Harriman's order in anticipation of the approval of the loan, was paid to National City Bank to pay off its loan to J. A. M. A. Corporation, another dummy corporation of Harriman; $200,000 took up an existing demand note of M. H. O. Company to the bank which had been secured by the Standard Oil shares; and $30,000 discharged an existing obligation of Harriman to the bank. None of the officers or employees of the bank who took part in the making of the loan, other than Harriman, were aware that the pledged securities had been procured from Munroe by fraud. Formally, the loan was approved by other officers acting as the loan committee of the bank. The District Court found as a fact that they were completely dominated by Harriman and habitually did whatever he requested.

At the outset it should be observed that Munroe did not deal with Harriman as an agent of the bank. Harriman's request was that the securities be lent to him personally, and so they were. Nor was Harriman acting as the bank's agent in borrowing them. Hence his fraudulent representations in procuring them cannot be attributed to the bank. Indeed, no contention is made that they can. The dispute is whether Harriman's knowledge of his prior fraud upon Munroe, and of the latter's resulting equitable claim to recover possession of the borrowed stock, must as a matter of law be imputed to the bank, when it accepted the pledge of the stock from Harriman's dummy, M. H. O. Company.

Aside from the effect of Harriman's "domination," to be discussed hereafter, it is clear that the bank would not be charged with knowledge of Munroe's claim. The principal is not affected by the knowledge of an agent as to matters involved in a transaction in which an agent deals with the principal or another agent of the principal as, or on account of, an adverse party. American Law Institute, Restatement, Agency, § 279. The rules for determining when an agent's knowledge will or will not be imputed to his principal are frequently stated in terms of presumptions. Thus, in *Distilled Spirits*, 11 Wall. 356, 367, Justice Bradley said that it is an agent's duty to communicate to his principal the knowledge he has concerning the subject of negotiation and there is a presumption that he will perform that duty. Similarly, in *American Nat'l Bank v. Miller*, 229 U.S. 517, 522, where the agent's knowledge was not imputed, the reason assigned was that the law does not presume that he has performed his duty of communication when his interest is to conceal the facts. Harriman's interest required concealment from the bank of the defect in title of the securities offered in pledge. But to explain the cases in terms of presumptions is not a rational analysis. The presumption of communication is a pure fiction, contrary to the fact, for it is only when the agent has failed to communicate his knowledge that any occasion arises for imputing it to the principal. The rational explanation of the *Distilled Spirits* Case is that common justice requires that one who puts forward an agent to do his business should not escape the consequences of notice to, or knowledge of, his agent. But the general rule is subject to equally well established exceptions (Mechem, *ibid.* § 1813), one of which is that an agent's knowledge is not imputed when he is acting adversely to his principal, as in the *Miller* Case. The real basis for this exception was stated by Judge Taft in *Thomson-Houston Electric Co. v. Capitol Electric Co.*, 65 F. 341, 343 (C.C.A.6): "The truth is that where an agent, though ostensibly acting in the business of the principal, is really committing a fraud, for his own benefit, he is acting outside of the scope of his agency, and it would therefore be most unjust to charge the principal with knowledge of it." But the injustice disappears if the principal adopts the unauthorized act of his agent in order to retain a benefit for himself. Thus, in *Curtis, Collins & Holbrook Co. v. United States*, 262 U.S. 215, an agent employed to procure title to land, contrary to instructions procured it with knowledge of a fraud practiced on the owner. Although the agent had an interest adverse to his principal to conceal the defect in title because his own profits would increase with the number of titles procured, his knowledge was imputed to the principal. He was the sole actor for the corporate principal in procuring the fraudulent patents. In such a case the principal is impaled on the horns of a dilemma. If he disclaims the agent's acceptance of the property for him as unauthorized, he has no ground to retain it; on the other hand, if he retains the property, he adopts the agent's act in procuring it and must in fairness take the accompanying burden of the agent's knowledge.

The situation just discussed must be carefully distinguished, however, from one where the principal buys property from an agent as an adverse party. In such case the principal's title may be traced through his own purchase or through the act of another agent, and he will have the status of a bona fide purchaser for value. Thus we reach the controlling issue in the case at bar, namely, whether Harriman's domination of the loan committee was such that, although he acted as an adversary party in offering the securities as collateral for the loan, he was also the sole representative of the bank in accepting the pledge.

The loan committee consisted of Messrs. Austin, Turner, Burke, and Jordan, in addition to Harriman. Formally, they all approved the loan by initialling the page in the committee book upon which it was recorded, but actually the loan was put through upon Harriman's instructions before it was ever brought to the attention of the committee members. Subsequently the executive committee and the board of directors confirmed the loan. With respect to loans to Harriman, or his personal corporations, the other officers and employees of the bank did without question whatever he requested, and the District Court found that they were completely dominated by him. This finding the appellants apparently do not question, nor could they do so successfully. . . . Harriman's domination was exerted to affect the action of the bank with respect to the particular transaction. His will alone caused the making of the loan and the acceptance of the collateral. Therefore he should be treated as the sole actor on behalf of the bank as fully as though he had physically placed the borrower's note and securities in the bank's vault and paid over the borrowed money without the knowledge of any other officer. In such case, as already pointed out, the corporation can claim title only by virtue of the sole actor's act and must accept it burdened with his knowledge of the defect in title.

It would prolong this opinion unduly to discuss all of the cases cited by opposing counsel. It may be admitted that they cannot all be reconciled, but there is substantial authority in support of the "sole actor" doctrine. For reasons already stated we think it is sound.

. . . .

Judgment affirmed.

Notes

1. The sole actor doctrine was at issue in *First Nat'l Bank of Cicero v. Lewco Securities Corp.*, 860 F.2d 1407 (7th Cir. 1988). The bank sued to recover bond certificates that it had accepted as collateral for $2,500,000 in loans. The bonds had been stolen. The true owners pointed to the participation by an officer of the bank (Giova) in the illegal loan and collateral transactions, arguing that this destroyed the bank's claim to bona fide purchaser status. The bank invoked the adverse interest exception to the imputation of Giova's knowledge to it. The owners then invoked the sole actor rule as an exception to the exception. The court stated, "This 'sole actor' exception is founded on the notion that, where a principal cannot embrace a transaction except through the acts of an unsupervised agent, the principal must accept the consequences of the agent's misconduct because it was the principal who allowed the agent to operate without accountability. Surprisingly, there is little case law addressing the specifics of how participation in a transaction may render an agent a sole actor. Courts have found an agent to be a sole actor when 'the whole procedure was entrusted by [the principal] to the initiation and execution of the agent. . . .'" The court remanded for a factual determination of whether Giova possessed "such exclusive authority over the verification of the collateral that he was a 'sole actor'. . . ."

2. See Matthew G. Doré, *Presumed Innocent? Financial Institutions, Professional Malpractice Claims, and Defenses Based on Management Misconduct,* 1995 Colum. Bus. L. Rev. 127, 165, stating:

Despite the broad language used to describe the sole actor doctrine and its rationale, the rule is *not* a generous exemption from the adverse interest exception. Instead the rule merely applies principles of estoppel, ratification or restitution in cases involving claims to property. The rule has been applied where the principal's right (typically a claim of title) *derives entirely* from transactions conducted solely by an agent whose interests are adverse to the principal and, to this author's knowledge, has not been extended beyond that context.

Problems

1. Ace Dry Goods, Inc., has been enjoying a good year and has decided to branch out by purchasing some land east of the town in which it is located. Baker, a clerk in the store, recently inherited some land in that area from her grandfather and wishes to sell it. Baker knows there is an outstanding interest in the land held by Carr. (Baker's grandfather had borrowed some money from Carr and had given him a mortgage on the land, which Carr had failed to record. The loan was never repaid.)

a. Baker does not inform Ace of Carr's interest and sells the land to Ace. Does Ace hold title subject to the knowledge of Carr's interest because Baker is its employee?

b. Assume the facts in part a, except assume that Baker is the president of Ace. The transaction is handled by the vice-president in charge of planning and is approved by the board of directors of Ace, none of whom knows about Carr's interest. These individuals are not dominated by Baker. They deal with her as an adverse party. Does Ace hold title subject to Carr's interest because Baker is its president?

c. Finally, assume that Baker is the president as in part b, but assume further that she handled all the details of the transaction from Ace's side in her capacity as president of Ace. Is your answer to this part the same as your answer to part b?

2. Judy was a secretary at the Fairview Christian School where her husband, Donald, was a teacher. Donald was accused of sexually abusing a student at the school, who sued him and the school. As to the school, the plaintiff alleged that Judy was aware of Donald's tortious behavior and her knowledge should be imputed to the school. The school has responded that Judy failed to report her knowledge to the school's principal or to anyone else at the school and that her knowledge should not be imputed to the school because she was motivated to protect her husband from the adverse consequences of disclosure. Should Judy's knowledge be imputed to the school?

3. In September, Poynor, a contract-writing agent for the Gulf Insurance Company, executed a one-year policy insuring against fire loss a fraternity house in Norman, Oklahoma. The local chapter of the fraternity that rented the house had become inactive six months earlier, and the house was unoccupied thereafter. Poynor knew it was unoccupied. The insurance policy contained a standard clause saying the Company was not liable for any loss occurring while "a described building . . . is vacant or unoccupied beyond a period of 60 consecutive days."

At all pertinent times Poynor was a member of the fraternity owning the house and of its local Alumni Control Board. Poynor had agreed with the Board after the house became vacant to look after it, protect it from vandalism, keep it insured, and so forth. Also, the property was listed with him for sale.

In November the house was destroyed by fire. A claim under the fire policy was made by the fraternity. Gulf Insurance Company refused to pay the claim, pointing to the fact that the house had been vacant for more than 60 days.

What argument would you make on the fraternity's behalf? What defense would you expect from the Company?

Chapter 10

Termination of the Agency Relationship

As with all other matters concerning agency, one must observe the legal problems from two perspectives: the rights and duties between principal and agent, and the rights of outsiders. This chapter will approach termination of authority in that manner.

A. Termination Between the Parties to an Agency Relationship

1. Termination by Will

1. By an instrument in writing containing language saying revocation of the arrangement "shall be effective only if made in writing" *P* authorizes *A* to sell Blackacre at any time during the next 30 days. One week later, *P* sees *A* on the street and says, "Don't sell." Has *A*'s authority been terminated?

2. *P* authorizes *A* to sell Blackacre for $1,000. Subsequently *A* observes that *P* has built an expensive house on Blackacre. Is *A*'s authority terminated?

3. *A* writes a letter to *P*, her principal, saying that she will no longer work for him. After mailing the letter but before *P* receives it, *A* closes a deal in accordance with her original authority. Was *A*'s authority terminated at the time she closed the deal? (Ignore questions of apparent authority in the eyes of the third party with whom *A* was dealing.)

See § 119 of the Restatement (Second), from which the above questions were drawn, stating that the agent's authority was terminated in numbers 1 and 2 above, and not terminated in number 3. Can you explain why? See also Restatement (Third) § 3.10(1), which states the same principles and *Security Servs., Inc. v. K Mart Corp.*, 996 F.2d 1516, 1523 (3d Cir. 1993), stating as follows: "General agency law holds that '[a]uthority created in any manner terminates when either party in any manner manifests to the other dissent to its continuance . . .'" [quoting from Restatement (Second) § 119], and *Strategis Asset Valuation & Mgt. v. Pacific Mut. Life Ins. Co.*, 805 F. Supp. 1544, 1550 (D. Colo. 1992), stating that, "A principal has the power to terminate an agent's authority at any time, although the termination may breach its contract with the agent." The rationale underlying this principle doubtless includes the policy that it should be in the power of the principal to manage its own business and to determine who shall act on its behalf, subject to paying damages for breach of contract under appropriate circumstances. *See* W. SEAVEY, LAW OF AGENCY 87 (1966) ("The essence of agency is the agent's duty of obedience, that is, a duty not to act in the principal's affairs except in accordance with the principal's desires as he has manifested them to the agent.").

a. Some Consequences of Termination of an Agency Relationship

As noted above, it is a basic feature of the principal-agent relationship that each party has the power to sever the relationship at any time. This power is based on the reasoning that one person cannot be forced to work for another and that a person is entitled to decide who will act on his behalf.[1] This is to be distinguished from the issue of the legal right of one party to sever an agency relationship without incurring damages for breach of contract.

Termination can be accomplished without conflict between the parties when the object of the agency is accomplished, or when the term of the contract between principal and agent is completed. Conflict sometimes arises, however, when an at-will relationship involves full-time employment and the principal (employer) decides to end it against the wishes of the agent (employee).[2] One issue that is generating considerable controversy today is what limits should be placed on an employer's right to terminate an employment-at-will relationship.

The extensive litigation on this issue involves two separate legal theories. One theory involves contract analysis. The assumption is made that employment at-will is a contract.[3] It is accepted today that contracts include an implied term of good faith. This provides the basis for an argument that every employment at will contains an implied term of good faith and fair dealing, which is interpreted in this context to mean that discharge can be made only for good cause. *See Morriss v. Coleman Co.*, 738 P.2d 841 (Kan. 1987) (listing the states on both sides of this issue). Many courts hesitate to create such an implied term, perhaps because they fear that by doing so they would in effect be imposing tenure (by another name) on all private employment contracts. Tenure is a common feature of university life, but rarely is it spoken

---

1. A distinction might usefully be drawn between representation and employment. A person always should be able to choose who can represent him in transactions entered on his behalf. But employment law includes restrictions on the rights of employers to discharge employees under some circumstances. Labor law is one illustration of this, and public employment is another.

2. It may seem awkward to call employees "agents." One tends to think of an agent as someone who enters into contracts on behalf of another. The duties of many employees are far removed from that. Yet conceptually all employees are agents, owing fiduciary duties (no matter how limited in scope) to their employers, because the employment relationship fits the core definition of agency of one person acting on behalf of and subject to the control of another.

3. The assumption that at-will employment is a contract can itself be debated. The essence of contract is promise, which involves commitment. The conventional understanding in employment at will is that there is no commitment, with either party free to end the relationship at any time.

of without a recognition that it comes at a real cost, admittedly one that universities have voluntarily imposed upon themselves. To impose tenure (in effect) by judicial declaration for all private, non-union employment contracts is quite another matter in the eyes of many courts.[4] *Murphy v. American Home Prods. Corp.*, 448 N.E.2d 86 (N.Y. 1983), is a frequently cited case that declined to create an implied covenant of good faith and fair dealing for an employment-at-will relationship.

The other theory that frequently is litigated is the relatively new tort of wrongful discharge. This approach is discussed in carefully reasoned majority and dissenting opinions in *Sheets v. Teddy's Frosted Foods, Inc.*, 427 A.2d 385 (Conn. 1980). The majority opinion endorses tort liability if a discharge is violative of public policy. In *Sheets*, the plaintiff employee alleged that he was discharged for insisting on compliance by the employer with the Connecticut Food and Drug Act. The majority held that this satisfied the public policy element. The dissent argued that this is a legislative matter, in part because the definition of "public policy" is difficult and open-ended. *See also Phung v. Waste Mgt.*, 491 N.E.2d 1114 (Ohio 1986) (resolving that this is a matter for the legislature).

The topic of wrongful discharge, if defined as any discharge without good cause, as some argue (thus blending the implied term and tort arguments), can evoke strong emotions. If conceptualized as a tort, damages for discharge without good cause can become alarmingly high because damages for mental pain and suffering are available, as are punitive damages. One of the difficulties created by recognizing such a tort is that ambiguity and uncertainty revolve around almost any human relationship of some duration and complexity, and a plausible story can be told on either side of almost any dispute involving termination of employment. This invites abuse once a large verdict has been achieved in litigation, some argue, by making possible coercive settlements through the threat of litigation with its risk of a high and unfair jury verdict. It also makes hiring people on a full-time basis risky and increases the incentive to use only temporary or part-time labor, some contend, which may result in the unintended consequence of reducing opportunities for employees.

For a time, California came close to recognizing the tort of wrongful discharge in this broad sense, but the California Supreme Court in *Foley v. Interactive Data Corp.*, 765 P.2d 373 (Cal. 1988), held that a tort remedy was not warranted for breach of the implied covenant of good faith and fair dealing. The Montana Supreme Court did recognize a tort remedy in this setting. *Gates v. Life of Montana Ins. Co.*, 668 P.2d 213 (1983). Legislation subsequently was passed in Montana limiting the remedy for a

---

4. The state of Montana has by statute restricted discharge of at-will employees by requiring employers to prove good cause, coupled with a limitation on damages. Mont. Code Ann. §39-2-901. One can argue that the legislature is a proper forum for the resolution of a question having such broad dimensions, since legislation can be tailored in a way a court decision cannot. Also, the legislative process provides for hearings and debate by different political interests in a way that a court suit, involving resolution of a specific dispute between particular parties, never can.

wrongfully terminated employee to a maximum of four years' wages, in most cases. Mont. Code Ann. § 39-2-901.

The following case deals with another potential consequence for a principal when an agency relationship for an indefinite term is terminated by the principal.

Want v. Century Supply Co.
Court of Appeals of Missouri
508 S.W.2d 515 (1974)

Clemens, Judge.

The trial court dismissed plaintiff's petition with prejudice upon defendant's motion that the petition did not state a claim on which relief could be granted. . . .

Plaintiff's petition alleged in substance that the parties agreed plaintiff was to work for defendant to obtain for defendant prior customers of plaintiff; that plaintiff would have "as long as he wanted," "whatever time [was] necessary . . . regardless of the length of time necessary," and "no deadline was placed thereon"; that plaintiff would advance costs himself, and "when plaintiff succeeded in said efforts" he would get a five per cent commission on the business he brought defendant; that a notice by defendant proclaimed to plaintiff's business associates plaintiff was "now affiliated with defendant"; that plaintiff performed his obligations for seven months, brought to defendant a monthly average of $10,000 in business and spent $3,600 in expenses; that after seven months defendant discharged plaintiff without good cause. Plaintiff prayed for an accounting from the date of employment to the filing of petition for a five per cent commission on all business obtained from plaintiff's geographic sales area for the same period of time and "a lump sum representing future commissions," to be held in constructive trust; and for such other and further relief as to the court might seem just and proper. . . .

[W]e determine the petition did state facts warranting relief. Giving plaintiff's petition a liberal construction, as we must, we need not construe it simply as an action for damages arising from a breach of contract. Instead, the petition may properly be construed as an action in *quantum meruit* for damages arising from the termination of an agency. As will be shown, a principal's rightful termination of agency may, under certain circumstances, subject the principal to damages suffered by his agent.

Agreements between principal and agent for an indefinite time generally may be terminated at the will of either party.

As in *Red-E-Gas Co. v. Meadows*, 360 S.W.2d 236 [7] (Mo. App. 1962), the agreement between plaintiff and defendant was "for an indefinite period of time, its duration was not fixed expressly or impliedly, and its expiration did not depend on the completion of a given undertaking." The agreement was therefore terminable at the will of either party but there is a limitation on the power to terminate an agency.

This limitation on the right to terminate an agency was spelled out in the oft-cited case of *Beebe v. Columbia Axle Co.*, 233 Mo. App. 212, 117 S.W.2d 624 (1938) where defendant discharged plaintiff as its sales agent. The court said: "The limitation is that, in any case of an indefinite agency where it is revoked by the principal, if it appears that the agent, induced by his appointment has in good faith incurred expense and devoted time and labor in the matter of the agency without having had a sufficient opportunity to recoup such from the undertaking, the principal will be required to compensate him in that behalf; for the law will not permit one thus to deprive another of value without awarding just compensation. The just principle acted upon by the courts in the circumstances suggested requires no more than that, in every instance, the agent shall be afforded a reasonable opportunity to avail himself of the primary expenditures and efforts put forth to the end of executing the authority conferred upon him and that, if such opportunity is denied him, the principal shall compensate him accordingly." . . .

Also pertinent to our case is *Gibbs v. Bardahl Oil Co.*, 331 S.W.2d 614 (Mo. 1960), where the parties entered a sales distributor agreement expressly terminable by either party on thirty days' notice. While plaintiff was in the process of building up a sales organization defendant discharged him. In upholding plaintiff's claim for the reasonable value of his services, the court . . . ruled: "Respondent's action is not an action for damages for breach of any contract by untimely cancellation. The cancellation of the contract by written notice is admitted and the right of cancellation is fully conceded. . . . We cannot construe the provisions of the agreement with reference to termination as necessarily implying that upon the termination of the distributorship under the circumstances here shown the appellant could retain and appropriate without liability that portion of respondent's investment of labor and expenses which respondent had not had a reasonable opportunity to recoup by way of commissions."

So, plaintiff's petition did state facts which if proven will warrant relief.[5]

We reverse the judgment dismissing plaintiff's petition and remand the cause with directions to grant plaintiff leave to amend his petition.

WEIER, ACTING P.J., MCMILLIAN, J., and JOHN M. CAVE, SPECIAL JUDGE, concur.

b. Irrevocable Powers Phrased in Agency Terms

1. The above materials have dealt in large part with termination of agency powers. Would the principles there identified lead to an effective revocation by *P* in the following situation? *P* authorizes *A*, in return for some services *A* rendered on *P*'s behalf, to sell a painting and pay herself out of the proceeds, returning the surplus to *P*. P. MECHEM, OUTLINES OF AGENCY 177 (4th ed. 1952), states that revocation is not available in such a situation since this is "not in reality a case of agency at all. In

---

5. [1] This opinion is not to be construed as holding plaintiff may recover "a lump sum representing *future* commissions."

a genuine agency case the power is given to the agent to enable him to do something for the principal; here it is given him to enable him to do something for himself." *See also* Restatement (Third) § 3.13.

2. Statutes in many states make the Secretary of State of the particular state the agent for service of process on a nonresident motorist driving in the state with regard to accidents occurring in the state. Suppose a motorist expressly revokes this appointment. Courts everywhere have said that the motorist-principal cannot do this. Do you see why this cannot be done?

2. Termination by Operation of Law

a. Death

Think back to the question raised in Part 1 of the material immediately above, dealing with termination of irrevocable powers phrased in agency terms. Should it make a difference if death of the principal is the intervening factor, rather than a change of mind? Draw your own conclusion, and then consider the answer given below in a famous case that has troubled courts and commentators for over 175 years.

Hunt v. Rousmanier's Administrators

Supreme Court of the United States
21 U.S. (8 Wheat.) 174 (1823)

Appeal from the Circuit Court of Rhode Island.

The original bill, filed by the appellant, Hunt, stated, that Lewis Rousmanier, the intestate of the defendants, applied to the plaintiff, in January, 1820, for the loan of 1450 dollars, offering to give, in addition to his notes, a bill of sale, or a mortgage of his interest in the brig Nereus, then at sea, as collateral security for the repayment of the money. The sum requested was lent; and, on the 11th of January, the said Rousmanier executed two notes for the amount; and, on the 15th of the same month, he executed a power of attorney, authorizing the plaintiff to make and execute a bill of sale of three fourths of the said vessel to himself, or to any other person; and, in the event of the said vessel, or her freight, being lost, to collect the money which should become due on a policy by which the vessel and freight were insured. This instrument contained, also, a proviso, reciting, that the power was given for collateral security for the payment of the notes already mentioned, and was to be void on their payment; on the failure to do which, the plaintiff was to pay the amount thereof, and all expenses, out of the proceeds of the said property, and to return the residue to the said Rousmanier.

The bill further stated, that on the 21st of March, 1820, the plaintiff lent to the said Rousmanier the additional sum of 700 dollars, taking his note for payment, and a similar power to dispose of his interest in the schooner Industry, then also at sea. The bill then charged, that on the 6th of May, 1820, the said Rousmanier died insolvent, having paid only 200 dollars on the said notes. The plaintiff gave notice of his claim; and, on the return of the Nereus and Industry, took possession of them, and offered the intestate's interest in them for sale. The defendants forbade the sale; and this bill was brought to compel them to join in it.

The defendants demurred generally, and the Court sustained the demurrer; but gave the plaintiff leave to amend his bill.

The amended bill stated, that it was expressly agreed between the parties, that Rousmanier was to give specific security on the Nereus and Industry; and that he offered to execute a mortgage on them. That counsel was consulted on the subject, who advised, that a power of attorney, such as was actually executed, should be taken in preference to a mortgage, because it was equally valid and effectual as a security, and would prevent the necessity of changing the papers of the vessels, or of taking possession of them on their arrival in port. The powers were, accordingly, executed, with the full belief that they would, and with the intention that they should, give the plaintiff as full and perfect security as would be given by a deed of mortgage. The bill prayed, that the defendants might be decreed to join in a sale of the interest of their intestate in the Nereus and Industry, or to sell the same themselves, and pay out of the proceeds the debt due to the plaintiff. To this amended bill, also, the defendants demurred, and on argument the demurrer was sustained. . . .

Mr. Chief Justice Marshall delivered the opinion of the Court.

The counsel for the appellant objects to the decree of the Circuit Court on two grounds. He contends,

1. That this power of attorney does, by its own operation, entitle the plaintiff, for the satisfaction of his debt, to the interest of Rousmanier in the Nereus and the Industry.

2. Or, if this be not so, that a Court of Chancery will, the conveyance being defective, lend its aid to carry the contract into execution, according to the intention of the parties.

We will consider, 1. The effect of the power of attorney.

This instrument contains no words of conveyance or of assignment, but is a simple power to sell and convey. As the power of one man to act for another, depends on the will and license of that other, the power ceases when the will, or this permission, is withdrawn. The general rule, therefore, is, that a letter of attorney may, at any time, be revoked by the party who makes it; and is revoked by his death. But this general rule, which results from the nature of the act, has sustained some modification. Where a letter of attorney forms a part of a contract, and is a security for money, or for the performance of any act which is deemed valuable, it is generally made irrevocable in terms, or if not so, is deemed irrevocable in law. Although a letter of attorney depends, from its nature, on the will of the person making it, and may, in general, be recalled at his will; yet, if he binds himself for a consideration, in terms, or by the nature of his contract, not to change his will, the law will not permit him to change it. Rousmanier, therefore, could not, during his life, by any act of his own, have revoked this letter of attorney. But does it retain its efficacy after his death? We think it does not. We think it well settled, that a power of attorney, though irrevocable during the life of the party, becomes extinct by his death.

This principle is asserted in *Littleton* (sec. 66) by Lord Coke, in his commentary on that section (52 b.), and in *Willes' Reports* (105, note, and 565). The legal reason of the rule is a plain one. It seems founded on the presumption, that the substitute acts by virtue of the authority of his principal, existing at the time the act is performed; and on the manner in which he must execute his authority, as stated in *Coombes'* case. In that case it was resolved, that "when one has authority as attorney to do any act, he ought to do it in his name who gave the authority." The reason of this resolution is obvious. The title can, regularly, pass out of the person in whom it is vested, only by a conveyance in his own name; and this cannot be executed by another for him, when it could not, in law, be executed by himself. A conveyance in the name of a person who was dead at the time, would be a manifest absurdity.

This general doctrine, that a power must be executed in the name of a person who gives it, a doctrine founded on the nature of the transaction, is most usually engrafted in the power itself. Its usual language is, that the substitute shall do that which he is empowered to do *in the name of his principal.* He is put in the place and stead of his principal, and is to act in his name. This accustomed form is observed in the instrument under consideration. Hunt is constituted the attorney, and is authorized to make, and execute, a regular bill of sale in the name of Rousmanier. Now, as an authority must be pursued, in order to make the act of the substitute the act of the principal, it is necessary that this bill of sale should be in the name of Rousmanier; and it would be a gross absurdity, that a deed should purport to be executed by him, even by attorney, after his death; for, the attorney is in the place of the principal, capable of doing that alone which the principal might do.

This general rule, that a power ceases with the life of the person giving it, admits of one exception. If a power be coupled with an "interest," it survives the person giving it, and may be executed after his death.

As this proposition is laid down too positively in the books to be controverted, it becomes necessary to inquire what is meant by the expression, "a power coupled with an interest"? Is it an interest in the subject on which the power is to be exercised, or is it an interest in that which is produced by the exercise of the power? We hold it to be clear, that the interest which can protect a power after the death of a person who creates it, must be an interest in the thing itself. In other words, the power must be engrafted on an estate in the thing.

The words themselves would seem to import this meaning. "A power coupled with an interest," is a power which accompanies, or is connected with, an interest. The power and the interest are united in the same person. But if we are to understand by the word "interest," an interest in that which is to be produced by the exercise of the power, then they are never united. The power, to produce the interest, must be exercised, and by its exercise, is extinguished. The power ceases when the interest commences, and, therefore, cannot, in accurate law language, be said to be "coupled" with it.

But the substantial basis of the opinion of the Court on this point, is found in the legal reason of the principle. The interest or title in the thing being vested in the person who gives the power, remains in him, unless it be conveyed with the power, and can pass out of him only by a regular act in his own name. The act of the substitute, therefore, which, in such a case, is the act of the principal, to be legally effectual, must be in his name, must be such an act as the principal himself would be capable of performing, and which would be valid if performed by him. Such a power necessarily ceases with the life of the person making it. But if the interest, or estate, passes with the power, and vests in the person by whom the power is to be exercised, such person acts in his own name. The estate, being in him, passes from him by a conveyance in his own name. He is no longer a substitute, acting in the place and name of another, but is a principal acting in his own name, in pursuance of powers which limit his estate. The legal reason which limits a power to the life of the person giving it, exists no longer, and the rule ceases with the reason on which it is founded. The intention of the instrument may be effected without violating any legal principle. . . .

It is, then, deemed perfectly clear, that the power given in this case, is a naked power, not coupled with an interest, which, though irrevocable by Rousmanier himself, expired on his death.

Affirmed.

Notes

1. Plaintiff's counsel as an alternative argument appealed to the equity powers of the court to reform the instruments due to a mistake being made by the parties to the transaction. The court, however, drew a distinction between mistakes of law and mistakes of fact, holding that this constituted a mistake of law and thus was irremediable. *Hunt v. Rousmanier's Adm'rs*, 26 U.S. (1 Pet.) 13 (1828).

2. Courts have found the rule articulated by Justice Marshall in *Hunt* a difficult one to apply. One situation where the *Hunt* test applies with clarity, however, is where a mortgage provides that the mortgagee (lender) shall have a power of sale in the event of default by the mortgagor (borrower). In title-theory states, where title is actually conveyed to the mortgagee subject to a condition subsequent (payment of the mortgage debt), the power obviously is coupled with a present interest and hence survives the death of the mortgagor. Although irrevocability might be more debatable in states where a mortgage constitutes only a lien, and thus the mortgagee would have to act in the name of a deceased mortgagor, courts in this area have been unaffected by such doctrinal refinements. See G.E. OSBORNE, MORTGAGES §338 (2nd ed. 1970), arguing that the mortgagee's power of sale is *sui generis* and should be treated as independent of agency concepts, citing to cases treating the power as irrevocable regardless of the underlying theory. Osborne's argument is consistent

with the analysis of Mechem noted above, stating that this is in reality not a case of agency at all, and with §§ 138 and 139 of the Restatement (Second) (see Note 3 below), which recognize that such powers are not agency powers.

3. Sections 138 and 139 of the Restatement (Second) of Agency address the *Hunt* problem. A jurisdiction adopting the Restatement (Second) approach would enforce the power involved in *Hunt* despite the death of the maker of the power and despite the lack of transfer of any present interest to the creditor. This is because the test for irrevocability is framed in different terms by the Restatement (Second). Instead of a formalistic concern about a conveyance in the name of a deceased person, the test focuses on for whose benefit the power exists. If it is for the benefit of the power holder, it is characterized as a power "given as security" and is irrevocable because it is not an agency power.

The relevant language of § 138 is as follows:

A power given as security is a power to affect the legal relations of another, created in the form of an agency authority, but held for the benefit of the power holder or a third person and given to secure the performance of a duty or to protect a title, either legal or equitable, such power being given when the duty or title is created or given for consideration.

Section 139 declares that such power is not terminated either by revocation or death of the creator of the power. *See* Warren A. Seavey, *Termination by Death of Proprietary Powers of Attorney*, 31 YALE L.J. 283 (1922), *reprinted in* W. SEAVEY, STUDIES IN AGENCY 109–27 (1949).

4. The approach of Mechem and the Restatement (Second) seem sensible and straightforward, yet the language of Justice Marshall in *Hunt* has proven remarkably durable. Some courts today still search for a "power coupled with an interest" and cite to and quote from *Hunt*. See, e.g., *Pacific Landmark Hotel v. Marriott Hotels*, 23 Cal. Rptr. 2d 555 (Cal. App. 1993), quoting from *Hunt* and working at length with the power coupled with an interest language in a dispute concerning revocation of a management contract.

b. Loss of Capacity

It is commonly held that loss of capacity of either the agent or the principal will terminate the relationship. The reasoning behind this rule is described in the following case.

In re Berry's Estate

Surrogate Court of New York, Queens County
329 N.Y.S.2d 915 (1972)

LOUIS D. LAURINO, SURROGATE.

In this contested accounting proceeding, the objectors move to file amended objections based on information discovered at the pre-trial examinations. From the pleadings and moving papers the court gleans the following allegations, all of which are subject, of course, to proof on the trial.

The decedent, Margaret Berry, was admitted to the hospital in February 1970. On March 26, 1970 she executed a power of attorney designating her niece, Irene Montanye, as her agent. Thereafter the decedent was discharged from the hospital. On April 29, 1970 the decedent suffered "a cerebral accident" (apparently a euphemism for apoplexy or a stroke) and was readmitted to the hospital. She remained in a comatose or semi-comatose condition until her death on June 30, 1971. On April 30th Mrs. Montanye, acting under the power of attorney, transferred some $109,000 of the decedent's funds into a Totten Trust account in the name of the decedent in trust for Anne R. Scully. Mrs. Scully is the mother of Mrs. Montanye and the sister of the decedent. She is the administratrix of this estate.

The thrust of the original objections filed by the other distributees of the decedent and their assignees was that the alleged agency created by the power of attorney was void because the decedent did not understand what she was doing and that the transfer of the funds to the Totten Trust was void as being beyond the scope of any agency created.

Having examined the hospital records and the decedent's physician, the objectors move to amend their objections to include one to the effect that the transfer of the funds was void because at the time of the transfer and thereafter the decedent was mentally incompetent by reason of being in a comatose or semi-comatose state and, therefore, the agency was suspended or revoked. The attorney for the administratrix opposes the amendment of the objections on the grounds that at law the objection raises no triable fact. He contends that a revocation of the power of attorney could only be accomplished by an act of the principal, or an agreement between the principal and agent, or by operation of law. He limits operation of law, as far as it is applicable in this matter, to the death of the principal or to a judicial declaration of the incompetency of the principal.

This Court disagrees. [Comment (b) of] the Restatement of the Law of Agency Section 122, states:

> The power of the agent terminates although he has no notice of the principal's loss of capacity or of the event causing it. It also terminates although the contingency has been provided for and it has been agreed that the authority would not thereupon terminate.

C.J.S. Agency § 88 states:

> Because the principal is said at all times to have a right of supervision over the agency, his insanity or mental incapacity before performance by the agent of his duties ordinarily terminates the agency as a matter of law, and the lunacy or mental incapacity of the principal will have this effect whether or not he has in fact been adjudged insane. . . .

Again, while there is no direct New York law in the matter, *Merritt v. Merritt*, 27 A.D. 208, 50 N.Y.S. 604, which is the leading case in New York on the proposition that insanity suspends an agency, quotes with approval *Davis v. Lane*, 10 N.H. 156.

In the *Davis* case the decedent's wife, who had been his general agent for several years, conducted business on his behalf, while he was lying entirely senseless upon his death bed. In holding the transaction void, the New Hampshire Court stated:

> We are of the opinion, however, that the authority of the agent, where the agency is revocable [i.e., not coupled with an interest] must cease, or be suspended, by an act of providence depriving the constituent of all mind and ability to act for himself, and that this doctrine can be sustained by very satisfactory principles.
>
> An authority to do an act for and in the name of another presupposed a power in the individual to do the act himself, if present. The act to be done is not the act of the agent but the act of the principal, and the agent can do no act in the name of the principal which the principal might not himself do if he were personally present. . . . But it would be preposterous, where the power is in its nature revocable, to hold that the principal was, in contemplation of law, present, making a contract or acknowledging a deed, when he was in fact lying insensible on his death bed, and this fact well known to those who undertook to act with and for him. . . .

Accordingly, if the objectors prove that at the time of the agent's transfer of the funds, and thereafter, that the decedent was mentally incompetent or incapacitated by reason of her alleged comatose or semi-comatose state, then the agency would have been suspended or revoked. The court, therefore, finds that the proposed amended objections raise a valid issue of law and fact.

Permission is given to file verified amended objections within 10 days of the date of the order to be entered hereon.

Campbell v. United States

United States Court of Claims
657 F.2d 1174 (1981)

Before FRIEDMAN, CHIEF JUDGE, and DAVIS and KUNZIG, JUDGES.

Opinion

FRIEDMAN, CHIEF JUDGE:

This is another chapter in the continuing saga of attempts by the Internal Revenue Service to limit the use of "flower bonds" to pay federal estate taxes. Flower bonds are United States Treasury bonds (1) that were issued a number of years ago at interest rates substantially below current ones and therefore sell significantly below par, but (2) that may be redeemed at par before maturity to pay federal estate taxes.

In the present case, as in a number of others, the bonds were purchased for the decedent soon after he became comatose and shortly before he died, pursuant to a power of attorney executed several years earlier. The government contends that the power of attorney lapsed when the decedent became comatose, that the purchase of the bonds on his behalf was ineffective, and that the decedent therefore was not the "owner" of the bonds when he died which, under the governing regulation, is a condition to the early redemption of the flower bonds at par to pay estate taxes. We reject this contention and hold that the decedent's estate was entitled to have the flower bonds redeemed at par for the payment of estate taxes.

I

The pertinent facts, which are stipulated, are as follows:

In 1965, the decedent, Lionel L. Campbell ("Campbell"), while in good health, gave his son ("Campbell Junior") "a full and universal power of attorney" authorizing Campbell Junior "to do any and every act, and exercise any and every power" that Campbell could do or exercise through any other person. On December 9, 1976, Campbell, then 73 years old, was "stricken with a cerebral hemorrhage, and became permanently and irreversibly mentally incompetent, remaining so until his death." He died 24 days later on January 2, 1977.

On December 10, the day after Campbell was stricken, Campbell Junior purchased, at a substantial discount and with Campbell's funds, a United States Treasury bond, in the face amount of $200,000, bearing interest at 3½ percent per annum, and maturing on November 15, 1998. In purchasing the bond, Campbell Junior intended to act as agent and attorney for his father, although he was fully aware of his father's medical condition.

The plaintiff, the executrix of Campbell's estate, filed with the appropriate Federal Reserve Bank an application to redeem at par the portion of the flower bond that was required to satisfy Campbell's federal estate tax liability. The Internal Revenue Service subsequently determined that that liability was $103,219. The United States, acting through the Commissioner of the Bureau of Public Debt, refused to redeem at par any portion of the bond. The Bureau holds $106,000 face amount of the bond, pending our final determination whether "an appropriate part of the subject bond was eligible for early redemption in satisfaction of decedent's estate tax liability." The plaintiff states that as of December 7, 1979, the approximate market value of the $106,000 face amount of the bond was $81,885.

The present suit seeks damages of approximately $35,000. This represents (1) the difference between the par and market value of the $106,000 face amount of the bond, plus (2) the difference in interest between the 3½ percent the bond earns and the statutory interest upon unpaid federal estate taxes, and (3) $5,000 in administrative costs the estate allegedly incurred because of the government's refusal to redeem the bond at par. The United States has filed a counterclaim for $103,219, the amount of the allegedly unpaid estate tax. Plaintiff does not dispute the amount of the assessment, but contends that the balance of the estate tax remains unpaid because the government refuses to redeem the flower bond.

II

. . . .

The only question before us is whether the bonds were actually owned by Campbell at his death. The government contends that when Campbell became "permanently and irreversibly mentally incompetent" following his stroke, the effect was to terminate Campbell Junior's "authority to act on decedent's behalf in effecting a bond purchase." Under the government's theory, therefore, Campbell Junior's purchase of the bond for his father was ineffective. . . .

Although there is no Texas authority dealing with this specific question, Texas law indicates that Texas courts would hold that when Campbell became comatose, the power of attorney did not immediately terminate but rather continued effective for some brief period, subject to disaffirmance by Campbell's executrix after his death. This is also the view of most of the federal courts that have considered the question under the laws of other states. . . .

The government relies heavily upon the Restatement (Second) of Agency. Section 122(1) of the Restatement states:

> Except as stated in the caveat, the loss of capacity by the principal has the same effect upon the authority of the agent during the period of incapacity as has the principal's death.

The caveat states that "[t]he Institute expresses no opinion as to the effect of the principal's temporary incapacity due to a mental disease." The comments add little to defining temporary incapacity:

> [T]he agent of one who becomes mentally incompetent to act on his own account or to appoint an agent does not necessarily lose authority to act for the principal. Very brief periods of insanity caused by temporary mental or physical illness of the principal do not destroy the power of a previously appointed agent to act in his behalf. . . . The matter is too amorphous for a statement of a definite rule.

Comment on Caveat

In refusing to accept the Restatement as a basis for holding in a flower bond case that under New York law a power of attorney was terminated when the decedent became comatose shortly before the bonds were purchased, the Second Circuit pointed out in *[United States v.] Manny, supra*[, 645 F.2d 163 (2d Cir. 1981)]:

> The difficulty with the Restatement analysis is that at the time of acting the agent cannot tell whether the incapacity will be temporary or permanent. Even in these [two] cases [consolidated on appeal], decedents could have recovered from their comatose conditions and survived. We are persuaded that the Restatement provisions are best construed as depriving agents of capacity only where the incapacity of their principals is known

to be permanent from the outset; mental or physical incapacity which does not preclude recovery should render the interim acts of the agent voidable rather than void. This reading is wholly consistent with the weight of New York cases in point and preserves the salutary principle that those temporarily unable to act for themselves should be able to benefit from favorable acts which their agents take during their incapacity.

645 F.2d at 168.

In *Manny*, which involved two consolidated cases similar to the present case, the court held that in both cases the disability resulting from the decedent's comatose state rendered the purchase of flower bonds voidable and not void and that since the executors had not rejected the purchase by the agent, the decedent was the owner of the bonds when he died. . . .

We agree with the reasoning of *Manny* and follow it. Although *Manny* dealt with New York rather than Texas law, there is no reason to think that the two states would reach different conclusions on this issue. . . .

The government stresses the stipulation in the present case that when Campbell suffered his stroke and became comatose, he "became permanently and irreversibly mentally incompetent, remaining so until his death." When Campbell suffered his stroke, however, his son could not then have been certain that his father's incapacity was permanent. Here, as was the case when the bonds were purchased in *Manny*, Campbell Junior, when he purchased the bond one day after his father's stroke, could not know whether incapacity would be permanent or only temporary. . . .

Since Campbell's estate did not repudiate the purchase and, in fact, ratified it by submitting the bond for early redemption, the purchase remained valid and enforceable. Consequently, under Texas law, Campbell was the owner of the bond at his death.

In so holding, we decide only this case, in which the bond was purchased the day after the decedent became comatose and less than 4 weeks before he died. We express no opinion on whether the result would be the same if the purchase was not made until a substantial time after the decedent became comatose, during which period a guardian could have been appointed, or if the decedent survived the purchase for an extended time.

Conclusion

The plaintiff is entitled to recover. . . .

Notes

1. The Restatement (Third) § 3.08(1) agrees with the *Campbell* decision, thus rejecting the rule stated in *In re Berry's Estate* and in Restatement (Second) § 122. The Restatement (Third) § 3.08(1) provides:

An individual principal's loss of capacity to do an act terminates the agent's actual authority to do the act. The termination is effective only when the agent has notice that the principal's loss of capacity is permanent or that the principal has been adjudicated to lack capacity. The termination is also effective as against a third party with whom the agent deals when the third party has notice that the principal's loss of capacity is permanent or that the principal has been adjudicated to lack capacity.

The drafters of Restatement (Third) observed that most recent cases reject the rule of Restatement (Second) § 122, and in Comment b provide these reasons for rejecting the rule:

> First, the rule made transactions on behalf of a principal automatically void, thereby denying the principal, or the principal's estate, the benefit of transactions that advance the principal's interests in conformity with the agent's reasonable understanding of them. Moreover, loss of legal capacity, unlike death, is not always final and its occurrence is often not precisely associated with a particular moment or event. When no judicial proceeding has determined a principal's lack of capacity, its loss may be difficult for the agent, the principal, or the third party to ascertain. Finally, the rule of automatic voidness can operate to benefit parties to the detriment of the principal's estate, in ways directly contrary to the principal's expressed intentions. For example, a rule making transactions automatically void disqualifies the principal's estate from benefiting from tax advantages associated with financial instruments that confer estate-tax benefits on the owner's estate if the instruments were purchased by an agent at a time when, in retrospect, it could be demonstrated that the principal lacked capacity.

> Second, the rule making such transactions automatically void creates substantial risks for agents acting in good faith, as well as for third parties. Widespread adoption of legislation mitigating such risks suggests that it is not necessary or desirable to treat as automatically void the transactions of an agent on behalf of a principal who lacks capacity at the time of the transaction. Several types of legislation are relevant. U.C.C. § 4-405 protects banks when a customer loses capacity but the bank does not have actual knowledge of an adjudication of incompetence. Under partnership legislation, a partner's loss of capacity does not automatically dissolve the partnership and terminate fellow partners' authority. Statutes that permit the creation of durable powers of attorney enable a principal to address, in advance of disability, the need to take legally consequential action should disability occur, when it is attractive to the principal to be able to do so without anticipating the appointment of a guardian or conservator. Separate from the creation of a durable power, statutes in many states provide, in substantial conformity with § 4(b) of the Uniform Durable Power of Attorney Act, that the disability or incapacity of a principal who has previously executed a power of attorney that is not a durable power does not terminate the agency as to the holder of the power or other person who deals in good faith without actual knowledge of the principal's disability or

incapacity. A majority of states have adopted statutes in substantial conformity with § 4(b).

2. What is the agent's risk of personal liability for breach of the warranty of authority under the rules of the *Campbell* and *Berry's Estate* cases?

3. The Model Probate Code provides for a "durable power of attorney," which is a
written power of attorney that is not revoked by incompetency if the maker so specifies. *See, e.g.,* Colo. Rev. Stat. § 15-14-501 (2006). It is of interest that a companion
provision (§ 15-14-502) provides that an agency created by any other written power
of attorney is not revoked by a principal's death, disability or incompetency if the
agent acts in good faith under the power of attorney without actual knowledge of
the death, disability or incompetency, unless the instrument specifies otherwise. *See*
Carolyn L. Dessin, *Acting as Agent under a Financial Durable Power of Attorney: An
Unscripted Role*, 75 Neb. L. Rev. 574 (1996); B. Kyle Childress, *Minding the Future,
How to Advise on Durable Powers of Attorney*, Bus. L. Today 52–56 (July/Aug. 1997).

c. Bankruptcy

This event terminates the power of an agent to deal with the assets of a bankrupt
principal even though the agent does not have notice of the bankruptcy. Restatement (Second) § 114, cmt. c. The agent's authority to bind the principal personally,
however, is terminated only upon notice to the agent. *Id.*

d. War

The effect of the outbreak of war has occasioned differing judicial responses. Several courts have held that such an event automatically terminates the agency where
the principal and agent are residents or nationals of the two countries at war. *See
Mutzenbecher v. Ballard*, 195 N.E. 206 (N.Y. 1935), noted in 3 U. Chi. L. Rev. 137
(1935). *See also* Note, 31 Harv. L. Rev. 637 (1918). Other courts have held that automatic revocation depends on whether the agency involves communication with the
enemy; if not, and if it is in "the manifest interest of the principal that the agency,
constituted before the war, should continue, the assent of the principal will be presumed." *Aldridge v. Franco-Wyoming Sec. Corp.*, 27 Del. Ch. 80, 89, 31 A.2d 246, 251
(1943) (the question in this case was whether a proxy to vote stock in a Delaware
corporation was revoked by the fact that the principals subsequently became alien
enemies).

B. Notice of Termination to Third Parties

1. Termination by Will

If you tell *T* that *A* is authorized to act on your behalf in some sort of continuing
relationship, doubtless you would make an effort to inform *T* when your agent's
authority is terminated in order to avoid the risk of "lingering apparent authority."

The problems involved in properly notifying third parties can be substantial, however, and they increase with the size of an organization and the extent to which it delegates authority.

Does the distinction between general and special agents have any bearing on the issue of notice to third parties? Can one argue sensibly that notice of revocation of authority is always unnecessary with a special agent, and is always necessary with a general agent? Should it make any difference whether the revocation is by will rather than by operation of law?

Under ordinary circumstances, no notice of revocation is necessary for a special agent because third parties could not be relying on any custom of dealing with the agent as such, and there is no appearance of continuing authority. One can, however, posit situations that challenge this generalization. Suppose, for example, that a principal has given her special agent a power of attorney or other indicia of authority. Notice of withdrawal of the power is necessary under this circumstance, of course. What happens if *P*, desiring to revoke, is unable to retrieve the power of attorney? See *Morgan v. Harper*, 236 S.W. 71 (Tex. Comm'n App. 1922), placing the risk of recapture on the principal and stating that if the agent refused to return the document, the principal "was under the duty to give notice of his revocation of the purported authority." How would you advise someone in this position to give notice? For one approach, see *Peterson v. Peterson*, 700 P.2d 585 (Kan. App. 1985), where the principal (who had granted a power of attorney, apparently in broad form, to her son) "filed a petition" in the district court asking that the power of attorney be nullified. The court held that filing the petition was adequate notice of revocation. The litigation in *Peterson* was between the mother and son, however. The court did not have before it a good faith claim by a third person. It may be that the reasonable expectations of the third party ordinarily will prevail under the circumstance where a principal has placed indicia of authority in the hands of an agent, whether special or general, and the third party relied on that. See also *Herbert Constr. Co. v. Continental Ins. Co.*, 931 F.2d 989 (2d Cir. 1990), set forth in Chapter 4, containing an extensive discussion of retrieval of powers of attorney and bond forms in the hands of a dishonest former agent.

With regard to general agents, the law requires that *P* give notice of termination of the agent's authority in order to protect those who relied on the agent's authority in the past or who may rely on an appearance of continuing authority. Does this mean, however, that the principal must give each party who falls in those categories personal notice of revocation of authority? The law does not carry liability so far. In general, the principal must give actual notice to those who in the past had given or received credit (presumably their names and addresses would be on the books of the business), and give public notice to all others, which is usually done in a local newspaper or other reasonable means of public notice. With respect to many persons this latter requirement will be fictional in terms of their actually receiving notice. It serves, however, as a convenient cut-off point for liability. Is there a better way to resolve the conflicting interests of protecting the expectancy interest of third parties and confining the liability of a principal who does not know all the people a general agent may have dealt with?

The expectations of the third party must be reasonable, of course. Apparent authority is terminated when the third party knows or has reason to know that the principal does not consent to the act the agent is purporting to have authority to do. An illustration of this is provided in the case of *D & G Equip. Co. v. First Nat'l Bank*, 764 F.2d 950, 955 (3d Cir. 1985), where the court cites with approval the following decision:

> [W]here corporation informed bank by resolution that named individuals were authorized to deposit and withdraw funds to and from a corporate account and where that resolution was not officially revoked, but second resolution showing change of corporate officers and designating new persons to have authority to do banking was furnished to bank, the bank had sufficient notice that authority of first officers to deposit and withdraw funds was withdrawn.

2. Termination by Operation of Law

As noted earlier, it is everywhere agreed that death of either of the parties to an agency relationship automatically terminates the relationship. Thus, the actual authority of an agent to act on behalf of the principal terminates on death. Is the same true with respect to the agent's apparent authority?

The decision of a clear majority of the courts which have been faced with this question is that, outside of the area of power coupled with an interest, termination of *all* authority is automatic upon death. No notice to third parties relying in good faith on the apparent authority of an agent is required. Restatement (Second) § 120.

This rule was described as "shocking" by Warren Seavey when Reporter for the first Restatement of Agency, but it is contained in § 120 of both the first and second Restatements on the reasoning that the function of the Restatement was to restate, not reform, the law. 11 ALI PROCEEDINGS 85 (1932–1934). As an example of this rule, a debtor can pay an agent in good faith without notice of the death of the principal yet be liable again to the estate of the deceased principal. Also, an agent while acting in good faith can incur liability under the warranty of authority. The rule constitutes a major exception to the principle of realization of reasonable expectations that underlies most of the law in the contractual area of agency.

A few jurisdictions have changed the common law rule by decision or by statute. And in every state there are statutes protecting banks against liabilities for cashing checks or forwarding checks for collection after the unknown death of a depositor. *See* UCC § 4-405(1).

The New York Law Revision Commission considered the problem of automatic termination of authority on death in 1939 and came to the following conclusion:

> Upon completion of a study of the question, transmitted herewith, the Commission has concluded that a remedial statute changing the law would not be desirable, for several reasons. The instances of injustice under the present law are extremely rare and there is consequently little demand for a change. The New York rule is in accord with the majority of jurisdictions.
>
> A changed rule would give rise to the possibility of fraud or collusion between the agent and a third person and there would be danger of injustice in holding the principal's estate on contracts made by agents who, unknown to the representative of the estate, have authority outstanding and whose authority cannot be disproved by the representative. Any extension of the time during which an agent's authority is valid as to third persons without notice, for a period after death, would not necessarily eliminate the possibility of injustice, but would merely extend the period and set another arbitrary date after which injustice might also be done. Furthermore, there are procedural difficulties to be considered, such as delay in the settlement of estates and in the final accountings of executors and administrators, difficulties in proof, [and] conflict in jurisdiction between the Supreme Court and the Surrogate's Court.

N.Y. Law Revision Comm'n Report 687 (1939).

As mentioned above, there is common law authority on the other side of this question. See the following statement against the automatic revocation rule contained in *Cassiday v. McKenzie*, 4 Watts & S. 282, 285, 39 Am. Dec. 76, 79 (Pa. 1842):

> Thus, if a man is the notorious agent for another to collect debts, it is but reasonable that debtors should be protected in payments to the agent until they are informed that the agency has terminated. But this, it is said, is only true of an agency terminated by express revocation, and does not hold, of an implied revocation by the death of the principal. It would puzzle the most acute man to give any reason why it should be a mispayment when revoked by death, and a good payment when expressly revoked by the party in his lifetime.

Notwithstanding the paucity of cases that are contrary to Restatement (Second) § 120, the drafters of the Restatement (Third) rejected the rule that the death of the principal revokes the authority of the agent to act on the principal's behalf. Section 3.07(2) of Restatement (Third) makes clear that, while an agent's actual authority terminates on the death of the principal, that "termination is effective only when the agent has notice of the principal's death." Similarly, in § 3.11(1), the drafters have provided that an agent's apparent authority may continue even if the agent's actual authority has terminated due to the death of the principal. The drafters justified this change not by a trend in the case law, but rather due to legislative changes, writing in Comment d to § 3.07 that:

> [l]egislation has long mitigated the common-law result. Widespread adoption of consistent legislation of general applicability is a reliable measure of contemporary policy. The residual common-law rule should reflect the policy judgments reflected in legislation such as the Uniform Commercial Code, the Uniform Durable Power of Attorney Act, and contemporary partnership statutes. Banks are protected by the provisions of U.C.C. § 4-405, which continue a bank's actual authority to pay or otherwise handle items when the bank does not know that its customer has died. Under § 4(a) of the Uniform Durable Power of Attorney Act, when a principal has executed any power of attorney, whether or not durable (see § 3.08(2)), the principal's death does not revoke the power of an agent whose authority is stated in the power and as to other persons, if they deal under the power in good faith and without actual knowledge of the principal's death. A majority of states have adopted statutes based on or comparable in effect to § 4(a).

It remains to be seen, of course, whether the drafters attempt to alter the law, as opposed to restating it, will find success in the courts.

Little case authority exists on whether the other instances of termination by operation of law (insanity, bankruptcy and war) are also terminable without notice. There is some case authority to the effect that termination does not operate without notice. *See* Mechem, *supra*, at 195, n73.

Problems

1. *P* has secured by entry the right to register a corporation in a certain name. *A* desires to organize a corporation and to use the same name. *A* proposes to *P* that if *P* will consent to the withdrawal of his entry so that *A* can properly use the name, *A* will pay *P* $1,000 in cash and give him 10 shares in the corporation. *P* agrees. *A* pays him the money and executes an agreement for the shares, and *P* gives *A* power of attorney, irrevocable in terms, authorizing *A* to execute and file in *P*'s name a relinquishment of *P*'s entry. *A* spends time and money in completing her organization and is ready to file her papers when *P* informs *A* that he revokes the power of attorney. Is the revocation effective? *P* then dies. Does that change your analysis?

a. Would it affect your analysis if *P* had given *A* the power of attorney gratuitously, saying "I don't need that name anymore," and then changed his mind or died before *A* had completed the transfer?

b. How would you as *A*'s lawyer advise her to cast this transaction, assuming your advice was sought in the beginning stages?

2. A patient in a hospital is dying of tuberculosis. He is totally disabled but is not incompetent mentally. The attorney for the hospital is called upon to arrange payment of the accumulated bills, which are substantial, from the patient's life insurance policy. The attorney is pressured for time, so she dictates a power of attorney for the patient to sign, authorizing the hospital to collect the insurance and apply it to the hospital bill. The patient dies soon thereafter. Will the hospital be able to make effective use of the power of attorney?

a. Suppose the policy contained both death benefits and total disability benefits. Would that fact strengthen the case for the hospital? If so, why?

b. Can you think of a better way the attorney could have cast the form of the document?

3. Martin Gough died intestate on July 27. He was survived by Margaret, a woman who lived with him for 25 years and claimed to be his widow, and three brothers, Luke, Frank and James. The three brothers were concerned about the disposition of Martin's assets to his widow, so they entered into a written agreement on August 16 "in consideration of the covenants hereinafter set forth" appointing Luke to negotiate with Margaret "to settle any claim she has against the estate of Martin Gough and to act as administrator of said estate, and as trustee of a proposed trust for the benefit of said Margaret," and agreeing "that we will approve any settlement made by him for our benefit." This was the substance of the agreement.

Luke thereafter negotiated a settlement with Margaret, providing her $495 monthly for the remainder of her life in consideration of her relinquishment of all claims against the estate. The money would be paid by Luke, who was to become trustee under a trust established with the assets of Martin's estate.

Two instruments were prepared and dated August 18, one a contract setting forth the above agreement with Margaret and the other an indenture of trust. They were signed by Luke, Frank and Margaret. James did not sign either instrument. Luke, at some later time, signed both instruments as attorney for James. On August 23 Luke's attorney received a letter from the attorney of James revoking the August 16 power of attorney.

Luke filed a petition for the administration of Martin's estate. James filed a similar petition and objected to the allowance of the petition filed by Luke. Luke then filed a bill in equity to obtain specific performance of the August 18 contract and indenture of trust.

What arguments would you make as attorney for Luke, using the material contained in this chapter? What defense would you anticipate James making? What difference does it make, if any, whether Luke signed James's name before or after August 23? *MacDonald v. Gough*, 326 Mass. 93, 93 N.E.2d 260 (1950).

Chapter 11

The Creation of a Partnership

A. Introduction

A general partnership is easy to form and operate. It can be created by oral agreement and can be run with considerable informality. No documents are filed as part of the creation of a partnership. If two or more people associate as co-owners to carry on a business for profit and take no steps to formalize their relationship in any other way, they have created a partnership. This is "the fundamental characteristic" that distinguishes partnerships "from every other business association. All other business associations are statutory in origin. They are formed by the happening of an event designated in a statute as necessary to their formation. . . . Partnership is a residuum. . . ."[1]

As we shall see, persons can create a partnership relationship among themselves without even realizing they are doing so, sometimes with unfortunate consequences. Despite the informality that is possible in the partnership form of doing business, thoughtful and imaginative legal advice is helpful to even the simplest partnership.

The partnership form of doing business is widely used. According to Census data, as of 2006, there were 2,947,000 active partnerships in this country.[2] This included substantial numbers of partnerships in every category of industry, with the bulk of them in services, finance, insurance, real estate, and wholesale and retail trade.

The tax law discussion contained below briefly summarizes partnership income tax advantages; also, the informality involved in the creation and operation of a partnership, plus its widespread and centuries-old use, making precedent available for many issues, may serve in part to explain the continuing vitality of this form of doing business when multiple ownership is involved. In addition, its function as a residual category for the joint ownership of business means that the law of partnership will always play the important role of governing the relations of those who do not wish to engage in the planning and expense involved in choosing another form of doing business, or who are unaware of other choices.

---

1. William Draper Lewis, *The Uniform Partnership Act*, 24 YALE L.J. 617, 622 (1915). Lewis was the draftsman for the Uniform Partnership Act (1914). The partnership is often described today as a "default" form of doing business, in the sense that if no other form of doing business is chosen by co-owners, one "defaults" to the partnership form.

2. Http//www.census.gov/compendia/statab/2010/tables/10s0728.pdf.

B. The Limited Liability Partnership (LLP)

The limited liability partnership ("LLP") is relatively new in the law of partnership and has a significant advantage over the traditional general partnership, as the LLP provides for limited liability of partners in a general partnership upon the filing of a document with the state. The material contained in the Introduction preceding Chapter 1, *supra*, will be developed at this point, with the view of providing the reader an understanding of the LLP prior to exposure to the law of the general partnership. Also, discussion of the LLP is incorporated where appropriate throughout the general partnership materials. An LLP is, after all, a partnership, which means that the concepts introduced below apply to it, with the exception of the vicarious liability of partners.

As noted in the Introduction, protection from the risk of vicarious liability for the debts[3] of a business plays an important role in the planning of most co-owners of a business. This protection first became available outside of the corporate context with the advent of the limited liability company ("LLC"), which is an unincorporated form of doing business that provides limited liability for all its owners in all 50 states.[4] The LLP followed soon thereafter. Advocates for limited liability for partners argued by analogy from the LLC, observing that states already had recognized limited liability for active owners in an unincorporated form of business that enjoys partnership taxation when they created the LLC, so why not extend the same privilege to partners? This argument proved persuasive, and the LLP is now available to partners in all states.[5] Without this option to obtain protection for partners from vicarious liability, the partnership form might eventually have been relegated largely to use in its default status.

Any existing partnership and any new partnership can create LLP status for itself by a simple filing with the appropriate state office. In "full shield" states, where there is no vicarious liability of partners for the contractual and tort liabilities of their partnership, partners enjoy protection similar to shareholders of a corporation.[6]

---

3. As noted in the Introduction, the word "debt" is used in its broadest sense, to include contractual obligations and tort liability.

4. The limited partnership provides limited liability in an unincorporated business form in all 50 states, as noted in the Introduction, but only for some of its owners. The general partners in a limited partnership are liable for the debts of the business. The limited partnership is covered in Chapter 14, the LLC in Chapter 15.

5. See Robert W. Hamilton, *Registered Limited Liability Partnerships: Present at the Birth (Nearly)*, 66 U. Colo. L. Rev. 1065 (1995), advancing the additional argument that the LLP came about as a response to huge damages awards against accounting and law partnerships stemming from the Savings & Loan crisis (which occurred from 1986 to 1995), among other events.

6. The liability being addressed above is vicarious in nature. Like shareholders in a corporation or members of an LLC, an individual partner in an LLP can incur liability by personally guaranteeing a partnership contract or by engaging in personal tortious conduct. Such liability is direct, not vicarious, in nature.

This neutralizes the beguiling attractions of the LLC, especially for the professions of law and accounting, whose practitioners prefer to refer to themselves as "partners" rather than as "members" of an LLC, a point that will be developed in Chapter 12 when discussing the doctrine of partner liability by estoppel.

In general, "partial shield" states provide protection only from vicarious tort liability or limit the availability of the LLP only to certain businesses, or both. To the extent one can identify a trend, it seems clearly to be in the direction of full shield protection. A major impetus in this regard is the Uniform Limited Liability Partnership Act (1996) ("ULLPA"), which provides full shield protection. ULLPA was promulgated by the National Conference of Commissioners on Uniform State Laws ("NCCUSL") in 1996, as an amendment to the revised Uniform Partnership Act of 1994 ("RUPA"), which will be discussed below when the text turns to the statutory definition of partnership. Subsequently, RUPA was retitled as the Uniform Partnership Act (1997), with ULLPA integrated into the law.

Some states require LLPs to maintain minimum insurance requirements. ULLPA does not require this. Nearly all states and ULLPA require that an LLP identify itself as a limited liability entity by including the initials "LLP" or their equivalent in the name of the partnership. ULLPA and many states require that LLPs file annual reports. Failure to file a renewal of a limited liability partnership registration in Texas, for instance, results in the loss of limited liability for the partners. *See Apcar Investment Partners VI, Ltd. v. Gaus*, 161 S.W.3d 137 (Tex. App. 2005).

Finally, some states provide in their LLP statutes that a partner will be liable for the tortious misconduct of "persons under the partner's direct supervision and control." The New York partnership law (§ 26) mandates such liability for LLPs that render "professional services." This language is not in ULLPA and raises potential problems of interpretation. For example, is the liability under this language direct or vicarious? It would seem most sensible for it to be interpreted as direct, addressing the negligent exercise of control. To hold that the liability is vicarious would be to impose vicarious liability on a co-agency relationship under RUPA, which makes no sense. And even under UPA, to impose vicarious liability would be to subvert the limited liability protections of the statute. But to interpret the phrase as imposing direct liability for the negligent exercise of control also is odd because a partner remains liable for personal wrongdoing under the LLP, and thus the language would be redundant.

It is conceivable that the phrase could have the counterproductive incentive of discouraging partners from close supervision of others, at least without indemnity protection from the firm. Although in the context of law firms it is possible that courts might create a duty of partners to supervise not only associate attorneys and staff, but also fellow partners, see Susan Fortney, *Am I My Partner's Keeper? Peer Review in Law Firms*, 66 U. Colo. L. Rev. 329 (1995), that seems unlikely. See, in general, Carol R. Goforth, *Limiting the Liability of General Partners in LLPs: An Analysis of Statutory Alternatives*, 75 Or. L. Rev. 1139 (1996), discussing the supervision and control issue, among others, at length.

C. The Partnership Relationship Defined and Distinguished from Other Relationships

1. Historical Background

The general partnership appeared very early in English commercial law through recognition of the Societas, a form of general partnership well known in the law merchant of Europe in the Middle Ages. The Societas was recognized by the English mercantile courts, described below.

A considerable amount of trade in medieval England was carried on at fairs, where merchants from many countries gathered. When disputes arose, there was a need for prompt adjudication according to the customs and usages that were familiar to the traders. Special courts, known as mercantile courts, were provided for merchants in towns with active markets, known as staple towns. The mercantile courts, which applied the law merchant rather than the common law, received sanction from Parliament by the Statute of the Staple, 27 Edw. III, Stat. 2 (1353).

Several principles of partnership law were established by the mercantile courts' recognition of the Societas. These included the right to account between partners; the rule that each partner represented the other partners and could bind them by contracts made on behalf of the firm; and the rule that each partner was personally liable to creditors of the firm for firm obligations. 8 W. Holdsworth, A History of English Law 197 (1926).

Gradually the law of partnership was drawn into the regular courts of England, initially in the equity courts, which heard mercantile cases and recognized mercantile customs. Equity established the principles that partners are fiduciaries of each other and have a right to have partnership property applied to partnership purposes. Eventually the law courts also recognized partnership matters, with the influence of Lord Mansfield playing a major role in the latter part of the eighteenth century in the recognition and application of mercantile customs.

Curiously, one question that was not settled early in English law was the definition of a partnership. There was doubt late into the nineteenth century about the standards for deciding under what circumstances a particular business arrangement between persons created a partnership. Important consequences attended this issue in view of the personal liability of partners.

2. An Early Test of Partnership

Waugh v. Carver, 2 H. Bl. 235, 126 Eng. Rep. 525 (Common Pleas 1793), is a case involving two ship agents who contracted to refer business to each other and to split the profits generated by the referrals. Their contract made it clear that neither party would be responsible for the losses of the other. One of the two was sued on a claim of partnership liability for the debts of the other relating to the referral business. In holding for the plaintiff, the court acknowledged that the ship agents had no intention to be partners. They nevertheless were held to be partners as to third persons for the following reason: "[U]pon the authority of *Grace v. Smith* (2 Black. 998), he who takes a moiety of all the profits indefinitely, shall, by operation of law, be made liable to losses, if losses arise, upon the principle that by taking a part of the profits, he takes from the creditors a part of that fund which is the proper security to them for the payment of their debts."

Questions

1. Assume that each member of the crew of a whaling ship agrees before the voyage to take as compensation a percentage of the profits obtained from the voyage. Does the holding of the *Waugh* case mean that the members of the crew are partners with the owners of the ship? Courts refused to take the rule of *Waugh* so far. A distinction was drawn between taking profits "as profits" and taking profits "as wages." Story described the distinction of profits "as profits" as subtle and refined, and noted that it was further defined as the status of having an interest in profits "as a principal trader." J. STORY, COMMENTARIES ON THE LAW OF PARTNERSHIP 50 (7th ed. 1881).

2. Does the explanation advanced in *Waugh* that one who takes a share in the profits should be liable as a partner because "he takes from the creditors a part of that fund which is the proper security for the payment of their debts" make sense to you? Story comments on that rationale, *supra* Note 1, at 55 (footnote), as follows:

> Creditors neither can nor do rely on profits for payment. Profits do not exist until creditors are paid. . . . In fact, what a creditor does rely on as a fund of payment are the gross returns, not the net profits.

Story also argues that the premise of *Waugh* is inequitable because defendant's liability is not limited to the extent of the profits received by him. Instead, he is liable for all the debts of the business whether or not he received any profits.

3. The Uniform Partnership Act (1914), the Revised Uniform Partnership Act (1997) and the 2013 Amendments to RUPA

The definition of a partnership is now statutory in all states. Section 6(1) of the Uniform Partnership Act ("UPA") defines a partnership as "an association of two or more persons to carry on as co-owners a business for profit." UPA was promulgated by NCCUSL in 1914. Some of its provisions seem patterned on the English Partnership Act, drafted by Sir Frederick Pollock and enacted in England in 1890. UPA is contained in volume 6 of Uniform Laws Annotated. The English Act is reproduced as Appendix B in 1 REED ROWLEY, ROWLEY ON PARTNERSHIP (2nd ed. 1960).

At one time UPA was enacted into law in all states except Louisiana. It still is law in a handful of states. The remaining states and the District of Columbia have adopted the Revised Uniform Partnership Act (1997) ("RUPA")[7] or earlier versions thereof. There is no substantive change in the definition of a partnership in RUPA § 202.

Both UPA and RUPA are set forth in a separate statutory supplement that is available from the publisher of this book. In 2013, RUPA was further amended, primarily to "harmonize" the language of RUPA with other uniform business entity acts. This revision also included some substantive changes and some improvements to the language of the Act. The amendments have been adopted in only a few jurisdictions. To the extent that this chapter includes references to RUPA, those references correspond to the 1997 version without the 2013 amendments. That version is also the version included in the current statutory supplement to this casebook.

RUPA makes a number of changes in partnership law. Also, it is much longer and more detailed than UPA, making express much of what is implied in UPA. The origins of RUPA may be found in a report by an American Bar Association committee that recommended extensive changes to UPA. See *Should the Uniform Partnership Act Be Revised?*, 43 Bus. Law. 121 (1987), containing the report. NCCUSL promptly appointed a committee to revise UPA and adopted RUPA in 1992. It then made changes to it and readopted it in 1993, 1996 and 1997. A summary of the major changes made by RUPA is contained in Donald J. Weidner & John W. Larson, *The Revised Uniform Partnership Act: The Reporters' Overview*, 49 Bus. Law. 1 (1993).

When adopting RUPA, many states included fairly extensive revisions. In that sense, RUPA has been treated by some states as more a model act than a uniform act. The relatively recent adoptions of RUPA and the availability of the limited liability company as a form of organization have limited the number of judicial decisions interpreting RUPA. By contrast, UPA, which was adopted by the states with almost no changes and is one of the few truly uniform acts, has generated considerable case authority in the past 100 years. Except where otherwise indicated, the issues resolved in the UPA cases included in this casebook would likely have been resolved the same way had RUPA been the applicable statute. Thus, the bulk of the materials in Chapters 11–13 involve litigation under UPA. The major changes made by RUPA will be identified throughout these materials and compared to the counterpart provisions in UPA.

UPA serves a dual function. It establishes certain basic principles of law which operate regardless of any agreement between the partners ("mandatory rules"), such as §§ 11–15, which state when a partnership is bound by admissions of or notice to a partner and define the nature of a partner's liability. It also establishes

---

7. As noted earlier, RUPA's official title is Uniform Partnership Act (1997). It was referred to as the "revised" Uniform Partnership Act throughout its drafting history and in nearly all the literature on the Act. The acronym "RUPA" has remained popular, perhaps because it is an easily pronounced, shorthand reference to what indeed is a revised (in a substantial way) Uniform Partnership Act, and it will be so identified in these materials. RUPA is contained in volume 6 of Uniform Laws Annotated.

certain principles that function only in the absence of agreement between the partners ("default rules"), such as § 18, which sets forth rules determining rights and duties of partners in relation to each other.

RUPA follows the same pattern. It makes the default function of the Act especially clear in its § 103, which provides that all the provisions of the Act are default rules except nine mandatory rules listed in § 103(b).

The elements of § 6(1) of UPA and § 202 of RUPA defining a partnership can be broken down as follows:

(i) "association"—This element has been construed to require voluntary agreement of the parties, express or implied, involving *delectus personae* (choice of the person). The personal liability of a partner for the obligations of the business doubtless provides much of the rationale for the concept of *delectus personae* because one partner can create liabilities for the others. In addition, each partner is a general agent of the firm, has management rights, information rights, and dissolution powers, all leading to a certain amount of understandable caution when choosing one's partners. Sections 18(g) of UPA and 401(i) of RUPA ("[a] person may become a partner only with the consent of all of the partners") reinforce this reading. Note that the right of *delectus personae* can be waived by agreement, as recognized in the first clause of § 18 of UPA and in § 103(a) of RUPA, which means that a partner can by express or implied agreement leave the choice of future partners up to the other partners or to an executive committee or whatever other arrangement is desired or casually fallen into.

(ii) "persons"—This word is defined in § 2 of UPA and in § 101(10) of RUPA. Note that a corporation or another partnership can be a partner. Capacity to contract is required since the partnership agreement is itself a contract. Incompetent persons cannot become partners and infants can disaffirm the partnership contract. Finally, partnerships require the association of at least two persons. If one partner withdraws from a two-person partnership, for whatever reason, the partnership dissolves. *Corrales v. Corrales*, 198 Cal. App. 4th 221 (2011).

(iii) "to carry on as co-owners a business"—Ownership is defined in the comments to § 6 of UPA and § 202 of RUPA as involving "the power of ultimate control."[8] It is ownership of the business that is referred to. Capital

---

8. See William Draper Lewis, *The Uniform Partnership Act*, 24 Yale L.J. 617, 620 (1915), stating: Ownership . . . involves the idea of control; but the degree of control necessary is incapable of exact definition." As noted earlier, Lewis was the draftsman for UPA. See also, *Papp v. Rocky Mountain Oil & Minerals*, 769 P.2d 1249 (Mont. 1989), where the court said the following in response to an argument that defendant should not be liable because it did not have an equal share in the venture being sued and was not actively involved in its business affairs: "However, we have established that the parties can choose to delegate management duties to one venturer and still establish the equal right to control.

can be contributed by just one partner. "Business" is defined in § 2 of UPA and § 101(1) of RUPA as "every trade, occupation or profession" and consists of "a series of acts directed toward an end." Comment to § 6 of UPA. The same language is contained in Comment 1 to § 202 of RUPA.

(iv) "for profit" — "A partnership is a creature of the law merchant . . ." *Teed v. Parsons*, 202 Ill. 455, 66 N.E. 1044 (1903). It "is a branch of our commercial law"; thus, "the operation of the act should be confined to associations organized for profit." Comment to Section 6 of UPA.

Section 7 of UPA sets forth rules for determining the existence of a partnership. Section 7(4) states that the "receipt by a person of a share in the profits of a business is prima facie evidence that he is a partner in the business." The section lists five situations in which "no such inference shall be drawn," however. The situations include the receipt of profits as wages of an employee, as rent to a landlord or as interest on a loan. Note also that a distinction is drawn in § 7(3) between the sharing of gross returns and the receipt of profits.

RUPA combines §§ 6 and 7 of UPA in its § 202, using nearly identical language for determining the existence of a partnership. It adds language designed to protect shared-appreciation mortgages "and other equity participation arrangements by clarifying that contingent payments do not automatically convert lending arrangements into partnerships." § 202(c)(v) cmt.

The "for-profit" limitation precluded partnership status — and the right to maintain a lawsuit — for a group of foreign investors formed to prosecute a claim for securities fraud. While the group, or association, might be characterized as a business, the court reasoned that it was not a "for-profit" organization. *Asociation de Prejudcicos v. Citibank, F.S.B.*, 770 So. 2d 1267 (Fla. App. 2000).

Joint Ventures

Is there a distinction between joint ventures and partnerships? A joint venture is described and placed in its modern context in RICHARD D. HARROCH, PARTNERSHIP & JOINT VENTURE AGREEMENTS § 7.01 (1997):

Joint ventures — arrangements in which two or more parties combine forces to engage in a specific economic activity — are quite common in the business world. Businesses form joint ventures because they believe that a combined effort will allow them to be more successful than if they act separately. For example, . . . a company that wishes to enter a foreign market may attempt to establish a toehold by forming a venture with a company that is already engaging in business in that market.

New York courts, however, have adopted a more nuanced definition of joint venture, summarized in *In re Cohen*, 422 B.R. 350, 377 (E.D.N.Y. 2010):

A joint venture is "'an association of two or more persons to carry out a single business enterprise for profit, for which purpose they combine their property, money, effects, skill and knowledge.'" A party seeking to establish the existence of a joint venture under New York law must demonstrate the following elements: (1) the existence of a specific agreement between two or more persons to carry on an enterprise for profit; (2) evidence in the agreement of the parties' intent to be joint venturers; (3) a contribution of property, financing, skill, knowledge, or effort by each party to the joint venture; (4) some degree of joint control over the venture by each party; and (5) the existence of a provision for the sharing of both profits and losses. The existence of a joint venture is generally a question of fact. The party asserting the existence of the joint venture bears the burden of proof to establish these elements. Failure to establish any element of the joint venture will be fatal to the party asserting the existence of the joint venture.

See also ALAN R. BROMBERG & LARRY E. RIBSTEIN, BROMBERG & RIBSTEIN ON PARTNERSHIP 2:74.1, § 2.06.a, observing that "most courts have chosen to distinguish between isolated transactions and continuing enterprises by classifying the former as joint ventures and applying partnership law with little or no modification." The fact that courts apply partnership law to joint venture situations minimizes the practical significance of distinguishing between joint ventures and partnerships, with the exception that the contractual and tort liability of members of a joint venture may be more limited than that of partners due to the narrower scope of the activities of a joint venture. This distinction may bear some similarity to the distinction drawn by many authorities between general and special agents, discussed in Chapter 4 of these materials.

Effective Date of RUPA

The official draft of RUPA contemplated that states adopting RUPA would not have the act immediately effective as to all partnerships. Rather, it would apply immediately to newly-formed partnerships and to all partnerships at some future date. In the interim, partnerships existing on the date of enactment could elect to be governed by its provisions. A few cases have arisen on the applicability of RUPA. In *Della Ratta v. Larkin*, 856 A.2d 643 (Md. 2004), for instance, the court considered whether a statutory provision that terminated UPA on a certain date would require a court to apply RUPA to a controversy pending on that termination date. The Maryland Supreme Court ruled that under those circumstances, the trial court should continue to apply UPA.

Notes and Questions

1. Betsy and Tom recently inherited some vacant land from their grandmother. The land is close to a growing city. They decide to hold onto the land and sell it in several years for a profit to be divided between them. In the meantime, they will split expenses, such as real estate taxes and liability insurance. Are Betsy and Tom partners concerning this project, thus owing each other fiduciary duties and each having the power to bind the other contractually in some situations?

Suppose Betsy and Tom decide to increase the value of their land by subdividing it and installing a sewer and water system and streets. In what way, if at all, would that affect your analysis of the facts cited above?

2. While a partnership may be created by an oral agreement, the one-year provision of the Statute of Frauds may render that agreement unenforceable. For instance, if the partners orally agreed to have a partnership for a period of, say, three years, that agreement may fall within the Statute of Frauds and be held unenforceable. On the other hand, if the parties orally agreed to a partnership of indefinite duration (even one that contemplated a long-term endeavor), the agreement would not violate the one-year provision of the Statute of Frauds because a partner may die within a year. *See, e.g., Leon v. Kelly*, 618 F. Supp. 2d 1334 (D.N.M. 2008) (citing New Mexico law).

3. Assume that an old and respected partnership in investment banking, a high-risk enterprise, is about to fail. Some close friends of one of the partners decide to try to help but definitely do not want to become partners of the business in its existing critical condition. They will be putting in substantial sums of money and want to make sure it is not mishandled. They therefore want some control over the business decisions. Also, if they do succeed in saving the business, they want the option to become partners of the firm. Finally, if they decide not to become partners after the business has returned to profitability, they would like to receive the profits attributable to the money they let the firm use.

What risks do they run if they get everything they want? Assume that they have come to you as an attorney and want you to draft an agreement protecting their interests. How would you go about doing so? As you know, RUPA is an immediate point of reference in nearly all jurisdictions. Section 202 is, of course. And you will want to check §308, dealing with liability as a partner by estoppel, as well. Draw your own conclusions after consulting those sections, and then observe how first a law firm and then a court dealt with a similar problem.

Martin v. Peyton[9]

Court of Appeals of New York 158 N.E. 77 (1927)

ANDREWS, J.

Much ancient learning as to partnership is obsolete. Today only those who are partners between themselves may be charged for partnership debts by others. (Partnership Law [Cons. Laws, ch. 39], sec. 11) [UPA §7.] There is one exception. Now and then a recovery is allowed where in truth such relationship is absent. This is because the debtor may not deny the claim. [UPA §16.]

Partnership results from contract, express or implied. If denied it may be proved by the production of some written instrument; by testimony as to some

---

9. Noted in 2 Ala. L.J. 193 (1926–27), 2 St. John's L. Rev. 51 (1927).

conversation; by circumstantial evidence. If nothing else appears the receipt by the defendant of a share of the profits of the business is enough. [Citing UPA § 7.]

Assuming some written contract between the parties the question may arise whether it creates a partnership. If it be complete; if it expresses in good faith the full understanding and obligation of the parties, then it is for the court to say whether a partnership exists. It may, however, be a mere sham intended to hide the real relationship. Then other results follow. In passing upon it effect is to be given to each provision. Mere words will not blind us to realities. Statements that no partnership is intended are not conclusive. If as a whole a contract contemplates an association of two or more persons to carry on as co-owners a business for profit a partnership there is. On the other hand, if it be less than this no partnership exists. Passing on the contract as a whole, an arrangement for sharing profits is to be considered. It is to be given its due weight. But it is to be weighed in connection with all the rest. It is not decisive. It may be merely the method adopted to pay a debt or wages, as interest on a loan or for other reasons.

An existing contract may be modified later by subsequent agreement, oral or written. A partnership may be so created where there was none before. And again, that the original agreement has been so modified may be proved by circumstantial evidence — by showing the conduct of the parties.

In the case before us the claim that the defendants became partners in the firm of Knauth, Nachod & Kuhne, doing business as bankers and brokers, depends upon the interpretation of certain instruments. There is nothing in their subsequent acts determinative of or indeed material upon this question. And we are relieved of questions that sometimes arise. "The plaintiff's position is not," we are told, "that the agreements of June 4, 1921, were a false expression or incomplete expression of the intention of the parties. We say that they express defendants' intention and that that intention was to create a relationship which as a matter of law constitutes a partnership." Nor may the claim of the plaintiff be rested on any question of estoppel. "The plaintiff's claim," he stipulates, "is a claim of actual partnership, not of partnership by estoppel, and liability is not sought to be predicated upon [UPA § 16]."

Remitted then, as we are, to the documents themselves, we refer to circumstances surrounding their execution only so far as is necessary to make them intelligible. And we are to remember that although the intention of the parties to avoid liability as partners is clear, although in language precise and definite they deny any design to then join the firm of K. N. & K.; although they say their interests in profits should be construed merely as a measure of compensation for loans, not an interest in profits as such; although they provide that they shall not be liable for any losses or treated as partners, the question still remains whether in fact they agree to so associate themselves with the firm as to "carry on as co-owners a business for profit."

In the spring of 1921 the firm of K. N. & K. found itself in financial difficulties. John R. Hall was one of the partners. He was a friend of Mr. Peyton. From him he obtained the loan of almost $500,000 of Liberty bonds, which K. N. & K. might use as collateral to secure bank advances. This, however, was not sufficient. The firm and its members had engaged in unwise speculations, and it was deeply involved. Mr. Hall was also intimately acquainted with George W. Perkins, Jr., and with Edward W. Freeman. He also knew Mrs. Peyton and Mrs. Perkins and Mrs. Freeman. All were anxious to help him. He, therefore, representing K. N. & K., entered into negotiations with them. While they were pending a proposition was made that Mr. Peyton, Mr. Perkins and Mr. Freeman or some of them should become partners. It met a decided refusal. Finally an agreement was reached. It is expressed in three documents, executed on the same day, all a part of the one transaction. They were drawn with care and are unambiguous. We shall refer to them as "the agreement," "the indenture" and "the option."

We have no doubt as to their general purpose. The respondents were to loan K. & K. $2,500,000 worth of liquid securities, which were to be returned to them on or before April 15, 1923. The firm might hypothecate them to secure loans totalling $2,000,000, using the proceeds as its business necessities required. To insure respondents against loss K. N. & K. were to turn over to them a large number of their own securities which may have been valuable, but which were of so speculative a nature that they could not be used as collateral for bank loans. In compensation for the loan the respondents were to receive 40 per cent of the profits of the firm until the return was made, not exceeding, however, $500,000 and not less than $100,000. Merely because the transaction involved the transfer of securities and not of cash does not prevent its being a loan within the meaning of [UPA § 7]. The respondents also were given an option to join the firm if they or any of them expressed a desire to do so before June 4, 1923.

Many other detailed agreements are contained in the papers. Are they such as may be properly inserted to protect the lenders? Or do they go further? Whatever their purpose, did they in truth associate the respondents with the firm so that they and it together thereafter carried on as co-owners a business for profit? The answer depends upon an analysis of these various provisions.

As representing the lenders, Mr. Peyton and Mr. Freeman are called "trustees." The loaned securities when used as collateral are not to be mingled with other securities of K. N. & K., and the trustees at all times are to be kept informed of all transactions affecting them. To them shall be paid all dividends and income accruing therefrom. They may also substitute for any of the securities loaned securities of equal value. With their consent the firm may sell any of its securities held by the respondents, the proceeds to go, however, to the trustees. In other similar ways the trustees may deal with these same securities, but the securities loaned shall always be sufficient in value to permit of their hypothecation for $2,000,000. If they rise in price the excess may be withdrawn by the defendants. If they fall they shall make good the deficiency.

So far there is no hint that the transaction is not a loan of securities with a provision for compensation. Later a somewhat closer connection with the firm appears. Until the securities are returned the directing management of the firm is to be in the hands of John R. Hall, and his life is to be insured for $1,000,000, and the policies are to be assigned as further collateral security to the trustees. These requirements are not unnatural. Hall was the one known and trusted by the defendants. Their acquaintance with the other members of the firm was of the slightest. These others had brought an old and established business to the verge of bankruptcy. As the respondents knew, they also had engaged in unsafe speculation. The respondents were about to loan $2,500,000 of good securities. As collateral they were to receive others of problematical value. What they required seems but ordinary caution. Nor does it imply an association in the business.

The trustees are to be kept advised as to the conduct of the business and consulted as to important matters. They may inspect the firm books and are entitled to any information they think important. Finally they may veto any business they think highly speculative or injurious. Again we hold this but a proper precaution to safeguard the loan. The trustees may not initiate any transaction as a partner may do. They may not bind the firm by any action of their own. Under the circumstances the safety of the loan depended upon the business success of K. N. & K. This success was likely to be compromised by the inclination of its members to engage in speculation. No longer, if the respondents were to be protected, should it be allowed. The trustees, therefore, might prohibit it, and that their prohibition might be effective, information was to be furnished them. Not dissimilar agreements have been held proper to guard the interests of the lender.

As further security each member of K. N. & K. is to assign to the trustees their interest in the firm. No loan by the firm to any member is permitted and the amount each may draw is fixed. No other distribution of profits is to be made. So that realized profits may be calculated the existing capital is stated to be $700,000, and profits are to be realized as promptly as good business practice will permit. In case the trustees think this is not done, the question is left to them and to Mr. Hall, and if they differ then to an arbitrator. There is no obligation that the firm shall continue the business. It may dissolve at any time. Again we conclude there is nothing here not properly adapted to secure the interest of the respondents as lenders. If their compensation is dependent on a percentage of the profits still provision must be made to define what these profits shall be.

The "indenture" is substantially a mortgage of the collateral delivered by K. N. & K. to the trustees to secure the performance of the "agreement." It certainly does not strengthen the claim that the respondents were partners.

Finally we have the "option." It permits the respondents or any of them or their assignees or nominees to enter the firm at a later date if they desire to do so by buying 50 per cent or less of the interests therein of all or any of the members at a stated price. Or a corporation may, if the respondents and the members agree, be formed in place of the firm. Meanwhile, apparently with the design of protecting the firm business against improper or ill-judged action which might render the option valueless, each member of the firm is to place his resignation in the hands of Mr. Hall. If at any time he and the trustees agree that such resignation should be accepted, that member shall then retire, receiving the value of his interest calculated as of the date of such retirement.

This last provision is somewhat unusual, yet it is not enough in itself to show that on June 4, 1921, a present partnership was created nor taking these various papers as a whole do we reach such a result. It is quite true that even if one or two or three like provisions contained in such a contract do not require this conclusion, yet it is also true that when taken together a point may come where stipulations immaterial separately cover so wide a field that we should hold a partnership exists. As in other branches of the law a question of degree is often the determining factor. Here that point has not been reached.

The judgment appealed from should be affirmed, with costs.

Cardozo, Ch. J., Pound, Crane, Lehman, Kellogg and O'Brien, JJ., concur.

Notes

1. In a widely cited article, William O. Douglas, *Vicarious Liability and the Administration of Risk*, 38 YALE L.J. 720 (1929), the thesis is advanced that the risk of partnership liability should be placed on those parties in an enterprise who share the power to set prices and to control costs of the enterprise, since such persons can best distribute the risk of loss. Douglas thus isolates control as the key element for consideration and by this he apparently means more than the power to prevent actions of the enterprise, as was given the creditors in *Martin v. Peyton*. Would the emphasis solely on control be as simplistic as the emphasis solely on sharing profits was in the 19th century? *See* J. Dennis Hynes, *Lender Liability: The Dilemma of the Controlling Creditor*, 58 TENN. L. REV. 635, 659–62 (1991).

2. Occasionally, parties will enter into an agreement labeled "partnership agreement" and include all of the "trappings" of a partnership in that agreement but, at some later point, argue that, in fact, they did not form a partnership because, for instance, they were not "co-owners of a business," as required by RUPA § 202. As an example, the parties may enter into a partnership agreement to obtain favorable tax treatment for distributions from the "partnership," but not co-own and manage the underlying assets generating the income. In such a case, the court may rule that the parties have not formed a partnership. *See Cunningham v. BHP Petroleum Great Britain PLC*, 427 F.3d 1238 (10th Cir. 2005) (on remand to the state court, the Colorado state district court, in an unreported decision, concluded that the parties had not formed a partnership, despite entering into a formal partnership agreement, filing partnership tax returns and referring to one another as "partners," because the partnership did not own the income-generating assets, which were profit distributions from oil and gas operations conducted by the "partners" employer). If, however, the partnership incurs a liability (in the BHP case, for instance, by retaining lawyers and accountants), the "partners" would be jointly and severally liable if the partnership was unable to discharge the liability and they would be estopped to deny the existence of a partnership.

Byker v. Mannes

Supreme Court of Michigan 641 N.W.2d 210 (2002)

Markman, J.

This case arises out of an alleged partnership between plaintiff David Byker and defendant Tom Mannes. In 1985, plaintiff was doing accounting work for defendant. The two individuals talked about going into business together because they had complementary business skills-defendant could locate certain properties because of his real estate background and plaintiff could raise money for their property purchases. Indeed, the parties stipulated the following:

> The Plaintiff . . . and Defendant . . . agreed to engage in an ongoing business enterprise, to furnish capital, labor and/or skill to such enterprise, to raise investment funds and to share equally in the profits, losses and expenses of such enterprise. . . . In order to facilitate investment of limited partners, Byker and Mannes created separate entities wherein they were general partners or shareholders for the purposes of operating each separate entity.

Over a period of several years, the parties pursued various business enterprises. They have stipulated that the following business entities were created during this time:

a. A 100% general partner interest in M & B Properties Limited Partnership, a Michigan limited partnership, which limited partnership owns a 50% partnership interest in Hall Street Partners, a Michigan partnership.

b. A 100% general partner interest in M & B Properties Limited Partnership-II, a Michigan limited partnership, which limited partnership owns a 50% partnership interest in Breton Commercial Properties, a Michigan partnership.

c. A 66-2/3% of the issued and outstanding shares of the common stock of JTD Properties, Inc., a Michigan corporation, which is the general partner of JTD Properties Limited Partnership I, a Michigan limited partnership, and which is also the general partner of M & B Properties Limited Partnership III, a Michigan limited partnership. The interest was later increased to 100% when John Noel left the partnership. A 66-2/3% of the issued and outstanding shares of the common stock of Pier 1000 Ltd., a Michigan corporation. The interest was later increased to 100% when John Noel left the partnership.

d. A 66-2/3% of the issued and outstanding shares of the common stock of Pier 1000 Ltd., a Michigan corporation. The interest was later increased to 100% when John Noel left the partnership.

e. A 66-2/3% general partner interest in BMW Properties, a Michigan partnership.

With regard to these entities, the parties shared equally in the commissions, financing fees, and termination costs. The parties also personally guaranteed loans from several financial institutions.

The business relationship between the parties began to deteriorate after the creation of Pier 1000 Ltd., which was created to own and manage a marina. Shortly after the creation of Pier 1000 Ltd., the marina encountered serious financial difficulties. To address these difficulties, the parties placed their profits from M & B Limited Partnership II into Pier 1000 Ltd. and borrowed money from several financial institutions.

Eventually, defendant refused to make any additional monetary contributions. Plaintiff, however, continued to make loan payments and incurred accounting fees on behalf of Pier 1000 Ltd., as well as on behalf of other business entities. Plaintiff also entered into several individual loans for the benefit of Pier 1000 Ltd. These business transactions were performed without defendant's knowledge.

The marina was eventually returned to its previous owners in exchange for their assumption of plaintiff's and defendant's business obligations. At this point, the business ventures between plaintiff and defendant ceased.

Plaintiff then approached defendant with regard to equalizing payments as a result of the losses incurred from the various entities. Defendant testified that this was the first time that he had received notice from plaintiff concerning any outstanding payments, and that he was "absolutely dumbfounded" by plaintiff's request for money.

After unsuccessfully seeking reimbursement from defendant, plaintiff filed suit for the recovery of the money on the basis that the parties had entered into a partnership.[10] Specifically, plaintiff asserted that the obligations between him and defendant were not limited to their formal business relationships established by the individual partnerships and corporate entities, but that there was a "general" partnership underlying all their business affairs. In response, defendant asserted that he merely invested in separate business ventures with plaintiff and that there were no other understandings between them.

The case proceeded to a bench trial where the trial court determined that the parties had created a general partnership.[11] The court observed that, although Michigan had not formally adopted § 202 of the 1994 Uniform Partnership Act (1994 UPA) [RUPA], the law in Michigan is that parties must merely have an intent to carry on a business for profit, not a subjective intent to create a partnership. On

---

10. [1] The parties stipulated that the alleged partnership was never memorialized in a written partnership agreement, had no formal name, no tax identification number, and no income tax filings.

11. [2] The trial court and the Court of Appeals termed the alleged partnership at issue a "super" partnership. The trial court defined such a partnership as one that, although not entailing a formal business relationship by the parties, is a "general partnership between them underlying all of their business affairs." Because the statutory and case law merely define a "partnership," this Court will simply use that term without embellishment.

this basis, the trial court concluded that the parties had maintained a business relationship that constituted a partnership. It stated:

> Having weighed the credibility of the witnesses, principally plaintiff and defendant, we conclude that they began their relationship with a general agreement that they were partners and would share profits and losses equally. Whether understood or not they had a general or super partnership. The evidence supports that both understood it.

Defendant appealed to the Court of Appeals, which reversed. In part, the Court of Appeals stated that the trial court incorrectly relied on §202 "for the proposition that 'the association of two or more persons to carry on as co-owners of business for profit forms a partnership, *whether or not the persons intend to form a partnership.*'" Further, it stated that "[t]he absence of intent to form a partnership contradicts the established law in this state that the *mutual* intent of the parties is of *prime* importance in ascertaining whether a partnership exists." (emphasis in original). Upon review of the facts, the Court of Appeals determined that the parties clearly did not intend to form a partnership.[12] Judge White dissented. She stated that, although Michigan had not adopted §202, the trial court correctly recognized that Michigan's existing definition of partnership was consistent with that provision. Pursuant to Michigan law, "intent of the parties is determinative, whether or not they attached the term 'partnership' to that intent." *Id.* at 2. Thus, in Judge White's view, "[t]here is no necessity that the parties attach the label 'partnership' to their relationship as long as they in fact both mutually agree to assume a relationship that falls within the definition of a partnership." We agree with Judge White's reasoning.

In 1917, the Michigan Legislature drafted the Michigan Uniform Partnership Act. 1917 PA 72. In this act, a partnership was defined as "an association of two [2] or more persons to carry on as co-owners a business for profit. . . ." *Id.* at §6, codified in 1929 CL 9846. Over the years, the definition has remained essentially constant. At present, partnership is defined as "an association of 2 or more persons, which may consist of husband and wife, to carry on as co-owners a business for profit. . . ." M.C.L. §449.6(1). This definition, as well as its predecessors, was modeled after the definition of partnership set forth in the 1914 UPA.

In 1994, however, the UPA definition of partnership was amended by the National Conference of Commissioners [sic]. The amended definition stated that "the association of two or more persons to carry on as co-owners a business for profit forms a partnership, *whether or not the persons intend to form a partnership.*" Section 202 (emphasis added). Although the commissioners were apparently satisfied with the existing judicial construction of the definition of partnership, the commissioners added the new language "whether or not the persons intend to form a partnership"

---

12. [4] A significant factor in the Court of Appeals finding was the fact that the parties were unaware that they had formed a partnership until nine years after the parties entered into their informal relationship.

in order to "codif[y] the universal judicial construction of UPA Section 6(1) that a partnership is created by the association of persons whose intent is to carry on as co-owners a business for profit, regardless of their subjective intention to be 'partners.'" Section 202 (Comment 1). The commissioners emphasized that "[n]o substantive change in the law" was intended by the amendment of §6. *Id*. To date, Michigan has not adopted the amended definition of partnership.

Although Michigan has not adopted the amended definition of partnership as set forth in §202 of the Uniform Partnership Act of 1994, we believe nonetheless that M.C.L. §449.6 is consistent with that amendment.

As already noted, a partnership in Michigan is statutorily defined as "an association of 2 or more persons, which may consist of husband and wife, to carry on as co-owners a business for profit. . . ." M.C.L. §449.6(1). That is, if the parties associate themselves to "carry on" as co-owners a business for profit, they will be deemed to have formed a partnership relationship regardless of their subjective intent to form such a legal relationship. The statutory language is devoid of any requirement that the individuals have the subjective intent to create a partnership. Stated more plainly, the statute does not require partners to be aware of their status as "partners" in order to have a legal partnership.

Further, the Court of Appeals emphasis upon subjective intent as being of "prime importance in ascertaining whether a partnership exists," belies the absence in the statute of even a reference to such "intent" as a factor for consideration. Indeed, §449.7, entitled "Rules for determining existence of a partnership," contains a listing of items to be specifically considered in this process and the subjective intent of the parties is conspicuously absent.

Although the provisions of M.C.L. §449.6(1) set forth the standard for determining whether a partnership has been formed, we note that the Court of Appeals relied heavily on several of our earlier cases that, in the Court's view, focused this inquiry on whether the parties mutually intended to form a partnership. However, upon further examination of these cases, we respectfully disagree with the Court of Appeals. Rather, we find that, despite language that could potentially lead to such a conclusion, these cases, in fact, contemplated an examination of all the parties' acts and conduct in determining the existence of a partnership.

When the Legislature initially drafted M.C.L. §449.6(1) the definition of partnership was well established in our common law, and is consistent with the interpretation that we give it today. Indeed, judicial interpretations of the Michigan Uniform Partnership Act have regularly referenced the common-law definition.

Pursuant to this common law, individuals would be found to have formed a partnership if they acted as partners, regardless of their subjective intent to form a partnership. Speaking through Justice Cooley, this Court stated the following with regard to the law of partnership:

> If parties intend no partnership the courts should give effect to their intent, unless somebody has been deceived by their acting or assuming to act as

partners; and any such case must stand upon its peculiar facts, and upon special equities.

It is nevertheless possible for parties to intend no partnership and yet to form one. If they agree upon an arrangement which is a partnership in fact, it is of no importance that they call it something else, or that they even expressly declare that they are not to be partners. The law must declare what is the legal import of their agreements, and names go for nothing when the substance of the arrangement shows them to be inapplicable.

Justice Cooley's statements clearly express that, in determining the existence of a partnership, the focus of inquiry is on the parties' actual conduct in their business arrangements, as opposed to whether the parties subjectively intend that such arrangements give rise to a partnership. Thus, one analyzes whether the parties acted as partners, not whether they subjectively intended to create, or not to create, a partnership. The Court of Appeals in the instant case rejected the trial court's reliance on the proposition that a partnership may be created where persons carry on as co-owners a business for profit regardless of their subjective intent to be partners. The Court emphasized that "[t]he absence of intent to form a partnership contradicts the established law in this state that the *mutual* intent of the parties is of *prime* importance in ascertaining whether a partnership exists." However, the cases relied on by the Court of Appeals do not hold that, standing alone, the absence of subjective intent to create a partnership is determinative of the question of the existence of a legal partnership. Rather, it is one factor to consider in deciding if the parties did, in fact, carry on as co-owners a business for profit.

This proposition has been consistently adhered to by this Court, although our decisions on occasion have utilized imprecise language and, therefore, created the possibility for some confusion.

. . . .

Accordingly, we believe that our prior case law has, consistent with M.C.L. §449.6(1), properly examined the requirements of a legal partnership by focusing on whether the parties intentionally *acted* as co-owners of a business for profit, and not on whether they consciously intended to create the legal relationship of "partnership."

We remand this matter to the Court of Appeals for analysis under the proper test for determining the existence of a partnership under the Michigan Uniform Partnership Act.

CORRIGAN, C.J., and CAVANAGH, WEAVER, KELLY, TAYLOR, YOUNG, and MARKMAN, JJ., concurred.

Notes

1. On remand, the Court of Appeals reaffirmed its earlier decision, with one judge dissenting. *Byker v. Mannes*, 2003 WL 550011 (Feb. 25, 2003) (White, J., dissenting).

On appeal to the Michigan Supreme Court, that Court reversed, adopting the dissenting opinion of the appellate Court. *Byker v. Mannes*, 668 N.W.2d 909 (Mich. 2003).

2. The Texas and Oregon legislatures have modified RUPA by providing a list of factors that indicate whether a partnership has been created:

>　(1) receipt or right to receive a share of profits of the business;
>
>　(2) expression of an intent to be partners in the business;
>
>　(3) participation or right to participate in control of the business; sharing or agreeing to share:
>
>>　(A) losses of the business; or
>>
>>　(B) liability for claims by third parties against the business; and
>
>　(4) contributing or agreeing to contribute money or property to the business.

Texas Rev. Civ. Stat. art. 6132b-2.03(a); Or. Rev. Stat. § 67.055.

The Texas Supreme Court provided this guidance on how these factors should be weighed:

> The TRPA [Texas Revised Partnership Act] factors seem to serve as a proxy for the common law requirement of intent to form a partnership by identifying conduct that logically suggests a collaboration of a business's purpose and resources to make a profit as partners. After examining the statutory language and considering that TRPA abrogated the common law's requirement of proof of all five factors, we determine that the issue of whether a partnership exists should be decided considering all of the evidence bearing on the TRPA partnership factors. While proof of all five common law factors was a prerequisite to partnership formation under the common law, the totality-of-the-circumstances test was, in some respect, foreshadowed in Texas case law.

Ingram v. Deere, 288 S.W.3d 886, 896 (Tex. 2009).

　How, if at all, does this approach differ, in substance, from the approach of RUPA?

3. Many aspects of the spousal relationship resemble a partnership, particularly when one of the spouses conducts a business as a sole proprietor with the support of the other spouse. *Lampe v. Williamson*, 331 F.3d 750 (10th Cir. 2003), which arose in a bankruptcy setting, considered the claim by the Trustee in bankruptcy that a farm run by the husband was actually owned by a partnership consisting of both spouses when the wife argued that she co-owned the farm equipment. The court rejected the Trustee's arguments under § 202 of RUPA, focusing on the intent of the parties:

> The Lampes co-owned the farm equipment, jointly participated in the work, and shared the profits. Thus, their farm operation reflects some elements of a partnership. But the existence of a partnership where the alleged partners are spouses raises complex legal issues. The usual indicia

of a partnership are blurred by the marital relationship. The co-owning of property, sharing of profits, and the apparent authority for one spouse to act on behalf of the other are all common to the marital relationship even absent a business. . . .

The Trustee bears the burden of proving an exemption is improperly claimed. . . . Thus, the Trustee bears the burden of proving a partnership relationship existed between the Lampes in this case. Both Donald and Shelia Lampe testified that no partnership was intended, and they filed their joint tax returns reflecting that the farming business was a sole proprietorship. Although the Lampes deposited profits in a joint account, no evidence suggested this arrangement was required by an agreement to share profits as partners rather than the voluntary co-mingling of funds as spouses. The Trustee has not directed us to any evidence the Lampes held themselves out to creditors or customers as a legal partnership. Absent a showing of some other indicia of a partnership beyond those incident to the marital relationship, the Trustee has not met its burden of proving a partnership existed, and Shelia Lampe therefore is entitled to claim the "tools of the trade" exemption.

Does the court focus on the parties' subjective intent? Should it?

Note on Non-Equity Partners

Members of a partnership, particularly, but not exclusively, law partnerships, sometimes include in their partnership agreements the option of designating a person as a "non-equity" partner. Such non-equity partners typically are not required to make a capital contribution to the partnership nor do they own an equity interest in the partnership. When the partnership liquidates and dissolves, they receive nothing. The reasons for creating a class of non-equity partners vary, but often the partnership would like to recognize the achievements or importance of an employee or associate of the partnership, but not "elevate" that person to full partnership status. But given the definition of a partnership as an "association of two or more persons to carry on as co-owners a business for profit," is the non-equity partner a partner under the law? Does a non-equity partner have the same potential liability, fiduciary duties, etc. of a traditional equity partner? The answer is unclear. *See Zito v. Fischbein Badillo Wagner Harding*, 809 N.Y.S.2d 444 (Sup. Ct. 2007) ("contract partner" not a partner). *But see* Douglas R. Richmond, *The Partnership Paradigm and Law Firm Non-Equity Partners*, 58 U. Kan. L. Rev. 507 (2010) (arguing that non-equity partners should be deemed partners).

The Colorado partnership law was amended in 2010 to specifically provide that a person may be a non-equity partner:

§ 7-64-205. Admission without contribution or transferrable interest

A person may be admitted as a partner to a partnership either upon formation of the partnership or thereafter without making a contribution or being obligated to make a contribution to the partnership, and a person may be admitted as a partner to a partnership either upon formation of the partnership or thereafter without acquiring a transferrable interest, if in either case such admission is pursuant to a written partnership agreement or other writing confirming the admission.

Presumably, under Colorado law a person admitted to the partnership under the above provision would have all of the rights and liabilities of a partner, subject to the terms of the partnership agreement. Note that the Colorado statute requires that admission of a non-equity partner must be pursuant to a writing, although otherwise under Colorado law and RUPA the terms of partnership may be oral. Why did the drafters insist on a writing?

Delaware has a similar provision, Del Code § 15-205, but does not require a writing and expressly cross-references the liability provision, making it clear that "non-equity partners" (the statute does not use that term) are liable for partnership obligations as are conventional partners.

D. The Underlying Theory of Partnership — Aggregate or Entity?

The underlying theory of the nature of a partnership was under debate for most of the last century. Is it an entity separate from the partners? Or is it a mere aggregate of the persons who are partners? One would assume that a question so fundamental would have been settled long ago. As a compelling example of the uncertainty, the two uniform acts are drafted on diametrically opposing theories. UPA is based on the aggregate theory with some compromises, as developed below. RUPA is based on the entity theory. The clear position taken by RUPA will come to dominate the law in view of its simplicity, as developed below, and the increasing rate of enactment of RUPA by the states, although it would be a mistake to assume that the entity theory will always provide simple answers to issues that involve the underlying nature of partnerships.

The literature on the drafting and scope of UPA, including its underlying theory, is substantial. In addition to a number of articles by people involved in the drafting of the Act,[13] there exists an exchange on the appropriate theory of partnership between William Draper Lewis, who completed drafting the Act after the death of Professor James Barr Ames, the initial draftsman (who prepared the initial draft of UPA on the entity theory), and Judson Crane, a professor at George Washington Law School at the time, who later wrote a hornbook on partnership law. *See* Crane,

---

13. *See* Lewis, *The Uniform Partnership Act*, 24 YALE L.J. 617 (1915); Williston, *The Uniform Partnership Act, With Some Remarks on Other Uniform Commercial Laws*, 63 U. PA. L. REV. 196 (1915); Lewis, *The Desirability of Expressing the Law of Partnership in Statutory Form*, 60 U. PA. L. REV. 93 (1911).

The Uniform Partnership Act—A Criticism, 28 Harv. L. Rev. 762 (1915); Lewis, *The Uniform Partnership Act—A Reply to Mr. Crane's Criticism*, 29 Harv. L. Rev. 158, 291 (1915); Crane, *The Uniform Partnership Act and Legal Persons*, 29 Harv. L. Rev. 838 (1916).

The essence of Crane's criticism was that the Act did not fully adopt the theory, widely accepted by the civil law and known as the mercantile theory, that a partnership is itself a distinct legal entity. Instead, the Act was drawn largely on the aggregate theory, known sometimes as the common law theory, with some modifications of traditional doctrine that will be covered in the materials to follow.

The aggregate theory is that a partnership is, in its essence, an aggregate of persons acting with a common purpose, sharing profits and losses, and holding partnership assets in joint ownership. A partnership is in existence only so long as its exact aggregate of partners exists. If one partner leaves or dies, or a new partner joins, the partnership is dissolved.[14] If the remaining partners continue the business in partnership form, they do so in a partnership that is different from the former partnership because the cast of persons is different. The remaining partners may continue to operate under the prior agreement to the extent applicable. This will often happen by implication if nothing express is said (see, analogously, UPA § 23). This is permissible, but the remaining partners nevertheless are a new and distinct partnership.

Crane argued that authority existed that could not be reconciled with the aggregate theory and which had to be explained on the theory that a partnership was itself a legal "person." Among the examples supporting his thesis, Crane cited cases upholding the validity of a contract between a firm and one of its members or between two firms having a common member. In using these cases to support his entity thesis, Crane relied on the "rule of law . . . that one person cannot be both a party obligor and a party obligee to a joint contract," citing a half-dozen cases subscribing to such a rule, including several cases holding such contracts invalid under the aggregate theory. 29 Harv. L. Rev. 843, notes (1916). Crane also argued that some decisions expressly declared a partnership to be a legal person as such and reached their result on that theory, including cases giving legal validity to a transfer of property between two firms, both comprised of the same partners. It was Crane's thesis that this authority proved that it was impossible for courts to apply consistently the aggregate theory of partnership.

Lewis responded at length to Crane's thesis in the articles cited above. He defined the issue as follows:

> The issue is whether the group of activities carried on by the partners should be regarded as being carried on by them—which is the actual

---

14. It is important to distinguish between dissolution of the *partnership* and termination of the *business*. Termination of the business does not necessarily (or even usually) follow from dissolution of the partnership. This point will be developed in the materials to come.

fact—or as being carried on by a legal personality distinct from the legal personalities of the partners. Thus under the aggregate theory the partners own in common the partnership property, and they are all joint principals in partnership transactions. Under the legal person theory the partnership legal person owns the partnership property, and the partners are merely its agents.

29 HARV. L. REV. at 162.

Lewis argued that existing practice would be changed by adopting the entity theory because persons would no longer be dealing with partners as principals. Persons dealing with the firm would deal with the entity itself, and not the partners as such, who under the entity theory would be merely agents of the firm. In order to realize on firm obligations, therefore, the creditors would first have to sue the firm, exhaust firm assets, and then proceed "by legal or equitable process" to levy on the separate property of the partners. Second, Lewis argued that if the entity theory was adopted it would be necessary to have some efficient system for the registration of all partnerships. "If a partnership is a legal person it should only be sued under its name. To ascertain beyond possibility of dispute what the name is, every partnership doing business in the state should register its name in a public office." *Id.* at 167. Lewis noted that universal registration would be difficult to enforce.

Lewis's draft, which rejected the entity approach taken by Professor Ames, was discussed at a meeting of a committee of the uniform law commissioners, law teachers and practitioners. A shift to the aggregate theory was unanimously approved. The aggregate theory proved difficult to administer and had unintended consequences, as the *Fairway Development* case, below, demonstrates. Those problems helped spur the approval of RUPA.

Fairway Development Co. v. Title Insurance Co. of Minnesota

United States District Court, Northern District of Ohio 621 F. Supp. 120 (1985)

DOWD, DISTRICT JUDGE.

Before the Court are the motions of the plaintiff, Fairway Development Company, and the defendant, Title Insurance Company of Minnesota, for summary judgment. . . . For the reasons which follow, the motion of the plaintiff is denied and the motion of the defendant is granted.

Plaintiff filed this action against the defendant alleging breach of contract under a title guarantee insurance policy. Plaintiff avers that under that policy, "defendant agreed to insure plaintiff against any loss sustained by it by reason of any defects, liens or encumbrances in the title of the insured to [the real property in question]." Plaintiff avers that defendant failed to reference on the exception sheet to the title policy issued by the defendant an easement granted in favor of The East Ohio Gas

Company for the purpose of maintaining a gas line over the property in question. Plaintiff claims that the easement "is a defect and encumbrance in plaintiff's title to the Property." Plaintiff avers that it gave notice to the defendant of the existence of the defect and encumbrance in the title to the property, and made a demand upon the defendant for payment of damages which it sustained as a result thereof. Plaintiff avers that defendant failed to pay plaintiff for losses sustained. . . .

. . . First, defendant asserts that it is liable under the title guaranty policy in question only to the named party guaranteed. Defendant asserts that it originally guaranteed a general partnership, which it refers to as Fairway Development I, consisting of three partners: Thomas M. Bernabei, James V. Serra, Jr., and Howard

J. Wenger. Defendant states that each of these three men contributed to the partnership's capital and shared in the partnership's profits and losses equally. Defendant argues that Fairway Development I commenced on October 15, 1979 and terminated on May 20, 1981, when two partners in Fairway Development I, Bernabei and Serra, sold and transferred their respective undivided one-third interests in the partnership to the remaining partner, Wenger, and a third-party purchaser, James E. Valentine. Defendant argues that a new partnership resulted from this sale, called Fairway Development II. Defendant concludes that it cannot be held liable to the plaintiff since it is not in privity with the plaintiff as the named party guaranteed. . . .

. . . Plaintiff states that in the instant case, the facts are clear that there was an intent between the partners of what defendant calls Fairway Development I and II to continue the operation of the Fairway Development Company following the sale by Bernabei and Serra of their interests to Wenger and Valentine without dissolving the partnership. Plaintiff states that in deciding this case, the Court's focus should be upon the intent of the parties. Lastly, plaintiff argues that Fairway Development II has continued to carry on the stated purpose of Fairway Development I, which is really just an expansion of the purpose set forth in the partnership agreement for Fairway Development I, the acquisition and development of real estate. . . .

The resolution of this case is governed by the law of the forum state, Ohio. Ohio has adopted the Uniform Partnership Law. . . . Ohio follows the common law aggregate theory of partnership, under which a partnership is regarded as the sum of the persons who comprise the partnership, versus the legal entity theory of partnership, under which the . . . partnership is regarded as an entity in itself. Three sections of the Ohio Uniform Partnership Law are particularly applicable to this case, and are set forth in relevant part, as follows:

[The court quotes UPA §§ 27 (Assignment of partner's interest) and 29 (dissolution defined) and the following Ohio statute.]

§ 1777.03 *New certificate on change in membership.*

On every change of the members of a partnership transacting business in this state under a fictitious name or under a designation that does not

show the names of the persons interested as partners in the business . . . ,
a new certificate shall be filed for record with the county recorder as
required by section 1777.02 of the Revised Code on the formation of such
partnership. . . .

Under Ohio Rev. Code § 1777.03, where members of a general partnership
change, the partnership must file a new certificate of partnership, unlike a limited
partnership, which simply may amend its certificate of partnership. The fact that
the Uniform Partnership Law makes this distinction[15] supports a finding that the
authors of the Uniform Partnership Act recognized that a change of the members
of a general partnership in fact changes the original partnership and creates a new
partnership requiring a new certificate, as opposed to an amendment to the original
certificate.

Likewise, [UPA § 29] provides that any change in the relation of the partners will
dissolve a partnership. . . . Further, the terms of Uniform Partnership Act § 41(1)
provide that:

> When any new partner is admitted into an existing partnership, or when
> any partner retires and assigns . . . his rights in partnership property to two
> or more of the partners, or to one or more of the partners, and one or more
> third persons, if the business is continued with[out] liquidation of the part-
> nership affairs, creditors of the first or dissolved partnership are also credi-
> tors of the partnership so continuing the business.

This section seems to assume that a dissolution occurs upon the admission of
a new partner or the retirement of an old partner. The official comment to § 41(1)
notes that: "It is universally admitted that any change in membership dissolves a
partnership, and creates a new partnership. This section, as drafted, does not alter
that rule."

These sections above discussed all support . . . a finding that when Fairway
Development II was formed, Fairway Development I dissolved, and a new partnership was formed. Defendant [Plaintiff?], however, argues that the language of [UPA
§ 27] cannot be reconciled with this analysis.

The terms of [UPA § 27] permit a partner to assign his interest to another and
allow the assignee to receive the assigning partner's interest in the partnership upon
dissolution, but limit the assignee from taking part in the management of partnership affairs. However, under [UPA § 24], a partner's property rights consist of "his
rights in specific partnership property, his interest in the partnership, and his right
to participate in the management." A "partner's interest" is defined in [UPA § 26] as
"his share of the profits and surplus, and the same is personal property." A partner's
interest is thus a subset of a partner's entire partnership rights.

---

15. [The court is in error on this point. UPA does not contain a section that requires filing any
document. — Eds.]

. . . The official comment to Section 27 of the Uniform Partnership Act points to early case law stating:

> *These authorities on the whole state that the mere assignment dissolves the partnership. Many such assignments, however, are merely by way of collateral security for a loan, the assigning partner in no wise intending to end the partnership relation.* If he neglects his personal relation, the other partners may dissolve the partnership under section 31 of this act. But the mere fact of assignment without more should not be said in all cases to be an act of dissolution. The change in the existing law follows a similar change of the English law embodied in section 31 of the English Partnership Act. [Emphasis added.]

These sections indicate that the provision of [UPA § 27] that a partner may convey his interest without dissolving the partnership enables a partner to transfer *some*, and not all, of his partnership rights without transferring management rights and without dissolving the partnership. [It] is thus not dispositive of the instant case where not one but two partners have transferred not just their interest in the partnership, i.e., their respective shares of profits and surplus, but their entire respective bundles of partnership rights. See *Agreement of Sale* (buyers agree to purchase "all right, title and interest" of the sellers). The Court's conclusion accords with the aggregate theory of partnership, which, applied to this case, recognizes Fairway Development I not as an entity in itself, but as a partnership made up of three members, Bernabei, Serra, and Wenger. That partnership ceased when the membership of the partnership changed.

. . . Plaintiff concedes that when Fairway Development II was formed, a new partnership [certificate] was required under the terms of Ohio Rev. Code § 1777.03. Plaintiff states that the fact that it filed an amended partnership certificate, notwithstanding the fact that it is not in compliance with law, indicates its intent to continue the original Fairway Development partnership. However, in the section entitled "Recital" of the partnership agreement between Wenger and Valentine, the partners of Fairway Development Company recognize that they are forming and creating a new general partnership, versus continuing Fairway Development I. In Article 3 of the same agreement, under the section entitled "Term," Valentine and Wenger address the commencement of the partnership, and state that it "shall *commence* upon the execution of this Agreement (emphasis)." Further, the terms of the partnership agreement broadened and changed the terms of the original agreement. Also, both partnership agreements provide that the partners are to own the partnership in equal shares, although an equal division of the partnership interests of Bernabei and Serra between Wenger and Valentine under the agreement of sale would have left Wenger owning a two-thirds interest in the partnership, and Valentine owning a one-third interest in the partnership.

. . . Fairway Development I, being a separate entity from Fairway Development II, the current plaintiff, the Court holds that the terms of the title guaranty extended only to the named party guaranteed, that party being Fairway Development I, and that Fairway Development II therefore has no standing to sue the defendant for breach of the contract in question. Defendant's motion for summary judgment is therefore granted.

It is so ordered.

Notes

1. The *Fairway Development* case caused consternation in legal circles and apparently added substantially to the impetus to adopt RUPA, as noted above. The concern was that *Fairway* took the aggregate theory too far, rendering uncertain the reliability of long term contracts entered into by a partnership. In part for this reason, RUPA adopts the entity theory. See § 201, stating simply, "A partnership is an entity." The Comment to § 201 states that this "will avoid the result in cases such as *Fairway Development....*" For a skeptical reaction to that statement, see Robert W. Hillman, *RUPA and Former Partners: Cutting the Gordian Knot with Continuing Partnership Entities*, 58 LAW & CONTEMP. PROBS. 7, 14 (1995) ("The Comment itself makes a huge assumption concerning the scope of RUPA's continuity provisions. . . . Absent some agreement that would change RUPA's default mode, the withdrawals from the original *Fairway Development* partnership [assuming the partnership was at will] would cause a dissolution of the original partnership under RUPA, as it did under the UPA."). The topic of dissolution under UPA and RUPA will be covered in Chapter 13. RUPA § 201 takes the law full circle back to the proposal of James Barr Ames. The costs of moving to the entity theory expressed by William Draper Lewis did not impress those drafting RUPA. No provision is made for registration of all partnerships, despite Lewis's fears that such would be required if the entity theory was adopted. The concerns expressed by Lewis for creditors who are trying to realize on firm obligations under the entity theory perhaps were more justified, depending on how one views the provisions in RUPA limiting the rights of creditors to proceed against partners, to be developed in Chapter 12.

2. Commenting on whether the entity theory, as embraced in RUPA, resolves the problem that partners face in situations like that in *Fairway Development*, Bromberg and Ribstein observe that "[e]ven if a partnership were clearly an entity, this would not necessarily change the result in *Fairway*, since dissociation would probably cause dissolution under RUPA which, in turn, would have the effect of creating a new entity. In short, the courts should focus on the policy and other considerations that are relevant to the results rather than the often irrelevant nature of partnership." BROMBERG & RIBSTEIN ON PARTNERSHIP 1:60–61.

3. Does the shift to the entity theory by RUPA raise any prospect that this could weaken the shared sense of moral obligation between partners that may exist when they are themselves the principals? It is of interest that William Draper Lewis, the draftsman for UPA, as noted earlier, apparently thought so. In his article *The Uniform Partnership Act — A Reply to Mr. Crane's Criticism*, 29 HARV. L. REV. 158, 173 (1915), he stated: "It should also be added that those with the largest practical experience present were opposed to regarding the partnership as a 'legal person' because of the effect of the theory in lessening the partner's sense of moral responsibility for partnership acts." Could it be fairly argued that operating as an LLP might have a similar effect?

4. The entity theory raises the prospect of a partnership with one, or even no, partner. Arguably, as the entity is separate from its partners, its existence ought not to be dependent on the number of partners, unless the partnership agreement so provides. RUPA, however, seems to require at least two partners, because a partnership is defined in § 101(9) as "an association of two or more persons. . . ." In addition, Comment 6 to § 302(d) suggests that when there is only one partner remaining, the partnership becomes a "sole proprietorship." It may, however, be possible to draft around this result, and provide in the partnership agreement that the sole remaining partner can continue the business of the partnership. *See* Wortham, *Revised Uniform Partnership Act: Anomalies of a Simplified, Modernized Partnership Law*, 92 Ky. L.J. 1083 (2003–2004).

E. Income Tax Considerations — A Brief Summary

Unlike corporations, partnerships do not pay federal income tax on the income generated by partnership business. Instead, each individual partner is taxed directly on his share of the partnership's taxable income. He also takes losses directly into his personal return. Internal Revenue Code (IRC) § 701. In this important respect the Code adopts the aggregate theory of partnership law. This can create desirable tax consequences, since the income that is passed through directly to the partners retains its original character (as tax exempt, for example); the same is true with losses, including losses generated solely on paper, such as depreciation.

The partnership does play a role as an entity under federal tax laws, however. It is required to file a tax return, setting forth its income and losses. IRC § 6031. The return serves informational purposes and also is the vehicle through which elections affecting the computation of taxable income derived by a partner from the partnership are made. This includes methods of accounting, computation of depreciation, deduction of intangible drilling and development costs, and so forth. If a partnership fails to make a favorable tax election, the individual partners are powerless to change that by taking action in their individual returns. The treatment of a partnership as an entity under the federal income tax laws for some purposes thus can have an impact on the individual partner's tax liability.

The desirable income tax consequences of operating in partnership form were for a period of time (from 1969 until the early 1980s) counterbalanced in some businesses by the favorable treatment given corporations in the area of retirement plan tax benefits. Partnerships of professional persons, for example, would incorporate in order to classify the owners as employees and take advantage of income tax deductions for contributions to the retirement plans of employees. These tax benefits were not as fully available to self-employed persons. A series of statutes adopted since 1982, however, has substantially reduced the retirement plan tax differences between partnerships and corporations.

F. Contributions of Property to the Partnership

1. Ambiguities Concerning Ownership of Particular Property

As noted earlier, a partnership can be created and operated with considerable informality. This informality sometimes leads to confusion as to who owns what, particularly in small businesses. Sections 8(1) and (2) address this issue, but in quite general terms. Section 8(1) states that property brought into partnership stock or purchased on account of the partnership is partnership property, but sometimes that simply restates the question because the very point at issue is whether it was intended that certain property was brought into partnership stock. Section 8(2) speaks more directly to the confused ownership issue, stating, "Unless the contrary intention appears, property acquired with partnership funds is partnership property." This establishes a presumption that may be useful in some confused ownership cases. It may not be easy, however, to identify the exact source of funds in some small, informally run businesses. *See Quinn v. Leidinger*, 107 N.J. Eq. 188, 152 A. 249 (1930) ("The section [8(2)] is perhaps not controlling since it is undisputed that these partners were in the habit of indiscriminately paying individual obligations with partnership funds").

The following language may prove helpful in dealing with confused ownership cases when the language of UPA does not provide guidance: "When the intention of the partners to convert [individually owned property] into firm property is inferred from circumstances, the circumstances must be such as do not admit of any other equally reasonable and satisfactory explanation." *Robinson Bank v. Miller*, 153 Ill. 244, 38 N.E. 1078, 1080 (1894).

RUPA covers the above concepts in §§ 203 and 204, where more detail is provided than in UPA but the approach is fundamentally the same. RUPA establishes two presumptions: one is that property purchased with partnership funds is partnership property, and the other that property acquired in the name of one or more of the partners without an indication of their status as partners and without the use of partnership funds is presumed to be the partners' separate property, even if used for partnership purposes. The first RUPA presumption applies even if the partnership provided only part of the purchase price for the property. *Mogensen v. Mogensen*, 729 N.W.2d 44 (Neb. 2007).

The second RUPA presumption, relating to the source of the funding for the purchase, was illustrated in *McCormick v. Brevig*, 96 P.3d 697 (Mont. 2004), where a mother deeded 10 head of Charolais cattle to her son Clark and his two sons. At the time, Clark had a ranching partnership with his sister Joan, who subsequently claimed that the cattle were partnership property, in part because these cattle were listed and treated as partnership property for all tax purposes, and proceeds from the sale of the cattle's offspring were placed into a partnership account. The Montana Supreme Court overruled a special master's treatment of the cattle as partnership assets in his accounting, a conclusion that had been endorsed by the Montana District Court. The Supreme Court's opinion read, in part, as follows:

> At trial, Clark argued that the Charolais cattle should be regarded as separate property due to the fact that his mother, who was not a partner, had gifted the cattle to Clark and his two sons, neither of whom are partners. The District Court concluded, however, that since Clark had signed tax returns indicating that the cattle were Partnership property, and had placed proceeds from the sale of calves into Partnership accounts, the cattle should be treated as Partnership assets.
>
> On cross-appeal, Clark challenges the District Court's characterization of the Charolais cattle as Partnership assets, and argues that the mere inclusion of the cattle in the Partnership tax returns is legally insufficient to transfer title of the cattle to the Partnership. We agree.
>
> As reflected in the statute [RUPA § 204], property purchased with partnership assets, or transferred in the partnership's name, or to one or more of the partners in their capacity as partners of the partnership, is presumed to be partnership property. On the other hand, property acquired in the name of a partner without an indication that the property is being transferred to that person in his or her capacity as a partner of the partnership is presumed to be separate property, even if used for partnership purposes.
>
> In the present case, [the] special master . . . included the cattle as partnership assets in his accounting because they were listed on the partnership tax returns. However, nothing in the record suggests that the Charolais cattle were purchased with Partnership assets or transferred to Clark and his two sons in their capacity as partners of the Partnership. Nor has their [sic] been any assignment of the cattle to the Partnership. Therefore, despite the fact that the cattle were included in the Partnership tax returns, and proceeds from the sale of the cattle's offspring placed in Partnership accounts, the cattle are to be presumed separate property pursuant to [RUPA § 204(d)].
>
> As Joan correctly points out, this presumption is a rebuttable one. Nonetheless, Joan did not introduce any evidence to overcome the presumption but, rather, has relied on appeal upon the District Court's findings that money from the sale of calves had been placed into Partnership accounts, and that the cattle had been listed on Partnership tax returns. However, we have previously considered and rejected arguments that a third party acquires an interest in cattle simply by feeding, watering, and pasturing them . . . Joan has not demonstrated any equitable interest in

the cattle by virtue of the Partnership's care and feeding of the cattle, nor has she provided any authority which would compel the conclusion that ownership of the cattle passed to the Partnership. Because the presumption established by [RUPA § 204(d)] has not been overcome by evidence to the contrary, we conclude the District Court erred in categorizing the Charolais cattle as Partnership assets, and reverse the court's determination in that regard.

Did the Montana Supreme Court consider the facts that Clark "had signed tax returns indicating that the cattle were Partnership property, and had placed proceeds from the sale of calves into Partnership accounts," evidence that the cattle were partnership property?

The presumption at issue in *McCormick* was overcome in *In the Matter of the Estate of Liike*, 776 N.W.2d 662, 665–66 (Iowa 2009). This case involved a farming partnership of two brothers (William and John). After the death of one (John), his widow claimed that the land used by the partnership was owned by the two brothers as tenants in common because that is how title was held. The court concluded that the presumption that favored the widow was overcome:

> It is agreed here that the deed conveying the 120 acres to the brothers gave the farm to them as tenants in common and there are no other recorded deeds changing the manner the real estate was titled. With this admission, under the statute a presumption is created that the land was not a partnership asset. . . . From the record before us, there is clear, convincing, and persuasive evidence to rebut the statutory presumption.

> The land was treated as a partnership asset from the time it was transferred to the brothers. The brothers signed a partnership agreement showing it was an asset of the partnership as of December 31, 1970. The testimony of William was that it always was a partnership asset. The testimony of the executor and a man who lived in the neighborhood where the land was located, both of whom knew the brothers, was that they treated it as a partnership asset and that John related on occasion that the farm was in a partnership.

Notes

1. Curtis Cyrus wrote his brother Charles in North Dakota urging him to come to Minnesota to go into partnership in a resort venture. Curtis recently had purchased a 60-acre tract of land in Minnesota with his own funds and in his own name. Charles, a skilled carpenter, found the idea attractive and moved his family to a rented house near the tract. He built a cabin on the tract and moved his family into it. He thereafter built six other cabins that were operated as a resort. The expense of building the cabins was paid for out of operating earnings. Curtis personally paid the taxes on the land and purchased the boats used in the business. It is unclear whether he was reimbursed for these expenditures out of resort earnings.

Charles received the living expenses for his family out of resort earnings. He contributed his labor to the project, his wife did all the washing, ironing and cleaning, and their three children, the oldest of whom was 18, helped with the resort work. Curtis remained regularly employed in Minneapolis. He did not contribute any personal work to the operation of the resort other than to build an occasional cabin shelf while on his vacation. The earnings of the resort were accounted for every fall and Curtis was given his one-half share.

Charles died recently, 10 years after the venture began. His widow is not interested in remaining at the resort, and would like her share of the business evaluated and paid to her. She wants one-half of the entire value of the resort business, including the fair market value of the land. Curtis objects to this, claiming that the land is his and not property of the partnership. If you were representing the widow, what arguments would you make on her behalf and on what authority? *See Cyrus v. Cyrus*, 242 Minn. 180, 64 N.W.2d 538, 45 A.L.R.2d 1002 (1954).

a. In what manner, if at all, would it alter your analysis if Charles had died after building only the first cabin?

b. Would it affect your analysis of the main problem if Curtis had purchased the 60-acre tract of land already complete with buildings, boats, and so forth, and the arrangement between the parties was otherwise the same?

2. The necessity for clearly spelling out ownership interests in a partnership agreement can be brought closer to home by considering the case of an established lawyer with a substantial library who forms a partnership with a young lawyer. Nothing is said about the library in their informal, oral agreement. They practice together for five years, during which time various supplements and other publications are purchased. The partnership then dissolves, by mutual but acrimonious agreement of the two partners. Does the older lawyer run a serious risk of losing one-half the value of her library to the younger lawyer?

3. The statute of frauds. In *In re Estate of Grosboll*, 315 P.3d 1284, 1290 (Colo. Ct. App. 2013), the Colorado appellate court held that real property could be deemed to be partnership property even absent a conveyance to the partnership that satisfied the statute of frauds. Rather, the question is what did the parties intend. In that regard, the court wrote:

> Factors a court should consider in determining the parties' intent to contribute individually held property to a partnership include (1) the language of any partnership agreement; (2) the use of the property in the partnership business; (3) the listing of the property as an asset and of its mortgage as a liability in the partnership books and tax returns; (4) the construction of improvements on the property at partnership expense; (5) the payment of taxes and insurance premiums on the property out of partnership funds; (6) a party's declaration of intent, such as by letter or will, accompanying his act of entering the partnership; and, generally, (7) the parties' conduct with respect to the property.

2. The Special Matter of Title to Real Property

The partnership form of business had great difficulty adjusting to the traditional rules of real estate law. At common law a conveyance of land to the partnership of Smith and Company ran afoul of the rule that a partnership was not an entity (not a "person") and title to real property had to be in a person. Courts responded in different ways to this, some saying legal title was in Smith in trust for all the partners. And if the partnership name was something like "Denver Supply Co." some courts held legal title did not pass at all. The partners did have equitable title, but ran the risk of losing this to a subsequent bona fide purchaser. As a result, conveyances were usually made to all the partners as individuals. This raised problems as to the legal status of the property vis-à-vis the partners and creditors of the partnership. The problems were compounded when the membership of the partnership changed during the period of ownership of the property. Similar problems were not encountered with the ownership of personal property and choses in action.

Problems also arose upon the death of a partner because, under the common law, property in which a partner held legal title descended directly to the heirs of the partner without regard to payment of outstanding debts of the firm. Equity responded by creating the fiction of "equitable conversion." The realty was deemed in equity converted into personalty to facilitate satisfaction of legitimate claims.

Finally, what of conveyances *from* the partnership? In what manner could the partners convey property held in the firm name? As can be expected, the answer at common law varied with the way in which title was taken in the first place.

This is an area in which UPA made substantial and sound change. *See* UPA §§ 8(3), 8(4), 10. These sections provide for acquisition by a partnership of title to real property and deal extensively with conveyances of real property both to and from the partnership. In this respect UPA treats a partnership as an entity, a sensible solution to a difficult problem.

RUPA § 302 is the counterpart to § 10 of UPA. As part of its effort to simplify the transfer of real property from a partnership, RUPA introduced in § 303 the option of filing and recording a statement of authority specifying the authority of partners to execute instruments transferring real property held in the name of the partnership.

3. The Property Rights of a Partner

The treatment in UPA of the property rights of a partner is subtle and complex. In part the reason for this is the desire of those drafting the act to stay as consistent as possible with the aggregate theory of partnership and yet at the same time resolve the confusion at common law concerning the rights of partners in partnership property.

The confusion began in 1693 with the case of *Heydon v. Heydon*, 1 Salk. 392, 91 Eng. Rep. 340 (1693), per Lord Holt, where partners were classified as co-owners of partnership property holding as joint tenants.[16] A traditional common law concept was thus applied to the partnership relationship, which is understandable, but it had bizarre consequences. Execution of judgments at common law could reach only tangible physical assets. The method for executing on an individual partner's interest, once the joint tenant nature of partnership property was established, was by physically seizing specific partnership property and selling it. The purchaser became a tenant in common with the other partners, to their disadvantage. Also, the remaining partners lost possession of the property while the process of levy and execution was taking place. Equity intervened and established a right of the other partners to apply partnership property to partnership obligations, but property rights nevertheless were not clearly defined and varied in theory and application from state to state. In addition, assignments and sales by partners, either of an interest in specific partnership property or of an entire partnership interest, created difficulties for the other partners in the firm.

The desire to clear up confusion regarding property rights was a major impetus for uniform legislation on partnerships. Section 25 of UPA creates a unique "tenancy in partnership" for individual partners, as explained in the following case. (The case also is one of the few modern cases to take a careful look at the relationship between a partnership and a joint venture.)

Groff v. Citizens Bank of Clovis

United States Court of Appeals, Tenth Circuit 898 F.2d 1475 (1990)

LOGAN, CIRCUIT JUDGE.

Citizens Bank of Clovis (Citizens Bank) appeals adverse rulings in both the bankruptcy and district courts in this priority dispute. Both courts determined that Citizens Bank had no interest in certain cattle held by a joint venture in which Lee Groff, a bankruptcy debtor, participated. The central issue on appeal is whether the rules governing partners' interests in partnership assets also apply to joint ventures. We hold that they do and, therefore, affirm the district court's decision.

To secure a debt of Lee and Gwen Groff, Citizens Bank took a security interest in specified cattle the Groffs owned and all cattle "after acquired." Unbeknownst to Citizens Bank, Lee Groff was about to enter a cattle-feeding venture with Ed Pickering. On several subsequent occasions, Groff and Pickering purchased cattle from Agri-Tech Services, Inc. (Agri-Tech), with Morgan County Feeders, Inc. (Morgan County) providing purchase money financing.

When Lee and Gwen Groff filed a bankruptcy petition, the question arose concerning creditors' rights to the Groff-Pickering cattle. Citizens Bank argued that the cattle came within the after-acquired property clause of their security agreement

---

16. They were regarded as tenants in common of real property, and joint tenants with right of survivorship to the surviving partners (for the purpose of winding up) of personal property. *See* BROMBERG & RIBSTEIN ON PARTNERSHIP 3:35, 3:78.

with the Groffs. The bankruptcy court held that (1) Groff and Pickering were engaged in a joint venture, (2) the cattle were property of the joint venture, (3) in this context, New Mexico partnership law applies to joint ventures, and (4) under New Mexico partnership law, Citizens Bank, as a creditor of the Groffs in their individual capacities only, had no interest in the Groff-Pickering cattle. Consequently, the bankruptcy court ruled that the Groffs' bankruptcy estate did not contain the Groff-Pickering cattle; the estate contained only "the debtors' interest in the Groff-Pickering joint venture as determined under the New Mexico substantive law of partnerships." The district court affirmed. On this appeal, Citizens Bank does not contest the first two issues listed above. Our review of the remaining issues is de novo.

Citizens Bank's principal contention on appeal is that in view of the bankruptcy court's finding that Groff and Pickering were engaged in a joint venture, it was inconsistent and erroneous to apply partnership law to the joint venture's property. This argument, however, ignores the essential nature of a joint venture.

The joint venture as a legal organization was unknown to the early common law; it is a creature of the American judiciary, dating from the late nineteenth century. Although its history is not entirely clear, apparently the joint venture concept was developed to extend principles of partnership law to organizations that did not meet the technical requirements of a partnership.

Today, the sole characteristic distinguishing a joint venture from a partnership is the joint venture's more limited purpose or scope: a joint venture is usually limited to carrying out a single transaction or a series of related transactions, while a partnership is for the purpose of carrying on a continuing business. Delineating the activity level beyond which a joint venture becomes a partnership can be a challenging task, but in most cases this is unnecessary, because "[a]s a general rule the substantive law of partnerships is applicable in determining the rights and liabilities of joint venturers and third parties."

As a matter of fact, "the present trend is to include joint ventures as a recognized type of partnership, rather than a distinct but analogous business entity." The Uniform Partnership Act itself applies to "a partnership for a fixed term or particular undertaking." UPA § 23(1) Any departure from partnership law in the context of joint ventures should be justified on the basis of the joint venture's more limited scope. Keeping this in mind, we examine partnership law governing partners' rights in partnership property.

Before the Uniform Partnership Act, the courts struggled in their attempts to apply traditional concepts of joint ownership to partnership property because none of these approaches were well suited to the partnership's business context. The resulting confusion and inconsistencies were the principal catalysts behind the creation of the Uniform Partnership Act (UPA) in 1914.

The UPA provides that the partnership owns property as an entity, separate and distinct from the partners. See UPA § 8. The rights of the partners in specific partnership property [are] as co-owners, holding as tenants in partnership. UPA § 25(1).

But "[a] partner's right in specific partnership property is not assignable except in connection with the assignment of rights of all the partners in the same property," UPA § 25(2)(b), and "[a] partner's right in specific partnership property is not subject to attachment or execution, except on a claim against the partnership," UPA § 25(2)(c). Individual partners can only assign their residual interests in the entire partnership. This is also the only partnership interest that the partners' individual creditors can reach; only partnership creditors can attach partnership property. UPA §§ 26–28. On dissolution of the partnership, partnership creditors have priority in the distribution of partnership property. If an individual partner becomes insolvent, that partner's individual creditors have priority over partnership creditors with regard to his separate property. UPA §§ 38(1), 40(h)–(i). So the UPA treats the partnership and its assets and liabilities as a separate entity, distinct from the assets and liabilities of its owners. This scheme is necessary to prevent disruption of, and facilitate credit for, the partnership business. It is equally necessary in the context of joint ventures.

In this case, because the Groffs purported to act solely on their own behalf in granting a lien on their cattle to Citizens Bank, they could transfer no interest in the Groff-Pickering cattle. The Groff-Pickering cattle could not enter the Groffs' bankruptcy estate under 11 U.S.C. § 541; only the Groffs' residual interest in the Groff-Pickering joint venture became property of the estate.

Affirmed.

Notes

1. The bankruptcy court in New Mexico considered the same issue under RUPA, reaching the same conclusion as the *Groff* court. *In re Shephard*, 2007 WL 1385725 (D.N.M. 2007).

2. As noted in *Groff*, the interest of a partner *in partnership property* is narrowly defined, limited largely to a right to possess partnership property for partnership purposes. Nearly all of the usual property rights are in fact held by the partnership. This indirect adoption of an entity approach was done with the objective of putting to rest the danger of intrusion by creditors or assignees into the partnership business. The interest of a partner *in the partnership* is defined in § 26 of UPA, thus sharply distinguishing the interest of a partner in specific partnership property from the interest of a partner in the partnership.

3. As *Groff* indicates, UPA applies to joint ventures and, in comment 2 to § 202, the drafters of RUPA wrote that "[r]elationships that are called 'joint ventures' are partnerships if they otherwise meet the definition of a partnership." Presumably, all of the provisions of RUPA would apply to such joint ventures. Nevertheless, the Idaho Supreme Court, in *Costa v. Borges*, 179 P.3d 316, 321 (Idaho 2008), held that unlike a RUPA partnership, a RUPA joint venture is not an entity separate and apart from its members. Therefore, the court concluded, "[t]hat portion of RUPA providing for the continuation of a partnership as a separate legal entity after dissociation

of a partner has no application to a joint venture." In dictum (because there were only two venturers), the court said that "even if the joint venture had three members it could not continue doing business after the withdrawal of one member." As support, the court cited a pre-RUPA joint venture decision, but did not cite to any provision of RUPA as support. Was the court on solid ground? Is there a reason to distinguish a joint venture from a partnership?

4. Another aspect of partnership property was at issue in *Putnam v. Shoaf*, 620 S.W.2d 510 (Tenn. App. 1981), which involved the sale by the plaintiff of a 50 percent partnership interest. For reasons that are unclear, the parties used a quitclaim deed that conveyed a "one-half (½) undivided interest" in the partnership's real and personal property (which were described in the deed). Subsequent to the conveyance, the partnership learned that it had been the victim of embezzlement and it brought suit against the embezzler and the bank that cashed the checks. The partnership was successful and the plaintiff made a claim against the proceeds, arguing that the possible recovery was not listed among the assets included in the quitclaim deed. Therefore, she said, she retained that "asset." What result? (She lost.)

5. In *Faegre & Benson, LLP v. R & R Investors*, 772 N.W.2d 846 (Ct. App. Minn. 2013), the four partners of R & R Investors transferred their partnership interests to David and Mary Klug in February 2000. The Klugs continued the business of the partnership under the same name and, in 2004, transferred their partnership interests to Strangis and Kass. One asset of the partnership that pre-dated the Klugs' acquisition was a claim against the federal government for breach of contract. That claim arose in 1997, but was dismissed by the U.S. Court of Federal Claims in 1999. The U.S. Supreme Court reinstated the claim in 2002 and it was settled in 2006. The Minnesota appellate court held that the claim remained an asset of R & R Investors throughout the relevant time period agreed, finding that the same result would obtain under both UPA and RUPA. The court noted that under UPA, when the Klugs acquired their interests in R & R Investors, technically a new partnership was created. But under UPA "absent an agreement to the contrary, the partnership property of the dissolved partnership became the property of the partnership continuing the business without the need for a separate devise." *Id.* at 855.

Because it adopts the entity theory, RUPA has a simpler approach to partnership property and the interest of individual partners. RUPA § 501 states, "A partner is not a co-owner of partnership property and has no interest in partnership property which can be transferred, either voluntarily or involuntarily." The Comment to § 501 notes that this "abolishes the UPA § 25(1) concept of tenants in partnership and reflects the adoption of the entity theory. Partnership property is owned by the entity and not by the individual partners."

The approach of UPA § 24, defining three separate interests of a partner as property rights, underwent a major change in RUPA. Section 502 states, "The only transferable interest of a partner in the partnership is the partner's interest in distributions. The interest is personal property." Although the Comments to §§ 501 and

502 do not mention §24, RUPA indirectly addresses the interests defined in §24 by denying a partner rights in specific partnership property and by saying nothing about classifying a partner's right to participate in management as a property right. The third property right recognized in §24, the interest in distributions, is addressed in §502.

Problems

1. Fred Bunch entered into business for himself under the name of Central Pump and Supply Company. He rented a building for his company from Johnson. Bunch eventually got in arrears on an account with Perry Corp., relating to equipment purchases by Central Pump. He gave a check to Perry on the account for a sizeable sum which was not honored due to insufficient funds. About this time, Bunch made overtures to Johnson with reference to Johnson getting into the business. Johnson borrowed money from his bank. The money was credited to Central Pump, and a portion of it was immediately transmitted to Perry to cover the bad check.

Johnson became involved in the general business affairs of Central Pump to the extent that he spent some time nearly every day in the company office, which was about one block from his regular business activity of running a motel. On infrequent occasions he went into the field where the company was involved in irrigation work. He ordered and returned some supplies from Perry. He signed some company checks and bought certain equipment and supplies from others on behalf of Central Pump.

Eventually the company went out of business. Johnson sold certain of its assets and applied the same to its obligations. Also, he paid two small local bills with his own funds. Other more sizeable company accounts presented to Johnson for payment were rejected by him, including $18,125.61 owed to Perry, all for equipment purchases. There were no profits during the time Johnson was involved with the business. Perry is seeking to collect on the amount owed to it.

Johnson claims that he was merely assisting Bunch in the business affairs of the company and was running errands for Bunch; that he was interested in getting into the business, but only as a corporation in which he would own a majority of the stock, and he advanced money and assisted Bunch in the operation of his business on this basis; that Bunch became ill and was unable to be about during the liquidation above mentioned, which Johnson did at the specific request of Bunch. Johnson claims that he paid the two small bills out of his own funds because they were owed to local merchants and, in light of their nuisance value, it was better to pay them rather than litigate the question of his liability for them.

Finally, in checking around, Perry discovered that one Adams, who worked full time for Central Pump holding a management position relating to the sales aspect of the business, had a contract with Bunch that provided that she got $1,500 per month plus fifteen percent of the profits, and was liable for fifteen percent of the losses incurred by activities under her direct control. The contract provided that

Adams could not make an advance draw on either salary or profits, and that Adams was to maintain a reserve fund of $5,000 in order to protect Central Pump from losses incurred by sales aspects of the business. Adams's share of profits was to be credited to this account, and she was allowed to draw on it, but not below $5,000. The contract also provided as follows:

> The relation of the parties hereto is principal as to the first party and agent as to the second party [Adams], and notwithstanding the provisions herein for sharing of profit and losses, nothing herein contained shall be construed as a relation of partnership or joint adventure between the parties, and second party shall not have the right to bind first party as a partner or co-adventurer, either as between the immediate parties, or as to third persons; and all of the rights, duties and obligations of the parties hereto shall be measured and controlled by the principles applicable to the relation of principal and agent.

Perry Corp. plans to sue Johnson and Adams for the full amount on its account. What are the arguments for and against Perry's claims?

2. *Minute Maid Corp. v. United Foods, Inc.*, 291 F.2d 577 (5th Cir. 1961), noted in 40 N.C. L. REV. 355 (1962), involved an elaborate arrangement that was tested judicially on whether it was a partnership or a creditor-bailee relationship. United Foods, Inc. ("United") was an authorized direct buyer of frozen food products from Minute Maid Corporation. Minute Maid's terms of sale to direct buyers included discounts based on volume. United did not have the financial ability to enable it to carry a large inventory of frozen food products and thus obtain the maximum discounts. Cold Storage Corporation ("Storage"), which owned and operated a cold storage warehouse in Dallas, did have the financial resources and the storage space.

United and Storage entered into a formal written agreement providing that Storage would loan United up to $300,000 on purchases of frozen foods to be stored in its facilities. Storage received a six per cent note on each loan. The notes were secured by the commodities stored if they were acceptable to Storage. Storage also billed United for warehouse charges and insurance.

The warehouse charges, interest and insurance were all charged to a "Special Account" established on the books of Storage. The Account also accumulated as credits all discounts and other special allowances received by United as a result of being able to buy in larger quantities. The agreement also provided that the Account was to be closed at the end of the calendar year, and

> a. If there is a credit balance, one-half thereof shall be paid by Storage to United, and the remainder shall be retained by Storage as its property.

> b. If there is a debit balance, Storage shall so notify United, who will pay Storage one-half the amount of such debit balance within 20 days of notification.

Another clause in the agreement provided that "In case of pending price increase, Storage and United may agree on the volume to be purchased by United, and Storage will loan, upon receipt of product in storage, the cost to United." The responsible officer for United testified at trial that, "they [Storage] could have stepped in and written me [United] off pretty . . . fast."

Minute Maid found itself with $143,000 of unpaid invoices to United. Apparently United was insolvent, so Minute Maid sought to hold Storage liable for the debt as a partner. It admitted that it had not known of the relationship between United and Storage at the time it extended credit to United.

The trial court, sitting without a jury, found that a partnership did not exist and denied Minute Maid's claim. On appeal, the judgment of the trial court was reversed (2 to 1) on the ground that, as a matter of law, a partnership existed. Can you articulate the basis for the court's decision?

3. Newton, Emmons and Miller each acquired a one-third interest in a parcel of four acres upon which stood a flour mill. Later they orally formed a partnership to engage in the business of milling grain. The business was conducted in the mill upon the land, and new machinery was placed in the mill from partnership funds. There was no agreement as to whether the mill remained the property of the individual partners or was capital of the partnership.

Thereafter, Emmons and Miller mortgaged their interests in the land for personal debts. Later the partnership became heavily indebted to the Robinson Bank and deeded the land, at the Bank's request, to one Woolworth as trustee for the benefit of the Bank. The partnership became insolvent and the Bank brought suit in equity to set aside the individual mortgages, claiming the land was partnership property. What result? What additional matters, if any, should be inquired into?

4. Able and Baker, both of whom are real estate brokers, formed a partnership in order to pool their capital and expertise and purchase land for development. They had known each other for years, were both respected and financially secure members of their community, and trusted each other completely. They thus did not bother to go to a lawyer, and made simply an oral agreement.

During the succeeding five years they bought a large number of parcels of land, some of which they held for speculation and some of which they started developing. Their acquisition of title to the land was done as casually as was their entering into the partnership. Some parcels were purchased in Able's name, some in the name of the Able and Baker partnership, and some in the name of "Able and Baker." All of these purchases were made with partnership funds.

a. Assume that your client has signed a contract with Able for sale to her of some of the land owned by the partnership, calling for deeds conveying title to your client in the same name in which title was taken by the partnership, as described below.

(i) Those parcels held in the name of the Able and Baker partnership.

(ii) Those parcels held in Able's name.

(iii) Those parcels held in the name of "Able and Baker."

What sections of UPA and RUPA would you consult in deciding whether this was the best approach? What additional documentation, if any, would you insist upon?

b. Alternatively, assume Baker died recently. Able is selling all the land owned by the partnership and retiring. Assume that your client has signed a contract with Able for the sale of the land to her. Again, in what form would you want to see title coming to your client, what sections of UPA or RUPA would you consult and what additional documentation, if any, would you require?

Chapter 12

The Operation of a Partnership

A. Contractual Powers of Partners

Partners are regarded as agents of their partnership when dealing on behalf of the firm. *See* UPA § 4(3) ("The law of agency shall apply under this act") and UPA § 9 ("Every partner is an agent of the partnership. . . ."). In addition, UPA § 18 is important to resolve questions of actual authority and management rights. The counterpart to § 9 in RUPA is § 301; the counterpart to § 18 is RUPA § 401. Thus, the actual authority, apparent authority, estoppel, and inherent agency power concepts addressed in Chapter 4 apply to the actions of partners, who are general agents, as well as to employees of a partnership.

RUPA § 303 is an innovation in partnership law. It provides a partnership the option of filing a statement of authority with the Secretary of State of the state where the partnership is located. Section 303 distinguishes between authority concerning transfers of real property held in the name of the partnership and other transactions. With regard to real property, a grant of authority contained in a certified copy of a filed statement recorded in the office for recording transfers of that property is conclusive in favor of a person who gives value without knowledge to the contrary, so long as a limitation on that authority is not recorded. With regard to other transactions, a statement can "state the authority, or limitations on the authority, of some or all of the partners to enter into other transactions on behalf of the partnership and any other matter." *Id.* at § 303(a)(2).

The Comment to RUPA § 303 states, "Since § 301 confers authority on all partners to act for the partnership in ordinary matters, the real import of [a statement of authority] is to grant extraordinary authority, or to limit the ordinary authority, of some or all of the partners." A properly filed *grant* of authority is conclusive in favor of a person who gives value without knowledge to the contrary, unless limited by another filed statement. Filing a *limitation* of authority does not operate as constructive notice to third persons, however, except with regard to real property and then only if a certified copy of the filed statement is *recorded* in the office for recording transfers of that property. RUPA § 303(e). RUPA provides for constructive notice from filed statements in two other situations: 90 days after a statement of dissociation is filed (§ 704) and 90 days after a statement of dissolution is filed (§ 805), cutting off lingering apparent authority in both instances, as noted in Chapter 13.

1. Actual Authority

Elle v. Babbitt

Supreme Court of Oregon
488 P. 440 (1971)

Before O'Connell, Chief Justice, and McAllister, Holman, Howell and Bryson, Justices.

Affirmed as modified.

McAllister, J.

This suit for an accounting was brought against Beall Pipe and Tank Corporation by three partners of a partnership known as The Pipe Machinery Co., for the benefit of all the partners thereof. The other 16 partners were named as defendants. The dispute arose out of the leasing of two pipe mills by the partnership to Beall and the termination of the lease. Beall appeals from the decree of the trial court.

Beall Pipe and Tank Corporation is a family-owned corporation, which for many years has been engaged in making pipe in Portland. John E. Beall was president and chief executive officer of the corporation and owned about 55 percent of its stock. His cousin, Franklin Beall, was the executive vice president and owned about 40 percent of the corporate stock. We will refer herein to Beall Pipe and Tank Corporation as the corporation or as Beall and to the individual Bealls by their full names. We will refer to The Pipe Machinery Co. as the partnership.

Beall formerly manufactured pipe by the "can" method. In 1953, Beall decided that it should acquire a modern tube mill for making welded steel pipe. In such a mill a continuous sheet of steel is fed into a machine which gradually bends the steel into a circle and welds it into a tube which is then cut into desired lengths. The rolls and guides which bend the sheet steel into a tube are known as "tooling." Pipe of various dimensions can be made by changing the tooling.

Beall did not have enough capital to buy a tube mill and John Beall proposed that a partnership be organized to buy the tube mill and lease it to the corporation. The partnership was formed on April 1, 1954, and was comprised of John Beall, Franklin Beall and five employees of the corporation. Later in 1954, eight additional partners were added, all of whom were Beall employees, except W. H. Kipp, Jr., who was a Beall customer. . . .

The first pipe mill was built in the Beall plant by the Monarch Forge Company of Portland and paid for by the partnership. As built, the mill was designed to make pipe from 6 to 16 inches in diameter. The mill was leased by the partnership to Beall for a royalty of one cent per inch of diameter for each lineal foot of pipe produced by the mill. A written lease was entered into under date of April 1, 1954, with an initial term of one year giving Beall the option to extend the lease from year to year for 10 years.

Later the partnership purchased a second mill known as the "through-put" mill designed for the manufacture of pipe from 16 to 42 inches in diameter and leased it to the corporation. . . .

Sometime prior to April 1, 1965, Beall decided to terminate its lease of the partnership mills and offered to buy both mills from the partnership. The offer was refused by some of the partners and while the parties were negotiating about the price a new lease was executed dated April 1, 1965. . . .

When Beall's final offer to purchase the mills was rejected, the corporation decided to build a new mill. . . .

The next question concerns a claim for unpaid royalties in the amount of $8,289.62, which the trial court allowed. This claim arose out of the following circumstances. In May, 1963, Beall was preparing a bid on a large job for Cascade Natural Gas. It was known that competition would be keen, and that a low bid would be necessary in order to get the job. Ralph Elle, one of the plaintiffs, worked for Beall at that time as its chief engineer and estimator. He testified that he prepared the estimates upon which this particular bid was based, and that it appeared that Beall's bid could not be low enough to get the job unless the royalties paid to the partnership were cut in half. This was discussed at a meeting held at the Beall plant, attended by John Beall, Franklin Beall, plaintiff Elle and Ben Wilkins, Beall's sales manager, who was also a partner. It was decided to bid on the basis of a 50 per cent royalty and Beall obtained the job. For the pipe produced for this job, the partnership was paid only half the usual royalty and plaintiffs claim the other half of these royalties on behalf of the partnership in the amount of $8,289.62.

No meeting of all the members of the partnership was called to discuss this cut in royalty, nor were the other partners formally notified or their agreement sought. When some of the other partners learned what had happened they complained to Elle, who referred them to John Beall. There is no evidence that any complaints were ever made to Mr. Beall.

Plaintiffs do not contend that there was any fraud or bad faith involved, but vigorously contend that the partners who decided to reduce the partnership royalties on the Cascade job were, in fact, acting for Beall, and that they had no authority to agree to the reduced royalty payments on behalf of the partnership.

The management of partnership affairs in its dealings with third parties is governed in part by statute.

[The court quotes UPA § 18(e) ("All partners have equal rights in the management and conduct of the partnership business") and (h) (". . . no act in contravention of any agreement between the partners may be done rightfully without the consent of all the partners.")]. The power of a single partner to bind the partnership in dealings with third parties is covered by [UPA § 9(1) and (4), which the court quotes]. Plaintiffs claim that the partners who were not consulted about the royalty reduction were deprived of their right to participate equally in the management of the partnership business. The rule stating this right is, however, subject to any agreement among the partners. [UPA § 18.] The members of a partnership may, if they wish, agree to leave the management of the business in the hands of a single managing partner. Such an agreement may be implied from the parties' course of conduct.

It is clear from the testimony in this case that most of the partners never concerned themselves with the management of partnership affairs. The following is quoted from the testimony of William Kipp, Jr., one of the plaintiffs:

> Q And insofar as you know, during this period of time, that there was no meetings of the partnership from 1958 to 1965, do you know of any other of the partners who had any   did anything affirmatively for the benefit of the partnership other than Mr. Elle possibly or Mr. Beall— John Beall?
>
> A No.
>
> Q In other words, all the partners did, the eighteen or nineteen partners during this period of time were to put up the money initially for their original investment and receive the profits each year, is that right?
>
> A It sounds a little ridiculous but that is the facts.

During the years the partnership leased the pipe mills to Beall the partnership's affairs were handled by those partners who were management-level employees and officers of Beall under the direction of John Beall. None of the partners ever objected to this manner of conducting the partnership business; John Beall became, by tacit agreement among all the partners, the managing partner with authority to conduct the ordinary business of the partnership. . . . In the present case the decision to agree on behalf of the partnership to a temporary reduction in royalty in order to enable Beall to make a successful bid on a large job was clearly part of the ongoing management of the partnership's business affairs. John Beall, by virtue of the other partners' long acquiescence in his exercise of management, had the authority to make that decision and to bind his copartners by agreement with Beall. It is also significant that the plaintiff Elle agreed to the reduction in royalty and so testified. It appears that the other partner Wilkins either agreed or did not object.

The award of $8,289.62 for unpaid royalties was in error.

[As modified, the trial court decree was affirmed.]

Summers v. Dooley

Supreme Court of Idaho
481 P.2d 318 (1971)

DONALDSON, JUSTICE.

This lawsuit, tried in the district court, involves a claim by one partner against the other for $6,000. . . .

The pertinent facts leading to this lawsuit are as follows. Summers entered a partnership agreement with Dooley (defendant-respondent) in 1958 for the purpose of operating a trash collection business. The business was operated by the two men and when either was unable to work, the non-working partner provided a replacement at his own expense. . . . In July, 1966, Summers approached his partner Dooley regarding the hiring of an additional employee but Dooley refused. Nevertheless, on his own initiative, Summers hired the man and paid him out of his own pocket. Dooley, upon discovering that Summers had hired an additional man, objected, stating that he did not feel additional labor was necessary and refused to pay for the new employee out of the partnership funds. Summers continued to operate the business using the third man and in October of 1967 instituted suit in the district court for $6,000 against his partner, the gravamen of the complaint being that Summers has been required to pay out more than $11,000 in expenses, incurred in the hiring of the additional man, without any reimbursement from either the partnership funds or his partner. [The trial court denied Summers the reimbursement he sought for expenses related to hiring extra help, and he appealed.]

The principal thrust of appellant's contention is that in spite of the fact that one of the two partners refused to consent to the hiring of additional help, nonetheless, the non-consenting partner retained profits earned by the labors of the third man and therefore the non-consenting partner should be estopped from denying the need and value of the employee, and has by his behavior ratified the act of the other partner who hired the additional man.

The issue presented for decision by this appeal is whether an equal partner in a two man partnership has the authority to hire a new employee in disregard of the objection of the other partner and then attempt to charge the dissenting partner with the costs incurred as a result of his unilateral decision. . . .

An application of the relevant statutory provisions and pertinent case law to the factual situation presented by the instant case indicates that the trial court was correct in its disposal of the issue since a majority of the partners did not consent to the hiring of the third man. [UPA § 18(h)] provides:

> Any difference arising as to ordinary matters connected with the partnership business may be decided by a *majority of the partners*. . . . (emphasis supplied).

The intent of the legislature may be implied from the language used, or inferred on grounds of policy or reasonableness. A careful reading of the statutory provision indicates that [UPA § 18(e)] bestows *equal rights in the management and conduct of the partnership business* upon all of the partners.[1] The concept of equality between partners with respect to management of business affairs is a central theme and recurs throughout the Uniform Partnership law, which has been enacted in this jurisdiction. Thus the only reasonable interpretation of [UPA § 18(h)] is that

---

1. [4] In the absence of an agreement to the contrary. . . . In the case at bar, there is no such agreement. . . .

business differences must be decided by a majority of the partners provided no other agreement between the partners speaks to the issues.

A noted scholar has dealt precisely with the issue to be decided.

> [I]f the partners are equally divided, those who forbid a change must have their way. Walter B. Lindley, A Treatise on the Law of Partnership, Ch. II, § III, ¶ 24-8, p. 403 (1924).

In the case at bar one of the partners continually voiced objection to the hiring of the third man. He did not sit idly by and acquiesce in the actions of his partner. Under these circumstances it is manifestly unjust to permit recovery of an expense which was incurred individually and not for the benefit of the partnership but rather for the benefit of one partner.

Judgment affirmed. Costs to respondent.

McQUADE, C. J., and McFADDEN, SHEPARD and SPEAR, JJ., concur.

National Biscuit Co. v. Stroud[2]

Supreme Court of North Carolina
106 S.E.2d 692 (1959)

Appeal by defendant Stroud from PARKER (JOSEPH W.), J., June Civil Term, 1958, of Carteret.

The case was heard in the Superior Court upon the following agreed statement of facts:

On 13 September 1956 the National Biscuit Company had a Justice of the Peace to issue summons against C. N. Stroud and Earl Freeman, a partnership trading as Stroud's Food Center, for the nonpayment of $171.04 for goods sold and delivered. After a hearing the Justice of the Peace rendered judgment for plaintiff against both defendants for $171.04 with interest and costs. Stroud appealed to the Superior Court: Freeman did not.

In March 1953 C. N. Stroud and Earl Freeman entered into a general partnership to sell groceries under the name of Stroud's Food Center. Thereafter plaintiff sold bread regularly to the partnership. Several months prior to February 1956 the defendant Stroud advised an agent of plaintiff that he personally would not be responsible for any additional bread sold by plaintiff to Stroud's Food Center. From 6 February 1956 to 25 February 1956 plaintiff through this same agent, at the request of the defendant Freeman, sold and delivered bread in the amount of $171.04 to Stroud's Food Center. Stroud and Freeman by agreement dissolved the partnership at the close of business on 25 February 1956, and notice of such dissolution was published in a newspaper in Carteret County 6–27 March 1956. . . .

---

2. Noted in 1960 Duke L.J. 150.

Stroud has paid all of the partnership obligations amounting to $12,014.45, except the amount of $171.04 claimed by plaintiff. To pay such obligations Stroud exhausted all the partnership assets he could reduce to money amounting to $4,307.08, of which $2,028.64 was derived from accounts receivable and $2,278.44 from a sale of merchandise and fixtures, and used over $7,700.00 of his personal money. Stroud has left of the partnership assets only uncollected accounts in the sum of $2,868.77, practically all of which are considered uncollectible.

Stroud has not attempted to rescind the dissolution agreement, and has tendered plaintiff, and still tenders it, one-half of the $171.04 claimed by it.

From a judgment that plaintiff recover from the defendants $171.04 with interest and costs, Stroud appeals to the Supreme Court.

PARKER, J. C. N.

Stroud and Earl Freeman entered into a general partnership to sell groceries under the firm name of Stroud's Food Center. There is nothing in the agreed statement of facts to indicate or suggest that Freeman's power and authority as a general partner were in any way restricted or limited by the articles of partnership in respect to the ordinary and legitimate business of the partnership. Certainly, the purchase and sale of bread were ordinary and legitimate business of Stroud's Food Center during its continuance as a going concern. . . .

In *Johnson v. Bernheim*, 76 N.C. 139, this Court said: "A and B are general partners to do some given business; the partnership is, by operation of law, a power to each to bind the partnership in any manner legitimate to the business. If one partner go to a third person to buy an article on time for the partnership, the other partner cannot prevent it by writing to the third person not to sell to him on time; or, if one party attempt to buy for cash, the other has no right to require that it shall be on time. And what is true in regard to buying is true in regard to selling. What either partner does with a third person is binding on the partnership. It is otherwise where the partnership is not general, but is upon special terms, as that purchases and sales must be with and for cash. There the power to each is special, in regard to all dealings with third persons at least who have notice of the terms." There is contrary authority: 68 C.J.S., Partnership, pp. 578–579. However, this text of C.J.S. does not mention the effect of the provisions of the Uniform Partnership Act.

The General Assembly of North Carolina in 1941 enacted a Uniform Partnership Act, which became effective 15 March 1941.

[The court quotes UPA §§ 9(1), 9(4), 15 and 18(e) and (h)].

Freeman as a general partner with Stroud, with no restrictions on his authority to act within the scope of the partnership business so far as the agreed statement of facts shows, had under the Uniform Partnership Act "equal rights in the management and conduct of the partnership business." Under [UPA § 18(h)] Stroud, his co-partner, could not restrict the power and authority of Freeman to buy bread for the partnership as a going concern, for such a purchase was an "ordinary matter connected with the partnership business," for the purpose of its business and within its scope, because in the very nature of things Stroud was not, and could not be, a majority of the partners. Therefore, Freeman's purchases of bread from plaintiff for Stroud's Food Center as a going concern bound the partnership and his co-partner Stroud. The quoted provisions of our Uniform Partnership Act, in respect to the particular facts here, are in accord with the principle of law stated in *Johnson v. Bernheim, supra*; same case 86 N.C. 339.

In Crane on Partnership, 2nd Ed., p. 277, it is said: "In cases of an even division of the partners as to whether or not an act within the scope of the business should be done, of which disagreement a third person has knowledge, it seems that logically no restriction can be placed upon the power to act. The partnership being a going concern, activities within the scope of the business should not be limited, save by the expressed will of the majority deciding a disputed question; half of the members are not a majority."

Sladen v. Lance, 151 N.C. 492, 66 S.E. 449, is distinguishable. That was a case where the terms of the partnership imposed special restrictions on the power of the partner who made the contract. . . .

The judgment of the court below is *Affirmed.*

RODMAN, J., dissents.

Notes

1. Is *National Biscuit* inconsistent with *Summers*? In one case, one of two partners objected to a particular act and the objection was effective (*Summers*); in the other case, one of two partners objected to a particular act and the objection was ineffective (*National Biscuit*). Are the two courts reading UPA § 18 differently?

2. It is often stated that partners are agents of each other and that many partnership questions are really just questions of agency law. If so, *National Biscuit* represents an example of an agency power that seems very unusual. In this instance the party who was bound expressly disapproved *and* communicated his disapproval to the third party prior to the making of the contract at issue. Does the special nature of the partnership relationship lead to such a result? If so, what is it about the partnership relationship that is distinctive from the ordinary agency relationship?

3. What alternatives are open to a partner in a situation similar to that faced by Stroud? Apparently only dissolution under § 31 or § 32 of UPA is available. One could argue, however, that this is appropriate. The dissenting partner agreed upon joining the partnership to be bound to decisions made in the ordinary course of business. This exposure to liability can be avoided only by leaving the business. Is *Summers* inconsistent with this argument?

4. For a discussion of other issues raised by UPA § 18(e), see Hillman, *Power Shared and Power Denied: A Look at Participatory Rights in the Management of General Partnerships*, 1984 U. ILL. L. REV. 865.

5. RUPA § 401(f), containing virtually identical language, is the counterpart to UPA § 18(e). Comment 7 to § 401 acknowledges that § 401(f) is based on UPA § 18(e), "which has been interpreted broadly to mean that, absent contrary agreement, each partner has a continuing right to participate in the management of the partnership and to be informed about the partnership business, even if his assent to partnership business decisions is not required."

2. Apparent Authority

Burns v. Gonzalez

Court of Civil Appeals of Texas
439 S.W.2d 128 (1969)

CADENA, JUSTICE

Plaintiff, William G. Burns, sued Arturo C. Gonzalez and Ramon D. Bosquez, individually and as sole partners in Inter-American Advertising Agency (herein called "the partnership"), to recover on a $40,000.00 promissory note executed by Bosquez in his own name and in the name of the partnership. After an interlocutory default judgment had been entered in favor of plaintiff against Bosquez, the trial court, sitting without a jury, entered the judgment appealed from, denying Burns any recovery against Gonzalez.

The sole business of the partnership was the sale, on a commission basis, of broadcast time on XERF, a radio station located in Ciudad Acuna, Mexico, and owned and operated by a Mexican corporation, Compania Radiodifusora de Coahuila, S.A. (herein called "Radiodifusora"). Bosquez and Gonzalez each owned 50% of the Radiodifusora stock, with Bosquez acting as president of the corporation.

The events culminating in this litigation began in 1957 when a written contract was entered into between Radiodifusora and the partnership, on the one hand, and Roloff Evangelistic Enterprises, Inc., and Burns, on the other. Under this contract, Radiodifusora and the partnership, in consideration of the payment of $100,000.00 by Roloff and Burns, agreed to make available to them two 15-minute segments of broadcast time daily over XERF so long as the franchise of the radio station remained in force, beginning July 1, 1957. In accordance with the terms of the contract, Roloff and Burns paid the $100,000.00 in four equal installments on July 1, 1957, November 1, 1957, March 1, 1958, and July 1, 1958, with Burns retaining 15% of such payments as his commission, as he had a right to do under the terms of the contract.

Subsequently, Roloff assigned all of its rights under this contract to Burns, effective June 16, 1962. Both Radiodifusora and the partnership approved such assignment.

Because of labor disputes and other circumstances, the radio station was shut down at various times. With some exceptions, the broadcast periods described in the 1957 contract were not made available to Burns or to persons to whom he sold such broadcast periods, after June 16, 1962.

On November 28, 1962, Bosquez, purporting to act on his own behalf and on behalf of the partnership, executed the note in question, payable to Burns on November 28, 1964. According to a separate instrument signed by Bosquez on the same date, the radio station was in receivership and it was unlikely that the broadcast periods to which Burns was entitled under the 1957 contract would be made available to him for the two-year period ending November 28, 1964, the date on which the note was payable. This instrument recited that since Burns would derive an income of $20,000.00 a year from sale of such broadcast periods, the note in the amount of $40,000.00 had been executed and delivered to Burns to compensate him for the income which he would have derived during the two-year period ending November 28, 1964. Bosquez testified, and Burns does not deny, that "one of the reasons" why he executed the note was the promise by Burns not to sue Radiodifusora. . . .

Although Gonzalez denied under oath the authority of Bosquez to execute the 1962 note, the trial court held that the note was an obligation of the partnership. The judgment in favor of Gonzalez was based on the theory that he had been relieved of liability on the note as a result of [a subsequent] agreement.

Under Sec. 9(1), U. P. A.:

> Every partner is an agent of the partnership for the purpose of its business, and the act of every partner, including the execution in the partnership name of any instrument, *for apparently carrying on in the usual way the business of the partnership* of which he is a member binds the partnership, unless the partner so acting has in fact no authority to act for the partnership in the particular matter, and the person with whom he is dealing has knowledge of the fact that he has no such authority. (Emphasis added.)

In this case, in fact, Bosquez had no authority to bind the partnership by executing a negotiable instrument. But, since this express limitation on the authority of Bosquez was unknown to Burns, then, under the language of Sec. 9(1), his act in executing the note would bind the partnership if such act can be classified as an act "for apparently carrying on in the usual way the business of the partnership."

As we interpret Sec. 9(1), the act of a partner binds the firm, absent an express limitation of authority known to the party dealing with such partner, if such act is for the purpose of "apparently carrying on" the business of the partnership in the way in which other firms engaged in the same business in the locality usually transact business, or in the way in which the particular partnership usually transacts its business. In this case, there is no evidence relating to the manner in which firms engaged in the sale of advertising time on radio stations usually transact business. Specifically, there is no evidence as to whether or not the borrowing of money, or the execution of negotiable instruments, was incidental to the transaction of business, "in the usual way," by other advertising agencies or by this partnership,

Inter-American Advertising Agency. It becomes important, therefore, to determine the location of the burden of proof concerning the "usual way" of transacting business by advertising agencies.

Sec. 9(1) states that the act of a partner "for apparently carrying on in the usual way the business of the partnership" binds the firm. This language does not place the burden of proof on the non-participating partner to establish the nonexistence of the facts which operate to impose liability on the firm. If the Legislature had intended to place the burden of proof on the non-participating partner, it could have done so easily. The statute could have been drafted to declare that the act of a partner binds the firm "unless it is shown that such act was not for apparently carrying on in the usual way the business of the partnership." Actually, the liability-imposing language of Sec. 9(1) indicates that the burden of proof is on the person seeking to hold the non-participating partner accountable. It is not couched in terms appropriate for the establishment of a presumption, "administrative" or otherwise. The language relating to carrying on in the usual way the business of the partnership is no more than a statement of the rule concerning vicarious liability based on "apparent" authority. . . .

We conclude that, under a reasonable interpretation of the language of Sec. 9(1), the burden of proving the "usual way" in which advertising agencies transact business was upon Burns.

Our conclusion is supported by the fact that the liability of partners with respect to third persons is largely determined by reference to the principles of the law of agency. Restatement 2d, Agency Sec. 14 (1958); U. P. A., Sec. 4(3). One who asserts that the particular act of an agent is within the scope of the agent's authority has the burden of proving the extent of such authority. We recognize, of course, that there are aspects in which the partner-agent differs from the "ordinary" agent. But we know of no distinction which compels application of different rules concerning the burden of proof in connection with establishment of the extent of the agent's power. The principle for imposing liability on the nonacting party, be he partner or ordinary principal, is that he has "held out" the actor as being empowered to perform acts of the nature of the act in question. If A seeks to impose liability on B for the act of C on the theory that B held C out as having power to do such act, clearly the burden of establishing the facts which constitute such holding out is on A.

In the case of an ordinary agent, "holding out" is established by showing that the principal placed the agent in a position which ordinarily carries with it generally recognized powers. The agent will then have, as far as third parties are concerned, the power to do the things ordinarily done by one occupying such a position, unless the third party has knowledge of limitations on the powers of the agent. In *Collins v. Cooper*, 65 Tex. 460, 464 (1886), the Supreme Court said that in determining the extent of an agent's power, it "becomes necessary, to consider the character of the business, the manner in which it is usual to carry on such a business, and, where the agency has continued for a long time, the manner in which the particular business was carried on. . . ." This is the same principle which is made applicable to problems concerning the powers of partners by Sec. 9(1).

There are many statements to the effect that members of a "trading" partnership have implied authority to bind the partnership by issuing commercial paper, while members of a "nontrading" partnership have no such implied authority. But we do not base our holding on the ground that the partnership here was of the nontrading type. It is apparent that the attempted distinction between the two types of partnership is nothing more than a shorthand rendition of the notion that B is liable for the act of C if B has "held out" to other persons that C is empowered to perform acts of that particular nature. The nature of the distinction is revealed by the language of Chief Justice Stayton in *Randall v. Meredith*, 76 Tex. 669, 13 S.W. 576, 582–583 (1890):

> "If the partnership contemplates the periodical or continuous or frequent purchasing, not as incidental to an occupation, but for the purpose of selling again the thing purchased, either in its original or manufactured state, it is a trading partnership; otherwise, it is not." . . . There is no doubt that all partnerships which fall within this definition are trading partnerships, and it may be that it is broad enough to cover all that should be so classed. If these were not embraced within this definition, in which each partner is clothed with power to borrow money, they may be recognized by the character of the business pursued, which makes frequent resort to borrowing a necessity, not existing by reason of embarrassments, or on account of some fortuitous event, but for the advantageous prosecution of even a prosperous business. . . .

> . . . An act may be necessary for the carrying on of the business of a partnership, but when done by one partner the firm cannot be bound by it, unless he has express or implied power to do the act. Whether he has the implied power depends on whether the act be "necessary to carry on the business in the ordinary way. A partner's power is to do only what is usual, and not what is unusual because necessary." . . .

It appears that the tests announced in Randall for determining whether a partnership is to be classed as trading or nontrading is exactly the same test for imposition of liability embodied in Sec. 9(1). This explains the fact that the U. P. A. makes no mention of the distinction between trading and nontrading firms.

We are aware of the language in *Crozier, Rhea & Co. v. Kirker*, 4 Tex. 252, 258–259 (1849), to the effect that every partner has implied power to bind his copartners by executing notes for commercial purposes consistent with the object of the partnership. Similar language is found in [two other Texas cases]. But in each of these cases the partnership business contemplated "the periodical or continuous or frequent purchasing, not as incidental to an occupation, but for the purpose of selling again the thing purchased." Where the partnership business is of that nature, it is usual and customary to purchase on credit and to execute paper evidencing the existence of the partnership debt. That is, to use the language of Sec. 9(1), in such partnership, "carrying on in the usual way the business of the partnership" involves borrowing and the issuance of commercial paper. Or, to use the language of *Randall*, the nature of such a partnership "makes frequent resort to borrowing a necessity, not existing by reason of embarrassments, or on account of some fortuitous event, but for the advantageous prosecution of even a prosperous business." The statements in *Crozier* [and the other two cases] relating to implied authority of a partner to issue negotiable paper must be construed as being applicable to the types of partnerships there involved. If not so limited, then the assertions that every partner has implied authority to bind the firm by executing negotiable instruments must be disregarded as incorrect, irreconcilable with the analysis of the problem in *Randall*, and inconsistent with the plain language of Sec. 9(1). The power of a partner to issue commercial paper arises not from the existence of the partnership, but from the nature of the partnership business and the manner in which such business is usually conducted. This is the plain meaning of Sec. 9(1).

The only thing we know of the nature of the partnership here is that it was restricted to the sale of broadcast time over XERF on a commission basis. There is nothing to show that the transaction of such business required "periodical or continuous or frequent purchasing" or made "frequent resort to borrowing a necessity, not existing by reason of embarrassments, or on account of some fortuitous event, but for the advantageous prosecution of even a prosperous business." The assets of the partnership consisted of a few desks, chairs, typewriters and office supplies.

We disagree with the contention put forward by Burns to the effect that Bosquez was the managing partner. At best, the record reflects that both Bosquez and Gonzalez were active in the management of the business. As a matter of fact, with the exception of the transactions involving the 1962 note and the 1963 agreement, the record discloses that all instruments significantly affecting the relations between the partners and Burns were signed by both Bosquez and Gonzalez.

Since the evidence does not disclose that Bosquez, in executing the 1962 note, was performing an act "for apparently carrying on in the usual way the business of the partnership," there is no basis for holding that the note sued on was a partnership obligation. . . .

The judgment of the trial court is affirmed.

Notes

1. For a somewhat different view of the trading, nontrading distinction, see *Owens v. Palos Verdes Monaco*, 191 Cal. Rptr. 381, 388 (Cal. App. 1983), involving a suit to prevent the sale of partnership (MLH) real property on the ground that the contract was signed by only one partner, where the court in rejecting this argument stated as follows:

A number of reported decisions, including *Petrikis v. Hanges* (1952) 245 P.2d 39, cited by appellants, hold that the sale of a partnership's only asset is beyond the scope of usual partnership business and thus cannot be effected by a single partner. In *Petrikis*, the seller of real property, Mr. Petrikis, sold the partnership's only asset, a cocktail lounge, without written authority from his partners. The court of appeal held that Petrikis had not bound the partnership because he had acted beyond the scope of usual business in selling the partnership's only asset. *Petrikis* is distinguishable from the present case in that *Petrikis* involved a trading partnership. Petrikis' partnership was in the business of running a bar, not the business of holding a bar in anticipation of its eventual sale. In the case at bench, MLH had a singular purpose. It existed solely to hold and sell a piece of real property. The business of MLH was selling its land. Thus, the sale was in the ordinary course of MLH's business.

2. With regard to matters of authority, as noted earlier, § 303 of RUPA provides for the filing of a statement of authority. If the statement is recorded in the appropriate office for recording interests in land, it can serve as notice of authority or the lack thereof to persons dealing with partnership real property, a matter that could prove useful in situations like those involved in *Owens* and *Petrikis* discussed in Note 1.

3. The following case discusses the apparent authority of partners in the context of transfers of firm property. See *Ditzel v. Kent*, 131 Mont. 129, 308 P.2d 628, 632 (1957):

> Likewise the sale of all the property of a partnership is not the carrying on in the usual way of the business of a partnership within the meaning of [UPA § 9]. These statutes [UPA §§ 9 and 10] though relating to deeds and conveyances are not substantially different from those considered by the court in *Ridgely v. First National Bank, C.C.*, 75 F. 808, 809, relating to mortgages of real property where the court said:
>
>> There can be no valid mortgage of co-partnership property except by an instrument which shall be executed by all members of the co-partnership. . . . A mortgage which on its face is made to be a mortgage of the entire partnership property, and is signed by some of the members of the partnership, but not all, is, in my judgment, under this statute, a void instrument, of no force and effect, either of the partnership property, or the interest of the persons signing it in the partnership property.

Although, as the *Owens* case indicates, one may wish to temper this language depending on the nature of the partnership business, nevertheless it is useful to be aware of the restrictive attitude of many courts toward this kind of transaction under UPA, and perhaps also under RUPA when no statement of authority is recorded.

4. With regard to the apparent authority of a partner, UPA and RUPA have similar, though not identical, language. Under UPA § 9(1), a partner binds the partnership when his act is "for apparently carrying on *in the usual way* the business of the partnership," while under RUPA § 301, the key language is, "for apparently carrying on *in the ordinary course* the partnership business or *business of the kind carried on* *by the partnership*" (emphasis added). RUPA thus makes two changes to UPA, but the comment to RUPA indicates that the change from "in the usual way" to "in the ordinary course" was not a substantive change, and the courts have treated the two phrases identically. *See Baltrusch v. Baltrusch*, 83 P.3d 256, 262 (Mt. 2003). As to the broader language of RUPA, which recognizes a partner's apparent authority if his act is in the ordinary course of a business of the kind carried on by the partnership, RUPA drafters sought to clarify UPA, thereby statutorily recognizing a number of cases, including *Burns v. Gonzales*.

5. Is commencing litigation to collect an obligation owed to the partnership within the ordinary course of the partnership business? In *Casey Ranch LP v. Casey*, 773 N.W.2d 816 (S.D. 2009), the South Dakota Supreme Court concluded that it was, at least where the underlying obligation giving rise to the obligation arose in the ordinary course of the partnership's business. In *Casey*, the underlying obligation was a lease of the partnership's ranch to a third party for grazing purposes. Because the partnership agreement provided that the purpose of the partnership included the leasing of the partnership's real property, the lease was in the ordinary course of the partnership's business and, therefore, so was a suit to enforce the lease. Is this logical?

The Relationship of the General and Limited Partnership Statutes

The general partnership statutes (UPA and RUPA) are linked to the limited partnership statute (the Uniform Limited Partnership Act, or ULPA, and the Revised Uniform Limited Partnership Statute, RULPA, both of which will be covered in Chapter 14, *infra*). This linkage is set forth in the limited partnership statutes; both ULPA and RULPA provide, in nearly identical language, that a general partner in a limited partnership has the rights and powers and is subject to the liabilities of a partner in a general partnership (ULPA § 9; RULPA § 403). By this shorthand provision, the drafters of the limited partnership statutes avoided having to incorporate many of the provisions of UPA and RUPA relating to the authority of a general partner, liability to co-partners and third parties, etc. Thus, limited partnership cases that consider the authority of a general partner, as does the following case, may provide important interpretations of RUPA or UPA.

RNR Investments Limited Partnership v. Peoples First Community Bank

Court of Appeal of Florida
812 So. 2d 561 (2002)

VAN NORTWICK, J.

RNR Investments Limited Partnership (RNR) appeals a summary judgment of foreclosure granted in favor of appellee, Peoples First Community Bank (the Bank). RNR argues that the trial court erred in granting summary judgment because disputed issues of material fact remained with respect to one of RNR's affirmative defenses. In that affirmative defense, RNR alleged that the Bank was negligent in lending $960,000 to RNR without consent of the limited partners when, under RNR's Agreement of Limited Partnership, the authority of RNR's general partner was limited to obtaining financing up to $650,000. Under section 620.8301(a), Florida Statutes (2000), however, the Bank could rely upon the general partner's apparent authority to bind RNR, unless the Bank had actual knowledge or notice of his restricted authority. In opposing summary judgment, RNR produced no evidence showing that the Bank had actual knowledge or notice of restrictions imposed on the authority of RNR's general partner. Accordingly, no issues of material facts are in dispute and we affirm.

Factual and Procedural History

RNR is a Florida limited partnership formed pursuant to chapter 620, Florida Statutes, to purchase vacant land in Destin, Florida, and to construct a house on the land for resale. Bernard Roeger was RNR's general partner and Heinz Rapp, Claus North, and S.E. Waltz, Inc., were limited partners. The agreement of limited partnership provides for various restrictions on the authority of the general partner. Paragraph 4.1 of the agreement required the general partner to prepare a budget covering the cost of acquisition and construction of the project (defined as the "Approved Budget") and further provided, in pertinent part, as follows:

> The Approved Budget for the Partnership is attached hereto as Exhibit "C" and is approved by evidence of the signatures of the Partners on the signature pages of this Agreement. . . . In no event, without Limited Partner Consent, shall the Approved Budget be exceeded by more than five percent (5%), nor shall any line item thereof be exceeded by more than ten percent (10%). . . .

Paragraph 4.3 restricted the general partner's ability to borrow, spend partnership funds and encumber partnership assets, if not specifically provided for in the Approved Budget. Finally, with respect to the development of the partnership project, paragraph 2.2(b) provided:

> The General Partner shall not incur debts, liabilities or obligations of the Partnership which will cause any line item in the Approved Budget to be exceeded by more than ten percent (10%) or which will cause the aggregate Approved Budget to be exceed [sic] by more than five percent (5%) unless the General Partner shall receive the prior written consent of the Limited Partner.

In June 1998, RNR, through its general partner, entered into a construction loan agreement, note and mortgage in the principal amount of $990,000. From June 25, 1998 through Mar. 13, 2000, the bank disbursed the aggregate sum of $952,699, by transfers into RNR's bank account. All draws were approved by an architect, who certified that the work had progressed as indicated and that the quality of the work was in accordance with the construction contract. No representative of RNR objected to any draw of funds or asserted that the amounts disbursed were not associated with the construction of the house.

RNR defaulted under the terms of the note and mortgage by failing to make payments due in July 2000 and all monthly payments due thereafter. The Bank filed a complaint seeking foreclosure. RNR filed an answer and affirmative defenses. In its first affirmative defense, RNR alleged that the Bank had failed to review the limitations on the general partner's authority in RNR's limited partnership agreement. RNR asserted that the Bank had negligently failed to investigate and to realize that the general partner had no authority to execute notes, a mortgage and a construction loan agreement and was estopped from foreclosing. The Bank filed a motion for summary judgment with supporting affidavits attesting to the amounts due and owing and the amount of disbursements under the loan.

In opposition to the summary judgment motion, RNR filed the affidavit of Stephen E. Waltz, the president one of RNR's limited partners, S.E. Waltz, Inc. In that affidavit, Mr. Waltz stated that the partners anticipated that RNR would need to finance the construction of the residence, but that paragraph 2.2(b) of the partnership agreement limited the amount of any loan the general partner could obtain on behalf of RNR to an amount that would not exceed by more than 10% the approved budget on any one line item or exceed the aggregate approved budget by more than 5%, unless the general partner received the prior written consent of the limited partners. Waltz alleged that the limited partners understood and orally agreed that the general partner would seek financing in the approximate amount of $650,000. Further, Waltz stated:

> Even though the limited partners had orally agreed to this amount, a written consent was never memorialized, and to my surprise, the [Bank], either through its employees or attorney, . . . never requested the same from any of the limited partners at any time prior to [or] after the closing on the loan from the [Bank] to RNR.

Waltz alleged that the partners learned in the spring of 2000 that, instead of obtaining a loan for $650,000, Roeger had obtained a loan for $990,000, which was secured by RNR's property. He stated that the limited partners did not consent to Roeger obtaining a loan from the Bank in the amount of $990,000 either orally or in writing and that the limited partners were never contacted by the Bank as to whether they had consented to a loan amount of $990,000.

RNR asserts that a copy of the limited partnership agreement was maintained at its offices. Nevertheless, the record contains no copy of an Approved Budget of the partnership or any evidence that would show that a copy of RNR's partnership agreement or any partnership budget was given to the Bank or that any notice of the general partner's restricted authority was provided to the Bank.

. . .

[T]he trial court entered a summary final judgment of foreclosure in favor of the Bank. The foreclosure sale has been stayed pending the outcome of this appeal.

Apparent Authority of the General Partner

Although the agency concept of apparent authority was applied to partnerships under the common law, in Florida the extent to which the partnership is bound by the acts of a partner acting within the apparent authority is now governed by statute. Section [301(11)], a part of the Florida Revised Uniform Partnership Act (FRUPA), provides:

> Each partner is an agent of the partnership for the purpose of its business. An act of a partner, including the execution of an instrument in the partnership name, for apparently carrying on in the ordinary scope of partnership business or business of the kind carried on by the partnership, in the geographic area in which the partnership operates, binds the partnership unless the partner had no authority to act for the partnership in the particular manner and the person with whom the partner was dealing knew or had received notification that the partner lacked authority.

Thus, even if a general partner's actual authority is restricted by the terms of the partnership agreement, the general partner possesses the apparent authority to bind the partnership in the ordinary course of partnership business or in the business of the kind carried on by the partnership, unless the third party "knew or had received a notification that the partner lacked authority." *Id.* "Knowledge" and "notice" under FRUPA are defined in section [RUPA § 102]. That section provides that "[a] person knows a fact if the person has actual knowledge of the fact." Further, a third party has notice of a fact if that party "(a) [k]nows of the fact; (b) [h]as received notification of the fact; or (c) [h]as reason to know the fact exists from all other facts known to the person at the time in question." [RUPA § 102(2)]. Finally, under [RUPA § 303] a partnership may file a statement of partnership authority setting forth any restrictions in a general partner's authority.

Commentators have described the purpose of these knowledge and notice provisions, as follows:

> Under RUPA, the term knew is confined to actual knowledge, which is cognitive awareness. . . . Therefore, despite the similarity in language, RUPA provides greater protection [than the Uniform Partnership Act (UPA)] to third persons dealing with partners, who may rely on the partner's apparent authority absent actual knowledge or notification of a restriction in this regard. RUPA effects a slight reallocation of the risk of unauthorized agency power in favor of third parties. That is consistent with notions of the expanded liability of principals since the UPA was drafted.

> RUPA attempts to balance its shift toward greater protection of third parties by providing several new ways for partners to protect themselves against unauthorized actions by a rogue partner. First, the partnership may notify a third party of a partner's lack of authority. Such notification is effective upon receipt, whether or not the third party actually learns of

it. More significantly, the partnership may file a statement of partnership authority restricting a partner's authority.

Donald J. Weidner & John W. Larson, *The Revised Uniform Partnership Act: The Reporters' Overview*, 49 Bus. Law 1, 31–32 (1993) (footnotes omitted). "Absent actual knowledge, third parties have no duty to inspect the partnership agreement or inquire otherwise to ascertain the extent of a partner's actual authority in the ordinary course of business, . . . even if they have some reason to question it." *Id.* at 32 n. 200. The apparent authority provisions of section [RUPA § 301(1)], reflect a policy by the drafters that "the risk of loss from partner misconduct more appropriately belongs on the partnership than on third parties who do not knowingly participate in or take advantage of the misconduct . . ." J. Dennis Hynes, *Notice and Notification Under the Revised Uniform Partnership Act: Some Suggested Changes*, 2 J. Small & Emerging Bus. L. 299, 308 (1998).

Analysis

Under [RUPA § 301(1)], the determination of whether a partner is acting with authority to bind the partnership involves a two-step analysis. The first step is to determine whether the partner purporting to bind the partnership apparently is carrying on the partnership business in the usual way or a business of the kind carried on by the partnership. An affirmative answer on this step ends the inquiry, unless it is shown that the person with whom the partner is dealing actually knew or had received a notification that the partner lacked authority. Here, it is undisputed that, in entering into the loan, the general partner was carrying on the business of RNR in the usual way. The dispositive question in this appeal is whether there are issues of material fact as to whether the Bank had actual knowledge or notice of restrictions on the general partner's authority.

RNR argues that, as a result of the restrictions on the general partner's authority in the partnership agreement, the Bank had constructive knowledge of the restrictions and was obligated to inquire as to the general partner's specific authority to bind RNR in the construction loan. We cannot agree. Under [RUPA § 301], the Bank could rely on the general partner's apparent authority, unless it had *actual knowledge* or *notice* of restrictions on that authority. While the RNR partners may have agreed upon restrictions that would limit the general partner to borrowing no more than $650,000 on behalf of the partnership, RNR does not contend and nothing before us would show that the Bank had actual knowledge or notice of any restrictions on the general partner's authority. Here, the partnership could have protected itself by filing a statement pursuant to [RUPA § 303] or by providing notice to the Bank of the specific restrictions on the authority of the general partner.

Because there is no disputed issue of fact concerning whether the Bank had actual knowledge or notice of restrictions on the general partner's authority to borrow, summary judgment was proper.

Affirmed.

Miner and Wolf, JJ., concur.

Note

Would *RNR Investments* be decided the same way under UPA?

3. Liability of Purported Partner

It is not unusual for lawyers who are solo practitioners to share office space and support staff, e.g., receptionist, secretaries, etc., with other similarly situated lawyers. In these arrangements, there is a risk that a third party might assume that the lawyers in this arrangement are partners of one another. Are the lawyers at risk? Section 308 of RUPA addresses this risk:

(a) If a person, by words or conduct, purports to be a partner, or consents to being represented by another as a partner, in a partnership or with one or more persons not partners, the purported partner is liable to a person to whom the representation is made, if that person, relying on the representation, enters into a transaction with the actual or purported partnership. If the representation, either by the purported partner or by a person with the purported partner's consent, is made in a public manner, the purported partner is liable to a person who relies upon the purported partnership even if the purported partner is not aware of being held out as a partner to the claimant. If partnership liability results, the purported partner is liable with respect to that liability as if the purported partner were a partner. If no partnership liability results, the purported partner is liable with respect to that liability jointly and severally with any other person consenting to the representation.

(b) If a person is thus represented to be a partner in an existing partnership, or with one or more persons not partners, the purported partner is an agent of persons consenting to the representation to bind them to the same extent and in the same manner as if the purported partner were a partner, with respect to persons who enter into transactions in reliance upon the representation. If all of the partners of the existing partnership consent to the representation, a partnership act or obligation results. If fewer than all of the partners of the existing partnership consent to the representation, the person acting and the partners consenting to the representation are jointly and severally liable.

[(c)–(e) omitted.]

This RUPA section is similar to the concept of apparent agency or agency by estoppel. (See, *supra*, Chapter 4, Section C, and Restatement (Third) § 2.05, which is set forth in those materials.) Thus, there are important factual questions as to whether the "purported partner" made or allowed others to hold him out as a partner and whether the third party relied on such representations. There may also be a question as to whether such holding out was "made in a public manner," because, if so, the purported partner may be liable even if he is not aware of being held out to the claimant.

Returning to the hypothetical situation raised above, the lawyers sharing office space have to take care not to refer to one another as "partners" or otherwise give the impression to third parties that they are partners. In *Atlas Tack Corp. v. DiMasi*, 637 N.E.2d 230 (Mass. Ct. App. 1994), the plaintiff retained a lawyer (Donabed) to handle a matter. Donabed shared office space with two other lawyers (DiMasi and Karll), the three shared the cost of a receptionist for the office, and had office stationery entitled "Law Offices of DiMasi, Donabed & Karll, A Professional Association." Plaintiff alleged that Donabed mishandled its case and sued all three lawyers for malpractice. DiMasi and Karll moved for summary judgment, submitting affidavits that stated that "they did not hold themselves out to be partners, never represented to the plaintiff or anyone else that they were partners and did not consent to any such representation." On this basis, the trial court granted summary judgment in favor of the defendants. On appeal, the Massachusetts Appellate Court reversed.

The appellate court noted that in their opposition to defendants motion, the plaintiff's president "averred that his corporation needed an attorney to handle a dispute relating to the cost of clean up of a hazardous waste site it owned and was referred to this law office; that it was the corporation's business practice to hire law firms with multiple personnel and financial resources; that he assumed that he was hiring the law firm of DiMasi, Donabed & Karll when he spoke to Donabed; that all the correspondence and invoices received by the plaintiff from Donabed bore the letterhead of 'Law Offices of DiMasi, Donabed & Karll, A Professional Association,' and listed a roll of attorneys in the left hand margin; and that the checks issued by the plaintiff in payment for legal services were made payable to DiMasi, Donabed & Karll." Thus, the court concluded, there was a question of fact as to whether "Donabed held himself out as a partner of the defendants and whether the holding out was done with the defendants' consent." Summary judgment was, therefore, inappropriate.

It may have been the case that the defendants wanted to give the impression that they were part of a firm while maintaining their separate practices. If so, they ran the risk that they would be treated as a partnership by a court and it does seem obvious from the facts that plaintiff could have so believed.

Section 16 of UPA is similar to RUPA §308, but uses the term "estoppel" to describe the concept:

§ 16. *Partner by estoppel*

(1) When a person, by words spoken or written or by conduct, represents himself, or consents to another representing him to any one, as a partner in an existing partnership or with one or more persons not actual partners, he is liable to any such person to whom such representation has been made, who has, on the faith of such representation, given credit to the actual or apparent partnership, and if he has made such representation or consented to its being made in a public manner he is liable to such person, whether the representation has or has not been made or communicated to such person

so giving credit by or with the knowledge of the apparent partner making the representation or consenting to its being made. [The rest of § 16 is omitted.]

a. Is There a Duty to Speak?

Under both RUPA and UPA, a question arises as to whether the law requires one to act in order to correct impressions that he did not create. The official comment to RUPA states that "As under the UPA, there is no duty of denial, and thus a person held out by another as a partner is not liable unless he actually consents to the representation." The comment to § 16 of UPA is similar: "the weight of authority is to the effect that to be held as a partner he must consent to the holding and that consent is a matter of fact. The act as drafted follows this weight of authority and better reasoning."

Those who drafted the comment did not elaborate on their reference to better reasoning in the last sentence of the above quotation, but perhaps they found the no duty to rescue and consideration doctrines more persuasive than the estoppel against owners' doctrine.

Nevertheless, remaining silent while being represented as a partner has its risks. See *J & J Builders Supply v. Caffin*, 248 Cal. App. 2d 292, (1967), stating: "However, declarations [to plaintiff] of partnership by Jeffrey in Caffin's presence [stating, 'This is my new partner, Caffin'] under circumstances in which Caffin must have known that a response negativing Jeffrey's representation should be made to avoid misleading plaintiff, are properly received as adoptive admissions of Caffin." UPA was adopted in California in 1929. See also *McBriety v. Phillips*, 26 A.2d 400, 405 (Md. 1942), stating: "If a person knows that he is held out as a partner by another, he is just as liable as though he had called himself a partner, unless he does all that a reasonable and honest man would do under similar circumstances to assert his denial in order to remove the impression and prevent innocent parties from being misled." UPA was adopted in Maryland in 1916.

b. The Reliance Conundrum

Subsection (1) of § 16 consists of one long, complex sentence. It draws a distinction between the private and public holding out of a person as a partner. A quick reading of that sentence has led some to conclude that if a representation is made in a public manner, proof of reliance on the representation is not part of a creditor's case, apparently because the phrase "on the faith of such representation," which is included in the private holding out portion of (1), is not repeated expressly in the public holding out portion of (1). *Brown & Bigelow v. Roy*, 132 N.E.2d 755 (Ohio Ct. App. 1955), provides support for this reading. The case involved the public posting of a license identifying defendant as a partner. Defendant claimed he was a creditor, not a partner. There was no evidence that plaintiff knew about the posting of the license. The court, in an opinion that did not work closely with the language of the statute, held that reliance did not need to be proved by the plaintiff creditor.

A different perspective on the language of § 16(1) is contained in *Reisen Lumber & Millwork Co. v. Simonelli*, 237 A.2d 303 (N.J. Super. Ct. 1967). The public holding out in *Simonelli* consisted of the filing with a public official of a business name certificate that identified defendant as a partner. Defendant had since left the partnership, which had never dealt with plaintiff creditor during the time defendant was a partner. Plaintiff admitted that it did not know of the certificate and had never previously heard of the partnership, but nevertheless sought to hold defendant liable as a partner by estoppel under § 16 because of the public holding out and the lack of public notice of dissolution of the partnership. The court found the absence of reliance determinative and held for defendant.

Section 308 of RUPA, the counterpart to § 16, has been rewritten to resolve the difficulty created by the awkward language of § 16. It continues the public-private distinction but makes it clear that reliance is required in either instance.

c. The Release Conundrum

Suppose a purported partner commits a tort and settles with the claimant. Can the claimant still maintain an action against other persons that claimant believed were the tortfeasor's partners? After summary judgments were entered for the defendants in the *Atlas Tack Corp.* case, the plaintiff settled his claim against Donabed and executed a release discharging him from all liability growing out of his legal representation but excepted from the provisions of that release its claims against DiMasi and Karll. They argued that since they were only vicariously liable, the release of the tortfeasor should operate to release them as well, notwithstanding the terms of the release. The court rejected this argument, noting that giving effect to a reservation in a settlement encourages settlements. Not all courts agree with this. See, Annotation, *"Release of, or Covenant Not to Sue, One Primarily Liable for Tort, but Expressly Reserving Rights Against One Secondarily Liable, as Bar to Recovery Against Latter,"* 24 A.L.R. 4th 547 (1983), for a collection of cases.

Note

Nearly all states have legislation requiring registration when an assumed or fictitious name is used in business. The use of surnames in a partnership name is not deemed fictitious in most jurisdictions, so long as the surnames are those of living partners. Probably the names of all the partners must be included in order to prevent the name from being fictitious. Noncompliance today usually will not prevent suit by a partnership if it complies prior to filing suit, nor affect the enforceability of contracts, but may expose the firm to liability for a fine. The assumed name statutes have been held not to apply to out-of-state partnerships if only an isolated business transaction within the state is involved.

B. Tort Liability for the Wrongs of Partners

1. In General

Section 13 of UPA establishes partnership liability for the wrongs of a partner acting in the ordinary course of the business of the firm. This concept was noted briefly in Chapter 3. Sections 14 (partnership bound by partner's breach of trust) and 15 (all partners are jointly and severally liable for everything chargeable to the partnership under §§ 13 and 14) also are relevant to this topic.

RUPA establishes the same basic standards of liability in its §§ 305 and 306. Section 305 picks up both §§ 13 and 14 of UPA in its subsections (a), establishing partnership liability for the actionable conduct of partners, and (b) establishing partnership liability for misapplication of money or property received by a partner from a third party. As explained in the Comment to § 305, the phrase "actionable conduct" was chosen to broaden the wording to include expressly liability for no-fault torts. Section 306 declares that partners are jointly and severally liable for all of the obligations of the partnership. This is a change from UPA, which distinguished between contract obligations (joint liability) and tort liabilities (joint and several liability). The distinction between the two kinds of liability will be covered shortly.

RUPA § 305 also provides that the partnership is liable for "any penalty incurred." Does this include punitive damages? While there is some contrary authority, the prevailing view is that the partnership is liable for punitive damages assessed against a partner for her wrongful or actionable conduct. *See Act II Jewelry, LLC v. Mu Ying Zhu*, 2010 U.S. Dist. LEXIS 70185 (E.D. Va. June 7, 2010).

As noted previously, the LLP plays an important role in this area. Protection from tort liability is a central feature of LLP legislation in all states, unlike the issue of contractual liability, where the states divide into full and partial shield approaches. Language in ULLPA making limited liability for partnership obligations available (in full shield capacity) is added as a new subsection (c) to RUPA § 306.

2. The Fraudulent Partner

Section 14(a) of UPA states that a partnership is bound to make good the loss where "one partner acting within the scope of his apparent authority receives money or property of a third person and misapplies it." RUPA § 305(a) covers the same doctrine, less clearly, by stating that a partnership is liable for a partner's wrongful act done "with authority of the partnership." The Comment to § 305 states that this "is intended to include a partner's apparent, as well as actual, authority." Fraud is the misconduct that generates nearly all of the litigation falling within these provisions.

a. The Traditional View

Rouse v. Pollard

Court of Errors & Appeals of New Jersey
21 A.2d 801 (1941)

CASE, JUSTICE.

This is an appeal by the complainant from a final decree in Chancery dismissing the bill as to all of the partners formerly of the law firm of Riker and Riker except Thomas E. Fitzsimmons against whom the decree ran as a judgment in the amount of $20,500 with interest and costs. The suit was to charge all of the members of the firm with liability for what was, in effect, an embezzlement of complainant's funds by the defendant Fitzsimmons in the above named amount. . . .

Complainant sought a separation from her husband. In or about the month of June, 1927, she went to the firm of Riker and Riker, stated her case and was referred to Fitzsimmons, a member of the firm. The separation agreement was signed, and there were a few other legal services rendered. In the course of the incidental conferences Fitzsimmons asked Mrs. Rouse what money she possessed and was informed by her of the amount thereof and the manner in which it was invested. According to Mrs. Rouse:

> He said the securities was a bad thing for a woman in my position to have and he suggested that I turn over my securities and sell them and turn the money over to the firm, that they dealt in gilt edge mortgage bonds, as he said. He said that they did that for their clients and it was perfectly secure. . . .

Mrs. Rouse wrote to her brokers directing them to sell her securities and to "forward a check for the same payable to me to my attorney, Mr. Thomas E. Fitzsimmons, c/o Riker & Riker, 24 Commerce Street, Newark, N.J." A check for $28,252.67 was sent as directed, was endorsed by Mrs. Rouse "Pay to the order of Thos. E. Fitzsimmons" and was deposited by Fitzsimmons in his personal bank account. No part ever came to the firm except $350, or thereabouts, which was paid by Fitzsimmons to the firm for the legal services rendered, and no member of the firm, other than Fitzsimmons, knew of the transaction. . . .

The experience of Mrs. Rouse is tragic and painful, but we must get, as best we may, at the facts. Her testimony reveals a faulty memory and a frail grasp upon the essentials of a business transaction. . . . Perhaps the initial respect which Mrs. Rouse entertained for Fitzsimmons' business sagacity and investment acumen was seeded in the fact that he was a member of the Riker firm; but he was a member of that firm for the practice of law, and that membership did not per se create liability by his partners for his acts outside the general scope of the practice of law. . . .

[I]f Fitzsimmons, as appellant now understands the fact to be, represented to her that the firm of Riker and Riker undertook to accept money in bulk from clients for future investment by and at the discretion of the attorneys in undesignated securities, and would do that for her, we are then confronted with the question whether Fitzsimmons, as a member of a firm of lawyers, bound together simply by an oral agreement "for the practice of law," could obligate his partners to such a venture. When Mrs. Rouse went to the offices of Riker and Riker in reliance upon their reputation as a law firm, stated the purpose of her visit, which was to obtain a legal service, and was introduced to Fitzsimmons as a member of the firm who would render the desired service, she had no justification therein for relying upon the responsibility of the partnership for any disconnected service assumed by Fitzsimmons outside one that was characteristically within the practice of law.

Appellant contends that the investment of the funds in mortgages was within the scope of the defendant law firm's practice or within the scope of Fitzsimmons' apparent authority. The proofs do not sustain the implication that the practice of this particular firm embraced the acceptance of clients' money to be placed at the firm's discretion in investments thereafter to be ascertained and selected, whether in first mortgages or otherwise. . . .

It has long been a recognized incident to the general practice of law, more extensively developed in some offices than in others, to make note of such clients as have moneys to invest on bond and mortgage, to bring the attention of those clients to the applications of proposed borrowers and, after the principals come to an agreement, to search the title, draw the necessary documents, even hold the money against the event, place the recordable papers on record and in general superintend the closing of the transaction. But we do not understand that it is a characteristic function of the practice of law to accept clients' money for deposit and future investment in unspecified securities at the discretion of the attorney, and we find to the contrary. It is possible that attorneys in isolated instances have done this; just as it is possible that a person of any profession or occupation has done so. It has not, however, been done by lawyers, in this jurisdiction at least, with such frequency or appropriateness as to become a phase of the practice. . . .

We have found that the incident sued upon, that is, the placing of money for the purposes named, is not a function of the practice of law and that it was not a part of any practice indulged in by the respondents; but beyond this appellant contends that it was within Fitzsimmons' apparent authority and so seeks to fasten liability upon respondents under that well known rule in the law of agency. The facts for the application of the principle do not exist. The respondents did nothing to indicate that Fitzsimmons had any authority to act in their behalf outside the practice of law.

Another point is that respondents should be made to answer for the loss upon the theory that inasmuch as they and the complainant were both innocent the burden should rest upon them because they put Fitzsimmons in the position where he was able to perpetrate the fraud upon complainant; and, yet another, that the respondents received a part of the funds and so are estopped from denying the authority of Fitzsimmons. These contentions also rest upon a warped view of the facts. The paying over of the money to Fitzsimmons not only was not an act in the practice of law, it was not a part of or connected with any transaction which Fitzsimmons was conducting or was authorized to conduct for the firm. The amount of $350 did not go to respondents as a participation in a tortious transaction but from money that belonged to Mrs. Rouse and in payment of legal services that were performed by the firm for her. The existence of the debt and the propriety of the charge were not in dispute. The money was paid to them in ignorance on their part, then and for many years thereafter, of any wrongdoing by Fitzsimmons, and without facts in their knowledge, or chargeable to their knowledge, which served to put them on notice. We find no element of estoppel.

The decree in the court below will be affirmed.

b. A Conflicting View

Cook v. Brundidge, Fountain, Elliott & Churchill

Supreme Court of Texas
533 S.W.2d 751 (1976)

STEAKLEY, JUSTICE.

As this case reaches us, it is a suit by Betty L. Cook, et al., against Brundidge, Fountain, Elliott & Churchill, a partnership for the practice of law. The suit sought to recover actual and exemplary damages against the law firm arising from alleged breaches of fiduciary duty in the attorney-client relationship, and from alleged fraudulent acts. The breaches and fraudulent acts were alleged to have been committed by Warren C. Lyon, a partner in the firm at the times in question. The motion of the law firm for summary judgment was granted by the trial court and this has been affirmed by the Court of Civil Appeals, 522 S.W.2d 740. The question for decision is whether the law firm established conclusively that it is not liable for the acts of Lyon. We hold that it did not and so reverse the judgments below and remand the cause for trial.

We learn the following from the summary judgment record. Brundidge, Fountain, Elliott & Churchill is a partnership engaged in the practice of law in Dallas, Texas. Warren C. Lyon was a partner of the law firm at the times in question. As such, in 1969, he represented the plaintiff Betty L. Cook in a divorce proceeding; he also prepared a will for her and for Isabelle Griffin, another plaintiff. Fees were charged by the law firm for these services and paid by Betty L. Cook and Isabelle Griffin. Lyon was also engaged in the real estate business and was an officer and stockholder in Texas Yummers, a Texas corporation. He also owned stock in a California company known as United States Franchise Corporation which assisted with the organization of Texas Yummers. Fees were also paid to the law firm by Texas Yummers.

Sometime in 1969, during a conference with Lyon concerning her divorce, Betty L. Cook informed Lyon that she, together with her aunt, Mrs. Isabelle Griffin, and her sister, Winifred Baker, were receiving approximately $60,000 from the sale of some property which had come to them from an estate in Illinois. Betty L.

Cook asked Lyon if he knew of someone with whom they could consult concerning the investment of this money in some real estate in Texas. Lyon told her he was a silent partner in a real estate firm and might be able to help her. He suggested several investments and then told her about Yummers, a fast-food franchise operation based in California, in which he had invested at, he said, substantial profit. Lyon said he had obtained a Yummers franchise and was in the process of forming a Texas corporation to handle it.

Betty L. Cook, et al., decided to invest in Yummers. They directed their attorney in Illinois to send Lyon a check for the proceeds of the sale of the land in Illinois, which he did. The check was dated July 3, 1969, and was in the sum of $60,343.25; it was made payable to "Warren Lyon as Attorney for Isabelle M. Griffin, Winifred Baker and Betty Cook." The check was mailed to and received by Lyon at the office of the law firm but there is no showing that the funds were deposited in or handled by or through any account of the law firm. [The funds were first loaned to Texas Yummers under a contract signed by Lyon as president of the corporation. Plaintiff alleged that Lyon had represented to her] that he had prepared the contract, that it was a good and valid mortgage contract and that as their attorney he could assure them that their interests were well-protected.... [Plaintiffs later exchanged their rights under the contract for stock. Texas Yummers went bankrupt]....

The affidavit of Lyon was ... that in all transactions with Betty L. Cook, other than with respect to the divorce proceeding and the preparation of a will for her, he was acting in his individual and personal capacity, for which the law firm received no fee or payment from Betty L. Cook.

The affidavit of Churchill [a senior partner] was to the effect that the firm is engaged exclusively in the practice of law; that Lyon as a partner was not authorized to act as an investment counselor, securities broker or dealer, or to act as a real estate broker, dealer or agent, and that Lyon was not a partner in the performance of any such services performed for Betty L. Cook; that the only service Lyon performed as a partner was the handling of a divorce for Betty L. Cook and the preparation of a will for her and perhaps a will for one of the other plaintiffs; that Lyon was acting in his individual capacity with respect to his real estate business and as a stockholder in United States Franchise Corporation, and in the corporation known as Yummers; and that "this firm received no fee, payment, commission, or profit in any of such transactions." ...

[Mrs. Cook] filed an affidavit in support of her response to the motion of the law firm for summary judgment. In this she stated:

> At no time in my dealings with Defendant Lyon did he indicate that he was acting in any capacity other than as my attorney at law or separate from the law firm of which he was a partner....

There was also filed by Betty L. Cook, et al., the affidavit of Stuart M. Mamer, their attorney in Champaign, Illinois. His activities, with particular reference to the law firm in Texas, were described as follows:

I was informed by telephone calls and correspondence from each of the three Plaintiffs herein that they were represented by counsel in Dallas, Texas. They informed me that their attorney was Warren C. Lyon, a member of the Dallas law firm of Brundidge, Fountain, Elliott & Churchill.

... On July 3, 1969, I drew a check to the order of "Warren Lyon, as Attorney for Isabelle M. Griffin, Winifred Baker and Betty Cook."

I received a letter dated July 14, 1969, from the law firm of Brundidge, Fountain, Elliott & Churchill bearing the signature "Warren Lyon." I received a letter dated August 12, 1969, in the same style. The first of these letters showed that copies thereof had been sent to Mmes. Cook, Baker, and Griffin.

As requested in the law firm's letter of July 14, 1969, I did indeed compute the capital gains taxes and prepared the necessary schedules for the 1969 income tax returns of Mmes. Cook, Baker, and Griffin.

... Vicarious liability of the law firm for the alleged damages suffered by Betty L. Cook, et al., is not claimed on the basis of any negligence or breach of duty on the part of the other members of the law firm; nor is it claimed that the other members of the law firm became cognizant of the acts of Lyon, or in anywise consented to or ratified his course of dealings with Betty L. Cook, et al. There is no claim, on the other hand, that Lyon or the law firm gave notice to Betty L. Cook, et al., that Lyon's authority as a partner was limited in any respect, or, more specifically, that any act of Lyon for his individual profit, or in which he had a personal interest, would be outside his authority as a member of the partnership.

The question of the liability of a professional partnership of attorneys for the acts of a partner not strictly legal in nature, but which occur during the existence of the attorney-client relationship in recognized legal matters, is of first impression in our jurisdiction. Other jurisdictions have dealt with the problem of determining the scope of business of a professional partnership in various ways. *Rouse v. Pollard* [is cited and described.]

In *Douglas Reservoirs Water Users Ass'n v. Maurer & Garst*, 398 P.2d 74 (Wyo. 1965), Maurer, a partner in the law firm, misappropriated a $10,000 check given to him by the Water Users Association, of which he was a member and the treasurer [and attorney]; the funds were supposed to be used to purchase a bond in the name of the association. The Wyoming Supreme Court affirmed a summary judgment in favor of the law partnership, holding that Maurer was not acting within the ordinary scope of the partnership business as a matter of law when he misappropriated the funds:

There is nothing to indicate that legal work had been involved in collecting money from the United States for Douglas Reservoirs Water Users Association, or that the $10,000 check had been entrusted to Maurer for a transaction ordinarily performed by lawyers.

In *Blackmon v. Hale*, 1 Cal. 3d 548, 83 Cal. Rptr. 194, 463 P.2d 418 (1970), the plaintiff gave an attorney a check payable to the attorney's partnership trust account, in order that funds would be available to the attorney in negotiations for plaintiff's purchase of a note and mortgage on some real property. The partner misappropriated the funds, and plaintiff sued the partnership for their recovery. [T]he California Supreme Court held that the partnership was liable for the partner's malfeasance on the ground that the partner was acting within the scope of his apparent authority in accepting plaintiff's funds. . . .

In *Zimmerman v. Hogg & Allen, P. A.*, 286 N.C. 24, 209 S.E.2d 795 (1974), Greene, who was a principal shareholder in Hogg & Allen, a professional association for the practice of law, represented Zimmerman, who was an officer and employee of a company which had engaged Hogg & Allen as its general counsel, in some personal legal matters. Zimmerman sent Greene $24,000 to be used in the purchase of shares of Kentucky Fried Chicken. Zimmerman sued Greene and Hogg & Allen for misappropriation of his money. Reversing the trial court's summary judgment in favor of Hogg & Allen, the North Carolina Supreme Court held that there was a fact question whether, in accepting Zimmerman's money, Greene was acting within the normal scope of business of the professional association.[3]

It is doubtful if the treatment of the problem by these various jurisdictions, and the rationale applied for solutions, can be harmonized; or that an accepted rule can be said to appear. A stricter view against the liability of a professional partnership for the misdeeds of a partner with a client is indicated in *Rouse* and *Douglas Reservoirs*; a more liberal view is indicated in *Blackmon, Zimmerman* and *Croisant.* Surprisingly, also, only two of the jurisdictions, California and Wyoming, considered the problem in the light of their respective uniform partnership acts which, in our view are particularly relevant, if not controlling. [The court quotes §§ 9, 13, and 14 of UPA.]

We have recently spoken of apparent authority in terms of estoppel, and have said that one seeking to charge a principal through apparent authority of an agent must prove such conduct on the part of the principal as would lead a reasonable prudent person to suppose that the agent had the authority he purports to exercise. The extent of authority of a partner is determined essentially by the same principles as those measuring the scope of the authority of an agent. In *Randall v. Meredith*, 76 Tex. 669, 13 S.W. 576 (1890), this Court wrote of the implied powers possessed by a partner:

> Third persons dealing with a member of a firm in reference to partnership matters, in the absence of power expressly conferred, must recognize the fact that the partner's power to bind his firm is restricted to the doing

---

3. [The fifth and final case described by the court is *Croisant v. Watrud*, 432 P.2d (Ore. 1967), where the court held an accounting partnership liable for the mishandling of funds entrusted to a partner by plaintiff, a client of the firm. —Eds.]

of such things as are within the scope of the particular business. Between the partners themselves, and between the firm and persons dealing with it through a partner, there is no doubt that the usages of firms engaged in the same character of business in the same country, as well as the general usage of the firm in the conduct of its business, may be looked to ascertain the implied powers possessed by a partner. . . .

As stated before, it is not claimed either that Lyon was authorized by the partnership to act as he did in the Yummers matter or that Betty L. Cook, et al., had notice or knowledge that Lyon had no authority to act for the partnership in what he did. Assuming misapplication of the funds, the crucial consideration in determining whether the law firm is bound by the acts of Lyon by force of the statutory provisions is whether in receiving the funds of Betty L. Cook, et al., in the sum of $60,343.25, Lyon was "apparently carrying on in the usual way the business of the partnership" (Sec. 9); or, as also expressed, whether he was "acting in the ordinary course of the business of the partnership" (Sec. 13). If so, it would follow that Lyon was "acting within the scope of his apparent authority" when he received the money and property of Betty L. Cook, et al.; and that the law firm is "bound to make good the loss" from his misapplication of the funds (Sec. 14).

It was the burden of the law firm as the defendant-movant for summary judgment to establish as a matter of law that no fact issue stands in the way of judgment in its favor. The summary judgment burden was that of establishing the negative of the statutory issues, namely, that Lyon was not apparently carrying on in the usual way the business of the law firm, i.e., was not acting in the ordinary course of its business and hence was not acting within the scope of apparent authority by force of statute. . . .

As noted earlier, the thrust of the affidavits of Churchill and Lyon in support of the motion for summary judgment was that the law firm is engaged exclusively in the practice of law, and that Lyon was not acting for the partnership in performing the services in question. But at the least, the acceptance by Lyon of the check of $60,343.25 payable to "Warren Lyon as Attorney for" Betty L. Cook, et al., together with the deposition testimony of Betty L. Cook upon which the motion of the law firm for summary judgment also relied for support, and, further, the affidavit of Betty L. Cook and that of the Illinois attorney, demonstrate the existence of fact issues with respect to the statutory conditions to liability of the partnership. This being so, the record does not establish conclusively that the law firm is not accountable to Betty L. Cook, et al., for the acts of Lyon.

The judgments of the trial court and of the Court of Civil Appeals are reversed and the cause is remanded for trial.

Dissenting opinion by McGee, J., in which Greenhill, C. J., joins.

McGee, Justice.

I respectfully dissent. I would hold that in this case the summary judgment proof established as a matter of law that Lyon had neither the actual nor the apparent authority to represent the law firm in the fraud perpetrated upon the petitioners. Further, no liability should rest upon the law firm under any of the controlling provisions of the Texas Uniform Partnership Act.

The record clearly reveals that Mrs. Cook initially asked Lyon whether he knew of someone to whom she could speak concerning the possible investment of certain monies in Texas properties. Thus, aside from her legal problems Mrs. Cook inquired of Lyon whether he knew of someone she could discuss investments with — apparently realizing that any discussion relative to legal matters had ceased. She specifically inquired as to whether he knew of "either an investment counselor or a real estate person." Lyon's answer was that he was a silent partner in a different field   a real estate firm, and that he could therefore be of some service to her in that separate capacity. . . . [I]t is clear that the investment counseling by Lyon was done without the knowledge of anyone else in the law firm and that the firm neither received a fee, nor profited in any way by Lyon's actions. The end result is that the pleadings, affidavits and depositions reveal that the activities out of which the defalcations arose did not constitute a partnership endeavor.

In *Randall v. Meredith*, 76 Tex. 669, 13 S.W. 576, 581 (1890), the court stated:

> Third persons dealing with a member of a firm in reference to partnership matters, in the absence of power expressly conferred, must recognize the fact that the partner's power to bind his firm is restricted to the doing of such things as are within the scope of the particular business.

Nevertheless, the majority has held that the liability of the law firm may ultimately be established under the applicable provisions of the Texas Uniform Partnership Act. . . .

[A]s viewed by the majority, the key is obviously the receipt of the funds. Though I would not limit the construction of the Act simply to the mere receipt of the funds, and aside from the confusion inherent in the majority's statement, I maintain that the liability provisions of the act are clear and well defined. . . .

. . . Perhaps the initial respect which Mrs. Cook entertained for Lyon's business sagacity and investment acumen was seeded in the fact that he was a member of that particular law firm; but he was a member of that firm for the practice of law, and that membership did not per se create liability by his partners for his acts outside the general scope of the practice of law. *Rouse v. Pollard*, 130 N.J. Eq. 204, 21 A.2d 801 (1941). . . .

When Mrs. Cook went to the offices of Brundidge, Fountain, Elliott & Churchill in reliance upon their reputation as a law firm to obtain legal advice and met with Lyon as a member of the firm who would render the desired service, she had no justification therein for relying upon the responsibility of the partnership for any disconnected service assumed by Lyon outside one that was characteristically within the practice of law. When Lyon volunteered himself as a real estate and investment counselor in the present case due to Mrs. Cook's instigating inquiry he was not "apparently carrying on in the usual way the business of the partnership," nor was he "acting in the ordinary course of the business of the partnership" within the meaning of the Partnership Act. In this case Lyon was acting in a private, nonlegal advisory capacity, and he was therefore entirely outside the scope of his authority and without the scope of the business carried on by this law firm. Such actions were not incidental to the business of a firm engaged exclusively in the practice of law . . . .

. . . In the instant case we find no actions by the principal law firm that would induce Mrs. Cook to believe that Lyon was authorized to act for the firm as a real estate broker or investment counselor. The firm did nothing to indicate to Mrs. Cook that Lyon was authorized to act in their behalf outside of the practice of law. Mrs. Cook herself stated in her affidavit and deposition that she had no contact with any other member of the law firm beyond greeting Mr. Churchill briefly on a few occasions. The mere fact that the law firm had conferred upon Lyon the authority to practice law within the scope of their partnership would not create the apparent authority to engage in investment counseling transactions as a service disconnected from the practice of law.

As a final note, I maintain that it is clearly evident that the majority has failed in its duty to lend a guiding hand to the trial court below. For instance, in what fashion do the three statutory liability provisions interrelate so as to possibly affix liability to the law firm? Since the ultimate outcome is dependent upon these pertinent liability provisions, what are the special issues that should be submitted in such cases? Whose viewpoint or actions determine the existence or nonexistence of liability? What does "apparently carrying on in the usual way the business of the partnership" mean? It is inevitable that the jury will require some form of instruction as to these matters. And, since the term "apparent authority" as set out in the statute has obviously not received its traditional interpretation, that concept will also require further specification and delineation. That problems and confusion are created is evident. The questions which arise call for and deserve answers. This case presents the initial instance in which the partnership liability provisions have been directly confronted and analyzed in such a fashion, and therefore, further guidance is essential.

C. The Nature of a Partner's Liability — Joint as Opposed to Joint and Several Liability

Sections 15 of UPA and 306 of RUPA deal with this subject. As noted earlier, both acts state that each partner is personally liable to outsiders for the debts and obligations of the firm. The personal liability of an incoming partner does not, however, absent consent, extend to partnership obligations incurred prior to the time of joining the firm, as covered below. And a partner who is held personally liable to an outsider for a partnership obligation ordinarily has indemnity rights under UPA

§ 18(b) and RUPA § 401(c) against the partnership. Nevertheless, the broad personal liability of partners is a key feature of partnership status, assuming that there has been no LLP filing by the partnership in the particular case.[4]

The distinction between "joint and several" obligations under UPA § 15(a) (tort liabilities) and "joint" obligations under § 15(b) (contract liabilities) raises procedural and substantive problems that have troubled partnership law for some time. UPA simply declares the general nature of a partner's liability, leaving the procedural effect of this declaration up to local law. See the Commissioner's Notes to § 15, 6 Uniform Laws Annotated. Although this issue is mooted in RUPA § 306, which declares all liabilities, both tort and contract, to be joint and several, many states have UPA as their governing law (at least with respect to some partnerships organized in those states), and thus it is important to address the distinction between joint obligations and joint and several obligations.

Ask yourself what the consequences would be if Jones, a tort claimant injured by a partner acting within the ordinary course of the partnership's business, sued only one of three partners in the partnership. Could she successfully do so? If so, and she obtains a judgment and executes on it, receiving only one-half the amount of the judgment, can she then sue the other two partners and execute against their assets? If so, would she have to relitigate the question of liability or would the first judgment be res judicata in the subsequent suit?

The clear impression from the language of § 15 is that tort claims fall under § 15(a). The argument that an unliquidated tort claim was a "debt" under § 15(b) and thus only joint liability was involved was litigated and lost in *Soberg v. Sanders*, 220 N.W. 781 (Mich. 1928).

Assuming, therefore, that joint and several liability applies, the normal procedural rules come into play and give us the answers to the questions asked above. See Bromberg & Ribstein on Partnership 5:111–12, § 5.11(d), stating that the other partners remain liable for the satisfaction of the claim and that res judicata does not apply to the subsequent suit. Res judicata would not apply because the other partners were not parties to the first action and have not had their day in court. *See* Restatement (Second) of Judgments § 60 (1982). In some jurisdictions, however, the issue of the liability of the partnership is considered settled by the first suit because the partner joined in that suit "had adequate representative capacity

---

4. This includes the "dormant" or "secret" partner, whose association with the firm is not generally known. The dormant or secret partner is nevertheless a full partner, subject to all partnership liabilities, with the only distinction in status being that the consequences of a failure to give proper notice upon retirement from the firm may not be so severe as for the other partners. Some distinction has been drawn between the secret and dormant partner on the ground that, while the identity of both types of partners is unknown to people outside the partnership, the secret partner is actively engaged in the management of the business, while a dormant partner is totally inactive. *See* UPA § 35(2)(b). "Silent" partners are defined, in I Rowley on Partnership 102 (1960), as actual members of the firm, known to be partners to outsiders, who nevertheless take no part in the management of the business. Their liabilities are the same as those of active partners.

for the partnership to be bound" (CRANE & BROMBERG ON PARTNERSHIP 350), with issues in the second suit focusing on whether the defendants indeed were partners or otherwise had personal defenses to the suit.

The procedural consequences of pursuing a joint obligation under § 15(b) are more complex. Assume that your client wants to sue a partnership of five people on a contractual obligation. The partnership is located in New York and three of the five partners reside there. Two reside out of state, one in Florida and one in Oregon. Assume that you could get service of process over them under the New York long arm statute but your client prefers not to incur the delay and expense in doing so. You are satisfied that the three in New York are financially responsible and, since each person bound by a joint obligation is bound for the whole obligation, are not concerned about the other two. Realizing this, can you successfully sue only the three in New York? The answer at common law is a decisive no. The three partners could plead "in abatement" and the action would be dismissed. Joint obligors must be sued jointly, subject to an exception where jurisdiction over all cannot be obtained. If they do not plead in abatement, the defense is deemed waived and the suit can continue to judgment, although many jurisdictions hold at common law that the cause of action merges with the judgment, with the result that the plaintiff could no longer recover against the two not joined.[5] In *PNC Bank, N.A. v. Farinacci*, 964 N.E.2d 1124 (Ohio Ct. App. 2011), however, the court held that "joint" liability under UPA § 15(b) meant that each partner in an eight-person partnership was liable for 1/8 of the debt to a bank under a line of credit.

Is it possible to avoid the abatement plea by suing the partnership and executing against the partnership assets? The answer in many states under UPA was no because a partnership is not a legal entity. Suits affecting partnership matters had to be brought against or by all the members of the firm. This result has been changed nearly everywhere by statute, as noted below.

In addition, the release of one joint obligor releases all at common law. Further, the death of a partner shifted liability to the remaining partners when a joint

---

5. For a clear expression of these distinctions, see *Cunard Line Ltd. v. Abney*, 540 F. Supp. 657, 659 (S.D.N.Y. 1982), where the court stated as follows:

> The joint nature of the obligation does not imply that the joint obligor is immune from being sued individually. It only gives the joint obligor the right to insist that the plaintiff join other such obligors if joinder is possible. . . . [A] plaintiff may hold a joint obligor personally liable on a joint obligation.

In a footnote the court stated:

> The individual joint obligor is a necessary party (not an indispensable one) in an action against one or more of the joint individual obligors. By contrast, if the obligors are also "severally" liable—as in the case of partners charged with a partnership tort liability— then they are merely proper parties to an action against them individually. Consequently, they don't even have the right to insist on joinder and the plaintiff may freely "pick his target."

obligation was involved. Equity intervened against application of this latter rule when the surviving partner or partners were insolvent.

The response to this unsatisfactory situation varied greatly in the different states. One form of legislation, known as the joint debtor act, allows actions against joint debtors to proceed against fewer than all the debtors if all the debtors are named as defendants, with the judgment enforceable against the joint property of all and the separate property of the debtors actually served with process. A different response was legislation permitting suit against a partnership in its own name, again with the judgment binding the joint property of all partners and the individual property of the partners actually served. Such statutes are known as common name statutes. Another response was legislation declaring that all contracts joint at common law are to be regarded as joint and several. Also, § 36(4) of UPA makes the individual property of a deceased partner liable for partnership obligations incurred while the deceased was a partner, whether or not the other partners are insolvent.

Assuming that the three partners were served with process under one of the above statutes and paid the ensuing judgment, do they have a right of contribution against the other partners not joined? Does it make any difference whether the liability is joint or is joint and several? What is your common-sense response to this? See § 18(b) of the UPA and, if the partnership is unable to indemnify, §§ 40(d) and 40(b)(II).

As mentioned above, RUPA declares all liability joint and several, whether tort or contractual in origin, in § 306. Thus, the above issues will not arise in jurisdictions adopting RUPA. Moreover, in *Segars v. McCormick*, 55 P.3d 470 (Okla. App. 2002), the court held that under RUPA a plaintiff may name any partners as individual defendants in an action against the partnership although, of course, subject to RUPA § 307, plaintiff may not reach the personal assets of an individual partner until exhausting the partnership assets. On the other hand, if an injured party claims that an individual partner's negligence was the cause of loss suffered, the partnership is not an indispensable party to the action. *Gildon v. Simon Property Group, Inc.*, 145 P.3d 1169 (Wash. 2006).

D. Suits against the Partnership

As mentioned above, a partnership is viewed as an aggregate of persons under UPA. It thus is not suable in its own name at common law since only legal persons may be named as parties to litigation. Suits affecting partnership matters have to be brought against the members of the firm in states that have not adopted legislation on this matter. This raises the joint obligor problems mentioned above when a claim is based on contractual grounds. If the suit is based on tort liability, there is no need to serve all partners. But in neither event can the firm itself be sued.

Many jurisdictions by separate statute now allow suit against a partnership in the partnership name, as noted earlier. UPA does not have a provision on this matter, on the ground that it is procedural in nature. The problem does not exist under

RUPA because of the entity status of a partnership. See § 307, stating, "A partnership may sue and be sued in the name of the partnership."

E. Suits by the Partnership

The common law, consistent with the aggregate theory, also does not recognize suit by the partnership in the firm name. With some exceptions, at common law suits to enforce partnership rights must be brought in the names of all partners since only legal persons may be named as parties to litigation. Many states have provided by statute that actions may be brought in the partnership name. *See* REUS-CHLEIN & GREGORY, AGENCY AND PARTNERSHIP 313–15. UPA does not have a provision on this. As noted above, the problem does not exist under RUPA because a partnership is defined as an entity.

In all entities—corporations, general partnerships, limited partnerships, and limited liability companies—a question arises as to whether an equity owner of the entity can maintain an action for damages allegedly suffered by the entity if those in control of the entity refuse to do so. Equity courts have long permitted corporate shareholders, under certain well-developed criteria, to maintain an action on behalf of the corporation when the directors of the corporation (who would normally have the exclusive authority to authorize such actions) fail to do so. Such actions are commonly called "derivative actions." The problem for general partnerships is unique because each of the partners is, by definition, an agent of the partnership and, arguably has the agency authority to initiate the action. When a state has amended its statutes to permit partnerships to maintain an action in its own name, courts must still decide who can maintain that action, as the next case demonstrates.

Adams v. Land Services, Inc.

Colorado Court of Appeals
194 P.3d 429 (2008)

Opinion by JUDGE VOGT

Plaintiffs, Lief Adams, Lewis Caricato, Bette Caricato, Lloyd Herren, Elizabeth McGill, James McGill, Suzanne Strickland, Gayeski Capital Equities, LLC, The Milton W. Fonay Trust, SabaColo, LLC, and Brighton Farms, LLP, appeal the trial court's summary judgments dismissing their claims against defendants, Land Services, Inc. (LSI), Douglas A. Barnes, and The Barnes Family Foundation (BFF). We affirm the judgment of dismissal based on lack of standing and therefore do not reach the merits of the trial court's earlier dismissal of plaintiffs' civil theft and false representation claims.

Plaintiff Brighton Farms, LLP, was formed in 1972 for the purpose of acquiring and holding for appreciation a parcel of land in Adams County, Colorado. (Although it retains the "LLP" designation in its name, Brighton Farms has been a general partnership since its limited liability status was revoked for failure to file a periodic report in 1999.) The other plaintiffs are general partners owning some 47% of the Brighton Farms partnership interests.

In 1998, Brighton Farms hired LSI and Barnes to manage and find a purchaser for the Adams County property. In 2004, Brighton Farms and LSI entered into a "platting agreement"-approved by the Brighton Farms partners holding a majority of the partnership interests, but opposed by some of the plaintiffs in this case-which provided that LSI would undertake various services to increase the value of the property, in exchange for which it would receive 40% of any net sales proceeds above the property's then-current market value of $24,000 per acre.

Brighton Farms subsequently received and accepted an offer to purchase the property for approximately $43,560 per acre. Upon sale of the property, LSI received its real estate broker's commission pursuant to the parties' listing agreement and its 40% share of the increased property value pursuant to the platting agreement. The balance of the net sale proceeds was distributed to the Brighton Farms partners, and the partnership was dissolved.

Plaintiffs then filed this action, alleging that LSI and Barnes had procured the platting agreement by fraud and that they had failed to perform the services that would have entitled them to compensation under the agreement. Plaintiffs asserted claims against LSI and Barnes for civil theft, breach of fiduciary duty, unjust enrichment, deceit by nondisclosure, false representation, money had and received, and breach of contract. They also sought a declaratory judgment and an accounting. BFF was added as a defendant on an additional equitable claim based on its alleged status as a donee or gratuitous transferee of property belonging to plaintiffs.

All the parties filed motions for summary judgment. The trial court entered summary judgment for defendants on plaintiffs' civil theft and false representation claims. Thereafter, it ruled that plaintiffs lacked standing to bring any of their claims, either as a derivative action on behalf of the Brighton Farms partnership or as individuals, and it therefore dismissed all the remaining claims on this basis.

I. Standing

Plaintiffs contend the trial court erred in ruling that they had no right to file a derivative action on behalf of Brighton Farms and lacked standing to sue as individuals. We disagree.

Standing is a threshold issue that must be satisfied before a case may be decided on the merits. To establish standing, a plaintiff must show that he or she has suffered an injury-in-fact to a legally protected interest. Because standing is a question of law, we review the trial court's resolution of the issue de novo.

A. Plaintiffs' Right to Sue on Behalf of Brighton Farms

We first address whether plaintiffs, as general partners holding a minority of the interests in a general partnership, may bring this action on behalf of the partnership. The trial court concluded that this action was "clearly a derivative action," and that

Colorado law did not afford general partners the derivative action remedy available to corporate shareholders pursuant to C.R.C.P. 23.1 and to limited partners pursuant to section 7-62-1001, C.R.S.2007. Plaintiffs agree that general partnership law does not recognize derivative actions and state that they make "no pretense of asserting claims derivatively"; rather, they argue that they may sue in the name of and on behalf of Brighton Farms because of their status as co-owners of partnership property and agents of the partnership. We are not persuaded.

1. Applicable Legal Principles

Plaintiffs' rights and status as general partners of Brighton Farms are determined under Colorado's version of UPA, which governs here because Brighton Farms was formed before 1998, and, therefore, RUPA does not apply.

The [UPA] provides certain remedies to individual general partners who are dissatisfied with actions taken by the partnership. [UPA § 22] entitles any partner to "a formal account as to partnership affairs" in certain enumerated circumstances, and [UPA § 32(1)] permits a partner to seek a judicial dissolution of the partnership where another partner has been guilty of conduct prejudicing the partnership business or has otherwise acted in a manner as to render a dissolution equitable.

However, the [UPA] includes no provision analogous to C.R.C.P. 23.1 or section 7-62-1001 that would give a general partner the right to bring a derivative action. In *Kline Hotel Partners v. Aircoa Equity Interests, Inc.*, 708 F.Supp. 1193, 1195 (D.Colo.1989), relied on by the trial court here, the federal district court cited the availability of other remedies for general partners under the [UPA], as well as the lack of any statutory provision permitting derivative actions on behalf of general partnerships, in concluding that, "in Colorado, a general partner has no capacity or standing to bring a derivative action on behalf of a general partnership."

There appear to be no Colorado cases, other than *Kline*, addressing the issue presented here. The general rule in other jurisdictions is that a partner cannot maintain a suit to enforce a partnership claim if a majority of the partners do not agree to do so.

Some courts have recognized an exception to the rule set forth above and would permit individual general partners to sue on behalf of the partnership when there are "exceptional circumstances" rendering other available remedies inadequate. In the case most frequently cited for that proposition, *Cates v. International Telephone & Telegraph Corp.*, 756 F.2d 1161 (5th Cir. 1985), the Fifth Circuit explained the circumstances that might permit a general partner to bring an action in the name of the partnership or in the partner's own name:

> We do not hold that Texas law would necessarily allow a derivative action on the part of a minority partner or an owner of a partnership interest. What we do hold is that in a proper case-one where the controlling partners, for improper, ulterior motives and not because of what they in good faith believe to be the best interests of the partnership, decline to sue on a valid, valuable partnership cause of action which it is advantageous to the partnership to

pursue-Texas law would afford *some* remedy to the minority partner or partnership interest owner *other than merely* a damage or accounting suit against the controlling partners, at least where the latter would not be reasonably effective to protect the substantial rights of the minority.

Id. at 1178 (emphasis in original).

2. Application to this Case

There is no indication in the record here that the partners owning a majority of the interests in Brighton Farms authorized plaintiffs to bring this action. Thus, under the general rule set forth in [omitted cases cited by the court] with which we agree, plaintiffs may not sue on behalf of Brighton Farms.

We further conclude that this case does not present the sort of "exceptional circumstances" that, under *Cates*, would permit plaintiffs to assert claims on behalf of the partnership.

The rights and duties of partners under the [UPA] are subject to any agreement among them. Under the Brighton Farms partnership agreement, management of the day-to-day business of the partnership was delegated to a management committee consisting of a maximum of five managing general partners. The managing general partners could execute any instruments necessary to effectuate the purposes of the agreement and were authorized to act on behalf of Brighton Farms on partnership business matters, including the conveyance of partnership property.

It is undisputed that the transactions with defendants at issue in this case were authorized and approved by the managing general partners, after the objections of the minority partners had been considered. Thus, the minority partners who disagreed with the managing general partners' actions were nevertheless bound by them.

Further, the record discloses no basis for concluding that the decision to enter into the challenged transactions with defendants was anything other than a good faith business decision on the part of the managing general partners. Thus, even those jurisdictions that permit minority general partners to sue in the name of the partnership in exceptional circumstances would not allow them to do so here. *See Cates*, 756 F.2d at 1177–78 (recognizing right of partners to sue on "a valid, valuable partnership cause of action" in some cases where controlling partners have refused to do so for improper, ulterior motives, but not in cases where controlling partners acted in what they in good faith believed to be in the best interests of the partnership).

We are not persuaded to reach a contrary conclusion based on plaintiffs' argument that, under section 9 of the [UPA], they are agents of the partnership and, as such, may assert claims on behalf of the partnership. As set forth above, the agency principle in § 9 is subject to the terms of the partnership agreement, in which plaintiffs delegated to the managing general partners the right to enter into the transactions with defendants. Further, even assuming plaintiffs were agents of Brighton Farms for some purposes, they were not authorized to bring this action as Brighton Farms' agents where their principal did not authorize such an action.

We are similarly unpersuaded by plaintiffs' reliance on Colorado cases, which have recognized that partners may sue in certain circumstances without joining the partnership or the other partners as parties. These cases addressed whether partners or partnerships were proper or indispensable parties.

In sum, we are aware of no theory that would allow plaintiffs, minority partners acting without the authorization of the partnership or of the majority partners, to seek redress on behalf of Brighton Farms for injuries allegedly resulting from Brighton Farms' transactions with defendants. Thus, because plaintiffs could not show that they suffered an injury-in-fact to a legally protected interest, the trial court properly concluded that they lacked standing to bring this action on behalf of Brighton Farms.

B. Plaintiffs' Standing to Sue as Individuals

We also reject plaintiffs' related contention that, as co-owners of partnership property pursuant to [UPA] section 25, they had standing to sue as individuals for injury to their individual interests in the partnership property.

Under the Brighton Farms partnership agreement, the Adams County parcel was partnership property, titled in the name of the partnership. Plaintiffs' complaint alleges that Brighton Farms sustained losses in connection with the sale of that property because of defendants' actions and inactions, but it does not allege that any individual plaintiff suffered unique losses not shared by the other partners. In such circumstances, claims for redress belong to the partnership and cannot be asserted by a partner in his or her individual capacity. As explained by the Fifth Circuit in *Cates*, in rejecting the minority partner's contention that he could assert individual claims distinct from partnership claims:

> [T]he record conclusively shows that the agreements sued on were between the partnerships and the defendants, that Cates individually was not a party thereto, and that the businesses which were the subject matter of the agreements were the businesses of the partnerships, not of Cates individually. Accordingly, any claims for damages which Cates suffered by reason of diminution in value of his partnership interest, or his share of partnership income, . . . by reason of breach of such agreements . . . are in effect subsumed within the causes of action of the partnerships and do not afford Cates . . . a separate, individual cause of action.

756 F.2d at 1181 (footnote omitted).

The principle applied in these cases is consistent with Colorado cases recognizing that corporate shareholders may not assert individual claims based on wrongs to the corporation where they did not suffer injuries separate and distinct from the injury to the corporation or the other shareholders.

Thus, the trial court did not err in concluding that plaintiffs also lacked standing to assert their claims as individuals.

The judgment is affirmed.

Note

The result in *Adams* would likely be the same had RUPA applied. Comment 2 following section 405 of RUPA notes that "RUPA does not authorize derivative actions. . . ." By contrast, most limited partnership and limited liability company statutes do expressly authorize derivative actions.

F. Notice and Notification to the Partnership

Sections 3 and 12 of UPA contain language concerning notice that is generally reflective of the common law. Section 102 of RUPA is the counterpart of §§ 3 and 12. It is based largely on § 1-201(25) of the Uniform Commercial Code and thus is more elaborate than UPA, but no major changes were made.

Federal Deposit Insurance Corp. v. Braemoor Assocs.

United States Court of Appeals, Seventh Circuit
686 F.2d 550 (1982)

POSNER, CIRCUIT JUDGE.

The Federal Deposit Insurance Corporation, as successor in interest to a defunct Illinois state bank, the State Bank of Clearing, brought this suit against Braemoor Associates, a joint venture, and against five individuals who are the surviving joint venturers in Braemoor, seeking to recover bank monies that the bank's president, Paul Bere, had funneled to Braemoor in breach of his fiduciary obligations to the bank. . . .

Braemoor Associates was formed in 1970 by several individuals, including Paul Bere, the president and board chairman of the State Bank of Clearing, to develop real estate. (Bere died before this suit was brought, and neither he nor his estate is a defendant.) . . . Although it is not unlawful per se for an Illinois bank to make a loan to its officers, or to enterprises which the officers control or actively manage, such loans, if they exceed $10,000, . . . require the approval of the bank's board of directors, and implicitly therefore disclosure of the conflict of interest to the board. . . .

Ringbloom, a real estate entrepreneur with whom Paul Bere had extensive business dealings, owned a company called Western. Bere and Ringbloom agreed that Western would purchase some land owned by Braemoor but the terms of payment were left somewhat indefinite. Late in 1971 Braemoor found itself owing a $60,000 installment payment to one of its contractors. Braemoor had less than $2000 in its bank account. Bere asked Ringbloom to pay Braemoor $60,000 on account of Western's land purchase so that Braemoor could pay the contractor, but Ringbloom said that Western did not have the money. Bere thereupon had the State Bank of Clearing lend Ringbloom $60,000 and Ringbloom immediately made out a check drawn on Western's bank account in the State Bank of Clearing for the same amount, payable to Braemoor. Ringbloom handed the check to Bere, who had it deposited in Braemoor's bank account. Braemoor then paid the contractor $60,000. The fact that the actual destination of the $60,000 loan from the State Bank of Clearing to Ringbloom was an enterprise controlled by Bere was not disclosed to the bank's board of directors. It is the first of the two loan transactions at issue in this case.

Several months later Braemoor needed to pay another installment to one of its contractors, this one for $240,000. Braemoor had only $16,000 in its bank account. Again Bere turned to Ringbloom, though Western was not due to make a payment to Braemoor on its land purchase agreement at that time. Again Western did not have the money, and again Bere stepped into the breach with a loan from his bank. . . .

The $60,000 loan to Western that found its way into Braemoor's pockets and the $240,000 portion of the second loan that also found its way into Braemoor's pockets were made in violation of Paul Bere's fiduciary obligations to his bank under the Illinois Banking Act; and the question is whether this breach of trust may be imputed to Braemoor. If so, it is not disputed that the FDIC may recover the proceeds of the breach in the hands of Braemoor; and since the principles of partnership law apply to joint ventures of individuals, there is also no question that if Braemoor is liable so are the individual defendants.

The district court found that the FDIC had failed to prove that the defendants had either (1) actual knowledge of Paul Bere's breach of trust or (2) knowledge of such facts as would lead a reasonable man to inquire whether Bere was committing a breach of trust; and the court concluded that without such proof the FDIC could not prevail. The FDIC does not challenge the finding that the defendants had no actual knowledge of the breach of trust, but it argues that the finding that they had no constructive notice is clearly erroneous. . . .

We need not decide whether either fact-finding is clearly erroneous. The FDIC's right to recover the proceeds of the two payments to Braemoor under the provisions of the Uniform Partnership Act (adopted in Illinois) is independent of what the other joint venturers knew, or as reasonable men should have known, about Paul Bere's breach of trust. Although the district court did not discuss the defendants' liability under the Uniform Partnership Act, the defendants do not contend that this theory of liability was not before the district court and should not be considered by us.

A joint venture of individuals is subject to the Uniform Partnership Act. . . . Section 12 of the Act provides that "the knowledge of the partner acting in the particular matter, acquired while a partner or then present to his mind, . . . operate[s] as . . . knowledge of the partnership, except in the case of a fraud on the partnership committed by or with the consent of that partner." Paul Bere, a partner in Braemoor, knew that in funneling $300,000 of his bank's money to Braemoor through Ringbloom he was violating his fiduciary duty to the bank. . . . Section 12 of the Uniform Partnership Act "imputed" that knowledge to the other joint venturers, which is to say made them and Braemoor, despite their lack of knowledge, fully liable for the breach of trust and hence constructive trustees of the proceeds of that breach for the benefit of the bank and its successor in interest, the FDIC, just as Paul Bere would have been if the FDIC had sued him. The exception in section 12 of the Uniform Partnership Act for frauds on the partnership is not applicable to this case, because Paul Bere was committing fraud on behalf of rather than against the partnership. We neither see, nor desire to concoct, any escape from the language of section 12. "The rule which imposes civil liability upon an 'innocent' partner for bad faith dealing of a co-partner is most pointedly applicable where the co-partner participates in the benefits derived from the dealing in bad faith." *Higgins v. Shenango Pottery*, 256 F.2d 504, 509 (3d Cir. 1958). We reach the same conclusion by an alternative route [under] Section 13 of the Uniform Partnership Act. . . .

. . . The district court erred by limiting its analysis to the distinct principles that govern cases where property that has been obtained in breach of trust comes into the hands of a third party who is not the principal or agent or partner of the person who committed the breach or is otherwise linked to him by a preexisting relationship, but is a stranger, and the question is whether the stranger has sufficient notice of the breach of trust to be forced to disgorge the property. The law imposes greater duties on people with regard to the acts of their agents and partners than with regard to the acts of strangers, presumably to give people an incentive to choose carefully with whom to enter into ventures that may injure innocent third parties.

[Judgment reversed and case remanded.]

Notes

1. If a partner raises the defense under § 12 of UPA (or under § 102(f) of RUPA, which is substantially the same) that a fraud had been committed on the partnership, who should bear the burden of proving that the fraud was on the partnership?

2. UPA § 12 and RUPA § 102(f) incorporate the "adverse interest exception" to imputation of knowledge or notice. (See Chapter 9, Section D, *supra*.) *Grassmueck v. American Shorthorn Assoc.*, 402 F.3d 833 (8th Cir. 2005), held that the sole actor doctrine applied in the partnership context.

3. RUPA did make one change to the notice provisions of UPA, which provides in § 3 that "knowledge" of a fact includes not only "actual knowledge," but also "knowledge of such fact as in the circumstances shows bad faith." By comparison, RUPA § 102(a) limits "knowledge" to "actual knowledge," thus doing away with UPA's inclusion of inquiry notice. *See Blankenship v. Smalley*, 324 P.3d 573 (Ore. App. 2014).

G. Keeping Track of Things—A Brief Look at Partnership Accounting

The financial condition of a partnership customarily is described by two distinct documents: the income statement and the balance sheet. The income statement, which also is known as the profit and loss statement, covers a defined period of time. The balance sheet shows the financial condition of a partnership at one particular point in time. It is important to read the two statements together to get a true picture of the financial condition of a business.

The income statement. This statement sets forth the revenues and the expenses of a business during an accounting period. An illustrative income statement for a retail business might read as follows:

Able and Baker Partnership Income Statement
for the Year Ending December 31, 2018

Sales		$150,000
Less returns and allowances		5,000
Net sales		$145,000
Cost of goods sold		60,000
Gross profit		85,000
Operating expenses		
Advertising	$5,000	
Depreciation	10,000	
Employee salaries	20,000	
	35,000	
Net income		$50,000

The income statement does not show an income tax because a partnership is not regarded as a separate entity for purposes of income taxation. As mentioned in Chapter 11, the partnership files only an information return.

Balance sheet. The balance sheet is a statement of assets, liabilities and the owners' equities at a given point in time. Usually the assets are shown on the left-hand side of the page and the liabilities, representing the amount owed by the business, on the right-hand side. An illustrative balance sheet is presented below.

Able and Baker Partnership Balance Sheet
December 31, 2018

Assets:		Liabilities:	
Cash	$10,000	Accounts payable	$20,000
Accounts receivable	20,000	Equity:	
Inventory	20,000	Able, capital	8,000
		Baker, capital	22,000
Total:	$50,000	Total:	$50,000

The capital account. The capital account of each partner shows the equity of the partner in the business. At the formation of the business it consists solely of the capital contribution of the partner. Conventional accounting practice adds undistributed net profits to the capital accounts of the partners at the end of each accounting period (usually a calendar year), and deducts from capital any withdrawals made during the accounting period.

UPA says nothing about accounts of the partners. RUPA states in §401, the counterpart section to §18 of UPA, that "[e]ach partner is deemed to have an account" that is credited with the net amount of the contribution and share of profits of the partner and charged with distributions to and the share of losses of the partner. An illustrative description of capital accounts is presented below.

Capital accounts	Able	Baker	Total
Investments, January 1, 2018	$10,000	$15,000	$25,000
Add:			
Additional investments	-0-	2,000	2,000
Net income for the year	$25,000	$25,000	$50,000
Totals	$35,000	$42,000	$77,000
Withdrawals	27,000	20,000	47,000
Balances, December 31, 2018	$8,000	$22,000	$30,000

In a business with more formal accounting procedures each partner would have a separate drawing account that is closed to the capital account at the end of the accounting period. Also, this illustration shows the partners dividing the net income equally. This can be varied by agreement. If retention of capital is important to the business, for example, the partners may wish to divide income in the ratio of capital accounts at the end of the year, which would discourage withdrawals. Capital accounts are regarded as debts of the firm. *See* UPA §40(b)(III). In general, see H. FINNEY & H. MILLER, PRINCIPLES OF ACCOUNTING, ADVANCED 1–16 (5th ed. 1960), on which the above illustrations were patterned.

H. Rights and Duties Among Partners

1. Fiduciary Duties

Section 21 of UPA is the starting point for addressing the fiduciary duties of partners to each other, with §20 (duty of partners to render information) and §22 (right to an account) adding to the definition of rights among partners. Although §21 is terse, focusing on personal appropriation of partnership benefits, and contains the word "fiduciary" only in its title, courts have developed a substantial body of law dealing with the fiduciary responsibilities of partners.

Section 404 of RUPA is the counterpart to UPA §21. It is a far more elaborate and complete statement of the fiduciary duties of partners, as developed below. Section 403, detailing a partner's rights and duties with respect to information, is the counterpart to UPA § 20. The right to an account is established in RUPA § 405(b). For more on the contrasting approach of UPA and RUPA on fiduciary duties, see, Mark J. Loewenstein, *Fiduciary Duties and Unincorporated Business Entities: In Defense of the "Manifestly Unreasonable" Standard*, 41 Tulsa L. Rev. 411, 412–13 (2006).

a. The Duty of Loyalty

i. Duty During Formation of Partnership

Corley v. Ott

Supreme Court of South Carolina
485 S.E.2d 97 (1997)

Moore, Justice.

This is an appeal of a final accounting between partners and an award of judgment for breach of a fiduciary duty. . . .

Appellant Ott held an option to purchase a tract of land known as Lakewood Estates. Without disclosing his option, Ott approached respondent Corley about providing the capital to purchase the land and "making some money on it." Corley agreed. On March 30, 1979, Ott signed a contract to individually purchase Lakewood Estates including 128 lots, a 34.68 acre lot called the "pond tract," and a water plant, for a purchase price of $171,200. Ott had the property transferred to a third party as trustee in order to conceal this purchase from Corley. That same day, the trustee contracted to convey the property to Ott and Corley "trading as Lakewood Associates of South Carolina, a general partnership." The purchase price was $198,200 for the same property conveyed earlier that day to Ott but without the 34.68 acre pond tract.

Both contracts called for annual installment payments on the same day. Each time an installment was paid by the Ott and Corley partnership, Ott received from the trustee the difference between the amount due on his contract and the amount due on the partnership contract. Ott received a total of $27,000 under this arrangement. He also received the 34.68 acre pond tract which was valued at $41,000 at the time of its conveyance to him.

The parties memorialized their partnership in a written partnership agreement dated September 28, 1979. In 1990, Corley commenced this action for dissolution of the partnership. Sometime during litigation, Corley discovered Ott's purchase contract and amended his complaint to allege a breach of fiduciary duty. . . .

Upon dissolution of a partnership, the liabilities of the partnership rank in order of payment as follows: third-party debts, debts to partners, return of capital to partners, profits to partners. [UPA § 40(b).] Ott contends his contributions of time and labor in improving Lakewood Estates should be credited to him as capital contributions.

[UPA § 18(f)] provides that no partner is entitled to remuneration for acting in the partnership business. Applying this provision of the Uniform Partnership Act, other courts have held that in the absence of an agreement to the contrary, a partner's services are not considered capital contributions upon dissolution. We adopt this same rule. In this case, there is no evidence of any agreement between the partners that Ott's services should be credited as capital contributions. Accordingly, the trial judge properly refused to credit them as such.

The trial judge found Ott breached his fiduciary duty to Corley by failing to disclose to Corley that he, Ott, had individually purchased Lakewood Estates, including the pond tract, for $27,000 less than the partnership paid on the same day for the same property minus the pond tract. The trial judge found Corley, who provided the capital for the purchase, was damaged in the amount of $27,000, the difference in the purchase price, plus $41,000, the value of the pond tract, for a total of $68,000.

Ott contends he breached no fiduciary duty on March 30, 1979, the date of the purchase contract, because the partnership did not yet exist as evidenced by the written partnership agreement signed September 28, 1979. We disagree.

A partnership may be found to exist by implication from the parties' conduct. On March 30, 1979, Corley and Ott entered into the purchase agreement as "Lakewood Associates of South Carolina, a general partnership." This evidence indicates the partnership was formed, at the latest, concurrently with that transaction on March 30.

Further, under [UPA § 21], a partner must account to the partnership for any benefit from any transaction connected with the formation of the partnership. In this case, Ott's prior undisclosed purchase of the property was intimately connected with the formation of the partnership and purchase of the property on March 30. Accordingly, this evidence supports the trial judge's finding that Ott breached his fiduciary duty as a partner.

Ott's remaining arguments are without merit. . . .

Affirmed.

Finney, C.J., and Toal, Waller and Burnett, JJ., concur.

Note

One of the controversial decisions made when drafting RUPA was to delete the word "formation" when describing the scope of a partner's fiduciary duties. Section 404(b)(1), which contains language closely patterned on UPA § 21, requires a partner to account for any benefit "derived by the partner in the conduct or winding up of the partnership business. . . ." By contrast, as applied in *Corley*, UPA § 21 requires a partner to account for any benefit . . . connected with the formation, conduct, or liquidation of the partnership. . . ." The explanation for the decision to delete "formation" in RUPA is contained in the Comment to § 401, stating:

"Reference to the 'formation' of the partnership has been eliminated by RUPA because of concern that the duty of loyalty could be inappropriately extended to the pre-formation period when the parties are really negotiating at arm's length. Once a partnership is agreed to, each partner becomes a fiduciary in the 'conduct' of the business."

ii. Pre-Empting Business Opportunities

Meinhard v. Salmon[6]

Court of Appeals of New York
164 N.E. 545 (1928)

Cardozo, Ch. J.

On April 10, 1902, Louisa M. Gerry leased to the defendant Walter J. Salmon the premises known as the Hotel Bristol at the northwest corner of Forty-second street and Fifth avenue in the city of New York. The lease was for a term of twenty years, commencing May 1, 1902, and ending April 30, 1922. The lessee undertook to change the hotel building for use as shops and offices at a cost of $200,000. Alterations and additions were to be accretions to the land.

Salmon, while in course of treaty with the lessor as to the execution of the lease, was in course of treaty with Meinhard, the plaintiff, for the necessary funds. The result was a joint venture with terms embodied in a writing. Meinhard was to pay to Salmon half of the moneys requisite to reconstruct, alter, manage and operate the property. Salmon was to pay to Meinhard 40 per cent of the net profits for the first five years of the lease and 50 per cent for the years thereafter. If there were losses, each party was to bear them equally. Salmon, however, was to have sole power to "manage, lease, underlet and operate" the building. There were to be certain preemptive rights for each in the contingency of death.

The two were coadventurers, subject to fiduciary duties akin to those of partners (*King v. Barnes*, 109 N.Y. 267). As to this we are all agreed. The heavier weight of duty rested, however, upon Salmon. He was a coadventurer with Meinhard, but he was manager as well. During the early years of the enterprise, the building, reconstructed, was operated at a loss. If the relation had then ended, Meinhard as well as Salmon would have carried a heavy burden. Later the profits became large with the result that for each of the investors there came a rich return. For each, the venture had its phases of fair weather and of foul. The two were in it jointly, for better or for worse.

When the lease was near its end, Elbridge T. Gerry had become the owner of the reversion. He owned much other property in the neighborhood, one lot adjoining the Bristol Building on Fifth avenue and four lots on Forty-second street. He had a plan to lease the entire tract for a long term to some one who would destroy the

---

6. Noted in 29 Colum. L. Rev. 367 (1929), 42 Harv. L. Rev. 953 (1929), 38 Yale L. Rev. 782 (1929).

buildings then existing, and put up another in their place. In the latter part of 1921, he submitted such a project to several capitalists and dealers. He was unable to carry it through with any of them. Then, in January, 1922, with less than four months of the lease to run, he approached the defendant Salmon. The result was a new lease to the Midpoint Realty Company, which is owned and controlled by Salmon, a lease covering the whole tract, and involving a huge outlay. The term is to be twenty years, but successive covenants for renewal will extend it to a maximum of eighty years at the will of either party. The existing buildings may remain unchanged for seven years. They are then to be torn down, and a new building to cost $3,000,000 is to be placed upon the site. The rental, which under the Bristol lease was only $55,000, is to be from $350,000 to $475,000 for the properties so combined. Salmon personally guaranteed the performance by the lessee of the covenants of the new lease until such time as the new building had been completed and fully paid for.

The lease between Gerry and the Midpoint Realty Company was signed and delivered on January 25, 1922. Salmon had not told Meinhard anything about it. Whatever his motive may have been, he had kept the negotiations to himself. Meinhard was not informed even of the bare existence of a project. The first that he knew of it was in February when the lease was an accomplished fact. He then made demand on the defendants that the lease be held in trust as an asset of the venture, making offer upon the trial to share the personal obligations incidental to the guaranty. The demand was followed by refusal, and later by this suit. A referee gave judgment for the plaintiff, limiting the plaintiff's interest in the lease, however, to 25 per cent. The limitation was on the theory that the plaintiff's equity was to be restricted to one-half of so much of the value of the lease as was contributed or represented by the occupation of the Bristol site. Upon cross-appeals to the Appellate Division, the judgment was modified so as to enlarge the equitable interest to one-half of the whole lease. With this enlargement of plaintiff's interest, there went, of course, a corresponding enlargement of his attendant obligations. The case is now here on an appeal by the defendants.

Joint adventurers, like copartners, owe to one another, while the enterprise continues, the duty of the finest loyalty. Many forms of conduct permissible in a workaday world for those acting at arm's length, are forbidden to those bound by fiduciary ties. A trustee is held to something stricter than the morals of the market place. Not honesty alone, but the punctilio of an honor the most sensitive, is then the standard of behavior. As to this there has developed a tradition that is unbending and inveterate. Uncompromising rigidity has been the attitude of courts of equity when petitioned to undermine the rule of undivided loyalty by the "disintegrating erosion" of particular exceptions (*Wendt v. Fischer*, 243 N.Y. 439, 444). Only thus has the level of conduct for fiduciaries been kept at a level higher than that trodden by the crowd. It will not consciously be lowered by any judgment of this court.

The owner of the reversion, Mr. Gerry, had vainly striven to find a tenant who would favor his ambitious scheme of demolition and construction. Baffled in the search, he turned to the defendant Salmon in possession of the Bristol, the keystone of the project. He figured to himself beyond a doubt that the man in possession would prove a likely customer. To the eye of an observer, Salmon held the lease as owner in his own right, for himself and no one else. In fact he held it as a fiduciary, for himself and another, sharers in a common venture. If this fact had been proclaimed, if the lease by its terms had run in favor of a partnership, Mr. Gerry, we may fairly assume, would have laid before the partners, and not merely before one of them, his plan of reconstruction. The pre-emptive privilege, or, better, the preemptive opportunity, that was thus an incident of the enterprise, Salmon appropriated to himself in secrecy and silence. He might have warned Meinhard that the plan had been submitted, and that either would be free to compete for the award. If he had done this, we do not need to say whether he would have been under a duty, if successful in the competition, to hold the lease so acquired for the benefit of a venture then about to end, and thus prolong by indirection its responsibilities and duties. The trouble about his conduct is that he excluded his coadventurer from any chance to compete, from any chance to enjoy the opportunity for benefit that had come to him alone by virtue of his agency. This chance, if nothing more, he was under a duty to concede. The price of its denial is an extension of the trust at the option and for the benefit of the one whom he excluded.

No answer is it to say that the chance would have been of little value even if seasonably offered. Such a calculus of probabilities is beyond the science of the chancery.... The very fact that Salmon was in control with exclusive powers of direction charged him the more obviously with the duty of disclosure, since only through disclosure could opportunity be equalized. If he might cut off renewal by a purchase for his own benefit when four months were to pass before the lease would have an end, he might do so with equal right while there remained as many years (cf. *Mitchell v. Reed*, 61 N.Y. 123, 127). He might steal a march on his comrade under cover of the darkness, and then hold the captured ground. Loyalty and comradeship are not so easily abjured....

We have no thought to hold that Salmon was guilty of a conscious purpose to defraud. Very likely he assumed in all good faith that with the approaching end of the venture he might ignore his coadventurer and take the extension for himself. He had given to the enterprise time and labor as well as money. He had made it a success. Meinhard, who had given money, but neither time nor labor, had already been richly paid. There might seem to be something grasping in his insistence upon more. Such recriminations are not unusual when coadventurers fall out. They are not without their force if conduct is to be judged by the common standards of competitors. That is not to say that they have pertinency here. Salmon had put himself in a position in which thought of self was to be renounced, however hard the abnegation. He was much more than a coadventurer. He was a managing coadventurer. For him and for those like him, the rule of undivided loyalty is relentless and supreme. A different question would be here if there were lacking any nexus of relation between the business conducted by the manager and the opportunity brought to him as an incident of management. For this problem, as for most, there are distinctions of degree. If Salmon had received from Gerry a proposition to lease a building at a location far removed, he might have held for himself the privilege thus acquired, or so we shall assume. Here the subject-matter of the new lease was an extension and enlargement of the subject-matter of the old one. A managing coadventurer appropriating the benefit of such a lease without warning to his partner might fairly expect to be reproached with conduct that was underhand, or lacking, to say the least, in reasonable candor, if the partner were to surprise him in the act of signing the new instrument. Conduct subject to that reproach does not receive from equity a healing benediction.

A question remains as to the form and extent of the equitable interest to be allotted to the plaintiff. The trust as declared has been held to attach to the lease which was in the name of the defendant corporation. We think it ought to attach at the option of the defendant Salmon to the shares of stock which were owned by him or were under his control. The difference may be important if the lessee shall wish to execute an assignment of the lease, as it ought to be free to do with the consent of the lessor. On the other hand, an equal division of the shares might lead to other hardships. It might take away from Salmon the power of control and management which under the plan of the joint venture he was to have from first to last. The number of shares to be allotted to the plaintiff should, therefore, be reduced to such an extent as may be necessary to preserve to the defendant Salmon the expected measure of dominion. To that end an extra share should be added to his half. . . .

ANDREWS, J. (dissenting)

. . . I am of the opinion that the issue here is simple. Was the transaction in view of all the circumstances surrounding it unfair and inequitable? I reach this conclusion for two reasons. There was no general partnership, merely a joint venture for a limited object, to end at a fixed time. The new lease, covering additional property, containing many new and unusual terms and conditions, with a possible duration of eighty years, was more nearly the purchase of the reversion than the ordinary renewal with which the authorities are concerned. . . .

Were this a general partnership between Mr. Salmon and Mr. Meinhard I should have little doubt as to the correctness of this result assuming the new lease to be an offshoot of the old. Such a situation involves questions of trust and confidence to a high degree; it involves questions of good will; many other considerations. As has been said, rarely if ever may one partner without the knowledge of the other acquire for himself the renewal of a lease held by the firm, even if the new lease is to begin after the firm is dissolved. Warning of such an intent, if he is managing partner, may not be sufficient to prevent the application of this rule. We have here a different situation governed by less drastic principles. . . .

It seems to me that the venture so inaugurated had in view a limited object and was to end at a limited time. There was no intent to expand it into a far greater undertaking lasting for many years. The design was to exploit a particular lease. Doubtless in it Mr. Meinhard had an equitable interest, but in it alone. This interest terminated when the joint adventure terminated. There was no intent that for the benefit of both any advantage should be taken of the chance of renewal—that the adventure should be continued beyond that date. Mr. Salmon has done all he promised to do in return for Mr. Meinhard's undertaking when he distributed profits up to May 1, 1922. Suppose this lease, non-assignable without the consent of the lessor, had contained a renewal option. Could Mr. Meinhard have exercised it? Could he have insisted that Mr. Salmon do so? Had Mr. Salmon done so could he insist that the agreement to share losses still existed or could Mr. Meinhard have claimed that the joint adventure was still to continue for twenty or eighty years? I do not think so. The adventure by its express terms ended on May 1, 1922. The contract by its language and by its whole import excluded the idea that the tenant's expectancy was to subsist for the benefit of the plaintiff. On that date whatever there was left of value in the lease reverted to Mr. Salmon, as it would had the lease been for thirty years instead of twenty. Any equity which Mr. Meinhard possessed was in the particular lease itself, not in any possibility of renewal. There was nothing unfair in Mr. Salmon's conduct.

I might go further were it necessary. Under the circumstances here presented had the lease run to both the parties I doubt whether the taking by one of a renewal without the knowledge of the other would cause interference by a court of equity. An illustration may clarify my thought. A and B enter into a joint venture to resurface a highway between Albany and Schenectady. They rent a parcel of land for the storage of materials. A, unknown to B, agrees with the lessor to rent that parcel and one adjoining it after the venture is finished, for an iron foundry. Is the act unfair? Would any general statements, scattered here and there through opinions dealing with other circumstance, be thought applicable? In other words, the mere fact that the joint venturers rent property together does not call for the strict rule that applies to general partners. Many things may excuse what is there forbidden. Nor here does any possibility of renewal exist as part of the venture. The nature of the undertaking excludes such an idea.

So far I have treated the new lease as if it were a renewal of the old. As already indicated, I do not take that view. Such a renewal could not be obtained. Any expectancy that it might be had vanished. What Mr. Salmon obtained was not a graft springing from the Bristol lease, but something distinct and different—as distinct as if for a building across Fifth avenue. I think also that in the absence of some fraudulent or unfair act the secret purchase of the reversion even by one partner is rightful. Substantially this is such a purchase. Because of the mere label of a transaction we do not place it on one side of the line or the other. Here is involved the possession of a large and most valuable unit of property for eighty years, the destruction of all existing structures and the erection of a new and expensive building covering the whole. No fraud, no deceit, no calculated secrecy is found. Simply that the arrangement was made without the knowledge of Mr. Meinhard. I think this not enough. . . .

Pound, Crane and Lehman, JJ., concur with Cardozo, Ch. J., for modification of the judgment appealed from and affirmance as modified; Andrews, J., dissents in opinion in which Kellogg and O'Brien, JJ., concur.

Notes

1. It may be of interest to the reader that the building in the *Meinhard* case was not completed until after the stock market crash of 1929 and the resulting depression. As stated in *Salmon v. Commissioner*, 126 F.2d 203, 204 (2d Cir. 1942), this had the following consequences for Meinhard's estate:

> The old building had been profitable but by the time the new one was ready in 1931 the fall in the value of real estate made its operation impossible except at a loss, and Salmon and Meinhard were either compelled to pay the deficits, or to suffer the property to become unoccupied and perhaps to pass out of their hands. Meinhard had died and his estate paid to Salmon his part of the deficits. . . .

2. The duty of loyalty limits the ability of a partner to hire his or her spouse. The New York court explained that such a partner's "financial relationship with his wife conflicted with his duty to [his co-partners] and therefore violated the precept of undiluted trust at the core of his responsibilities as a fiduciary." The court said that full disclosure and consent were necessary under these circumstances. *Birnbaum v. Birnbaum*, 73 N.Y.2d 461, 541 N.Y.S.2d 746, 539 N.E.2d 574 (1989).

3. The characterization of a partner as a trustee in the majority opinion in *Meinhard* was not fully embraced by the drafters of RUPA. Their decision to draw a distinction between a partner and a trustee has generated controversy, as will be noted below.

4. In *Levy & Surrick v. Surrick*, 524 A.2d 993, 994 (Pa. Super. 1987), Surrick, a 50 percent shareholder in a professional corporation for the practice of law, purchased for private investment a mini-mall that had a long-term lease with one of the clients of the law firm. Levy, the other shareholder, brought suit in the name of the corporation alleging breach of fiduciary duty by Surrick for secretly pre-empting a business opportunity. The court held for Surrick, stating that the purchase was not within the scope of the agency relationship. "[N]othing in the record suggests that the corporation existed for any purpose other than to practice law. It was not in the land acquisition business." *See also Fuqua v. Taylor*, 683 S.W.2d 735, 738 (Tex. App. 1984) (joint venturer was under duty to inform fellow venturers of opportunity to reacquire lapsed oil and gas lease, but under no duty to inform them of acquisition of another lease two miles from the site of the lapsed lease which was outside the scope of their fiduciary relationship. "Appellees have not cited, nor have we discovered, any authority holding that mere proximity is sufficient to extend a fiduciary duty from property within the scope of a fiduciary relationship to other property."); *Dixon v. Trinity Joint Venture*, 431 A.2d 1364 (Md. App. 1981) (general partner breached fiduciary duty to inform limited partnership of opportunity to buy 10 acres of land adjacent to land partnership was developing). See also *Triple Five of Minnesota, Inc. v. Simon*, 280 F. Supp. 2d 895 (D. Minn. 2003), a case involving the Mall of America, in which plaintiff (one of the owners of the mall) successfully complained that its partner (and the individuals who controlled it) breached a fiduciary duty to plaintiff by acquiring the partnership interest of another partner without providing plaintiff the opportunity to participate in the acquisition. A few aspects of *Triple Five* are worth noting. First, the person that actually acquired the partnership interest in question was technically not plaintiff's partner. The court had little trouble with this defense because the acquirer was controlled by the same people who controlled the defendant partner, holding that a "fiduciary duty may be imputed to officers and directors of the general partner company." *Id.* at 900. Second, the partnership agreement provided that no partner would be liable to any other partner except in the case of fraud or gross negligence, and the defendant argued that the plaintiff alleged neither. The court agreed with the defendant, but held that while partners can structure their relationship as they desire, "they are not free to destroy its fiduciary character." *Id.* at 901. The disclaimer of fiduciary duties is considered later in this section. Finally, on plaintiff's usurpation claim, the court held that plaintiff bore the burden of proving that it had the financial wherewithal to participate in the acquisition, rejecting the argument that lack of financial ability was an affirmative defense. In this case, however, the evidence clearly established plaintiff's financial ability, rendering moot the procedural question of who bore the burden of proof. On appeal, the court of appeals affirmed the district court's holding on breach of fiduciary duty, but reversed and remanded on the issue of remedy. *Triple Five of Minnesota, Inc. v. Simon*, 404 F.3d 1088 (8th Cir. 2005).

5. Judge Cardozo's emphasis on Salmon's greater responsibilities as managing partner is supported by other authorities. *See, e.g., Wirum & Case Architects v. Cash*, 837 P.2d 692 (Alaska 1992) (extensive treatment of the duties of a managing partner). *See also Pohl v. National Benefits Consultants, Inc.*, 956 F.2d 126, 128–29 (7th Cir. 1992) ("A fiduciary is an agent who is required to treat his principal with utmost loyalty and care — treat him, indeed, as if the principal were himself. The reason for the duty is clearest when the agent has a broad discretion the exercise of which the principal cannot feasibly supervise, so that the principal is at the agent's mercy.").

6. It was noted earlier that in the view of the reporter for UPA, based on the observation of those with "the largest practical experience" present at a meeting to discuss the theory of UPA, a shift to the entity theory would result "in lessening the partner's sense of moral responsibility for partnership acts." It can be argued that operating in LLP form would intensify that concern. If so, with regard to internal relations, would this intensify or weaken the need to have strong fiduciary duties?

7. Fiduciary duties can be created by contract. For instance, in *Deloitte LLP v. Flanagan*, 2009 Del. Ch. LEXIS 220 (Dec. 29, 2009), the partners in an accounting firm agreed not to trade in the securities of the firm's audit clients. The defendant in this action breached that agreement as well as a companion provision that required him to accurately report his holdings in such securities. The court concluded that defendant's "conduct here-in particular, his misrepresentations with respect to his holdings-suffices to constitute a breach of his duty to be 'just and faithful to the Partnership' [as the agreement provided]. Thus, Deloitte's motion for summary judgment on its breach of fiduciary duty claim is granted."

iii. Leaving the Business

A well-known case, *Meehan v. Shaughnessy*, 535 N.E.2d 1255 (Mass. 1989), involved extensive treatment of the fiduciary duties of partners leaving a law partnership. In this case two partners (Meehan and Boyle) left a law firm (Parker Coulter), taking with them several associates and 142 of the 350 contingent fee cases pending at the time. Prior to leaving, they denied their intent to leave. Also, once they announced their intent to leave, the remaining partners asked them for a list of the cases they intended to remove. They stalled in responding to this request and in the meantime vigorously solicited the clients involved. Litigation ensued between the firm and its former partners. In its opinion, the court stated the following with regard to the fiduciary duty implications of Meehan's and Boyle's conduct:

> ... Parker Coulter argues ... that Meehan and Boyle breached their fiduciary duties by unfairly acquiring consent from clients to remove cases from Parker Coulter. We agree that Meehan and Boyle, through their preparation for obtaining clients consent, their secrecy concerning which clients they intended to take, and the substance and method of their communications with clients, obtained an unfair advantage over their former partners in breach of their fiduciary duties.

> A partner has an obligation to "render on demand true and full information of all things affecting the partnership to any partner." [UPA] § 20. On three separate occasions Meehan affirmatively denied to his partners, on their demand, that he had any plans for leaving the partnership. During this period of secrecy, Meehan and Boyle made preparations for obtaining removal authorizations from clients. ...

> On giving their notice, Meehan and Boyle continued to use their position of trust and confidence to the disadvantage of Parker Coulter. The two immediately began communicating with clients and referring attorneys. Boyle delayed providing his partners with a list of clients he intended to solicit until mid-December, by which time he had obtained authorization from a majority of the clients.

> Finally, the content of the letter sent to the clients was unfairly prejudicial to Parker Coulter. [The trial judge] found that the notice did not "clearly present to the clients the choice they had between remaining at Parker Coulter or moving to the new firm." By sending a one-side announcement, on Parker Coulter letterhead, so soon after notice of their departure, Meehan and Boyle excluded their partners from effectively presenting their services as an alternative to those of Meehan and Boyle.

Meehan and Boyle could have foreseen that the news of their departure would cause a certain amount of confusion and disruption among their partners. The speed and preemptive character of their campaign to acquire clients' consent took advantage of their partners' confusion. By engaging in these preemptive tactics, Meehan and Boyle violated the duty of utmost good faith and loyalty which they owed their partners. . . .

In these circumstances, it is appropriate to place on the party who improperly removed the case the burden of proving that the client would have consented to removal in the absence of any breach of duty. . . . [R]equiring [Meehan and Boyle] to disprove causation will encourage partners in the future to disclose seasonably and fully any plans to remove cases. This disclosure will allow the partnership and the departing partner an equal opportunity to present to clients the option of continuing with the partnership or retaining the departing partner individually.[7]

. . . .

Meehan and Boyle breached the duty they owed to Parker Coulter. If the judge determines that, as a result of this breach, certain clients left the firm, Meehan and Boyle must account to the partnership for any profits they receive on these cases pursuant to [UPA § 21]. . . .

Id. at 1263–70; *see* Robert W. Hillman, *Loyalty in the Firm: A Statement of General Principles on the Duties of Partners Withdrawing from Law Firms*, 55 WASH. & LEE L. REV. 997 (1998).

Note

In *Phil Watson, P.C. v. Peterson*, 650 N.W.2d 562 (Iowa 2002), an associate (Peterson) left a law firm (Watson) and persuaded a number of clients for whom he was handling matters (both contingent fee and hourly matters) to retain him when he moved to his new firm (EVP). Watson claimed that Peterson and EVP owed him his lost profits on the cases that Peterson took: "the fees it would have realized if the clients had not left the firm, less Peterson's salary and expenses the firm would have incurred in earning the fees." *Id.* at 567. While the trial court agreed with this argument, and awarded plaintiff Watson approximately $115,000, the Iowa Supreme Court reversed, holding that Watson was entitled only to a quantum meruit recovery, and "the proper way to calculate the division of the contingency fees is to award Watson a percentage of each fee based on the percentage of time Peterson spent on each case at Watson compared to the time spent on the case at EVP." Id. The court calculated that, based on this formula, Watson's share of contingent fee cases would

---

7. [16] As between the attorneys, a mutual letter, from both the partnership and the departing partner, outlining the separation plans and the clients' right to choose, would be an appropriate means of opening the discussion between the attorneys and their clients concerning the clients' choice of continuing representation.

be $34,240 and on the noncontingent fee cases (which were billed on an hourly rate), $16,726.

Gibbs v. Breed, Abbott & Morgan

Supreme Court of New York, Appellate Division
710 N.Y.S.2d 578 (2000)

Ernst H. Rosenberger, J.P., Angela M. Mazzarelli, Richard W. Wallach, Alfred D. Lerner and David B. Saxe, JJ.

Mazzarelli, J.

Plaintiffs Charles Gibbs and Robert Sheehan are former partners of Breed Abbott & Morgan ("BAM") who specialize in trust and estate law. They withdrew from BAM in July 1991 to join Chadbourne & Parke ("Chadbourne"), and brought this action for monies due to them under their BAM partnership agreement. Defendants asserted various counterclaims alleging that plaintiffs breached their fiduciary duty to BAM. The counterclaims were severed and tried without a jury. Plaintiffs appeal from the trial court's determination [693 N.Y.S.2d 426] that, in the course of both partners' planning and eventually implementing their withdrawal from BAM, they breached their fiduciary duty to the partnership. Plaintiffs also appeal from the trial court's determination that $1,861,045 in damages resulted from these transgressions.

From January 1991 until July 1991, plaintiffs were the only partners in the Trusts and Estates department ("T/E") at BAM; plaintiff Gibbs was the head of the department. A third partner, Paul Lambert, had been the former head of the department, and he had obtained many, if not most of the department's clients. In 1989 he had left the firm to become the United States Ambassador to Ecuador and was still on leave in 1991. Lambert intended to return to the firm upon completion of his term as ambassador. The BAM trusts and estates department also employed three associate attorneys, Warren Whitaker (fifteenth year), Austin Wilkie (fourth year), and Joseph Scorese (first year); two accountants, Lois Wetzel and Ellen Furst; and two paralegals, Lee Ann Riley and Ruth Kramer.

Gibbs had become dissatisfied with BAM, and in January 1991 he began interviews to locate a new affiliation. He also approached Sheehan to persuade him to move with him. Sheehan and Gibbs subsequently conducted a number of joint interviews with prospective employers. In May 1991, Ambassador Lambert visited BAM, and Gibbs told him that he had been interviewing. Lambert relayed this information to the other partners. In early June, plaintiffs informed the executive committee that they had received an offer from two firms: McDermott, Will & Emory and Bryan Cave.

On June 19, 1991, both plaintiffs informed Stephen Lang, BAM's presiding partner, that they had accepted offers to join Chadbourne. Lang asked Gibbs not to discuss his departure with any of the T/E associates, and Gibbs agreed not to do so. On

June 20, 1991, Lawrence Warble, a BAM partner who was named temporary head of the T/E department, met with its associates and non-legal personnel to inform them that plaintiffs were leaving the firm.

On June 24, 1991, Gibbs and Sheehan sent Chadbourne a memo listing the names of the personnel in the T/E department of BAM, their respective salaries, their annual billable hours, and the rate at which BAM billed out these employees to clients. The memo included other information about the attorneys, including the colleges and law schools they attended, and their bar admissions. This list had been prepared by Sheehan on April 26, 1991, months before the partners announced they were leaving. Sheehan specifically testified that the memo was prepared in anticipation of discussions with prospective firms, and both Gibbs and Sheehan testified at trial that the recruitment of certain associates and support personnel was discussed with different firms between March and May, as the partners were considering various affiliations. While Gibbs and Sheehan were still partners at BAM, Chadbourne interviewed four BAM employees that Gibbs had indicated he was interested in bringing to Chadbourne with him. On June 27, 1991, plaintiffs submitted their written resignations. Before Gibbs and Sheehan left BAM, they wrote letters to clients served by them, advising that they were leaving BAM and that other attorneys at BAM could serve them. These letters did not mention the fact that the two partners were moving to Chadbourne. Although the partnership agreement required 45 days notice of an intention to withdraw, BAM waived this provision upon plaintiffs' production of their final billings for work previously performed.[8] Gibbs left BAM on July 9, 1991, and Sheehan left on July 11, 1991, both taking various documents, including their respective "chronology" or desk files.[9] With the assistance of his chronology file, Gibbs began to contact his former clients on July 11, 1991. On July 11th, Chadbourne made employment offers to Whitaker, Wilkie, Wetzel, and Riley. Wilkie, Wetzel, and Riley accepted that same day; Whitaker accepted on July 15, 1991. In the following weeks, 92 of the 201 BAM T/E clients moved their business to Chadbourne.

After hearing all the testimony and the parties' arguments, the trial court determined that Gibbs' actions in persuading his partner Sheehan to leave BAM, "and the way in which the leave was orchestrated, were done, at least partially, with the

---

8. [1] BAM did not attempt to prepare a joint letter with Gibbs and Sheehan, announcing their departure, as recommended by the American Bar Association Committee on Ethics and Professional Responsibility (see, ABA Comm. on Ethics and Professional Responsibility, Informal Op. 1457 (1980)).

9. [2] The "chronology" or desk files contained copies of every letter written by the respective attorneys during the previous years. The letters included those written to adversaries about pending legal matters, letters written to clients, and letters written to others about ongoing BAM matters. These letters were duplicates of those kept in BAM's regular client files, but defendants allege that due to the fact that the files are arranged chronologically, active matters are more easily referenced. The original correspondences, left with the firm, have been filed by client and are dispersed throughout the department.

intention of crippling BAM's Trusts and Estates ("T/E") department", and constituted a breach of loyalty to BAM. The court also found that Gibbs and Sheehan had breached their fiduciary duties to BAM by sending Chadbourne the April 26, 1991 memo detailing personal information about the individuals in the T/E Department at BAM, because this gave Chadbourne a competitive advantage in offering employment to other members of the department. Finally, the court found that Gibbs and Sheehan breached their fiduciary duties to BAM by taking their chronology files with them to Chadbourne. Specifically, the court concluded that by taking their respective chronology files, the partners "to a large degree hobbled their former partners in their effort to rebuild the Trusts and Estates department, in order to maintain a viable department, and in their ability to serve clients without undue disruption."

With respect to damages, the court concluded that both Gibbs and Sheehan were entitled to recover their share of BAM profits accruing until the end of July 1991, and that Sheehan was entitled to the remainder of his capital account with the firm. Although there was no evidence that the partners had improperly solicited former BAM clients, the court found that despite BAM's efforts to mitigate damages by hiring a new partner and two associates into the T/E Department, that department suffered financial losses as a result of plaintiffs' conduct, and concluded that it was entitled to recover lost profits for a reasonable period following plaintiffs' departure. The court directed that lost profits be calculated from July 1991, when the partners left the firm, to November 1993, when BAM dissolved. Gibbs and Sheehan were held jointly and severally liable for $1,861,045. The court also awarded defendants prejudgment interest and attorneys' fees. The court's liability finding should be modified, the damage award vacated, and the matter remanded for a determination of the financial loss, if any, occasioned by plaintiffs' disloyal act of supplying competitors with BAM's confidential employee data.

The members of a partnership owe each other a duty of loyalty and good faith, and "[a]s a fiduciary, a partner must consider his or her partners' welfare, and refrain from acting for purely private gain" (*Meehan v. Shaughnessy*, 404 Mass. 419, 434, 535 N.E.2d 1255). Partners are constrained by such duties throughout the life of the partnership and "[t]he manner in which partners plan for and implement withdrawals . . . is [still] subject to the constraints imposed on them by virtue of their status as fiduciaries" (Robert Hillman, *Loyalty in the Firm: A Statement of General Principles on the Duties of Partners Withdrawing From Law Firms*, 55 WASH & LEE L. REV. 997 [1998]). According the trial court's findings on issues of fact and credibility appropriate deference, we uphold that portion of the court's liability determination which found that plaintiffs breached their fiduciary duty as partners of the firm they were about to leave by supplying confidential employee information to Chadbourne while still partners at BAM. However, we find no breach with respect to Gibbs' interactions with Sheehan, or with respect to either partner's removal of his desk files from BAM.

Defendants did not establish that Gibbs breached any duty to BAM by discussing with Sheehan a joint move to another firm, or that Sheehan's decision was based upon anything other than his own personal interests. In addition, while in certain situations "[A] lawyer's removal or copying, without the firm's consent, of materials from a law firm that do not belong to the lawyer, that are the property of the law firm, and that are intended by the lawyer to be used in his new affiliation, could constitute dishonesty, which is professional misconduct under [Model] Rule 8.4(c)" (D.C. Bar Legal Ethics Comm. Op. 273 at 192), here, the partners took their desk copies of recent correspondence with the good faith belief that they were entitled to do so.

Contrary to the finding of the trial court, and applying the principle that "[t]he distinction between motive and process is critical to a realistic application of fiduciary duties" (*Hillman, supra* at 999), we find no breach of duty in plaintiffs' taking their desk files. These were comprised of duplicates of material maintained in individual client files, the partnership agreement was silent as to these documents, and removal was apparently common practice for departing attorneys (*compare, Graubard, supra* [86 N.Y.2d 112] at 121, 629 N.Y.S.2d 1009, 653 N.E.2d 1179 ["abandoning the firm on short notice (taking clients and files) would not be consistent with a partner's fiduciary duties"]; *Kaufman v. IBM*, 97 A.D.2d 925, 470 N.Y.S.2d 720, *affd*. 61 N.Y.2d 930, 474 N.Y.S.2d 721, 463 N.E.2d 37 [employee who had been working with trade secrets and had signed an agreement that his files belonged to his employer denied injunction barring firm from keeping certain documents from him upon his termination]; *Matter of Cupples*, 952 S.W.2d 226; 1997 Mo. LEXIS 71 [attorney committed professional misconduct by secreting client litigation files from his partners, and appropriating cases to himself in preparation for withdrawal]).

However, the record supports the court's finding that both partners committed a breach of their fiduciary duty to the BAM partners by supplying Chadbourne, and presumably the other partnerships they considered joining, with the April 26, 1991 memorandum describing the members of BAM's T/E department, their salaries, and other confidential information such as billing rates and average billable hours, taken from personnel files. Moreover, a closer examination of the record does not support the dissent's conclusion that these partners did not engage in surreptitious recruiting. The partners may not have discussed with firm employees the possibility of moving with them prior to June 20, 1991, but they indicated to Chadbourne the employees they were interested in prior to this date, and Gibbs specifically testified that he refrained from telling one of his partners, to whom he had a duty of loyalty, about his future plans to recruit specific associates and support staff from the partnership.

There is no evidence of improper client solicitation in this case, nor is it an issue on this appeal. Although the analogy could be useful in concluding that Gibbs did not breach his fiduciary duty to the partnership by working with Sheehan to find a new affiliation, the fiduciary restraints upon a partner with respect to client solicitation are not analogous to those applicable to employee recruitment. By contrast to the lawyer-client relationship, a partner does not have a fiduciary duty to the employees of a firm which would limit its duty of loyalty to the partnership. Thus, recruitment of firm employees has been viewed as distinct and "permissible on a more limited basis than . . . solicitation of clients" (*Hillman, supra* at 1031). Pre-withdrawal recruitment is generally allowed "only after the firm has been given notice of the lawyer's intention to withdraw" (*id.*).

However, here, Sheehan prepared a memo in April of 1991, well in advance of even deciding, much less informing his partners, of his intention to withdraw. There is ample support in the record for the trial court's finding that the preparation and sending of the April 26, 1991 memo, combined with the subsequent hiring of certain trusts and estates personnel, constituted an egregious breach of plaintiff's fiduciary duty to BAM. Moreover, it is not speculative to infer more widespread dissemination given Sheehan's trial testimony that the memo "was prepared in connection with talking to other firms", and that "he was sure the subject of staffing was discussed at firms other than Chadbourne". Sheehan's disclosure of confidential BAM data to even one firm was a direct breach of his duty of loyalty to his partners. Because the memo gave Chadbourne confidential BAM employment data as well as other information reflecting BAM's valuation of each employee, Chadbourne was made privy to information calculated to give it an unfair advantage in recruiting certain employees (*see, Bancroft-Whitney Co. v. Glen*, 64 Cal.2d 327, 49 Cal. Rptr. 825, 411 P.2d 921 [breach of fiduciary duty for corporate officer to surreptitiously provide competitor with selective list of qualified employees and their salaries]).

While partners may not be restrained from inviting qualified personnel to change firms with them (*see, Denburg v. Parker Chapin Flattau & Klimpl*, 82 N.Y.2d 375, 382, 604 N.Y.S.2d 900, 624 N.E.2d 995 [striking down provision which would restrain partner from competing with his former firm] *citing, Jacob v. Norris, McLaughlin & Marcus*, 128 N.J. 10, 607 A.2d 142 [striking down provision which would prohibit partner form soliciting firm employees for a year after leaving the firm]), here Gibbs and Sheehan began their recruiting while still members of the firm and prior to serving notice of their intent to withdraw. They did so without informing their partners that they were disseminating confidential firm data to competitors. Their actions, while still members of the firm, were intended to and did place BAM in the position of not knowing which of their employees were targets and what steps would be appropriate for them to take in order to retain these critical employees. The dissent's analysis, that once the firm was notified of the partners' departure, there was no breach of fiduciary duty, is flawed. The breach occurred in April of 1991 and could not be cured by any after-the-fact notification by the fiduciary who committed the breach that he was withdrawing from the firm. Chadbourne still had the unfair advantage of the confidential information from the April 1991 memo, and still had the upper hand, which was manifested by its ability to tailor its offers and incentives to the BAM recruits.

Contrary to the dissent, I would characterize the memo distributed to prospective competitors as confidential. The data was obtained from BAM personnel files which Sheehan had unique access to as a BAM partner. The dissent's statement that such financial information is generally known to "headhunters" is without foundation. While the broad outlines of the partners' profits at a select number of large

New York firms and the incremental increases in the base compensation of young associates at some firms are published in professional publications such as the New York Law Journal, or known to some recruitment firms, the available figures often vary substantially from the actual compensation received by specific individuals.

For example, the BAM partnership agreement, which is included in the record, reveals that the approximately 40 partners in the firm earn substantially different percentages of the firm's earnings. No professional publication would be privy to these financials. With respect to the specific associates and support staff whose compensation was disseminated in the April 1991 memo, the information disclosed to Chadbourne incorporated these individuals' bonuses. Bonus payments are confidential, often voted by the partnership, based upon the unique quality of an individual's work, the number of hours billed, and many other intangible factors. These lump sum payments often constitute a substantial portion of an associate's salary, and the payments are certainly not available to the public. Finally, support staff also receive bonuses paid to them at the discretion of the individual partners, from their personal accounts. This information is highly individualized and also privileged. Sheehan abused his fiduciary duty to the partnership by accessing personnel files to obtain the actual gross compensation of the associates and support staff he and Gibbs wished to bring with them, including bonuses, and disclosing this information to Chadbourne.

Moreover, the memo contained more than a list of salaries. It itemized each of the employees' annual billable hours, and the rates at which BAM billed these employees out to their clients, information which was not otherwise publicly available. These facts go directly to a potential employee's value and were accessible only to members of the BAM partnership. Selected partners providing BAM's confidential information, which they were able to obtain by virtue of their position as fiduciaries, to Chadbourne was an act of disloyalty to their partnership. The confidential information placed Chadbourne, as a competing prospective employer, in the advantageous position of conducting interviews of the associates and support staff with more knowledge than any firm could obtain through independent research, as well as providing it with information BAM partners did not know it had, thereby prejudicing their own efforts to retain their associates and support staff.

The calculation of damages in cases such as this is difficult. "[B]reaches of a fiduciary relationship in any context comprise a special breed of cases that often loosen normally stringent requirements of causation and damages" (*Milbank, Tweed, Hadley & McCloy v. Boon*, 13 F.3d 537, 543 [2d Cir. 1994]. This is because the purpose of this type of action "'is not merely to *compensate* the plaintiff for wrongs committed . . . [but also] to *prevent* them, by removing from agents and trustees all inducement to attempt dealing for their own benefit in matters which they have undertaken for others, or to which their agency or trust relates'" (*Diamond v. Oreamuno*, 24 N.Y.2d 494, 498, 301 N.Y.S.2d 78, 248 N.E.2d 910, [emphasis in original]. However, the proponent of a claim for a breach of fiduciary duty must, at a minimum, establish that the offending parties' actions were "a substantial factor" in causing an identifiable loss (*see, Milbank, supra*).

A reasonable assessment of lost profits has been deemed an appropriate measure of damages in cases where there was evidence that the fiduciary improperly solicited clients to move with him or her (*see, Meehan, supra* at 435, 535 N.E.2d 1255), or where the fiduciary's acts could otherwise be connected to a subsequent loss of business. Here, the court based its damage award on what it believed to be a series of disloyal acts. Defendants did not establish how the only act of plaintiffs which this Court finds to be disloyal, that of supplying employee information to Chadbourne, in and of itself, was a substantial cause of BAM's lost profits. We therefore vacate the court's award to defendants of the total profits lost by BAM between the time of plaintiffs' departure in July 1991 and BAM's dissolution in November 1993, and remand for consideration of the issue of whether plaintiffs' disloyal act of sending Chadbourne the April 26, 1991 memorandum was a significant cause of any identifiable loss, and, if so, the amount of such loss.

Accordingly, the order, Supreme Court, New York County (Herman Cahn, J.), entered October 1, 1998, which, after a nonjury trial on defendants' counterclaims, determined that plaintiffs had breached their fiduciary duty to defendants, should be modified, on the law, to limit such conclusion to the act of disseminating confidential employee information, and otherwise affirmed, without costs. Order, same court and Justice, entered on or about June 29, 1999, which, to the extent appealed from as limited by the parties' briefs, directed that defendants shall recover $1,861,045, plus pre-judgment interest, on their counterclaims, should be reversed, on the law, without costs, the damage award vacated, and the matter remanded for recalculation of damages in accordance with this Opinion.

All concur except WALLACH and SAXE, JJ. who concur in part and dissent in part in an Opinion by SAXE, J.

iv. Dealing with Conflicts of Interest

RUPA §404(b) provides that a partner's duty of loyalty is *limited* to three specified duties: the duty to account for partnership property, the duty to refrain from dealing with the partnership as or on behalf of an adverse party, and the duty to refrain from competing with the partnership. Some states, including California, altered the language of §404 to provide that a partner's duty of loyalty *included* those three duties, implying that the duty of loyalty may include other duties. The California Court of Appeals, in *Enea v. Superior Court*, 132 Cal. App. 4th 1559 (Cal. App. 2005), so held in a case in which a partner leased partnership property to himself at less than fair market value. Analyzing the official and California versions of RUPA, the court wrote:

> Despite the numerous diversions offered by defendants, the case presents a very simple set of facts and issues. For present purposes it must be assumed that defendants in fact leased the property to themselves, or associated entities, at below-market rents. Defendants made no attempt to establish otherwise, let alone to establish the absence of triable issues of fact on the point. Therefore the sole question presented is whether defendants

were categorically entitled to lease partnership property to themselves, or associated entities (or for that matter, to anyone) at less than it could yield in the open market. Remarkably, we have found no case squarely addressing this precise question. We are satisfied, however, that the answer is a resounding "No."

The defining characteristic of a partnership is the combination of two or more persons to jointly conduct business. It is hornbook law that in forming such an arrangement the partners obligate themselves to share risks and benefits and to carry out the enterprise with the highest good faith toward one another—in short, with the loyalty and care of a fiduciary. "'Partnership is a fiduciary relationship, and partners are held to the standards and duties of a trustee in their dealings with each other. . . . [I]n all proceedings connected with the conduct of the partnership every partner is bound to act in the highest good faith to his copartner and may not obtain any advantage over him in the partnership affairs by the slightest misrepresentation, concealment, threat or adverse pressure of any kind.' [Citations.]'" (*BT-I v. Equitable Life Assurance Society* (1999) 75 Cal.App.4th 1406, 1410–1411, 89 Cal.Rptr.2d 811, quoting *Leff v. Gunter* (1983) 33 Cal.3d 508, 514, 189 Cal. Rptr. 377, 658 P.2d 740.) Or to put the point more succinctly, "Partnership is a fiduciary relationship, and partners may not take advantages for themselves at the expense of the partnership." (*Jones v. Wells Fargo Bank* (2003) 112 Cal.App.4th 1527, 1540, 5 Cal.Rptr.3d 835; see *Jones v. H.F. Ahmanson & Co.* (1969) 1 Cal.3d 93, 108, 111, 81 Cal.Rptr. 592, 460 P.2d 464.)

Here the facts as assumed by the parties and the trial court plainly depict defendants taking advantages for themselves from partnership property *at the expense of the partnership*. The advantage consisted of occupying partnership property at below-market rates, i.e., less than they would be required to pay to an independent landlord for equivalent premises. The cost to the partnership was the additional rent thereby rendered unavailable for collection from an independent tenant willing to pay the property's value.

Defendants' objections to this reasoning ring hollow. Their main argument appears to be that their conduct was authorized by [the California version of RUPA § 404], which codifies the fiduciary duties of a partner under California law. The implication of such an argument is that [the California version of RUPA § 404] provides the *exclusive* statement of a partner's obligation to the partnership and to other partners. This premise would be correct if California had adopted, in its proposed form, the uniform law on which [the California version of RUPA § 404] is based. Section 404 of the Uniform Partnership Act (1997), also known as the Revised Uniform Partnership Act or RUPA, contains an explicitly exclusive enumeration of a partner's duties. After noting that a partner owes fiduciary duties of loyalty and care, the uniform Act declares that those duties are "limited to" obligations listed there. [RUPA, §404(b) and (c)] While [the California version of RUPA §404] retains this language with respect to the duty of care, it repudiates it with respect to the duty of loyalty, stating instead that "... [a] partner's duty of loyalty to the partnership and the other partners *includes* all of the following: ..." (Italics added.)

The leading treatise on RUPA confirms that by altering the proposed language, the California Legislature rejected one of the "fundamental" changes the drafters sought to bring to partnership law, i.e., "an exclusive statutory treatment of partners' fiduciary duties." (Hillman, et al., The Revised Uniform Partnership Act (2004 ed.), p. 202.) The proposed uniform version "[b]y its terms ... comprises an exclusive statement of the fiduciary duties of partners among themselves and to the partnership. The formulation is exclusive in two ways; the duties of loyalty and care are the only components of the partners' fiduciary duties, and the duties themselves are exclusively defined." (*Ibid.*, fns. omitted.) But several states, *most clearly California*, balked at the latter restriction, leaving the articulation of the duty of loyalty to traditional common law processes. "Some adopting states ... modified the RUPA language in ways which make, or arguably make, the fiduciary duty formulation non-exclusive. [Citation.] The available California legislative history states that: '[the California version of RUPA §404] establishes a *comprehensive, but not exhaustive, definition* of partnership fiduciary duties. A partner owes *at least two* duties to other partners and the partnership: a duty of loyalty and a duty of care. In addition, an obligation of good faith and fair dealing is imposed on partners.' [Citation] This reading is also supported by the drafters' conclusion in the legislative history that 'the new fiduciary duty section makes no substantive change from prior law.' [Citation.]" (*Ibid.*, fn. 5, quoting Senate Rules Com., Off. of Sen. Floor Analyses, 3d reading analysis of Assem. Bill No. 583 (1995–1996 Reg. Sess.) as amended Aug. 23, 1996, p. 6, some italics added.)

Further, even if the statutory enumeration of duties were exclusive it would not entitle defendants to rent partnership property to themselves at below-market rates. The first duty listed in the statute is "[t]o account to the partnership and hold as trustee for it *any property, profit, or benefit* derived by the partner in the conduct ... of the partnership business or *derived from a use by the partner of partnership property. ...*"

Defendants persuaded the trial court that the conduct challenged by plaintiff was authorized by [the California version of RUPA §404], which states, "A partner does not violate a duty or obligation under this chapter or under the partnership agreement merely because the partner's conduct furthers the partner's own interest." The apparent purpose of this provision, which is drawn verbatim from RUPA section 404(e), is to excuse partners from accounting for incidental benefits obtained in the course of partnership activities *without detriment to the partnership.*[10] It does not by its terms authorize the kind of conduct at issue here, which did not "merely" further defendants' own interests but did so by depriving the partnership of valuable assets, i.e., the space which would otherwise have been rented at market rates. Here, the statute entitled defendants to lease partnership property *at the same rent another tenant would have paid.* It did not empower them to occupy partnership property for their own exclusive benefit at partnership expense, in effect converting partnership assets to their own and appropriating the value it would otherwise have realized as distributable profits. Defendants' argument to the contrary seems conceptually indistinguishable from a claim that if a partnership's "primary purpose" is to purchase and hold investments, individual partners may freely pilfer its office supplies.

Defendants also persuaded the trial court that they had no duty to collect market rents in the absence of a contract expressly requiring them to do so. This argument turns partnership law on its head. Nowhere does the law declare that partners owe each other only those duties they explicitly assume by contract. On the contrary, the fiduciary duties at issue here are *imposed by law,* and their breach sounds in tort. We have no occasion here to consider the extent to which partners might effectively limit or modify those delictual duties by an explicit agreement or whether the partnership agreement in fact required market rents by its terms. There is no suggestion that it purported to affirmatively *excuse* defendants from the delictual duty not to engage in self-dealing. Instead, their argument is predicated on the wholly untenable notion that they were entitled to do so unless the agreement explicitly declared otherwise.

Defendants also assert, and the trial court found, that the "primary purpose" of the partnership was to hold the building for appreciation and eventual sale. This premise hardly justified summary adjudication. If the partners had explicitly agreed *not* to derive market rents from the property, but to let it be used for the exclusive advantage of some of them indefinitely,

---

10. [3] The authors of the above-cited treatise note that this provision has received "two very different interpretations . . . , one rather narrow and the other quite broad. Under the narrow interpretation, Section 404(e) is essentially an evidentiary rule which could be paraphrased as 'the fact that a partner directly personally benefits from the partner's conduct in the partnership context does not, without more, establish a violation of the partner's duties or obligations under RUPA or the partnership agreement.' Under the broad interpretation, Section 404(e) means that partners are free to pursue their short-term, individual self-interest without notice to or the consent of the partnership, subject only to the specific restrictions contained in the Section 404(b) duty of loyalty—in effect that the pursuit of self-interest cannot be a violation of the non-fiduciary obligation of good faith and fair dealing." (Hillman, et al., *supra,* p. 207.) We need not decide which of these views, if either, prevails in California. Even under the broader reading, section 16404, subdivision (e), does not authorize a partner to exploit partnership property for personal advantage at partnership expense.

there would be some basis to contend that defendants were entitled to conduct themselves as they did—or at least that plaintiff was estopped to complain. But the mere anticipation of eventual capital gains as the main economic benefit to be derived from the venture has no tendency whatsoever to entitle individual partners to divert to their own advantage benefits that would otherwise flow to the partnership.

132 Cal. App. 4th at 1563–67.

J & J Celcom v. AT&T Wireless Services, Inc.

Supreme Court of Washington
169 P.3d 823 (2007)

C. Johnson, J.

This case involves a certified question from the United States Court of Appeals for the Ninth Circuit. We are asked to determine whether, under the Revised Uniform Partnership Act, a controlling partner violates the duty of loyalty where the controlling partner causes the partnership to sell its assets to an affiliated party. We answer the certified question in the negative.

Facts and Procedural History

While certain facts may remain disputed in the federal court proceedings, the Ninth Circuit provided the following description of the parties, their partnerships, and those facts we consider for our analysis. J & J Celcom and other former partners (minority partners) acquired their fractional interests in nine regional cellular telephone partnerships through a lottery. The key asset in each partnership included the right to own licenses for various cellular radio frequencies. At the time of the asset sales at issue in this case, the minority partners owned less than five percent of each partnership, and AT&T Wireless Services (AWS) owned the remainder. AWS provided wireless service to the customers and all technical and administrative services related to the partnerships.

To eliminate the expense of the administrative services related to the partnerships, AWS invoked its majority interest in each partnership and voted to buy out the minority partners. Initially, AWS offered to buy out the minority partners at a price slightly higher than the third party appraisal of four of the nine partnerships. AWS sent letters to the minority partners offering an opportunity to sell voluntarily. The letters stated that, if any minority partner declined the offer, AWS would vote to sell the assets of its partnership to an affiliated entity at the appraised value, dissolve the partnership, and pay the minority partners their pro rata share of the purchase price. Several minority partners accepted the offer but because some declined, AWS proceeded with the asset sales. The Ninth Circuit ruled that the asset sale transactions at issue were based on prices that were fair as a matter of law. *J & J Celcom v. AT&T Wireless Servs., Inc.*, 481 F.3d 1138 (9th Cir.2007).

Certified Question

Does a controlling partner violate the duty of loyalty to the partnership or to dissenting minority partners where the controlling partner causes the partnership to sell all its assets to an affiliated party at a price determined by a third party appraisal, when the appraisal and the parties to the transaction are disclosed and the partnership agreement allows for sale of assets upon majority or supermajority vote, but the partnership agreement is silent on the subject of sale to a related party?

Analysis

The relevant portion of the Washington Revised Uniform Partnership Act (RUPA) provides:

> [The court quotes RUPA § 404(a)-(e).]

Here, as the federal district court held, the partnership agreement expressly allows for sale of partnership assets by majority vote. The federal district court and Ninth Circuit ruled that when AWS sold the partnership assets, it disclosed material information, paid fair consideration, and acted in good faith as a matter of law. Also, the minority partners have offered no proof of damages as a result of AWS's sale of the partnership's assets. Therefore, we find nothing in Washington's RUPA, when applied to the present case, that indicates that AWS violated the duty of loyalty to the partnership.

In addition to Washington's RUPA, our finding is supported by Washington case law. We recognized in *Karle v. Seder*, 35 Wash.2d 542, 550, 214 P.2d 684 (1950) that a partner may lawfully purchase partnership assets from another partner, provided they act in good faith, pay fair consideration, and disclose material information. In *Bassan v. Investment Exchange Corp.*, 83 Wash.2d 922, 524 P.2d 233 (1974) we held that a partner has a duty to account for any benefit of [sic-or] profit held by the partner relating to any aspect of the partnership.

It is of interest to note that the Ninth Circuit perceived our holdings in *Karle* and *Bassan* as pointing "in different directions." *J & J Celcom*, 481 F.3d at 1142. However, we fail to see how the holdings conflict. The cases simply addressed different issues on completely different sets of facts. *Karle* concerned the unlawful concealment of material information by a partner and *Bassan* concerned a partner's lawful requirement to account for any profit derived from transactions on behalf of the partnership. Neither of these concerns are presented under the facts of the case before us.

In *Karle*, two partners decided to sell a tavern, which was their partnership asset. One partner accepted an offer without disclosing to the other partner the actual price or the material details of the sale. We affirmed the trial court judgment that the partner committed fraud by failing to disclose his agreement to sell the tavern for $25,000 while representing to his partner that he sold the tavern for $20,000. No such fraud exists in the present case, which would implicate the holding of *Karle*.

In *Bassan*, we reversed the trial court's dismissal of an action for an accounting and dissolution of the partnership, and we determined that the general partner was accountable to the partnership for profits realized when it received a markup on land it sold to the partnership without the consent of the partners. The partnership agreement was silent on whether consent was required. In the case before us, the federal district court has determined, as a matter of law, that the sale of partnership assets was made at a fair market value.

In the context of the certified question, the holdings of *Karle* and *Bassan* do not conflict. In this case, the partnership agreement does not preclude the sale of the assets; the price paid was fair at the time as a matter of law and no bad faith exists as a matter of law.

Conclusion

Based on the narrow issue posed by the certified question, and the procedural posture underlying our analysis, we answer the certified question no.

We Concur: Chief Justice Gerry L. Alexander, Tom Chambers, Susan Owens, Mary E. Fairhurst, Richard B. Sanders, James M. Johnson and Bobbe J. Bridge, JJ.

Madsen, J. (concurring).

I agree with the majority that the question posed by the certified question from the Ninth Circuit Court of Appeals should be answered no. The majority is correct that *Karle v. Seder*, 35 Wash.2d 542, 214 P.2d 684 (1950) and *Bassan v. Investment Exchange Corp.*, 83 Wash.2d 922, 524 P.2d 233 (1974) are factually different and address different issues . . . However, the majority does not address the fact that *Karle* and *Bassan* were decided under the UPA, not the Revised Uniform Partnership Act (RUPA), a point which the Ninth Circuit considered "critical."[11]

As stated by the Ninth Circuit, the central issue here is "the scope of a partner's fiduciary duty of loyalty in the context of a self-dealing transaction that was disclosed but not specifically authorized by the partnership agreement." *J & J Celcom*, 481 F.3d at 1141. In particular, the Ninth Circuit asked this court to decide whether the language in the partnership agreements authorizing dissolution of the partnership upon majority vote is sufficiently specific to contract around AT&T's duty of loyalty, which encompasses the duty to refrain from self-dealing. In order to provide a useful answer, I believe the court should analyze this question in light of changes in the law since *Karle* and *Bassan* were decided. Therefore, I concur.

Discussion

RUPA represents a major overhaul in the nature of the fiduciary duties imposed on partners. There are two general views of the partnership relation: one emphasizes the fiduciary nature of the relationship and the other emphasizes the contractual nature of the relationship.[12] The common law and UPA are based on the

---

11. [1] The legislature adopted RUPA in 1998.

12. [2] *See generally* Michael Haynes, *Partners Owe to One Another a Duty of the Finest Loyalty . . . or Do They? An Analysis of the Extent to Which Partners May Limit Their Duty of Loyalty to One Another*, 37 Tex. Tech L. Rev. 433, 449 (2005).

fiduciary view, the fundamental principle of which is that partners must subordinate their own interests to the collective interest, absent consent of all the partners. Thus, under the common law and UPA, the duty of loyalty prevented a partner from benefiting, directly or indirectly, from the partnership, more than any of the other partners. The broad approach from the Restatement of Agency, incorporated into partnership law, was that the duty of loyalty required a partner to act solely for the benefit of the partnership in all matters connected to the partnership. This required partners to disgorge any profits made without consent of the other partners, the rule applied in *Bassan*.

RUPA represents a major shift away from the fiduciary view and toward the "libertarian" or "contractarian" view, by (a) expressly limiting fiduciary duties, (b) sanctioning a partner's pursuit of self-interest, and (c) allowing partners to waive most fiduciary duties by contract. RUPA was intended to bring the law of partnership into the "modern age," to make partnerships more rational, efficient, and stable business entities.

Under UPA [§ 21], the partner's fiduciary duty was embodied in the following provision:

> Every partner must account to the partnership for any benefit, and hold as trustee for it any profits derived by him without the consent of the other partners from any transaction connected with the formation, conduct, or liquidation of the partnership, or from any use by him of any of its property.

This was the sole mention of the partner's fiduciary duties and provided the basis for a broad duty of loyalty, as reflected in *Bassan*.

In contrast, the duty of loyalty in RUPA consists only of three subduties. RUPA provides: "(1) The *only* fiduciary duties a partner owes to the partnership and the other partners are the duty of loyalty and the duty of care set forth in subsections (b) and (c) of this section." (emphasis added).[13]

Our state legislature has adopted RUPA, and under its provisions, fiduciary duties are specifically set forth as explained below. First, a partner has a duty

> [t]o account to the partnership and hold as trustee for it any property, profit, or benefit derived by the partner in the conduct and winding up of the partnership business or derived from a use by the partner of partnership property, including the appropriation of a partnership opportunity;

---

13. [3] Indeed, commentators have criticized the act's reformulation of the fiduciary duties owed by partners to other partners, describing the revisions as "'a pinched and almost mean-spirited vision of the duty of loyalty'" that is "'a radical degradation of the duty of loyalty generally . . . and the present Act.'" Allan W. Vestal, *Fundamental Contractarian Error in the Revised Uniform Partnership Act of 1992*, 73 B.U.L. REV. 523, 573–74 (1993) (alterations in original) (footnote omitted) (quoting letter from Melvin A. Eisenberg to Comm'rs on Uniform Laws (July 27, 1992) (on file with the *Boston University Law Review*)). Many states have not adopted RUPA and continue to view the duty of loyalty as inherent in the partnership relationship.

[RUPA §404(b)(1)]. This section reflects the classic duty of loyalty, carried forward from the UPA, which requires a partner to refrain from taking more than its fair share of profits. In this case, no breach of loyalty occurred under this provision because AT&T only took its pro rata share of the profits, fully disclosed the profits, and sold the assets at fair market value. The Ninth Circuit found that, as a matter of law, AT&T had not been aware at the time of the sale that the partnership assets would later be sold to Cingular Wireless LLC at a great profit. *J & J Celcom*, 481 F.3d 1138.

Next, a partner has a duty

[t]o refrain from dealing with the partnership in the conduct or winding up of the partnership business as or on behalf of a party having an interest adverse to the partnership;

[RUPA §404(b)(2)]. This duty is drawn from the *Restatement (Third) Agency* §8.03 (2006).

Addressing this provision, a law review commentator has stated:

When dealing with the partnership as an adverse party without consent of the partnership, the partner must deal fairly with the partnership and disclose all facts which the partner "knows or should know would reasonably affect the [partner's] judgment." This means that a partner may transact with the partnership for his own benefit so long as (1) the partner makes a full disclosure of all relevant facts to the partnership, (2) the partnership agrees to the transaction, and (3) the partner does not take unfair advantage of the partnership. *The important principle is disclosure* because even in situations where the court would allow a limit to the duty of loyalty, incomplete or inadequate disclosure results in the application of traditional fiduciary duties. The obligation of disclosure is equally important when a partner seeks to compete with the partnership or has an interest that conflicts with the partnership.

Michael Haynes, *Partners Owe to One Another a Duty of the Finest Loyalty... or Do They? An Analysis of the Extent to Which Partners May Limit Their Duty of Loyalty to One Another*, 37 Tex. Tech L. Rev. 433, 445–46 (2005) (emphasis added) (alteration in original) (footnotes omitted).

In this case, these requirements are met. AT&T made full disclosure of all relevant facts, the partnership "agreed" to the transaction, by approving it in compliance with partnership formalities, and AT&T did not take unfair advantage of the partnership, since the partnership was purchased at fair market value.

Next, a partner has a duty

[t]o refrain from competing with the partnership in the conduct of the partnership business before the dissolution of the partnership.

[RUPA § 404 (b) (3)]. The drafter's comment to this provision provides that

[t]he duty not to compete applies only to the "conduct" of the partnership business; it does not extend to winding up the business, as do the other loyalty rules. Thus, a partner is free to compete immediately upon an event of dissolution under Section 801, unless the partnership agreement otherwise provides.

Unif. P'Ship Act (1997) § 404, 6 U.L.A. 145 cmt. 2 (2001).

Upon dissolution, AT&T had the right to purchase the partnership assets for its own account, without violating the duty of loyalty. Thus, nothing prohibited AT&T from causing the partnership assets to be sold to an affiliated entity.

The act also provides that

[a] partner does not violate a duty or obligation under this chapter or under the partnership agreement merely because the partner's conduct furthers the partner's own interest.

[RUPA § 404 (e)].

This language has been characterized as a "rejection of the fiduciary essence of the partnership relationship in favor of the contractarian premise." Allan W. Vestal, *Fundamental Contractarian Error in the Revised Uniform Partnership Act of 1992*, 73 B.U.L. REV. 523, 535 (1993) (describing the duty of loyalty in the context of fiduciary duties as a whole). This provision starkly contrasts with the duty of loyalty that existed under UPA, which required a partner to disgorge profits obtained from "any transaction" connected with the partnership "without the consent of the other partners." Former RCW 25.04.210(1). Under RUPA, partners need not obtain the consent of their copartners as a precondition for pursuing their own self-interest.

Finally, the act allows that

[a] partner may lend money to and transact other business with the partnership, and as to each loan or transaction the rights and obligations of the partner are the same as those of a person who is not a partner, subject to other applicable law.

[RUPA § 404(f)]. The drafter's comment to this provision states:

The rights and obligations of a partner doing business with the partnership as an outsider are expressly made subject to the usual laws governing those transactions. . . .

It is unclear under the UPA whether a partner may, for the partner's own account, purchase the assets of the partnership at a foreclosure sale or upon the liquidation of the partnership. Those purchases are clearly within subsection (f)'s broad approval. It is also clear under that subsection that a partner may purchase partnership assets at a foreclosure sale, whether the partner is the mortgagee or the mortgagee is an unrelated third party. Similarly, a partner may purchase partnership property at a tax sale. The obligation of good faith requires disclosure of the partner's interest in the transaction, however.

Unif. P'Ship Act (1997) § 404, 6 U.L.A. 146 cmt. 6 (2001).

[RUPA § 404(f)] allows a partner to "transact business" with the partnership on the same terms as may a third party. This encompasses the right to purchase partnership assets upon dissolution. A partner does not violate a duty or obligation merely by furthering its own interest and may transact business with the partnership on the same basis as a third party "subject to applicable law."

The partnership may waive the duty of loyalty, unless "manifestly unreasonable," in two ways:

The partnership agreement may identify specific types or categories of activities that do not violate the duty of loyalty.

[RUPA § 103(b)(3)(i)].

All of the partners or *a number or percentage specified in the partnership agreement* may authorize or ratify, after full disclosure of all material facts, a specific act or transaction that otherwise would violate the duty of loyalty.

[RUPA § 103(b)(3)(ii)] (emphasis added).

Although the partnership agreement does not specifically authorize AT&T to sell the partnership assets to an affiliated entity, it does expressly allow for sale and/or dissolution of the partnership by majority vote. AT&T complied with the partnership agreement and partnership formalities in selling the partnership assets and dissolving the partnership. Upon dissolution, AT&T had the right to purchase the partnership assets for its own account, without violating the duty of loyalty. Nothing prohibited AT&T from causing the partnership assets to be sold to an affiliated entity. Because the certified question and the record indicate that AT&T acted in good faith, paid fair market value, and fully disclosed the nature of its self-dealing transaction, the transaction was not "manifestly unreasonable" within the meaning of [RUPA § 103(b)(3)]. Thus, the majority correctly answers the question in the negative. *Karle* and *Bassan*, which were decided before the changes in RUPA, do not require a different answer.

Note

The concurring opinion indicates near the end of its analysis that the "transaction" in question was not "manifestly unreasonable." But the "manifestly unreasonable" test in § 103(b)(3) refers to a provision in the partnership agreement, and the opinion acknowledged the partnership agreement did not authorize AT&T to sell partnership assets to an affiliate. In any event, would the transaction in question have survived a challenge under UPA?

v. Fiduciary Duties and Freedom of Contract

The first of the following two cases involves a suit by limited partners against the general partners of a limited partnership. A considerable amount of recent litigation defining or applying fiduciary duties involves suits arising in this context. Section 9(1) of the Uniform Limited Partnership Act, the governing law in the following case, makes general partners "subject to all the restrictions and liabilities of a partner in a partnership without limited partners."[14] The fiduciary obligation is especially obvious in the limited partnership context because most limited partners play a passive role in the business, as will be developed in Chapter 14, and thus are particularly vulnerable to abuse of managerial power.

One question pursued in the next two cases is the extent to which partners can define by agreement the fiduciary duties they owe each other. This topic also is addressed by RUPA, as noted above and as more fully developed below.

Labovitz v. Dolan
Appellate Court of Illinois
545 N.E.2d 304 (1989)

Before BILANDIC, P.J., and HARTMAN, J.

SCARIANO, J.

We have for decision in this case the issue, as posited by the plaintiffs, of whether management discretion granted solely and exclusively to a general partner in a limited partnership agreement authorizes the general partner to use economic coercion to cause his limited partner investors to sell their interests to him at a bargain price.

Plaintiffs as limited partners invested over $12 million dollars in a cablevision programming limited partnership sponsored and syndicated by defendant general partner Dolan. In 1985 the partnership reported earnings of over $34 million dollars, and in 1986 it had earnings of just under $18 million dollars, as a result of which each of the limited partners was required to report his prorata share on his personal income tax returns for those years. Plaintiffs claim that although the partnership had cash available to fund the limited partners' tax obligations, Dolan elected to make only a nominal distribution of cash to cover such liability; accordingly, in 1985 and in 1986 the limited partners were required to pay taxes almost entirely from their own funds on income retained by the partnership. In late November of 1986 an affiliate owned and controlled by Dolan offered to buy out the interests of the limited partners for approximately two-thirds of their book value. Over 90% of the limited partners accepted the offer, but simultaneously filed suit claiming Dolan's tactics to be a breach of his fiduciary duty to them. The circuit court dismissed plaintiffs' complaint with prejudice . . . holding that Dolan's acts were

---

14. Similar language is contained in §403 of the Revised Uniform Limited Partnership Act (1976), except that it is preceded by the following language: "Except as provided in the Act or in the partnership agreement. . . ." The 1985 amendments to the 1976 RULPA did not change §403.

within the broad discretion granted him under the terms of the partnership agreement. Plaintiffs appeal from that ruling.

The limited partnership in this case, Cablevision Programming Investments (CPI) was organized for the purpose of investing in entities that produce and acquire programming for marketing and distribution to cable and other pay television services. . . .

The [Private Placement Memorandum (PPM)] . . . advised investors that their rights and obligations "are governed by the Articles of Limited Partnership" (the Articles), which were bound as an exhibit to the PPM, and added, in a section entitled "Projected Results of Operations of Cablevision Programming Investments," that:

> "The Partnership, Cablevision and its affiliates' intended policy is to make cash distributions to partners each year in an amount approximating the amount of taxable income reflected each year, after providing for adequate working capital requirements deemed necessary by the General Partners. Although the projections assume that this policy can be followed in the future, there are significant contingencies relating to many factors which, from time to time, may prohibit any distributions, including, but not limited to cash, cash availability, general working capital requirements, lending restrictions and revised costs and capital requirements."

The Articles provided that Dolan will have "full responsibility and exclusive and complete discretion in the management and control of the business and affairs of the partnership"; that "Dolan in his sole discretion shall determine the availability of Cash Flow for distribution to partners"; that they "contain the entire understanding among the partners and supersede any prior understanding and/or written or oral agreements among them"; and that Dolan would be liable to the limited partners for his willful misconduct but not for "errors in judgment or for any acts or omissions that do not constitute willful misconduct."

CPI limited partnership interests were offered and sold only to "wealthy and sophisticated investors." . . . The offering of 85 units was fully subscribed.

The articles provided also that net profits, net losses and cash flow were to be allocated as follows: Dolan.5%, CMC[15].5%, and limited partners 99%. In 1985, the partnership earned $34,101,000; in 1986 it earned $17,842,000. As noted above, the limited partners were required to pay taxes on these earnings, but Dolan did not distribute cash in an amount sufficient to cover their tax liability. Dolan did, however, lend CPI money to other companies he controlled. . . .

On November 25, 1986 Cablevision Systems Corporation (CSC), owned and controlled by Dolan, made an offer to purchase all of the CPI limited partnership interests for $271,870 per unit, payable $90,623 in cash and the remainder was to

---

15. [A general partner owned and controlled by Dolan.—Eds.]

be paid either in 9% notes due on June 30, 1988, and June 30, 1989, or in CSC Class A common stock. The offer disclosed that "Dolan and his affiliates would derive substantial benefits in connection with the offer" and that "although the partnership was potentially very valuable . . . it was extremely difficult to determine its true value since it was likely that current assumptions would not materialize and that unanticipated events and circumstances would occur." . . . More than 90% of the limited partners elected to accept CSC's offer and sold their interests in CPI to CSC.

On December 1, 1986, plaintiff Joel Labovitz, who had owned three units, filed a class action complaint, but after other former owners joined in his suit as individual plaintiffs, that complaint was withdrawn and this action was substituted. . . .

Opinion

It is abundantly clear, as defendants point out, that Dolan was granted rather wide latitude in deciding whether or not to distribute cash to the limited partners; the Articles grant him "sole discretion" in the matter, and do not mention any distribution for the purpose of meeting the limited partners' tax obligations. Even in the PPM, where distributions of cash approximating the amount of taxable income each year are projected in tabulated form, the language is far from precise and gives the general partner rather liberal discretionary powers as to such distribution.

It is also clear, however, that despite having such broad discretion, Dolan still owed his limited partners a fiduciary duty, which necessarily encompasses the duty of exercising good faith, honesty, and fairness in his dealings with them and the funds of the partnership. It is no answer to the claim that plaintiffs make in this case that partners have the right to establish among themselves their rights, duties and obligations, as though the exercise of that right releases, waives or delimits somehow, the high fiduciary duty owed to them by the general partner—a gloss we do not find anywhere in our law. On the contrary, the fiduciary duty exists concurrently with the obligations set forth in the partnership agreement whether or not expressed therein. Indeed, at least one of the authorities relied upon by defendants is clear that although "partners are free to vary many aspects of their relationship *inter se*, . . . they are not free to destroy its fiduciary character." *Saballus [v. Timke]*, 122 Ill.App.3d [109] 116 [(1983)].

Thus, the language in the Articles standing alone does not deprive plaintiffs of the trial they seek against Dolan for breach of fiduciary duty. We therefore agree with plaintiffs that the trial court did not give due consideration to Dolan's duty as general partner to exercise the highest degree of honesty and good faith in his handling of partnership assets, and instead treated the parties as arm's length strangers holding that no inquiry could be made into the fairness of the transactions at issue because of the language in the Articles regarding Dolan's discretion. Yet "in any fiduciary relationship, the burden of proof shifts to the fiduciary to show by clear and convincing evidence that a transaction is equitable and just." (*Bandringa v. Bandringa* (1960), 20 Ill.2d 167, 170 N.E.2d 116; *Schueler v. Blomstrand* (1946), 394 Ill. 600, 69 N.E.2d 328; *Grossberg v. Haffenberg* (1937), 367 Ill. 284, 11 N.E.2d 359.)

Indeed, cases cited and relied upon by defendants hold that "where there is a question of breach of a fiduciary duty of a *managing partner*, all doubts will be resolved against him, and the managing partner has the burden of proving his innocence." *Saballus*, 122 Ill.App.3d at 117–18, 77 Ill.Dec. 451, 460 N.E.2d 755, citing *Bakalis v. Bressler* (1953), 1 Ill.2d 72, 78, 115 N.E.2d 323. (Emphasis supplied.). . . .

Defendants prevailed in the trial court on their . . . motion on the ground that the claim is defeated by affirmative matter, namely, Dolan's sole discretion in the matter of distributing cash flow. As to such affirmative defense, defendants choose to remain completely oblivious to the fact that although the Articles clearly gave the general partner the sole discretion to distribute cash as he deemed appropriate, that discretion was encumbered by a supreme fiduciary duty of fairness, honesty, good faith and loyalty to his partners. Language in an agreement such as "sole discretion" does not metamorphose the document into an unrestricted license to engage in self-dealing at the expense of those to whom the managing partner owes such a duty. Defendants cite no authority, and we find none, for the proposition that there can be an *a priori* waiver of fiduciary duties in a partnership-be it general or limited. Nor is the practice of imposing purported advance waivers of fiduciary duties in limited partnership enterprises to be given judicial recognition on the basis of the facts developed in this case. Defendants' argument that the good faith doctrine protects only the reasonable expectations of the contracting parties is, we think, aptly answered by plaintiffs' statement to the trial judge at the hearing on defendants' motion to dismiss: ". . . the risk we took was that the business would not succeed. We did not take the risk that the business would succeed so well that the general partner would squeeze us out and take the investment for himself," an argument, by the way, that sets forth a precise formulation of the exact issue in this case.

Our courts are not bound to endow it as doctrine that where the general partner obtains an agreement from his limited partner investors that he is to be the sole arbiter with respect to the flow that the cash of the enterprise takes, and thereby creates conditions favorable to his decision that the business is too good for them and contrives to appropriate it to himself, the articles of partnership constitute an impervious armor against any attack on the transaction short of actual fraud. That is not and cannot be the law. And that is precisely the gravamen of plaintiffs' complaint: that the general partner refused unreasonably to distribute cash and thereby forced plaintiffs to continually dip into their own resources in order to pay heavy taxes on large earnings in a calculated effort to force them to sell their interests to an entity which Dolan owned and controlled at a price well below at least the book value of those interests. . . .

Plaintiffs therefore correctly maintain that they "were entitled to a trial in which Dolan must prove he acted fairly and not as his limited partners' business adversary." Accordingly, we hold that the trial judge incorrectly granted the defendants' . . . motion, and that plaintiffs were entitled to a trial on the issues formulated in this case.

REVERSED AND REMANDED.

Question

Does *Labovitz* represent a failure on the part to Dolan's counsel to draft appropriate language to permit Dolan to act as he did, or is there no way counsel could accomplish such a purpose under Illinois law?

Singer v. Singer

Court of Appeals of Oklahoma
634 P.2d 766 (1981)

BOYDSTON, JUDGE.

This appeal is from [a] judgment of district court declaring land purchased by defendants is to be held in constructive trust for . . . Josaline Production Co., a partnership. . . . All parties to this action are related through family ties, intricate partnerships and trusts. . . .

The Singer family formed an oil production partnership in the late 1930's. Through inheritance and assignments, partnership interests have been conveyed and passed down to other family members, fractionalizing the ownership.

The original partnership was called Josaline Production Co. . . . Between 1962 and 1977 intrafamily assignments resulted in Andrea and her brother Stanley becoming partners. . . . In 1977, the parties re-drafted the partnership agreement, carefully defining duties and rights of the parties and restating the current ownership percentages. . . .

The 1977 restated partnership agreement contained the following paragraph:

> 8. *Each partner shall be free to enter into business and other transactions for his or her own separate individual account,* even though such business or other transaction may be in conflict with and/or competition with the business of this partnership. Neither the partnership nor any individual member of this partnership shall be entitled to claim or receive any part of or interest in such transactions, *it being the intention and agreement* that any *partner will be free to deal on his or her own account to the same extent and with the same force and effect as if he or she were not and never had been members of this partnership.* (emphasis supplied)

On July 25, 1979, the Josaline partners held a meeting in Oklahoma City which was attended by several members of the Josaline partnership. . . . At the meeting several investment opportunities were raised, but the meeting was mainly held to discuss routine business of Josaline. One item of interest on the agenda was the possible purchase . . . of 95 acres of land in the Britton area owned by Investors Diversified Services (IDS). The proposed purchase included 45 acres of minerals and was listed for sale at a purchase price of one and one-half million dollars.

Prior to the meeting, Joe L. [Singer] requested Stanley to look into the possibility of purchasing the land through the listing realtor. At the meeting the IDS land was briefly discussed but the decision of whether to purchase was deferred.

After the meeting, defendants Stanley and Andrea formed a general partnership, Gemini Realty Company (Gemini), and on September 25, 1979, purchased the IDS land, taking title in Gemini's name without further consultation with any of the Josaline partners. . . .

Within a short time, Joe L. learned of the transaction and demanded Singer Bros. partnership be permitted to purchase 50 percent of the property. Initially, Stanley offered to give Singer Bros. 16.66 percent but withdrew the offer before it had been accepted. No other member of the Singer family requested or was permitted to participate and this suit resulted. . . .

After having identified the true parties in interest,[16] resolution of the dispute—Josaline's contention that by reason of the fiduciary aspects of partnership it is entitled to participate in the purchase of the IDS land—is simplified. We would agree with Josaline's contention except for paragraph 8 of the partnership contract.

We find the defendants had a contract right to do precisely what they did, namely, compete with the partners of Josaline and with Josaline itself "as if there never had been a partnership." Because of paragraph 8, the fact that the land is in an area of partnership interest does not preclude intra-partnership competition. A special area of interest is just another way of labeling and describing an investment area where competition is ordinarily not permitted between partners, absent agreement.[17] Josaline contracted away its right to expect a noncompetitive fiduciary relationship with any of its partners.

We find paragraph 8 is designed to allow and is uniquely drafted to promote spirited, if not outright predatory competition between the partners. Its strong wording leaves no doubt in our minds that its drafters intended to effect such a result. This is reinforced by the fact the partners repeated the same clause in two successive contracts. We construe it to legitimize and extend free competition between the partners to partnership prospects and opportunities, including the Britton area of interest and the IDS land.

From a fiduciary aspect, the permissible boundaries of intra-partnership competition, under paragraph 8, are limited only after the threshold of actual partnership acquisition has been crossed. Had Stanley and Andrea pirated an existing partnership asset or used partnership funds or encumbered Josaline financially, our decision would be different.

---

16. [The case has been edited to remove a complex discussion involving the interests of other parties.—Eds.]

17. [16] Absent fraud, illegality or overreaching in the *procurement* of written contract, parties rights are fixed by the contract.

... Further, there is a complete absence of proof the partners waived paragraph 8 rights by their post-1977 conduct. . . .

We hereby reverse and remand to trial court with instructions to vacate the judgment rendered below and order judgment be rendered in favor of defendants. Costs of appeal and trial taxed against plaintiffs.

BACON, P. J., and BRIGHTMIRE, J., concur.

Notes

1. As noted in *Enea*, the duty of loyalty is treated at length in RUPA. It is described in § 404(a) as one of only two fiduciary duties,[18] and then is limited in (b) to the following three rules: a partner must account for profits derived from the business, including the appropriation of a partnership opportunity; must refrain from dealing as or on behalf of an adverse party; and must refrain from competing with the partnership before dissolution. Section 103(b)(3) of RUPA states that the duty of loyalty may not be eliminated by the partnership agreement, but "the partners by agreement may identify specific types or categories of activities that do not violate the duty of loyalty, if not manifestly unreasonable." Would the *Singer* case likely come out the same in a RUPA jurisdiction?

In addition, in § 404(e) RUPA provides that, "A partner does not violate a duty or obligation under this Act or under the partnership agreement merely because the partner's conduct furthers the partner's own interest." Comment 1 to § 404 states that, "[a]rguably, the term 'fiduciary' is inappropriate when used to describe the duties of a partner because a partner may legitimately pursue self-interest and not solely the interest of the partnership and the other partners, as must a true trustee. Nevertheless, partners have long been characterized as fiduciaries." This idea is developed in Comment 5, which states, "That admonition [in § 404(e)] has particular application to the duty of loyalty and the obligation of good faith and fair dealing. It underscores the partner's rights as owner and principal in the enterprise, which must always be balanced against his duties and obligations as an agent and fiduciary."

This approach of RUPA has drawn fire from two different perspectives. One perspective is represented by Allan W. Vestal, *Fundamental Contractarian Error in the Revised Uniform Partnership Act of 1992*, 73 BOSTON U. L. REV. 523, 535 (1993) ("The Revised Act turns the world upside down with respect to the fiduciary relations of partners *inter se*. The engine of this error is the drafters' rejection of the fiduciary essence of the partnership relationship in favor of the contractarian premise. . . . This shift is breathtaking. In one stroke of the pen [referring to § 404(e)] the drafters have made the partners adversaries, whereas before they were bound by 'the duty of the finest loyalty' . . ."). *See also* Claire Moore Dickerson, *Is It Appropriate to Appropriate Corporate Concepts: Fiduciary Duties and the Revised Uniform*

---

18. The other is the duty of care, to be discussed shortly.

Partnership Act, 64 U. Colo. L. Rev. 111, 155–56 (1993) ("Once the partnership form has been chosen, there would be no purpose in wasting time—and transaction costs—on negotiating the terms of a fiduciary duty. I do not agree with contractarian commentators who maintain that the traditional fiduciary duties are so vague and aspirational as to be meaningless.... Far from being naively aspirational, those duties serve to guide the parties to a standard of behavior that reduces the need to monitor.").

The other perspective is represented by Larry E. Ribstein, *The Revised Uniform Partnership Act: Not Ready for Prime Time*, 49 Bus. Law. 45, 52–54 (1993), stating in part as follows:

> *Fiduciary duty* is a type of contractual term courts supply because the parties themselves would have contracted for the duties if it were not so costly to contract in detail.... Because fiduciary duties are contractual 'gap-fillers,' the precise nature of the duties that exist in any particular contractual relationship depends on the express and implied terms of the relevant contract.... The UPA prohibition on unilateral benefit without co-partners' consent [§ 21] gives courts the flexibility to fill gaps in partnership contracts by determining who owns what and the partners' duties regarding partnership property. Because the extensive case law under the UPA's simple language recognizes a full range of fiduciary duties, there was no need for further detail. Yet RUPA perversely attempts to spell out a set of duties that exists in all partnerships under all circumstances.... While partners may have a duty to act unselfishly in partnership affairs, RUPA errs in making this duty part of every partnership contract. Partners often do not contract to be strict fiduciaries in the typical agency or trust sense of one who controls the property of another. In other words, partners are not necessarily comparable to directors or executives of publicly-held corporations. Instead, partners may be self-seeking co-venturers who are constrained from the worst kinds of misconduct by their contingent compensation, personal liability for debts, and their co-partners' close monitoring and power to withdraw at any time.

See also J. Dennis Hynes, *Freedom of Contract, Fiduciary Duties, and Partnerships: The Bargain Principle and the Law of Agency*, 54 Wash. & Lee L. Rev. 439 (1997); Allan W. Vestal, *Advancing the Search for Compromise: A Response to Professor Hynes*, 58 Law & Contemp. Probs. 55 (Spring 1995); J. William Callison, *Blind Men and Elephants: Fiduciary Duties Under the Revised Uniform Partnership Act, Uniform Limited Liability Company Act, and Beyond*, 1 J. Small & Emerging Bus. L. 109 (1997).

2. The language of RUPA § 103 raises some unavoidable issues. For example, what is the meaning of "eliminate" and "manifestly unreasonable" in § 103(b)(3)? What is meant by "specific types or categories of activities" in § 103(b)(3)(i)? *See*, Mark J. Loewenstein, *Fiduciary Duties and the Unincorporated Buisness Entities: In Defense of the "Manifestly Unreasonable" Standard*, 41 Tulsa L. Rev. 411 (2006).

b. The Duty of Care

Duffy v. Piazza Construction, Inc.

Court of Appeals of Washington
815 P.2d 267 (1991)

COLEMAN, CHIEF JUDGE.

Richard and James Duffy appeal the trial court's order granting summary judgment in favor of Piazza Construction and dismissing their complaint, arguing that under the circumstances of this case, an action for negligence of one joint venturer against the other should be allowed. We affirm.

On July 5, 1983, brothers Richard and James Duffy signed a letter of agreement with John Piazza, president of Piazza Construction, Inc., regarding a United States Forest Service request for proposals for office facilities in Sedro Woolley, Washington. The letter stated as follows:

It is agreed between the parties that Richard and James Duffy, et. al., shall joint venture with John J. Piazza in submitting a proposal for office space upon the following terms and conditions:

(A) Mr. Piazza shall supply all necessary drawings, building specifications and necessary cost items to prepare a proposal for said Office Building.

(B) James and Richard Duffy, et al., shall make available the Land for said proposal.

(C) Each Joint Venture Partner shall contribute at his cost the above mentioned items and shall be allocated a partnership percentage of Ownership and a return on said Ownership based on the fair market value of each contribution.

The letter of agreement outlined two proposals that the parties intended to submit. Additionally, the letter stated that "[a]ll parties agree to work for the acceptance of one of these proposals and the final offering shall be agreed to by all parties before final submission."

The bid specifications provided by the Forest Service in its original solicitation for offers indicated that proposals should include at least 15,500 square feet of net usable office space. Piazza's first two proposals both contained plans that provided 15,645 square feet of net usable office space. Its final proposal, however, included only 15,000 square feet of net usable office space. Piazza reduced the amount of net usable office space in its final proposal based upon a diagram of a suggested floor plan provided by the Forest Service.

On July 13, 1984, the Forest Service informed Piazza that another bidder's offer had been accepted. Piazza's bid had been rejected as nonresponsive because its proposal did not meet the minimum square footage requirement.

The Duffys filed a complaint against Piazza, apparently alleging that Piazza was negligent in the preparation of its bid and that it was liable to them for the lost profits that they had expected. On March 12, 1990, Piazza filed a motion for summary judgment. In its memorandum in support of the motion, Piazza argued that a joint venture partner may not maintain an action for negligence against another joint venture partner when the alleged negligence (1) was committed within the scope of the joint venture business, (2) was not the result of bad faith, and (3) did not result in physical injury to person or property. Piazza's motion was granted, and the Duffys' complaint against Piazza was dismissed. This appeal followed.

The sole issue on appeal is whether the trial court erred when it granted summary judgment in favor of Piazza and dismissed the Duffys' complaint with prejudice.

The relationship between joint venturers is like that of partners in a partnership. The associations are so similar that their rights, duties, and liabilities generally are subject to the same rules. Each participant in a joint venture has a duty of good faith, fairness, candid disclosure, and honesty. Generally, there is no liability of one partner to another for negligence in the management of a joint venture. An action for negligence may lie between partners or joint venturers when the negligence results in injury to the person or property of the one seeking to recover damages.

. . . .

[W]e hold as a matter of law that negligence in the management of the affairs of a general partnership or joint venture does not create any right of action against that partner by other members of the partnership. It is only when there is a breach of trust, such as when one partner or joint venturer holds property or assets belonging to the partnership or venture, and converts such to his own use, would such action lie. In the ordinary management and operation of a general partnership or joint venture there is no liability to the other partners or joint venturers for the negligence in the management or operation of the affairs of the enterprise.

The Duffys do not allege that Piazza breached its duty of good faith or that its negligence resulted in physical injury to the Duffys or their property. Therefore, although Piazza may have been negligent when it submitted a bid that included less than the required amount of net usable office space, the trial court correctly granted summary judgment in favor of Piazza and dismissed the Duffys' complaint.

The decision of the trial court is affirmed.

PEKELIS and BAKER, JJ., concur.

Notes

1. Courts typically apply the business judgment rule to decisions made by partners. The business judgment rule is the standard by which judgments of the board of directors are reviewed by the courts. In the partnership context, see, for example, *Kuznik v. Bees Ferry Associates*, 538 S.E.2d 15, 27 (S.C. Ct. App. 2000); *Starr v. Fordham*, 648 N.E.2d 1261, 1265–66 (Mass. 1995). Under the Delaware corporate law formulation of the business judgment rule, which is followed by many courts when the business decisions of partners or managers of a limited liability company are challenged, the courts will presume that the directors acted in good faith, with due care and in the best interests of the corporation. The burden of proof is on those challenging the decision to overcome such presumptions. If the challengers meet that burden, the directors then bear the burden of proving the fairness of their decision. *See, e.g., Cede & Co. v. Technicolor, Inc.*, 634 A.2d 345, 361 (Del. 1993). This formulation of the business judgment rule is intended to and does provides a measure of protection to the decision maker, placing a burden of proof on those mounting a challenge.

2. In Chapter 2 it was noted that a paid agent is subject to a duty to the principal to act with the standard of care and skill accepted in the locality for the kind of work involved and, in addition, to exercise any special skills the agent has or purports to have. As noted in *Duffy*, this standard does not apply to partners. Instead, partners are not liable to other partners for mere negligence in the operation of the business. *See also* BROMBERG & RIBSTEIN ON PARTNERSHIP 6:141–45, §6.07(f). Why the different treatment for partners? Perhaps it can be explained in part by the special incentive partners have, stemming from personal liability for the debts of the business, to act with care and to monitor the behavior of fellow partners. If this explanation is accurate, should the standard of care be increased for partners in an LLP, where there is no liability for the debts of the business?

UPA does not specifically address the duty of care partners owe to each other. It specifies that, subject to contrary agreement, losses are shared according to the sharing of profits. Presumably this includes losses caused by a partner's negligence, unless agreed otherwise.

RUPA directly addresses a partner's standard of care, stating in §404(c) that, "A partner's duty of care to the partnership and the other partners in the conduct and winding up of the partnership business is limited to refraining from engaging in grossly negligent or reckless conduct, intentional misconduct, or a knowing violation of law." By this approach, RUPA declined to create a special default rule for losses caused by the negligence of partners. Instead, such losses are treated in the same way as losses caused by the negligence of a nonpartner agent. (One would not want to push this analogy too far, however. The common law of agency requires an agent to indemnify the principal for losses caused by the agent's negligence, as noted in Chapter 2, while partners generally do not have such an obligation, as developed in the *Moren* case below.) The drafters assumed that most partners would agree to share losses equally, reasoning that negligence is inevitable and likely to occur at random among partners. The Comments to §404(c) are terse, but this point is made by the Reporter for RUPA in Donald J. Weidner, *Three Policy Decisions Animate Revision of Uniform Partnership Act*, 46 BUS. LAW. 427, 464–68 (1991).

3. For a thoughtful commentary on the appropriateness of a gross negligence standard for a partner's duty of care, see J. William Callison, *"The Law Does Not Perfectly Comprehend": The Inadequacy of the Gross Negligence Duty of Care Standard in Unincorporated Business Organizations*, 94 KY. L.J. 451 (2005–2006) (arguing that a gross negligence standard is inappropriate in some circumstances and that the RUPA drafters should not have attempted to articulate a single standard for all cases).

Moren v. Jax Restaurant

Court of Appeals of Minnesota
679 N.W.2d 165 (2004)

CRIPPEN, JUDGE

Facts

Jax Restaurant, the partnership, operates its business in Foley, Minnesota. One afternoon in October 2000, Nicole Moren, one of the Jax partners, completed her day shift at Jax at 4:00 p.m. and left to pick up her two-year-old son Remington from day care. At about 5:30, Moren returned to the restaurant with Remington after learning that her sister and partner, Amy Benedetti, needed help. Moren called her husband who told her that he would pick Remington up in about 20 minutes.

Because Nicole Moren did not want Remington running around the restaurant, she brought him into the kitchen with her, set him on top of the counter, and began rolling out pizza dough using the dough-pressing machine. As she was making pizzas, Remington reached his hand into the dough press. His hand was crushed, and he sustained permanent injuries.

Through his father, Remington commenced a negligence action against the partnership. The partnership served a third-party complaint on Nicole Moren, arguing that, in the event it was obligated to compensate Remington, the partnership was entitled to indemnity or contribution from Moren for her negligence. The district court's summary judgment was premised on a legal conclusion that Moren has no obligation to indemnify Jax Restaurant so long as the injury occurred while she was engaged in ordinary business conduct. The district court rejected the partnership's argument that its obligation to compensate Remington is diminished in proportion to the predominating negligence of Moren as a mother, although it is responsible for her conduct as a business owner. This appeal followed.

Issue

Does Jax Restaurant have an indemnity right against Nicole Moren in the circumstances of this case?

Analysis

Under Minnesota's Uniform Partnership Act of 1994 [RUPA], a partnership is an entity distinct from its partners, and as such, a partnership may sue and be sued in the name of the partnership. "A partnership is liable for loss or injury caused to a person . . . as a result of a wrongful act or omission, or other actionable conduct, of a partner acting in the ordinary course of business of the partnership or with authority of the partnership." [RUPA § 305] Accordingly, a "partnership shall . . . indemnify a partner for liabilities incurred by the partner in the ordinary course of the business of the partnership. . . ." [RUPA § 401(c)]. Stated conversely, an "act of a partner which is not apparently for carrying on in the ordinary course the partnership business or business of the kind carried on by the partnership binds the partnership only if the act was authorized by the other partners." [RUPA § 301(2)]. Thus, under the plain language of the [RUPA], a partner has a right to indemnity from the partnership, but the partnership's claim of indemnity from a partner is not authorized or required.

The district court correctly concluded that Nicole Moren's conduct was in the ordinary course of business of the partnership and, as a result, indemnity by the partner to the partnership was inappropriate. It is undisputed that one of the cooks scheduled to work that evening did not come in, and that Moren's partner asked her to help in the kitchen. It also is undisputed that Moren was making pizzas for the partnership when her son was injured. Because her conduct at the time of the injury was in the ordinary course of business of the partnership, under the [RUPA], her conduct bound the partnership and it owes indemnity to her for her negligence. [RUPA §§ 305(a) and 401(c)].

Appellant heavily relies on one foreign case for the proposition that a partnership is entitled to a contribution or indemnity from a partner who is negligent. *See Flynn v. Reaves*, 135 Ga.App. 651, 218 S.E.2d 661 (1975). In *Flynn*, the Georgia Court of Appeals held that "where a partner is sued individually by a plaintiff injured by the partner's sole negligence, the partner cannot seek contribution from his co-partners even though the negligent act occurred in the course of the partnership business." *Id.* at 663. But this case is inapplicable because the Georgia court applied common law partnership and agency principles and, like appellant, makes no mention of the RUPA, which is the law in Minnesota.

Appellant also claims that because Nicole Moren's action of bringing Remington into the kitchen was partly motivated by personal reasons, her conduct was outside the ordinary course of business. Because it has not been previously addressed, there is no Minnesota authority regarding this issue. But there are two cases from outside of Minnesota that address the issue in a persuasive fashion. *Grotelueschen v. Am. Family Ins. Co.*, 171 Wis.2d 437, 492 N.W.2d 131, 137 (1992) (An "act can further part personal and part business purposes and still occur in the ordinary course of the partnership."); *Wolfe v. Harms*, 413 S.W.2d 204, 215 (Mo.1967) ("[E]ven if the predominant motive of the partner was to benefit himself or third persons, such does not prevent the concurrent business purpose from being within the scope of the partnership."). Adopting this rationale, we conclude that the conduct of Nicole Moren was no less in the ordinary course of business because it also served personal purposes. It is undisputed that Moren was acting for the benefit of the partnership by making pizzas when her son was injured, and even though she was simultaneously acting in her role as a mother, her conduct remained in the ordinary course of the partnership business.

Decision

Because Minnesota law requires a partnership to indemnify its partners for the result of their negligence, the district court properly granted summary judgment to respondent Nicole Moren. In addition, we conclude that the conduct of a partner may be partly motivated by personal reasons and still occur in the ordinary course of business of the partnership.

Affirmed.

Note

In *Moren*, the court holds that a negligent partner is not liable to indemnify the partnership for the liability it incurred as a result of her negligence. Is the court's rationale convincing?

c. The Duty of Full Disclosure

It is unclear whether the duty of disclosure is regarded as a separate fiduciary duty or as simply part of the duties of care and loyalty. RUPA treats it as the latter. *See* RUPA § 404(a) ("The only fiduciary duties a partner owes to the partnership and the other partners are the duty of loyalty and the duty of care."). The duty of disclosure is mentioned only in Comment 2 to § 404, which states that "the other partners can consent to conduct otherwise proscribed by the rule [of loyalty]. To be effective, their consent must be predicated on full disclosure of . . . all material facts regarding the transaction to be approved." Nevertheless, the duty of disclosure frequently receives separate treatment, as in the following case.

Walter v. Holiday Inns, Inc.

United States Court of Appeals, Third Circuit
985 F.2d 1232 (1993)

SLOVITER, CHIEF JUDGE.

Plaintiffs are several individuals and a corporation who formed a 50-50 partnership with Holiday Inns, Inc. (Holiday) in 1979 to develop and operate Harrah's Marina Hotel and Casino in Atlantic City, New Jersey. In 1981, plaintiffs sold their 49% interest in the partnership to Holiday. In 1983, plaintiffs sold their remaining 1% interest to Holiday. In 1985, four years after the first sale, by which time the hotel/casino complex had become highly profitable, they filed this suit claiming that in the buy-out transaction Holiday . . . breached the fiduciary duty it owed to plaintiffs. After plaintiffs presented their case, the district court granted Holiday's motion for judgment as a matter of law on the breach of fiduciary duty claim. Plaintiffs appeal. . . .

. . . Although the complaint refers to "defendants' fraudulent misrepresentations and concealment of material facts and . . . breach of fiduciary duties owed to plaintiffs," the essence of plaintiffs' claims is that Holiday failed to provide them with certain information that they needed to negotiate the buy-out transaction from an equal position with Holiday. . . . As to the fiduciary duty claim, the district court noted the "tense, if not hostile, environment between the parties," and concluded based on dictum in *Fravega v. Security Savings & Loan Ass'n*, 469 A.2d 531 (Ch. Div. 1983), questioning the application of a fiduciary standard "to transactions where the relationship between the parties is, by nature, adversarial," that New Jersey would apply a limited "adverse interest" exception when "partners are dealing with one another at arm's length." The court thus concluded that "[g]iven the environment in which the parties were operating, it seems clear that traditional notions of fiduciary duty were inapplicable." The court held, however, that even assuming *arguendo* that a fiduciary duty existed and was breached, judgment as a matter of law for Holiday was appropriate because plaintiffs had failed to prove that the alleged misstatements and omissions would have been material to their decision to sell their partnership interest or that they would have relied on the non-disclosed information. . . .

Plaintiffs contend that the district court erred in granting judgment for Holiday as a matter of law on plaintiffs' claim of breach of a fiduciary duty because the court interpreted New Jersey law as recognizing an "adverse-interest" exception to the fiduciary duty between partners in the buy-out context. . . . Plaintiffs argue that the majority of state courts, including New Jersey, have held that fiduciary principles apply with full force during partnership buy-out transactions. Plaintiffs ask us to predict that the Supreme Court of New Jersey would reject the dictum in *Fravega* and would align itself with this majority rule.

Plaintiffs also ask us to decide which party bears the burden of proof when such inter-partner transactions are alleged to be infected by fraud, another unsettled issue in New Jersey. . . . Although the existence of persuasive authority supporting the application of fiduciary principles even when partners act as adversaries makes it likely that *Fravega* was too slender a reed on which to decide this case, we need not engage in the difficult predictive function of state law that diversity jurisdiction would require if we can base our ruling on a more settled ground.

Since the mid-19th century, New Jersey courts have recognized that in order to set aside the sale of a partnership interest on the ground of breach of fiduciary duty, "it is essential that the misrepresentation or concealment should be . . . in regard to a fact material to the contract." The district court's alternate basis for its grant of Holiday's motion for judgment as a matter of law was that Holiday did not withhold or misstate any material facts. Even if Holiday had some fiduciary obligation to plaintiffs and Holiday had the burden of proving that this duty was not breached, if the evidence plaintiffs produced at trial showed that under the circumstances none of the alleged misstatements or omissions would have been material to their decision to sell their partnership interest to Holiday or that Holiday had no obligation to do more than it did, we must affirm.

Materiality cannot be determined in a vacuum. In business transactions, what is material must be evaluated in the context in which the statements or omissions occurred. This is true as well in partnership buy-outs. Bromberg and Ribstein on Partnership at 6:64 (1988) (in partnership buy-out transactions, "[e]ven if a partner was subject to a duty of full disclosure and failed to disclose every fact in connection with a particular transaction, there is no liability unless the nondisclosed facts were such as might be expected to have induced action or forbearance by the other partners—that is, were material").

As a general proposition courts and commentators have recognized that in determining whether a fiduciary duty has been breached by a material misstatement or by a failure to disclose a material fact, the sophistication of the complaining partner and the degree of access to partnership records are key factors to be considered. See, e.g., *Burke v. Farrell*, 656 P.2d 1015, 1017 (Utah 1982) (although selling partner did not disclose value of partnership interest, no breach of fiduciary duty where acquiring partner had "ample access to information about the value of his partnership interest" and had "ready access to the records of the partnership"); *Coleman v. Lofgren*, 593 P.2d 632, 633, 635–637 (Alaska 1979) (where purchasing partner "at all times had access to the partnership records," seller of partnership business did not breach fiduciary duty owed to purchasing partner where seller failed to disclose insolvency of business, even though purchaser relied on seller to inform him of partnership affairs). . . .

The plaintiffs stipulated that at the relevant times "each of the plaintiffs was a highly sophisticated and experienced investor," and the record amply bears that out. In light of this concession we need only examine the extent of plaintiffs' access to the partnership records.

Plaintiffs contend that they were passive partners while Holiday was the managing partner with exclusive control over all financial information concerning the casino. If that were in fact the case, we believe that New Jersey would hold Holiday to a more stringent fiduciary standard in connection with the buy-out than if the partners bargained from equal positions. . . . However, we find insufficient evidence in the record to support plaintiffs' factual assertion, even viewing the facts in the light most favorable to the plaintiffs.

Those portions of the record that plaintiffs have cited to support their claim of passivity reveal that although the day-to-day operations of the casino were under Holiday's control through its subsidiary, Harrah's, Inc., the most important decisions regarding the planning and financial management remained with the partnership's Executive Committee on which plaintiffs served equally with defendants. . . . The record also shows that plaintiffs requested and received volumes of financial data . . . that provided them with ample data by which to assess the partnership's financial situation. . . .

With these general principles in mind, we proceed with an item by item analysis of the specific facts that plaintiffs claim would have been material to their decision to sell their half share of the casino to Holiday. We do so mindful of our prior assertion that "[o]nly when the disclosures or omissions are so clearly unimportant that reasonable minds could not differ should the ultimate issue of materiality be decided as a matter of law."

Plaintiffs have devoted considerable argument to Holiday's failure to provide them with copies of the financial projections contained in the Boxer Report. The Report, prepared prior to the 1981 buy-out, was a 35 year financial forecast prepared by the defendants, based on the current financial statements and projected growth, which projected large cash flows and high profits for the hotel/casino project. It also contained two ten-year projections of substantial, albeit differing, profits. . . . [T]he Boxer Report was simply a projection based on the volumes of financial information already in plaintiffs' possession. Of course, we recognize that every negotiator would like to have all the information upon which his or her counterpart is proceeding, but that is a far cry from materiality in the legal sense. That depends, instead, on whether plaintiffs had access to the raw data upon which they could make their own projections. The record shows they did. . . .

We conclude therefore that the record fails to support plaintiffs' argument that Holiday made any material misrepresentations or omitted providing material facts that it had a duty to disclose to plaintiffs. Thus we conclude that the district court did not err in granting judgment as a matter of law on plaintiffs' claim of breach of fiduciary duty.

d. The Duty of Good Faith and Fair Dealing

It might seem odd for the reader to see this duty discussed in a section dealing with a partner's fiduciary duties. The duty of good faith is well established in the law and applies to many relationships that can hardly be characterized as fiduciary in nature. See § 1-203 of the Uniform Commercial Code ("Every contract or duty within this Act imposes an obligation of good faith in its performance or enforcement.") and § 205 of the Restatement of Contracts ("Every contract imposes upon each party a duty of good faith and fair dealing in its performance and its enforcement."). Nevertheless, the duty of good faith and fair dealing plays a major role in partnership law, particularly under RUPA, as will be seen below.

Nothing is said about good faith in § 21, the basic fiduciary section of UPA. Only § 31(1)(d) of UPA mandates a duty of good faith (by use of the words "bona fide") and then only in the narrow context of expulsion of a partner. Nevertheless, the duty of good faith is closely related to the basic fiduciary duties. See Bromberg & Ribstein on Partnership 6:111, 6.07(a)(1), stating, "The main elements of the partners' fiduciary duties have been summarized as good faith, fairness, and loyalty."

RUPA takes a different approach. It includes a duty of good faith and fair dealing in § 404(d) and applies it to all partnership dealings. The phrase "good faith and fair dealing" is not defined in RUPA.

The duty of good faith and fair dealing is one of the duties listed in RUPA § 103(b) that cannot be eliminated by the partnership contract. It is not classified as a fiduciary duty, however. As noted earlier, § 404(a) states: "The only fiduciary duties a partner owes to the partnership and the other partners are the duty of loyalty and the duty of care set forth in subsections (b) and (c)." The Comment to § 404(d) states that the duty of good faith and fair dealing "is not a fiduciary duty. Nor is it a separate and independent obligation. It is an ancillary obligation that applies whenever a partner discharges a duty or exercises a right under the partnership agreement or Act."

What does "good faith" mean in the partnership context? What impact does it have on the agreements and conduct of partners? A typical example of the good faith concept in the context of a partnership agreement is set forth in *Oregon RSA No. 6, Inc. v. Castle Rock Cellular of Oregon Limited Partnership*, 840 F. Supp. 770 (D. Ore. 1993). In this case, each partner had the right of first refusal if any partner wished to convey its partnership interest to any third party other than an affiliate of the partner. The partnership consisted of three partners, each of which had several affiliates. The owner of one of the partners agreed to sell the partner to an affiliate of one of the other two partners. The third partner cried foul, seeing this as an end around the right of first refusal. The court agreed. While, technically, no partner sold a partnership interest in violation of the agreement, practically that is what happened. The covenant of good faith and fair dealing protects the reasonable contractual expectations of the parties, the court said, and defendants' actions in this case ran afoul of those expectations. This doctrine also explains the *Labovitz* case, *supra*.

As mentioned above, the duty of good faith is expressly applied under UPA to expulsion of partners under a power conferred by the partnership agreement. That language has generated considerable litigation, particularly in the context of law partnership, as the following cases indicate.

Holman v. Coie

Court of Appeals of Washington
522 P.2d 515 (1974)

MUNSON, JUDGE. . . .

Plaintiff Francis Holman joined the defendant law firm, of which his father was a senior partner, in 1941. He was made a partner in 1954 and has worked almost exclusively upon legal matters for Boeing, a firm client. Plaintiff William M. Holman joined the firm in 1949, and became a partner in 1957. During his early tenure he had done legal work for Boeing, but he had not done so for many years preceding the plaintiffs' expulsion from the law firm. Plaintiffs' father retired from the law firm in 1962, after a distinguished legal career.

The law firm, at the time of commencement of this action, consisted of 22 partners and other associates. Various partnership agreements had been entered into by the partners over the lifetime of this firm. Both plaintiffs were signators to the agreement controlling this action which was effective January 1, 1968. It provided, as had other previous agreements, that the business affairs of the partnership would be administered by an executive committee, comprised of 10 named partners. Both plaintiffs were members of this committee, which had the right to name new members and expel present members from the firm. The possibility of expulsion is mentioned in over a dozen different places throughout the partnership agreement. The agreement states that "any member may be expelled from the Firm by a majority vote of the Executive Committee," but does not specify whether expulsion shall be with or without cause or list any of the grounds for expulsion.

. . . There was testimony by [a] member of the executive committee that, prior to the admission of William Holman to the executive committee, the committee's meetings had been pleasant, friendly, and characterized by a spirit of unselfishness and devotion to the best interests of the firm. However, after admission of the Holmans, there appeared to develop a polarization among the committee, with the Holmans on one side and the remainder of the committee on the other. There is also testimony which would indicate that a number of years prior to the expulsion some consideration had been given to requesting the Holmans to leave the firm. . . .

In mid-April, 1969, Francis Holman made a speech before the State Senate regarding personal property tax legislation which was then before the Senate. There may have been some misstatement in the speech or in the reporting of it; in any event, the speech apparently served to aggravate several of the top officials of Boeing. . . . In April, preceding the speech, the president of Boeing advised the managing partner of the law firm that they desired Francis Holman to do no further legal work on their behalf. . . .

On May 7, 1969, the executive committee—the only absent members being plaintiffs and one other member who was on a European trip—met for 9½ hours in the Olympic Hotel. . . . Francis Holman was not notified of the meeting; William Holman had been informed earlier that there would be no executive committee meeting on May 7. The seven partners present discussed in detail whether the Holmans should be expelled from the law firm; the record shows the consensus favored expulsion, although neither a formal vote nor formal action was taken.

[On May 13] Francis Holman . . . was advised by his brother, William, of an executive committee meeting scheduled for 4 P.M. which had been recessed until 8 P.M. because of Francis Holman's absence; and that he had been advised it was particularly important that both Holmans be present. William Holman surmised that they were about to be expelled, an impression which became a harsh reality when they appeared at the 8 P.M. meeting. The meeting was convened by the managing partner, who then read aloud a resolution which, without giving cause or reasons, expelled them from the partnership. When they asked the reasons for the resolution, none were stated. A vote was taken; by a 7-2 result the partners were expelled. It is this action which serves as the basis for the suit brought against the law firm. . . .

It is the general contention of the plaintiffs that the defendant partners breached the partnership agreement by the act of expulsion in (a) failing to give proper notice to the plaintiffs of executive committee meetings on May 7 and May 13, 1969; (b) expelling plaintiffs without cause; (c) failing to state the reasons for expulsion; and (d) failing to allow plaintiffs an opportunity to be heard. . . .

Paragraph 2.3 of the partnership agreement provides that notice is not a requisite to the validity of any meeting of the executive committee; consequently, the fact that plaintiffs had no advance notice of the meeting is of no effect. . . .

As stated in A. Bromberg, Crane and Bromberg on Partnership, § 74(d), at 426 (1968); "Expulsion provisions are rare because of each partner's fear that the others may gang up on him." As a consequence, there is very little law on the subject of expulsion. There is, however, case law involving partnership agreements which substantiates the proposition that additional requirements should not be added to unambiguous expulsion provisions. . . .

We find this partnership agreement to [be] unambiguous, and not to require notice, reasons, or an opportunity to be heard. To inject those issues would be to rewrite the agreement of the parties, a function we neither presume nor assume.

Plaintiffs also challenge the expulsion on the basis that there was substantial evidence that it was not bona fide, or in good faith, and contend such a requirement should be implied.

[UPA § 31(1)(d)] states: "Dissolution is caused: (1) . . . (d) By the expulsion of any partner from the business bona fide in accordance with such a power conferred by the agreement between the partners; . . ." The partnership agreement here at issue merely states that a partner may be expelled by majority vote of the executive committee with no provisions for cause, reasons, notice or hearing. "Bona fide" is defined as: "In or with good faith; honestly, openly, and sincerely; without deceit or fraud." Black's Law Dictionary 223 (4th ed. 1951).

Undoubtedly, the general rule of law is that the partners in their dealings with each other must exercise good faith. . . . However, the personal relationships between partners to which the terms "bona fide" and "good faith" relate are those which have a bearing upon the business aspects or property of the partnership and prohibit a partner, to-wit, a [fiduciary] from taking any personal advantage touching those subjects. Plaintiffs' claims do not relate to the business aspects or property rights of this partnership. There is no evidence the purpose of the severance was to gain any business or property advantage to the remaining partners. Consequently, in that context, there has been no showing of breach of the duty of good faith toward plaintiffs.

There is authority for plaintiffs' contention that the term "bona fide" or "good faith" requires more, i.e., compliance with basic procedural due process standards. While courts do not rewrite contracts for the parties, they do presume to interpret them in accordance with what the court finds to be the parties' intent. "Good faith" is defined as: "An honest intention to abstain from taking any unconscientious advantage of another, even through technicalities of law, together with an absence of all information, notice or benefit or belief of facts which would render transaction unconscientious." Black's Law Dictionary 822 (4th ed. 1951).

An article in B. Davies, 33 Conveyance & Property Lawyer (n.s.), *Good Faith Principle and the Expulsion Clause in Partnership Law* 32, 42 (1969), published in England, states in part:

> [S]hould the situation be one involving an "expulsion" ... and the dispute ... is determined by the majority of partners, it is submitted that the application of the rules of natural justice are an essential legal prerequisite in the determination of the partnership dispute. This is so because partners in this circumstance are acting as a "tribunal or body of persons invested with authority to adjudicate upon matters involving civil consequences to individuals."

The article concludes that prior to expulsion, a partner is entitled to notice, the reasons, and a hearing, much as has been found by our courts under the phrase "due process of law."

We choose not to follow Mr. Davies. These parties in writing the partnership clauses dealing with expulsion, and the defendants who carried them out, chose to adopt the guillotine approach, rather than a more diplomatic approach, to the expulsion of partners. The actions of defendants were within the contemplation of the agreement. While this course of action may shock the sensibilities of some, to others it may be that once the initial decision is made, the traumatic reaction to that decision is more quickly overcome and the end result more merciful. However that course of action may appear to the reader, the possibility of exactly such action occurring is clear from reading the agreement. None of the partners had any reason to believe the agreement required anything more prior to abruptly and brusquely terminating their services.

Plaintiffs contend there was substantial evidence indicating the individual partners breached fiduciary duties they owed to plaintiffs as members of the Bar. In view of our holding that the executive committee had the right to expel plaintiffs without stating reason or cause pursuant to the partnership agreement, there was no breach of any fiduciary duty.

We conclude that these parties contractually agreed to the very method of expulsion exercised by the defendants, i.e., a clean, quick, and expeditious severance, with a clear method of accounting. It is not difficult to understand why parties to such a professional relationship would find this method desirable. This case, which has consumed nearly 4 years of litigation, and the attendant publicity, illustrates the virtues of this method of expulsion. The foundation of a professional relationship is personal confidence and trust. Once a schism develops, its magnitude may be exaggerated rightfully or wrongfully to the point of destroying a harmonious accord. When such occurs, an expeditious severance is desirable. To imply terms not expressed in this partnership agreement frustrates the unambiguous language of the agreement and the result contemplated.

We affirm the trial court's dismissal of the defendant partners.

GREEN, C.J., and MCINTURFF, J., concur.

Note

See also *Lawlis v. Kightlinger & Gray*, 562 N.E.2d 435, 442 (Ind. App. 1990), where a law firm senior partner (Lawlis), who struggled with alcoholism, was expelled after he had cured his problem and requested a return to the economic level he was at prior to receiving treatment. The firm had an expulsion clause similar to that in *Holman*, with no procedural standards or requirement of cause. Lawlis fought the expulsion, arguing that his fellow partners had "a predatory purpose" for expelling him because "the easiest way to increase the top partners' salaries is to eliminate a senior partner." The court responded as follows:

> From the time Lawlis's addiction to alcohol became known to the partnership's Finance Committee, it sought to assist and aid him through his medical crisis, even though he was taking substantial amounts of time off from his work to attempt cures in sanatoriums and had concealed the fact of his alcoholism from his partners for many months.... Also,... the Finance Committee, instead of recommending Lawlis's immediate expulsion as a method of increasing its lawyer to partner ratio, proposed he remain a partner for a maximum total of an additional eight months to give him time to find other employment and retain insurance coverage while so engaged. During that period it proposed he be permitted ... to draw up to $25,000 while he sought other employment. Such proposal again clearly negates a partnership "predatory purpose" for Lawlis's expulsion. Thus, there is no "genuine" issue as to whether the partnership acted in good faith when it expelled Lawlis because it can be foreclosed by reference to the undisputed facts here.
>
> Where the remaining partners in a firm deem it necessary to expel a partner under a no cause expulsion clause in a partnership agreement freely negotiated and entered into, the expelling partners act in "good faith" regardless of motivation if that act does not cause a wrongful withholding of money or property legally due the expelled partner at the time he is expelled. Used in this context, "good faith" means
>
>> a state of mind indicating honesty and lawfulness of purpose: belief in one's legal title or right: belief that one's conduct is not unconscionable ...: absence of fraud, deceit, collusion, or gross negligence....
>
> Webster's Third New International Dictionary, G. & C. Merriam and Co., 1976. Clearly, the senior partners acted in the belief they had the legal right to do so under the partnership agreement, as they did. That they recommended a step-down severance over six months rather than the "guillotine" severance permitted them under the agreement demonstrates a compassionate, not greedy, purpose. If we were to hold otherwise, we would be engrafting a "for cause" requirement upon this agreement when such was not the intent of the parties at the time they entered into their agreement. Lawlis's argument is without merit....

Bohatch v. Butler & Binion

Supreme Court of Texas
977 S.W.2d 543 (1998)

ENOCH, JUSTICE, delivered the opinion of the Court, in which GONZALEZ, OWEN, BAKER, and HANKINSON, JUSTICES, join.

Partnerships exist by the agreement of the partners; partners have no duty to remain partners. The issue in this case is whether we should create an exception to this rule by holding that a partnership has a duty not to expel a partner for reporting suspected overbilling by another partner. The trial court rendered judgment for Colette Bohatch on her breach of fiduciary duty claim against Butler & Binion and several of its partners (collectively, "the firm"). The court of appeals held that there was no evidence that the firm breached a fiduciary duty and reversed the trial court's tort judgment; however, the court of appeals found evidence of a breach of the partnership agreement and rendered judgment for Bohatch on this ground. 905 S.W.2d 597. We affirm the court of appeals' judgment.

I. Facts

Bohatch became an associate in the Washington, D.C., office of Butler & Binion in 1986 after working for several years as Deputy Assistant General Counsel at the Federal Energy Regulatory Commission. John McDonald, the managing partner of the office, and Richard Powers, a partner, were the only other attorneys in the Washington office. The office did work for Pennzoil almost exclusively.

Bohatch was made partner in February 1990. She then began receiving internal firm reports showing the number of hours each attorney worked, billed, and collected. From her review of these reports, Bohatch became concerned that McDonald was overbilling Pennzoil and discussed the matter with Powers. Together they reviewed and copied portions of McDonald's time diary. Bohatch's review of McDonald's time entries increased her concern.

On July 15, 1990, Bohatch met with Louis Paine, the firm's managing partner, to report her concern that McDonald was overbilling Pennzoil. Paine said he would investigate. Later that day, Bohatch told Powers about her conversation with Paine.

The following day, McDonald met with Bohatch and informed her that Pennzoil was not satisfied with her work and wanted her work to be supervised. Bohatch testified that this was the first time she had ever heard criticism of her work for Pennzoil.

The next day, Bohatch repeated her concerns to Paine and to R. Hayden Burns and Marion E. McDaniel, two other members of the firm's management committee, in a telephone conversation. Over the next month, Paine and Burns investigated Bohatch's complaint. They reviewed the Pennzoil bills and supporting computer print-outs for those bills. They then discussed the allegations with Pennzoil in-house counsel John Chapman, the firm's primary contact with Pennzoil. Chapman, who had a long-standing relationship with McDonald, responded that Pennzoil was satisfied that the bills were reasonable.

In August, Paine met with Bohatch and told her that the firm's investigation revealed no basis for her contentions. He added that she should begin looking for other employment, but that the firm would continue to provide her a monthly draw, insurance coverage, office space, and a secretary. After this meeting, Bohatch received no further work assignments from the firm.

In January 1991, the firm denied Bohatch a year-end partnership distribution for 1990 and reduced her tentative distribution share for 1991 to zero. In June, the firm paid Bohatch her monthly draw and told her that this draw would be her last. Finally, in August, the firm gave Bohatch until November to vacate her office.

By September, Bohatch had found new employment. She filed this suit on October 18, 1991, and the firm voted formally to expel her from the partnership three days later, October 21, 1991.

The trial court granted partial summary judgment for the firm on Bohatch's wrongful discharge claim, and also on her breach of fiduciary duty and breach of the duty of good faith and fair dealing claims for any conduct occurring after October 21, 1991 (the date Bohatch was formally expelled from the firm). The trial court denied the firm's summary judgment motion on Bohatch's breach of fiduciary duty and breach of the duty of good faith and fair dealing claims for conduct occurring before October 21, 1991. The breach of fiduciary duty claim and a breach of contract claim were tried to a jury. The jury found that the firm breached the partnership agreement and its fiduciary duty. It awarded Bohatch $57,000 for past lost wages, $250,000 for past mental anguish, $4,000,000 total in punitive damages (this amount was apportioned against several defendants), and attorney's fees. The trial court rendered judgment for Bohatch in the amounts found by the jury, except it disallowed attorney's fees because the judgment was based in tort. After suggesting remittitur, which Bohatch accepted, the trial court reduced the punitive damages to around $237,000.

All parties appealed. The court of appeals held that the firm's only duty to Bohatch was not to expel her in bad faith. The court of appeals stated that "'[b]ad faith' in this context means only that partners cannot expel another partner for self-gain." Finding no evidence that the firm expelled Bohatch for self-gain, the court concluded that Bohatch could not recover for breach of fiduciary duty. However, the court concluded that the firm breached the partnership agreement when it reduced Bohatch's tentative partnership distribution for 1991 to zero without notice, and when it terminated her draw three months before she left. The court concluded that Bohatch was entitled to recover $35,000 in lost earnings for 1991 but none for 1990, and no mental anguish damages. Accordingly, the court rendered judgment for Bohatch for $35,000 plus $225,000 in attorney's fees.

II. Breach of Fiduciary Duty

We have long recognized as a matter of common law that "[t]he relationship between . . . partners . . . is fiduciary in character, and imposes upon all the participants the obligation of loyalty to the joint concern and of the utmost good faith, fairness, and honesty in their dealings with each other with respect to matters pertaining to the enterprise." *Fitz-Gerald v. Hull*, 150 Tex. 39, 237 S.W.2d 256, 264 (1951) (quotation omitted). Yet, partners have no obligation to remain partners; "at the heart of the partnership concept is the principle that partners may choose with whom they wish to be associated." *Gelder Med. Group v. Webber*, 41 N.Y.2d 680, 394 N.Y.S.2d 867, 870–71, 363 N.E.2d 573, 577 (1977). The issue presented, one of first impression, is whether the fiduciary relationship between and among partners creates an exception to the at-will nature of partnerships; that is, in this case, whether it gives rise to a duty not to expel a partner who reports suspected overbilling by another partner.

At the outset, we note that no party questions that the obligations of lawyers licensed to practice in the District of Columbia — including McDonald and Bohatch — were prescribed by the District of Columbia Code of Professional Responsibility in effect in 1990, and that in all other respects Texas law applies. Further, neither statutory nor contract law principles answer the question of whether the firm owed Bohatch a duty not to expel her. The Texas Uniform Partnership Act addresses expulsion of a partner only in the context of dissolution of the partnership. *See* [UPA] §§ 31, 38. In this case, as provided by the partnership agreement, Bohatch's expulsion did not dissolve the partnership. Additionally, the new Texas Revised Partnership Act [RUPA] does not have retroactive effect and thus does not apply. Finally, the partnership agreement contemplates expulsion of a partner and prescribes procedures to be followed, but it does not specify or limit the grounds for expulsion. Thus, while Bohatch's claim that she was expelled in an *improper way* is governed by the partnership agreement, her claim that she was expelled for an *improper reason* is not. Therefore, we look to the common law to find the principles governing Bohatch's claim that the firm breached a duty when it expelled her.

Courts in other states have held that a partnership may expel a partner for purely business reasons. [citations omitted] Further, courts recognize that a law firm can expel a partner to protect relationships both within the firm and with clients. Finally, many courts have held that a partnership can expel a partner without breaching any duty in order to resolve a "fundamental schism." *See Waite*, 560 A.2d [619] at 623 [(N.H. 1989)] (concluding that in removing partner as managing partner "the partners acted in good faith to resolve the 'fundamental schism' between them"); *Heller v. Pillsbury Madison & Sutro*, 50 Cal.App.4th 1367, 58 Cal.Rptr.2d 336, 348 (1996) (holding that law firm did not breach fiduciary duty when it expelled partner who was not as productive as firm expected and who was offensive to some of firm's major clients); *Levy v. Nassau Queens Med. Group*, 102 A.D.2d 845, 476 N.Y.S.2d 613, 614 (1984) (concluding that expelling partner because of "[p]olicy disagreements" is not "bad faith").

The fiduciary duty that partners owe one another does not encompass a duty to remain partners or else answer in tort damages. Nonetheless, Bohatch and several distinguished legal scholars urge this Court to recognize that public policy requires a limited duty to remain partners—*i.e.*, a partnership must retain a whistleblower partner. They argue that such an extension of a partner's fiduciary duty is necessary because permitting a law firm to retaliate against a partner who in good faith reports suspected overbilling would discourage compliance with rules of professional conduct and thereby hurt clients.

While this argument is not without some force, we must reject it. A partnership exists solely because the partners choose to place personal confidence and trust in one another. Just as a partner can be expelled, without a breach of any common law duty, over disagreements about firm policy or to resolve some other "fundamental schism," a partner can be expelled for accusing another partner of overbilling without subjecting the partnership to tort damages. Such charges, whether true or not, may have a profound effect on the personal confidence and trust essential to the partner relationship. Once such charges are made, partners may find it impossible to continue to work together to their mutual benefit and the benefit of their clients.

We are sensitive to the concern expressed by the dissenting Justices that "retaliation against a partner who tries in good faith to correct or report perceived misconduct virtually assures that others will not take these appropriate steps in the future." 977 S.W.2d at 561 (Spector, J., dissenting). However, the dissenting Justices do not explain how the trust relationship necessary both for the firm's existence and for representing clients can survive such serious accusations by one partner against another. The threat of tort liability for expulsion would tend to force partners to remain in untenable circumstance—suspicious of and angry with each other—to their own detriment and that of their clients whose matters are neglected by lawyers distracted with intra-firm frictions.

Although concurring in the Court's judgment, Justice Hecht criticizes the Court for failing to "address amici's concerns that failing to impose liability will discourage attorneys from reporting unethical conduct." To address the scholars' concerns, he proposes that a whistleblower be protected from expulsion, but only if the report, irrespective of being made in good faith, is proved to be correct. We fail to see how such an approach encourages compliance with ethical rules more than the approach we adopt today. Furthermore, the amici's position is that a reporting attorney must be in good faith, not that the attorney must be right. In short, Justice Hecht's approach ignores the question Bohatch presents, the amici write about, and the firm challenges—whether a partnership violates a fiduciary duty when it expels a partner who in good faith reports suspected ethical violations. The concerns of the amici are best addressed by a rule that clearly demarcates an attorney's ethical duties and the parameters of tort liability, rather than redefining "whistleblower."

We emphasize that our refusal to create an exception to the at-will nature of partnerships in no way obviates the ethical duties of lawyers. Such duties sometimes necessitate difficult decisions, as when a lawyer suspects overbilling by a colleague.

The fact that the ethical duty to report may create an irreparable schism between partners neither excuses failure to report nor transforms expulsion as a means of resolving that schism into a tort.

We hold that the firm did not owe Bohatch a duty not to expel her for reporting suspected overbilling by another partner.

III. Breach of the Partnership Agreement

The court of appeals concluded that the firm breached the partnership agreement by reducing Bohatch's tentative distribution for 1991 to zero without the requisite notice. The firm contests this finding on the ground that the management committee had the right to set tentative and year-end bonuses. However, the partnership agreement guarantees a monthly draw of $7,500 per month regardless of the tentative distribution. Moreover, the firm's right to reduce the bonus was contingent upon providing proper notice to Bohatch. The firm does not dispute that it did not give Bohatch notice that the firm was reducing her tentative distribution. Accordingly, the court of appeals did not err in finding the firm liable for breach of the partnership agreement. Moreover, because Bohatch's damages sound in contract, and because she sought attorney's fees at trial under section 38.001(8) of the Texas Civil Practice and Remedies Code, we affirm the court of appeals' award of Bohatch's attorney's fees.

We affirm the court of appeals' judgment.

HECHT, JUSTICE, filed a concurring opinion.

SPECTOR, JUSTICE, filed a dissenting opinion, in which PHILLIPS, CHIEF JUSTICE, joined.

HECHT, JUSTICE, concurring in the judgment.

. . . .

I respond briefly to the Court's opinion and to the dissent. . . .

[T]he Court mischaracterizes my position, just as it does the amici's arguments. It simply is not true that I "propose[ ] that a whistle blower be protected from expulsion, but only if the report, irrespective of being made in good faith, is proved to be correct." As I have explained, I would not attempt to define when a law firm partner expelled for reporting unethical conduct can recover damages because I do not regard it as essential to the disposition of this case to do so. I would not hold that being correct is enough, only that being incorrect precludes recovery, at least in these circumstances. My criticism of the Court is not that another bright-line rule—one based on whether a report was correct—would be better, but that no bright-line rule should be adopted when the full ramifications of so broad a rule have not been adequately considered. It should come as no surprise to anyone that a lawyer can be fired for being incorrect, albeit in good faith. A lawyer can always be terminated for being incorrect about legal matters. It is, after all, a lawyer's judgment that is important, not her sincerity. Bohatch's charges were not merely an innocent mistake. They caused the expenditure of a significant amount of time in investigation, the report of possible overbilling to one of the firm's major clients, potentially jeopardizing that relationship, and an impossible strain on three lawyers working together on the same business for the same client in a small but important office of the firm.

Without offering a solution to the problems the amici raise, the Court adopts an absolute rule: a law firm that expels a partner for reporting ethics violations has no liability to the partner under any circumstances. The rule is ill-advised, particularly when it is far broader than necessary to address Bohatch's claims. . . .

The dissent finds no support in any authority in any jurisdiction. Furthermore, the argument that allowing expulsion of a partner who incorrectly reports unethical conduct impairs Rule 8.03(a) of the Texas Disciplinary Rules of Professional Conduct is equally unfounded. That rule states in part that "a lawyer having knowledge that another lawyer has committed a violation of applicable rules of professional conduct that raises a substantial question as to that lawyer's honesty, trustworthiness or fitness as a lawyer in other respects, shall inform the appropriate disciplinary authority." A lawyer's duty under this rule is only triggered by (1) knowledge of (2) a rules violation that (3) raises a substantial question about a lawyer's honesty, trustworthiness, or fitness. Bohatch's suspicions do not meet these requirements.

Even if they did, the dissent fails to make a convincing argument for liability in every situation in which a lawyer reports a suspected ethical violation. The dissent does not even acknowledge the tensions that would plainly arise between partners making and denying charges of unethical behavior. These tensions might easily prevent proper representation of clients. "[P]artners have a right not to continue a partnership with someone against their will," the dissent concedes, but if their will is based on a partner's assertions of unethical conduct, then they must pay to exert it. Not even lawyers should be forced to choose *in every instance* between maintaining an untenable partnership and paying for its termination over ethical disagreements however serious and sincere.

The dissent's reference to Twain to say that the "wages" of "right" and "wrong" in disagreements over ethics "is just the same" is clever, but it ignores the practicalities of maintaining a relationship of trust and confidence, and it glibly expresses a much too cynical view of the entire problem presented here. Acknowledging that some law partnerships cannot legitimately be expected to survive internecine quarrels over ethics simply does not spell the end of an attorney's responsibility to professional obligations and standards. Thus it is just not true, as the dissent asserts, that "this case sends an inappropriate signal to lawyers and to the public that the rules of professional responsibility are subordinate to a law firm's other interests." The matter is not so simple. A lawyer cannot simply enshroud any complaint against his colleagues in the mantle of obedience to rules of professional responsibility. The toll such a complaint makes is also important. The dissent's added charge that the result in this case "leave[s] an attorney who acts ethically and in good faith without recourse", assumes incorrectly that the only "recourse" is an action for damages. Twain suggests that righteousness has its own rewards. The dissent argues that those rewards must be monetary to be real. . . .

Spector, joined by Phillips, Chief Justice, dissenting.

> [W]hat's the use you learning to do right when it's troublesome to do right and ain't no trouble to do wrong, and the wages is just the same?
>
> *— The Adventures of Huckleberry Finn*

The issue in this appeal is whether law partners violate a fiduciary duty by retaliating against one partner for questioning the billing practices of another partner. I would hold that partners violate their fiduciary duty to one another by punishing compliance with the Disciplinary Rules of Professional Conduct. Accordingly, I dissent. . . .

It is true that no high court has considered the issue of whether expulsion of a partner for complying with ethical rules violates law partners' fiduciary duty. The dearth of authority in this area does not, however, diminish the significance of this case. Instead, the scarcity of guiding case law only heightens the importance of this Court's decision. . . .

In light of this Court's role in setting standards to govern attorney's conduct, it is particularly inappropriate for the Court to deny recourse to attorneys wronged for adhering to the Disciplinary Rules. I would hold that in this case the law partners violated their fiduciary duty by retaliating against a fellow partner who made a good faith effort to alert her partners to the possible overbilling of a client.

The duty to prevent overbilling and other misconduct exists for the protection of the client. Even if a report turns out to be mistaken or a client ultimately consents to the behavior in question, as in this case, retaliation against a partner who tries in good faith to correct or report perceived misconduct virtually assures that others will not take these appropriate steps in the future. Although I agree with the majority that partners have a right not to continue a partnership with someone against their will, they may still be liable for damages directly resulting from terminating that relationship.

The Court's writing in this case sends an inappropriate signal to lawyers and to the public that the rules of professional responsibility are subordinate to a law firm's other interests. Under the majority opinion's vision for the legal profession, the wages would not even be the same for "doing right"; they diminish considerably and leave an attorney who acts ethically and in good faith without recourse. Accordingly, I respectfully dissent.

Cadwalader, Wickersham & Taft v. Beasley

Court of Appeal of Florida
728 So. 2d 253 (1998)

On Rehearing

Polen, Judge. . . .

Cadwalader, Wickersham & Taft (CW & T), a New York law firm, appeals from a final judgment awarding return of capital, interest, profits, and punitive damages to its former partner, James Beasley (Beasley), for wrongful expulsion. CW & T appeals all aspects of the award except for the return of the paid-in capital with interest. Beasley cross-appeals the court's refusal to award him any interest in the firm's goodwill. CW & T appeals from an award of attorney's fees and costs to Beasley. . . . We reverse as to the award of profits, attorney's fees and costs, but affirm as to all other points raised by both parties.

Beasley laterally transferred to become a partner at CW & T in its Palm Beach office in 1989. After his arrival, the Palm Beach office suffered from internal discord and, by 1994, the office was operating at a loss. In response to this situation, the firm's management committee began discussions regarding the termination of up to 30 partners nationwide, including the Palm Beach partners. During this time, and allegedly unbeknownst to CW & T, Beasley was planning to leave the firm. He met secretly with associates in CW & T's Palm Beach office about leaving with him.

The management committee eventually held a day-long meeting on August 7, 1994. Prior to the meeting, the committee members were asked to submit lists of less productive partners to be considered for possible termination. All of the Palm Beach partners were identified on the lists actually submitted. A tentative vote was reached at that meeting and, later that month, the committee formally decided to close its Palm Beach office by year-end 1994. It informed its partners, including Beasley, of its decision on August 30, 1994.

After the announcement, Beasley retained Professor Robert Hillman, who opined that CW & T, pursuant to the partnership agreement, lacked the legal authority to expel him from the partnership. In response to this opinion, CW & T sent a memorandum to Beasley informing him that he was still a partner in the firm. It then offered Beasley either relocation within the firm but in the New York or Washington, D.C. offices, or, a compensation/severance package which included his return of capital, departure bonus, and full shares through December 31, 1994. He was presented with a written withdrawal agreement confirming the same. Beasley, a member of both the Florida and New York bars, rejected the same as impractical.

Settlement negotiations between CW & T and Beasley then continued. On November 9, he sued the firm for fraud and breach of fiduciary duty, among other counts. On November 10, 1994, CW & T sent a letter to Beasley informing him to vacate the premises by 5:00 p.m. the next day. The letter specifically prohibited him from continuing to represent himself as associated with the firm.

After a nine-day bench trial, Judge Cook authored a meticulous and, we believe, exceptionally well-reasoned final judgment. He found that CW & T was authorized to close the Palm Beach office pursuant to the partnership agreement, and that Beasley would have voluntarily left CW & T by year-end 1994 in any event. Nevertheless, since the partnership agreement lacked provisions for the expulsion of a partner except in one limited situation,[19] he found that CW & T had anticipatorily breached the partnership agreement when it announced its plans to close the Palm Beach office in August, and then actually breached the agreement when it sent him the November 10, 1994 letter. The final judgment awarded Beasley his paid-in capital plus interest (which CW & T does not dispute), his percentage interest in the firm's accounts receivables and assets and interest thereon, and punitive damages, all totaling $2.5+ million. The later judgment awarded Beasley's attorneys fees and costs. These amounts are broken down as follows:

— Beasley's paid-in capital of $194,193, plus interest at the rate as defined in the partnership agreement to the date of judgment [$42,199] $236,392.00

— his percentage interest in the firm's accounts receivable, work-in-progress, office building and other assets $867,110.00

— his profits attributable to the use of his right in the property of the dissolved partnership $935,261.52

— punitive damages $500,000.00

— attorney's fees and costs $1,108,247.92

The court, however, rejected Beasley's claims for future lost income and retirement benefits. The appeals and cross-appeal, as set forth above, ensued.

I. Whether Beasley was Expelled or Voluntarily Withdrew

Under New York Partnership Law's adoption of the Uniform Partnership Act (UPA), partners have no common law or statutory right to expel or dismiss another partner from the partnership; they may, however, provide in their partnership agreement for expulsion under prescribed conditions which must be strictly applied. Absent such a provision, as here, the removal of a partner may be accomplished only through dissolution of the firm. *Dawson v. White & Case*, 88 N.Y.2d 666, 649 N.Y.S.2d 364, 672 N.E.2d 589 (1996).

The evidence supports Judge Cook's finding that CW & T intended to remove Beasley as a partner in the firm when it announced it was closing its Palm Beach office by year-end 1994. This finding, in turn, supports the conclusion that CW & T anticipatorily expelled Beasley from the firm.

In reaching this conclusion, we necessarily reject CW & T's argument that Beasley voluntary withdrew from the firm rather than having been expelled. Beasley had been practicing exclusively in South Florida for 22 years, where he built a substantial client base. As the trial court observed, to suddenly uproot to New York or Washington and leave his clients and contacts behind, as the court suggested, would have severely diminished his rainmaking abilities. Under these circumstances, we

---

19. [1] Paragraph F(4) of the agreement provided for expulsion where a partner experienced sudden and total disability, a provision not implicated in this case.

conclude that his rejecting the offer as impractical was not tantamount to a voluntary withdrawal.

Even assuming that CW & T did not anticipatorily breach the agreement on August 29, 1994, we conclude that the November 10, 1994 letter actually expelled him. Even though CW & T notes that Beasley planned on eventually leaving the firm even before it announced the decision to close the Palm Beach office, and that he most likely would not have stayed past 1994, the record does not reflect that he actually had definite plans to leave.

We further reject CW & T's argument that Beasley's suing the firm on November 9, 1994 was tantamount to a voluntary withdrawal. Since CW & T does not dispute the lack of frivolousness of Beasley's lawsuit, but merely takes issue with its allegations, we find its argument unpersuasive.

II. The Award of Interest

CW & T then argues the trial court erred in finding that a dissolution occurred and contends that, as a "withdrawn partner" pursuant to the agreement, Beasley was entitled to only his paid-in capital. Even if dissolution had occurred, it argues he still only would be entitled to an amount significantly less than that awarded to him. Beasley disputes that he was a "withdrawn" partner pursuant to the agreement, and contends that dissolution was mandated.

Under the partnership agreement, a "withdrawn Partner" is anyone "who was a Partner under this or a prior Firm Agreement." More specifically, the agreement provides that a partner, upon 60 days written notice, may withdraw from the firm at the end of any fiscal year. CW & T argues that, under these provisions, Beasley was technically a withdrawn partner and, thus, was only entitled to his capital contribution plus interest under Paragraph F(2)(a)(i) of the agreement. We, instead, agree with Judge Cook that the term "withdrawn" neither contemplated nor encompassed a partner expelled in the same manner as Beasley, especially since Beasley never provided any written notice of a voluntary withdrawal, and since CW & T conceded at trial that it did not treat Beasley as a "withdrawn partner" after his departure.

Antidissolution Provision

CW & T then argues that concluding a dissolution occurred would conflict with that portion of the agreement which states, "Neither withdrawal of a Partner nor the death of a Partner, nor *any other event* shall cause dissolution of the Firm [unless 75% of the remaining partners agreed in writing]." (Emphasis added.) It reasons that expulsion of a partner, however wrongful, is an "event" for purposes of this antidissolution clause. We disagree, for to construe this anti-dissolution provision strictly would recognize an implicit expulsion provision where no provision exists. Such an interpretation would be inconsistent with existing law.

Even if the provision were broad enough to cover expulsions, we believe Beasley would still be allowed to seek dissolution of the partnership. Under New York law, any partner has the right to a formal accounting as to partnership affairs if he is wrongfully excluded from the partnership business or possession of its property by his co-partners, or "[w]henever other circumstances render it just and reasonable." [UPA § 22] Thus, a wrongful exclusion of one partner by a co-partner from participation in the conduct of the business may be grounds for judicial dissolution. *See Karrick v. Hannaman*, 168 U.S. 328, 18 S. Ct. 135, 42 L. Ed. 484 (1897) (holding that an antidissolution provision in partnership agreement should not prevent dissolution when one partner wrongfully excludes the other); *see also Clark v. Gunn*, 134 N.Y.S.2d 206, 207 (App. Div. 1954) (holding that, where the partnership agreement in question contained no provisions for the majority's expulsion of the minority, and that is what the plaintiffs attempted to do, the partnership may be dissolved under partnership law); *Bailly v. Betti*, 241 N.Y. 22, 148 N.E. 776 (1925) (holding an attempted exclusion of partner from the firm business warranted an action for an accounting though the time of dissolution fixed by the articles had not arrived and no dissolution was asked).

Since Beasley was expelled, his damages are to be assessed under § 71 of New York Partnership Law [UPA § 40], and not under the partnership agreement. Since there is competent, substantial evidence in the record to support both the method and result used to calculate his interest in the firm's assets, we affirm the award of interest in the firm's assets in the amount of $867,110.00.

III. The Award of Profits

Under New York law, when a partnership continues following the expulsion of a partner, that partner has the right to receive the value of his partnership interest as of the date of dissolution, either with interest from the date of dissolution, *or*, at his election, the profits attributable to the use of his right in the property of the dissolved partnership. [UPA § 42]

Strictly construing this statute, Beasley was entitled to either interest *on the value* of his interest in the dissolved partnership ($867,110) *or* profits attributable to the use of his right in the property of the firm *on top of* the $867,110. Beasley elected to receive the profits attributable to his use through the date of judgment instead of interest at 3% over prime (as defined in the agreement). Based on his expert, Mr. Burgher, having calculated the profits attributable to the use of his right in the property based on the firm's total earnings to reflect what Beasley's total income would have been had he stayed at the firm from November, 1994 through May, 1996, the court awarded Beasley profits in the amount of $935,261.52.

CW & T argues that, as a matter of law, awarding Beasley $935,261.52 in "profits" based on this calculation was incorrect. Relying on *Kirsch v. Leventhal*, 181 A.D.2d 222, 586 N.Y.S.2d 330 (1992), it reasons that Beasley should not be entitled to profits resulting from the postdissolution services of the remaining partners. We agree. To the extent that some of the firm's postdissolution profits may be attributable to the postdissolution efforts, skill, and diligence of the remaining partners, the firm's fee as a result of those services should not be proportionately attributable to the use of the departing partner's right in the property of the dissolved partnership. As the record does not clarify what portion, if any, of the postdissolution profits earned on services (as opposed to firm assets) was attributable to Beasley, we find that Beasley failed to carry his burden of showing what the quantum meruit value of his services was after he left the firm.

Beasley tries to distinguish *Kirsch* and the other cases upon which CW & T relies based on the fact that the partners in those cases were not wrongfully expelled. If recognized, this distinction may help justify the court's award, but it would seem to be an impermissible extension of [UPA § 42]. As an equitable consideration, although the facts underlying Beasley's departure appear much more egregious than in the cases CW & T cites, Beasley still had "dirt under his fingernails."[20] While CW & T should not be unjustly enriched through its wrongful expulsion of Beasley, neither should Beasley be unjustly enriched by reaping the rewards of other partners' individual efforts. Accordingly, we reverse this portion of the award and remand the case to the trial court to calculate Beasley's interest on $867,110 at 3% over prime, the defined rate pursuant to the agreement, under [UPA § 42].

IV. The Imposition of Punitive Damages

CW & T then argues that the court's award of punitive damages was both unwarranted and erroneous as a matter of law. It asserts that the court's failure to award Beasley compensatory damages on his breach of fiduciary duty claim barred an award of punitive damages under New York law. Under New York law, the nature of the conduct which justifies an award of punitive damages is conduct having a high degree of moral culpability, or, in other words, conduct which shows a "conscious disregard of the rights of others or conduct so reckless as to amount to such disregard." (citations omitted). CW & T is correct in arguing that punitive damages are generally recovered only after compensatory damages have been awarded; however, since the purpose of punitive damages is to both punish the wrongdoer and deter others from such wrongful behavior, as a matter of policy, courts have the discretion to award punitive damages even where compensatory damages are found lacking.

We believe CW & T should not be insulated from the consequences of its wrongdoing simply because Beasley suffered no compensatory damages. As the court found, CW & T "was participating in a clandestine plan to wrongfully expel some partners for the financial gain of other partners. Such activity cannot be said to be honorable, much less to comport with the 'punctilio of an honor.'" Because these findings establish that CW & T consciously disregarded the rights of Beasley, we affirm the award of punitive damages.

V. The Award of Attorney's Fees, Expert Witness Costs and Trial Costs

As to the trial court's award of attorney's fees and costs, CW & T argues that *Chapel v. Mitchell*, 84 N.Y.2d 345, 618 N.Y.S.2d 626, 642 N.E.2d 1082 (1994) and

---

20. [3] The final judgment clearly shows Judge Cook's determination of the relative equities of the parties' positions when he found, "If Beasley has dirt under his fingernails, CW & T was up to its' (sic) elbows in the dung heap."

A.G. Ship Maintenance Corp. v. Lezak, 69 N.Y.2d 1, 511 N.Y.S.2d 216, 503 N.E.2d 681 (1986) support the "American Rule" which dictates that attorney's fees cannot be awarded absent a statute or contract authorizing the same. As such, it correctly maintains that the trial court misapplied this law in ordering that CW & T recompense Beasley for his attorney's fees and costs. . . . As such, we reverse.

Moreover, we reverse the award of costs. Under New York law, these costs, including expert witness fees, are not recoverable absent statutory authorization. . . .

VI. Whether CW & T Had Valuable Goodwill

Beasley argues on cross-appeal that the trial court's acceptance of CW & T's expert's "junk accounting" caused it to wrongfully find the firm had no valuable goodwill. We disagree, as there is competent, substantial evidence in the record to support Judge Cook's finding. Beasley's assertions that the court was "hoodwinked" simply is not supported by the evidence.

AFFIRMED in part; REVERSED in part and REMANDED for further proceedings in accordance with this opinion.

STEVENSON and SHAHOOD, JJ., concur.

Note

See Donald J. Weidner, Cadwalader, *RUPA and Fiduciary Duty*, 54 WASH. & LEE L. REV. 877, 892 (1997), commenting on the lower court decision in *Cadwalader*. Dean Weidner stated in part as follows with regard to the decision, affirmed on appeal, to find Cadwalader liable to Beasley:

> Cadwalader appears to equate an attempt to dissociate from a problematic partner with an attempt to appropriate a contingent fee. . . . Cadwalader shifts the focus from where it belongs, which is on the reasonable expectations under the partnership agreement, to the motivation behind the decision to dissolve. The court suggests that the very decision to dissolve is actionable if profit is a motivator. In so doing, Cadwalader represents a problematic addition to the line of cases recognizing a cause of action for bad faith dissolution of an at-will partnership.

2. The Right to an Accounting and Suits Among Partners

The right of a partner to a formal account as to partnership matters has been recognized for centuries. At common law the right existed only at dissolution or if a partner was excluded from participation in the business, unless provided for in the partnership agreement. UPA §22 recognized and expanded the common law right to an accounting. The expansion is contained in part (d) of §22, which allows an accounting whenever circumstances "render it just and reasonable." RUPA §405 also makes an accounting available during the term of the partnership as well as upon dissolution.

The excerpts contained below from two cases may prove useful in introducing the process involved in an accounting. In *Schane v. Conrad*, 386 N.E.2d 431, 433 (Ill. 1979), the following was stated:

> A suit for an accounting involves two separate and distinct determinations; i.e., that an accounting is required and that a sum certain is due to plaintiff as a result and, traditionally, these determinations have been made in separate hearings. See 1 Ill. L. & Prac. *Accounting* § 34 (1953), where the following was stated:
>
> > The well-settled practice, after determining that the right to an accounting exists, where the account consists of many items covering a great length of time, and the testimony is conflicting, is to enter an interlocutory decree to account, declaring the rights of the parties, and the basis or rule to be adopted in stating the account, and then refer the cause to a master.

In *Polikoff v. Levy*, 270 N.E.2d 540, 546–547 (Ill. App. Ct. 1971), the court described the accounting process as follows:

> The cross and separate appeals in this case attack that portion of the trial-court decree which approved defendants' accounting. Defendants filed 20 documents as an accounting for the co-venture operations. These documents consisted of balance sheets, financial statements and monthly reports prepared by accountants. The accountants' letters accompanying some of the various documents stated that the accountants expressed no opinion on the financial statements and in certain instances that the documents were prepared from the books and records without audit or other examination. . . .
>
> An accounting is a statement of receipts and disbursements. A final account of a partnership or co-venture should show all of the detailed financial transactions of the business and the true status of the firm's assets. In *Wylie v. Bushnell*, 277 Ill. 484, 115 N.E. 618 (1917), the court, in passing on a trustee's report, said (277 Ill. at 491, 115 N.E. at 622):
>
> > Of course, there can be no question as to the duty of a trustee to keep regular and accurate accounts during the whole course of his trusteeship, from which it can be ascertained what property has come into his hands, what has passed out, and what remains therein, including all receipts and disbursements in cash, and the sources from which they came, to whom paid and for what purpose paid. (Citing authorities.)
>
> In an accounting on dissolution of a partnership or co-venture, the same type of account is required as that of a trustee. The account should list all receipts and disbursements made and the original vouchers, bills and cancelled checks should be tendered or available for inspection to support the items listed. It should include a listing of original contributions and current assets and liabilities.

While it is apparent that the account in the instant case must cover many years, will consist of many items, and will require production of many documents, yet in order for the account to be of any value or to fulfill the duty of accounting it cannot be merely a summary or lump listing of types of items. Simply because a matter has become complicated or voluminous does not excuse the duty of giving "true and full information." While the burden may be considerable, this does not eliminate the requirement of a proper account where a duty to account exists. That which was filed as an account does not comply with the duty to account. The decree of the circuit court, in so far as it approved the accounting, was in error and must be reversed.

One of the questions raised when partners sue each other is whether an accounting is required as part of the suit. Under the common law and UPA, an accounting was a necessary prerequisite to such a suit. The policy behind the accounting rule is well explained in *Schuler v. Birnbaum*, 62 A.D.2d 461, 462–463 (N.Y. App. Div. 1978), as follows:

> Generally, courts will not interfere in internal disputes between members of a partnership, preferring instead that the partners settle their differences among themselves or else dissolve and go out of business settling their affairs at that time by a final and full accounting with all partners joined. In this way, premature piece-meal judgments between partners which may later require adjustment when all the business of the partnership is reviewed are avoided. Thus, it is the general rule that partners cannot sue each other at law for acts relating to the partnership unless there is an accounting, prior settlement, or adjustment of the partnership affairs.

Smith v. Manchester Mgt. Corp., 373 A.2d 361, 363 (N.H. 1977), provides an example of the traditional approach to a suit between partners. In *Smith*, the plaintiff (Smith) sued his partner prior to termination of the partnership and thus before the customary final accounting on winding up and termination. He alleged that defendant mismanaged partnership affairs, failed to meet its capital obligation to the partnership, and engaged in a pattern of self-dealing. Smith asked for a jury trial. His request was denied on the reasoning that an accounting, which is equitable in nature, was a necessary part of his suit. This judgment was affirmed on appeal, the court stating:

> It is well-settled law that in the absence of statutory permission an action at law, as distinguished from an action in equity, is not maintainable between partners with respect to partnership transactions, unless there has been an accounting or settlement of the partnership affairs. . . . Plaintiff's principal argument in avoidance of this well established rule is that his claims do not involve partnership affairs, but rather direct contractual obligations between the parties in their individual capacities. We find this characterization by plaintiff to be inapposite. . . . The partnership relation here has existed over a considerable period of time and has undoubtedly involved

numerous transactions. No accounting has been had. Plaintiff's complaints go to the heart of the conduct of the partnership affairs. We conclude the court did not err in concluding that plaintiff was not entitled to a jury trial.

The *Schuler*, case cited above, sets out a key exception to the UPA accounting rule:

> One exception to this rule permits a partner to maintain an action at law against his co-partner when no complex accounting is required or when only one transaction is involved which is fully closed but unadjusted. The evidence before the court upon the motion for summary judgment established that the parties had formed a partnership to operate a nursing home, that the partnership was abandoned after it failed to obtain a state license, and that the retention of the architects and filing of the license application was the sole business transacted by the partnership. This was not rebutted by defendants by factual allegations establishing the need for an accounting, nor did defendants counterclaim for an accounting as they could have. Accordingly, this action at law may be maintained.
>
> . . . .

405 N.Y.S.2d at 351.

RUPA § 405, is less insistent on the necessity of an accounting than the common law or UPA. Section 405(b) states, "A partner may maintain an action against the partnership or another partner for legal or equitable relief, including an accounting as to partnership business, to enforce a right under the partnership agreement, a right under this Act . . . , or enforce the rights and otherwise protect the interests of the partner, including rights and interests arising independently of the partnership relationship." Comment 2 to § 405 states that § 405(b) "reflects a new policy choice that partners should have access to the courts during the term of the partnership to resolve claims against the partnership and the other partners, leaving broad judicial discretion to fashion appropriate remedies. Under RUPA an accounting is not a prerequisite to the availability of the other remedies a partner may have against the partnership or the other partners."

Courts interpreting RUPA § 405 have, in fact, been allowing suits between partners to go forward without an accounting. In *Simpson v. Thorslund*, 211 P.3d 469 (Wash. Ct. App. 2009), for instance, two individuals formed a partnership to build homes. (They had planned to form a corporation, but failed to sign the necessary paperwork, so the court found a de facto partnership.) One partner (Thorslund) handled the business side, while the other (Simpson) was, essentially, a laborer who had been promised regular compensation. Thorslund allegedly mismanaged the business, misappropriated partnership funds, and failed to pay Simpson his compensation or repay a loan that Simpson had made to the business. Simpson brought suit against Thorslund to recover these amounts. The trial court held that a formal accounting was not necessary and the appellate court affirmed: "an accounting was required under the common law and was a precondition to an action between partners, including de facto partners. Since the adoption of RUPA in 1998, however, Washington law no longer requires such an accounting." *See also Berry v. Ostrom*, 163 P.3d 247 (Idaho Ct. App. 2007).

Question

Can parties to a partnership agreement contract way their rights to an accounting under RUPA § 405?

I. Claims by Creditors of the Partnership

1. Rights Against Partnership Assets

It has never been doubted that partnership creditors have rights against partnership assets. But how does an unpaid, unsecured creditor realize its rights under UPA? Can the creditor sue the partnership, obtain a judgment, and execute against the partnership assets? The aggregate theory makes this impossible because, as noted earlier, a partnership is not a person and cannot be sued. As mentioned previously, many states by statute have authorized suits against a partnership and execution against the partnership assets, as well as the individual assets of any partner personally joined and served with process. For those jurisdictions that do not provide for this, a creditor must sue the individual partners, obtain judgment, and execute against the partnership assets by virtue of the equity described immediately below.

The Rowley treatise (§ 38.0-C) indicates that a creditor's rights are purely derivative from a partner's rights under § 38 of the UPA to have partnership property paid to discharge partnership liabilities. This is referred to as a partner's "equity" because this right historically was first recognized in the equity courts. The recognition in UPA § 25(2)(c) that partnership property can be attached for a partnership debt, coupled with the rule in § 25(2)(b) that a partner's right in specific partnership property is not assignable unless the rights of all partners in the property are assigned, reinforce the notion that creditors have the right to have partnership property applied to the payment of partnership debts.

A creditor's rights against partnership assets are more simply defined in RUPA due to the adoption of the entity theory. *See* §§ 307(a) ("A partnership may sue and be sued in the name of the partnership") and 501 ("A partner is not co-owner of partnership property . . .").

The rights of firm creditors when the partnership sells out or merges into a new partnership are discussed in Chapter 13.

2. Rights Against the Personal Assets of Individual Partners

The personal liability of each partner for the debts of the partnership is set forth in § 15 of UPA. In the majority of states, a creditor of a joint and several obligation can obtain a judgment against any partner it chooses, or against the partnership (assuming a common name statute or its equivalent), or both. The creditor can execute against the personal assets of the partner it has chosen until satisfaction of the underlying claim is achieved without having first to execute against partnership assets. As noted earlier, a partner who pays a firm obligation is entitled to indemnity under UPA § 18(b), which softens the impact of the above rule.

Some states disagree with the above rule and insist on exhaustion of partnership assets before personal assets of partners can be reached. *See* Reuschlein & Gregory, Agency and Partnership 317 (2nd ed. 1990). The authorities are more divided when the liability is joint rather than joint and several in nature.

RUPA, which in § 306 retains personal liability for each partner despite its adoption of the entity theory, has made a substantial change in this area. Section § 307(d) states that a judgment creditor "may not levy execution against the assets of a partner to satisfy a judgment based on a claim against the partnership unless a judgment on the same claim has been obtained against the partnership and a writ of execution on the judgment has been returned unsatisfied in whole or in part . . . [a creditor need not first exhaust partnership assets if the partner so agrees; also, the statute provides for court permission to levy execution first against the assets of a partner as an exercise of the court's equitable powers]." Comment 4 to § 307 states that the rule of (d) "respects the concept of the partnership as an entity and makes partners more in the nature of guarantors than principal debtors on every partnership debt."

The above change has drawn some criticism on the ground that the burden of clarification of guarantor status should be placed on the partners, not imposed by statute on creditors. Partners are the owners of the business who enjoy its profits, are liable for its debts, and are the people whose reputations for reliability and solvency frequently play a role in the extension of credit, especially for small businesses. Also, economically the burden of clarification is best imposed on the partners in the interest of making credit and collection of debts less costly, it is argued. *See* J. Dennis Hynes, *The Revised Uniform Partnership Act: Some Comments on the Latest Draft of RUPA*, 19 Fla. St. U. L. Rev. 727, 737–38 (1992). It is important to note that the coverage in this section is focusing on partnerships that have not filed for LLP status.

The matter of priority among the creditors of an insolvent individual partner is addressed in § 40(h) and (i) of UPA. The rule of § 40 that partnership creditors have priority in partnership assets and individual creditors in individual assets is known as the "dual priorities" rule or the "jingle" rule. *See* MacLachlan, Bankruptcy 424 (1956).

RUPA indirectly addresses this issue in § 807(a), which states, "In winding up a partnership's business, the assets of the partnership must be applied to discharge its obligations to creditors, including partners who are creditors." Comment 2 to § 807 states, "RUPA in effect abolishes the 'dual priority' or 'jingle' rule of UPA. . . . Under . . . RUPA, partnership creditors share pro rata with the partners' individual creditors in the assets of the partners' estates."

These provisions of the partnership statutes are, of course, subject to any contrary provisions in federal bankruptcy law, a topic that is beyond the scope of this book.

J. Claims by Personal Creditors of a Partner against the Partnership Interest of the Partner

Can the personal creditors of a partner initiate legal proceedings against the partner's interest in the partnership? That may in some cases constitute a substantial part of the assets of the debtor partner and thus be of real interest to an unpaid personal creditor.

As noted earlier, § 25 of UPA effectively seals specific partnership property against the claims of creditors of individual partners, making a change from the common law. A remedy has been provided for creditors under § 28, however, in the form of a "charging order" which may be imposed by court order against "the interest" of the debtor partner on due application by a judgment creditor. The interest of a partner in a partnership is defined in § 26 as "his share of the profits and surplus." The meaning of profits is obvious; "surplus" is not defined in UPA but usually means the excess of partnership assets over partnership liabilities. Would liabilities in this context include the capital accounts of the firm? See § 40(b) of the UPA, defining "liabilities" in the context of distribution of assets after dissolution. What arguments can be made for and against the inclusion of capital accounts?

Although § 28 does not so specify, all payments, including distributions of earnings and withdrawal of capital, that would otherwise go to the debtor partner can be redirected to the creditor. The creditor should ask for language to that effect when obtaining the charging order.

Section 28(2) of UPA provides that a creditor may foreclose on the interest of a partner. Courts have restricted exercise of the foreclosure power to circumstances where the creditor would not otherwise obtain payment of the debt within a reasonable time through partnership distributions pursuant to a charging order. See J. Dennis Hynes, *The Charging Order: Conflicts Between Partners and Creditors*, 25 Pac. L.J. 1 (1993), discussing court restrictions on foreclosure and sale of a partner's interest.

The purchaser at a foreclosure sale does not buy the privilege to exercise managerial powers, but does acquire the power to dissolve the partnership under § 32(2) if it is one at will, or at the termination of the specified term. Presumably this power would encourage the other partners to purchase the interest at the sale or to redeem it before the sale, which they can do under § 28(2). *See* J. Gordon Gose, *The Charging Order Under the Uniform Partnership Act*, 28 Wash. L. Rev. 1 (1953); Elliot Axelrod, *The Charging Order—Rights of a Partner's Creditor*, 36 Ark. L. Rev. 81 (1983).

RUPA embraces the charging order concept in § 504. It makes only minor changes from UPA.

Tupper v. Kroc

Supreme Court of Nevada
494 P.2d 1275 (1972)

Batjer, Justice.

These two cases were consolidated for the purpose of appeal because the same legal issues are involved in each.

Lloyd G. Tupper, appellant, and Ray A. Kroc, respondent, entered into three limited partnerships for the purpose of holding title to and leasing parcels of real estate. Tupper was the general partner, Kroc was the limited partner and each held a fifty per cent interest.

Kroc filed an action alleging that Tupper had mismanaged and misappropriated funds from these partnerships and requested that they be dissolved and that a receiver be appointed. Pending the final outcome of that action the trial court appointed a receiver to manage the three business organizations. Prior to the date on which the complaint for dissolution had been filed, Tupper had on several occasions been unable to pay his share of the partnerships' obligations. Kroc on those occasions personally contributed the total amounts owed by the partnerships, and in return accepted interest bearing notes from Tupper in amounts equal to one-half of the partnerships' debts paid by him. Kroc thereafter filed an action against Tupper to recover on those notes and was awarded a summary judgment in the amount of $54,609.02.

In an effort to collect on that judgment, Kroc filed a motion pursuant to [UPA § 28] requesting the district court to charge Tupper's interest in the partnerships with payment of the judgment and for the sale of Tupper's interest to satisfy the judgment. On June 12, 1969, a charging order was entered directing the sheriff to sell all of Tupper's "right, title and interest" in the three partnerships and to apply the proceeds against the unsatisfied amount of the judgment. Tupper was served with notice of the sale, but he took no action to redeem his interest. The sale was held on June 27, 1969, and Kroc purchased Tupper's interest for $2,500.

Kroc filed a motion to terminate the receivership on March 12, 1970, contending that he was the sole owner of the partnerships and that the need for a receiver had ceased. On May 18, 1970, the appellants filed an objection to the respondents' motion to terminate the receivership, and a motion to set aside the sale conducted pursuant to the charging order. The trial court denied the appellants' motion to set aside the sale, and granted the respondents' motion to terminate the receivership and discharge the receiver. It is from these two orders that this appeal is taken.

The appellants contend that the trial court erred when it confirmed the sale of Tupper's interest in the three partnerships because (1) Kroc failed to affirmatively show that a sale of Tupper's interest in the partnerships was necessary; (2) a partner's interest in a partnership is not subject to a sale in satisfaction of a judgment; (3) it was improper to nominate the sheriff to conduct the sale which was irregularly and improperly held; (4) the sheriff's sale was inequitable in that the price paid for Tupper's partnership interest was grossly inadequate; (5) it was impermissible to conduct the sale of Tupper's interest in the partnerships while they were in receivership; and (6) the sale was in violation of the partnerships' agreements. Furthermore, the appellants contend that it was improper to discharge the receiver because Tupper retained such an equity in the partnership business and assets as to compel continuation of the receivership. . . .

The charging order was properly entered by the district court against Tupper's interest in the three partnerships. UPA § 28; *Balaban v. Bank of Nevada*, 86 Nev. 862, 477 P.2d 860 (1970); *State v. Elsbury*, 63 Nev. 463, 175 P.2d 430 (1946). The district court also was authorized, in aid of the charging order, to make all orders and directions as the case required. UPA § 28(1). Pursuant to the provisions of this statute the district court was authorized to appoint a receiver to act as a repository for Tupper's share of the profits and surplus for the benefit of Kroc, or as the court did here, order the sale of Tupper's interest. UPA §§ 28(1), (2) and 32(2). In Kroc's application for the order charging Tupper's interest in the partnerships he requested an order directing a sale of that interest. Likewise in the notice to Tupper and his attorneys they were advised that Kroc was seeking a sale of Tupper's interest. The application and notice afforded Tupper an opportunity to take whatever steps he deemed necessary to either limit the charging order or prevent the sale.[21] Tupper was allowed thirty days to file an appeal from the order charging his interest in the partnerships and ordering the sale. NRCP 73. He did not appeal from that order, but instead waited nearly a year after the sale was made before filing a motion to set it aside. The appellants are now estopped to question the propriety of the charging order.

Although the appellants concede that the charging order is not under attack they continue a collateral attack by insisting that the sale of Tupper's interest in the partnerships authorized by the charging order was void. One of those contentions of irregularity is based upon the fact that an accounting "to determine the nature and extent of the interest to be sold" was not required by the district court before it entered its order authorizing the sale. In support of this contention the appellants rely upon *Balaban v. Bank of Nevada, supra*. Although we declared the sale in that case to be void and ordered an accounting, it is inapposite to support a claim that the sale in this case is void. In *Balaban* the notice of sale advised that "said sale will

21. [2] If only a charging order had been entered or had the court in the charging order appointed a receiver under NRS 87.280 [UPA § 28], to receive Tupper's share of the partnerships' profits or upon dissolution his share of the surplus instead of ordering a sale, then upon receipt by Kroc of an amount sufficient to satisfy the judgment against Tupper entered on April 30, 1969, Tupper would have been restored to his right to receive his share of the profits or upon dissolution his share of the surplus; however, when his interest in the partnerships was sold he was forever foreclosed from receiving any profits or surplus from the three partnerships.

include all physical assets." This was impermissible and for that reason we set the sale aside. Furthermore, *Balaban* concerned a dissolution of a partnership by death, its winding up and the interplay of the Uniform Partnership Act and the probate code.

Within those chapters are found special provisions and requirements for an accounting (UPA § 43) which are not found in the statute authorizing the charging order (UPA § 28). An accounting prior to the sale of Tupper's interest was not compelled in this case.

The appellants also contend that Tupper's interest in the partnership was inadequately described. Anyone reading or relying on the notice of sale was, as a matter of law, deemed to understand that by statute the sale of Tupper's interest in the partnerships consisted of a sale of his share of the profits and surplus and no more. UPA §§ 24, 26 and 28. Any further or more extensive description would have been confusing or redundant. An accounting might have revealed the amount of current profits, if any, or the estimated value of the surplus, if any, but it would not have added anything to the description of Tupper's interest beyond that found in UPA § 26.

Pursuant to UPA § 28(1) the district court was authorized to make any order which the circumstances of the case required. The statute authorized the appointment of the sheriff of Clark County to sell Tupper's interest in the partnerships, and authorized Tupper's interest to be sold in accordance with the provisions of NRS 21.130(2)[22] at a time certain on June 27, 1969. Because this was a judicial sale authorized by NRS Ch. 87, and not an execution sale, the district court was not bound to have Tupper's partnership interest sold in strict compliance with NRS 21.130(2) but the court was free, pursuant to UPA § 28(1), to order any notice procedure that it deemed reasonable. Therefore, it was authorized to modify the notice requirements of NRS 21.130(2) by requiring that Tupper's interest be sold at 9:00 A.M. on June 27, 1969. The fact that the sale was conducted fourteen days after the notice of sale was posted by the sheriff has no effect upon the validity of the sale and can be construed to have inured to the benefit of Tupper.

The appellants' contention that the price paid by Kroc for Tupper's interest in the three partnerships is inadequate, is without merit. The mode for determining the value of Tupper's interest in the partnerships was by a public sale. See *McMillan v. United Mortgage Co.*, 82 Nev. 117, 412 P.2d 604 (1966). The fair market value of $2,500 was established by Kroc's bid at the sheriff's sale. The respondents were under no duty or obligation to support or justify that price and the entire burden

---

22. [3] NRS 21.130(2): "In case of other personal property, by posting a similar notice in 3 public places of the township or city where the sale is to take place, not less than 5 nor more than 10 days before sale, and, in case of sale on execution issuing out of a district court, by the publication of a copy of the notice in a newspaper, if there be one in the county, at least twice, the first publication being not less than 10 days before date of sale."

was upon the appellants to prove its inadequacy. Thus it became a question of fact to be determined by the trial judge who heard the testimony and observed the witnesses.

We will not substitute our judgment for that of the trial judge as to the weight given to evidence.

The appellants contend that the sale amounted to an involuntary assignment of Tupper's interest in the partnerships and is in violation of the partnership agreements which preclude a partner from assigning his interest. We do not agree. A sale made pursuant to a charging order of a partner's interest in a partnership is not an assignment of an interest in a partnership. See UPA § 27. Furthermore, the partnership agreements could not divest the district court of its powers provided by statute to charge and sell an interest of a partner in a partnership.

Finally the appellants contend that because Tupper retained an equity in the partnerships' business and assets, the district court erred when it discharged the receiver. Unfortunately for the appellants this is not true. After Kroc bought all of Tupper's interest in the partnerships, i.e., all of his right and title to the profits and surplus, Kroc was entitled to all of the profits and all of the surplus. "Surplus" is the excess of assets over liabilities. *Balaban v. Bank of Nevada, supra*; *State v. Elsbury, supra*; *Anderson v. United States*, 131 F. Supp. 501 (S.D. Cal. 1954). After the sale Tupper had no immediate or future rights to any profits or surplus or any equity whatever in the partnership property, and therefore he had no valid reason to insist on a continuation of the receivership.

Although as a matter of law the respondents were entitled to have the receivership terminated and the receiver discharged, the wisdom of that request, short of the dissolution of the partnerships, is questionable, for as soon as the receiver was discharged Tupper had the authority under the UPA, as well as the partnerships' agreements, to assert his right to participate in the management. By purchasing Tupper's interest in the partnerships Kroc did not divest Tupper of his other property rights (UPA § 24).

The receiver was appointed at the request of Kroc, now Tupper wants the receiver to be reappointed to protect Tupper as a general partner from liability that might be incurred through excessive partnership debts. At a glance it might seem that Tupper's fears have some merit. However, as a matter of law, at the moment the receiver was discharged Tupper's right to participate in the management of the partnerships (UPA § 24) was restored, and as the general partner he would, at least theoretically, be able to prevent the partnerships from incurring liabilities in excess of assets.

The orders of the district court from which these appeals have been taken are affirmed.

Zenoff, C.J., and Mowbray, Thompson and Gunderson, JJ., concur.

Notes

1. The *Tupper* opinion contains a careful and thorough discussion of the difficult subject of foreclosure under a charging order. As mentioned above, there is no substantive difference between UPA § 28 and RUPA § 504, and thus the discussion in *Tupper* retains significance in jurisdictions that have adopted RUPA. The partnerships in *Tupper* were limited partnerships, which means that today the operative section for beginning analysis would be § 703 of the Revised Uniform Limited Partnership Act, which is derived from § 22 of the original Uniform Limited Partnership Act, both contained in the statutory supplement to this book. Both sections are sketchy, especially § 703. Both limited partnership acts depend on UPA to fill in gaps in coverage, as evidenced by the *Tupper* opinion, which relied heavily on UPA. Re-RULPA § 703 incorporates RUPA § 504 and thus continues the law as reflected in *Tupper*.

2. The status of a purchaser of a partner's interest upon foreclosure of a charging order is that of an assignee (by operation of law) of the partner's interest. 2 BROMBERG & RIBSTEIN ON PARTNERSHIP 3:105, § 3.05(d)(3)(v). The rights of an assignee are thus a matter of interest to a person contemplating purchase at a foreclosure sale. The following case addresses that topic.

Bauer v. Blomfield Co./Holden Joint Venture

Supreme Court of Alaska

849 P.2d 1365 (1993)

BURKE, JUSTICE.

William J. Bauer, assignee of a partnership interest, sued the partnership and the individual partners, claiming that partnership profits were wrongfully withheld from him. The superior court granted summary judgment to the partnership and individual partners, and dismissed Bauer's complaint with prejudice. We affirm.

In 1986 William Bauer loaned $800,000 to Richard Holden and Judith Holden. To secure the loan, the Holdens assigned to Bauer "all of their right, title and interest" in a partnership known as the Blomfield Company/Holden Joint Venture. The other members of the partnership consented to the assignment. . . .

When the Holdens defaulted on the loan, Bauer sent the following notice to the partnership members: "William Bauer hereby gives notice that he is exercising his rights to receive all distributions of income and principal from the Blomfield Company/Holden Joint Venture Partnership." Thereafter, for a time, the partnership income share payable to the Holdens was paid monthly to Bauer.

In January, 1989 the partners stopped making income payments to Bauer. They, instead, agreed to use the income of the partnership to pay an $877,000 "commission" to partner Chuck Blomfield. Bauer was not a party to this agreement; he was notified of the agreement after the fact by means of a letter dated January 10, 1989. Bauer was not asked to consent to the agreement, and he never agreed to forego payment of his assigned partnership income share or to pay part of the "commission" to Blomfield. The amount Bauer would have received, had the "commission" not been paid, was $207,567. Blomfield's $877,000 commission represented five percent of the increased gross rental income earned by the partnership from lease extensions obtained from the state by Blomfield on partnership properties leased by the state. . . .

Insisting that his assigned right to the Holdens' share of the partnership's income had been violated, Bauer filed suit in superior court against the partnership and all of the partners except the Holdens. Bauer sought declaratory and injunctive relief, and damages. His various claims were dismissed, with prejudice, when the court concluded that Bauer's assignment from the Holdens did not make him a member of the partnership. Therefore, he was not entitled to complain about a decision made with the consent of all the partners. This appeal followed. . . .

As the Holdens' assignee, Bauer was not entitled "to interfere in the management or administration of the partnership business or affairs, or to require any information or account of partnership transactions or to inspect the partnership books." [UPA § 27(1)].[23]

The "interest" that was assigned to Bauer was the Holdens' "share of the [partnership's] profits and surplus." [UPA § 26]. The assignment only entitled Bauer to "*receive . . . the [partnership] profits to which the [Holdens] would otherwise be entitled.*" [UPA § 27(1)] (emphasis added). Because all of The Blomfield Company/ Holden Joint Venture partners agreed that Chuck Blomfield was entitled to receive an $877,000 commission, to be paid out of partnership income, we agree with the superior court's conclusion that there were no partnership profits which the Holdens, and thus Bauer, were entitled to receive until the commission was fully paid.

Affirmed.

Matthews, Justice, with whom Rabinowitz, Chief Justice, joins, dissenting.

It is a well-settled principle of contract law that an assignee steps into the shoes of an assignor as to the rights assigned. Today, the court summarily dismisses this principle in a footnote and leaves the assignee barefoot. . . .

The court is correct to state that Bauer's assignment entitles him to nothing if the partnership decides to forego a distribution. However, this statement leaves

---

23. [2] We are unwilling to hold that partners owe a duty of good faith and fair dealing to assignees of a partner's interest. To do so would undermine the clear intent of [UPA § 27(1)]. Partners should be able to manage their partnership without regard for the concerns of an assignee, who may have little interest in the partnership venture. As commentators have explained:

> The U.P.A. rules concerning assignment of partnership interests and the rights of assignees balance the interests of assignees, assignors, and nonassigning partners in a way that is suited to the very closely held business. Although the assignee's impotence obviously limits the market value of the partners' interest, the partners need to be protected from interference by unwanted strangers.

Alan R. Bromberg & Larry E. Ribstein, *Partnership* § 3:61 (1988).

unanswered the crucial question that must first be asked: was the partners' decision to pay Blomfield a "commission," thereby depleting profits for distribution, a decision made in good faith? Until this question is answered, we cannot know if Bauer was unjustly deprived of that to which he is entitled.

. . . The court is correct in noting that Bauer has no management rights in the partnership. Bauer's attempt to enforce his right to profits under the assignment is not, however, an interference with the management of the partnership. Requiring the partners to make decisions regarding distributions in good faith does not interfere with management, It merely requires that the partners fulfill their existing contractual duties to act in good faith.

I further disagree with the court's interpretation of the intent of the statute. The statute's intent is to assure that an assignee does not interfere in the management of the partnership while receiving "the profits to which the assigning partner would otherwise be entitled." [UPA § 27(1)]. As interpreted by the court, the statute now allows partners to deprive an assignee of profits to which he is entitled by law for whatever outrageous motive or reason. The court's opinion essentially leaves the assignee of a partnership interest without remedy to enforce his right.[24]

Upon formation of the Blomfield Company/Holden Joint Venture, a contractual relationship arose among the partners.[25] This court has held that a covenant of good faith and fair dealing is implied in all contracts. . . .

One element of the contract between the Holdens and the partnership is the Holdens' right to receive their share of profits when a distribution is made. As an element of the partnership contract, this right is accompanied by the duty of the parties to deal fairly and in good faith. The partnership has a right to decide not to make a distribution, but in making this decision, the partnership must act in good faith.

The Holdens assigned to Bauer that part of the partnership contract that entitled the Holdens to receive distributions. Under the law of assignments, Bauer steps into the shoes of the Holdens as to this distribution right. Accompanying this contract right is the partners' duty to act in good faith. Thus, as the assignee of that element of the contract, the partners owe Bauer a duty of good faith and fair dealing in deciding whether to make a distribution.

---

24. [2] The court notes that the Uniform Partnership Act balances the rights of assignees, assignors, and nonassigning partners. One of the ways in which the U.P.A. accomplishes this is to provide the assignee with the right to petition a court for dissolution of the partnership. The U.P.A. states that upon application of an assignee, the court must decree a dissolution if the partnership was a partnership at will at the time of assignment. U.P.A. § 32(2)(b). Although the Alaska Partnership Act was copied from the U.P.A., due to an error in cross-referencing, it is unclear that an assignee in Alaska has the right to apply for a dissolution. Thus he may be deprived of one of the "balances" that the U.P.A. sets up for his protection.

25. [3] See Alan A. Bromberg & Larry E. Ribstein, *Partnership* § 1.01, at 1:11 (1988) ("Fundamentally, general partnership is a contractual relationship among the partners.") . . .

Holding that, as a matter of law, the partners owe Bauer a duty of good faith when deciding whether to make a distribution does not resolve the dispute in this case. Whether the decision to pay the "commission" in lieu of making a distribution was made in good faith is a factual question. As the moving party on a motion for summary judgment, the burden is on the partnership to demonstrate that no genuine issue existed as to whether the decision to pay the 5% "commission" was made in good faith. The partnership presented little to no evidence on this issue.[26] This court should thus remand to the superior court for a factual determination of whether or not the decision by the partners to pay Blomfield's "commission" was made in good faith.

The court's decision today effectively leaves an assignee with no remedy to enforce his right to receive partnership profits. Without such a remedy, his assignment becomes worthless. As I believe this result is contrary to basic contract and assignment law, I dissent from the court's opinion.

K. The LLP Shield

As noted in the introductory materials at the beginning of Chapter 11, general partnerships can now take advantage of a statutory provision that removes, or at least greatly limits, the exposure of partners to vicarious liability for the debts or obligations of the partnership. Limited liability partnerships are now quite common, but cases testing the effectiveness of the liability shield are not. The following New York case reflects what may prove to be an important exception to the liability shield.

Ederer v. Gursky

Court of Appeals of New York
881 N.E.2d 204 (2007)

[The parties to this litigation were partners in Gursky & Ederer, LLP (the LLP), a limited liability partnership registered in 2001. Ederer withdrew as a partner in June, 2003 and] on June 26, 2003, Ederer entered into a withdrawal agreement with the LLP, which Gursky signed as a partner in the LLP. Under this agreement, Ederer agreed to remain a partner in the LLP so as to serve as lead counsel for a trial scheduled to commence in Georgia on June 30, 2003, although he was not obligated to delay his withdrawal from the LLP beyond July 8. In exchange, the LLP agreed to

---

26. [7] In support of its contention that the decision to pay the "commission" was fair, the partnership argued that the amount paid to Blomfield was the "standard" rate. The only evidence presented by the partnership was the testimony of Blomfield himself that a 5% "commission" was standard. One should view this with some skepticism as Blomfield was dealing with a tenant who was already in the building and did not have to be located or persuaded to move in. Furthermore, the rate Blomfield received is greater than 5% as the rent on which the "commission" is based is a future stream of income, not a present lump sum. After discounting future rental income to its present value, Blomfield's "commission" is greater than 5%.

"continue to pay [Ederer his] regular draw and other compensation through the date of [his] withdrawal from the [LLP]"; to have files on which he was working transferred to his new firm upon the client's request; to give him the opportunity to review his clients' bills before the LLP asked for payment; and to allow him and/ or his representatives (including accountants) access to the LLP's books and records after his withdrawal from the LLP.

Ederer withdrew from the LLP on or about July 4, 2003 after having helped secure a $2 million verdict in the Georgia trial, which generated a $600,000 contingency fee for the LLP. After Ederer's departure, the LLP continued in business under the name Gursky & Partners, LLP until March 1, 2005, when it ceased operations.

In December 2003, Ederer commenced this action against the LLP, Gursky & Partners, LLP and Gursky, Stern, Feinberg and Levine [the remaining partners after Ederer's withdrawal], seeking an accounting and asserting breach of the withdrawal agreement. In his amended verified complaint dated November 1, 2005, Ederer sought an accounting of his interest in the LLP and asserted causes of action for breach of contract relating to the June 2003 written agreement to pay him for the two weeks he tried the Georgia case for the LLP, among other claims.

In their verified answer dated November 7, 2005, defendants denied the gravamen of Ederer's complaint; and interposed numerous affirmative defenses as well as various counterclaims.

On November 7, 2005, defendants moved to dismiss the complaint as to defendants Gursky, Stern, Feinberg and Levine. . . . As relevant to this appeal, defendants argued that Ederer's complaint set forth no cognizable causes of action upon which relief could be granted against the individual defendants because Partnership Law § 26(b) shielded them from any personal liability.

Supreme Court determined that Ederer was entitled to an accounting against all defendants because Partnership Law § 26, which places limits on the personal liability of partners in an LLP applies "to debts of the partnership or the partners to third parties" and "has nothing to do with a partner's fiduciary obligation to account to his partners for the assets of the partnership." . . .

The Appellate Division affirmed Supreme Court's order on December 5, 2006.

This appeal comes down to a dispute over the effect of the Legislature's 1994 amendments to section 26 of the Partnership Law. As originally adopted by the Legislature in 1919, section 26 was identical to section 15 of the Uniform Partnership Act (UPA). Prior to its amendment in 1994, section 26 provided that

"[a]ll partners are liable

"1. Jointly and severally for everything chargeable to the partnership under sections twenty-four and twenty-five.

"2. Jointly for all other debts and obligations of the partnership; but any partner may enter into a separate obligation to perform a partnership contract."

Section 24 [UPA § 13] specifies that

"[w]here, by any wrongful act or omission of any partner acting in the ordinary course of the business of the partnership, or with the authority of his copartners, loss or injury is caused to any person, not being a partner in the partnership, or any penalty is incurred, the partnership is liable therefor to the same extent as the partner so acting or omitting to act."

Section 25 [UPA § 14] binds the partnership to "make good the loss"

"1. Where one partner acting within the scope of his apparent authority receives money or property of a third person and misapplies it; and

"2. Where the partnership in the course of its business receives money or property of a third person and the money or property so received is misapplied by any partner while it is in the custody of the partnership."

Partnership Law § 26, as originally enacted, and its prototype, section 15 of the UPA, have always been understood to mean what they plainly say: general partners are jointly and severally liable to nonpartner creditors for all wrongful acts and breaches of trust committed by their partners in carrying out the partnership's business, and jointly liable for all other debts to third parties. This proposition follows naturally from the very nature of a partnership, which is based on the law of principal and agent. Just as a principal is liable for the acts of its agents, each partner is personally responsible for the acts of other partners in the ordinary course of the partnership's business. In addition to this vicarious liability to nonpartner creditors, each partner concomitantly has an obligation to share or bear the losses of the partnership through contribution and indemnification in the context of an ongoing partnership; and contribution upon dissolution and winding up.

The nationwide initiative to create a new business entity combining the flexibility of a partnership without the onus of this traditional vicarious liability originated with a law adopted

"in Texas in 1991, following the savings and loan crisis. At that time, a number of legal and accounting firms faced potentially ruinous judgments arising out of their professional services for banks and thrifts which thereafter failed. Because these professional firms were typically organized as general partnerships, this liability also threatened the personal assets of their constituent partners. The Texas LLP statute protected such partners (at least prospectively) from this unlimited personal exposure without requiring a reorganization of their business structure."

In New York, the Legislature enacted limited liability partnership legislation as a rider to the New York Limited Liability Company Law (*see* Walker § 14:2, at 344). This legislation eliminated the vicarious liability of a general partner in a registered limited liability partnership by amending section 26 of the Partnership Law, and making conforming changes to sections 40(1), (2), 65 and 71(d). Specifically, new section 26(b) creates an exception to the vicarious liability otherwise applicable by virtue of section 26(a) (original section 26 [section 15 of the UPA]), by providing that

> "[e]xcept as provided by subdivisions (c) and (d) of this section, no partner of a partnership which is a registered limited liability partnership is liable or accountable, directly or indirectly (including by way of indemnification, contribution or otherwise), for any debts, obligations or liabilities of, or chargeable to, the registered limited liability partnership or each other, whether arising in tort, contract or otherwise, which are incurred, created or assumed by such partnership while such partnership is a registered limited liability partnership, solely by reason of being such a partner."

Section 26(c) excludes from section 26(b)'s liability shield "any negligent or wrongful act or misconduct committed by [a partner] or by any person under his or her direct supervision and control while rendering professional services on behalf of [the] registered limited liability partnership." Section 26(d) allows partners to opt out from or reduce the reach of section 26(b)'s protection from vicarious liability.

As one commentator has noted, by "expressly provid[ing] that limited liability includes liability by way of indemnification or contribution," section 26(b) precludes the potential for a plaintiff to "attempt an end-run around the liability shield of [section 26(b)] by first asserting a claim against the [limited liability partnership] and then arguing that the general partnership statute requires the [limited liability partnership] partners to make contributions to the [limited liability partnership]" (Johnson, *Limited Liability for Lawyers: General Partners Need Not Apply*, 51 Bus. Law. 85, 110 [1995]). The Legislature further expressed its intention to negate a partner's indemnification or contribution obligations with respect to liabilities for which the partner was not vicariously liable by making sections 40(1), (2), 65 and 71(d) subject to section 26(b).

Defendants point out that section 26(b) eliminates the liability of a partner in a limited liability partnership for "any debts" without distinguishing between debts owed to a third party or to the partnership or each other. As a result, they contend, the Legislature did not "leave open to conjecture whether §26(b) was intended to cover debts which may be owed by the [limited liability partnership] (or one partner) to other partners." This argument ignores, however, that the phrase "any debts" is part of a provision (section 26) that has always governed only a partner's liability to third parties, and, in fact, is part of article 3 of the Partnership Law ("Relations of Partners to Persons Dealing with the Partnership"), not article 4 ("Relations of Partners to One Another"). The logical inference, therefore, is that "any debts" refers to any debts owed a third party, absent very clear legislative direction to the contrary.

Defendants also note that chapter 576's legislative history illustrates the desire to enact liability protection for partners in limited liability partnerships that is "the same as that accorded to shareholders of a professional corporation organized under the [Business Corporation Law] [and] as that accorded to members of a professional LLC" (Senate Introducer Mem in Support, Bill Jacket, L. 1994, ch. 576). They point out that "the legislative history of the LLP Act plainly indicates that the Legislature intended to provide an *even greater shield* of individual liability to partners in LLPs than that enacted by other states as of the date of the legislation."

These observations are correct, but do not advance defendants' cause. Chapter 576 does, in fact, afford limited liability partners the same protection from third-party claims as New York law provides shareholders in professional corporations or professional limited liability companies. And unlike New York, most states "have adopted a partial liability shield protecting the partners only from vicarious personal liability for all partnership obligations arising from negligence, wrongful acts or misconduct, whether characterized as tort, contract or otherwise, committed while the partnership is an LLP" (*see* Prefatory Note Addendum to Uniform Partnership Act [1997] [explaining that RUPA, by contrast, "provid(es) for a corporate-styled liability shield which protects partners from vicarious personal liability for all partnership obligations incurred while a partnership is a limited liability partnership"]; *see also* Walker § 14:5, at 346 ["The type of LLP generally permitted by the states (other than Minnesota and New York) . . . offers less insulation against personal liability than many other types of organization"]). Nowhere in the voluminous commentary on limited liability partnerships has anyone suggested that New York (or any other state) has adopted a statute expanding the concept of limited liability in the way asserted by defendants.

. . . .

[The court held the individual partners liable.]

SMITH, J. (dissenting).

The text of Partnership Law § 26(b) seems clear to me: "no partner of a partnership which is a registered limited liability partnership is liable . . . for any debts, obligations or liabilities of . . . the registered limited liability partnership . . . whether arising in tort, contract or otherwise." The statute contains two specific exceptions, applicable when a partner acts wrongfully or when partners agree to vary the liability scheme (Partnership Law § 26[c], [d]), but there is no exception for liabilities to former partners claiming a share of the partnership's net assets. We should not create an exception that the Legislature did not. The majority draws a distinction between liability to "third parties" and liabilities to former partners—but a *former* partner is a third party where the partnership is concerned, and there is no good reason to treat him more favorably than any other third party.

No one suggests that section 26(b) exempts partners from any of their fiduciary duties; if a partner has diverted partnership funds to himself, or otherwise received more than his fair share, he will not escape liability and his former partners, as well as his existing partners, will be made whole. The issue is whether a former partner claiming his partnership share may reach the personal assets of partners who are no more blameworthy, and have no more been unjustly enriched, than he has.

I can think of two situations in which this issue may be important. First, without any fault by any partner, the business of the partnership may go badly after a partner withdraws from the firm but before he is paid his share, leaving the firm without enough assets to satisfy his claim. (This is apparently what happened here.) Secondly, the partnership's insolvency may result from the fault of a partner who is himself insolvent; in that case, the question is whether the former partner can proceed against the innocent remaining partners.

In the first case, there is no apparent reason why a former partner should be allowed to collect his debt when other third-party creditors may not; in fact, the Partnership Law provides in another context that debts to nonpartners have a preferred status (UPA § 40). In the second case, the rule adopted by the majority can produce even more clearly perverse results. Take an extreme example: Suppose there are three partners, two with a 49% interest each and one with a 2% interest. One of the 49% partners withdraws, and is entitled to 49% of the firm's assets. Before he can be paid, however, it is found that the other 49% partner has stolen all of those assets, lost them at a casino and gone bankrupt. Why should the innocent 2% partner have to make good the former partner's large loss?

JUDGES CIPARICK, GRAFFEO, PIGOTT and JONES concur with JUDGE READ; JUDGE SMITH dissents in a separate opinion in which CHIEF JUDGE KAYE CONCURS.

Order, insofar as appealed from, affirmed, etc.

Notes

1. A partner withdrawing from an LLP is treated differently than a shareholder whose shares are redeemed by a corporation or a member of an LLC whose membership interest is redeemed by the LLC. In the absence of a personal guarantee, the withdrawing shareholder or LLC member can only look to the firm's assets for satisfaction of amounts due to him, while under the *Ederer* opinion, the withdrawing partner can hold his former partners personally liable, even in the absence of an express agreement to that effect. Can you rationalize this difference in treatment? Although not mentioning the *Ederer* case, the California Appellate Court reached a contrary conclusion in *Rappaport v. Gelfand*, 197 Cal. App. 4th 1213 (2011), holding that the trial court erred when it held the remaining partners in a limited liability partnership liable for the buy-out price due a dissociating partner. The California Appellate Court relied on the plain language of RUPA § 306.

2. As noted in the introduction to Chapter 11, *supra*, the LLP statutory shield in New York is less protective than the RUPA provision. Section 26(c) of the New York Partnership Law provides, in relevant part:

> Notwithstanding the provisions of subdivision (b) of this section [the shield provision], (i) each partner, employee or agent of a partnership which is a registered limited liability partnership shall be personally and fully liable and accountable for any negligent or wrongful act or misconduct committed by him or her or by any person under his or her direct supervision and

control while rendering professional services on behalf of such registered limited liability partnership. . . .

3. Some states, in their rules of professional conduct, require lawyers practicing as an LLP to maintain professional liability insurance. *See, e.g.*, N.J. Rules of Court 1:21-1C. What happens if a firm fails to maintain that insurance? Does it convert to a general partnership, making each partner liable for claims against the firm? The New Jersey Supreme Court, when faced with this issue, held that it did not, for two reasons. First, the Rule contains no such conversion provision; rather, it authorizes the Supreme Court to "terminate or suspend the limited liability partnership's right to practice law or otherwise discipline it." Second, the New Jersey partnership statute (like RUPA) contained no provision that would terminate LLP status for failure to maintain such insurance. *Mortgage Grader, Inc. v. Ward & Olivio, L.L.P.*, 139 A.3d 30 (N.J. 2016).

Problems

1. Riveredge Plaza Associates ("Plaza"), a general partnership, was formed by Riveredge and Metropolitan for the purpose of acquiring and developing real estate located at 25 Vreeland Road in Morris County, New Jersey. Two office buildings have been constructed by the partnership on the property. Riveredge owns a 30 percent interest in the partnership and Metropolitan 70 percent. Riveredge is a small investment company, owned by several individuals. Metropolitan is a large, nationally known insurance company with extensive real estate holdings. The Plaza partnership agreement provides that Riveredge and Metropolitan together will control the business and affairs of the partnership.

In addition to its status as general partner, Metropolitan is the holder of a first mortgage on the partnership property in the principal amount of $11,500,000. The mortgage carries an interest rate of 15.125 percent. The note and mortgage provide for prepayment without penalty after 14 years. There is a five percent penalty if the mortgage is accelerated due to default during the 14-year period.

Assume that it is now five years after the partnership was formed. Interest rates are currently available at less than 10 percent. Riveredge, in its capacity as partner, has requested Metropolitan, in its capacity as partner and as lender, to allow refinancing of the mortgage. Plaza is in a tight situation with regard to cash flow and could benefit greatly by a mortgage at the current market interest rate. Even if it paid the five percent prepayment fee, it would be better off refinancing the mortgage. Metropolitan has refused to refinance with or without a five percent penalty. Riveredge has brought a suit to compel Metropolitan to accept prepayment under a theory of fiduciary duty. What are the arguments on both sides? Does it make any difference whether the note and mortgage are interpreted to allow a right to prepay upon payment of the five percent penalty? *Riveredge Assocs. v. Metropolitan Life Ins. Co.*, 774 F. Supp. 892 (D.N.J. 1991).

2. Parr is a general partner of a three-person partnership that owns a commercial building. The building is subject to two mortgages and is not paying for

itself. The partnership has looked diligently for a buyer and for refinancing, without success. Foreclosure on the first mortgage is imminent. The bank holding the second mortgage plans to redeem and then wants to sell the building at cost to Parr. It has promised financing to Parr. Parr has come to you for advice. She is concerned about liability to her two partners. How would you handle this problem?

3. Templeton and Sheets went into partnership to establish a stock farm. They acquired a herd of brood mares for that purpose. Without the knowledge or consent of Sheets, Templeton sold the entire herd to Lowman, and gambled away the substantial down payment given him by Lowman. Sheets refused to surrender the herd and Lowman brought replevin. What result? *Cf. Lowman v. Sheets*, 124 Ind. 416, 24 N.E. 351 (1890); *In re Messenger*, 32 F. Supp. 490 (E.D. Pa. 1940) (where a member of a partnership engaged in the plumbing business sold the firm's truck without the consent of his co-partner).

4. The Smith & Samson partnership, in which there are two partners, is engaged in the newspaper business. Samson, one of the partners, suffered a heart attack and has spent the last 18 months at home convalescing. During the time he was gone Smith, the other partner, ordered pianos from plaintiff on stationery using the partnership letterhead, which set forth just the name and address of the firm. Several months went by. Smith then ordered some more pianos, again using the partnership letterhead and stating in his letter, "We have a prospect of selling two or three more if we have them." The plaintiff shipped the pianos but was not paid. He sues Smith and Samson. As the lawyer for Samson, what defense would you make on his behalf? And as the lawyer for plaintiff, how would you rebut it? *Cf. Boardman v. Adams*, 5 Iowa 224 (1857). Would it affect your analysis if the letterhead used had also contained the following language directly underneath the names: "50 years in the newspaper business"?

5. Charles and Sonny are brothers who formed a partnership 10 years ago for the purpose of hauling milk. The relationship between them deteriorated such that Sonny no longer desired to continue the partnership. On July 1, he notified Charles of his intent to dissolve the partnership. The next day he wrote to Dairymen, Inc. ("DI"), party to the main milk hauling contract of the partnership, to tell it the partnership was not going to renew the contract at its annual renewal date on September 1. Sonny also informed DI that he wanted to apply for the right to haul milk for DI after the expiration of the partnership's contract. On August 1, Sonny and Charles agreed to hold a private "auction" between themselves for all the assets of the partnership "including equipment and milk routes." Charles was the successful bidder at the auction held on August 15, bidding $86,000. Without the DI contract the value of the assets was $22,000.

On the same day as the auction DI called a producers' meeting and those present voted not to approve Charles as their hauler. Instead, they voted to have Sonny haul their milk. The DI field representative stated that DI could not work with Charles, and the drivers stated they would quit before driving for Charles. Sonny accepted the offer and is now hauling milk for DI. Charles is angry about this turn of events. Does he have a claim against Sonny? *Monin v. Monin*, 785 S.W.2d 499 (Ky. App. 1990).

Chapter 13

Dissociation of a Partner and Dissolution of a Partnership

The title of this chapter draws a distinction between dissociation of a partner and dissolution of a partnership. The concept of "dissociation" was introduced into partnership law by RUPA. It is part of the reformulation of the underlying theory of partnership by those drafting RUPA, with the goal of stabilizing the partnership form of doing business. A partnership is expressly declared to be an entity in RUPA § 201, and it is specified in § 601 that a partner "dissociates" under some circumstances, an event that does not always or even usually result in dissolution of the partnership. This is a sharp departure from the theory underlying UPA, where any change in the membership of partners resulted in an automatic dissolution of the partnership.

UPA. Section 29 of UPA defines the legal event of dissolution as "the change in the relation of the partners caused by any partner ceasing to be associated in the carrying on . . . of the business," such as the withdrawal, death or bankruptcy of a partner. The language of § 29, reflecting the aggregate theory, makes the existence of any partnership seem fragile and apt to be drastically disrupted at any time by events beyond the partners' control. Consider a large law firm, for example. One of 50 partners withdraws, dies or goes bankrupt. Is the partnership, a successful and well-known firm of years' standing, now "dissolved" and the remaining partners forced to "terminate" the business? That does not make any sense, does it?

Under UPA termination of the business does not follow from dissolution if there has been planning ahead of time or if an agreement is made to continue the business after dissolution has taken place, although cooperation may not be as easy to come by in the latter situation. See UPA § 38(1), setting the stage for termination of the business but also recognizing that the partners can agree otherwise. For example, the partnership agreement can anticipate dissolution and provide for continuing the business and evaluating and distributing the departing partner's interest in a way that is convenient to the business (such as a payout over a period of time) and fair to the partner. Also, § 38(2) provides a statutory right for the remaining partners to continue the business when a partner wrongfully dissolves the partnership.

Sections 41 and 42 of UPA deal with rights and liabilities when the business is continued. We will address the matter of continuing the business and the problems involved in forming a new business following treatment of the causes of dissolution.

RUPA. RUPA devotes three articles to breakups of personnel in a partnership. Article 6 defines the events that result in dissociation of a partner. Article 7 sets the standards for the buyout of a partner, subject to agreement otherwise. Article 8 covers dissolution and winding up of the business.

Dissociation under RUPA. As noted above, dissociation is a new concept introduced by RUPA. It is intended to recognize that there are circumstances in which a partner can leave the partnership without causing dissolution of the firm. RUPA §601 lists 10 events that will cause dissociation, including the express will, expulsion, bankruptcy, or death of a partner. Most dissociations result in a buyout of the dissociating partner's interest under Article 7.[1]

Dissolution under RUPA. The dissolution provisions of RUPA are contained in §801. They are largely default in nature; with several narrow exceptions, they are not included in the list of mandatory terms in §103. Thus, similar to UPA, partners under RUPA have the contractual freedom to avoid termination of the business. The way in which they accomplish this is different, however, because they can simply deny the event of dissolution, something unavailable under UPA. The end result is the same in many cases, however. The business continues and the departing partner is paid out.

Liquidation Rights

Unless otherwise agreed, dissolution creates liquidation rights in "each partner, as against his co-partners." UPA §38(1). RUPA also recognizes the liquidation right. See §807(a) (distribution "in cash" to partners) and (b) ("Each partner is entitled to a settlement of all partnership accounts upon winding up the partnership business."), which continue the rule of §38(1) of UPA, although it applies to a narrower range of circumstances under RUPA. It is useful at this stage to see the liquidation right in operation.

Dreifuerst v. Dreifuerst

Court of Appeals of Wisconsin
280 N.W.2d 335 (1979)

BROWN, PRESIDING JUDGE.

The plaintiffs and the defendant, all brothers, formed a partnership. The partnership operated two feed mills, one located at St. Cloud, Wisconsin and one located at Elkhart Lake, Wisconsin. There were no written Articles of Partnership governing this partnership.

On October 4, 1975, the plaintiffs served the defendant with a notice of dissolution and wind-up of the partnership. The action for dissolution and wind-up was

---

1. A partner's dissociation "will always result in either a buyout of the dissociated partner's interest or a dissolution and winding up of the partnership business." §603 cmt. 1.

commenced on January 27, 1976. . . . The parties were unable, however, to agree to a winding-up of the partnership.

[T]he defendant requested that the partnership be sold pursuant to [UPA § 38(1)], and that the court allow a sale, at which time the partners would bid on the entire property. By such sale, the plaintiffs could continue to run the business under a new partnership, and the defendant's partnership equity could be satisfied in cash.

[T]he trial court, by written decision, denied the defendant's request for a sale and instead divided the partnership assets in-kind according to the valuation presented by the plaintiffs. The plaintiffs were given the physical assets from the Elkhart Lake mill, and the defendant was given the physical assets from the St. Cloud mill. The defendant appeals this order and judgment dividing the assets in-kind. . . . The sole question in this case is whether, in the absence of a written agreement to the contrary, a partner, upon dissolution and wind-up of the partnership, can force a sale of the partnership assets.

At the outset, we note, and the parties agree, that the appellant was not in contravention of the partnership agreement since there was no partnership agreement. The partnership was a partnership at will. They also agree there was no written agreement governing distribution of partnership assets upon dissolution and wind-up. The dispute, in this case, is over the authority of the trial court to order in-kind distribution in the absence of any agreement of the partners.

[UPA § 38(1)] provides:

> When dissolution is caused in any way, except in contravention of the partnership agreement, each partner, as against his co-partners and all persons claiming through them in respect to their interests in the partnership, *unless otherwise agreed*, may have the partnership property applied to discharge its liabilities, and the surplus applied to pay *in cash* the net amount owing to the respective partners. (Emphasis supplied.)

The appellant contends this statute grants him the right to force a sale of the partnership assets in order to obtain his fair share of the partnership assets in cash upon dissolution. He claims that in the absence of an agreement of the partners to in-kind distribution, the trial court had no authority to distribute the assets in-kind. He is entitled to an in-cash settlement after judicial sale. The respondents contend the statute does not entitle the appellant to force a sale and grants the trial court the power to distribute the assets in-kind if in-kind distribution is equitably possible and doesn't jeopardize the rights of creditors. . . .

A partnership at will is a partnership which has no definite term or particular undertaking and can rightfully be dissolved by the express will of any partner. In the present case, the respondents wanted to dissolve the partnership. This being a partnership at will, they could rightfully dissolve this partnership with or without the consent of the appellant. In addition, the respondents have never claimed the appellant was in violation of any partnership agreement. Therefore, neither the appellant nor the respondents have wrongfully dissolved the partnership.

Unless otherwise agreed, partners who have not wrongfully dissolved a partnership have a right to wind up the partnership. [UPA 37] Winding-up is the process of settling partnership affairs after dissolution. Winding-up is often called liquidation and involves reducing the assets to cash to pay creditors and distribute to partners the value of their respective interests. Thus, lawful dissolution (or dissolution which is caused in any way except in contravention of the partnership agreement) gives each partner the right to have the business liquidated and his share of the surplus paid *in cash*. In-kind distribution is permissible only in very limited circumstances. If the partnership agreement permits in-kind distribution upon dissolution or wind-up or if, at any time prior to wind-up, all partners agree to in-kind distribution, the court may order in-kind distribution. While at least one court has permitted in-kind distribution, absent an agreement by all partners, *Rinke v. Rinke*, 330 Mich. 615, 48 N.W.2d 201 (1951), the court's holding in that case was limited. In *Rinke*, the court stated:

> The decree of the trial court provided for dividing the assets of the partnerships rather than for the sale thereof and the distribution of cash proceeds. Appellants insist that such method of procedure is erroneous. . . . Attention is directed to Section 38 of [UPA]. [I]t was not the intention of the legislature in the enactment of the Uniform Partnership Act to impose a mandatory requirement that, under all circumstances, the assets of a dissolved partnership shall be sold and the money received therefor divided among those entitled to it, particularly so, as in the case at bar, where there are no debts to be paid from the proceeds. *The situation disclosed by the record in the present case is somewhat unusual in that no one other than the former partners is interested in the assets of the businesses. In view of this situation and of the nature of the assets*, we think that the trial court was correct in apportioning them to the parties. There is no showing that appellants have been prejudiced thereby. (Emphasis supplied.) 330 Mich. at 628, 48 N.W.2d at 207.

The Michigan court's holding was limited to situations where: (1) there were no creditors to be paid from the proceeds, (2) ordering a sale would be senseless since no one other than the partners would be interested in the assets of the business, and (3) an in-kind distribution was fair to all partners.

That is not the case here. There was no showing that there were no creditors who would be paid from the proceeds, nor was there a showing that no one other than the partners would be interested in the assets. These factors are important if an in-kind distribution is to be allowed. Section [38 of UPA is] intended to protect creditors as well as partners. In-kind distributions may affect a creditor's right to collect the debt owed since the assets of the partnership, as a whole, may be worth more than the assets once divided up. Thus, the creditor's ability to collect from the individual partners may be jeopardized. Secondly, if others are interested in the assets, a sale provides a more accurate means of establishing the market value of the assets and, thus, better assuring each partner his share in the value of the assets.

Where only the partners are interested in the assets, a fair value can be determined without the necessity of a sale. The sale would be merely the partners bidding with each other without any competition. This process could be accomplished through negotiations or at trial with the court as a final arbitrator of the value of the assets. With these policy considerations in mind, we think the Michigan court's holding in *Rinke* was limited to the facts of that case. Those facts not being present in this case, we do not feel an in-kind distribution in this case was proper.

However, even assuming the respondents in this case can show that there are no creditors to be paid, no one other than the partners are interested in the assets, and in-kind distribution would be fair to all partners, we cannot read § 38 of the Uniform Partnership Act as permitting an in-kind distribution under any circumstances, unless all partners agree. The statute and § 38 of the Uniform Partnership Act are quite clear that if a partner may force liquidation, he is entitled to his share of the partnership assets, after creditors are paid *in cash*. To the extent that *Rinke v. Rinke, supra*, creates an exception to cash distribution, we decline to adopt that exception. We, therefore, must hold the trial court erred in ordering an in-kind distribution of the assets of the partnership.

The last question that arises is whether the appellant can force an actual sale of the assets or whether the trial court can determine the fair market value of the assets and order the respondents to pay the appellant in cash an amount equal to his share in the assets.

As discussed above, a sale is the best means of determining the true fair market value of the assets. Generally, liquidation envisions some form of sale. Since the statutes provide that, unless otherwise agreed, any partner who has not wrongfully dissolved the partnership has the right to wind up the partnership and force liquidation, he likewise has a right to force a sale, unless otherwise agreed. While judicial sales in some instances may cause economic hardships, these hardships can be avoided by the use of partnership agreements.

Judgment reversed and cause remanded for further proceedings not inconsistent with this opinion.

Notes

1. As noted in *Dreifuerst*, the *Rinke* court reads a judicial gloss onto § 38(1), providing for judicial distribution in kind under certain circumstances. For another case taking a similar approach, see *Nicholes v. Hunt*, 541 P.2d 820 (Or. 1975). In that case Hunt, who had operated a small manufacturing business as a sole proprietor, took in Nicholes as a partner in order to obtain needed capital. Hunt and Nicholes did not get along, and Hunt decided to dissolve the partnership. Nicholes sought a judicial sale under § 38(1) so that he could bid against Hunt for ownership of the assets of the partnership. The trial court refused to order a sale, instead distributing the assets to Hunt and giving Nicholes the cash value of his interest. This was affirmed on appeal in an opinion stating that "the equities lie with the defendant [Hunt]. . . .

The defendant conceived and designed the machinery and the method of operation, which was successfully operated for a number of years before formation of the partnership at will. Plaintiff is not precluded from engaging in a like or similar business." *Id.* at 828. The *Rinke* and *Nicholes* cases are unusual, however. In most situations, the *Dreifuerst* approach prevails.

2. *Creel v. Lilly*, 354 Md. 77, 729 A.2d 385 (1999), reflects a judicial resistance to the UPA requirement that the partnership liquidate the assets on the death of a partner, unless the agreement otherwise provides or the estate consents to the continuation. In *Creel*, the court interpreted a crudely drafted agreement to allow the surviving partners to continue the business of the partnership, despite the objections of the personal representatives of the deceased partner. Apparently, recognizing that its reading of the partnership agreement was on weak grounds, the court went on to say that UPA doesn't require a liquidation of the partnership's assets, which the court characterized as a "fire sale." The court supported this conclusion by relying, in part, on the legislative enactment of RUPA, which clearly would not require liquidation under these circumstances. This enactment, the court suggested, should influence the way in which the partnership agreement is interpreted, giving a preference to an interpretation that would permit the surviving partners to continue the business. In a remarkable statement, however, the court gave even greater weight to the effect of adopting RUPA: "Even if there were no partnership agreement governing this case, however, we hold that Maryland's UPA—particularly in light of the legislature's recent adoption of RUPA—does not grant the estate of a deceased partner the right to demand liquidation of a partnership where the partnership agreement does not expressly provide for continuation of the partnership and where the estate does not consent to the continuation." *Id.* at 401–02.

3. The split of the courts in the interpretation of UPA, as reflected in the *Dreifuerst* and *Rinke* cases, has carried over to RUPA. In *McCormick v. Brevig*, 96 P.3d 697, 704 (Mont. 2004), the court held that under RUPA, when a dissolution results from a court order, "the partnership assets necessarily must be reduced to cash. . . ." *See also Pankratz Farms, Inc. v. Pankratz*, 95 P.3d 671 (Mont. 2004); *Mock v. Bigale*, 867 So. 2d 1259 (Fla. App. 2004). Taking a contrary view was the court in *Horne v. Aune*, 121 P.3d 1227, 1233–34 (Wash. App. 2005), a case involving a residence owned and occupied by two partners (Aune and Horne). One partner, Aune, moved out of the residence, dissolved the partnership and sought to require a sale of the residence, while the other partner (Horne) desired to continue to reside there with her son. The court rejected Aune's argument that a sale was required:

> We decline Aune's invitation to follow the Montana Supreme Court's reasoning in *McCormick*. Instead, we adopt Maryland's approach in *Creel*. Contrary to *McCormick*, the winding-up statute does not plainly mean forced sale. Thus, in our view, the trial court's resort to the dictionary in *McCormick* was appropriate. According to Black's Law Dictionary, "liquidate" means:

1. To settle (an obligation) by payment or other adjustment; to extinguish (a debt). 2. To ascertain the precise amount of (debt, damages, etc.) by litigation or agreement. 3. To determine the liabilities and distribute the assets of (an entity), esp. in bankruptcy or dissolution. 4. To convert (a non-liquid asset) into cash. 5. To wind up the affairs of (a corporation, business, etc.).

As used in [RUPA § 807(b)], the phrase "liquidation of the partnership assets," guarantees partners the right to receive, in cash, the fair value of their property interest upon winding up and dissolution of the partnership. But that result may be achieved by means other than forced sale. Historically, liquidation equaled forced sale because that was deemed the most accurate method of valuing partnership assets. But where, as here, the parties stipulate to the partnership assets' value, there is no reason to equate liquidation with forced sale. . . .

Although the court's equitable discretion is subject to partnership statutes, RUPA does not do away altogether with equitable considerations. "Unless displaced by particular provisions of this chapter, the principles of law and equity supplement this chapter." [RUPA § 104(a)] The court's exercise of equitable discretion to grant Horne the right to purchase the property is not inconsistent with the winding-up statute.

Opinions consistent with *Horne* include *Investment Management, Inc. v. Jordan Realty, Inc.*, C3-01-2162, 2002 Minn. App. LEXIS 925 (July 30, 2002). Were the *Investment Management* and *Horne* courts on solid ground citing equitable principles in the face of the statutory provision? Consider, as well, RUPA § 402: "A partner has no right to receive, and may not be required to accept, a distribution in kind."

A. Causes of Dissolution Under UPA and RUPA

UPA. The causes of dissolution under UPA are set forth in § 31, as amplified by § 32, and bear careful reading. These sections largely codify and clarify the rules formulated at common law.

Note that § 31 is divided into three parts: (i) dissolution caused without violation of the partnership agreement, such as arrival of the agreed termination date of the partnership, or by the will of any partner if no term was agreed upon; (ii) dissolution caused in violation of the partnership agreement (observe, therefore, that a partner always has the *power* to terminate a partnership, even though there is no contractual *right* to do so); and, finally, (iii) four circumstances where it does not seem to make any difference what the partnership agreement provides with respect to the timing and existence of an event of dissolution.

RUPA. As noted earlier, dissolution is a less frequent event under RUPA. The specific dissolution provisions of RUPA will be identified in the cases and notes below.

1. Dissolution at Will

Girard Bank v. Haley

Supreme Court of Pennsylvania
332 A.2d 443 (1975)

Pomeroy, Justice.

This suit in equity was brought by appellants' decedent, Anna Reid, who averred in her complaint that she had dissolved a partnership between herself and the defendants, and prayed that the business of the firm be wound-up and its assets distributed. During the course of the proceedings Mrs. Reid died and the executors of her estate were substituted as parties plaintiff. The principal question for decision is whether the partnership was dissolved during Mrs. Reid's lifetime, as she averred and her personal representatives urge, or upon her death, as the trial court found.

The following facts are not in dispute. On September 28, 1958, Mrs. Reid and the three defendants, appellees here, entered into a written partnership agreement for the purpose of leasing for profit certain real property located in Montgomery County, Pennsylvania. Mrs. Reid was to manage the property, and the defendants were to perform the physical labor necessary to maintain the premises in good condition. The initial partnership assets consisted of real estate valued at $50,000 and $10,000 in cash, both contributed by Mrs. Reid, and an additional sum of $10,000 in cash contributed in equal shares by the three other partners. By letter addressed to her partners, the defendants, Mrs. Reid notified them that she was dissolving the partnership and requested that the partnership assets be liquidated as soon as possible.[2] Meetings between the partners following receipt of this letter failed to produce agreement for a plan for liquidation or as to the respective rights of the parties in the assets of the partnership. This suit praying for a winding up of the affairs of the partnership and a liquidation of its assets was then brought.

The chancellor found that the partnership had been dissolved, not by Mrs. Reid's letter, but rather by her death, and concluded that the defendants, as surviving partners, were entitled to exercise their option under the partnership agreement to purchase the interest of the deceased partner.[3] . . . This appeal followed.

None of the parties disputes the chancellor's conclusion that the partnership has been dissolved; the dispute, as indicated at the outset, is when that event occurred. Dissolution of a partnership is statutorily defined as "the change in the relation of the partners caused by any partner ceasing to be associated in the carrying on, as distinguished from the winding up, of the business." Uniform Partnership Act § 29 ("the Act"). There is no doubt that dissolution of a partnership will be caused by the death of any partner, § 31(4) of the Act, and if Mrs. Reid's death was the cause of the

---

2. [1] The letter was undated, but the record establishes that it was sent on February 10, 1971. . . .
3. [The agreement provided a method for evaluation of a deceased partner's interest, and for payment over a 10-year period for Mrs. Reid's interest in the event of her death.—Eds.]

dissolution here involved, the chancellor was quite correct in looking to the agreement as defining the rights and obligations of the surviving partners on the one hand and the estate of the deceased partner on the other. If, however, dissolution occurred during the lifetime of Mrs. Reid, those portions of the agreement, which are concerned solely with the effect of the death of a partner, are not germane. The agreement being otherwise silent as to winding up and liquidation, the provisions of the Act will control.

The chancellor was impressed with the fact that the decedent "was a strong willed person" who dominated the partnership enterprise, that the defendant partners had each contributed many thousands of hours of hard work and planning to the "joint venture," and that neither Mrs. Reid (who testified at the first hearing, but who then, according to the adjudication, "appeared confused and feeble") nor her personal representatives had offered "evidence to justify a termination." In supposing that justification was necessary the learned court below fell into error. Dissolution of a partnership is caused, under § 31 of the Act, "by the express will of any partner." The expression of that will need not be supported by any justification. If no "definite term or particular undertaking [is] specified in the partnership agreement," such an at-will dissolution does not violate the agreement between the partners; indeed, an expression of a will to dissolve is effective as a dissolution even if in contravention of the agreement. *Ibid.*[4] We have recognized the generality of a dissolution at will. . . .

There is no doubt in our minds that Mrs. Reid's letter effectively dissolved the partnership between her and her three partners. It was definite and unequivocal: "I am terminating the partnership which the four of us entered into on the 28th day of September, 1958." The effective termination date is therefore February 10, 1971, and Mrs. Reid's subsequent death after this litigation was in progress is an irrelevant factor in determining the rights of the parties.

The remaining question is whether or not the unilateral dissolution made by Mrs. Reid violated the partnership agreement. The agreement contains no provision fixing a definite term, and the sole "undertaking" to which it refers is that of maintaining and leasing real property.[5] This statement is merely one of general purpose,

---

4. [6] The Official Comment by the Commissioners on Uniform State Laws to Section 31 of the Act states the rationale for this rule as follows:

> The relation of partners is one of agency. The agency is such a personal one that equity cannot enforce it even where the agreement provides that the partnership shall continue for a definite time. The power of any partner to terminate the relation, even though in doing so he breaks a contract, should, it is submitted, be recognized.
>
> The rights of the parties upon a dissolution in contravention of the agreement are safeguarded by section 38(2), *infra.*

6 Uniform Laws Annotated 377 (1969).

5. [8] The pertinent language is contained in paragraph 1. of the agreement: "This agreement . . . has for its object the operation, management, cultivation, maintenance, leasing for profit a tract of land with the buildings and improvements thereon erected. . . ."

however, and cannot be said to set forth a "particular undertaking" within the meaning of that phrase as it is used in the Act. A "particular undertaking" under the statute must be capable of accomplishment at some time, although the exact time may be unknown and unascertainable at the date of the agreement. Leasing property, like many other trades or businesses, involves entering into a business relationship which may continue indefinitely; there is nothing "particular" about it.[6] We thus conclude, on the record before us, that the dissolution of the partnership was not in contravention of the agreement.

In light of our conclusion that an inter-vivos dissolution took place, the provisions of the Act rather than the post-mortem provisions of the agreement, will govern the winding-up of the partnership affairs and the distribution of its assets. . . .

Decree vacated; case remanded for further proceedings consistent with this opinion. Each party to pay own costs.

Page v. Page

Supreme Court of California
359 P.2d 41 (1961)

TRAYNOR, J.

Plaintiff and defendant are partners in a linen supply business in Santa Maria, California. Plaintiff appeals from a judgment declaring the partnership to be for a term rather than at will.

The partners entered into an oral partnership agreement in 1949. Within the first two years each partner contributed approximately $43,000 for the purchase of land, machinery, and linen needed to begin the business. From 1949 to 1957 the enterprise was unprofitable, losing approximately $62,000. The partnership's major creditor is a corporation, wholly owned by plaintiff, that supplies the linen and machinery necessary for the day-to-day operation of the business. This corporation holds a $47,000 demand note of the partnership. The partnership operations began to improve in 1958. The partnership earned $3,824.41 in that year and $2,282.30 in the first three months of 1959. Despite this improvement plaintiff wishes to terminate the partnership.

The Uniform Partnership Act provides that a partnership may be dissolved "By the express will of any partner when no definite term or particular undertaking is specified." UPA § 31(1)(b). The trial court found that the partnership is for a term, namely, "such reasonable time as is necessary to enable said partnership to repay from partnership profits, indebtedness incurred for the purchase of land, buildings, laundry and delivery equipment and linen for the operation of such business. . . ." Plaintiff correctly contends that this finding is without support in the evidence.

---

6. [9] In contrast, a partnership formed for the purpose of developing and selling a particular tract of land would be one for a particular undertaking, and hence not rightfully terminable at will until the purpose was accomplished.

Defendant testified that the terms of the partnership were to be similar to former partnerships of plaintiff and defendant, and that the understanding of these partnerships was that "we went into partnership to start the business and let the business operation pay for itself, — put in so much money, and let the business pay itself out." There was also testimony that one of the former partnership agreements provided in writing that the profits were to be retained until all obligations were paid.

Upon cross-examination defendant admitted that the former partnership in which the earnings were to be retained until the obligations were repaid was substantially different from the present partnership. The former partnership was a limited partnership and provided for a definite term of five years and a partnership at will thereafter. Defendant insists, however, that the method of operation of the former partnership showed an understanding that all obligations were to be repaid from profits. He nevertheless concedes that there was no understanding as to the term of the present partnership in the event of losses. He was asked: "[W]as there any discussion with reference to the continuation of the business in the event of losses?" He replied, "Not that I can remember." He was then asked, "Did you have any understanding with Mr. Page, your brother, the plaintiff in this action, as to how the obligations were to be paid if there were losses?" He replied, "Not that I can remember. I can't remember discussing that at all. We never figured on losing, I guess."

Viewing this evidence most favorably for defendant, it proves only that the partners expected to meet current expenses from current income and to recoup their investment if the business were successful.

Defendant contends that such an expectation is sufficient to create a partnership for a term under the rule of *Owen v. Cohen*, 19 Cal. 2d 147, 150 [119 P.2d 713]. In that case we held that when a partner advances a sum of money to a partnership with the understanding that the amount contributed was to be a loan to the partnership and was to be repaid as soon as feasible from the prospective profits of the business, the partnership is for the term reasonably required to repay the loan. It is true that *Owen v. Cohen, supra,* and other cases hold that partners may impliedly agree to continue in business until a certain sum of money is earned (*Mervyn Investment Co. v. Biber*, 184 Cal. 637, 641–642 [194 P. 1037]), or one or more partners recoup their investments (*Vangel v. Vangel*, 116 Cal. App. 2d 615, 625 [254 P.2d 919]), or until certain debts are paid (*Owen v. Cohen, supra*, at p. 150), or until certain property could be disposed of on favorable terms (*Shannon v. Hudson*, 161 Cal. App. 2d 44, 48 [325 P.2d 1022]). In each of these cases, however, the implied agreement found support in the evidence.

In *Owen v. Cohen, supra,* the partners borrowed substantial amounts of money to launch the enterprise and there was an understanding that the loans would be repaid from partnership profits. In *Vangel v. Vangel, supra,* one partner loaned his copartner money to invest in the partnership with the understanding that the money would be repaid from partnership profits. In *Mervyn Investment Co. v. Biber, supra,* one partner contributed all the capital, the other contributed his services, and it was understood that upon the repayment of the contributed capital from partnership profits the partner who contributed his services would receive a one-third interest in the partnership assets. In each of these cases the court properly held that the partners impliedly promised to continue the partnership for a term reasonably required to allow the partnership to earn sufficient money to accomplish the understood objective. In *Shannon v. Hudson, supra,* the parties entered into a joint venture to build and operate a motel until it could be sold upon favorable and mutually satisfactory terms, and the court held that the joint venture was for a reasonable term sufficient to accomplish the purpose of the joint venture.

In the instant case, however, defendant failed to prove any facts from which an agreement to continue the partnership for a term may be implied. The understanding to which defendant testified was no more than a common hope that the partnership earnings would pay for all the necessary expenses. Such a hope does not establish even by implication a "definite term or particular undertaking" as required by [UPA § 31(1) (b)].

All partnerships are ordinarily entered into with the hope that they will be profitable, but that alone does not make them all partnerships for a term and obligate the partners to continue in the partnerships until all of the losses over a period of many years have been recovered.

Defendant contends that plaintiff is acting in bad faith and is attempting to use his superior financial position to appropriate the now profitable business of the partnership. Defendant has invested $43,000 in the firm, and owing to the long period of losses his interest in the partnership assets is very small. The fact that plaintiff's wholly owned corporation holds a $47,000 demand note of the partnership may make it difficult to sell the business as a going concern. Defendant fears that upon dissolution he will receive very little and that plaintiff, who is the managing partner and knows how to conduct the operations of the partnership, will receive a business that has become very profitable because of the establishment of Vandenberg Air Force Base in its vicinity. Defendant charges that plaintiff has been content to share the losses but now that the business has become profitable he wishes to keep all the gains.

There is no showing in the record of bad faith or that the improved profit situation is more than temporary. In any event these contentions are irrelevant to the issue whether the partnership is for a term or at will. Since, however, this action is for a declaratory judgment and will be the basis for future action by the parties, it is appropriate to point out that defendant is amply protected by the fiduciary duties of copartners.

Even though the Uniform Partnership Act provides that a partnership at will may be dissolved by the express will of any partner (UPA § 31(1) (b)), this power, like any other power held by a fiduciary, must be exercised in good faith.

We have often stated that "Partners are trustees for each other, and in all proceedings connected with the conduct of the partnership every partner is bound to act in the highest good faith to his copartner and may not obtain any advantage over him in the partnership affairs by the slightest misrepresentation, concealment, threat or adverse pressure of any kind." Although Civil Code, section 2411, embodying the foregoing language, was repealed upon the adoption of the Uniform Partnership Act, it was not intended by the adoption of that act to diminish the fiduciary duties between partners. (UPA § 21)

A partner at will is not bound to remain in a partnership, regardless of whether the business is profitable or unprofitable. A partner may not, however, by use of adverse pressure "freeze out" a copartner and appropriate the business to his own use. A partner may not dissolve a partnership to gain the benefits of the business for himself, unless he fully compensates his copartner for his share of the prospective business opportunity. . . .

Likewise in the instant case, plaintiff has the power to dissolve the partnership by express notice to defendant. If, however, it is proved that plaintiff acted in bad faith and violated his fiduciary duties by attempting to appropriate to his own use the new prosperity of the partnership without adequate compensation to his copartner, the dissolution would be wrongful and the plaintiff would be liable as provided by subdivision (2) (a) of UPA § 38 (rights of partners upon wrongful dissolution) for violation of the implied agreement not to exclude defendant wrongfully from the partnership business opportunity.

The judgment is reversed.

GIBSON, C.J., McCOMB, J., PETERS, J., WHITE, J., DOOLING, J., and WOOD (PARKER), J. pro tem., concurred.

Notes

1. See Robert W. Hillman, *Private Ordering Within Partnerships*, 41 U. MIAMI L. REV. 425 (1987), discussing the relationship of fiduciary duties and dissolution rights.

2. Both *Girard Bank* and *Page* demonstrate the vulnerability of partnerships at will. With regard to the policy underlying the rule that any partner has the right to dissolve a partnership at will at any time, the Comment to § 34 of UPA, addressing notice of dissolution among partners, states that a partner has the "right to terminate a relationship which must necessarily depend on mutual good will and confidence." Also, the language in footnote 6 in *Girard*, quoting the Comment to § 31, is instructive.

3. *Causes of dissolution under RUPA.* Unless otherwise agreed, under RUPA § 801 dissolution occurs when (i) a partnership is at will and a partner gives notice of intent to withdraw, (ii) the term of a partnership expires, (iii) during the existence of a term partnership certain events of dissociation (such as the death or wrongful dissociation of a partner) take place and within 90 days a majority of the remaining partners elect to wind up the partnership business, (iv) a court decrees dissolution under specified circumstances, and (v) upon several other events, including application to a court by a transferee of a partner's interest if the partnership is at will or has concluded its term.

As stated in Comment 3 to § 801, "Section 801 continues two basic rules that have been the law for more than 75 years. First, it continues the UPA rule that any member of an *at-will* partnership has the right to force a liquidation.[7] Second, by negative implication, it continues the rule that the partners who wish to continue the business of a *term* partnership cannot be forced to liquidate the business by a partner who withdraws prematurely in violation of the partnership agreement."

Section 802(b) specifies that

> [a]t any time after the dissolution of a partnership and before the winding up of its business is completed, all of the partners, including any dissociating partner other than a wrongfully dissociating partner, may waive the right to have the partnership business wound up and the partnership terminated. In that event, the partnership resumes carrying on its business as if dissolution had never occurred.

In the colorful phrase of Professor Hillman, § 802(b) makes possible "unringing the dissolution bell."[8]

As noted above, RUPA in § 801 continues to recognize (as a default rule) the rule of *Girard Bank* and *Page* that any partner of a partnership at will can dissolve the partnership and force liquidation. This language in § 801 has not gone uncriticized, perhaps in part because it seems inconsistent with the numerous other provisions of RUPA that are designed to promote the stability of partnerships. It can be argued that Article 7 of RUPA, which is designed to protect a departing partner from subsequent liabilities incurred by the firm and defines in some detail the buyout rights of a departing partner, provides sufficient protection for the departing partner and thus there is no need for dissolution powers. The October 1993 Supplemental Report of the Subcommittee on RUPA of the Committee on Partnerships and Unincorporated Business Organizations of the American Bar Association's Section on Business Law objected strongly to § 801, asserting that the Comments do not present "sufficient justification for the single partner bust-up rule" and noting that Texas adopted RUPA without that rule.

---

7. It is important to note that under RUPA the partners can agree to avoid dissolution in this circumstance, unlike UPA. Thus, the partners in an at-will partnership can agree that the partnership will continue until a majority of partners vote to dissolve it. See ROBERT W. HILLMAN ET AL., GENERAL AND LIMITED LIABILITY PARTNERSHIPS UNDER THE REVISED UNIFORM PARTNERSHIP ACT 247 (1996), noting that such an agreement "should prove particularly popular for professional service partnerships."

8. Robert W. Hillman, *RUPA and Former Partners: Cutting the Gordian Knot with Continuing Partnership Entities*, 58 LAW & CONTEMP. PROBS. 7, 12 (1995).

2. Judicial Dissolution

Horizon/CMS Healthcare Corp. v. Southern Oaks Health Care, Inc.

Court of Appeal of Florida
732 So. 2d 1156 (1999)

GOSHORN, J.

Horizon/CMS Healthcare (hereinafter "Horizon") appeals the final judgment in favor of Southern Oaks Health Care, Inc. (hereinafter "Southern Oaks") in the multi-million dollar breach of contract case filed by Southern Oaks. Of the numerous issues argued in the appeal and cross appeal, only one issue merits discussion.

Horizon is a large, publicly traded provider of both nursing home facilities and management for nursing home facilities. It wanted to expand into Osceola County in 1993. Southern Oaks was already operating in Osceola County; it owned the Southern Oaks Health Care Center and a Certificate of Need issued by the Florida Agency for Health Care Administration for a new 120-bed facility in Kissimmee. Horizon and Southern Oaks decided to form a partnership to own the proposed Kissimmee facility, which was ultimately named Royal Oaks, and agreed that Horizon would manage both the Southern Oaks facility and the new Royal Oaks facility. To that end, Southern Oaks and Horizon entered into several partnership and management contracts in 1993.

In 1996, Southern Oaks filed suit alleging numerous defaults and breaches of the twenty-year agreements. The case was tried in two parts. Following the bench trial, the trial court found largely in favor of Southern Oaks, concluding that Horizon breached its obligations under two different partnership agreements. The jury likewise found, inter alia, that Horizon had breached several management contracts. Thereafter, the court ordered that the partnerships be dissolved, finding that "the parties to the various agreements which are the subject of this lawsuit are now incapable of continuing to operate in business together" and that because it was dissolving the partnerships, "there is no entitlement to future damages. . . ." In its cross appeal, Southern Oaks asserts that because Horizon unilaterally and wrongfully sought dissolution of the partnerships, Southern Oaks should receive a damage award for the loss of the partnerships' seventeen remaining years' worth of future profits. We reject its argument.

Southern Oaks argues Horizon wrongfully caused the dissolution because the basis for dissolution cited by the court is not one of the grounds for which the parties contracted. The pertinent contracts provided in section 7.3 "Causes of Dissolution":

> In addition to the causes for dissolution set forth in Section 7.2(c),[9] the Partnership shall be dissolved in the event that: (a) the Partners mutually

---

9. [2] Section 7.2(c), referred to in section 7.3, provides that if a party defaults under the contract and does not cure the default, the non-defaulting party may elect to purchase the defaulter's entire partnership interest or elect to dissolve the partnership. It continues, "If the Non-Defaulter

agree to terminate the Partnership; (b) the Partnership ceases to maintain any interest (which term shall include, but not be limited to, a security interest) in the Facility; (c) the Partnership, by its terms as set forth in this Agreement, is terminated; (d) upon thirty (30) days prior written notice to the other Partner, either Partner elects to dissolve the Partnership on account of an Irreconcilable Difference which arises and cannot, after good faith efforts, be resolved; (e) the Partners determine, based on the opinion of Partnership counsel, that the Partnership cannot legally remain in existence or continue its business operations without material detriment under 42 U.S.C. §§ 1320a-7 and 1320a-7b(b) and regulations promulgated or proposed pursuant thereto, or any other federal or similar state laws; (f) the Transferring Partner sells its Partnership Interest to the Purchasing Partner; (g) pursuant to a court decree; or (h) on the date specified in Section 2.4.

The term "irreconcilable difference" used in the above quote is defined in the contracts as

[A] reasonable and good faith difference of opinion between the Partners where either (i) the existence of the difference of opinion has a material and adverse impact on the conduct of the Partnerships' Business, or (ii) such difference is as to (x) the quality of services which is or should be provided at the long-term care facilities owned by the Partnership, (y) the adoption of a budget for a future fiscal year, or (z) any matter requiring unanimous approval of the Partners under the terms of this Agreement.

Southern Oaks argues that what Horizon relied on at trial as showing irreconcilable differences—the decisions of how profits were to be determined and divided—were not "good faith differences of opinion," nor did they have "a material and adverse impact on the conduct of the Partnerships' Business." Horizon's refusal to pay Southern Oaks according to the terms of the contracts was not an "irreconcilable difference" as defined by the contract, Southern Oaks asserts, pointing out that Horizon's acts were held to be breaches of the contracts. Because there was no contract basis for dissolution, Horizon's assertion of dissolution was wrongful, Southern Oaks concludes.

Southern Oaks contends further that not only were there no contractual grounds for dissolution, dissolution was also wrongful under the Florida Statutes. Southern Oaks argues that pursuant to [RUPA § 602],[10] Horizon had the power to dissociate from the partnership, but, in the absence of contract grounds for

---

does not elect to acquire the Partnership Interest of the Defaulter or is precluded from doing so, the Partnership shall be dissolved and terminated pursuant to Section 7.4 of this Agreement by written notice to the Defaulter."

10. [3] Section 620.8602, Florida Statutes (1997) [RUPA § 602] provides:
   620.8692. Partner's power to dissociate; wrongful dissociation.

the dissociation, Horizon wrongfully dissociated. It asserts that it is entitled to lost future profits under Florida's partnership law,[11] relying on [RUPA § 602(3)]. Southern Oaks also cites . . . 59A Am. Jur. 2d *Partnership* § 565 (1987) ("The right of actions for damages from a partnership dissolution depends on the fact that the dissolution is brought about in violation of the contract between the partners."). Southern Oaks states that its claim is *not* for wrongful dissolution, but rather arises under applicable contract law.

We find Southern Oaks' argument without merit. First, the trial court's finding that the parties are incapable of continuing to operate in business together *is* a finding of "irreconcilable differences," a permissible reason for dissolving the partnerships under the express terms of the partnership agreements. Thus, dissolution was not "wrongful," assuming there can be "wrongful" dissolutions, and Southern Oaks was not entitled to damages for lost future profits. Additionally, the partnership contracts also permit dissolution by "judicial decree." Although neither party cites this provision, it appears that pursuant thereto, the parties agreed that dissolution would be proper if done by a trial court for whatever reason the court found sufficient to warrant dissolution.

Second, even assuming the partnership was dissolved for a reason not provided for in the partnership agreements, damages were properly denied. Under RUPA, it is clear that wrongful *dissociation* triggers liability for lost future profits. *See* § 602(3) ("A partner who wrongfully dissociates is liable to the partnership and to the other partners for damages caused by the dissociation. The liability is in addition to any other obligation of the partner to the partnership or to the other partners."). However, RUPA does *not* contain a similar provision for dissolution; RUPA does not

---

(1) A partner has the power to dissociate at any time, rightfully or wrongfully, by express will pursuant to § 601(1).

(2) A partner's dissociation is wrongful only if:

   (a) It is in breach of an express provision of the partnership agreement; or

   (b) In the case of a partnership for a definite term or particular undertaking, before the expiration of the term or the completion of the undertaking:

      1. The partner withdraws by express will, unless the withdrawal follows within 90 days after another partner's dissociation by death or otherwise under § 601(6)–(10) or wrongful dissociation under this subsection;

      2. The partner is expelled by judicial determination under § 601(5);

      3. The partner is dissociated by becoming a debtor in bankruptcy; or

      4. In the case of a partner who is not an individual, trust other than a business trust, or estate, the partner is expelled or otherwise dissociated because the partner willfully dissolved or terminated.

(3) A partner who wrongfully dissociates is liable to the partnership and to the other partners for damages caused by the dissociation. The liability is in addition to any other obligation of the partner to the partnership or to the other partners.

11. [4] In 1995, Florida enacted the Revised Uniform Partnership Act (RUPA), effective January 1, 1996 for general partnerships formed on or after that date. However, RUPA applies retroactively to all general partnerships, whenever they were initially formed, beginning January 1, 1998. The prior partnership law, the Uniform Partnership Act, was repealed effective January 1, 1998.

refer to the dissolutions as rightful or wrongful. Section 801, "Events causing dissolution and winding up of partnership business," outlines the events causing dissolution without any provision for liability for damages. Under subsection 801(5), the statute recognizes judicial dissolution:

> A partnership is dissolved, and its business must be wound up, only upon the occurrence of any of the following events:
>
> . . . .
>
> (5) On application by a partner, a judicial determination that:
>
> > (a) The economic purpose of the partnership is likely to be unreasonably frustrated;
> >
> > (b) Another partner has engaged in conduct relating to the partnership business which makes it not reasonably practicable to carry on the business in partnership with such partner; or
> >
> > (c) It is not otherwise reasonably practicable to carry on the partnership business in conformity with the partnership agreement; . . .

Paragraph (5)(c) provides the basis for the trial court's dissolution in this case. While "reasonably practicable" is not defined in RUPA, the term is broad enough to encompass the inability of partners to continue working together, which is what the court found.

Certainly the law predating RUPA allowed for recovery of lost profits upon the wrongful dissolution of a partnership. *See generally A.J. Richey Corp. v. Garvey*, 132 Fla. 602, 182 So. 216 (1938) (holding that where co-partners breached contract, the third partner was entitled to dissolution of the contract and to recover his share of anticipated profits assuming he could establish same); 59A Am.Jur.2d *Partnership* § 566 (1987) ("In case of a breach of the partnership contract by wrongful dissolution, the damages recoverable include the value of the profits which the plaintiff otherwise would have received, or the value to him of the continuance of the agreement during the term provided by contract, meaning the prospective or anticipated profits of the partnership, or the profits that would have accrued to the injured partner had the partnership not been wrongfully dissolved.") (footnotes omitted). However, RUPA brought significant changes to partnership law, among which was the adoption of the term "dissociation." Although the term is undefined in RUPA, dissociation appears to have taken the place of "dissolution" as that word was used pre-RUPA.[12] "Dissolution" under RUPA has a different meaning, although the term

---

12. [5] *See* Arnold M. Wensinger, Note, *The Revised Uniform Partnership at Breakup Provisions: Stability or Headache?*, 50 WASH. & LEE L. REV. 905, 933 (1993) ("The meaning of the RUPA's 'dissociation' is analogous to the present UPA definition of dissolution. The dissolution of a partnership under the UPA indicates a change in the relationship between the partners. Although dissociation is not expressly defined in the RUPA, the various 'events' of dissociation indicate the meaning behind the term.") (footnotes omitted).

is undefined in RUPA.[13] It follows that the pre-RUPA cases providing for future damages upon wrongful dissolution are no longer applicable to a partnership dissolution. In other words a "wrongful dissolution" referred to in the pre-RUPA case law is now, under RUPA, known as "wrongful dissociation." Simply stated, under section 602, only when a partner *dissociates* and the dissociation is wrongful can the remaining partners sue for damages.[14] When a partnership is *dissolved*, RUPA at section 806 provides the parameters of liability of the partners upon dissolution:

(1) Except as otherwise provided in subsection (2), after dissolution, a partner is liable to the other partners for the partner's share of any partnership liability incurred under § 804.

(2) A partner who, with knowledge of the dissolution, incurs a partnership liability under § 804(2) by an act that is not appropriate for winding up the partnership business is liable to the partnership for any damage caused to the partnership arising from the liability.

Southern Oaks' attempt to bring the instant dissolution under the statute applicable to dissociation is rejected. The trial court ordered dissolution of the partnership, not the dissociation of Horizon for wrongful conduct. There no longer appears to be "wrongful" dissolution—either dissolution is provided for by contract or statute or the dissolution was improper and the dissolution order should be reversed.[15] In the instant case, because the dissolution either came within the terms of the partnership agreements or [RUPA § 801(5)(c) (judicial dissolution where it

---

13. [6] One note writer recognized:

Dean Weidner [Reporter for RUPA] believed the continued use of dissolution in the RUPA will cause further confusion because the term "dissolution" always has caused confusion and the RUPA now defines dissolution in a different manner. However, the new RUPA terminology will increase confusion not only for the causes noted by Dean Weidner, but also for the following reasons: (1) the RUPA adds a new term, dissociation, to the primary lexicon of partnership law; (2) the RUPA, while redefining dissolution, substitutes dissociation for dissolution as the primary trigger to the breakup provisions; and (3) the distinction between a dissociation that definitely effects a buyout and one that results in a termination of the partnership is not always clear.

Id. at 933–34 (footnotes omitted). *See also* James W. Beasley, Jr., *10 . . . 9 . . . 8 . . . RUPA's Retroactive Liftoff,* Fla. B.J., Dec. 1997, at 38, 43 ("Under the UPA, the departure of a partner caused a dissolution of the partnership. UPA § 29. Under RUPA, departure of a partner is called a "dissociation" (§ 601); a dissociation may lead to a cash buyout of the partner under Article 7, or to dissolution and winding up of the partnership under Article 8. The term "dissolution," which has an uncommon and confusing definition under the UPA, is unfortunately used again in RUPA, but in yet another way. (§ 805).").

14. [7] Dissociation is not a condition precedent to dissolution under RUPA. *See* Weiner & Larson, *The Revised Uniform Partnership Act: The Reporters' Overview,* 49 Bus. Law 1, 9 (1993) ("Most dissolution events are dissociations. On the other hand, it is not necessary to have a dissociation to cause a dissolution and winding up.").

15. [8] Interestingly, Southern Oaks has not argued that reversal of the dissolution is required. It appears, however, that if the facts and circumstances do not warrant dissolution under the contracts or under RUPA, it would be error to order dissolution and the remedy would be reversal, not damages for "wrongful" dissolution.

is not reasonably practicable to carry on the partnership business), Southern Oaks' claim for lost future profits is without merit.

Affirmed.

Cobb and Antoon, JJ., concur.

Note

Courts have found that one partner's failure to provide an accounting provides grounds for judicial dissolution under UPA and RUPA. *See Aegis Corp. v. United Builders of Washington, Inc.*, 112 Wn. App. 1021 (2002); *Fisher v. Fisher*, 227 N.E.2d 334 (Mass. 1967); *Schroer v. Schroer*, 248 S.W.2d 617 (Mo. 1952).

3. Wrongful Dissociation

Saint Alphonsus Diversified Care, Inc. v. MRI Associates, LLP

Supreme Court of Idaho
224 P.3d 1068 (2009)

Eismann, Chief Justice.

This is an appeal from a judgment against a general partner for wrongful dissociation. . . .

Background

Doctors of Magnetic Resonance, Inc.; Saint Alphonsus Diversified Care, Inc.; Mednow, Inc.; and HCA of Idaho, Inc., formed a general partnership named MRI Associates (MRIA). The parties executed a written partnership agreement that was effective on April 26, 1985. The purpose of the partnership was to acquire and operate diagnostic and therapeutic devices, equipment, and accessories [and related purposes]. . . .

On February 24, 2004, Saint Alphonsus Diversified Care, Inc. gave notice to MRIA that it would dissociate from the partnership effective on April 1, 2004, and on October 18, 2004, it filed this lawsuit seeking a judicial determination of the amount it was entitled to receive for its interest in MRIA. MRIA responded by filing a multi-count counterclaim against Saint Alphonsus Diversified Care, Inc., and against St. Alphonsus [Regional Medical Center] (both herein called St. Alphonsus). . . . [St. Alphonsus withdrew from the partnership so that it could compete with the partnership for medical imaging business. The trial court instructed the jury that this withdrawal was a wrongful dissociation as a matter of law.]

Ultimately, the case went to a jury trial on the remaining causes of action in MRIA's counterclaim alleging causes of action for wrongful dissociation. . . . The jury found St. Alphonsus liable on all causes of action, and awarded damages of $63.5 million. The district court reduced the verdict to $36.3 million after determining that the jury had totaled damage awards on two alternative theories. The court also denied St. Alphonsus's motions for a judgment notwithstanding the verdict or a new trial. St. Alphonsus then timely appealed. . . .

St. Alphonsus dissociated from MRIA on April 1, 2004. MRIA included in its counterclaim a cause of action for wrongful dissociation alleged under two theories: (a) the dissociation breached an express provision of the partnership agreement and (b) the partnership agreement had a definite term and the dissociation occurred prior to the expiration of that term. MRIA and St. Alphonsus both filed motions for partial summary judgment on that cause of action. The district court granted MRIA's motion for summary judgment, holding that St. Alphonsus's dissociation was wrongful because it breached an express provision of the partnership agreement. The court did not discuss the alternative theory that the dissociation occurred prior to the expiration of the definite term of the partnership. St. Alphonsus contends the district court erred in granting the partial summary judgment.

"A partner who wrongfully dissociates is liable to the partnership and to the other partners for damages caused by the dissociation." RUPA § 602(c). A partner's dissociation is wrongful if "[i]t is in breach of an express provision of the partnership agreement." RUPA § 602(b)(1). Whether there is an express provision in the partnership agreement that was breached by the dissociation is an issue of law over which we will exercise free review. . . .

Under the RUPA, "[a] partnership is an entity distinct from its partners." RUPA § 201(a). An association of two or more persons to carry on as co-owners a business for profit *forms* a partnership; they are not the partnership. RUPA § 202(a). A partner who chooses to withdraw from the partnership is dissociated, RUPA § 601(1), but "[t]he dissociation of the partner does not require the dissolution of the partnership and the winding up of its affairs." *Costa v. Borges*, 145 Idaho 353, 357, 179 P.3d 316, 320 (2008). A partner has the power to dissociate at any time, rightfully or wrongfully. RUPA § 602(a). If a partner wrongfully dissociates, a majority in interest of the remaining partners can, within ninety days, agree to continue the partnership, RUPA § 801(1) & (2)(i), but they will have to purchase the dissociating partner's interest. RUPA § 701.

 . . . . Under the RUPA, a partner can give notice of the partner's express will to withdraw as a partner, which terminates the partner's right to participate in the management and conduct of the partnership business. RUPA §§ 601(1) and 603(a). . . . Thus, the issue is whether St. Alphonsus's withdrawal from the partnership breached an express provision of the partnership agreement. . . .

The relevant provision of the partnership agreement is as follows:

Article 6 Withdrawal of Hospital Partner

6.1 *Conditions for withdrawal.* Any Hospital Partner may withdraw from the Partnership at any time if, in a Hospital Partner's reasonable judgment, continued participation in this Partnership: (i) jeopardizes the tax-exempt status of such Hospital Partner or its parent or their subsidiaries; or

(ii) jeopardizes medicare/medicaid or insurance reimbursements or participations; (iii) if the business activities of the Partnership are contrary to the ethical principles of the Roman Catholic Church as designated from time to time; or (iv) is or may be in violation of any local, state or federal laws, rules or regulations. In the event that a Hospital Partner withdraws, such Hospital Partner's interest in the Partnership shall terminate on the date of withdrawal, and that interest, including, without limitation, the Hospital Partner's vote on the Board of Partners and its interest in the Partnership management fee, shall be reallocated among the remaining Hospital Partners. (If there are no remaining Hospital Partners, the reallocation shall be among the remaining Partners). Unless otherwise agreed, the withdrawing Hospital Partner shall only be entitled to receive for its interest in the Partnership an amount: which is equal to the balance in such Hospital Partner's capital account at the time of withdrawal. . . .

When deciding whether St. Alphonsus's dissociation was wrongful, the district court considered only the first sentence in section 6.1 of the agreement. It concluded that the words "Any Hospital Partner may withdraw from the Partnership at any time if" followed by four defined circumstances was an express provision limiting the circumstances under which St. Alphonsus could rightfully dissociate. The court reasoned as follows:

> When reading contract terms, the Court must apply the ordinary and plain meaning to the words used. The word "if" is commonly defined as "a: in the event that, b: allowing that, c: on the assumption that, d: on condition that." Substituting one of these definitions into the contract language, section 6.1 allows the Hospital Partners to withdraw *on the condition that* one of the listed events occurs. In the reverse, if one of the four reasons is not present, the Hospital Partners *may not* withdraw from the partnership rightfully. In the Court's view, the use of "only" before "if" would be redundant in this context. The section, "Conditions for Withdrawal" lends further support to the Court's finding that "if" was expressly conditional language. (Emphases in original; citation and footnote omitted.)

The district court picked one definition of the word "if" ("on condition that") and concluded that section 6.1 established the conditions that must exist before a hospital partner could withdraw from the partnership without breaching the agreement. Another definition rejected by the court would also be consistent with the context. The sentence could be read to state that the hospital partner may withdraw *in the event that* one of the listed events occurs. For example, the second sentence of the section begins, "In the event that a Hospital Partner withdraws. . . ." It would not change the meaning to substitute "If" for "In the event that." The district court found some support for its interpretation by the section title, "Conditions for Withdrawal." However, the word "conditions" is synonymous with "circumstances." *Roget's II: The New Thesaurus* 164 (Houghton Mifflin Co.1988). With "if" and "conditions" given these alternative meanings, the section is not an *express* provision limiting the circumstances under which St. Alphonsus could withdraw without breaching the partnership agreement.

With these meanings, the section would provide that St. Alphonsus could withdraw from the partnership in the event that any of four circumstances occurred. To conclude it prohibited withdrawal unless one of those four circumstances occurred, one would have to apply the maxim *expressio unius est exclusio alterius* (the expression of one thing is the exclusion of another). "When certain persons or things are specified in a law, contract, or will, an intention to exclude all others from its operation may be inferred." *Black's Law Dictionary* 581 (6th ed. 1990). Application of the maxim is not mandatory. However, even if that maxim were applied to *infer* that these four circumstances were exclusive, that would not be an *express* provision limiting the circumstances in which St. Alphonsus could rightfully dissociate. . . .

RUPA §602(b)(1) provides that a dissociation is wrongful if it is "in breach of an express provision of the partnership agreement." The statute does not simply provide that dissociation is wrongful if it is in breach of the partnership agreement, or if it is in breach of a provision in the partnership agreement. It is only wrongful if it breaches an *express* provision of the partnership agreement. We have defined the word "express" as follows: "Black's Law Dictionary defines 'express' as, '[c]lear; definite; explicit; plain; direct; unmistakable; not dubious or ambiguous. Declared in terms; set forth in words. Directly and distinctly stated. Made known distinctly and explicitly, and not left to inference. 'Express' means 'manifested by direct and appropriate language.'" *Sweeney v. Otter*, 119 Idaho 135, 140, 804 P.2d 308, 313 (1990) (citations omitted). Because the provision limiting the right to withdraw rightfully must be an express provision, any doubt as to the meaning of the provision at issue must be resolved in favor of not limiting the right to withdraw. The provision of the partnership agreement at issue does not contain any prohibitive language. For example, it does not state that a hospital partner *shall not* withdraw from the partnership *except* under the specified circumstances. Likewise, it does not state that a hospital partner may *only* withdraw from the partnership under the specified circumstances. We hold that the provision is not an express provision limiting the right to dissociate rightfully.

St. Alphonsus was clearly prejudiced by the district court's determination that it had wrongfully dissociated from the partnership. . . .

Conclusion

We vacate the judgment and verdict and remand this case for further proceedings that are consistent with this opinion. We award costs on appeal to appellant.

JUSTICES BURDICK, J. JONES, HORTON and JUSTICE PRO TEM KIDWELL Concur.

Notes

1. The Idaho Supreme Court reads the partnership article on withdrawal as setting forth a nonexclusive list of the "events" that may motivate a party to withdraw. If

this listing of events was not intended to be an exclusive list of the circumstances under which a partner could withdraw, what was the purpose of the list?

2. One might conclude from the opinion that, as a policy matter, the court believes that restrictions on dissociation should be read narrowly or, put differently, that there is a presumption that a partner is free to dissociate without incurring liability therefore. Is such a reading a fair reading? If so, is the underlying policy a good policy?

4. Judicial Expulsion

RUPA §601(5) provides that, if a partner engages in certain misconduct, a court has the power to expel that partner and, under §801(5), to dissolve the partnership. If partners proceed under §601 instead of §801, expulsion will mean that the expelled partner has been dissociated from the partnership, with the normal consequences of dissociation. By contrast, under UPA such misconduct could be the basis only for judicial dissolution of the partnership, as the statute provides no way short of dissolution to expel a partner. (Of course, the partnership agreement could provide a mechanism for expulsion.) One of the grounds for judicial dissolution under UPA and judicial expulsion under RUPA is that the partner's conduct makes it "not reasonably practicable to carry on the business in partnership with [that partner]." Under UPA, this conduct must be the partner's willful or consistent breach of the partnership agreement, while under RUPA any conduct relating to the partnership business that makes it not reasonably practicable to carry on the business in partnership with the offending partner is sufficient for either dissociation of the offending partner or dissolution. The next case is a RUPA expulsion case (under RUPA §601).

Brennan v. Brennan Associates

Supreme Court of Connecticut
977 A.2d 107 (2009)

Before NORCOTT, KATZ, PALMER, ZARELLA and SILBERT, Js.

KATZ, J.

As aptly described by the trial court, "[t]his particular case is the unhappy story of a financially successful [partnership] that became an environment of distrust, rancor and paralysis after the untimely death of [one of the four partners]." On one side is the plaintiff, Thomas Brennan, one of the partnership's founding members. On the other side are the defendants: the named defendant, the partnership of Brennan Associates (partnership); the two other surviving partners; and the four coadministrators (administrators) of the estate of the deceased partner, Richard Aiello (decedent). The plaintiff appeals from the trial court's judgment granting the counterclaim filed by the defendant partners, Alexander Aiello and Serge Mihaly, seeking the plaintiff's expulsion from the partnership, pursuant to [RUPA §601(5)(iii)]. . . . We affirm the trial court's judgment.

The record reveals the following undisputed facts and procedural history. In 1984, the plaintiff, the decedent, Aiello and Mihaly executed an agreement whereby they formed the partnership, principally for the management and operation of a shopping center they owned in Trumbull. The plaintiff and the decedent each held a 32 percent interest in the partnership, Aiello held a 25 percent interest and Mihaly held an 11 percent interest. Because each partner's number of votes was equal to his partnership interest, and a 70 percent vote was necessary for any business initiative proposed, the plaintiff and the decedent each held a sufficient interest to veto any proposed initiative.

Until his death in December, 2004, the decedent essentially ran the partnership. He negotiated all of the leases, performed all of the improvements and paid all of the bills. He kept the partnership books at an office where he also kept records for two other partnerships. The plaintiff, Aiello and Mihaly were essentially silent partners and were fully content with the decedent's management of the partnership.

After the decedent's death, in January, 2005, his attorney, Thomas Welch, held a meeting with the three surviving partners and others who had an interest in the disposition of the decedent's partnership interest pursuant to the decedent's will. The will directed the sale of the decedent's interest in the partnership to his cousins, the defendants Peter DiNardo and Leonard DiNardo. Welch informed those present that he hoped to transfer the decedent's interest as soon as feasible, with no one expressing opposition at that time. Welch later was replaced as administrator, on his own motion, by another attorney, the defendant David Lehn. Lehn later obtained permission to have Peter DiNardo, Leonard DiNardo and their father, the defendant Salvatore DiNardo, added as administrators of the decedent's estate.

Shortly after the reading of the will, the harmony between the surviving partners deteriorated. They reached an impasse over many issues, including check signing authority, control over and access to partnership books, and decisions relating to the management of the shopping center. The plaintiff also came to believe that Aiello and Salvatore DiNardo had committed insurance fraud in relation to claims that had been submitted to the partnership's insurance company. At some point, the plaintiff made an offer to buy the decedent's share of the partnership, which Lehn rejected. . . .

[Plaintiff asserts various claims and] [t]he administrators, Aiello and Mihaly thereafter each filed counterclaims against the plaintiff. . . . Aiello and Mihaly sought a judicial determination expelling the plaintiff from the partnership pursuant to [§ 601(5)]. They claimed that the plaintiff's conduct constituted grounds for dissociation under each of the three subparagraphs of that statute. . . .

[After trial,] the court granted the application of Aiello and Mihaly to expel the plaintiff from the partnership under [RUPA § 601(5)(iii)], and therefore did not consider whether dissociation was warranted under the other subparagraphs alleged. Among the evidence that the trial court relied on was the plaintiff's 1989 federal felony conviction for tax fraud. Because of the plaintiff's lack of candor with his partners about the basis for the conviction, his unwillingness before the court in the present action to recognize the depth and significance of his past wrongdoing, and his recent actions and acrimony toward the partners, including an unfounded accusation of insurance fraud, the court found that Aiello and Mihaly reasonably no longer felt that they could trust the plaintiff. In sum, the court concluded that, because the plaintiff no longer could do business with Aiello and Mihaly and vice versa, the appropriate remedy was dissociation of the plaintiff pursuant to [§ RUPA 601(5)(iii)]. . . .

We begin with the issue in the plaintiff's appeal as to whether the trial court properly granted the application by Aiello and Mihaly for the plaintiff's expulsion pursuant to [§ 601(5)(iii)]. That section permits the court to grant an application for expulsion if "the partner engaged in conduct relating to the partnership business which makes it not reasonably practicable to carry on the business in partnership with the partner. . . ." [RUPA § 601(5)(iii)]. The plaintiff first claims that expulsion is not authorized under [RUPA § 601(5)(iii)] for a long past, public conviction based on conduct unrelated to the partnership's business. . . . We conclude that, in light of the totality of circumstances, including the plaintiff's past conviction as it related to the present events, the trial court properly ordered expulsion under [RUPA § 601(5) (iii)]. . . .

Prior to addressing the question of whether the plaintiff should be dissociated from the partnership, the trial court made numerous factual findings relating to certain conflicts between the plaintiff and the defendants that had arisen since the decedent's death. First, the court addressed disputes over check signing authority, which had been limited under the partnership agreement to the plaintiff and the decedent. The court found that Aiello had signed checks for the partnership for two months following the decedent's death because of problems with the plaintiff's authorization, which thereafter were resolved. The court further found that the plaintiff had resisted the efforts by Aiello and Mihaly to vest Aiello with check signing authority to facilitate partnership business and by the administrators to exercise the decedent's check signing authority as they rightfully were entitled to do. The court found, in sum, that the plaintiff had "sought to maintain himself as the sole signatory to exercise individual control over the finances of the business" and had "engaged in a steady campaign of obstructing anything that he perceived to be the wishes of the DiNardos."

Next, the court addressed disputes over tenants and related issues. Although one of the retail tenants had complained about the manner in which Salvatore DiNardo had addressed the tenant when Salvatore DiNardo and Aiello came to the tenant's place of business, the court found that the plaintiff "[had] cultivated this witness to complain against [Salvatore] DiNardo, and in exchange [the plaintiff] forbore on the rent, so that [the tenant] was allowed to fall between $7000 and $12,000 behind in his rental payments." The court also pointed to other instances in which the plaintiff was unable to agree with the defendants about various decisions relating to partnership business.

Finally, the court addressed an accusation the plaintiff had levied against Aiello and Salvatore DiNardo, namely, that they falsely had inflated invoices submitted to the partnership's insurance company for water damage that had occurred at the partnership premises. The court found that the plaintiff never had produced any evidence to the court or to Aiello and Mihaly in support of this accusation. The court further found that the plaintiff had declined to follow Mihaly's suggestion to return the insurance payment if the plaintiff had evidence of such fraud, instead depositing the money in the partnership's account. Thus, the trial court found that the plaintiff had created "an atmosphere of tension by inferring fraud and wrongdoing by a partner," despite a lack of proof.

Before turning to the question of the plaintiff's expulsion, the court also addressed the relevance of the plaintiff's 1989 tax fraud conviction. The trial court noted that the plaintiff had misrepresented the true nature and extent of his criminal conduct to his partners, both at the time of his conviction and during the course of the present litigation. The court further noted that the plaintiff had made similar misrepresentations to the court, with the additional claim that he had relied on the advice of his accountant when he engaged in the criminal conduct. Because the plaintiff had refused to acknowledge to the trial court in the present matter the full extent of this wrongdoing, the court concluded that the plaintiff "presently continues to be unable to recognize the depth of and significance of his wrongdoing. Therefore, the remoteness in time, which might normally be significant, is not here. It is unfair to ask partners to trust [the plaintiff] with their finances and decisions when his past significant culpable conduct regarding money in business matters is soft pedaled and rationalized to the present day."

The trial court thereafter turned to the issue of whether the standard for dissociation had been met. Although Aiello and Mihaly had alleged that dissociation was warranted under either subparagraphs [(i), (ii) or (iii) of RUPA § 601(5)], the trial court rested its conclusion on subparagraph (iii), which, as we previously have noted, permits the court to grant an application for expulsion if "the partner engaged in conduct relating to the partnership business which makes it not reasonably practicable to carry on the business in partnership with the partner. . . ." Because the concept of dissociation is a relatively new one under Connecticut law, the court was guided in its decision by case law addressing the more established, and in its view analogous, standard for dissolution. . . .

The crux of the plaintiff's challenge to the trial court's conclusion is that the grounds for his expulsion were improper under [RUPA § 601(5)(iii)] because: (1) his conviction was not "conduct *relating to* the partnership" under that statute (emphasis added); and (2) although the inability of one partner to work with the other partners because of acrimony and mistrust that has developed can be a proper basis for *dissolution*, it is not a proper basis for *dissociation* of the one partner who is the source of these problems. We disagree.

. . . .

We would agree with the plaintiff that, had the trial court based its decision to expel him *solely* on his 1989 conviction and the defendants' recent discovery of the actual nature of the conviction, such a ground might be too attenuated to constitute "conduct *relating to* the partnership business. . . ." (Emphasis added.) § [RUPA 601(5) (iii)]. Although the term "relating to" uniformly has been given a broad meaning, a recent discovery by partners of a past lie regarding past conduct concerning an unrelated enterprise likely would not meet this standard. We disagree, however, with the plaintiff's characterization of the trial court's reliance on his criminal conviction.

Although the plaintiff views the court's reliance on his conviction in isolation, our review of its decision demonstrates that the court incorporated this fact into a broader mosaic. Read in context, the court clearly found the conviction as relating to the partnership's business because of several *current* factors. First, since the decedent's death, the plaintiff had engaged in a pattern of adversarial conduct with Aiello and Mihaly that had caused them to mistrust him, including besmirching Aiello's reputation with a false accusation of fraud. Second, the decedent's death had placed the plaintiff in a position of control over the partnership that he previously had not enjoyed, and the plaintiff thereafter engaged in conduct to maintain such control to the exclusion of everyone else. Although, at oral argument to this court, the plaintiff contended that actions such as seeking to preclude others from obtaining check signing authority were simply an attempt to maintain the "status quo," the status prior to the decedent's death was that this authority was not exclusive to the plaintiff. Moreover, it is ironic that the plaintiff claimed to be seeking to protect the status quo when, according to Aiello and Mihaly, it was the plaintiff who wanted to make substantial changes in the way the partnership was being conducted. Third, the plaintiff was not fully forthcoming about his conviction, either to the court or to the defendants, when confronted in the present proceedings with the belated discovery by Aiello and Mihaly of the true nature of the conviction. In sum, although the plaintiff's 1989 conviction, standing alone, might not constitute conduct relating to the partnership that would warrant his dissociation, it properly could inform the court's view of the plaintiff's current conduct relating to the partnership as to whether Aiello and Mihaly's mistrust was justified and whether the plaintiff's explanations as to his intent were credible. Such factors undoubtedly were relevant to whether the acrimony was so pervasive and entrenched that dissociation was warranted.

The case law cited by the trial court in support of its decision, as well as that submitted to this court by the defendants and revealed in our independent research, confirms that an irreparable deterioration of a relationship between partners is a valid basis to order dissolution, and, therefore, is a valid basis for the alternative remedy of dissociation. The plaintiff has proffered no case law to the contrary. Rather, the plaintiff asserts that, because dissociation connotes wrongdoing by the ousted partner, whereas dissolution does not, the ground for dissociation provision in [RUPA § 601(5)(iii)] should be construed more strictly. We disagree.

Under [UPA] one of the grounds for dissolution is identically worded to the ground in [RUPA § 601(5)(iii)], namely, that "another partner has engaged in conduct relating to the partnership business which makes it not reasonably practicable to carry on the business in partnership with that partner. . . ." Thus, there is no textual basis for imposing a higher burden of proof for dissociation than dissolution. Prior to Connecticut's adoption of [RUPA], the sole mechanism for relief under the present circumstances would have been for Aiello and Mihaly to obtain a dissolution of the partnership, which in turn would have left them free to reformulate a new partnership without the plaintiff. Under [RUPA], a partnership now has a choice, either to dissolve the partnership or to seek the dissociation of a partner who has made it not reasonably practicable to carry on the partnership with him. The new remedy of dissociation permits a financially viable partnership to remain intact without dissolving the partnership and reconstituting it. As the commentary to the revised partnership act notes: "[The revised partnership act] dramatically changes the law governing partnership breakups and dissolution. An entirely new concept, 'dissociation,' is used in lieu of the [partnership act] term 'dissolution' to denote the change in the relationship caused by a partner's ceasing to be associated in the carrying on of the business." Rev. Unif. Partnership Act of 1997, § 601, comment (1), 6 U.L.A., Pt. 1, p. 164 (2001); see id., comment (6) (noting that conduct that satisfies ground at issue in this case also may satisfy same ground under dissolution provision). We, therefore, conclude that the trial court properly considered the conviction in connection with the plaintiff's conduct relating to the partnership and properly determined that, under all of the circumstances, the plaintiff's dissociation was an appropriate remedy. . . .

The judgment is affirmed.

In this opinion the other justices concurred.

Notes

1. In *Robertson v. Jacobs Cattle Co.*, 830 N.W.2d 191 (Neb. 2013), the trial court ordered the dissociation (expulsion) of certain partners whose conduct, the court found, frustrated the economic purpose of the partnership and rendered it not reasonably practicable to carry on the partnership business. The Nebraska Supreme Court affirmed. The factual basis for this legal conclusion was, however, less than convincing. The partnership was in the business of leasing farmland and the partners were also the lessees. The dissociated partners defaulted on their lease payments and, on that basis, the trial court concluded that they should be expelled. Their default, however, was not in their capacities as *partners*. The partnership presumably could have terminated the leases for nonpayment and leased the property to other lessees. The Nebraska courts thus gave a fairly broad and generous (to the partnership) reading of the Nebraska equivalent of RUPA § 601(5).

2. Courts often express reluctance to order judicial dissolution, opining that differences and discord should be settled by the partners themselves. "Equity is not a referee of partnership quarrels." *Potter v. Brown*, 195 A. 901, 904 (Pa. 1938). This expresses a widely shared judicial sentiment, but there are limits to this principle, as in all matters. See, for example, the following language in *Steckroth v. Ferguson*, 281 Mich. 279, 274 N.W. 792 (1937):

> It is not alone large affairs which cause trouble. The continuance of dis-
> agreeable and annoying petty treatment is serious in its cumulative disrup-
> tive character. . . . One partner cannot continually minimize the other and
> bring him into disrepute or contempt without destroying the basic status
> upon which a successful partnership rests.

See also Owen v. Cohen, 19 Cal. 2d 147, 119 P.2d 713 (1941) ("an aggregate" of separately trivial acts "can destroy all the confidence and cooperation between the partners"). For an example of dissension between partners, in this case siblings, that, in
the court's view, justified judicial dissolution, see *Russell Realty Associates v. Russell*,
724 S.E.2d 690 (Va. 2012). *See generally* Robert W. Hillman, *Misconduct as a Basis
for Excluding or Expelling a Partner: Effecting Commercial Divorce and Securing Custody of the Business*, 78 Nw. U. L. Rev. 527 (1983).

Should the reluctance to order judicial dissolution, expressed in *Potter* and other
cases, carry over to a reluctance to order expulsion? Should there be a higher standard for a judicial dissociation (i.e., expulsion) under RUPA §601(5) than for judicial dissolution under RUPA §801(5)?

3. Under UPA, if the court orders judicial dissolution, the partners seeking dissolution must, if they desire to continue the business of the partnership, purchase the
interests of the partner or partners whose wrongful conduct caused the judicial dissolution. UPA §38(2)(b) defines a buyout, stating that the parties continuing the
business must pay (or secure payment by bond) to any partner who has caused the
dissolution wrongfully "the value of his interest, less any damages recoverable [for
breach of the agreement] and in like manner indemnify him against all present or
future partnership liabilities."

4. *Buyouts under RUPA.* Section 701 ("Purchase of Dissociated Partner's Interest") addresses this topic, elaborating upon the standards set forth in UPA §38(2).
It applies to all dissociations, whether wrongful or non-wrongful. Subsection (h)
states that a wrongfully dissociating partner is not entitled to payment until the end
of the term, unless a court finds that an earlier payment will not cause undue hardship to the firm.

5. *RUPA and wrongful dissolution.* See §801(5)(ii), addressing this issue. Section 801(5) is one of the dissolution provisions that cannot be varied in the partnership agreement. *See* §103(b)(8). Note, as well, that under RUPA §103(b)(7) the
power of a court to expel a partner cannot be varied by the partnership agreement.

B. Notice of Dissolution and Termination of Authority among Partners

1. Termination of Authority

UPA. Sections 33 and 34 of UPA address termination of authority by dissolution.
The first sentence of §33 declares that dissolution "terminates all authority of any

partner to act for the partnership" except "so far as may be necessary to wind up partnership affairs or to complete transactions begun but not then finished."

A distinction is drawn in §§ 33 and 34 between a dissolution by act of a partner and dissolution by bankruptcy or death. If by act, an unknowing partner who contracts for new business after dissolution can call upon her fellow partners for contribution. Only personal knowledge of the dissolution cuts off this right. If the dissolution is by death or bankruptcy, however, the right of contribution of a partner who contracts for new business is cut off if she had knowledge or notice of the event (see § 3 for the definition of knowledge and notice). The assumption underlying this distinction apparently is that a partner can be held to greater responsibility to be alert to involuntary circumstances, but is entitled to be personally informed before losing contribution rights against other partners if the event of dissolution is the voluntary act of another partner.

RUPA. Section 806 of RUPA is the counterpart to §§ 33 and 34 of UPA. It does not distinguish among kinds of dissolution, instead declaring contribution available to partners for post-dissolution liabilities incurred by the partnership under § 804, which includes acts appropriate for winding up the partnership business. A partner who with knowledge of the dissolution does an act that binds the partnership but is not appropriate for winding up is declared liable to the partnership for damages by § 806(b).

With regard to the distinct act of dissociation under RUPA, Sections 702 and 703 address the dissociated partner's power to bind the partnership and the dissociated partner's liability to other persons. Both sections confine liability to persons who did not have notice of the dissociation (§ 704 provides for filing a statement of dissociation as a means of giving constructive notice 90 days after a statement is filed) and establish a two-year limitation period for exposure to liability even if no notice is given. Article 8 contains similar provisions relating to dissolution.

2. Notice of Dissolution — Lingering Apparent Authority

UPA. Section 35 of UPA deals with the effect of dissolution upon third parties, addressing the lingering apparent authority of partners following dissolution of the partnership. It distinguishes between third parties who had extended credit to the partnership prior to dissolution and those who merely had known of the partnership prior to dissolution. Those who extended credit are entitled to more individualized notice; those who merely knew of the firm are held to notice by publication in a newspaper of general circulation in each place the partnership business was carried on.

RUPA. In RUPA, notice of dissolution is covered in §§ 804 and 805, which allow the partnership and any partner who has not wrongfully dissociated to file a statement of dissolution. The effect of the statement is to put third parties on constructive notice of dissolution 90 days after the statement is filed. As stated in the Comments to § 805, "Thus, after 90 days the statement of dissolution operates as constructive notice conclusively limiting the apparent authority of partners to transactions which are appropriate for winding up the business."

Those sections read as follows:

§ 804. Partner's Power to Bind Partnership After Dissolution.

Subject to Section 805, a partnership is bound by a partner's act after dissolution that:

(1) is appropriate for winding up the partnership business, or

(2) would have bound the partnership under Section 301 before dissolution, if the other party to the transaction did not have notice of the dissolution.

§ 805. Statement of Dissolution.

(a) After dissolution, a partner who has not wrongfully dissociated may file a statement of dissolution stating the name of the partnership and that the partnership has dissolved and is winding up its business.

(b) A statement of dissolution cancels a filed statement of partnership authority for the purposes of Section 303(d) and is a limitation on authority for the purposes of Section 303(e).

(c) For the purposes of Sections 301 and 804, a person not a partner is deemed to have notice of the dissolution and the limitation on the partners' authority as a result of the statement of dissolution 90 days after it is filed.

(d) After filing and, if appropriate, recording a statement of dissolution, a dissolved partnership may file and, if appropriate, record a statement of partnership authority which will operate with respect to a person not a partner as provided in Section 303(d) and (e) in any transaction, whether or not the transaction is appropriate for winding up the partnership business.

Note

Incorporation of partnership. A common situation that raises the notice of dissolution problem is incorporation of a partnership. An argument sometimes is made that the use of corporate checks is sufficient to constitute notice of dissolution. One court, *Jensen Sound Lab. v. Long*, 113 Ill. App. 331, 447 N.E.2d 464, 465–66, 69 Ill. Dec. 247 (1983), evaluated that argument in the following terms:

As a general rule, actual notice of the dissolution of a partnership must be given to persons who have dealt with the firm and who have no knowledge of the dissolution in order to relieve the partners of debts incurred after the dissolution in the name of the partnership. Partnership liability will be incurred under this rule, however, only if, when an existing partnership is incorporated, the firm continues dealing in the same way and the change of name does not convey information of the incorporation. . . . In the instant case, the evidence upon which the trial court made its ruling indicated that the plaintiff was in receipt of corporate checks for almost two years from the time of the defendants' incorporation. The name of the corporation, Long's Sound Systems, Inc., was significantly different from that of the partnership, Long's Auto Sound, and contained an appropriate indicium of corporateness. . . . On this record, then, we cannot say that the trial court erred in finding that the plaintiff was sufficiently notified of the defendants' incorporation.

C. Continuing the Business

1. The Buy-Sell Agreement

Estate of Cohen, Ex rel. Perelman v. Booth Computers

Superior Court of New Jersey, Appellate Division
22 A.3d 991 (2011)

Before Carchman, Graves and St. John, Js.

Carchman, P.J.A.D.

In this appeal, we address the question of whether, under the facts presented, a family partnership agreement that provides for a buyout based on net book value may be enforced where the disparity between book value and market value is significant. In deciding this issue, we consider the difference between book value and market value as well as addressing the issue of whether the disparity between the two renders the agreement unconscionable and unenforceable.

We conclude, as did the trial judge, that the formula utilized in calculating net book value was appropriate, the buyout agreement was enforceable, and the disparity between book value and market value does not render the agreement unconscionable.

Plaintiff Estate of Claudia Cohen, by its executor, Ronald Perelman, appeals from a judgment awarding $178,000 for Claudia's interest in defendant Booth Computers (Booth), a family partnership in which her brother, defendant James Cohen, was also a partner. Plaintiff argues that the trial judge erred in finding that, under the buyout provision of Booth's partnership agreement, it was entitled to only the net book value of Claudia's interest in the partnership, as reflected in Booth's financial statement at the time of Claudia's death, rather than the fair market value of that interest, which plaintiff claims was $11,526,162.

. . . .

I.

These are the relevant facts developed during the trial of this dispute.

Robert Cohen, Claudia and James's father, amassed a considerable fortune through his ownership and control of various business entities, including the

Hudson News group of companies, a distributor of newspapers and magazines. He and his wife, Harriet, were the parents of three children—Claudia, Michael and James.

According to James, Robert requested a partnership agreement be prepared for the benefit of his children. The agreement was not negotiated but presented to the children for signature. Apparently, the partnership was formed by Robert to purchase and lease computer equipment, but this never came to fruition. At the time of Booth's formation, Claudia was twenty-seven, Michael twenty-one, and James nineteen.

James did not know who drafted the agreement but assumed that it was his father's attorney. He received the document from his father but did not recall whether he understood all its provisions, including paragraph sixteen, which governed buyouts of the partners. He did understand that the general concept of the partnership was to create a vehicle to produce income for the children. Neither he nor his siblings consulted an attorney before signing the agreement.

The agreement created Booth Computers and provided in part:

> 11. The Partnership shall maintain books and records setting forth its financial operations and said books and records shall reveal all monies received and expended on behalf of the Partnership. Such books shall be kept on a calendar year basis and shall be closed and balanced at the end of each year. An audit shall be made at the end of each year, or more often, as desired by the Partners.
>
>   . . . .
>
> 13. Each of the Partners recognizes and agrees that one of the reasons he has entered into this Partnership is the personal and family relationship which exists among all Partners and that none of the partners wishes to enter into a partnership with non-family members. In furtherance of the foregoing, each of the Partners covenants and agrees that during his lifetime he shall not sell, assign, transfer, mortgage, pledge, encumber or otherwise dispose of all or any part of his interest in the Partnership, except upon the terms and conditions and subject to the limitations as hereinafter set forth in Paragraphs 14 and 15 of this Agreement.

The agreement also contained a buyout provision, to be implemented under certain conditions:

> 15. In the event of the divorce or separation of any Partner who is married, and upon the death of any Partner, the remaining or surviving Partners shall be obligated to purchase, in equal shares, and the divorced Partner or Partner whose marriage is being terminated, or the estate of a deceased Partner, as the case may be, shall be obligated to sell the entire interest in the Partnership theretofore owned by such Partner at the price and upon the terms and conditions hereinafter set forth in this Paragraph 15;

(A) The price at which such Partnership interest shall be sold shall be the value thereof, determined in accordance with the provisions of Paragraph 16;

. . . .

16. The purchase price of any part or all of a Partner's interest in the Partnership shall be its value determined as follows:

(A) Each of the Partners has considered the various factors entering into the valuation of the Partnership and has considered the value of its tangible and intangible assets and the value of any goodwill which may be present. With the foregoing in mind, each of the Partners has determined that the full and true value of the Partnership is equal to its net worth plus the sum of FIFTY THOUSAND ($50,000.00) DOLLARS. The term "net worth" has been determined to be net book value as shown on the most recent Partnership financial statement at the end of the month ending with or immediately preceding the date of valuation;

(B) The value of any interest in the Partnership which is sold and transferred under the terms of this Agreement shall be determined by multiplying the full and true value of the Partnership as above determined by that percentage of the capital of the Partnership which is being sold and purchased hereunder.

. . . .

Claudia died on June 15, 2007. On July 13, 2007, Ronald Kochman, another of Robert's attorneys, sent a letter on James's behalf implementing the buyout in the sum of $177,808.50 [based on the formulas in the partnership agreement].

We now address the issue of valuation. Plaintiff asserts that the trial judge erred in finding that defendants were entitled to specific performance of the buyout provision based on book value rather than fair market value.

. . . .

To establish a right to specific performance, the party seeking the relief must demonstrate that the contract in question is valid and enforceable at law, and that the terms of the contract are clear. Here, defendants claim that the buyout provision is clear so that they are entitled to specific performance of the buyout provision of the partnership agreement.

Book value is defined as:

Accounting terminology which gives a going-concern-value for a company. It is arrived at by adding all assets and deducting all liabilities and dividing that sum by the number of shares of common stock outstanding. . . . The valuation at which assets are carried on the books, that is, cost less reserve for depreciation. [*Black's Law Dictionary* 165 (5th ed. 1979).]

Fair market value is defined as "[t]he amount at which property would change hands between a willing buyer and a willing seller, neither being under any compulsion to buy or sell and both having reasonable knowledge of the relevant facts . . . in the open market. . . ." *Black's Law Dictionary* 537 (5th ed. 1979).

While book value reflects the cost of the asset as reflected on the entity's books, fair market value reflects the asset's value in the open market. It is not unusual for the two values to vary and in many instances, as here, differ substantially.

We recognize the disparity between net book and fair market value, yet the controlling factor as to which buyout method is applicable is the language of the partnership agreement.

Plaintiff further asserts that the language of the buyout clause at issue here called for fair market value, not book value. It contends that the clause equated "net book value" with "full and true value," and that the latter contemplated market value. However, the term "full and true value" was merely a descriptive phrase indicating that what followed was full and true value, specifically, net book value. We will not torture the language of a contract to create an ambiguity.

Plaintiff also suggests that fair market value should have been utilized because the language of the buyout provision was ambiguous. There is no single definition of book value that can be applied in all cases. In this instance, use of the term "net worth" in addition to "book value" did create some confusion. Yet, these terms have been found to be synonymous. *See N.J.S.A.* 54:10A-4(d) (providing that net worth means the aggregate of the values disclosed by the books of the corporation). Moreover, the partnership agreement specifically states that "the term 'net worth' has been determined to be net book value. . . ."

. . . .

The trial judge's determination that Claudia's shares should be bought out at book value, rather than fair market value, was supported by both substantial credible evidence and the applicable law. The judge did not err in holding that defendants established their entitlement to specific performance of the buyout provision as a matter of law.

. . . .

Plaintiff contends that the trial judge erred in not finding defendants' buyout price to be unconscionable given the "gross disparity" between the cost approach they utilized and the fair market value approach plaintiff seeks. It points to the result of the judgment, whereby James will take sole possession of an asset worth sixty times greater than the amount paid to Claudia's estate.

. . . .

The first factor, procedural unconscionability, includes age, literacy, lack of sophistication, hidden or unduly complex contract terms and bargaining tactics. The second factor, substantive unconscionability, "simply suggests the exchange of obligations so one-sided as to shock the court's conscience."

New Jersey case law "clearly include[s] both the procedural and substantive unconscionability concepts," but those concepts are applied flexibly.

. . . .

While there is a dearth of authority in New Jersey addressing the issue of uncon-scionability in the context of price disparity, other jurisdictions generally hold that disparity in price alone does not constitute unconscionability.

. . . .

Disparity in price between book value and fair market value, where a buyout provision is clear, is not sufficient to "shock the judicial conscience" and to warrant application of the doctrine of unconscionability. This view is consistent with the basic principle that where the terms of the contract are clear, it is not the court's function to make a better contract for either of the parties.

We reiterate what is critical about this agreement and its terms. This was a family partnership created by and funded (except for the modest contributions by the children) by Robert for the benefit of his children according to his terms. He intended the beneficiaries to be family members and understood that the buyouts would require the children to provide funds to the other children. The possibil-ity or even probability that a surviving child would be the ultimate beneficiary of the assets of the partnership was apparent on the face of the agreement. Judge Contillo did not abuse his discretion by finding that the buyout provision was not unconscionable.

Affirmed.

Note

Buy-sell agreements can be structured in various ways, for instance, fixing the price of the dissociated partner's interest at fair market value; book value; a multiple of the earnings of the partnership; or a price agreed upon annually by the partners. The last method is particularly fraught with difficulties, as the partners, despite their best intentions, often fail to fix a new price after having established one in their initial agreement. Courts then are left with the choice of enforcing the agree-ment of the parties, which seems unfair to the dissociated partner, or fashioning a new agreement for the parties. As might be expected, when the initially agreed-upon price is unfair to the dissociated partner, the courts often opt for the latter. *See, e.g., In re Estate of Bolinger*, 292 Mont. 97, 971 P.2d 767 (Mont. 1998).

2. Continuation Clauses

Drafters of UPA partnership agreements often sought to avoid dissolution of the partnership upon the death or withdrawal of a partner by including a "continua-tion clause" in the agreement. Such clauses typically said something to the effect that the death or retirement of a partner "shall not dissolve the partnership and the partnership shall be reconstituted and continued as though such death or retire-ment had not taken place." *See, e.g., Hunter v. Straube*, 543 P.2d 278 (Ore. 1975). The agreement also provided for a buyout of the interest of the deceased or retired partner. In effect, such continuation clauses sought to accomplish what RUPA provides. Although common, such clauses did not accomplish much, because UPA expressly declares, without qualification, that such an event *does* dissolve the partnership. Note that UPA does anticipate that the partners of a dissolved partnership may form a new partnership to carry on the business of the dissolved partnership. Consider also the following language in *Wilzig v. Sisselman*, 442 A.2d 1021, 1025, 1029 (N.J. Super. 1982), *aff'd*, 506 A.2d 1238 (N.J. 1986), addressing this point:

> In other words, [§ 31] deems the death of a partner cause for dissolution without regard for the terms of the partnership agreement.... [This does] not preclude the remaining partners from carrying on the business pursuant to a prior agreement, with or without the addition of new partners. The UPA expressly contemplates the continuation of partnership business without liquidation.... [Section 41 protects creditors when the business is continued without liquidation. An agreement for continuing the business thus] would be enforced as "in effect a type of winding up without the necessity of discontinuing the day-to-day business." ... In this case the formation of the new partnership and assumption of liabilities of the old ... constituted the automatic winding up of the affairs of its predecessor.

One reason that lawyers included a continuation clause in a partnership agreement was that it might avoid the result of the *Fairway Development* case, *supra*, Chapter 11. See Alan R. Bromberg, *Partnership Dissolution — Causes, Consequences and Cures*, 43 Tex. L. Rev. 631 (1965), arguing that a continuation clause in a partnership agreement can avoid dissolution under UPA § 31. See also Robert W. Hillman, *Indissoluble Partnerships*, 37 U. Fla. L. Rev. 691 (1985), arguing that partners should be able to prevent dissolution by agreement.

3. Liability of an Incoming Partner

Sections 17 and 41(7) of UPA address this question, specifying that an incoming partner is liable for existing debts of the business but that such liability "shall be satisfied only out of partnership property." RUPA § 306(b) adopts the same approach.

Under UPA § 17 and RUPA § 306(b), is a partner who joins a partnership after a long-term obligation was undertaken by the firm but who subsequently enjoys the benefits of the executory portion of the contract, like possession under a long-term lease, liable for the obligations arising after the date of admission to the firm? Case authority is split on this, but substantial authority exists that finds personal liability under this circumstance. See Bromberg & Ribstein on Partnership 7:268–69, § 7.18(b), citing case authority upholding liability for the executory portion of the contract, and stating that this is logical. "U.P.A. § 17 provides that a new partner's liability 'for all the obligations of the partnership arising before his admission' is satisfied only out of partnership property. This could be interpreted as limiting the new partner's personal liability only as to the portion that was executed prior to the new partner's admission. However, both continuing partners and creditors arguably would expect the new partners to assume responsibility for obligations that benefit the firm during their tenure." When, however, a person becomes a partner subsequent to the execution of a lease (and thus is not in privity of contract with the landlord) and ceases to be a partner before a breach, that person is generally not liable to the landlord on that breach. *8182 Maryland Assoc. v. Sheehan*, 14 S.W.3d 576 (Mo. 2000) (the "privity of estate" between the landlord and a person who became a partner after the execution of the lease ends when that person ceases to be a partner). Note that if the partnership is an LLP in a full shield state, there would be no liability for the incoming partner even under the executory portion of the contract, absent an assumption of liability.

4. Liability of a Withdrawing Partner

What is the relationship of a withdrawing partner to the creditors of the former firm, including persons with whom the firm is in a contractual relationship? Assuming the business is continued, does the withdrawing partner remain indefinitely liable for the obligations of the dissolved partnership? What is the effect of an assumption of partnership liabilities by the remaining partners, made at the time accounts were settled between the withdrawing partner and the remaining partners? See § 36(1)–(3) of UPA, stating that the rights of creditors are not affected by agreements among the partners to which the creditor is not a party. Also, suretyship concepts are invoked in § 36(3) with regard to the effect of material alterations of the original debt without the consent of the withdrawing partner. RUPA § 703 follows the same approach.

Redman v. Walters
California Court of Appeal
88 Cal. App. 3d 448 (1979)

ELKINGTON, ASSOCIATE JUSTICE.

The superior court, on defendant William Walters' motion for summary judgment against plaintiff Fred Redman, entered an order that "the motion herein be and it is granted," and that plaintiff's "complaint herein be and it is dismissed and that judgment be entered for defendant (Walters)." We treat the order as an appealable order dismissing plaintiff's action insofar as it relates to defendant Walters. . . .

In 1969 plaintiff Redman employed legal representation of the "Law Offices," or partnership, or association, or some other arrangement of attorneys, known as "MacDonald, Brunsell & Walters." The purpose was the commencement and maintenance of a lawsuit for Redman, who advanced "the sum of $1,000.00 to cover actual costs." The lawsuit was thereafter filed, with "MacDonald, Brunsell & Walters" as Redman's attorneys of record. William Walters, the instant respondent, was the person designated as "Walters" of "MacDonald, Brunsell & Walters."

In 1970 Walters severed his relationship with the other attorneys of the above described grouping and commenced practicing law elsewhere. He had "never met"

Redman, nor was he "aware he existed," nor had he "ever discussed or in any way participated in any review of the (subject) legal services. . . ." Nor had he a "communication of any nature from any party or any attorney on this lawsuit, and to my knowledge I have not participated in nor received any compensation whatsoever for any services purportedly rendered on behalf of Fred Redman." All of Redman's dealings in relation to his lawsuit had been with Attorney Brunsell.

After Walters' departure, the law practice arrangement, or a similar one, continued under the name of "MacDonald & Brunsell" and later, "MacDonald, Brunsell & Caton," which entitlements appeared, without formal substitution, as attorneys of record for Redman in the lawsuit. Redman was never advised of the changed names, or attorneys, except that he may have observed them in a notice of deposition or other communications or information. But he had never consented to any change or substitution of attorneys.

In late 1974, Redman's lawsuit was dismissed for failure to bring it to trial within five years. Upon learning of this, Redman commenced an action for damages including as defendants therein "MacDonald, Brunsell & Walters, a Partnership," and "William Walters." The cause of action alleged was that "defendants, and each of them, failed to exercise reasonable care and skill in representing the plaintiff in such action. . . .

On Walters' motion for summary judgment the parties' affidavits conclusively established, and the superior court properly concluded as a matter of law, (1) that "MacDonald, Brunsell & Walters" held itself, or themselves, out to the public and to Redman as a partnership consisting of the three named persons, and (2) that Redman reasonably believed that he had engaged such partnership to commence and prosecute his lawsuit.

From this it necessarily followed, and the trial court properly assumed, that in its relations with Redman, "MacDonald, Brunsell & Walters" was a partnership or its equivalent, an ostensible partnership or partnership by estoppel. For the purposes of both of Redman's actions "MacDonald, Brunsell & Walters" must and will be deemed by us, a "partnership."

In its "Memorandum Decision" the superior court expressed the following conclusions. Although a "partnership" had existed, because of its "dissolution" in 1970 "defendant Walters was not the attorney of record for the plaintiff (Redman) on October 14, 1974, the date of the alleged negligent act, and the relation of attorney and client not existing defendant Walters had no duty to perform and as such there was no negligence on his part." Further, upon the "dissolution," "MacDonald & Brunsell" (without Walters) became Redman's attorneys and attorneys of record, *and thus* his agents. As his agents they had knowledge of the "dissolution" and that they alone had become Redman's attorneys. This knowledge, by operation of law, was "imputed" to Redman, the principal. The court reasoned: "It is a general rule of agency that notice to or knowledge possessed by an agent is imputed to the principal which rule applies for certain purposes in the relation of attorney and client. The rule rests on the premise that the agent has acquired knowledge which it is his duty to communicate to his principal and the presumption that he has performed that duty. Under our law the presumption is deemed conclusive for the purposes of civil action."

We disagree with the rationale and conclusions of the superior court.... As noted, the "partnership" of "MacDonald, Brunsell & Walters" had accepted employment from Redman to commence and prosecute his lawsuit. Upon its "dissolution" 10 months later the "partnership" was not terminated in respect of its duty to fulfill its contractual obligation to Redman. For: "On dissolution the partnership is not terminated, but continues until the winding up of partnership affairs is completed." [UPA § 30].

Among the partnership affairs of "MacDonald, Brunsell & Walters" to be "wound up" was the performance of its agreement with Redman, or that party's consent, express or implied, or perhaps by estoppel, to nonrepresentation by the outgoing partner, Walters. As said in *Cotten v. Perishable Air Conditioners*, 116 P.2d 603, 604: "In general a dissolution operates only with respect to future transactions; as to everything past the partnership continues until all pre-existing matters are terminated." And: "The dissolution of the partnership does not of itself discharge the existing liability of any partner." [UPA § 36(1), and §§ 13 and 15] An individual partner's liability in such a case will not be terminated except by performance of an agreement creating the liability, or by express or implied consent of the other contracting party that he need not so perform.

It follows that in respect of Redman, unless he had in some manner consented (or was estopped to claim otherwise) to nonrepresentation by Walters, "MacDonald, Brunsell & Walters" continued as a partnership and Walters as a partner. And as such a partner Walters would, of course, be responsible also for the negligent act of the partnership or one or more of his partners. [Citing UPA § 13.]

No validity whatever is found in Walters' contention, and the superior court's conclusion, that because of the principal and agent relationship inherent in that of client and attorney, knowledge of the dissolution was imputed to Redman who thereby was conclusively presumed to have consented to substitution of MacDonald & Brunsell as his attorneys in the earlier litigation....

"The knowledge of the agent is considered and imputed as the knowledge of the principal only when the former acquires it in the course of his agency. If he does not acquire it while acting within the scope of his authority, the knowledge is no more to be imputed to the principal than to an utter stranger." (*Palo Alto Ass'n v. First Nat'l Bank*, 164 P. 1124, 1129.) Here, the unilateral decision of the partnership to dissolve, and continue the representation of Redman by two of its members, was patently not within the authority granted it by Redman.

Moreover, such a rule of presumed knowledge of the principal will apply only in respect of a *third person* dealing with the agent.... And even were we to presume, *arguendo*, such notice to Redman, it does not reasonably follow that he had consented, or had as a matter of law waived objection, or been estopped to object, to a change in the partnership's obligation to represent him. . . .

In situations such as that before us, law firms or related associations would be well advised to heed the rules stated by [UPA § 36, which the court quotes].

The order granting the motion for summary judgment and dismissing plaintiff's complaint is reversed.

RACANELLI, P. J., and NEWSOM, J., concur.

Note

The withdrawing partner needs to be concerned about more than the existing debts of the partnership. As noted above, notice of dissociation or dissolution is required in order to cut off liability of the withdrawing partner to third persons who deal with the firm thereafter. In this regard, consider *Eisenberg v. Redd*, 38 S.W. 3d 409 (Mo. 2001), where the court held that a lawyer who withdrew from a law firm was not covered by a mutual release entered into between the firm and the plaintiff after the lawyer withdrew from the firm.

5. Creditors' Claims

If all or substantially all of the assets of a partnership are sold, is the purchaser responsible for the liabilities of the selling partnership? Should the answer be different if the purchaser is itself a partnership and one or more of the partners of the seller are also partners of the purchaser? As a general matter, under UPA § 41 if the business of the partnership is continued with one or more partners of the seller, the creditors of the dissolved partnership remain creditors of the new partnership. If no partner of the seller is a partner of the purchaser, but the purchaser promises the seller to pay the debts of the seller, the creditors of the dissolved partnership remain creditors of the purchaser. The implication of these provisions is that if the seller and purchaser have no common partners (or the purchaser is not a partnership), and the purchaser does not assume the seller's liabilities, creditors of the seller must look to it for payments of amounts due to them.

RUPA is simpler, as the following language in the Comment to § 703 of RUPA indicates:

> In general under RUPA, as a result of the adoption of the entity theory, relationships between a partnership and its creditors are not affected by the dissociation of a partner or by the addition of a new partner, unless otherwise agreed. Therefore, there is not the same need under RUPA as there is under the UPA for an elaborate provision deeming the new partnership to assume the liabilities of the old partnership. See UPA Section 41.

A comment in a prior draft of RUPA elaborates on this point as follows:

> The question is whether the group that purchases the assets [of a partnership] should be deemed to assume the continuing liabilities of the old

partnership simply because one original partner is a member of the group. Under this draft, the answer is no. The Committee should first consider whether the answer should be no. Given that the original partners remain personally liable, given that this draft makes them jointly and severally liable and given that the law of fraudulent transfers still applies, why should the new partnership be considered a continuation of the old partnership after an asset purchase in every case in which one of the purchasers, no matter how small his interest, was an original partner?

Comment to § 605, the successor to UPA § 41, in the 1991 draft of RUPA. The Comment to § 703 in the 1992 draft (§ 605 having disappeared) states, "The same rule [no liability for the new partnership absent assumption] should apply whether the new partnership takes over by a purchase of the assets or a purchase of the partnership interests."

There is an important exception to the general rule that the purchaser of the assets of RUPA partnership (or, for that matter, the purchaser of the assets of a corporation or other entity such as a limited liability company) is not liable for the liabilities of the seller. That exception is sometimes called "successor liability" and is the basis for the claim in the following case.

Case v. Paul Troester Maschinenfabrik

United States District Court, Western District of New York
139 F. Supp. 2d 428 (2001)

Larimer, Chief Judge.

Introduction

On January 8, 1998, plaintiff George Case ("plaintiff" or "Case"), a sheeter operator at Garlock, Inc., suffered injuries when his right arm became entangled in a Model KD-IT-45/15 calender machine[16] that he was operating during the course of his employment. Troester Maschinenbau GmbH & Co. ("TMG"), a German partnership, manufactured the machine in question in 1982. George Case and his wife, Anna Case (collectively "plaintiffs"), commenced the present action, against defendants Paul Troester Maschinenfabrik ("PTM"), another German partnership, and Troester Machinery, Ltd. ("TML"), an American corporation based in Ohio. Plaintiffs assert claims of breach of express and implied warranties of merchantability and fitness for a particular purpose, strict products liability for design defects and failure to warn, negligence stemming from a manufacturing defect, gross negligence, and, on behalf of Anna Case, loss of consortium. Presently before the Court is defendants' motion for summary judgment, and plaintiffs' cross-motion to amend the complaint and for additional discovery.

---

16. [1] A machine that prepares material used in the manufacture of gaskets.

Factual Background

A principal element of defendants' motion for summary judgment is their contention that neither of them manufactured the machine plaintiff was operating when he was injured. Instead, they contend that they had no relationship to TMG, the German entity that manufactured the machine. A brief review of the nature and history of these entities is, therefore, appropriate.

TMG was founded in 1969, and based in Sontra, Germany. Defendants maintain that TMG produced only manufacturing mills and calenders. In 1994, it terminated business operations, was dissolved and liquidated, and, according to defendants, ceased to exist as a legal entity under German law. Defendants further submit that at the same time, TMG's real estate and "nearly all" of its production machines were sold to third parties, but certain raw materials, two or three used machines and certain furniture were purchased by PTM. The proceeds from the liquidation of TMG's assets were utilized to satisfy its debts, and the remaining balance was distributed to TMG's partners.

PTM has been a partnership based in Hanover, Germany since 1892. Between 1969 and 1994, during TMG's existence, PTM manufactured only vulcanizing plants, rubber extruders, plastic extruders and complete production lines. Defendants maintain that there is no legal relationship between PTM and TMG, and PTM is not the successor-in-interest to TMG. They maintain that PTM is a "completely separate, unrelated and distinct company from TMG." At the same time, defendants concede that "some, but not all, of TMG's former partners, management and/or shareholders now serve as partners and/or in management of PTM." Defendants also concede that since 1994, PTM has produced two calender machines, but they consider them different in design and operation from those previously produced by TMG. PTM further asserts that it never assumed TMG's tort liabilities or any of its debts.

TML was established as an Ohio corporation in 1995 for the sole purpose of selling rubber and plastic extrusion machines in the United States. It has never manufactured any products. TML's management, personnel, assets and partners are all different from TMG.

Plaintiffs maintain that Troester is a trade name used by a partnership that has produced various machines for use in the manufacture of gaskets since 1892. They also assert that the machine involved in the accident was assembled pursuant to a cooperation agreement between TMG and PTM, and that "various kinds of calenders" were among the machines that TMG and PTM manufactured together. The manufacture of the machine in question was performed under the engineering, technical, and design direction of Hans Johzhim Golish, who was the technical director of both TMG and PTM and a PTM employee for 23 years. Moreover, all partners of TMG were partners in PTM.

Plaintiffs also assert that prior to 1970 the KD-IT-45/15 calender machine was produced at PTM's location in Hannover. During TMG's existence, the same model calender machine was produced by TMG in Sontra. Upon its dissolution in 1994, all of TMG's patents, design drawings, drafts, technical information, engineering plans, histories of modifications, customer lists and sales information were transferred to PTM. Finally, plaintiffs assert that since TMG's dissolution, PTM continues to service TMG's former customers.

Discussion

Successor Liability

In support of their motion for summary judgment, defendants' principal argument is that plaintiffs cannot establish that either PTM or TML are successors-in-interest to TMG, and no successor liability exists.

Under New York law, the general rule is that a corporation that acquires the assets of another corporation is not liable for the torts of its predecessor. However, there are established exceptions to the general rule, and a successor business entity may be held liable for the torts of its predecessor if (1) it expressly or impliedly assumed the predecessor's tort liability, (2) there was a consolidation or merger of seller and purchaser, (3) the purchaser was a mere continuation of the seller, or (4) the transaction is entered into fraudulently to escape such obligations. The New York Court of Appeals has previously noted that "[t]he second and third items are based on the concept that a successor that effectively takes over a company in its entirety should carry its predecessor's liabilities as a concomitant to the benefits that it derives from the good will purchased. This is consistent with the desire to ensure that a source remains to pay for the victim's injuries." *Grant-Howard Assocs. v. General Housewares Corp.*, 63 N.Y.2d 291, 295, 482 N.Y.S.2d 225, 227, 472 N.E.2d 1 (2d Cir.1984).

The distinction in the present case, of course, is that partnerships, rather than corporations, are involved. Plaintiffs initially attempted to argue that this distinction renders any successor liability analysis inapplicable. I disagree. The Second Circuit has held that "[t]he traditional rule of corporate successor liability and the exceptions to the rule are generally applied regardless of whether the predecessor or successor organization was a corporation or some other form of business organization." *Graham v. James*, 144 F.3d [229] at 240 [(2d Cir. 1998)]; *see also R.C.M. Executive Gallery Corp. v. Rols Capital Co.*, 1997 U.S. Dist. LEXIS 565, *5 n. 3 93-CV-8571 . . . (S.D.N.Y., Jan. 23, 1997) ("[t]he fact that in this case the 'predecessor company' was a partnership and not a corporation does not preclude the application of the traditional successor liability doctrine"); *Soo Line R.R. Co. v. B.J. Carney & Co.*, 797 F.Supp. 1472, 1482 n. 4 (D.Minn.1992) (rejecting argument that partnership cannot be held liable under any theory of successor liability).

. . .

Plaintiffs' next contention is that PTM and TML are carrying on the gasket sheet calender business previously operated by TMG, and that, therefore, PTM and TML are a mere continuation of TMG. Under the mere continuation exception to the general rule, courts have examined various factors including whether the successor (1) retained the same employees, supervisory personnel, the same production facilities in the same location and the same business name, (2) continued production of the same products, (3) maintained the same assets and general business operations and (4) held itself out to the public as the continuation of the previous enterprise.

Here, certain of these factors are unquestionably satisfied. It is undisputed that TMG was created in 1969 by a group of partners who, at that time, were also partners of PTM. Peter Schmidt further testified that TMG was created to extend PTM's capacity. When TMG was dissolved in 1994, PTM retained most of the managerial personnel and certain of the employees of TMG, at least for some period of time. In further support of their position, plaintiffs have submitted evidence that some of TMG's assets and customers have been transferred to PTM's partners. In addition, defendants concede that at least some of the former partners of TMG were or are partners in PTM. PTM's assertion that it did not design the machine at issue is undermined by the fact that, at the relevant time, PTM and TMG had an agreement in place, which gave PTM exclusive access to TMG's designs.

There is also at least a question of fact with respect to whether PTM continued production to some extent of TMG's products. The machine involved in the accident was a KD-IT-45/15, and it bore the Troester label. PTM admits that it has manufactured calenders since TMG's dissolution. Notably, although TMG was dissolved some seven years ago, PTM has recently advertised its Troester KD-45/15 gasket sheet calender, virtually the same model number that had been used by TMG. Moreover, PTM's Hans-Johzhim Golisch testified: "I had the overall technical responsibility [for the Troester KD-IT-45/15]; that is to say, all-important matters were coordinated with me."

There is a further question of fact with respect to whether PTM and TMG held themselves out to the public as the same business. Notwithstanding defendants' contention that PTM and TMG were entirely distinct entities, plaintiffs maintain that, prior to TMG's dissolution, both TMG and PTM were referenced in the same business brochures as simply Troester. In support, they have submitted a joint Troester advertisement referencing both PTM and TMG. The phrases "*Our* plant in Hannover" (PTM's base) and "*Our* plant Sontra" (TMG's base) (emphasis added) could be construed to suggest joint business operations under the Troester name. It is also established that PTM and TML, like TMG, have used the same trade name—Troester. The obvious similarity between the two entities' names suggests to the general public as well that there was some affiliation between them.

I find this evidence to be sufficient to defeat defendants' motion.

Plaintiffs also assert that successor liability exists based upon the so-called product line exception to the general rule. This exception provides that "when a corporation buys substantially all of the assets of a corporate manufacturer and thereafter continues essentially the same manufacturing operation it may be strictly liable for defects in products in the same line even though they were in fact made by the predecessor." *LaFountain v. Webb Industries Corporation*, 951 F.2d 544, 547 (3d Cir.1991); *see also Roll v. Tracor, Inc.*, 26 F.Supp.2d 482, 488–489 (W.D.N.Y.1998). Defendants maintain that in order to invoke the product line exception, plaintiffs bear the burden of proving: (1) their remedy against the original manufacturer was virtually destroyed by the successor's acquisition of substantially all of predecessor's assets; (2) the successor entity continued to manufacture essentially the same product line as its predecessor; (3) the succeeding entity had the ability to assume the original manufacturer's risk-spreading role; and (4) the successor benefitted from the original manufacturer's good will. *Gavette v. Warner & Swasey Co.*, 1999 WL 118438, *9 [, 1999 U.S. Dist. LEXIS 2541] (N.D.N.Y., Mar. 5, 1999). Because there exist questions of fact regarding whether PTM was a mere continuation of TMG, I need not determine this issue.

Plaintiffs' attempt to impose liability on TML because it is a subsidiary of PTM is attenuated at best, and their theory of liability does not withstand scrutiny under the aforementioned principles. TML is a separate corporation with separate management based in a separate country. It does not manufacture any products; it merely sells them in the United States. Indeed, TML was not even incorporated until 1995, some thirteen years after the machine at issue was manufactured, and a year after TMG was dissolved. Moreover, TML has neither expressly nor impliedly agreed to assume TMG's debts, and TML was not a party to the cooperation agreement between PTM and TMG. Plaintiffs have failed to demonstrate any adequate connection between these two entities to survive the pending motion for summary judgment.

For all of these reasons, defendants' motion for summary judgment based upon successor liability grounds is denied with respect to PTM, but granted with respect to TML.

6. The Treatment of Goodwill

When a partner's interest is purchased by the partnership, a question of valuation immediately arises. One asset of the partnership may be its goodwill. Should the partnership interest of the withdrawing partner, or of a deceased partner, include a pro rata portion of goodwill?

Dawson v. White & Case

Court of Appeals of New York
672 N.E.2d 589 (1996)

CIPARICK, JUDGE.

In 1988, the law firm of White & Case dissolved and then re-formed without one of its partners, Evan R. Dawson. This appeal presents two questions arising from an accounting pursuant to Partnership Law §74 [UPA §43] of Dawson's interest in White & Case: (i) whether the law firm possesses goodwill that can be distributed in an accounting proceeding; . . . [17]

---

17. [The second question dealt with whether an unfunded pension plan was a liability for dissolution accounting purposes. The Court of Appeals agreed with the courts below that it was not. — Eds.]

Plaintiff Evan R. Dawson was a partner at the Manhattan law firm of White & Case for nearly 20 years. Sometime before 1988, the firm commenced negotiations with Dawson to persuade him to withdraw as a partner. When the talks reached an impasse, White & Case voted to dissolve the partnership and re-form without Dawson, effective July 1, 1988.

Dawson commenced this action against the partnership in dissolution and successor firm, alleging he was wrongfully terminated. In an amended complaint, Dawson asserted causes of action for an accounting, interference with prospective economic advantage, breach of fiduciary duty, conversion, trespass, invasion of privacy, and breach of contract. Dawson moved by order to show cause for a preliminary injunction to prohibit White & Case from interfering with his office and files. White & Case cross-moved to dismiss the accounting cause of action, contending that article SIXTH of the partnership agreement provided a mechanism for the distribution of Dawson's interest, and further moved for summary judgment on two of the tort causes of action.

Supreme Court, in granting Dawson's motion in part and denying White & Case's cross motion, enjoined White & Case from impeding Dawson's access to his client files and ruled that summary judgment on the tort causes of action was premature. In addition, the court ordered an accounting pursuant to [UPA §43], concluding that article SIXTH was not controlling with respect to Dawson's financial entitlement because it dealt only with the voluntary withdrawal, death or retirement of a partner, not to a partner's expulsion.

After a hearing, the Special Referee valued the assets of White & Case, including the firm's goodwill as an asset. . . . Supreme Court confirmed the report and entered judgment in Dawson's favor. . . .

The Appellate Division affirmed, concluding that the partnership possessed distributable goodwill (see *Dawson v. White & Case*, 622 N.Y.S.2d 269). The Court noted: "Indeed, that defendant's remaining partners, after dissolving defendant in order to exclude plaintiff as a partner, immediately reconstituted themselves as a new firm using the same name, address, facilities and client list as the dissolved firm, evidences that defendant in fact had good will to distribute" (622 N.Y.S.2d 269). . . .

Before turning to the specific issues on appeal, it is useful to review certain elemental principles of partnership law. Foremost among these, indeed "at the heart of the partnership concept," is "the principle that partners may choose with whom they wish to be associated" (*Gelder Med. Group v. Webber*, 363 N.E.2d 573). In recognition of this principle, we have held that a partnership agreement may contain a termination provision or some other mechanism by which to remove a partner. Absent such a mechanism, however, the removal of a partner can be accomplished only through dissolution of the firm, defined as a "change in the relation of the partners caused by any partner ceasing to be associated in the carrying on . . . of the business" [UPA §29]. The White & Case partnership agreement did not contain an express termination provision, and so, in order to remove Dawson, the partners voted to dissolve the firm and then to immediately re-form without him.[18]

This act of dissolution conferred on Dawson the "right to an account of his interest . . . as against the . . . partnership continuing the business" [UPA §43]. When, as in this case, the partnership business is continued after dissolution, the accounting is performed by computing the firm's assets less its liabilities, with the balance hypothetically apportioned among the partners to fix the former partner's share of the partnership [UPA §40(c)]. . . .

The first issue is whether White & Case possessed goodwill that was capable of distribution upon dissolution. When applied to law firms, the term "goodwill" refers to the "ability to attract clients as [a] result of [the] firm's name, location, or the reputation of [its] lawyers" (Black's Law Dictionary 695 [6th ed.]).[19] We conclude that the Special Referee erred in including goodwill as an asset of White & Case in the partnership accounting.

Analysis begins with the statutory instruction that "[i]n settling accounts between the partners after dissolution, . . . *subject to any agreement to the contrary* . . . [t]he assets of the partnership" include the "partnership property" [UPA §40[a][I] [emphasis added]. By statute, then, the partners are free to exclude particular items from the class of distributable partnership property, and such an agreement will be enforced in an accounting proceeding. . . .

In [*In re*] *Brown* [150 N.E. 581], the issue was whether a brokerage company was obligated to account to a former partner for the company's goodwill even though goodwill was not mentioned in the partnership agreement or in the company's books, incoming members paid nothing for goodwill, and a recently retired partner did not receive compensation for goodwill. The Court concluded that the trier of fact might infer "from the course of dealing between the partners when new members came in and old ones went out that by tacit understanding there was to be no accounting for good will" (*id.* at 7). The same conclusion was reached in the context of a law firm dissolution in the case of *Siddall v. Keating*, 185 N.Y.S.2d 630, *aff'd*, 164 N.E.2d 860.

The pertinent facts of this case are similar to those of *Brown* and *Siddall*: new White & Case partners never paid anything for goodwill; departing partners never received a payment for goodwill; and goodwill was not listed as an asset in the firm's

---

18. [1] While partners are statutorily empowered to dissolve the partnership at any time [UPA §31(2)], wrongfully dissolving partners may be liable to the expelled partner for breach of the partnership agreement when the partnership is not at will [UPA §38(2)]. Whether such a breach occurred in this case is not raised on appeal.

19. [2] The term "goodwill" represents an elusive concept, but is broadly defined as "the advantage or benefit, which is acquired by an establishment, beyond the mere value of the capital, stock, funds, or property employed therein, in consequence of the general public patronage and encouragement, which it receives from constant or habitual customers, on account of its local position, or common celebrity, or reputation for skill or affluence, or punctuality, or from other accidental circumstances or necessities, or even from ancient partialities or prejudices" (Story, Partnership §99, at 170).

financial statements. Indeed, the partners' intention not to credit goodwill is even more apparent in this case than in either *Brown* or *Siddall*. The White & Case partnership agreement contained the following provisions: . . . "The computation of the amount with which a Former Partner shall be charged or credited . . . shall exclude any value for the good will of the partnership or the Firm name, as such items are deemed to be of no value" (art. SIXTH [d]).

Dawson attempts to avoid these provisions by claiming they are inapplicable. He contends . . . that article SIXTH only applies in the event of a partner's withdrawal, retirement or death, not to this expulsion situation. We disagree and find that the partnership agreement reflects the binding written expression of the terms under which these partners assented to associate with each other and evinces their intention that goodwill be deemed "of no value." Its provisions reinforce our holding that, for purposes of this partnership accounting, White & Case lacks distributable goodwill.

We note that the holding in this case is based on the specific facts presented, and should not be construed as a prohibition against the valuation, in the appropriate case, of law firm goodwill. In addition, the existence of law firm goodwill has been recognized in conjunction with the recent promulgation of Code of Professional Responsibility DR 2-111(A), which authorizes the sale of "a law practice, including good will," by a "lawyer retiring from a private practice of law, [or] a law firm one or more members of which are retiring from the private practice of law with the firm."

To the extent that dictum in *Siddall* stands for the proposition that a professional business, as a matter of law, cannot have any goodwill apart from the goodwill of its constituent members, we note that this rationale has been rejected by this Court in a different context (see *Spaulding v. Benenati*, 442 N.E.2d 1244 [enforcing sale of dentistry practice goodwill]; and has been superseded by the economic realities of the contemporary practice of law, illustrated by attorney advertising, internationalization of law firms, and other professional developments. In short, the ethical constraints against the sale of a law practice's goodwill by a practicing attorney no longer warrant a blanket prohibition against the valuation of law firm goodwill when those ethical concerns are absent. . . .

Accordingly, the judgment appealed from and order of the Appellate Division brought up for review should be modified, without costs, and the case remitted to Supreme Court, New York County, for further proceedings in accordance with the opinion herein and, as so modified, affirmed.

SIMONS, TITONE, BELLACOSA and SMITH, JJ., concur.

KAYE, C.J., and LEVINE, J., took no part.

Notes

1. See REUSCHLEIN & GREGORY, AGENCY AND PARTNERSHIP 341, § 226 (1979), noting that in recent times courts have been reluctant to deny categorically the existence of goodwill in professional partnerships. *See also Stefanski v. Gonnella*, 446 N.E.2d 734

(Mass. App. 1983) (treating the existence of goodwill in a professional partnership as a question of fact, and citing cases on both sides of this issue).

2. The above materials highlight the importance of drafting language in the partnership agreement (and, if the business is sold, in the contract of sale) specifying the manner in which goodwill is to be treated by the firm. This should include providing a method for evaluation of this asset, if it is to be taken into account at all, particularly since it may be years before an event requiring evaluation will arise. Clauses recognizing and evaluating goodwill typically are accompanied by covenants not to compete.

3. Under RUPA § 701(b), the buyout price that a dissociated partner is entitled to receive is based on the value of the assets, assuming that the assets "were sold at a price equal to the greater of the liquidation value or the value of the entire business as a going concern without the dissociated partner. . . ." Presumably, then, the going concern value would include any value attributable to the continuing partners. This is confirmed in the Comments to § 701: "[U]nless the partnership's goodwill is damaged by the wrongful dissociation, the value of the dissociated partner's interest will include any goodwill value of the partnership."

4. Calculating goodwill is more an art than a science. In *Dixon v. Crawford, McGilliard, Peterson & Yelish*, 262 P.3d 108 (Wash. Ct. App. 2012), the appellate court accepted the trial court's use of the "excess earnings method" of valuing goodwill in a law partnership. The court described the method as follows:

> The capitalization of the difference between [the earnings of the partners] and the sum of the remaining partners' individual replacement values provides an accurate reflection of the goodwill value of the firm as a whole.

This formulation leaves many questions unanswered. For instance, if the "earnings of the partners" includes the earnings of the dissociating partner, would that not overvalue goodwill unless that partner's replacement value is also subtracted? And what factors enter into "capitalization"? The lower court considered future risk and growth. But how are these amounts to be determined? Finally, how would one calculate the "replacement value" of a lawyer? These uncertainties also indicate the importance of careful drafting.

5. Recall the *Cadwalader* case, *supra* Chapter 12, where the trial court concluded that the firm had no valuable goodwill and its decision was affirmed on appeal.

7. Calculation of Buy-out Price Under RUPA § 701

In *Robertson v. Jacobs Cattle Co.*, 830 N.W.2d 191 (Neb. 2013), the Nebraska Supreme Court upheld the decision of the trial court to expel various partners on the basis that their conduct made it not reasonably practical to carry on the business of the partnership with them. The expelled partners were the plaintiffs in the trial court, seeking dissolution of the partnership. The defendants counterclaimed, seeking to expel the plaintiffs. The defendants prevailed in the trial court and were the appellees before the Wyoming Supreme Court. In the portion of the opinion set forth below, the Wyoming Supreme Court considered the proper way to calculate the buy-out price for the appellants' partnership interests, applying RUPA § 701(b). Of interest in this case is the interplay between the provisions of RUPA and the partnership agreement, in which the allocation of profits did not necessarily track the partners' relative interest in partnership capital. The court wrote:

> The remaining issues pertain to the district court's calculation of the buy-out price which the dissociated partners are to receive for their interests in the partnership. This price is governed by [RUPA § 701(b)], which provides:
>
>> The buyout price of a dissociated partner's interest is the amount that would have been distributable to the dissociating partner [RUPA § 807(b)] if, on the date of dissociation, the assets of the partnership were sold at a price equal to the greater of the liquidation value or the value based on a sale of the entire business as a going concern without the dissociated partner and the partnership were wound up as of that date. Interest must be paid from the date of dissociation to the date of payment.
>
> [RUPA § 807(b)] provides in pertinent part:
>
>> Each partner is entitled to a settlement of all partnership accounts upon winding up the partnership business. In settling accounts among the partners, profits and losses that result from the liquidation of the partnership assets must be credited and charged to the partners' accounts. The partnership shall make a distribution to a partner in an amount equal to any excess of the credits over the charges in the partner's account. A partner shall contribute to the partnership an amount equal to any excess of the charges over the credits in the partner's account but excluding from the calculation charges attributable to an obligation for which the partner is not personally liable under [section 306].
>
> [The court then determined that the date of dissociation was the date that the trial court entered its order granting the defendants' counterclaim seeking expulsion of the complaining partners.]
>
> The land owned by the partnership is a capital asset. Under the operative partnership agreement, the partners each had a capital account. The value of the capital account was "directly proportionate to [each partner's] original Capital contributions as later adjusted for draws taken from the Partnership." At the time of dissociation, the capital account of each appellant was approximately 5.33 percent of the total capital in the partnership.
>
> Each partner also had an income account under the partnership agreement. Net profits and net losses of the partnership were to be "credited or debited to the individual income accounts [of each partner] as soon as practicable after the close of each fiscal year." The agreement provided that the "term[s] 'net profits' and 'net losses' shall mean the net profits and net losses of the Partnership as determined by generally accepted accounting principles." It further noted that "[t]he net profits and net losses of the

Partnership" were distributable or chargeable "to each of the Partners in proportion to the votes they have." Under the agreement, [appellants had] a total of eight votes. Thus, appellants each had a 12.5 percent share of net profits and losses in their income account.

The district court expressly found that appellants' "interests in the partnership shall be purchased by the partnership as required by [RUPA § 701(b)]." In its ruling, the district court considered the value of the partnership's assets, including the appreciated value of the land, less the partnership's liabilities, and arrived at a liquidation value for the partnership. It then accepted appellees' argument that the proper buyout price was calculated by applying each partner's capital account percentage to the partnership's total liquidation value.

On appeal, appellants agree the buyout was to be calculated pursuant to [RUPA § 701)] and agree with the district court's liquidation value of the partnership. But they argue the district court erred in calculating the buyout price because it did not consider how the hypothetical capital gain realized from treating the land as though it had been sold on the date of dissociation would flow to each partner based on the partnership agreement's allocation of net profits and losses. Appellants contend the proper calculation results in each of them receiving a buyout equal to 12.5 percent of the liquidation value of the partnership.

Appellants' argument rests on two premises: (1) that a capital gain would be realized upon a hypothetical selling of the partnership land pursuant to [RUPA § 701(b)], which would constitute "profits" within the meaning of [RUPA § 807(b)], that the hypothetical profit would constitute "net profits" within the meaning of paragraph 11 of the partnership agreement.

[RUPA § 701(b)] provides that the buyout price of a dissociated partner's interest is to be based on the amount that "would have been distributable to the dissociating partner" under [RUPA § 807(b)] "if, on the date of dissociation, the assets of the partnership were sold at . . . liquidation value . . . and the partnership were wound up as of that date." [RUPA § 807(b)] then provides that "profits and losses that result from [such] liquidation of the partnership assets must be credited and charged to the partners' accounts."

It is clear from the plain language of [RUPA § 701(b)] that the proper calculation must be based upon the assumption that the partnership assets, here the land, were sold on the date of dissociation, even though no actual sale occurs. Here, the initial question is whether selling the partnership land on the date of dissociation would result in a capital gain and "profits" in the context of [RUPA § 807(b)]. We consider this to be a question of statutory interpretation.

The term "capital gain" means "profit realized when a capital asset is sold or exchanged." The term "profit" is generally defined as the "excess of revenues over expenditures in a business transaction." We are required to give the language of a statute its plain and ordinary meaning. Accordingly, we conclude that the capital gain which would be realized upon a hypothetical liquidation of the partnership's land on the date of dissociation (as required by [RUPA § 701(b)]) would constitute "profits" within the meaning of the phrase in [RUPA § 807(b)].

The remaining question is how those "profits" should be "credited and charged to the partners' accounts" in this particular situation. Appellants contend that it must be done pursuant to paragraph 11 of the partnership agreement, which specifically states how "net profits" and "net losses" "as determined by generally accepted accounting principles" are to be distributed to the partners. But there is no expert testimony equating this type of capital gain to "net profits" under "generally accepted accounting principles." . . . We conclude that the district court erred in refusing to consider evidence on this issue, and we reverse that portion of its order calculating the amount of the buyouts and remand the cause with directions for the court to reconsider the buyout calculations after receiving appellants' evidence on this issue. In this respect, we note that RUPA eliminates the distinction in [the original Uniform Partnership Act] between the liability owing to a partner in respect of capital and the liability owing in respect of profits. Section 807(b) [of RUPA] speaks simply of the right of a partner to a liquidating distribution. That implements the logic of RUPA Sections 401(a) and 502 under which *contributions to capital and shares in profits and losses combine to determine the right to distributions.*

Id. at 873–78.

Notes

1. Calculating the buy-out price for lawyer dissociating from a law firm presents distinct challenges. In *Rappaport v. Gelfand*, 197 Cal. App. 4th 1213 (2011), the appellate court was faced with an appeal from the trial court's decision valuing two assets of the law firm, a contingent fee for a case on appeal and, in a second case, a fee for which the firm had a lien but faced litigation from the client. In both instances, the court said that the applicable test was "the sale price of the separate assets based upon their market value as determined by a willing and knowledgeable buyer and a willing and knowledgeable seller, neither of which is under any compulsion to buy or sell." To determine this "market value," the appellate court held that it was appropriate to consider expert testimony. With respect to valuing the contingent fee for the case on appeal, for instance, the expert for the dissociated lawyer opined that the case, for which the trial court awarded $900,000 in damages, was worth between 85 percent and 95 percent of that amount. He chose a settlement value of 90 percent, or a 10 percent discount from the award. He then discounted the contingent fee to which the firm would be entitled by the same amount. The trial court accepted this calculation and the appellate court affirmed.

2. If a partnership fails to pay the buyout price set forth in the partnership agreement, does the partnership dissolve as a result? Two partners who withdrew from a partnership claimed that the failure to pay the buyout price meant that the partnership was dissolved. The Nebraska Supreme Court did not agree, because neither the partnership agreement nor did the Nebraska version of RUPA so provided. *Shoemaker v. Shoemaker*, 745 N.W.2d 299 (Neb. 2008).

D. Winding Up; Liquidation; Terminating the Business

1. Winding Up and Liquidation

Winding up. The Comment to UPA § 29 states in part as follows: "In this act dissolution designates the point in time when the partners cease to carry on the business together; termination is the point in time when all the partnership affairs are wound up; winding up, the process of settling partnership affairs after dissolution." Section 37 of UPA focuses on the right to wind up, stating that, subject to agreement, "the partners who have not wrongfully dissolved" have the right to wind up, "provided, however, that any partner, his legal representative or his assignee, upon cause shown, may obtain winding up by the court." Section 803 of RUPA is the counterpart to § 37. It defines the right to wind up in similar terms, except that it adds a provision delineating some of the rights of the person winding up the business.

Liquidation. *Beals v. Superior Welding Co.*, 653 N.E.2d 430, 438 (Ill. App. 1995), states the following with regard to liquidation:

> Plaintiff presents no authority to support her claim that the partnership of Hall and Schwartz was not "liquidated" within the meaning of section 41 [of UPA]. The term "liquidation" is not defined in [UPA] but it appears to be used interchangeably with the term "winding up" of partnership affairs referenced in sections 29 and 37 of the Partnership Act. . . . Schwartz purchased Hall's interest in the firm, notified clients and the public of the dissolution, acknowledged the completion of all projects and receipt of all accounts receivable, and agreed not to transact any business on behalf of the former partnership when he commenced business as a proprietorship. Under these facts, nothing more was required to wind up or liquidate the partnership.

Resnick v. Kaplan

Court of Special Appeals of Maryland
434 A.2d 582 (1981)

Argued before MORTON, MOYLAN and MOORE, JJ.

MOORE, JUDGE.

This appeal represents only a part of the extensive litigation between former law partners which was spawned by the dissolution of their law firm in October, 1972.

The action below was for an accounting by the appellees—the four partners ("the Kaplan group") who continued in practice together—against the appellant ("Resnick"), their erstwhile partner who left and opened his own office. The Circuit Court for Baltimore City (Karwacki, J.) granted the Kaplan group's motion for partial summary judgment, entering judgment for them in the amount of $207,871.94. Partial summary judgment was also entered in favor of Resnick for $29,861.56. All other matters were ordered to be the subject of further proceedings. . . .

The primary dispute thus resolved by the lower court was the method of allocation of fees received by the parties after dissolution; and it was decided that the allocation should be made on the basis of their respective percentage interests in the partnership, not on the basis of the time spent on individual cases after dissolution. Resnick contends that summary judgment was improper. We affirm. . . .

The partnership agreement in this case does not provide for the rights of the parties upon dissolution. It recites that the partnership "shall commence on January 1, 1969, and continue from year to year thereafter until it is dissolved in accordance with the terms hereof." Then, it simply states:

> To the extent that dissolution is not covered by the terms of this Agreement, it shall be in accordance with the laws of the State of Maryland.

The Uniform Partnership Act, [UPA § 29], defines dissolution as

> the change in the relation of the partners caused by any partner ceasing to be associated *in the carrying on as distinguished from the winding up of the business.* (Emphasis added.)

The statute also provides that the partnership is *not* terminated on dissolution *"but continues until the winding up of partnership affairs is completed."* [UPA § 30.] (Emphasis added.)

Resnick participated in the winding up of the partnership affairs pertaining to the 150 cases upon which he worked. Kaplan et al. handled the remaining cases of the firm. These were contractual, professional obligations and it was the duty of the respective partners to see to their completion. In the performance of these contracts, the fiduciary character of their relationship as partners continued.

The Uniform Act conferred no right upon either side to compensation for services rendered in this winding up process, *cf.* UPA § 37 and, in the absence of any provision in the partnership document, it was correctly held that the aggregate of the fees collected should be allocated according to the percentages specified in the agreement for the distribution of profits and losses.

Directly on point is the case of *Frates v. Nichols*, 167 So. 2d 77 (Fla. 3d DCA 1964). Following the dissolution of a law firm, one of the partners, Frates, took with him ten negligence cases of the old firm, having secured retainer agreements from the clients. The completion of the work on these cases resulted in the payment of contingent fees in excess of $200,000. Frates contended that upon dissolution the firm's retainer agreements expired and that, on the basis of the new retainers which he had obtained, he was entitled to retain all the fees except a *quantum meruit* payment to the old firm for services rendered prior to the dissolution. The court rejected this contention, concluding that these fees in their entirety were assets of the firm and that Frates was entitled to receive only his partnership interest therein. In reaching this conclusion, the court stated:

> Although never having been passed on by a Florida court, the proposition is universally accepted that a law partner in dissolution owes a duty to his old firm to wind up the old firm's pending business, and that he is not entitled to any extra compensation therefor.
>
> The dissolution date of February 28, 1961 did not put an immediate end to the partnership, it continued for the purpose of winding up its affairs, and inasmuch as Frates had a duty to wind up the affairs of the partnership, *his signing of a retainer agreement with an already existing client was without consideration and void.*
>
> . . . .
>
> We adopt the rule recognized by our sister states that the retention of a law firm obligates every member thereof to fulfilling that contract, and that upon a dissolution any of the partners is obligated to complete that obligation without extra compensation. (Footnotes omitted.) (Emphasis added.)

Finally, we reject the notion, suggested by appellant, that different rules are to be applied to the winding up of professional partnerships as distinguished from "business" partnerships. The definition of "business" in the Act as including "profession," UPA § 2, negates the possibility of any such distinction. . . .

Order . . . affirmed.

Notes

1. As the *Resnick* case makes clear, a partner who winds up the affairs of a dissolved partnership is not entitled to compensation for such efforts. UPA § 18(f) provides an exception to this rule: a "surviving partner is entitled to reasonable compensation for his services in winding up the partnership affairs." UPA does not define a "surviving partner," but a Texas decision cited this common-sense definition: "A surviving partner is that partner who, during the existence of the partnership, outlives the other or others, and the relation necessarily arises only when one of an existing partnership outlives or survives in life the other." *Kahn v. Seely,* 980 S.W.2d 794, 798 (Tex. App. 1998)(citing several earlier Texas decisions).

2. In recent years, a number of law firms, including prominent national and international firms, have experienced financial difficulties resulting in bankruptcy. Often, partners in a failing firm agree to amend their partnership agreement to include a "*Jewel* Waiver," which reverses the outcome reflected in *Resnick.* (The concept of such a waiver emanates from *Jewel v. Boxer,* 156 Cal. App. 3d 171 (1984), where the court held that, absent an agreement to the contrary, profits derived from a law firm's unfinished business are owed to the former partners in proportion to their

partnership interests.) An example of a *Jewel* Waiver and its effect were at issue in *In re Thelen LLP*, 20 N.E.3d 264 (N.Y. 2014), a case involving a New York law firm that dissolved and filed for bankruptcy. The waiver provided:

> [n]either the Partners nor the Partnership shall have any claim or entitle-ment to clients, cases or matters ongoing at the time of the dissolution of the Partnership other than the entitlement for collection of amounts due for work performed by the Partners and other Partnership personnel prior to their departure from the Partnership. The provisions of this [section] are intended to expressly waive, opt out of and be in lieu of any rights any Partner of the Partnership may have to "unfinished business" of the Part-nership, as the term is defined in Jewel v. Boxer, 156 Cal. App.3d 171 [203 Cal. Rptr. 13] (Cal. App. 1 Dist. 1984), or as otherwise might be provided in the absence of this provision through the interpretation of the [California Uniform Partnership Act of 1994, as amended].

The Trustee in bankruptcy sought to avoid the waiver and recover fees earned by partners who completed pending matters while affiliated with other law firms. The New York Court of Appeals, responding to questions posed to it by the United States Court of Appeals for the Second Circuit, upheld the waiver, holding that "pending hourly fee matters are not partnership 'property' or 'unfinished business' within the meaning of New York's Partnership Law. A law firm does not own a client or an engagement, and is only entitled to be paid for services actually rendered." The New York Court's opinion is written so broadly that if applied to a fact pattern such as that in *Resnick*, a different result would ensue in that case. At the least, *In re Thelen LLP* is an important endorsement of a *Jewel* Waiver. *See also Heller Ehrman LLP v. Davis Wright Tremaine LLP*, 4 Cal. 5th 467 (Cal. 2018) (reaching the same result responding to a question certified by the Ninth Circuit Court of Appeals).

3. In *Bushard v. Reisman*, 800 N.W.2d 373 (Wis. 2011), the plaintiff (Bushard), one of two partners, sent a notice of dissolution to his co-partner (Reisman), who con-tinued to operate the business for several years thereafter. Reisman sent regular dis-tributions of profits to Bushard and, after a period of time, started to pay himself a salary. Bushard challenged the appropriateness of Reisman's drawing a salary and prevailed. Reisman argued that the court should make an equitable exception to the "no compensation" rule, but the court declined to do so, finding that UPA was clear on this point and left no room for judicial creativity. In addition, the court found that Bushard had never consented to a continuation of the business, so that the value of the business would not be fixed at the date of dissolution (which occurred when Bushard sent his notice). Consequently, Reisman could not credit those distribu-tions against a hypothetical valuation of the business as of the date of dissolution. If and when Reisman finally wound-up the business, Bushard would be entitled to half of the proceeds realized in the liquidation.

4. Section 401(h) of RUPA broadens the UPA rule, and it provides that partner who renders services in winding up the business of the partnership is entitled to "reason-able compensation."

Marr v. Langhoff

Court of Appeals of Maryland
589 A.2d 470 (1991)

RODOWSKY, JUDGE.

This case is a sequel to *Moniodis v. Cook*. . . . When the litigation was finally resolved very substantial fees were received by plaintiffs' counsel. One of these counsel was Stephen D. Langhoff (Langhoff), formerly a shareholder in the professional services corporation now named Michael E. Marr, P.C. (Marr P.C.), which initially had represented the plaintiffs in *Cook*. In this action Marr P.C. claims Langhoff's share of the *Cook* fee, together with prejudgment interest, for a total claim in excess of $800,000. . . .

[Langhoff, Marr and Bennett joined together in practice under the name Marr, Langhoff & Bennett (ML & B)]. [I]n the fall of 1981 serious differences arose between Marr and Langhoff [with the consequence that] Marr considered "the firm to be dissolved." . . . It is undisputed that the effective date when Langhoff "would no longer be a member of the firm of [ML & B]" was January 1, 1982.

On or about December 31, 1981, Langhoff's last day with ML & B, Bennett and Langhoff discussed ML & B's work in progress for clients and physical assets. Apparently without difficulty, they reached a very simple agreement. Bennett testified, "I broached the topic, whatever is yours is yours, and whatever is ours is ours. . . . Steve [Langhoff] indicated that he was agreeing with that, basically." Langhoff's recollection of the conversation was similar. He said, "[W]e . . . were . . . going to go our separate ways and continue on or basically as we were before [the merger of the practices]." . . .

When Langhoff moved out of the Marr & Bennett, P.A. offices on March 6, 1982, he took the *Cook* file with him. His explanation of this conduct is that he intended to carry out whatever the clients' wishes were concerning their representation. Shortly thereafter Bennett sought to review the *Cook* file, searched for it, and realized that it was missing. Bennett telephoned Langhoff who acknowledged that he had the file. . . . [The *Cook* client decided to retain Langhoff. After conclusion of the *Cook* litigation, Marr sued Langhoff on a claim of breach of fiduciary duty]. . . .

Marr P.C.'s legal argument in support of its breach of fiduciary duty claim involved three steps. First, although ML & B was a professional services corporation, the plaintiff urged that the legal relationship between Marr, Langhoff and Bennett should be the same as between partners on dissolution of their partnership. Secondly, during the winding up of the partnership business following dissolution partners continue to owe one another fiduciary duties with respect to the business of the dissolved partnership. In this respect Marr P.C. relied on *Resnick v. Kaplan*. Thirdly, Marr P.C. viewed the violation of fiduciary duty as a tort, relying on Restatement (Second) of Torts § 874 (1977) ("One standing in a fiduciary relation with another is subject to liability to the other for harm resulting from a breach of duty imposed by the relation."). . . . [Marr recovered a judgment of $812,027.22 at trial. The judgment was reversed by the Court of Special Appeals on the ground that the corporate model applied to the relationships; the court remanded for a determination of Langhoff's post-termination duties in that context. Certiorari was granted by the Court of Appeals.]

We do not reach . . . the ground of decision relied upon by the Court of Special Appeals. . . . [T]he special agreement reached between Bennett and Langhoff on or about December 31, 1981, extinguished any continuing duty of loyalty to Marr P.C. which Langhoff might otherwise have had and which necessarily was the foundation of the tort sued upon. As a result, the remand which the Court of Special Appeals ordered is unnecessary. . . .

We construe the Langhoff-Bennett contract to have effected an immediate winding up of ML & B. . . . Whether we view Marr and Bennett as having expressly willed a dissolution, or as having expelled Langhoff, ML & B was dissolved December 31, 1981. See [UPA § 30] "On dissolution, the partnership is not terminated, but continues until the winding up of partnership affairs is completed." [UPA § 38(1)] addresses the rights of partners in the application of the partnership property on dissolution. [The court quotes § 38(1).]

The accrual of a right to an account is addressed in [UPA § 43] which reads:

> "The right to an account of his interest shall accrue to any partner . . . as against the winding up partners . . . at the date of dissolution, in the absence of any agreement to the contrary."

Title 9 is the Maryland Uniform Partnership Act (UPA). The UPA has been applied to the dissolution of legal services partnerships. Work in progress at the time of dissolution is an asset of the dissolved firm and the partners of the dissolved firm have an obligation to complete the work in progress. . . . [M]utual fiduciary duties [exist] during winding up because the parties remained partners in the dissolved firm until termination. But the mutual fiduciary duties cease when the winding up is completed. . . . The trial court . . . did not give the correct legal effect to the Langhoff-Bennett contract.

Meehan v. Shaughnessy, 404 Mass. 419, 535 N.E.2d 1255 (1989), illustrates the effect of a contract provision addressing partnership dissolution. . . . In lieu of "waiting for the unfinished business to be 'wound up' and liquidated" in accordance with Massachusetts statutes dealing with partnerships, the partnership agreement gave a withdrawing partner "the right to remove any case which came to the firm 'through the personal effort or connection' of the partner, if the partner compensate[d] the dissolved partnership 'for the services to and expenditures for the client.'" . . . The court held:

> "Under the agreement, the old firm's unfinished business is, in effect, 'wound up' immediately; the departing partner takes certain of the unfinished business of the old, dissolved [firm] on the payment of a 'fair charge,' and the new, surviving [firm] takes the remainder of the old partnership's unfinished business. The two entities surviving after the dissolution possess

'new business,' unconnected with that of the old firm, and the former partners no longer have a continuing fiduciary obligation to windup for the benefit of each other the business they shared in their former partnership."

The Langhoff-Bennett contract effected, contemporaneously with the dissolution of ML & B, the same legal result as did the dissolution provision of the partnership contract in *Meehan v. Shaughnessy*. Faced with dissolution Marr, acting through Bennett, and Bennett agreed with Langhoff to eliminate a period of winding up and to cut directly to termination of the partnership. The right to compel liquidation after dissolution under [UPA § 38(1)] exists "unless otherwise agreed." . . .

. . . The Langhoff-Bennett contract is not simply an allocation of work in progress as the initial component of a winding up. . . . For the same reasons the Langhoff-Bennett contract extinguishes the fiduciary duties, if any, between the shareholders in ML & B, even if the correct analysis here proceeds on a corporate model. . . .

The Langhoff-Bennett contract substituted for the fiduciary duty. Langhoff may well have breached the Langhoff-Bennett contract by physically taking the *Cook* file, but Marr P.C. has not sued on that express contract. The assumpsit count of the complaint which was dismissed with prejudice was not a claim on that express contract. The assumpsit count rested on restitutionary principles which, in turn, rested on fiduciary duty. . . .

Judgment of the Court of Special Appeals Vacated. Case Remanded to That Court for the Entry of a Judgment Reversing the Judgment of the Circuit Court for Baltimore City and Remanding This Case to the Circuit Court for Baltimore City for the Entry of a Judgment in Favor of the Defendant, Stephen D. Langhoff.

Ohlendorf v. Feinstein

Court of Appeals of Missouri
636 S.W.2d 687 (1982)

PUDLOWSKI, JUDGE.

Plaintiff, Howard C. Ohlendorf, is appealing a judgment against him in a court tried case on a cross-claim to wind up a partnership in which the plaintiff and the defendants, Bernard Feinstein and Fred Whaley, were partners. The facts are as follows:

On May 23, 1974, the Missouri State Highway Commission offered seven tracts of land in Jefferson County for sale at auction. Defendant Feinstein submitted the highest bid for all seven tracts. This bid of $568,703.25 was subsequently accepted by the State Highway Commission. Feinstein signed a sales agreement on May 23, and delivered a check for ten percent of the purchase price ($56,870.32) to the State Highway Commission. Immediately after the bidding, Ohlendorf, Feinstein and Whaley discussed the formation of a partnership. On May 25, 1974, all three parties executed a notice of assignment documenting the partnership agreement. Ohlendorf subsequently recorded this assignment. Pursuant to the formation of the partnership Ohlendorf and Whaley each transferred $18,956.77 to Feinstein. The purpose of the partnership was to obtain purchasers (including themselves) for the seven tracts, so that when the purchase from the State Highway Department was closed, the partnership could immediately resell the tracts for a profit. The three partners were to share equally in the expenses and profits of the partnership.

The parties endeavored to find individual buyers for the tracts. Ohlendorf undertook to purchase tract 3 himself, for $150,000. Prior to August, 1974, the parties were partially successful at finding buyers for the other tracts. In August, however, there was a falling out among the parties. Ohlendorf informed the other parties that the partnership was dead as far as he was concerned. Ohlendorf stated that he had no intention of purchasing tract 3. He subsequently notified the State Highway Commission that the partnership would not complete the purchase of the seven tracts. There is no doubt that Ohlendorf wrongfully breached the partnership agreement causing a dissolution of the partnership.

Ohlendorf filed suit against Feinstein and Whaley seeking recovery of the $18,956.77 he transferred to Feinstein at the inception of the partnership. Defendants filed a cross-claim to wind up the joint venture pursuant to [UPA § 37]. Defendants sought damages in the form of lost profits for Ohlendorf's wrongful breach of the partnership agreement. [UPA § 38]. The trial judge dissolved the partnership under [UPA § 32]. Judgment was entered in favor of Feinstein against Ohlendorf in the amount of $50,932.25, and in favor of Whaley against Ohlendorf in the same amount. This appeal followed.

In his first point on appeal plaintiff contends that the defendants failed to prove that the lost profits were a direct and proximate result of plaintiff's breach of the partnership agreement. This position is based upon the assertion that the defendants would not have suffered any damages if they had proceeded with the purchase and sale of the seven tracts on their own account. We find plaintiff's position unpersuasive.

Dissolution of a partnership results when any partner ceases to be associated with the carrying on of the partnership business. [UPA § 29.] In this case, dissolution was recognized by decree of the trial court upon its finding that the plaintiff willfully breached the partnership agreement. [UPA § 32.] Dissolution, however, is not a termination of the partnership business. The partnership business continues until the winding up of the partnership affairs is complete. [UPA § 30.] The partners who have not wrongfully dissolved the partnership have the *right* to wind up the partnership business. [UPA § 37.] The partners, however, are not required to exercise their right to wind up the business. "The Uniform Partnership Law contemplates that dissolved partnerships may continue in business for a short, long or indefinite period of time, . . . so long as none of the partners insist on a winding up and final termination of the partnership business." *Schoeller v. Schoeller*, 497 S.W.2d 860, 867 (Mo. App. 1973). Thus, when a dissolution is caused by the wrongful act of a partner, the innocent partner(s) have an election of remedies. They may: wind up the partnership business, and seek damages from the wrongful partner; continue the business in the same name, either by themselves or jointly with others, or, continue the business and seek damages. [UPA § 38.]

This review of the law clearly demonstrates that when a partnership is dissolved due to the wrongful conduct of a partner, the innocent partner(s) have the option of winding up the partnership business or continuing it. By statute, the right to terminate the business and seek damages is unconditional. [UPA § 37.] Plaintiff's position here is really a backhanded attempt to impose a limitation upon the defendants' right to wind up the partnership. Plaintiff asserts that the defendants' damages are not a proximate result of his wrongful conduct, because the defendants would have obtained their profits if they had continued the business. The practical effect of adopting this position would be to impose a duty upon the defendants to continue the partnership business if there is a reasonable certainty that it will be profitable. We refuse to impose a duty which is clearly contrary to the provisions of the Uniform Partnership Law. Thus, the defendants' damages in this case become a direct and proximate consequence of the plaintiff's wrongful conduct, once the defendants elected to wind up the partnership business. . . .

The trial court's findings of fact and award of damages for tracts 1, 2 and 6 is reversed and remanded for further proceedings to determine the lost profits, if any, for those tracts. In all other respects the decision of the trial court is affirmed.

Smith, P.J., and Satz, J., concur.

2. Termination

The order of distribution of assets is specified by UPA § 40(b). Creditors outside of the partnership are paid first, then the claims of partners other than for capital contributions or profits, then capital is returned and finally the remaining balance, if any, is distributed as profits. If the partnership property is insufficient to repay capital contributions, the loss is to be shared by the solvent partners in the proportions in which they share profits. UPA §§ 18(a), 40(d). The statutory rules of distribution may be varied by agreement of the partners (UPA § 40, first clause), except that the rights of third persons cannot be affected without their consent.

Section 807 of RUPA is the counterpart provision to § 40. It abolishes the priority rules of § 40(b) and (c) that subordinate inside debt (partners as creditors of the firm) to outside debt. The Comment to § 807 states, however, that this decision is largely formal in nature because partners are personally liable for unsatisfied outside debt. (The Comment was drafted prior to the appearance of the full shield LLP, which undermines the "largely formal" explanation in the Comment. One could argue that creditors are always free to negotiate priorities upon dissolution and thus the abolition of the UPA priority rules is insignificant, but that would seem true, in a practical way, only for substantial debts.) Also, § 807 abolishes the "dual priority" rule in § 40(h) and (i). In all other significant respects §§ 40 and 807 are in agreement.

As noted above, until the partnership is "terminated," it continues for the purpose of winding-up its affairs. But what constitutes "termination"? This issue arose in *Curley v. Kaiser*, 962 A.2d 167 (Conn. App. Ct. 2009), where the court noted that merely liquidating the assets of the partnership was not enough. The assets had to be distributed before the partnership could be deemed terminated.

a. Settlement of Accounts

On liquidation of the partnership, the creditors of the partnership must be paid first. Any remaining proceeds are paid to the partners, first to discharge any obligations of the partnership to the partners (including the partners' capital accounts, which are considered obligations of the partnership), and then any balance is distributed equally, subject to any contrary agreement of the partners. If, on the other hand, the proceeds of liquidation are inadequate to discharge obligations to creditors, the partners are liable, equally, to fund the difference, again subject to a contrary agreement the partners might have had. *See, e.g., Mahan v. Mahan*, 107 Ariz. 517, 489 P.2d 1197 (1971).

The court in *Farnsworth v. Deaver*, 147 S.W.3d 662 (Tex. Ct. App. 2004), gave a succinct illustration of how a liquidation works under RUPA when there are insufficient assets to repay the partners' capital contributions:

> In winding up the affairs of a partnership, creditors of the entity are not the only ones entitled to payment. So too "shall [the partnership] make a distribution to a partner in an amount equal to the partner's positive balance in the partner's capital account." Given this, capital accounts having a positive balance are debts of the partnership. Being debts, they must be included within the liabilities for which the partners are ultimately responsible.
>
> Next, if the debts of the partnership exceed its assets (which also include the value assigned to each capital account) it can be said that the partners have suffered a capital loss. And, these losses, like all other debts, must be satisfied by the partners in direct proportion to their share of the profits. For example, let us assume that three partners contributed $10,000, $5000, and $2000, respectively, to capitalize Partnership X and agreed to share profits equally. Let us also assume that upon dissolution of the partnership only $5000 remained after paying all creditors other than partners who are creditors in their capacity as partners. Since each partner is entitled to repayment of his capital, Partnership X has a loss of $12,000, *i.e.* the $17,000 representing the sum of the capital due each partner less the $5000 remaining after payment of all obligations other than those owed the partners as partners. Dividing the $12,000 loss between the partners in proportion to their share of the profits, *i.e.* one-third each, would result in each partner owing $4000 to the partnership. And, once this $4000 is offset against the sums due from the partners as reflected by their respective capital accounts, the partner who initially paid $10,000 in capital would have a positive

balance of $6000 in his capital account. The one who paid $5000 would have a positive balance of $1000, while the one who paid $2000 would have a negative balance of $2000. Thus, the partner with the negative balance would be obligated to pay $2000 to the partnership to remove his capital account from its negative position.

b. The Losing Venture: Claims Among Partners

Kovacik v. Reed

Supreme Court of California
315 P.2d 314 (1957)

SCHAUER, JUSTICE.

In this suit for dissolution of a joint venture and for an accounting, defendant appeals from a judgment that plaintiff recover from defendant one half the losses of the venture. We have concluded that inasmuch as the parties agreed that plaintiff was to supply the money and defendant the labor to carry on the venture, defendant is correct in his contention that the trial court erred in holding him liable for one half the monetary losses, and that the judgment should therefore be reversed.

[P]laintiff, a licensed building contractor in San Francisco, operated his contracting business as a sole proprietorship under the fictitious name of "Asbestos Siding Company." Defendant had for a number of years worked for various building contractors in that city as a job superintendent and estimator.

Early in November, 1952 [the court quotes from the proceedings below]:

> Kovacik [plaintiff] told Reed [defendant] that Kovacik had an opportunity to do kitchen remodeling work for Sears Roebuck Company in San Francisco and asked Reed to become his job superintendent and estimator in this venture. Kovacik said that he had about $10,000.00 to invest in the venture and that, if Reed would superintend and estimate the jobs, Kovacik would share the profits with Reed on a 50-50 basis. Kovacik did not ask Reed to agree to share any loss that might result and Reed did not offer to share any such loss. The subject of a possible loss was not discussed in the inception of this venture. Reed accepted Kovacik's proposal and commenced work for the venture shortly after November 1, 1952. . . . Reed's only contribution was his own labor. Kovacik provided all of the venture's financing through the credit of Asbestos Siding Company, although at times Reed purchased materials for the jobs in his own name or on his account for which he was reimbursed. . . .

> The venture bid on and was awarded a number of . . . remodeling jobs . . . in San Francisco. Reed worked on all of the jobs as job superintendent. . . . During . . . August, 1953, Kovacik, who at that time had all of the financial records of the venture in his possession, . . . informed Reed that the venture had been unprofitable and demanded contribution from Reed as to

amounts which Kovacik claimed to have advanced in excess of the income received from the venture. Reed at no time promised, represented or agreed that he was liable for any of the venture's losses and he consistently and without exception refused to contribute to or pay any of the loss resulting from the venture. . . . The venture was terminated on August 31, 1953.

Kovacik thereafter instituted this proceeding, seeking an accounting of the affairs of the venture and to recover from Reed one half of the losses. Despite the evidence above set forth from the statement of the oral proceedings, showing that at no time had defendant agreed to be liable for any of the losses, the trial court "found"— more accurately, we think, concluded as a matter of law—that "plaintiff and defendant were to share equally all their joint venture profits and losses between them," and that defendant "agreed to share equally in the profits and losses of said joint venture." Following an accounting taken by a referee appointed by the court, judgment was rendered awarding plaintiff recovery against defendant of some $4,340, as one half of the monetary losses[20] found by the referee to have been sustained by the joint venture.

It is the general rule that in the absence of an agreement to the contrary the law presumes that partners and joint adventurers intended to participate equally in the profits and losses of the common enterprise, irrespective of any inequality in the amounts each contributed to the capital employed in the venture, with the losses being shared by them in the same proportions as they share the profits. [The court cites UPA § 18 and a dozen California cases.]

However, it appears that in the cases in which the above stated general rule has been applied, each of the parties had contributed capital consisting of either money or land or other tangible property, or else was to receive compensation for services rendered to the common undertaking which was to be paid before computation of the profits or losses. Where, however, as in the present case, one partner or joint adventurer contributes the money capital as against the other's skill and labor, all the cases cited, and which our research has discovered, hold that neither party is liable to the other for contribution for any loss sustained. Thus, upon loss of the money the party who contributed it is not entitled to recover any part of it from the party who contributed only services. The rationale of this rule is that where one party contributes money and the other contributes services, then in the event of a loss each would lose his own capital—the one his money and the other his labor.

---

20. [1] The record is silent as to the factors taken into account by the referee in determining the "loss" suffered by the venture. However, there is no contention that defendant's services were ascribed any value whatsoever. It may also be noted that the trial court "found" that "neither plaintiff nor defendant was to receive compensation for their services rendered to said joint venture, but plaintiff and defendant were to share equally all their joint venture profits and losses between them." Neither party suggests that plaintiff actually rendered services to the venture in the same sense that defendant did. And, as is clear from the settled statement, plaintiff's proposition to defendant was that plaintiff would provide the money as against defendant's contribution of services as estimator and superintendent.

Another view would be that in such a situation the parties have, by their agreement to share equally in profits, agreed that the value of their contributions — the money on the one hand and the labor on the other — were likewise equal; it would follow that upon the loss, as here, of both money and labor, the parties have shared equally in the losses. Actually, of course, plaintiff here lost only some $8,680 — or somewhat less than the $10,000 which he originally proposed and agreed to invest. . . .

It follows that the conclusion of law upon which the judgment in favor of plaintiff for recovery from defendant of one half the monetary losses depends is untenable, and that the judgment should be reversed. Consequently, it is unnecessary to dispose of defendant's further contention that plaintiff could not in any event recover, because the joint venture did not hold or apply for a general contractor's license or any other license, and was thus tainted with illegality.

The judgment is reversed.

GIBSON, C.J., and SHENK, CARTER, TRAYNOR, SPENCE, and McCOMB, JJ., concur.

Notes

1. Not all courts would agree with *Kovacik*. *See, e.g., Richert v. Handly*, 311 P.2d 417 (Wash. 1957); *see also* MELVIN A. EISENBERG, AN INTRODUCTION TO AGENCY AND PARTNERSHIP 52 (2nd ed. 1995). Eisenberg argues in support of *Kovacik* as follows:

> The line taken in *Kovacik* is sound. If a services-only partner has been fully compensated for his services, it is hard to see why he should not be required to contribute toward making up a capital loss. Otherwise, a capital partner would bear all the partnership's loss and the services-only partner would bear none. But if a services-only partner has not been compensated for his services, then if he must contribute toward the capital loss he would lose all the value of his services while the capital partner would lose only part of the value of his capital. It is unlikely that the parties would have agreed to this result if they had negotiated on the issue when the partnership was formed. As *Kovacik* suggests, therefore, where the services-only partner has not been compensated for his services, the partners should normally be deemed to have impliedly agreed that he need not contribute to a capital loss.

For a contrasting view, applying a contractarian approach, see Stephen M. Bainbridge, *Contractarianism in the Business Associations Classroom:* Kovacik v. Reed *and the Allocation of Capital Losses in Service Partnerships*, 34 GA. L. REV. 631 (2000).

2. RUPA § 401(b) states that "[a] partnership shall charge each partner's account with a share of the partnership losses, whether capital or operating, in proportion to the partner's share of the profits." This continues the rule in UPA § 18(a). The Comment to § 401 acknowledges that this rejects the *Kovacik* approach and that this "may seem unfair," stating that "[i]n entering a partnership with such a capital structure, the partners should foresee that application of the default rule may bring about unusual results and take advantage of their power to vary by agreement the allocation of capital losses. On the other hand, as a practical matter, the working partner's obligation to contribute anything beyond his original investment may be illusory. The partner who contributes little or no capital may be without resources to share losses and is, in that case, execution proof."

Problems

1. Clare Childers' husband, Hal Childers, was killed in a plane crash on January 2. Mrs. Childers employed the law firm of Brown, Kronzer, and Steely to represent her in a suit against the Federal Aviation Administration (FAA) for the alleged negligence of its employees in causing her husband's death. The case was assigned to Robert Steely, a partner of the firm, because of his expertise in aircraft litigation. On May 1, Steely filed a claim with the FAA. In response to the FAA's request for a statement of authority, Mrs. Childers stated in a written document that she had employed the above law firm and Mr. Steely as her attorney to represent her in the claim.

On November 10, Steely was killed in a plane crash. On November 22, the FAA, unaware of this, denied Mrs. Childers' tort claim by certified letter, return receipt requested, addressed to Steely at the law firm's address. In the confusion following Steely's death, the letter, which was receipted for by the receptionist of the firm, was placed in the "evidence" file of the case without any member of the firm seeing it. Federal regulations provide that final denial can be sent to the claimant's legal representative. Six months later, the statute of limitations under 28 U.S.C.A. § 2401 for appeal from denial of an FAA claim expired.

Mrs. Childers has discovered the above facts and has come to you for help. Can you, by promptly filing suit, save her claim? What arguments would you make on her behalf?

2. The partnership between Brown and Casey, doing business as the Connecticut Hay & Grain Co., employed Rose as an agent to buy hay for them in the New York State area. Brown subsequently withdrew from the business, effective January 1. No notice of dissolution was given. On May 2, pursuant to the order of Casey, Rose purchased hay from Todd, purporting to act wholly on his own account and on his own credit, but actually acting on behalf of the partnership. On July 22, Rose was notified of the withdrawal of Brown.

Rose died in August. Prior to his death he told Todd that he had purchased the hay as agent for the partnership. Todd had sold hay on credit to Connecticut Hay on several prior occasions.

Todd did not get paid for her hay. She initiated suit against Brown, the only solvent person in the picture. Brown defends on the ground that he had withdrawn from the partnership prior to the purchase of the hay. How would you analyze the rights between the parties? *Cf. Morris v. Brown*, 115 Conn. 389, 162 A. 1 (1932); Restatement of Agency § 7, cmt. d; § 110, cmt. c; § 119. In what respect, if at all, is the Restatement doctrine affected by the fact that the principal in this case is a partnership?

a. Would it change your analysis if Brown had been an inactive partner who had not participated in the business and was unknown to Rose and to Todd?

b. Would it affect your response if Rose had told Todd he was acting on behalf of Connecticut Hay & Grain Co. prior to the purchase of the hay, and this was the first time the partnership had dealt with Todd?

3. *A* and *B* orally formed a partnership at will, each contributing $1,000 capital. The partnership made a $7,000 net profit the first year, which was not withdrawn by the partners. Then *C* joined the partnership, contributing $1,000. The partnership lost $4,000 in the next year. *A* has decided to leave the business. What return of capital is she entitled to? Assume nothing was said about this matter when the partnership was formed.

4. *A* and *B* orally formed a partnership for a three-year term. As part of their capital contributions *A* transferred to the partnership 1,000 shares of *X* corporation stock, and *B* transferred 1,000 shares of *Y* corporation stock. The shares were of approximately equal value. The shares were put in the partnership name in order to facilitate their use by the firm as collateral security for loans, the proceeds of which were used to start the business. None of the stock was sold. The three-year term has come to an end. *A*'s stock has increased fivefold in value, and *B*'s has declined by 70 percent. *A* wants to take her stock back, and *B* wants all stock to be sold and the proceeds divided equally. Assume this matter was not covered in the partnership agreement. Who should prevail?

5. After two years with the firm, Guinand, an employee of the partnership of Walton and Kearns, was granted an interest in the partnership under the following terms, which were contained in a letter to him:

Dear Mr. Guinand:

This letter is to confirm your ownership of an undivided ten per cent (10%) interest in WALTON-KEARNS, a co-partnership composed of Paul T. Walton and Thomas F. Kearns. This interest includes and is not in addition to the various interests from time to time heretofore acquired by you.

Upon termination of your employment with the partnership for any cause whatsoever your interest in the partnership will be determined and discharged as of said time without resulting in a dissolution of the partnership; and such interest as may have theretofore been vested in you in specific properties shall become your separate property, subject to adjustments incident to your proportionate share of the then partnership indebtedness.

(Signed by the partners, Paul T. Walton and Thomas F. Kearns.)

Do you see any problems of interpretation in the above letter? If you were drafting the letter for the partners, in what manner, if at all, would you vary the language? *See Guinand v. Walton*, 25 Utah 2d 253, 480 P.2d 137 (1971).

6. Mocquot applied for work at the Cotton Gin Company. He was informed that they had no work for him, but that one Meadows needed someone to run his gin for him. Mocquot went to Meadows and told him he had no money but, at the suggestion of Meadows, agreed he would go in partnership with Meadows and run the gin for the season, including buying, receiving, ginning and shipping the cotton, for half the net profit. Meadows agreed to contribute $10,000 capital. Nothing else was spelled out in the agreement. Mocquot worked for the season (approximately eight months), and received nothing for his services because the business lost money due to a severe fluctuation in the cotton market. Meadows paid the resulting loss of $5,000. The partnership has dissolved and Meadows now seeks to recover one-half the loss of his capital from Mocquot. What result?

7. On December 1, 1993, plaintiff and the three defendants entered into a partnership for the purpose of giving musical performances under the firm name of Flonzaley Quartet. The agreement contained no provision with respect to good will. The partnership was for a fixed term, to expire June 1, 1998. The Quartet gave performances and made records for four years. The defendants in December 1997 served notice on plaintiff that they would not continue with him after June 1, 1998, and contended his only interest was in some music sheets. They plan to continue the quartet by simply replacing plaintiff. Plaintiff sued to dissolve the partnership and demanded a 25 percent interest in good will. What result? *See Bailly v. Betti*, 241 N.Y. 22, 148 N.E. 776 (1925) (noted in 11 CORNELL L.Q. 256, and 35 YALE L.J. 496). For subsequent litigation on the same matter, see *Bailly v. Betti*, 126 Misc. 45, 212 N.Y.S. 455 (Sup. Ct., NY Co. 1925).

Chapter 14

The Limited Partnership

The limited partnership is a form of doing business made available by statute. It is created by filing with the state a certificate for a partnership consisting of at least one general partner and one limited partner. It allows an investor who is a limited partner to participate in profits in an ownership capacity in a partnership without personal liability for the obligations of the partnership. As noted in Chapter 11, there are income tax advantages to operating in partnership form. These advantages are available to limited partners. Limited partners are not exposed to personal liability so long as the partnership is properly formed and, depending on the jurisdiction, the limited partners are careful not to exercise control over the business, as developed below.

At one time, the limited partnership was the only convenient form of doing business that combined the advantages of partnership taxation with the benefits of limited liability. With the advent of the LLC, the LLP, and the check-the-box change in taxation (see Chapter 15), that is no longer true. Nevertheless, the limited partnership continues to be used, in part because of its convenient and well-defined distinction between general and limited partners, making the limited partnership "hard-wired." That feature makes it a favorite, among other things, for estate planning, where a family may want to include children in a partnership without sharing control with them. There are other ways of achieving this objective, like the creation of two categories of members in an LLC with only one category possessing managerial powers. Nevertheless, there is a comfort level with the limited partnership, which has been a prominent part of the law for well over one hundred years, generating a considerable body of precedent on many issues.

The familiarity and convenience of the limited partnership may account for its continued use despite the availability of other limited liability unincorporated entities. In addition, the recent appearance of the limited liability limited partnership (LLLP), which extends limited liability to general partners, may add to the use of the limited partnership. Under the LLLP all owners enjoy limited liability, similar to the corporation, the LLC, and the LLP. This avoids the inconvenience of having to create a corporate general partner in order to ensure limited liability for all owners, which many limited partnerships do today.

ULPA. The uniform act that served as the source for the creation of limited partnerships until 1976 is the Uniform Limited Partnership Act ("ULPA"). It was promulgated by NCCUSL in 1916 and at one time was adopted in all states except Louisiana. It is set forth in the statutory supplement to this book.

RULPA (1976). In 1976, NCCUSL promulgated a revised version of ULPA in response to the increasingly frequent use of limited partnerships for large-scale economic enterprises such as commercial real estate and oil and gas exploration, drilling, and production. A major incentive for this use was that limited partnerships were effective tax shelter vehicles due to the pass-through nature of partnership taxation, allowing tax losses such as interest expense in highly leveraged transactions, depreciation, and depletion allowances to be passed directly through to the limited partners. ULPA needed modernization in order to make the limited partnership a more convenient vehicle for these large-scale projects owned by numerous limited partners. The Revised Uniform Limited Partnership Act ("RULPA") (1976) increased flexibility of operation for limited partnerships by, among other things, replacing the certificate of limited partnership with the partnership agreement as the important governing document and reducing the circumstances under which a limited partner ran the risk of liability because of the exercise of control by adding a list of "safe harbors" for limited partners. It has been adopted in nearly all states, and is contained in the statutory supplement to this book.

The 1985 amendments to RULPA. In 1985, the Commissioners promulgated substantial amendments to the 1976 Act, further increasing the flexibility and ease of use of the limited partnership by, for example, greatly simplifying the filing requirements and further reducing the risks for limited partners who want to be active in the business. Nearly all states have adopted the 1985 amendments or significant portions of those amendments. The 1985 amendments are set forth in the statutory supplement to this book by deletion and addition to the text of RULPA (1976), which is the format used in 6 Uniform Laws Annotated, along with a list of the states adopting the amendments.

ULPA is still the law in a handful of states, with most of those states allowing limited partnerships existing at the time of the enactment of RULPA to continue to be governed by ULPA but also to have the right to elect to be governed by RULPA. Those states chose this route rather than displacing ULPA with RULPA, which keeps ULPA alive for those partnerships formed prior to adoption of RULPA that have not made an election to be governed by RULPA.

The 1976 Act with the 1985 amendments will be referred to in these materials as RULPA. The 1976 Act without amendments will be referred to as RULPA (1976).

For commentary on the 1916 Act, see William D. Lewis, *The Uniform Limited Partnership Act*, 65 U. Pa. L. Rev. 715 (1917). For some of the commentary on RULPA, see Edwin W. Hecker, *The Revised Uniform Limited Partnership Act: Provisions Governing Financial Affairs*, 46 Mo. L. Rev. 577 (1981); Edwin W. Hecker, *Limited Partners' Derivative Suits Under the Revised Uniform Limited Partnership Act*, 33 Vand. L. Rev. 343 (1980); Edwin W. Hecker, *The Revised Uniform Limited Partnership Act: Provisions Affecting the Relationship of the Firm and Its Members to Third*

Parties, 27 U. Kan. L. Rev. 1 (1978); Robert A. Kessler, *The New Uniform Limited Partnership Act: A Critique*, 48 Fordham L. Rev. 159 (1979).

Re-RULPA. In August 2001, the National Conference of Commissioners on Uniform State Laws approved a new act to govern limited partnerships. Although simply entitled "Uniform Limited Partnership Act (2001)," this book will refer to the proposed act as "Re-RULPA," as it is known in much of the scholarly comment and to differentiate it from prior uniform laws relating to limited partnerships. The fact that three uniform laws relating to limited partnerships were approved by NCCUSL in the span of 25 years, while the original act stood for 60 years, speaks to the continuing importance of, and interest in, limited partnerships as a form of business. Re-RULPA makes several important changes to RULPA, including the following:

- *De-linking*. Re-RULPA de-links limited partnership law from UPA. Section 1105 of RULPA provides that, "in any case not provided for in this [Act] the provisions of the Uniform Partnership Act shall govern." This linkage caused considerable confusion and was one of the primary motivating forces behind the Re-RULPA project. Because Re-RULPA is now a stand-alone act governing limited partnerships, it is considerably longer than its predecessor acts.[1]

- *Limited liability for the general partner.* Re-RULPA recognizes the growing popularity of the limited liability limited partnership (LLLP), that is, a limited partnership in which neither the general partners nor the limited partners are liable for partnership obligations. Thus, LLLPs are to limited partnerships what an LLP is to a general partnership. Re-RULPA allows a limited partnership to elect LLLP status through a simple statement in the certificate of limited partnership. *See* §§ 102(9), 201(a)(4), 404(c).

- *Liability Shield for Limited Partners.* Several cases in this section of the book will focus on the important question of whether a limited partner might become liable for the obligations of the limited partnership. As we shall see, that is the case under RULPA and ULPA if the limited partner engages in certain activities on behalf of the partnership (although those two Acts differ on just what activities are sufficient to result in a loss of protection for the limited partner). Section 303 of Re-RULPA abandons that approach and provides, simply, that a limited partner is not liable for the obligation of the limited partnership, "even if the limited partner participates in the management and control of the limited partnership."

In 2013, Re-RULPA was further amended, primarily to "harmonize" the language of Re-RULPA with other uniform business entity acts. This revision also included some substantive changes and some improvements to the language of the Act. The 2013 Act has been adopted in only a few jurisdictions. To the extent that

---

1. Some states had already amended their partnership laws to accomplish de-linking. See, e.g., California Corporations Code § 16101(7), explained in *Mieuli v. DeBartolo*, No. C-00-3225 JCS, 2001 U.S. Dist. LEXIS 22519 (N.D. Cal. May 7, 2001).

this chapter includes references to Re-RULPA, those references correspond to the 2001 version, which has been somewhat more widely adopted. That version is also the version included in the current statutory supplement to this casebook.

The limited partnership has proved to be an attractive device for raising capital, sometimes on a very large scale. This was particularly true prior to the Tax Reform Act of 1986, noted below. The use of the limited partnership to raise capital on a large scale can create complex tax and securities problems. While such problems are beyond the scope of this book, it nevertheless may be useful to refer briefly to several matters that occur frequently.

Securities law issues. The interest of a limited partner is regarded as a "security" under applicable federal and state law under many circumstances. Unless an exemption applies, or the limited partner takes an active role in the management of the business, it may be necessary to register the interest as a security with the Securities and Exchange Commission or with the state securities commissioners. *See* Note, *Modern Partnership Interests as Securities: The Effect of RUPA, RULPA, and LLP Statutes on Investment Contract Analysis*, 55 WASH. & LEE. L. REV. 955 (1998); Conrad E.J. Everhard, *The Limited Partnership Interest: Is It a Security? Changing Times*, 17 Del. J. Corp. L. 441 (1992).

Taxation issues. The enactment of the Tax Reform Act of 1986 had a substantial negative impact on tax shelters by, among other things, mandating passive activity loss restrictions specifying that passive losses be offset only against passive income. IRC §469. This applies to limited partners, who are generally deemed to be engaging in a passive activity. Also, in 1988 Congress responded to the use of limited partnerships as potential substitutes for doubly-taxed publicly traded corporations by enacting legislation mandating that "a publicly traded partnership shall be treated as a corporation" unless 90% of its income is passive income, such as income from rent, interest, dividends, or sale of property. I.R.C. §7704.

A. Historical Background

The following quoted material from *Rathke v. Griffith*, 36 Wash. 2d 394, 396–99, 218 P.2d 757, 758–60, 18 A.L.R.2d 1349, 1353 (1950), gives a useful account of the historical background of the limited partnership in this country, which commenced in 1822 when New York adopted a statute patterned on French law.

> In this connection, it is pertinent to consider briefly the history of the concept of the limited partnership in the United States.

> This form of association, though common on the continent of Europe since the middle ages, was unknown to the common law of England and the United States, and was originally borrowed from the civil law of France. *Ames v. Downing*, 1 Bradford (N. Y.) 321, includes an interesting account of the historical background of the limited partnership. From their earliest

inception (in New York and Connecticut in 1822), limited partnership statutes, being in derogation of the common law, were strictly construed by most courts. The view was commonly taken that the special or limited partner was essentially a general partner, with immunity from personal liability only on condition of full and exact compliance with the statutory requirements as to the details of formation of the association. . . .

Thus, the statutes often provided that, at the time of filing the certificate of partnership, one of the general partners should file an affidavit stating that sums specified in the certificate of partnership to have been contributed by each of the special partners had actually been paid in cash; and they commonly further provided that any false statement in this affidavit would result in the alleged special partners being held liable as general partners. The earlier cases held that a statement that the payment had been made in cash when it had actually been made by check (and the check had not been presented for payment at the time of the filing of the affidavit), was a false statement within the meaning of the latter proviso, and rendered all parties to the transaction liable as general partners. Later cases, in recognition of the fact that payment by check is commonly accepted as payment in cash, relaxed this rule, and, expressing the view that, in the situation described, it would be unreasonable to hold the special partner to general liability, refused to do so. But such liberality was by no means universal. . . .

But it was coming to be recognized that the strict interpretation being given to the limited partnership statutes by the courts, though it unquestionably carried out the intent of those responsible for the adoption of these statutes, was rendering this form of association commercially impracticable. The limited partnership statutes were quite commonly coming to be regarded as a trap. . . . Accordingly, in 1916, a uniform limited partnership act was drafted in order to remedy these deficiencies. . . . Mr. William Lewis, the draftsman of the new act, has written of it as follows:

"Practically all the differences between the new Uniform Act and the existing statutes are due to the desire of the Conference to present to the legislatures of the several states an act, under which a person willing to invest his money in a business for a share in the profits, may become a limited partner, with the same sense of security from any possibility of unlimited liability as the subscribers to the shares of a corporation." William D. Lewis, *The Uniform Limited Partnership Act*, 65 U. Pa. L. Rev. 715, 723.

B. Organizational Defects

As with all business entities authorized by statute, it is necessary to comply with the statutory requirements when creating a limited partnership. See *Direct Mail Specialist, Inc. v. Brown*, 673 F. Supp. 1540 (D. Mont. 1987), where the organizers of a limited partnership filed a certificate of limited partnership (containing several defects) in a county clerk's office instead of the office required by the statute, that of the secretary of state of Montana. An application for registration of an assumed business name was filed with the secretary of state, but it failed to identify the business as a limited partnership. Plaintiff, a creditor of the partnership, sued the limited partners for personal liability for the debt. The court held that there was not substantial compliance with the organizational requirements of ULPA, the governing statute at the time, which meant that all the limited partners were general partners and thus personally liable for the debt. They were general partners because they were co-owners of a business for profit that had not successfully filed under a state statute for different status. The litigation involved the effort by one limited partner to escape liability under § 11 of ULPA, but she had renounced her interest three years after learning that plaintiff intended to hold her liable as a general partner. The court held that her renunciation was as a matter of law not "promptly" made, as required by § 11.

The following case does not involve an organizational defect in the sense addressed by *Direct Mail*. It nevertheless deals extensively with § 304 of RULPA, the counterpart provision to ULPA § 11, and the key provision in such matters today.

Briargate Condominium Ass'n v. Carpenter

United States Court of Appeals, Fourth Circuit
976 F.2d 868 (1992)

HAMILTON, CIRCUIT JUDGE:

Judith Carpenter appeals the decision of the district court, entered after a trial to the bench, holding her liable as a general partner for debts of the Briargate Homes partnership (Briargate Homes or the Partnership) to Briargate Condominium Association, Incorporated (the Association). Carpenter asserts that the district court erred in concluding that she had not effectively withdrawn from the Partnership pursuant to [RULPA] § 304. . . .

This is a collection action. Briargate Homes was a North Carolina partnership which purchased several units in the Briargate Condominium complex in Richland County, South Carolina. . . . The Partnership failed to pay assessed fees in the amount of $85,106.08 as of December 1, 1988, some of which accrued prior to February 1988 and some afterward. Five of Carpenter's six individual codefendants in this collection action settled with the Association for a total sum of $25,000, which was credited against the indebtedness.[2] At the time of the district court's order of December 4, 1991, the total amount of fees and interest assessed against Carpenter individually and the Partnership was $104,146.75.

Briargate Homes was formed in the latter part of 1984 when William E. Goodall, Jr., Carpenter's accountant at that time, induced her and other of his clients to

---

2. [1] The sixth codefendant, Porter Hicks, Carpenter's ex-husband, is in bankruptcy.

invest in the Partnership as a tax shelter. Goodall received funds from Carpenter and her then-husband Hicks to purchase units in the Briargate Condominium complex on behalf of the Partnership. While Carpenter contends that she believed she was investing in a limited partnership, Briargate Homes operated as a general partnership from its inception. . . .

At trial, there was extensive testimony concerning Carpenter's knowledge and belief about the status of the Partnership. Carpenter did not sign the Briargate Homes partnership agreement. She contends, and the district court so concluded, that she never personally saw copies of the K-1 partnership tax forms, which clearly identified her as a general partner in Briargate Homes. . . .

On February 5, 1988, only days after a deposition in another case in which she was informed that she might be liable as a general partner, Carpenter notified the other partners and the Association by mail that she was withdrawing from any equity participation and renouncing any interest in the profits of Briargate Homes. Carpenter is an experienced businesswoman, serves on the board of directors of a bank, and has ready access to legal and other professional advice. . . . [The court quotes § 304].[3]

[W]e turn to the language of the statute. Subsection (a) specifies that a person who has contributed to a business enterprise "is not a general partner in the enterprise and is not bound by its obligations" [except under circumstances specified in subsection (b)] if two conditions are met.

First, at the time the person contributes to the business, the person must have a "good faith" belief "that he has become a limited partner" in the enterprise rather than a general partner. If there is no good faith basis for believing that a business is a limited partnership at the time of contribution, then there is no basis for obtaining relief under the statute. . . .

Second, the person must "on ascertaining the mistake" take one of two courses of action. He may correct the mistake in the form of the enterprise by filing an appropriate certificate of limited partnership. Under this option, the person may continue in the business with the limited liability he believed he possessed at the time of contribution. In the alternative, the person may give notice[4] and withdraw

---

3. [6] At oral argument, counsel for the Association contended that § 304 might not be applicable to a case like this where the enterprise, Briargate Homes, was founded as and always existed as a general partnership. Counsel particularly noted that in *Vette v. Giles*, 281 F. 928 (7th Cir. 1922), the courts, in applying § 11 of the Uniform Limited Partnership Act of 1916 were dealing with a situation where the parties attempted to form a limited partnership, but did so in a defective manner. As the Seventh Circuit noted, however, application of § 11 "is not limited to instances where there has been an attempted compliance with the provision of the new act. It includes in its terms any person who at any time contributed to a partnership, erroneously believing himself to be a limited partner." *Vette*, 281 F. at 935. We conclude that North Carolina would apply § 304 broadly, as suggested by *Vette* with respect to § 11.

4. [8] The statute does not specify the form of such notice or the procedures by which such notice is to be served. See *Graybar Electric Co. v. Lowe*, 462 P.2d 413, 416 (1969) (holding that

completely from future equity participation in the business. Unlike the predecessor statute, § 304 provides no specific time frame for pursuing either course of action.

If the two elements are met — a good faith belief at the time of contribution and either a proper certificate is filed or notice of withdrawal is given — then the person is liable only as a limited partner with respect to third parties dealing with the enterprise. Satisfaction of the two elements in subsection (a) effectively cuts off all personal liability as a general partner, unless subsection (b) applies.

Subsection (b) sets forth the only circumstances under which a person who meets the requirements of subsection (a) may incur liability like a general partner. Personal liability to third parties arises when the third party transacts business with the enterprise before the person files a proper certificate or withdraws. Imposition of liability is limited, however, by the requirement that at the time he transacts business, the third party "actually believed in good faith that the person was a general partner at the time of the transaction." Reliance on the part of the third party in the resources of the defendant as a general partner is absolutely essential before liability may be imposed for transactions occurring before withdrawal.

Unlike its predecessor statute, [ULPA § 11], § 304 does not specify how quickly a proper certificate or notice of withdrawal must be filed after a person ascertains he is not a limited partner. The current statute deleted the word "promptly" contained in the prior statute. The present statute also added the language in subsection (b) regarding reliance by the third party as a prerequisite for imposing liability. This difference in the old and new statutes is significant. It reflects a shift in emphasis away from the speed with which withdrawal is effected to an emphasis on protection of reliance by third parties doing business with the enterprise. The key to liability is no longer, therefore, how quickly the first party corrects the error, but rather reliance by the third party on that person's apparent status as a general partner in transacting business with the enterprise.[5]

---

written notice of withdrawal to the creditor is sufficient notice of withdrawal as to that creditor under statute based on § 11 of the Uniform Partnership Act of 1916). See also N.C. Gen. Stat. §§ 59-33(b)(2), 59-36 (stating that notice provisions of Uniform Partnership Act apply to limited partnerships and that a written statement of fact delivered by mail is sufficient notice). Plaintiff has not contested the form of the notice given in this case.

5. [9] Because the application of the Revised Uniform Statute is not, by its terms, contingent on how soon a renunciation is filed, there exists the possibility that an individual could contribute with a good faith belief that a limited partnership existed, discover the mistake, and choose to sit on such knowledge. The individual could then bail out of the business when it appeared that some third party might believe he was a general partner and might look to that person's assets when transacting business with the enterprise. The fact that a person could act in such manner does not, however, necessarily harm the third party where there is in fact no reliance on the supposed status of the first party as a general partner. The possibility that an individual could reap profits or benefits from the enterprise prior to withdrawing was recognized in the cases applying old § 11 of the Uniform Act. There was debate as to whether the word "renounces" in the statute required disgorgement of all past benefits received from the enterprise. See *Giles*, 263 U.S. [553] at 563 [(1924)] (noting that individuals returned all dividends acquired, but reserving question

The change in the statute to delete the word "promptly" and add a reliance requirement distinguishes this case from *Vidricksen v. Grover*, 363 F.2d 372 (9th Cir. 1966) and *Direct Mail Specialist, Inc. v. Brown*, cases which the Association and the district court cite to assert that Carpenter's withdrawal was untimely. Both cases involved statutes patterned after § 11 of the old Uniform Limited Partnership Act with the requirement that withdrawal be effected "promptly." Both cases found the purported limited partner liable because withdrawal was not effected within some fixed period of time, not because some third party had relied mistakenly on the person being a general partner. Section 304 specifically deleted the time limitation and substituted a reliance test; therefore, inserting a time limitation on withdrawal by implication would appear to contravene the statute.

This interpretation of § 304 is sensible. It comports with the remedial purpose of the statute to relieve persons from strict liability as general partners, as occurred under prior law, when they erroneously believe themselves limited partners. Furthermore, it provides adequate security to third parties who deal with the business entity by recognizing their right to recovery where valuable consideration has been extended to the enterprise in reliance on the ability to hold the first party liable as a general partner for the debt incurred.

Given this interpretation of the statute, we believe the judgment of the district court must be vacated, and the case remanded to the district court for additional findings.

First, the district court must determine whether or not Carpenter held a "good faith" belief that she was a limited partner at the time she initially joined and contributed to the Briargate Homes venture.[6] . . . The district court did not conclusively state whether or not Carpenter had a "good faith" belief that she was becoming a limited partner at that time. The district court did conclude that by at least mid-1986 Carpenter could not have held a good faith belief she was a limited partner,

of whether return necessary); *Gilman Paint & Varnish Co. v. Legum*, 197 Md. 665, 80 A.2d 906, 910–11 (1951) (holding no obligation to return past profits under facts of case). In adopting § 304, the legislature resolved this dilemma by eliminating the word "renounce" and choosing language specifically requiring withdrawal only from "future equity participation." . . . Thus, where a person does not act promptly upon ascertaining the mistake, this provides no basis for recovery to a third party. While such conduct might appear inequitable, it is not inequitable as to third parties without reliance as set forth in § 304(b). Cf. *Giles*, 263 U.S. at 561 (applying § 11 and holding that to allow recovery "would give creditors what they are not entitled to have" because they were in no worse position because of defendants' acts). . . .

6. [10] We do not hold that the protection of § 304 is only available to those who held a good faith belief they were limited partners at the time of their initial contribution to the enterprise. The statute speaks only of contribution generally. Though not presented on the facts of this case, one could conceivably initially invest as a general partner, but be persuaded at the time of a subsequent contribution that he is a limited partner. The rules governing personal liability discussed above, and the "good faith" requirements would apply. In this particular case, Carpenter contends she believed she was a limited partner from the beginning; therefore, the inquiry must focus on her belief at the time of her initial contribution.

but the key date, for purposes of the statute, is the date of the contribution to the enterprise. Should the district court conclude that Carpenter did not have a good faith belief that she was a limited partner at the time of the initial contribution, then the statute affords her no relief.

Second, assuming Carpenter demonstrates a good faith belief at the time she invested, then her notice of withdrawal effectively cut off liability for any fees accrued after such notice. To hold Carpenter liable for fees accrued prior to the notice, the district court must determine if and when the Association "actually believed in good faith that the person [Carpenter] was a general partner." § 304(b). . . .[7]

Carpenter also contends that the district court misapplied the "good faith" belief component of § 304 by adopting an objective, rather than a subjective, test for assessing good faith belief. Because the issue of good faith belief must be decided on remand, we address this issue below.

We believe that the North Carolina Supreme Court would adopt an objective standard when applying the good faith requirement in § 304. The statutory language itself suggests that a purely subjective approach to assessing what a person claiming the protection of § 304 believes is inappropriate. Protection is not afforded for just any subjective belief, no matter how unreasonable, but rather only for a "good faith" belief. Good faith encompasses "freedom from knowledge of circumstances which ought to put the holder on inquiry . . . [and] being faithful to one's duty or obligation." Black's Law Dictionary 623–24 (5th ed. 1979). Thus, while the inquiry necessarily entails determining what the individual person seeking to withdraw believed at the time he contributed to the enterprise, the inquiry must go further and ask whether such a belief was reasonable under the circumstances facing that particular individual.

Case law construing application of § 11 of the Uniform Limited Partnership Act provides some guidance on this issue. Though § 11 does not qualify the term "believing" with the term "good faith," courts applying § 11 assessed the alleged erroneous belief for objective indicia of good faith rather than accepting the mere protestations of the individual defendant. . . .

Carpenter asserts that other provisions of the North Carolina Revised Uniform Limited Partnership Act use language such as "knew or should have known," to indicate when an objective standard should be employed; therefore, the use of the phrase "in good faith believes" in § 304(a) must be subjective. See [RULPA] § 207(1). We are not persuaded, however. The term "good faith" necessarily qualifies the term

---

7. [12] The statute obviously creates something of a burden on a business to investigate other enterprises with whom it will conduct a transaction to determine who may be responsible for any debt incurred. In this case, if the Association had investigated the records and found no certificate of limited partnership, as required by statute, and had inquired of any of the partners concerning the members of the Partnership, there would presumably be a good faith basis for believing that Briargate Homes was a general partnership and Carpenter was a general partner. Such evidence, if it exists, may be presented to the district court on remand.

"believes" to exclude a belief that is utterly foolish when evaluated in light of the circumstances facing a particular individual at the time they formed or held such belief. To adopt the position of Carpenter would drain the phrase "good faith" of all meaning and, in fact, redefine the term to protect a party's deliberate indifference to his or her personal and financial affairs. . . .

In conclusion, we vacate the judgment of the district court and remand for further proceedings in accordance with this opinion.

Vacated and remanded.

C. The Agreement of Limited Partnership

The parties to a limited partnership typically set forth their understandings in a written agreement, although, strictly speaking, that is not necessary. RULPA acknowledges that the agreement may be oral. ["Partnership agreement means any valid agreement, written or oral, of the partners as to the affairs of a limited partnership and the conduct of its business." RULPA § 101(9).] Under ULPA, the certificate of limited partnership required extensive disclosures of the arrangements of the parties, and could itself serve as an agreement. RULPA and its amendments severely reduced the amount of disclosure, so that a modern certificate of limited partnership includes very little information and could not serve as an agreement.

Assuming a written agreement is entered into, a question arises as to the rules that apply to interpreting that agreement. If ambiguous, for instance, is extrinsic evidence admissible? The Delaware Supreme Court addressed this issue in *SI Management L.P. v. Wininger*, 707 A.2d 37 (Del. 1998):

> Here, the setting in which the Limited Partnership came into existence appears on this record to be quite different from that in *Eagle* [*Industries, Inc. v. DeVilbiss Health Care*, 702 A.2d 1228 (Del. 1997)]. This was not a bilateral negotiated agreement. Rather, it appears that the General Partner solicited and signed on 1,850 investors to the Agreement that those investors had no hand in drafting. Based on that premise, the principle of *contra proferentem* applies. Accordingly, ambiguous terms in the Agreement should be construed against the General Partner as the entity solely responsible for the articulation of those terms. On remand and final hearing on a permanent injunction, the trial court should determine whether these plaintiffs actually did engage in negotiations with the General Partner on the issues in question here.
>
> A court considering extrinsic evidence assumes that there is some connection between the expectations of contracting parties revealed by that evidence and the way contract terms were articulated by those parties. Therefore, unless extrinsic evidence can speak to the intent of *all* parties to a contract, it provides an incomplete guide with which to interpret

contractual language. Thus, it is proper to consider extrinsic evidence of bilateral negotiations when there is an ambiguous contract that was the product of those negotiations, as in *Eagle*.

On the limited record before us in this case, however, it appears that the 1,850 investors comprising the limited partnership reacted to a "take it or leave it" proposal by the General Partner without meaningful individualized negotiations. Because the articulation of contract terms in this case appears to have been entirely within the control of *one party*—the General Partner—that party bears full responsibility for the effect of those terms. Accordingly, extrinsic evidence is irrelevant to the intent of *all parties* at the time they entered into the agreement.

Note

Suppose the general partner involved in a dispute with the limited partners over the meaning of a provision in the partnership agreement became the general partner after the agreement was in existence. Would it make sense to construe the agreement against such a general partner? Suppose, instead, that the partnership agreement provided that the rule of *contra proferentem* would not apply to any disputes regarding the interpretation of the partnership agreement. Would such a provision be enforceable?

D. The Limited Partner

1. The Control Question

a. In General

Holzman v. DeEscamilla

Court of Appeal of California
195 P.2d 833 (1948)

MARKS, J.—

This is an appeal by James L. Russell and H. W. Andrews from a judgment decreeing they were general partners in Hacienda Farms Limited, a limited partnership, from February 27 to December 1, 1943, and as such were liable as general partners to the creditors of the partnership.

Early in 1943, Hacienda Farms Limited was organized as a limited partnership (Civ. Code, § 2477 et seq.), with Ricardo de Escamilla as the general partner and James L. Russell and H. W. Andrews as limited partners.

The partnership went into bankruptcy in December, 1943, and Lawrence Holzman was appointed and qualified as trustee of the estate of the bankrupt. On November 13, 1944, he brought this action for the purpose of determining that

Russell and Andrews, by taking part in the control of the partnership business, had become liable as general partners to the creditors of the partnership. The trial court found in favor of the plaintiff on this issue and rendered judgment to the effect that the three defendants were liable as general partners.

The findings supporting the judgment are so fully supported by the testimony of certain witnesses, although contradicted by Russell and Andrews, that we need mention but a small part of it. We will not mention conflicting evidence as conflicts in the evidence are settled in the trial court and not here.

De Escamilla was raising beans on farm lands near Escondido at the time the partnership was formed. The partnership continued raising vegetable and truck crops which were marketed principally through a produce concern controlled by Andrews.

The record shows the following testimony of de Escamilla:

> A. We put in some tomatoes. Q. Did you have a conversation or conversations with Mr. Andrews or Mr. Russell before planting the tomatoes? A. We always conferred and agreed as to what crops we would put in. . . . Q. Who determined that it was advisable to plant watermelons? A. Mr. Andrews. . . . Q. Who determined that string beans should be planted? A. All of us. There was never any planting done—except the first crop that was put into the partnership as an asset by myself, there was never any crop that was planted or contemplated in planting that wasn't thoroughly discussed and agreed upon by the three of us; particularly Andrews and myself.

De Escamilla further testified that Russell and Andrews came to the farms about twice a week and consulted about the crops to be planted. He did not want to plant peppers or egg plant because, as he said, "I don't like that country for peppers or egg plant; no, sir," but he was overruled and those crops were planted. The same is true of the watermelons.

Shortly before October 15, 1943, Andrews and Russell requested de Escamilla to resign as manager, which he did, and Harry Miller was appointed in his place.

Hacienda Farms Limited maintained two bank accounts, one in a San Diego bank and another in an Escondido bank. It was provided that checks could be drawn on the signatures of any two of the three partners. It is stated in plaintiff's brief, without any contradiction (the checks are not before us) that money was withdrawn on 20 checks signed by Russell and Andrews and that all other checks except three bore the signatures of de Escamilla, the general partner, and one of the other defendants. The general partner had no power to withdraw money without the signature of one of the limited partners.

[ULPA § 7] provides as follows:

> A limited partner shall not become liable as a general partner unless, in addition to the exercise of his rights and powers as a limited partner, he takes part in the control of the business.

The foregoing illustrations sufficiently show that Russell and Andrews both took "part in the control of the business." The manner of withdrawing money from the bank accounts is particularly illuminating. The two men had absolute power to withdraw all the partnership funds in the banks without the knowledge or consent of the general partner. Either Russell or Andrews could take control of the business from de Escamilla by refusing to sign checks for bills contracted by him and thus limit his activities in the management of the business. They required him to resign as manager and selected his successor. They were active in dictating the crops to be planted, some of them against the wish of de Escamilla. This clearly shows they took part in the control of the business of the partnership and thus became liable as general partners.

Judgment affirmed.

Barnard, P. J., concurred.

Note

See *Weil v. Diversified Props.*, 319 F. Supp. 778, 782 (D.C. Cir. 1970), refusing to allow a general partner to invoke §7 against his limited partners who had, he alleged, taken over the business during a financial crisis. The court in the alternative stated that even if a general partner could sue under §7, "[c]ertainly common sense dictates that in times of severe financial crisis all partners in such an enterprise, limited or general, will become actively interested in any effort to keep the enterprise afloat. . . ."

With regard to the definition of control, see *Mount Vernon Sav. & Loan v. Partridge Assocs.*, 679 F. Supp. 522, 528 (D. Md. 1987), where the court stated,

> a limited partner may be actively involved in the day to day operation of the partnership's affairs, provided that he does not have ultimate decision making responsibility. Thus, the question is not whether [limited partner] provided advice and counsel to [general partner], but whether it exercised at least an equal voice in making partnership decisions so as, in effect, to be a general partner.

On a separate topic, the court in *Mount Vernon* decided that it did not need to resolve the threshold question of whether ULPA §7 or RULPA §303 (which is the counterpart to §7) governed the suit before it because, with regard to the control question, "the new Act merely clarifies what was inchoate in the old."

Gateway Potato Sales v. G.B. Investment Co.

Court of Appeals of Arizona
822 P.2d 490 (1991)

Taylor, Judge.

Gateway Potato Sales (Gateway), a creditor of Sunworth Packing Limited Partnership (Sunworth Packing), brought suit to recover payment for goods it had supplied to the limited partnership. Gateway sought recovery from Sunworth Packing, from Sunworth Corporation as general partner, and from G.B. Investment Company (G.B. Investment) as a limited partner, pursuant to Arizona Revised Statutes Annotated [RULPA § 303]. Under § [303], a limited partner may become liable for the obligations of the limited partnership under certain circumstances in which the limited partner has taken part in the control of the business.

G.B. Investment moved for summary judgment, urging that there was no evidence that the circumstances described in [§ 303] had occurred in this case. It argued that, as a limited partner, it was not liable to the creditors of the limited partnership except to the extent of its investment. The trial court agreed, granting G.B. Investment's motion for summary judgment.

Gateway appeals from the judgment and the denial of its motion for reconsideration, arguing the existence of conflicting evidence of material facts relating to the participation of the limited partner in the control of the partnership business. We agree and reverse the grant of summary judgment. . . .

In late 1985, Robert C. Ellsworth, the president of Sunworth Corporation, called Robert Pribula, the owner of Gateway, located in Minnesota, to see if Gateway would supply Sunworth Packing with seed potatoes. Pribula hesitated to supply the seed potatoes without receiving assurance of payment because Pribula was aware that Ellsworth had previously undergone bankruptcy. Pribula, however, decided to sell the seed potatoes to Sunworth Packing after being assured by Ellsworth that he was in partnership with a large financial institution, G.B. Investment Company, and that G.B. Investment was providing the financing, was actively involved in the operation of the business, and had approved the purchase of the seed potatoes. Thereafter, from February 1986 through April 1986, Gateway sold substantial quantities of seed potatoes to Sunworth Packing.

While supplying the seed potatoes, Pribula believed that he was doing business with a general partnership (i.e., Sunworth Packing Company, formed by Sunworth Corporation and G.B. Investment Company). The sales documents used by the parties specified "Sunworth Packing Company" as the name of the partnership. Pribula was neither aware of the true name of the partnership nor that it was a limited partnership.

All of Gateway's dealings were with Ellsworth. Pribula neither contacted G.B. Investment prior to selling the seed potatoes to the limited partnership nor did he otherwise attempt to verify any of the statements Ellsworth had made about G.B. Investment's involvement. The only direct contact between G.B. Investment and Gateway occurred some time after the sale of the seed potatoes. . . .

G.B. Investment's vice-president, Darl Anderson, testified in his affidavit that G.B. Investment had exerted no control over the daily management and operation of the limited partnership, Sunworth Packing. This testimony was contradicted, however, by the affidavit testimony of Ellsworth which was presented by Gateway in opposing G.B. Investment's motion for summary judgment. According to Ellsworth,

G.B. Investment's employees, Darl Anderson and Thomas McHolm, controlled the day-to-day affairs of the limited partnership and made Ellsworth account to them for nearly everything he did. This day-to-day contact included but was not limited to approval of most of the significant operational decisions and expenditures and the use and management of partnership funds without Ellsworth's involvement.[8]

Ellsworth testified further that he had described G.B. Investment's control of the business operation to Pribula. Pribula confirmed that Ellsworth had informed him that G.B. Investment's employees, McHolm and Anderson, were at the partnership's office on a frequent basis, that Ellsworth reported directly to them, that daily operations of the partnership were reviewed by representatives of G.B. Investment, and that Ellsworth had to get their approval before making certain business decisions. . . . [The court quotes RULPA 303 (a)]:

[A] limited partner is not liable for the obligations of a limited partnership unless he is also a general partner or, in addition to the exercise of his rights and powers as a limited partner, he takes part in the control of the business. However, if the limited partner's participation in the control of the business is not substantially the same as the exercise of the powers of a general partner, he is liable only to persons who transact business with the limited partnership with actual knowledge of his participation in control.

. . . Gateway argued that the statute imposes liability on a limited partner whose participation in the control of the business is substantially the same as the exercised power of a general partner. Gateway further argued that even if the person transacting business with the limited partnership did not know of the limited partner's participation in control, there is liability. Alternatively, Gateway argued that the statute imposes liability when the powers exercised in controlling the business might fall short of being "substantially the same as the exercise of powers of a general partner,"

---

8. [1] Ellsworth described with some specificity the ways in which G.B. Investment's control was exerted:

a. During the early months of the Partnership, Thomas McHolm and/or Darl Anderson were at the Partnership's offices on a daily basis directing the operation of the Partnership, and thereafter, they were at the Partnership's offices at least 2–3 times per week reviewing the operations of the business, directing changes in operations, and instructing me to make certain changes in operating the Partnership's affairs. . . .

d. Prior to constructing improvements to the packaging facilities of the Partnership, Thomas McHolm and/or Darl Anderson had to approve all construction bids, individually selected some of the suppliers and subcontractors, and individually selected the equipment to be installed. . . .

f. During a great portion of the duration of the Partnership, Thomas McHolm and/or Darl Anderson oversaw the daily operations of the Partnership because I had to have all expenditures approved by Thomas McHolm and/or Darl Anderson and Darl Anderson had to approve and sign checks issued by the Partnership, including without limitation payroll checks and invoices for telephone charges, utilities, publications, interest payments, bank card charges, supplies, etc. Copies of a sampling of the invoices and the corresponding checks are attached hereto as Exhibit 2. . . .

but the person transacting business with the limited partnership had actual knowledge of the participation in control. Gateway asserted that the evidence it was presenting in response to the motion for summary judgment raised issues of material fact as to whether either of these situations had occurred. If either had occurred, Gateway argued, it would be entitled to recover from the limited partner, G.B. Investment.

In granting G.B. Investment's motion for summary judgment, the trial court conclud[ed] that G.B. Investment could not be found liable under [§ 303] as a matter of law. [A]s we interpret the trial court's comments, it read the statute as having a threshold requirement — that is, under all circumstances, a creditor of the limited partnership must have contact with the limited partner in order to impose liability on the limited partner. The evidence before the trial court showed that Gateway merely relied upon the statements made by Ellsworth, president of the general partner, and that Gateway did not contact G.B. Investment prior to transacting business with the limited partnership. Based upon these facts, the trial court concluded that liability could not be imposed upon G.B. Investment. . . .

To the extent that the trial court's ruling may have been based on a belief that a limited partner could never be liable under the statute unless the creditor had contact with the limited partner and learned directly from him of his participation and control of the business, we believe that ruling to be in error. In [§ 303] the legislature stopped short of expressly stating that if the limited partner's participation in the control of the business is substantially the same as the exercise of the powers of a general partner, he is liable to persons who transact business with a limited partnership even though they have no knowledge of his participation and control. It has made this statement by implication, though, by stating to the opposite effect that "if the limited partner's participation in the control of the business is not substantially the same as the exercise of the powers of a general partner, he is liable only to persons who transact business with the limited partnership with actual knowledge of his participation in control." [§ 303(a).]

We believe this interpretation is strengthened by an examination of the legislative history of Arizona's limited partnership statute. It is further strengthened by the legislature's refusal to modify this statute to correspond to the Revised Uniform Limited Partnership Act, as amended in 1985. . . . In 1985, the drafters of the RULPA backtracked from the position taken in section 303(a) of the 1976 Act. The new amendments reflect a reluctance to hold a limited partner liable if the limited partner had no direct contact with the creditor. The 1985 revised RULPA section 303(a) was amended to provide as follows:

> Except as provided in Subsection (d), a limited partner is not liable for the obligations of a limited partnership unless he is also a general partner or, in addition to the exercise of his rights and powers as a limited partner, he participates in the control of the business. *However, if the limited partner participates in the control of the business, he is liable only to persons*

who transact business with the limited partnership reasonably believing, based upon the limited partner's conduct, that the limited partner is a general partner. (Emphasis added.)

The Arizona legislature, however, has not revised [RULPA] to correspond to the [1985] amendments. . . . It follows then that no contact between the creditor and the limited partner is required to impose liability.

Moreover, whereas section 303 of the RULPA [1985 amendments] states that the creditor's reasonable belief must be "based upon the limited partner's conduct," under [§ 303] the only requirement is that the creditor has had "actual knowledge of [the limited partner's] participation in control." The statute does not state that this knowledge must be based upon the limited partner's conduct. . . . Under the facts presented in this case, Gateway had no direct contact with G.B. Investment until after the sales were concluded. We conclude, therefore, that G.B. Investment would be liable only if the "substantially the same as" test was met.

Whether a limited partner has exercised the degree of control that will make him liable to a creditor has always been a factual question. This is so regardless of whether the particular statute involved is patterned after section 7 of the ULPA or after section 303 of the RULPA. Our current Arizona statute lists activities that a limited partner may undertake without participating in controlling the business. It also states that other activities may be excluded from the definition of such control. Where activities do not fall within the "safe harbor" of § 303(b), it is necessary for a trier-of-fact to determine whether such activities amount to "control." In the absence of actual knowledge of the limited partner's participation in the control of the partnership business, there must be evidence from which a trier-of-fact might find not only control, but control that is "substantially the same as the exercise of powers of a general partner." . . .

Viewing the facts in the light most favorable to Gateway, we cannot say as a matter of law that G.B. Investment was entitled to summary judgment. We conclude that Gateway is entitled to a determination by trial of the extent of control exercised by G.B. Investment over Sunworth Packing.

For the foregoing reasons, we reverse the judgment of the trial court and remand for further proceedings.

EHRLICH, P.J., and CLABORNE, J., concur.

Notes

1. Suppose a limited partner controls the limited partnership, but the creditor knows that the limited partner is not the general partner. It would seem that under RULPA § 303(a) the creditor could not prevail against the limited partner, for how could such a creditor "reasonably believe" that the limited partner was a general partner? Nevertheless, the bankruptcy court in the Southern District of New York found otherwise. *In re Adelphia Communications Corp.*, 376 B.R. 87, 93-105 (S.D.N.Y. 2007). Consider whether the court's reasoning is persuasive:

At the heart of ACC's [the debtor] summary judgment motion is its contention that Lucent [the creditor] had actual knowledge that ACC was the limited partner of Devon [the limited partnership], defeating Lucent's claim that it had a reasonable belief that ACC was a general partner. ACC contends that Lucent's "actual knowledge" is not disputed, making its own alleged conduct irrelevant. Section 17-208 of Delaware's Revised Uniform Limited Partnership Act states:

> § 17-208. Notice
>
> The fact that a certificate of limited partnership is on file in the Office of the Secretary of State is notice that the partnership is a limited partnership and is notice of all other facts set forth therein which are required to be set forth in a certificate of limited partnership by § 17-201(a)(1)-(3) and by § 17-202(f) of this title and which are permitted to be set forth in a certificate of limited partnership by § 17-218(b) of this title.

The parties agree that ACC was listed as a limited partner in the "Agreement of Limited Partnership of Devon Mobile Communications, L.P." dated November 3, 1995, and that Devon filed a Certificate of Limited Partnership with the Secretary of State for the State of Delaware on June 13, 1995. It appears that Lucent had actual knowledge of ACC's status as a limited partner, and for the purposes of this ruling the Court assumes Lucent did have actual knowledge.

Adelphia's contention that Lucent's actual knowledge is fatal might be correct if [ULPA § 303(a)] stated that limited partners who participate in control will be liable only to persons who transact business with the limited partnership "reasonably believing . . . that the limited partner is a general partner." If that was all that [ULPA § 303(a)] said, the Court would be free to consider all factors that had a bearing on a third party's reasonable belief, including the third party's actual knowledge. ACC's reading, however, omits six important words in [ULPA § 303(a)] following "reasonable belief." The reasonable belief is to be "based upon the limited partner's conduct." Thus, [ULPA § 303(a)] requires the Court to determine Lucent's reasonable belief based upon conduct of ACC, not Lucent.

Important to the analysis is the focus of [ULPA § 303(a)] is at all times on the conduct of the limited partner. At first glance, it may seem illogical to ignore the actual knowledge of the third party. Under this interpretation of [ULPA § 303(a)], a third party could be held to have a "reasonable belief" that a limited partner was acting as the *de facto* general partner notwithstanding the fact that third party actually knew of the limited partner's status in public filings. Yet that is what the plain language of [ULPA § 303(a)] mandates by inclusion of the words "reasonably believing, *based upon the limited partner's conduct,* that the limited partner is a general partner." (emphasis added).

2. In contrast to *Adelphia*, consider *Shimko v. Guenther*, 505 F.3d 987 (9th Cir. 2007). In this case, the plaintiff, a lawyer, sued his former client for unpaid legal fees. The court first determined that the services were rendered to the limited partnership of which the defendant was a limited partner. The court then considered the finding of the district court that due to defendant's substantial involvement in the business of the limited partnership, it was reasonable for plaintiff to believe that defendant was a general partner. The appellate court concluded that because plaintiff had been asked to advise the defendant and others connected with the business on their potential liability, in the exercise of due care plaintiff should have consulted the limited partnership agreement, where he would have learned of defendant's "actual status as a limited partner." *Id*. at 992. Knowing that, the court held, plaintiff "could not have reasonably believed that [defendant] was a general partner, whatever role [defendant] played in the control of the business." *Id*.

3. Section 303 of Re-RULPA represents a significant change from prior law. It flatly states that a limited partner is not liable for obligations of the limited partnership "solely by reason of being a limited partner, even if the limited partner participates in the management and control of the limited partnership." This section thus completes the evolution evident in the two earlier versions of RULPA, where the drafters permitted a greater role for limited partners without incurring liability for such a role. Suppose a limited partner manages the business of the partnership and a creditor assumes that the limited partner is the general partner. Would the limited partner be liable, assuming the limited partner was aware of the creditor's misperception and did nothing to disabuse the creditor of that understanding?

b. Control of the Corporate General Partner

Zeiger v. Wilf

Superior Court of New Jersey, Appellate Division
755 A.2d 608 (2000)

LESEMANN, J.A.D.

This case offers a virtual primer in the Byzantine relationships among various forms of business organizations employed in a modern venture capital project. It includes a limited partnership, a corporation, a general partnership and several sophisticated individuals all involved in the proposed redevelopment of a hotel/office building in downtown Trenton. It also demonstrates the significance of limited individual liability which is a key reason for employing some of those entities, and the inevitable risk that anticipated rewards from such a venture may not be realized.

At issue here is an agreement by which plaintiff, a seller of the property to be renovated, was to receive a "consultant fee" of $23,000 per year for sixteen years. The payments, however, ceased after two years. A jury found the redevelopers (a limited partnership and a corporation) liable for those payments, and an appeal by those entities has now been abandoned. As a result, the matter now focuses on plaintiff's claim that Joseph Wilf, the individual who led the various defendant entities, should be held personally liable for the consultant payments and that such liability should also be imposed on a general partnership owned by Wilf and members of his family.

There is no claim that Wilf personally, or his general partnership, ever guaranteed the consultant payments or that plaintiff ever believed Wilf had made such guarantees. Nor is there a claim that plaintiff did not understand at all times that he was contracting only with a limited partnership and/or a corporation, and not with Wilf personally or with his general partnership. For those reasons, and also because we find no merit in various other theories of individual liability advanced by plaintiff, we affirm the summary judgment entered in favor of Wilf individually, and we reverse the judgment against Wilf's family-owned general partnership. . . .

[The property was sold to Trenton, Inc., a corporation (the "corporation"), which was originally obligated on the consulting contract. That contract and the corporation's property rights were subsequently assigned to Trenton, L.P., a limited partnership (the "limited partnership"). The general partner of the limited partnership was Trenton, Inc. and the principle limited partner was CPA, a general partnership controlled by the defendant Wilf. CPA also owned 50% of the stock of Trenton, Inc. Wilf handled the renovations on behalf of the limited partnership as an officer of its corporate general partner.]

Eventually, the project failed. The limited partnership and the corporation filed bankruptcy. . . . On July 19, 1993, plaintiff sued Wilf, claiming that Wilf had become the "surviving partner and owner of the partnership assets" pertaining to the "purchase and transfer of" the hotel, and that he was in default respecting payment of plaintiff's consulting fees.

[The trial court granted summary judgment in favor of Wilf, dismissing the complaint as to him. Subsequently,] a jury returned a $456,801 verdict against the limited partnership and the corporation, to which sum the trial court added prejudgment interest. However, while the trial court had submitted to the jury the liability issue as to the limited partnership and the corporation, it had withheld for determination by the court plaintiff's claim against CPA. On December 4, 1997, the court found that CPA was also liable to plaintiff for the aforesaid $456,801, and entered judgment against it for that amount.

This appeal was initially filed by plaintiff, seeking reversal of the judgment in favor of Joseph Wilf. A cross-appeal was then filed by CPA, by Trenton, L.P. and by Trenton, Inc. . . . [B]ecause of the intervening bankruptcy proceedings, defendants have advised that no "useful purpose is served by continuing to process this appeal" on behalf of the limited partnership or the corporation. Thus, defendants have argued for reversal only as against CPA while, of course, also maintaining that the dismissal as to defendant Wilf should be affirmed. . . .

[P]laintiff claims the limited partnership statute imposes general partner liability on Wilf because he functioned as the operating head of the parties' renovation project. We find the claim inconsistent with both the policy and the language of the statute.

A basic principle of [RULPA] is a differentiation between the broad liability of a general partner for the obligations of a limited partnership (see [RULPA § 404]), and the non-liability of a limited partner for such obligations. *See* [RULPA § 303(a)]. Preservation of that distinction and protection against imposing unwarranted liability on a limited partner has been a consistent concern of the drafters of the Uniform Act on which our New Jersey statute is based, and has been described as "the single most difficult issue facing lawyers who use the limited partnership form of organization." *See Revised Unif. Limited Partnership Act,* Prefatory Note preceding § 101, U.L.A. (1976) (hereinafter "Commissioners' Report"). Indeed, the history of the Uniform Limited Partnership Act, and thus the evolution of our New Jersey statute, shows a consistent movement to insure certainty and predictability respecting the obligations and potential liability of limited partners. The framers of the Act have accomplished that by consistently reducing and restricting the bases on which a general partner's unrestricted liability can be imposed on a limited partner. Under the present version of the Uniform Act, the imposition of such liability (absent fraud or misleading) is severely limited. Our New Jersey statute (as discussed below) reflects that same philosophy in the provisions of [RULPA § 303(a)].

The original version of the ULPA was adopted in 1916. That enactment dealt with the question of a limited partner's liability in one short provision. In Section 7 it said,

> A limited partner shall not become liable as a general partner unless, in addition to the exercise of his rights and powers as a limited partner, he takes part in the control of the business.

In 1976, the original ULPA was substantially replaced by a revised version (on which the New Jersey statute is based) which "was intended to modernize the prior uniform law." *See* Commissioners Report Prefatory Note preceding Section 101. One of the ways that modernization was effected was by a new Section 303, which replaced the old Section 7, and was adopted virtually verbatim as Section 27 of the New Jersey statute. Section 303 reads as follows:

> [A] limited partner is not liable for the obligations of a limited partnership unless . . . , in addition to the exercise of his [or her] rights and powers as a limited partner, he [or she] takes part in the control of the business. However, if the limited partner's participation in the control of the business is not substantially the same as the exercise of the powers of a general partner, he [or she] is liable only to persons who transact business with the limited partnership with actual knowledge of his participation in control.

The Commissioners' Report in the comment to Section 303 states:

> Section 303 makes several important changes in Section 7 of the 1916 Act . . . .
> The second sentence of Section 303(a) reflects a wholly new concept . . . .
> It was adopted partly because . . . it was thought unfair to impose general

partner's liability on a limited partner except to the extent that a third party had knowledge of his participation in control of the business . . . , but also (and more importantly) because of a determination that it is not sound public policy to hold a limited partner who is not also a general partner liable for the obligations of the partnership except to persons who have done business with the limited partnership reasonably believing, based on the limited partner's conduct, that he is a general partner.

Following that 1976 version, more limitations on a limited partner's liability came in 1988, with a series of "Safe Harbor" amendments, virtually all of which were adopted in New Jersey. See [RULPA §303(b)]. The Commissioners' Report explained the reason for those additions to Section 303 of the Uniform Act:

Paragraph (b) is intended to provide a "Safe Harbor" by enumerating certain activities which a limited partner may carry on for the partnership without being deemed to have taken part in control of the business. This "Safe Harbor" list has been expanded beyond that set out in the 1976 Act to reflect case law and statutory developments and more clearly to assure that limited partners are not subjected to general liability where such liability is inappropriate.

Although plaintiff argues that [RULPA §303] imposes a general partner's liability on Wilf (and CPA) because Wilf took "part in the control of the business," we are satisfied that the argument has no merit. To accept it, and impose such liability on the facts presented here, would reverse the evolution described above and create precisely the instability and uncertainty that the drafters of the RULPA (and the New Jersey Act) were determined to avoid.

Plaintiff's argument rests on Wilf's key role in the renovation project. Wilf acknowledges that role, but argues that his actions were taken as a vice president of Trenton, Inc.—the corporation which was the sole general partner of Trenton, L.P. Wilf argues that since the corporation is an artificial entity, it can only function through its officers, see *Printing Mart-Morristown v. Sharp Electronics Corp.*, 116 N.J. 739, 761, 563 A. 2d 31 (1989), and that is precisely what he was doing at all times when he acted concerning this enterprise. Wilf also points to the "Safe Harbor" provisions of [RULPA §303(b)] to reinforce his claim that his actions here did not impose general partner liability upon him.

We agree with that analysis. As noted, the 1988 "Safe Harbor" provisions set out a number of activities which, under the statute, do not constitute participating in "the control of" a business so as to impose a general partner's liability on a limited partner. The provision to which Wilf particularly refers is [RULPA §303(b)(1)], which provides that,

b. A limited partner does not participate in the control of the business within the meaning of subsection a. solely by[,]

[1] Serving as an officer, director or shareholder of a corporate general partner;

That provision clearly applies here and essentially undercuts plaintiff's argument: while plaintiff claims that Wilf's activities constitute "control" of the activities of Trenton, L.P., the statute says, in just so many words, that those activities do *not* constitute the exercise of control.

In addition to the "Safe Harbor" protections, [RULPA § 303(a)] itself sharply limits the circumstances under which the exercise of "control" could lead to imposition of general partner liability on a limited partner. It first provides that if a limited partner's control activities are so extensive as to be "substantially the same as" those of a general partner, that control, by itself, is sufficient to impose liability: *i.e.*, if a limited partner acts "the same as" a general partner, he will be treated as a general partner. However, but for that extreme case, mere participation in control does not impose liability on a limited partner. Such liability may be imposed only as to "persons who," in essence, rely on the limited partner's participation in control and thus regard him as a general partner.

That limitation of liability to those who rely on a limited partner's exercise of control is critical to a sound reading of the statute. It is consistent with the series of amendments from 1916 to now, which have been designed to insure predictability and certainty in the use of the limited partnership form of business organization. To reject plaintiff's claim of liability would be consistent with that view of the statute. To accept the claim would inject precisely the instability and uncertainty which the statute is designed to avoid.

Here, there was none of the "reliance" which is a necessary basis for a limited partner's liability. It bears repeating that plaintiff, an insider in the project, does not claim he was ever misled as to the entities with whom he was dealing. Plaintiff is described as a sophisticated, experienced developer and businessman. He does not deny that description. He does not claim that he ever sought or obtained any individual guarantee or promise of payment from Wilf, and certainly not from CPA. Nor does plaintiff deny that he understood completely that he was dealing with a limited partnership and a corporation. He does not deny his understanding that those entities, by their very nature, provide limited resources and limited recourse for parties with whom they contract. *See Frank Rizzo, Inc. v. Alatsas*, 27 N.J. 400, 402, 142 A. 2d 861 (1958), where the court, speaking of a corporation but employing language equally applicable to a limited partnership, noted that,

> [o]rdinarily we do not think in terms of the possibility of individual liability of corporate officers for obligations incurred by the entity in the usual course of business. Such personal liability is inconsistent with the existence of a body corporate at common law and can emanate only from some positive legislative fiat.

In short, there is no claim that plaintiff was misled, or that he relied on some impression that Wilf was a general partner of Trenton, L.P., and thus there is no basis for any finding of personal liability against Wilf under [RULPA § 303(a)].

The only other possible statutory basis for imposing liability on Wilf is the provision which would impose such liability if Wilf's activities were "substantially the same as the exercise of the powers of a general partner" of Trenton, L.P. While that phrase is less than precise, and we are aware of no helpful decision interpreting or applying it, we see no basis for its application here.

First, recall that Wilf's activities as an officer of Trenton, Inc., are specifically sanctioned by the "Safe Harbor" provisions. With the other corporate officers having abrogated their responsibilities, it is difficult to see, first, what other choice was available to Wilf; and second, why his actions should have any adverse effect on him under the Limited Partnership Act.

Further, it is significant that plaintiff does not rest his argument so much on the powers and functions exercised by Wilf, as on the manner in which he exercised those functions. That is, the argument points mainly to Wilf's carelessness in not consistently and specifically identifying himself as an officer of Trenton, Inc., when he acted on behalf of Trenton, L.P. or signed documents on behalf of the limited partnership. The argument, in short, refers more to form than to substance. It lacks force because, regardless of Wilf's alleged carelessness, plaintiff was at all times fully aware of what Wilf was doing and how he was doing it. A failure to comply with some designated formality might have had some significance if, at any time or in any way, it misled plaintiff or prejudiced him. But, as we have noted several times, that is simply not the case.[9]

Plaintiff cites three out-of-state cases in support of his argument against Wilf and CPA. We find all of them either distinguishable or, for other reasons, non-persuasive.

. . . .

We are satisfied that, were we to find individual liability against Wilf because of his "control" here, we would be encouraging precisely the instability and uncertainty which are anathema to widespread use of the limited partnership as a business entity. The modern, sound view, epitomized by [RULPA], the New Jersey statute and the well reasoned decisions discussed above is in the other direction: to curtail the threat of personal liability unless there is some "reliance on the part of

---

9. [7] The 1976 version of the Uniform Act was amended in 1985, to eliminate entirely the reference to a limited partner's control activities being "substantially the same as the exercise of the powers of a general partner." Thus, the present version projects liability on a limited partner *only* if an outsider "reasonably [believed], based upon the limited partner's conduct, that the limited partner is a general partner." The purpose of the amendment, quite clearly, is to make even clearer the points noted in the comments quoted above: it "is not sound public policy" to hold a limited partner to a general partner's liability, unless he has misled others into believing he was a general partner. *See Revised Unif. Limited Partnership Act, supra*, Prefatory Note preceding Section 101. Although New Jersey has not (yet) adopted the 1985 amendment, neither has it rejected the proposal, and there is no reason to conclude that New Jersey's Section 27 is not consistent with both the presently existing Section 101 and its earlier version.

the outsider dealing with the limited partnership." There was no such reliance here, and there is no basis for imposing personal liability on Wilf. . . .

The summary judgment in favor of defendant Wilf is affirmed, as is the judgment against Trenton, L.P. and Trenton, Inc. The judgment against defendant CPA is reversed. . . .

c. Piercing the Veil of a Limited Partnership

A widely accepted principle in corporate law is that the "veil" of a corporation may be "pierced," meaning that, under certain circumstances, the limited liability (the veil) that is afforded to shareholders and others may be ignored (pierced). Veil-piercing is an equitable doctrine developed by the courts to address situations in which shareholders or others affiliated with a corporation have "abused" the privilege of operating in a corporate form by using the corporation to perpetrate a fraud or injustice. *See, generally,* Peter B. Oh, *Veil-Piercing Unbound*, 93 B.U.L. REV. 89 (2013); Mark J. Loewenstein, *Veil Piercing to Non-owners: A Practical and Theoretical Inquiry*, 41 SETON HALL L. REV. 839 (2011). The courts have considered whether this doctrine should be applied to limited partnerships so that limited partners may be held liable for the debts and obligations of the partnership, essentially adding to RULPA § 303 circumstances under which a limited partner may be liable to third parties. In the following case, the New Jersey court embraced the doctrine.

Canter v. Lakewood of Voorhees

Superior Court of New Jersey, Appellate Division
22 A.3d 68 (2011)

SIMONELLI, J.A.D.

This is a nursing home negligence action arising from injuries sustained by plaintiff Sanford Canter at the Lakewood of Voorhees Nursing Home, a New Jersey licensed long-term care facility (the nursing home). By leave granted, defendant Seniors Healthcare, Inc. (SHI) appeals from the denial of its motions for partial summary judgment and reconsideration on the issue of whether corporate veil-piercing principles apply to a New Jersey limited partnership, or alternatively, whether there is a genuine issue of material fact as to whether plaintiff established the veil-piercing factors.

We hold that equitable principles, such as veil piercing, may apply to a New Jersey limited partnership but in limited circumstances, such as where a limited partner takes or attempts action not within the safe harbor of N.J.S.A. 42:2A-27b, or dominates and uses the limited partnership to perpetrate a fraud, injustice, or otherwise circumvent the law. Because the record does not establish such circumstances, we reverse.

We begin by explaining the relationship between the various entities and individuals involved in this matter. Defendant Lakewood of Voorhees Associates LP

(Lakewood) is a limited partnership formed in 1978 pursuant to the New Jersey Uniform Limited Partnership Law (1976) (NJULPL), N.J.S.A. 42:2A-1 to -73. At its inception, Lakewood was capitalized with at least $600,000. Lakewood owns and operates the nursing home.

SHI is a Pennsylvania corporation incorporated in 1996. It is a limited partner of Lakewood and holds an 84.12% interest in the partnership. It also is the sole shareholder of defendant Ozal of Lakewood, Inc. (Ozal) and defendant Seniors Management-North, Inc. (SMN).

Ozal is a New Jersey corporation incorporated in 1999. Ozal is Lakewood's general partner and holds a 1% interest in the partnership.

SMN is a New Jersey corporation incorporated in 2000. SMN provides accounting, billing, group purchasing, support and professional-consulting services to the nursing home pursuant to a management agreement. Its employee, Cherly Carnes, is the nursing home's administrator who controls the nursing home's day-to-day operations. SMN has no ownership interest in Lakewood, but receives a management fee pursuant to the management agreement. SMN also manages nine other nursing homes in New Jersey, Pennsylvania and the District of Columbia.

Defendant Steven Lazovitz is Ozal's sole director. He is also a director, officer and majority shareholder of SHI. He is a former general and limited partner of Lakewood and former officer of SMN. Lazovitz executed the original management agreement on behalf of Lakewood when he was the general partner.

Lenard Brown and Robert Sall are directors and employees of SHI and former officers of SMN. SMN paid the salaries of Brown, Sall and Lazovitz until they were placed on SHI's payroll. SHI pays their salaries from the corporate overhead fees it receives from SMN.

Plaintiff's expert opined, in part, that Lakewood, SHI and SMN "operate as one seamless long[-]term care organization," and SHI and SMN "exercised significant control" over Lakewood's operation. Realizing that plaintiff may use this opinion to impose liability on SHI for Lakewood's negligence, SHI filed a motion for partial summary judgment contending, in part, that corporate veil-piercing principles do not apply to a limited partnership, such as Lakewood, and the NJULPL alone governs a limited partner's liability to third parties.[10] Alternatively, SHI contended that even if corporate veil-piercing principles could apply to a limited partnership, there was no genuine issue of material fact that SHI did not dominate Lakewood or use Lakewood to perpetrate a fraud, injustice, or otherwise circumvent the law.

Focusing on the interrelationship between the various entities and individuals, the motion judge applied corporate veil-piercing principles to a limited partnership. The judge concluded there was a genuine issue of material fact as to whether SHI

---

10. Although all defendants moved for partial summary judgment, only SHI sought leave to appeal. Thus, we limit this opinion to SHI.

controlled Lakewood, sufficient to hold SHI, Lakewood's limited partner, liable to third parties for Lakewood's negligence. The judge made the following findings to support this conclusion: (1) SHI is SMN's and Ozal's sole shareholder; (2) SHI owns approximately 84% of Lakewood, whereas Ozal only owns 1%; (3) the entities did not observe corporate formalities; (4) there is "extensive commonality of ownership and of officer involvement" among the entities; and (5) Lakewood did not carry liability insurance, regardless of whether it was required to have such insurance. The judge also concluded,

> Because of various factors . . . the nature and extent of the control here exhibited ultimately by [SMN] and the interconnection between these various entities and the persons involved with respect to them, I am left to conclude that, in terms of [SHI's] role as a limited partner, there is a genuine issue of material fact as to its overall role in this enterprise and specifically whether it, [SHI], is effectively the general partner . . . of Lakewood . . . or the equivalent thereof.
>
> Again, I acknowledge the respect that is to be afforded to corporate [form] or the equivalent thereof in the context of a limited partnership . . . and yet, when there is direct involvement in the conduct, I am satisfied that [SHI] is not entitled to . . . summary judgment . . . because I am not convinced, as a matter of law, that that's the case. [SHI] may be effectively a general partner, given the nature of this arrangement and, . . . otherwise, because of the interrelationship with all the other entities—and I say this with respect to all these entities—summary judgment in its favor is not appropriate.

Notably, the judge did not find that SHI was substantially involved in Lakewood's day-to-day operations; rather, he found that SMN and its employees are involved in Lakewood's day-to-day operations. Also, the judge made no finding whether SHI used Lakewood to perpetrate a fraud, injustice, or otherwise circumvent the law.

The judge subsequently denied SHI's motion for reconsideration. SHI then filed a motion for leave to appeal from the denial of both motions, which we granted. On appeal, SHI contends the judge erred in applying corporate veil-piercing principles to Lakewood, a limited partnership. It argues that only the NJULPL applies in this case and its "safe harbor" provision, N.J.S.A. 42:2A-27b, shields SHI from any liability for Lakewood's negligence. Alternatively, SHI contends that even if corporate veil-piercing principles could apply to a limited partnership, the judge: (1) erroneously found there was a genuine issue of material fact as to the first prong of the corporate veil-piercing test, that is, that SHI dominated Lakewood; and (2) failed to find the second prong, that is, that SHI used Lakewood to perpetrate a fraud, injustice, or circumvent the law.

. . . .

[W]e are satisfied the judge properly concluded that corporate veil-piercing principles can apply to a limited partnership; however, the record does not support veil piercing in this case.

N.J.S.A. 42:2A-27a shields a limited partner from liability for the limited partnership's obligations except under two circumstances: (1) where the limited partner is "also a general partner," or (2) where a limited partner "participat[es] in the control of the business[.]" N.J.S.A. 42:2A-27a. However, where "the limited partner's participation in the control of the business is not substantially the same as the exercise of the powers of a general partner, he is liable only to persons who transact business with the limited partnership with actual knowledge of, and reliance on, his participation in control." *Ibid.*

N.J.S.A. 42:2A-27a is modeled after § 303(a) of the Revised Uniform Limited Partnership Act (1976) (RULPA), which effected changes to the original 1916 Act

> because of a determination that it is not sound public policy to hold a limited partner who is not also a general partner liable for the obligations of the partnership except to persons who have done business with the limited partnership reasonably believing, based on the limited partner's conduct, that he is a general partner. [Uniform Limited Partnership Act (1976) § 303 Comment, 6B U.L.A. 182 (2008).]

N.J.S.A. 42:2A-27a "sharply limits the circumstances under which the exercise of 'control' could lead to imposition of general partner liability on a limited partner." *Zeiger v. Wilf*, 333 N.J. Super. 258, 276, 755 A.2d 608 (App. Div.), *certif. denied*, 165 N.J. 676, 762 A.2d 657 (2000).

Consistent with the sharp limitations of N.J.S.A. 42:2A-27a, N.J.S.A. 42:2A-27b provides a "safe harbor" provision.[11] It establishes certain activities, in which a limited partner may engage, which do not constitute participation in control of the limited partnership's business within the meaning of N.J.S.A. 42:2A-27a. Included within those safe harbor activities are: (1) being or serving as a shareholder of a general partner; (2) "[c]onsulting with or advising a general partner with respect to any matter, including the business of the limited partnership"; or (3) being a contractor, an agent or employee of the limited partnership. N.J.S.A. 42:2A-27b(1)–(2), (6).

New Jersey has not addressed whether corporate veil-piercing principles can apply to a limited partnership. However, N.J.S.A. 42:2A-2 provides that the NJULPL "shall be so interpreted and construed as to effect its general purpose to make uniform the law of those states which enact it." Accordingly, we look to other states that have adopted the RULPA to see how they apply corporate veil piercing in the limited partnership context.

---

11. N.J.S.A. 42:2A-27b is modeled after § 303(b) of the RULPA, which "is intended to provide a 'safe harbor' by enumerating certain activities which a limited partner may carry on for the partnership without being deemed to have taken part in control of the business." Uniform Limited Partnership Act (1976) § 303 Comment, *supra*, at 182. Since 1976, the safe harbor list has expanded over the years to reflect case law and recent developments demonstrating when limited partners should not be subjected to general liability. *Ibid.*

Absent authority in this State, we consult Delaware corporate law for guidance. [Citing Delaware law, the court concluded that Delaware would apply corporate veil-piercing principles to a Delaware limited partnership.]

We agree that corporate veil-piercing principles can be applied to a New Jersey limited partnership under appropriate circumstances. However, to pierce the veil there must be evidence that the limited partner participated in the control of the limited partnership's business by taking or attempting action not within the safe harbor of N.J.S.A. 42:2A-27b or dominated the limited partnership and used the limited partnership to perpetrate a fraud or injustice, or otherwise circumvent the law. Both prongs of the domination test must be established by clear and convincing evidence.

To determine the issue of dominance in the veil-piercing context, "courts consider whether 'the parent so dominated the subsidiary that it had no separate existence but was merely a conduit for the parent.'" In making this determination, "courts engage in a fact-specific inquiry considering whether the subsidiary was grossly undercapitalized, the day-to-day involvement of the parent's directors, officers and personnel, and whether the subsidiary fails to observe corporate formalities, pays no dividends, is insolvent, lacks corporate records, or is merely a facade." "As a general principle, . . . the control issue frequently boils down to the limited partner's role in the day-to-day functioning of the business and that partner's decision-making authority versus the role of the general partner."

Ownership alone is not enough for piercing. In addition, "the mere fact that several corporations may be subsidiaries of one parent does not prevent their individual identities from being respected." This court has previously observed that a limited partner of a limited partnership does not assume general partner liability even if the partnership's limited partners were also the sole shareholders, officers and directors of a corporate general partner, and by acting on behalf of the general partner they controlled the activities of the limited partnership.

It is only when one entity owns an interest in another entity "'for the purpose of control, so that the subsidiary company may be used as a mere agency or instrumentality for the [holding] company, [that the owner] will be liable for injuries due to the negligence of the subsidiary.'" The hallmarks of domination for an illegitimate purpose "are typically the engagement of the subsidiary [here, the limited partnership] in no independent business of its own but exclusively the performance of a service for the parent [or here, the majority limited partner] and, even more importantly, the undercapitalization of the subsidiary [limited partnership] rendering it judgment-proof."

Undercapitalization means

"capitalization very small in relation to the nature of the business of the corporation and the risks . . . attendant to such businesses. The adequacy of capital is to be measured as of the time of formation of the corporation. A corporation that was adequately capitalized when formed, but which subsequently suffers financial reverse is not undercapitalized. . . . Adequate capitalization is a question of fact that turns on the nature of the business of the particular corporation. . . ."

The undercapitalization factor is key "in determining corporate dominance" because it provides an inference as to whether the business entity "'was established to defraud its creditors or other improper purpose[s] such as avoiding the risks known to be attendant to a type of business.'"

Contrary to the judge's findings, SHI does not participate in the control of Lakewood's business within the meaning of N.J.S.A. 42:2A-27a by being or serving as a shareholder of Ozal. *See* N.J.S.A. 42:2A-27b(1), (6). Nor does SHI participate in the control of Lakewood's business because it owns SMN, which controls Lakewood's day-to-day operations. SHI's mere ownership of SMN, without more, does not demonstrate SHI's involvement in Lakewood's day-to-day operations, nor does it demonstrate domination. Also, even if SMN's control of Lakewood could somehow be imputed to SHI, being a contractor for Lakewood does not constitute participation in the control of Lakewood's business.

Further, the commonality of ownership and officer involvement does not establish participation in the control of Lakewood's business. There is nothing wrong with Lazovitz being or serving as Ozal's officer or director, while at the same time being or serving as SHI's officer, director, or shareholder.

There is also nothing wrong with the structuring of the various entities in this case. Where individuals set up "legitimate business structures to further their personal and business plans" and "d[o] not use their partnerships to commit fraud or defeat the ends of justice[,]" the veil-piercing doctrine will not apply.

Finally, there is no evidence demonstrating that plaintiff believed, let alone knew, that SHI controlled either Lakewood or the nursing home, or that plaintiff had any dealings with SHI that may justify a finding of liability under N.J.S.A. 42:2A-27a. By contrast, in *OTR [Assoc. v. IBC Servs.*, 801 A.2d 407 (App. DW.)], *supra*, this court held that veil piercing was appropriate where (1) the parent company's domination and control of the subsidiary company was patently clear, (2) the plaintiff believed it was dealing with the parent company and not the subsidiary and did not discover the fact of separate corporate entities until much later in the business dealings, and (3) the subsidiary affirmatively and intentionally led the plaintiff to believe it was transacting business with the parent company. In *OTR*, "in every functional and operational sense, the subsidiary had no separate identity [from the parent company]." *Id.* at 56, 801 A.2d 407. Here, however, there is no evidence that Lakewood had no separate identity from SHI. Thus, no liability can be imposed on SHI.

The question then is whether there is other evidence establishing that SHI dominated Lakewood and used Lakewood to perpetuate a fraud, injustice, or otherwise circumvent the law. There is no evidence that SHI dominated Lakewood and used Lakewood to perpetuate a fraud or injustice, or otherwise circumvent the law. To the contrary, it is clear that Lakewood was sufficiently capitalized at its inception and has a separate existence from SHI. Long before SHI and SMN were organized in 1996 and 2000, respectively, Lakewood was organized as a limited partnership in 1978 for the legitimate business purpose of owning and operating a nursing home. Lakewood is not insolvent and has assets and income; it has a license to operate the nursing home, owns the property on which the nursing home is located, and earns income from the nursing home's clients. Lakewood also has approximately 240 employees, independent certified public accountants that prepared its financial statements, its own bank accounts, and it enters into contracts in its own name. It also has the right to terminate the management agreement with SMN

There also is no evidence of a commingling of funds. There is also no evidence that Lakewood failed to observe limited partnership formalities (as opposed to corporate formalities). Neither the limited partnership agreement, nor the NJULPL, require annual meetings. *Compare* N.J.S.A. 42:2A (not requiring annual meetings of a limited partnership), *with* N.J.S.A. 14A:5-2 (requiring annual meetings of the shareholders of a corporation). Also, unlike corporation law, which requires corporations to "keep books and records of account and minutes of the proceedings of its shareholders," N.J.S.A. 14A:5-28(1), the NJULPL has no such requirement, *see* N.J.S.A. 42:2A-9. Therefore, it is irrelevant that Lakewood had no annual meetings.

We conclude that the judge erred in denying summary judgment to SHI. . . .

The evidence in this case, even taken in a light most favorable to plaintiff, is insufficient to establish a genuine issue of any material fact such that Lakewood's veil should be pierced to impose liability on SHI for Lakewood's negligence.

Reversed.

Question

Should the court have added, essentially, another basis for liability for a limited partner when the statute already addressed the issue of the potential liability of a limited partner?

2. Removal of the General Partner by the Limited Partners for Cause

DV Realty Advisors v. Policemen's Annuity

Supreme Court of Delaware

75 A.3d 101 (2013)

Before Steele, Chief Justice, Holland, Berger, Jacobs and Ridgely, Justices (constituting the Court en Banc).

Holland, Justice:

[DV Realty, the general partner of the limited partnership, was required by the terms of the limited partnership agreement (LPA) to provide an annual audited financial statement to the limited partners. For various reasons, it completed the

2009 statement in March, 2011, some 313 days after the due date mandated by § 11.5 of the LPA. Earlier statements were also delivered late. As a result (and for other reasons not relevant to the opinion in this case), the limited partners all voted to remove the general partner pursuant to § 3.10(a)(ii) of the LPA, which provided:

> [The general partner] may be removed without Cause by an affirmative vote or consent of the Limited Partners holding in excess of 75% of the [Limited] Partnership Interests then held by all Limited Partners; provided that consenting Limited Partners in *good faith* determine that such removal is necessary for the *best interest* of the [Limited] Partnership. (emphasis added by the court).]

. . . .

The Court of Chancery ruled that the Limited Partners bore the burden of proof to demonstrate action in good faith under § 3.10(a)(ii). The Court of Chancery noted that "The LPA . . . does not define good faith, and good faith can sometimes include objective, as well as subjective, elements." Looking to the language of section 3.10(a)(ii), the Court of Chancery found that the term "good faith" was ambiguous.

To resolve that ambiguity, the Court of Chancery turned to the Uniform Commercial Code ("UCC") definition of good faith found in title 6, section 1-201(20) of the Delaware Code, which states: "'Good faith', except as otherwise provided in Article 5 [which deals with letters of credit], means honesty in fact and the observance of reasonable commercial standards of fair dealing." The Court of Chancery also examined the common law, noting that good faith usually meant subjective good faith, but "there is likely some conduct which is so unreasonable that [the Court of Chancery] will necessarily determine that it could not have been undertaken in good faith." The Court of Chancery decided to use the UCC definition of "good faith" because it was "at least" as broad as the common law definition.

The Court of Chancery then concluded that the Limited Partners determined in good faith that the removal of DV Realty was "necessary for the best interest of the Limited Partnership." The court found that the Limited Partners had removed DV Realty in subjective good faith:

> Ultimately, the court determines that the [limited partners] have shown that [DV Realty's] continuous failure to have the Limited Partnership's audited [f]inancial statements completed in the time prescribed by Section 11.5 provided them with a good faith belief that [DV Realty] needed to be removed for the best interest of the Limited Partnership.

The Court of Chancery also found that it was objectively reasonable for the Limited Partners to believe that it was necessary in the best interest of the Limited Partnership for DV Realty to provide timely audited financial statements. The court explained:

> Annual audited financial statements provide significant value to a business. Thus, when a limited partnership agreement places, on a general partner,

the duty of having the limited partnership's audited financials completed by a specific time, and the general partner consistently fails to meet that duty, it is objectively reasonable to believe that [it] is necessary in the best interest of the limited partnership to replace that general partner.

Thus, the Court of Chancery held the Limited Partners acted in good faith, both subjectively and objectively, and therefore complied with the requirements of section 3.10(a)(ii).

. . . .

The LPA's contractual duty encompasses a concept of "good faith" that is different from the good faith concept addressed by the implied covenant of good faith and fair dealing.

Good Faith Undefined

The language of the LPA does not define good faith. For that reason, the Court of Chancery decided to use the UCC definition of "good faith" because it is "at least" as broad at the common law definition. This Court has never held that the UCC definition of good faith applies to limited partnership agreements.

The UCC applies to specific kinds of contracts, but not to limited partnerships. If the parties wanted to use the UCC definition of good faith, they could have so provided in the LPA or incorporated it as a defined term by reference. Because neither alternative was chosen by the parties to the LPA, the Court of Chancery inappropriately applied the UCC definition of good faith to the LPA.

The "good faith" provision in LPA section 3.10(a)(ii) provides the standard by which to measure the Limited Partners' actions. The LPA's contractual duty requires the Limited Partners "in good faith [to] determine that such removal is necessary for the best interest of the [Limited] Partnership." To determine whether the Limited Partners breached the LPA's contractual duty of good faith, we must first analyze what standard the LPA imposes.

. . . In the LPA before us, the use of the term "good faith" is in the context of ensuring the Limited Partners do not arbitrarily or capriciously remove the General Partner.

Good Faith/Bad Faith

Many centuries ago, Aristotle observed that we "often gain knowledge of (a) a characteristic by the opposite characteristic, and (b) of characteristics by those things in which they are exhibited." It follows, Aristotle then noted, that if one term in a pair of opposites is used in more than one sense, the other term will also be used in more than one sense. Good faith and bad faith are illustrative examples of opposite characteristics—as described by Aristotle—in that each is used in more than one sense and thereby informs our understanding of each other. . . .

In our recent opinion in *Brinckerhoff v. Enbridge Energy Company, Inc.*, [67 A.3d 369 (Del. 2013)], we defined the characteristic of good faith by its opposite characteristic—bad faith. We applied a traditional common law definition of the business judgment rule to define a limited partnership agreement's good faith requirement. We used the formula describing conduct that falls outside business judgment protection, namely, an action "so far beyond the bounds of reasonable judgment that it seems essentially inexplicable on any ground other than bad faith." That definition of good faith, as set forth in *Brinckerhoff*, is appropriately applied in this case as well.

Record Supports Removal

Section 3.10(a)(ii) required the Limited Partners to determine in good faith that the removal of DV Realty was "necessary in the best interest of the Limited Partnership." Applying the definition in *Brinckerhoff*, that determination will be considered to be in good faith unless the Limited Partners went "so far beyond the bounds of reasonable judgment that it seems essentially inexplicable on any ground other than bad faith." The record establishes that, as the Managing Partner, DV Realty had repeatedly breached its obligation under section 11.5(a) of the LPA to deliver to the Limited Partners audited financial statements on time—by April 30 following the close of each year. The audited financial statements for 2008 were delivered 173 days late (on October 20, 2009); the audited financial statements for 2009 were delivered 303 days late (on March 9, 2011); and the audited financial statements for 2010 were 337 days late as of the time trial commenced (April 2, 2012).

Given these undisputed facts, the Court of Chancery correctly found that the Limited Partners "have shown that the Managing Partner's continuous failure to have the Limited Partnership's audited [f]inancial statements completed in the time prescribed by section 11.5 provided them with a good faith belief that the Managing Partner needed to be removed for the best interest of the Limited Partnership." As the Court of Chancery explained, "when a limited partnership agreement places, on a general partner, the duty of having the limited partnership's audited financials completed by a specific time, and the general partner consistently fails to meet that duty, it is objectively reasonable to believe that [it] is necessary in the best interest of the limited partnership to replace that general partner." The Court of Chancery also found DV Realty's rebuttal—that the timely issuance of audited financial statements would result in the auditor's "going concern" qualification—did not excuse DV Realty's failure, as the Managing Partner, to timely provide audited financial statements as the LPA required.

The proper good faith standard called for by section 3.10(a)(ii) of the LPA is purely subjective. Therefore, the Court of Chancery ruled incorrectly that "good faith" as used in the LPA, includes both subjective good faith—"honesty in fact"—and an element of objectivity—"reasonable commercial standards of fair dealing" as provided in the UCC. Nevertheless, applying the subjective standard of good faith to the evidence in the record, we hold that the Court of Chancery properly concluded that the Limited Partners met the contractual standard for removal of the Managing Partner "without Cause" set forth in section 3.10(a)(ii) of the LPA.

That is, the Limited Partners "in good faith determine[d] that such removal [was] necessary for the best interest of the [Limited] Partnership."

3. Suits by Limited Partners

In *Klebanow v. New York Produce Exch.*, 344 F.2d 294, 297 (2d Cir. 1965), the court was presented with the question whether limited partners can sue on behalf of the partnership when the partnership and its liquidating partner allegedly have rendered themselves unable to sue. In a well-known and highly regarded opinion, Judge Friendly decided that a suit of this nature was maintainable, despite § 26 of ULPA. A brief excerpt from the opinion is contained below:

> A limited partner, barred from using his name in the firm title, said to lack "property rights" in partnership assets, and presumed to have priority over other partners in the distribution of assets, does have some resemblance to a creditor. However, in the main, a limited partner is more like a shareholder, often expecting a share of the profits, subordinated to general creditors, having some control over direction of the enterprise by his veto on the admission of new partners, and able to examine books and "have on demand true and full information of all things affecting the partnership. . . ." See [ULPA §§ 9, 10, 23]. That the limited partner is immune to personal liability for partnership debts save for his original investment, is not thought to be an "owner" of partnership property, and does not manage the business may distinguish him from general partners but strengthens his resemblance to the stockholder; and even as to his preference in dissolution, he resembles the preferred stockholder. Indeed, it makes considerably greater sense to clothe the instant appellants with whatever descriptive phrase is necessary to enable them to sue on behalf of the partnership than to entertain derivative suits by persons owning a few shares in giant corporations, especially if the shares are non-participating redeemable preferred. . . .
>
> The district judge was influenced to a contrary view by the limited partner's right to have a "dissolution and winding up by decree of court," N.Y. Partnership Law [10(1)(c)], presumably for the same causes as a general partner, [citing UPA § 32] in which the court may, in its discretion, appoint a receiver. But we see no reason why such possibilities should prevent the speedier and more effective remedy of suit by a limited partner, any more than the beneficiary's right to ask that a trustee be instructed or removed prevents suit by him when the trustee has wrongfully refused. We would indeed expect that the New York courts would require strong allegations and proof of disqualification or wrongful refusal by the general partners before allowing a limited partner to sue on the partnership's behalf—a mere difference of opinion would be nowhere near enough. . . .

In *CML V, LLC v. Bax*, 6 A.3d 238 (Del. Ch. 2010), the Delaware Chancery Court was faced with the question of whether a creditor of an LLC had standing to maintain a derivative action. The court ultimately ruled that it did not, in an opinion that is excerpted in Chapter 15 below. In the course of that opinion, the court discussed whether creditors of a limited partnership have standing to maintain a derivative action on behalf of the partnership, writing:

> The debate over limited partner derivative standing dates back over a century. In 1822, New York adopted the country's first limited partnership statute. In 1916, the National Conference of Commissioners on Uniform State Laws ("NCCUSL") promulgated the original Uniform Limited Partnership Act ("ULPA"). *Id.* Every state except Louisiana eventually adopted it in some form, with Delaware following suit in 1973.

> ULPA did not explicitly authorize derivative actions, and courts split on whether a limited partner could sue derivatively. The majority rule recognized that limited partners could sue derivatively by analogizing them to stockholders and trust beneficiaries. . . .

> In 1973, Delaware was the last state to adopt ULPA. While taking much from the uniform act, the Delaware drafters included a number of unique provisions, including express statutory authorization for limited partner derivative actions.

> . . . .

> Comparing Section 1732 of the LP Act [authorizing limited partners to bring derivative actions] with Section 327 of the DGCL [Delaware General Corporation Law] reveals close parallels. Both are non-exclusive statutes. Section 1732(a) establishes a non-exclusive right of a limited partner to sue derivatively ("An action *may* be brought in the right of a limited partnership to procure a judgment in its favor by a limited partner."). In language paralleling Section 327, Section 1732(b) then provides that "[i]n any such action"-*i.e.*, an action in which the plaintiff is a limited partner-the contemporaneous ownership requirement must be met. Delaware's original foray into derivative standing for alternative entities thus tracked Section 327, authorized limited partner derivative actions and imposed restrictions on them, but did not otherwise purport to limit who could sue derivatively.

> In 1976, NCCUSL promulgated RULPA, which was "intended to modernize the prior uniform law while retaining the special character of limited partnerships . . . Following Delaware's example, RULPA added provisions addressing a limited partner's right to maintain a derivative action, which became RULPA Sections 1001 to 1004. Section 1001, entitled "Right of Action," stated:

> A limited partner may bring an action in the right of a limited partnership to recover a judgment in its favor if general partners with authority to do so have refused to bring the action or if an effort to cause those general partners to bring the action is not likely to succeed.

RULPA, *supra*, § 1001, 6B U.L.A. 370. Section 1002, entitled "Proper Plaintiff," provided:

> In a derivative action, the plaintiff must be a partner at the time of bringing the action and (i) at the time of the transaction of which he complains or (ii) his status as a partner had devolved upon him by operation of law or pursuant to the terms of the partnership agreement from a person who was a partner at the time of the transaction.

RULPA, *supra*, § 1002, 6B U.L.A. 378. NCCUSL's derivative standing provisions mark the first use of exclusive language.

I have not been able to discern why NCCUSL drafted the derivative standing provisions in this fashion. The prefatory note to the 1976 version of RULPA states simply that "Article 10 of the Act authorizes derivative actions to be brought by limited partners." RULPA, *supra*, Prefatory Note, 6B U.L.A. 5. The commentary to Sections 1001 and 1002 remarks only that the respective sections are "new." RULPA, *supra*, §§ 1001, 1002, 6B U.L.A. 370, 378.

To a reader aware of Section 327 and the contemporaneous ownership requirement, it is not immediately clear that NCCUSL intended Sections 1001 and 1002 to be exclusive. Read literally, Section 1001 is not exclusive. It states only that "[a] limited partner *may* bring an action in the right of a limited partnership." It does not say that no one else can sue in the name of the limited partnership, only that a limited partner *may* sue if the general partners with authority to sue have refused, or if efforts to make them sue would not be likely to succeed. If anything, Section 1001 appears geared towards adopting the corporate requirement of demand futility [that is, demand is excused if it would futile to make a demand]. Section 1002 follows immediately after Section 1001 and limits the circumstances under which a partner can sue by imposing the contemporaneous ownership requirement. Although it stated that a plaintiff "must be a partner," Section 1002 focuses principally on the *timing* of ownership. Of the section's 66 words, 56 address this subject.

Given the close connection between Sections 1001 and 1002 and the obvious intent to transplant the demand and contemporaneous ownership requirements into the LP corpus, one could readily imagine that the NCCUSL scribes did not consciously intend to change the rules of derivative standing. They simply may have wanted a straightforward, actively voiced provision. In other words, rather than pondering the subtleties of standing, they may have been heeding the guidance of grammarians.

When presented with NCCUSL's work, however, the architects of the Delaware LP Act faced a clear choice. Unlike NCCUSL, which was writing on a blank slate, the LP Act already had a derivative action standing provision. Section 1732 was non-exclusive and closely tracked Section 327. The drafters did not have to go the RULPA route. When they presented Delaware's proposed version of RULPA to the General Assembly in 1982, it again included uniquely Delawarean sections. Yet the drafters chose to replace Section 1732 with the facially exclusive RULPA versions. In New York, the only other jurisdiction with a pre-RULPA derivative standing provision, the legislators retained their non-exclusive language. *See* N.Y. P'ship Law § 115-a. At least for Delaware, the decision to implement the RULPA provisions suggests a conscious intent to make statutory standing exclusive.

In the decades since *Klebanow* was decided, corporate derivative actions became more common and the considerable jurisprudence that developed has influenced a parallel, though not identical, development for limited partnerships, as the next case demonstrates.

Anglo American Security Fund v. S.R. Global International Fund

Court of Chancery of Delaware
829 A.2d 143 (2003)

CHANDLER, CHANCELLOR.

Plaintiffs, Anglo American Security Fund, L.P., Diversified Long Term Growth Fund, L.P., Sterling Grace Capital Management, L.P., Drake Associates, L.P., The Lorraine G. Grace Trust 1487, and Oliver R. Grace Junior Trust 90 II, bring this action against defendants, S.R. Global International Fund, L.P. (the "Fund") Sloane Robinson Investment (Cayman), Ltd., ("Sloane") the general partner of the Fund, and Ernst & Young LLP, ("E & Y") the Fund's independent auditors. Plaintiffs allege that Sloane breached its fiduciary duties to the limited partners of the Fund; that the Fund and Sloane breached the Fund's limited partnership agreement ("Agreement") and were negligent; that E & Y made negligent misrepresentations in the Fund's audited financial statements and aided and abetted Sloane's breach of fiduciary duty; and that all defendants engaged in fraud against the limited partners of the Fund. The defendants challenge the standing of the plaintiffs to bring these claims and have moved to dismiss the complaint under Court of Chancery Rule 12(b)(6) for failure to state a claim and under Court of Chancery Rule 9(b) for failure to state with particularity the circumstances constituting the alleged fraud.

I. Statement of Facts

The plaintiffs each became limited partners of the Fund in or about August 1997, with initial capital investments ranging from over $0.4 million to approximately $11.9 million. The Fund is a Delaware limited partnership created "to serve as a fund through which the assets of its Partners may be utilized" in investing in various types of securities and other financial instruments or to act as what is commonly termed a hedge fund. The Fund establishes in its books a capital account for each partner consisting of the partner's original capital contribution, plus any additional capital contributions, minus any capital withdrawals, and adjusted at the end of each fiscal period for the partner's proportional share of net profits and losses. The Fund is obligated to provide the partners with unaudited quarterly reports and an audited annual financial statement as well as information necessary for federal income tax purposes. Limited partners of the Fund are not permitted to assign their interests without written consent of the general partner and must provide written notice to the Fund thirty business days prior to making any capital withdrawal. Sloane, the general partner of the Fund, is a company organized under the laws of the Cayman Islands. E & Y, the Fund's auditor, is a Delaware limited liability partnership.

As of December 31, 1999, Sloane's capital account in the Fund was credited with $22,350,704 or 15% of the net profits to the limited partners in 1999.[12] On February 18, 2000, Sloane withdrew $22,350,704 from its capital account. The credit to Sloane's capital account was recorded in the Fund's audited 1999 financial statement ("1999 Statement"). The 1999 Statement was provided to the limited partners in March 2000. Although it did report other post-year-end capital contributions and withdrawals as "Subsequent Events," the 1999 Statement did not report Sloane's February 18 withdrawal. This withdrawal was reported in the Fund's quarterly statement for the first quarter of 2000, which statement was received by the limited partners on May 9, 2000.

The plaintiffs take issue with the withdrawal on the bases that (1) the withdrawal overdrew Sloane's capital account because substantial losses sustained by the Fund during January and February 2000 had reduced the available balance in Sloane's capital account below $22,350,704; (2) the Agreement permits the general partner to withdraw funds only on the last day of the month; and (3) the withdrawal should have been disclosed as a Subsequent Event in the 1999 Statement.

III. Analysis

A. Standing of Plaintiffs

Defendants move to dismiss all claims on the basis that they are derivative in nature and the plaintiffs do not have standing to bring a derivative claim. Delaware partnership law requires in a derivative action that the plaintiff be a partner (or assignee of one) at the time of bringing the action and at the time of the challenged transaction. The Court is entreated to take judicial notice of Fund records indicating that all plaintiffs had withdrawn from the fund by the time this action was filed. These records are not integral to and are not incorporated by reference into the complaint and the Court has not considered them in ruling on these motions to dismiss. Nonetheless, if I determine that the action is derivative in nature the

---

12. [4] Section 9.01(b) of the Agreement provides that when the net profits exceed net losses in any fiscal year, 15% of the excess is to be debited from the capital accounts of the limited partners and "shall be credited as of the end of the fiscal year to the Capital Account of the General Partner."

Court may then consider extrinsic documents presented by the defendants indicating that the plaintiffs lack standing to bring a derivative action, thereby converting the motion to one for summary judgment under Rule 56. Therefore, I now turn to the defendants' argument that the claims in this case are derivative.

The test for distinguishing direct from derivative claims in the context of a limited partnership is substantially the same as that used when the underlying entity is a corporation. In both instances the determination is made by careful application of a rather nuanced test.[13] The test looks to the nature of the injury and to the nature of remedy that could result if the plaintiffs are successful. When a plaintiff alleges either an injury that is different from what is suffered by other shareholders (or partners) or one that involves a contractual right of shareholders (or partners) that is independent of the entity's rights, the claim is direct. If the injury is one that affects all partners proportionally to their *pro rata* interests in the corporation, the claim is derivative. In a derivative action the plaintiff sues for an injury done to the partnership and any recovery of damages is paid to the partnership. Conversely, in a direct action the plaintiff sues to redress an injury suffered by the individual plaintiff and damages recovered are paid directly to the plaintiff who was injured. In every case the court must determine from the complaint whether the claims are direct or derivative and may not rely on either party's characterization. Because harm to the entity will almost inevitably harm the stakeholders and because the entity itself is in some ways no more than an amalgamation of a certain subset of stakeholders' interests, differentiation of direct from derivative claims can be elusive.

To further complicate matters, whereas corporations are largely creatures of statute with some limited contractual flexibility, limited partnerships offer greater contractual flexibility with only a few statutory constraints. Consequently, the structure and function of a limited partnership is sometimes analogous to the corporate model with the limited partners having similar rights and responsibilities as corporate shareholders and the general partner acting in much the same capacity as a corporate board of directors—but not necessarily so. Application of corporate law rules to disputes related to a limited partnership necessitates a bit of flexibility. This is true because the facts unique to a limited partnership dispute include the contents of the limited partnership agreement—how it specifies or modifies the entity's function and structure and the rights and responsibilities of the general and limited partners. In his opinion in *In re Cencom Cable Income Partners, L.P. Litigation*, then-Vice Chancellor Steele noted that, "In the partnership context, the relationships among the parties may be so simple and the circumstances so clear-cut that the distinction between direct and derivative claims becomes irrelevant."[14]

---

13. [14] *See In re Cencom Cable Income Partners, L.P. Litig.*, 2000 Del. Ch. Lexis 10 at *7 (Del. Ch.) (citing Donald J. Wolfe, Jr. & Michael A. Pittenger, Corporate and Commercial Practice in the Delaware Court of Chancery § 9-2(a), at 517 (1998) [hereinafter Wolfe & Pittenger]).

14. [22] *In re Cencom Cable Income Partners, L.P. Litig.*, 2000 Del. Ch. Lexis 10, at *8.

Similarly, in some instances, the relationships among the parties and the function and structure of the partnership itself may diverge from the corporate model so dramatically that some claims, which in a corporate context might be classified as derivative, *must* be brought as direct claims in order to enable the injured parties to recover while preventing a windfall to individuals or entities whose interests were not injured.

The essence of the plaintiffs' claims is that Sloane withdrew funds from its capital account in violation of the partnership agreement; that this withdrawal exceeded the balance in the account; and that timely disclosure of the withdrawal was not given to the limited partners. It is undisputed that on February 18, 2000, Sloane withdrew $22,350,704 from its capital account. The plaintiffs contend that this withdrawal breached the Agreement, which permits the general partner to make withdrawals only on the last day of the month. When the 1999 Statement was prepared and distributed to the limited partners, it disclosed (as "Subsequent Events") information about deposits and distributions related to the capital accounts of limited partners that occurred after December 31, 1999, but did not disclose that on February 18, 2000, the general partner withdrew over $22 million from its capital account. Plaintiffs claim that this withdrawal is material because it amounts to the general partner having "bailed out" of the Fund. Indeed, the plaintiffs contend that due to losses sustained by the Fund in January and February 2000, the balance of the capital account of the general partner, as of February 18, 2000, would have been less than the amount that was withdrawn, causing a negative balance in the account. Because the 1999 Statement contained other information of a similar nature (post-year-end withdrawals by limited partners) and because the withdrawal was material, the failure to disclose it in the 1999 Statement rendered the statement materially false and misleading.

The defendants point out that the various claims made by the plaintiffs allege only two distinct types of injury, either diminution in value of the fund or misdisclosure of the withdrawal, each of which constitute derivative rather than direct claims. All claims with respect to the fact of the February 18 withdrawal, according to the defendants, state merely a diminution in value of the Funds assets, which injures the limited partners only in proportion to their *pro rata* interest in the Fund. All claims related to the failure to report the withdrawal in the 1999 Statement, defendants argue, are similarly derivative under the recent Court of Chancery ruling in *Manzo v. Rite Aid Corp.*[15]

1. Diminution of Value of the Fund

Delaware corporate and limited partnership cases have agreed that a diminution of the value of a business entity is classically derivative in nature. In *Cencom*, however, then-Vice Chancellor Steele held that two claims, which "at first appear derivative in nature since the alleged injury devalues the partnership's assets," were nonetheless direct claims due to special circumstances present in the context of that

---

15. [23] 2002 Del. Ch. Lexis 147 (Del. Ch.).

limited partnership.[16] Similarly, for reasons discussed below, I conclude that the operation and function of the Fund as specified in the Agreement diverge so radically from the traditional corporate model that the claims made in the complaint must be brought as direct claims.

Cencom provides an instructive analytical framework for categorizing the claims at issue here. That opinion held that "superimposing derivative pleading requirements . . . serves no useful or meaningful public policy purpose" in the context of certain narrow factual situations that may arise with respect to an alternative (non-corporate) entity.[17] The court identified two discernable purposes for classifying claims as derivative: (1) to ensure that any remedy accrues to the entity that sustained the injury but does not confer benefits on wrongdoers nor provide windfalls to the uninjured and (2) to provide a gatekeeping function that will both promote corporate resolution of internal problems and deter strike suits.[18] Because, in *Cencom*, (1) there was no ongoing conduct (the partnership being in liquidation); (2) the only two parties to the partnership (the class of limited partners and the general partner) were clearly adversaries in the pending litigation; and (3) the claims had proven to be sufficiently meritorious to survive a motion for summary judgment, the court determined that imposition of derivative requirements would impede efficient and final resolution of the claims and would simply "make[ ] no sense."[19]

Due to the structure and operation of the Fund, whenever the value of the Fund is reduced, the injury accrues irrevocably and almost immediately to the current partners but will not harm those who later become partners. Although other types of injuries could harm the Fund as an entity in ways that appropriately could be challenged in a derivative action,[20] injuries that result in a direct reduction of the Fund's assets will effect an almost immediate reduction in the capital accounts of each of the existing partners. Such losses confer only a fleeting injury to the Fund, one that is immediately and irrevocably passed through to the partners. When an injured partner withdraws from the partnership, the partner's capital account has already been diminished by any and all diminutions of value to the Fund from the time of entering the partnership until the time of withdrawal. There are no successors in interest to partners so injured because there are no "shares" sold to someone

---

16. [26] 2000 Del. Ch. Lexis 10, at *12.

17. *Id.* at *9.

18. [28] *Id.* at *13–17.

19. [29] *Id.* at *13.

20. [30] For example, if the general partner violated § 3.03 of the Agreement and invested in a company for the purpose of exercising control, thereby possibly exposing the Fund to liability as a controlling shareholder, this theoretically could form the basis of a claim that may be derivative in nature. Similarly, if the general partner were to engage in some (perhaps illegal) activities that led to restrictions being placed on the Fund's ability to engage in certain types of potentially beneficial investment transactions, the harm would accrue more directly to the Fund as an entity. Any harm to the investors would be indirect and would cease when an investor withdrew from the Fund. Such a scenario suggests another theoretical basis for a derivative claim.

else, any withdrawing partner's interest in the entity is liquidated. Any recovery obtained by the Fund in a derivative action cannot provide a remedy to wronged former partners nor to their (non-existent) successors in interest. If additional partners are later admitted, they suffer no injury from previous reductions in the value of the fund because their capital accounts will reflect the full amount of their initial investments adjusted only for events occurring after their admission as partners. Such newly admitted limited partners would receive a windfall if the Fund were to recover damages for diminution of Fund value prior to their admission as limited partners. Characterizing the plaintiffs' claims as derivative would thus have the perverse effect of denying standing (and therefore recovery) to parties who were actually injured by the challenged transactions while granting ultimate recovery (and therefore a windfall) to parties who were not.[21] This result is antithetical to the first purpose of derivative litigation identified in *Cencom*, does nothing to further the gatekeeping functions of derivative litigation requirements, and, in the words of Vice Chancellor Steele, "makes no sense." I hold that the plaintiffs' claims related to Sloane's February 18, 2000, withdrawal, are direct claims.

2. Misdisclosure in the 1999 Statement

In support of their contention that claims related to non-disclosure of the withdrawal in the Fund's 1999 Statement are derivative, the defendants argue that if the plaintiffs' allegations were true, the plaintiffs have alleged, as did the plaintiff in *Manzo*, only that they "experienced an injury suffered by all [investors] in proportion to their pro rata ownership interest." At first blush, *Manzo* appears to be apposite. The plaintiff in *Manzo* challenged omissions and false disclosures in annual financial statements and other information disclosed to the Securities Exchange Commission, the shareholders, and the public over a period of three years. The specific injury alleged was unclear, but the plaintiff suggested that the misdisclosures resulted, at the very least, in depriving her and a class of similarly situated shareholders of accurate financial information upon which to base decisions to buy, sell, or hold shares in the corporation. The Court held in *Manzo* that this injury was shared equally by *all* stockholders and any injury would derive to them only in proportion to their *pro rata* ownership interest and did not implicate any contractual right of shareholders that was not similarly a right of the corporation as a whole. Therefore the claim was derivative. Here, plaintiffs allege that at least one effect of the two-month delay in disclosing to the limited partners that the general partner had bailed out of the Fund was to deprive the limited partners of the same opportunity to "cut their losses" promptly before the value of the Fund's investments declined further. Nonetheless, the structure and function of the Fund, as described

---

21. [31] Although limited partners admitted to partnership after the injury would not have standing to bring a derivative claim because they were not partners at the time of the challenged transaction, 6 *Del. C.* § 17-1002, they would reap the rewards if the claim were brought derivatively by a limited partner that did have standing because the recovery would derive to the Fund and, therefore, to all of the partners in proportion to their *pro rata* interests.

in the terms of the Agreement, is so dissimilar to the corporate structure in which the *Manzo* claims were brought, that the reasoning and policy of that opinion are inapposite to the claims made in the complaint and, in any event, the disclosure claim seems to implicate a contractual right of the limited partners that is not similarly a right of the Fund itself.

Under the terms of the Agreement, the limited partners have absolutely no control over the governance and management of the Fund; the limited partners are entitled to very limited routine disclosures regarding the activities and performance of the Fund; the limited partners' interests in the Fund are not freely transferable or tradable; the liquidity of the limited partners' investment is somewhat restricted and, perhaps, most importantly for purposes of this motion to dismiss, the Fund exists solely to utilize "the assets of its Partners" in various investment vehicles and maintains its books to account separately for the value of each partner's assets at all times. The Fund operates more like a bank with the individual partners each having accounts—albeit accounts that are not federally insured or afforded virtually any regulatory protections against loss of the assets invested. This is not a typical corporate business venture in which the value to the investors is based not only upon the physical assets of the entity but also upon the speculative value of the entity as a going concern. Other than a general partner's interest in management fees, there is no going-concern value. Yet, the limited partners have no capacity to replace a general partner that fails properly to represent the limited partners' interests. The only alternative available to a dissatisfied limited partner is to withdraw from the Fund.

Even the choice of withdrawing is impossible to implement instantaneously because the Agreement provides that limited partners may withdraw only on the last day of the month and only after giving thirty business days notice. This is six weeks at a minimum. The Fund is designed for the purpose of engaging in some highly speculative investments. This can be very rewarding as the partners found in fiscal year 1999 and highly risky as was discovered in 2000. In every event, such investments tend to be highly volatile and a delay of six or more weeks in withdrawing one's funds from such a vehicle can lead to massive changes to the value of the account from the date the decision is made to withdraw until the funds may actually be withdrawn.

The plaintiff limited partners each appear to be sophisticated parties that understood and voluntarily accepted the terms of the Agreement and assumed the risks of investing in the Fund in order potentially to reap the rewards of undertaking such risks. As such, these sophisticated investors reasonably expected that the general partner would fulfill at least the obligations it voluntarily accepted under the Agreement and as a fiduciary. As the defendants correctly point out, Section 12.05 of the Agreement specifies the obligations of the general partner to report to the limited partners—unaudited quarterly reports of the fund performance, an audited financial report annually, and a year-end report to each partner indicating the necessary gain and loss information for Federal income tax purposes. Thus, the 1999

Statement was contractually required to be provided to the partners and any claims that it was incomplete, or materially false or misleading would state a direct claim.

. . . .

[The court denied the defendants' motion to dismiss for failure to state a claim.]

Notes

1. The ability of limited partners to bring a derivative suit is expressly recognized in Article 10 of RULPA.

2. Rules of civil procedure require corporate shareholders, before bringing a derivative action, to make a demand on the board of directors or allege with particularity why such a demand would be futile. *See, e.g.,* Rule 23.1 of the Federal Rules of Civil Procedure. These provisions apply to derivative actions filed by limited partners as well. *See, e.g., Diamond v. Pappathanasi,* 935 N.E.2d 340 (Mass. Ct. App. 2010).

3. As noted above, courts look to corporate precedents to determine the parameters of the derivative action. For instance, in *Hirsch v. Jones Intercable, Inc.,* 984 P.2d 629 (Colo. 1999), the Colorado Supreme Court considered whether the general partner of a limited partnership could cause the action to be dismissed in the same way that a corporate board can cause the dismissal of a corporate derivative suit. *Hirsch* involved a derivative action brought by the limited partners in three limited partnerships against Jones Intercable, Inc., the general partner for all three partnerships. The partnerships had entered into a joint venture among themselves ("Venture") for the purpose of investing in the cable TV business. The partnership agreements provided that Jones as general partner could purchase cable systems from Venture and that the price paid would be the average of three separate independent appraisals of the property involved. Jones purchased a cable system from Venture, paying the appraised price. Nevertheless, the limited partners brought suit alleging breach of fiduciary duty because the price "grossly undervalued" the system sold. Jones moved to dismiss, alleging that a demand was not made upon it prior to the suit being brought. The trial court denied that motion and ordered that Jones appoint an independent counsel, subject to court approval, "to review, consider, and report on the demand." The board of directors of Jones appointed an attorney to investigate plaintiffs' claims. Plaintiffs did not object to the individual appointed and the trial court approved the appointment. The Independent Counsel's report concluded that plaintiffs' claims were not meritorious and that it would not be appropriate or desirable for Jones's board to pursue the claims. Nevertheless, the trial court denied Jones's motion for summary judgment based on the report and an appeal followed. After agreeing that a demand upon Jones would be futile in this case because Jones would be suing itself, the Colorado Supreme Court stated as follows:

> ... We further conclude that under the Colorado Uniform Limited Partnership Act of 1981, the rights of the parties as to derivative actions are much like those of shareholders. We evaluate the action accordingly, and follow the New York approach governing court involvement in corporate

derivative actions. That is, once a special litigation committee (SLC) is duly appointed by the general partner and acts on behalf of the partnership in seeking to dismiss the action brought in the name of the partnership, the trial court's role is limited to determining the authority, independence, and good faith of the SLC. Because no Colorado case had set out this standard previously, the trial court did not make such an inquiry and findings here. Accordingly, we return the case to the trial court for that inquiry and for further proceedings consistent with this opinion.

Id. at 631.

The court contrasted its approach with the Delaware approach, where "even if the court is satisfied that the SLC is disinterested and independent, the court then applies its own business judgment to determine whether the claim should be dismissed." *Id.* at 637. The court stated instead that, "We agree with the Court of Appeals of New York that because most courts 'are ill equipped and infrequently called on to evaluate what are and must be essentially business judgments,'... the role of a Colorado trial court in reviewing an SLC's decision regarding derivative litigation should be limited to inquiring into the independence and good faith of the committee." *Id.* at 638.

4. A subsequent decision of the Colorado Court of Appeals, *Day v. Parachute Invest. Holdings, LLC*, 251 P.3d 1225, 1228 (Colo. Ct. App. 2010), made clear that the party seeking dismissal on the basis of a report by a special litigation committee bears the burden of persuasion:

> Consistent with the majority view, we will impose the burden of persuasion on those seeking dismissal based on an SLC's report. Such a motion is not, strictly speaking, a summary judgment motion because it does not address the merits of the claims. Rather, it is "a hybrid motion" with a standard "akin to summary judgment."

> The moving party has the "ultimate burden of persuasion" in showing that "there is no genuine issue as to any material fact and that the moving party is entitled to judgment as a matter of law."

5. In an action at law between limited partners, unless modified by statute, the "accounting rule" (discussed, *supra*, Chapter 12, Section H.2) applies. See *Drenis v. Haligiannis*, 452 F. Supp. 2d 418 (S.D.N.Y. 2006), where the court applied the rule.

4. Limitations on Distributions and Transfer of Interests

Distributions. RULPA provides in §§ 503 and 504 that, unless otherwise agreed, partners share profits, losses, and distributions "on the basis of the value of the contributions made by each partner." This differs from the default rule under UPA, where profits, losses, and surplus are shared equally unless otherwise agreed. Do you see why the limited partnership act might have established a different rule? It is useful to note that, as a practical matter, the allocations almost always will be established in the agreement of the partners. Re-RULPA continues this rule only as to distributions. Re-RULPA § 503 provides that distributions will be shared on the basis of the value of contributions made to the limited partnership by each partner. It contains no provision allocating profits and losses among partners. *See* § 503 cmt.

RULPA contains statutory restrictions on distributions to limited partners in its §§ 607 and 608. Section 607 contains a solvency limitation, and § 608 mandates the return of contributions received even while the firm was solvent if they are necessary to pay pre-distribution creditors (but the exposure to this liability is only up to one year for the latter situation; it is six years if the distribution was wrongful). The policy underlying these limitations probably is that this protection for creditors is the price one must pay for the privilege of limited liability. Similar restrictions apply to the LLC (see Chapter 15) and to most (but not all) LLPs. The concept of limitations on distributions may be starting to break down in the face of the arguments that they create uncertainty for limited partners and members of LLCs and LLPs, and that creditors already enjoy protection under the prohibition against fraudulent conveyances that exists generally by separate statute.

While Re-RULPA continues the solvency requirement found in RULPA, Re-RULPA does not include § 608's mandate that contributions be returned to pay pre-distribution creditors. *See* Re-RULPA §§ 508, 509.

Transfers of interest. Under what circumstances may limited partners transfer their interests? Section 702 of RULPA addresses the topic of assignment of partnership interest. Does it allow limited partners to transfer their partnership status to others, or just their rights to income and other distributions? If one cannot (in the absence of agreement of the other partners) transfer full partnership status, what is the reasoning behind this default rule, considering the passive role most limited partners play?

Temple v. White Lakes Plaza Assocs., Ltd.

Court of Appeals of Kansas
816 P.2d 399 (1991)

Before ELLIOTT, P.J., and LARSON and RULON, JJ.

RULON, JUDGE:

White Lakes Plaza Associates, Ltd. (White Lakes), defendant, appeals a district court judgment ordering that Marianna V. Temple, plaintiff, be made a limited partner in that partnership. . . .

On February 1, 1977, John Temple became a limited partner in White Lakes, a Kansas limited partnership formed for the purpose of operating the White Lakes Plaza apartment complex in Topeka, Kansas. . . . John's interest in the partnership's net income and losses was 5%. His wife Marianna signed the partnership agreement, consenting to its terms.

The partnership agreement gives the limited partners no authority to act for or bind the partnership. The agreement further provides that all limited partners and the general partner must consent to (1) a termination of the partnership other than in accordance with the agreement; (2) amendment of the agreement; and (3) sale of all or substantially all of the partnership's assets.

The certificate of limited partnership contains the following provision:

> "A Limited Partner may sell, assign or transfer his limited partnership interest; however, any such purchaser shall only be entitled to be admitted as a Substituted Limited Partner if the Assignor so designates his intention in the instrument of assignment, and the General Partner consents thereto, the denial or granting of which shall be at the sole discretion of the General Partner. The General Partner does not have the right to admit additional Limited Partners without the consent of the Limited Partners."

. . . On January 23, 1986, a decree was filed by a Florida court dissolving the marriage of John and Marianna. As part of the property settlement, the Florida court awarded Marianna "100% of the interest of [John] in the . . . limited partnership[ ] known as . . . White Lakes Plaza." . . .

In late January 1986, John executed an assignment of his partnership interest to Marianna. The assignment provided that John intended Marianna to become a substituted limited partner. . . .

In a letter to general partner Fritz Duda, John acknowledged that Duda had told him the partnership interest transfer would not be allowed "because of the uniqueness of this partnership and particularly the unanimous vote of the limited partners needed for ultimate sale." . . . After further correspondence among Marianna, John, and Duda, Marianna ultimately filed suit in Shawnee District Court. . . .

During the bench trial, Marianna testified that she wished to become a limited partner in White Lakes for advantageous treatment under the tax laws. She stated the partnership was a passive income generator that she could use to offset passive losses. . . .

During his testimony, Duda . . . testified that from her behavior in the divorce proceeding, her filing of the instant litigation, and his discussions with John, he believed Marianna "would be litigious, would be conceivably an obstructionist." . . .

The district court essentially balanced honoring the Florida property award under full faith and credit against preservation of the integrity of a Kansas limited partnership, and found "no overwhelming legitimate reason exists" not to give the property award full faith and credit. The district court specifically stated "[t]he limited partnership will suffer no irreparable harm by reason of admission of Marianna Temple as an investor" and ordered Marianna be made a substituted limited partner without having "to comply with the specific requirements of the limited partnership agreement and the Kansas Limited Partnership Act." . . .

Before us, White Lakes argues that the partnership certificate and agreement, as permitted by Kansas statute, place restrictions on the admission of substituted limited partners. Consistent with his power granted by the partnership agreement, Duda as general partner denied Marianna admission as a substituted limited partner, properly exercising his discretion. White Lakes further contends that in ordering Marianna to be given partner status, the district court improperly substituted its discretion for that of general partner Duda. . . .

In resolving this issue, the applicable statutory framework for our review is the Kansas Revised Uniform Limited Partnership Act (RULPA). [The court quotes §§ 702 and 704]. . . . RULPA does not prohibit the grant of such authority to a general partner.

Marianna argues that the above RULPA provisions allowing for restrictions on the admission of substituted limited partners should not be applied to a partner's involuntary assignment of his or her interest, such as that ordered by a divorce decree. Any such ruling, however, would be contrary to principles developed in general partnership law. The Uniform Partnership Act and case law developed thereunder have been applied to limited partnerships. . . . A distinguishing feature of a partnership is the rule of *delectus personae* or choice of the person. . . .

To support her argument, Marianna cites cases where courts have held that restrictions on transfer of corporate stock apply only to voluntary transfers: . . . Corporate law has been applied to limited partnerships. 59A Am. Jur. 2d, *Partnership* § 1236. However, application of the above cases [cases cited by plaintiff omitted] dealing with transfers of corporate stock to allow the assignee of a limited partnership interest under a divorce decree to become a substituted limited partner would unfavorably affect the distinctive nature of the partnership form of business association. The remaining partners in the limited partnership should not have an individual forced on them as a partner. Furthermore, the ability of a limited partner in White Lakes to transfer or assign his or her interest is not being contested by the partnership. Only the right of Marianna, an assignee, to become a limited partner merely by virtue of the assignment is being challenged.

We agree the nature of a limited partner's role in the management of the partnership's business differs from that of a general partner in either a general or limited partnership. However, in the instant case, White Lakes is composed of a comparatively small group of limited partners who, along with the general partner, are experienced in the business of the partnership — real estate investment and management. Under the partnership agreement, each limited partner has the authority to veto a decision "affecting the basic structure of the [p]artnership": termination, amendment of the agreement, and sale of assets. It would be contrary to the principles of partnership law to require White Lakes to accept as a substituted limited partner someone who has been rejected under the partnership agreement's provisions for becoming a substituted limited partner. We believe Marianna is an assignee of John's interest and therefore has the rights due an assignee under the agreement, but she cannot be made a substituted limited partner outside of the agreement or in contravention of RULPA.

Consistent with RULPA, the partnership agreement, and the divorce decree, John could and did transfer his share of profits and losses and the right to receive distributions. As an assignee, Marianna is also entitled to receive such allocation of income, gain, loss, deduction, or credit to which John was entitled. John, having transferred all his interest, ceased to be a partner. . . .

We affirm that portion of the district court judgment which awarded Marianna the earnings from the assigned partnership interest being held in escrow, but reverse the portion of the judgment making Marianna a substituted limited partner in the partnership.

5. Duties of Limited Partners

KE Property Management, Inc. v. 275 Madison Management Corp.[22]

Court of Chancery of Delaware
No. 12683, 1993 Del. Ch. LEXIS 147 (July 21, 1993)

Memorandum Opinion

HARTNETT, VICE CHANCELLOR.

Although the procedural posture in this suit is complex, the gravamen of the suit is quite simple. The issue is the control of a limited partnership based in New York and whether, under the Partnership Agreement and New York law, the fraud by the agent of the managing general partner justified the general partner's removal by a limited partner.

There is no disputed fact that prevents summary judgment for the plaintiff, a general partner, on its claim that, as a matter of law, a limited partner affiliated with it was justified in removing the general managing partner because of the fraud committed by the agent of the partner that was removed. . . .

The original plaintiff, KE Property Management, Inc. ("KE Property"), one of the general partners of 275 Madison Associates L.P., a Delaware limited partnership ("the Partnership"), seeks a declaratory judgment that the purported removal of 275 Madison Management Corp. ("275 Madison Corp."), the managing general partner of the Partnership, by KJ Capital Management, Inc. ("KJ Capital") an affiliate of plaintiff was effective. It therefore seeks to enjoin 275 Madison Corp. from purporting to act as the managing general partner. . . .

---

22. Noted in 19 Del. J. Corp. L. 805 (1993).

The essential facts are undisputed. The Partnership was formed in October 1987 for the purpose of owning a building and a ground lease at 275 Madison Avenue in New York City. Originally, there were three general partners: Harry Skydell, Udi Toledano and Joseph Mizrachi. Skydell was the original managing general partner and he arranged for the Partnership to retain Hudson Park Management Co. ("Hudson Park"), an entity controlled by Skydell, to manage the building.

In 1988, KJ Capital invested $4 million in the Partnership and was admitted as a limited partner and its affiliate KE Property [the "Kawasaki Partners"] became a general partner. Two entities owned by the Nasser family, R.A.J.N. Corp. and Belmor Co., Inc. ("the Nasser Limited Partners"), invested $6 million in the Partnership and also became limited partners.

In February 1989, the Partnership borrowed $70 million from [Kawasaki Leasing International, Inc.] ("Kawasaki Lender") to refinance its existing obligations. This loan was secured by a mortgage on the building and ground lease. Portions of this loan were sold to [seven other entities that purchased the loan] ("the Loan Participants").

That same month, 275 Madison Corp. was formed to serve as managing general partner of the Partnership in lieu of Skydell. . . . [Skydell owned a majority of the shares of 275 Madison Corp.]

The original partnership agreement was revised in July 1989 to reflect the changes made among the partners. The Revised Partnership Agreement contemplated that Hudson Park, an entity controlled by Skydell, would continue to manage the building.

Between January and May 1990, Skydell misappropriated $2 million of Partnership funds by diverting money from the Partnership's accounts at Chase Manhattan Bank. 275 Madison Corp. claims that, although Skydell was its President at the time, he committed the fraud through Hudson Park, the manager of the building, rather than in his capacity as part-owner and officer of 275 Madison Corp. However, the signature cards for the Partnership's accounts from which the funds were siphoned showed, and a representative from Chase testified, that Skydell was authorized to sign in his capacity as a representative of the managing partner. . . .

On August 15, 1990, the Nassers purchased Skydell's interest in 275 Madison Corp. for $200,000 and in November 1990 they caused 275 Madison Corp. to terminate Hudson Park's management contract. In April 1991, an audit uncovered Skydell's defalcations.

In 1990 and 1991 the Partnership experienced financial difficulties and the Nassers negotiated with the Kawasaki Lender for a restructuring of the finances of the Partnership. On July 9, 1991, on behalf of itself and the Loan Participants, the Kawasaki Lender notified the Partnership that it was in default of the loan agreement and at risk of foreclosure. 275 Madison Corp. took the position that it would be in the best interests of the Partnership for the Partnership to seek protection from its creditors under the federal bankruptcy laws. However, KE Property refused to agree, allegedly because of improper loyalty to its affiliate the Kawasaki Lender in alleged violation of its fiduciary duty to the other partners.

On August 20, 1991, KJ Capital, an affiliate of KE Property, as one of the limited partners, sent 275 Madison Corp. a letter purportedly removing it as managing general partner. Paragraph 5.07(d) of the Partnership Agreement provides, in relevant part, that "the Limited Partners may . . . by a vote of not less than 25% of the Units then outstanding, expel any General Partner if he has . . . injured the Partnership as a result of his fraud or willful misconduct in the performance of his duties as a General Partner." KJ Capital claimed that Skydell's misappropriation of $2 million constituted fraud or willful misconduct on the part of 275 Madison Corp. in its capacity as the managing general partner of the Partnership. It is not disputed that 25% of the units outstanding favored the expulsion.

275 Madison Corp., however, claims that KJ Capital used Skydell's fraud as a pretext to remove it from its position as managing general partner to prevent 275 Madison Corp. from filing for bankruptcy on behalf of the Partnership. KJ Capital allegedly acted at the behest of the Kawasaki Lender in so doing. . . . KE Property then brought this action seeking a declaratory judgment that the purported removal of 275 Madison Corp. as managing general partner by KJ Capital was effective and seeking an injunction prohibiting 275 Madison Corp. from acting on behalf of the Partnership. . . .

In addition to its other defenses, 275 Madison Corp. argues that summary judgment should be denied because the Kawasaki [Partners] acted in "bad faith" in that their real motivation in removing 275 Madison Corp. was to prevent it from taking the partnership into bankruptcy to block the foreclosure of the mortgage. Because there is a presumption that the Kawasaki [Partners] acted in good faith, defendant bears the burden of rebutting the presumption by showing the existence of bad faith.

275 Madison Corp.'s allegation of bad faith is predicated upon KJ Capital having owed a fiduciary duty to it. A general partner owes a fiduciary duty to its partners. It was, however, KJ Capital, a limited partner (rather than KE Property, a General Partner) that acted to remove 275 Madison Corp. as managing general partner.

KJ Capital, a limited partner, is controlled by the same entity that controls KE Property, a general partner. This might be sufficient to impose on KJ Capital the same fiduciary duty that KE Property has as a general partner. It is not necessary to decide that issue, however, because although the Delaware Revised Uniform Limited Partnership Act does not specifically state that a limited partner owes a fiduciary duty to a general partner it, by reference to the Delaware Uniform Partnership Act [referring to the equivalent of UPA §6(2)], [the fiduciary obligations under UPA §21 are available and can be invoked under appropriate circumstances].

Under the Delaware Uniform Partnership Law all partners owe each other fiduciary obligations. Therefore, to the extent that a partnership agreement empowers a limited partner with discretion to take actions affecting the governance of the limited partnership, the limited partner may be subject to the obligations of a fiduciary, including the obligation to act in good faith as to the other partners.

The Partnership Agreement does not leave the decision as to the removal of 275 Madison Corp. to the unlimited discretion of KJ Capital or any other partner, however. Instead, it provides that removal can only occur upon "fraud or willful conduct" injurious to the Partnership. As previously discussed [in an omitted portion], 275 Madison Corp. was legally guilty of "fraud or willful conduct" injurious to the Partnership because of the acts of its agent Skydell that are imputed to it.

An allegation of bad faith "raises essentially a question of fact," which means that such an allegation generally is sufficient to defeat a motion to dismiss or a motion for judgment on the pleadings. However, allegations unsupported by any competent evidence cannot defeat a motion for summary judgment. Where the non-moving party bears the burden of persuasion at trial, as 275 Madison Corp. does here as to overcoming the presumption of good faith, the non-moving party, after adequate opportunity for discovery, must introduce competent evidence which, if true, would rebut the presumption or summary judgment will be granted against it.

As noted above, the parties conducted extensive discovery on the issue of the propriety of 275 Madison Corp.'s removal in the bankruptcy proceedings. 275 Madison Corp. has not adduced any competent evidence to overcome the presumption of good faith of the Kawasaki Partners in removing 275 Madison Corp. All that 275 Madison Corp. has proffered is mere speculation as to what the Kawasaki Partners might do if they gain control of the enterprise. Such speculation cannot prevent the Kawasaki Partners from exerting their lawful right under the Partnership Agreement to remove 275 Madison Corp. for willful misconduct.

Summary judgment therefore must be granted to KE Property on its claim against 275 Madison Corp. . . .

Note

In *Cantor Fitzgerald, L.P. v. Cantor*, No. 16297, 2000 Del. Ch. LEXIS 43 (Mar. 13, 2000), the court decided that express duties of loyalty imposed on a limited partner under the terms of a limited partnership agreement were enforceable even if such duties do not exist separately at law or equity. The court cited the Delaware RULPA provision that emphasizes the freedom of contract.

6. Rights of Personal Creditors of Partners

1. In *Lauer Const., Inc. v. Schrift*, 716 A.2d 1096 (Md. App. 1998), the court held that a creditor could charge the interest of the general partner and that a court could order a forced sale of that debtor partner's partnership interest.

2. A creditor of a limited partner may obtain a charging order against that partner's partnership interest to satisfy a judgment against the limited partner. The charging order entitles the creditor to receive the share of partnership profits that would otherwise be distributed to the judgment debtor partner. The creditor, however,

succeeds to no other rights of the debtor partner. For instance, in *Green v. Bellerive Condos. Ltd. Pshp.*, 763 A.2d 252 (Md. App. 2000), the court held that the creditor was not entitled to receive notice of a potential partnership opportunity, even though the debtor partner was entitled to such notice under the partnership agreement. In *Baybank v. Catamount Construction, Inc.*, 693 A.2d 1163 (N.H. 1997), the court made clear that a judgment creditor with a charging order against the limited partnership interest of a judgment debtor lacks standing to obtain an order dissolving the limited partnership. Under RULPA § 802, only a partner can apply for judicial dissolution and even then dissolution can only be ordered when the court concludes that "it is not reasonably practicable to carry on the business in conformity with the partnership agreement." Plaintiff in *Baybank* could not satisfy that test.

7. Withdrawal Rights of a Limited Partner

The right of a limited partner to withdraw from the partnership and receive the value of his partnership interest is a right that has changed with different versions of the uniform limited partnership act. In the original ULPA, a limited partner "may rightfully demand the return of his contribution . . . after he has given six months notice in writing. . . ." (ULPA § 16(2)). RULPA similarly allowed withdrawal on six months written notice (RULPA § 603) and provides that after a reasonable time thereafter, the withdrawing limited partner is entitled to receive the fair value of his interest in the partnership. By contrast, Re-RULPA denies the limited partner the right to dissociate, but does recognize the power to dissociate. (Re-RULPA § 602). Re-RULPA provides in § 505 that the dissociating limited partner has no right to "receive a distribution on account of dissociation." Thus, under Re-RULPA a withdrawing or dissociating limited partner has the status of a transferee of his own interest. *See* comment to Re-RULPA § 505. Under any of these statutes, the limited partnership agreement may provide otherwise and could deny or limit withdrawal rights. *See Della Ratta v. Larkin*, 856 A.2d 643 (Md. App. 2004) (the limited partnership agreement had provisions dealing with transfers of a partnership interest, a partner's incompetency or bankruptcy, liens on partnership interests and a partner's failure to satisfy a capital call, but none of these constitutes withdrawal under RULPA; thus, the default provision of § 603 on withdrawal applies).

8. Merger of a Limited Partnership into Another Entity

Statutes in many states allow the merger of any two or more entities, including any combination of partnerships (both general and limited), corporations, and limited liability companies. The partnership agreement of, say, a limited partnership can, of course, prohibit or limit such transactions. In the absence of such an agreement, however, the relevant statute typically specifies the required procedure to approve and effectuate the merger. A party who controls a limited partnership may use a merger to squeeze out the limited partners, and this raises the question as to whether such a transaction constitutes a breach of that partner's fiduciary duties.

A related question is whether partners who object to the consideration that they will receive pursuant to the terms of the merger can insist that an independent appraiser be appointed, as is often the case in corporate statutes.

9. Inspection Rights of Limited Partners

Limited partnership statutes typically provide that limited partners may inspect certain books and records of the partnership. *See, e.g.,* Re-RULPA, § 304. This right to inspect is further protected in § 110, which provides that the partnership agreement may not "unreasonably restrict the right to information under Section[] 304," but the agreement "may impose reasonable restrictions on the availability and use of information obtained. . . ." Consistent with its philosophy that a partnership is essentially contractual, Delaware law permits the partnership agreement "to restrict" the rights of a limited partner to obtain information. 6 Del. C. § 17-305(f). As to what information a limited partner may request (assuming the partnership agreement does not otherwise limit inspection rights), see *Madison Avenue Investment Partners, LLC v. America First Real Estate Investment Partners, L.P.,* 806 A.2d 165 (Del. Ch. 2002) (information relating to value of interest) and *Forsythe v. CIBC Employee Private Equity Fund* (U.S.) I, L.P., 2005 Del. Ch. LEXIS 104 (information relating to mismanagement).

10. Dissolution of a Limited Partnership

ULPA provides that a limited partnership dissolves on the retirement, death, or insanity of a general partner, unless the certificate permitted the remaining general partners to continue the business or all partners consent to the continuance of the business (ULPA § 20). Under RULPA, dissolution is covered in Article 8. It provides for nonjudicial dissolution in § 801(e.g., at the time specified in the certificate of limited partnership; on the occurrence of events specified in the limited partnership agreement; on written consent of all partners; and, under certain circumstances, on the withdrawal of a general partner). Under § 802, a court may dissolve a limited partnership on application by a partner "whenever it is not reasonably practicable to carry on the business in conformity with the partnership agreement." This latter provision has been interpreted to mean that judicial dissolution is improper if the business can be conducted profitably even if there is dissension among the partners. *See, e.g., Valone v. Valone,* 2010 U.S. Dist. LEXIS 115892 (N.D. Ga. Nov. 1, 2010).

E. The General Partner

1. Powers of a General Partner

The general partner in a limited partnership has all of the rights and powers of a partner in a general partnership. (RULPA § 403; Re-RULPA § 406) This broad grant of authority, combined with the fact that unless the limited partnership agreement provides otherwise, the limited partners are powerless to act, gives the general partners considerable discretion in managing the business of the partnership. Nevertheless, as in a general partnership, the managing partners of a limited partnership are constrained by fiduciary duties and cannot, for instance, pledge assets of the limited partnership to benefit the general partner. *Luddington v. Bodenvest Ltd.*, 855 P.2d 204 (Utah 1993). This is more fully developed below.

2. Fiduciary Duty of the General Partner

Appletree Square I Limited Partnership v. Investmark, Inc.

Court of Appeals of Minnesota
494 N.W.2d 889 (1993)

CRIPPEN, JUDGE.

Appletree Square One Limited Partnership purchased a commercial office building which is contaminated with asbestos fireproofing materials. Purchasers sued the sellers on various theories of fraud for failing to disclose the presence and hazards of asbestos. Purchasers appeal from summary judgment dismissing each of their claims. We reverse.

Appletree Square I Limited Partnership was formed September 21, 1981, to purchase and operate One Appletree Square, a 15-story office building. The partnership was organized under the 1976 Uniform Limited Partnership Act. Appellants represent the partnership and its affiliates who purchased the property (purchasers). Respondents represent the builders and sellers of the property (sellers), who held interests in the partnership when sale transactions occurred.

This suit is based on two transactions. The building sale occurred in 1981. In 1985, a further acquisition was made by sale of a 25 percent interest in the Appletree partnership. An affiliate of the purchasers, CRI, represented them in both transactions; CRI is a real estate syndication firm. During negotiations for the sale of the property in 1981, CRI wrote a letter to sellers requesting "any information that you have not already sent to us which would be material to our investors' participation in this development." In response, CRI was told to inspect the building and the records, because the sellers "ha[d] no way of knowing what information would be material to your investors' participation."

In 1986, the purchasers learned that the structural steel in the building had been coated with asbestos-based fireproofing, which was deteriorating and releasing fibers. The cost of abatement was estimated at ten million dollars. In their subsequent suit, the purchasers alleged that the sellers were liable for failing to disclose the presence and danger of asbestos. . . .

. . . The [trial] court stated that under [RULPA § 305] and the partnership agreement, the partners' fiduciary duties were only to render, on demand, true and full information. Because appellants had not demanded information about asbestos, respondents had not breached their fiduciary duty of disclosure. Additionally, the environmental liability statute [an additional claim made by plaintiffs] did not apply because it took effect after the 1981 transaction and because it applies to the sale of real estate, not partnership interests. . . .

This appeal turns on whether respondents had a fiduciary duty to disclose to appellants the presence and danger of asbestos. If such a fiduciary duty existed, the trial court must address triable issues on appellants' claims of breach of duty to disclose. . . .

Common Law Duty of Disclosure

Absent a fiduciary relationship, one party to a transaction has "no duty to disclose material facts to the other." In this case, appellants and respondents were partners in a limited partnership. The relationship of partners is fiduciary and partners are held to high standards of integrity in their dealings with each other. Parties in a fiduciary relationship must disclose material facts to each other. Where a fiduciary relationship exists, silence may constitute fraud. Under the common law, respondents had a duty to disclose information regarding asbestos if they knew about it.

Uniform Limited Partnership Act and Duties of Disclosure

The trial court held that the Uniform Limited Partnership Act changed the common law duties of disclosure. [RULPA §305](2) states that limited partners have the right, "upon reasonable demand," to obtain information from the general partners. This statute mirrors the disclosure requirement in the Uniform Partnership Act and should be interpreted similarly. The trial court held that because appellants did not demand information about asbestos, respondents had no obligation to disclose the information.

The trial court's holding is contradicted by a proper interpretation of the disclosure statute. [RULPA §305](2) addresses the narrow duty of partners to respond to requests for information. It does not negate a partner's broad common law duty to disclose all material facts. See H. Reuschlein and W. Gregory, Handbook on the Law of Agency and Partnership, 285 (1979) (the duty to render information is not the same as the duty to disclose). This view has been accepted by other jurisdictions that have adopted the uniform acts governing general and limited partnerships. See *Band v. Livonia Assocs.*, 439 N.W.2d 285, 294 (Mich. App. 1989) ("section 20 [of the Uniform Partnership Act] has been broadly interpreted as imposing a duty to disclose all known information that is significant and material to the affairs or property of the partnership"). . . . [RULPA §305](2) did not eliminate respondents' common law duty to disclose material information to their partners.

Contractual Duties of Disclosure

The trial court also held that the parties limited their duties of disclosure in their contract. The contract stated that the general partners would "provide the partners with all information that may reasonably be requested." Again, appellants never requested information.

Partners may change their common law and statutory duties by incorporating such changes in their partnership agreement. However, where the major purpose of a contract clause is to shield wrongdoers from liability, the clause will be set aside as against public policy. Additionally, while "partners are free to vary many aspects of their relationship ... they are not free to destroy its fiduciary character." H. Reuschlein and W. Gregory, Handbook on the Law of Agency and Partnership, 268 (1979).

To hold that partners may replace their broad duty of disclosure with a narrow duty to render information upon demand would destroy the fiduciary character of their relationship, and it would also invite fraud. Unless partners knew what questions to ask, they would have no right to know material information about the business. In this case, if respondents knew the building was contaminated with asbestos and if they reasonably should have known their partners did not know about the asbestos, they may have breached their fiduciary duty of disclosure. . . .

Justifiable Reliance

. . . The trial court held as a matter of law that appellants were not justified in relying on respondents to disclose the presence and danger of asbestos. The court based its decision on the fact that respondents told appellants to conduct their own investigation and on its finding that appellants were sophisticated buyers. A fiduciary's duty is defined "with reference to the experience and intelligence of the person to whom the duty is owed." *Perranoski*, 299 N.W.2d [404] at 413 [(Minn. 1980)]. . . .

There is no compelling evidence that either the building specifications or a visual inspection of the building should have revealed the asbestos. Moreover, although the purchasers had partnership authority over management of the building prior to the 1985 partnership interest buyout, respondents were managers in fact from 1972 (when the building was constructed) to 1985. To discover asbestos on their own, appellants would have had to know enough to ask about it or know enough to have various building materials tested.

Finally, the fact that respondents told appellants to investigate did not make appellants' reliance unreasonable as a matter of law. Respondents' statement did not specifically tell appellants not to rely on them. Moreover, even if respondents had told appellants not to rely on them, that statement would not necessarily make reliance unreasonable. Evidence in the record permits a finding that respondents had superior knowledge and knew appellants did not know about the asbestos. These are fact questions which must be answered to determine whether respondents neglected their fiduciary duty to inform appellants. . . .

The trial court erred in holding that respondents' common law duties of disclosure were limited by the Uniform Limited Partnership Act and by the partnership agreement. The court also erred in determining issues of material fact regarding appellants' reliance on disclosures of respondents and in determining reasonable diligence. We reverse summary judgments for respondents. Further proceedings are to occur in accordance with this opinion.

Reversed.

Notes

1. Although the opinion is not entirely clear on the facts regarding the relationship of the parties, it can be read as a case involving the sale by general partners of partnership property to limited partners. With regard to the duty of general partners toward limited partners, the material in Chapter 12 regarding the fiduciary duties partners owe one another applies here, of course. That includes the duty of good faith and fair dealing, which is also considered more fully below.

2. For a case discussing the duty of good faith of a general partner in a limited partnership, see *Desert Equities v. Morgan Stanley Leveraged Fund II*, 624 A.2d 1199 (Del. 1993). In that case, Desert Equities, a limited partner, sued the general partner alleging that it acted in bad faith in exercising its authority under the partnership agreement to exclude Desert from participating in investments of the partnership. Desert alleged that the general partner did this in retaliation for Desert's act of filing a suit against affiliates of the general partner in a different limited partnership. The court, in allowing the case to go to the finder of fact, stated that "a claim of bad faith hinges on a party's tortious state of mind." It quoted as follows from Black's Law Dictionary in support of its conclusion that bad faith is a state of mind: "[The] term 'bad faith' is not simply bad judgment or negligence, but rather it implies the conscious doing of a wrong because of dishonest purpose or moral obliquity; it is different from the negative idea of negligence in that it contemplates a state of mind affirmatively operating with furtive design or ill will." In *Della Ratta v. Larkin*, 856 A.2d 643 (Md. Ct. App. 2004), the court found that a general partner, who was presumed to have the authority to make a capital call on the limited partners, acted in bad faith when he made the call to "force out" the limited partners. The general partner had the opportunity to pursue third-party financing and good faith required that he do so.

3. While the trend of the law seems to allow parties to limit or waive fiduciary duties in their partnership agreement, and the Delaware courts generally enforce such waivers (e.g., *Sonet v. Plum Creek Timber Co.*, 722 A.2d 319, 322 (Del. Ch. 1998) ("[P]rinciples of contract preempt fiduciary principles where the parties to a limited partnership have made their intentions to do so plain"), not all courts agree. *See, e.g., BT-I v. Equitable Assurance Society of the United States*, 76 Cal. App. 4th 1406, 89 Cal. Rptr. 2d 811 (1999). In this case, the partnership was in default on its loan. The general partner bought the loan and subsequently foreclosed on the property. The limited partner claimed such actions breached the fiduciary duty of the general partner, who defended on the basis of a provision in the partnership agreement that gave it broad powers to refinance and restructure partnership debt. The general partner also relied on a provision of RUPA §404(f), applicable in California, that states: "a partner may lend money to and transact other business with the limited partnership and, subject to applicable law, has the same rights and obligations with respect thereto as a person who is not a partner." The court was unconvinced and held in favor of the limited partner. *See also 1515 North Wells, L.P. v. 1513 North Wells, L.L.C.*, 913 N.E.2d 1 (Ill. App. 2009) (noting that the Illinois limited partnership statute does not permit the parties to a partnership agreement to "eliminate or reduce a partner's fiduciary duties").

4. Consistent with the philosophy of Re-RULPA to de-link UPA and ULPA, Re-RULPA contains a provision (§408) that tracks RUPA §404, specifying the duties of a general partner.

5. The Delaware version of RULPA contains this provision limiting the liability of the general partner under certain circumstances:

> (e) Unless otherwise provided in a partnership agreement, a partner or other person shall not be liable to a limited partnership or to another partner or to another person that is a party to or is otherwise bound by a partnership agreement for breach of fiduciary duty for the partner's or other person's good faith reliance on the provisions of the partnership agreement.

6 Del. C. §17-1101(e).

Because many publicly held partnerships are organized under Delaware law, and because a provision similar to §17-1101 is in the Delaware LLC Act and in other statutes in other jurisdictions (e.g., Washington, RCWA 25.15.040; Massachusetts, M.G.L.A. 156C §63) a judicial interpretation of this section is important. The Chancery Court of Delaware, which is the most important court in the United States in terms of corporate law and, probably, in terms of partnership law as well (at least with regard to publicly held partnerships) considered the meaning of a predecessor of this section in the next case.

Gotham Partners, L.P. v. Hallwood Realty Partners, L.P.

Court of Chancery of Delaware
795 A.2d 1 (2001)

[This case involved a publicly held limited partnership controlled by a corporate general partner, Hallwood Realty Corporation. The general partner was, in turn, controlled by another corporation, The Hallwood Group Incorporated ("HGI"). For various reasons, the general partner determined to engage in a series of transactions that resulted in a reduction of the number of partnership units held by the limited partners and an increase in the number of units held by HGI. For instance, the general partner caused the partnership to engage in a reverse split, pursuant to which every five partnership units owned by a partner would be converted to one unit, with fractional units acquired for cash by HGI. Another such transaction was an odd-lot offer. In this transaction, the partnership offered to purchase from limited partners blocks of fewer than 100 units, so-called "odd-lots," and resell the purchased units to HGI. The purported rationale for the reverse split was to increase the trading price of partnership units, thereby encouraging ownership by institutional holders (who were otherwise reluctant to make investments in low priced units) and to eliminate the risk that the partnership units would be delisted from the American Stock Exchange because of the low selling price of the units. The purported rationale for making the odd-lot offer was also two-fold: first, the offer would reduce the number of partners, thus reducing the partnership's administrative costs; and second, the offer would allow the odd-lot holders to sell at market price without incurring brokerage costs.

Regardless of the partnership's stated reasons for engaging in these and other transactions, their effect was to increase the control of the general partner and virtually eliminate the possibility that the general partner could be ousted by a vote of the limited partners.

One of the limited partners, Gotham Partners, L.P. ("Gotham") challenged these transactions in a derivative action, claiming, among other things, that the process employed by the general partner to approve the transactions was in violation of the partnership agreement. Plaintiff was a substantial minority partner who had an interest in taking over control of the partnership. To accomplish that, it had to reduce the voting power of the general partner and its affiliates. It sought to do so by seeking judicial rescission of HGI's acquisition of units under the reverse stock split, odd-lot purchase and other transactions (the "Challenged Transactions").]

I. The Critical Contractual Provisions

The facts of this case are best read in light of the critical contractual dispute between the parties. For its part, Gotham contends that the Challenged Transactions—in particular, the Odd Lot Offer—involved the simple sale of units from the Partnership to HGI. As a result, it asserts that those Transactions were governed by §§ 7.05, 7.09, and 7.10(a) of the Partnership Agreement. Section 7.05 states that the Partnership "*is expressly permitted to enter into transactions with the General Partner or any affiliate thereof provided that the terms of any such transaction are substantially equivalent to terms obtainable by the Partnership from a comparable unaffiliated third party.*"[23] Section 7.09 provides in pertinent part that "the General Partner may, on behalf of and for the account of the Partnership, purchase or otherwise acquire Units and following any such purchase or acquisition, may sell or otherwise dispose of such Units. . . ." Section 7.10(a), meanwhile, states that the General Partner shall "form an Audit Committee . . . comprised of two members of the board of directors who are not affiliated with the General Partner or its Affiliates except by reason of such directorship. . . . *The function[ ] of the Audit Committee shall be to*

---

23. [3] Emphasis added.

review and approve . . . transactions between the Partnership and the General Partner and any of its Affiliates."[24]

The defendants argue that §§ 7.05 and 7.10(a) are inapposite to the Challenged Transactions, because each of those transactions supposedly involved the "issuance" of Partnership units to HGI. Issuances, say the defendants, are governed by § 9.01 of the Partnership Agreement, which is inconsistent with the entire fairness approach of §§ 7.05 and 7.10(a). The relevant parts of § 9.01 follow:

> (a) Subject to Sections 9.01(b) and (c) hereof, the General Partner is authorized to cause the Partnership to issue Units at any time or from time to time to the General Partner, to Limited Partners or to other Persons . . . without any consent or approval of the Limited Partners or Assignees. . . . *Subject to Section 9.01(b) hereof, the General Partner shall have sole and complete discretion in determining the rights, powers, preferences and duties . . . and the consideration and terms and conditions with respect to any future issuance of Units. . . .*
>
> (b) The General Partner or any Affiliate thereof may, but is not obligated to, make Capital Contributions to the Partnership in the form of cash or other property in exchange for Units. *Except as set forth above, the number of Units issued to the General Partner or any such Affiliate in exchange for any Capital Contribution shall not exceed the Net Agreed Value of the contributed property or the amount of cash, as the case may be, divided by the Unit Price of a Unit as of the day of such issuance.*[25]

The defendants claim that the Transactions were in fact carried out as issuances under § 9.01 and that the price paid by HGI complied with the floor set by § 9.01(b) for issuances to affiliates of the General Partner, which is based on a five-day market average tied to the date of issuance. Noting that, subject to this floor price, § 9.01(a) vests "sole and complete" discretion in the General Partner to set the terms of issuances, the defendants claim that the plain language of the Partnership Agreement precludes the operation of §§ 7.05 and 7.10(a). In further support of this argument, the defendants note that § 7.10(c) provides:

> Whenever in this Agreement . . . the General Partner is permitted or required to make a decision (i) *in its "sole discretion" or "discretion" or under a similar grant of authority or latitude, the General Partner shall be entitled to consider only such interests and factors as it desires and shall have no duty or obligation to give any consideration to any interest of or factors affecting the Partnership, . . . the Limited Partners or the Assignees,* or (ii) in its "good faith" or under another express standard, *the General Partner shall act under such express standard and shall not be subject to any other or different standards imposed by this Agreement, . . . or any other agreement contemplated*

---

24. [4] Emphasis added.
25. [5] Partnership Agreement § 9.01 (emphasis added).

> *herein or therein. Each Limited Partner or Assignee hereby agrees that any*
> *standard of care or duty imposed in this Agreement, . . . or any other agree-*
> *ment contemplated herein or under the Delaware RULPA or any other appli-*
> *cable law, rule or regulation shall be modified, waived or limited in each case*
> *as required to permit the General Partner to act under this Agreement, . . . or*
> *any other agreement contemplated herein and to make any decision pursuant*
> *to the authority prescribed in this Section 7.10(c) so long as such action or deci-*
> *sion does not constitute willful misconduct and is reasonably believed by the*
> *General Partner to be consistent with the overall purposes of the Partnership*

To superimpose either the substantive requirement of § 7.05 or the procedural requirement of § 7.10(a) on § 9.01 transactions, the defendants contend, would conflict with the clear mandate of § 7.10(c) by fettering the General Partner's complete discretion with conflicting substantive and procedural "standards" and by requiring it to consider "interest[s] of or factors affecting the . . . Limited Partners."[26] Rather, the only duty of the General Partner was to ensure that HGI paid a price in compliance with § 9.01(b) and that duty was carried out. . . .

[After concluding that the nature of the odd-lot offer was such that it fell under §§ 7.05 and 7.10(a) and not § 9.10, the court considered the defendants' argument that § 1101(d) of the Delaware version of RULPA ("DRULPA") exculpated them from liability:]

D. Do Provisions Of The DRULPA Or The Partnership Agreement Exculpate The Defendants' Breach?

The defendants have asserted certain affirmative defenses that allegedly insulate them from liability. I begin with their reliance on § 17-1101(d)(1) of DRULPA, which states in pertinent part that:

> To the extent that, at law or in equity, a partner or other person has
> duties (including fiduciary duties) and liabilities relating thereto to a lim-
> ited partnership or to another partner . . . (1) any such partner or other
> person acting under the partnership agreement shall not be liable to the
> limited partnership or to any such other partner . . . for the partner's or
> other person's good faith reliance on the provisions of the partnership
> agreement . . . .

The parties vigorously contest the meaning of § 17-1101(d)(1). For their part, the defendants view the statute as immunizing any breach of a partnership agreement, so long as the breach resulted from a good faith misreading of even an unambiguous provision. According to the defendants: (i) § 17-1101(d)(2) of DRULPA allows a Partnership Agreement to occupy the territory covered by traditional fiduciary duties by specifying the standards that will replace such duties, thus creating a

---

26. [6] *Id.* § 7.10(c) (emphasis added).

safe-harbor from traditional fiduciary liability; and (ii) § 17-1101(d)(1) of DRULPA permits fiduciaries to violate the contractual standards that supplanted their fiduciary duties without redress so long as the contractual violation was made in good faith.

Gotham argues that the defendants' interpretation of the statute produces an absurd and unreasonable result. Given that § 17-1101(c) says that the DRULPA is supposed to provide maximal contractual freedom and *enforceability*, Gotham contends that it cannot be construed to force limited partners to rely upon partnership agreements as their sole protection and simultaneously strip them of any right for redress when their fiduciaries breach those agreements. Such a reading, Gotham argues, renders any protections for investors wholly illusory. Instead of ambiguities being construed in favor of the reasonable expectations of investors, even unambiguous provisions of agreements are unenforceable against fiduciaries if the fiduciaries can prove that they made a good faith mistake. Can this really be what the General Assembly intended? Gotham says no, and that § 17-1101(d)(1) must be limited to exculpating good faith breaches of fiduciary duty, and as not applying to breach of contract claims.

The parties' arguments raise important public policy concerns, which warrant careful attention by the General Assembly and by the relevant committees of the Delaware State Bar Association. Fortunately, I need not answer all these questions to resolve this case.

The broad language of § 17-1101(d)(1) can arguably be read to apply to claims of breach of contract, as Chancellor Chandler adverted to in *Continental Ins. Co. v. Rutledge & Co., Inc.*[27] and as I acknowledged in my summary judgment opinion in this case. In the summary judgment opinion, I declined to resolve the defendants' § 17-1101(d)(1) defense until a fuller record was developed and the parties could look for legislative history that might illuminate the General Assembly's intent. Unfortunately, that deferral did not yield any useful legislative history.

In view of the lack of clarity regarding the statute's scope and the important public policy issues at stake, I adhere to a minimalist approach and do not propose to decide definitively whether § 17-1101(d)(1) can exculpate a breach of the Partnership Agreement itself. For purposes of resolving this case, I need only apply Chancellor Chandler's approach in the *Rutledge* case. *Rutledge* states that § 17-1101(d)(1) might be read to insulate a general partner from liability if the general partner breached an ambiguous agreement provision in good faith, but could not be read to immunize a breach of an unambiguous statute [sic—agreement provision?].[28] Under that approach, the limited partners would bear the burden of plausible uncertainty in an agreement in situations where the general partner could prove that it made a good faith mistake.

---

27. [36] Del. Ch., 750 A.2d 1219 (2000).
28. [39] 750 A.2d at 1239–40.

In this case, the Agreement provisions relevant to the Odd Lot resales are not ambiguous. Because those resales did not involve an issuance, §§ 7.05, 7.09, and 7.10(a) applied; § 9.01 did not. The record is consistent with the conclusion that the General Partner intentionally advertised the Odd Lot Offer as involving a resale to avoid the burdens that would have attended an issuance. As such, it did not rely in good faith on an ambiguous provision of the Agreement. Indeed, it did not act at all under the provision of the Agreement, § 9.01, upon which it purported to rely in good faith. Instead, it intentionally structured a transaction that was unambiguously covered by §§ 7.05 and 7.10(c), and then failed to comply with the provisions of those sections. As a result, the defendants' § 17-1101(d)(1) defense is denied, even assuming that § 17-1101(d)(1) may be read to exculpate contractual breaches.

The weakness of defendants' position is also buttressed by another factor, which is well exemplified in this case. As noted, § 17-1101(d)(2) permits a partnership agreement to restrict or expand fiduciary duties, so long as it does so clearly and unambiguously.[29] There are two methods by which courts conclude that an unambiguous contractual alteration has occurred. The first involves a situation where the agreement plainly states that it is modifying the general partner's fiduciary duties, *e.g.*, by stating that the general partner may compete with the partnership. The second and more difficult interpretative method is when the partnership agreement so specifically covers a topic that there is no room for the operation of traditional fiduciary duties. Compliance with the substitute contractual provision is said in such a case to create a safe harbor from fiduciary liability.[30] If DRULPA were read to permit a fiduciary to avoid fiduciary liability because a contract provision created a substitute standard, and then not comply with that standard because of a misreading, an arguably inequitable and illogical framework would emerge. Such would be the case here.

Under § 7.06 of the Agreement:

> The General Partner, its Affiliates and all officers, directors, partners, employees and agents of the General Partner and its Affiliates shall not be liable to the Partnership, any Limited Partner, Assignee or any other Person who has acquired an interest to the Partnership for any losses sustained or liabilities incurred, including monetary damages, as a result of any act or omission, unless such act or omission constitutes (a) a breach of any duty of loyalty to the Partnership, (b) an act or omission in bad faith which involves intentional misconduct or a knowing violation of law, or (c) a transaction from which an improper personal benefit is derived.

The defendants argue that § 7.06 insulates them from liability. But § 7.06 is modeled on exculpatory charter provisions authorized under § 102(b)(7) of the Delaware

---

29. [40] *Id.* at 1235.

30. [41] *In re Cencom Cable Income Partners, L.P. Litig.*, 1996 Del. Ch. LEXIS 17, *11, C.A. No. 14634, Steele, V.C. (Feb. 15, 1996).

General Corporation Law, which exculpates defendants only from liability for violations of the duty of care. All of the remaining defendants here—the General Partner, HGI, and the HGI directors—had a self-interest in ensuring that the General Partner retained control of the Partnership and had an interest in HGI obtaining favorable price terms. Thus, § 7.06 does not protect them from liability.

Given this reality, an apparent anomaly that would arise if § 17-1101(d)(1) were held to insulate the defendants from liability for their contractual breach, *after they have argued that the contractual standards supplant traditional fiduciary duties.* It is only because the Agreement imposes specific standards of conduct that default fiduciary duties were held not to apply to the General Partner's actions in effecting the Challenged Transactions. The safe harbor for the General Partner from fiduciary liability is thus compliance with the Agreement. If § 17-1101(d)(1) were interpreted as the defendants would have it, the General Partner is free to escape fiduciary liability in a self-interested context that would not fall within the exculpatory clause in § 7.06 if it mistakenly misread the Agreement in its own conflicted favor.

There are at least two logical ways to resolve this anomaly. One is to follow the teaching of *Rutledge*, and to limit the exculpating effect of § 17-1101(d)(1) to situations where a general partner's breach of the partnership agreement involved a good faith misreading of an ambiguous provision.

Another approach is less favorable to general partners, more protective of investors, and in keeping with the traditional approach of construing exculpatory provisions narrowly.[31] That approach would hold a general partner and other fiduciaries responsible under traditional fiduciary principles when they did not comply with the contractual provisions that supplanted such duties. That is, to the extent that the general partner and other interested fiduciaries do not properly avail themselves of a contractual safe harbor in implementing a conflict transaction, they would suffer liability unless they could prove fairness. Stated a bit differently, § 17-1101(d)(1) would only avail a defendant when the defendant accurately read, applied, and relied on an agreement provision in taking action. As so read, § 17-1101(d) would therefore protect a general partner from a fiduciary duty or other non-contractual claim only where its actions were contractually authorized. This narrower construction would be consistent with the commentators' almost exclusive focus on § 17-1101(d)(1) as a provision that addresses fiduciary duty claims. Because the defendants' § 17-1101(d)(1) defense fails even under *Rutledge*, I need not determine which approach is most faithful to § 17-1101 as a whole. . . .

. . .

---

31. [44] *See, e.g., Blum v. Kauffman*, Del. Supr., 297 A.2d 48, 49 (1972) (stating that the policy of Supreme Court is to read exculpatory clauses narrowly and construe them as not conferring immunity if that is reasonably possible). The traditional cautious approach to exculpatory provisions is reflected in this court's decision in *Walker v. Resource Dev. Co.*, Del. Ch., Lamb, V.C., 791 A.2d 799, 817–18 (2000), which construed 6 *Del. C.* § 18-1101 the LLC's statute's equivalent to § 17-1101(d).

F. What Is The Appropriate Remedy?

[The court concluded that HGI underpaid for the Odd Lot units, but that rescission was not an appropriate remedy because (1) the plaintiff unjustifiably delayed in challenging the transactions, and (2) the defendants did not undertake the Challenged Transactions to entrench the General Partner's control or enrich HGI. The court went on to award the plaintiff damages of $3,417,422.50.]

Notes

1. On appeal, the Delaware Supreme Court reversed on the question of damages, ruling that while the defendants may not have intended to entrench the general partner, that was the effect and the remedy must compensate the plaintiff for that loss. The defendants are liable for the "control premium" that was not reflected in the price of the odd lot units. *Gotham Partners, L.P. v. Hallwood Realty Partners, L.P.*, 817 A.2d 160 (Del. 2002). In response to dictum in the Delaware Supreme Court's opinion in *Gotham* that suggested that the drafters of a limited partnership agreement could restrict, but not eliminate, fiduciary duties, the Delaware legislature amended its alternative entity statutes (partnership and LLC statutes) to make clear that fiduciary duties could be eliminated. For instance, § 17-1101(d) of the Delaware version of RULPA now provides:

> To the extent that, at law or in equity, a partner or other person has duties (including fiduciary duties) to a limited partnership or to another partner or to another person that is a party to or is otherwise bound by a partnership agreement, the partner's or other person's duties may be expanded or restricted or eliminated by provisions in the partnership agreement; provided that the partnership agreement may not eliminate the implied contractual covenant of good faith and fair dealing.

2. In *Miller v. American Real Estate Partners, L.P.*, No. 16788, 2001 Del. Ch. LEXIS 116 (Sept. 6, 2001), the court considered a partnership provision, similar to that in *Gotham Partners*, that the defendants contended eliminated any default fiduciary duty of loyalty owed by the general partner to the partnership. The applicable provision in *Miller*, § 6.13(d), read as follows:

> Whenever in this Agreement the General Partner is permitted or required to make a decision (i) in its "sole discretion" or "discretion", with "absolute discretion" or under a grant of similar authority or latitude, the General Partner shall be entitled to consider only such interests and factors as it desires and shall have no duty or obligation to give any consideration to any interest of or factors affecting the Partnership, the Operating Partnership or the Record Holders, or (ii) in its "good faith" or under another express standard, the General Partner shall act under such express standard and shall not be subject to any other or different standards imposed by this Agreement or any other agreement contemplated herein.

Id. at *19–20.

The court distinguished this language from that in *Gotham Partners*:

> This case presents a twist on *Gotham Partners* and *Gelfman v. Weeden Investors, L.P.* [792 A.2d 977 (2001)]. Like the provisions in *Gotham Partners* and *Gelfman*, § 6.13(d) sets forth a sole discretion standard that appears to be quite different from the duty of a fiduciary to act with procedural and substantive fairness in a conflict situation. What is different about § 6.13(d), however, is that it does not expressly state that default provisions of law must give way if they hinder the General Partner's ability to act under the sole discretion standard. Rather, § 6.13(d) merely states that other standards in the Agreement or agreements contemplated by the agreement give way to the sole discretion standard. By its own terms, § 6.13(d) says nothing about default principles of law being subordinated when the sole discretion standard applies.

> This omission is of legal significance. In prior cases, this court has held that default principles of fiduciary duty will apply unless a partnership agreement plainly provides otherwise. As the defendants would have it, when the Partnership Agreement says that the General Partner has sole discretion, it means that the General Partner has unreviewable power to act in any manner whatsoever, however advantageous to the General Partner and however disadvantageous to the Partnership. According to the defendants, the General Partner could choose to invest Partnership funds in a failing venture solely to ensure that the General Partner's own investment in that venture is not lost, and turn its back on a less risky and more profitable opportunity for the Partnership.

> This court has made clear that it will not [be] tempted by the piteous pleas of limited partners who are seeking to escape the consequences of their own decisions to become investors in a partnership whose general partner has clearly exempted itself from traditional fiduciary duties. The DRULPA puts investors on notice that fiduciary duties may be altered by partnership agreements, and therefore that investors should be careful to read partnership agreements before buying units. In large measure, the DRULPA reflects the doctrine of *caveat emptor*, as is fitting given that investors in limited partnerships have countless other investment opportunities available to them that involve less risk and/or more legal protection. For example, any investor who wishes to retain the protection of traditional fiduciary duties can always invest in corporate stock.

> But just as investors must use due care, so must the drafter of a partnership agreement who wishes to supplant the operation of traditional fiduciary duties. In view of the great freedom afforded to such drafters and the reality that most publicly traded limited partnerships are governed by agreements drafted exclusively by the original general partner, it is fair to

expect that restrictions on fiduciary duties be set forth clearly and unambiguously. A topic as important as this should not be addressed coyly.

Here, I conclude that the Partnership Agreement fails to preclude the operation of the fiduciary duty of loyalty with sufficient clarity, even in situations when the General Partner has the contractual power to act in its sole discretion. The reasons I reach this conclusion are several. First, I again note the absence of any express indication that default principles of law must give way when the sole discretion standard applies. This absence is striking given the prevalence of such express provisions, and their use in concert with contractual language markedly similar to § 6.13(d). The drafter's decision to preempt conflicting provisions of the Agreement and of other contracts, but not those of default law can thus be viewed as intentional.

Id. at *25–29 (footnotes omitted).

3. While the Delaware courts' interpretation of § 1101(d) in *Gotham Partners* and *Miller* provides limited guidance, the Delaware Supreme Court decision in *United States Cellular Investment Co. of Allentown v. Bell Atlantic Mobile Systems, Inc.*, 677 A.2d 497 (Del. 1996), demonstrates the potential reach of the section. In this case, the defendant was the general partner and a limited partner in a partnership that allowed limited partners, but not the general partner, to compete with the partnership (by acquiring licenses in areas adjoining the area in which the partnership had a license to operate a cellular telephone service). The general partner allegedly breached the agreement and its fiduciary duties by obtaining a license in an area that was prohibited to it. The general partner defended on the basis that it was also a limited partner and, as such, free to obtain the competing license. The Delaware Supreme Court held in favor of the defendant general partner, affirming a lower court ruling dismissing the complaint. The Court ruled that, under § 1101(d), the plaintiff must allege that defendant acted "in knowing breach of the Agreement"; that is, that the defendant acted in bad faith. It was not enough, the Court said, that plaintiff alleged that defendant's actions were "intentional."

4. Delaware courts have embraced corporate notions in resolving fiduciary duty disputes between the general partner and limited partners. For instance, as in corporate law, if a majority of the limited partners approve, after full disclosure, a transaction in which the general partner has a conflict of interest, the Delaware courts will not examine the transaction to determine its fairness to the limited partners. *See, e.g., R.S.M. Inc. v. Capital Management Holdings L.P.*, 790 A.2d 478, 498 (Del. Ch. 2001).

5. One commentator has expressed doubts about the constitutionality, under the Delaware constitution, of Delaware statutes allowing waiver of fiduciary duties. *See* Lyman Johnson, *Delaware's Nonwaivable Duties*, 91 B.U. Law Rev. 701 (2011) (arguing that the Delaware legislature cannot limit the Delaware Chancery Court from recognizing fiduciary duties in unincorporated entities).

Brickell Partners v. Wise

Court of Chancery of Delaware
794 A.2d 1 (2001)

STRINE, VICE CHANCELLOR.

Plaintiff Brickell Partners brought this action challenging the acquisition of Crystal Gas Storage, Inc. by El Paso Energy Partners, L.P. ("El Paso" or the "Partnership"). Brickell Partners is a limited partner in El Paso and has sued derivatively on its behalf. Crystal Gas is owned by El Paso Energy Corp. ("Energy"), which also owns and controls El Paso's general partner, DeepTech International, Inc. Energy also holds 34.5% of El Paso's units, which are traded on the New York Stock Exchange.

El Paso purchased Crystal Gas for $170 million in newly issued El Paso preference units. The complaint alleges that this consideration exceeded "the value of Crystal Gas, its assets and businesses" and that the transaction is therefore substantively unfair to El Paso. By way of support for this assertion, the complaint simply notes that "for the quarter ended September 30, 1999, Crystal Gas reported a decline in revenues of $1.2 million and a decline for the nine months of that fiscal year of about $3.5 million."

The complaint also challenges the procedures used to effect this "conflict" transaction. The only procedural protection used by El Paso to ensure the interests of unitholders other than Energy was to subject the transaction to "Special Approval" by DeepTech's "Conflicts and Audit Committee." The two members of that Committee were defendant Michael B. Bracy, a director of DeepTech and a former employee of Energy, and defendant H. Douglas Church, another director of DeepTech.

The complaint alleges that the process was "irreparably impaired" because Bracy and Church owed fiduciary duties to DeepTech as DeepTech directors, and thus could not fairly opine on a transaction in which DeepTech and El Paso had conflicting interests. The complaint also charges that Bracy's former status as an employee in an unspecified position at Energy compromised him further.

The defendants—principally DeepTech and its directors—have filed a motion to dismiss the complaint. According to the defendants, the El Paso Partnership Agreement precludes the plaintiff's claims for breach of fiduciary duty in connection with the Crystal Gas acquisition. In particular, the defendants emphasize the following provision of the Partnership Agreement:

> 6.9 *Resolution of Conflicts of Interest.* (a) Unless otherwise expressly provided in this Agreement . . . *whenever a potential conflict of interest exists or arises between the General Partner or any of its Affiliates, on the one hand, and the Partnership,* the Operating Companies, any Partner or any Assignee, *on the other hand, any resolution or course of action in respect of such conflict of interest* shall be permitted and deemed approved by all Partners, *and*

shall not constitute a breach of this Agreement, of the Operating Companies Agreements, of any agreement contemplated herein or therein, *or of any duty stated or implied by law or equity, if the resolution or course of action is or, by operation of this Agreement, is deemed to be, fair and reasonable to the Partnership. The General Partner shall be authorized*, but not required in connection with its resolution of such conflict of interest, to seek *Special Approval of a resolution of such conflict or course of action. Any conflict of interest and any resolution of such conflict of interest shall be conclusively deemed fair and reasonable to the Partnership if such conflict of interest or resolution is (i) approved by Special Approval*, (ii) on whole, on terms no less favorable to the Partnership than those generally being provided to or available from unrelated third parties *or* (iii) fair to the Partnership, taking into account the totality of the relationships between the parties involved (including other transactions that may be particularly favorable or advantageous to the Partnership). . . . The General Partner (including the Conflicts and Audit Committee in connection with Special Approval) shall be authorized in connection with its determination of the "fair and reasonable" nature of any transaction or arrangement and in its resolution of any conflict of interest to consider (i) the relative interests of any party to such conflict, agreement, transaction or situation and the benefits and burdens relating to such interest; (ii) any customary or accepted industry practices and any customary or historical dealings with a particular Person; (iii) any applicable generally accepted accounting or engineering practices or principles; and (iv) such additional factors as the General Partner or such Conflicts and Audit Committee determines in its sole discretion to be relevant, reasonable or appropriate under the circumstances. Nothing contained in this Agreement, however, is intended to nor shall it be construed to require the General Partner or such Conflicts and Audit Committee to consider the interests of any Person other than the Partnership. In the absence of bad faith by the General Partner, the resolution, action or terms so made, taken or provided by the General Partner with respect to such matter shall not constitute a breach of this Agreement or any other agreement contemplated herein or a breach of any standard of care or duty imposed herein or therein or under the Delaware Act or any other law, rule or regulation.[32]

Pursuant to the Agreement, "Special Approval" means "approval of a majority of the members of the Conflicts and Audit Committee of the Partnership."[33] Such Special Approval was obtained for the Crystal Gas transaction.

The defendants argue that § 6.9 of the Agreement supplants the traditional default fiduciary duties that would otherwise apply to the Crystal Gas deal in the absence of contractual modification. The fiduciary duty of loyalty would, if unmodified,

---

32. [4] Partnership Agreement § 6.9 (emphasis added).
33. [5] *Id.* at A-10.

have required the defendants to demonstrate that the Crystal Gas acquisition was entirely fair. The defendants note that 6 *Del. C.* § 17-1101(c) statutorily authorized the parties to the Partnership Agreement to restrict the fiduciary duties owed to El Paso by DeepTech and the other defendants. As this court has noted many times in recent years, "principles of contract preempt fiduciary principles where the parties to a limited partnership have made their intentions to do so plain."[34]

Here, the plain and unambiguous language of § 6.9 of the Partnership Agreement displaces traditional fiduciary duty principles. In place of such principles, the Agreement provides limited partners solely with the protection of Conflicts and Audit Committee Review when DeepTech decides to seek "Special Approval" of a conflict transaction, as it did here. Such "Special Approval" is "conclusive [ ]" evidence of the "fair[ness] and reasonable[ness]" of a conflict transaction, and bars any challenge to the transaction based on the Agreement, other contracts, or default principles of law or equity.[35] As a result, the plain language of the Agreement appears to compel a dismissal of the complaint, assuming the plaintiff has not pled facts suggesting that the defendants did not comply with § 6.9 itself.

To meet this challenge, the plaintiff has argued that § 6.9 is ambiguous because the Agreement never defines precisely who shall serve on the Conflicts and Audit Committee. According to plaintiff, the reasonable expectation of a limited partner would be that the Committee would be comprised of persons with no relation or duty at all to DeepTech. Because the two members were both DeepTech directors, the plaintiff argues that the Committee process did not accord with that supposed expectation and therefore that the defendants may not rely upon the "Special Approval" safe harbor.

The problem for the plaintiff is that its argument (which sounds somewhat plausible in the abstract) has little force in the precise context governed by the Partnership Agreement. As this court has noted elsewhere, directors of corporate general partners occupy a strange and unsettling position. By definition, they find themselves in a position of on-going conflict because they owe fiduciary duties to the corporate general partner (on whose board they serve) and fiduciary duties to the limited partnership governed by the corporate general partner. Even when such directors have no material self-interest in the success of the corporate general partner as an entity or the partnership itself, they owe duties to two entities with potentially conflicting interests. Thus, their situation is subtly but critically different from the position of an outside, "independent" director of a corporation. An ideal corporate independent director owes her fidelity only to the corporation and its stockholders, to the exclusion of any potentially conflicting constituency. That can never be so with the director of a corporate general partner forced to opine on a transaction between an affiliate of the corporate general partner and the partnership.

---

34. [6] *Sonet v. Timber Co.*, Del.Ch., 722 A.2d 319, 322 (1998).
35. [7] Partnership Agreement § 6.9.

This reality, however, dissipates the force of the plaintiff's argument. Although the Partnership Agreement does not define the Conflicts and Audit Committee of DeepTech, the very use of the term Committee implies that the group will be comprised of directors of DeepTech. It may be that the Agreement's use of the term Conflicts and Audit Committee and its conferral of certain types of authority on that Committee would lead a reasonable investor to conclude that the Committee would be comprised solely of *non-management directors* of DeepTech. What it cannot be reasonably read as implying is that the Committee would be comprised of members with no relationship to DeepTech at all.

Neither Bracy nor Church is alleged to be a current member of the management of DeepTech. Neither is alleged to be a stockholder of Energy (or even of DeepTech for that matter). At most, the plaintiff avers that Bracy used to work for Energy. When and for how long the plaintiff does not say. Even more important, the plaintiff does not allege facts from which it can be inferred that Bracy was beholden to Energy for material, personal reasons separate and apart from the structural conflict he inherently faced as a DeepTech director.[36]

Therefore, the plaintiff has failed to plead facts that indicate that the defendants' conduct is not insulated from challenge because of the Conflicts and Audit Committee's Special Approval of the Crystal Gas transaction. For that reason the plaintiff's complaint is dismissed with prejudice.

Notes

1. In *Brickell Partners*, a committee appointed by the corporate general partner approved the acquisition by the partnership of a corporation that was owned by an affiliate of the corporate general partner, a classic conflict of interest situation. The plaintiff limited partner challenged the transaction, but the court dismissed the action because the limited partnership agreement expressly permitted this process. Suppose, however, that the plaintiffs alleged that the members of the committee were significant shareholders of El Paso Energy Corp., the seller. Would that have affected the outcome of the case? What if committee members were corporate officers of DeepTech International, Inc., the corporate general partner, but not shareholders of El Paso Energy?

2. As the *Brickell Partners* case indicates, the Delaware courts have held that the directors of a corporate general partner of a Delaware limited partnership owe fiduciary duties to the limited partners. *In re USACafes, L.P. Litigation*, 600 A.2d 43 (Del. Ch. 1991). In this case, the plaintiff, a limited partner, alleged that the directors of the corporate general partner approved a sale of the partnership's assets and received "side payments" from the buyer to obtain their approval. Such allegations, the court held, were sufficient to state a claim upon which relief could be granted.

---

36. [9] The complaint is also devoid of even a conclusory allegation that DeepTech or any other defendant tainted the Special Approval process by defrauding or otherwise tainting the work of the Conflicts and Audit Committee.

The principle of *USACafes* is widely accepted, but has been criticized as a "needless doctrine," because other doctrines, such as veil piercing, are adequate to address the concerns that *USACafes* addresses. *See* Mohsen Manesh, *The Case Against Fiduciary Entity Veil Piercing*, 72 Bus. Law. 61 (2016).

3. The General Partner's Obligations Under the Implied Covenant of Good Faith and Fair Dealing

The Delaware courts have revisited the question of what constitutes good faith in a number of decisions, and the law has become increasingly nuanced in this area. Attorneys representing promoters of limited partnerships and limited liability companies follow these decisions closely and shape their agreements accordingly. The challenge these attorneys face is to give considerable freedom of action to the general partner or manager of these companies (particularly in related party transactions), but still make the deal marketable. The solution, generally speaking, is to provide that the general partner or manager must act in good faith and then to clearly define what constitutes good faith.

In *Norton v. K-Sea Transp. Partners L.P.*, 67 A.3d 354 (Del. 2013), which is typical of these cases, the Delaware Supreme Court considered a carefully drawn limited partnership agreement in the context of a challenge to an acquisition of the partnership. The plaintiff (Norton), a limited partner, complained about the way the consideration in the deal ($329 million) was divided between the general partner and the limited partners. The record suggested that the general partner's interest may have been worth as little as $100,000, yet it received $18 million in the deal.

The limited partnership agreement (LPA) required, among other things, that the general partner approve such a transaction and, in doing so, act in good faith. Under the LPA, the general partner acts in "good faith" if it reasonably believes that its action is in the best interest of, or at least not inconsistent with, the best interests of the partnership. In accordance with a provision of the agreement, a committee of the board of directors of the partnership obtained an opinion from an investment banker (Stifel, Nicolaus & Co.) that the proposed deal was fair to the limited partners, but the opinion expressly did not consider the fairness of the consideration paid to the general partner. The general partner relied on this fairness opinion in recommending the deal to the limited partners and the court concluded that the general partner was "therefore conclusively presumed to have acted in good faith" when it approved the deal and submitted it to the limited partners for their approval. The court concluded its opinion with this observation:

> Norton [the plaintiff] willingly invested in a limited partnership that provided fewer protections to limited partners than those provided under corporate fiduciary duty principles. He is bound by his investment decision. Here, the LPA did not require [the general partner] to consider separately the . . . fairness [of the amount of consideration paid to it], but granted [the

general partner] broad discretion to approve a merger, so long as it exercised that discretion in "good faith." Reliance on Stifel's opinion satisfied this standard. By opining that the consideration Kirby [the acquirer] paid to the unaffiliated unitholders [limited partners] was fair, Stifel's opinion addressed the fairness [of the payment to the general partner], albeit indirectly. Kirby presumably was willing to pay a fixed amount for the entire Partnership. If [the general partner] diverted too much value to itself, at some point the consideration paid to the unaffiliated unitholders would no longer be "fair."

Furthermore, the LPA does not leave ... unitholders unprotected. [The general partner's] approval merely triggered submission of the Merger to the unitholders for a majority vote. If the unitholders were dissatisfied with the Merger's terms, "their remedy [was] the ballot box, not the courthouse." Here [the general partner] is conclusively presumed to have approved the Merger in good faith, and a majority of the unitholders voted to consummate it. The LPA required nothing more.

In *Gerber v. Enterprise Products Holdings, LLC*, 67 A.3d 400 (Del. 2013) the Delaware Supreme Court similarly faced a fact pattern in which the general partner apparently complied with the terms of the limited partnership agreement in a related party transaction, but the transaction seemed, on its face, to be unfair to the limited partners. The limited partner challenging the transaction prevailed, in part because the court distinguished between the general partner's contractual fiduciary duty of good faith (which, like the provision in *Norton*, was clearly set out in the agreement) and the implied covenant of good faith and fair dealing (which, by statute cannot be disclaimed). In the course of its lengthy opinion, the Supreme Court quoted from an earlier, unrelated Chancery Court decision (*ASB Allegiance Real Estate Fund v. Scion Breckenridge Managing Member, LLC*, 50 A.3d 434, 440–42 (Del. Ch. 2012)) that distinguished between these two concepts of good faith:

The implied covenant seeks to enforce the parties' contractual bargain by implying only those terms that the parties would have agreed to during their original negotiations if they had thought to address them. Under Delaware law, a court confronting an implied covenant claim asks whether it is clear from what was expressly agreed upon that the parties who negotiated the express terms of the contract would have agreed to proscribe the act later complained of as a breach of the implied covenant of good faith—had they thought to negotiate with respect to that matter. While this test requires resort to a counterfactual world—what if—it is nevertheless appropriately restrictive and commonsensical.

The temporal focus is critical. Under a fiduciary duty or tort analysis, a court examines the parties as situated at the time of the wrong. The court determines whether the defendant owed the plaintiff a duty, considers the defendant's obligations (if any) in light of that duty, and then evaluates whether the duty was breached. Temporally, each inquiry turns on the parties' relationship as it existed at the time of the wrong. The nature of the parties' relationship may turn on historical events, and past dealings necessarily will inform the court's analysis, but liability depends on the parties' relationship when the alleged breach occurred, not on the relationship as it existed in the past.

An implied covenant claim, by contrast, looks to the past. It is not a free-floating duty unattached to the underlying legal documents. It does not ask what duty the law should impose on the parties given their relationship at the time of the wrong, but rather what the parties would have agreed to themselves had they considered the issue in their original bargaining positions at the time of contracting. "Fair dealing" is not akin to the fair process component of entire fairness, i.e., whether the fiduciary acted fairly when engaging in the challenged transaction as measured by duties of loyalty and care whose contours are mapped out by Delaware precedents. It is rather a commitment to deal "fairly" in the sense of consistently with the terms of the parties' agreement and its purpose. Likewise "good faith" does not envision loyalty to the contractual counterparty, but rather faithfulness to the scope, purpose, and terms of the parties' contract. Both necessarily turn on the contract itself and what the parties would have agreed upon had the issue arisen when they were bargaining originally.

The retrospective focus applies equally to a party's discretionary rights. The implied covenant requires that a party refrain from arbitrary or unreasonable conduct which has the effect of preventing the other party to the contract from receiving the fruits of its bargain. When exercising a discretionary right, a party to the contract must exercise its discretion reasonably. The contract may identify factors that the decision-maker can consider, and it may provide a contractual standard for evaluating the decision. Express contractual provisions always supersede the implied covenant, but even the most carefully drafted agreement will harbor residual nooks and crannies for the implied covenant to fill. In those situations, what is "arbitrary" or "unreasonable"—or conversely "reasonable"—depends on the parties' original contractual expectations, not a "free-floating" duty applied at the time of the wrong.

As a result of these decisions, counsel must be aware of three different concepts of good faith: the fiduciary duty of good faith, the contractual fiduciary duty of good faith, and the implied covenant of good faith and fair dealing. In *Gerber*, the court concluded that the general partner did satisfy the contractual fiduciary duty of good faith, but not the implied covenant of good faith and fair dealing. In short, a committee of the general partnership had approved the transaction relying on an allegedly flawed opinion of an investment banker, a procedure that a limited partner could not have anticipated and, therefore, a violation of the implied covenant of good faith and fair dealing.

Without so stating, the *Gerber* opinion implied that the contractual fiduciary duty of good faith displaced the common law fiduciary duty of good faith, although that is far from certain. In any event, the *Gerber* decision is an excellent example of the Court's willingness to employ the implied covenant to protect minority investors when those in control have satisfied the express terms of the agreement.

4. Withdrawal of General Partner

Under §602 of RULPA, a general partner may withdraw from the limited partnership, but the section recognizes that if the withdrawal violates the limited partnership agreement, the general partner will be liable for damages. Under §702, unless the partnership agreement otherwise provides, a general partner may assign his or her partnership interest, but the assignee is only entitled to the distributions to which the assignor would be entitled. Under §402, a general partner who withdraws or assigns his interest ceases to be a general partner. Finally, as noted in section D.2 above, if the limited partnership is without a general partner, it may be dissolved, subject to the provisions of §801. These provisions were at play in *Della Ratta v. Larkin*, 856 A.2d 643 (Md. 2004), where, in violation of an unambiguous anti-assignment provision in the partnership agreement, the sole general partner assigned his partnership interest to a trust, apparently to avoid some estate taxes. When a dispute subsequently arose between the general partner and certain of the limited partners, the limited partners claimed that the assignment caused the general partner to cease to be a partner and dissolved the partnership. The issue was then the effect of an assignment in violation of an anti-assignment clause. The Maryland court concluded that the assignment "was invalid and unenforceable from its inception." As there was no effective assignment, the general partner had not withdrawn and the partnership was not dissolved.

Problems

1. A group of individuals wish to invest capital in an enterprise that will engage in investment activities. The group is divided roughly into two categories: those with money, and those with (or who purport to have) investment skills. The money group decides, on legal advice, to invest through the limited partnership form as limited partners. They have chosen this form because of the limited liability, which is important because some of the investments may expose the partnership to liability, and because of the flow-through feature under the tax laws of losses and gains.

The limited partner group will contribute 95 percent of the capital and will receive 80 percent of the partnership profits and losses. The group with investment skills will contribute five percent of the capital, will receive 20 percent of the profits, and will be the general partners. They will manage the enterprise, including making the day-to-day investment decisions.

The limited partners want to protect their investment and have asked you whether the following protective measures present any legal problems:

a. Although the general partners will manage the ordinary investment activities, it is unlikely as a practical matter that major commitments of capital will be made without informing the limited partners and perhaps obtaining their consent. The limited partners are entirely content with this. What risks, if any, does this create?

b. The limited partners want the power reserved in the agreement:

(i) to limit the salaries paid to the general partners;

(ii) to prevent the general partners from becoming partners or directors in other businesses; and

(iii) to prevent the general partners from acting as accommodation endorsers or guarantors of the commercial instruments of others.

What risks are run under these circumstances? Does the cumulative effect of reserving all three of the above limitations pose a different problem than each limitation treated alone? Assume that the partnership is subject to (1) ULPA; (2) RULPA (1976); (3) the 1985 amendments to RULPA; and (4) Re-RULPA. To what extent does your analysis differ under each Act?

See Feld, *The "Control" Test for Limited Partnership*, 82 HARV. L. REV. 1471 (1969), from which the above problem is adapted.

2. On April 9, 1998, a document entitled "Amendment of Certificate of Limited Partnership" was executed and filed in the appropriate state office by the Marlbeck Motor Company, reciting that Albert Antoyan was being added as a limited partner to the firm. The document stated that Antoyan had contributed $1,000, and that he had loaned the Company $50,000, to be repaid in installments of $750 per month or 10 percent of the profits, whichever was greater. Upon satisfaction of the loan he would continue to get 10 percent of the profits. The loan was secured by a chattel mortgage on the inventory of the Company.

Antoyan was employed by Marlbeck Motor Company from January 1, 1996, to approximately April of 2000. In 1997 he became sales manager. He sold new cars, had an office and had sales personnel working under him. He had no authority to hire or fire the people under him or to order new cars without the consent of Mr. Marlbeck. He followed a formula set by Mr. Marlbeck for calculating trade-in allowances to customers purchasing new cars. He had nothing to do with the used car aspect of the business, nor with running the general office.

In April 1998, Antoyan was authorized to co-sign checks of the Company. He did so only when Mr. Marlbeck was out of town or indisposed.

In April 2000, Antoyan left the employ of the Company and never returned to work for them. Soon thereafter the Company went bankrupt and Antoyan was sued by the creditors, who claimed he was liable for the debts of the firm. What result? *See Grainger v. Antoyan*, 48 Cal. 2d 805, 313 P.2d 848 (1957) (noted in 56 MICH. L. REV. 285 (1957)). As with Problem 1, assume that the applicable law is (1) ULPA; (2) RULPA (1976); (3) the 1985 amendments to RULPA; and (4) Re-RULPA. To what extent, if at all, does your analysis differ under each Act?

Chapter 15

The Limited Liability Company

A. Introduction

The limited liability company ("LLC") is a relatively new form of doing business. It was first created by statute in Wyoming in 1977, patterned on a European model. It is designed to offer co-owners of an unincorporated business who make a proper filing with the state freedom from personal liability for the debts of the business, the option to manage the business, and the tax advantage of partnership status, which provides that the income of a business will pass through directly to its owners, without separate taxation at the entity level.

The owners of an LLC enjoy limited liability. This means that owners, while remaining liable for personal wrongdoing, are not vicariously liable for the contract or tort obligations of the business. In this sense, owners of an LLC enjoy the same immunity from the liabilities of the business that shareholders of a corporation enjoy.

The LLC is a flexible form of doing business. Management of an LLC bears none of the formalities of the corporate form of business unless the owners choose to introduce formalities. Similar to partners, the owners of an LLC can structure management as they wish. Many states provide for a choice of management upon forming an LLC: it can be member-managed (and thus very similar in informality and flexibility to a limited liability partnership), or the LLC can be manager-managed, where the owners who are not also managers play a largely passive role, similar to limited partners in a limited liability limited partnership.

The LLC is viewed by some investors as an improvement over the limited partnership because it allows for the exercise of managerial powers without the risk of personal liability for the debts of the business, a status which the limited partner does not fully enjoy even today under the 1985 amendments to RULPA, but does under Re-RULPA. Also, in the LLC all owners enjoy limited liability, as contrasted with the limited partnership, where the general partners are liable for all obligations of the partnership. (The recent appearance of the LLLP would change this in states adopting LLLP legislation.)

The LLC is viewed as an improvement over the general partnership because there is no personal liability for the debts of the business. The fact that, unlike a partnership, documents have to be prepared and filed in order to create an LLC is of little concern to the sophisticated investor. (The recent emergence of the LLP would change this, particularly in full-shield states.)

The LLC is an improvement over the corporation in some situations because it can be run more informally and the double taxation of operating in corporate form is avoided. It is regarded as an improvement over the Subchapter S corporation because its organization and operation are far less restricted.

These advantages created a powerful incentive for states to pass enabling legislation allowing people to adopt this form of doing business once the Internal Revenue Service approved partnership tax status for a properly formed LLC. That step was taken in 1988, when the IRS approved partnership status for a Wyoming LLC. Adoption of LLC enabling statutes by other states accelerated rapidly thereafter, with the great bulk of states adopting such legislation in 1991 and 1992. All 50 states now have LLC enabling legislation.

The LLC is now the clear choice for new businesses in the United States.[1] In 2017, for instance, 143,996 new LLCs were formed in Delaware, compared with only 41,553 new corporations and 11,517 partnerships. This is particularly remarkable, inasmuch as Delaware is a state that has depended on new incorporations as an important source of revenue for the state and lawyers from across the country routinely advise their clients to form their corporations under Delaware law. With just a few exceptions, more LLCs are formed in each state than are corporations, and new LLCs dwarf the number of new partnerships. Moreover, the trend is strongly in favor of LLCs. In 2004, for instance, a total of 1,041,811 new LLCs were formed in the United States, compared to 899,238 corporations. By 2007, 1,375,148 new LLCs were formed, compared to 747,533 new corporations. LLCs now likely account for roughly 70 percent of new business entity formations. Despite the dramatic decline in new partnership formations, partnership law, particularly RUPA, remains important as LLC acts are typically patterned after RUPA and bear a strong resemblance to it.

ULLCA. The above legislative avalanche took place without the impetus of a model or uniform act promulgated by NCCUSL. This is unusual in modern law, as evidenced by the uniform partnership and limited partnership acts, which preceded and strongly influenced state legislation. Perhaps this can be explained by the fact that the prospect of limited liability plus pass-through taxation was too tempting

---

1. Statistics are from the web site of the International Association of Commercial Administrators (https://www.iaca.org/annual-reports/ and from the Secretary of State of Delaware). For an in-depth statistical analysis, see Rodney D. Chrisman, *LLCs Are the New King of the Hill: An Empirical Study of the Number of New LLCs, Corporations, and LPs formed in the United States between 2004–2007 and How LLCs Were Taxed for Tax Years 2002–2006*, 15 FORDHAM J. CORP. & FIN. L. 459 (2010).

to wait for the promulgation of a uniform act, and states were pressured into hasty action. Also, the competitive pressure of not losing local filings to states that had already adopted enabling legislation doubtless influenced some states to move quickly. A uniform act is now available, however. In 1995, NCCUSL promulgated the Uniform Limited Liability Company Act (1995) ("ULLCA"). ULLCA was amended in 1996 to reflect the check-the-box regulations described below and substantially re-worked in 2006 (the Revised Uniform Limited Liability Company Act or "RUL-LCA"). In 2013, RULLCA was further amended, primarily to "harmonize" the language of RULLCA with other uniform business entity acts. This revision also included some substantive changes and some improvements to the language of the Act. The 2013 Act has been adopted in only a few jurisdictions. To the extent that this chapter includes references to RULLCA, those references correspond to the 2006 version, which has been somewhat more widely adopted. That version is also the version included in the current statutory supplement to this casebook.

ULLCA and RULLCA as amended are contained in the statutory supplement to this book, including all comments. The comments are helpful because they discuss the different approaches in the various states to the LLC and explain the choices made while drafting ULLCA and RULLCA. ULLCA and RULLCA are designed to maximize flexibility for the owners of an LLC. ULLCA was adopted in nine states and has influenced amendments to LLC legislation in a number of other states. RULLCA has been adopted in 12 states to date. However, there remains a great deal of diversity among the states in their LLC legislation.

The interest in the LLC is such that the field has generated several substantial treatises and form books. *See, e.g.,* J. William Callison & Maureen A. Sullivan, Limited Liability Companies: State Statutes and Federal Materials (2006); Larry E. Ribstein & Robert R. Keatinge, Limited Liability Companies (2006); Carter G. Bishop & Daniel S. Kleinberger, Limited Liability Companies (2006); Philip P. Whynott, The Limited Liability Company (2005) (a distinctive feature of this book is that it includes a large number of sample forms, plus several case studies analyzing drafting challenges for the attorney, including an oil and gas venture, a law firm, and a car dealership); Michael A. Bamberger & Arthur J. Jacobson, State Limited Liability Company and Partnership Laws (2006). Among the many articles published in the area, see Murdock, *Limited Liability Companies in the Decade of the 1990s: Legislative and Case Law Developments and Their Implications for the Future*, 56 Bus. Law. 499–590 (2001); J. William Callison, *Venture Capital and Corporate Governance: Evolving the Limited Liability Company to Finance the Entrepreneurial Business*, 26 Iowa L. Rev. 97 (2000); Wayne M. Gazur & Neil M. Goff, *Assessing the Limited Liability Company*, 41 Case W. Res. L. Rev. 387 (1991) (one of the first articles written on the LLC); Robert R. Keatinge et al., *The Limited Liability Company: A Study of the Emerging Entity*, 47 Bus. Law. 378 (1992); Wayne M. Gazur, *The Limited Liability Company Experiment: Unlimited Flexibility, Uncertain Role*, 58 Law & Contemp. Probs. 135 (1995).

B. Tax Matters

1. The Kintner Regulations

For many years taxation of unincorporated business associations was governed by the Kintner regulations, which have now been superseded by the check-the-box regulations described below. Under the Kintner regulations the Internal Revenue Service determined whether a particular organization qualified for partnership tax status by looking at the following four characteristics of a corporation: continuity of life, centralized management, free transferability of interests, and limited liability. If an organization had more than two of those characteristics, it was taxed as a corporation, which is why the recent availability of limited liability in the unincorporated association form was of tax significance.

As one can imagine, a great deal of the planning and drafting for unincorporated organizations centered around the challenge posed by the Kintner regulations. Also, the early LLC statutes were drafted with the danger of falling into corporate status in mind. For example, some of the early statutes, including Wyoming's statute, were "bullet proof" in the sense that a drafting attorney could not unwittingly create tax liability by overlooking the four characteristics. Wyoming accomplished this by mandating that unanimous consent was required for continuation of an LLC upon an event of dissolution and that membership interests could not be transferred without unanimous consent of all other members. Even before the advent of check-the-box, other states were moving to "default" statutes, allowing more flexibility and trust in the drafting skills of persons organizing LLCs to themselves avoid the corporate tax trap. All of this has changed with the adoption of the revolutionary check-the-box proposal put forth by the IRS.

2. The Check-the-Box Regulations

On January 1, 1997, the Treasury's check-the-box regulations were promulgated in final form. Treas. Reg. § 301.7701-1. They permit LLCs to enjoy all four corporate characteristics and still qualify for partnership taxation. LLCs now qualify as partnerships for tax purposes as a default rule, without the necessity of affirmatively filing a check-the-box election. Also, the check-the-box regulations clarify the status of the one-member LLC, disregarding it as an entity separate from its owner in the absence of an election to be treated as a corporation. Accordingly, the one-member LLC can offer limited liability and yet be treated as a sole proprietorship (if the member is an individual) or an unincorporated division (if the member is a corporation).

This change has had a major impact on tax planning, simplifying matters considerably. It seems a safe assumption that many attorneys today will look first to using the LLC or LLP in a full-shield state when advising clients who are considering the formation of a closely held[2] business. The inconvenience of operating in corporate form is avoided, as is the difficulty of double taxation.

C. Securities Laws Issues

An important question is whether an investment in an LLC is a "security" under federal and state securities laws. If so, the LLC has to undertake expensive and time-consuming registration and disclosure processes before selling membership interests, or find an exemption from registration. In general, answering the question of whether a membership interest in an LLC is a security depends largely on whether members rely upon the efforts of others to generate profits. If so, the membership interest may be characterized as an "investment contract," which is a type of security. *See SEC v. W.J. Howey Co.*, 328 U.S. 293, 299 (1946) ("an investment contract for purposes of the Securities Act means a contract, transaction or scheme whereby a person invests his money in a common enterprise and is led to expect profits solely from the efforts of a promoter or a third party."). *See* Elaine Wells, *Limited Liability Company Interests as Securities*, 4 LLC Rep. 96-610 (1996). Under this test, general partnership interests usually are regarded as outside of the securities laws because each partner has management rights, while limited partnership interests usually are regarded as securities due to the passive role of most limited partners. With regard to LLCs, the answer turns on how the entity is structured and what role the members play. If members do not rely "solely on the efforts of others," presumably they will not have to worry about the securities laws. Thus, the manager-managed LLC might pose some risk for a need to register, and the member-managed LLC ordinarily would not. *Compare Robinson v. Glynn*, 349 F.3d 166 (4th Cir. 2003), *and Tschetter v. Berven*, 621 N.W. 2d 372 (2001) (investment units in LLC were not securities), *with Ak's Daks Communications, Inc. v. Maryland Securities Division*, 771 A.2d 487 (Md. Ct. Spec. App. 2001) (LLC interest was an "investment contract" and therefore a "security"). Partnership interests in an LLP might also be considered securities if the partners do not play a meaningful role in the management of the LLP. This is often the case when ownership of the LLP is widespread and at least some of the partners are unsophisticated in the business of the LLP. *See SEC v. Lowery*, 633 F. Supp. 466 (W.D. Mich. 2009); *SEC v. Shiner*, 268 F. Supp. 2d 1333 (S.D. Fla. 2003); *Toothman v. Freeborn & Peters*, 80 P.3d 804 (Colo. App. 2002).

D. The Creation of an LLC

It is necessary to file a document, generally called articles of organization, with the state in order to create an LLC. In many states an LLC can be formed and owned

---

2. "Closely held" means a limited number of owners, as contrasted with a publicly held business. "Small business" is another phrase used to describe the closely held business, although some closely held businesses are far from small in size and influence.

by one person. (The taxation of an LLC under such circumstance is similar to that of a sole proprietorship rather than a partnership, since a partnership necessarily involves co-owners.) Although the details vary considerably among the states, the articles of organization contain, as a minimum, provisions describing the name and identification of the firm as a limited liability company, the address of the principal place of business or registered office, and the name and address of the registered agent for service of process. Owners of an LLC are called "members" in nearly all jurisdictions. The name of an LLC must contain the initials "LLC" or some equivalent thereof, to warn persons that they are dealing with a limited liability entity. In most jurisdictions LLCs must file annual reports with the state, on pain of administrative dissolution if they fail to do so. *See, e.g.,* ULLCA § 809(2).

After filing the articles of organization, the organizers typically enter into an "operating agreement," which, like a partnership agreement, details the relationship among the members. (The statutory supplement to this book contains a sample operating agreement.) The lack of an operating agreement, however, is not fatal to the existence of an LLC. See § 103 of ULLCA, providing that "all members of a limited liability company *may* enter into an operating agreement." (Emphasis added.) The LLC statutes contain numerous "default" provisions that apply in the absence of contrary provisions in the operating agreement. It is nevertheless true that the operating agreement is a very important part of the LLC documentation. Finally, the LLC is typically funded by contributions from members, which may include "tangible or intangible property or other benefit to the company, including . . . contracts for services to be performed." *See* ULLCA § 401.

While the members of a limited liability company have a great deal of freedom in fashioning the provisions of the operating agreement, there are limits to what they can do. If there is a gap in the operating agreement, the court may fill that gap with the implied covenant of good faith, discussed above in the context of partnership and limited partnership agreements and below in the context of operating agreements. In addition, courts will sometimes resist a literal interpretation of an operating agreement. For instance, in *Leight v. Osteosymbionics, L.L.C.,* 2016 WL 193511 (Ohio App. Jan. 14, 2016), the operating agreement empowered the majority member to amend the agreement and she did so, adding an arbitration provision. The minority members subsequently sued her and she invoked the newly added arbitration provision. The Ohio appellate court rejected her claim that the controversy was subject to arbitration because the plaintiffs had not agreed to arbitration.

One way to form an LLC is to convert another existing entity or sole proprietorship into an LLC. A number of states have legislation allowing the conversion of any entity into any other kind of entity.

Notes

1. Not surprisingly, courts are adopting corporate principles in deciding whether parties that contract with a promoter of an LLC not yet in existence are estopped to deny the existence of the LLC after it is formed and ratifies the contract. In *P.D. 2000, L.L.C. v. First Financial Planners, Inc.*, 998 S.W.2d 108, 111 (Mo. Ct. App. 1999) the contract in question was entered into between the defendant and the plaintiff LLC, which was actually formed some two and a half months after the contract was executed. Nonetheless, the court held that the LLC could enforce the agreement "on the basis of the doctrine of estoppel." The plaintiff knew that the LLC was not yet in existence and the contract stated that the LLC was in the process of organization. Moreover, the LLC immediately undertook performance of the agreement. By comparison, see *Brcka v. Falcon Electric Corp.*, C8-00-1434, 2001 Minn. App. LEXIS 649 (June 12, 2001), where the court held that in the absence of any reliance factors, the failure to file articles of organization results in a finding that the promoters would be treated as partners of a general partnership.

2. Another doctrine from corporate law, the concept of a "de facto" corporation, has found its way into LLC law. The concept is that an entity may not have taken all of the steps necessary to become a "de jure" entity, yet it has made an attempt to do so and should be considered a "de facto" entity. A de facto corporation is recognized as a corporation for legal purposes. *In re Hausman*, 921 N.E.2d 191 (N.Y. 2009) recognized that the de facto doctrine applied to limited liability companies, but that the elements of the doctrine had not been satisfied in that case: (1) a law under which the limited liability company might be organized, (2) an attempt to organize it, and (3) an exercise of company powers thereafter. The second prong was not satisfied because the organizers of the LLC failed to make a "colorable attempt" to file the articles of organization, which the court said was necessary to satisfy the second prong.

In *Duray Development, LLC v. Perrin*, 792 N.W.2d 749 (Mich. Ct. App. 2010), the defendant entered into a contract on behalf of Outlaw Excavating, LLC to provide excavation services to the plaintiff. The contract was entered into on October 27 and the articles of organization for Outlaw were executed the same day. Michigan law provides, however, that the articles of organization must be delivered to the administrator of the Michigan Department of Energy, Labor and Economic Growth. After the articles are delivered, the administrator "shall endorse upon it the word 'filed'" and the articles become effective when so endorsed. This did not occur until November 29. Nevertheless, the court held that the de facto doctrine applied and the LLC, not its member, was liable on the contract.

Elf Atochem North America, Inc. v. Jaffari

Supreme Court of Delaware
727 A.2d 286 (1999)

VEASEY, CHIEF JUSTICE:

This is a case of first impression before this Court involving the Delaware Limited Liability Company Act (the "Act"). The limited liability company ("LLC") is a relatively new entity that has emerged in recent years as an attractive vehicle to facilitate business relationships and transactions. The wording and architecture of the Act is somewhat complicated, but it is designed to achieve what is seemingly a simple concept — to permit persons or entities ("members") to join together in an environment of private ordering to form and operate the enterprise under an LLC agreement with tax benefits akin to a partnership and limited liability akin to the corporate form.

This is a purported derivative suit brought on behalf of a Delaware LLC calling into question whether: (1) the LLC, which did not itself execute the LLC agreement in this case ("the Agreement") defining its governance and operation, is nevertheless bound by the Agreement; and (2) contractual provisions directing that all disputes be resolved exclusively by arbitration or court proceedings in California are valid under the Act. Resolution of these issues requires us to examine the applicability and scope of certain provisions of the Act in light of the Agreement.

We hold that: (1) the Agreement is binding on the LLC as well as the members; and (2) since the Act does not prohibit the members of an LLC from vesting exclusive subject matter jurisdiction in arbitration proceedings (or court enforcement of arbitration) in California to resolve disputes, the contractual forum selection provisions must govern.

Accordingly, we affirm the judgment of the Court of Chancery dismissing the action brought in that court on the ground that the Agreement validly predetermined the fora in which disputes would be resolved, thus stripping the Court of Chancery of subject matter jurisdiction.

Plaintiff below-appellant Elf Atochem North America, Inc., a Pennsylvania Corporation ("Elf"), manufactures and distributes solvent-based maskants to the aerospace and aviation industries throughout the world. Defendant below-appellee Cyrus A. Jaffari is the president of Malek, Inc., a California Corporation. Jaffari had developed an innovative, environmentally-friendly alternative to the solvent-based maskants that presently dominate the market.

For decades, the aerospace and aviation industries have used solvent-based maskants in the chemical milling process. Recently, however, the Environmental Protection Agency ("EPA") classified solvent-based maskants as hazardous chemicals and air contaminants. To avoid conflict with EPA regulations, Elf considered developing or distributing a maskant less harmful to the environment.

In the mid-nineties, Elf approached Jaffari and proposed investing in his product and assisting in its marketing. Jaffari found the proposal attractive since his company, Malek, Inc., possessed limited resources and little international sales expertise. Elf and Jaffari agreed to undertake a joint venture that was to be carried out using a limited liability company as the vehicle.

On October 29, 1996, Malek, Inc. caused to be filed a Certificate of Formation with the Delaware Secretary of State, thus forming Malek LLC, a Delaware limited liability company under the Act. The certificate of formation is a relatively brief and formal document that is the first statutory step in creating the LLC as a separate legal entity. The certificate does not contain a comprehensive agreement among the parties, and the statute contemplates that the certificate of formation is to be complemented by the terms of the Agreement.

Next, Elf, Jaffari and Malek, Inc. entered into a series of agreements providing for the governance and operation of the joint venture. Of particular importance to this litigation, Elf, Malek, Inc., and Jaffari entered into the Agreement, a comprehensive and integrated document of 38 single-spaced pages setting forth detailed provisions for the governance of Malek LLC, which is not itself a signatory to the Agreement. Elf and Malek LLC entered into an Exclusive Distributorship Agreement in which Elf would be the exclusive, worldwide distributor for Malek LLC. The Agreement provides that Jaffari will be the manager of Malek LLC. Jaffari and Malek LLC entered into an employment agreement providing for Jaffari's employment as chief executive officer of Malek LLC.

The Agreement is the operative document for purposes of this Opinion, however. Under the Agreement, Elf contributed $1 million in exchange for a 30 percent interest in Malek LLC. Malek, Inc. contributed its rights to the water-based maskant in exchange for a 70 percent interest in Malek LLC.

The Agreement contains an arbitration clause covering all disputes. The clause, Section 13.8, provides that "any controversy or dispute arising out of this Agreement, the interpretation of any of the provisions hereof, or the action or inaction of any Member or Manager hereunder shall be submitted to arbitration in San Francisco, California. . . ." Section 13.8 further provides: "No action . . . based upon any claim arising out of or related to this Agreement shall be instituted in any court by any Member except (a) an action to compel arbitration . . . or (b) an action to enforce an award obtained in an arbitration proceeding. . . ." The Agreement also contains a forum selection clause, Section 13.7, providing that all members consent to: "exclusive jurisdiction of the state and federal courts sitting in California in any action on a claim arising out of, under or in connection with this Agreement or the transactions contemplated by this Agreement, provided such claim is not required to be arbitrated pursuant to Section 13.8"; and personal jurisdiction in California. The Distribution Agreement contains no forum selection or arbitration clause.

Elf's Suit in the Court of Chancery

On April 27, 1998, Elf sued Jaffari and Malek LLC, individually and derivatively on behalf of Malek LLC, in the Delaware Court of Chancery, seeking equitable remedies. Among other claims, Elf alleged that Jaffari breached his fiduciary duty to Malek LLC, pushed Malek LLC to the brink of insolvency by withdrawing funds for personal use, interfered with business opportunities, failed to make disclosures to Elf, and threatened to make poor quality maskant and to violate environmental regulations. Elf also alleged breach of contract, tortious interference with prospective business relations, and (solely as to Jaffari) fraud.

The Court of Chancery granted defendants' motion to dismiss based on lack of subject matter jurisdiction. The court held that Elf's claims arose under the Agreement, or the transactions contemplated by the agreement, and were directly related to Jaffari's actions as manager of Malek LLC. Therefore, the court found that the Agreement governed the question of jurisdiction and that only a court of law or arbitrator in California is empowered to decide these claims. Elf now appeals the order of the Court of Chancery dismissing the complaint. . . .

The phenomenon of business arrangements using "alternative entities" has been developing rapidly over the past several years. Long gone are the days when business planners were confined to corporate or partnership structures.

The Delaware Act was adopted in October 1992. . . . To date, the Act has been amended six times with a view to modernization. The LLC is an attractive form of business entity because it combines corporate-type limited liability with partnership-type flexibility and tax advantages. The Act can be characterized as a "flexible statute" because it generally permits members to engage in private ordering with substantial freedom of contract to govern their relationship, provided they do not contravene any mandatory provisions of the Act. . . .

The basic approach of the Delaware Act is to provide members with broad discretion in drafting the Agreement and to furnish default provisions when the members' agreement is silent. The Act is replete with fundamental provisions made subject to modification in the Agreement (*e.g.* "unless otherwise provided in a limited liability company agreement . . .").

Although business planners may find comfort in working with the Act in structuring transactions and relationships, it is a somewhat awkward document for this Court to construe and apply in this case. To understand the overall structure and thrust of the Act, one must wade through provisions that are prolix, sometimes oddly organized, and do not always flow evenly. Be that as it may as a problem in mastering the Act as a whole, one returns to the narrow and discrete issues presented in this case.

Section 18-1101(b) of the Act . . . provides that "[i]t is the policy of [the Act] to give the maximum effect to the principle of freedom of contract and to the enforceability of limited liability company agreements." . . .

In general, the commentators observe that only where the agreement is inconsistent with mandatory statutory provisions will the members' agreement be invalidated. Such statutory provisions are likely to be those intended to protect third parties, not necessarily the contracting members. As a framework for decision, we apply that principle to the issues before us, without expressing any views more broadly. . . .

Malek LLC's Failure to Sign the Agreement does not Affect the Members' Agreement Governing Dispute Resolution

Elf argues that Malek LLC came into existence on October 29, 1996, when the parties filed its Certificate of Formation with the Delaware Secretary of State. The parties did not sign the Agreement until November 4, 1996. Elf contends that Malek LLC existed as an LLC as of October 29, 1996, but never agreed to the Agreement because it did not sign it. Because Malek LLC never expressly assented to the arbitration and forum selection clauses within the Agreement, Elf argues it can sue derivatively on behalf of Malek LLC pursuant to 6 Del. C. § 18-1001.[3]

We are not persuaded by this argument. Section 18-101(7) defines the limited liability company agreement as "any agreement, written or oral, *of the member or members* as to the affairs of a limited liability company and the conduct of its business." Here, Malek, Inc. and Elf, the members of Malek LLC, executed the Agreement to carry out the affairs and business of Malek LLC and to provide for arbitration and forum selection.

Notwithstanding Malek LLC's failure to sign the Agreement, Elf's claims are subject to the arbitration and forum selection clauses of the Agreement. The Act is a statute designed to permit members maximum flexibility in entering into an agreement to govern their relationship. It is the members who are the real parties in interest. The LLC is simply their joint business vehicle. This is the contemplation of the statute in prescribing the outlines of a limited liability company agreement.

Classification by Elf of its Claims as Derivative is Irrelevant

Elf argues that the Court of Chancery erred in failing to classify its claims against Malek LLC as derivative. Elf contends that, had the court properly characterized its claims as derivative instead of direct, the arbitration and forum selection clauses would not have applied to bar adjudication in Delaware.

In the corporate context, "the derivative form of action permits an individual shareholder to bring 'suit to enforce a corporate cause of action against officers, directors and third parties.'" The derivative suit is a corporate concept grafted onto the limited liability company form. The Act expressly allows for a derivative suit, providing that "a member . . . may bring an action in the Court of Chancery in the right of a limited liability company to recover a judgment in its favor if managers or members with authority to do so have refused to bring the action or if an effort to cause those managers or members to bring the action is not likely to succeed." [§ 18-1001] Notwithstanding the Agreement to the contrary, Elf argues that [§ 18-1001] permits the assertion of derivative claims of Malek LLC against Malek LLC's manager, Jaffari.

Although Elf correctly points out that Delaware law allows for derivative suits against management of an LLC, Elf contracted away its right to bring such an action in Delaware and agreed instead to dispute resolution in California. That is, Section 13.8 of the Agreement specifically provides that the parties (*i.e.*, Elf) agree to

---

3. [35] 6 Del. C. § 18-1001 provides: "Right to bring action. A member may . . . bring an action in the Court of Chancery in the right of a limited liability company to recover a judgment in its favor if managers or members with authority to do so have refused to bring the action or if an effort to cause those managers or members to bring the action is not likely to succeed."

institute "[n]o action at law or in equity based upon *any* claim arising out of or related to this Agreement" except an action to compel arbitration or to enforce an arbitration award. Furthermore, under Section 13.7 of the Agreement, each member (*i.e.,* Elf) "consent[ed] to the exclusive jurisdiction of the state and federal courts sitting in California in *any* action on a claim arising out of, under or in connection with this Agreement or the transactions contemplated by this Agreement."

Sections 13.7 and 13.8 of the Agreement do not distinguish between direct and derivative claims. They simply state that the members may not initiate *any* claims outside of California. Elf initiated this action in the Court of Chancery in contravention of its own contractual agreement. As a result, the Court of Chancery correctly held that all claims, whether derivative or direct, arose under, out of, or in connection with the Agreement, and thus are covered by the arbitration and forum selection clauses.

This prohibition is so broad that it is dispositive of Elf's claims (counts IV, V and VI of the amended complaint) that purport to be under the Distributorship Agreement that has no choice of forum provision. Notwithstanding the fact that the Distributorship Agreement is a separate document, in reality these counts are all subsumed under the rubric of the Agreement's forum selection clause for any claim "arising out of" and those that are "in connection with" the Agreement or transactions "contemplated by" or "related to" that Agreement under Sections 13.7 and 13.8. We agree with the Court of Chancery's decision that:

> plaintiff's claims arise under the LLC Agreement or the transactions contemplated by the Agreement, and are directly related to Jaffari's "action or inaction" in connection with his role as the manager of Malek. Plainly, all of plaintiff's claims revolve around Jaffari's conduct (or misconduct) as Malek's manager. Virtually all the remedies that plaintiff seeks bear directly on Jaffari's duties and obligations under the LLC Agreement. Plaintiff's complaint that "Jaffari ... has totally disregarded his obligations under the *LLC Agreement*" also lends support to my conclusion.

The Court of Chancery was correct in holding that Elf's claims bear directly on Jaffari's duties and obligations under the Agreement. Thus, we decline to disturb its holding.

The Argument that Chancery Has "Special" Jurisdiction for Derivative Claims Must Fail

Elf claims that 6 Del. C. §§ 18-110(a), 18-111 and 18-1001 vest the Court of Chancery with subject matter jurisdiction over this dispute. According to Elf, the Act grants the Court of Chancery subject matter jurisdiction over its claims for breach of fiduciary duty and removal of Jaffari, even though the parties contracted to arbitrate all such claims in California. In effect, Elf argues that the Act affords the Court of Chancery "special" jurisdiction to adjudicate its claims, notwithstanding a clear contractual agreement to the contrary.

Again, we are not persuaded by Elf's argument. Elf is correct that 6 Del. C. §§ 18-110(a) and 18-111 vest jurisdiction with the Court of Chancery in actions involving removal of managers and interpreting, applying or enforcing LLC agreements respectively. As noted above, Section 18-1001 provides that a party may bring derivative actions in the Court of Chancery. Such a grant of jurisdiction may have been constitutionally necessary if the claims do not fall within the traditional equity jurisdiction. Nevertheless, for the purpose of designating a more convenient forum, we find no reason why the members cannot alter the default jurisdictional provisions of the statute and contract away their right to file suit in Delaware.

For example, Elf argues that Section 18-110(a), which grants the Court of Chancery jurisdiction to hear claims involving the election or removal of a manager of an LLC, applies to the case at bar because Elf is seeking removal of Jaffari. While Elf is correct on the substance of Section 18-110(a), Elf is unable to convince this Court that the parties may not contract to avoid the applicability of Section 18-110(a). We hold that, because the policy of the Act is to give the maximum effect to the principle of freedom of contract and to the enforceability of LLC agreements, the parties may contract to avoid the applicability of Sections 18-110(a), 18-111, and 18-1001. Here, the parties contracted as clearly as practicable when they relegated to California in Section 13.7 "any" dispute "arising out of, under or in connection with [the] Agreement or the transactions contemplated by [the] Agreement. . . ." Likewise, in Section 13.8: "*[n]o action* at law or in equity based upon *any claim arising out of or related to*" the Agreement may be brought, except in California, and then only to enforce arbitration in California.

Our conclusion is bolstered by the fact that Delaware recognizes a strong public policy in favor of arbitration. Normally, doubts on the issue of whether a particular issue is arbitrable will be resolved in favor of arbitration. In the case at bar, we do not believe there is any doubt of the parties' intention to agree to arbitrate *all* disputed matters in California. If we were to hold otherwise, arbitration clauses in existing LLC agreements could be rendered meaningless. By resorting to the alleged "special" jurisdiction of the Court of Chancery, future plaintiffs could avoid their own arbitration agreements simply by couching their claims as derivative. Such a result could adversely affect many arbitration agreements already in existence in Delaware.

Validity of Section 13.7 of the Agreement under 6 Del. C. § 18-109(d)

Elf argues that Section 13.7 of the Agreement, which provides that each member of Malek LLC "consents to the exclusive jurisdiction of the state and federal courts sitting in California in any action on a claim arising out of, under or in connection with this Agreement or the transactions contemplated by this Agreement . . ." is invalid under Delaware law. Elf argues that Section 13.7 is invalid because it violates 6 Del. C. § 18-109(d).

Subsection 18-109(d) is part of Section 18-109 relating to "Service of process on managers and liquidating trustee." It provides:

In a written limited liability company agreement or other writing, a manager or member *may* consent to be subject to the nonexclusive jurisdiction of the courts of, or arbitration in, a specified jurisdiction, or the exclusive jurisdiction of the courts of the State of Delaware, or the exclusivity of arbitration in a specified jurisdiction or the State of Delaware. . . .

Section 18-109(d) does not expressly state that the parties are prohibited from agreeing to the *exclusive* subject matter jurisdiction of the courts or arbitration fora of a foreign jurisdiction. Thus, Elf contends that Section 18-109(d) prohibits vesting exclusive jurisdiction in a court outside of Delaware, which the parties have done in Section 13.7.

We decline to adopt such a strict reading of the statute. Assuming, without deciding, that Section 109(d) relates to subject matter jurisdiction and not merely *in personam* jurisdiction, it is permissive in that it provides that the parties "may" agree to the non-exclusive jurisdiction of the courts of a foreign jurisdiction or to submit to the exclusive jurisdiction of Delaware. In general, the legislature's use of "may" connotes the voluntary, not mandatory or exclusive, set of options. The permissive nature of Section 18-109(d) complements the overall policy of the Act to give maximum effect to the parties' freedom of contract. Although Section 18-109(d) fails to mention that the parties may agree to the *exclusive* jurisdiction of a foreign jurisdiction, the Act clearly does not state that the parties must agree to either one of the delineated options for subject matter jurisdiction. Had the General Assembly intended to prohibit the parties from vesting exclusive jurisdiction in arbitration or court proceedings in another state, it could have proscribed such an option. The Court of Chancery did not err in declining to strike down the validity of Section 13.7 or Section 13.8 of the Agreement.

We affirm the judgment of the Court of Chancery dismissing Elf Atochem's amended complaint for lack of subject matter jurisdiction.

Notes

1. Following the decision in *Elf Atochem*, the Delaware legislature amended the LLC statute to codify the holding in the case. *See* 6 Del. C. § 18-101(7) ("[a] limited liability company is not required to execute its limited liability company agreement. A limited liability company is bound by its limited liability company agreement whether or not the limited liability company executes the limited liability company agreement"). There is some authority contrary to *Elf Atochem*. *See Trover v. 419 OCR, Inc.*, 921 N.E.2d 1249 (Ill. App. Ct. 2010) (an arbitration agreement not binding on an LLC because it was not a party to it).

2. *Statute of Frauds.* In a decision handed down in 2009, the Delaware Supreme Court held that although an operating agreement may be oral, the statute of frauds still applied and rendered unenforceable that portion of the operating agreement which could not be performed within a year of its making. *Olson v. Halvorsen*, 986 A.2d 1150 (Del. 2009). The Delaware legislature promptly amended its limited

liability company act to overrule the decision. *See* 6 Del. C. § 18-101(7) ("A limited liability company agreement is not subject to any statute of frauds (including Section 2714 of this Title)").

E. The Entity Theory and the LLC

Litchfield Asset Management Corporation v. Howell

Appellate Court of Connecticut

799 A.2d 298 (2002) *overruled on other grounds by Robinson v. Coughlin,* 830 A.2d 1114 (Conn. 2003)

LAVERY, C.J.

The defendants appeal from the trial court's judgment awarding damages and injunctive relief to the plaintiff, Litchfield Asset Management Corporation. [The defendants are Jon Howell and Mary Ann Howell, who are husband and wife, and the two limited liability companies, Mary Ann Howell Interiors and Architectural Design, LLC, and Antiquities Associates, LLC, through which Mary Ann Howell managed her interior design business during the times relevant to this appeal.] . . .

The following facts and procedural history are relevant to our disposition of the appeal. Mary Ann Howell has worked for approximately thirty years in the field of interior design. In 1993, operating through the now defunct Mary Ann Howell Interiors, Inc. (Interiors), she entered into an agreement to perform services for the plaintiff at its facilities in Texas. In 1995, the plaintiff brought an action in a Texas court against Mary Ann Howell and Interiors based on disputes arising from the agreement. Mary Ann Howell and Interiors unsuccessfully objected to the Texas court's jurisdiction and, thereafter, failed to defend against the plaintiff's claims. In July, 1996, the Texas court entered a default judgment against Mary Ann Howell and Interiors in the amount of $657,207 plus interest. In December, 1996, the plaintiff brought an action in the Connecticut Superior Court to enforce the Texas judgment. In February, 1997, the Connecticut trial court rendered a judgment in favor of the plaintiff in the amount of $657,207 plus interest. That judgment was affirmed on appeal in December, 1997. *Litchfield Asset Management Corp. v. Howell,* 47 Conn. App. 920, 703 A.2d 1192 (1997).

While the aforementioned proceedings were unfolding, Mary Ann Howell and her family members formed two new limited liability companies, Mary Ann Howell Interiors and Architectural Design, LLC (Design), and Antiquities Associates, LLC (Antiquities). In May, 1996, Mary Ann Howell contributed $144,679, which she obtained by borrowing against her life insurance policies, in exchange for a 97 percent ownership interest in Design. Jon Howell and the couple's two daughters, Marla Howell and Wendi Howell, each contributed $10 in exchange for a 1 percent ownership interest. In November, 1997, Design contributed $102,901 for a 99 percent interest in Antiquities, and Mary Ann Howell contributed $10 for the remaining 1 percent.

On May 11, 1998, the plaintiff commenced the present action against Mary Ann Howell, Jon Howell, Design and Antiquities. The plaintiff alleged that Mary Ann Howell and Jon Howell had formed Design, a "mere shell," and used it "to perpetrate a fraud or promote injustice by preventing the plaintiff from collecting on its judgment against Mary Ann Howell." It also alleged that Mary Ann Howell and Jon Howell, by forming Antiquities and causing Design to transfer $102,901 to Antiquities, created another entity that "serv[ed] no legitimate purpose" but fraudulently or unjustly to prevent the collection of the plaintiff's judgment. Last, the plaintiff alleged that Mary Ann Howell and Jon Howell, by forming Design and Antiquities, and transferring Mary Ann Howell's personal assets into and between them, wilfully, wantonly and maliciously conspired to fraudulently divert those assets beyond the plaintiff's reach as a judgment creditor, resulting in monetary damage to the plaintiff.

On the first and second counts, the plaintiff sought a judgment declaring that Design and Antiquities were alter egos of Mary Ann Howell, "established and operated so as to avoid the just debt owed the plaintiff," and enjoining Design and Antiquities from transferring or encumbering their assets until the plaintiff's judgment is satisfied. On the third count, the plaintiff sought damages, punitive damages, attorney's fees and an order enjoining Mary Ann Howell and Jon Howell from transferring or encumbering the assets of, or income or profits derived from, Design or Antiquities.

The case was tried to the court on May 25, 2000, and May 31, 2000. The following facts were admitted, stipulated to by the parties or reasonably found by the court on the basis of the evidence presented. Mary Ann Howell is the general manager of both Design and Antiquities. Neither company has any employees; those who provide services for the companies have independent contractor status. Both companies operate out of a loft space above the garage at Jon Howell and Mary Ann Howell's personal residence. Neither company pays any rent to Jon Howell, owner of the premises, for its use. Mary Ann Howell exercised complete control over the policies, finances and business practices of Design and Antiquities; there is no indication in the record that Jon Howell, Wendi Howell or Marla Howell participated in their operation in any significant way.

Mary Ann Howell has never drawn a salary or received regular distributions from either Design or Antiquities, but consistently has used company funds to pay for many personal expenses and to provide substantial, interest free loans or gifts to family members. . . .

Although Design and Antiquities maintained separate bank accounts, payments for Antiquities' sales were deposited into Design's account without a corresponding reimbursement from Design to Antiquities. The records of the two companies were segregated to some extent for tax purposes, though tax returns were not filed for either company for the two years preceding trial.

After considering the evidence, the court concluded that the requisite legal tests had been satisfied such that Design and Antiquities were but alter egos of Mary

Ann Howell and thus were liable for her personal debt owed to the plaintiff. . . . The court granted the equitable relief requested by the plaintiff and awarded the plaintiff $163,260 in monetary damages and $21,682 in punitive damages. Additional facts will be set forth as necessary. . . .

The defendants . . . claim that the court improperly disregarded the corporate forms of Design and Antiquities so as to hold them liable for the personal debt of Mary Ann Howell. We disagree.

"A corporation is a separate legal entity, separate and apart from its stockholders. . . . It is an elementary principle of corporate law that a corporation and its stockholders are separate entities and that . . . corporate property is vested in the corporation and *not* in the owner of the corporate stock." (Citations omitted; emphasis in original; internal quotation marks omitted.) *State v. Radzvilowicz*, 47 Conn. App. 1, 18–19, 703 A.2d 767, cert. denied, 243 Conn. 955, 704 A.2d 806 (1997). That principle also is applicable to limited liability companies and their members. General Statutes § 34-133. The assets of a corporation or limited liability company, therefore, typically are not available to creditors seeking to recover amounts owed by a stockholder or member of that corporation or limited liability company.[4] Nonetheless, "[c]ourts will . . . disregard the fiction of a separate legal entity to pierce the shield of immunity afforded by the corporate structure in a situation in which the corporate entity has been so controlled and dominated that justice requires liability to be imposed. . . ." (Internal quotation marks omitted.) *Angelo Tomasso, Inc. v. Armor Construction & Paving, Inc.*, 187 Conn. 544, 552, 447 A.2d 406 (1982).

The court determined that the facts of this case warranted a disregard of Design's and Antiquities' limited liability structures so as to hold the companies liable for Mary Ann Howell's debt to the plaintiff. The court found sufficient evidence to pierce the corporate veils[5] under both the instrumentality rule; see Id., at 553, 447 A.2d 406; and the identity rule.[6] See Id., at 554, 447 A.2d 406. We will address in turn the court's application of each of these rules, mindful that both involve fact based determinations and that the ultimate "issue of whether the corporate veil [should be] pierced presents a question of fact"; Id., at 561, 447 A.2d 406; *Davenport v. Quinn*, 53 Conn. App. 282, 302, 730 A.2d 1184 (1999); such that we must defer to the court's findings unless they are clearly erroneous. . . .

---

4. [9] Pursuant to General Statutes § 34-171, however, a judgment creditor of a limited liability company member may apply to a court to "charge the member's limited liability company interest with payment of the unsatisfied amount of the judgment with interest. . . ." Thereafter, any distributions from the company to the member are available to satisfy the judgment debt. See, e.g., *PB Real Estate, Inc. v. DEM II Properties*, 50 Conn. App. 741, 719 A.2d 73 (1998).

5. [10] A court's disregard of an entity's structure is commonly known as "'piercing the corporate veil.'" 18 Am. Jur. 2d 841, Corporations § 43 (1985).

6. [11] Pursuant to Connecticut case law, however, a court may properly disregard a corporate entity if the elements of *either* the instrumentality rule or identity rule are satisfied. *Angelo Tomasso, Inc. v. Armor Construction & Paving, Inc.*, supra, 187 Conn. at 553, 447 A.2d 406; *Saphir v. Neustadt*, 177 Conn. 191, 209–10, 413 A.2d 843 (1979), *Zaist v. Olson*, 154 Conn. 563, 578, 227 A.2d 552 (1967).

We note at the outset that this case presents a fact pattern that, while not especially novel or uncommon, has not been considered by Connecticut's appellate courts. In the usual veil piercing case, a court is asked to disregard a corporate entity so as to make available the personal assets of its owners to satisfy a liability of the entity. In this case, an instance of what is known as "reverse piercing," the plaintiff argues the opposite, that the assets of the corporate entities should be made available to pay the personal debts of an owner.[7]

A guiding concept behind both standard and reverse veil piercing cases is the need for the court to "avoid an over-rigid preoccupation with questions of structure . . . and apply the preexisting and overarching principle that liability is imposed to reach an equitable result." (Citations omitted; internal quotation marks omitted.) *LiButti v. United States*, 107 F.3d 110, 119 (2d Cir. 1997). We consider this directive to be sensible and therefore recognize that under the appropriate circumstances, i.e., when the elements of the identity or instrumentality rule have been established, a reverse pierce is a viable remedy that a court may employ when necessary to achieve an equitable result and when unfair prejudice will not result.

We now review the court's application of the veil piercing rules to the facts of this case. "The instrumentality rule requires, in any case but an express agency, proof of three elements: (1) Control, not mere majority or complete stock control, but complete domination, not only of finances but of policy and business practice *in respect to the transaction attacked* so that the corporate entity as to this transaction had at the time no separate mind, will or existence of its own; (2) that such control must have been used by the defendant to commit fraud or wrong, to perpetrate the violation of a statutory or other positive legal duty, or a dishonest or unjust act in contravention of plaintiff's legal rights; *and* (3) that the aforesaid control and breach of duty must proximately cause the injury or unjust loss complained of." (Emphasis in original; internal quotation marks omitted.) *Davenport v. Quinn*, supra, 53 Conn. App. at 300, 730 A.2d 1184, quoting *Angelo Tomasso, Inc. v. Armor Construction & Paving, Inc.*, supra, 187 Conn. at 553, 447 A.2d 406.

We first consider whether the element of domination and control is present under the facts of this case. Specifically, we inquire as to whether the court properly found that Mary Ann Howell dominated and controlled Design directly, and that through extension of her control of Design, she also controlled Antiquities. Courts, in assessing whether an entity is dominated or controlled, have looked for the presence of a number of factors. Those include: "(1) the absence of corporate formalities; (2) inadequate capitalization; (3) whether funds are put in and taken out of the corporation for personal rather than corporate purposes; (4) overlapping ownership,

---

7. [13] The fact pattern before us has been more specifically described as "outsider reverse piercing," in that an outside third party pursuing a claim against a corporate insider is attempting to have the corporate entity disregarded. Conversely, in an "insider reverse piercing" claim, a corporate insider attempts to have the corporate entity disregarded. G. Crespi, "The Reverse Pierce Doctrine: Applying Appropriate Standards," 16 J. Corp. L. 33, 37 (1990).

officers, directors, personnel; (5) common office space, address, phones; (6) the amount of business discretion by the allegedly dominated corporation; (7) whether the corporations dealt with each other at arm's length; (8) whether the corporations are treated as independent profit centers; (9) payment or guarantee of debts of the dominated corporation; and (10) whether the corporation in question had property that was used by other of the corporations as if it were its own." *Hale Propeller, LLC v. Ryan Marine Products Pty., Ltd.*, 98 F. Supp. 2d 260, 265 (D. Conn. 2000), citing *William Passalacqua Builders, Inc. v. Resnick Developers South, Inc.*, 933 F.2d 131, 139 (2d Cir. 1991); see also *Northern Tankers (Cyprus) Ltd. v. Backstrom*, 967 F. Supp. 1391, 1401–1408 (D. Conn. 1997).

In this case, there is evidence of Mary Ann Howell's dominance and control to satisfy many of those elements. Regarding the third factor, the parties stipulated that Mary Ann Howell used company funds to pay in excess of $30,000 in personal expenses, to purchase gifts for and make interest free loans to family members and to pay the $8247 balance of a loan for a vehicle titled to Jon Howell. As to the fourth factor, the overlap in ownership between Design and Antiquities was nearly complete, in that Mary Ann Howell owned 97 percent of Design and together, Design and Mary Ann Howell owned the entirety of Antiquities. Further, Mary Ann Howell is the general manager of both companies, each of which has no employees but retains the same independent contractors. Design and Antiquities both operate out of the same office space, i.e., the loft over the Howells' garage, thereby satisfying the fifth factor. Regarding the seventh, eighth and tenth factors, Design's retention of revenue obtained through the sale of Antiquities' inventory evidences a lack of arm's length dealing between the two companies, a failure to treat Antiquities as an independent profit center and Design's treatment of Antiquities property as if it belonged to Design. Given the evidence, we cannot say that it was clearly erroneous for the court to have found that Mary Ann Howell exercised domination and control over Design and Antiquities.

We next consider whether the court properly found that Mary Ann Howell used that control and dominance to perpetrate a wrong. In 1995, the plaintiff initiated an action against Mary Ann Howell and Interiors, the corporation through which she previously had conducted business and, eventually, obtained a judgment of $657,270. Mary Ann Howell testified that in May, 1996, she formed Design using $144,659 of her own funds along with $30 of her family's funds. Mary Ann Howell testified that Jon Howell had no involvement in Design, other than to sign the paperwork for its formation, and that her daughters were made members of the company only in case anything ever happened to her. She stated that her daughters knew that she made whatever decisions were necessary to run the business, and that they never came to her and suggested that things be done any differently. Mary Ann Howell also testified that she was the only party with signatory powers on Design's bank account.

Some eighteen months later, in November, 1997, after the plaintiff had obtained its judgment in Texas and just before that judgment was recognized by the

Connecticut court, Mary Ann Howell, as general manager and 97 percent owner of Design, caused Design to fund the start-up of Antiquities with $102,901 of the money she previously had transferred to Design. Jon Howell, Marla Howell and Wendi Howell had no involvement in the operation of Antiquities.

After the formation of the two limited liability companies, Mary Ann Howell continued to utilize the transferred funds as if they were her own, as evidenced by the stipulations regarding the payment of her personal expenses. Moreover, by having Design pay her expenses directly, instead of paying her a salary or providing regular cash distributions, Mary Ann Howell deprived the plaintiff of any means of collecting the judgment against her. . . . Given the evidence before it, the court properly found that Mary Ann Howell had used her control of Design and Antiquities unjustly to avoid her personal debt to the plaintiff.

Last, we review the court's finding that Mary Ann Howell's transfer of her personal funds to Design, and then to Antiquities, proximately caused the loss of which the plaintiff complained. . . .

In this case, Mary Ann Howell, with knowledge that the plaintiff was pursuing a claim against her that she chose not to defend, transferred the cash value of her life insurance policies from herself to Design. That transfer prevented the plaintiff from securing collection of the judgment it eventually obtained against Mary Ann Howell. We conclude that the proximate causation requirement similarly is satisfied here. As such, the court was correct in finding that the elements of the instrumentality rule were satisfied. We turn now to its application of the identity rule.

"The identity rule has been stated as follows: If a plaintiff can show that there was such a unity of interest and ownership that the independence of the corporations had in effect ceased or had never begun, an adherence to the fiction of separate identity would serve only to defeat justice and equity by permitting the economic entity to escape liability arising out of an operation conducted by one corporation for the benefit of the whole enterprise." (Internal quotation marks omitted.) *Davenport v. Quinn,* supra, 53 Conn. App. at 300–301, 730 A.2d 1184, quoting *Angelo Tomasso, Inc. v. Armor Construction & Paving, Inc.,* supra, 187 Conn. at 554, 447 A.2d 406. . . .

In applying the identity rule, the court found that there was unity of interest between Mary Ann Howell and the two limited liability companies. It considered her large ownership interests in both Design and Antiquities and, more importantly, how she used her complete control of each company to manage their assets as if they were her own. The evidence presented at trial showed that Mary Ann Howell used company funds extensively to pay personal expenses, to make casual loans to family members and to buy gifts for family members, and that Mary Ann Howell conducted the operations of Design and Antiquities without any input from the other members. Although Design paid significant amounts toward the cost of a vehicle, that vehicle was titled to Jon Howell.

Little was presented to demonstrate the adherence to any corporate formalities other than some segregation of expenses for tax purposes. Mary Ann Howell used the same checking account and credit cards for both personal and business purposes, although the bills were paid entirely by the limited liability companies. Mary Ann Howell testified that items purchased by one company sometimes were paid for by the other and that she was unsure whether corresponding reimbursements were effected. Regular distributions were not made to members, nor were meetings held. Neither company leased office space, but operated out of the same area of the Howells' home. Antiquities was treated as an adjunct of Design, not as an independent entity with its own distinct interests. Given the evidence, it was not clearly erroneous for the court to have found that Mary Ann Howell conducted the business of the two companies no differently from the way she conducted her personal affairs and, thus, the identity rule was satisfied.

We therefore conclude that the court properly disregarded Design's and Antiquities' structures as limited liability companies so as to hold them liable for the personal debt of Mary Ann Howell.

Notes

1. Assuming that the transfers from Ms. Howell to the limited liability companies did not constitute fraudulent conveyances, should that not preclude reverse veil-piercing?

2. Courts routinely borrow from corporate law in developing veil-piercing doctrines for limited liability companies, as *Litchfield* illustrates. Is this justified? Corporations are characterized by statutes and traditions that give rise to certain "formalities," e.g., corporations have boards of directors that meet periodically and keep minutes of their actions, have shareholders that meet annually, issue stock certificates, etc. One of the advantages of using a limited liability company is to do away with these formalities; the operating agreement, which is not a public document, typically includes few such formalities. To the extent, then, that failure to adhere to corporate formalities is a linchpin of corporate veil-piercing, there is no real analog in the law of limited liability companies. The fact that courts, and legislatures, are sympathetic to the doctrine when it comes to limited liability companies suggests that failure to adhere to formalities in *corporate law* is less important than dictum from corporate veil piercing cases suggests. See *Kaycee Land and Livestock v. Flahive*, 46 P.3d 323, 328 (Wyo. 2002), recognizing this distinction: "Certainly, the various factors which would justify piercing an LLC veil would not be identical to the corporate situation for the obvious reason that many of organizational formalities applicable to corporations do not apply to LLCs."

3. Courts have applied the law relating to the liability of a parent corporation for the obligations of its subsidiary to a situation in which a corporation is the sole owner of an LLC. In *Andrews III v. Kerr McGee Corp.*, No. 1:00CV158-D-A, 2001 U.S. Dist. LEXIS 25973 (N.D. Miss., Dec. 4, 2001), the court, citing Delaware law, said that Kerr McGee, the parent corporation, would be liable for the torts of its wholly-owned LLC, KMC, if the plaintiffs could establish: "(1) complete dominion and control by Kerr McGee over KMC such that Kerr McGee and KMC actually

operate as a 'single economic entity'; and (2) deliberate and purposeful misuse of KMC's corporate form [sic] that will result in unfairness, injustice and injury to the plaintiffs if KMC's corporate veil [sic] is not pierced."

4. Some LLC statutes have provisions specifically addressing veil-piercing. See, for example, Colo. Rev. Stat. § 7-80-107, stating, "In any case in which a party seeks to hold the members of a limited liability company personally responsible for the alleged improper actions of the limited liability company, the court shall apply the case law which interprets the conditions and circumstances under which the corporate veil of a corporation may be pierced under Colorado law."

5. Who is potentially liable when the veil of a limited liability company is pierced? The veil-piercing theory typically only applies to members, so the member of a limited liability company who treats the company as his alter ego is the one who runs the risk of personal liability on a veil piercing theory. The Colorado appellate court, however, disagreed with this interpretation. Instead, the court, citing a case in which a corporate director was held liable on a veil-piercing theory, reasoned that "[w]hether the conduct in question is that of a corporate director . . . or an LLC manager . . . the injustice wrought by adherence to the corporate or LLC fiction is the same: the director's or manager's actions in using the corporate or LLC assets for personal gain would defeat a creditor's valid claim." *Sheffield Services Company v. Trowbridge*, 211 P.3d 714, 721 (Colo. App. Ct. 2009). *Sheffield* was overruled by *Weinstein v. Colborne Foodbotics, LLC*, 302 P.3d 263 (Colo. 2013), which read *Sheffield* as holding that managers of an LLC owe fiduciary duties to creditors, a notion that the *Weinstein* court rejected.

Of course, if a non-owner of an entity uses the entity's assets for personal purposes, the entity would have a claim against that person and, if the entity is insolvent, the creditors may be able to pursue that claim on behalf of the entity. *See, e.g., North American Catholic Educational Programming Foundation, Inc. v. Gheewalla*, 930 A.2d 92 (Del. 2007) (creditors of a corporation may protect their interests by bringing derivative claims on behalf of an insolvent corporation). *But see CML V, LLC v. Bax*, 6 A.3d 238 (Del. Ch. 2010) ("Section 18-1002 [of the LLC Act] limits standing to bring a derivative claim to holders of membership interests in a limited liability company and their assignees. Section 18-1002 does not grant standing to creditors.").

6. What law applies to a claim of veil-piercing? As a general matter, when deciding a question relating to the governance of an LLC, the courts apply the law of the state in which the LLC was organized. This is sometimes referred to as the "internal affairs doctrine." For instance, if a court must decide whether a certain act (say, the bankruptcy of a member) dissolves the LLC, it will look first to the LLC act of the state in which the LLC filed its articles of organization. In the case of veil-piercing, however, it is not clear whether the internal affairs doctrine applies; veil-piercing might be characterized as relating to the *external* affairs of the entity. *Compare, Ramlall v. MobilePro Corp.*, 30 A.3d 1003, 1009 (Md. 2011) (Maryland law applied to piercing claim against Delaware corporation under Maryland Wage Payment and Collection Law) and *Harrelson v. Lee*, 798 F. Supp. 2d 310 (D. Mass.

2011) (Massachusett's law would be applied in case raising issue of piercing the veil of a foreign corporation) with *Tyson Fresh Meats, Inc. v. Lauer Ltd. LLC*, 918 F. Supp. 2d 835, 850 (N.D. Iowa 2013) (Nebraska law would apply to claim of piercing the veil of a Nebraska LLC even though dispute occurred in Iowa and suit was filed there). The prevailing view is that the internal affairs doctrine applies to veil piercing claims. In any case, although the articulation of a veil-piercing claim varies from state to state, the substance of the claim does not differ greatly. The major exception to this observation is that some states, e.g., Texas (*Metroplex Mailing Services, LLC v. RR Donnelley & Sons Co.*, 410 S.W.3d 889 (Tex. App. 2013)) and Maryland (*Serio v. Baystate Properties, LLC*, 60 A.3d 475 (Md. 2013)), refuse to pierce the veil absent proof of fraud.

The entity theory also plays a substantial role in other issues, as evidenced by the next case.

Abrahim & Sons Enterprises v. Equilon Enterprises, LLC

United States Court of Appeals, Ninth Circuit
292 F.3d 958 (2002)

Before Pregerson, Rymer, and T.G. Nelson, Circuit Judges.

T.G. Nelson, Circuit Judge.

Appellants, a group of independent dealers who operate gas stations leased from Shell or Texaco, allege that the oil companies violated California law by transferring the gas stations to a limited liability company without first offering Appellants a chance to buy the stations. Appellees argue that California law does not apply to this situation because Appellees merely contributed their assets to a limited liability company that they controlled. The district court agreed with Appellees and granted their summary judgment motion. We reverse the district court.

I.

Appellants are forty-three independent dealers who operate Shell or Texaco gasoline stations in southern California. All appellants leased their stations from, and had dealer agreements with, Shell or Texaco. In 1998, Shell and Texaco addressed growing concerns about declining oil prices, declining profits, and increased competition by combining their retail marketing and refining activities into a limited liability company, called Equilon Enterprises. They contributed all of their western refining and marketing assets to Equilon and assigned the gas station leases and dealer agreements to Equilon as well. In exchange, Shell and Texaco, as the sole members of Equilon, received 100% of the ownership interests in the limited liability company.[8] The individual gas stations continued to sell Shell and Texaco products under their same leases and agreements.

---

8. [1] Shell owns 56% of Equilon and Texaco owns 44% based on the value of the assets they contributed.

Appellants claim that Shell and Texaco violated California Business & Professions Code § 20999.25(a) by transferring the gas stations to Equilon without offering Appellants a chance to purchase the stations. Section 20999.25(a) prohibits a franchisor from selling, transferring, or assigning an interest in a premises to another person unless he or she first makes a bona fide offer to sell that interest to the franchisee. Alternatively, if the franchisor receives an acceptable offer from another party to buy the premises, the franchisor must offer the franchisee a right of first refusal.[9]

After Appellants filed their claim in state court, Appellees removed the case to federal district court on the basis of diversity and moved for summary judgment. The district court granted the motion, holding that Shell and Texaco's contribution of the gas stations to Equilon was not a sale, transfer, or assignment of the stations to another person. Appellants appeal that decision. . . .

II.

We review a grant of summary judgment de novo. We must determine, viewing the evidence in the light most favorable to the nonmoving party, whether any genuine issues of material fact exist and whether the district court correctly applied the relevant substantive law.

III.

This case involves the statutory interpretation of California Business & Professions Code § 20999.25(a), which reads in relevant part:

> In the case of leased marketing premises as to which the franchisor owns a fee interest, the franchisor *shall not sell, transfer, or assign to another person* the franchisor's interest in the premises unless the franchisor has first . . . made a bona fide offer to sell, transfer, or assign to the franchisee the franchisor's interest in the premises. . . .[10]

No California cases interpret the phrase "sell, transfer, or assign to another person" within the meaning of this statute. Likewise, no cases interpret the identical language found in the Petroleum Marketing Practices Act,[11] after which the California statute is patterned. Therefore, we must decide how the California Supreme Court would interpret that phrase and whether the phrase encompasses the transaction at issue here.

When interpreting a statute, we attempt to "ascertain and effectuate legislative intent." In determining that intent, we must first look to the words of the statute, giving them their ordinary, common sense meaning. If the words of the statute are clear and unambiguous, there is no need to resort to other indicia of legislative intent. Only if the meaning is not clear will we turn to legislative history to help resolve the ambiguity.

---

9. [2] Cal. Bus. & Prof. Code § 20999.25(a).
10. [6] Cal. Bus. & Prof. Code § 20999.25(a) (emphasis added).
11. [7] 15 U.S.C. § 2802(b)(2)(E)(iii).

California Business & Professions Code § 20999.25 indisputably governs the parties' relationship. The question here is whether Shell and Texaco's contribution of assets to Equilon falls under Section 20999.25(a). To decide this question, we must determine whether: (1) Equilon is "another person" and (2) the contribution of assets was a sale, transfer, or assignment. We hold that the ordinary understanding of the words in Section 20999.25(a) encompasses the contribution of properties to Equilon in this case.

A. Another Person

We must first determine what types of entities fall within the meaning of "another person" under Section 20999.25(a). We believe that corporations and limited liability companies (LLCs) fall within that meaning. Corporations and LLCs are distinct legal entities, separate from their stockholders or members. The acts of a corporation or LLC are deemed independent of the acts of its members. For this reason, both corporations and LLCs are included within the definition of "person" in the California Corporations Code. The purpose of forming these types of businesses is to limit the liability of their shareholders and members.

LLCs were not a form of business entity at the time the California legislature enacted Section 20999.25(a). However, the legislature had already enacted the California Corporations Code. Thus, when it enacted Section 20999.25(a), the legislature understood that corporations were considered distinct legal entities. Considering the legislature's understanding of corporations at the time it enacted Section 20999.25(a), and the fact that LLCs are also treated as distinct legal entities, both corporations and LLCs fit within the meaning of "another person" as stated in Section 20999.25(a). Because Equilon is an LLC, it is distinct from its members Shell and Texaco and is "another person" under Section 20999.25(a).

Shell and Texaco argue that Equilon is not a distinct entity because they own and control Equilon. In essence, they ask us to disregard the corporate form they themselves created because the form does not benefit them here. We refuse to do so. Members own and control most LLCs, yet the LLCs remain separate and distinct from their members. Indeed, the separate and distinct nature of LLCs is their reason for existence. Just because it happens not to benefit Shell and Texaco here is no reason to disregard the formation of this entity. Based on the common understanding of how an LLC works, Equilon fits within the meaning of "another person."

Finally, common sense dictates that Equilon is not the same entity as Shell or Texaco individually. Equilon is owned jointly by Shell and Texaco. The gas stations, which previously were owned by only one oil company, now will be controlled and influenced by both companies. Therefore, the current owner of the gas stations is not identical to the previous owners. We conclude that Equilon is "another person" under Section 20999.25(a).

B. Sale, Transfer, or Assignment

The second part of our analysis is whether the oil companies' contribution of assets to Equilon was a sale, transfer, or assignment. The district court focused on the fact that the transaction was a "tax-free exchange" in holding that it was not a sale, transfer, or assignment. While the tax-free nature of the transaction indicates that the transaction was not a sale, we see no reason why such a transaction could not be a transfer.

According to the rules of statutory construction, transfer must mean something different than sale or assignment. In common, everyday parlance, transfer has a broad meaning. Webster's Dictionary defines "transfer" as "[t]o convey or make over the possession or legal title of (e.g., property) to another." Because Shell and Texaco relinquished their title, possession, and control of the gas stations to Equilon, it makes perfect sense to say they transferred the properties to Equilon.

In support of the idea that the oil companies transferred the gas stations, we note that the record contains a copy of a corporate grant deed, which shows that Shell transferred title of its properties to Equilon. The deed states that Shell, as grantor, granted Equilon all of Shell's rights, title, and interest in the gas stations. We assume that Texaco executed a similar deed. In addition, the individual oil companies did not maintain control of their properties. Both companies submitted forms to the Securities Exchange Commission (SEC) documenting the formation of the limited liability company. In Shell's SEC form, the company admitted that it does not exercise control over Equilon. Texaco's SEC form stated that Texaco and Shell jointly control Equilon. Therefore, neither company maintained complete control over its former properties.

Finally, under the California Corporations Code, Shell and Texaco have no interest in the property of Equilon. Once members contribute assets to an LLC, those assets become capital of the LLC and the members lose any interest they had in the assets.[12] Thus, once Shell and Texaco contributed the gas stations to Equilon, they no longer had an interest in the stations and could not individually exert control over them. The oil companies no longer had title, possession, or control over the properties. Therefore, their contribution was a transfer to Equilon.

Because the plain language of the statute is unambiguous, we do not need to resort to the legislative history. We hold that the transaction at issue here was a transfer to another person, Equilon, which triggered the duty to offer the gas stations to the franchisees first. We therefore reverse the district court and remand for further proceedings.

Reversed and remanded.

---

12. [21] Cal. Corp. Code § 17001(g) (defining contribution as any money, property, or service rendered that a member contributes to an LLC as capital); *id.* § 17300 ("A member or assignee has no interest in specific limited liability company property."). *See also* [*PacLinkCommunications Int'l, Inc v. Superior Court of Los Angeles County*], 90 Cal. App. 4th 958, 964, 109 Cal. Rptr. 2d 436 (2001) ("Because members of the LLC hold no direct ownership interest in the company's assets . . . , the members cannot be directly injured when the company is improperly deprived of those assets.")

Notes

1. Suppose that Texaco had assigned all of its fee interests to an LLC of which it was the sole member. Would that have triggered the right of first refusal? Should it have? Assuming that the right of first refusal would not have been triggered, suppose the LLC that received the fee interest then became a member of an LLC together with a Shell-created LLC that did likewise. Would that have triggered the right of first refusal? In *R.N.R. Oils, Inc. v. BP West Coast Products, LLC*, 2006 Cal. App. Unpub. LEXIS 6075 (July 13, 2006), the court considered the applicability of the California statute at issue in *Abrahim* to a transfer of leased premises within a single corporate structure. BP America was the sole owner of Atlantic Richfield and, indirectly, the sole owner of BP West Coast LLC. BP America caused Atlantic Richfield to transfer leased premises to BP West Coast as part of a corporate reorganization. An Atlantic Richfield franchisee claimed a right of first refusal under the statute. The court held the statute did not apply and distinguished *Abrahim* because Shell and Texaco were "distinct legal entities."

2. In *Frontier Traylor Shea, LLC v. Metropolitan Airports Commission*, 132 F. Supp. 2d 1193 (D. Minn. 2000), an LLC submitted the low bid on a construction project, but was not awarded the contract because in the pre-qualification materials the principals of the LLC represented that the "exact name" of the bidder was "Frontier/Traylor/Shea joint venture." The court held that the bidding authority did not abuse its discretion in determining that an LLC was not a joint venture because a joint venture is a "species of partnership" in which each of the venturers is liable for the debts of the undertaking. Thus, the actual bidder, an LLC, was substantially different from the entity represented in the pre-bid materials. The court's ruling might be questioned because, generically speaking, the principals were undertaking a joint venture, albeit in the form of an LLC. Moreover, the principals might have formed a joint venture of single member LLCs. Would that not have been consistent with the representation that the bidder would be a joint venture partnership?

3. Despite considerable authority that an LLC is a separate legal entity (e.g., § 201 of ULLCA states that an LLC is "a legal entity distinct from its members"), for purposes of diversity jurisdiction, most courts have held that an LLC is a citizen of the state or states of which its members are citizens. *Cosgrove v. Bartolotta*, 150 F.3d 729 (7th Cir. 1998). This follows the rule for limited partnerships. *Carden v. Arkoma Associates*, 494 U.S. 185 (1990). Corporations, however, are citizens of the state in which they are incorporated. 28 U.S.C. § 13329(c)(1). Does it make more sense to follow the rule for limited partnerships than corporations, especially considering how freely courts borrow from corporate law in the veil piercing cases?

4. Under § 501(a) of ULLCA, the property of the business of an LLC is owned by the LLC, not its members. An example of a court's failure to fully appreciate legal separateness is illustrated in the following case.

Turner v. Andrew

Supreme Court of Kentucky
413 S.W.3d 272 (2013)

Opinion of the Court by JUSTICE ABRAMSON

On April 16, 2007, Coy Turner was driving a feed-truck owned by his employer, M & W Milling, when a movable auger mounted on the vehicle swung loose into oncoming traffic, striking and seriously damaging a dump truck owned by Billy Andrew. The damaged truck was one of seven dump trucks owned by Andrew and operated by "Billy Andrew, Jr. Trucking, LLC." The LLC, of which Andrew was the sole member, was formed in January 2006, fifteen months prior to the accident. Andrew filed suit against Turner and M & W Milling in January 2008 claiming personal property damage to the truck as well as the loss of "income derived from the use of said motor vehicle owned by [Andrew] and used in the conduct of [Andrew's] business." The LLC was not named as a plaintiff in the lawsuit.

. . . .

The trial court granted final judgment in favor of M & W on December 7, 2009.

. . . .

The Court of Appeals reversed the trial court's judgment, concluding that Andrew could properly pursue the lost business claim in his own name because he is the sole owner of the LLC.

. . . .

Not surprisingly, courts across the country addressing limited liability statutes similar to our own have uniformly recognized the separateness of a limited liability company from its members even where there is only one member. . . .

The Court of Appeals reasoned that because Andrew was the sole owner of the business he was necessarily the real party in interest, a status that allowed him to properly advance the lost profits claim in his own name rather than in the name of the LLC. The theory of interchangeability underpinning this position was explicitly rejected by this Court in Miller v. Paducah Airport Corp., 551 S.W.2d 241 (Ky. 1977) in the context of a solely-owned corporation. In Miller, the president of a corporation that operated a cab service brought suit in his individual capacity against an airport challenging the legality of a lease. Id. at 242. The Court held that the corporation was "an entity, separate, apart and distinct from [Mr. Miller] himself," despite the fact that Mr. Miller owned the entirety of the corporation's stock. Id. This Court concluded that the corporation, and not Mr. Miller in his personal capacity as the corporation's president, was the real party in interest to the claim, declaring that such a distinction "is not trivial nor supertechnical." Id. at 243. The same conclusion is mandated here. The LLC and its solitary member, Andrew, are not legally interchangeable. Moreover, an LLC is not a legal coat that one slips on to protect the owner from liability but then discards or ignores altogether when it is time to pursue a damage claim. The law pertaining to limited liability companies simply does not work that way.

Andrew argued, and the Court of Appeals accepted, that because Andrew is the sole owner of the LLC and the business operated from his residence the LLC can be disregarded. While it is true that there are limited instances where an LLC's separate entity status may be disregarded in the interest of equity, this is not one of those cases. "Piercing the corporate veil is an equitable doctrine invoked by courts to allow a creditor recourse against the shareholders of a corporation." Inter-Tel Technologies, Inc. v. Linn Station Properties, LLC, 360 S.W.3d 152, 155 (Ky. 2012). The doctrine can also apply to limited liability companies. . . .

The facts before us bear no resemblance to the traditional veil-piercing scenario. This is not a situation where an unpaid LLC creditor seeks to pierce the veil of an LLC to reach the personal assets of its member. This is not even what is sometimes referred to as an "outsider reverse" piercing case where the creditor of an individual who is the sole member of an LLC seeks to pierce the veil to get at LLC assets to satisfy the member's personal debt. There is an "insider reverse" piercing theory, adopted by a very few states, but it is employed in that rare instance where equity is perceived to require disregard of the entity. Thus, the estate of a sole corporate shareholder/ LLC member may be allowed to recover as an "insured" under a policy issued to the entity, Roepke v. Western Nat'l Mutual Ins. Co., 302 N.W.2d 350 (Minn. 1981), or a sole shareholder or LLC member may be allowed to claim the protection of a usury statute even though the loan was to the entity, Gelber v. Kugel's Tavern, 10 N.J. 191, 89 A.2d 654 (1952). See generally Gregory Crespi, "The Reverse-Pierce Doctrine: Applying Appropriate Standards," 16 J. Corp. L. 33 (Fall 1990). In all of the limited number of insider reverse piercing cases, strong public policy considerations have been at the heart of the court's decision.

Here, Andrew created an LLC and it appears that it was conducting the trucking business at issue. By law, the only appropriate plaintiff to assert the lost business damages claim was the LLC, a point that was raised in M & W's answer in February, 2008, and then made repeatedly and explicitly throughout the litigation. Nevertheless, Andrew's counsel never moved to amend the complaint to add the LLC as plaintiff.

On remand, . . . the trial court should determine if the LCC was conducting the trucking business on April 16, 2007. If it was, M & W are entitled to summary judgment as a matter of law because Andrew personally had no standing to bring the business loss claim in his own name.

Questions

Did Andrew have standing to maintain a claim for damage to the truck (as opposed to a loss of business claim)? Why might Andrew's attorney have declined to name the LLC as a plaintiff with respect to the claim for loss of business?

Note

In *Premier Van Schaack Realty, Inc. v. Sieg*, 51 P.3d 24 (Utah Ct. App. 2002), the court affirmed a trial court decision that a real estate commission was not due following the transfer of the property to an LLC of which the transferor was a partial owner. The court characterized the transaction as one that was only a change in the form of ownership. *Premier* is in conflict with *Turner* and most cases that have dealt with this issue. Compare *Premier* with the decision in *Gebhardt Family Investment, L.L.C. v. Nations Title Insurance of New York, Inc.*, 752 A.2d 1222 (Md. App. 2000), for instance. In *Gebhardt*, a husband and wife transferred real property to a limited liability company of which they were the sole members. The transfer was made for estate planning purposes, and no money changed hands. Subsequent to the transfer, the Gebhardts, in their individual capacities, made a claim under their title insurance policy when they learned of a cloud on title to the property. The title insurer defended on the basis that the Gebhardts no longer owned the property and, therefore, had no standing to maintain a claim. The court ruled in favor of the insurer, rejecting the Gebhardts' argument that because they were the sole members of the L.L.C. the conveyance was, in effect, to themselves, and they still retained an interest in the property. Instead, the court found a transfer for value: "[U]pon executing the deed to the L.L.C., the Gebhardts reaped the limited liability and estate planning benefits conferred by the Virginia Limited Liability Company Act. Having accepted those benefits, it is disingenuous for the Gebhardts to now deny that the conveyance ever took place." *Id*. at 1227. See also *Hagan v. Adams Property Associates, Inc.*, 482 S.E.2d 805 (Va. 1997), where the court held that a transfer of real estate from the property owner to an LLC of which the transferor was one of three members was a "sale or exchange" for purposes of a brokerage agreement previously executed by the transferor. In response to the defendant's argument that there was no consideration and thus no sale or exchange, the court ruled that the assumption by the limited liability company of the debt secured by a first deed of trust and the agreement of the limited liability company to place a second lien the property to secure a note due the transferor constituted consideration. (The court did not indicate the identity of the obligor on the note. Presumably it was not the limited liability company, as that would more clearly indicate a sale to the limited liability company.) *See generally* 1 Ribstein and Keatinge on Limited Liability Cos. §3.8 (2006). Did the courts in *Turner*, *Gebhardt* and *Hagan* exalt form over substance, or should the *Premier* court be faulted for ignoring the separate legal identity of the limited liability company?

———————

Members of a limited liability company, like shareholders in a corporation and limited partners in a limited partnership, enjoy limited liability. They are not liable for the debts or obligations of the limited liability company, unless they personally guaranty those liabilities or are subject to veil piercing. However, members of a limited liability company (as well as shareholders and limited partners) are always liable for their own conduct. That said, determining whether a member bears personal liability for his or her conduct is not always an easy proposition. The following case illustrates the problem.

Weber v. U.S. Sterling Securities, Inc.

Supreme Court of Connecticut

924 A.2d 816 (2007)

BORDEN, NORCOTT, PALMER, VERTEFEUILLE and ZARELLA, Js.

VERTEFEUILLE, J.

The plaintiff initially filed a complaint against U.S. Sterling Securities, Inc. (U.S. Sterling), a resident of Brooklyn, New York, doing business as U.S. Sterling Capital Corporation, and Michelle Master Orr and Shawn Orr, both doing business for Retail Relief, LLC (Retail Relief), alleging that they had sent a one page unsolicited fax advertisement to the plaintiff in violation of [a federal] act.... The plaintiff alleged in his complaint that Shawn Orr sent a one page fax from Hauppauge, New York, to the plaintiff's residence in Brooklyn. The fax advertised the services of Retail Relief, a consulting firm that offers to help retail businesses negotiate gross margin agreements with vendors, that is, advises businesses on the correct price at which to sell their products in order to make a certain profit. Michelle Master Orr is identified in the advertisement as the firm's managing director; she and her husband, Shawn Orr, both reside in New Canaan, Connecticut.

The plaintiff brought the present action both in his individual capacity and as a class action on behalf of all persons and entities who had received similar unsolicited fax advertisements. In his complaint, the plaintiff alleged that the defendants sent the same unsolicited fax to 5000 class members. Pursuant to 47 U.S.C. § 227(b)(3)(A), the plaintiff sought injunctive relief and alleged that according to 47 U.S.C. § 227(b)(3)(B) and (C), violation of the act entitled him and the other class members to statutory damages in the amount of $500 for each unsolicited fax received and treble damages for wilful or knowing violations of the act.

Thereafter, the defendants moved for summary judgment, alleging inter alia that they could not be found personally liable because they were acting on behalf of a Delaware limited liability company. The trial court granted the defendants' motion, finding that no genuine issue of material fact existed as to any of the plaintiff's allegations and that the defendants are entitled to summary judgment as a matter of law. This appeal followed.

A brief description of the act provides context for the plaintiff's allegations. First enacted in 1991 in response to consumer complaints regarding the growing number of unsolicited telemarketing calls and fax advertisements, the act was intended to "protect the privacy interests of residential telephone subscribers by placing restrictions on unsolicited, automated telephone calls to the home and to facilitate interstate commerce by restricting certain uses of [fax] machines and automatic dialers." The act makes it unlawful "for any person within the United States ... to use any telephone [fax] machine, computer, or other device to send an unsolicited advertisement to a telephone [fax] machine. . . ." 47 U.S.C. § 227(b)(1)(C) (2000) . . . Claims under the act sound in tort regardless of whether they are construed as property or invasion of privacy tort claims . . .

The plaintiff first claims that the trial court improperly concluded that the defendants cannot be held personally liable for sending unsolicited faxes on behalf of Retail Relief, a Delaware limited liability company. Specifically, the plaintiff claims that the trial court improperly concluded that § 18-303(a) of title 6 of the Delaware Code Annotated exempts members of a limited liability company from personal tort liability. We agree.

The limited liability company shields owners and managers from personal liability for the debts and liabilities incurred by the limited liability company. "All the [limited liability company] statutes explicitly provide that neither the members nor managers of [a limited liability company] are liable for debts, obligations, or other liabilities of the [limited liability company]. Indeed, the ability to combine limited liability with partnership features is one of the most important advantages of the [limited liability company]." 2 L. Ribstein & R. Keatinge, Limited Liability Companies (2005) § 12:1, p. 12-1. Much like the liability protection offered to shareholders in a corporation, members of a limited liability company have been traditionally exempt from liability based on their membership in a limited liability company while they remain personally liable for their individual conduct. Generally, "[l]imited liability means only that a member or manager is not liable for debts and liabilities of the business solely by virtue of being such a member or manager. It does not protect the members or managers from direct individual liability for their own wrongs, such as torts and professional malpractice." Id., at § 12:4, p. 12-12.

Because Retail Relief was incorporated [sic] in Delaware, we look to Delaware law to determine the extent of the defendants' liability.

We begin our analysis with the text of § 18-303(a) of title 6 of the Delaware Code Annotated. Section 18-303(a) provides in relevant part: "Except as otherwise provided by this chapter, the debts, obligations and liabilities of a limited liability company, whether arising in contract, tort or otherwise, shall be solely the debts, obligations and liabilities of the limited liability company, and *no member or manager of a limited liability company shall be obligated personally for any such debt, obligation or liability of the limited liability company solely by reason of being a member or acting as a manager of the limited liability company.*" (Emphasis added.)

The plaintiff claims that § 18-303(a) does not shield limited liability company members from individual liability based on their personal conduct. In response, the defendants argue that their mere status as limited liability company members with Retail Relief exempts them from all personal liability and they rely in particular on the . . . language from the Delaware statute quoted above.

To resolve the plaintiff's claim, we must ascertain the meaning of the word "solely." . . . "[S]olely" is defined to mean "to the exclusion of alternate or competing things. . . ." Webster's Third New International Dictionary. Thus, the statute plainly provides that a limited liability company member cannot be held liable for the malfeasance of a limited liability company by virtue of his membership in the limited liability company alone; in other words, he must do more than merely be a member in order to be liable personally for an obligation of the limited liability company. The statute thus does not preclude individual liability for members of a limited liability company if that liability is not based simply on the member's affiliation with the company.

Several Delaware courts have reached this same conclusion. As the Delaware Court of Chancery has observed, "[§]18-303(a) protects members and managers of [a limited liability company] against liability for any obligations of the [limited liability company] solely by reason of being or acting as [company] members or managers. But, its phrase, 'solely by reason of being a member . . .' *does* imply that there are situations where [limited liability company] members and managers *would not* be shielded by this provision. . . .

"Under Delaware law, a limited liability company formed under the Delaware Limited Liability Company Act [Del. Code Ann tit. 6, § 18-101 et seq.] is treated for liability purposes like a corporation." *Wellman v. Dow Chemical Co.*, United States District Court, Docket No. 05-280-SLR, 2007 WL 842084, *2 (D. Del. March 20, 2007). According to *St. James Recreation, LLC v. Rieger Opportunity Partners, LLC*, Docket No. 19346, 2003 WL 22659875, *6–8 (Del. Ch.), 29 Del. J. Corp. L. 634 (November 5, 2003): "The default common-law rule is that corporate officials may be held individually liable for their tortious conduct, even if undertaken while acting in their official capacity. . . . [V]arious courts of [the state of Delaware] have recognized that executives, directors and officers of an entity can be held *individually* liable for the fraudulent or tortious acts which they, in their official capacities, commit, ratify or approve, despite the fact that they may have acted as an agent for or performed for the benefit of that entity at the time the fraudulent or tortious act was committed, ratified or approved." (Citations omitted; emphasis in original; internal quotation marks omitted.) Accordingly, we conclude that although § 18-303(a) of the Delaware Code Annotated shields the defendants from personal liability based solely on their affiliation with Retail Relief, it does not shield them from personal liability for their own tortious conduct.

As previously noted herein, claims under the act generally are viewed as sounding in tort. We agree with the cases that have characterized claims under the act as tortious in nature.

Because those claims sound in tort, and § 18-303(a) does not bar the defendants' liability for tortious conduct, we conclude that the trial court improperly rendered summary judgment in favor of the defendants on the issue of the defendants' personal liability for the plaintiff's claim.

Notes

1. *Weber* is one of a growing number of cases in which an injured party has sought to hold a member of an LLC liable for those injuries. For a comment on *Weber* and

other cases in which members are held liable, see Mark J. Loewenstein, *Veil Piercing to Non-owners: A Practical and Theoretical Inquiry*, 41 Seton Hall L. Rev. 839 (2011) (footnotes omitted):

> In some ways, *Weber* is an easy case—the individual defendants were alleged have actually committed the wrongful act. A bit more attenuated than *Weber* is *Estate of Countryman*, 679 N.W.2d 598 (Iowa 2004), where the defendant's wrongful act was more in the nature of nonfeasance than misfeasance. The case arose out of a residential natural gas explosion resulting in death. One of the defendants, the manager of the limited liability company that supplied the propane, allegedly was at least partially at fault for failing to properly warn the propane users. This negligence was enough, in the court's view, to hold the manager directly liable to the injured parties.
>
> The *Estate of Countryman* decision pushes the boundaries of direct liability for managers of a limited liability entity because the defendant, at least arguably, did not have a direct duty to the plaintiffs or their decedents. The manager owed a duty to the limited liability company that employed him and many courts have ruled that an agent is not liable for damages to a third party for a breach of the duty that the agent owes to the principal. That is, many courts have drawn a distinction between misfeasance and nonfeasance, with the former a basis for liability, but not the latter. The principal in the *Estate of Countryman*—the supplier of the propane—presumably owed a duty to warn and would, of course, be liable if it failed to discharge that duty, but arguably its agents did not. By contrast, if the agent had negligently damaged the plaintiff's premises while installing a heater, the agent's liability is clearer; the agent owed a duty to both its principal and to the customer to exercise due care while on the customer's premises. Nevertheless, the trend of the law seems to be in the direction of eliminating the distinction between misfeasance and nonfeasance in determining the liability of an agent and the court in *Estate of Countryman* did not even discuss the issue.

2. Despite fairly uniform interpretation of LLC acts to impose liability on managers and members who personally commit torts, the Illinois Appellate Court, in *Dass v. Yale*, 3 N.E.3d 858 (Ill. App. Ct. 2013), reached a contrary result. In this case, the plaintiffs, purchasers of a condominium unit, alleged that the managing member (Yale) of the LLC that sold the unit (Wolcott LLC), committed fraud against them. Yale moved to dismiss the complaint against him on the basis of the Illinois LLC Act, section 10-10 of which provided:

> (a) Except as otherwise provided in subsection (d) of this Section, the debts, obligations, and liabilities of a limited liability company, whether arising in contract, tort, or otherwise, are solely the debts, obligations, and liabilities of the company. A member or manager is not personally liable for a debt, obligation, or liability of the company solely by reason of being or acting as a member or manager.

(b) (Blank).

(c) The failure of a limited liability company to observe the usual company formalities or requirements relating to the exercise of its company powers or management of its business is not a ground for imposing personal liability on the members or managers for liabilities of the company.

(d) All or specified members of a limited liability company are liable in their capacity as members for all or specified debts, obligations, or liabilities of the company if:

(1) a provision to that effect is contained in the articles of organization; and

(2) a member so liable has consented in writing to the adoption of the provision or to be bound by the provision.

The Illinois court acknowledged the similarity between the uniform act and Illinois statute, but placed emphasis on subsection (d) of the Illinois act, which is not part of the uniform act. The court read the Illinois law as protecting Yale from liability because subsection (d) set forth the only basis on which liability could be found and plaintiffs failed to allege that those conditions were satisfied in this case. Was the Illinois court on sound grounds with this decision?

3. The separateness of an LLC from its members was pivotal in *Primary Investments, LLC v. Wee Tender III, Inc.*, 746 S.E.2d 823 (Ga. Ct. App. 2013). In this case, Primary LLC, which operated a day care facility, sold its assets to the plaintiff, which planned to operate a day-care facility on the same site. In the asset sale agreement, Primary LLC agreed that neither it nor its agents would open a competing facility within a 10-mile radius of the facility that it sold to plaintiff for a period of three years. The former members of Primary LLC (all of whom, admittedly, were agents of Primary LLC) did, however, open a competing day-care facility prior to the expiration of the three-year period and within 10 miles of the plaintiff's facility. The court held that while Primary LLC was bound by the noncompete, its members were not as they did not sign the asset sale agreement and the LLC could not bind them to the agreement without their consent.

F. The Operation of an LLC

1. The Management of an LLC

Pinnacle Data Services, Inc. v. Gillen

Court of Appeals of Texas
104 S.W.3d 188 (2003)

Opinion by CHIEF JUSTICE MORRISS.

In the present case, Pinnacle Data Services, Inc. (PDS) brought suit against Joseph Gillen, Charles Baldridge, and MJCM, L.L.C. (collectively referred to herein as GBM). PDS claimed GBM was guilty of unjust enrichment, member oppression, breach of contract, breach of fiduciary duty, breach of duty of loyalty, and civil conspiracy. PDS also claimed it was entitled to declaratory relief, as well as reformation. GBM filed a combination traditional and no-evidence motion for summary judgment, and the trial court granted the motion, dismissing all claims. On appeal, PDS brings the following points of error: (1) the trial court erred by granting summary judgment with respect to declaratory relief, member oppression, and unjust enrichment; and (2) the trial court erred by granting more relief than GBM requested in its motion for summary judgment.

In 1997 Max Horton, Morris Horton, Joseph Gillen, and Charles Baldridge formed MJCM, L.L.C. (herein MJCM). The parties agreed that Gillen and Baldridge would each own twenty-five percent of MJCM, and PDS would own the remaining fifty percent.[13] The Regulations[14] were signed by Gillen and Baldridge, individually, and by Max Horton, as president of PDS. The Articles of Organization (Articles) listed the original members as Gillen, Baldridge, and PDS. According to the Regulations and the Articles, MJCM was to be managed by its members. Further, the members agreed to receive payment in the form of profit distributions instead of salaries and bonuses. The distributions were made pursuant to the terms set forth in the Articles and Regulations.

However, as MJCM became more profitable, the members began to disagree over how the company should be managed. On August 29, 2000, the members convened for a meeting. At this meeting, Gillen proposed amendments to the Articles that would convert MJCM from member managed to manager managed, and Gillen would be named as manager. The Regulations provide that the Articles can only be amended by an affirmative vote of at least sixty-six and two-thirds percent of the *ownership interest*, while the Articles allow for their amendment by an affirmative vote of two-thirds of the *members*. The Regulations also provide that, to the extent the Regulations conflict with the Articles, the Articles control. Gillen and Baldridge voted to institute the proposed changes. After being named manager, Gillen relieved Max and Morris Horton of their duties with MJCM. Gillen also increased the number of employees and began paying himself and Baldridge salaries and bonuses. PDS brought suit, and the trial court granted summary judgment in favor of GBM, and PDS brings this appeal.

Declaratory Relief

PDS claimed it was entitled to the following declaratory relief:

(a) the Regulations control over the Articles with respect to member voting powers and procedures;

---

13. [1] PDS is owned by Max Horton. His brother, Morris Horton, participates in the management of PDS. Apparently, Max and Morris were under the impression that, despite technically not being members of MJCM, they would still have the right to participate in its management.

14. [Operating Agreement.—Eds.]

(b) the Amended Articles adopted on August 29, 2000 are void and of no effect;

(c) Pinnacle is a member-managed company;

(d) the election of Gillen as manager on August 29, 2000 is void and of no effect; and

(e) any amendments to the Articles and Regulations since August 29, 2000 are void.

It is undisputed that a determination of whether the Articles or the Regulations control will dispose of each claim for declaratory relief. The dispute arises from a conflict in the voting procedures set forth in the Regulations and the Articles. The Regulations provide in pertinent part:

At any meeting of Members, presence of Members entitled to cast at least sixty-six and two-thirds percent of the total votes of all Members entitled to vote at such meeting constitutes a quorum. Action on a matter is approved if the matter receives approval by at least sixty-six and two-thirds percent of the total number of votes entitled to be cast by all Members in the Company entitled to vote at such meeting or such greater number as may be required by law or the Articles for the particular matter under consideration.

On the other hand, the Articles provide:

Approval of 2/3 of the members is needed for (1) amending the articles of organization or the regulations; (2) changing the status of the Company from one in which management is reserved to the members to one in which management is vested in one or more managers, or vice versa;

. . . .

Therefore, if the Articles control, Gillen and Baldridge had the authority to amend the Articles and change the management structure of MJCM despite not having PDS's consent.

Under the Texas Limited Liability Company Act (TLLCA), the regulations of a limited liability company "may contain any provisions for the regulation and management of the affairs of the limited liability company *not inconsistent with law or the articles of organization.*" Tex. Rev. Civ. Stat. Ann. art. 1528n, § 2.09 (Vernon Supp. 2003) (emphasis added). Further, the first page of the Regulations provides:

These Regulations are subject to, and governed by, the Texas Limited Liability Company Act and the Articles [defined as the Articles of Organization]. In the event of a conflict between the provisions of these Regulations and the mandatory provisions of the Act or the provisions of the Articles, the provisions of the Act or the Articles control.

It is undisputed that Max Horton, as president of PDS, signed the Regulations, which included the above clause concerning conflict between the Articles and the Regulations. Further, Baldridge signed and filed the Articles with the Secretary of State on March 31, 1997, making them available to the public.

Despite the express terms of the TLLCA and the Regulations, PDS asserted several arguments in support of its contention that the Regulations control, none of which are supported by law or evidence. For example, PDS contended that, because the Regulations were signed by all parties, it constituted a contract, and under rules of contract interpretation, the Regulations control over the Articles. PDS cited no statutory or case law in support of this contention, and this Court has found none. In fact, such a holding would be in direct contradiction with the express language of the TLLCA and the Regulations. *See* Tex.Rev.Civ. Stat. Ann. art. 1528n, §2.09. PDS also contended it was not given a copy of the Articles until two years after the Regulations were signed, which made the Articles unenforceable. Again, PDS failed to cite authority for its contention. PDS has also failed to produce any evidence that it sought to obtain a copy of the Articles before that time, even though it signed Regulations that were expressly subordinate to the Articles. Further, the Articles were on file with the Secretary of State beginning March 31, 1997, and Max Horton admitted in his deposition that he kept a copy of the Articles in his desk. The terms set forth in the Regulations, Articles, and the TLLCA are not rendered inoperative because PDS failed to exercise diligence in obtaining a copy of the Articles before agreeing to their terms. . . . Therefore, PDS has not raised a genuine issue of fact, and the trial court did not err by granting summary judgment with respect to its claim for declaratory relief.

Note

As noted above, an LLC can be member managed or manager managed. A member-managed LLC strongly resembles an LLP: each member of the LLC has general agency authority, just as each partner in the LLP does. An LLC that is manager managed is similar to an LLLP. Only the general partners of the LLLP have general agency authority, and only the managers of the LLC do. As the *Pinnacle Data* case demonstrates, it is easy to convert a member-managed LLC to a manager-managed one.

a. Authority and Apparent Authority of Members

The authority of a member in a member-managed LLC and a manager in a manager-managed LLC track closely to the authority of a partner in a general partnership which, in turn, is based on agency law principles. *See* ULLCA §301. The drafters of ULLCA, drawing on RUPA, have distinguished between transactions involving real property and all other transactions. Thus, §301(c) of ULLCA provides:

> Unless the articles of organization limit their authority, any member of a member-managed company or manager of a manager-managed company may sign and deliver any instrument transferring or affecting the company's interest in real property. The instrument is conclusive in favor of a person who gives value without knowledge of the lack of authority of person signing and delivering the instrument.

This provision seems internally inconsistent. The first sentence allows the LLC to limit the authority of a member or manager (provided it does so in the articles of organization, not just the operating agreement), while the second sentence seems to create apparent authority for the person signing the instrument. The Comment says that if a limitation is included in the articles of organization, it is effective "even as to persons without knowledge of the agent's lack of authority." The "lack of authority" reference in the second sentence of the quoted provision may simply refer to a limitation of authority included in the operating agreement. Thus, the drafters of the ULLCA have made the policy determination that those dealing with an LLC are on notice as to at least certain of the provisions in its articles of organization. The wisdom of this policy choice might be questioned; it means that persons dealing with an LLC must review the articles of organization or bear the risk of its limitations.

Note

Is a lender deemed to have knowledge of the terms of an operating agreement provided to the bank by the limited liability company? The court in *Sunflower Bank, N.A. v. Airport Red Coach Inn of Wichita, L.L.C.*, 175 P.3d 883 (Kan. Ct. App. 2008) (unpublished) answered this question in the affirmative. In this case, the manager, Pyle, borrowed money on behalf of the LLC from the Bank, but was not expressly authorized to do so by the other members of the LLC. Section XI of the operating agreement provided as follows:

"A. Except as provided in subparagraph B of this section, all members shall have rights in the management of the LLC proportionate to their interest in the LLC. No member shall, without the consent of the other members, endorse any note or act as an accommodation party or otherwise become surety for any person in any transaction involved in the LLC. Without the consent of the LLC, no member shall on behalf of the LLC borrow or lend money, or make, deliver or accept any commercial paper, or execute any mortgage, security agreement, bond, or lease, purchase or contract to purchase, or sell or contract to sell any property for or of the LLC. No member shall, except with the consent of the other members, mortgage, grant a security interest in its share in the LLC or in the LLC capital assets or property, or do any act detrimental to the best interests of the LLC or which would make it impossible to carry on the ordinary purpose of the LLC. The term 'consent of the other members' as used in this paragraph means unanimous consent.

"B. The LLC may from time to time elect to designate one of its members as general manager for the LLC. Such person so designated shall have authority to execute all instruments in the name of the LLC as required for the construction of the facility."

The court noted the evidence in the case that established that paragraph B above was added to make clear that, despite paragraph A, not all members had to *sign* evidences of indebtedness; they only had to *approve* the incurrence of the indebtedness, which they did not do in this case. With that evidence, and the testimony of an "expert" that the term "execute" in paragraph B "was very different from the word 'borrow' used in paragraph A," the court concluded:

> The entirety of Section XI of the LLC's operating agreement is completely unambiguous. Given that we must give each phrase its proper meaning, the district court's reading of the operating agreement is the only one that makes sense. If the "execute" clause in Paragraph B gave the manager carte blanche power to borrow money, then most of Paragraph A of Section XI has no meaning. It would be nonsensical to have one paragraph cancel out another. Thus, execute must mean the power to sign loan instruments on behalf of the LLC, but only once the authority to borrow has come from all other LLC members. Given the letters contained in the record on appeal, this seems to be the LLC's intent. The district court correctly interpreted the operating agreement.

> The Bank also argues that Pyle had implied authority to borrow money because the LLC members allowed him to manage the company "very much as he pleased." The Bank believes Pyle's habit of borrowing money was a matter of "carrying on the usual business of the company." This argument is not valid because the testimony at the trial was that the other LLC members had no idea Pyle was borrowing this money. The LLC could not ratify something it did not realize existed.

> Finally, the Bank contends that K.S.A. 17-7614(c)(2) allowed the Bank to reasonably believe that the general manager had the authority to bind the company. This argument is based on the idea that the district court failed to focus on what the Bank actually knew at the time Pyle sought the loans subsequent to the initial construction loan.

K.S.A. 17-7614(c) reads in relevant part:

> "If the articles of organization provide that management of the limited liability company is vested in one or more managers: . . . (2) every manager is an agent of the limited liability company for the purpose of its business and affairs, and the act of any manager for apparently carrying on in the usual way of the business or affairs of the limited liability of which the manager is a manager binds the limited liability company, unless the manager so acting has, in fact, no authority to act for the limited liability company in the particular matter, and the person with whom the manager is dealing has knowledge of the fact that the manager has no such authority."

However, K.S.A. 17-7614(e) states:

> "No act of a member, manager or other agent of a limited liability company in contravention of a restriction on authority shall bind the limited liability company to persons having knowledge of the restriction."

The Bank's argument here is defeated by the plain language of the LLC's operating agreement and subsection (e) of K.S.A. 17-7614. Because the

Bank had a copy of the LLC's operating agreement before any money was loaned, it was clearly given written notice of the limits of Pyle's authority. We conclude that the district court properly ruled that [the loans in question were not] properly authorized by the LLC.

Notice how the court disposes of the argument that the members allowed Pyle, the manager, to act "very much as he pleased." The court treats this as a claim that the members ratified Pyle's borrowings, which the court says cannot be the case since the members were unaware of those borrowings. But the Bank's argument may have been that the members *acquiesced* in Pyle's authority, much as the partners in *Elle v. Babbitt, supra*, Chapter 12, "tacitly agreed" that Beall would manage the partnership. Assuming the other members of the limited liability company in *Sunflower Bank* gave Pyle freedom to act by their passivity, should the case have come out differently? In other words, can the parties to an operating agreement *implicitly* amend that agreement?

b. Fiduciary Duties of Members

What fiduciary duties do members owe each other and the LLC, if any? Are members like partners, who owe broad fiduciary duties? Or are they like limited partners, who owe no duties solely as a result of the status of being a limited partner? (Of course, a limited partner can become subject to, for example, a duty of good faith if it exercises its right to obtain information about the business and then uses the information against the business.) In general, fiduciary duties tend to arise when a person is given authority to act in the business, to exercise managerial powers, or otherwise to occupy a position of trust. Unsurprisingly, ULLCA breaks down fiduciary duties along these lines. See §409, distinguishing between member-managed and manager-managed companies. Following closely the language of RUPA §404, ULLCA states that "the only" fiduciary duties are those of loyalty and care, which it imposes on members of member-managed companies. With regard to members of manager-managed companies, however, §409(h)(1) states: "[A] member who is not also a manager owes no duties to the company or to the other members solely by reason of being a member." *See McGee v. Best*, 106 S.W.3d 48, 63–64 (Tenn. Ct. App. 2002). The manager is held to fiduciary duties, of course, like any other agent. *See generally* J. William Callison & Allan W. Vestal, *"They've Created a Lamb with Mandibles of Death": Secrecy, Disclosure, and Fiduciary Duties in Limited Liability Firms*, 76 IND. L.J. 271 (2001).

In *Pappas v. Tzolis*, 982 N.E.2d 576 (N.Y. 2012) (reproduced in Chapter 2, Section B.4.d.iii), the New York Court of Appeals upheld the terms of an operating agreement that protected what appeared to be sharp dealing by a member of an LLC who bought out his co-members. In the following case, the court confronted a provision that seemingly allowed unlimited competition, but consider whether that is a fair way to characterize the provision in question.

McConnell v. Hunt Sports Enterprises

Court of Appeals of Ohio
725 N.E.2d 1193 (1999)

TYACK, JUDGE.

In 1996, the National Hockey League ("NHL") determined it would be accepting applications for new hockey franchises. The deadline for applying for an NHL expansion franchise was November 1, 1996. [Lamar Hunt, John McConnell and others formed Columbus Hockey Limited, LLC ("CHL") for the purpose of seeking a franchise for Columbus, Ohio.] The members of CHL were McConnell, Wolfe Enterprises, Inc., Hunt Sports Group, Pizzuti Sports Limited, and Buckeye Hockey, L.L.C. Each member made an initial capital contribution of $25,000. CHL was subject to an operating agreement that set forth the terms between the members. Pursuant to section 2.1 of CHL's operating agreement, the general character of the business of CHL was to invest in and operate a franchise in the NHL.

On or about November 1, 1996, an application was filed with the NHL on behalf of the city of Columbus. In the application, the ownership group was identified as CHL. . . . A $100,000 check from CHL was included as the application fee. Also included within the application package was Columbus's plan for an arena to house the hockey games. There was no facility at the time, and the proposal was to build a facility that would be financed, in large part, by a three-year countywide one-half percent sales tax. The sales tax issue would be on the May 1997 ballot.

On May 6, 1997, the sales tax issue failed. . . . [O]n May 7, 1997, Dimon McPherson, chairman and chief executive officer of Nationwide Insurance Enterprise ("Nationwide"), met with Hunt, and they discussed the possibility of building the arena despite the failure of the sales tax issue. . . .

By May 28, 1997, Nationwide had come up with a plan to finance an arena privately and on such date, Nationwide representatives met with representatives of Hunt Sports Group. Hunt Sports Group did not accept Nationwide's lease proposal. [Hunt acted without consulting the other CHL investors. McPherson then approached McConnell.] McPherson told McConnell about [Hunt's] rejection of the lease proposal and discussed the NHL's [new] deadline. McConnell stated that if Hunt would not step up and lease the arena and, therefore, get the franchise, McConnell would. . . .

On June 9, 1997, a meeting [between Hunt, McConnell and other CHL investors] took place. . . . The NHL required that the ownership group be identified and that such ownership group sign a lease term sheet by June 9, 1997. [Hunt stated that he found Nationwide's lease offer unacceptable.] McConnell . . . accepted the term sheet and was signing it in his individual capacity. The term sheet contained a signature line for "Columbus Hockey Limited" as the franchise owner. [The name was eliminated.] McConnell then signed the term sheet as the owner of the franchise. . . .

On June 17, 1997, the NHL expansion committee recommended to the NHL board of governors that Columbus be awarded a franchise with McConnell's group as owner of the franchise. On the same date, the complaint in the case at bar was filed [by McConnell seeking a declaratory judgment that the ownership of the franchise by his group was proper]. On or about June 25, 1997, the NHL board of governors awarded Columbus a franchise with McConnell's group as owner.[15] Hunt Sports Group, Buckeye Hockey, L.L.C. and Ameritech have no ownership interest in the hockey franchise. . . . [The Hunt group filed an answer and counterclaim, in addition to a separate suit filed in New York.]

In their complaint, McConnell and Wolfe Enterprises, Inc. requested a declaration that section 3.3 of the CHL operating agreement allowed members of CHL to compete with CHL. Specifically, McConnell and Wolfe Enterprises, Inc. sought a declaration that under the operating agreement, they were permitted to participate in COLHOC and obtain the franchise. [A] second claim sought judicial dissolution of CHL. [The trial court rendered a judgment in favor of McConnell.] . . .

. . . Appellant [Hunt] asserts, in part, that the trial court's interpretation of section 3.3 was incorrect and that section 3.3 is ambiguous and subject to different interpretations. Therefore, appellant contends extrinsic evidence should have been considered, and such evidence would have shown the parties did not intend section 3.3 to mean members could compete against CHL and take away CHL's only purpose. . . .

Section 3.3 of the operating agreement states:

> "*Members May Compete.* Members shall not in any way be prohibited from or restricted in engaging or owning an interest in any other business venture of any nature, including any venture which might be competitive with the business of the Company."

Appellant emphasizes the word "other" in the above language and states, in essence, that it means any business venture that is different from the business of the company. Appellant points out that under section 2.1 of the operating agreement, the general character of the business is "to invest in and operate a franchise in the National Hockey League." Hence, appellant contends that members may only engage in or own an interest in a venture that is not in the business of investing in and operating a franchise with the NHL.

Appellant's interpretation of section 3.3 goes beyond the plain language of the agreement and adds words or meanings not stated in the provision. Section 3.3, for example, does not state "[m]embers shall not be prohibited from or restricted in engaging or owning an interest in any other business venture that is different from

---

15. [2] The ownership group is now formally known as COLHOC Limited Partnership ("COLHOC"). Portions of the record indicate COLHOC was formed before the June 9, 1997 meeting. JMAC, Inc. is the majority owner, and JMAC Hockey, L.L.C. is the general partner of COLHOC. JMAC Hockey, L.L.C. signed the general partnership agreement on June 26, 1997.

the business of the company." Rather, section 3.3 states: "any other business venture *of any nature*." (Emphasis added.) It then adds to this statement: "including any venture which might be competitive with the business of the Company." The words "any nature" could not be broader, and the inclusion of the words "any venture which might be competitive with the business of the Company" makes it clear that members were not prohibited from engaging in a venture that was competitive with CHL's investing in and operating an NHL franchise. Contrary to appellant's contention, the word "other" simply means a business venture other than CHL. The word "other" does not limit the type of business venture in which members may engage.

Hence, section 3.3 did not prohibit appellees from engaging in activities that may have been competitive with CHL, including appellees' participation in COLHOC. Accordingly, . . . appellees were entitled to a declaration that section 3.3 of the operating agreement permitted appellees to request and obtain an NHL hockey franchise to the exclusion of CHL. . . .

Before we can review the propriety of the directed verdict in this case, the law on fiduciary duty and interference with a prospective business relationship must be addressed. The term "fiduciary relationship" has been defined as a relationship in which special confidence and trust is reposed in the integrity and fidelity of another, and there is a resulting position of superiority or influence acquired by virtue of this special trust. In the case at bar, a limited liability company is involved which, like a partnership, involves a fiduciary relationship. Normally, the presence of such a relationship would preclude direct competition between members of the company. However, here we have an operating agreement that by its very terms allows members to compete with the business of the company. Hence, the question we are presented with is whether an operating agreement of a limited liability company may, in essence, limit or define the scope of the fiduciary duties imposed upon its members. We answer this question in the affirmative.

A fiduciary has been defined as a person having a duty, *created by his or her undertaking*, to act primarily for the benefit of another in matters *connected with such undertaking*. . . . These principles support our conclusion that a contract may define the scope of fiduciary duties between parties to the contract.

. . . The operating agreement constitutes the undertaking of the parties herein. In becoming members of CHL, appellant and appellees agreed to abide by the terms of the operating agreement, and such agreement specifically allowed competition with the company by its members. As such, the duties created pursuant to such undertaking did not include a duty not to compete. Therefore, there was no duty on the part of appellees to refrain from subjecting appellant to the injury complained of herein.

We find further support for our conclusion in case law concerning close corporations and partnerships. . . . The *Cruz* [*v. S. Dayton Urological Assocs., Inc.*, 121 Ohio App. 3d 655, 700 N.E.2d 675 (1997),] case stands for the proposition that close corporation employment agreements may limit the scope of fiduciary duties that otherwise would apply absent certain provisions in such agreements. The same principle has been applied in situations involving partnerships that are subject to partnership agreements. *See Spayd v. Turner, Granzow & Hollenkamp* (1985), 19 Ohio St. 3d 55, 59, 482 N.E.2d 1232, 1236, 19 OBR 54, 57–58 (the respective rights of partnership members depend primarily on the specific provisions contained within the partnership contract as recognized in [UPA § 18] which states that the rights and duties of partners are subject to any agreement between the partners).

"Operating agreement" is defined in R.C. 1705.01(J) as all of the valid written or oral agreements of the members as to the affairs of a limited liability company and the conduct of its business. . . . Indeed, many of the statutory provisions in R.C. Chapter 1705 governing limited liability companies indicate they are, in various ways, subject to and/or dependent upon related provisions in an operating agreement. Here, the operating agreement states in its opening paragraph that it evidences the mutual agreement of the members in consideration of their contributions and promises to each other. Such agreement specifically allowed its members to compete with the company.

Given the above, we conclude as a matter of law that it was not a breach of fiduciary duty for appellees to form, COLHOC and obtain an NHL franchise to the exclusion of CHL. In so concluding, we are not stating that *no* act related to such obtainment could be considered a breach of fiduciary duty. In general terms, members of limited liability companies owe one another the duty of utmost trust and loyalty. However, such general duty in this case must be considered in the context of members' ability, pursuant to operating agreement, to compete with the company.

Judgment affirmed in part and reversed in part.

BOWMAN, J., concurs.

PEGGY L. BRYANT, J., concurs in part and dissents in part [concerning the reversal of the award of attorney fees].

Notes

1. Suppose that ULLCA §§ 409(b)(3) and 103(b)(2)(i) applied to the facts of *McConnell*. Would the provision permitting competition be deemed a "manifestly unreasonable" activity in light of the duty of loyalty? Would the case have been decided differently if the McConnell group had submitted a proposal simultaneously with the initial proposal by CHL (the original group)? Perhaps a provision that permitted competition under that scenario would be manifestly unreasonable, but not one construed to permit competition in the fact situation in this case.

2. In *KMK Factoring, L.L.C. v. McKnew* (*In re William McKnew*), 270 B.R. 593 (E.D. Va. 2001), the court was faced with the issue of whether a manager of an LLC is a fiduciary for purposes of the federal bankruptcy code. The issue in this case arose under § 523 of the Bankruptcy Code, which prohibits the discharge of an individual debtor from any debt for fraud or defalcation *while acting in a fiduciary capacity*. 11 U.S.C. § 523(a)(4) (2001) (emphasis added). After noting that the issue was one of federal law, the court concluded that for purposes of § 523 a manger of an LLC is not a fiduciary: "[T]he imposition of a fiduciary relationship here would unnecessarily stretch the long imposed restriction of limiting such a relationship to an express or technical trust, and instead impose it to an instance where traditional concepts of embezzlement or larceny more nearly fit."

VGS, Inc. v. Castiel

Court of Chancery of Delaware
2000 Del. Ch. LEXIS 122 (Aug. 31, 2000)

STEELE, VICE CHANCELLOR.

One entity controlled by a single individual forms a one "member" limited liability company. Shortly thereafter, two other entities, one of which is controlled by the owner of the original member, become members of the LLC. The LLC Agreement creates a three-member Board of Managers with sweeping authority to govern the LLC. The individual owning the original member has the authority to name and remove two of the three managers. He also acts as CEO. The unaffiliated third member becomes disenchanted with the original member's leadership. Ultimately the third member's owner, also the third manager, convinces the original member's owner's appointed manager to join him in a clandestine strategic move to merge the LLC into a Delaware corporation. The appointed manager and the disaffected third member do not give the original member's owner, still a member of the LLC's board of managers, notice of their strategic move. After the merger, the original member finds himself relegated to a minority position in the surviving corporation. While a majority of the board acted by written consent, as all involved surely knew, had the original member's manager received notice beforehand that his appointed manager contemplated action against his interests he would have promptly attempted to remove him. Because the two managers acted without notice to the third manager under circumstances where they knew that with notice that he could have acted to protect his majority interest, they breached their duty of loyalty to the original member and their fellow manager by failing to act in good faith. The purported merger must therefore be declared invalid.

I. Facts

David Castiel formed Virtual Geosatellite LLC (the "LLC") on January 6, 1999 in order to pursue a Federal Communications Commission ("FCC") license to build and operate a satellite system which its proponents claim could dramatically increase the "real estate" in outer space capable of transmitting high speed internet traffic and other communications. When originally formed, it had only one Member—Virtual Geosatellite Holdings, Inc. ("Holdings"). On January 8, 1999, Ellipso, Inc. ("Ellipso") joined the LLC as its second Member. Several weeks later, on January 29, 1999, Sahagen Satellite Technology Group LLC ("Sahagen Satellite") became the third Member of the LLC. David Castiel controls both Holdings and Ellipso. Peter Sahagen, an aggressive and apparently successful venture capitalist, controls Sahagen Satellite.

Pursuant to the LLC Agreement, Holdings received 660 units (representing 63.46% of the total equity in the LLC), Sahagen Satellite received 260 units (representing 25%), and Ellipso received 120 units (representing 11.54%). The founders vested management of the LLC in a Board of Managers. As the majority unitholder, Castiel had the power to appoint, remove, and replace two of the three members of the Board of Managers. Castiel, therefore, had the power to prevent any Board decision with which he disagreed. Castiel named himself and Tom Quinn to the Board of Managers. Sahagen named himself as the third member of the Board.

Not long after the formation of the LLC, Castiel and Sahagen were at odds. Castiel contends that Sahagen wanted to control the LLC ever since he became involved, and that Sahagen repeatedly offered, unsuccessfully, to buy control of the LLC. Sahagen maintains that Castiel ran the LLC so poorly that its mission had become untracked, additional necessary capital could not be raised, and competent managers could not be attracted to join the enterprise. Further, Sahagen claims that Castiel directed LLC assets to Ellipso in order to prop up a failing, cash-strapped Ellipso. At trial, these issues and other similar accusations from both sides were explored in great detail. For our purposes here, all that need be concluded is the unarguable fact that Castiel and Sahagen had very different ideas about how the LLC should be managed and operated.

Sahagen ultimately convinced Quinn that Castiel must be ousted from leadership in order for the LLC to prosper. As a result, Quinn (Castiel's nominee) covertly "defected" to Sahagen's camp, and he and Sahagen decided to wrest control of the LLC from Castiel. Many LLC employees and even some of Castiel's lieutenants testified that they believed it to be in the LLC's best interest to take control from Castiel.

On April 14, 2000, without notice to Castiel, Quinn and Sahagen acted by written consent to merge the LLC under Delaware law into VGS, Inc. ("VGS"), a Delaware corporation. Accordingly, the LLC ceased to exist, its assets and liabilities passed to VGS, and VGS became the LLC's legal successor-in-interest. VGS's Board of Directors is comprised of Sahagen, Quinn, and Neel Howard. Of course, the incorporators did not name Castiel to VGS's Board.

On the day of the merger, Sahagen executed a promissory note to VGS in the amount of $10 million plus interest. In return, he received two million shares of VGS Series A Preferred Stock. VGS also issued 1,269,200 shares of common stock to Holdings, 230,800 shares of common stock to Ellipso, and 500,000 shares of common stock to Sahagen Satellite. Once one does the math, it is apparent that Holdings and Ellipso went from having a 75% controlling combined ownership interest in the LLC to having only a 37.5% interest in VGS. On the other hand, Sahagen and Sahagen Satellite went from owning 25% of the LLC to owning 62.5% of VGS.

There can be no doubt why Sahagen and Quinn, acting as a majority of the LLC's board of managers did not notify Castiel of the merger plan. Notice to Castiel would have immediately resulted in Quinn's removal from the board and a newly constituted majority which would thwart the effort to strip Castiel of control. Had he known in advance, Castiel surely would have attempted to replace Quinn with someone loyal to Castiel who would agree with his views. Clandestine machinations were, therefore, essential to the success of Quinn and Sahagen's plan.

II. Analysis

A. The Board of Managers did have authority to act by majority vote

The LLC Agreement does not expressly state whether the Board of Managers must act unanimously or by majority vote. Sahagen and Quinn contend that because a number of provisions would be rendered meaningless if a unanimous vote was required, a majority vote is implied. Castiel, however, maintains that a unanimous vote must be implied when the majority owner has blocking power.

Section 8.01(b)(i) of the LLC Agreement states that, "[t]he Board of Managers shall initially be composed of three (3) Managers." Sahagen Satellite has the right to designate one member of the initial board, and if the Board of Managers increased in number, Sahagen Satellite could "designate a number of representatives on the Board of Managers that is less than Sahagen's then current Percentage Interest." If unanimity were required, the number of managers would be irrelevant—Sahagen, and his minority interest, would have veto power in any event. The existence of language in the LLC Agreement discussing expansion of the Board is therefore quite telling. Also persuasive is the fact that Section 8.01(c) of the LLC Agreement, entitled "Matters Requiring Consent of Sahagen," provides that Sahagen's approval is needed for a merger, consolidation, or reorganization of the LLC. If a unanimity requirement indeed existed, there would have been no need to expressly list matters on which Sahagen's minority interest had veto power.

Section 12.01(a)(i) of the LLC Agreement also supports Sahagen's argument. This section provides that the LLC may be dissolved by written consent by either the Board of Managers or by Members holding two-thirds of the Common Units. The effect of this Section is to allow any combination of Holdings and Sahagen Satellite, or Holdings and Ellipso, as Members, to dissolve the LLC. It seems unlikely that the Members designed the LLC Agreement to permit Members holding two-thirds of the Common Units to dissolve the LLC but denied their appointed Managers the power to reach the same result unless the minority manager agreed.

Castiel takes the position that while the Members can act by majority vote, the Board of Managers can act only by unanimous vote. He maintains that if the Board fails to agree unanimously on an issue the issue should be put to an LLC Members' vote with the majority controlling. The practical effect of Castiel's interpretation would be that whenever Castiel and Sahagen disagreed, Castiel would prevail because the issue would be submitted to the Members where Castiel's controlling interest would carry the vote. If that were the case, both Sahagen's Board position and Quinn's Board position would be superfluous. I am confident that the parties never intended that result, or if they had so intended, that they would have included plain and simple language in the agreement spelling it out clearly.

B. By failing to give notice of their proposed action, Sahagen and Quinn failed to discharge their duty of loyalty to Castiel in good faith

Section 18-404(d) of the LLC Act states in pertinent part:

> Unless otherwise provided in a limited liability company agreement, on any matter that is to be voted on by managers, the managers may take such action without a meeting, *without prior notice* and without a vote if a consent or consents in writing, setting forth the action so taken, shall be signed by the managers having not less than the minimum number of votes that would be necessary to authorize such action at a meeting (emphasis added).

Therefore, the LLC Act, read literally, does not require notice to Castiel before Sahagen and Quinn could act by written consent. The LLC Agreement does not purport to modify the statute in this regard.

Those observations can not complete the analysis of Sahagen and Quinn's actions, however. Sahagen and Quinn knew what would happen if they notified Castiel of their intention to act by written consent to merge the LLC into VGS, Inc. Castiel would have attempted to remove Quinn, and block the planned action. Regardless of his motivation in doing so, removal of Quinn in that circumstance would have been within Castiel's rights as the LLC's controlling owner under the Agreement.

Section 18-404(d) has yet to be interpreted by this Court or the Supreme Court. Nonetheless, it seems clear that the purpose of permitting action by written consent without notice is to enable LLC managers to take quick, efficient action in situations where a minority of managers could not block or adversely affect the course set by the majority even if they were notified of the proposed action and objected to it. The General Assembly never intended, I am quite confident, to enable two managers to deprive, clandestinely and surreptitiously, a third manager representing the majority interest in the LLC of an opportunity to protect that interest by taking an action that the third manager's member would surely have opposed if he had knowledge of it. My reading of Section 18-404(d) is grounded in a classic maxim of equity—"Equity looks to the intent rather than to the form."[16] In this hopefully unique situation, this application of the maxim requires construction of the statute to allow action without notice only by a *constant or fixed majority*. It can not apply to an illusory, will-of-the wisp majority which would implode should notice be given. Nothing in the statute suggests that this court of equity should blind its eyes to a shallow, too clever by half, manipulative attempt to restructure an enterprise through an action taken by a "majority" that existed only so long as it could act in secrecy.

Sahagen and Quinn each owed a duty of loyalty to the LLC, its investors and Castiel, their fellow manager. Castiel or his entities owned a majority interest in the LLC and he sat as a member of the board representing entities and interests empowered by the Agreement to control the majority membership of the board. The

---

16. [3] DONALD J. WOLFE, JR. & MICHAEL A. PITTENGER, CORPORATE AND COMMERCIAL PRACTICE IN THE DELAWARE COURT OF CHANCERY, at vii (1998) (listing the maxims of equity) ...

majority investor protected his equity interest in the LLC through the mechanism of appointment to the board rather than by the statutorily sanctioned mechanism of approval by members owning a majority of the LLC's equity interests. It may seem somewhat incongruous, but this Agreement allows the action to merge, dissolve or change to corporate status to be taken by a simple majority vote of the board of managers rather than rely upon the default position of the statute which requires a majority vote of the equity interest. Instead the drafters made the critical assumption, known to all the players here, that the holder of the majority equity interest has the right to appoint and remove two managers, ostensibly guaranteeing control over a three member board. When Sahagen and Quinn, fully recognizing that this was Castiel's protection against actions adverse to his majority interest, acted in secret, without notice, they failed to discharge their duty of loyalty to him in good faith. They owed Castiel a duty to give him prior notice even if he would have interfered with a plan that they conscientiously believed to be in the best interest of the LLC.[17] Instead, they launched a preemptive strike that furtively converted Castiel's controlling interest in the LLC to a minority interest in VGS without affording Castiel a level playing field on which to defend his interest. "[Another] traditional maxim of equity holds that equity regards and treats that as done which in good conscience ought to be done."[18] In good conscience, under these circumstances, Sahagen and Quinn should have given Castiel prior notice.

Many hours were spent at trial focusing on contentions that Castiel has proved to be an ineffective leader in whom employees and investors have lost confidence. I listened to testimony regarding delayed FCC licensing, a suggested new management team for the LLC, and the alleged unlocked value of the LLC. A substantial record exists fully flushing out the rancorous relationships of the members and their wildly disparate views on the existing state of affairs as well as the LLC's prospects for the future. But the issue of who is best suited to run the LLC should not be resolved here but in board meetings where all managers are present and all members appropriately represented, and/or in future litigation, if it unfortunately becomes necessary.

Likewise, the parties spent much time and effort arguing over the standard to be applied to the actions taken by Sahagen and Quinn. Specifically, the parties debated whether the standard should be entire fairness or the business judgment rule. It should be clear that the actions of Sahagen and Quinn, in their capacity as managers constituted a breach of their duty of loyalty and that those actions do not, therefore, entitle them to the benefit or protection of the business judgment rule. They intentionally used a flawed process to merge the LLC into VGS, Inc., in an attempt to prevent the member with majority equity interest in the LLC from protecting his

---

17. [4] I make no ruling here as to whether I believe the merger and the resulting recapitalization of the LLC was in the LLC's best interests, nor do I rule here regarding the wisdom of Castiel's actions had he in fact been able to remove Quinn before the merger.

18. [5] WOLFE & PITTENGER, *supra*, at § 2-3(b)(1)(i), *citing* 2 JOHN NORTON POMEROY, A TREATISE ON EQUITY JURISPRUDENCE § 363 et seq. (5th ed. (1941)).

interests in the manner contemplated by the very LLC Agreement under which they purported to act. Analysis beyond a look at the process is clearly unnecessary. Perhaps, had notice been given and an attempt then made to block Castiel's anticipated action to replace Quinn, the allegedly disinterested and independent member that Castiel himself had appointed, the analysis might be different. However, this, as all cases must be reviewed as it is presented, not as it might have been.

III. Conclusion

For the reasons stated above, I find that a majority vote of the LLC's Board of Managers could properly effect a merger. But, I also find that Sahagen and Quinn failed to discharge their duty of loyalty to Castiel in good faith by failing to give him advance notice of their merger plans under the unique circumstances of this case and the structure of this LLC Agreement. Accordingly, I declare that the acts taken to merge the LLC into VGS, Inc. to be invalid and the merger is ordered rescinded.

Notes

1. The Vice Chancellor's opinion was affirmed on appeal. 781 A.2d 696 (Del. 2001).

2. Like corporate codes, LLC acts often include provisions that protect managers and member-managers who in good faith rely on information, opinions, etc., of legal counsel, accountants and others. *Flippo v. CSC Associates III, L.L.C.*, 262 Va. 48, 547 S.E.2d 216, 222 (2001), is a good example of the limits of such protective provisions. In *Flippo*, the defendant member-manager sought legal counsel to assist him gaining control of the assets of the LLC. Counsel recommended that the defendant convey the assets of the LLC to a joint venture with a corporation that the defendant controlled. Defendant followed this advice and faced a claim from the other members of the LLC that he breached his fiduciary duty. The lower court held in favor of the plaintiffs and the Virginia Supreme Court affirmed, rejecting the defense that the defendant relied in good faith on the advice of counsel: "The advice relied and acted upon in this case was given solely for the purpose of implementing the [defendant's] personal estate planning goals. Even if legal, the action was neither sought nor taken with the intent of benefiting [the LLC] and, in fact, had an adverse impact." Among other things, the defendant was found liable for substantial punitive damages for breach of fiduciary duty. Was the attorney guilty of professional malpractice for the advice?

3. As in veil-piercing cases, courts frequently rely on corporate concepts in defining fiduciary duties. In *Solar Cells, Inc. v. True North Partners, LLC*, No. 19477, 2002 Del. Ch. LEXIS 38 (Apr. 25, 2002), the Delaware Chancery Court applied familiar principles of corporate law in ruling that the member controlling an LLC had a fiduciary duty to the other member when engineering a merger of the LLC into an entity controlled by the defendant. Moreover, the defendant bore the burden of proving that the transaction was entirely fair to the plaintiff. A provision in the operating agreement waiving conflicts of interest and exculpating the controlling member (and the persons it designated as managers of the LLC) from liability did not compel a contrary result, the court ruled, because only injunctive relief was being sought. Similarly, in *Gottsacker v. Monnier*, 697 N.W.2d 436 (Wis. 2005), the Wisconsin Supreme Court, relying on principles of corporate law, ruled that while the majority owners of a limited liability company could vote to approve a sale of the limited liability company's assets to an entity that they controlled, they had to deal fairly with the squeezed out minority member. *See, also, William Penn Partnership v. Saliba*, 13 A.3d 749 (Del. 2011) (managers who engage in self-interested transactions bear the burden of proving the fairness of those transactions).

4. The management structure of publicly held limited liability companies is often identical to corporations, with boards of directors and officers. The courts apply the business judgment rule to actions of such directors, meaning that the courts will generally defer to the business judgments of the directors of an LLC unless the directors failed to act in good faith, acted without care (i.e., were allegedly grossly negligent) or had a conflict of interest. In *Blackmore Partners, L.P. v. Link Energy LLC*, 864 A.2d 80, 85–86 (Del. Ch. 2004), the unit holders, or members, of an LLC complained that the board of directors violated their fiduciary duties to the members when they sold all of the assets of the LLC (which they were empowered to do without a vote of the members) at a price that allowed the LLC to discharge its debts to its creditors, but provided no return to the unit holders. The plaintiffs did not specifically allege that the directors had a conflict of interest, acted with gross negligence or failed to act in good faith. Thus, it would seem that the directors' decision was "protected" by the business judgment rule. Nevertheless, the court declined to dismiss the action for failure to state a claim upon which relief may be granted:

> The complaint alleges, and for purposes of this motion the court assumes as true, that the Director Defendants approved a transaction that disadvantaged the holders of Link's equity units. Until the announcement of the transaction, the units had significant, if not substantial, trading value. Indeed, there is a basis in the complaint to infer that the value of Link's assets exceeded its liabilities by least $25 million. Moreover, the facts alleged support an inference that Link was neither insolvent nor on the verge of re-entering bankruptcy. Yet, as a result of the transaction at issue, those units were rendered valueless.
>
> In the circumstances, the allegation that the Defendant Directors approved a sale of substantially all of Link's assets and a resultant distribution of proceeds that went exclusively to the company's creditors raises a reasonable inference of disloyalty or intentional misconduct. Of course, it is also possible to infer (and the record at a later stage may well show) that the Director Defendants made a good faith judgment, after reasonable investigation, that there was no future for the business and no better alternative for the unit holders. Nevertheless, based only [on] the facts alleged and the reasonable inferences that the court must draw from them, it would appear that no transaction could have been worse for the unit holders and [it is] reasonable to infer, as the plaintiff argues, that a properly motivated board

of directors would not have agreed to a proposal that wiped out the value of the common equity and surrendered all of that value to the company's creditors.

> In an analogous case, Chancellor Allen recognized "[t]he broad principle that if directors take action directed against a class of securities they should be required to justify" their action. Thus, while on a more complete record, it may appear that the Director Defendants took no such action or were justified in acting as they did, this court cannot now conclude that the complaint does not state a claim for breach of the duty of loyalty or other misconduct not protected by the exculpatory provision in Link's operating agreement. For this reason, the Rule 12(b)(6) motion to dismiss must be denied.[19]

Is there any reason to treat the business judgments of the managers of an LLC different from the business judgments of corporate directors?

5. The member-managers of an LLC (or managers in a manager-managed LLC) are subject to the same duties as directors of a corporation with regard to business or "corporate" opportunities. ULLCA § 409(b)(1) provides that under the duty of loyalty the member-manager must account for any profit, etc. derived from "the use by the member of the company's property, including the company's opportunity." Similarly, § 409(b)(3) provides that a member-manager has a duty "to refrain from competing with the company in the conduct of the company's business before the dissolution of the company." Thus, to the extent that a member-manager pursues a business opportunity that competes with the LLC, such conduct violates this provision. Similarly, a member-manger would be prohibited from competing with the LLC to obtain the same business opportunity. The doctrine of corporate opportunities is generally covered in courses on corporate law. It is sufficient for present purposes to quote a succinct summary of the doctrine from a recent Delaware Chancery Court opinion:

> The corporate opportunity doctrine is a consequence of a fiduciary's duty of loyalty, and it exists to prevent officers or directors of a corporation — or, as in this case, a managing member of an LLC — from personally benefiting from opportunities belonging to the corporation. A corporate officer or director may not take a business opportunity as his own if:
>
> > (1) the corporation is financially able to exploit the opportunity; (2) the opportunity is within the corporation's line of business; (3) the corporation has an interest or expectancy in the opportunity; and (4) by taking the opportunity for his own, the corporate fiduciary will thereby be placed in a position inimicable to his duties to the corporation.

---

19. [Ultimately, the defendants did prevail. *Blackmore Partners, L.P. v. Link Energy LLC,* No. 454-N, 2005 Del.Ch. LEXIS 155 (Oct. 14, 2005). — Eds.]

Conversely, a director or officer may take personal advantage of a corporate opportunity if:

> (1) the opportunity is presented to the director or officer in his individual and not corporate capacity; (2) the opportunity is not essential to the corporation; (3) the corporation holds no interest or expectancy in the opportunity; and (4) the director or officer has not wrongfully employed the resources of the corporation in pursuing or exploiting the opportunity.

> Generally, for a corporation to have an expectant interest in any specific property, "there must be some tie between the property and the nature of the corporate business." An opportunity may be said to be in the corporation's line of business where the opportunity embraces "an activity as to which [the corporation] has fundamental knowledge, practical experience and ability to pursue, which, logically and naturally, is adaptable to its business, and . . . consonant with its reasonable needs and aspirations for expansion."

Grove v. Brown, 2013 Del. Ch. LEXIS 202 (Aug. 8, 2013).

Katris v. Carroll

Appellate Court of Illinois

842 N.E.2d 221 (2005)

PRESIDING JUSTICE MCNULTY delivered the opinion of the court:

This case concerns the applicability of fiduciary duties to a member of a manager-managed limited liability company under the Illinois Limited Liability Company Act (Act). Plaintiff-appellant Peter Katris, individually and in a derivative capacity on behalf of Viper Execution Systems, L.L.C. (the LLC), asserted a cause of action for collusion against defendants-appellees Patrick Carroll and Ernst & Company (Ernst). Katris, a manager of the LLC, contended that Carroll and Ernst colluded with a member of the LLC in the member's breach of his fiduciary duties to Katris and the LLC. The circuit court of Cook County granted summary judgment in favor of Carroll and Ernst, finding that the LLC member did not owe the LLC or Katris any fiduciary duty.

In affirming the circuit court's grant of summary judgment, we follow the plain meaning of section 15-3(g)(3) of the Act. This section imposes fiduciary duties only on a member of a manager-managed limited liability company who exercises some or all of the authority of a manager pursuant to the operating agreement. The facts in this case showed that the member did not exercise any such authority pursuant to the operating agreement. Accordingly, the member did not owe any fiduciary duties, and, as a result, the collusion claim fails and summary judgment was proper.

Background

In the early to mid-1990s, Stephen Doherty wrote a software program called "Viper" for Lester Szlendak. Subsequently, Katris and William Hamburg, both Ernst employees, expressed interest in Viper, and on February 14, 1997, they joined Szlendak and Doherty in forming the LLC to exploit the capabilities of the software. On that date, they filed the LLC's articles of organization with the Secretary of State. In it, they indicated that management of the LLC was vested in its managers, Katris and Hamburg, and not retained by its members.

Pursuant to the LLC's operating agreement, signed by the four members on February 14, 1997, each member held a 25% interest, and as a condition of the operating agreement, Szlendak and Doherty assigned their rights, interest and title to Viper to the LLC. The operating agreement provided that the "business and affairs of the [LLC] shall be managed by its [m]anagers" and that the members agreed to elect Katris and Hamburg as the "sole [m]anagers" of the LLC. The operating agreement also enumerated the powers of the managers and set forth the rights and obligations of the members. However, none of the provisions setting forth the rights and obligations of the members provided the members with any managerial authority. Pursuant to its terms, the operating agreement could "not be amended except by the affirmative vote of [m]embers holding a majority of the [p]articipating [p]ercentages."

Also on February 14, 1997, Katris and Hamburg, as managers of the LLC, prepared a written consent adopting certain resolutions in lieu of holding an initial meeting of the managers. They resolved, *inter alia*, to adopt the operating agreement dated February 14, 1997, as the operating agreement of the LLC and to elect the following: Hamburg as chief executive officer, Katris as chief financial officer, Szlendak as director of marketing, and Doherty as director of technical services. The written consent contained signature lines for Hamburg and Katris, who were identified as "all of the [m]anagers" of the LLC.

Prior to and at the time of the LLC's formation, Doherty worked as an independent contractor for Hamburg and Carroll (also an Ernst employee); however, in late 1997, Ernst hired Doherty to work for Carroll. As part of his duties for Carroll, Doherty worked with a programmer hired by Ernst to adapt a software program ultimately called "Worldwide Options Web (WWOW)."

Katris initiated this action on January 16, 2002, and ultimately asserted a breach of fiduciary duty claim against Doherty and a claim for collusion against Doherty, Carroll and Ernst. He alleged that WWOW was functionally similar to Viper and contended that Doherty usurped a corporate opportunity of the LLC by working in secret with Carroll and the programmer hired by Ernst to develop competing software for Ernst. He further contended that Carroll and Ernst colluded with Doherty in the breach of Doherty's fiduciary duties to the LLC.

Doherty subsequently settled with Katris, providing Katris with an affidavit setting forth his involvement in the case in exchange for his dismissal. As a result of Doherty's dismissal from the case, only Katris' claim for collusion against defendants-appellees Carroll and Ernst remained.

Carroll and Ernst filed a motion for summary judgment asserting, *inter alia*, that Katris' collusion claim failed because Doherty, as a nonmanager member of the manager-managed LLC, did not owe Katris or the LLC a fiduciary duty under section 15-3(g) of the Act, and thus they could not collude with Doherty to breach a fiduciary duty under that section.

In response, Katris filed an affidavit attaching the February 14, 1997, written consent. Katris stated that the written consent constituted an amendment to the operating agreement and that, pursuant to the terms of that amendment, Doherty was named "Director of Technology" and "given the sole management responsibility for developing, writing, revising and implementing the Viper software." According to Katris' affidavit, Doherty "was in charge of adapting the software to route options orders, in addition to stock orders," and the "LLC relied on him totally to develop the Viper software." Katris contended that pursuant to section 15-3(g)(3) of the Act, Doherty was thus subject to the standards of conduct imposed upon managers under the Act and breached those duties by usurping a corporate opportunity belonging to the LLC.

On October 1, 2004, the circuit court entered an order granting Carroll and Ernst's motion for summary judgment. The court subsequently denied Katris' motion for reconsideration, and this appeal follows.

Analysis

In this appeal, Katris contends that the trial court erred in granting summary judgment on his collusion claim against Carroll and Ernst.

Here, Katris asserted a cause of action for collusion against Carroll and Ernst. He contended that Carroll and Ernst colluded with Doherty in breaching Doherty's fiduciary duty to Katris and the LLC. Accordingly, Katris' claim against Carroll and Ernst depended upon a finding that Doherty owed Katris and the LLC a fiduciary duty. In this appeal, Katris contends that summary judgment was improper because Doherty owed Katris and the LLC such a fiduciary duty.

We look to the applicable provisions of the Act in determining the fiduciary duties owed by the managers and members of the LLC. The parties here agree that section 15-3(g) of the Act applies to determine Doherty's fiduciary duties.

Katris acknowledges that theirs was a manager-managed LLC and that, pursuant to the Act, a member of a manager-managed LLC "who is not also a manager owes no duties to the company or to the other members solely by reason of being a member." Katris thus concedes that Doherty did not owe any fiduciary duties solely by reason of being a member of the LLC.

Katris contends, however, that Doherty owed fiduciary duties to the LLC pursuant to section 15-3(g)(3) of the Act. Section 15-3(g)(3) provides:

> [A] member who pursuant to the operating agreement exercises some or
> all of the authority of a manager in the management and conduct of the

company's business is held to the standards of conduct in subsections (b), (c), (d), and (e) of this Section to the extent that the member exercises the managerial authority vested in a manager by this Act[.]

Katris contends that Doherty exercised some of the authority of a manager in his capacity as director of technology for the LLC and thus falls within the ambit of this section. Carroll and Ernst disagree, contending that pursuant to the plain terms of the statute, Doherty was only subject to fiduciary duties if he exercised managerial authority pursuant to the operating agreement. They maintain that Doherty did not have any such managerial authority under the operating agreement. We agree.

"'The cardinal rule of statutory construction is to ascertain and give effect to the intent of the legislature.'" *In re Application of the County Collector*, 826 N.E.2d 951 (2005). The plain meaning of the language used by the legislature is the best indication of legislative intent, and when the language is clear, this court should not look to extrinsic aids for construction. If possible, a statute should be construed so that no part is rendered superfluous or meaningless.

Looking at the plain language of section 15-3(g)(3) of the Act, Doherty was subject to fiduciary duties if he exercised some or all of the authority of a manager pursuant to the LLC's operating agreement. The Act provides for the creation of an operating agreement, stating that "[a]ll members of a limited liability company may enter into an operating agreement to regulate the affairs of the company and the conduct of its business and to govern relations among the members, managers, and company." The four members of the LLC here entered into such an operating agreement on February 14, 1997.

Looking to that operating agreement, it specifically provides that the business and affairs of the LLC "shall be managed by its [m]anagers," provides for the election of Katris and Hamburg as the "sole [m]anagers" of the LLC, and sets forth the powers of the managers of the LLC. Although the operating agreement also sets forth the rights and obligations of the members, these provisions do not provide for any managerial authority. Accordingly, Doherty did not exercise any managerial authority pursuant to the LLC's operating agreement.

Katris contends, however, that the managers amended the operating agreement by passing the February 14, 1997, written consent wherein they elected Doherty "Director of Technology." He contends that Doherty's designation as "Director of Technology" elevated him to a position beyond that of a mere member of the LLC and was sufficient to impart on him some managerial authority. This argument fails for two reasons.

First, Katris has provided no authority for his contention that the written consent constituted an amendment to the operating agreement. Pursuant to its own terms, an amendment to the operating agreement required the "affirmative vote of [m]embers holding a majority of the [p]articipating [p]ercentages." Katris and Hamburg were the sole participants to the February 14, 1997, written consent and held only a combined 50% interest in the LLC. They thus could not amend the operating agreement without an additional vote. Accordingly, the facts do not support Katris' contention that the written consent constituted an amendment to the operating agreement.

Second, even if the written consent were viewed as part of the operating agreement, it did not change and, indeed, it reaffirmed the terms of the operating agreement. Katris and Hamburg executed the written consent in their capacities as the managers of the LLC. In it, they specifically resolved to adopt the operating agreement the four members had executed that day as the operating agreement of the LLC. In the signature lines to the written consent, Katris and Hamburg designated themselves as "all of the [m]anagers" of the LLC. In light of these facts, something more than the managers' designation of Doherty as "Director of Technology" was required to change the terms of the operating agreement and grant Doherty managerial authority pursuant to it.

In reaching this conclusion, we find Katris' contentions in his affidavit, wherein he enumerates the managerial authority Doherty held as a result of being named "Director of Technology" in the written consent, inapposite under section 15-3(g)(3) of the Act. By its terms, that section applies where the non manager member exercises some or all of the authority of a manager *pursuant to the operating agreement*. To look beyond the operating agreement to Katris' affidavit would be to ignore the plain meaning of the statute and to render the express words used therein superfluous or meaningless. This we cannot do.

The undisputed facts of this case show that Doherty was a member of a manager-managed LLC and exercised no managerial authority pursuant to the LLC's operating agreement. Accordingly, the undisputed facts show that Doherty owed no fiduciary duties to Katris or the LLC pursuant to the Act and Katris' collusion claim against Carroll and Ernst fails as a matter of law. We therefore conclude that the circuit court properly granted the motion for summary judgment and affirm its judgment.

Affirmed.

Note

While Doherty may not have had fiduciary duties to the LLC by virtue of being a non-managing member, might he not have had fiduciary duties as an employee/agent of the LLC?

c. Use of Corporate Structure

It is not unusual for a limited liability company to be structured as a corporation; that is, the operating agreement for the LLC will provide for a board of directors, officers with the titles that are typical in a corporation (e.g., president, vice-president, etc.), membership interests that are called shares, etc. When an LLC is structured in this way, a question arises as to whether corporate law precedents—that is, judicial interpretations of corporate statutes—should be applied to legal questions that arise in the LLC. In an unreported, but well-known opinion (among lawyers for alternative entities), *Obeid v. Hogan*, 2016 WL 3356851, at *6 (Del. Ch.

June 10, 2016), Vice Chancellor Laster of the Delaware Chancery Court indicated that corporate law precedents would be consulted, writing:

> Using the contractual freedom that the LLC Act bestows, the drafters of an LLC agreement can create an LLC with bespoke governance features or design an LLC that mimics the governance features of another familiar type of entity. The choices that the drafters make have consequences. If the drafters have embraced the statutory default rule of a member-managed governance arrangement, which has strong functional and historical ties to the general partnership (albeit with limited liability for the members), then the parties should expect a court to draw on analogies to partnership law. If the drafters have opted for a single managing member with other generally passive, non-managing members, a structure closely resembling and often used as an alternative to a limited partnership, then the parties should expect a court to draw on analogies to limited partnership law. If the drafters have opted for a manager-managed entity, created a board of directors, and adopted other corporate features, then the parties to the agreement should expect a court to draw on analogies to corporate law.

The implications of this observation should not be overlooked by the drafters of the operating agreement. For instance, LLC statutes typically provide, as a default rule, that each manager in a manager-managed LLC has agency authority and can bind the company. By contrast, directors are not viewed as agents and can only act as a decision-making body in accordance with the corporate law statute and bylaws. The drafters of an operating agreement opting to use a corporate-like structure need to address any ambiguity that might arise as a result of adopting a structure not contemplated by the typical LLC act. *See* Bradley T. Borden, Christine Hurt, and Thomas E. Rutledge, *It's A Bird, It's A Plane, No, It's A Board-Managed LLC!*, Business Law Today (March, 2017). The *Obeid* case involved the question of whether the board of directors of an LLC could appoint an outsider (neither a member nor a director) as a special litigation committee. This is addressed below, following *Wood v. Baum*.

2. Claims Among Members

a. Derivative Claims

Wood v. Baum

Supreme Court of Delaware
953 A.2d 136 (2008)

Before Steele, Chief Justice, Holland and Jacobs, Justices.

Jacobs, Justice.

Paddy Wood, the plaintiff below, appeals from the dismissal by the Court of Chancery of her derivative action on behalf of Municipal Mortgage & Equity, LLC ("MME"). For the reasons set forth, we affirm.

Facts

MME, a Delaware limited liability company with its principal place of business in Baltimore, Maryland, "provides debt and equity financing to various parties, invests in tax-exempt bonds and other housing-related debt and equity investments, and is a tax credit syndicator that acquires and transfers low-income housing tax credits." MME has a ten-member Board of directors, of which two are inside directors [that is, officers of the company]. MME's Amended and Restated Certificate of Formation and Operating Agreement (the "Operating Agreement") exempts directors from any liability "except in the case of fraudulent or illegal conduct of such person."[20]

Plaintiff's complaint, filed on September 7, 2006, named as defendants the ten then-current members of MME's Board and one former director. Five of the defendants were also members of MME's Audit Committee. On October 20, 2006, the defendants moved under Court of Chancery Rule 23.1[21] to dismiss the initial complaint, for failure to make a pre-suit demand on the Board. Plaintiff subsequently filed an amended complaint (the "Complaint"). The Complaint set forth a myriad of allegations that are fairly summarized as follows:

(a) The defendants breached their fiduciary duties by causing MME to improperly value certain non-performing assets in violation of MME's internal policies, GAAP and SEC standards, in particular Financial Accounting Standard 115 ("FAS 115"). As a result, MME issued false financial statements concerning the value and performance of those assets.

(b) The defendants breached their fiduciary duties by causing MME to make improper charitable contributions, some of which were related-party transactions. The beneficiaries used those contributions to service debt held by MME, thereby concealing the deterioration of MME's tax-exempt bond portfolio.

(c) The defendants breached their fiduciary duties by causing MME to execute a series of "related party transactions involv[ing] transfers of the securitized property via deeds in lieu of foreclosures from affiliated companies followed by near simultaneous resales of the same property at enormous profits." The effect was significantly to inflate MME's financial performance.

---

20. [1] Section 8.1(a) of the Operating Agreement provides: "No director or officer of the Company shall be liable, responsible, or accountable in damages or otherwise to the Company or any Shareholders for any act or omission performed or omitted by him or her, or for any decision, except in the case of fraudulent or illegal conduct of such person." The corollary indemnification provisions are set out in Section 8.1(b) of the Operating Agreement.

21. [2] Ch. Ct. R. 23.1(a) relevantly provides: "In a derivative action brought by one or more shareholders or members to enforce a right of a corporation . . . the complaint shall allege . . . with particularity the efforts, if any, made by the plaintiff to obtain the action the plaintiff desires from the directors or comparable authority and the reasons for the plaintiff's failure to obtain the action or for not making the effort."

(d) The defendants breached their *Caremark* duties[22] by "fail[ing] properly to institute, administer and maintain adequate accounting and reporting controls, practices and procedures," which resulted in a "massive restatement process, an SEC investigation, and loss of substantial access to financial markets."

On March 21, 2007 and April 10, 2007, the defendants renewed their motion to dismiss the Complaint. After oral argument, the Court of Chancery, ruling from the bench, dismissed the Complaint for failure to allege particularized facts sufficient to establish that demand on the Board would have been futile. The Court of Chancery noted that "though the complaint is 80-some pages long and is a model of prolixity, it fails to state any basis on which the Court could reasonably conclude that the demand futility standard is met." This appeal followed.

Analysis

A stockholder may not pursue a derivative suit to assert a claim of the corporation unless the stockholder: (a) has first demanded that the directors pursue the corporate claim and the directors have wrongfully refused to do so; or (b) establishes that pre-suit demand is excused because the directors are deemed incapable of making an impartial decision regarding the pursuit of the litigation. Having failed to make a pre-suit demand upon MME's Board, plaintiff must establish demand futility.

The controlling legal standard for determining the sufficiency of a complaint to withstand dismissal based on a claim of demand futility under Court of Chancery Rule 23.1 is well-established. Two tests are available to determine whether demand is futile. The *Aronson* test applies to claims involving a contested transaction *i.e.*, where it is alleged that the directors made a conscious business decision in breach of their fiduciary duties. That test requires that the plaintiff allege particularized facts creating a reason to doubt that "(1) the directors are disinterested and independent [or that] (2) the challenged transaction was otherwise the product of a valid exercise of business judgment."[23] Only the second (and alternative) prong is implicated here because the plaintiff does not contest that a majority of the Board is generally independent and disinterested (except as discussed below). The second (*Rales*) test applies where the subject of a derivative suit is not a business decision of the Board but rather a violation of the Board's oversight duties. The *Rales* test requires that the plaintiff allege particularized facts establishing a reason to doubt that "the board of directors could have properly exercised its independent and disinterested business judgment in responding to a demand."[24]

---

22. [4] *See In re Caremark Int'l Inc. Deriv. Litig.*, 698 A.2d 959 (Del.Ch. 1996); *Stone ex rel. AmSouth Bancorporation v. Ritter*, 911 A.2d 362, 364 (Del.2006).

23. [8] *Aronson v. Lewis*, 473 A.2d 805, 814 (Del. 1984).

24. [9] *Rales v. Blasband*, 634 A.2d 927, 934 (Del. 1993).

To satisfy either test, a plaintiff must "comply with stringent requirements of factual particularity" of Court of Chancery Rule 23.1.[25] Here, the plaintiff attempted to create a "reasonable doubt" that the Board would have properly exercised its business judgment by alleging that the Board was disabled because of a substantial risk of personal liability.[26] In evaluating that claim, it must be kept in mind that the exculpation provision contained in MME's Operating Agreement exempts MME's directors from all liability except in case of "fraudulent or illegal conduct." Section 18-1101(e) of the Delaware Limited Liability Company Act ("LLCA") allows a limited liability company, such as MME, to "provide for the limitation or elimination of any and all liabilities . . . for breach of duties (including fiduciary duties) of a [director]," except that the LLC "may not limit or eliminate liability for any act or omission that constitutes a bad faith violation of the implied contractual covenant of good faith and fair dealing."[27] Therefore, under the Operating Agreement and the LLCA, the MME directors' exposure to liability is limited to claims of "fraudulent or illegal conduct," or "bad faith violation[s] of the implied contractual covenant of good faith and fair dealing."

Where directors are contractually or otherwise exculpated from liability for certain conduct, "then a serious threat of liability may only be found to exist if the plaintiff pleads a *non-exculpated* claim against the directors based on particularized facts."[28] Where, as here, directors are exculpated from liability except for claims based on "fraudulent," "illegal" or "bad faith" conduct, a plaintiff must also plead particularized facts that demonstrate that the directors acted with scienter, *i.e.*, that they had "actual or constructive knowledge" that their conduct was legally improper.[29] Therefore, the issue before us is whether the Complaint alleges particularized facts that, if proven, would show that a majority of the defendants knowingly engaged in "fraudulent" or "illegal" conduct or breached "in bad faith" the covenant of good faith and fair dealing. We conclude that the answer is no.

First, plaintiff has not pled with particularity any claim based on fraudulent conduct. The Complaint does not even purport to state a cause of action for fraud, let alone plead the specific facts required to support such a claim. Instead, the Complaint only alleges conclusorily that the defendants made "affirmative misrepresentations"

---

25. [10] *Brehm v. Eisner*, 746 A.2d 244, 254 (Del. 2000).

26. [11] In *Aronson*, this Court held that "the mere threat of personal liability . . . is insufficient to challenge either the independence or disinterestedness of directors" and that a reasonable doubt that a majority of directors is incapable of considering demand should only be found where "a substantial likelihood of personal liability exists." *Aronson*, 473 A.2d at 814. *See also Rales*, 634 A.2d at 936; *In re Baxter Int'l, Inc. S'holders Litig.*, 654 A.2d 1268, 1269 (Del. Ch. 1995).

27. [12] 6 Del. C. § 18-1101(e).

28. [13] *Guttman v. Huang*, 823 A.2d 492, 501 (Del. Ch. 2003) (citing *Baxter*, 654 A.2d at 1270) (emphasis in original). *Accord, Stone ex rel. AmSouth Bancorporation v. Ritter*, 911 A.2d 362, 367 (Del. 2006).

29. [14] *See, e.g., Malpiede v. Townson*, 780 A.2d 1075 (Del. 2001); *Emerald Partners v. Berlin*, 787 A.2d 85 (Del. 2001). *See also, e.g., Desimone v. Barrows*, 924 A.2d 908, at 933–35 (Del. Ch. 2007).

and "actively condoned and facilitated a campaign of deceit." Such assertions are insufficient to state an actionable claim for fraud.

Second, the Complaint alleges many violations of federal securities and tax laws but does not plead with particularity the specific conduct in which each defendant "knowingly" engaged, or that the defendants knew that such conduct was illegal. Before oral argument, this Court directed the plaintiff to identify "the particularized pleaded facts that, if true, would establish that the directors had actual or constructive knowledge that the various acts or omissions complained of were wrongful . . . [and] the paragraph [s] of the [C]omplaint where such knowledge is specifically alleged." The facts plaintiff identified in response to that request fell into four main categories: (a) the defendants executed MME's annual reports and other publicly filed financial reports; (b) the defendants authorized certain transactions; (c) five of the defendants served on MME's Audit Committee; and (d) other "red flags." None of the acts identified by plaintiff establish that the directors knowingly participated in illegal conduct.

The Board's execution of MME's financial reports, without more, is insufficient to create an inference that the directors had actual or constructive notice of any illegality. Plaintiff contends that the Court of Chancery should have inferred that the Board "had knowledge of certain transactions because [the Board] had to authorize the transactions." Specifically, plaintiff argues, such knowledge should be inferred because the alleged transactions were "related party transactions" that the Board was required to approve under MME's Operating Agreement. Delaware law on this point is clear: board approval of a transaction, even one that later proves to be improper, without more, is an insufficient basis to infer culpable knowledge or bad faith on the part of individual directors.[30] We conclude that the Court of Chancery correctly applied Delaware law in declining to infer from the Board's approval either that (i) each member of the Board knew that the alleged transactions were improper or that (ii) the Board consciously and in bad faith failed to discharge fiduciary or contractual responsibilities with respect to those transactions.

Plaintiff also asserts that membership on the Audit Committee is a sufficient basis to infer the requisite scienter. That assertion is contrary to well-settled Delaware law. In *Rattner v. Bidzos*, for example, the Court of Chancery declined to infer that the directors had a culpable state of mind based on allegations that certain board members served on an audit committee and, as a consequence, should have been aware of the facts on which the plaintiff premised her interpretation of "SEC rules and regulations, and FSAB and GAAP standards."[31]

---

30. [18] *Aronson v. Lewis*, 473 A.2d 805, 814 (Del. 1984) (holding that "mere directorial approval of a transaction, absent particularized facts supporting a breach of fiduciary duty claim, or otherwise establishing the lack of independence or disinterestedness of a majority of the directors, is insufficient to excuse demand").

31. [19] *Rattner v. Bidzos*, 2003 WL 22284323, at *12–*13 (Del. Ch. Ct.) (noting that "conspicuously absent from any of the Amended Complaint's allegations are particularized facts regarding

Finally, plaintiff claims that the Board knowingly ignored "red flags."[32] Under Delaware law, red flags "are only useful when they are either waved in one's face or displayed so that they are visible to the careful observer."[33] Here, the Court of Chancery correctly concluded that there were no cognizable "red flags" from which it could be inferred that the defendants knew that FAS 115 was being improperly applied, or that the defendants otherwise consciously and in bad faith ignored the improprieties alleged in the complaint.

. . . .

Given the broad exculpating provision contained in MME's Operating Agreement, the plaintiff's factual allegations are insufficient to establish demand futility.

Conclusion

For the reasons set forth above, the judgment of the Court of Chancery affirmed.

Notes

1. With regard to the availability of derivative suits to members of an LLC, *see* ULLCA §§ 1101–1104, establishing the right of members to bring derivative suits "if the members or managers having authority to do so have refused to commence the action or an effort to cause those members or managers to commence the action is not likely to succeed." Also, "the complaint must set forth with particularity the effort of the plaintiff to secure initiation of the action by a member or manager or the reasons for not making the effort." ULLCA § 1103.

2. Courts are increasingly facing the question of whether the claim made by a member of the LLC is derivative in nature, that is, a claim of the LLC, or a direct claim of the member bringing the suit. In resolving this question, courts have drawn on the extensive body of case law generated in the corporate area. As a general rule, courts look to a two-pronged test to determine if a claim is direct (and, therefore, may be maintained by the member free from interference of the LLC) or derivative (in which case the managers or other members have a role to play, as explained in *Wood*). This two-prong test looks first to who suffered the injury alleged in the complaint (if the member suffered the injury directly, the claim is direct, if indirectly, the claim is derivative) and, second, who will receive the benefit of any recovery or other remedy. See, e.g., *Tooley v. Donaldson, Lufkin & Jenrette, Inc.*, 845 A.2d 1031 (Del. 2004).

---

the Company's internal financial controls during the Relevant Period, notably the actions and practices of [the company's] audit committee" and "any facts regarding the Board's involvement in the preparation of the financial statements and the release of financial information to the market," and rejecting plaintiff's asserted inferences where the court was "unable to conclude that a majority of the Board faces a substantial likelihood of liability for failing to oversee [the company's] compliance with required accounting and disclosure standards").

32. [20] *See Stone ex rel. AmSouth Bancorporation v. Ritter*, 911 A.2d 362 (Del. 2006).
33. [21] *In re Citigroup Inc. S'holders Litig.*, 2003 WL 21384599, at *2 (Del. Ch. Ct.).

3. All jurisdictions recognize the right of a corporate shareholder, under proper circumstances and subject to varying constraints, to bring a derivative action on behalf of the corporation, but it may not be the case that LLC members have such a right. In New York, one court held that members do not have such a right, *Lio v. Zhong*, 814 N.Y.S.2d 562 (Sup. Ct. 2006) (member of an LLC may not maintain a derivative action under New York law), but this decision was overruled by the New York Court of Appeals in a subsequent case, *Tzolis v. Wolff*, 884 N.E.3d 1005 (N.Y. Ct. App. 2008). Some states permit the parties to preclude the availability of a derivative action in the operating agreement by failing to designate the statutory provisions as nonwaivable. *See, e.g.*, Colo. Rev. Stat. § 7-80-108 (2006). Interestingly, in *Lio*, while the court held that a member of an LLC could not maintain a derivative action (later overruled), it also held that a "cause of action for breach of fiduciary duty between LLC members is a legally cognizable personal claim of an LLC member." 814 N.Y.S.2d at 562. A similar claim brought by a corporate shareholder would likely be characterized as derivative. *See Phoenix Airline Svcs. v. Metro Airlines*, 397 S.E.2d 699 (Ga. 1990). Finally, some courts, drawing on corporate precedents, permit a member of a closely held limited liability company to maintain a breach of fiduciary duty claim as a direct cause of action as an exception to the normal rule. *Stoker v. Bellemeade*, LLC, 615 S.E.2d 1 (Ga. Ct. App. 2005). *See generally* Daniel S. Kleinberger, *Direct Versus Derivative and the Law of Limited Liability Companies*, 58 Baylor L. Rev. 63 (2006). See also *Anglo American Security Fund v. S.R. Global Intern'l Fund*, reproduced in Chapter 14, Section D.3., *supra*, a case in which the court considered how to characterize the claim of a limited partner.

4. When a derivative action is filed by a corporate shareholder, the corporate board will often appoint a "special litigation committee" of independent directors to investigate the matter and determine whether the action should go forward, be settled, or be dismissed. The law surrounding derivative actions and special litigation committees has been adopted in the context of limited partnerships and is discussed in Chapter 14, Section D, *supra*. Similarly, those precedents have been applied to derivative actions filed by members of LLCs. When an LLC elects a corporate-type structure, at least one court has looked to corporate law to decide whether the board members of the LLC could appoint an outsider (a retired federal judge who was neither a member nor a director of the LLC) to serve as the special litigation committee. In *Obeid v. Hogan*, 2016 WL 3356851 (Del. Ch. June 10, 2016), discussed above, the Delaware Chancery Court, citing corporate law, held that the board of directors of an LLC could *not* appoint a person who was not a director of the LLC to serve as the special litigation committee. While the operating agreement could have so provided, it did not and because the parties chose a corporate structure, the corporate rule—that only directors have such authority—would be applied.

5. In *LNYC Loft, LLC v. Hudson Opportunity Fund I, LLC,* 154 A.D.3d 109 (App. Div. 2017), the defendant manager sought to appoint a person who was neither a member nor a manager to serve as a "special litigation committee" to decide whether the derivative action should proceed. The plaintiff resisted the appointment and the New York court agreed, noting that the operating agreement for the company reserved "major decisions" to the members and the appointment of a special litigation committee was such a decision.

While the standing of a member of an LLC to maintain a derivative action is now well established, the standing of creditors to maintain an action is a matter of some controversy, as the next case indicates.

CML V, LLC v. BAX

Court of Chancery of Delaware
6 A.3d 238 (2010)

Laster, Vice Chancellor.

I. Factual Background

Plaintiff CML V, LLC ("CML") lent funds to JetDirect Aviation Holdings, LLC ("JetDirect" or the "Company").

JetDirect was a private jet management and charter company that, through subsidiaries, provided charter services, prepaid memberships for charter flights, aircraft management services, and maintenance and fuel services. Beginning in 2005, as part of a roll-up strategy, JetDirect acquired a number of small to mid-sized charter and service companies.

JetDirect's aggressive expansion left it with a highly leveraged balance sheet and volatile cash flows. In 2006, JetDirect's board of managers became aware of serious deficiencies in its accounting system. BKD LLP, JetDirect's auditor, informed the Individual Defendants of nineteen "material weaknesses," "significant deficiencies," and "control deficiencies" in JetDirect's internal controls. A year later, JetDirect's new auditor, Ernst & Young LLP ("E & Y") declined to complete its audit because JetDirect's internal controls lacked sufficient integrity for E & Y to rely on the Company's books. Most notable among these deficiencies was the failure of JetDirect's management to properly collect and account for financial data from JetDirect's subsidiaries.

JetDirect's internal control deficiencies were exacerbated when senior management attempted to consolidate the Company's billing operations. The project was botched, and JetDirect's billing cycle expanded dramatically. Accounts receivable increased more than six-fold, and it took up to sixteen weeks to gather financial data to report to the board.

In April 2007, CML loaned JetDirect $25,743,912, an amount later increased to $34,243,912. Despite lacking current information about JetDirect's financial condition, the Company's board approved four major acquisitions in late 2007. CML contends that if JetDirect's managers had possessed accurate financial data, they would have seen that JetDirect lacked the working capital to finance the acquisitions. CML also contends that senior management hid adverse information from the board.

In June 2007, JetDirect defaulted on its loan obligations to CML. By January 2008, JetDirect was insolvent. In late 2008, JetDirect's managers began liquidating some of JetDirect's holdings. According to CML, certain managers negotiated sales of Jet-Direct assets to entities they controlled, and the JetDirect board approved the interested sales without adequately reviewing their fairness.

Based on these allegations, CML asserts derivatively in Count I that the Individual Defendants breached their duty of care by approving the late 2007 acquisitions without informing themselves of critical information about JetDirect's financial condition. CML asserts derivatively in Count II that the Individual Defendants acted in bad faith by consciously failing to implement and monitor an adequate system of internal controls. Count II also alleges that a member of senior management hid critical information from the board. CML asserts derivatively in Count III that the Individual Defendants who benefited from the self-interested asset sales breached their duty of loyalty. In Count IV, CML asserts a direct claim against Jet-Direct for breach of its loan agreement with CML. If Counts I–III are successful, the Individual Defendants will pay damages to JetDirect, and CML can recover those funds under Count IV.

II. Legal Analysis

"[T]he creditors of an *insolvent* corporation have standing to maintain derivative claims against directors on behalf of the corporation for breaches of fiduciary duties." *N. Am. Catholic Educ. Programming Found., Inc. v. Gheewalla*, 930 A.2d 92, 101 (Del.2007) [hereinafter, "*Gheewalla*"]; *accord Prod. Res. Gp., L.L.C. v. NCT Gp., Inc.*, 863 A.2d 772, 776 (Del. Ch. 2004). When a corporation is insolvent, the creditors become "the principal constituency injured by any fiduciary breaches that diminish the firm's value." *Gheewalla*, 930 A.2d at 102 (quoting *Prod. Res.*, 863 A.2d at 792). Under these circumstances, "equitable considerations give creditors standing to pursue derivative claims against the directors of an insolvent corporation." *Id.*

CML argues that the same equitable considerations entitle creditors to sue derivatively on behalf of an insolvent LLC. The Individual Defendants respond that the Delaware LLC Act precludes creditor standing. As demonstrated by this Court's decisions and scholarly commentary, the standing provisions in the alternative entity statutes have not been widely understood as barring derivative claims by creditors of an insolvent entity. To the contrary, many have assumed that creditor derivative standing exists. Nevertheless, the literal terms of the LLC Act control, and they bar a creditor of an insolvent LLC from suing derivatively. Although this Court may depart from the literal reading of a statute where such a reading is so inconsistent with the statutory purpose as to produce an absurd result, this is not such a case.

A. The Plain Language Of The LLC Act

. . . "If the statute as a whole is unambiguous, there is no reasonable doubt as to the meaning of the words used and the Court's role is then limited to an application of the literal meaning of the words." *Coastal Barge Corp. v. Coastal Zone Indus. Control Bd.*, 492 A.2d 1242, 1246 (Del. 1985).

The LLC Act creates a statutory right to bring a derivative action. Section 18-1001, entitled "Right to Bring Action," states: "A member or an assignee of a limited liability company interest may bring an action in the Court of Chancery in the right of a limited liability company to recover a judgment in its favor if managers or members with authority to do so have refused to bring the action or if an effort to cause those managers or members to bring the action is not likely to succeed." 6 Del. C. § 18-1001. The following section, entitled "Proper Plaintiff," provides:

> In a derivative action, the plaintiff must be a member or an assignee of a limited liability company interest at the time of bringing the action and: (1) At the time of the transaction of which the plaintiff complains; or (2) The plaintiff's status as a member or an assignee of a limited liability company interest had devolved upon the plaintiff by operation of law or pursuant to the terms of a limited liability company agreement from a person who was a member or an assignee of a limited liability company interest at the time of the transaction. 6 Del. C. § 18-1002.

Under the plain language of Section 18-1002, a plaintiff "must be a member or an assignee." Section 18-1001 similarly refers only to "a member or an assignee." The only Delaware treatise to comment directly on how these provisions affect creditors states: "Under Sections 18-1001 and 18-1002, [an LLC] creditor is not a proper plaintiff in a derivative suit." Robert L. Symonds, Jr. & Matthew J. O'Toole, *Delaware Limited Liability Companies* § 9.09, at 9-61 n.270 (2007).

. . . .

The exclusive language of Section 18-1002 contrasts with the non-exclusive language of Section 327 of the Delaware General Corporation Law (the "DGCL"), 8 Del. C. § 327. Section 327 is the only provision in the DGCL that addresses derivative actions. It provides: "In any derivative suit instituted by a stockholder of a corporation, it shall be averred in the complaint that the plaintiff was a stockholder of the corporation at the time of the transaction of which such stockholder complains or that such stockholder's stock thereafter devolved upon such stockholder by operation of law." 8 Del. C. § 327.

. . . .

Under the plain language of Section 18-1002, standing to bring a derivative action is limited to "a member or an assignee." Read literally, Section 18-1002 denies derivative standing to creditors of an insolvent LLC.

B. A Dog That Has Not Barked

As compelling as a literal reading of Section 18-1002 might seem, it encounters an awkward fact: Despite the ostensibly obvious implications of the statute, virtually no one has construed the derivative standing provisions as barring creditors of an insolvent LLC from filing suit. Particularly in light of *Production Resources* and *Gheewalla*, an exclusive reading of Section 18-1002 would cause LLC derivative actions to differ markedly from their corporate cousins. If practitioners widely understood the derivative standing provisions to have this effect, one would expect treatises, articles, and commentaries to call attention to that fact. . . . In the years since *Production Resources* and *Gheewalla*, one also would expect courts to have encountered parties raising the statutory provisions as a defense. Yet the universe of authorities favoring the no-standing position consists of (i) a single sentence at the end of a footnote in one Delaware treatise, *see* Symonds & O'Toole, *supra*, § 9.09, at 9-61 n.270, and (ii) abbreviated treatment in an unreported district court decision.

. . . .

Many commentators, by contrast, have assumed that creditors of an insolvent LLC can sue derivatively. In light of this assumption, they have debated vigorously whether an LLC agreement can limit the fiduciary duties that the creditors would invoke. That question never arises if creditors lack standing to sue under Section 18-1002.

. . . .

C. Other Sources Of Authority

Delaware Supreme Court decisions empower this Court to resolve any apparent tension between the plain language of the LLC Act and the commonly held understanding of the provisions decisively in favor of the statutory language. "If a statute is unambiguous, there is no need for judicial interpretation, and the plain meaning of the statutory language controls." *Eliason v. Englehart*, 733 A.2d 944, 946 (Del. 1999). The derivative standing provisions of the LLC Act, however, are not uniquely Delawarean provisions, nor are they artifacts of the LLC statute. Rather they are part of widely adopted uniform acts where consistent interpretation and stable commercial expectations have particular salience. A context-free reading of those provisions risks a content-skewed result. Although I could resolve this case on plain meaning alone, I also have considered (i) how parallel provisions of other alternative entity statutes have been interpreted, (ii) the source and development of the alternative entity derivative standing provisions, and (iii) whether enforcing the plain meaning of Section 18-1002 would create an absurd result at odds with the overarching purpose and framework of the LLC Act. Each line of inquiry supports applying Section 18-1002 as an exclusive provision that limits derivative standing to LLC members and assignees.

1. The Comparable Provisions Of The LP Act

The Delaware Limited Partnership ("LP") Act contains derivative standing provisions phrased identically to Sections 18-1001 and 18-1002, except for substituting terms relevant to the entity covered, such as "partner" and "limited partnership" for "member" and "limited liability company." *See* 6 Del. C. §§ 17-1001 & 17-1002. This comes as no surprise. The LLC Act was "modeled on the popular Delaware LP Act." *Elf Atochem N. Am., Inc. v. Jaffari*, 727 A.2d 286, 290 (Del. 1999). "In fact, its architecture and much of its wording is almost identical to that of the Delaware LP Act." *Id.*

In framing derivative standing in exclusive terms, Sections 17-1001 and 17-1002 of the Delaware LP Act track the comparable derivative action provisions in the

Revised Uniform Limited Partnership Act ("RULPA"). A leading treatise on RULPA regards the derivative standing provisions as exclusive: "A person must be a limited partner to bring a derivative suit under R.U.L.P.A. § 1001. R.U.L.P.A. § 1002 restates this requirement ('must be a partner at the time of bringing the action'). . . ." Alan R. Bromberg & Larry E. Ribstein, 4 *Bromberg and Ribstein on Partnership* § 15.05(g), at 15:67 (2010-2 Supp.). . . . [The Court described the history of derivative actions in limited partnerships, reproduced in Chapter 14, Section D, above, concluding that creditors of a limited partnership lack standing to bring a derivative action.]

3. No Statutory Conflict

CML argues that I should disregard the literal language of Section 18-1002 because, under Delaware Supreme Court precedent, a statute will be deemed ambiguous "if a literal reading of the statute would lead to an unreasonable or absurd result not contemplated by the legislature." In addition, "the literal meaning of a statute is not to be followed when it departs from the true intent and purpose of the statute and to conclusions inconsistent with the general purpose of the act." *In re Opinions of the Justices*, 88 A.2d 128, 134 (Del. 1952); *accord Darling Apartment Co. v. Springer*, 22 A.2d 397, 402 (Del. 1941). CML argues that a plain reading of Section 18-1002 generates an absurd distinction between insolvent corporations, where creditors can sue derivatively, and insolvent LLCs, where they cannot. CML further contends that Sections 18-1001 and 18-1002 were so clearly intended to transport the demand and contemporaneous ownership requirements into the world of LLCs that it would be inconsistent with that more limited purpose to apply the statute more broadly as an exclusive provision.

I cannot agree. As a threshold matter, there is nothing absurd about different legal principles applying to corporations and LLCs. . . .

I also cannot conclude that the derivative standing provisions were adopted solely to transpose the corporate demand and contemporaneous ownership tunes into an alternative entity key. Delaware's decision to replace Section 1732 with the RULPA provisions suggests an intent to make standing exclusive, and this is how the provisions subsequently were interpreted when LP assignees attempted to sue. When the alternative entity statutes were amended in 1998, the drafters could have returned to the open-ended language of the Section 1732. The evolution of Delaware's derivative standing provisions suggests a conscious decision to make the statutes exclusive.

Nor does barring creditor derivative standing conflict with the overarching purpose or structure of the LLC Act. According to the LLC Act itself, "[i]t is the policy of this chapter to give the maximum effect to the principle of freedom of contract and to the enforceability of limited liability company agreements." 6 Del. C. § 18-1101(b). . . . Creditors generally are presumed to be "capable of protecting themselves through the contractual agreements that govern their relationships with firms." *Prod. Res.*, 863 A.2d at 787. "Creditors are often protected by strong covenants, liens on assets, and other negotiated contractual protections." *Id.* at 790. To limit creditors to their bargained-for rights and deny them the additional right to sue derivatively on behalf of an insolvent entity comports with the contractarian environment created by the LLC Act.

The LLC Act includes specific statutory features that appear designed (at least in part) with creditors in mind, and which creditors can use to obtain additional rights and protections. First, the LLC Act authorizes an LLC agreement to "provide rights to any person, including a person who is not a party to the [LLC] agreement, to the extent set forth therein." 6 Del. C. § 18-101(7). A creditor therefore can bargain for express contractual rights in the LLC agreement while remaining a nonparty to the agreement.

Creditors also can use Section 18-101(7) in other ways. In a departure from the contract law rule against penalty clauses, Section 18-306 of the LLC Act provides that members may be subjected "to specified penalties or specified consequences" for breaching the LLC Agreement or "[a]t the time or upon the happening of events specified in the [LLC] agreement." 6 Del. C. § 18-306. Combining this authority with Section 18-101(7) enables creditors to bargain for penalties and consequences for members upon the occurrence of specific events or if creditors' rights are breached. Other LLC Act provisions offer similar points of entry for creditor protections. *See, e.g.,* 6 Del. C. § 18-402 ("Unless otherwise provided in [an LLC] agreement, the management of [an LLC] shall be vested in its members. . . . [A] manager shall cease to be a manager as provided in [an LLC] agreement.").

Second, Section 18-1101 enables creditors to expand their available remedies. Under Section 18-1101(c), "[t]o the extent that, at law or in equity, a member or manager . . . has duties (including fiduciary duties) to a limited liability company . . . , the . . . duties may be *expanded* or restricted or eliminated by provisions in the [LLC] agreement." 6 Del. C. § 18-1101(c) (emphasis added). Although typically cited for authorizing the restriction or elimination of legal duties, this section likewise authorizes the expansion of legal duties. An LLC agreement conceivably could provide for duties triggered by insolvency that would include an obligation to preserve assets for creditors. If a creditor is willing to become a party to the LLC agreement, then it might be able to make creative use of Section 18-1101(c) of the LLC Act.

Third, other provisions of the LLC Act offer creditors additional opportunities to secure protection. Section 18-303(b) provides that notwithstanding the general protection of limited liability provided by the LLC Act, a member or manager may agree in the LLC agreement "or under another agreement" to be "obligated personally for any or all of the debts, obligations and liability of the limited liability company." 6 Del. C. § 18-303(b). This provision could be used in lieu of or to supplement personal guarantees for a particular debt. Similarly, Section 18-215 authorizes an LLC agreement to "establish or provide for the establishment of 1 or more designated series of . . . [LLC] . . . assets" that may carry "separate rights, powers or duties with respect to specified property or obligations of the [LLC] or profits and losses associated with specified property or obligations." 6 Del. C. § 18-215(a) & (b).

This provision could be used in lieu of or to supplement security interests in a particular asset.

In each of these cases, a creditor can protect its enhanced rights through a provision conditioning the approval of any amendment to the LLC agreement on creditor consent or the satisfaction of conditions. *See* 6 Del. C. § 18-302(e) ("If [an LLC] agreement provides for the manner in which it may be amended, including by requiring the approval of a person who is not a party to the [LLC] agreement or the satisfaction of conditions, it may be amended only in that manner or as otherwise permitted by law. . . .").

Fourth, and along different lines, a creditor of an LLC can protect itself by seeking the appointment of a receiver. . . .

Fifth, despite the lack of derivative standing, a creditor possesses a statutory right to enforce a member's obligation to make a contribution to the LLC. Subject to statutory limitations, if a creditor extends credit to an LLC in reliance on a member's obligation to make a contribution to the LLC or to return a distribution in violation of the LLC Act, then the creditor may enforce the obligation to the extent of the creditor's reasonable reliance. 6 Del. C. § 18-502(b). "Thus, in proper circumstances, [an LLC] creditor in effect may be placed in a position similar to that of the company itself in enforcing rights against members for contributions and returns." Symonds & O'Toole, *supra*, § 15.02, at 15-7. Under Section 18-505, usury is not a defense to an obligation of a member or manager to the LLC arising under the LLC agreement. *See* 6 Del. C. § 18-505. A member is obligated to make its required contributions to the LLC even if the member cannot perform because of death, disability, or some other reason. *See* 6 Del. C. § 18-502(a).

. . . .

In light of the expansive contractual and statutory remedies that creditors of an LLC possess, it does not create an absurd or unreasonable result to deny derivative standing to creditors of an insolvent LLC. The outcome does not frustrate any legislative purpose of the LLC Act; it rather fulfills the statute's contractarian spirit.

III. Conclusion

Counts I–III are dismissed because CML lacks derivative standing. Count IV is dismissed for lack of jurisdiction, subject to CML's right to transfer the action to the Delaware Superior Court. *See* 10 Del. C. § 1902. IT IS SO ORDERED.

Note

ULLCA § 1102, following corporate law, provides that the plaintiff in a derivative action "must be a member of the company when the action is commenced" and at the time of the transaction of which the plaintiff complains or the plaintiff must have obtained membership status by operation of law or "pursuant to the terms of the operating agreement from a person who was a member at the time of the transaction." RULLCA § 903 also requires that the plaintiff be a member of the LLC, but does not require that the plaintiff be a member at the time of the transaction complained of.

b. Direct Claim for Oppression

Pointer v. Castellani

Supreme Judicial Court of Massachusetts
918 N.E.2d 805 (2009)

Before Marshall, C.J., Ireland, Spina, Cowin, Cordy, & Botsford, JJ.

Ireland, J.

Fletcher Granite Company, LLC (FGC), was formed on February 25, 1999, by [Bernard] Pointer and defendants Victor Castellani, Paul Woodberry, and Kathleen Herbert to take ownership of the assets of a granite company we shall call Pioneer.... One of the pieces of real estate [owned by Pioneer] significant for our purposes was an approximately sixty-four acre parcel in Milford that contained wetlands and an abandoned quarry.

Pointer had been president of Pioneer, and his initial involvement in the sale of the business was in that capacity. Ultimately, however, he joined with Castellani, Woodberry, and Herbert. The group had agreed that, when FGC assumed ownership of Pioneer, they would continue to operate the quarry business and sell the real estate.

FGC's operating agreement provided that Castellani and Woodberry together would own a fifty-one per cent interest in the business and Pointer would own a forty-three per cent interest. Pointer, Castellani, Woodberry, and Herbert became members of FGC. Pointer, Castellani, and Herbert were the initial managers. The initial managers could not be removed except for a "willful or intentional violation or reckless disregard of the Manager's duties . . . [or] a material breach of the Operating Agreement without cure after twenty days notice [by] the Board of Managers." Pointer became FGC's president; he was the only one experienced in operating a granite business. Herbert acted as the chief financial officer, and Woodberry and Castellani, "for the most part, were merely passive investors."

Through a wholly owned subsidiary, Pioneer also owned a residential subdivision called Greystone Estates, Inc. (Greystone). Pioneer was unwilling to sell its granite business unless it also sold Greystone. Pointer and another individual, Lou Frank, had decided to purchase Greystone. To that end, just before FGC was formed, he and Frank formed Stone Ridge Investments, LLC (SRI), of which Pointer owned fifty per cent. The other members of FGC were interested only in the quarry business and not in Greystone. The other members knew Pointer was involved in SRI, as he conducted SRI business while he was president of FGC. Pointer told the others that he would assist Frank in the Greystone transaction, but Pointer did not disclose that he was a substantial (fifty per cent) owner. Implicit in the judge's findings however, which also has support in the record, is that the others knew he was a principal of SRI. The others learned of the extent of Pointer's ownership only after Pointer's employment was terminated. It is important to note that, as discussed *infra*, Pointer and Frank formed another entity, Stone Ridge Management, LLC (SRM), in 2000.

FGC closed on Pioneer's quarry, mill, and certain real estate on March 30, 1999. All but Woodberry were present at the closing. On April 1, 1999, SRI closed on Greystone. Pointer was the only member of FGC present.

The judge found that, at the time the parties entered into the transaction to acquire Pioneer's businesses, Pointer's intention was to stay with FGC as president and ultimately to control FGC. Pointer had a further expectation that he would be involved in the real estate development part of the transaction. The judge found that Castellani and Woodberry had expectations "primarily as investors in the FGC quarrying and granite sales business. They had little interest or expectation in actually running FGC." Herbert's expectations were that she continue her position as financial officer of FGC and own a "small piece of the company." The judge further found that neither Herbert, Castellani, nor Woodberry had any "interest in real estate purchase, sale or development."

We now provide some preliminary information about FGC's operating agreement and Pointer's employment contract. Under § 2.3 of the operating agreement, FGC was organized to "own and operate a quarry business and to engage in any other lawful act or activity permitted under the [l]aw." In addition, under § 5.1.4.7 of the operating agreement, the approval of 66.7 per cent of the managers was required for FGC to engage in any business other than that related to quarrying. Furthermore, § 5.4.3 of the operating agreement states:

> [N]othing in this Agreement shall be deemed to restrict in any way the rights of any Member, or any affiliate of any Member, to conduct any other business or activity whatsoever, and no Member shall be accountable to [FGC] or to any other Member with respect to that business or activity. The organization of [FGC] shall be without prejudice to the Members' respective rights (or the rights of their respective Affiliates) to maintain, expand, or diversify such other interests and activities and to receive and enjoy profits or compensation therefrom. Each Member waives any rights the Member might otherwise have to share or participate in such other interests or activities of any other Member or the Member's Affiliates."

The operating agreement explicitly anticipated that "the conduct of [FGC]'s business may involve business dealings and undertakings with Members and their Affiliates" and required that, "in those cases, . . . dealings and undertakings shall be at arm's length and on commercially reasonable terms."

Pointer's appointment as FGC's president was executed by an employment agreement on April 19, 1999. The agreement was for a specific, renewable term and stated, in relevant part, that Pointer could be removed without a requisite 360 days' notice only if, among other things, he engaged in dishonest or disloyal behavior, committed a material breach of the operating agreement, or substantially failed to perform a material duty. Although the employment agreement stated that Pointer had "to work exclusively for [FGC] and . . . not engage in any other business activity without the prior written consent of [FGC]," it also stated that Pointer could "perform services for SRI to such an extent as [Pointer] may reasonably determine." The judge also found that "everyone knew of Pointer's activities at the FGC offices for SRI/SRM, that all [SRI/SRM documents] plainly listed the same street address as that of FGC, that all of SRI/SRM documents were kept in unlocked files at the office, and that Pointer reimbursed FGC for the time his secretary expended on SRI/SRM matters [for which FGC sent Pointer invoices]."

The sale, in 2001, to SRM of FGC's approximately sixty-four acre parcel containing undeveloped land and an abandoned quarry in Milford is at the center of several issues raised in this case and thus requires elaboration. . . .

[The court explained that Frank (a developer) and Pointer planned to include the FCG parcel with other land Frank was acquiring. Pointer knew of these plans, but did not inform Castellani, Woodberry or Herbert of it. Frank had an option to acquire the FCG parcel, which pre-dated FCG's acquisition. Pointer, acting on behalf of FCG, extended this option several times, including once after it had expired. Eventually, Pointer and Frank acquired the parcel from FCG through SRM at a price of $300,000, considerably less than the option price of $475,000, but a price that the trial court found was a "commercially reasonable price." The price was negotiated by Castellani, acting for FCG, and Frank, acting for SRM. Pointer had information suggesting that the land was more valuable than the purchase price, but he did not share this information with Castellani, Woodberry or Herbert. Pointer and Frank then proceeded with their development plan.

The court also recounted various problems that arose under Pointer's leadership: deteriorating profits, improper accounting, and the payment of excessive interest on a loan to FCG from SRM. (Eventually, SRM refunded a portion of the excessive interest to FCG.)]

When Castellani and Woodberry learned of Pointer's actions, they were concerned about his judgment and ability to manage FGC, but they did not discuss their concerns with him. Instead, they concluded that Pointer deliberately reported the receivables to the bank and had concealed financial problems by borrowing from SRM. In addition, FGC, on a pure performance basis, was projecting a loss for 2003, and was in difficulties with its bank.

As majority owners, Castellani and Woodberry secretly decided to find someone to replace Pointer as the top executive of FGC. In November, 2003, the pair began communicating with the defendant Jonathan Maurer, culminating in Maurer's hiring in January, 2004, as FGC's chief executive officer. The contract Maurer signed stated that Castellani and Woodberry would "use their best efforts to cause the operating agreement to be modified" to allow Maurer to purchase shares up to forty per cent of FGC. Pointer was not informed of the decision to hire Maurer until February, 2004. In addition, Pointer and Castellani executed a memorandum, in

February, 2004, that provided that Pointer's employment agreement could continue until at least March 31, 2006. Maurer became a manager of FGC, and started working on March 15, 2004. The record shows that Maurer had Pointer removed from all of FGC's interoffice distribution lists as of March 18, 2004.

In March, 2004, two other actions by Pointer came to the attention of Castellani and Woodberry. During a four-year period, Pointer made political contributions in the amount of $4,825. He wrote personal checks for which he was reimbursed by FGC. This practice had the effect of concealing from Federal and State election authorities contributions by FGC, and predated the sale of the granite business to FGC. In March, 2004, Castellani and Woodberry learned about the contributions. However, the judge found that Pointer's practice was not hidden from FGC, and that in 2003, FGC instituted a company policy, drafted with the assistance of Castellani, that allowed such contributions if either the chairman or the president (i.e., Pointer) approved. The judge concluded that the political contributions were an "exceptionally minor issue." In any event, Pointer reimbursed FGC for the contributions.

The second action by Pointer involved a report done by FGC's accountants concerning the [improper accounting]. The judge found "although [the bank was] somewhat concerned [it] took no action other than to assist FGC and provide it with acceptable forms to accomplish the same thing. The bank never called its loan. . . ."

At a meeting on March 29, 2004, the managers and members tried to talk about these issues with Pointer, but he refused to participate because it was not on the agenda he had submitted for the meeting. Pointer was informed that he was suspended with full pay and benefits. He was also barred from the facility unless there was a prior arrangement with one of the managers.

Without notice to Pointer, the managers had a meeting where they terminated Pointer's employment as of June 30, 2004, by means of a resolution that set forth several allegations (resolution). Pointer was given no opportunity to respond. After Pointer's termination, Maurer told Pointer that he could no longer represent FGC in any official capacity and would not be allowed direct access to his FGC electronic mail messages.

Pointer sued the defendants, alleging, in relevant part, that the defendants engaged in a freeze-out, committed a breach of their fiduciary duty, violated his employment contract and the covenant of good faith and fair dealing, and interfered with an advantageous relationship. The judge found for Pointer on his claims, and on the defendants' counterclaims, which alleged, insofar as relevant here, breach of fiduciary duty by misappropriating a corporate opportunity and self-dealing; breach of contract; and breach of the implied covenant of good faith and fair dealing in relation to the operating agreement and his employment agreement. The judge found for SRI/SRM on the defendants' counterclaim charging aiding and abetting fiduciary breaches.

The defendants appealed, and Pointer cross-appealed concerning the appropriate remedy for the freeze-out.

It is uncontested that FGC is a close corporation in that it has "(1) a small number of stockholders; (2) no ready market for the corporate stock; and (3) substantial majority stockholder participation in the management, direction and operations of the corporation." See *Brodie v. Jordan*, 447 Mass. 866, 868–869, 857 N.E.2d 1076 (2006), quoting *Donahue v. Rodd Electrotype Co. of New England, Inc.*, 367 Mass. 578, 586, 328 N.E.2d 505 (1975). "Because of the fundamental resemblance . . . to [a] partnership . . . stockholders in the close corporation owe one another substantially the same fiduciary duty in the operation of the enterprise that partners owe to one another[, that is,] the 'utmost good faith and loyalty.'" *Donahue v. Rodd Electrotype Co. of New England, Inc., supra* at 592–593, 328 N.E.2d 505, quoting *Cardullo v. Landau*, 329 Mass. 5, 8, 105 N.E.2d 843 (1952).

1. *The freeze-out and termination of employment.* The defendants argue that the judge erred in finding for Pointer on his claims of a freeze-out and wrongful termination of his employment. There was no error.

Whatever the advantages of the corporate form, its very structure may "suppl[y] an opportunity for the majority stockholders to oppress or disadvantage minority stockholders [through] a variety of oppressive devices, termed 'freeze-outs.'" *Donahue v. Rodd Electrotype Co. of New England, Inc., supra* at 588, 328 N.E.2d 505. Means employed to effectuate a freeze-out include depriving the minority shareholder of offices or employment in the corporation. *Id.* at 589, 328 N.E.2d 505, quoting F.H. O'Neal & J. Derwin, Expulsion or Oppression of Business Associates 42 (1961). In *Wilkes v. Springside Nursing Home, Inc.*, 370 Mass. 842, 849–850, 353 N.E.2d 657 (1976), this court stated:

> "The denial of employment to the minority at the hands of the majority is especially pernicious in some instances. A guaranty of employment with the corporation may have been one of the 'basic reason[s] why a minority owner has invested capital in the firm.' . . . The minority stockholder typically depends on his salary as the principal return on his investment, since the 'earnings of a close corporation . . . are distributed in major part in salaries'. . . . Other noneconomic interests of the minority stockholder are likewise injuriously affected by barring him from corporate office. . . . In sum, by terminating a minority stockholder's employment . . . the majority effectively frustrate the minority stockholder's purposes in entering on the corporate venture and also deny him equal return on his investment."

Id. at 849–850, 353 N.E.2d 657, quoting Symposium-The Close Corporation, 52 Nw. U. L. Rev. 345, 392 (1957), and 1 F.H. O'Neal, Close Corporations § 1.07 (1971).

A breach of fiduciary duty through a freeze-out also occurs when the reasonable expectations of a shareholder are frustrated.

Nevertheless, majority shareholders "have certain rights to what has been termed 'selfish ownership' in the corporation which should be balanced against the concept of their fiduciary obligation to the minority" permitting them "room to maneuver" and "a large measure of discretion" in, among other things, hiring and firing corporate employees. *Wilkes v. Springside Nursing Home, Inc., supra* at 850–851, 353 N.E.2d 657, and authorities cited. Therefore, where there is an allegation of a breach of fiduciary duty, the court must allow the controlling group to demonstrate a "legitimate business purpose for its action." *Id.* at 851, 353 N.E.2d 657, and cases and authorities cited. The minority stockholder is then allowed to "demonstrate that the same legitimate objective could have been achieved through an alternative course less harmful to the minority's interest." *Id.* at 851–852, 353 N.E.2d 657, and authorities cited.

Applying these principles to the facts in this case, the judge did not err in concluding that Pointer was subject to a freeze-out when Castellani and Woodberry, in violation of their fiduciary duty, secretly hired Maurer in January, 2004, barred Pointer from the FGC, and ultimately fired him as president in June, 2004. In addition, for the reasons cited above, the judge also did not err in concluding that Pointer's actions did not require his termination because less harmful alternatives outweighed "any of the asserted business purposes for the actions that Castellani and Woodberry took in secretly engaging Maurer." The judge stated:

> "[Castellani and Woodberry] attempted to excuse this failure [to inform Pointer about discussions with Maurer] by expressing concern that Pointer would react badly to news that an effort was underway to find someone who would be senior to him in the operations of FGC. If Pointer were to leave before a new executive could be located, [they] knew that there was no one immediately able to step into his role. Certainly neither of them was equipped, nor interested, in doing so. Further, they were concerned that the bank might move their account to workout or call the loan if Pointer left the company."

There is no merit to the defendants' argument, without citation to authority, that they did not commit a breach of their fiduciary duty because, even though he was barred from FGC without an invitation from another manager, Pointer continued to be a manager and member, hold an equity interest, and receive detailed financial information. At the very least, as the judge found, the freeze-out frustrated Pointer's reasonable expectation that ultimately he would be able to be the owner of FGC. Moreover, Pointer did not have full access to his electronic mail messages or inter-office memoranda. There also is no merit to the defendants' argument that termination cannot be a freeze-out. Nor did the judge err in stating that Pointer had a reasonable expectation of employment as president. The judge found that when Castellani and Woodberry secretly decided to replace Pointer, one of the reasons they kept the information from Pointer was because they needed someone to run FGC in the interim and neither Castellani nor Woodberry was equipped or interested. Although it is true that the employment contract could be terminated and was extended only until March, 2006 . . . here it was wrongfully terminated and thus frustrated Pointer's reasonable expectation in remaining president.

The defendants claim that the judge also erred in holding that Pointer did not commit a breach of his employment contract. This argument has no merit.

The resolution terminating Pointer's employment enumerated the grounds on which that termination was based. In relevant part, it stated that Pointer had violated his employment agreement and the operating agreement, and engaged in acts of malfeasance that materially injured FGC by forming a fifty per cent ownership in SRI/SRM and engaging in certain real estate transactions; inadequately compensating for resources FGC provided to Pointer while he conducted SRI/SRM business; causing FGC to borrow $300,000 from SRM at exorbitant interest rates; including cut-and-store billing in the receivables that resulted in false reports to the bank; and reimbursing himself for political contributions. Given the judge's findings recited *supra*, he did not err in concluding, inter alia, that the $300,000 loan helped FGC; Pointer had a right, even under his employment contract, to conduct SRI/SRM business to the extent he reasonably determined was necessary and everyone at FGC was aware of this; the cut-and-store reporting was known to the bank and FGC was not harmed thereby; and, although the political contributions should not have been handled in the way they were, Pointer had the power to make contributions in FGC's behalf and all the other owners had to do was talk to Pointer about his practices.

The judge also did not err in determining that the defendants' claim that Pointer should have revealed to the other members and managers that the purchase of FGC's parcel was part of a larger real estate venture and that Pointer was a fifty per cent owner of SRI/SRM was contrived. The judge found that no one from FGC other than Pointer had any interest in real estate development; that under FGC's operating agreement, for FGC to engage in real estate transactions, approval of 66.7 per cent of the members was required, and the defendants presented no evidence that demonstrated that FGC was deviating from its operating agreement; and that Castellani knew that SRM was aggregating land for development. In fact, the others knew that there was discussion about using some land for a golf course. Castellani sent Pointer a newspaper article involving a golf course developer sued over "turtles."

The defendants argue that they could not have demonstrated that FGC was interested in real estate when they did not know that Pointer was a fifty per cent owner of SRM, and thus, they argue, they did not know that the opportunity was even available to them. However, the judge implicitly found that they knew Pointer was an owner of SRI and that SRM was buying the parcel; indeed, Pointer signed the purchase and sale agreement and deed for FGC's parcel as a manager of SRM.

As the judge found, Castellani, Woodberry, Herbert and Maurer owed Pointer, who was a forty-three per cent owner of FGC, "real substance and communication, including efforts to resolve *supposed* complaints by less drastic measures than termination. But such efforts never truly were attempted." (Emphasis added.) The judge called some of the charges "contrived" or not "credible," and concluded that, by the time the resolution was written, the others were simply trying "to find a way to get rid of Pointer."

The defendants argue that because Pointer was president under an employment contract, the terms of the contract control rather than their fiduciary duty. Even assuming that this assertion has merit, the cases on which the defendants rely are easily distinguished. . . .

2. *Usurpation of a corporate opportunity and self-dealing.* [The court affirmed the lower court's conclusion that the real estate development was not a "corporate opportunity" of FGC]. . . .

5. *Remedy for freeze-out.* Having found Castellani, Woodberry, Herbert, and Maurer individually liable to Pointer for a freeze-out, the judge gave the parties ninety days to try to reach a binding agreement under which one side or the other would buy out the shareholder interests of the other. Failing that, he ordered FGC to be liquidated by a receiver and each party to be awarded the net proceeds in accordance with their respective shareholder interests under the operating agreement.[34] The defendants appealed from the judge's entire judgment, including the remedy; Pointer did not appeal. The parties did not agree to a buyout. The judge stayed that portion of the judgment ordering liquidation, pending the appeal. In his order, the judge noted that he was aware of our decisions in *Brodie v. Jordan*, 447 Mass. 866, 870–871, 872–873, 857 N.E.2d 1076 (2006), quoting *Zimmerman v. Bogoff*, 402 Mass. 650, 661, 524 N.E.2d 849 (1988) (remedy for freeze-out is to put minority shareholder in same position he or she would have been in had freeze-out not occurred; absent agreement between shareholders, court cannot force buyout of minority shareholder's stock), and *Bernier v. Bernier*, 449 Mass. 774, 873 N.E.2d 216 (2007) (discussing valuation of shares of S corporation).

In July, 2008, approximately eight months after judgment entered, Pointer filed a motion for relief from judgment under Mass. R. Civ. P. 60(b)(5) or (6), 365 Mass. 828 (1974). He asked the judge to modify the remedy for the freeze-out because, he argued, FGC was insolvent and, therefore, a forced sale would yield him nothing. He requested that the remedy be modified to order the defendants to pay him approximately $3.6 million dollars, which, according to an expert who testified for Pointer at trial, was 43.3 per cent of the value of FGC when the freeze-out occurred. In return, Pointer would tender his stock.

Because the trial judge had retired, another judge ruled that the relief Pointer sought was contrary to the *Brodie* decision. As the judge stated, the operating agreement does not require any buyout during the lifetime of a shareholder.

Both sides make numerous arguments concerning the appropriate remedy for the freeze-out. We need not discuss them because we conclude that the trial judge's order for a forced sale of FGC violated our holding in the *Brodie* decision. Because we held that a forced buyout of a shareholder was improper without some authorization from shareholders, it would be inconsistent for us now to hold that a forced sale is proper. *Brodie v. Jordan, supra* at 873 n. 7, 857 N.E.2d 1076 (calling involuntary dissolution "drastic remedy"). Nevertheless, Pointer is entitled to damages or other equitable relief from Castellani, Woodberry, Herbert, and Maurer, which will

---

34. [29] The judge also ordered an alternative remedy, discussed *infra*.

put him in the position he would have been in had the freeze-out not occurred, and compensates him for the denial of his reasonable expectations.

Anticipating that this court would conclude that a forced sale of FGC violated the holding in the *Brodie* decision, the trial judge fashioned an alternative remedy, stating he "would grant to Pointer an order for his reinstatement as [p]resident of FGC, together with back pay for salary lost at the rate he was earning at the time of his discharge to the date of his reinstatement, indemnification for his reasonable attorney's fees and costs in litigating this action, along with appropriate injunctive relief to enable him to resume and continue in the future, under reasonable regulation by the FGC members and managers, in his position as [p]resident." However, since the trial judge fashioned this remedy, it appears that circumstances have changed, not the least of which is that FGC may have been sold. We are constrained in fashioning a remedy here, as Pointer sought both monetary damages and equitable relief, and the appropriate remedy depends on further factual findings. Therefore, the case is remanded for further proceedings to determine whether it is possible to implement the trial judge's alternative remedy. If not, the judge should fashion another remedy, one that presumably would include monetary damages and other equitable relief that the judge deems appropriate.

Conclusion. For the reasons set forth above, we affirm the decision of the trial judge insofar as he found for Pointer on his claims and on the defendants' counterclaims. We affirm the denial of Pointer's motion for relief from judgment that requested a forced buyout of his shares of FGC. The case is remanded for further proceedings consistent with this opinion concerning an appropriate remedy for the freeze-out.

So ordered.

Notes

1. To what extent were the motives of Castellani, et. al. for firing Pointer relevant to the court's decision? Should their motives be relevant?

2. Note that *Wood* and *Pointer* deal with different categories of fiduciary duties. *Wood* involves fiduciary duties that a person in control owes to the entity and, indirectly, to those who own the equity interests in the entity. The policy reason for this fiduciary duty is that investors who lack control place their trust and confidence in those who do exercise control. In contrast to *Wood*, cases like *Pointer* (and, in particular, the corporate law cases that it cites as precedent, such as *Wilkes v. Springside Nursing Home, Inc.*) involve the finding of a fiduciary duty among equity owners in situations in which they are acting in their capacity as owners. In these cases, the courts impose fiduciary duties not because of trust and confidence, but rather on the idea that in closely held entities the owners treat one another as partners and, as we have seen, in partnerships each partner owes a fiduciary duty to each co-partner. This raises the question of whether there are differences between a corporation and a limited liability company that support a different outcome in the *Pointer*. Are there?

3. *Pointer* (and the recognition of a claim for oppression) would not be followed in all states. In *Nixon v. Blackwell*, 626 A.2d 1366 (Del. 1993), for instance, the Delaware Supreme Court declined to adopt *Wilkes* in a dispute among close corporation shareholders and in *Nightingale & Associates, LLC v. Hopkins*, 2008 U.S. Dist. LEXIS 90204 (D.N.J., Nov. 5, 2008), the federal court concluded that Delaware law did not provide a cause of action on behalf of an "oppressed" member of an LLC against his co-members.

4. In many states, including, importantly, Delaware, the parties to a limited liability company operating agreement can "contract around" fiduciary duties; that is, limit or eliminate the sort of fiduciary duties at issue in *Wood*.

5. Delaware, unlike most states, does not specify default fiduciary duties that those in control of a limited liability company owe to the entity, and, for a time, there was a debate in Delaware as to whether, in fact, common law fiduciary duties would be recognized by the Delaware courts if the operating agreement was silent on the issue. In a few Chancery court decisions (e.g., *Auriga Capital Corp. v. Gatz Properties, LLC*, 40 A.3d 839 (Del. Ch. 2012); *Kelly v. Blum*, 2010 Del. Ch. LEXIS 31 (Feb. 24, 2010)) the courts did recognize that, unless disclaimed in the operating agreement, managers were subject to common law fiduciary duties. In 2013, the Delaware legislature amended the partnership and LLC statutes to codify the result in *Auriga*. For instance, with respect to LLCs, § 18-1104 of the Delaware code now reads as follows:

> In any case not provided for in this chapter, the rules of law and equity, including the rules of law and equity relating to fiduciary duties and the law merchant, shall govern.

6. *Implied covenant of good faith and fair dealing.* All contracts include an implied covenant of good faith and fair dealing. LLC statutes typically provide that while other duties may be modified or waived, the implied covenant of good faith and fair dealing may not be waived. ULLCA, for instance, provides that the operating agreement may not "eliminate the obligation of good faith and fair dealing, but may determine the standards by which the performance of the obligation is to be measured, if the standards are not manifestly unreasonable." In the *Kelly* case, noted above, the court described a cause of action based on the implied covenant:

> Under the LLC Act, the contracting parties to an LLC agreement may not waive the implied covenant of good faith and fair dealing. This implied covenant "inheres in every contract" and requires that contracting parties "refrain from arbitrary or unreasonable conduct which has the effect of preventing the other party from receiving the fruits of the contract." Nevertheless, the implied covenant is "only rarely invoked successfully" and may not "be invoked to override the express terms of the contract."
>
> To state a claim of breach of the implied covenant of good faith and fair dealing, a party "must allege [1] a specific implied contractual obligation, [2] a breach of that obligation by the defendant, and [3] resulting damage to the plaintiff." Because general allegations of bad faith do not satisfy

these elements, to state a cognizable claim a "plaintiff must allege a *specific implied contractual obligation* and allege how the violation of that obligation denied the plaintiff the fruits of the contract."

In this case, Kelly alleged that MBC Investment and MBC Lender breached the implied covenant by voting in favor of the Merger, not seeking additional, further, or different strategic alternatives for the Company, and allowing the Company to enter affiliated or self-interested transactions and affiliated indebtedness. He does not allege, however, any specific implied contractual obligation, how such an implied obligation was breached, or how his contractual interest may have been damaged by such a breach ... Thus, I grant Defendants' motion to dismiss Count III of Kelly's Complaint because he failed to state a claim "draw[ing] a sufficient connection between [any] alleged violations of the implied covenant and a specific implied obligation in the contract."

Kelly v. Blum, supra, at *57–60 (footnotes omitted). See, as well, the discussion in Chapter 14, Section E.3, *supra,* where the implied covenant is discussed in the context of partnership cases. The Delaware courts do not differentiate between partnership and LLC cases in considering the applicability of the implied covenant.

c. Direct Claim for Breach of Fiduciary Duty

Does a member of an LLC owe a duty directly to other members beyond the duty not to "oppress" that member, as described in *Pointer*? Remember, fiduciary duties are imposed on a person (a fiduciary) who has obligations to another (the beneficiary), when the beneficiary has placed his or her trust and confidence in the fiduciary and the fiduciary accepts that responsibility. This, of course, describes the typical principal-agent relationship, but also the relationship between a corporate director and the corporation or the manager of an LLC and the LLC. But does trust and confidence also describe the relationship among shareholders in a corporation or among members in an LLC, when not acting in a representative capacity? Typically, the answer is no. An LLC member (who is not acting as a manager in the transaction at issue) may act in his or her sole interest. The principle announced in *Pointer v. Castellani,* however, is one exception to that general rule. From time to time, however, courts have imposed fiduciary duties on members, without articulating why that duty is imposed. *VGS, Inc. v. Castiel, supra,* is one example. The following case presents another.

Feresi v. The Livery, LLC

Court of Appeals, California
232 Cal.App.4th 419 (2015)

BURKE, J.

The Commercial Code1 provides that "a financing statement must be filed to perfect all security interests. . . ." (§ 9310, subd. (a).) It further provides, "A perfected security interest . . . has priority over a conflicting unperfected security interest. . . ." (§ 9322, subd. (a)(2).) This order of priority is not immutable and in some circumstances must yield to principles of equity. Here two parties hold security interests in the same entity. One party perfected his security interest by breaching a fiduciary duty owed to the party whose security interest was unperfected. We conclude that equity compels the subordination of the perfected interest to the holder of the unperfected interest.

The security interests held by the parties to this dispute attach to James Mesa's (Mesa) membership share in The Livery, LLC (the LLC). The competing claimants are Mesa's former wife, Renee Feresi (Feresi) whose unperfected security interest was created in 2006, and Mark Hartley as Trustee of the Fitzgerald–Hartley Pension Plan (Hartley) whose perfected security interest was created in 2008. Hartley is the president and managing member of the LLC.

The LLC and Hartley appeal the trial court's judgment in favor of Feresi. Hartley contends his perfected security interest in Mesa's ownership share of the LLC has statutory priority over Feresi's preexisting but unperfected security interest. Feresi contends Hartley's security interest is invalid because he created the priority of his interest by breaching the fiduciary duty of good faith and fair dealing that he owed to her as the member of the LLC.

We modify the judgment to strike the references to "Mark Hartley, individually" and affirm the judgment as modified.

Procedural History and Facts

Feresi and Mesa married in 1995 and separated in 2002. During their marriage, the couple acquired a 25 percent interest in the LLC. The LLC began with four investors who owned equal shares. Hartley's family trust was an investor and he served as the LLC's president and managing member.

In May 2006, the court entered a judgment dissolving the marriage of Feresi and Mesa. The judgment incorporated the terms of a Marital Settlement Agreement (MSA) that awarded Feresi one-half of the community's interest in the LLC. Mesa was also required to make the monthly payments on Feresi's home mortgage and to pay it off within five years. Mesa's financial obligations to Feresi were secured by Mesa's interest in the LLC and other properties.

Feresi did not file a Uniform Commercial Code Financing Statement (UCC–1 financing statement) to "perfect" her security interest in Mesa's share of the LLC. She instead gave Hartley and the other members of the LLC written notice that the dissolution judgment awards her one-half of Mesa's share of the LLC and that Mesa pledged his retained share as security for his financial obligations to her. Amendments to the books and records of the LLC showed Feresi as a member with a 12.5 percent ownership interest. Corporate tax returns identify Feresi as an LLC member.

By 2008, Mesa was struggling financially and fell behind on his obligations to Feresi and other creditors. On October 7, 2008, Hartley made a short-term loan to Mesa of $200,000 from the Fitzgerald–Hartley Pension Plan. Although Hartley knew Mesa's membership share in the LLC secured his financial obligations to Feresi, Hartley nevertheless secured the loan from his pension plan by the same 12.5 percent membership share Mesa pledged to Feresi in 2006. Hartley did not disclose to Feresi either that his pension plan intended to loan money to Mesa or that it would be secured by Mesa's membership share.

On October 30, 2008, Feresi notified Hartley as president and manager of the LLC that she intended to enforce Mesa's obligations to her by taking the 12.5 percent share of the LLC and certain other properties he pledged. To this end, Feresi filed an Order to Show Cause (OSC) in the family law proceedings to compel Mesa to convey his 12.5 percent membership share in the LLC to her. While the OSC was pending, on November 12, 2008, Feresi filed a quiet title action against Mesa and the LLC to foreclose the "judicial liens" created by the MSA and dissolution judgment, and to obtain quiet title to Mesa's 12.5 percent membership share.

After he was notified of Mesa's failure to meet his obligations to Feresi and of her OSC and quiet title action, Hartley determined that Feresi had not filed a UCC–1 financing statement to perfect her security interest in Mesa's membership share of the LLC. Hartley took advantage of this circumstance to acquire priority for his own, conflicting security interest in the same membership share by filing a UCC–1 financing statement reflecting the loan made by his pension plan to Mesa.

On January 22, 2009, a "judgment" was entered on Feresi's OSC, ordering Mesa to "assign, convey and transfer" his remaining 12.5 percent interest in the LLC to Feresi. Mesa complied with that order on January 26, 2009. On the same day, Feresi notified Hartley and the other LLC members that Mesa's transfer was complete and that the LLC's records should be amended to identify her as the owner of a 25 percent membership interest.

On October 7, 2009, Mesa failed to repay the loan from Hartley's pension plan. On November 12, 2009, the pension plan published a "Notice of Disposition" announcing that Mesa's 12.5 percent membership interest in the LLC would be sold on November 23 to satisfy the debt. On November 19, 2009, Feresi filed this action for declaratory and injunctive relief.

After a trial in November 2012, the court issued its statement of decision and factually found: "[B]y 2007, Renee Feresi [was] recognized as a member of The Livery, LLC and [was] designated as a 12.5 [percent] member on The Livery LLC [corporate tax] returns for 2007." It also found that, when Hartley and Mesa perfected the security interest of Hartley's pension plan in Mesa's share of the LLC, Hartley had actual notice of Feresi's prior security interest, knew Mesa was in default on his obligations to Feresi, knew she was entitled to enforce her security interest by taking Mesa's share of the LLC, and knew that she had filed the OSC and quiet title action to do so. It also concluded that, once Hartley learned in October 2009 that Mesa had transferred his 12.5 percent membership interest to Feresi, Hartley was obligated to insure that the LLC's corporate records showed Feresi was the exclusive owner of a 25 percent membership interest in the LLC.

The trial court ruled that Hartley breached a fiduciary duty owed to Feresi and that the security interest created by Mesa and Hartley in October 2008 in favor of Hartley's pension plan was "null and void." The trial court declared that Feresi has a 25 percent membership interest in the LLC that is not encumbered by the claims of Hartley or his pension plan. Hartley, Hartley's family trust and his pension plan were enjoined from attempting to enforce their security interest in Mesa's share of the LLC.

Discussion

. . .

Despite the diversions offered by Hartley, this case presents a relatively simple set of facts and issues. If the trial court's factual findings are supported by substantial evidence, then the question presented is whether Hartley is categorically entitled to claim priority for the security interest in favor of his pension plan even if it extinguishes the preexisting security interest of his co-member Feresi by breaching a fiduciary duty he owes to her. We are satisfied the answer to that question is "No."

Feresi Has Been a Member of the LLC Since 2006.

First, we disagree with Hartley's contention that Feresi was not a member of the LLC and was therefore not a person to whom he owed a duty of good faith and fair dealing. The trial court concluded otherwise and substantial evidence supports that conclusion. Feresi and her counsel repeatedly gave oral and written notice to Hartley and the LLC that the MSA and judgment awarded Feresi a 12.5 percent membership share in the LLC and that Mesa had pledged his remaining 12.5 percent membership share as security for his financial obligations to Feresi. Hartley and the other LLC members acknowledged Feresi was also a member by, for example, identifying her as a member on the LLC's tax returns.

Hartley's Duties as a Fiduciary.

The manager of an LLC has a fiduciary duty and owes to the members of the LLC the same duties of loyalty and good faith as a partner owes to the partnership and its partners. Thus, Hartley is obligated to act with the utmost loyalty and in the highest good faith when dealing with any member of the LLC, including Feresi. He may not obtain any advantage over Feresi (or any other member of the LLC) by even the slightest misrepresentation or concealment. (Enea v. Superior Court (2005) 132 Cal. App.4th 1559, 1564, 34 Cal.Rptr.3d 513.

The animating principle of a fiduciary's duties to his charges is unfaltering loyalty and honesty. "Many forms of conduct permissible in a workaday world for those acting at arm's length, are forbidden to those bound by fiduciary ties. A trustee is held to something stricter than the morals of the market place. Not honesty alone, but the punctilio of an honor the most sensitive, is then the standard of behavior. As to this there has developed a tradition that is unbending and inveterate. Uncompromising rigidity has been the attitude of courts of equity when petitioned to undermine the rule of undivided loyalty by the 'disintegrating erosion' of particular exceptions [citation]. Only thus has the level of conduct for fiduciaries been kept at a level higher than that trodden by the crowd." (Meinhard v. Salmon (1928) 249 N.Y. 458, 464, 164 N.E. 545.)

Hartley Breached the Duty of Good Faith and Fair Dealing He Owed to Feresi.

Substantial evidence supports the trial court's conclusion that Hartley breached his fiduciary duty to Feresi by destroying the value of her security interest in Mesa's ownership share in the LLC to advance his own. Hartley had actual knowledge of Feresi's security interest in Mesa's LLC membership, knew that Mesa was in default on his obligations to Feresi and knew that Feresi's security interest was immediately enforceable. Hartley loaned money to Mesa, created a conflicting security interest in Mesa's membership share and then surreptitiously perfected it to gain an advantage over Feresi.

We reject Hartley's contention that filing of the UCC–1 financing statement was not a breach of his fiduciary duties because, "A partner does not violate a duty or obligation under this chapter or under the partnership agreement merely because the partner's conduct furthers the partner's own interest." (§ 16404, subd. (e).) "The apparent purpose of this provision . . . is to excuse partners from accounting for incidental benefits obtained in the course of partnership activities without detriment to the partnership. [Fn. omitted.]" (Enea v. Superior Court, supra, 132 Cal.App.4th at p. 1566, 34 Cal.Rptr.3d 513.) Hartley is not entitled to disregard his actual knowledge of Feresi's preexisting security interest in the same property and perfect his security interest at her expense. Hartley's filing of the UCC–1 financing statement was not without detriment to his partner, Feresi. It rendered her security interest worthless. Section 16404, subdivision (e) has no application under these circumstances.

Feresi had no reason to protect the priority of her own security interest in the same property because she was unaware that her partner held a conflicting interest. Hartley took advantage of Feresi's ignorance by concealing this from her, and betrayed her trust and confidence by perfecting his pension plan's security interest ahead of hers. In doing so, Hartley breached the fiduciary duties of loyalty and good faith he owed to Feresi. The primacy of Hartley's security interest in Mesa's share of the LLC must succumb to the infection of his duplicity and silence. The trial court properly refused to enforce the security interest held by Hartley's pension plan.

Notes

1. Note how the court uses the language from the *Meinhard* case (*supra*, Chapter 12, Section H) to support its conclusion as well as the concept of good faith and fair dealing. Is one rationale stronger than the other? Regarding the good faith and fair dealing rationale, note how the court characterizes good faith as a fiduciary duty, as opposed to an implied *contractual* term. (*See, e.g.,* the discussion *supra*, Chapter 14, Section E.3) As a fiduciary duty, it is rather formless and, perhaps, boundless. Indeed, a possible definition of the duty of good faith as used in *Feresi* may be a duty of "fairness."

2. Cases consistent with *Feresi* include *Patmon v. Hobbs*, 280 S.W.3d 589 (Ky. Ct. App. 2009) (managing member of LLC owes duty of loyalty to members); *Bushi v. Sage Health Care, PLLC*, 203 P.3d 694 (Idaho 2009) (summary judgment in favor of members of an LLC who amended operating agreement to allow expulsion and then expelled plaintiff reversed; if defendants acted in bad faith they would be liable to plaintiff). Compare, to *Feresi*, the Arizona appellate court decision in *TM2008 Investments, Inc. v. Procon Capital Corp.*, 323 P.3d 704 (Ariz. App. Ct. 2014), where the court rejected the idea that members of an LLC owe one another fiduciary duties. Instead, the court held, the Arizona LLC Act leaves it up to the operating agreement to set forth what duties, if any, members owe the company and one another:

> We decline in this case to mechanically apply fiduciary duty principles from the law of closely-held corporations or partnerships to a limited liability company created under Arizona law. The legislature did not explicitly outline any such duties for members of an LLC; instead, the LLC Act allows the members of an LLC to not only create an operating agreement, but also delineate in that agreement the duties members owe one another. See A.R.S. §29–682(B) ("An operating agreement governs relations among the members and the managers . . . and may contain any provision that is not contrary to law and that relates to . . . duties or powers of its members. . . ."). The members of Doveland Developments created a written operating agreement (the "Agreement") which does, as discussed below, outline reciprocal duties the members would owe each other. Therefore, the trial court erred by imputing, without reference to the Agreement, a fiduciary duty on the members of Doveland Developments to each other based solely on principles applicable to closely-held corporations and/or partnerships.

Id. at 707–08.

Similarly, the Virginia Supreme Court has held that a member of an LLC cannot maintain a direct action against a manager for breach of fiduciary duty. The court explained that in the analogous corporate context, directors of a corporation owe fiduciary duties to the entity and to shareholders "as a class," but not to individual shareholders. *Remora Investments, L.L.C. v. Orr*, 673 S.E.2d 845, 848 (Va. 2009). Thus, the law in this area is unsettled.

3. Limitations on Distributions

Nearly all states provide a solvency limitation on distributions to the members of an LLC. If an LLC is insolvent at the time of a distribution, the members receiving the distribution must return it to the LLC for payment of creditors. *See, e.g.*, ULLCA §§ 406, 407. The reason for this limitation probably is that the limited partnership served as an analogy for the LLC at the time the early LLC legislation was being debated and drafted. The uniform limited partnership acts contain similar limitations on distributions to limited partners, as do corporate codes with regard to distributions to shareholders.

Note that under these statutes the obligation of a member receiving an improper distribution is to return that distribution to the LLC and, therefore, presumably only the LLC has standing to sue to recover such a distribution. *Weinstein v. Colborne Foodbotics*, 302 P.3d 263 (Colo. 2013) (creditor lacks standing to sue for an improper distribution); *accord, Rev O, Inc. v. Woo*, 725 S.E.2d 45 (N.C. Ct. App. 2012).

An issue that has arisen several times in the context of an LLC is whether compensation paid to a member of an LLC for services rendered should be considered a distribution and subject to the limitations on distributions. Some courts have so held. E.g., *Steiner v. Coffee*, No. 06-CI-08253 (Ky. Cir. Ct. Feb. 2, 2007). In response to cases such as *Steiner*, a number of states have amended their LLC acts to provide that amounts paid as reasonable compensation to members of an LLC do not constitute distributions. *See, e.g.,* Texas Bus. Org. Code, § 101.206; Va. Code Ann. § 13.1-1035(e); Del. Code Ann. tit. 6, § 18-607(a), Colo. Rev. Stat. § 7-80-606; Ky. Rev. Stat. Ann. § 275.225(7).

4. Transferability of Interests

As noted above, early LLC acts were quite strict on transferability of membership interests because of concern about the corporate characteristic of free transferability of interest. Most recent legislation leaves the members free to make their own agreements, and the check-the-box regulations make this an unimportant issue today. Thus, the source of law today for most LLCs on this issue is their operating agreement.

Condo v. Conners

Supreme Court of Colorado
266 P.3d 1110 (2011)

CHIEF JUSTICE BENDER delivered the Opinion of the Court.

. . . .

This appeal arises out of Thomas Banner's attempted assignment of a portion of his membership interest in the Hut Group to his former wife, Elizabeth Condo. Banner was a member of the Hut Group with a one-third ownership interest. As part of Condo and Banner's divorce settlement, Banner agreed to assign Condo his right to receive monetary distributions from the Hut Group. Additionally, Banner and Condo agreed that Banner would vote against all issues that required unanimous consent, unless Condo directed him to do otherwise, effectively assigning Condo his voting interest in the Hut Group.

Before executing this assignment to Condo, however, Banner first sought approval from the other members of the Hut Group, Thomas Conners and George Roberts. Article 10.1 of the Hut Group's operating agreement expressly provides that "a Member shall not sell, assign, pledge or otherwise transfer any portion of its interest in [the Hut Group]" "without the prior written approval of all of the Members." Additionally, Article 10.2 states: "If at any time any Member proposes to sell, assign or otherwise dispose of all or any part of its interest in the [LLC], such Member . . . shall first obtain written approval of all of the Members to such transfer pursuant to [Article] 10.1. . . ."

Accordingly, Banner drafted an instrument assigning his right to distributions and effectively transferring his voting right to Condo and sought the approval of Conners and Roberts. This first draft of the assignment explicitly recognized the LLC's anti-assignment clause (Article 10.1) and provided that the instrument was "subject to and conditional upon the Company's delivery of its consent hereto" and that "[i]f such consent is not obtained . . . this assignment shall be of no further force and effect." Conners and Roberts refused to consent to the assignment.

In response, Banner and Condo drafted and executed a second instrument (the "Banner assignment"). This second draft similarly assigned Banner's right to receive distributions and effectively transferred Banner's voting interest to Condo. In contrast to the first draft, however, the second draft did not acknowledge the Operating Agreement's anti-assignment clause and was not contingent on the consent of the other members. Conners and Roberts did not receive notice that Banner and Condo executed this second draft of the assignment, and the Banner assignment was submitted to the divorce court without any showing that it was in compliance with Article 10.1 of the Operating Agreement.

When Conners and Roberts learned of the unapproved Banner assignment, they contacted Banner and expressed their concern that it violated the terms of the Operating Agreement. Conners and Roberts sent Banner a letter explaining their unease that the assignment would effectively make Banner a noncontributing member of the Hut Group and would eliminate any incentive Banner had to assist in the Hut Group's continued financial success. To resolve these issues, Conners and Roberts, allegedly with the aid of their attorney, Wendell Porterfield, offered to buy-out Banner's interest in the Hut Group. After some negotiation, Banner agreed to sell his entire interest to Conners and Roberts for $125,000.

Thereafter, Condo sued Conners, Roberts, and Porterfield for tortious interference with contract and civil conspiracy. Her claims were based on the theory that (1) she was validly assigned the right to receive distributions from the Hut Group and (2) the defendants had conspired with Banner in bad faith to buy his interest at a "fire-sale" price and thereby destroy the value of her right to receive Banner's monetary distributions. Thus, Condo alleged that the defendants had conspired to interfere with the Banner assignment.

In granting summary judgment for all defendants, the trial court reasoned that both of Condo's claims turned on the existence of a valid assignment predating Banner's sale to Conners and Roberts. It ruled that the Banner assignment was invalid because it was made without the consent of Conners and Roberts. The trial court held that Banner's assignment to Condo was void as against public policy because his failure to receive the consent of the other members constituted bad faith in corporate dealings.

Condo appealed, and the court of appeals affirmed on other grounds.

. . . .

Condo petitioned this court for certiorari review of the court of appeals' decision, and we granted her petition.

. . . .

A. Review under Contract Principles and the Terms of this Operating Agreement

Before addressing each of Condo's arguments on appeal, we address a threshold issue raised by the defendants, who claim that an LLC operating agreement should not be interpreted in accordance with prevailing contract law. The defendants argue that an LLC operating agreement more closely resembles a constitution or charter than a contract because it serves as an organic document for the LLC. Thus, the defendants assert that an operating agreement is much more than a multilateral agreement among the members and that it instead serves as a "super-contract" that explicitly restricts the power of any member to transfer any interest without complying with its express terms. Consequently, the defendants argue that Banner lacked the authority to assign his interest under the express terms of the Operating Agreement and any potential exception found within contract law is irrelevant. We disagree.

. . . .

[T]he Operating Agreement itself is framed in terms of a multilateral agreement among the members and it is appropriate to interpret it in light of prevailing principles of contract law.

Accordingly, we review the Operating Agreement in light of such principles. In interpreting a contract, our primary goal is to determine and effectuate the reasonable expectations of the parties. . . . When the terms of an operating agreement do not conflict with existing law, Colorado law mandates that we give "maximum effect to the principle of freedom of contract and to the enforceability of [the terms]."

In the present operating agreement, Article 10.1 expressly states that "a Member shall not sell, assign, pledge or otherwise transfer *any portion of its interest* in [the Hut Group]" "without the prior written approval of all of the Members." (Emphasis added). Similarly, Article 10.2 states: "If at any time any Member proposes to sell, assign or otherwise dispose of all or any part of its interest in the [LLC], such Member . . . shall first obtain written approval of all of the Members to such transfer. . . ." Condo does not dispute the language of Articles 10.1 and 10.2 of the Operating Agreement nor does she dispute that Conners and Roberts never consented to the Banner assignment.

Although Condo concedes that the assignment appears to contravene the terms of the anti-assignment clause, she makes two alternative arguments as to why the unapproved Banner assignment was legally effective. First, Condo asserts that the assignment did not violate the anti-assignment clause because the clause should be narrowly interpreted to prohibit only nonconforming assignments of contractual duties. Thus, she concludes, the anti-assignment clause does not apply to an assignment of contractual rights. Second, Condo alternatively argues that even if the Banner assignment did violate the anti-assignment clause, the nonconforming assignment is legally binding nonetheless. This argument, Condo contends, has its genesis in the modern approach to anti-assignment clauses, which Condo urges this court to adopt in light of the modern credit-based economy and the public policy in support of the alienability of contract rights. We address each of these arguments in turn.

B. Application of this Anti-Assignment Clause

Condo argues that we should narrowly interpret the Operating Agreement's anti-assignment clause such that it only applies to the assignment of membership *duties* and places no limit on the ability of a member to assign his or her membership *rights*. Condo claims that the present anti-assignment clause does not apply to the transfer of Banner's right to receive monetary distributions. Condo argues that unlike an assignment of Banner's duties to the Hut Group, the assignment of his right to distributions has no effect on the ownership interests of Conners and Roberts.

In the present context, however, this interpretation is too narrow given the plain meaning of the Hut Group's anti-assignment clause. Further, in the context of an LLC operating agreement, Colorado law compels us to give "maximum effect" to the terms of the operating agreement. § 7-80-108(4).

As mentioned, Article 10.1 of the Hut Group Operating Agreement expressly states that "a Member shall not sell, assign, pledge or otherwise transfer *any portion of its interest* in [the Hut Group]" "without the prior written approval of all of the Members." (Emphasis added). Under Colorado law, a membership interest in an LLC is statutorily defined to include the "right to receive distributions of such company's assets." § 7-80-102(10). Additionally, Article 4 of the Operating Agreement explicitly sets forth the manner and timing of the Hut Group's mandatory distributions, which thus creates a right that each member may enforce under the Operating Agreement. Because the right to receive distributions is a component of the membership interest, it is impossible to read Article 10.1's express limitation on the transfer of "any portion" of a membership interest as anything other than a restriction on the assignment of such a right. . . . [T]he present anti-assignment clause appears to have intentionally employed the broadest possible language to prevent the unconsented transfer of any membership interest.

Hence, we agree with the court of appeals that the right to receive distributions, which is statutorily and contractually defined to be a portion of the membership interest, falls within the express application of the anti-assignment clause to "any portion" of the membership interest. Any other result would fail to give "maximum effect" to the language selected by the members in Article 10.1.

C. Application of the Modern Approach to this Anti-Assignment Clause

Having concluded that the Operating Agreement's anti-assignment clause applies to the transfer of both rights and duties, we address whether the unapproved Banner assignment was void or whether it became legally effective despite its failure to comply with the anti-assignment clause. If the anti-assignment clause rendered Banner powerless to make a nonconforming assignment, the assignment was void and the present claims cannot stand. If, in contrast, Banner had the power but not the right to make the assignment, the assignment can be said to have occurred—albeit wrongfully—and Condo's present claims against the defendants may survive summary judgment.

As emphasized, under the LLC statutes, we give "maximum effect" to the terms of the Operating Agreement. The Operating Agreement's anti-assignment clause provides that: "without the prior written approval of all of the Members . . . a Member *shall not* sell, assign, pledge or otherwise transfer any portion of its interest in the Company." (Emphasis added.) Giving "maximum effect" to this clause does not resolve whether this anti-assignment clause functions as (1) a duty not to assign without consent or (2) renders each member powerless to assign without consent.

Accordingly, we resolve this issue by examining the classical and modern approaches to anti-assignment clauses. Ultimately, pursuant to prevailing Colorado case law and in light of the approach set forth in the Restatement (Second) of Contracts, we conclude that the language of the Operating Agreement and the context of the present dispute rendered Banner powerless to make the unapproved Banner assignment.

We first note that the court of appeals resolved this issue by looking to what it considered to be our application of the classical approach in *Parrish Chiropractic Centers, P.C. v. Progressive Casualty Insurance Co.*, 874 P.2d 1049, 1051 (Colo.1994), and extending this principle to the context of an anti-assignment clause in an LLC operating agreement. *Condo*, 271 P.3d at 524. Under the classical approach, an assignment made in violation of an express anti-assignment clause is void ab initio because the assignor is powerless to make a nonconforming transfer. *See id.*

Now, Condo urges us to depart from *Parrish Chiropractic* and adhere to the modern approach as set forth in *Rumbin v. Utica Mutual Insurance Co.*, 254 Conn. 259, 757 A.2d 526 (2000). Under the modern approach, an anti-assignment clause creates a duty by which a party is contractually obligated to refrain from making a nonconforming assignment, but does not restrict the power of a member to nevertheless do so. *Id.* at 530–31. Instead of classifying a nonconforming assignment as void, the modern approach treats this unlawful act as a breach of the duty not to assign, which can then be enforced by the other party or parties to the contract through a breach of contract action. *Id.* As adopted in *Rumbin*, the modern approach allows for parties to contractually restrict the power—again, as opposed to the right—to assign, but such a clause will only render the parties powerless to assign when it expressly states that any nonconforming assignment is "void" or "invalid." . . .

The Restatement, however, does not adopt the strict "magic words" approach, and instead states that whether an anti-assignment clause merely creates a duty not to assign turns on the language used and the context in which the contract is made. Restatement (Second) of Contracts § 322(2)(a) (1981). . . . Thus, although the Restatement is similar to *Rumbin* in that it creates a presumption in favor of treating an anti-assignment clause as a duty not to assign, given specific language in an anti-assignment clause and under the appropriate circumstances, it allows that an anti-assignment clause may render the parties powerless to assign, even in the absence of "magic words."

Applying our previous holding in *Parrish Chiropractic* and considering the rationale underlying the Restatement approach, we hold that the Operating Agreement rendered the parties powerless to assign any portion of the membership interest without the consent of all other members. Two of the rationales we applied in *Parrish Chiropractic* are pertinent to our resolution of the present matter. First, we highlighted the strong public policy in favor of freedom of contract—that is, the ability of a party to contractually restrict the ability of other parties to assign their rights and/or duties. *Parrish Chiropractic*, 874 P.2d at 1054. Second, we emphasized "the corollary right of the [nonassigning party] to deal only with whom it contracted." *Id.* at 1054–55. Thus, we applied the classical approach in *Parrish Chiropractic* to afford contracting parties the maximum flexibility to shape their contract within the confines of the law, while simultaneously allowing for the option of increased predictability and stability in contractual relations through the use of an anti-assignment clause. *See id.*

. . . .

Accordingly, and in light of the strong public policy favoring the freedom of contract, we agree that the plain meaning of the Operating Agreement's anti-assignment clause rendered Banner powerless to make the unapproved assignment to Condo.

Further, in the context of a closely-held LLC, such as the Hut Group, there is also a clear public policy in favor of allowing the members to tightly control who may receive either rights or duties under the operating agreement. . . .

Given these circumstances and the plain meaning of the Operating Agreement, we hold that the nonconforming Banner assignment had no legal effect and cannot support Condo's underlying claims of tortious interference with contract and civil conspiracy. Accordingly, summary judgment was appropriate.

In re Carlisle Etcetera LLC

Court of Chancery of Delaware
114 A.3d 592 (2015)

LASTER, Vice Chancellor

In 2012, petitioner Well Union Capital Limited ("WU Parent") and respondent Tom James Company ("James") formed Carlisle Etcetera LLC, a Delaware limited liability company ("Carlisle" or the "Company"). They executed a simple form of operating agreement (the "Initial LLC Agreement") in which they committed to work promptly on a more detailed operating agreement to replace the original one.

After the Company was formed, WU Parent transferred its member interest to a wholly owned subsidiary called Well Union U.S. Holdings, Inc. ("WU Sub"). James knew about the transfer, did not object, and treated WU Sub as a member from that point on. For purposes of the Delaware Limited Liability Company Act (the "LLC Act"), however, the transfer rendered WU Sub an assignee, rather than a member.

WU Parent and James never reached agreement on a replacement operating agreement. Other disputes arose, and the relationship deteriorated. Deadlock prevailed at the manager level, where the Initial LLC Agreement called for a board of directors (the "Board") to serve as the singular manager of the Company. The Board has four members, two appointed by WU Parent and two by James. They split 2–2 on key issues.

Both sides eventually recognized that they could not manage the Company jointly and that one side needed to buy out the other. Despite some initially positive signs, they could not agree on a buyout procedure or a price.

During the venture's halcyon days, the Board appointed a James executive as the Company's CEO. Through the CEO, James controls the Company's day-to-day operations. With the Board deadlocked, the CEO has been operating free of any oversight. Given its advantaged position, James does not see the deadlock as a problem and feels no urgency to alleviate it. During negotiations over the buyout, James sought to use its privileged position to extract concessions from WU Sub.

WU Sub turned to this court for assistance. It filed this action, in which it petitioned to dissolve the Company. James moved to dismiss on the grounds that WU Sub is an assignee, not a member, and that an assignee lacks standing to petition for statutory dissolution under Section 18–802 of the LLC Act. 6 Del. C. § 18–802. In an amended petition, WU Parent joined as a co-petitioner.

This decision holds that WU Parent and WU Sub lack standing to petition for statutory dissolution under Section 18–802. The motion is denied, however, because WU Sub has standing to seek dissolution in equity. [This second issue is covered in section J, *infra*.]

. . . .

A. Statutory Standing To Seek Dissolution Under Section 18–802

Section 18–802 of the LLC Act addresses dissolution. It states that "[o]n application by or for a member or manager the Court of Chancery may decree dissolution of a limited liability company whenever it is not reasonably practicable to carry on the business in conformity with a limited liability company agreement." 6 Del. C. § 18–802. By its terms, this language limits the right to seek statutory dissolution under Section 18–802 to members and managers of an LLC. As to this issue, James is correct.

B. WU Parent And WU Sub's Status As Members Or Managers

To petition for statutory dissolution under Section 18–802, WU Parent and WU Sub must be members or managers of the Company. Neither claims to be a manager. The Initial LLC Agreement makes clear that the Board, acting collectively, is the manager of the Company. WU Parent and WU Sub do claim to be members.

Taking the allegations of the petition as true, WU Parent cannot be a member. WU Parent was a member of the Company, but it assigned its interest to WU Sub. Under Section 18–702(a) of the LLC Act, "[a] limited liability company interest is assignable in whole or in part except as provided in a limited liability company agreement." Id. § 18–702(a). The Initial LLC Agreement was silent about assignability, so the interest was freely assignable.

WU Parent lost its status as a member of the Company when it assigned all of its interest in the Company to WU Sub. Under Section 702(b)(3) of the LLC Act, "[u]nless otherwise provided in a limited liability company agreement: . . . (3) [a] member ceases to be a member and to have the power to exercise any rights or powers of a member upon assignment of all of the member's limited liability company interest." Id. § 18–702(b)(3). By operation of law, once WU Parent assigned its interest in the Company to WU Sub, WU Parent "cease[d] to be a member" and could no longer exercise a member's right to seek statutory dissolution. Under the facts as pled, WU Parent cannot petition for statutory dissolution.

The analysis for WU Sub is more complex. As an initial matter, James is correct that WU Sub did not automatically become a member by receiving WU Parent's interest. Under Section 18–702(b)(1) of the LLC Act, "[u]nless otherwise provided in a limited liability company agreement: . . . (1) [a]n assignment of a limited liability company interest does not entitle the assignee to become . . . a member." 6 Del. C. § 18–702(b)(1). The Initial LLC Agreement did not provide otherwise, so under the facts as pled, the transfer of WU Parent's interest made WU Sub an assignee, not a member.

By default under the LLC Act, only a member can petition for statutory dissolution, not an assignee. Section 18–702(b)(1) reinforces this reading by stating that "[u]nless otherwise provided in a limited liability company agreement: . . . (1) [a]n assignment of a limited liability company interest does not entitle the assignee . . . to exercise any rights or powers of a member." Id. § 18–702(b)(1). Section 18–702(a) similarly provides that

> the assignee of a member's limited liability company interest shall have no right to participate in the management of the business and affairs of a limited liability company except as provided in a limited liability company agreement or, unless otherwise provided in the limited liability company agreement, upon the affirmative vote or written consent of all of the members of the limited liability company.

Id. § 18–702(a). The Initial LLC Agreement did not give assignees the right to seek statutory dissolution. Without more, therefore, WU Sub cannot claim to be a member or exercise the rights of a member, so WU Sub cannot seek statutory dissolution.

[WU Sub also argued that it became a de facto member of the LLC because it was treated as such in the records of the LLC. The court rejected this argument, ruling that under Delaware law, a person may only become a member as provide in the operating agreement (which was silent on whether assignees could become members) or "upon the affirmative vote or written consent of all of the members of the limited liability company." As to the latter, Delaware law contemplates that there will be "formal member action," either a meeting called with appropriate notice or a written consent. Neither occurred here, so that WU Sub did not become a member.]

The need for formal member action comports with the policies underlying this aspect of the statutory regime. As Chief Justice Strine observed, writing as a Vice Chancellor, "[t]here are likely two motivations for the statutory default rules in §§ 18–702, 18–704(a), and 18–301 concerning the assignment of a limited liability company interest and the assignee's possible (and subsequent) admission as a member of the LLC." Achaian, Inc. v. Leemon Family LLC, 25 A.3d 800, 804 n.14 (Del. Ch. 2011). The first was tax-related and is now outdated. The imposition of statutory limitations on the free alienability of LLC member interests formed a critical part of early attempts "to create an entity that, as a matter of tax law, is classified as a partnership with each owner treated as a partner, but whose owners are shielded by state law from automatic personal liability," an effort since rendered superfluous by the Treasury Department's adoption of the "check-the-box" tax classification regime. When the LLC Act was drafted, however, the tax implications were significant, so it is logical that the LLC Act would require formal member action to admit an assignee.

"The second reason for the default rules in the [LLC] Act regarding the transferability of [member] interests may rest on the notion that one generally is entitled to select his own business associates in a closely held enterprise, like an LLC." Achaian, 25 A.3d at 804 n.14. "The policy that underlies § 18–702(b)(3) is that 'it is far more tolerable to have to suffer a new passive co-investor one did not choose than to endure a new co-manager without consent.'" Eureka VIII LLC, 899 A.2d at 115 (quoting *601 Milford Power Co., LLC v. PDC Milford Power, LLC, 866 A.2d 738, 760 (Del. Ch. 2004)). It makes sense that the LLC Act would require formal member action to accept a new business partner, rather than contemplating de facto membership or the constructive admission of assignees. . . .

Based on the allegations of the petition, James is correct that WU Sub is not a member who can seek statutory dissolution. Neither petitioner can.

5. Exit Privileges

The privilege of a member to exit an LLC is largely governed by agreement today. The default provision in ULLCA is § 602, which states: "Unless otherwise provided in the operating agreement, a member has the power to dissociate from a limited liability company at any time, rightfully or wrongfully, by express will pursuant to Section 601(1)."

6. Expulsion of a Member

Walker v. Resource Development Company Limited, L.L.C.

Court of Chancery of Delaware
791 A.2d 799 (2000)

Plaintiff Randolph T. Walker is a cousin of former President Bush. Walker testified to having attended Windham College and to having participated in several courses offered by the Commercial Investment Real Estate Association. Walker also testified that his presence at various banking conferences as a non-attendee gave him experience in sophisticated financial consulting.

Defendant William J. Cox, Jr., before the events described herein, was an intelligence officer in the United States Navy. Defendant William C. Baron met Cox while serving as an intelligence officer for the Department of Defense. Prior to leaving the service, they spent time serving in the former Soviet Republic of Moldova. Both had certain technical expertise that would help them in working in the oil and gas industry, but had no significant business experience. Defendant William C. Liedtke, III, is an oil and gas attorney and is the son of William C. Liedtke, Jr. The elder Liedtke, along with his brother J. Hugh Liedtke, were partners and close associates of former President Bush in various oil and gas related business ventures. Liedtke has considerable legal and business sophistication, especially in the oil and gas industry.

Defendant Resource Development Company, Limited, L.L.C. ("REDECO") is a Delaware limited liability company founded by Cox and Baron. Between April 4 and August 23, 1995, at the very least, REDECO's members were defendants Cox, Baron and Liedtke (collectively, the "three Bills") and plaintiff Walker. Defendant REDECO Limited, LLC is a Texas entity that was created after the events relevant to this matter took place.

[In a long and detailed account, the court describes how Walker misrepresented his background and experience, leading the defendants to believe that he could obtain financing for an oil and gas exploration and production concession that they were seeking from the Moldovian government. Frustrated by Walker's drinking problems, financial irresponsibility, conflicts with principals and associates of REDECO and, finally, his inability to secure the financing that he had promised would be forthcoming, the three Bills expelled Walker from REDECO. The removal letter of August 24, 1995 provided:]

Your actions have constituted a breach of trust and have resulted in a loss of faith in your abilities to continue as a member of the Firm. Your actions over the past few months appear to violate Firm policies and prevent us from fulfilling our normal business responsibilities. Accordingly, we have mutually agreed that your membership must terminate immediately so it is clear you are not and cannot be acting on behalf of the Firm.

... [W]e hereby terminate your ownership interest in the Firm. In addition to the numerous actions constituting breach of trust, your financial obligations to the Firm remain outstanding. To this end, we have calculated your share of the Firm's total debt to be $4,179.43. Please pay this sum to the Firm on or before September 1, 1995.

Walker never acknowledged or returned the document to Cox. Instead, his counsel sent Cox a letter dated September 22, 1995, stating that because the Operating Agreement does not provide for involuntary withdrawal of a member, Walker remained an 18% owner of the business. With respect to amounts due, Walker's counsel explained that the Agreement does not require additional capital contributions except pursuant to an "enforceable promise" to pay. This letter requested "documentation of this alleged obligation." Cox made no response.

. . . .

REDECO eventually obtained financing from Costilla Corp., a company with which Liedtke's brother was affiliated. . . .

A series of financing transactions eventually led to the exchange of the three Bills' REDECO holdings (via interests in other companies) into shares of a Canadian corporation holding a 12.5% interest in any future profits that might be earned by REDECO from the Moldovan concession after various other investors receive their return. Specifically, REDECO Energy, Inc., a publicly traded corporation listed on the Alberta stock exchange, holds the 12.5% future profits interest. The three Bills' only remaining connection with REDECO is through shares in REDECO Energy, which, pursuant to Canadian law, are held in an escrow account and will remain in escrow until the company meets certain performance benchmarks. To date, the company has failed to meet any of those benchmarks. . . .

IV. Analysis

. . . .

B. The August 24, 1995 Removal Letter Did Not Remove Walker From His Membership In REDECO

The three Bills had no authority to unilaterally remove Walker from the LLC on August 24, 1995. Neither the Operating Agreement nor the law provides any mechanism for removal of a member in these circumstances.

1. The Operating Agreement Does Not Provide For Removal

Delaware's Limited Liability Company Act is codified at 6 Del. C. Ch. 18. "The basic approach of the Delaware Act is to provide members with broad discretion in drafting the [Operating] Agreement and to furnish default provisions when the members' agreement is silent."[35] "Once members exercise their contractual freedom in their limited liability company agreement, they can be virtually certain that the agreement will be enforced in accordance with its terms."[36]

As Chief Justice Veasey said *Elf Atochem*, "[T]he following observation relating to limited partnerships applies as well to limited liability companies:

> The Act's basic approach is to permit partners to have the broadest possible discretion in drafting their partnership agreements and to furnish answers only in situations where the partners have not expressly made provisions in their partnership agreement. Truly, the partnership agreement is the cornerstone of a Delaware limited partnership, and effectively constitutes the entire agreement among the partners with respect to the admission of partners to, and the creation, operation and termination of, the limited partnership. . . ."[37]

Thus, LLC members' rights begin with and typically end with the Operating Agreement. The Operating Agreement includes no provision that can be read to allow the three Bills to deprive Walker of his ownership interest in the circumstances presented in this case. Article X deals with removal of the Manager but makes clear that "removal shall be without prejudice to the [Manager's] contract rights," *implicitly including his ownership rights.* Article XXII, does address the voluntary and involuntary withdrawal from membership but identifies no instance even arguably applicable in this case. The absence of such a provision is surprising, considering what the three Bills knew about Walker at the time they entered into this agreement.[38] They knew that he had embarrassed the company, experienced bouts of drunkenness and alcohol abuse, misrepresented his sophistication in financing transactions *and borrowed money from the very person with whom he was supposed to be negotiating on REDECO's behalf.* Most importantly, they knew or had every reason to know that if the Appian[39] deal fell through, they could not rely on Walker to find an alternative source of financing for REDECO.

Thus, the three Bills could easily have protected themselves in the Operating Agreement against the failure of negotiations with Norris [principal of Appian— Eds.] by simply making Walker's REDECO interest contingent on successfully closing a deal with Appian. They failed to do so for reasons that are unexplained. Since

35. [48] *Elf Atochem North America, Inc. v. Jaffari*, Del. Supr., 727 A.2d 286, 291 (1999).

36. [49] 2 R.F. Balotti & J.A. Finkelstein, *The Delaware Law of Corporations & Business Organizations*, § 20.4 (2000) (hereinafter "Balotti & Finkelstein").

37. [50] *Elf Atochem*, 727 A.2d at 291 (quoting from Martin A. Lubaroff & Paul Altman, *Delaware Limited Partnerships*, § 1.2 (1999)).

38. [51] The absence of any provision tying Walker's continued equity participation to his success in obtaining financing also stands in contrast to the terms of . . . [an earlier] agreement, which included specific terms for termination and involuntary removal in the event Walker failed to obtain financing for REDECO.

39. [The court here refers to The Appian Group, a source of potential financing the Walker claimed would fund REDECO's operations.—Eds.]

the Operating Agreement does not justify Walker's removal, defendants are left to the default rules.

2. There is No Basis in the Law for Unilateral Removal of an LLC Member

Defendants make the troubling argument that, although there is no basis for doing so in the Operating Agreement, under applicable law the three Bills had the inherent power to remove Walker from the entity, taking away his ownership interests therein, due to his alleged breach of fiduciary duty.[40] In their post-trial brief, defendants identified virtually no legal support for this proposition. After I noted the lack of legal authority at oral argument, defendants directed my attention to *Lloyd v. Horn, Inc.*, an opinion of the United States Court of Appeals for the Tenth Circuit.[41]

Lloyd is plainly distinguishable from the present case and does not, in any case, support defendants' legal argument. In that case, Lloyd, who had acted as managing partner of the business for several years, announced soon after the partnership converted to a limited liability company that he would terminate his employment with the business (by declining to accept the position of Managing Member) but keep his ownership interest in the new entity. The other members then purported to remove him from the LLC and eliminate his ownership interest.

The prior partnership agreement in that case "expressly limited the amount Lloyd, as Managing Partner, could realize from his partnership interest should he withdraw or be fired from the partnership. Under the terms of the partnership agreement, if Lloyd withdrew or was fired as Managing Partner, his partnership interest would be valued at the amount of his capital account plus all undistributed earnings through the effective date of withdrawal or termination." The LLC operating agreement incorporated virtually the same restriction on the value of the Managing Member's interests, *but failed to require that Lloyd take that position.* Thus, a conflict arose when Lloyd refused to take the position from the outset and claimed a standard member's ownership interest.

The district court rescinded the LLC agreement, on the basis of unilateral mistake and constructive fraud, and determined that the parties' rights were still controlled by the prior partnership agreement, i.e., Lloyd's interest was based on his capital contributions. The court of appeals affirmed the district court's order for equitable rescission and its decision that the parties' rights rested on the prior partnership agreement. Neither court recognized any inherent right on the part of the other members to "fire" Lloyd from the entity or take away his ownership interest.

---

40. [The defendants alleged that Walker had an arrangement with The Appian Group that if Appian invested in REDECO, Appian would pay Walker a finder's fee. In an omitted portion of the opinion, the court concluded that defendants failed to prove that Walker had admitted to such an arrangement or that it in fact existed.—Eds.]

41. [52] 166 F.3d 1221 (10th Cir. 1998) (TABLE). *Lloyd* is not only an unpublished opinion, it includes an introductory note explaining that "[t]his order and judgment is not binding precedent, except under the doctrines of law of the case, res judicata, and collateral estoppel."

Defendants also claim that "both the Delaware statutes and authority from other jurisdictions provide that a Chancery Court should uphold the removal of a member or partner when the equities so dictate." For this they cite 8 Del. C. § 18-1104, which simply states that the rules of law and equity govern where the statute is silent, and two plainly distinguishable cases decided by New York state and federal courts.[42] None of these authorities vary the fundamental principle under Delaware law that a majority of the members (or stockholders) of a business entity, unless expressly granted such power by contract, have no right to take the property of other members (or stockholders). Other mechanisms may be available to them to recast their business relations to eliminate persons from the enterprise, such as the merger provisions of the various business entity laws. But, these provisions do not provide for the forfeiture of economic rights, requiring instead that the persons whose interests are eliminated are entitled to receive fair value therefor.

. . . .

[The court then considered defendants other arguments for expulsion: that Walker's interest in REDECO had been reduced to zero by his failure to make capital contributions and that Walker had induced the defendants to enter into the operating agreement as a result of fraudulent inducement. The court found factual and legal shortcomings with both arguments. Thus, expulsion was wrongful.]

. . . .

E. Walker's Remedy

Defendants raise in their supplemental post-trial brief, for the first time, the claim that the LLC statute protects the three Bills from personal liability for their effort to appropriate Walker's REDECO interests. In that regard, defendants cite to § 18-1101 of the LLC act, which provides that "[t]o the extent that . . . a member or manager or other person has duties . . . and liabilities relating thereto to a limited liability company or to another member or manager . . . [that person] shall not be liable . . . [for that person's] good faith reliance on the provisions of the limited liability company agreement."

Even if the three Bills believed that they were entitled to take away Walker's membership interest, they have failed to adduce any proof that they formed such a belief in reasonable reliance on any provision of the Operating Agreement. Indeed, no provision of that agreement could support such a belief.

---

42. [54] *Curley v. Brignoli Curley & Roberts Assoc.*, 746 F. Supp. 1208 (S.D. N.Y. 1989) (ordering removal of general partner who breached his fiduciary duties from managerial role, pending appointment of a receiver and limited partners' determination of whether to continue venture); *May v. Flowers*, 106 A.D.2d 873, 483 N.Y.S.2d 551 (N.Y.A.D.1984), *appeal dismissed*, 64 N.Y.2d 611, 491 N.Y.S.2d 1025, 480 N.E.2d 749 (1985) (granting dissolution of limited partnership and rescission of agreement based on breach of fiduciary duty by general partner rendering partnership's continued operation unfeasible).

I also have no doubt that the cited statute is not intended to bar Walker from recovering his property from those who purported to take it from him. First, all I conclude here is that the August 24, 1995 letter did not have the effect of depriving Walker of his interest in REDECO. Thus, when they later dealt with REDECO as if they owned 100% of its membership interest, the three Bills were each dealing with Walker's property in proportion to their relative ownership interests in REDECO. Thus, in concluding (as I do, *infra*) that they hold a portion of the property they have subsequently received in exchange for 100% of the equity interest in REDECO subject to a constructive trust in favor of Walker, I am not ordering them to relinquish anything that they ever owned.

Further, I must view the cited provision allowing members of an LLC to rely in good faith on the terms of the operating agreement in the context in which it appears in the statute, and with regard to the general tenor of the statute as a whole. This provision is intended, for example, to make clear that an apparent limit on liability for breach of fiduciary duty is to be interpreted broadly. I have no doubt that the legislature never intended this provision to allow the members of an LLC to misappropriate property from another member and avoid returning that property or otherwise compensating the wronged member.

As previously discussed, there is no proof before me of the value of Walker' 18% interest at any time. Thus, there is no basis on which to enter an award of damages. Nevertheless, this does not mean that Walker is not entitled to some remedy because the evidence at trial established that the value of 100% of REDECO's membership interest held as of August 24, 1995 by the three Bills and Walker is now represented by the shares of REDECO Energy, Inc. owned by the three Bills. Subject to the following discussion, Walker is entitled to 18% of those shares, from each of the Bills in proportion to his relative interest, and, to that end, I will impose a constructive trust on those shares in his favor.

Of course, the terms of such a trust must reflect the reality that in the period of time since Walker was purportedly expelled, the three Bills have had to meet substantial capital calls to maintain their (and Walker's) economic position. Had they not done so, Liedtke testified, they would have been "drilled out or squeezed out" of the deal. The evidence shows that the three Bills contributed $139,000 "net of everything" since August 24, 1995. Had Walker been allowed to retain his 18% share in REDECO, he would have had to pay his share of REDECO's accrued debt, both the $4,179.43 he owed prior to August 24, 1995, plus an additional $25,020.00, representing 18% of the $139,000 expended by the three Bills after that date, for a total of $29,199.43 plus interest. If he is to recover his proportionate share of the REDECO Energy stock, he will be required to pay that amount in exchange therefor.

V. Conclusion

For the reasons and to the extent set forth herein, I will enter judgment in favor of plaintiff and against the defendants. . . .

Note

While the Delaware LLC Act does not include a provision on expulsion of a member, the operating agreement could, of course, so provide. Some states specifically authorize expulsion, even making that right nonwaivable in the operating agreement. *See CCD, L.C. v. Millsap*, 116 P.3d 366 (Ut. 2005) (member's misappropriation of the LLC's trust fund warranted expulsion). Both of the uniform LLC Acts include provisions on expulsion by the members and pursuant to judicial decree. ULLCA § 601 and RULLCA § 602. Under ULLCA, the operating agreement cannot waive the right to judicial dissolution. ULLCA § 103(5). What policy reasons would justify making the expulsion right nonwaivable?

7. Claims of Creditors of Members

Creditors of members of an LLC are in a position similar to that of creditors of a limited partner. *See, e.g.,* ULLCA § 504. Thus, the remedies of a judgment creditor of a member did not include seizure and forced sale of the debtor-member's interest in the LLC. Rather, under the typical LLC act, a creditor of a member is limited to the remedy of a charging order. The North Carolina appellate court made clear that the judgment creditor has only the rights of an assignee of the debtor-member's interest; those rights do not include the management rights that the member may have had in the LLC. In addition, once the judgment creditor is paid in full, the economic interests that charging order covered revert back to the debtor-member. *First Bank v. S & R Grandview, L.L.C.*, 755 S.E.2d 393 (N.C. Ct. App. 2014). A charging order will reach payments made to the owners of an LLC, even if characterized as compensation. *PB Real Estate, Inc. v. DEM II Properties*, 50 Conn. App. 741, 719 A.2d 73 (1998).

Entrepreneurs often utilize a limited liability company as an "asset protection device." The theory is that a person can convey assets to the LLC and prevent that person's creditors from reaching those assets; if the creditor obtains a judgment, the creditor would be limited to the remedy of a charging order. Management rights would not inure to the benefit of the creditor and the judgment debtor would remain in control of the assets. The efficacy of the strategy depends on whether a charging order is the exclusive remedy of the judgment creditor. If the LLC statute so provides, as does, for instance, ULLCA § 504 (e), RULLCA § 503(g), and the Delaware LLC Act § 18-703(d), the issue is moot. In *Olmstead v. F.T.C.*, 44 So. 3d 76 (Fla. 2010), however, the Florida Supreme Court decided that the Florida statute did not provide an exclusive remedy and a judgment creditor could reach the entire interest of the LLC member in a single-member LLC. The court's decision drew a vigorous dissent, which argued that the logic of the decision would allow a creditor to reach the entire membership interest of a judgment debtor in a multimember LLC, thus subverting the intent of the LLC act to limit the remedy of a judgment creditor to a charging order. The dissent also argued that the majority's decision did not treat the LLC as a legal entity that is separate and distinct from the members of the LLC:

The interpretation of the statute advanced by the majority simply ignores the separation between the particular separate assets of an LLC and a member's specific membership interest in the LLC. The ability of a member to *voluntarily* assign his, her, or its interest does not subject the property of an LLC to execution on the judgment. Under the factual circumstances of the present case, the trial court forced the judgment debtors to *involuntarily* surrender their membership interests in the LLCs and then authorized a receiver to liquidate the specific LLC assets to satisfy the judgment. In doing so, the trial court ignored the clearly recognized legal separation between the specific assets of an LLC and a member's interest in profits or distributions from those assets.

Id. at 86.

In response to the *Olmstead* decision, the Florida legislature amended its LLC Act to, essentially, limit the reach of the decision to single-member LLCs. For multi-member LLCs, a charging order is the "sole and exclusive remedy by which a judgment creditor of a member or member's transferee may satisfy a judgment from the judgment debtor's interest in a limited liability company or rights to distributions from the limited liability company." F.S.A. § 605.050. Recent amendments proposed by the Uniform Law Commissioners to RULLCA have embraced the *Olmstead* decision. Proposed § 503(f) provides:

> (f) If a court orders foreclosure of a charging order lien against the sole member of a limited liability company: (1) the court shall confirm the sale; (2) the purchaser at the sale obtains the member's entire interest, not only the member's transferable interest; (3) the purchaser thereby becomes a member; and (4) the person whose interest was subject to the foreclosed charging order is dissociated as a member.

See also In re Albright, 291 B.R. 538 (D. Colo. 2003) (the trustee in bankruptcy succeeded to all of the rights—economic and management—of the sole member of an LLC upon her filing a petition in bankruptcy). *See generally* J. William Callison, *Charging Order Exclusivity: A Pragmatic Approach to Olmstead v. Federal Trade Commission*, 66 Bus. Law. 339 (2011); Thomas E. Geu, Thomas Rutledge, John W. DeBruyn, *To Be or Not to Be Exclusive: Statutory Construction of the Charging Order in the Single Member LLC*, 9 DePaul Bus. & Comm. L.J. 83 (2012).

8. Inspection of Books and Records

Like corporation statutes, LLC acts typically include provisions giving members and managers the right to inspect the books and records of the LLC, subject to certain limitations. In *Arbor Place, L.P. v. Encore Opportunity Fund, L.L.C.*, No. 18928, 2002 Del. Ch. LEXIS 102 (Jan. 29, 2002), the court limited the inspection rights of a member, holding that those rights did not include the right to inspect the records of subsidiaries of the LLC which were investment funds. The LLC itself was described by the court as a "feeder fund," providing funds for its subsidiaries. The court held that these subsidiaries were separate legal entities and plaintiff was unsuccessful in "piercing the veil" of these subsidiary funds under traditional tests.

9. Bankruptcy of a Member

LLC statutes and operating agreements typically provide that a person ceases to be a member of the LLC if the member files a voluntary petition in bankruptcy. (*See, e.g.*, 6 Del. C. § 18-304.) Such a provision, sometimes called an "ipso facto clause," raises a question under the federal bankruptcy code: "There is federal precedent that holds that an interest in an alternative entity—even a managing interest in a limited partnership—falls within the protective scope of § 365(e)(1) and that an ipso facto clause may not operate to divest a bankruptcy trustee from assuming that contract." *Milford Power Company, LLC v. PDC Milford Power, LLC*, 866 A.2d 738, 751 (Del. Ch. 2004) (citing *Summit Investment and Development Corp. v. Leroux*, 69 F.3d 608 (1st Cir. 1995)). In *Milford Power Company*, the Delaware Chancery Court upheld an ipso facto bankruptcy clause against a company that filed a Chapter 11 bankruptcy petition that was subsequently dismissed. However, the court held that while the member who filed the petition lost its membership interest and right to participate in the management of the LLC, it did not forfeit its economic interests, and would be treated as an assignee of a member's interest in the LLC.

G. Series LLCS

In 1996, Delaware amended the Delaware Limited Liability Company Act to allow the formation of a Series LLC. (In addition to Delaware, a growing number of states explicitly authorize series limited liability companies.) A Series LLC is an LLC partitioned into distinct series with each having its own assets, debts, obligations, liabilities, and rights separate from the other series. For example, a real estate investor could form a Series LLC to own and manage various properties with each property being a distinct series, and any loss or liability would only be enforceable against that particular series. Prior to Series LLCs, the investor would have needed to form separate LLCs for each property to accomplish the same result regarding potential losses and liabilities. The investor's use of a Series LLC could lower his or her costs because it would require only one filing fee and tax return compared to the costs of maintaining multiple LLCs.

To form and maintain a Series LLC in Delaware, notice must be given in the certificate of formation and separate and distinct records must be maintained for each series and its assets. Failure to properly manage the distinct series as separate entities may subject a series to the liabilities of another series. For example, joint ownership of assets or cross-collateralization between series may lead to a court to be reluctant to enforce the liability limitation provided for in the various statutes.

Series LLCs offer much of the same flexibility in management as a traditional LLC. Members and managers have the rights, powers, and duties that they contracted for in the LLC operating agreement. Absent an agreement, management is vested in the members based on a member's interest in the profits resulting from the particular series. In Delaware, fiduciary duties may also be eliminated between members of a Series LLC to the same extent as a traditional LLC, which only prohibits eliminating the implied duty of good faith and fair dealing. This could be particularly important for a member who is a manager of more than one series. The rules regarding dissolution and termination of Series LLCs and traditional LLCs are also very similar. It should be noted, however, that a series may be terminated without resulting in the dissolution of the LLC, but the termination of the LLC results in the dissolution of each series.

While Series LLCs are over two decades old, they are still relatively rare. This is because both attorneys and sophisticated clients seem to be more comfortable with traditional LLCs and other entity options. There is very little case law guiding attorneys on how courts are likely to hold on various liability issues between series, and it is also unclear how both tax and bankruptcy law will be applied to Series LLCs. As these issues become clearer, attorneys and investors may be more willing to take advantage of the Series LLC form. For further discussion, *see* Thomas E. Rutledge, *Again, for the Want of a Theory, the Challenge of the "Series" to Business Organization Law*, 46 Amer. Bus. L. J. 311 (2009); Dominick T. Gattuso, *Series LLCs*, Bus. L. Today, July–Aug. 2008, at 33; Norman M. Powell, *Delaware Alternative Entities*, Prob. & Prop., Jan.–Feb. 2009, at 11.

H. LLCs as Social Enterprise Vehicles: The L3C and the Benefit LLC

The most recent form of business entity is the low-profit limited liability company, referred to in the literature as the "L3C," and the benefit LLC. The idea behind the L3C is to take advantage of tax federal tax regulations that permit private foundations to invest in certain for-profit companies. (But for such provisions, private foundations are generally limited to making donations to tax-exempt, charitable institutions.) A qualifying investment is known as a program related investment (PRI) and L3C statutes have been drafted to facilitate compliance with these regulations. In short, an L3C subordinates the importance of profits to the accomplishment of some charitable purpose, such as education or improving the environment. When these objectives are consistent with the purposes of the private foundation, and certain other criteria are satisfied, the private foundation can "invest" in the L3C without jeopardizing its status as a tax-exempt organization or risking the imposition of a tax on the investment. L3C statutes are intended to mirror the tax regulations and several states have adopted L3C legislation. Despite carefully drawn statutes, however, a private foundation cannot be assured that its investment in an L3C will qualify as a program related investment merely because it has invested in an L3C. For that reason, L3C statutes are a trap for the unwary and a private foundation that invests in an L3C must still satisfy itself that it is in compliance with all applicable tax regulations. *See* Carter G. Bishop, *The Low-Profit LLC (L3C): Program Related Investment by Proxy or Perversion?*, 63 ARK. L. REV. 243 (2010); J. William Callison, *L3Cs: Useless Gadgets?*, 19 BUS. L. TODAY 55 (2009); Robert M. Lang, Jr., *The L3C: The New Way to Organize Socially Responsible and Mission Driven Organizations*, 36 A.L.I.-A.B.A CONTINUING LEGAL EDUC. 251 (2007), *available at* SN036 ALI-ABA 251. Perhaps for these reasons, at least one state (North Carolina) has already repealed provisions relating to the formation of L3Cs.

Benefit LLC legislation is patterned after benefit corporation laws. In the corporate context, benefit corporation statutes mandate, in various ways, that when a board of directors of a benefit corporation makes a decision it should take into account the effect of that decision on the environment and societal interests. In addition, the benefit corporation may elect to have a "specific public benefit" as a focus of its activities, thus sacrificing profit for an identified social good. Most states have now adopted amendments to their corporate codes to allow the formation of benefit corporations and some states have amended their LLC statutes to permit the formation of benefit LLCs. However, benefit LLCs really serve little purpose, as LLCs can be formed for any purpose and whatever a benefit LLC may do, a regular LLC may do as well. *See generally* Mohsen Manesh, *Introducing the Totally Unnecessary Benefit LLC*, 97 N.C. L. REV. (forthcoming 2019), available at: https://papers.ssrn.com/sol3/papers.cfm?abstract_id=3219956.

I. LLCs as Estate Planning Devices

Limited liability companies are being used increasingly as estate planning devices. (Limited partnerships and, in some states, Limited Partnership Associations, have traditionally been used for these purposes.) Families convey the family businesses and other assets into an LLC, with one generation maintaining control and next generation family members remaining passive. When those active in the business pass away, their membership interests are inherited by the younger generation(s). Because the inherited membership interests are typically minority interests, are subject to transfer restrictions, and do not have unlimited control, the value of those interests, relative to the value of the underlying assets of the LLC, will be discounted for estate tax purposes. A further exploration of these matters is best left to a course in estate planning.

J. Dissolution of an LLC

In the early LLC statutes, dissolution occurred on the death or withdrawal of a member, thus avoiding the corporate characteristic of continuity of life. Today most state statutes have been amended to make dissolution at the option of the members and to provide that the entity will continue automatically unless a certain percentage (the default rule is a majority) of the members vote to dissolve. Again, the check-the-box regulations have rendered the concern about continuity of life unimportant as a tax matter with regard to the income tax. It should be noted, however, that transferability of interests and continuity of life continue to play a role in terms of valuation discounts available under the federal estate and gift tax, as noted immediately above. *See generally* Andrew J. Williams, *Discounting Transfer Taxes with LLCs and Family Limited Partnerships*, 13 J. Tax'n of Investments 210 (1996).

The next cases, dealing with dissolution of an LLC, demonstrate the influence of corporate law and partnership law in interpreting LLC statutes.

1. Judicial Dissolution

Haley v. Talcott

Court of Chancery of Delaware
864 A.2d 86 (2004)

Strine, Vice Chancellor.

I. Factual Background

Haley and Talcott each have a 50% interest in Matt & Greg Real Estate, LLC, a Delaware limited liability company they formed in 2003. The creation of the company, however, is only a recent event in the history between the parties.

Haley and Talcott have known each other since the 1980s . . . In 2001, Haley found the location for what would become the Redfin Grill. Talcott contributed substantial start-up money and Haley managed the Redfin Grill without drawing a salary for the first year.

The structure of the agreements between the parties forming the Redfin Grill is complex and the subject of additional litigation before this court. For reasons that are not relevant, Haley and Talcott chose to create and operate the Redfin Grill as an entity solely owned by Talcott, with Haley's rights and obligations being defined by a series of contracts. Those agreements, all dated November 30, 2001, included an Employment Agreement, a Retention Bonus Agreement, and a Side Letter Agreement (together, the "Employment Contract"), as well as an Agreement regarding an option to purchase real estate (the "Real Estate Agreement").

The Employment Contract, although structured as an agreement between an employer and an employee, makes clear that the parties were operating the business as a joint venture. . . .

The equivalent nature of the parties' contributions is further confirmed by the Real Estate Agreement. In that agreement, Talcott granted Haley the right to participate in an option to purchase the property where the Redfin Grill was situated which is located at 1111 Highway One in Bethany Beach, Delaware (the "Property").

In 2003, the parties formed Matt & Greg Real Estate, LLC to take advantage of the option to purchase the Property that was the subject of the Real Estate Agreement.

The option price was $720,000 and the new LLC took out a mortgage from County Bank in Rehoboth Beach, Delaware, for that amount, exercised the option, and obtained the deed to the Property on or about May 23, 2003. Importantly, both Haley and Talcott, individually, signed personal guaranties for the entire amount of the mortgage in order to secure the loan. The Redfin Grill continued to operate at the site, paying the LLC $6,000 per month in rent, a payment sufficient to cover the LLC's monthly obligation under the mortgage. Thus by mid-2003, the parties appeared poised to reap the fruits of their labors; unfortunately, at that point their personal relationship began to deteriorate.

. . .

On or about October 27, 2003, the conflict that had been brewing between the parties led to some kind of confrontation. As a result, Talcott sent a letter of understanding to Haley dated October 27, 2003, purporting to accept his resignation and forbidding him to enter the premises of the Redfin Grill.

Haley responded on November 3, 2003 with two separate letters from his counsel to Talcott. In the first, Haley asserts that he did not resign, and that he regarded Talcott's October 27, 2003 letter of understanding as terminating him without cause in breach of the Employment Contract. Haley goes on to express his intent to pursue legal remedies, an intent that he acted upon in the related case in this court.

In his second November 3, 2003 letter, Haley purported to take several positions expressly as a 50% member in the LLC including: 1) rejecting the new lease proposed by Talcott for the Redfin Grill; 2) voting to revoke any consent to possession by the Redfin Grill and terminating any lease by which the Redfin Grill asserts the right to possession; and 3) voting that the Property be put up for sale on the open market.

Of course, as a 50% member, Haley could not force the LLC to take action on these proposals because Talcott opposed them. As a result, the pre-existing status quo continued by virtue of the stalemate—a result that Talcott favored. The Redfin Grill's lease has expired and, as a consequence, the Redfin Grill continues to pay $6,000 per month to the LLC in a month-to-month arrangement. The $6,000 rent exceeds the LLC's required mortgage payment by $800 per month, so the situation remains stable. With only a 50% ownership interest, Haley cannot force the termination of the Redfin Grill's lease and evict the Redfin Grill as a tenant; neither can he force the sale of the Property, land that was appraised as of June 14, 2004 at $1.8 million. In short, absent intervention by this court, Haley is stuck, unless he chooses to avail himself of the exit mechanism provided in the LLC Agreement.

That exit mechanism, like judicial dissolution, would provide Haley with his share of the fair market value of the LLC, including the Property. Section 18 of the LLC Agreement provides that upon written notice of election to "quit" the company, the remaining member may elect, in writing, to purchase the departing member's interest for fair market value. If the remaining member elects to purchase the departing member's interest, the parties may agree on fair value, or have the fair value determined by three arbitrators, one chosen by each member and a third chosen by the first two arbitrators. The departing member pays the reasonable expenses of the three arbitrators. Once a fair price is determined, it may be paid in cash, or over a term if secured by: 1) a note signed by the company and personally by the remaining member; 2) a security agreement; and 3) a recorded UCC lien. Only if the remaining member fails to elect to purchase the departing member's interest is the company to be liquidated.

The LLC agreement describes additional details regarding the term and interest rate of any installment payments and defines penalty, default, and acceleration terms to be contained in the securing note. Although these details are not critical to a comparison between a contractual separation under the LLC Agreement and a judicial dissolution, they demonstrate the level of detail that the parties considered in crafting the exit mechanism. But despite this level of detail, the exit provision does not expressly provide a release from the personal guaranties that both Haley and Talcott signed to secure the mortgage on the Property. Nor does the exit provision state that any member dissatisfied with the status quo must break an impasse by exit rather than a suit for dissolution.

Rather than use the exit mechanism, Haley has simultaneously sought: 1) dissolution of the LLC; and 2) relief in an employment litigation filed against Talcott and Redfin Grill, a case also pending in this court. Haley does not view himself as being obligated by the LLC Agreement to be the one who exits; moreover, he would bear the cost of the exit mechanism and that mechanism, as will be discussed, would not release him from the guaranty. . . .

Haley has moved on since leaving the Redfin Grill in an active capacity, and now operates another restaurant in Lewes, Delaware. Despite his shift in focus, Haley continues to be interested in the Redfin Grill, and has expressed his desire to buy Talcott out of both the LLC and the Redfin Grill itself if given the opportunity. Talcott, by urging the exit remedy provided in the LLC Agreement, has expressed his desire to buy Haley out of the LLC and has no interest in selling the Redfin Grill. Haley continues to refuse to use the exit mechanism.

Pragmatically, the current impasse arises because we have two willing buyers and no willing sellers. Haley alleges that, given this practical dilemma, and his evident inability to effect his desired direction for the LLC, judicial dissolution is his only practicable remedy.

. . .

III. Legal Analysis

A. Procedural Framework

Haley alleges that pursuant to 6 Del. C. § 18-802 the court should exercise its discretion and dissolve the LLC because it is not reasonably practicable for it to continue the business of the company in conformity with the LLC Agreement. Section 18-802 provides in its entirety:

> On application by or for a member or manager the Court of Chancery may decree dissolution of a limited liability company whenever it is not reasonably practicable to carry on the business in conformity with a limited liability company agreement.

Haley argues that dissolution is required because the two 50% managers cannot agree how to best utilize the sole asset of the LLC, the Property, because no provision exists for breaking a tie in the voting interests, and because the LLC cannot take any actions, such as entering contracts, borrowing or lending money, or buying or selling property, absent a majority vote of its members. Because this circumstance resembles corporate deadlock, Haley urges that 8 Del. C. § 273 provides a relevant parallel for analysis.

Here, the key facts about the parties' ability to work together are not rationally disputable. Therefore, my decision on the motion largely turns on two legal issues: 1) if the doctrine of corporate deadlock is an appropriate analogy for the analysis of a § 18-802 claim on these facts; and 2) if so, and if action to break the stalemate is necessary to permit the LLC to function, whether, because of the contract-law foundations of the Delaware LLC Act, Haley should be relegated to the contractual exit mechanism provided in the LLC Agreement.

B. Case Law Under § 273 of the Delaware General Corporate Law ("DGCL") Provides an Appropriate Framework For Analysis

Section 18-802 of the Delaware LLC Act is a relatively recent addition to our law, and, as a result, there have been few decisions interpreting it. Nevertheless, § 18-802 has the obvious purpose of providing an avenue of relief when an LLC cannot continue to function in accordance with its chartering agreement. Thus § 18-802 plays a role for LLCs similar to the role that § 273 of the DGCL [Delaware General Corporation Law] plays for joint venture corporations with only two stockholders. When a limited liability agreement provides for the company to be governed by its members, when there are only two members, and when those members are at permanent odds, § 273 provides relevant insight into what should happen. To wit, Section 273(a) provides, in relevant part, that:

> If the stockholders of a corporation of this state, having only 2 stockholders each of whom own 50% of the stock therein, shall be engaged in a joint venture and if such stockholders shall be unable to agree upon the desirability of discontinuing such joint venture and disposing of the assets used in such venture, either stockholder may, unless otherwise provided in the certificate of incorporation of the corporation or in a written agreement between stockholders, file with the Court of Chancery a petition stating that it desires to discontinue such joint venture and to dispose of the assets used in such venture in accordance with a plan to be agreed on by both stockholders or that, if no such plan shall be agreed upon by both stockholders, the corporation be dissolved.

Section 273 essentially sets forth three pre-requisites for a judicial order of dissolution: 1) the corporation must have two 50% stockholders, 2) those stockholders must be engaged in a joint venture, and 3) they must be unable to agree upon whether to discontinue the business or how to dispose of its assets. Here, by analogy, each of the three provisions is indisputably met.

First, there is no dispute that the parties are 50% members of the LLC. . . .

Second, there is no rational doubt that the parties intended to be and are engaged in a joint venture. While the standard for establishing a joint venture has evolved over time, it has always included the circumstances presented here, where two parties "agree[d] for their mutual benefit to combine their skills, property and knowledge, actively managing the business."[43] The relationship between Haley and Talcott indicates active involvement by both parties in creating a restaurant for their mutual benefit and profit, and the Employment Contract shows that Haley was to be the "Operations Director" of the Redfin Grill, a position that, according to the Side Letter Agreement, would only be terminated if the restaurant was sold. Haley was also entitled to a 50% share of the Redfin Grill's profits. In short, Haley and Talcott were in it together for as long as they owned the restaurant, equally sharing the profits as provided in the Employment Contract.

Most importantly, Haley never agreed to be a passive investor in the LLC who would be subject to Talcott's unilateral dominion. Instead, the LLC agreement provided that: "no member/managers may, *without the agreement of a majority vote of the managers' interest*, act on behalf of the company." Acts of the company expressly include: borrowing money in the company name; using company property as collateral; binding the company to any obligation such as a guarantor or surety; selling, mortgaging or encumbering any personal or real property of the company except for business purposes for proper consideration; lending company funds; contracting for any debt except for a proper company purpose; and drawing checks on the company account in excess of $5,000. Under these terms, as a 50% member/manager, no major action of the LLC could be taken without Haley's approval. Thus, Haley is entitled to a continuing say in the operation of the LLC.

Finally, the evidence clearly supports a finding of deadlock between the parties about the business strategy and future of the LLC. Haley's second letter of November 3, 2003 expresses his desire to end the lease of the Redfin Grill and sell the Property at fair market value. The very fact that dissolution has not occurred, combined with Talcott's opposition in this lawsuit, leads inevitably to the conclusion that Talcott opposes such a disposition of the assets. Neither is Talcott's opposition surprising given his economic interest in the continued success of the Redfin Grill, success that one must assume relies, in part, on a continuing favorable lease arrangement with the LLC.

---

43. [22] *Wah Chang Smelting & Ref. Co. of America, Inc. v. Cleveland Tungsten Inc.*, 1996 WL 487941, at *6 (Del. Ch. Aug. 19, 1996). . . .

Talcott suggests that Haley has merely voluntarily removed himself from the management process and that no express disagreement has arisen. This court, however, may consider the totality of the circumstances in determining whether the parties disagree, and only a rational dispute of fact will preclude the entry of summary judgment. Contrary to Talcott's assertion, it is not, at least in a § 273 suit, necessary that the parties formally attempt to reach an agreement before coming to court. In any event, it is clear that, through counsel, the parties have made efforts to resolve this impasse.

Moreover, there is no evidentiary support for Talcott's suggestion that the parties are not at an impasse. . . .

For all these reasons, if the LLC were a corporation, there would be no question that Haley's request to dissolve the entity would be granted. But this case regards an LLC, not a corporation, and more importantly, an LLC with a detailed exit provision. That distinguishing factor must and is considered next.

C. Even Given the Contractual Emphasis of the Delaware LLC Act, the Exit Remedy Provided in the LLC Agreement is an Insufficient Alternative to Dissolution

The Delaware LLC Act is grounded on principles of freedom of contract. For that reason, the presence of a reasonable exit mechanism bears on the propriety of ordering dissolution under 6 Del. C. § 18-802. When the agreement itself provides a fair opportunity for the dissenting member who disfavors the inertial status quo to exit and receive the fair market value of her interest, it is at least arguable that the limited liability company may still proceed to operate practicably under its contractual charter because the charter itself provides an equitable way to break the impasse.

Here, that reasoning might be thought apt because Haley has already "voted" as an LLC member to sell the LLC's only asset, the Property, presumably because he knew he could not secure sole control of both the LLC and the Redfin Grill. Given that reality, so long as Haley can actually extract himself fairly, it arguably makes sense for this court to stay its hand in an LLC case and allow the contract itself to solve the problem.

Notably, reasoning of this nature has been applied in the § 273 context. Even under § 273, this court's authority to order dissolution remains discretionary and may be influenced by the particular circumstances. Talcott rightly argues that the situation here is somewhat analogous to that in *In re Delaware Bay Surgical Services* where this court declined to dissolve a corporation under § 273 in part because a mechanism existed for the repurchase of the complaining member's 50% interest.[44]

But, this matter differs from *Surgical Services* in two important respects. First, in *Surgical Services*, the respondent doctor had owned the company before admitting

---

44. [32] *In re Delaware Bay Surgical Services*, C.A. No. 2121-S (Del. Ch. Jan. 28, 2002) (resolving cross summary judgment motions).

the petitioner to his practice as a 50% stakeholder. The court found that both parties clearly intended, upon entering the contract, that if the parties ended their contractual relationship, the respondent would be the one permitted to keep the company. By contrast, no such obvious priority of interest exists here. Haley and Talcott created the LLC together and while the detailed exit provision provided in the formative LLC Agreement allows either party to leave voluntarily, it provides no insight on who should retain the LLC if both parties would prefer to buy the other out, and neither party desires to leave. In and of itself, however, this lack of priority might not be found sufficient to require dissolution, because of a case-specific fact; namely, that Haley has proposed—as a member of the LLC—that the LLC's sole asset be sold. But I need not—and do not—determine how truly distinguishing that fact is, because forcing Haley to exercise the contractual exit mechanism would not permit the LLC to proceed in a practicable way that accords with the LLC Agreement, but would instead permit Talcott to penalize Haley without express contractual authorization.[45]

Why? Because the parties agree that exit mechanism in the LLC Agreement would not relieve Haley of his obligation under the personal guaranty that he signed to secure the mortgage from County Bank. If Haley is forced to use the exit mechanism, Talcott and he both believe that Haley would still be left holding the bag on the guaranty. It is therefore not equitable to force Haley to use the exit mechanism in this circumstance. While the exit mechanism may be workable in a friendly departure when both parties cooperate to reach an adequate alternative agreement with the bank, the bank cannot be compelled to accept the removal of Haley as a personal guarantor. Thus, the exit mechanism fails as an adequate remedy for Haley because it does not equitably effect the separation of the parties. Rather, it would leave Haley with no upside potential, and no protection over the considerable downside risk that he would have to make good on any future default by the LLC (over whose operations he would have no control) to its mortgage lender. Thus here, unlike in *Surgical Services*, the parties do not, in fact, "have at their disposal a far less drastic means to resolve their personal disagreement."[46]

---

45. [35] Stated plainly and putting aside Haley's proposal to sell the Property, it is an interesting question whether the 50% member of an LLC that operates an on-going business, and who does not favor inertial policy, must exit rather than force dissolution, particularly when the cost of the exit procedure would, as here, be borne solely by him. Arguably, it is economically more efficient—absent an explicit requirement that the party disfavoring inertia exit if he is dissatisfied—to order dissolution, and allow both parties to bid as purchasers, with the assets going to the highest bidder (inside or outside) who presumably will deploy the asset to its most valuable use. It is also concomitantly arguable that if parties wish to force the co-equal member disfavoring inertia to exit rather than seek dissolution, then they should explicitly contract upfront in the LLC agreement that exit (or the triggering of a buy-sell procedure, giving incentives for the business to be retained by the member willing to pay the highest value) is the required method of breaking any later-arising stalemate.

46. [37] *In re Delaware Bay Surgical Services*, C.A. No. 2121-S, at 5 (Del. Ch. Jan. 28, 2002).

IV. Conclusion

For the reasons discussed above, I find that it is not reasonably practicable for the LLC to continue to carry on business in conformity with the LLC Agreement. The parties shall confer and, within four weeks, submit a plan for the dissolution of the LLC. The plan shall include a procedure to sell the Property owned by the LLC within a commercially reasonable time frame. Either party may, of course, bid on the Property.

It is so ordered.

R & R Capital, LLC v. Buck & Doe Run Valley Farms, LLC

Court of Chancery of Delaware
2008 Del. Ch. LEXIS 115 (Aug. 19, 2008)

Memorandum Opinion

CHANDLER, CHANCELLOR.

For Shakespeare, it may have been the play, but for a Delaware limited liability company, *the contract's the thing.*[47] Ultimately, it is the contract that compels the Court's decision in this case because it is the contract that "defines the scope, structure, and personality of limited liability companies."[48] On June 2, 2008, two New York LLCs filed a petition with this Court seeking dissolution of nine separate Delaware LLCs. The respondent Delaware LLCs, some of which have had their certificates of formation canceled by the state pursuant to 6 Del. C. § 18-1108 for failure to pay their annual taxes, have moved to dismiss the petition. That motion is based primarily on two arguments. First, with respect to two of the respondent entities, the petitioners lack standing to seek dissolution because they are neither members nor managers. For reasons explained more fully below, I conclude that this argument is meritorious, but incomplete. Consequently, I grant respondent's motion to dismiss the claims against Pandora Farms, LLC and Pandora Racing, LLC pursuant to 6 Del. C. §§ 18-802 and 18-803, but cannot dismiss the claim pursuant to 6 Del. C. § 18-805. Second, with respect to the other respondent entities, of which the petitioners are members, the respondents argue that petitioners have waived their right to seek dissolution in the respective LLC Agreements. Again, for reasons explained at length below, I conclude that this argument is meritorious and that Delaware's strong policy in favor of freedom of contract in the LLC Agreements requires such a result.

---

47. [1] *Compare* WILLIAM SHAKESPEARE, HAMLET act 1, sc. 2, ln. 604 ("the play's the thing"), *with TravelCenters of Am., LLC v. Brog*, C.A. No. 3516-CC, 2008 WL 1746987, at *1 (Del. Ch. Apr. 3, 2008) ("Limited Liability Companies are creatures of contract").

48. [2] *Fisk Ventures, LLC v. Segal*, C.A. No. 3017-CC, 2008 WL 1961156, at *1 (Del. Ch. May 7, 2008).

I. Background

The factual background of this dispute is somewhat predictable; the procedural background, however, is a veritable nightmare. Generally, the respondent entities were formed years ago with capital contributions from the Russet brothers (presumably the Rs in R & R Capital) and Linda Merritt. The bulk of the capital (over $9.7 million) was provided by the petitioners, but Merritt had the sole and exclusive power to manage the entities. These respondent entities own land and race horses. Unfortunately, the relationship between the financiers, the Russets, and their appointed manager, Merritt, has deteriorated, and, perhaps predictably, the parties have turned to the courts.

. . . .

The June 2 petition for dissolution seeks, in the alternative, the winding up and dissolution of the respondent entities or the appointment of a receiver. The petitioners allege that most of the respondent entities have had their certificates of formation canceled for failing to designate a registered agent, for failing to pay annual taxes, or for both. They further allege that Merritt's attempts to revive the cancelled certificates are ineffective as a matter of law, that Merritt has refused to provide an accounting of the canceled entities, and that Merritt—along with her "long-time boyfriend" Leonard Pelullo—has defrauded the entities and orchestrated self-dealing transactions. Neither Merritt nor Pelullo, however, is a party to this action.

II. Analysis

A. The Pandora Entities

[The court concluded that petitioners did not have standing to seek dissolution of] Pandora Racing, LLC and Pandora Farms, LLC (collectively, the "Pandora Entities"), because the relevant statutory provisions, 6 Del. C. §§ 18-802, 18-803, and 18-802, provide, "[o]n application *by or for a member or manager,* the Court of Chancery may decree dissolution of a limited liability company whenever it is not reasonably practicable to carry on the business in conformity with a limited liability company agreement."

The petitioners, however, were neither members nor managers of the Pandora Entities. The sole member of the two Pandora Entities was PDF Properties, LLC and a member of an LLC which is itself a member of another LLC has no authority to seek dissolution or the winding up of the latter LLC.

B. The Waiver Entities

Petitioners are members of the other seven respondent entities, and there is no question, therefore, that they have statutory standing to seek relief under sections 18-802, 18-803, and 18-805. Nevertheless, Buck & Doe Run Valley Farms, LLC, Grays Ferry Properties, LLC, Hope Land, LLC, Merritt Land, LLC, Unionville Land, LLC, Moore Street, LLC, and PDF Properties, LLC (collectively, the "Waiver Entities") contend that the petitioners cannot pursue this action because they have waived their rights to seek dissolution or the appointment of a liquidator.

Specifically, the Waiver Entities point to provisions of their respective LLC Agreements in which the members purported to waive these rights. The petitioners concede that the contractual language purports to effect such a waiver, but nonetheless argue that the waiver is invalid as a matter of law. Because neither Delaware's LLC Act nor its policy precludes such a waiver, and because the waiver of such rights would not leave an LLC member inequitably remediless, this Court concludes that petitioners have indeed waived these rights and grants the Waiver Entities' motion to dismiss.

1. The LLC Agreements

The seven Waiver Entities have identical LLC Agreements and each one addresses dissolution explicitly. Specifically, their Agreements limit the events that shall cause dissolution to five events:

> (i) an Event of Withdrawal of a Member . . . ; (ii) the affirmative vote of all Members; (iii) upon the sale of all or substantially all of the Company's assets; (iv) the conversion of the Company into a corporation or other Person; or (v) upon the entry of a decree of judicial dissolution under Section 18-802 of the Act.

The Agreements, however, further provide that the Members have waived the right to seek dissolution under section 18-802. The seven LLC Agreements contain the following provision:

> *Waiver of Dissolution Rights.* The Members agree that irreparable damage would occur if any member should bring an action for judicial dissolution of the Company. Accordingly each member accepts the provisions under this Agreement as such Member's sole entitlement on Dissolution of the Company and waives and renounces such Member's right to seek a court decree of dissolution or to seek the appointment by a court of a liquidator for the Company.

2. Freedom of Contract and Limited Liability Companies

As this Court has noted, "Limited Liability Companies are creatures of contract, 'designed to afford the maximum amount of freedom of contract, private ordering and flexibility to the parties involved.'"[49] . . . .

The members of the Waiver Entities obviously availed themselves of this flexibility. Their respective LLC Agreements outline-often in great detail-the governance structure the members agreed would best serve the companies. Moreover, as noted above, the LLC Agreements also provide for the dissolution of the entities. In those Agreements, the members agreed that the initiation of a dissolution action would cause "irreparable damage," and they therefore agreed to waive their rights to seek

---

49. [18] *TravelCenters of Am., LLC v. Brog*, C.A. No. 3516-CC, 2008 WL 1746987, at *1 (Del. Ch. Apr. 3, 2008) (quoting *In re Grupo Dos Chiles, LLC*, C.A. No. 1447-N, 2006 WL 668443, at *2 (Del. Ch. Mar. 10, 2006)).

dissolution or the appointment of a liquidator. To the extent this waiver is enforceable under the statute and public policy, petitioners' suit against the Waiver Entities under sections 18-802, 18-803, and 18-805 is barred by contract and must be dismissed.

3. The LLC Act Does Not Prohibit Waiver of these Rights

. . . .

Petitioners argue that certain provisions of the LLC Act are mandatory and nonwaivable. As the Supreme Court has explained, "[t]he Act can be characterized as a 'flexible statute' because it generally permits members to engage in private ordering with substantial freedom of contract to govern their relationship, provided they do not contravene any mandatory provisions of the Act."[50] Generally, the mandatory provisions of the Act are "those intended to protect third parties, not necessarily the contracting members."[51] Finally, "[i]n general, the legislature's use of 'may' connotes the voluntary, not mandatory or exclusive, set of options."[52]

Petitioners proffer a far broader rule and argue that "[s]tatutory provisions that do not contain the qualification 'unless otherwise provided in a limited liability company agreement' (or a variation thereof) are mandatory and may not be waived." Petitioners, however, offer no authority for this assertion and, in fact, authorities they cite directly contradict it. In *Elf Atochem North America, Inc. v. Jaffari*, for example, a case on which petitioners heavily rely, the Supreme Court held that a provision of the LLC Act *not* containing petitioners' magical phrase was nonetheless permissive and subject to modification. Indeed, in *Elf*, the Supreme Court explicitly noted that the "unless otherwise provided" phrase was merely one example of the means by which a court could ascertain the intent of the General Assembly. Indeed, in other provisions, the General Assembly explicitly forbids waiver. For example, the Act overtly bars members from "eliminat[ing] the implied contractual covenant of good faith and fair dealing."[53]

Sections 18-802, 18-803, and 18-805 are not mandatory provisions of the LLC Act that cannot be modified by contract. First, the Act does not expressly say that these provisions cannot be supplanted by agreement, and, in fact, section 18-803 does include the "unless otherwise provided" phrase. Second, the provisions employ permissive rather than mandatory language. Section 18-802 states that the "Court of

---

50. [29] *Elf Atochem N. Am., Inc. v. Jaffari*, 727 A.2d 286, 290 (Del. 1999).

51. [30] *Id.* at 292; *see also* 1 Larry E. Ribstein and Robert R. Keatinge, Ribstein and Keatinge on Limited Liability Companies § 4:16, 4-36 to 4-47 ("The operating agreement generally controls except to the extent that it is inconsistent with mandatory statutory provisions. Such provisions include those . . . which are intended to protect third parties."); *Id.* § 4:16, 4-43 ("If an LLC statute provides that statutory rights may be varied by an operating agreement, the statute should specify that the operating agreement does not vary statutory rights of nonparties. LLC statutes do not allow the operating agreement to vary provisions that affect third-party creditors, or provide in general terms that an operating agreement governs only rights among the members.").

52. [31] *Elf*, 727 A.2d at 296.

53. [35] 6 Del. C. § 1101(c).

Chancery *may* decree dissolution"[54] and section 18-805 states that "the Court of Chancery . . . *may* either appoint" a trustee or receiver.[55] Finally, and most importantly, none of the rights conferred by these provisions that are waived in the LLC Agreement is designed to protect third parties. This Court has recognized that third parties have no interest in dissolution under section 18-802, and section 18-805 specifically permits creditors to petition the Court for the appointment of a receiver for a canceled limited liability company. The rights of third-party creditors under section 18-805 are not affected by the LLC Agreement. In sum, the LLC Act "expressly encourages 'made-to-order' structuring of limited liability companies" and "offers explicit assurance that contractual arrangements will be given effect to the fullest permissible extent."[56] Because the waiver of a member's right to petition for dissolution or the appointment of a receiver does not violate the LLC Act and does not interfere with the rights of third parties, the waiver is valid and enforceable under the statute.

4. Public Policy Does Not Prohibit Waiver of these Rights

Finally, petitioners argue that the Court should refuse to enforce their knowing, voluntary waiver of their right to seek dissolution or the appointment of a receiver because such waivers violate the public policy of Delaware and offend notions of equity. This argument too must fail. First, as discussed throughout this Opinion and others, in treatises, and in the LLC Act itself, the public policy of Delaware with respect to limited liability companies is freedom of contract. Second, there are legitimate business reasons why a firm would want to set up its governance structure so that its members could not petition the Court for dissolution. Finally, the LLC Act provides protections that cannot be waived; this Court need not exercise its equitable discretion and disregard a negotiated agreement among sophisticated parties to allow this action to proceed.

The hunt for legislative intent with respect to Delaware's LLC Act is rather simple, because the General Assembly explicitly stated that the "policy" of the Act is "to give the maximum effect to the principle of freedom of contract and to the enforceability of limited liability company agreements."[57] . . . .

Here, the LLC Agreement is a contract between sophisticated parties. The business relationships between the individuals behind the petitioners and Lynda Merritt is extensive; clearly these were parties who knew how to make use of the law of alternative entities. The mere fact that the business relationship has now soured cannot justify the petitioners' attempt to disregard the agreement they made. Therefore, contrary to petitioners' argument that Delaware's public policy will not

---

54. [36] 6 Del. C. § 18-802 (emphasis added).

55. [37] 6 Del. C. § 18-805 (emphasis added).

56. [39] Robert L. Symonds, Jr. & Matthew J. O'Toole, Symonds & O'Toole On Delaware Limited Liability Companies § 1.03[A][1] (2007).

57. [40] 6 Del. C. § 18-1101(b).

countenance their unambiguous contractual waiver, the state's policy mandates that this Court respect and enforce the parties' agreement.

In addition to Delaware's general policy promoting the freedom of contract, there are legitimate business reasons why members of a limited liability company may wish to waive their right to seek dissolution or the appointment of a receiver. For example, it is common for lenders to deem in loan agreements with limited liability companies that the filing of a petition for judicial dissolution will constitute a noncurable event of default. In such instances, it is necessary for all members to prospectively agree to waive their rights to judicial dissolution to protect the limited liability company. Otherwise, a disgruntled member could push the limited liability company into default on all of its outstanding loans simply by filing a petition with this Court. In fact, one of the petitioners here, R & R Capital, LLC, has acted as a lender to some of the Waiver Entities and included such a provision in its loan agreement with respondent Unionville Land, LLC.

Finally, petitioners' plea to this Court's sense of equity is misplaced. The LLC Act does not abandon petitioners with no recourse as they "sit idly by while Merritt (the manager) seeks to continue operating seven entities that have had their certificates of formation canceled and two entities whose narrow purposes have been fulfilled."[58] Instead, the LLC Act preserves the implied covenant of good faith and fair dealing.[59] The petition filed is replete with allegations about the unbecoming conduct of Merritt, and petitioners' brief opposing the motion to dismiss likewise criticizes her. Petitioners, however, have not named Merritt as a party in this action. Although, fairly construed, the petition may allege a breach of the implied covenant, the petitioners unambiguously have failed to state a claim upon which relief can be granted because they have not named the alleged bad-faith actor in their petition. It is the unwaivable protection of the implied covenant that allows the vast majority of the remainder of the LLC Act to be so flexible. There is no threat to equity in allowing members to waive their right to seek dissolution, because there is no chance that some members will be trapped in a limited liability company at the mercy of others acting unfairly and in bad faith.

III. Conclusion

When parties wish to launch a new enterprise, the form of the limited liability company offers a highly customizable vehicle in which to do so. The flexibility of such an entity springs from its roots in contract; the parties have "the broadest possible discretion" to set the structure of the limited liability company.[60] ... The allure of the limited liability company, however, would be eviscerated if the parties could simply petition this court to renegotiate their agreements when relationships sour. Here, the sophisticated members of the seven Waiver Entities knowingly,

58. [48] Petitioners' Answering Br. at 11.
59. [49] *See* 6 Del. C. § 1101(c).
60. [51] *Elf Atochem N. Am., Inc. v. Jaffari*, 727 A.2d 286, 291 (Del. 1999).

voluntarily, and unambiguously waived their rights to petition this Court for dissolution or the appointment of a receiver under the LLC Act. This waiver is permissible and enforceable because it contravenes neither the Act itself nor the public policy of the state. Moreover, with respect to the two other respondent entities-the Pandora Entities-the petitioners lack statutory standing to seek dissolution or the winding up of the entities.

These parties have cases pending in both state and federal courts in Delaware, Pennsylvania, and New York. These parties, however, originally came together and negotiated a series of agreements that led to the nine entities presently before the Court; perhaps the most prudent resolution to their problems is once again negotiation-a negotiated settlement. With Shakespeare this Opinion began, and with Shakespeare it too shall end:

> Recall—lest another court these parties try—"Our remedies oft in ourselves do lie."[61]

Notes

1. Section 10.1 of the operating agreement in *R & R Capital* provides that one means by which dissolution of the limited liability company will occur is the "entry of a decree of judicial dissolution under Section 18-802 of the Act." Section 13.1 of the operating agreement, however, appears to prohibit members from seeking the entry of such a decree. Can these two provisions of the operating agreement be squared? If not, how should a court deal with this conflict?

2. Depending on the LLC statute in question, judicial dissolution is available under various circumstances, often similar to the corporate grounds, as suggested in *Haley*, and the grounds listed in limited partnership statutes. A common provision in these statutes for judicial dissolution arises when, in the context of a limited liability company, a member demonstrates that the conduct of another member makes it "not reasonably practicable to carry on the [limited liability] company's business in conformity with the articles of organization and operating agreement." *See, e.g.,* ULLCA §801(4)(b). In *Horning v. Horning Construction, LLC*, 816 N.Y.S.2d 877 (Sup. Ct. 2006), the plaintiff, who had a successful construction business, started a limited liability company and brought in two former employees as equal members. The plaintiff was unhappy with this arrangement. He complained that his co-members did not live-up to their responsibilities and the parties never agreed to an operating agreement. These and other disputes motivated plaintiff to seek a buyout from the other members and, when that failed, dissolution of the company using the "not reasonably practicable" provision. The court refused to dissolve the limited liability company, noting that the statutory provision sets a "stringent standard" for those seeking to invoke it, a standard that plaintiff failed to satisfy. In short, judicial

---

61. [55] William Shakespeare, All'S Well That Ends Well act 1, sc. 1, ln. 231.

dissolution, the court said, is not a substitute for an exit provision that could have been provided in the operating agreement.

A more typical example where the court did order dissolution is *Venture Sales, LLC v. Perkins*, 86 So.3d 910, 916 (Miss. 2012). The LLC was formed in 2000 to develop raw land that the parties contributed to the LLC. For various reasons, no development had taken place by 2010, when one of the members sought judicial dissolution. The trial court concluded that it was not reasonably practicable to carry on the business of the LLC in conformity with its articles of organization or operating agreement and, therefore, dissolution was appropriate under the Mississippi LLC act. The Mississippi Supreme Court agreed, noting that because the property remained undeveloped for 10 years and the defendants presented no evidence that development would occur within the foreseeable future, the LLC could not "meet the purpose for which it was formed." What is noteworthy is that the courts did not take a theoretical and abstract perspective as to the meaning of "reasonably practicable" and opted instead to determine whether it was likely that the LLC would achieve its purpose.

The Delaware Chancery Court has decided a few cases recently interpreting the Delaware act containing a similar provision. In *Fisk Ventures, LLC v. Segal*, 2009 Del. Ch. LEXIS 7 (Jan. 13, 2009), the court set forth three factual scenarios to consider under this provision: "1) whether the members' vote is deadlocked at the Board level; 2) whether there exists a mechanism within the operating agreement to resolve this deadlock; and 3) whether there is still a business to operate based on the company's financial condition." In applying these factors in a subsequent case, the court noted that "the relevant inquiry is not whether the Company cannot possibly continue its business in accord with the Operating Agreement, but rather whether to do so would be reasonably practicable." *Lola Cars Int'l Ltd. v. Krohn Racing, Lola Cars Intern. Ltd. v. Krohn Racing, LLC*, 2009 Del. Ch. LEXIS 193 (Nov. 12, 2009) (allegations of deadlock on the board of an LLC states claim for judicial dissolution).

3. Another common ground for judicial dissolution, borrowed from corporate codes, is "deadlock." The Kansas limited liability company act, for instance, provides that a member owning at least 25 percent of the interests of the LLC can obtain judicial dissolution upon a showing that "the business of the limited liability company is suffering or is threatened with irreparable injury because the members of a limited liability company, or the managers of a limited liability company having more than one manager, are so deadlocked respecting the management of the affairs of the limited liability company that the requisite vote for action cannot be obtained and the members are unable to terminate such deadlock. . . ." K.S.A. 17-76, 117.

4. The Chancellor's opinion in the *R & R Capital* case is another example of the penchant of the Delaware courts to emphasize and honor freedom of contract. The court hedges a bit, however, noting how the petitioners are not left without a remedy and that, as a business matter, the waiver of the right to seek dissolution contained in the operating agreement makes perfect sense. Put differently, this was not a difficult case. A more difficult fact situation presented itself in the following case, *In* *re Carlisle*, a portion of which is covered above. Recall that in the excerpted portion of the case in Section F.4, *supra*, the Delaware Chancery Court carefully considered whether an assignee of a membership interest became a member itself. The Court decided that it did not and, therefore, the assignee lacked standing to seek judicial dissolution under the Delaware LLC Act. The Court went on to consider whether it had the equitable power to afford the assignee standing. Its analysis follows below.

In re Carlisle Etcetera LLC
Court of Chancery of Delaware
114 A.3d 592 (2015)

LASTER, Vice Chancellor

[For a summary of the facts of this case and the court's disposition of the plaintiffs' argument that they had standing to seek dissolution of the LLC under the Delaware LLC Act or the operating agreement, see Section F.4.]

. . . .

C. Equitable Standing To Seek Dissolution

James argues that because neither WU Parent nor WU Sub can seek statutory dissolution under Section 18–802, this case must be dismissed. In my view, James errs in contending that Section 18–802 is the exclusive extra-contractual means of obtaining dissolution of an LLC. Under the facts of this case, WU Sub has standing to seek dissolution in equity.

"[T]his Court, as a court of equity, has the power to order the dissolution of a solvent company and appoint a receiver to administer the winding up of those assets." Weir v. JMACK, Inc., 2008 WL 4379592, at *2 (Del. Ch. Sept. 23, 2008). Justice Story described the "power to dissolve the partnership during the term for which it is stipulated" as one of the "strongest cases to illustrate the beneficial operation of the jurisdiction" of a court of equity. 2 Joseph Story, Commentaries on Equity Jurisprudence §915 (W.H. Lyon, Jr. ed., 14th ed. 1918) [hereinafter Story]. The implementation of a dissolution decree would require the appointment of a receiver, which is likewise an equitable remedy that forms part of this court's equitable powers. Courts of equity have long had the power to appoint receivers in cases "where the partners themselves are wholly unable to agree as to the management of the property and the settlement of the partnership affairs." 4 John Norton Pomeroy, Equity Jurisprudence §1333(1) (Spencer W. Symons ed., 5th ed. 1941) [hereinafter Pomeroy]. Justice Story viewed the appointment of a receiver favorably in suits for dissolution when "one [partner] has wrongfully excluded the other from participation" in the management of the business. 2 Story §914 n. 1.

For Section 18–802 to provide the exclusive method of dissolving an LLC, it would have to divest this court of a significant aspect of its traditional equitable jurisdiction. Section 18–802 does not state that it establishes an exclusive means to obtain dissolution, nor does it contain language overriding this court's equitable authority. To the contrary, the LLC Act elsewhere recognizes that equity backstops the LLC structure by providing generally that "the rules of law and equity" shall govern in "any case not provided for in this chapter." 6 Del. C. § 18–1104.

If Section 18–802 did purport to establish an exclusive means to obtain dissolution and override a significant portion of this court's traditional equitable jurisdiction, then the validity of that aspect of the provision would raise serious constitutional questions. . . .

Although this court's equitable jurisdiction is measured by the "the general equity jurisdiction of the High Court of Chancery of Great Britain as it existed prior to the separation of the colonies," the Delaware Supreme Court has recognized that the scope of that jurisdiction is not limited by the extent of British scientific, technological, and legal knowledge at the time of the handover. "Historically, equity jurisdiction 'has taken its shape and its substance from the perceived inadequacies of the common law and the changing demands of a developing nation.'" Schoon v. Smith, 953 A.2d 196, 204 (Del.2008) (quoting Donald J. Wolfe, Jr. & Michael A. Pittenger, Corporate and Commercial Practice in the Delaware Court Of Chancery § 2–2[a], at 2–2 (2006)). "It cannot be said too forcefully that the general powers of the Court of Chancery refers to that complete system of equity as administered by the High Court of Chancery of Great Britain." Glanding v. Indus. Trust Co., 45 A.2d 553, 558–59 (Del.1945) (emphasis added). It is the "complete system" of equity that this court inherited and administers, not the temporally specific subject matter of eighteenth century cases.

To stress this point, the Delaware Supreme Court in Schoon quoted from a wide range of sources that demonstrate the continuing and evolving role of equity. The high court started with Pomeroy:

> [T]he Chancellor always has had, and always must have, a certain power and freedom of action, not possessed by the courts of law, of adapting the doctrines which he administers. He can extend those doctrines to new relations, and shape his remedies to new circumstances, if the relations and circumstances come within the principles of equity, where a court of law in analogous cases would be powerless to give any relief.

Id. at 204–205 (quoting 1 Pomeroy § 60). The Schoon court similarly quoted from Justice Story, who explained that equity "has an expansive power, to meet new exigencies; and the sole question, applicable to the point of jurisdiction, must from time to time be[ ] whether such rights and wrongs do exist, and whether the remedies [therefore] in other courts, and especially in the courts of common law, are full, and adequate to redress." Id. (quoting 1 Story § 53). The high court also cited McClintock on Equity for the proposition that "the chancellors could adapt their system to meet changing needs without resorting to the fiction that they were merely interpreting and applying former rules, but the tendency to follow the path laid out by former chancellors was strong." Id. at 205 (quoting McClintock on Equity § 4 (2d ed. 1948)). . . .

Given the weight of these authorities, the extensive discussion in Schoon, and the decisions in DuPont and Glanding, I cannot accept the contention that because the nascent practice of entity law as it existed at the time of the colonies' separation had not yet envisioned LLCs, they fall outside the domain of equity. Decisions addressing the dissolution of LLCs have recognized the continuing role of equity. Most notably, in Haley [reproduced above], this court reviewed a contractual exit mechanism in a two-member operating agreement and determined that it did not provide the exiting member with "an adequate remedy." 864 A.2d at 88. Chief Justice Strine, writing as a Vice Chancellor, explained that the existence of an exit mechanism was not sufficient; it had to be a "reasonable exit mechanism" that provided "a fair opportunity for the dissenting member who disfavors the inertial status quo to exit." Id. at 96. On the facts of the case, the Chief Justice found that it was "not equitable to force [the locked-out member] to use the exit mechanism" and ordered dissolution. Id. at 98.

This case also differs from Bax [reproduced in Section F.2.a, above], where the Delaware Supreme Court affirmed a decision of this court holding that creditors of an insolvent LLC lacked standing to sue derivatively under Section 18–1002 of the LLC Act. On appeal, the plaintiff-appellant contended that the LLC Act could not deprive the Court of Chancery of jurisdiction to recognize a creditor's standing in equity to sue derivatively. The Delaware Supreme Court rejected that argument for a series of reasons, culminating in its recognition that creditors of an LLC have ample remedies available at law. Bax, 28 A.3d at 1046. As Chief Justice Strine had explained while a member of this court, the premise of granting creditors equitable standing to sue derivatively is not unproblematic. Arguably, it involves using the law of fiduciary duty to fill gaps that do not exist. Creditors are often protected by strong covenants, liens on assets, and other negotiated contractual protections. The implied covenant of good faith and fair dealing also protects creditors. So does the law of fraudulent conveyance. With these protections, when creditors are unable to prove that a corporation or its directors breached any of the specific legal duties owed to them, one would think that the conceptual room for concluding that the creditors were somehow, nevertheless, injured by inequitable conduct would be extremely small, if extant. . . .

This court has held that the parties to an LLC agreement can waive by contract the right to seek statutory dissolution under Section 18–802. See R & R Capital, LLC v. Buck & Doe Run Valley Farms, LLC, 2008 WL 3846318, *4 (Del. Ch. Aug. 19, 2008). In my view, the ability to waive dissolution under Section 18–802 does not extend to a party's standing to seek dissolution in equity.

In concluding that parties to an LLC agreement could waive the right to seek dissolution under Section 18–802, the R & R Capital decision relied heavily on arguments by commentators to the effect that a Delaware LLC should be viewed as a purely contractual entity to which principles of equity (including fiduciary duties) do not apply. Reasonable minds could disagree about that proposition. But whatever one's personal thoughts might have been on the matter, the General Assembly in 2013 adopted an amendment to the LLC Act inconsistent with the purely contractarian view.[62]

Of particular relevance to dissolution, the purely contractarian view discounts core attributes of the LLC that only the sovereign can authorize, such as its separate legal existence, potentially perpetual life, and limited liability for its members. See 6 Del. C. §§ 18–201, 18–303. To my mind, when a sovereign makes available an entity with attributes that contracting parties cannot grant themselves by agreement, the entity is not purely contractual. Because the entity has taken advantage of benefits that the sovereign has provided, the sovereign retains an interest in that entity. That interest in turn calls for preserving the ability of the sovereign's courts to oversee and, if necessary, dissolve the entity. Put more directly, an LLC agreement is not an exclusively private contract among its members precisely because the LLC has powers that only the State of Delaware can confer. Those powers affect the rights of third parties, who at a minimum must take into account the LLC's separate legal existence and its members' limited liability shield. Just as LLCs are not purely private entities, dissolution is not a purely private affair. It involves third party claims, which have priority in the dissolution process. See id. §§ 18–803, 18–804 (describing winding up and priorities for distribution of assets). Because an LLC takes advantage of benefits that the State of Delaware provides, and because dissolution is not an exclusively private matter, the State of Delaware retains an interest in having the Court of Chancery available, when equity demands, to hear a petition to dissolve an LLC.

This approach finds support in Huatuco v. Satellite Healthcare and Satellite Dialysis of Tracy, LLC, 2013 WL 6460898 (Del. Ch. Dec. 9, 2013), aff'd, 93 A.3d 654 (Del.2014) (ORDER). The Huatuco opinion followed R & R Capital in holding that the members of an LLC had waived their right to seek statutory dissolution under Section 18-802 when they "specifically considered, and addressed, dissolution and dissolution rights." Id. at *5. But the Huatuco court reserved decision on "[w]hether the parties may, by contract, divest this Court of its authority to order a dissolution in all circumstances, even where it appears manifest that equity so requires—leaving, for instance, irreconcilable members locked away together forever like some alternative entity version of Sartre's Huis Clos." Id. at *1 n. 2. The Huatuco court did not have to answer that question because "considerations fundamental to equity [were] absent." Id.

This case presents the type of situation anticipated in Huatuco where equity should intervene. If the opportunities for dissolution are limited to Section 18-802 and the specific terms of the Initial LLC Agreement, then dissolution is not an

---

62. [8] See H.B. 126, 147th Gen. Assemb. (Del. 2013) (amending 6 Del. C. § 18–1104 to provide that "In any case not provided for in this chapter, the rules of law and equity, including the rules of law and equity relating to fiduciary duties and the law merchant, shall govern"); Miller, supra, at 314 (noting that the debate over the purely contractual status of LLCs "was resolved by legislation that was signed into law on June 30, 2013").

option. WU Parent and WU Sub lack standing to seek it, and James does not want it. The Company will continue, with Royal Spirit locked-in as a silent and powerless passive investor.

That situation is contrary to the bargain the parties struck. WU Parent and James formed the Company as equal business partners. They contributed equal amounts of capital and brought comparable expertise, with one side acting as a major supplier and the other as a day-to-day manager. Desiring to seize the opportunity to buy Connaught's assets quickly, they agreed to start with a basic operating agreement in which they committed to negotiate a more detailed replacement agreement. As reflected by the Proposed LLC Agreement, the terms of that more detailed agreement contemplate that an affiliate transfer from WU Parent to WU Sub would result in the automatic admission of WU Sub as a substitute member. In other words, had the parties finalized the Proposed LLC Agreement, or acted in accordance with their agreement in principle, then WU Sub would be a member and have standing to seek dissolution under Section 18-802. Based on the allegations of the petition, WU Parent engaged in the affiliate transfer with James' knowledge and participation, and James subsequently treated WU Sub as a member.

"Equity always attempts to . . . ascertain, uphold, and enforce rights and duties which spring from the real relations of parties." 2 Pomeroy § 378 (emphasis in original). "[E]quity regards substance rather than form." Monroe Park v. Metro. Life Ins. Co., 457 A.2d 734, 737 (Del.1983). Equity also "regards that as done which in good conscience ought to be done." Id. The real relationship between the parties is a joint venture in which they are equal participants. Neither party intended to be a "passive investor . . . subject to [the other party's] unilateral dominion." Haley, 864 A.2d at 95. In good conscience, WU Sub should be regarded as a member with the power to seek dissolution.

Likewise, the "real relations" of the parties point to a scenario warranting dissolution. For a time, both sides recognized the need to go their separate ways. James only changed its mind because of its fortuitous position as the entity's de facto manager. But that reality does not make the status quo a satisfactory alternative. "Although the LLC is technically functioning at this point, this operation is purely a residual, inertial status quo that just happens to exclusively benefit one of the 50% members. . . ." Id. at 96. The Initial LLC Agreement made the Board the singular manager of the Company. Because its four members are deadlocked, the duly authorized manager of the Company cannot exercise its statutory and contractual authority or carry out its obligation to manage and direct the business and affairs of the entity. Brubaker may be managing the Company because of the power vacuum created by the deadlock, but Brubaker is not the Board. Under the prevailing state of affairs, the Company is operating contrary to the governance structure set forth in its constitutive agreement.

When considering whether holders of equity in other entities can pursue equitable causes of action, despite their lack of formal record ownership status, this court has relied on the substance of the relationship and permitted the suits to proceed.

The same reasoning employed by Chancellor Seitz in Burry Biscuit supports recognizing an assignee's standing to sue in equity for dissolution: "Here we have an equitable owner . . . suing in a court of equity," asserting a cause of action that "must in this state be brought in equity," and in a suit that "does involve an equitable remedy." 60 A.2d at 112. Consequently, I believe that WU Sub has standing in equity, as an assignee, to seek dissolution of the Company under the facts alleged in the petition.

If *In re Carlisle* stands as good law in Delaware (and the case was not appealed to the Delaware Supreme Court), one might argue that Delaware LLCs are not quite "contractual entities," an argument that Vice Chancellor Laster seemed to embrace in this decision. As you read the following case, consider whether the Ohio Supreme Court is relying on equitable principles or the statute.

Holdeman v. Epperson

Supreme Court of Ohio
857 N.E.2d 583 (2006)

LANZINGER, J.

In this case, accepted on a discretionary appeal, we are asked to determine what rights an executor of the estate of a deceased member of a limited liability company is entitled to exercise. Louise Epperson and Daniel Holdeman formed Holdeman-Eros, L.L.C. on May 3, 2002. They also executed an operating agreement that set forth their respective ownership interests and management authority for the business. Pursuant to the agreement, Daniel Holdeman was a member and director and held a 51 percent interest in the company and Louise Epperson, the other member and director, held a 49 percent interest in the company.

Shortly after the company was formed, Holdeman died, and his widow, Jo Ann Holdeman, was appointed executor of his estate. As the executor, pursuant to Section 12 of the operating agreement, Mrs. Holdeman became Holdeman's successor-in-interest. Under the agreement's terms, a successor-in-interest shall be admitted as a member only upon the written consent of the company. When Mrs. Holdeman asked for consent to become a member, Epperson refused.

Mrs. Holdeman then filed a declaratory-judgment action against Epperson and the company, requesting a declaration that she should be given all the rights of a member during the estate's administration. Epperson and the company counterclaimed, seeking a declaration that because Holdeman ceased to be a member of the company when he died, Mrs. Holdeman, though the assignee of his membership interest, was not a member.

The Clark County Court of Common Pleas awarded a declaratory judgment to Mrs. Holdeman, holding that she, as executor of her husband's estate and successor-in-interest, should be accorded all rights as a member of the company, including, but not limited to, the full rights of profits and distributions, full access to all business records, and full rights of operation and control of the company "with due regard for and with the purpose of timely administering the estate."

The Second District Court of Appeals affirmed the judgment of the trial court, stating that as R.C. 1705.21(A) conflicts with the operating agreement's provisions dealing with the death of a member, the statute takes precedence. In concluding that "Mrs. Holdeman is entitled to exercise all the member rights that Daniel Holdeman possessed before his death," the court of appeals stressed that Mrs. Holdeman could exercise her member rights only during the period of administration of the estate, for purposes of settling the estate.

The proposition as framed by the appellants is whether "[t]he legal representative of a withdrawing member of a limited liability company has the legal rights of an assignee and not a member." Restated, the principal issue in this case is the extent to which an executor of an estate of a deceased member may exercise "member" rights in a limited liability company.

The appellants, Epperson and the company, argue that Mrs. Holdeman, as a successor-in-interest and executor, has only the legal rights as an assignee of the economic interest of the member in the company, rather than the full rights of a member. They contend that the operating agreement does not conflict with the statute and thus the operating agreement controls the outcome. Appellee, Mrs. Holdeman, asserts that R.C. 1705.21(A) conflicts with and therefore overrides the provisions of the operating agreement. Both the statute and operating agreement must be examined.

The Operating Agreement

The operating agreement of the company states that the company is a "member-managed limited liability company. All of the authority of the Company shall be exercised by or under the Company's Board of Directors, which shall consist of all of the Members of the Company." The board of directors consisted of Epperson and Daniel Holdeman. Because Daniel Holdeman owned the larger percentage interest in the company, he was the managing member of the company and presided over the meetings of the board of directors. The term "member" is not specifically defined in the operating agreement.

Section 10 deals with restrictions on transfer of a member's interest. Section 10.1 states, "Except as specifically provided otherwise in this Operating Agreement, no Member shall assign or otherwise transfer all or any part of any interest in the Company, or withdraw from the Company, without the consent of a Majority-in-Interest (other than the Member attempting to transfer the interest)." If a member seeks to assign his or her interest, the assignee may be admitted as a member only after complying with certain requirements, including that "[t]he Company shall consent in writing to the admission of the assignee as a Member, which consent may be withheld for any reason."

The provision of specific interest in resolving the issue before us is Section 11, entitled "Death of a Member." This section states that when a member dies, the successor-in-interest of the deceased member "shall immediately succeed to the interest of such member in the Company. Such Successor-in-Interest shall not become a Member of the Company unless admitted as a Member in accordance with Section 10 of this Agreement." A successor-in-interest is defined in Section 12 as "such person as the Member shall, from time to time, have designated in a notice to the Company. . . . In the event that a Member has failed to designate a Successor in Interest, or if the person designated is not then living or for any reason renounces, disclaims or is unable to succeed to such interest, the Successor in Interest shall be the executor or administrator of the deceased Member's estate, who shall hold or distribute such interest in accordance with applicable fiduciary law." The section also directs that a successor-in-interest shall not become a full member unless the company consents.

Since Daniel Holdeman never executed a notice to the company designating a successor-in-interest, his widow, as executor of his estate, automatically became the successor-in-interest pursuant to Section 12. Mrs. Holdeman could not become a full member of the company without consent from the company, which the company declined to give. Thus, the language of the operating agreement implicitly restricted Mrs. Holdeman to a membership interest rather than the status of a member of the company.

Typically, once an operating agreement is reviewed and it appears that the terms of the contract dictate the status of the parties, the inquiry ends because "courts presume that the intent of the parties to a contract resides in language they chose to employ in the agreement." *Shifrin v. Forest City Ents., Inc.* (1992), 64 Ohio St.3d 635, 638, 597 N.E.2d 499. Furthermore, when "the terms in a contract are unambiguous, courts will not in effect create a new contract by finding an intent not expressed in the clear language employed by the parties." Id. Nevertheless, in this case, both the trial court and the court of appeals examined R.C. Chapter 1705 and found that the General Assembly has preempted this area by enacting R.C. 1705.21(A).

Statutory Provisions

R.C. 1705.21(A) provides, "If a member who is an individual dies or is adjudged an incompetent, his executor, administrator, guardian, or other legal representative may exercise all of his rights as a member for the purpose of settling his estate or administering his property, including any authority that he had to give an assignee the right to become a member."

In examining this statute, both the trial court and appellate court looked at the definitions of "member" and "membership interest" set forth in the Limited Liability Company Act, R.C. Chapter 1705. "Member" is defined as a "person whose name appears on the records of the limited liability company as the owner of a membership interest in that company." R.C. 1705.01(G). A "membership interest" is defined as "a member's share of the profits and losses of a limited liability company and the right to receive distributions from that company." R.C. 1705.01(H).

The terms are distinguishable in that a "member" possesses management rights, and one holding merely a "membership interest" possesses limited, economic rights. R.C. 1705.22 gives members the right to obtain "[t]rue and full information" regarding the status of the business and financial condition of the company, while R.C. 1705.18 limits the assignee of a membership interest to receiving profits, losses, and allocations of the company and specifically directs that the assignee is not "to become or to exercise any rights of a member."

The appellants contend that the company's operating agreement explicitly limits a member's successor-in-interest to possession of an economic interest in the company unless consent is given. Nevertheless, while it is true that the operating agreement restricts Mrs. Holdeman as the successor-in-interest to economic rights only, R.C. 1705.21(A) expressly grants the executor of an estate the right to exercise "*all of [the decedent's] rights as a member* for the purposes of settling his estate." (Emphasis added.)

Although the operating agreement seems inconsistent with the statute, Epperson and the company assert that R.C. Chapter 1705, read in its entirety, does not conflict with the terms of the operating agreement, because the General Assembly intended to limit an executor to the exercise of economic rights that the decedent held at death. They also state that other sections of R.C. Chapter 1705 considered in conjunction with R.C. 1705.21(A) show that the General Assembly did not intend to give an executor the rights of a member. They point out that under R.C. 1705.15, a member ceases to be a member upon an event of withdrawal, and death is one of the listed events. R.C. 1705.15(E). R.C. 1705.18 states that an assignee of a membership interest is not entitled to exercise the rights of a member, and R.C. 1705.20 provides the procedures by which an assignee can become a member of a limited liability company. Appellants assert that these sections plainly show that on his death, Holdeman withdrew from the company. He therefore had retained only the membership rights of an assignee, and Mrs. Holdeman is entitled to exercise only those rights.

Statutory Precedence

We have held, "It is elementary that no valid contract may be made contrary to statute, and that valid, applicable statutory provisions are parts of every contract." *Bell v. N. Ohio Tel. Co.* (1948), 149 Ohio St. 157, 158, 36 O.O. 501, 78 N.E.2d 42. This maxim is codified in R.C. Chapter 1705. R.C. 1705.04(A) sets forth the requirements for a company's articles of organization. Besides setting forth the name of the company and the period of its duration, the articles of organization can include any other provisions "that are not inconsistent with applicable law." As a result, to the extent the operating agreement is in conflict with the statute, the statute takes precedence.

The statutory provisions that Epperson and the company rely upon, R.C. 1705.15, 1705.18, and 1705.20, contain the limiting words, "[u]nless," "if," or "except as otherwise provided in the operating agreement." They all discuss in general terms the rights of assignees of membership interests. These sections do not appear to be inconsistent with the operating agreement.

R.C. 1705.21(A), on the other hand, specifically sets forth the rights of legal representatives for a deceased member and grants the executor "all of [the deceased's] rights as a member for the purpose of settling his estate or administering his property." Because this section does not state "except as otherwise provided in the operating agreement," we can infer that the General Assembly did not intend R.C. 1705.21(A) to be restricted by contrary language within an operating agreement.

Furthermore, as the court of appeals so aptly remarked, "R.C. 1705.21(A) refers to member rights in the past tense. In this regard, the statute specifically says that an executor may exercise all the decedent's rights as a member, 'including any authority he [the decedent] *had* to give an assignee the right to become a member.' * * * If the legislature intended to restrict executors to member rights that a decedent possesses after death, the legislature would have used the present tense. In such a situation, the legislature would have said that executors may exercise a decedent's rights, including the authority the decedent 'has' to give assignees the right to become members. However, this is not the language the legislature used." (Emphasis and bracketed material added by the court of appeals.) *Holdeman*, 107 Ohio St.3d 1681, 2005-Ohio-6480, 839 N.E.2d 402, ¶ 29.

In enacting R.C. 1705.21(A), the General Assembly ensured that the legal representative of a decedent's estate has the ability to carry out an executor's fiduciary obligations to the estate's beneficiaries. The membership rights granted are limited in time and in purpose for settlement of the estate.

Accordingly, we affirm the judgment of the Clark County Court of Appeals and hold that an executor of the estate of a deceased member of a limited liability company has all rights that the member had prior to death, for the limited purpose of settling the member's estate or administering his property.

Judgment affirmed.

MOYER, C.J., RESNICK, PFEIFER and O'CONNOR, JJ., concur.

LUNDBERG STRATTON and O'DONNELL, JJ., dissent.

LUNDBERG STRATTON, J., dissenting.

I respectfully dissent. I believe that in enacting R.C. 1705.21, the General Assembly simply intended to clarify what rights an executor is entitled to exercise in situations that the operating agreement may not have addressed. Any broader interpretation flies in the face of limited-liability operating agreements. If the operating agreement already defines the rights of the parties upon a member's death, then no statute can interfere with those contract rights. Therefore, I would reverse the judgment of the court of appeals and hold that the operating agreement of a limited liability company controls the relationship of the remaining members and the executor.

In this case, Epperson owned a 49 percent interest in Holdeman-Eros, L.L.C., and the decedent owned a 51 percent interest. Thus, in his capacity as the majority member, the decedent had been the managing member and presided over meetings of the board of directors. Through the majority's interpretation, Mrs. Holdeman, who was never intended by Epperson or the decedent to become a controlling member of the company, effectively becomes a majority member and presumably is permitted to exercise all the rights of a majority member, including presiding over meetings of the board of directors and exercising her majority vote to control the future course of the company. I do not believe that this result was intended by the General Assembly in enacting R.C. Chapter 1705.

I believe that the majority's interpretation of R.C. 1705.21(A) is contrary to the express language contained in other sections of R.C. Chapter 1705, which delineates the conditions under which one may exercise the right to participate in the management of a limited liability company. See R.C. 1705.12, 1705.14, 1705.15, 1705.18, and 1705.20. Interpreting R.C. 1705.21(A) in pari materia with the remaining sections of R.C. Chapter 1705 mandates the conclusion that an executor has only the rights of an assignee of a member and not the full rights of a member unless the operating agreement provides otherwise.

For example, R.C. 1705.15(E) addresses the effect of the death of a member:

> "Except as approved by the specific written consent of all members at the time, *a person ceases to be a member of a limited liability company upon the occurrence of any of the following events of withdrawal:*
>
>   . . . .
>
> "(E) Unless otherwise provided in writing in the operating agreement, *a member who is an individual dies*, or is adjudicated an incompetent." (Emphasis added.)

Thus, as of the date of his death, the decedent is considered by statute to have withdrawn from the company and to have lost his membership status.

In the event that, unlike here, no operating agreement exists, I agree that pursuant to R.C. 1705.21(A), the executor of an estate of a deceased member of a limited liability company has all rights that the member had prior to death, "for the limited purpose of settling the member's estate or administering his property." But by merely reciting the language of the statute, the majority fails to determine the actual rights of an executor in this situation and therefore fails to delineate the full effect of exercising those rights.

If R.C. 1705.21(A) controls over the operating agreement, then the parties need guidance as to the last phrase of the statute, "for the purpose of settling [the member's] estate or administering his property." Does this language mean merely collecting assets, assessing value, and determining the amount due the estate, which are essentially similar to the economic rights as an assignee and are duties of an executor? Or can the executor, especially if the decedent was a member who had majority control, make decisions that go to the heart of the company's operations, such as changing the direction of the business, hiring or firing other employees, and suing other parties, all under the guise of "administering his property"? After all, under the majority's interpretation, the executor is now a majority member of the board with authority to control the company, even though the executor may be unqualified for the task.

I believe that by failing to clarify the statutory language, we duck the real controversy in this case, which is what actions are allowed in the executor's role of settling the estate of a deceased member of a limited liability company. We give no guidance to the executor in this situation, and in essence by assigning full membership rights to the executor, we give our blessing to any actions that she might take. I believe that we should define the statutory phrase "settling the member's estate or administering his property" as taking only those actions necessary to collect, evaluate, and distribute the assets due the estate, which is, effectively, fulfilling the duties of an executor.

. . . .

O'DONNELL, J., concurs in the foregoing dissenting opinion.

2. Winding Up

Hurwitz v. Padden

Court of Appeals of Minnesota
581 N.W.2d 359 (1998)

Considered and decided by SHORT, P.J., and HUSPENI and WILLIS, JJ.

SHORT, JUDGE.

Michael B. Padden seeks a quantum meruit recovery of legal fees from lawsuits acquired prior to the dissolution of the firm, Hurwitz & Padden, PLC. On appeal from the trial court's equal division of those fees, Padden argues the trial court erred in applying partnership principles to the law firm's dissolution.

In September 1991, Thomas R. Hurwitz and Michael B. Padden formed a two-person law firm, Hurwitz & Padden, PLC ("firm"), but failed to enter into a written partnership agreement. The partners shared all firm proceeds on a 50-50 basis, and reported all income as partnership income. In January 1993, Hurwitz filed articles of organization, which established the firm as a limited liability company with the Secretary of State. . . .

On February 15, 1996, Padden notified Hurwitz that he wanted to dissolve their professional relationship as of March 1, 1996. The parties successfully resolved all business issues involving their relationship, except for the division of attorney fees from several of the firm's contingency fee cases. In August 1996, Hurwitz filed this declaratory judgment action against Padden seeking a formal dissolution, a post-dissolution distribution of attorney fees on a 50-50 basis, and injunctive relief. By counterclaim, Padden requested a full accounting and an award of defense costs and fees. Both parties filed cross-motions for partial summary judgment. The trial court found in favor of Hurwitz, deciding the contingency fees should be divided equally, and submitted all accounting matters to a referee. After adopting the referee's findings, the trial court entered judgment in favor of Hurwitz for $101,750. . . .

As a partnership moves toward termination, it conducts a "winding up" of its affairs. When a partnership is in this "winding up" stage, the UPA confers no right of compensation for services rendered by the partners in furtherance of the partnership business. *Resnick v. Kaplan*, 49 Md. App. 499, 434 A.2d 582, 587 (1981). . . . During the period between dissolution and termination, partnership distributions continue to be made according to pre-dissolution rules. . . . Pending contingency files are uncompleted transactions of the partnership, and the fees obtained from such cases are assets of the firm subject to distribution under the UPA.

Padden argues the trial court erred in applying partnership principles to the dissolution of a limited liability company. However, the Minnesota Limited Liability Company Act specifically incorporates the definition and use of the term "dissolution" from the Uniform Partnership Act. *See* Minn. Stat. § 322B.03, subd. 15 (1996) (stating dissolution "obligates the limited liability company to wind up its affairs and to terminate its existence as legal entity"). Under both statutes, the entity is not terminated upon dissolution, but continues until all business issues are resolved. Thus, the UPA provides guidance when examining the end stages of either entity's life. Moreover, the mere fact that the parties filed a limited liability company document with the state does not foreclose an examination of partnership law. *See Fox v. Abrams*, 163 Cal. App. 3d 610, 210 Cal. Rptr. 260, 263 (1985) (applying no-compensation rule to professional corporations); *Sullivan, Bodney & Hammond v. Bodney*, 16 Kan. App. 2d 208, 820 P.2d 1248, 1251 (1991) (holding in dissolution of law firm corporation, partners only entitled to receive payment from pending contingency fee cases according to their interest in the firm prior to dissolution); *cf. Harris v. Mardan Business Sys., Inc.*, 421 N.W.2d 350, 353 (Minn. App. 1988) (stating reliance on partnership principles is appropriate when enforcing fiduciary duty among shareholders in close corporations because many close corporations are partnerships in a different name), *review denied* (Minn. May 18, 1988).

It is undisputed: (1) the firm had no written or oral agreement regarding the division of contingency fees upon dissolution; (2) the firm existed for approximately five-and-a-half years before Padden requested dissolution; (3) a little over five months elapsed between the date of dissolution and the date the parties cross-claimed to settle the firm's remaining issues; (4) the firm's contingency fee cases were acquired before the firm's dissolution; (5) prior to its dissolution, the firm divided fees equally between the parties; and (6) at the time the parties filed suit, the firm was in a winding-up phase. Under these circumstances, partnership principles, including the "no-compensation rule," govern the division of fees obtained from pre-dissolution contingency fee files. . . .

Padden also argues the Minnesota Rules of Professional Conduct prohibit an equal division of the contingency fees because the parties failed to strictly comply with the fee-splitting requirements. However, the Model Rules of Professional Conduct "regulate the manner in which lawyers from *different* firms may split a fee." . . . Until the firm's affairs are wound-up, the entity remains intact for the purposes of completing its affairs, and lawyers remain in the same firm until that process is completed. . . . Under these circumstances, the equal division of fees does not violate Minnesota's Rules of Professional Conduct. . . .

Affirmed.

Notes

1. One issue that has arisen at least a few times is whether a member who withdraws from an LLC and causes its dissolution is entitled to participate in the winding-up. In *Investcorp, L.P. v. Simpson Investment Co., L.C.*, 267 Kan. 840, 983 P.2d 265 (1999), the court, after parsing the language of various provisions in the operating agreement and LLC statute, concluded that the withdrawing members could participate. In contrast, see *Lindsay, Marcel, Harris & Pugh v. Harris*, 752 So. 2d 335 (La. Ct. App. 2000), where the Louisiana court held that an attorney who had withdrawn from his law firm organized as an LLC was no longer a "member" of the LLC entitled to seek judicial dissolution of the LLC. Would it make sense to differentiate between withdrawal as a member of the LLC and a member of the law practice?

2. Like RUPA, the typical limited liability company act provides for a liquidation on dissolution without an option on the part of either party to buy-out the other. Of course, the operating agreement could provide for a buy-out option. Nevertheless, at least one court has recognized an equitable power to order a buy-out in lieu of liquidation. *In re Superior Vending, LLC*, 71 A.D.3d 1153, 898 N.Y.S.2d 191 (App. Div. 2010). As noted in Chapter 13, *supra*, the courts have followed a similar tact under RUPA.

3. Business entity statutes typically require periodic filings with, and the payment of a fee to, the secretary of state of the jurisdiction where the entity was formed. Failure to comply with this requirement results in "administrative dissolution." While sometimes intentional, the failure to comply is often unintentional. As a result, business entity statutes often allow the administratively dissolved entity to file a form with the secretary of state, pay fees and penalties, and become reinstated, usually retroactively to the date of dissolution. The effect of retroactive reinstatement may be to protect the agents of the entity who acted for the entity during the period that it was administratively dissolved. Recall that under agency law, a person acting for a nonexistent principal is personally liable on any transactions entered into on behalf of that nonexistent principal; a dissolved business entity is, at least arguably, a nonexistent entity. These questions were explored in great depth in *Pannell v. Shannon*, 425 S.W.3d 58, 76 (Ky. 2014). In this case, an LLC was administratively dissolved and, before it was reinstated, the managing member of the LLC entered into a lease on behalf of the entity. When the LLC subsequently defaulted (which was after it was reinstated), the lessor sued the managing member personally. The applicable Kentucky statute that allowed for reinstatement provided (as many do) for retroactive effect. The Court held in favor of the defendant:

> The strong principle of favoring limited liability informs our understanding of the law applicable to limited liability companies. From it, we can even more readily conclude that the legislature intended the relation-back, effective-date, and as-if-the-administrative-dissolution-had-never-occurred language to create a seamless company functionality that protects the members of the LLC from personal liability for actions occurring during a period of administrative dissolution, as long as reinstatement occurs.... [T]his would comport with the general rule in most jurisdictions that business-entity owners (usually shareholders of a corporation but sometimes, as in this case, members of a limited liability company) are not personally liable for actions during a period of dissolution followed by reinstatement.

Such relation-back provisions, however, have their limits. In *CF SBC Pledgor 1 2012-1 Trust v. Clark/School, LLC*, 78 N.E.3d 381 (Ill. App. 2016), a mortgage agreement provided that it was an event of default if the mortgagor, a limited liability company, failed to maintain its good standing as an LLC. When the mortgagor was administratively dissolved, the mortgagee brought a foreclosure action. Illinois LLC Act, 805 ILCS 180/35-40(d) provided:

> Upon the filing of the application for reinstatement, the limited liability company existence shall be deemed to have continued without interruption from the date of the issuance of the notice of dissolution, and the limited liability company shall stand revived with the powers, duties, and obligations as if it had not been dissolved; and all acts and proceedings of its members, managers, officers, employees, and agents, acting or purporting to act in that capacity, and which would have been legal and valid but for the dissolution, shall stand ratified and confirmed.

The Illinois court held that the reinstatement by the mortgagor was ineffective to avoid foreclosure: "The relation-back provision allows a reinstated LLC to ratify actions taken on its behalf while it was dissolved but, like the relation-back provision in the Business Corporation Act, cannot impose a legal fiction that belies actual, real world facts." 78 N.E.3d at 387.

Problems

The purpose of the following problems and questions, some of which involve issues raised here for the first time, is to encourage the reader to take a thorough look at ULLCA and to acquire familiarity with it. Although ULLCA will not always supply an easy answer, it (or the counterpart statute in the jurisdiction in which the reader will be practicing law) is always a good place to start analysis of an LLC problem.

1. Able, Baker, and Carr, the three partners of the ABC partnership, have operated as a partnership in the waste disposal business for years. Recently they formed an

LLC named "ABC Ltd.," and continued their business in this new form. The filing that created ABC Ltd. is a matter of public record. Also, the business with its new name has been heavily advertised in the local press and on television. Dunn, a creditor of the ABC partnership for many years, continues extending credit to the business without formal notice of the change. Are Able, Baker, and Carr personally liable to Dunn for the debts incurred by the LLC?

2. Farr, a valuable employee of ABC LLC, recently has received an offer from a competing business. Can the LLC offer him a 15 percent interest in the company without requiring any contribution from him? Can it give Farr a 15 percent interest in the profits but withhold any management rights from him? Suppose that Farr incurs a substantial debt on behalf of the business after he has become a member, in an area unrelated to the work he does but within the scope of the business. The debt is unauthorized. Can an argument be made that the firm will be liable for the debt? If nothing is said when Farr is brought into the business, and he thereafter decides to sell his interest to another, can he do so without informing Able, Baker, and Carr and obtaining their consent?

3. Grace, who recently has been appointed sole manager of ABC LLC, begins dumping toxic waste material in illegal places. The dumping is discovered, and the LLC is fined by the state and sued for damages by persons owning the land on which the waste was dumped. Carr knew about Grace's activities but said nothing. Is Carr liable to the owners of the land? Are Able and Baker liable for Carr's or Grace's behavior? Assume alternatively that none of the members knew about the dumping but that if they had been conscientiously reviewing documents and keeping track of accounts they would have discovered it. Is there any personal liability?

4. Assume that Carr thereafter becomes bankrupt. Does she remain a member of the LLC? If not, what are the rights of her creditors to get the cash value of her interest? Would it include good will? If the other members wanted to keep Carr as a member, could they?

5. Suppose the members of ABC LLC decided to put the management of the firm solely in the hands of Able. Thereafter Able decides not to distribute earnings for several years. The other two members, Baker and Carr, are angry about this and want to make a claim against Able. Can they do this? On what basis? (It is useful to note that annual profits are treated for tax purposes as if received by each member of an LLC, whether or not the profits are actually distributed, similar to partners in a partnership.) Assume alternatively that Baker and Carr are worried that Able has not been pursuing valid claims that the LLC has against third parties. Do they have any remedy for this?

6. Suppose several investors form an LLC to bid on a professional basketball franchise. The operating agreement designates the promoter, Smith, as the sole manager of the LLC. One of the investor/members, Jones, thinks Smith is making strategic errors and is thinking of organizing a new group to make a bid. The operating agreement has no provisions that would either restrict or permit Jones from organizing

a rival group and making a bid. It would mean the loss of several thousand dollars that Jones invested in the LLC, but Jones is willing to risk that loss. Jones would like to know whether there are any legal restrictions on his ability to form a competing group and bid on the franchise. What would you advise?

Index

[References are to sections.]

A

Agency Relationship
Contractual powers (See Contracts)
Corporate relationships
  Generally, 1[G][4]
  Agency status of corporate directors,
    1[G][4][a]
  Mere instrumentality/alter ego
    doctrine contrasted with tradi-
    tional agency liability, 1[G][4][b]
Debtor-creditor relationship, 1[B]
Dual agency, 1[E]; 1[E][1]
Duty (See DUTY)
Escrow holder, 1[D]
Franchise relationship, 1[G][1]
History of, 1[H]
Liability to third parties (See Liability
  of Agent to Third Parties)
Limited liability companies (LLCs)
  (See Limited Liability Companies
  (LLCs))
Marriage relationship, 1[G][2]
Partnerships (See Partnerships)
Property relationships
  Generally, 1[G][3]
  Co-ownership, 1[G][3][a]
  Landlord-tenant, 1[G][3][b]
Sale of goods, 1[A]
Termination of (See Termination of
  Agency Relationship)
Tort liability (See Tort Liability)
Trusts, law of, 1[C]
Unscrupulous agent, 5[A]
Vicarious tort liability
  (See Vicarious Tort Liability)

Ambiguous Principal Problem
Generally, 1[E]; 1[E][2]
History of, 1[H]

B

Business Trusts
Generally, Intro [B][2]

C

Contracts
Authority of agent to bind principal
  Generally, 4[A][2]
  Apparent authority, 4[B]
  Delegation of authority,
    4[A][2][a]
  Express authority, 4[A][1]
  Implied authority
  Incidental authority, 4[A][2][b]
  Inherent agency power, 4[D]
Estoppel, 4[C]
Liability of agent to third parties
  (See Liability of Agent to Third
  Parties, subhead: Contract, on)
Ratification doctrine
  (See Ratification Doctrine)
Undisclosed principal
  (See Undisclosed Principal)

Co-Ownership
Agency versus, 1[G][3][a]

Corporate Relationships (See Agency
  Relationship, subhead: Corporate
  relationships)

Corporations
Generally, Intro [A]
Agency relationship (See Agency

Relationship, subhead: Corporate relationships)

D

Damages, Punitive
Generally, 3[A][4][b][iv]
Debtor-Creditor Relationship
Generally, 1[B]
Limited liability companies (LLCs), 15[F][7]; 15[F][9]
Dual Agency, 1[E]; 1[E][1]
Duty
Agent's duties to principal
Generally, 2[B]
Accounting, 2[B][3]
Fiduciary duty (See Fiduciary Duty, subhead: Agent's duty to principal)
Good conduct, 2[B][1]
Indemnification for loss/misconduct, 2[B][2]
Obedience, 2[B][1]
Care, duty of, 2[A][3]
Compensation, duty to pay , 2[A][2]
Fiduciary duty (See Fiduciary Duty)
Principal's duties to agent
Care, duty of, 2[A][3]
Compensation, duty to pay , 2[A][2]
Deal fairly and in good faith, 2[A][5]
Exoneration, 2[A][1]
Indemnification, 2[A][1]
Social legislation
Generally, 2[A][4][b]
Worker's compensation legislation, 2[A][4][a]
Social legislation
Generally, 2[A][4][b]
Worker's compensation legislation, 2[A][4][a]

E

Escrow Holder
Generally, 1[D]
Exoneration

Principal's duties to agent, 2[A][1]

F

Fiduciary Duty
Agent's duty to principal
Care, 2[B][4][b]
Commencement of, 2[B][4][a]
Disclosure, 2[B][4][c]
Loyalty (See subhead: Loyalty, duty to)
Limited liability company members, 15[F][1][b]
Loyalty, duty to
Generally, 2[B][4][d]
Arm's length, dealing at, 2[B][4][d][iii]
During relationship, 2[B][4][d][i]
Post-termination competition, 2[B][4][d][ii]
Franchise
Agency versus, 1[G][1]
Fraud
Limitations on liability, 5[B]
Unscrupulous agent, 5[A]

I

Imputed Knowledge
Generally, 9[C]
Indemnification
Agent's indemnification to principal, 2[B][2]
Misconduct of agent, 2[B][2]
Principal's indemnification to agent, 2[A][1]

L

Landlord-Tenant
Agency versus, 1[G][3][b]
Liability of Agent to Third Parties
Contract, on
Fully disclosed principal, 7[A][2]
Partially disclosed principal, 7[A][3]
Principal
Fully disclosed, 7[A][2]

Partially disclosed, 7[A][3]
Unintentionally disclosed,
    7[A][1]
Unintentionally disclosed principal,
    7[A][1]
Economic harm, 7[C]
Tort liability, 7[D]
Warranty of authority, agent's, 7[B]
Limited Liability Companies (LLCs)
Generally, 15[A]; Intro [B][7]
Authority and apparent authority of
    members, 15[F][1][a]
Bankruptcy of member, 15[F][9]
Benefit LLCs, 15[H]
Claims among members
    Derivative claims, 15[F][2][a]
    Direct claim for oppression,
        15[F][2][b]
Creation of, 15[D]
Creditors' claims
    Generally, 15[F][7]
    Bankruptcy of member, 15[F][9]
Dissolution, 15[J]
    Judicial, 15[J][1]
    Winding up, 15[J][2]
Entity theory, 15[E]
Estate planning devices, as, 15[I]
Exit privileges, 15[F][5]
Expulsion of member, 15[F][6]
Fiduciary duties of members,
    15[F][1][b]
Inspection of books and records by
    members, 15[F][8]
Limitations on distributions, 15[F][3]
Low-profit limited liability companies
    (L3C), 15[H]
Management of
    Generally, 15[F][1]
    Authority and apparent authority of
        members, 15[F][1][a]
    Fiduciary duties of members,
        15[F][1][b]
Securities laws issues, 15[C]
Series LLCs, 15[G]

Social enterprise vehicle, as, 15[H]
    Benefit LLC, 15[H]
    L3C, 15[H]
Tax matters
    Check-the-box regulations, 15[B][2]
    Kintner regulations, 15[B][1]
Transferability of interests, 15[F][4]
**Limited Liability Limited Partnerships
(LLLPs)**
Generally, Intro [B][6]
Limited Liability Partnerships (LLPs)
Generally, 11[B]; Intro [B][4]
Limited Partnerships
Generally, Intro [B][5]
Agreements, 14[C]
Dissolution of, 14[D][10]
General partner
    Control by limited partners,
        14[D][1][b]
    Fair dealing, obligations under
        implied covenant of, 14[E][3]
    Fiduciary duty, 14[E][2]
    Good faith and fair dealing, obliga-
        tions under implied covenant of,
        14[E][3]
    Powers, 14[E][1]
    Removal of
        Generally, 14[D][2]
        Limited partners for cause,
            removal by, 14[D][2][a]
        Revised Uniform Partnership Act
            (RUPA) Section 801(4),
            problem of, 14[D][2][b]
    Withdrawal of, 14[E][4]
Historical background, 14[A]
Limited partners
    Control
        Generally, 14[D][1][a]
        Corporate general partner,
            control over, 14[D][1][b]
        General partner (See subhead:
            General partner)
        Piercing veil of limited partner-
            ship, 14[D][1][c]

Distributions, 14[D][4]

Duties, 14[D][5]

Inspection rights of, 14[D][9]

Suits by, 14[D][3]

Transfers of interests, 14[D][4]

Withdrawal rights, 14[D][7]

Merger of limited partnership into
another entity, 14[D][8]

Organization defects, 14[B]

LLCs (See Limited Liability Companies
(LLCs))

LLLPs (See Limited Liability Limited
Partnerships (LLLPs))

LLPs (See Limited Liability
Partnerships (LLPs))

M

Marriage

Agency versus, 1[G][2]

Misconduct

Agent's indemnification to principal,
2[B][2]

N

Negligence

Imputed contributory negligence,
3[A][1][d]

Negligent Acts

Vicarious tort liability, 3[A][4][a]

Nonprofit Associations (See
Vicarious Tort Liability, subhead:
Unincorporated nonprofit associa-
tion relationship)

Notice, Notification and Knowledge

Generally, 9[A]

Adverse interest qualification, 9[D]

Imputed knowledge, 9[C]

Notification, 9[B]

Partnerships, 12[F]

Sole actor doctrine, 9[E]

P

Partnerships

Generally, Intro [B][3]

Accounting

Partner's right to accounting,
12[H][2]

Principles, 12[G]

Aggregate theory, 11[D]

Continuing business

Buy-out price calculation, 13[C][7]

Buy-sell agreements, 13[C][1]

Continuation clauses, 13[C][2]

Creditors' claims, 13[C][5]

Goodwill, 13[C][6]

Liability, assumption of

Incoming partners, 13[C][3]

Withdrawing partners, 13[C][4]

Contractual powers of partners

Generally, 12[A]

Actual authority, 12[A][1]

Apparent authority, 12[A][2]

Liability of purported partner
(See subhead: Liability of
purported partner)

Contributions of property

Ownership of particular property,
ambiguities concerning, 11[G][1]

Property rights, 11[G][3]

Title to property, 11[G][2]

Creation of

Generally, 11[A]

Aggregate theory, 11[D]

Contributions of property
(See subhead: Contributions
of property)

Entity theory, 11[D]

Historical background, 11[C][1]

Income tax considerations, 11[E]

Limited liability partnerships (LLPs),
11[B]

Revised Uniform Partnership Act
(RUPA), 11[C][3]

2013 amendments, 11[C][3]

Test for partnership, 11[C][2]

Uniform Partnership Act (UPA),
11[C][3]

Creditors' claims

Creditors' rights against, 14[D][6]

Limited liability partnership (LLP) shield, 12[K]

Partners, 14[D][6]

Personal creditors of partners against partnership interests, 12[J]

Rights

    Assets, against partnership, 12[I][1]

    Personal assets of individual partners, rights against, 12[I][2]

Dissociation, wrongful, 13[A][3]

Dissolution

    Generally, 13[A]

    Judicial dissolution, 13[A][2]

    Notice of dissolution, 13[B][2]

    Termination of authority, 13[B][1]

    Will, at, 13[A][1]

Duty

    Care, 12[H][1][b]

    Fiduciary duty (See subhead: Fiduciary duty)

    Full disclosure, 12[H][1][c]

    Good faith and fair dealing, 12[H][1][d]

Entity theory, 11[D]

Fiduciary duty

    Generally, 12[H][1]

    Freedom to contract and, 12[H][1][a][v]

    General partner, 14[E][2]

    Loyalty

        Conflicts of interest, 12[H][1][a][iv]

        Formation of partnership, during, 12[H][1][a][i]

        Leaving business, 12[H][1][a][iii]

        Pre-empting business opportunities, 12[H][1][a][ii]

Fraudulent partner

    Generally, 12[B][2]

    Conflicting view, 12[B][2][b]

Traditional view, 12[B][2][a]

Historical background, 11[C][1]

Income tax considerations, 11[E]

Joint and several liability, 12[C]

Judicial expulsion, 13[A][4]

Liability of purported partner

    Generally, 12[A][3]

    Duty to speak, 12[A][3][a]

    Release conundrum, 12[A][3][c]

    Reliance conundrum, 12[A][3][b]

Limited liability partnerships (LLPs), 11[B]; Intro [B][4]

Limited partnerships (See Limited Partnerships)

Liquidation of business, 13[D][1]

Notice and notification to, 12[F]

Partners, suits among, 12[H][2]

Revised Uniform Partnership Act (RUPA), 11[C][3]

    2013 amendments, 11[C][3]

Rights and duties among partners

    Accounting, right to, 12[H][2]

    Fiduciary duty (See subhead: Fiduciary duty)

    Suits among partners, 12[H][2]

Suits against partnership, 12[D]

Suits by partnership, 12[E]

Termination of business

    Generally, 13[D][2]

    Claims among partners, 13[D][2][b]

    Settlement of accounts, 13[D][2][a]

Test for partnership, 11[C][2]

Tort liability for wrongs of partners

    Generally, 12[B][1]

    Fraudulent partner (See subhead: Fraudulent partner)

Uniform Partnership Act (UPA), 11[C][3]

Vicarious tort liability, 3[B]

Winding up business, 13[D][1]

Wrongful dissociation, 13[A][3]

Punitive Damages

Generally, 3[A][4][b][iv]

R

Ratification Doctrine
Generally, 8[A]
Changed circumstances, 8[E]
Implied ratification, 8[A][2]
Justification for concept, 8[A][1]
Knowledge requirement, 8[B]
No partial ratification rule, 8[D]
Silence as affirmation, 8[C]

Revised Uniform Partnership Act (RUPA)
Generally, 11[C][3]
2013 Amendments, 11[C][3]
RUPA (See Revised Uniform Partnership Act (RUPA))

S

Social Legislation
Generally, 2[A][4][b]
Worker's compensation legislation, 2[A][4][a]

Sole Actor Doctrine
Generally, 9[E]

Sole Proprietorships
Generally, Intro [B][1]

Subagency
Generally, 1[F]
History of, 1[H]

T

Termination of Agency Relationship
Notice to third parties
Operation of law, termination by, 10[B][2]
Will, termination by, 10[B][1]
Operation of law, by
Bankruptcy, 10[A][2][c]
Death, 10[A][2][a]
Incapacity, 10[A][2][b]
War, 10[A][2][d]
Will, by
Generally, 10[A][1]
Consequences, 10[A][1][a]

Irrevocable powers phrased in agency terms, 10[A][1][b]

Third Parties
Liability of agent to third parties (See Liability of Agent to Third Parties)
Payments, 6[C][1]; 6[C][2]
Remedies of third party, 6[B][1][a]
Termination of agency relationship, notice to third parties in
Operation of law, termination by, 10[B][2]
Will, termination by, 10[B][1]

Tort Liability
Agent to third parties, to, 7[D]
Ratification doctrine (See Ratification Doctrine)
Vicarious tort liability (See Vicarious Tort Liability)
Wrongs of partners, for
Generally, 12[B][1]
Fraudulent partner (See Partnerships, subhead: Fraudulent partner)

Trusts
Agency and law of trusts, 1[C]
Business trusts, Intro [B][2]

U

Undisclosed Principal
Liabilities of
Authorized transactions
Generally, 6[B][1]
Election rule, 6[B][1][b]
Remedies of third party, 6[B][1][a]
Third party, remedies of, 6[B][1][a]
Unauthorized transactions, 6[B][2]
Rights of
Generally, 6[A]
Assertion of rights, 6[A][1]
Exceptions, 6[A][4]

Parol evidence rule, 6[A][2]
  Sealed contracts, 6[A][3]
Setoff, 6[C][3]
Third party payments, 6[C][1];
  6[C][2]
Uniform Partnership Act (UPA)
Generally, 11[C][3]
**Unincorporated Nonprofit Association
  Relationship** (See Vicarious Tort
  Liability, subhead: Unincorporated
  nonprofit association relationship)
UPA (See Uniform Partnership Act
  (UPA))

V

Vicarious Tort Liability
Direct liability of employer,
  3[A][1][f]
Employment limitation, scope of
  Generally, 3[A][4]
  Intentional torts (See subhead:
    Intentional torts)
  Negligent acts, 3[A][4][a]
Estoppel, by, 3[D][1]
Family car doctrine, 3[D][2]
Imputed contributory negligence,
  3[A][1][d]
Independent contractor exception in
  the modern economy
  Generally, 3[A][2][a]
  Limitations to, 3[A][2][b]
Intentional torts
  Generally, 3[A][4][b]
  Assault on section 228(1)(c),
    3[A][4][b][i]
  Implied contract theory,
    3[A][4][b][iii]
  Non-physical torts, 3[A][4][b][v]
  Punitive damages, 3[A][4][b][iv]
  Restatement section 219(2)(d),
    3[A][4][b][ii]
Losses caused by tortious behavior,
  limitation to, 3[A][1][e]

Master-servant relationship
  Generally, 3[A][1]
  Borrowed servants, 3[A][3]
  Direct liability of employer,
    3[A][1][f]
  Employment limitation, scope of
    (See subhead: Employment
    limitation, scope of)
  Imputed contributory negligence,
    3[A][1][d]
  Independent contractor exception in
    the modern economy
    Generally, 3[A][2][a]
    Limitations to, 3[A][2][b]
  Losses caused by tortious behavior,
    limitation to, 3[A][1][e]
  Respondeat superior liability
    (See subhead: Respondeat
    superior liability)
Negligent acts, 3[A][4][a]
Owner consent and other legislation,
  3[D][3]
Partnership relationship, 3[B]
Respondeat superior liability
  Employment relationship,
    3[A][1][b]
  Holmes thesis, 3[A][1][a][i]
  Rationale for respondeat superior
    Generally, 3[A][1][c]
    Arguments questioning theory,
      3[A][1][c][i]
    Favor of/explanations for theory,
      arguments in, 3[A][1][c][ii]
  Wigmore rebuttal, 3[A][1][a][ii]
Unincorporated nonprofit association
  relationship
  Generally, 3[C]
  Association, liability of
    Generally, 3[C][2][a]
    Actions of affiliates and chapters,
      3[C][2][b]
    Members, to, 3[C][2][c]
  Members, liability of, 3[C][1]